STREET ATLAS
Edinburgh
and East Central Scotland

Contents

III Key to map symbols

IV-V Key to map pages

VI-VII Route planning

VIII Administrative and post code boundaries

1 Street maps

232 Extra-large-scale map of Edinburgh town centre

234 Index of hospitals, industrial estates, railway stations, schools, shopping centres, street names and universities

PHILIP'S

First edition published 1995
First colour edition published 1999 by

Ordnance Survey®   and   George Philip Ltd., a division of
Romsey Road   Octopus Publishing Group Ltd
Maybush   2-4 Heron Quays
Southampton   London
SO16 4GU   E14 4JB

ISBN 0-540-07653 8 (hardback)
ISBN 0-540-07654 6 (spiral)

**The mapping between pages 1 and 233 (inclusive) in this atlas is
derived from Ordnance Survey® Large Scale and Landranger®
mapping, and revised using OSCAR® and Land-Line® data.**

Ordnance Survey, OSCAR, Land-line and Landranger are registered trade
marks of Ordnance Survey, the national mapping agency of Great Britain.

Printed and bound in Spain by Cayfosa

Digital Data

The exceptionally high-quality mapping
found in this book is available as digital
data in TIFF format, which is easily
convertible to other bit-mapped (raster)
image formats.

The index is also available in digital form
as a standard database table. It contains
all the details found in the printed index
together with the National Grid reference
for the map square in which each entry
is named and feature codes for places
of interest in eight categories such as
education and health.

For further information and to discuss
your requirements, please contact the
Ordnance Survey Solutions Centre on
01703 792929.

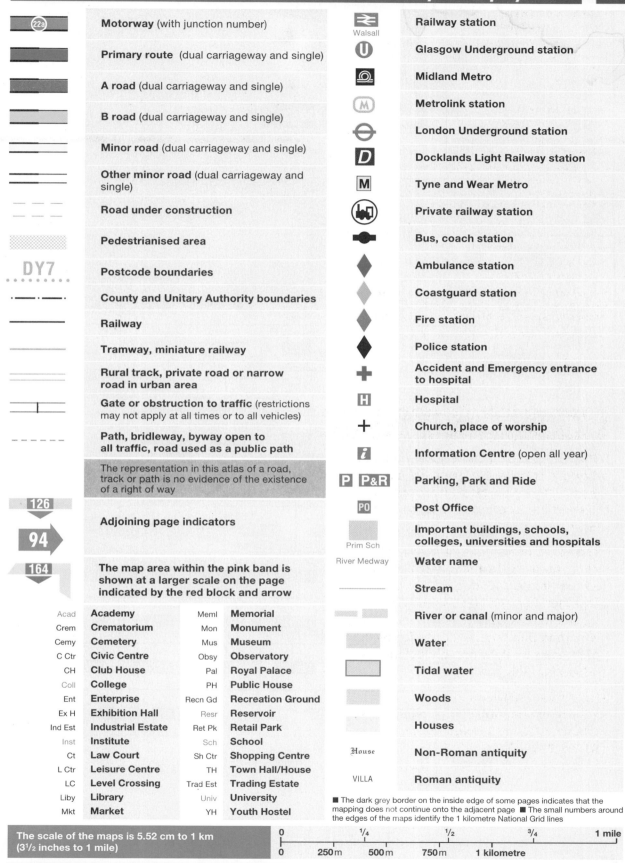

Motorway (with junction number)	
Primary route (dual carriageway and single)	
A road (dual carriageway and single)	
B road (dual carriageway and single)	
Minor road (dual carriageway and single)	
Other minor road (dual carriageway and single)	
Road under construction	
Pedestrianised area	
Postcode boundaries	
County and Unitary Authority boundaries	
Railway	
Tramway, miniature railway	
Rural track, private road or narrow road in urban area	
Gate or obstruction to traffic (restrictions may not apply at all times or to all vehicles)	
Path, bridleway, byway open to all traffic, road used as a public path	
The representation in this atlas of a road, track or path is no evidence of the existence of a right of way	
Adjoining page indicators	
The map area within the pink band is shown at a larger scale on the page indicated by the red block and arrow	

Acad	Academy	Meml	Memorial
Crem	Crematorium	Mon	Monument
Cemy	Cemetery	Mus	Museum
C Ctr	Civic Centre	Obsy	Observatory
CH	Club House	Pal	Royal Palace
Coll	College	PH	Public House
Ent	Enterprise	Recn Gd	Recreation Ground
Ex H	Exhibition Hall	Resr	Reservoir
Ind Est	Industrial Estate	Ret Pk	Retail Park
Inst	Institute	Sch	School
Ct	Law Court	Sh Ctr	Shopping Centre
L Ctr	Leisure Centre	TH	Town Hall/House
LC	Level Crossing	Trad Est	Trading Estate
Liby	Library	Univ	University
Mkt	Market	YH	Youth Hostel

Railway station	Walsall
Glasgow Underground station	
Midland Metro	
Metrolink station	
London Underground station	
Docklands Light Railway station	
Tyne and Wear Metro	
Private railway station	
Bus, coach station	
Ambulance station	
Coastguard station	
Fire station	
Police station	
Accident and Emergency entrance to hospital	
Hospital	
Church, place of worship	
Information Centre (open all year)	
Parking, Park and Ride	
Post Office	
Important buildings, schools, colleges, universities and hospitals	Prim Sch
Water name	River Medway
Stream	
River or canal (minor and major)	
Water	
Tidal water	
Woods	
Houses	
Non-Roman antiquity	House
Roman antiquity	VILLA

■ The dark grey border on the inside edge of some pages indicates that the mapping does not continue onto the adjacent page ■ The small numbers around the edges of the maps identify the 1 kilometre National Grid lines

The scale of the maps is 5.52 cm to 1 km (3½ inches to 1 mile)

0		¼		½		¾		1 mile

| 0 | 250m | 500m | 750m | 1 kilometre | | | | |

The scale of the maps on pages numbered in red is 11.04 cm to 1 km (7 inches to 1 mile)

0		220 yards		440 yards		660 yards		½ mile

| 0 | 125m | 250m | 375m | ½ kilometre | | | | |

Key to map pages

Page Scale

115	These pages are at 3½ inches to the mile
233	These pages are at 7 inches to the mile

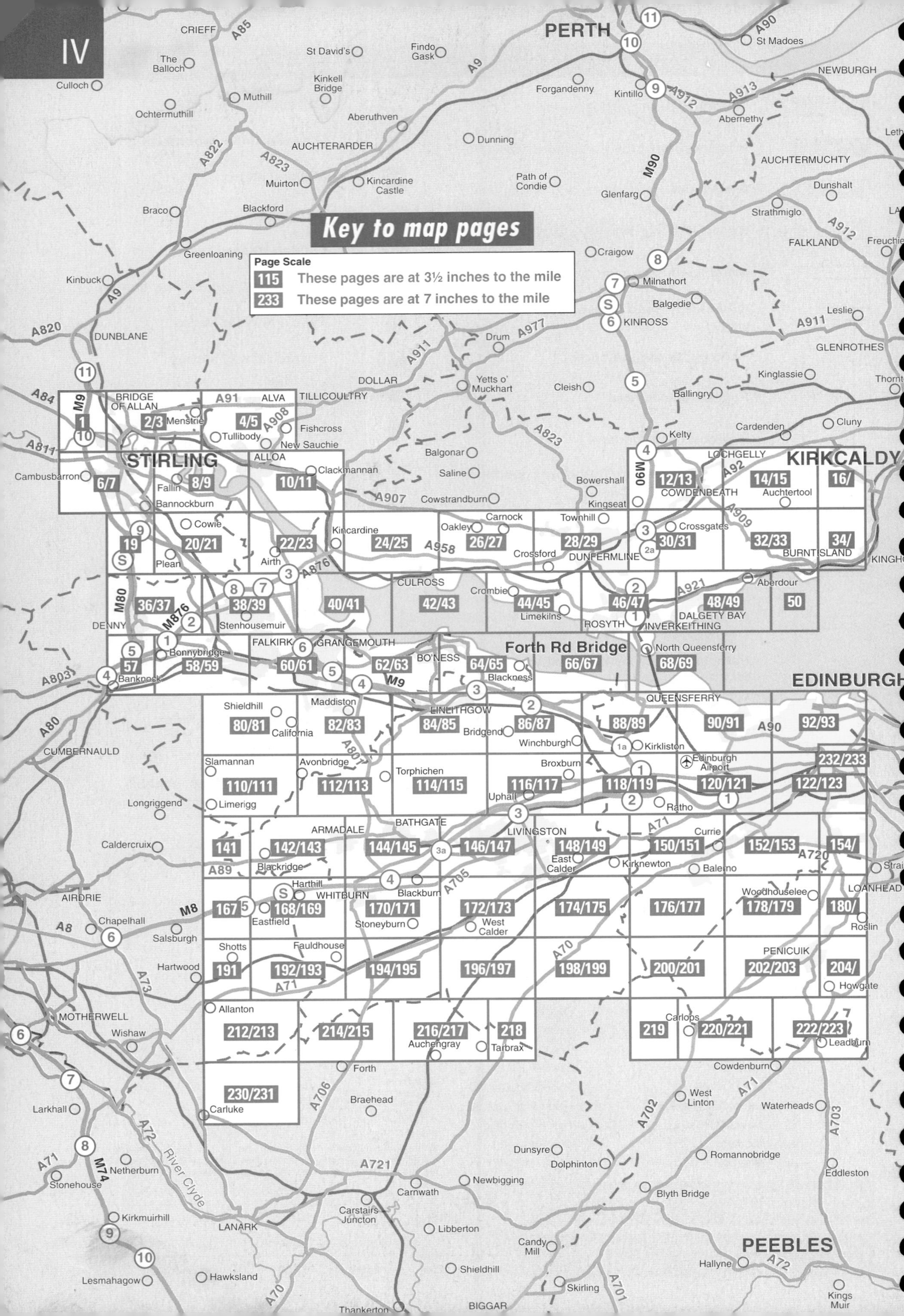

CRIEFF
A85
PERTH
A90
St Madoes
The Balloch
St David's
Findo Gask
A9
NEWBURGH
Culloch
Kinkell Bridge
Muthill
Forgandenny
Kintillo
A912
A913
Abernethy
Ochtermuthill
Aberuthven
Dunning
A822
AUCHTERARDER
A823
M90
AUCHTERMUCHTY
Muirton
Kincardine Castle
Path of Condie
Glenfarg
Dunshalt
Braco
Blackford
Strathmiglo
Greenloaning
Craigow
FALKLAND
Freuchie
Kinbuck
Milnathort
Balgedie
KINROSS
Leslie
A820
DUNBLANE
Drum
A977
A911
GLENROTHES
DOLLAR
Yetts o' Muckhart
Cleish
Kinglassie
Thornton
A84
M9
BRIDGE OF ALLAN
A91
ALVA
TILLICOULTRY
Ballingry
Menstrie
Tullibody
A908
Fishcross
New Sauchie
Cluny
Cardenden
Kelty
Balgonar
A811
STIRLING
ALLOA
Clackmannan
Saline
LOCHGELLY
KIRKCALDY
Cambusbarron
Fallin
Bowershall
A92
COWDENBEATH
Auchtertool
Bannockburn
A907
Cowstrandburn
Kingseat
Cowie
Kincardine
Oakley
Carnock
Townhill
Crossgates
A909
Plean
Airth
A876
A958
Crossford
DUNFERMLINE
BURNTISLAND
KINGHORN
CULROSS
Crombie
A921
Aberdour
M80
M876
DENNY
Stenhousemuir
Limekilns
ROSYTH
DALGETY BAY
INVERKEITHING
FALKIRK
GRANGEMOUTH
Forth Rd Bridge
North Queensferry
Bonnybridge
BO'NESS
Blackness
A803
Banknock
EDINBURGH
QUEENSFERRY
Shieldhill
Maddiston
LINLITHGOW
California
Bridgend
Winchburgh
Kirkliston
A90
A80
CUMBERNAULD
A801
Edinburgh Airport
Slamannan
Avonbridge
Torphichen
Broxburn
Longriggend
Limerigg
Uphall
Ratho
BATHGATE
ARMADALE
LIVINGSTON
A71
Currie
Caldercruix
Blackridge
A89
East Calder
Kirknewton
Balerno
A720
Straiton
Harthill
LOANHEAD
AIRDRIE
WHITBURN
Blackburn
A705
Woodhouselee
M8
Chapelhall
A8
Eastfield
Stoneyburn
West Calder
Roslin
Salsburgh
Shotts
Fauldhouse
PENICUIK
Hartwood
A73
A71
A70
Howgate
MOTHERWELL
Allanton
Carlops
Wishaw
Auchengray
Tarbrax
Leadburn
Forth
Cowdenburn
West Linton
Carluke
A706
Braehead
A702
Waterheads
A703
Larkhall
A72
River Clyde
M74
Netherburn
A71
Stonehouse
A721
Dunsyre
Dolphinton
Romannobridge
Eddleston
Carnwath
Newbigging
Blyth Bridge
Kirkmuirhill
Carstairs Junction
LANARK
Libberton
Candy Mill
PEEBLES
Lesmahagow
Hawksland
Shieldhill
Hallyne
A72
A70
Skirling
A701
Kings Muir
Thankerton
BIGGAR
1
2/3
4/5
6/7
8/9
10/11
12/13
14/15
16/
19
20/21
22/23
24/25
26/27
28/29
30/31
32/33
34/
36/37
38/39
40/41
42/43
44/45
46/47
48/49
50
57
58/59
60/61
62/63
64/65
66/67
68/69
80/81
82/83
84/85
86/87
88/89
90/91
92/93
110/111
112/113
114/115
116/117
118/119
120/121
122/123
232/233
141
142/143
144/145
146/147
148/149
150/151
152/153
154/
167
168/169
170/171
172/173
174/175
176/177
178/179
180/
191
192/193
194/195
196/197
198/199
200/201
202/203
204/
212/213
214/215
216/217
218
219
220/221
222/223
230/231

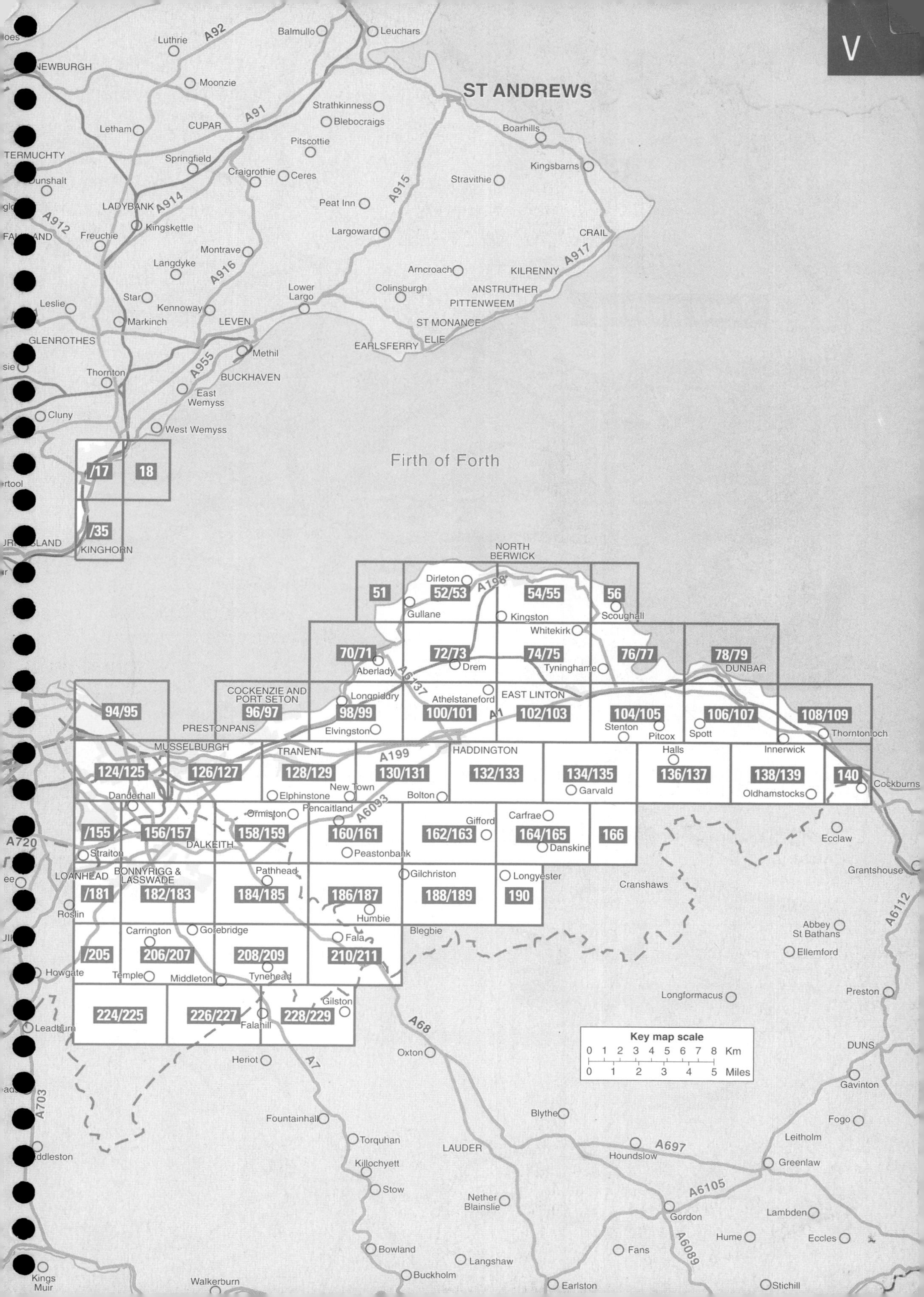

Luthrie • Balmullo • • Leuchars
A92
• Moonzie
NEWBURGH •
• Strathkinness • Blebocraigs
ST ANDREWS
Letham • CUPAR • Pitscottie • Boarhills
A91
TERMUCHTY • Springfield • Kingsbarns
Dunshalt • Craigrothie • Ceres • Peat Inn • Stravithie
A912 LADYBANK A914 • Largoward CRAIL
FALKLAND • Freuchie • Kingskettle A915
Montrave • Arncroach • KILRENNY A917
Langdyke A916 • Colinsburgh ANSTRUTHER PITTENWEEM
Leslie • Star • Lower Largo ST MONANCE
Kennoway ELIE
Markinch • LEVEN EARLSFERRY
GLENROTHES • Methil
A955 BUCKHAVEN
Thornton • East Wemyss
Cluny • West Wemyss

Firth of Forth

/17 | 18
/35
KINGHORN

NORTH BERWICK
51 | 52/53 | 54/55 | 56
Dirleton A198
Gullane Kingston Scoughall
Whitekirk
70/71 | 72/73 | 74/75 | 76/77 | 78/79
Aberlady A6137 Drem Tyninghame DUNBAR
COCKENZIE AND PORT SETON Longniddry Athelstaneford EAST LINTON
94/95 | 96/97 | 98/99 | 100/101 | 102/103 | 104/105 | 106/107 | 108/109
PRESTONPANS Elvingston A1 Stenton Spott Thorntonloch
MUSSELBURGH Pitcox
124/125 | 126/127 | TRANENT 128/129 | 130/131 | HADDINGTON 132/133 | 134/135 | Halls 136/137 | Innerwick 138/139 | 140
Danderhall New Town Bolton Garvald Oldhamstocks Cockburns
Elphinstone
Ormiston Pencaitland A6093 Gifford Carfrae
/155 | 156/157 | 158/159 | 160/161 | 162/163 | 164/165 | 166
DALKEITH Peastonbank Danskine Ecclaw
Straiton Gilchriston Longyester Grantshouse
LOANHEAD BONNYRIGG & LASSWADE Pathhead Cranshaws
/181 | 182/183 | 184/185 | 186/187 | 188/189 | 190
Roslin Humbie Abbey St Bathans
Carrington Gorebridge Fala Blegbie Ellemford
/205 | 206/207 | 208/209 | 210/211
Howgate Temple Middleton Tynehead Longformacus Preston
Leadburn Gilston DUNS
224/225 | 226/227 | 228/229
Falahill Gavinton
Heriot A7 Oxton Fogo
A703 Leitholm
Fountainhall Blythe Greenlaw
Torquhan A697
iddleston LAUDER Houndslow A6105
Killochyett A6089
Stow Nether Blainslie Gordon Lambden
Kings Muir Hume Eccles
Walkerburn Bowland Langshaw Buckholm Earlston Stichill

Key map scale
0 1 2 3 4 5 6 7 8 Km
0 1 2 3 4 5 Miles

Route planning

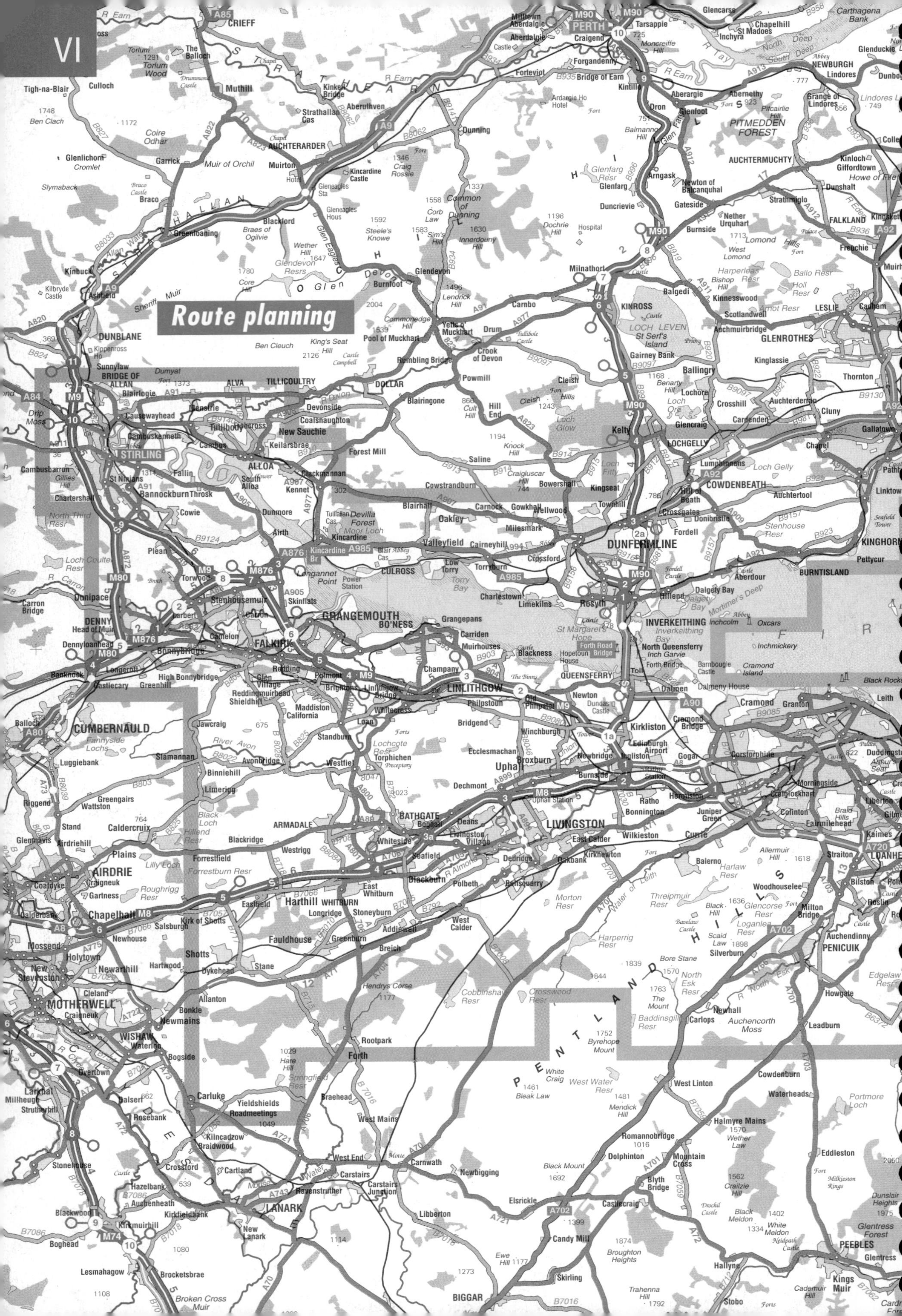

CRIEFF
PERTH
M90
Bridge of Earn
STRATHEARN
Muthill
AUCHTERARDER
Gleneagles
Dunning
Glen Eagles
OCHIL HILLS
Glen Devon
PITMEDDEN FOREST
AUCHTERMUCHTY
NEWBURGH
FALKLAND
Milnathort
KINROSS
LOCH LEVEN
GLENROTHES
LESLIE
DUNBLANE
BRIDGE OF ALLAN
ALVA
TILLICOULTRY
DOLLAR
STIRLING
ALLOA
Clackmannan
Kincardine
CULROSS
DUNFERMLINE
COWDENBEATH
LOCHGELLY
Rosyth
INVERKEITHING
BURNTISLAND
KINGHORN
FIRTH OF FORTH
Forth Road Bridge
QUEENSFERRY
GRANGEMOUTH
BO'NESS
FALKIRK
LINLITHGOW
CUMBERNAULD
M9
M8
M80
M876
A9
A92
A90
AIRDRIE
Chapelhall
BATHGATE
LIVINGSTON
Uphall
Kirkliston
Edinburgh Airport
Cramond
Leith
Corstorphine
PENICUIK
LOANHEAD
PENTLAND HILLS
Harthill
WHITBURN
Shotts
Fauldhouse
West Calder
MOTHERWELL
WISHAW
Carluke
LANARK
Carstairs
Carnwath
West Linton
Romannobridge
PEEBLES
BIGGAR
Lesmahagow

Carthagena Bank · Kilmany · Leuchars · Eden Mouth · ST ANDREWS BAY
Rathillet · Balmull · Guardbridge · St Andrews
NEWBURGH · Lindores · Glenduckie · Norman's Law · Kincaple · Strathkinness · ST ANDREWS · Kinkell Ness · Buddo Ness
Dunbog · Lindores Loch · Kilmaron Cas · Dairsie or Osnaburgh · Biebocraigs · Prior Muir · Boarhills · Babbet Ness
Lindores · Fernie · Lotham · CUPAR · Bridgend · Pitscottie · Cameron Resr · Stravithie · Kingsbarns · Cambo Ness
Collessie · Bow of Fife · Ceres · Baldinnie · Radernie · Dunino · Carr Brigs · Tullybothy Craigs
Kinloch · Giffordtown · Howe of Fife · LADYBANK · Craigrothie · Peat Inn · Lathones · FIFE NESS
Dunshalt · Pitlessie · Balmalcolm · Montrave · Largoward · Kellie Law · CRAIL · West Ness
FALKLAND · Kingskettle · Kettlebridge · Clatto Resr · Largo Law · Wester Newburn · Arncroach · KILRENNY · ANSTRUTHER
Frenchie · Muirhead · Bonnybank · Lundin Links · Upper Largo · Colinsburgh · Abercrombie · PITTENWEEM
Ballo Resr · Kennoway · LARGO BAY · Drumeldrie · Kilconquhar · Kilconquhar Loch · ST MONANS
LESLIE · Cadham · MARKINCH · Milton of Balgonie · Lower Largo · Ruddons Point · EARLSFERRY · ELIE · Sauchar Point
ROTHES · Thornton · Windygates · LEVEN · Innerleven · METHIL · Chapel Ness · Isle of May
Cluny · Coaltown of Balgonie · BUCKHAVEN · Macduff's Castle
Gallatown · Coaltown of Wemyss · East Wemyss · West Wemyss
KIRKCALDY · Pathhead · Dysart · Linktown · FIRTH OF FORTH
KINGHORN · Pettycur · Inchkeith
BURNTISLAND · Black Rocks

Fidra · Craigleith · Bass Rock
Eyebroughy · NORTH BERWICK
Dirleton · North Berwick Law · Auldhame · St Baldred's Boat · Tantallon Castle
Gullane · Gullane Bay · Kingston · Whitekirk · St Baldred's Cradle · Tyne Mouth
Aberlady · Aberlady Bay · Drem · DUNBAR · West Barns · Broxburn · Barns Ness
EDINBURGH · Leith · Portobello · COCKENZIE AND PORT SETON · Gosford Bay · Spittal · Ballencrieff · Athelstaneford · Tyninghame · Skateraw · Power Station
Duddingston · Arthur's Seat · PRESTONPANS · Longniddry · Garleton Hills · EAST LINTON · Pitcox · Innerwick · Thorntonloch
MUSSELBURGH · Inveresk · Wallyford · Elvingston · Huntington · R Tyne · Hailes Castle · Stenton · Brunt Hill · Reed Point
Craigmillar · Liberton · TRANENT · Gladsmuir · HADDINGTON · Papple · Whitelaw Hill · Cockburnspath · Pease Bay
Morningside · Gilmerton · Millerhill · Macmerry · Samuelston · Garvald · Cocklaw Hill
Braid Hills · Kaimes · DALKEITH · New Winton · New Town · Bolton · Danskine · Dunbar Common · Bransly Hill
Fairmilehead · LOANHEAD · BONNYRIGG AND LASSWADE · Cousland · East Saltoun · Gifford · Yaste House · WHITEADDER WATER · Spartleton Edge · Heart Law · Blackburn Rig
Straiton · Bilston · Bolton · Mayfield · Pencaitland · Humbie · Hopes · Meikle Says Law · Cranshaws · Grantshaws
Roslin · Rosewell · Arniston · Newtongrange · Newlandrig · Crichton · Fala Dam · Lammer Law · Whiteadder Resr · Cranshaws Hill · Ellemford · Marygold
PENICUIK · Auchendinny · Gorebridge · Fala · Fala Moor · Crib Law · WHITEADDER · Longformacus · Preston
Howgate · Temple · North Middleton · Tynehead · Soutra · Hunt Law · Blythe Edge · Watch Water Resr · DUNS
Edgelaw Resr · Rosebery Resr · Middleton · Falahill · Gilston · Hogs Law · Dirrington Great Law · Gavinton
Gladhouse · MOORFOOT HILLS · Heriot · Oxton · Hotel · Scoured Rig · Dirrington Little Law · Polwarth
Portmore Loch · Dun Law · Ladyside Height · Fountainhall · Collie Law · Edgarhope Wood · Westruther · Halliburton · Fogo · Hule Moss
Eddleston · Blackhope Scar · Whitehope Law · Torquhan · LAUDER · Blythe · Thirlestane · Houndslow · Greenlaw · Swintonmill
Milkieston Rings · Dunslair Heights · Windlestraw Law · Killochyett · Lauder Common · Gordon · Hume · Leitholm
Glentress Forest · Black Law · Great Law · Stow · Bowland · Buckholm · Sweethope House · Mellerstain House · Stichill · Ednam
PEEBLES · Glentress · Cardrona · Lee Pen · Walkburn · Knowes Hill · Earlston · Nenthorn · Carham
Kings Muir · Cardrona Forest · GALASHIELS

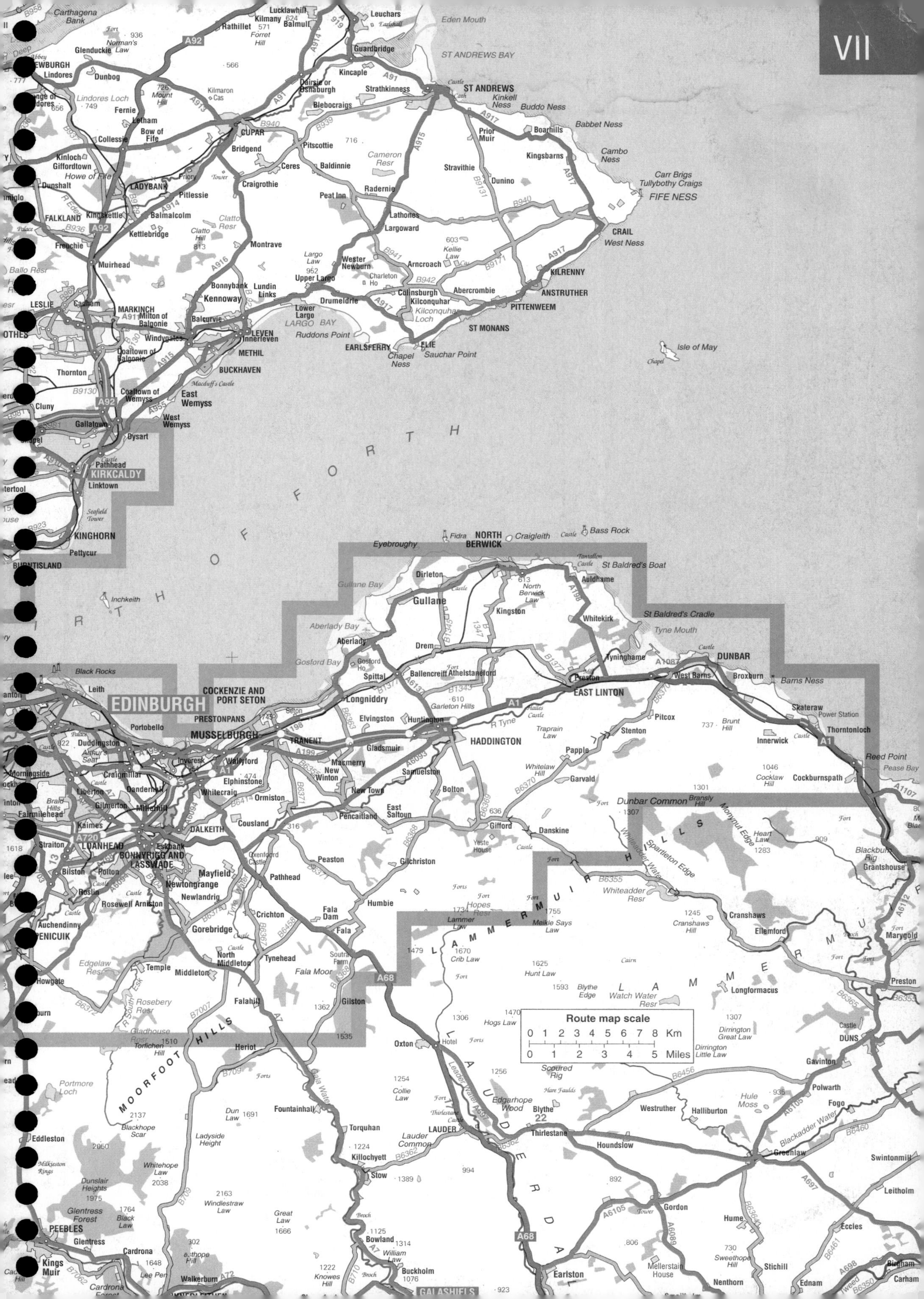

Route map scale
0 1 2 3 4 5 6 7 8 Km
0 1 2 3 4 5 Miles

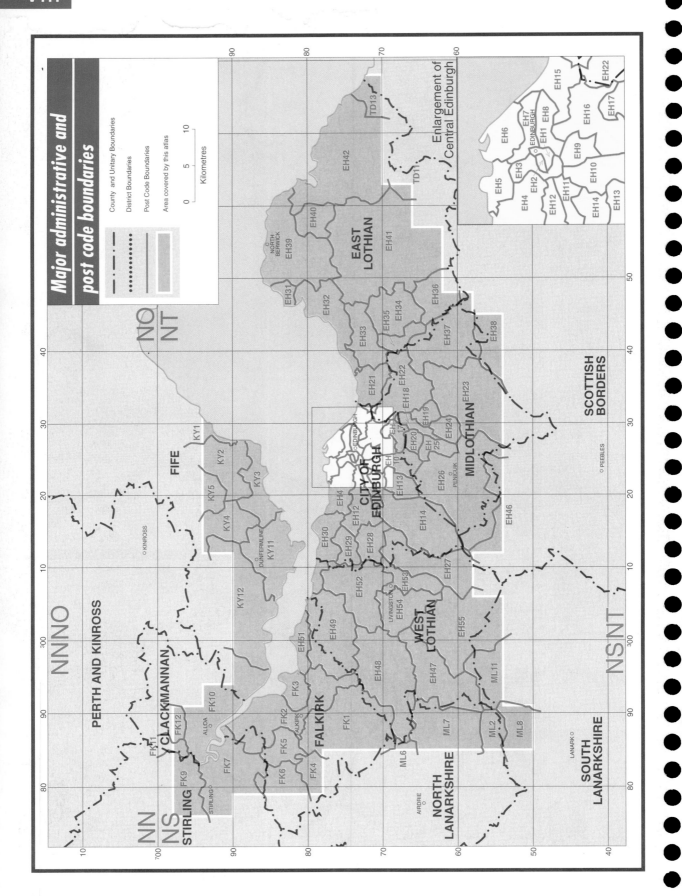

Major administrative and post code boundaries

County and Unitary Boundaries
District Boundaries
Post Code Boundaries
Area covered by this atlas

Kilometres
0 5 10

Enlargement of Central Edinburgh

EH1 EDINBURGH
EH2 EH3 EH4 EH5 EH6 EH7 EH8 EH9 EH10 EH11 EH12 EH13 EH14 EH15 EH16 EH17 EH22

PERTH AND KINROSS

NN NO
NS NT

CLACKMANNAN

STIRLING

FIFE

KINROSS

DUNFERMLINE

ALLOA

STIRLING

FALKIRK

FALKIRK

KY1 KY2 KY3 KY4 KY5 KY11 KY12

FK1 FK2 FK3 FK4 FK5 FK6 FK7 FK9 FK10 FK11 FK12

CITY OF EDINBURGH

EDINBURGH

EAST LOTHIAN

NORTH BERWICK

EH31 EH32 EH33 EH34 EH35 EH36 EH37 EH38 EH39 EH40 EH41 EH42

TD13
TD1

MIDLOTHIAN

PENICUIK

PEEBLES

WEST LOTHIAN

LIVINGSTON

EH21 EH18 EH22 EH19 EH20 EH24 EH25 EH26 EH23 EH46 EH30 EH29 EH28 EH27 EH12 EH4 EH14 EH13 EH52 EH53 EH54 EH55 EH49 EH51 EH48 EH47

NORTH LANARKSHIRE

AIRDRIE

SOUTH LANARKSHIRE

LANARK

SCOTTISH BORDERS

ML2 ML6 ML7 ML8 ML11

NN NO
NS NT

2

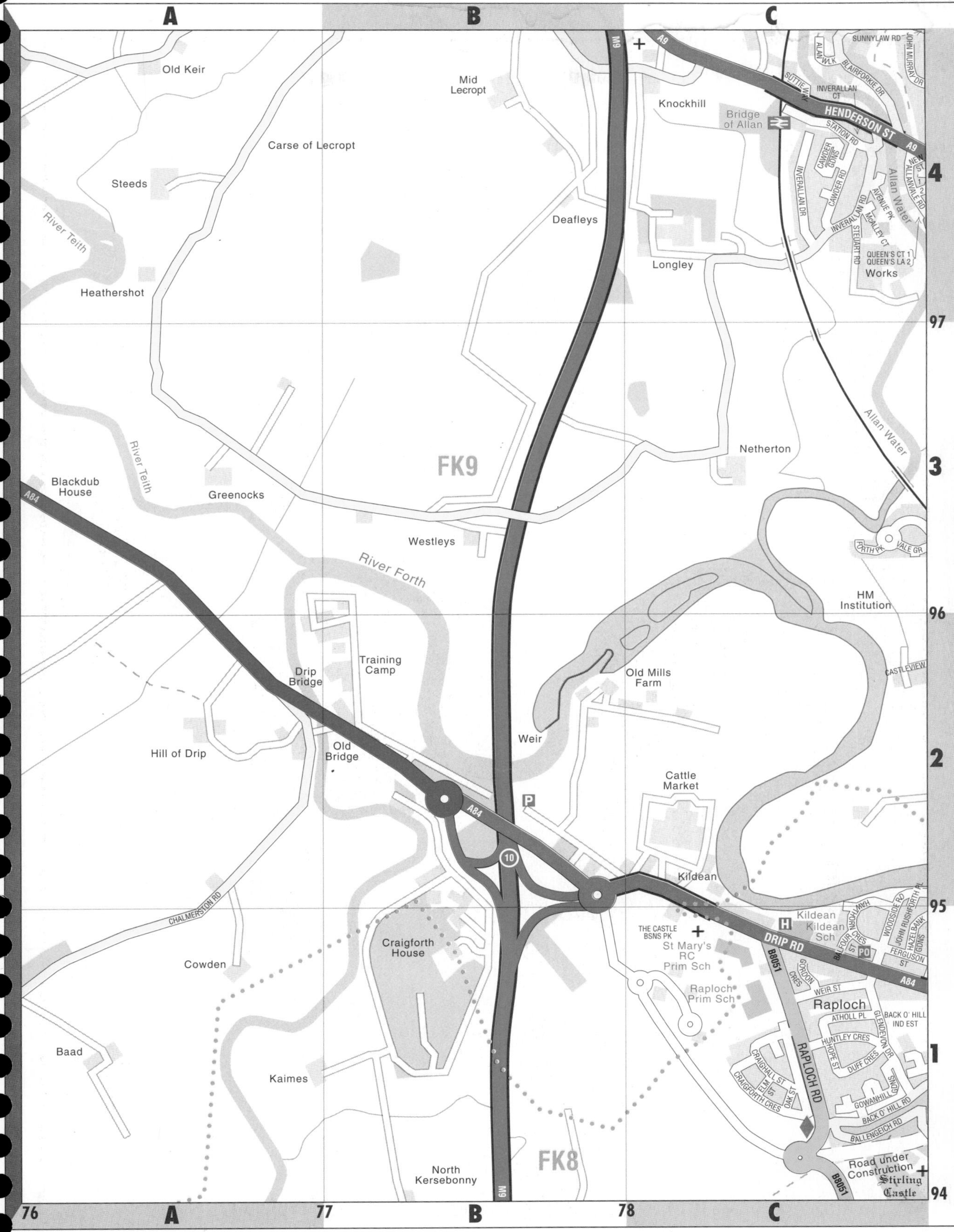

A
B
C
Old Keir
Mid Lecropt
Knockhill
Bridge of Allan
Carse of Lecropt
Steeds
River Teith
Deafleys
Longley
Works
Heathershot
97
FK9
Netherton
Allan Water
3
Blackdub House
River Teith
Greenocks
Westleys
River Forth
HM Institution
96
Training Camp
Drip Bridge
Old Mills Farm
Weir
Old Bridge
Hill of Drip
2
Cattle Market
A84
A9
M9
HENDERSON ST
STATION RD
INVERALLAN DR
CAWDER RD
SUNNYLAW RD
JOHN MURRAY DR
BLAIRFORKIE DR
ALLANVALE RD
FORTH PK
VALE GR
CASTLEVIEW
10
Kildean
95
CHALMERSTON RD
Craigforth House
THE CASTLE BSNS PK
St Mary's RC Prim Sch
Kildean Sch
DRIP RD
B8051
Raploch Prim Sch
Raploch
Cowden
WEIR ST
ATHOLL PL
BACK O' HILL IND EST
HUNTLEY CRES
DUFF CRES
GLENDEVON DR
RAPLOCH RD
CRAIGHALL ST
CRAIGFORTH CRES
GOWANHILL GDNS
BALLENGEICH RD
1
Baad
Kaimes
FK8
North Kersebonny
Road under Construction
Stirling Castle
94
76
A
77
B
78
C

6

2

1

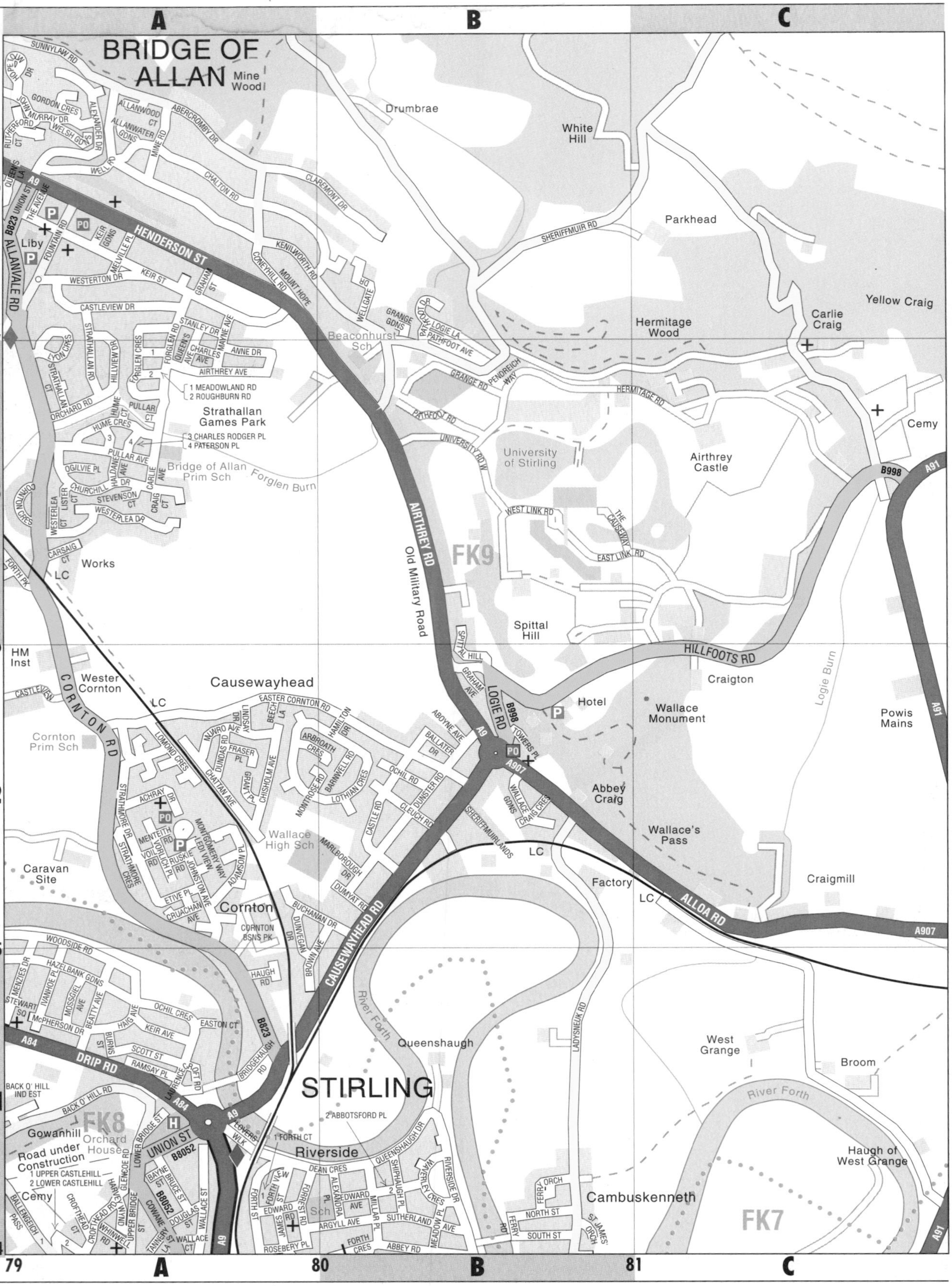
A
B
C
BRIDGE OF ALLAN
Mine Wood
Drumbrae
White Hill
Parkhead
Yellow Craig
Carlie Craig
Hermitage Wood
Beaconhurst Sch
Strathallan Games Park
Bridge of Allan Prim Sch
Forglen Burn
University of Stirling
Airthrey Castle
Cemy
FK9
Works
LC
Spittal Hill
HM Inst
Wester Cornton
Causewayhead
Cornton Prim Sch
Craigton
Hotel
Wallace Monument
Powis Mains
Logie Burn
Abbey Craig
Wallace's Pass
Wallace High Sch
Caravan Site
Factory
Craigmill
Cornton
CORNTON BSNS PK
Queenshaugh
River Forth
West Grange
Broom
STIRLING
Riverside
Cambuskenneth
Haugh of West Grange
FK7
FK8
Gowanhill
Orchard House
Road under Construction
1 UPPER CASTLEHILL
2 LOWER CASTLEHILL
BACK O' HILL IND EST
1 MEADOWLAND RD
2 ROUGHBURN RD
3 CHARLES RODGER PL
4 PATERSON PL
2 ABBOTSFORD PL
1 FORTH CT
SUNNYLAW RD
GORDON CRES
JOHN MURRAY DR
WELSH GDNS
ALEXANDER DR
ALLANWOOD CT
ALLANWATER GDNS
ABERCROMBY DR
MINE RD
WELL RD
CHALTON RD
CLAREMONT DR
HENDERSON ST
UNION ST
THE AVENUE
FOUNTAIN RD
KEIR GDNS
MELVILLE PL
KEIR ST
GRAHAM ST
WESTERTON DR
ALLANVALE RD
CASTLEVIEW DR
CONEYHILL RD
MOUNT HOPE
KENILWORTH RD
WELLGATE DR
GRANGE GDNS
LOGIE LA
PATHFOOT AVE
SHERIFFMUIR RD
HERMITAGE RD
PENDREICH WAY
GRANGE RD
PATHFOOT RD
UNIVERSITY RD W
WEST LINK RD
THE CAUSEWAY
EAST LINK RD
HILLFOOTS RD
STANLEY DR
MAYNE AVE
QUEEN'S AVE
CHARLES AVE
ANNE DR
AIRTHREY AVE
FORGLEN RD
FORGLEN CRES
HILLVIEW DR
STRATHALLAN RD
STRATHALLAN CT
LYON CRES
ORCHARD RD
HUME CT
HUME CRES
PULLAR CT
PULLAR AVE
HALDANE AVE
OGILVIE PL
CHURCHILL DR
STEVENSON CT
WESTERLEA CT
LISTER CT
WESTERLEA DR
CARLIE AVE
CRAIG CT
CORNTON CRES
CARSAIG CT
FORTH PK
AIRTHREY RD
Old Military Road
SPITTAL HILL
GRAHAM AVE
LOGIE RD
B998
TOWERS PL
A907
A91
A9
B823
CASTLEVIEW
CORNTON RD
EASTER CORNTON RD
LINDSAY DR
BEECH LA
HAMILTON DR
ABOYNE AVE
BALLATER DR
ARBROATH CRES
BARNWELL RD
LOMOND CRES
MUNRO AVE
DUNDAS RD
FRASER PL
CHATTAN AVE
GRANT PL
CHISHOLM AVE
MONTROSE RD
LOTHIAN CRES
OCHIL RD
DUNSTER RD
CASTLE RD
CLEUCH RD
SHERIFFMUIRLANDS
WALLACE GDNS
CRAIG CRES
STRATHMORE DR
STRATHMORE CRES
ACHRAY DR
MENTEITH RD
VOIL RD
VORLICH PL
RUSKIE RD
MONTGOMERY WAY
LEDI VIEW
JOHNSTON AVE
ADAMSON PL
ETIVE PL
CRUACHAN AVE
MARLBOROUGH DR
DUMYAT RD
BUCHANAN DR
DUNVEGAN DR
BROWN AVE
HAUGH RD
CAUSEWAYHEAD RD
ALLOA RD
LADYSNEUK RD
WOODSIDE RD
MENZIES DR
HAZELBANK GDNS
IVANHOE PL
MOSSGIEL AVE
BEATTY AVE
STEWART SQ
McPHERSON DR
OCHIL CRES
EASTON CT
KEIR AVE
HAIG AVE
BURNS ST
SCOTT ST
RAMSAY PL
LAURENCRE CROFT RD
BRIDGEHAUGH RD
A84
DRIP RD
BACK O' HILL RD
LOWER BRIDGE ST
UNION ST
B8052
LOVERS WLK
BAYNE ST
BRUCE ST
COWANE ST
DOUGLAS ST
WALLACE ST
WALLACE CT
TANNERY LA
UPPER BRIDGE ST
GLENCOE RD
HARVEY WYND
WHINWELL RD
CROFTHEAD RD
CROFTHEAD CT
BALLENGEICH PASS
FORTH VIEW
FORTH ST
EDWARD RD
JAMES ST
FORREST RD
DEAN CRES
ALEXANDRA PL
EDWARD AVE
ARGYLL AVE
MILLAR PL
SHIPHAUGH PL
QUEENSHAUGH DR
WAVERLEY CRES
RIVERSIDE DR
SUTHERLAND AVE
MEADOW PL
FORTH CRES
ABBEY RD
ROSEBERY PL
FERRY ORCH
NORTH ST
SOUTH ST
FERRY RD
ST JAMES' ORCH
4
97
3
96
2
95
1
94
79
80
81

1
7

4

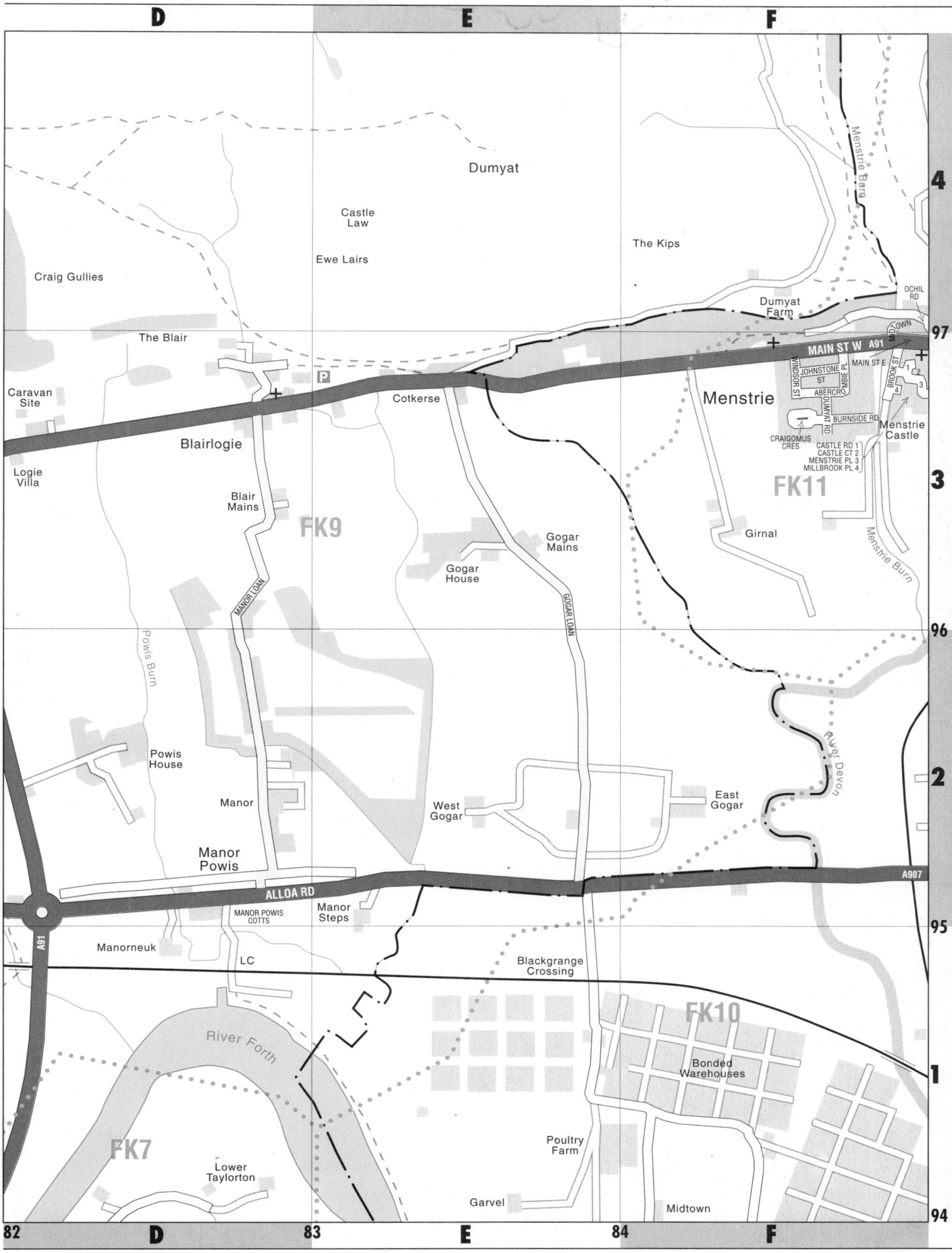
D
E
F
Dumyat
Castle
Law
Ewe Lairs
The Kips
Craig Gullies
Dumyat
Farm
OCHIL
RD
The Blair
MAIN ST W
A91
MAIN ST E
JOHNSTONE
ST
WINDSOR ST
ABERCRO
MBIE PL
DUMYAT RD
BURNSIDE RD
BROOK ST
Menstrie Burn
Caravan
Site
Cotkerse
Menstrie
Menstrie
Castle
CRAIGOMUS
CRES
CASTLE RD 1
CASTLE CT 2
MENSTRIE PL 3
MILLBROOK PL 4
Blairlogie
Logie
Villa
FK11
Blair
Mains
FK9
Gogar
Mains
Girnal
Gogar
House
MANOR LOAN
GOGAR LOAN
Powis Burn
River Devon
Powis
House
East
Gogar
West
Gogar
Manor
Manor
Powis
ALLOA RD
A907
MANOR POWIS
COTTS
Manor
Steps
A91
Manorneuk
LC
Blackgrange
Crossing
River Forth
FK10
Bonded
Warehouses
FK7
Lower
Taylorton
Poultry
Farm
Garvel
Midtown
4
3
2
1
97
96
95
94
82
83
84

8

4

3

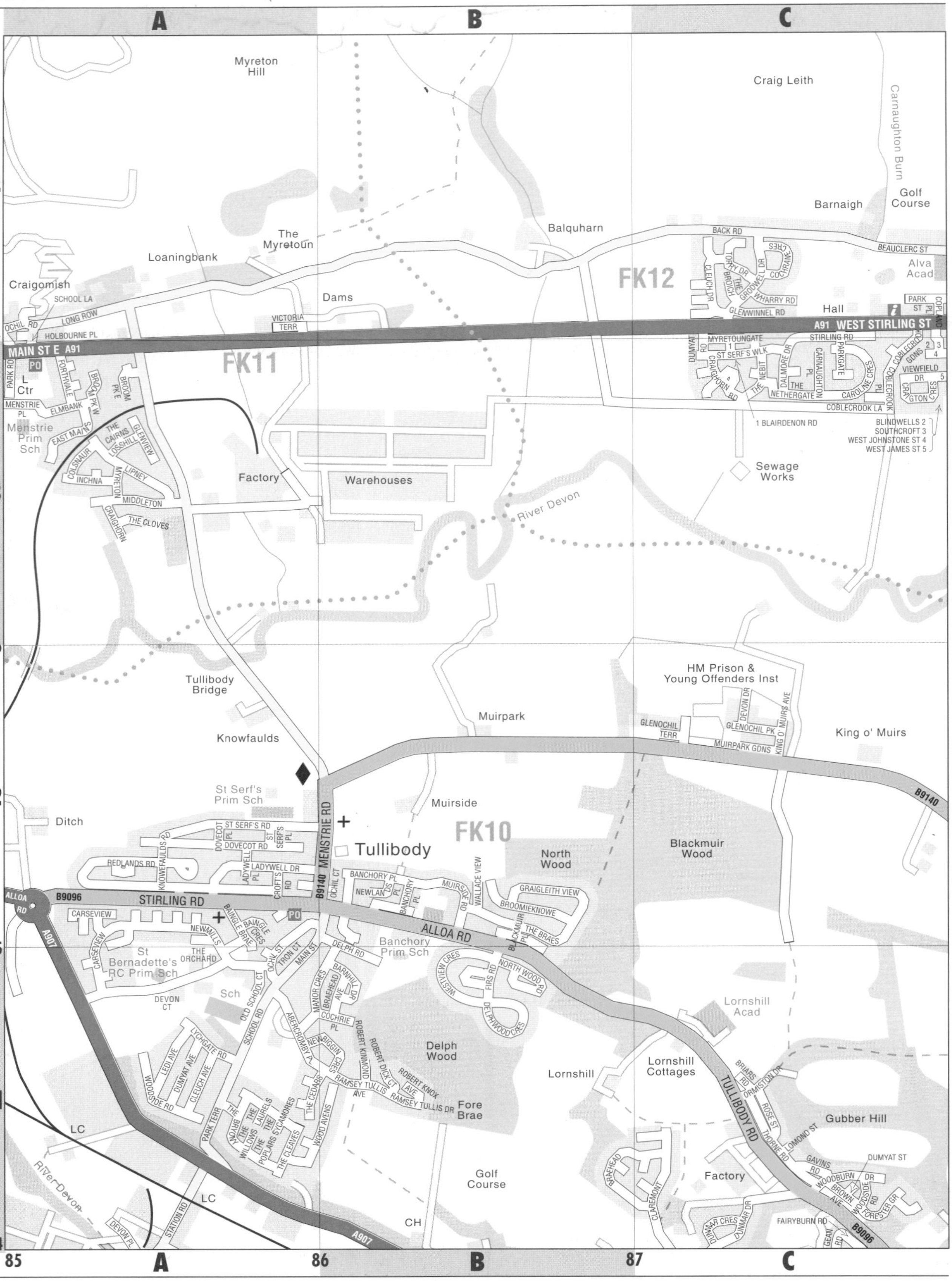
A
B
C
Myreton Hill
Craig Leith
Carnaughton Burn
Golf Course
Barnaigh
Balquharn
The Myretoun
Loaningbank
Craigomish
SCHOOL LA
LONG ROW
OCHIL RD
HOLBOURNE PL
Dams
VICTORIA TERR
FK12
BACK RD
BEAUCLERC ST
Alva Acad
PARK ST
Hall
A91 WEST STIRLING ST
MAIN ST E A91
FK11
PO
L Ctr
MENSTRIE PL
ELMBANK
Menstrie Prim Sch
EAST MAINS
THE CAIRNS
GLENVIEW
COLSNAUR
INCHNA
LIPNEY
MYRETON
MIDDLETON
CRAIGHORN
THE CLOVES
Factory
Warehouses
River Devon
Sewage Works
MYRETOUNGATE
ST SERF'S WLK
STIRLING RD
COBLECROOK LA
1 BLAIRDENON RD
BLINDWELLS 2
SOUTHCROFT 3
WEST JOHNSTONE ST 4
WEST JAMES ST 5
VIEWFIELD
GLENWINNEL RD
WHARRY RD
4
3
97
96
95
2
1
94
HM Prison & Young Offenders Inst
Tullibody Bridge
Knowfaulds
Muirpark
King o' Muirs
GLENOCHIL TERR
GLENOCHIL PK
MUIRPARK GDNS
MUIRS AVE
B9140
St Serf's Prim Sch
Muirside
FK10
Tullibody
Ditch
ST SERF'S RD
DOVECOT RD
REDLANDS RD
LADYWELL DR
MENSTRIE RD
Blackmuir Wood
North Wood
ALLOA RD
B9096
STIRLING RD
CARSEVIEW
ALLOA RD
A907
St Bernadette's RC Prim Sch
THE ORCHARD
Sch
DEVON CT
Banchory Prim Sch
BANCHORY PL
NEWLAN
WALLACE VIEW
GRAIGLEITH VIEW
BROOMIEKNOWE
THE BRAES
WESTVIEW CRES
FIRS RD
NORTH WOOD RD
DELPHWOOD CRES
Delph Wood
Lornshill Acad
Lornshill
Lornshill Cottages
TULLIBODY RD
Gubber Hill
Fore Brae
RAMSEY TULLIS DR
Golf Course
Factory
CH
LC
LC
River Devon
STATION RD
DEVON PL
A907
DUMYAT ST
FAIRYBURN RD
DUMMAR CRES
85
86
87

3
9

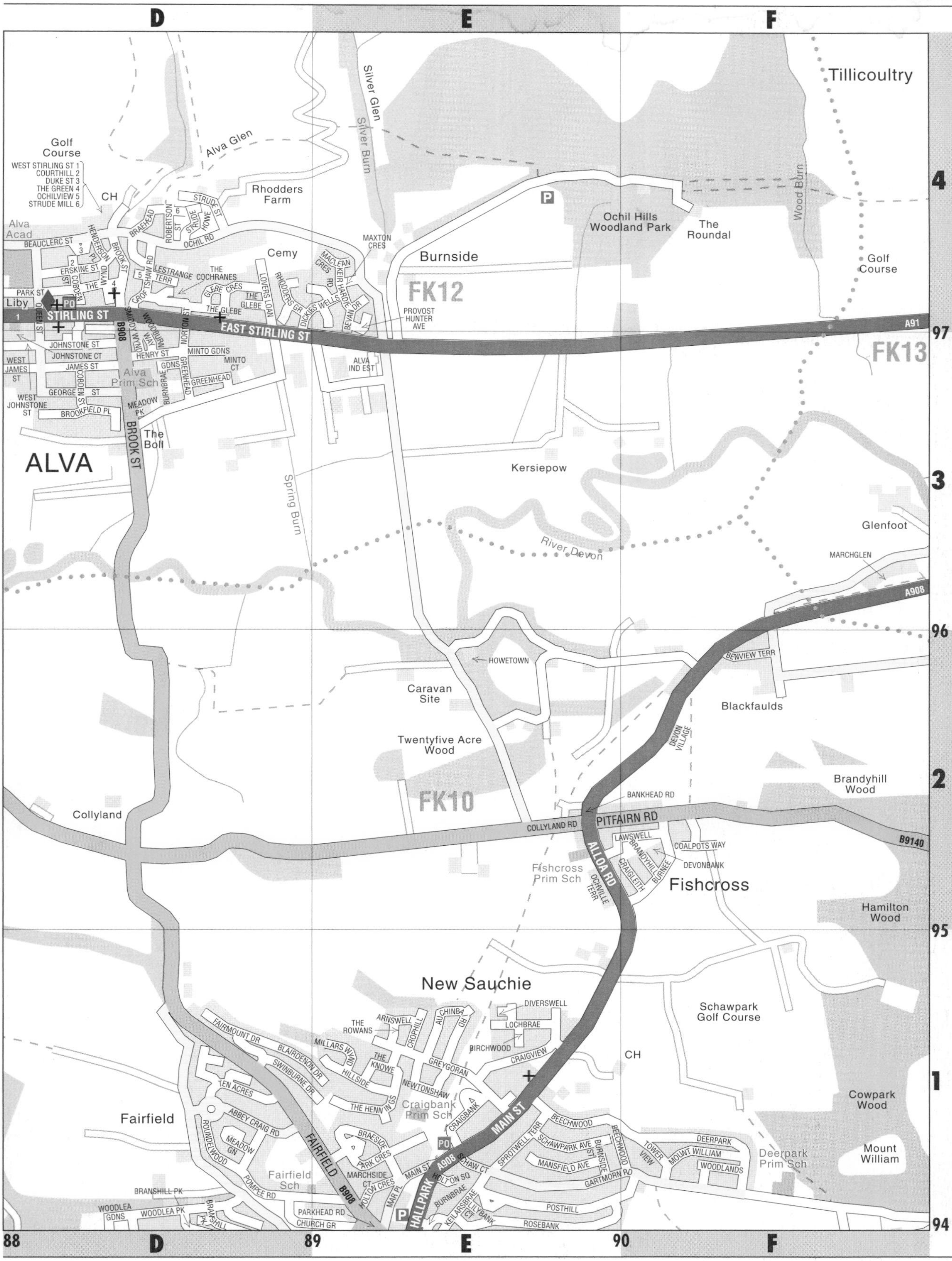
D
E
F
4
97
3
96
2
95
1
94
88
89
90
Tillicoultry
Golf Course
WEST STIRLING ST 1
COURTHILL 2
DUKE ST 3
THE GREEN 4
OCHILVIEW 5
STRUDE MILL 6
CH
Alva Acad
Alva Glen
Silver Glen
Silver Burn
Wood Burn
Rhodders Farm
Ochil Hills Woodland Park
The Roundal
Golf Course
Cemy
Burnside
FK12
FK13
MAXTON CRES
PROVOST HUNTER AVE
STIRLING ST
EAST STIRLING ST
A91
B908
Liby
PO
ALVA IND EST
Alva Prim Sch
BROOK ST
The Boll
ALVA
Kersiepow
Spring Burn
River Devon
Glenfoot
MARCHGLEN
A908
HOWETOWN
Caravan Site
BENVIEW TERR
Blackfaulds
DEVON VILLAGE
Twentyfive Acre Wood
Brandyhill Wood
FK10
BANKHEAD RD
Collyland
COLLYLAND RD
PITFAIRN RD
B9140
ALLOA RD
LAWSWELL
COALPOTS WAY
DEVONBANK
Fishcross Prim Sch
Fishcross
Hamilton Wood
New Sauchie
DIVERSWELL
LOCHBRAE
Schawpark Golf Course
THE ROWANS
BIRCHWOOD
CRAIGVIEW
CH
FAIRMOUNT DR
BLAIRDENON DR
SWINBURNE DR
TEN ACRES
THE HENNINGS
Craigbank Prim Sch
MAIN ST
Cowpark Wood
Fairfield
ABBEY CRAIG RD
MEADOW GN
ROUNDELWOOD
FAIRFIELD
BEECHWOOD
SCHAWPARK AVE
MANSFIELD AVE
GARTMORN RD
TOWER VIEW
MOUNT WILLIAM
DEERPARK
WOODLANDS
Deerpark Prim Sch
Mount William
Fairfield Sch
POMPEE RD
BRANSHILL PK
WOODLEA GDNS
WOODLEA PK
PARKHEAD RD
CHURCH GR
HALLPARK
POSTHILL
ROSEBANK
BURNBRAE
SHAW CT
SPROTWELL TERR

10

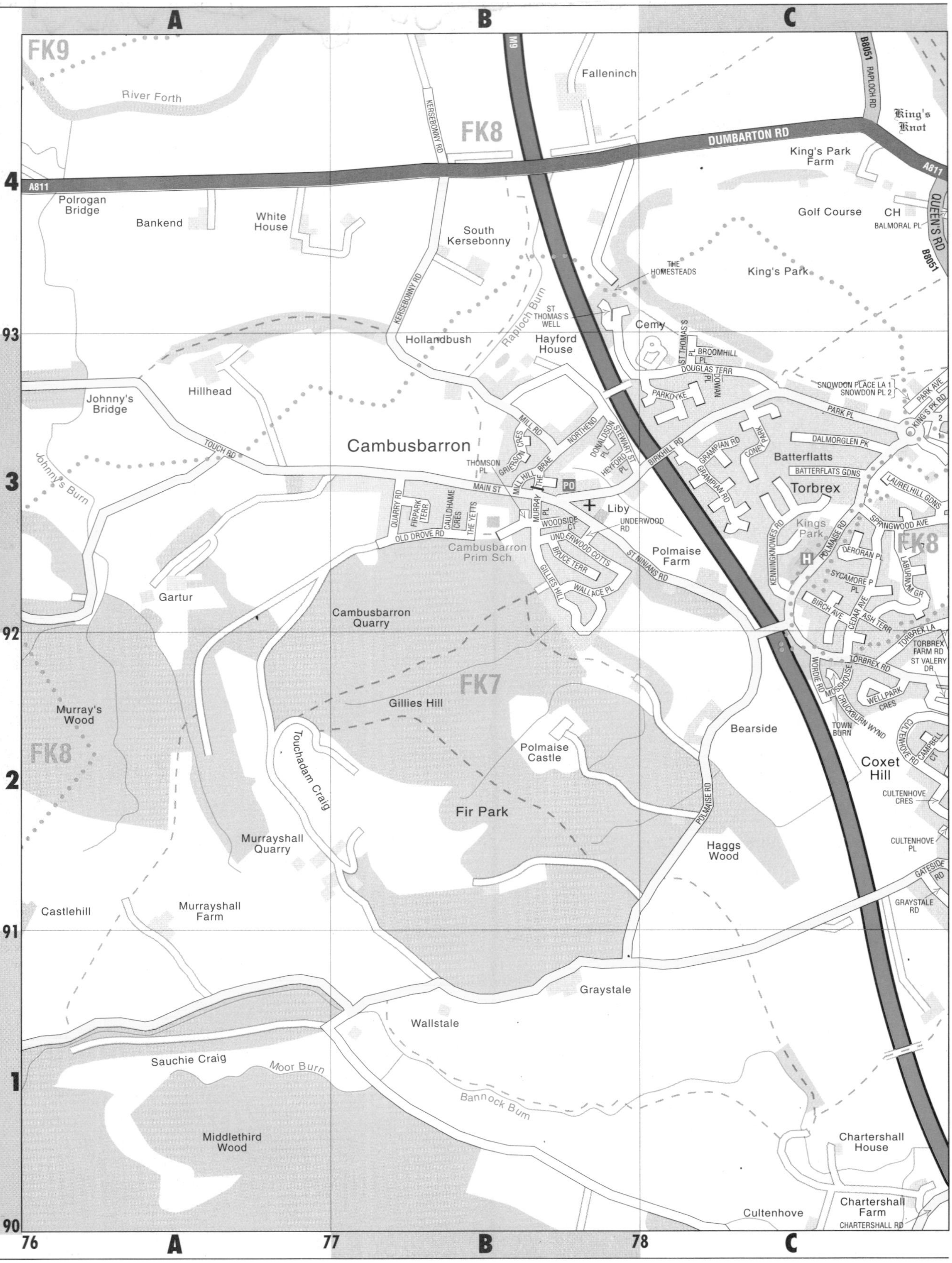

A   B   C

FK9

River Forth

Falleninch

KERSEBONNY RD

FK8

B8051 RAPLOCH RD

King's Knot

DUMBARTON RD

A811

QUEEN'S RD

B8051

4

A811

Polrogan Bridge

Bankend

White House

South Kersebonny

King's Park Farm

Golf Course   CH

BALMORAL PL

THE HOMESTEADS

King's Park

Raploch Burn

ST THOMAS'S WELL

Cemy

ST THOMAS'S

93

Hollandbush

Hayford House

BROOMHILL PL

Douglas TERR

PARKDYKE

SNOWDON PLACE LA 1
SNOWDON PL 2

PARK AVE

Johnny's Bridge

Hillhead

MILL RD

NORTHEND

STEWART ST

DONALDSON PL

BIRKHILL RD

GRAMPIAN RD

CONEY

KIPP

PARK RD

KING'S PK RD

DALMORGLEN PK

Batterflatts

BATTERFLATS GDNS

LAURELHILL GDNS

TOUCH RD

Cambusbarron

THOMSON PL

GRIESPY CRES

HEYFORD PL

GRAMPIAN RD

Torbrex

SPRINGWOOD AVE

FK8

3

Johnny's Burn

MAIN ST

MILL HILL BRAE

THE

MURRAY ST

PO

Liby

UNDERWOOD RD

Kings Park

POLMAISE RD

DERORAN PL

LAURELHILL

QUARRY RD

FIRPARK TERR

CAULDHAME CRES

THE YETTS

WOODSIDE CT

UNDERWOOD COTTS

ST NINIANS RD

Polmaise Farm

KENNINGKNOWES RD

SYCAMORE P

ASH TERR

TORBREX LA

Gartur

OLD DROVE RD

Cambusbarron Prim Sch

BRUCE TERR

GILLIES HILL

WALLACE PL

BIRCH AVE

CEDAR AVE

TORBREX RD

TORBREX FARM RD

ST VALERY DR

92

Cambusbarron Quarry

WORDIE RD

MOSSHOUSE

CRECKBURN WYND

WELLPARK

GATESIDE RD

Murray's Wood

FK7

Gillies Hill

TOWN BURN

Coxet Hill

CULTENHOVE CRES

FK8

Touchadam Craig

Polmaise Castle

Bearside

CULTENHOVE PL

2

Murrayshall Quarry

Fir Park

POLMAISE RD

Haggs Wood

GATESIDE

Castlehill

Murrayshall Farm

GRAYSTALE RD

91

Graystale

Bannock Burn

Chartershall House

1

Sauchie Craig

Moor Burn

Wallstale

Cultenhove

Chartershall Farm

CHARTERSHALL RD

Middlethird Wood

90

76   A   77   B   78   C

2
8

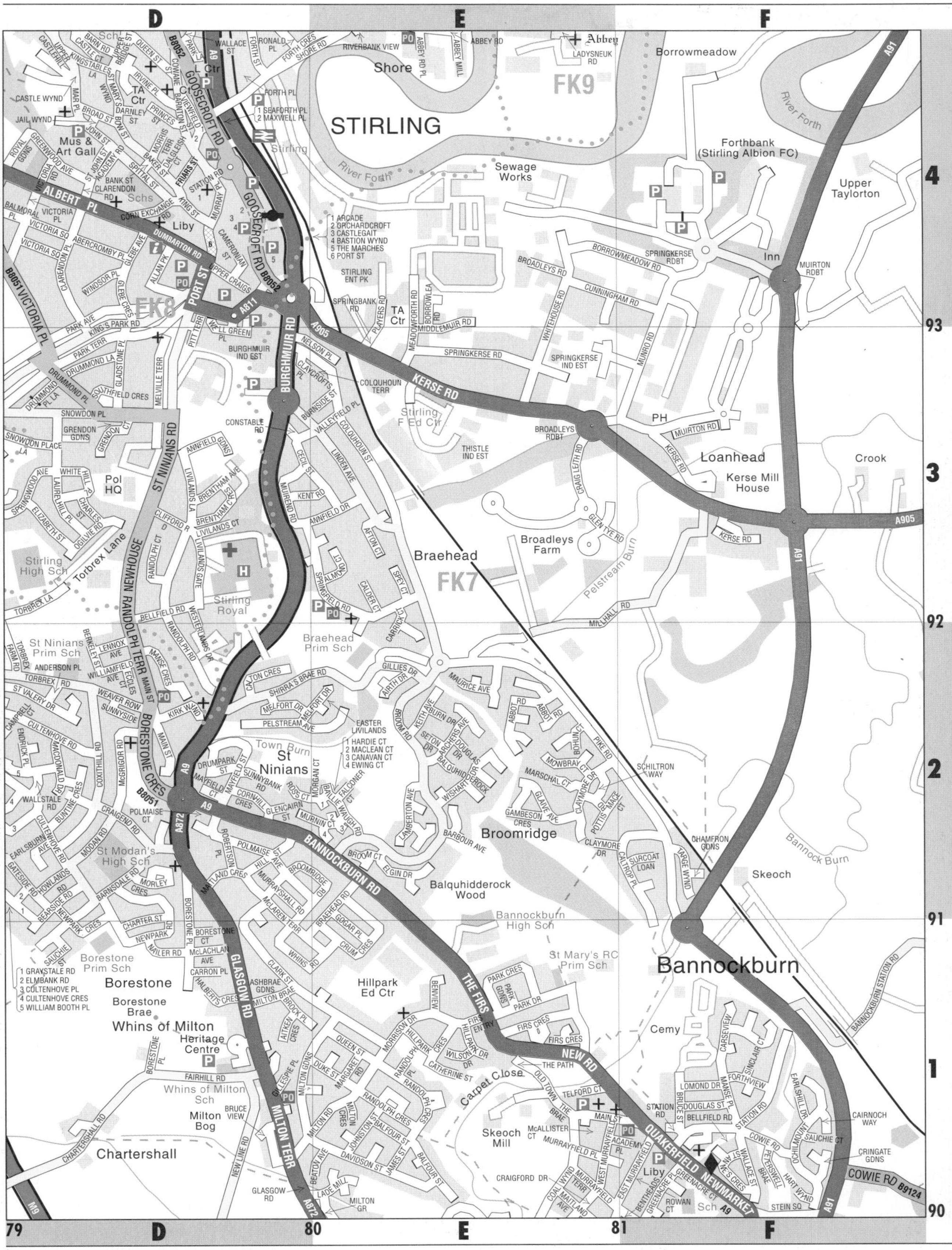
D
E
F
STIRLING
Shore
Abbey
Borrowmeadow
FK9
River Forth
Forthbank
(Stirling Albion FC)
Sewage
Works
Upper
Taylorton
Mus &
Art Gall
TA
Ctr
L Ctr
Liby
Schs
ALBERT PL
DUMBARTON RD
GOOSECROFT RD
FK8
PORT ST
BURGHMUIR RD
KERSE RD
A905
A91
A9
A811
B8052
B8051
Stirling
Inn
MUIRTON RDBT
SPRINGKERSE RDBT
BROADLEYS RDBT
BORROWMEADOW RD
CUNNINGHAM RD
SPRINGKERSE RD
SPRINGKERSE IND EST
BURGHMUIR IND EST
STIRLING ENT PK
TA
Ctr
THISTLE IND EST
Stirling
F Ed Ctr
PH
Loanhead
Crook
Kerse Mill
House
Broadleys
Farm
Braehead
FK7
Pelstream Burn
MILLHALL RD
Pol
HQ
ST NINIANS RD
Stirling
High Sch
Torbrex Lane
Stirling
Royal
NEWHOUSE
RANDOLPH TERR
Braehead
Prim Sch
St Ninians
Prim Sch
St
Ninians
Town Burn
BORESTONE CRES
Broomridge
Balquhidderock
Wood
St Modan's
High Sch
BANNOCKBURN RD
Bannock Burn
Skeoch
Bannockburn
High Sch
Bannockburn
St Mary's RC
Prim Sch
Hillpark
Ed Ctr
THE FIRS
NEW RD
Borestone
Prim Sch
Borestone
Borestone
Brae
Whins of Milton
Heritage
Centre
GLASGOW RD
Whins of Milton
Sch
Milton
Bog
Chartershall
MILTON TERR
Carpet Close
Skeoch
Mill
Cemy
Liby
QUAKERFIELD
NEWMARKET
COWIE RD B9124
BANNOCKBURN STATION RD
M9
A872
4
93
3
92
2
91
1
90
79
80
81

19
8

7
3

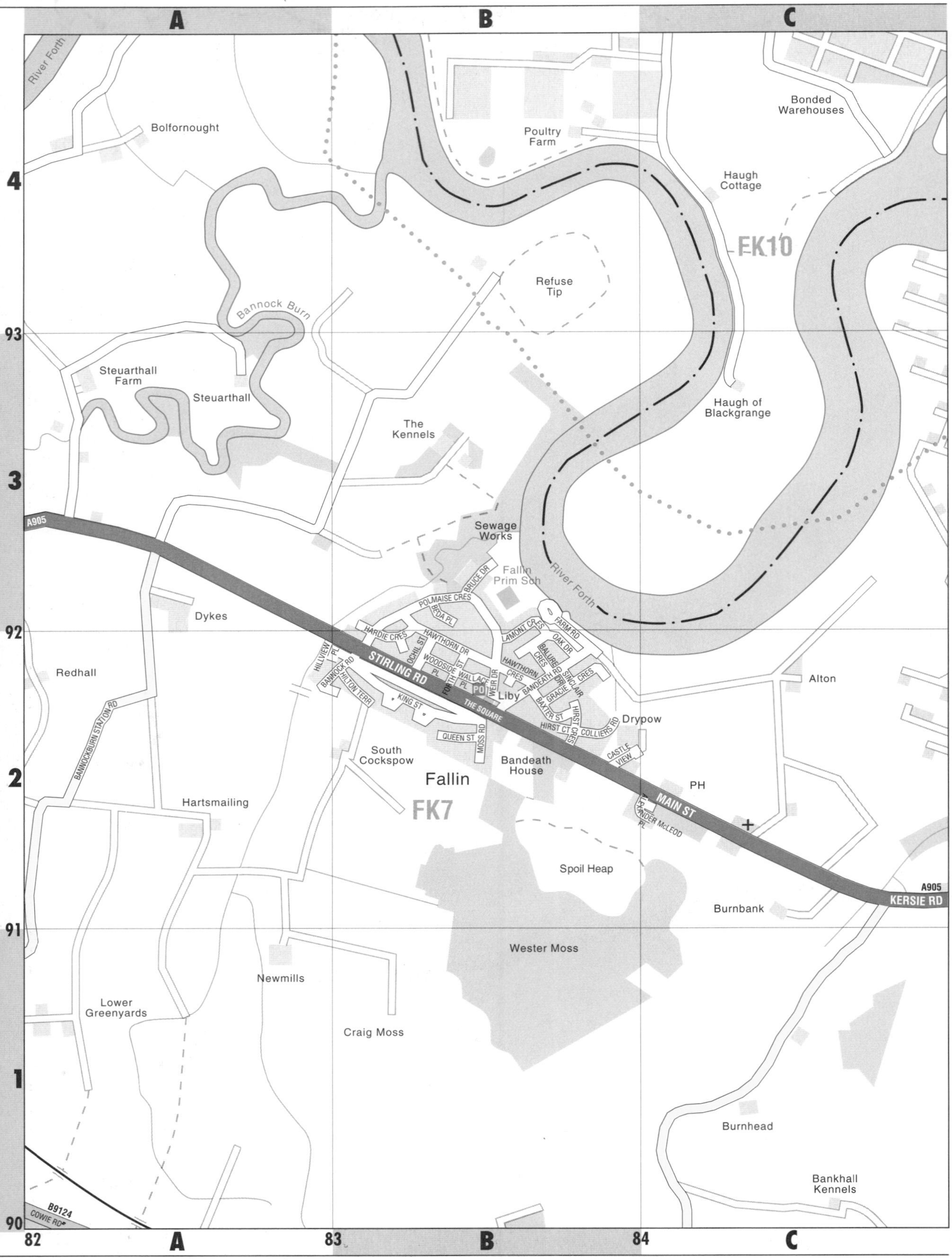
A
B
C
River Forth
Bolfornought
Poultry Farm
Bonded Warehouses
Haugh Cottage
FK10
Refuse Tip
Bannock Burn
Steuarthall Farm
Steuarthall
The Kennels
Haugh of Blackgrange
Sewage Works
Fallin Prim Sch
River Forth
A905
Dykes
Redhall
POLMAISE CRES
BRUCE DR
BRIDA PL
HARDIE CRES
HAWTHORN DR
LAMONT CRES
FARM RD
OAK DR
BALURE CRES
HILLVIEW PL
OCHIL ST
WOODSIDE PL
STIRLING RD
BANNOCK RD
HILTON TERR
KING ST
FORTH ST
WALLACE PL
WEIR DR
HAWTHORN CRES
BANDEATH RD
SINCLAIR CRES
GRACIE
BAXTER ST
HIRST CRES
HIRST CT
COLLIERS RD
PO
Liby
THE SQUARE
QUEEN ST
MOSS RD
Alton
Drypow
CASTLE VIEW
BANNOCKBURN STATION RD
South Cockspow
Bandeath House
Fallin
FK7
PH
MAIN ST
ALEXANDER McLEOD PL
Hartsmailing
Spoil Heap
A905
KERSIE RD
Burnbank
Wester Moss
Newmills
Lower Greenyards
Craig Moss
Burnhead
Bankhall Kennels
B9124
COWIE RD
4
93
3
92
2
91
1
90
82
83
84

7
20

D E F

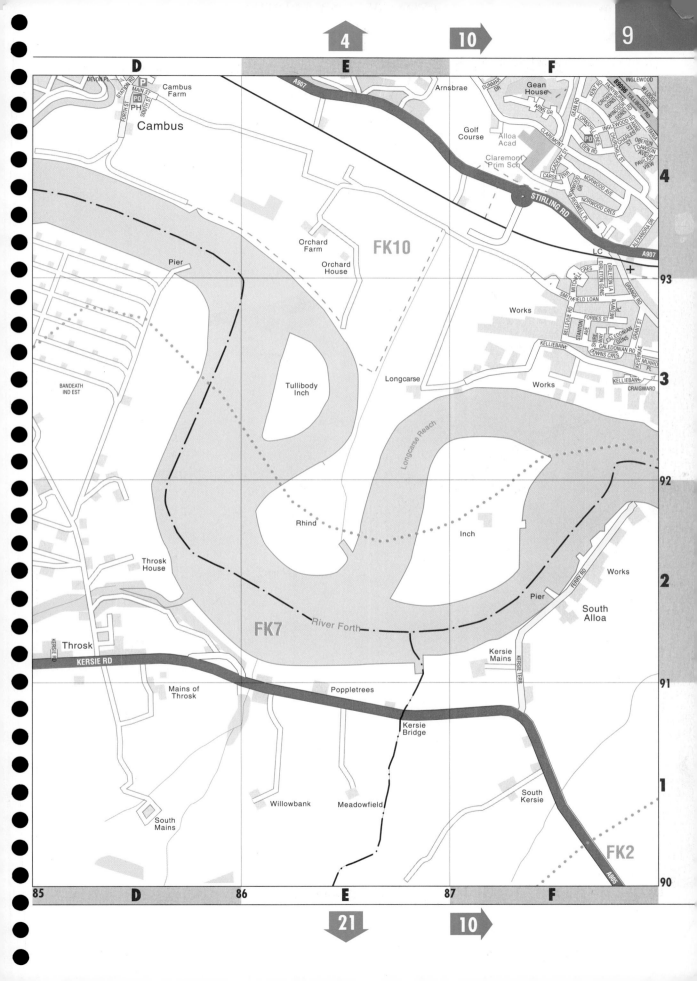
DEVON PL
STATION RD
P
MAIN ST
PO
PH
SOUTH ST
FORTH ST
Cambus Farm
Cambus
A907
Arnsbrae
DUNMAR DR
Gean House
ARNS GR
GEAN RD
KENT RD
FAIRYBURN RD
CROWN GDNS
B9096
TULLIBODY RD
INGLEWOOD
W LODGE GDNS
WINDSOR GDNS
LORNSHILL CRES
INGLEWOOD RD
ST ANNE
TITANIA
Golf Course
Alloa Acad
CLAREMONT
EDEN RD
PO
CHURCHILL ST
CHARLES ST
OBERON
DAWSON AVE
PAVILION VIEW
Claremont Prim Sch
ACADEMY ST
CARSE TERR
NORWOOD GR
NORWOOD AVE
NORWOOD CRES
REDWELL PL
STIRLING RD
ALEXANDRA DR
A907
LC
FK10
Orchard Farm
Orchard House
Pier
MITCHELL CRES
DIRLETON GDNS
DIRLETON LA
GRANGE RD
SMITHFIELD LOAN
Works
BELLEVUE RD
MEDWYN PL
FORBES ST
STANTON AVE
SHIRE WAY
CALEDONIAN GDNS
GRANT ST
CALEDONIAN RD
DOWNS CRES
KELLIEBANK
KEVERKAE
MUNRO PL
KELLIEBANK
CRAIGWARD
Longcarse
Works
BANDEATH IND EST
Tullibody Inch
Longcarse Reach
Rhind
Inch
Throsk House
Works
FERRY RD
Pier
South Alloa
FK7
River Forth
KERSIE RD
Throsk
KERSIE RD
Kersie Mains
KERSIE TERR
Mains of Throsk
Poppletrees
Kersie Bridge
South Kersie
Willowbank
Meadowfield
South Mains
FK2
A905

93
92
91
90
4
3
2
1

85 D 86 E 87 F

9
5

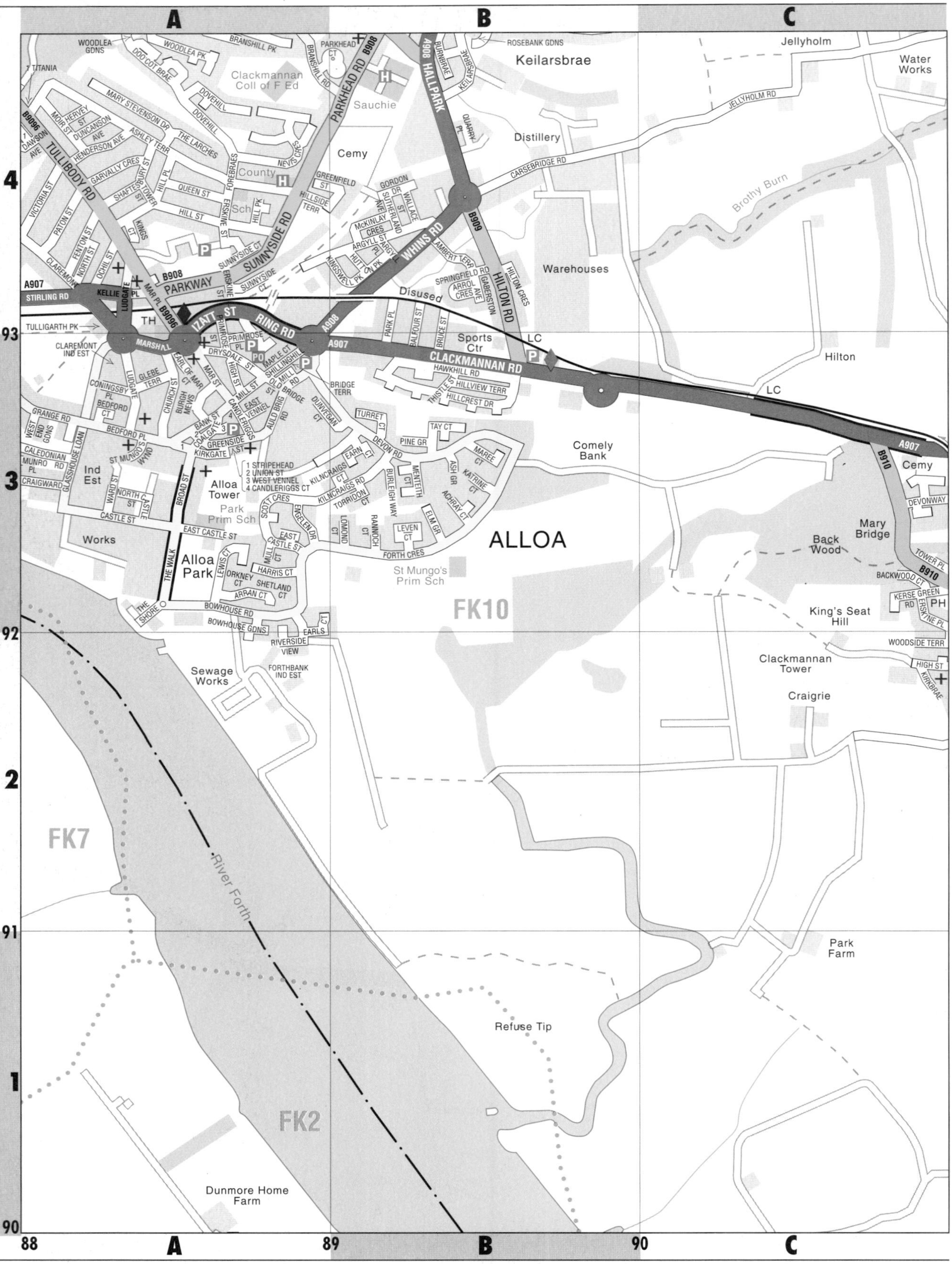
A
B
C
4
93
3
92
2
91
1
90
88
89
90
Jellyholm
Water Works
Keilarsbrae
ROSEBANK GDNS
JELLYHOLM RD
Distillery
CARSEBRIDGE RD
Brothy Burn
Warehouses
Hilton
LC
Clackmannan Coll of F Ed
Sauchie
Cemy
County
Sch
PARKHEAD
HALLPARK
A908
B909
HILTON RD
WHINS RD
SUNNYSIDE RD
PARKHEAD RD
B908
TULLIBODY RD
B9096
A907
STIRLING RD
PARKWAY
KELLIE PL
LUDGATE
Disused
ZATT ST
RING RD
CLACKMANNAN RD
Sports Ctr
TH
MARSHALL
CLAREMONT IND EST
TULLIGARTH PK
Ind Est
Works
Alloa Tower
Park Prim Sch
Alloa Park
THE WALK
BROAD ST
EAST CASTLE ST
CASTLE ST
BOWHOUSE RD
BOWHOUSE GDNS
RIVERSIDE VIEW
FORTHBANK IND EST
Sewage Works
1 STRIPEHEAD
2 UNION ST
3 WEST VENNEL
4 CANDLERIGGS CT
St Mungo's Prim Sch
ALLOA
FK10
Comely Bank
Cemy
B910
Mary Bridge
Back Wood
King's Seat Hill
Clackmannan Tower
Craigrie
Park Farm
Refuse Tip
FK7
River Forth
FK2
Dunmore Home Farm

9
22

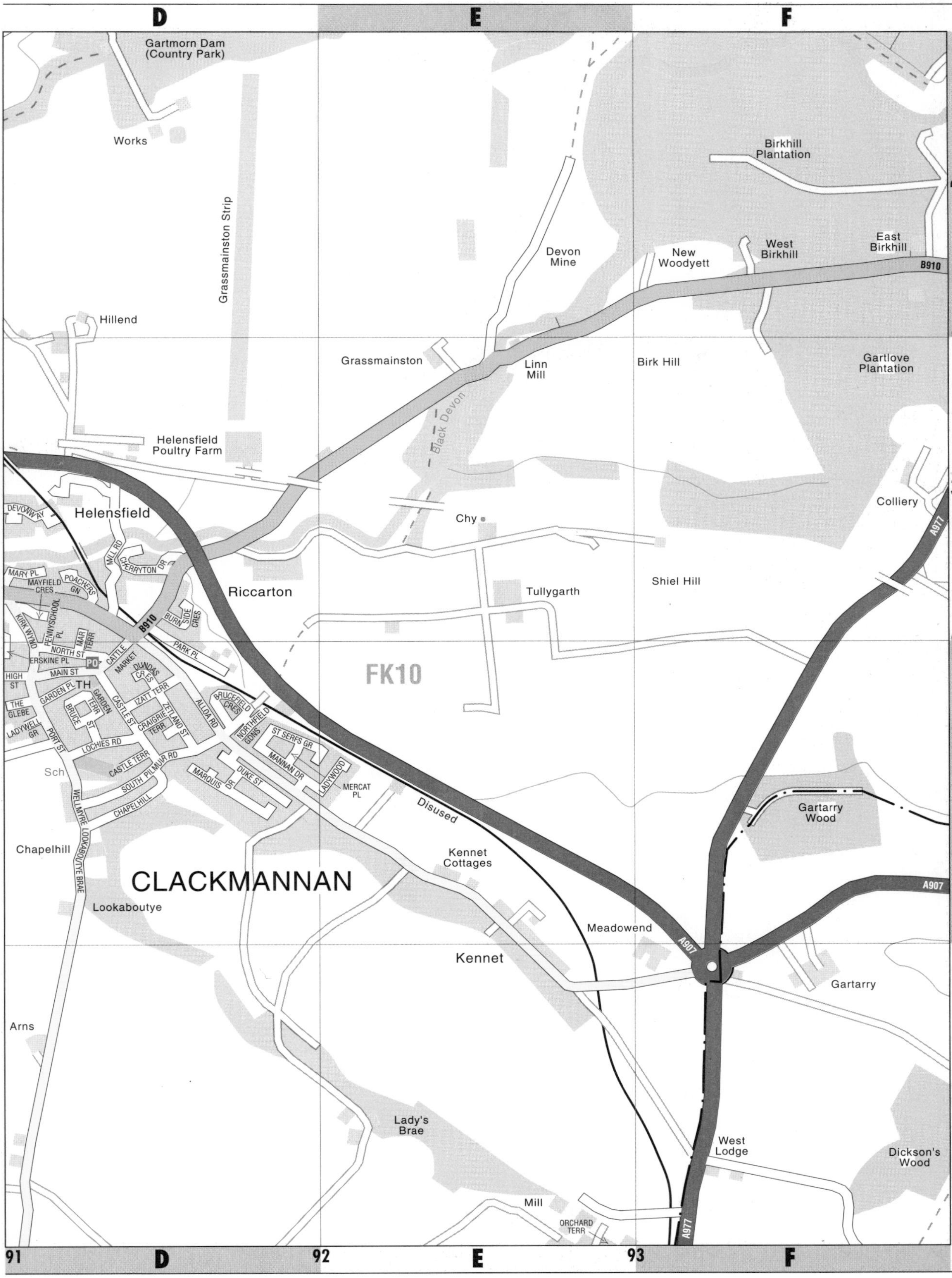
D
E
F
Gartmorn Dam (Country Park)
Works
Grassmainston Strip
Birkhill Plantation
4
Devon Mine
New Woodyett
West Birkhill
East Birkhill
B910
Hillend
93
Grassmainston
Linn Mill
Birk Hill
Gartlove Plantation
Black Devon
Helensfield Poultry Farm
3
Helensfield
Chy
Colliery
A977
Riccarton
Tullygarth
Shiel Hill
92
FK10
TH
PO
Sch
2
Disused
MERCAT PL
Gartarry Wood
Chapelhill
Kennet Cottages
CLACKMANNAN
A907
Lookaboutye
Meadowend
91
Kennet
Gartarry
Arns
1
Lady's Brae
West Lodge
Dickson's Wood
Mill
ORCHARD TERR
90
91
92
93

23

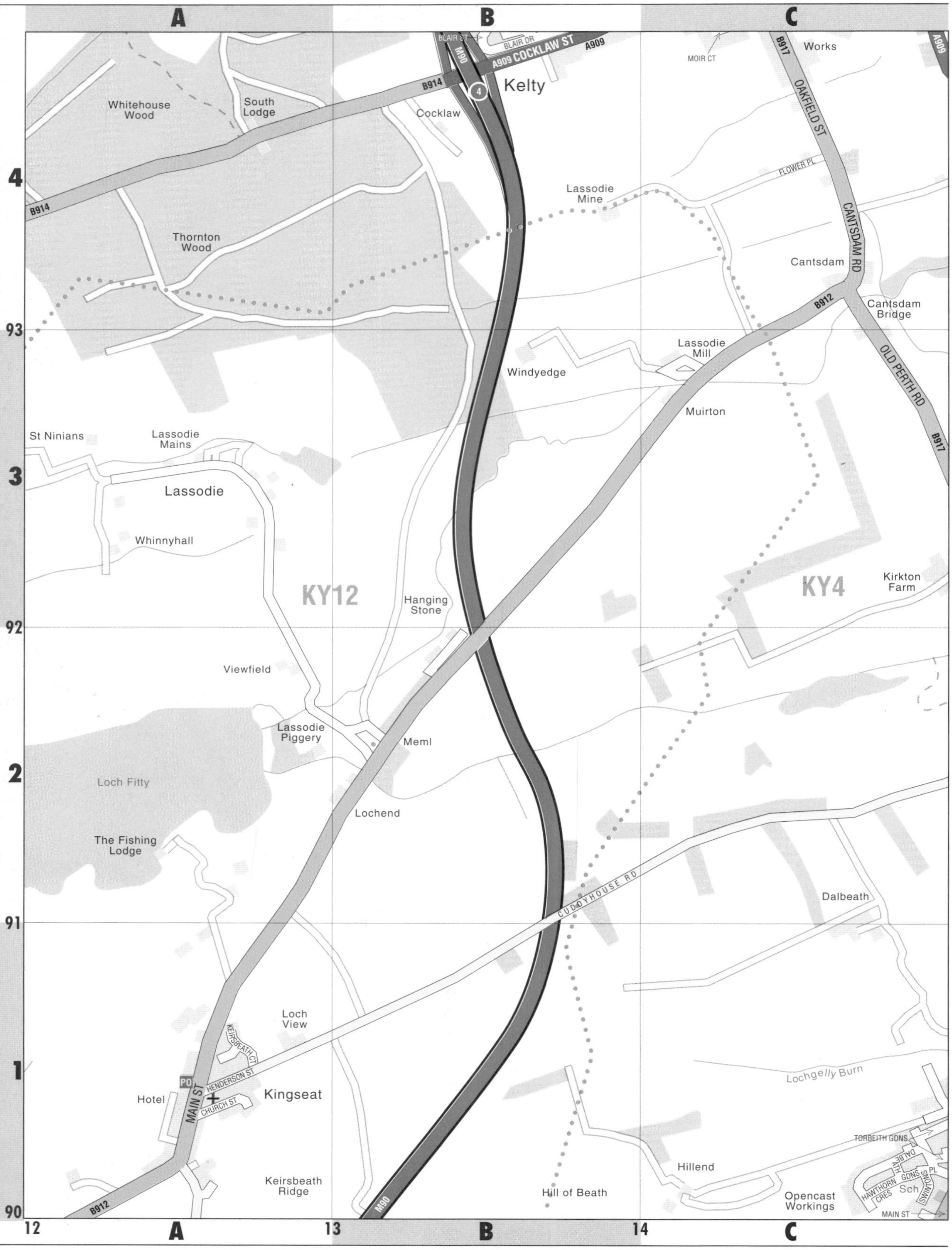
A
B
C
4
93
3
92
2
91
1
90
12
13
14
BLAIR ST
BLAIR DR
A909 COCKLAW ST
A909
M90
B914
Kelty
Cocklaw
MOIR CT
B917
Works
OAKFIELD ST
FLOWER PL
Whitehouse Wood
South Lodge
Thornton Wood
Lassodie Mine
CANTSDAM RD
Cantsdam
B912
Cantsdam Bridge
Lassodie Mill
Windyedge
OLD PERTH RD
Muirton
St Ninians
Lassodie Mains
Lassodie
Whinnyhall
KY12
Hanging Stone
KY4
Kirkton Farm
Viewfield
Lassodie Piggery
Meml
Loch Fitty
Lochend
The Fishing Lodge
CUDDYHOUSE RD
Dalbeath
Loch View
KEIRSBEATH CT
HENDERSON ST
PO
MAIN ST
CHURCH ST
Hotel
Kingseat
Lochgelly Burn
TORBEITH GDNS
Keirsbeath Ridge
Hill of Beath
Hillend
Opencast Workings
HAWTHORN CRES
Sch
MAIN ST

30

14

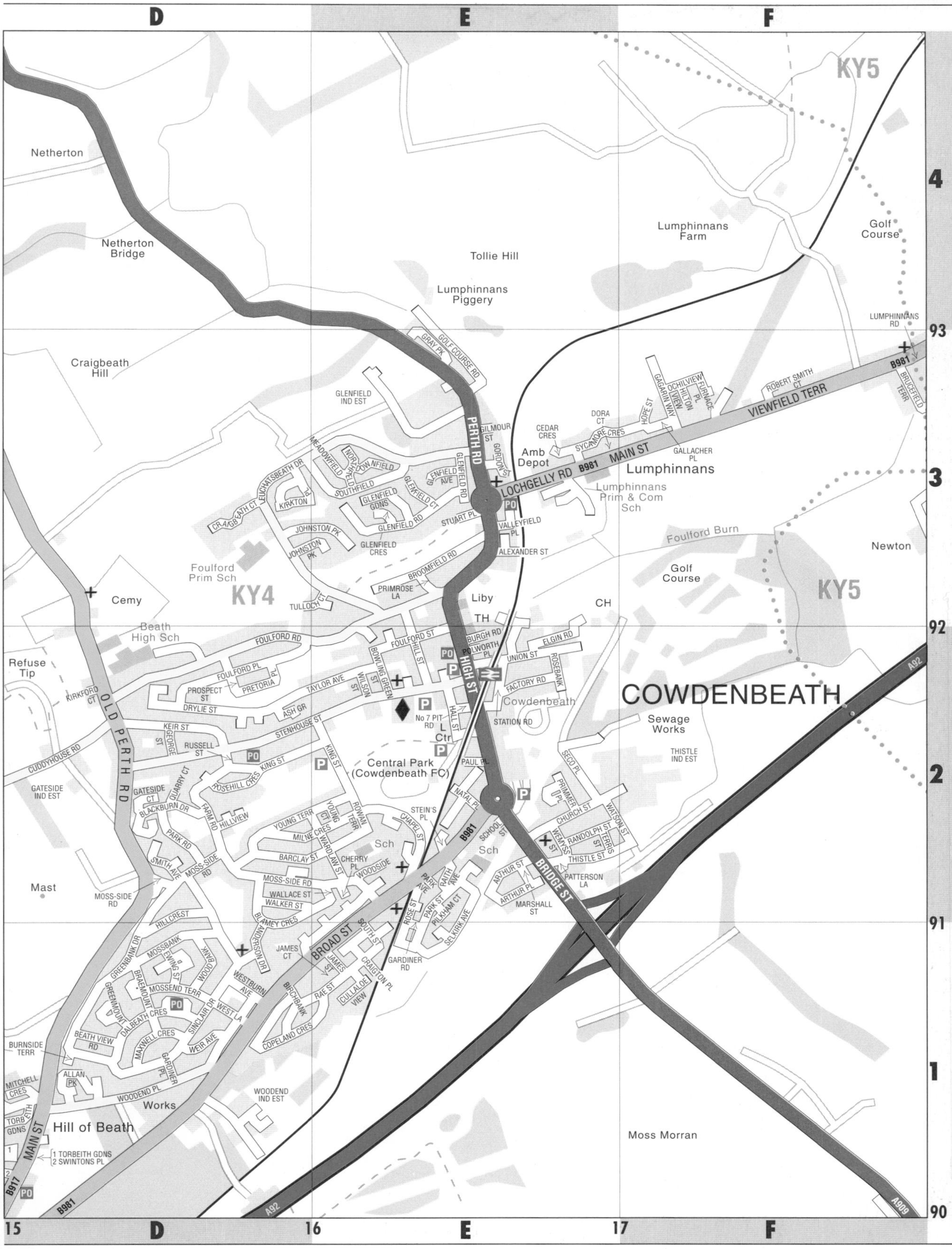
D
E
F
KY5
Netherton
4
Netherton Bridge
Tollie Hill
Lumphinnans Farm
Golf Course
Lumphinnans Piggery
Craigbeath Hill
93
LUMPHINNANS RD
GOLF COURSE RD
GRAY PK
GLENFIELD IND EST
PERTH RD
GILMOUR ST
GORDON ST
CEDAR CRES
DORA CT
SYCAMORE CRES
HOPE ST
GAGARIN WAY
OCHILVIEW
HILTON VIEW
FURNACE PL
ROBERT SMITH CT
VIEWFIELD TERR
B981
BRUCEFIELD TERR
GALLACHER PL
Amb Depot
MAIN ST
Lumphinnans
Lumphinnans Prim & Com Sch
LOCHGELLY RD
3
MEADOWFIELD
NORTHFIELD
DOWNFIELD
SOUTHFIELD
GLENFIELD AVE
GLENFIELD CT
GLENFIELD GDNS
GLENFIELD RD
GLENFIELD CRES
STUART PL
VALLEYFIELD PL
ALEXANDER ST
CRAIGBEATH CT
LEUCHATSBEATH DR
KIRKTON
JOHNSTON PK
Foulford Burn
Newton
Foulford Prim Sch
BROOMFIELD RD
Golf Course
KY4
KY5
Cemy
PRIMROSE LA
TULLOCH CT
Liby
TH
CH
Beath High Sch
92
FOULFORD RD
FOULFORD ST
BURGH RD
POLWORTH PL
ELGIN RD
UNION ST
ROSEBANK
Refuse Tip
FOULFORD PL
PRETORIA
BOWLING GREEN
HILL ST
HIGH ST
FACTORY RD
PROSPECT ST
KIRKFORD CT
TAYLOR AVE
WILSON ST
COWDENBEATH
Cowdenbeath
DRYLIE ST
ASH GR
No 7 PIT RD
HALL ST
STATION RD
Sewage Works
KEIR ST
STENHOUSE ST
L Ctr
A92
GEORGE ST
RUSSELL ST
THISTLE IND EST
OLD PERTH RD
CUDDYHOUSE RD
KING ST
Central Park (Cowdenbeath FC)
PAUL PL
SECO PL
GATESIDE IND EST
GATESIDE CT
QUARRY CT
ROSEHILL CRES
2
BLACKBURN DR
FARM RD
HILLVIEW
NATAL PL
PRIMMER PL
YOUNG TERR
YOUNG CT
ROWAN TERR
STEIN'S PL
CHAPEL ST
SCHOOL ST
CHURCH ST
WATSON ST
PARK RD
MILNE CRES
WARDLAW ST
Sch
B981
WEMYSS ST
RANDOLPH ST
TERRIS ST
BARCLAY ST
CHERRY PL
Sch
THISTLE ST
SMITH AVE
MOSS-SIDE RD
WOODSIDE
ARTHUR ST
ARTHUR PL
PATTERSON LA
Mast
MOSS-SIDE RD
MOSS-SIDE RD
WALLACE ST
WALKER ST
PARK AVE
RAITH AVE
BRIDGE ST
MARSHALL ST
HILLCREST
BLAMEY CRES
ROSE ST
PARK ST
PILKHAM CT
SELKIRK AVE
91
GREENBANK DR
MOSSBANK
ANDERSON DR
JAMES CT
SOUTH ST
BROAD ST
GARDINER RD
EWING ST
WOOD BANK
BRAEMOUNT
MOSSEND TERR
WESTBURN AVE
JAMES ST
CRAIGTON PL
GREENMOUNT
DALBEATH CRES
SINCLAIR DR
WEST LA
BIRCHBANK
RAE ST
CULLALOE VIEW
BEATH VIEW RD
MAXWELL CRES
WEIR AVE
COPELAND CRES
BURNSIDE TERR
GARDINER PL
1
MITCHELL CRES
ALLAN PK
WOODEND PL
Works
WOODEND IND EST
TORBEITH GDNS
Hill of Beath
MAIN ST
Moss Morran
1 TORBEITH GDNS
2 SWINTONS PL
B917
B981
A92
A909
90
15
16
17

31

14

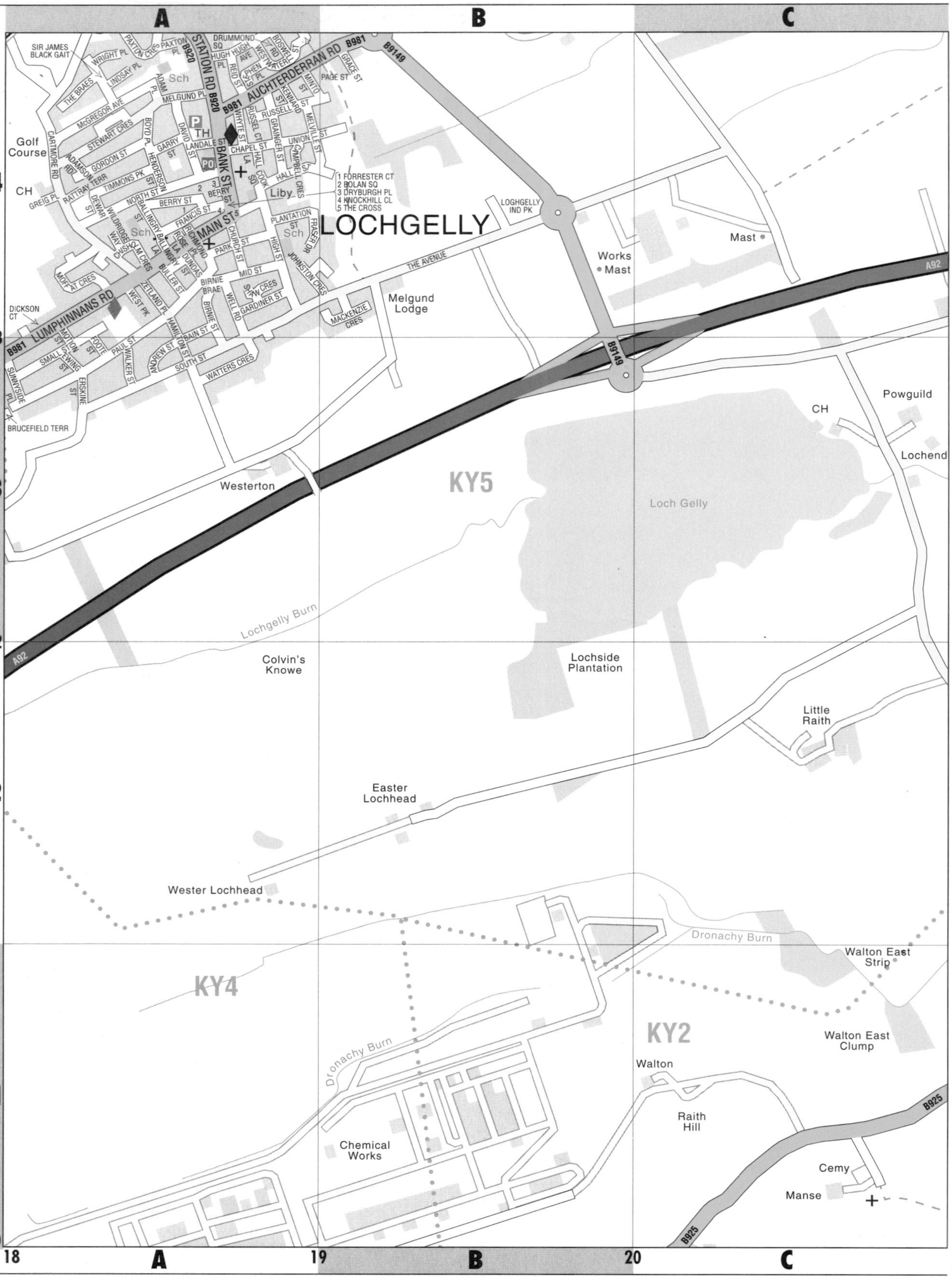

A B C

4

93

3

2

92

2

91

1

90

18 A 19 B 20 C

LOCHGELLY

KY5

KY4

KY2

Loch Gelly

Golf Course

CH

SIR JAMES BLACK GAIT

THE BRAES
WRIGHT PL
LINDSAY PL
PAXTON PL
PAXTON CRES
DRUMMOND SQ
HUGH PL
WEST WYND
REID ST
BOSWELL ST
GRACE ST
STATION RD
B920
B981

McGREGOR AVE
STEWART CRES
GORDON ST
MELGUND PL
B920
B981
TH
BANK ST
PO

AUCHTERDERRAN RD

B981
B9149

CARTMORE RD
ADMIRAL ST
RATTRAY ST
GREIG PL
BOYD ST
DAVID ST
GARRY ST
HENDERSON
LANDALE ST
CHAPEL ST
LA
CHAPEL HILL
RUSSELL ST
GRAINGER ST
MELVILLE ST
CAMPBELL ST
UNION ST

PAGE ST

LOCHGELLY IND PK

NORTH ALL PK
BERRY ST
FRANCIS ST
MAIN ST
BERRY ST
Liby

1 FORRESTER CT
2 ROLAN SQ
3 DRYBURGH PL
4 KNOCKHILL CL
5 THE CROSS

Works
Mast

Mast

CH

Powguild

Lochend

DEWAR
WILD
BALL
CHURCH ST
PLANTATION ST
HIGH ST
JOHNSTON CRES
FRASER DR
Sch
THE AVENUE

Sch
Sch

LUMPHINNANS RD
MOSSAT CRES
WEST PK
MID ST
SOUTH CRES
WELL RD
GARDINER ST
Melgund Lodge

DICKSON CT
SMALL ST
SWING
COTT
PAUL ST
WALKER ST
ANDREW ST
MAIN ST
BIRNIE ST
WATERS CRES
MACKENZIE CRES

B981
HAMILTON
ERSKINE
SUNNYSIDE
SOUTH ST

BRUCEFIELD TERR

Westerton

A92

B9149

Colvin's Knowe

Lochgelly Burn

Lochside Plantation

Little Raith

Easter Lochhead

Wester Lochhead

Dronachy Burn

Walton East Strip

Walton East Clump

Walton

Raith Hill

Chemical Works

Dronachy Burn

B925

Cemy

Manse

B925

A92

16

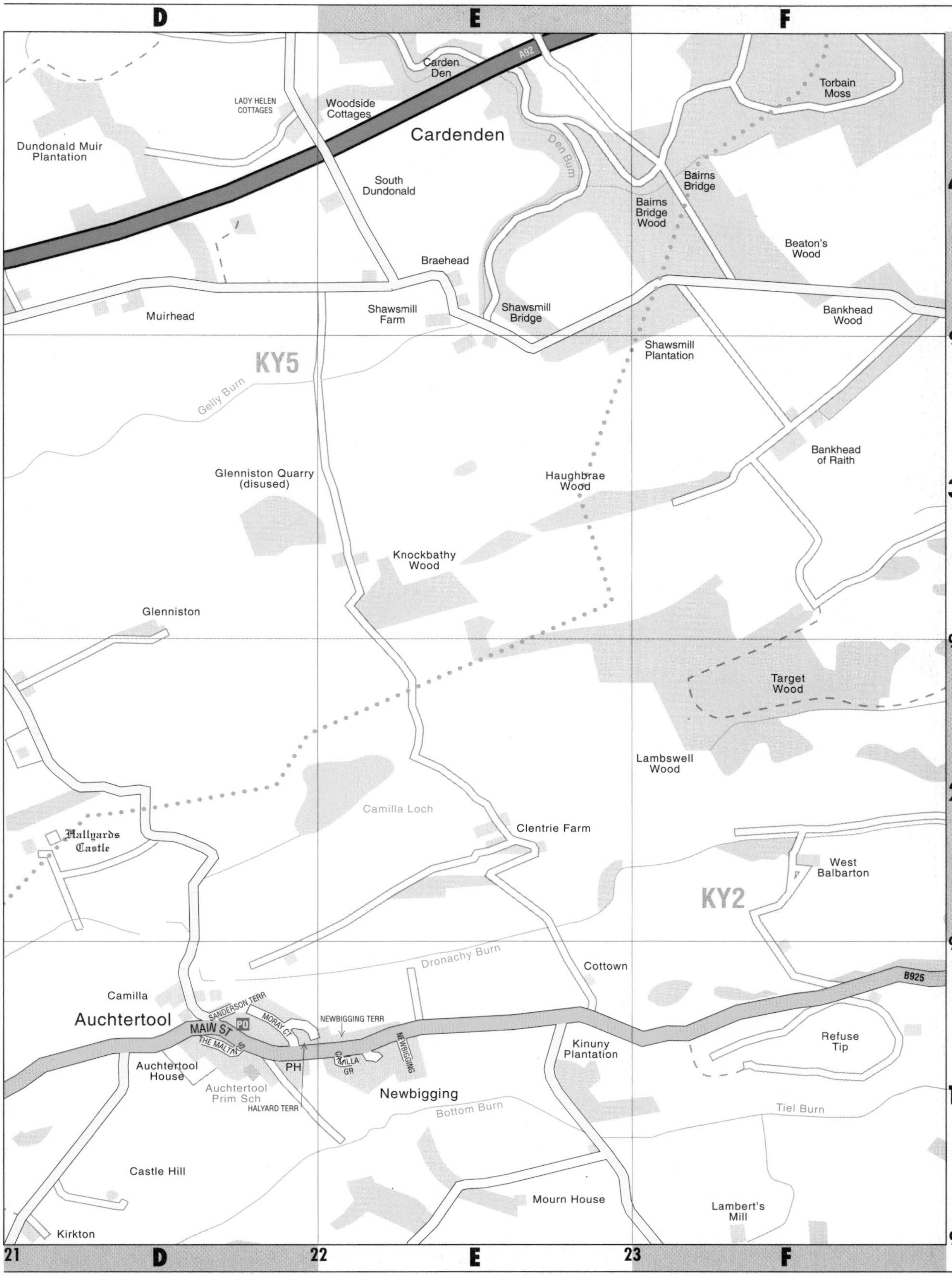
D
E
F
A92
Carden
Den
Torbain
Moss
LADY HELEN
COTTAGES
Woodside
Cottages
Cardenden
Den Burn
Dundonald Muir
Plantation
South
Dundonald
Bairns
Bridge
Bairns
Bridge
Wood
Beaton's
Wood
Braehead
Muirhead
Shawsmill
Farm
Shawsmill
Bridge
Bankhead
Wood
Shawsmill
Plantation
KY5
Gelly Burn
Bankhead
of Raith
Glenniston Quarry
(disused)
Haughbrae
Wood
Knockbathy
Wood
Glenniston
Target
Wood
Lambswell
Wood
Camilla Loch
Hallyards
Castle
Clentrie Farm
West
Balbarton
KY2
Dronachy Burn
Cottown
B925
Camilla
SANDERSON TERR
MORAY CT
NEWBIGGING TERR
Auchtertool
MAIN ST
PO
THE MALTINGS
CAMILLA GR
NEWBIGGING
Kinuny
Plantation
Refuse
Tip
Auchtertool
House
PH
Auchtertool
Prim Sch
HALYARD TERR
Newbigging
Bottom Burn
Tiel Burn
Castle Hill
Mourn House
Lambert's
Mill
Kirkton
4
93
3
92
2
91
1
90
21
22
23

33
16

15

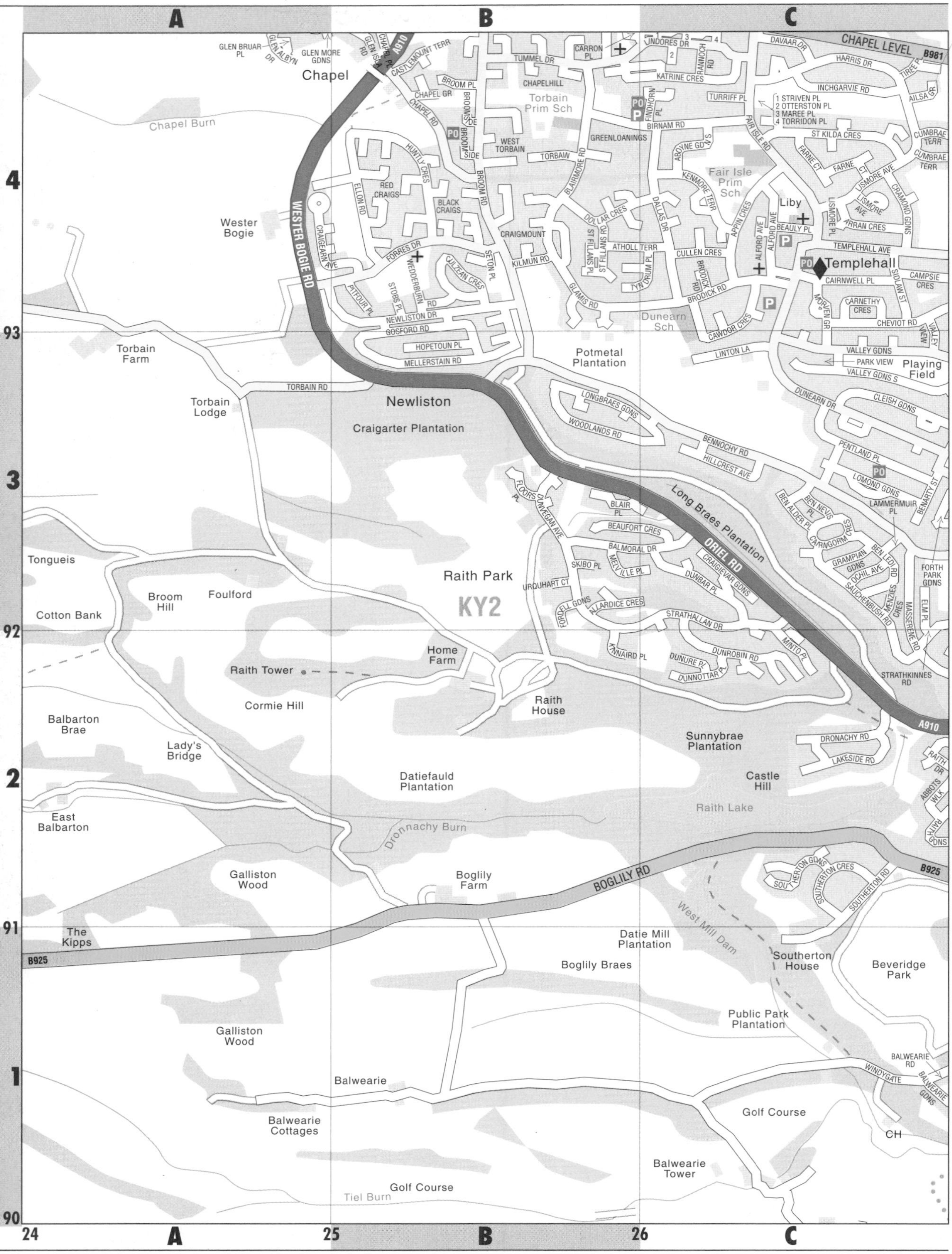

A
B
C
4
93
3
92
2
91
1
90
24
25
26
Chapel
Chapel Burn
GLEN BRUAR PL
GLEN ALBYN DR
GLEN MORE GDNS
GLEN ISLA RD
CHAPEL PL
A910
CASTLEMOUNT TERR
CHAPEL LEVEL
B981
DAVAAR DR
HARRIS DR
TIREE PL
INCHGARVIE RD
AILSA GR
TUMMEL DR
CARRON PL
INDORES DR
RANNOCH RD
KATRINE CRES
TURRIFF PL
1 STRIVEN PL
2 OTTERSTON PL
3 MAREE PL
4 TORRIDON PL
BROOM PL
CHAPELHILL
Torbain Prim Sch
CHAPEL GR
CHAPEL RD
BROOMSIDE
FINDHORN PL
BIRNAM RD
FAIR ISLE RD
ST KILDA CRES
CUMBRAE TERR
WEST TORBAIN
GREENLOANINGS
ABOYNE GDNS
TORBAIN
BLAIRMORE RD
HUNTLY CRES
Fair Isle Prim Sch
FARNE CT
FARNE
LISMORE AVE
CRAMOND GDNS
Wester Bogie
WESTER BOGIE RD
ELLON RD
RED CRAIGS
BLACK CRAIGS
BROOM RD
KENMORE TERR
DOLLAR CRES
DALLAS DR
APPIN CRES
Liby
LISMORE PL
ARRAN CRES
BEAULY PL
CRAIGEARN AVE
FORRES DR
WEDDERBURN RD
CRAIGMOUNT
ST FILLANS RD
ST FILLANS PL
ATHOLL TERR
CULLEN CRES
ALFORD AVE
TEMPLEHALL AVE
Templehall
CULZEAN CRES
SETON PL
KILMUN RD
TYNDRUM PL
BRODICK RD
BRODICK
CAIRNWELL PL
CAMPSIE CRES
SIDLAW ST
PITFOUR PL
STOBS PL
GLAMIS RD
CAWDOR CRES
MORVEN GR
CARNETHY CRES
CHEVIOT RD
NEWLISTON DR
GOSFORD RD
Dunearn Sch
VALLEY VIEW
HOPETOUN PL
VALLEY GDNS
LINTON LA
PARK VIEW
Playing Field
MELLERSTAIN RD
Potmetal Plantation
VALLEY GDNS S
Torbain Farm
TORBAIN RD
Torbain Lodge
Newliston
Craigarter Plantation
LONGBRAES GDNS
WOODLANDS RD
DUNEARN DR
CLEISH GDNS
BENNOCHY RD
HILLCREST AVE
PENTLAND PL
LOMOND GDNS
FLOORS PL
DUNVEGAN AVE
BLAIR PL
Long Braes Plantation
BEN ALDER PL
BEN NEVIS PL
LAMMERMUIR PL
BENARTY ST
BEAUFORT CRES
ORIEL RD
CAIRNGORM CRES
Tongueis
BALMORAL DR
CRAIGIEVAR GDNS
GRAMPIAN GDNS
BEN LEDI RD
FORTH PARK GDNS
Raith Park
SKIBO PL
MELVILLE PL
DUNBAR PL
OCHIL AVE
Broom Hill
Foulford
URQUHART CT
SAUCHENBUSH RD
MENZIES CRES
MASSERENE RD
ELM PL
Cotton Bank
KY2
FORDELL GDNS
ALLARDICE CRES
STRATHALLAN DR
KINNAIRD PL
DUNROBIN RD
MINTO PL
Home Farm
DUNURE PL
DUNNOTTAR PL
STRATHKINNES RD
Raith Tower
Cormie Hill
Raith House
A910
Balbarton Brae
Sunnybrae Plantation
DRONACHY RD
Lady's Bridge
LAKESIDE RD
RAITH DR
Datiefauld Plantation
Castle Hill
ABBOTS WLK
Raith Lake
East Balbarton
RAITH GDNS
Dronnachy Burn
B925
Galliston Wood
Boglily Farm
BOGLILY RD
SOUTHERTON GDNS
SOUTHERTON CRES
SOUTHERTON RD
West Mill Dam
The Kipps
B925
Datie Mill Plantation
Southerton House
Beveridge Park
Boglily Braes
Public Park Plantation
Galliston Wood
BALWEARIE RD
WINDYGATE
BALWEARIE GDNS
Balwearie
Golf Course
Balwearie Cottages
CH
Balwearie Tower
Golf Course
Tiel Burn

15

34

18

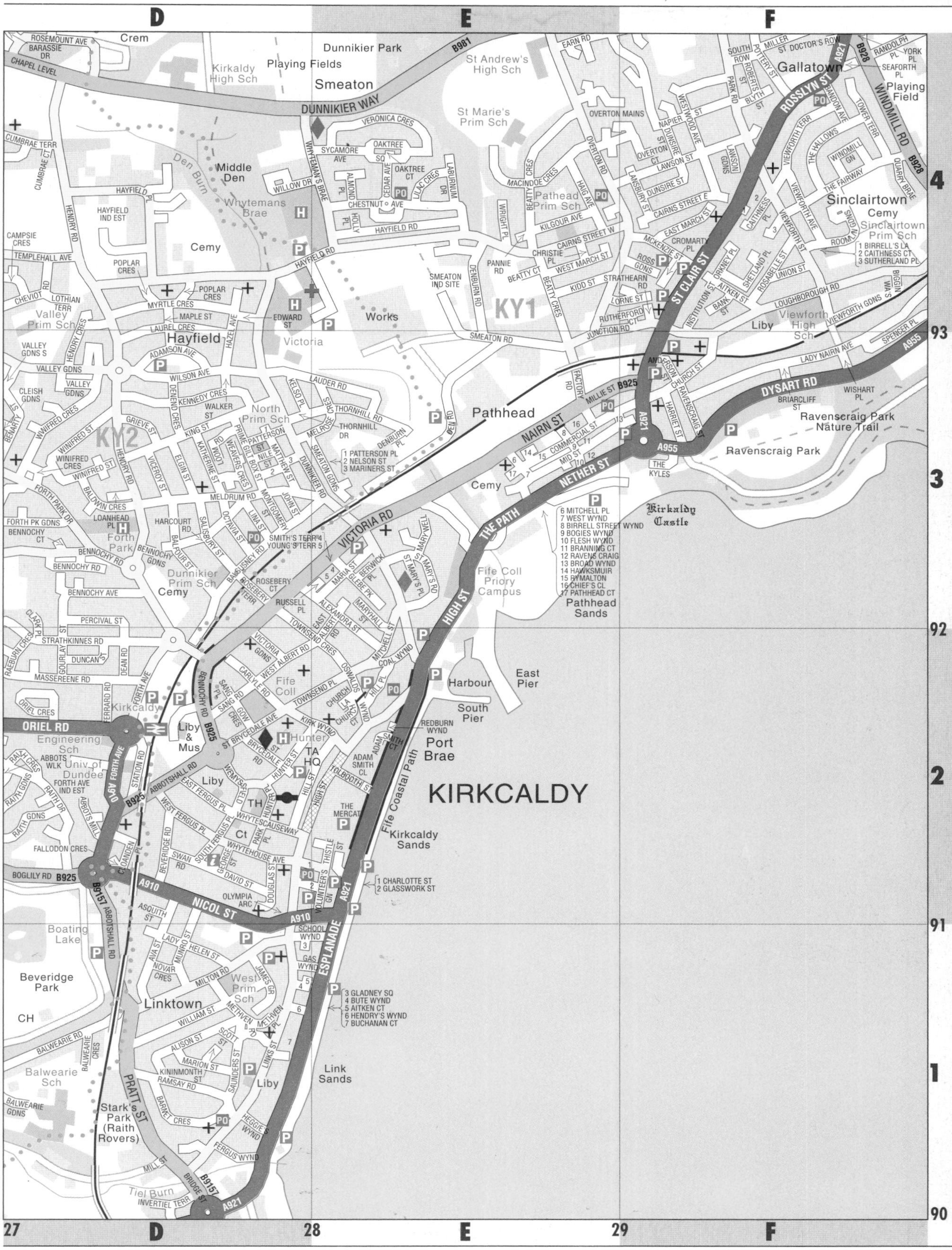
D
E
F
KIRKCALDY
Crem
Dunnikier Park
Playing Fields
Smeaton
Kirkaldy High Sch
St Andrew's High Sch
St Marie's Prim Sch
DUNNIKIER WAY
B981
CHAPEL LEVEL
ROSEMOUNT AVE
BARASSIE DR
CUMBRAE TERR
Middle Den
Den Burn
Whytemans Brae
Cemy
HAYFIELD RD
HAYFIELD IND EST
HENDRY RD
CAMPSIE CRES
TEMPLEHALL AVE
POPLAR CRES
LOTHIAN TERR
CHEVIOT RD
Valley Prim Sch
MYRTLE CRES
MAPLE ST
LAUREL CRES
Hayfield
EDWARD ST
Victoria
Works
SMEATON RD
SMEATON IND SITE
DENBURN RD
KY1
KY2
Pathhead Prim Sch
Pathhead
OVERTON MAINS
OVERTON RD
Gallatown
ROSSLYN ST
WINDMILL RD
B928
A921
Playing Field
Sinclairtown
Sinclairtown Prim Sch
1 BIRRELL'S LA
2 CAITHNESS CT
3 SUTHERLAND PL
ST CLAIR ST
Liby
Viewforth High Sch
LOUGHBOROUGH RD
VIEWFORTH GDNS
SPENCER PL
LADY NAIRN AVE
A955
DYSART RD
WISHART PL
BRIARCLIFF ST
Ravenscraig Park Nature Trail
Ravenscraig Park
THE KYLES
NAIRN ST
B925
MILLIE ST
NETHER ST
COMMERCIAL ST
MID ST
THE PATH
HIGH ST
Kirkaldy Castle
6 MITCHELL PL
7 WEST WYND
8 BIRRELL STREET WYND
9 BOGIES WYND
10 FLESH WYND
11 BRANNING CT
12 RAVENS CRAIG
13 BROAD WYND
14 HAWKSMUIR
15 RYMALTON
16 CHIEF'S CL
17 PATHHEAD CT
Pathhead Sands
Fife Coll Priory Campus
North Prim Sch
1 PATTERSON PL
2 NELSON ST
3 MARINERS ST
VICTORIA RD
SMITH'S TERR 4
YOUNG'S TERR 5
Forth Park
Dunnikier Prim Sch
BENNOCHY RD
PERCIVAL ST
STRATHKINNES RD
DUNCAN ST
MASSEREENE RD
ORIEL RD
ORIEL CRES
Kirkcaldy
Engineering Sch
Univ of Dundee
FORTH AVE IND EST
Liby & Mus
Fife Coll
Hunter
TA HQ
Harbour
East Pier
South Pier
Port Brae
Fife Coastal Path
Kirkcaldy Sands
TH
Liby
A910
NICOL ST
BOGLILY RD
B9157
A915
FALLODON CRES
ESPLANADE
1 CHARLOTTE ST
2 GLASSWORK ST
Boating Lake
Beveridge Park
West Prim Sch
Linktown
3 GLADNEY SQ
4 BUTE WYND
5 AITKEN CT
6 HENDRY'S WYND
7 BUCHANAN CT
CH
Balwearie Sch
Link Sands
Stark's Park (Raith Rovers)
PRATT ST
Tiel Burn
INVERTIEL TERR
BRIDGE ST
93
92
91
90
4
3
2
1
27
28
29

35

18

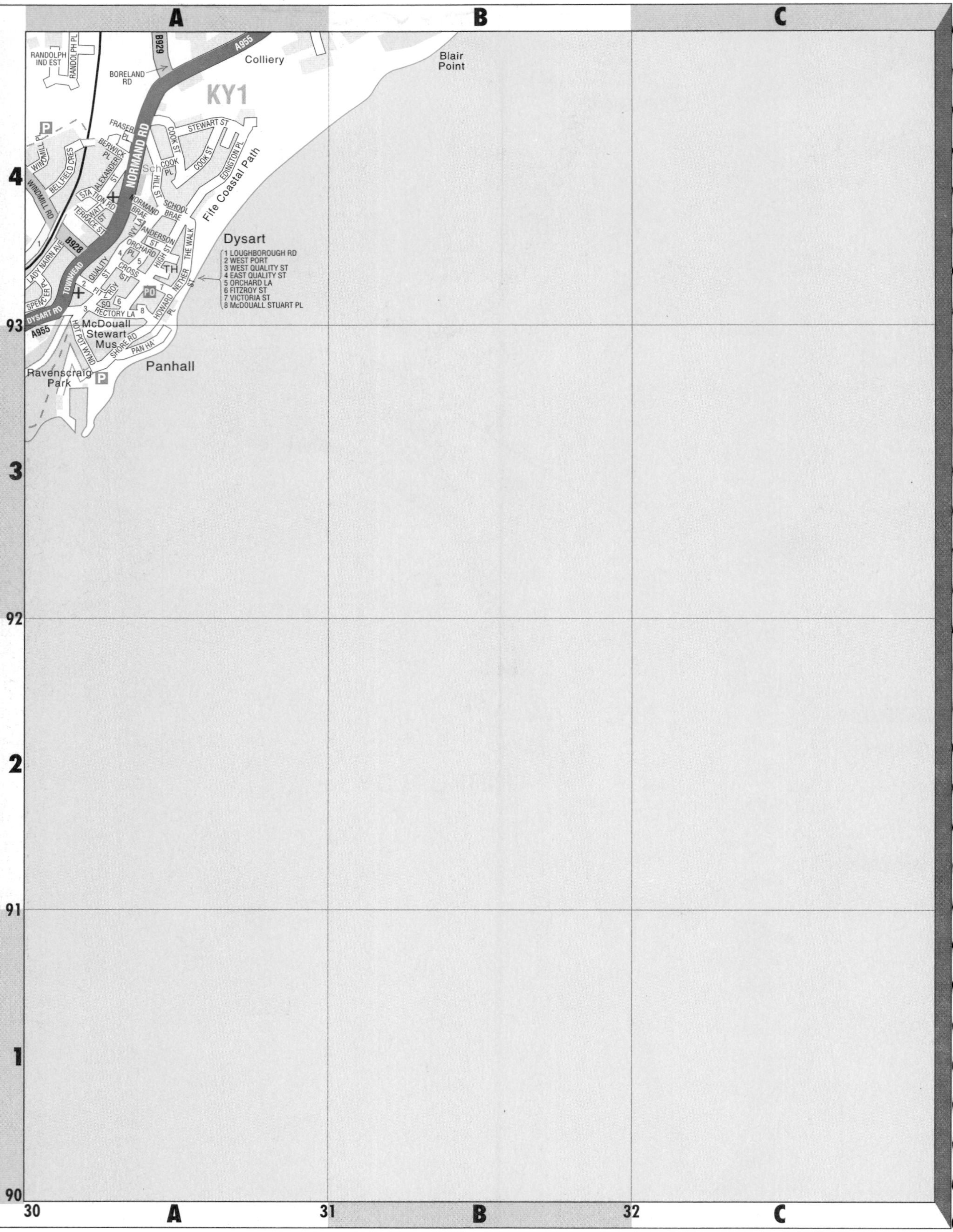

Colliery

Blair
Point

KY1

RANDOLPH
IND EST

BORELAND
RD

STEWART ST

Fife Coastal Path

Dysart

1 LOUGHBOROUGH RD
2 WEST PORT
3 WEST QUALITY ST
4 EAST QUALITY ST
5 ORCHARD LA
6 FITZROY ST
7 VICTORIA ST
8 McDOUALL STUART PL

McDouall
Stewart
Mus.

Ravenscraig
Park

Panhall

7
20

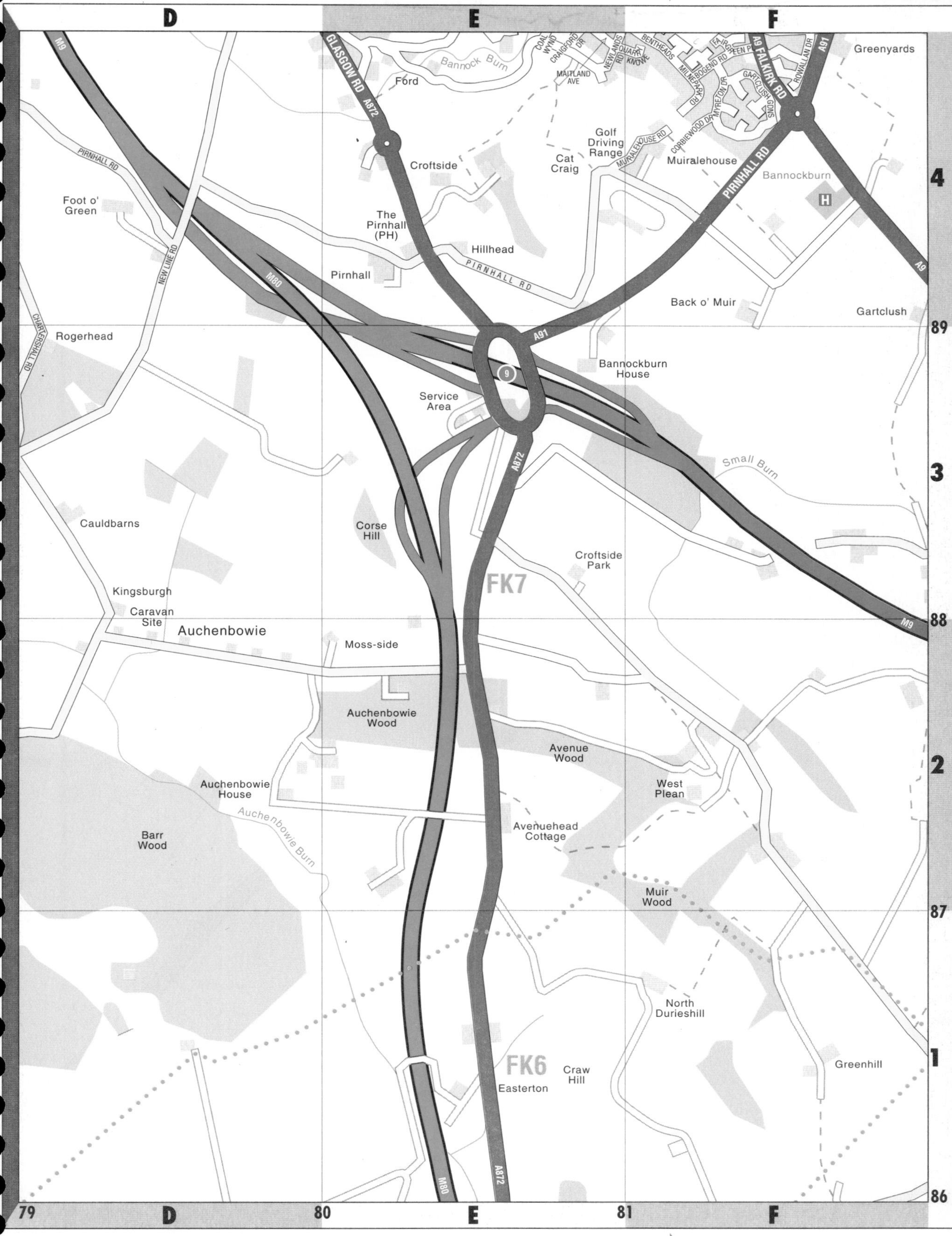
D
E
F
79
80
81
86
87
88
89
1
2
3
4
M9
GLASGOW RD
A872
Bannock Burn
Ford
COAL WYND
CRAIGFORD DR
MAITLAND AVE
NEWLANDS RD
QUARRY KNOWE
BENTHEADS
MILNEPARK RD
BOGEND RD
MYRETON DR
GARTCLUSH GDNS
CORBIEWOOD DR
A9 FALKIRK RD
ROWALLAN DR
A91
Greenyards
Golf Driving Range
Cat Craig
MURALEHOUSE RD
Muiralehouse
PIRNHALL RD
Bannockburn
H
Croftside
PIRNHALL RD
Foot o' Green
The Pirnhall (PH)
Hillhead
PIRNHALL RD
Pirnhall
M80
NEW LINE RD
A9
Back o' Muir
Gartclush
CHARTERSHALL RD
Rogerhead
A91
Bannockburn House
9
Service Area
A872
Small Burn
Cauldbarns
Corse Hill
Croftside Park
FK7
Kingsburgh
Caravan Site
Auchenbowie
Moss-side
M9
Auchenbowie Wood
Avenue Wood
West Plean
Auchenbowie House
Auchenbowie Burn
Barr Wood
Avenuehead Cottage
Muir Wood
North Durieshill
Greenhill
FK6
Craw Hill
Easterton
M80
A872

36
20

A B C

COWIE RD B9124
Westerton of Cowie
Sewage Works
Easter Greenyards
Hilton Farm
Cowiehall RD
WESTERTON
CARNOCK PARK ST
HILTON
SCOTSTOUN RD
BANNOCKBURN RD
St Margaret's RC Prim Sch
Cowie Prim Sch
Cowiehall
BERRYHILL
Berry Hills
MAIN ST
Cowie
MOUNT OLIPHANT
EASTERTON DR
EASTERTON GR
PO
ISSUE AVE
ALLOWAY DR
ARMOUR
BRIG
STANTER DR
KYLE AVE
KYLEDOON GR
OCHILVIEW
BURNS TERR
Liby

4

89
Gartclush
A9
Sink
Station RD
Works

3
Plean Farm
FK7
Plean Junction
Gallamuir Wood
B9124
Sauchenford Smallholdings
GALLAMUIR RD

88
M9
Gallamuir
B9124
FK2
Pleanbank Wood
Sauchinford Burn

2
Pleanbank Farm
BURNSIDE CRES
PO
Liby
WALLACE CRES
LOANFOOT GDNS
PARKSIDE CT
PRESIDENT
KENNEDY DR
CARBRIDGE
CRES
GLENHILL
CRES
STIRLING PL
OAK CRES
BRUCE ST
BRUCE CRES
BEECH AVE
CARBROOK DR
SPENQUARTER DR
BALFOUR CT
TORBURN AVE
GALLAM
Sewage Works
FK5

Gartwhinnie Farm
Works
Plean
East Plean Prim Sch
MAIN ST
Cushenquarter

87
P
CADGERS LOAN
Plean House
GILLESPIE TERR
CARDROWAN RD
GLEN RD

1
Muirmailing
Plean Burn
A9
Plean Country Park
Carbrook Mains
M9

86

82 A 83 B 84 C

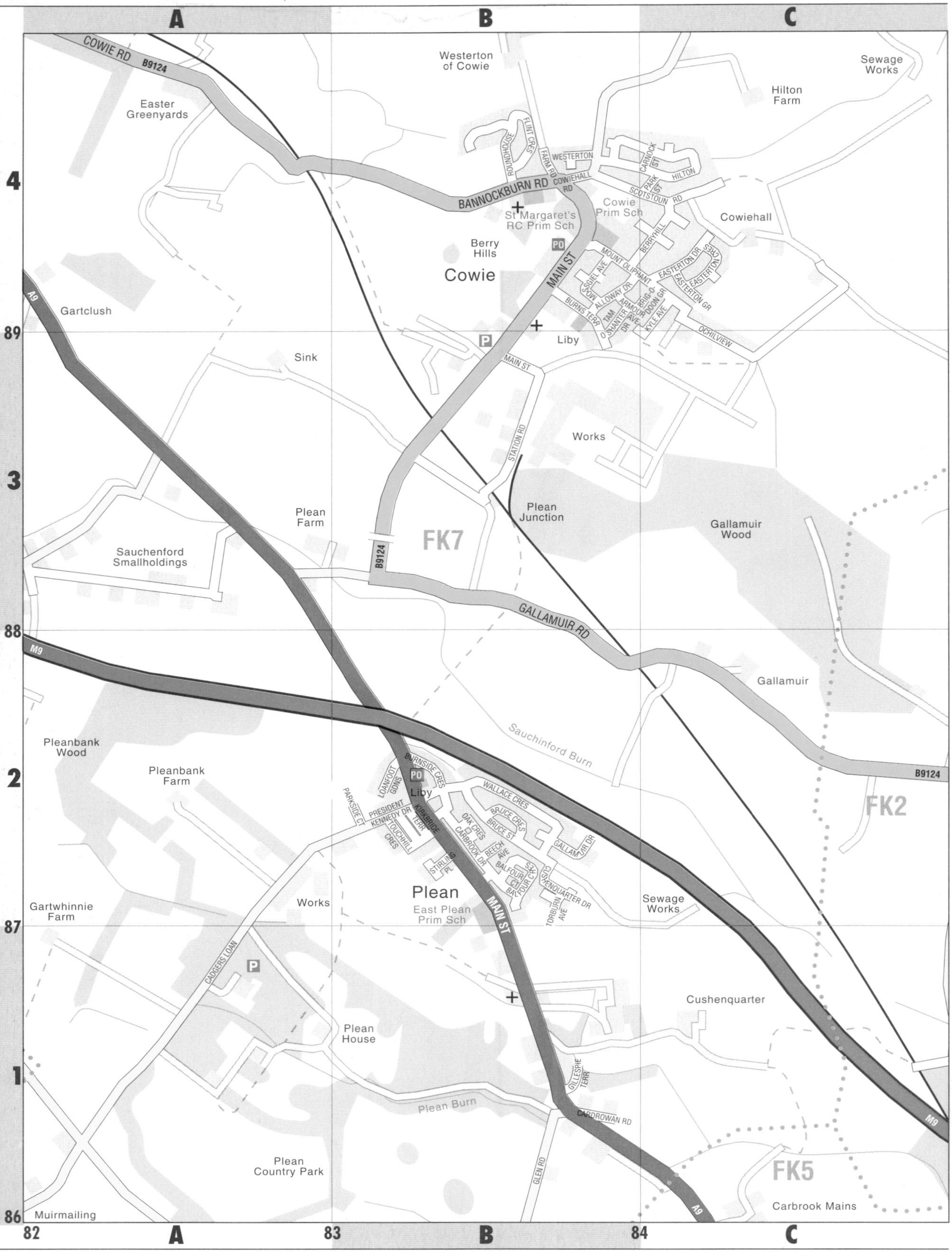

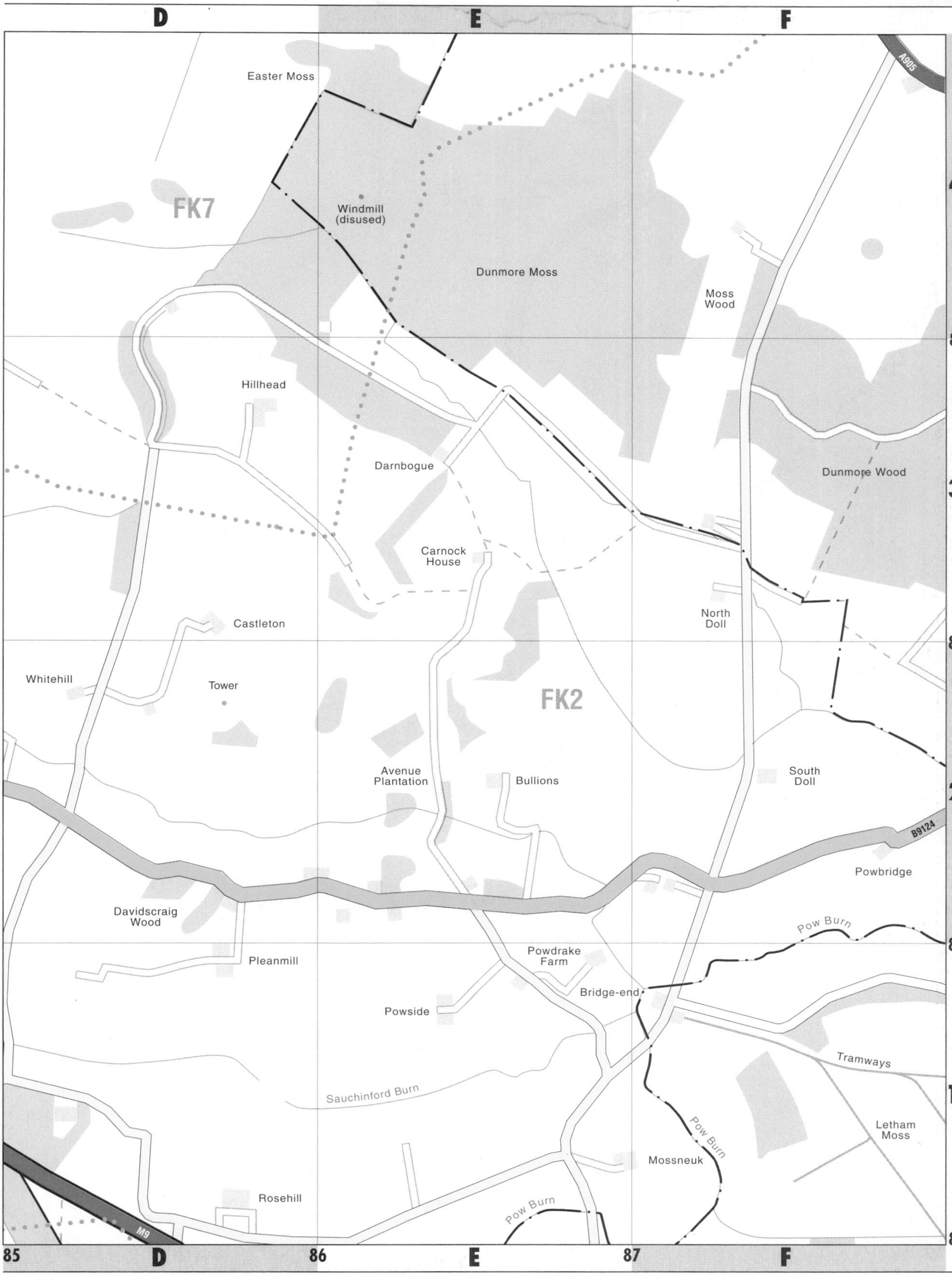
D
E
F
Easter Moss
FK7
Windmill
(disused)
Dunmore Moss
Moss
Wood
A905
4
89
Hillhead
Darnbogue
Dunmore Wood
3
Carnock
House
Castleton
North
Doll
88
Whitehill
Tower
FK2
Avenue
Plantation
Bullions
South
Doll
2
B9124
Powbridge
Davidscraig
Wood
Pow Burn
87
Pleanmill
Powdrake
Farm
Bridge-end
Powside
Tramways
Sauchinford Burn
1
Letham
Moss
Pow Burn
Mossneuk
Rosehill
Pow Burn
M9
86
85
86
87

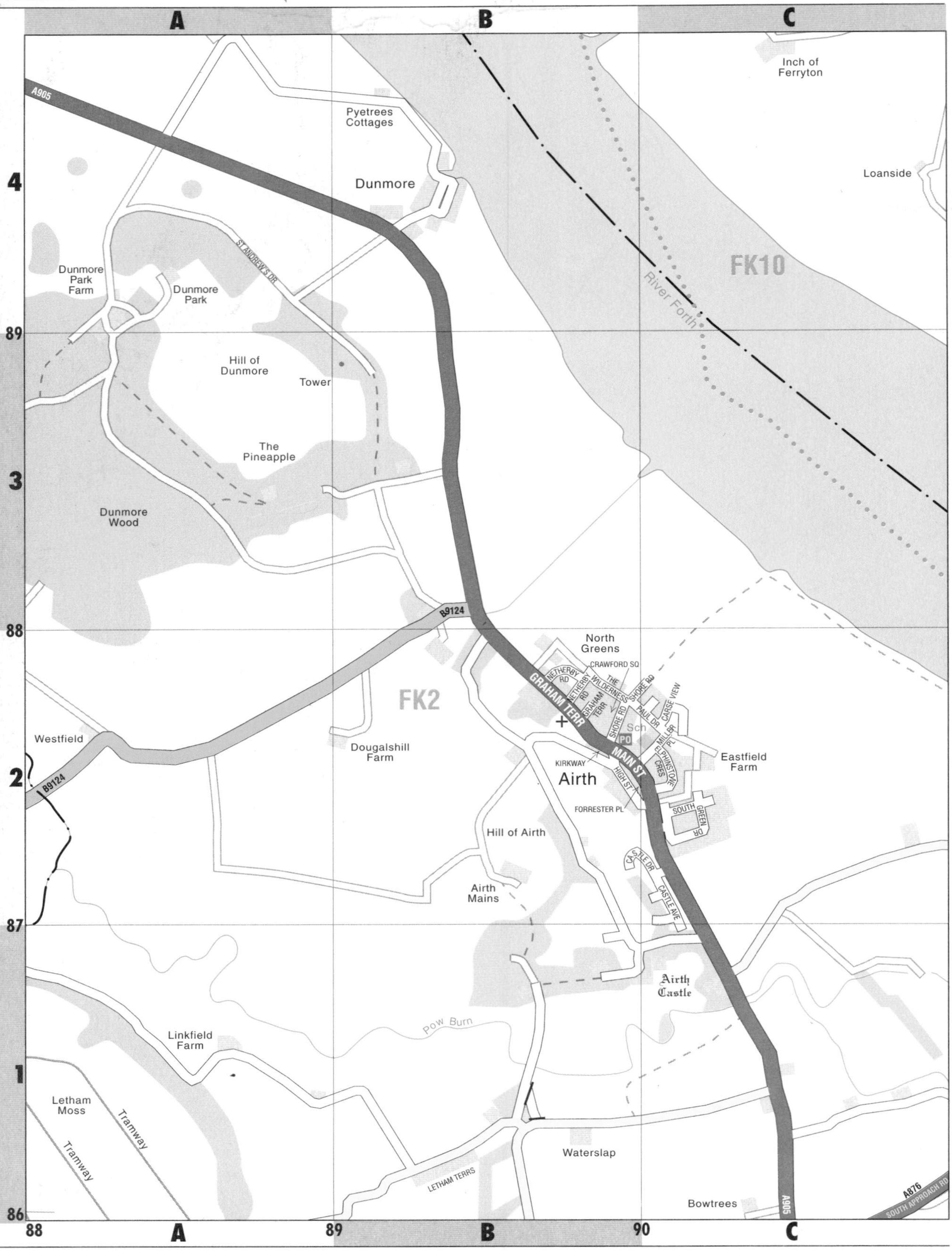

A   B   C

4

89

3

88

2

87

1

86

A905

Pyetrees
Cottages

Dunmore

FK10

Inch of
Ferryton

Loanside

River Forth

Dunmore
Park Farm

Dunmore Park

ST ANDREW'S DR.

Hill of
Dunmore

Tower

The
Pineapple

Dunmore
Wood

B9124

North
Greens

CRAWFORD SQ

NETHERBY RD
NETHERBY RD
THE WILDERNESS
SHORE RD
GRAHAM TERR
CARSE VIEW
PAUL DR

FK2

GRAHAM TERR

MAIN ST
PO
Sch
MILLER PL
ELPHINSTONE CRES

Westfield

B9124

Dougalshill
Farm

Airth

KIRKWAY

HIGH ST

Eastfield
Farm

FORRESTER PL

SOUTH GREEN RD

Hill of Airth

Airth
Mains

CASTLE DR

CASTLE AVE

Airth
Castle

Pow Burn

Linkfield
Farm

Letham
Moss

Tramway

Tramway

Tramway

LETHAM TERRS

Waterslap

Bowtrees

A905

A876
SOUTH APPROACH RD

88   A   89   B   90   C

11
24

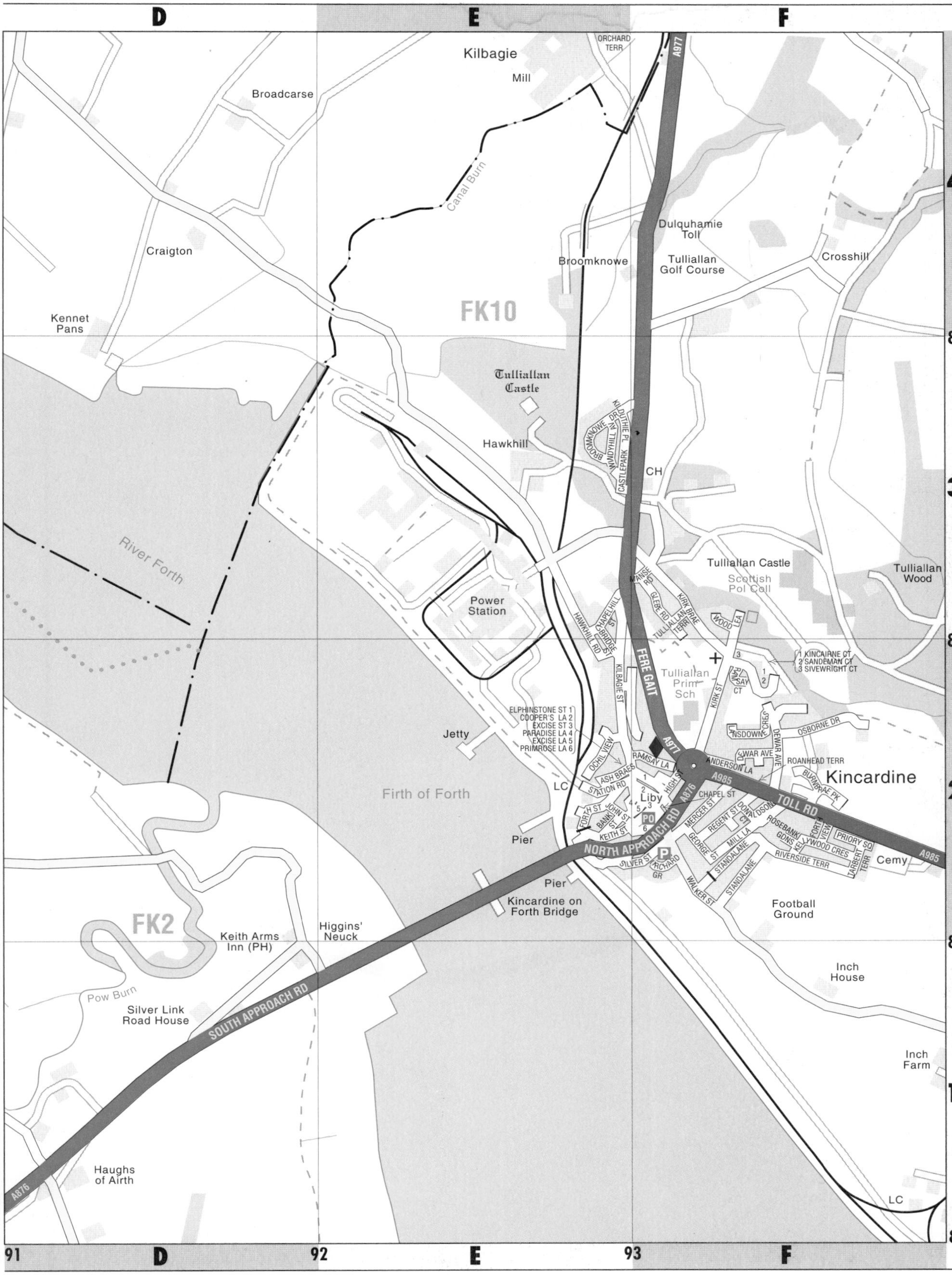
D
E
F
Kilbagie
Mill
ORCHARD TERR
A977
Broadcarse
Canal Burn
4
Dulquhamie Toll
Tulliallan Golf Course
Crosshill
Craigton
Broomknowe
FK10
Kennet Pans
89
Tulliallan Castle
Hawkhill
BROOMKNOWE DR
KILDUTHIE PL
WINDYHILL AV
CASTLEPARK
CH
3
River Forth
Tulliallan Castle
Scottish Pol Coll
Tulliallan Wood
Power Station
MANSE RD
CHAPEL HILL
GLEBE RD
KIRK BRAE
WOOD LEA
TULLIALLAN TERR
HAWKHILL RD
BRIDGE ST
88
FERE GAIT
1 KINCAIRNE CT
2 SANDEMAN CT
3 SIVEWRIGHT CT
Tulliallan Prim Sch
KILBAGIE ST
KIRK ST
RAMSAY CT
ELPHINSTONE ST 1
COOPER'S LA 2
EXCISE ST 3
PARADISE LA 4
EXCISE LA 5
PRIMROSE LA 6
LANSDOWNE CRES
OSBORNE DR
Jetty
OCHIL VIEW
DEWAR AVE
WAR AVE
RAMSAY LA
ANDERSON LA
ROANHEAD TERR
ASH BRAES
A985
BURNBRAE PK
Kincardine
STATION RD
HIGH ST
CHAPEL ST
TOLL RD
2
LC
Firth of Forth
Liby
A876
FORTH ST
JOHN ST
BANK ST
KEITH ST
PO
MERCER ST
REGENT ST
DONALDSON CT
ROSEBANK GDNS
FORTH VIEW
KELLYWOOD CRES
PRIORY SQ
TARBERT TERR
MILL LA
GEORGE ST
RIVERSIDE TERR
Pier
NORTH APPROACH RD
P
SILVER ST
ORCHARD GR
STANDALANE
WALKER ST
Cemy
A985
Pier
Kincardine on Forth Bridge
Football Ground
FK2
Keith Arms Inn (PH)
Higgins' Neuck
87
Inch House
Pow Burn
Silver Link Road House
SOUTH APPROACH RD
Inch Farm
1
Haughs of Airth
A876
LC
86
91
D
92
E
93
F

40
24

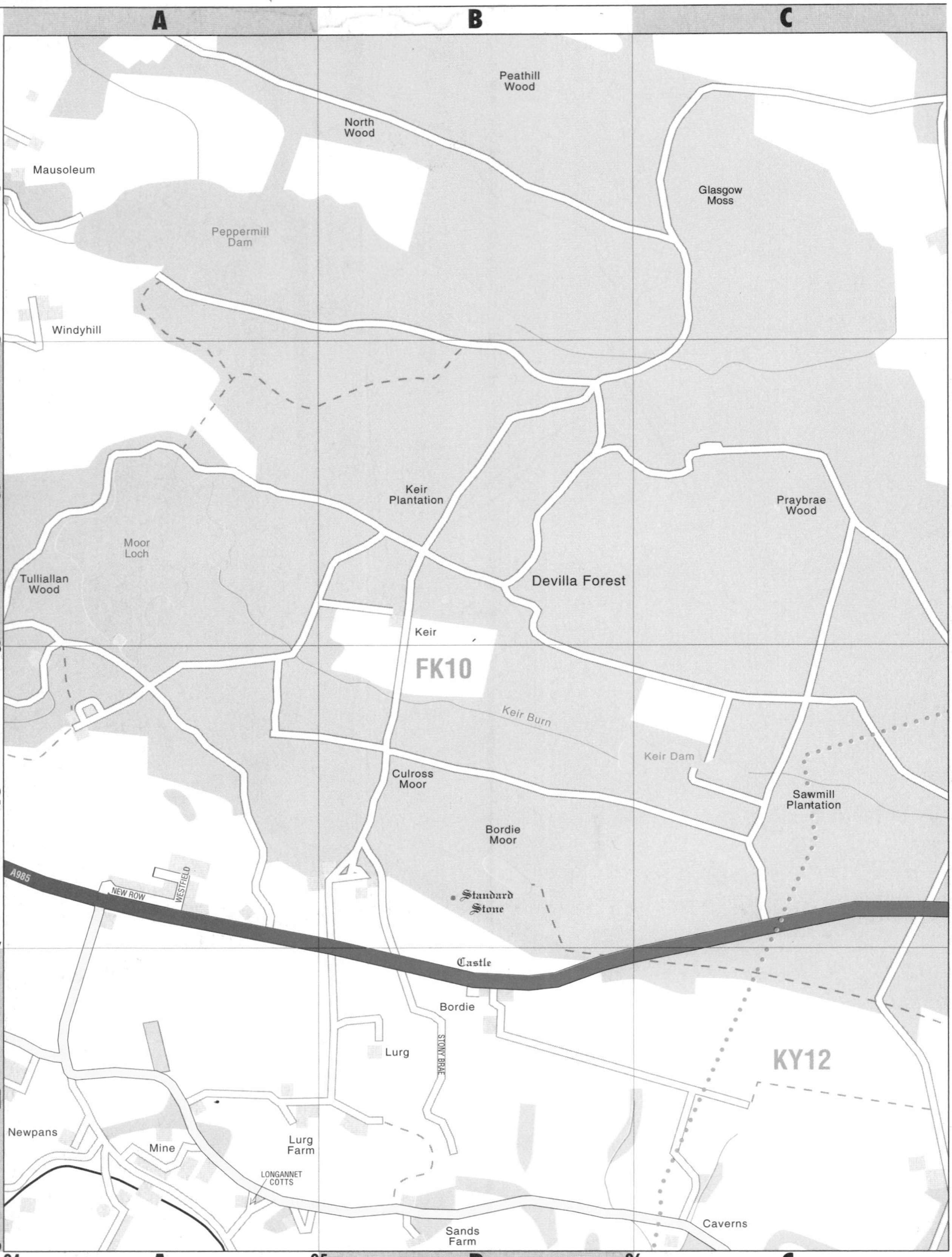

A
B
C

4

Mausoleum

North
Wood

Peathill
Wood

Glasgow
Moss

Peppermill
Dam

89

Windyhill

3

Keir
Plantation

Praybrae
Wood

Moor
Loch

Devilla Forest

Tulliallan
Wood

88

Keir

FK10

Keir Burn

Keir Dam

2

Culross
Moor

Sawmill
Plantation

A985

NEW ROW

WESTFIELD

Bordie
Moor

Standard
Stone

87

Castle

Bordie

1

Lurg

STONY BRAE

KY12

Newpans

Mine

Lurg
Farm

LONGANNET
COTTS

Caverns

86

94

A

95

B

96

C

26

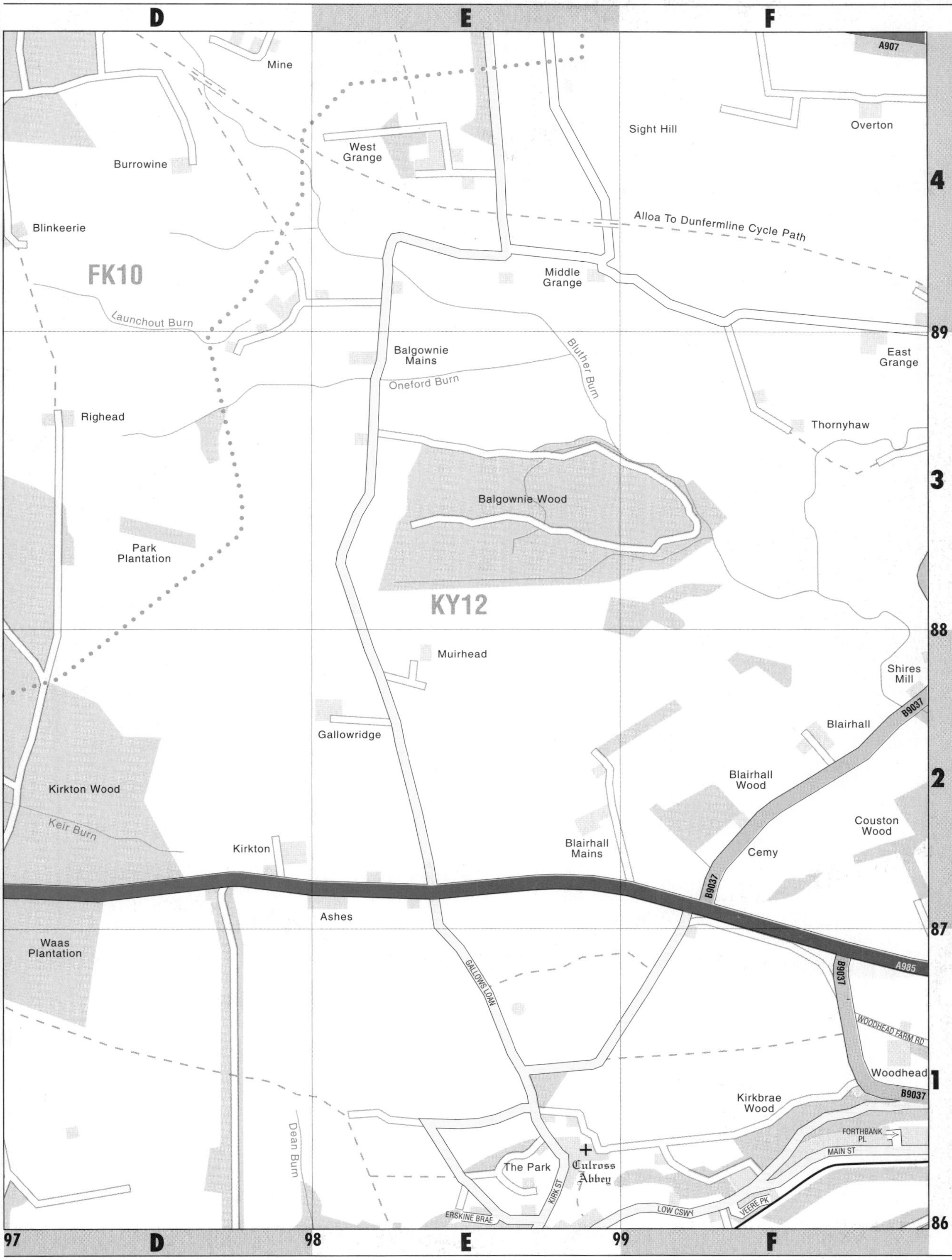
D
E
F
A907
Mine
Sight Hill
Overton
West Grange
Burrowine
4
Alloa To Dunfermline Cycle Path
Blinkeerie
FK10
Middle Grange
Launchout Burn
89
Balgownie Mains
East Grange
Oneford Burn
Bluther Burn
Righead
Thornyhaw
3
Balgownie Wood
Park Plantation
KY12
88
Muirhead
Shires Mill
B9037
Blairhall
Gallowridge
2
Blairhall Wood
Kirkton Wood
Couston Wood
Keir Burn
Kirkton
Blairhall Mains
Cemy
Ashes
87
Waas Plantation
A985
GALLOWS LOAN
WOODHEAD FARM RD
Woodhead
1
Kirkbrae Wood
Dean Burn
FORTHBANK PL
MAIN ST
The Park
Culross Abbey
KIRK ST
LOW CSWY
VEERE PK
ERSKINE BRAE
86
97
98
99

42
26

25

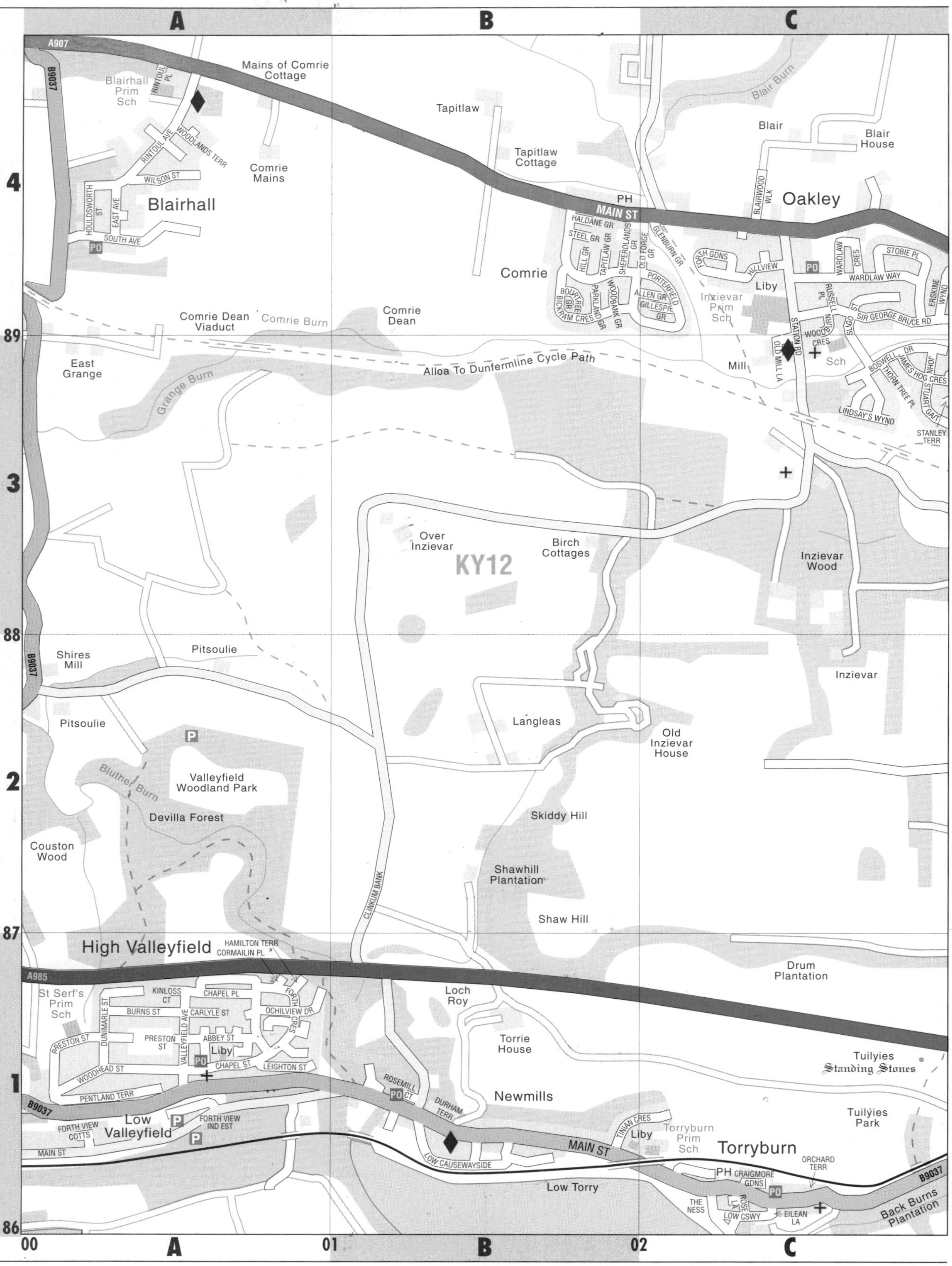
A
B
C
A907
B9037
Blairhall Prim Sch
RINTOUL PL
Mains of Comrie Cottage
Tapitlaw
Blair Burn
Blair
Blair House
RINTOUL AVE
WOODLANDS TERR
Comrie Mains
Tapitlaw Cottage
WILSON ST
HOULDSWORTH ST
EAST AVE
Blairhall
PH
MAIN ST
BLAIRWOOD WLK
Oakley
SOUTH AVE
PO
HALDANE GR
STEEL GR
HILL GR
TAPITLAW GR
SHEPERDLANDS GR
OLD FORGE GR
GLENBURN GR
FORTH GDNS
HILLVIEW
PO
WARDLAW CRES
STOBIE PL
WARDLAW WAY
ERSKINE WYND
Comrie
Liby
BOUSTREE GR
BICKRAM CRES
PARKLAND GR
WOODBANK GR
PORTERFIELD
ALLEN GR
GILLESPIE GR
Inzievar Prim Sch
RUSSELL PL
SLIGO ST
SIR GEORGE BRUCE RD
Comrie Dean Viaduct
Comrie Burn
Comrie Dean
STATION RD
WOODBURN CRES
89
East Grange
Alloa To Dunfermline Cycle Path
OLD MILL LA
Mill
Sch
BOSWELL DR
JAMES HOG CRES
JOHN STUART GAIT
THORN TREE PL
Grange Burn
LINDSAY'S WYND
STANLEY TERR
3
Over Inzievar
Birch Cottages
KY12
Inzievar Wood
88
Shires Mill
Pitsoulie
Inzievar
Langleas
Pitsoulie
Old Inzievar House
P
Valleyfield Woodland Park
2
Bluther Burn
Devilla Forest
Skiddy Hill
Couston Wood
Shawhill Plantation
CLINKUM BANK
Shaw Hill
87
High Valleyfield
HAMILTON TERR
CORMAILIN PL
Drum Plantation
A985
St Serf's Prim Sch
KINLOSS CT
CHAPEL PL
FORTH CRES
Loch Roy
BURNS ST
CARLYLE ST
OCHILVIEW DR
DUNIMARLE ST
PRESTON ST
PRESTON ST
VALLEYFIELD AVE
ABBEY ST
Torrie House
Liby
PO
Tuilyies Standing Stones
WOODHEAD ST
CHAPEL ST
LEIGHTON ST
1
ROSEMILL CT
PENTLAND TERR
PO
Newmills
B9037
DURHAM TERR
Low Valleyfield
P
FORTH VIEW IND EST
Tuilyies Park
FORTH VIEW COTTS
P
TINIAN CRES
Torryburn Prim Sch
MAIN ST
Liby
Torryburn
LOW CAUSEWAYSIDE
PH
CRAIGMORE GDNS
ORCHARD TERR
Low Torry
B9037
THE NESS
ROSE LA
PO
LOW CSWY
EILEAN LA
Back Burns Plantation
86
00
A
01
B
02
C

25

43

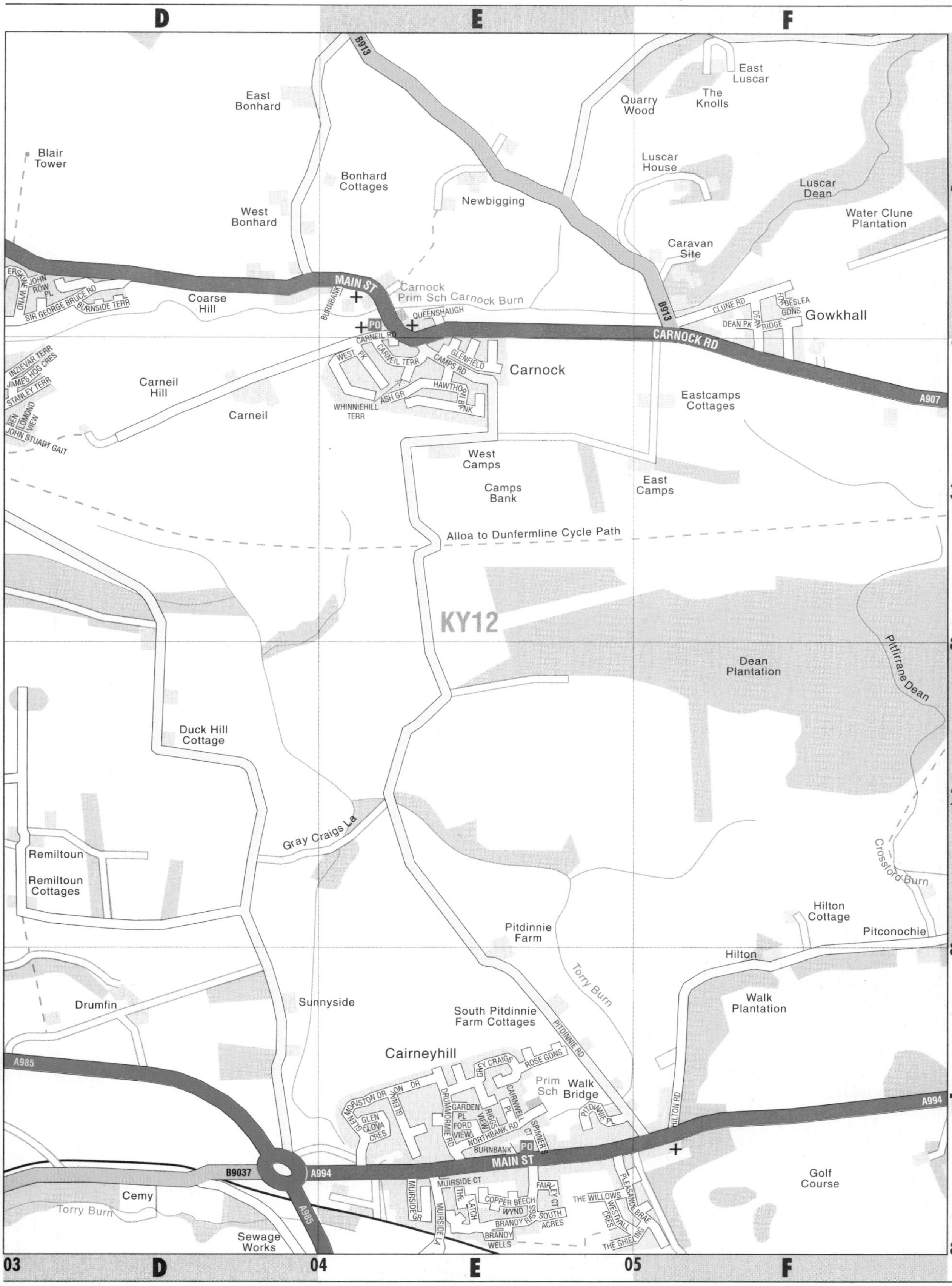

D   E   F

B913

Blair Tower

East Bonhard

Quarry Wood

East Luscar

The Knolls

Bonhard Cottages

Luscar House

Luscar Dean

Water Clune Plantation

4

West Bonhard

Newbigging

Caravan Site

ERSKINE WYND
JOHN ROW PL
SIR GEORGE BRUCE RD
BURNSIDE TERR

Coarse Hill

MAIN ST

BURNBANK

Carnock Prim Sch   Carnock Burn

QUEENSHAUGH

B913

CLUNE RD
DEAN PK
DET RIDGE
FORBESLEA GDNS

Gowkhall

CARNOCK RD

A907

89

PO

CARNEIL RD

WEST PK
CARNEIL TERR
GLENFIELD
CAMPS RD

INZIEVAR TERR
JAMES HOG CRES
STANLEY TERR
BEN BHORAID
JOHN STUART GAIT

Carneil Hill

Carneil

WHINNIEHILL TERR
ASH GR
HAWTHORN
BANK

Carnock

Eastcamps Cottages

West Camps

Camps Bank

East Camps

3

Alloa to Dunfermline Cycle Path

KY12

Dean Plantation

Pitfirrane Dean

88

Duck Hill Cottage

2

Remiltoun

Remiltoun Cottages

Gray Craigs La

Crossford Burn

Hilton Cottage

Pitconochie

Pitdinnie Farm

Hilton

87

Drumfin

Sunnyside

South Pitdinnie Farm Cottages

Torry Burn

Walk Plantation

A985

Cairneyhill

MONASTON DR
JOHN RD
GLEN GLOVA CRES
GARDEN PL
FORD VIEW
INGGAL PL
DRUMMOND RD
NORTHBANK RD
GREY CRAIGS
CAIRNWELL VIEW
ROSE GDNS
SPINNERS CT

Walk Bridge

Prim Sch

PITDINNIE RD

HILTON RD

A994

1

B9037

A994

MAIN ST

BURNBANK

Golf Course

Cemy

Torry Burn

A985

MUIRSIDE CT
MUIRSIDE GR
MUIRSIDE LA

THE LATCH
COPPER BEECH WYND
BRANDY RES
SOUTH ACRES
BRANDY WELLS

FAIRLEY CT
THE WILLOWS
PLEASANCE BRAE
WESTHALL CRES
THE SHIELINGS

Sewage Works

86

27

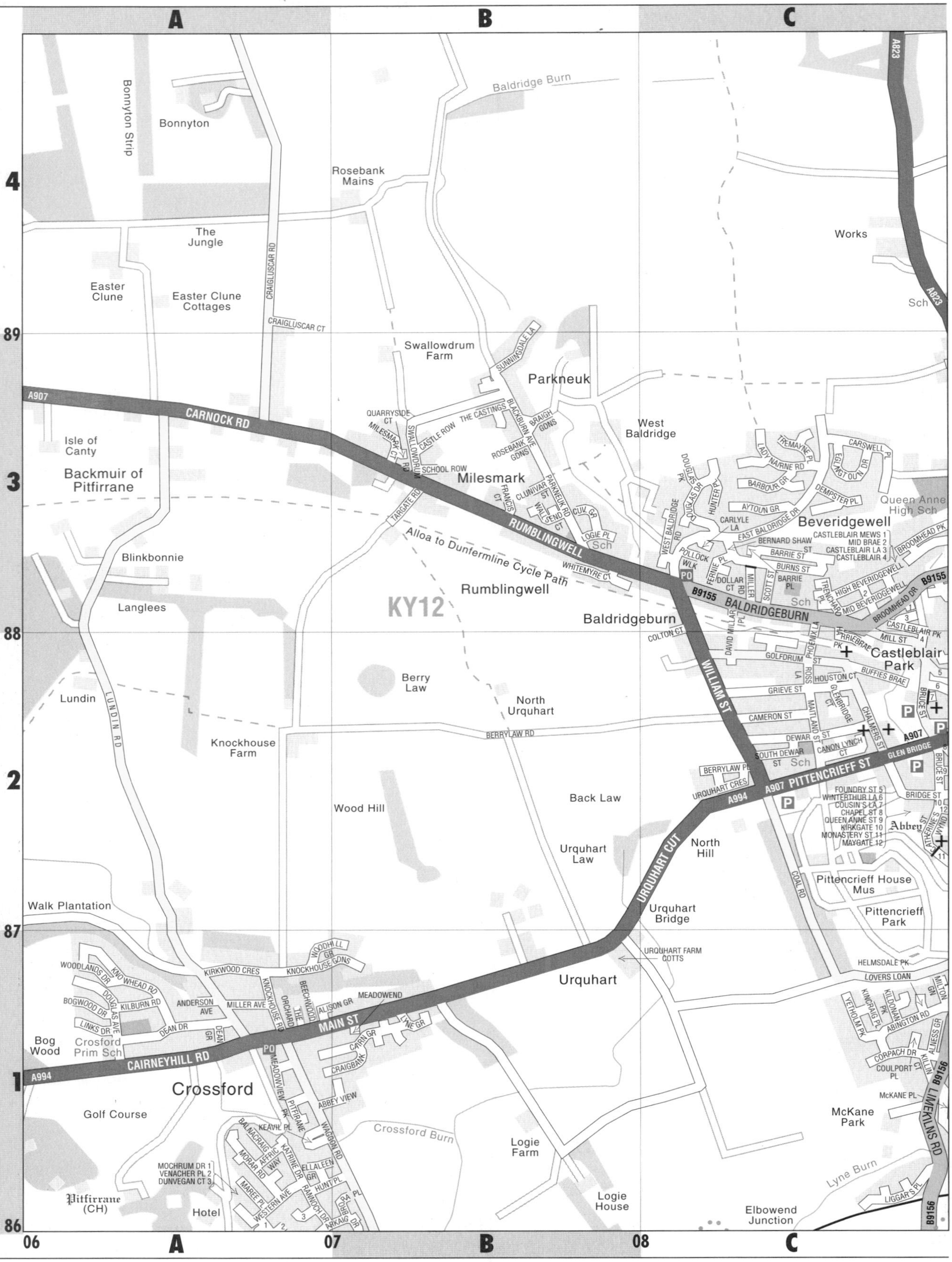
A
B
C
4
89
3
88
2
87
1
86
06
07
08
Bonnyton Strip
Bonnyton
Baldridge Burn
Rosebank Mains
The Jungle
Easter Clune
Easter Clune Cottages
CRAIGLUSCAR RD
CRAIGLUSCAR CT
Works
Sch
A823
Swallowdrum Farm
Parkneuk
SUNNINGDALE LA
A907
CARNOCK RD
Isle of Canty
Backmuir of Pitfirrane
QUARRYSIDE CT
MILESMARK CT
SWALLOWDRUM RD
CASTLE ROW
THE CASTINGS
BLACKBURN AVE
BRAIGH GDNS
ROSEBANK GDNS
SCHOOL ROW
Milesmark
West Baldridge
TARGATE RD
FRANCIS CT
CLUNIVAR ST
PARKNEUK RD
WALLSEND CT
CUIL GR
LOGIE PL
Sch
RUMBLINGWELL
Alloa to Dunfermline Cycle Path
WHITEMYRE CT
Rumblingwell
Blinkbonnie
Langlees
KY12
Baldridgeburn
COLTON CT
Berry Law
North Urquhart
Lundin
LUNDIN RD
Knockhouse Farm
BERRYLAW RD
WILLIAM ST
Back Law
Wood Hill
Urquhart Law
URQUHART CUT
North Hill
Urquhart Bridge
URQUHART FARM COTTS
Walk Plantation
Urquhart
DOUGLAS PK
DOUGLAS DR
HUNTER PL
TREMAYNE PL
LADY NAIRNE RD
CARSWELL PL
EGLINGTOUN DR
BARBOUR GR
DEMPSTER PL
Queen Anne High Sch
AYTOUN GR
Beveridgewell
WEST BALDRIDGE RD
CARLYLE LA
EAST BALDRIDGE DR
BERNARD SHAW ST
CASTLEBLAIR MEWS 1
MID BRAE 2
CASTLEBLAIR LA 3
CASTLEBLAIR 4
BROOMHEAD PK
BARRIE ST
BURNS ST
POLLOCK WLK
FERNIE PL
DOLLAR CT
MILLER RD
SCOTT ST
BARRIE PL
TRENCHARD PL
HIGH BEVERIDGEWELL
MID BEVERIDGEWELL
B9155
PO
B9155 BALDRIDGEBURN
Sch
BROOMHEAD DR
CASTLEBLAIR PK
MILL ST
DAVID MILLAR PL
PHOENIX LA
HARRIEBRAE PK
Castleblair Park
GOLFDRUM ST
ROSS LA
HOUSTON CT
BUFFIES BRAE
GRIEVE ST
MAITLAND ST
GLENBRIDGE CT
CHALMERS ST
BRUCE ST
CAMERON ST
DEWAR ST
CANON LYNCH CT
SOUTH DEWAR ST
Sch
A907
GLEN BRIDGE
BERRYLAW PL
URQUHART CRES
A994
A907 PITTENCRIEFF ST
FOUNDRY ST 5
WINTERTHUR LA 6
COUSIN'S LA 7
CHAPEL ST 8
QUEEN ANNE ST 9
KIRKGATE 10
MONASTERY ST 11
MAYGATE 12
BRIDGE ST
Abbey
ST CATHERINE'S WYND
COAL RD
Pittencrieff House Mus
Pittencrieff Park
HELMSDALE PK
LOVERS LOAN
MILTON GN
YETHOLM PK
KINCRAIG PL
KILDONAN PK
ABINGTON RD
ALNESS GR
CORPACH DR
KILLIN CT
COULPORT PL
McKANE PL
B9156
LIMEKILNS RD
McKane Park
Lyne Burn
LIGGAR'S PL
Elbowend Junction
WOODLANDS DR
KNOWHEAD RD
KIRKWOOD CRES
KNOCKHOUSE GDNS
WOODHILL GR
BOGWOOD DR
KILBURN RD
DOUGLAS AVE
ANDERSON AVE
MILLER AVE
KNOCKHOUSE RD
ORCHARD
THE
BEECHWOOD
ALISON GR
MEADOWEND
LINKS DR
DEAN DR
GR
DEAN
MAIN ST
LYNE GR
CAIRN GR
Bog Wood
Crosford Prim Sch
CAIRNEYHILL RD
PO
A994
MEADOWVIEW PK
CRAIGBANK
Crossford
Golf Course
PITFIRRANE PK
ABBEY VIEW
WAGGON RD
KEAVIL PL
BALNACRAIG
AFFRIC WAY
MORAR RD
KATRINE DR
Crossford Burn
ELLALEEN GR
MOCHRUM DR 1
VENACHER PL 2
DUNVEGAN CT 3
HUNT PL
MAREE PL
WESTERN AVE
RANNOCH DR
ORA PL
ARKAIG DR
Pitfirrane (CH)
Hotel
Logie Farm
Logie House

27

45

30

D E F

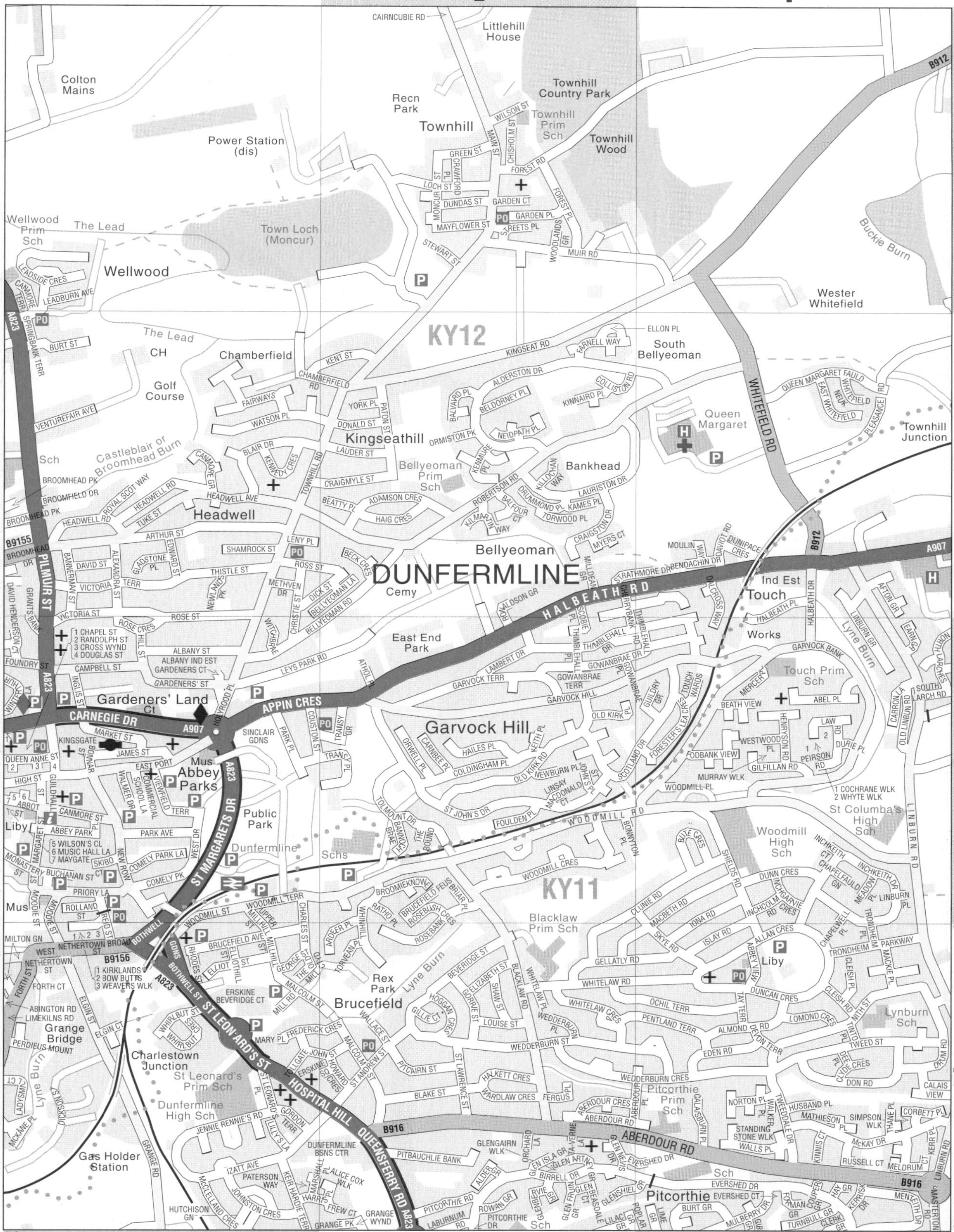

Colton Mains
Littlehill House
Townhill Country Park
Recn Park
Townhill
Townhill Prim Sch
Townhill Wood
Power Station (dis)
Wellwood Prim Sch
The Lead
Town Loch (Moncur)
Wellwood
Buckie Burn
Wester Whitefield
KY12
South Bellyeoman
CH
Chamberfield
Golf Course
Queen Margaret
Townhill Junction
Kingseathill
Castleblair or Broomhead Burn
Sch
Bellyeoman Prim Sch
Bankhead
Headwell
Bellyeoman
DUNFERMLINE
Cemy
Ind Est
Touch
Works
East End Park
Touch Prim Sch
Gardeners' Land
Garvock Hill
Mus
Abbey Parks
Public Park
Dunfermline
Schs
Woodmill High Sch
St Columba's High Sch
KY11
Liby
Mus
Blacklaw Prim Sch
Liby
Rex Park
Lyne Burn
Brucefield
Grange Bridge
Charlestown Junction
St Leonard's Prim Sch
Dunfermline High Sch
Lynburn Sch
Pitcorthie Prim Sch
Gas Holder Station
Sch
Pitcorthie
PITCORTHIE DR
B912
A907
B9155
A823
B9156
B916
PILMUIR ST
CARNEGIE DR
APPIN CRES
HALBEATH RD
WHITEFIELD RD
ST MARGARETS DR
ST LEONARD'S ST
HOSPITAL HILL
QUEENSFERRY RD
ABERDOUR RD
WOODMILL RD
KINGSEAT RD
MUIR RD
FOREST RD
HALBEATH DR
LINBURN RD
GARVOCK HILL
WEDDERBURN ST
PITCAIRN ST
ROSE ST
VICTORIA ST
LEYS PARK RD
BEVERIDGE ST
ELIZABETH ST
LOUISE ST
BLAKE ST
09
10
11
86
87
88
89
1
2
3
4

D E F

46

30

29
12

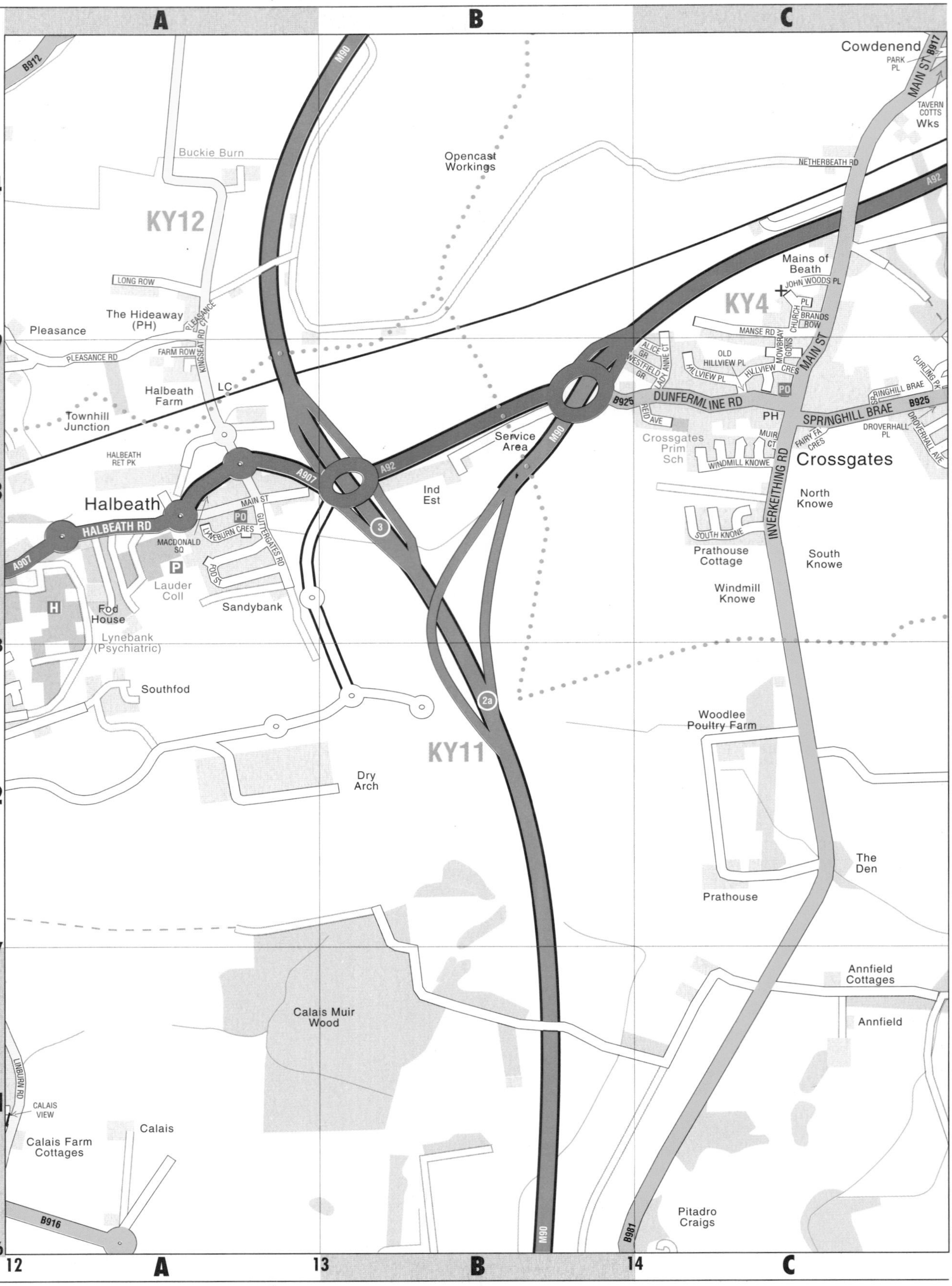
A
B
C
Cowdenend
PARK PL
MAIN ST
B917
TAVERN COTTS
Wks
B912
M90
Buckie Burn
Opencast Workings
NETHERBEATH RD
A92
KY12
Mains of Beath
JOHN WOODS PL
KY4
PL
BRANDS ROW
CHURCH
LONG ROW
The Hideaway (PH)
PLEASANCE
Pleasance
MANSE RD
MOWBRAY GDNS
MAIN ST
PLEASANCE RD
FARM ROW
KINGSEAT RD
ALICE GR
WESTFIELD GR
LADY ANNE CT
OLD HILLVIEW PL
HILLVIEW PL
HILLVIEW CRES
CURLING PK
Halbeath Farm
LC
B925
DUNFERMLINE RD
PO
RINGHILL BRAE
B925
Townhill Junction
REID AVE
PH
SPRINGHILL BRAE
Service Area
DROVERHALL PL
HALBEATH RET PK
A907
A92
Crossgates Prim Sch
MUIR CT
FAIRY FA CRES
DROVERHALL AVE
WINDMILL KNOWE
Crossgates
Ind Est
Halbeath
MAIN ST
INVERKEITHING RD
North Knowe
HALBEATH RD
PO
LYNEBURN CRES
GUTTERGATES RD
3
SOUTH KNOWE
A907
MACDONALD SQ
P
FOD ST
Prathouse Cottage
South Knowe
Lauder Coll
H
Windmill Knowe
Fod House
Sandybank
Lynebank (Psychiatric)
Southfod
2a
Woodlee Poultry Farm
KY11
Dry Arch
The Den
Prathouse
Annfield Cottages
Calais Muir Wood
Annfield
LINBURN RD
CALAIS VIEW
Calais
Calais Farm Cottages
B916
M90
B981
Pitadro Craigs
4
89
3
88
2
87
1
86
12
13
14
A
B
C

29
47

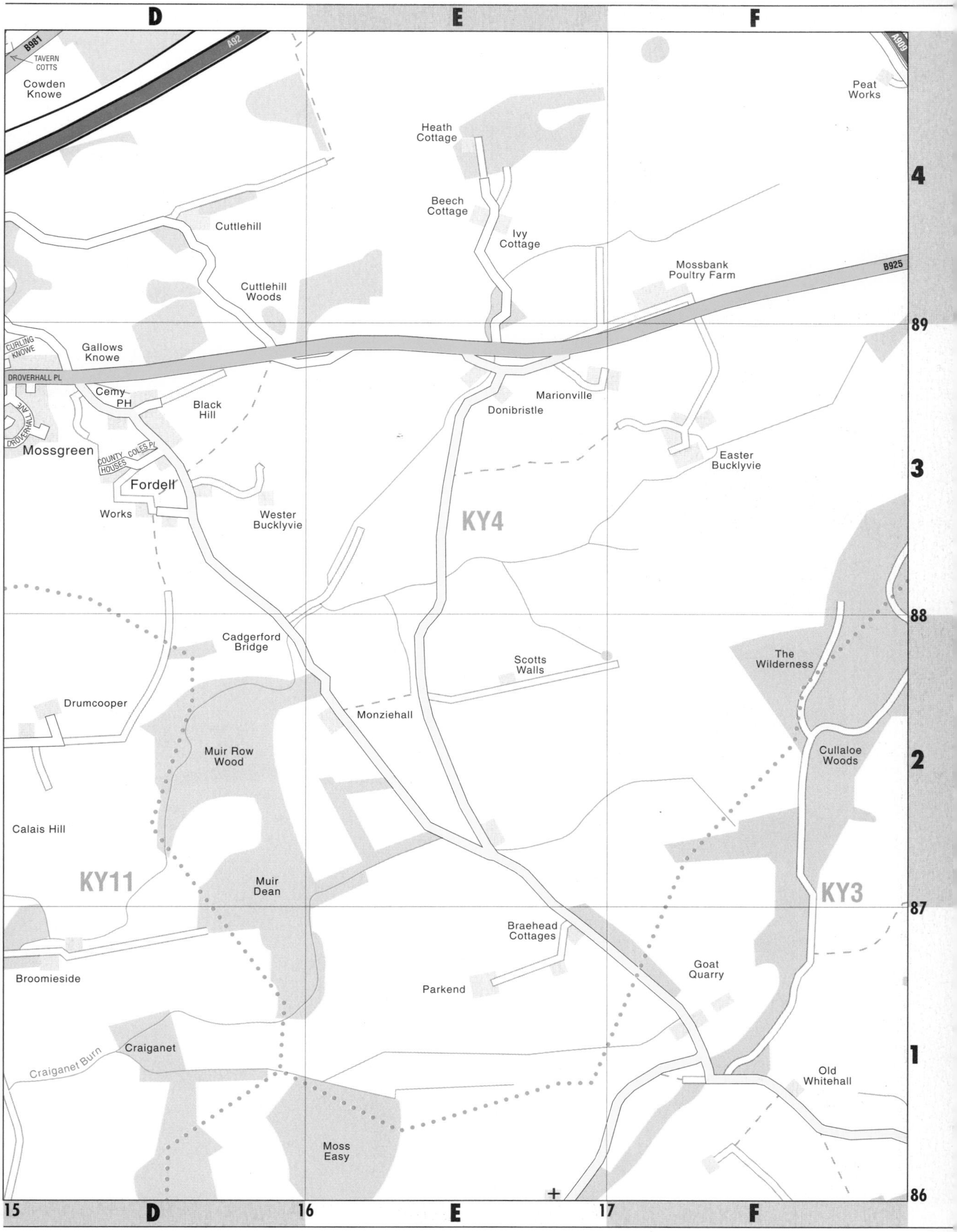

D

E

F

B981

TAVERN COTTS

Cowden Knowe

A92

Peat Works

A909

Heath Cottage

4

Cuttlehill

Beech Cottage

Ivy Cottage

Cuttlehill Woods

Mossbank Poultry Farm

B925

89

CURLING KNOWE

Gallows Knowe

DROVERHALL PL

Marionville

Cemy PH

Black Hill

Donibristle

DROVERHALL AVE

Mossgreen

COUNTY HOUSES

COLES PL

Easter Bucklyvie

Fordell

Works

Wester Bucklyvie

KY4

3

Cadgerford Bridge

88

Scotts Walls

The Wilderness

Drumcooper

Monziehall

Cullaloe Woods

Muir Row Wood

2

Calais Hill

KY11

Muir Dean

KY3

87

Braehead Cottages

Broomieside

Parkend

Goat Quarry

Craiganet Burn

Craiganet

1

Old Whitehall

Moss Easy

86

15

D

16

E

17

F

31
14

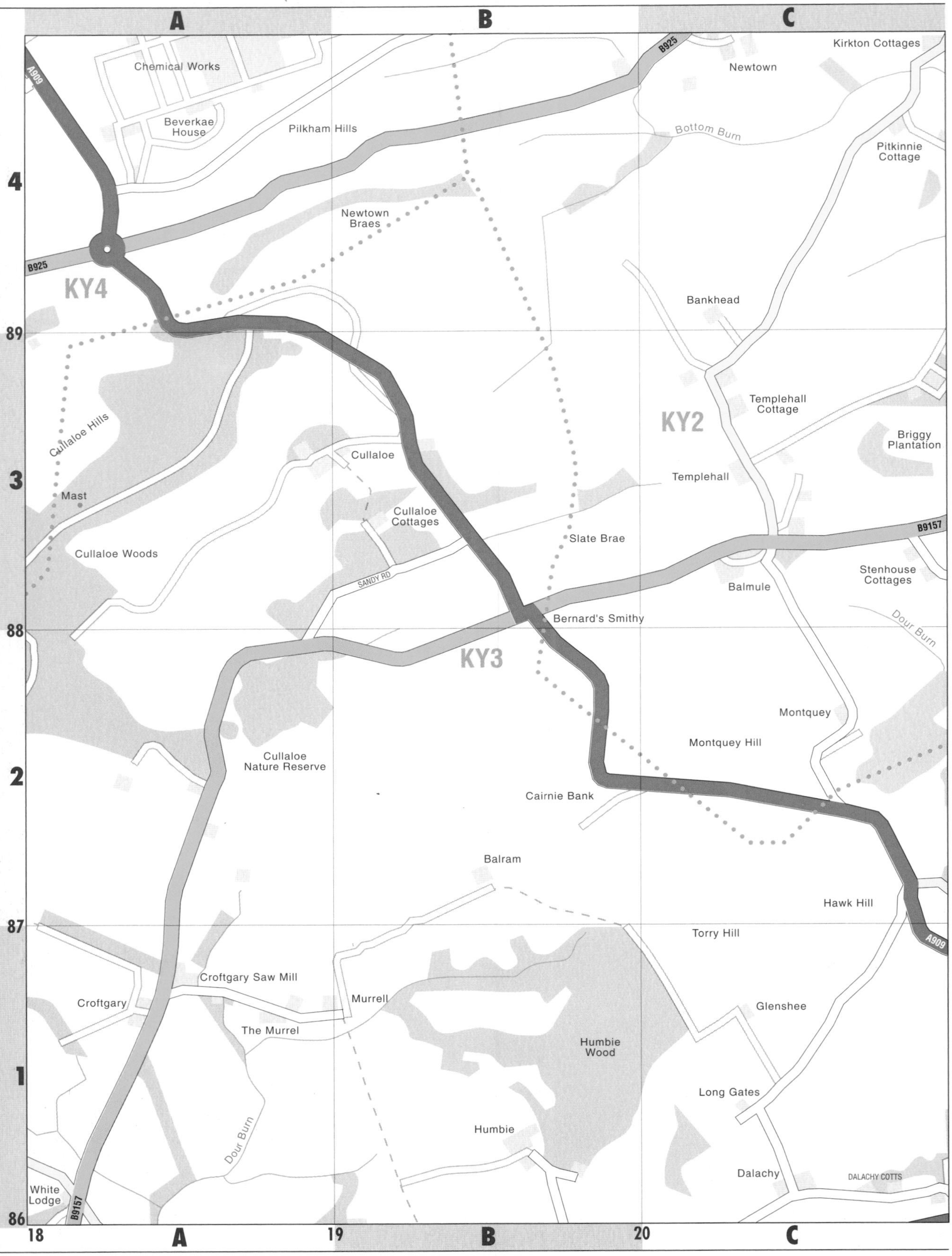

A   B   C

Chemical Works

Beverkae House

Pilkham Hills

B925

Newtown

Kirkton Cottages

Bottom Burn

Pitkinnie Cottage

Newtown Braes

KY4

Bankhead

KY2

Templehall Cottage

Cullaloe Hills

Briggy Plantation

Cullaloe

Mast

Templehall

Cullaloe Cottages

Slate Brae

Cullaloe Woods

B9157

SANDY RD

Stenhouse Cottages

Balmule

Dour Burn

Bernard's Smithy

KY3

Montquey

Cullaloe Nature Reserve

Montquey Hill

Cairnie Bank

Balram

Hawk Hill

Torry Hill

A909

Croftgary Saw Mill

Glenshee

Croftgary

Murrell

The Murrel

Humbie Wood

Long Gates

Humbie

Dour Burn

Dalachy

DALACHY COTTS

White Lodge

B9157

18   A   19   B   20   C

31
49

15
34

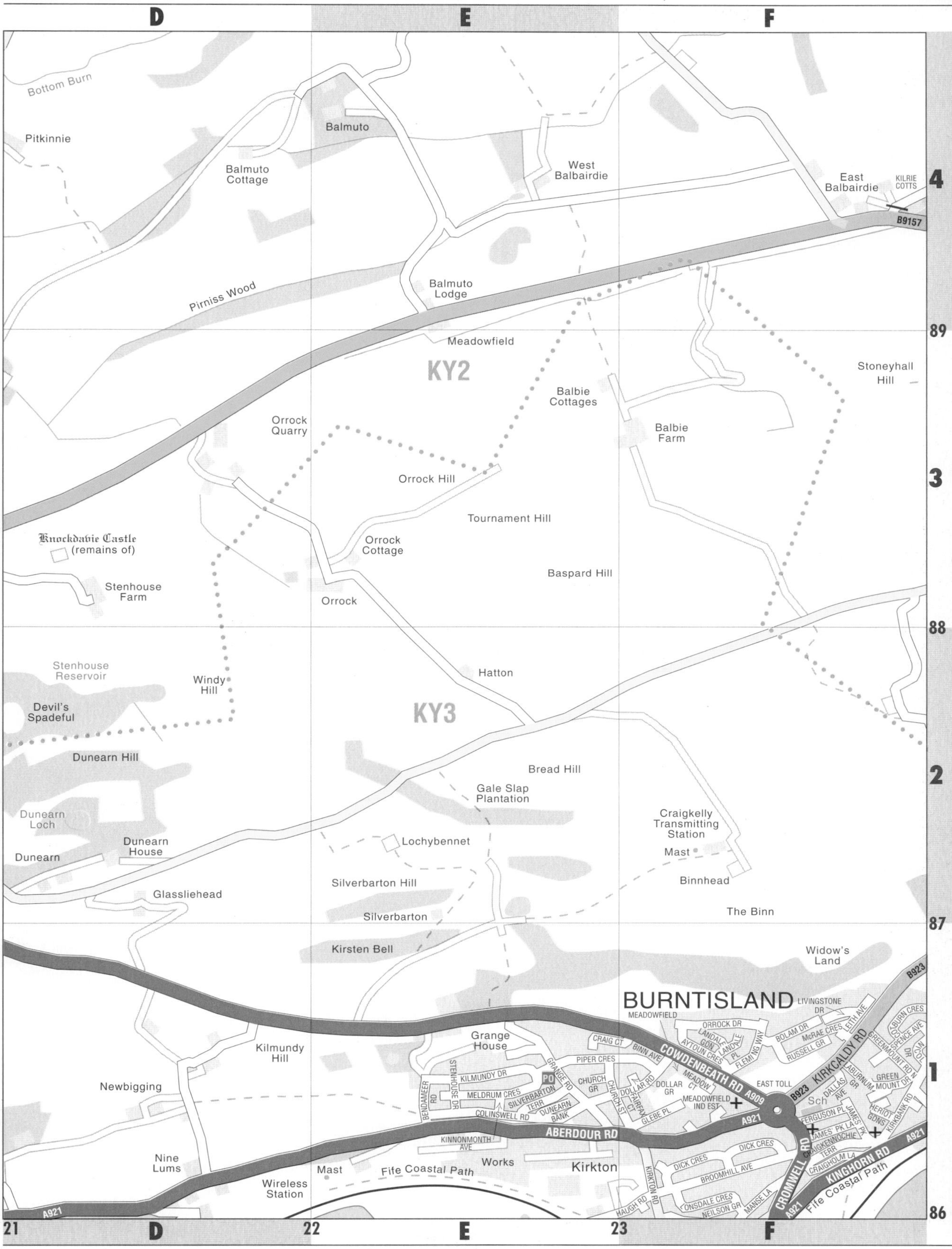
D
E
F
Bottom Burn
Pitkinnie
Balmuto
Balmuto Cottage
West Balbairdie
East Balbairdie
KILRIE COTTS
B9157
4
Pirniss Wood
Balmuto Lodge
Meadowfield
89
KY2
Stoneyhall Hill
Balbie Cottages
Balbie Farm
Orrock Quarry
Orrock Hill
3
Tournament Hill
Knockdavie Castle (remains of)
Orrock Cottage
Baspard Hill
Stenhouse Farm
Orrock
88
Stenhouse Reservoir
Windy Hill
Hatton
Devil's Spadeful
KY3
Dunearn Hill
Bread Hill
2
Gale Slap Plantation
Dunearn Loch
Craigkelly Transmitting Station
Dunearn
Dunearn House
Lochybennet
Mast
Binnhead
Silverbarton Hill
Glassliehead
The Binn
Silverbarton
87
Kirsten Bell
Widow's Land
B923
BURNTISLAND
MEADOWFIELD
LIVINGSTONE DR
Grange House
Kilmundy Hill
CRAIG CT
BINN AVE
COWDENBEATH RD
A909
KIRKCALDY RD
Newbigging
PIPER CRES
CHURCH GR
KILMUNDY DR
STENHOUSE DR
GRANGE RD
PO
DOLLAR GR
MEADOWFIELD IND EST
EAST TOLL
1
BENDAMEER RD
MELDRUM CRES
SILVERBARTON TERR
DUNEARN BANK
COLINSWELL RD
GLEBE PL
A921
FERGUSON PL
JAMES' PK LA
CRAIGKENNOCHIE TERR
ABERDOUR RD
KINNONMONTH AVE
DICK CRES
CRAIGHOLM LA
KINGHORN RD
Nine Lums
Works
Mast
Fife Coastal Path
Kirkton
KIRKTON RD
BROOMHILL AVE
CROMWELL RD
Wireless Station
HAUGH RD
LONSDALE CRES
NEILSON GR
MANSE LA
Fife Coastal Path
A921
86
21
22
23

33
16

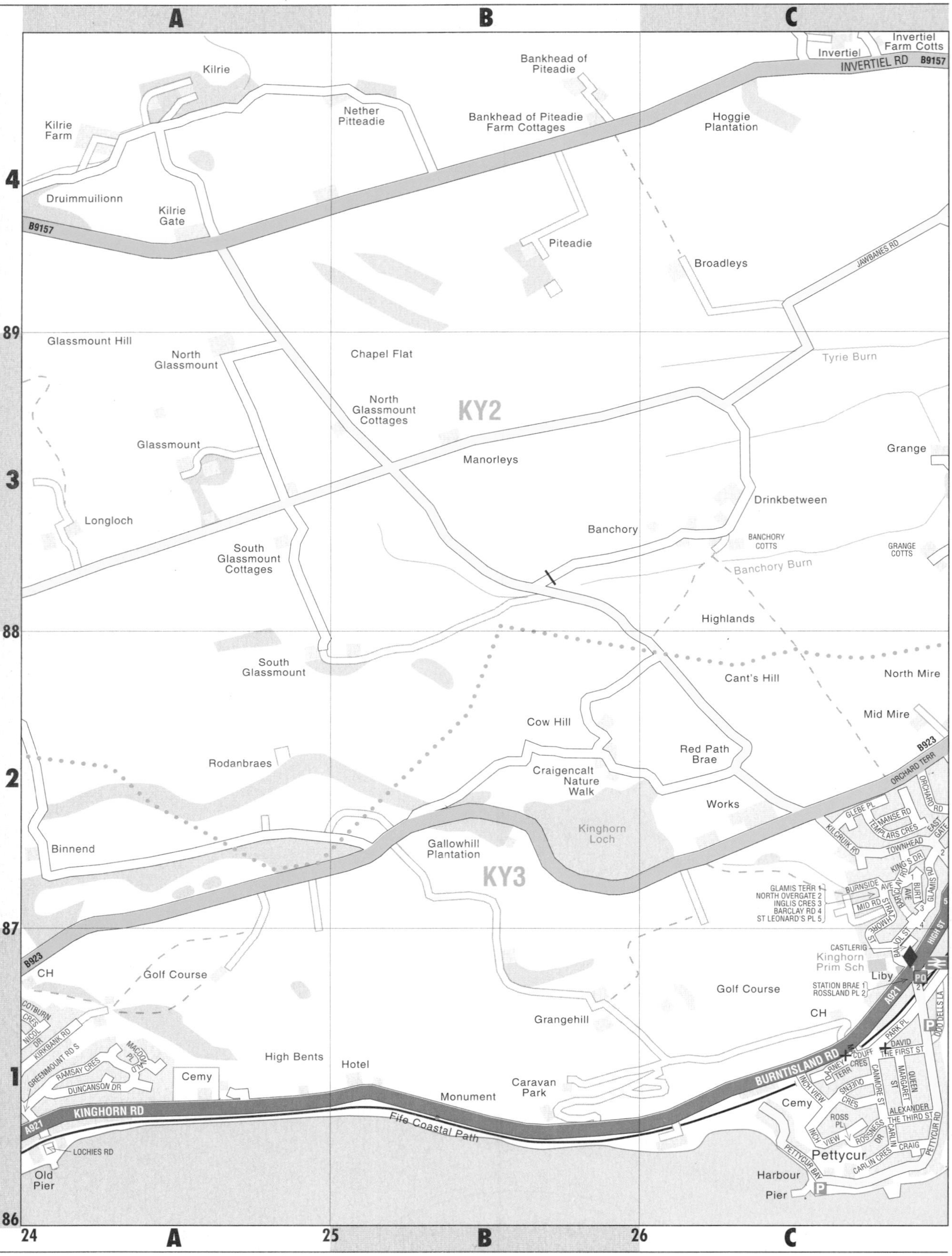
A
B
C
Invertiel
Invertiel Farm Cotts
INVERTIEL RD
B9157
Kilrie
Bankhead of Piteadie
Nether Pitteadie
Bankhead of Piteadie Farm Cottages
Hoggie Plantation
Kilrie Farm
4
Druimmuilionn
Kilrie Gate
B9157
Piteadie
Broadleys
JAWBANES RD
89
Glassmount Hill
North Glassmount
Chapel Flat
Tyrie Burn
North Glassmount Cottages
KY2
Glassmount
Manorleys
Grange
3
Drinkbetween
Longloch
Banchory
BANCHORY COTTS
GRANGE COTTS
South Glassmount Cottages
Banchory Burn
Highlands
88
South Glassmount
Cant's Hill
North Mire
Cow Hill
Mid Mire
Red Path Brae
Rodanbraes
B923
2
Craigencalt Nature Walk
ORCHARD TERR
Works
Kinghorn Loch
Binnend
Gallowhill Plantation
KY3
GLEBE PL
MANSE RD
TEMPLARS CRES
KILCRUIK RD
TOWNHEAD
EAST GATE
KING'S DR
GLAMIS TERR 1
NORTH OVERGATE 2
INGLIS CRES 3
BARCLAY RD 4
ST LEONARD'S PL 5
BURNSIDE
MID RD
87
CASTLERIG
Kinghorn Prim Sch
HIGH ST
B923
CH
Golf Course
Liby
PO
STATION BRAE 1
ROSSLAND PL 2
Golf Course
A921
CH
COTBURN CRES
NICOL DR
KIRKBANK RD
GREENMOUNT RD S
RAMSAY CRES
Grangehill
PARK PL
DAVID THE FIRST ST
High Bents
Hotel
BURNTISLAND RD
1
Cemy
DUNCANSON DR
Caravan Park
Monument
INCH VIEW
CANMORE ST
MARGARET ST
QUEEN
KINGHORN RD
Cemy
ALEXANDER THE THIRD ST
A921
Fife Coastal Path
ROSS PL
ROSSNESS DR
PETTYCUR RD
LOCHIES RD
PETTYCUR BAY
Pettycur
CARLIN CRES
CRAIG
Old Pier
Harbour
Pier
P
86
24
A
25
B
26
C

33

17

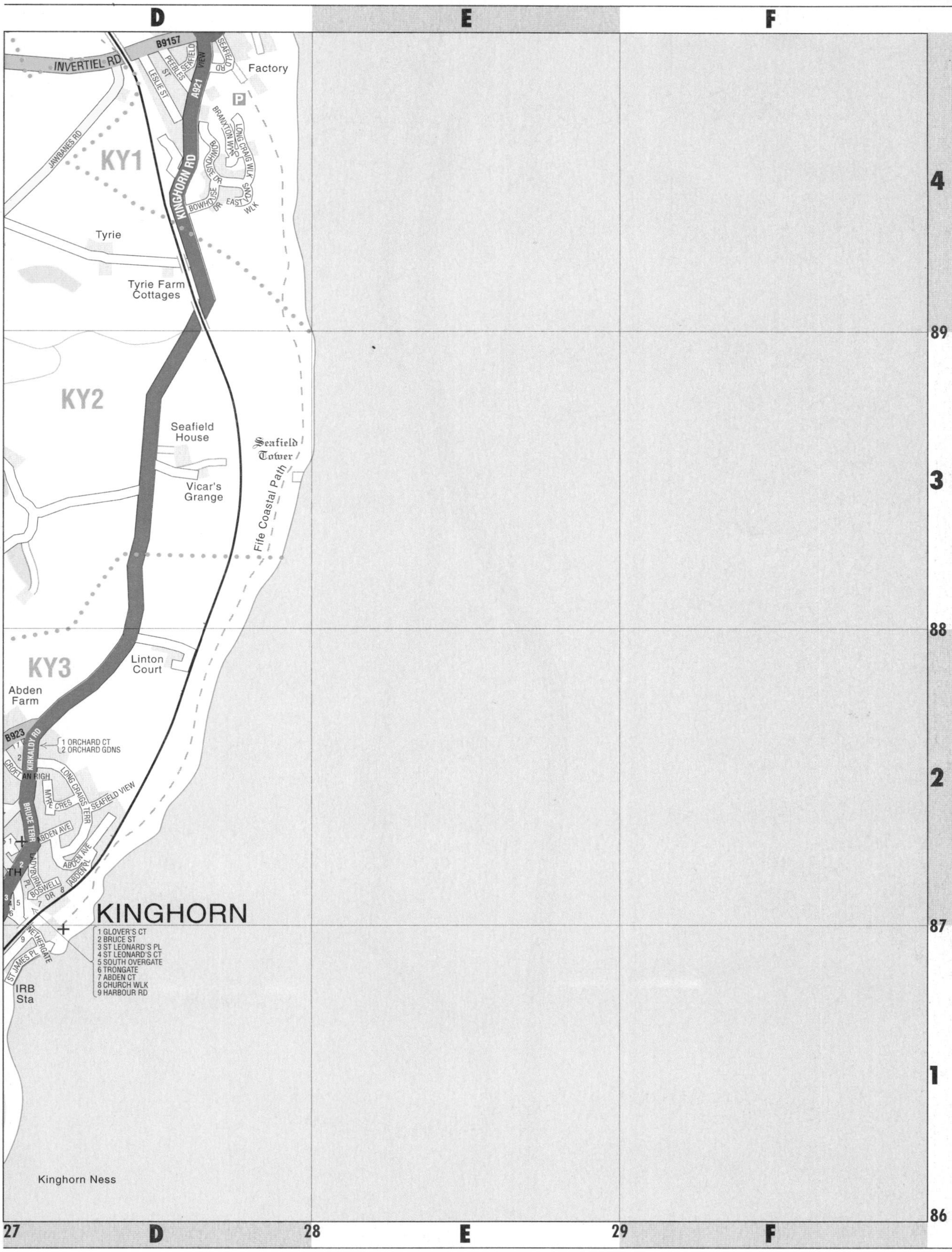
D
E
F
B9157
INVERTIEL RD
LESLIE ST
PEEBLES ST
SEAFIELD VIEW
SEAFIELD RD
Factory
A921
JAWBANES RD
KY1
BRANKTON WYND
LONG CRAIG WLK
KINGHORN RD
BOWHOUSE DR
BOWHOUSE DR
EAST WLK
Tyrie
Tyrie Farm Cottages
KY2
Seafield House
Seafield Tower
Vicar's Grange
Fife Coastal Path
KY3
Linton Court
Abden Farm
B923
KIRKALDY RD
1 ORCHARD CT
2 ORCHARD GDNS
CROFT AN RIGH
LONG CRAIGS TERR
SEAFIELD VIEW
BRUCE TERR
ABDEN AVE
ABDEN AVE
ABDEN PL
LADYBURN PL
BOSWELL DR
TH
KINGHORN
1 GLOVER'S CT
2 BRUCE ST
3 ST LEONARD'S PL
4 ST LEONARD'S CT
5 SOUTH OVERGATE
6 TRONGATE
7 ABDEN CT
8 CHURCH WLK
9 HARBOUR RD
NETHERGATE
ST JAMES PL
IRB Sta
Kinghorn Ness
4
89
3
88
2
87
1
86
27
28
29

19

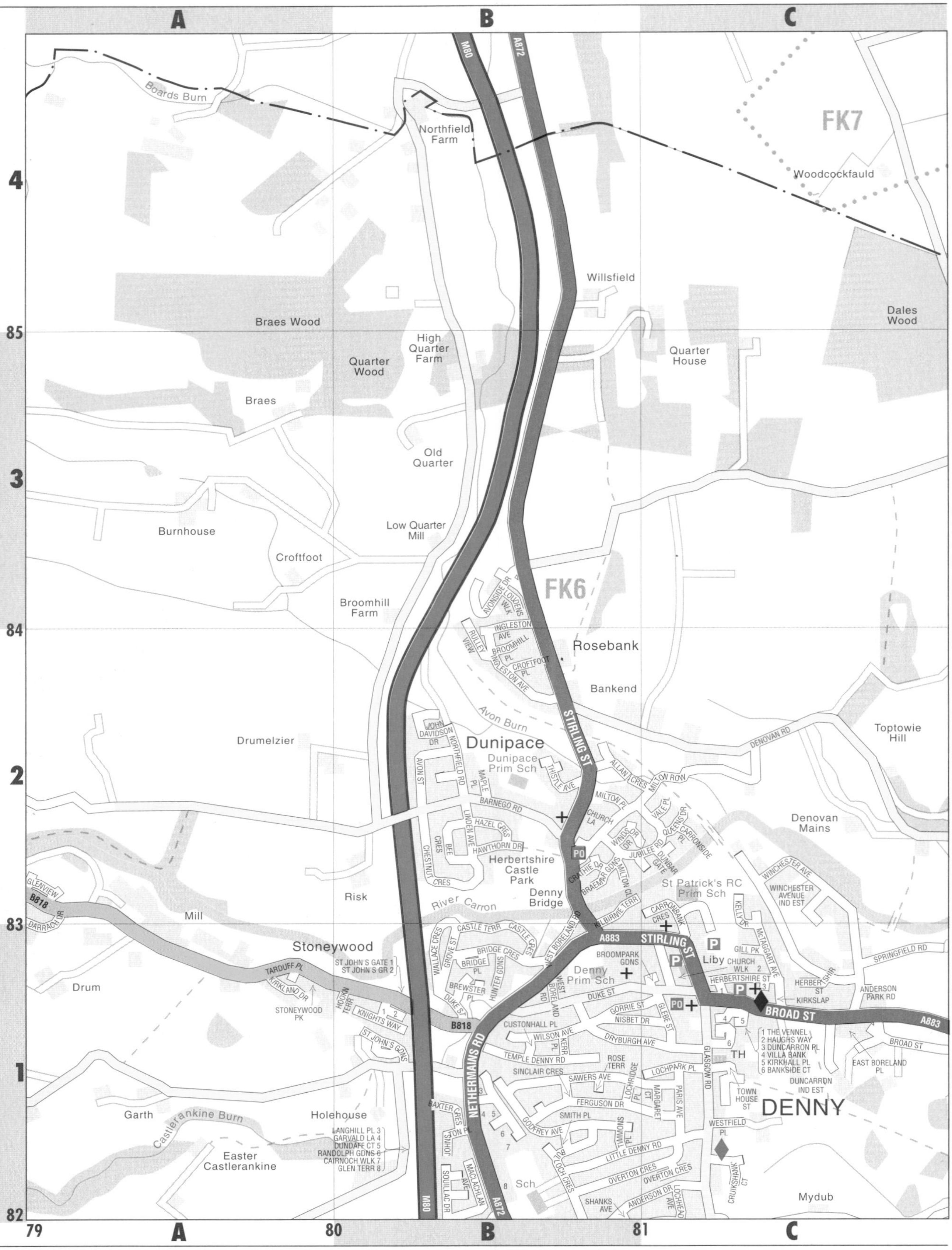

A
B
C
4
85
3
84
2
83
1
82
79
80
81
M80
A872
Boards Burn
Northfield Farm
FK7
Woodcockfauld
Willsfield
Dales Wood
Braes Wood
High Quarter Farm
Quarter Wood
Quarter House
Braes
Old Quarter
Burnhouse
Croftfoot
Low Quarter Mill
Broomhill Farm
FK6
Rosebank
Bankend
Avon Burn
Drumelzier
Dunipace
Dunipace Prim Sch
STIRLING ST
DENOVAN RD
Toptowie Hill
Denovan Mains
Herbertshire Castle Park
Denny Bridge
St Patrick's RC Prim Sch
River Carron
Risk
Mill
B818
Stoneywood
Drum
STONEYWOOD PK
A883
BROAD ST
Liby
Denny Prim Sch
TH
TOWN HOUSE ST
DENNY
DUNCARRON IND EST
NETHERMAINS RD
Garth
Castlerankine Burn
Holehouse
Easter Castlerankine
Sch
Mydub
1 THE VENNEL
2 HAUGHS WAY
3 DUNCARRON PL
4 VILLA BANK
5 KIRKHALL PL
6 BANKSIDE CT
LANGHILL PL 3
GARVALD LA 4
DUNDAFF CT 5
RANDOLPH GDNS 6
CAIRNOCH WLK 7
GLEN TERR 8
ST JOHN'S GATE 1
ST JOHN'S GR 2

57

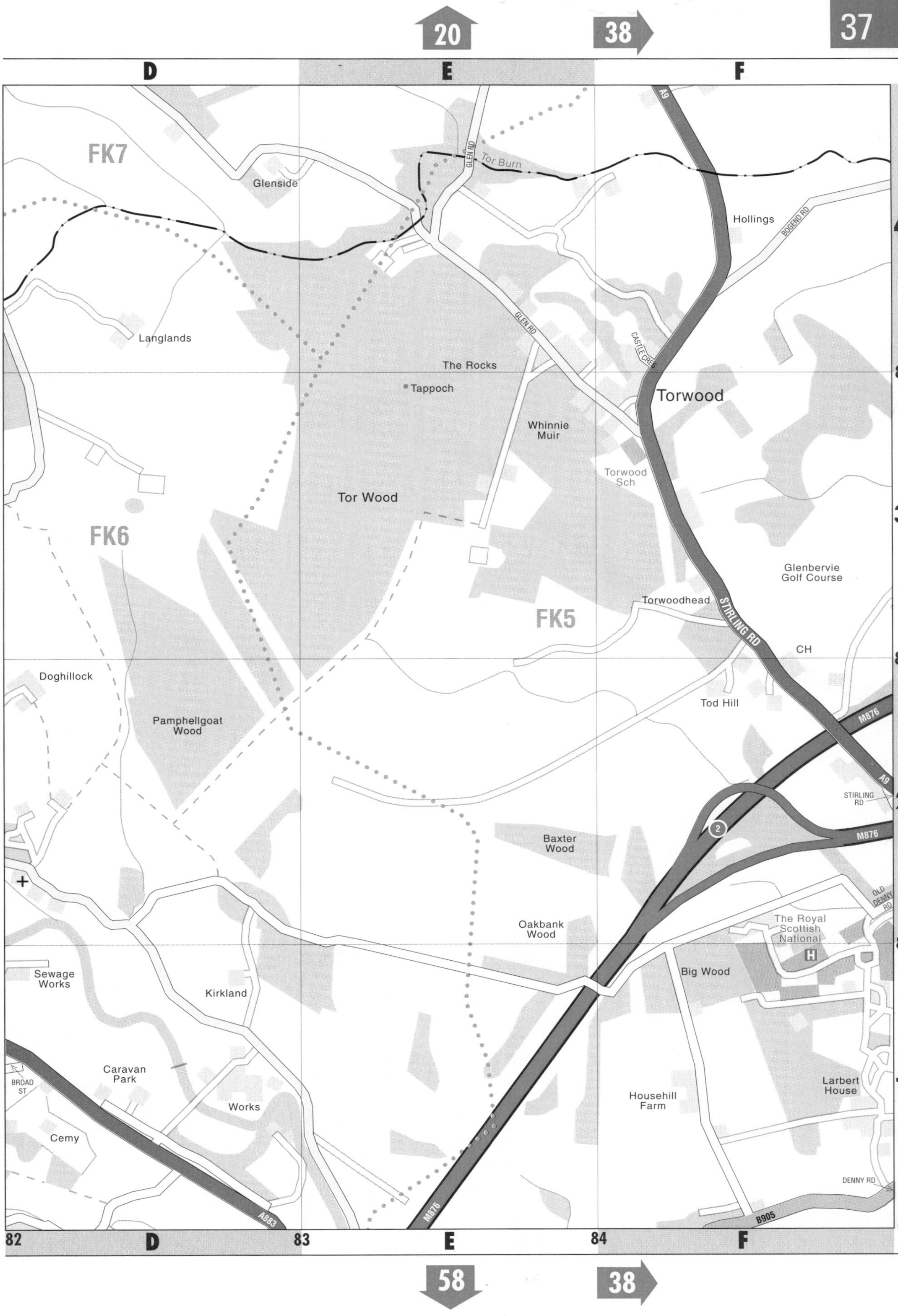
20
38
D
E
F
FK7
Glenside
GLEN RD
Tor Burn
A9
Hollings
BOGEND RD
4
Langlands
GLEN RD
CASTLE CRES
The Rocks
85
Tappoch
Torwood
Whinnie Muir
Torwood Sch
Tor Wood
3
FK6
Glenbervie Golf Course
Torwoodhead
STIRLING RD
FK5
CH
84
Doghillock
Tod Hill
Pamphellgoat Wood
M876
A9
STIRLING RD
2
2
M876
Baxter Wood
OLD DENNY RD
Oakbank Wood
The Royal Scottish National
H
83
Sewage Works
Big Wood
Kirkland
Caravan Park
BROAD ST
Larbert House
1
Househill Farm
Works
Cemy
DENNY RD
A883
M876
B905
82
82
D
83
E
84
F
58
38

37
21

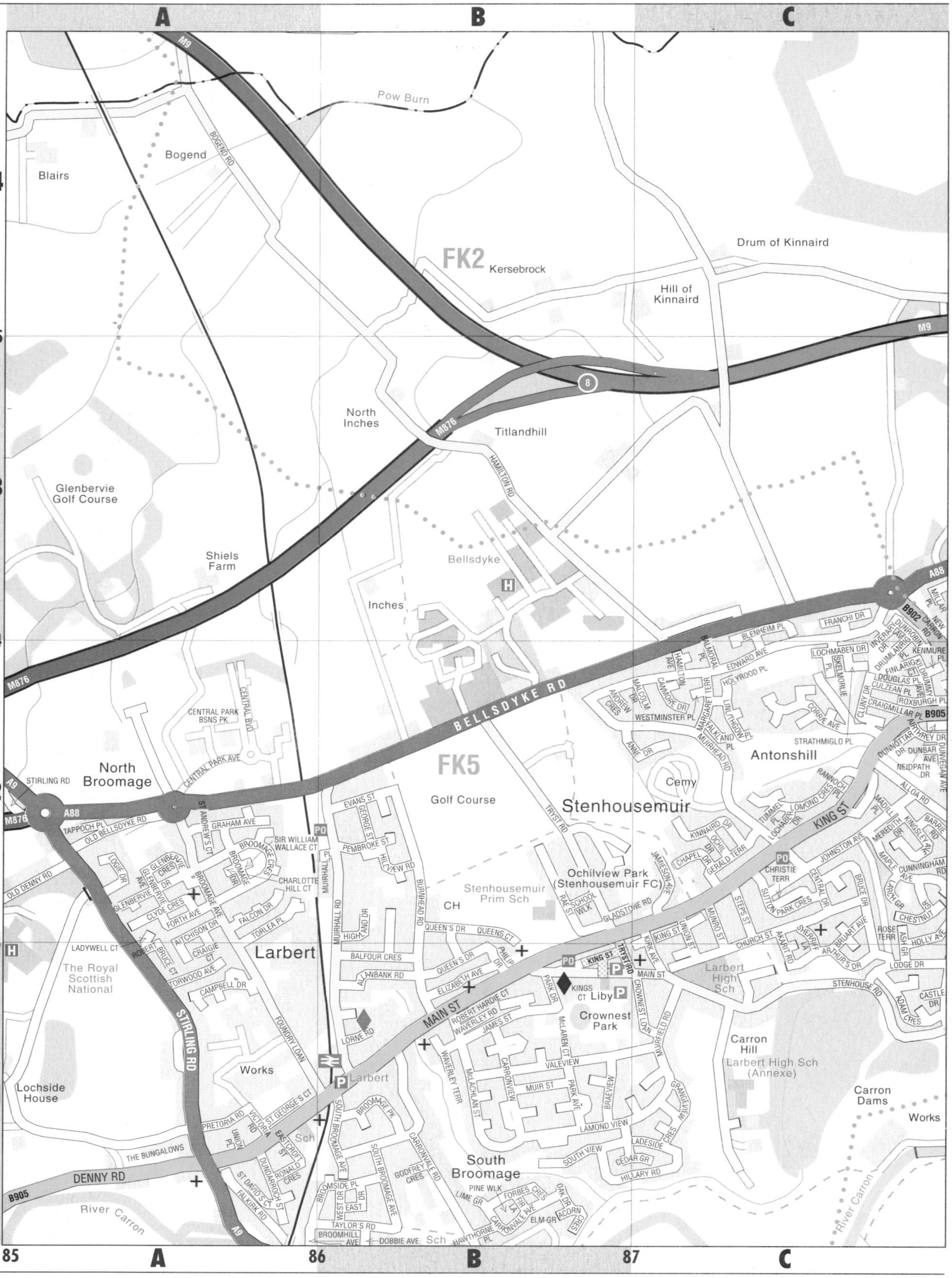
A
B
C
Pow Burn
Bogend
Blairs
BOGEND RD
M9
FK2
Kersebrock
Drum of Kinnaird
Hill of
Kinnaird
North
Inches
Titlandhill
M876
HAMILTON RD
Glenbervie
Golf Course
Shiels
Farm
Bellsdyke
Inches
A88
B902
FRANCHI DR
BLENHEIM PL
BELLSDYKE RD
CENTRAL PARK
BSNS PK
CENTRAL BVD
CENTRAL PARK AVE
North
Broomage
STIRLING RD
A9
FK5
Golf Course
Stenhousemuir
Antonshill
Cemy
STRATHMIGLO PL
KING ST
MAIN ST
Ochilview Park
(Stenhousemuir FC)
Stenhousemuir
Prim Sch
CH
Larbert
The Royal
Scottish
National
Larbert
High
Sch
Crownest
Park
Liby
Carron
Hill
Larbert High Sch
(Annexe)
Carron
Dams
Works
Lochside
House
Works
Larbert
South
Broomage
DENNY RD
B905
River Carron
THE BUNGALOWS
STIRLING RD
4
85
3
84
2
83
1
82
86
87

22
40

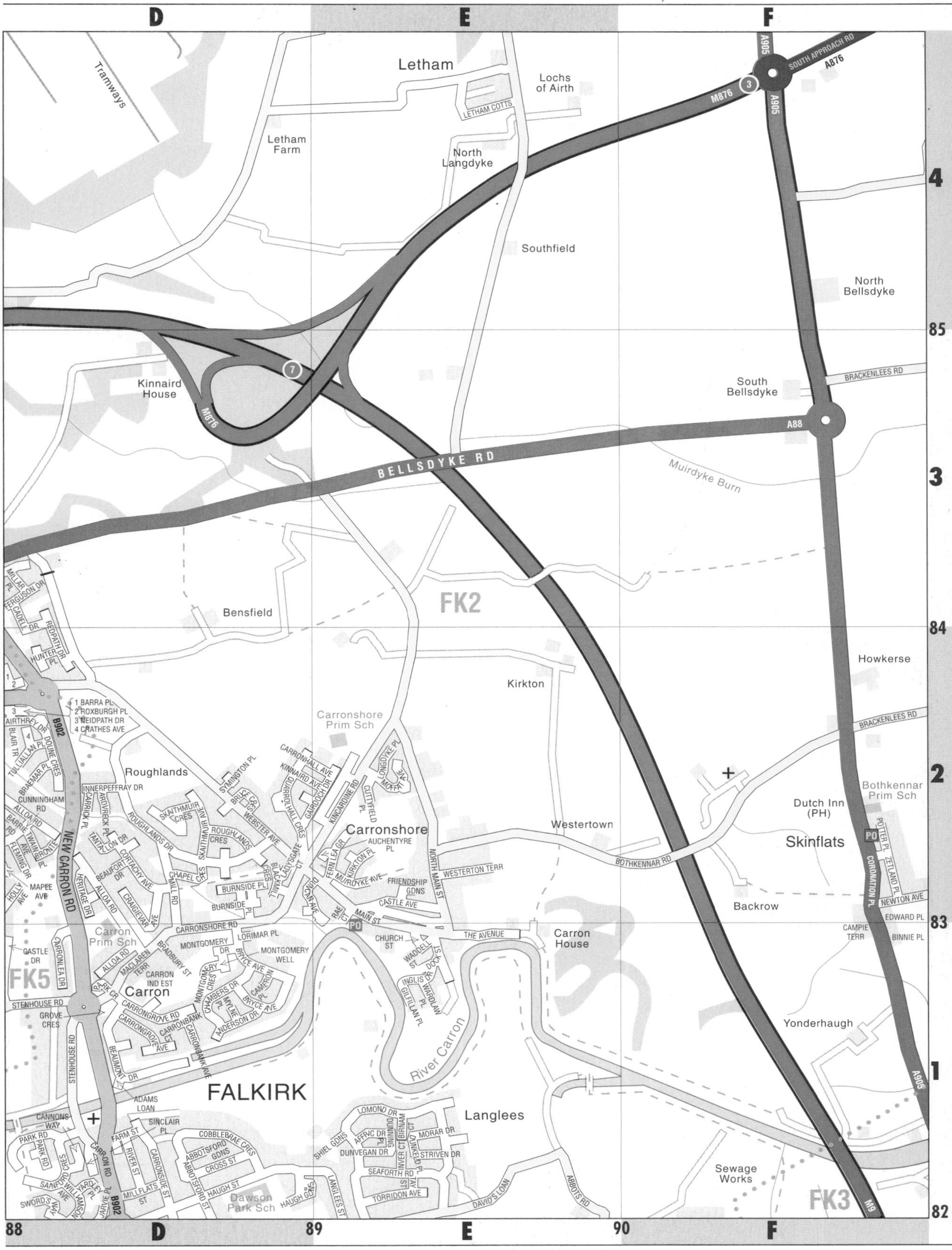
D
E
F
Tramways
Letham
Lochs of Airth
LETHAM COTTS
Letham Farm
North Langdyke
M876
A905
SOUTH APPROACH RD
A876
4
Southfield
North Bellsdyke
85
Kinnaird House
South Bellsdyke
BRACKENLEES RD
A88
BELLSDYKE RD
Muirdyke Burn
3
FK2
Bensfield
84
Kirkton
Howkerse
Carronshore Prim Sch
1 BARRA PL
2 ROXBURGH PL
3 NEIDPATH DR
4 CRATHES AVE
B902
Roughlands
2
Bothkennar Prim Sch
Dutch Inn (PH)
Westertown
Carronshore
Skinflats
AUCHENTYRE PL
BOTHKENNAR RD
WESTERTON TERR
POTTER PL
ZETLAND PL
CORONATION PL
NEW CARRON RD
MAPLE AVE
FRIENDSHIP GDNS
CASTLE AVE
MAIN ST
Backrow
NEWTON AVE
EDWARD PL
CAMPIE TERR
BINNIE PL
83
Carron Prim Sch
CARRONSHORE RD
LORIMAR PL
MONTGOMERY WELL
CHURCH ST
THE AVENUE
Carron House
FK5
CARRON IND EST
Carron
STENHOUSE RD
GROVE CRES
River Carron
Yonderhaugh
1
FALKIRK
ADAMS LOAN
SINCLAIR PL
Langlees
COBBLEBRAE CRES
ABBOTSFORD GDNS
CROSS ST
DUNVEGAN DR
STRIVEN DR
SEAFORTH RD
TORRIDON AVE
Sewage Works
FK3
M9
Dawson Park Sch
HAUGH GDNS
LANGLEES ST
DAVID'S LOAN
ABBOTS RD
82
88
89
90

60
40

A   B   C

4

Greendyke

Powfoulis
Manor Hotel

Mains of
Powfoulis

Pocknave

Brackenlees

85

Hardlands

Stonehouse
Farm

Firth of Forth

3

FK2

BRACKENLEES RD

Orchardhead

84

Newton Mains
Farm

2

Skinflats

NEWTON AVE

NEWTON RD

83

Grangemouth Harbour
& Docks

NORTH SHORE RD

River Carron

Carron Dock

CENTRAL DOCK RD

Western Channel

1

LC

MIDDLE ST LA

NORTH BRIDGE ST

SOUTH BRIDGE ST

GRANGE LA

FK3

1 YORK LA
2 YORK SQ
3 YORK ARC
4 LA PORTE PREC
5 LIBRARY LA
6 CHARING CROSS

1 BELL CT
2 TAYLOR CT
3 NELSON GDNS

LC's

Glensburgh

A905

GLENSBURGH RD

DEVON ST

BANK ST

WEST CHURCH ST

DALGRAIN RD

SOUTH SHORE RD

GRANGEBURN RD

ALLAN CT

NAISMITH CT

PARIS ST

NELSON ST

GEORGE...

ROWDRAKE RD

AVON ST

DON ST

TWEED ST

CLYDE ST

STATION RD

A904

UNION RD

EARL'S RD

PO

TH

Liby

BO'NESS RD

DOCK RD

A904

TAY ST

KELVIN ST

82

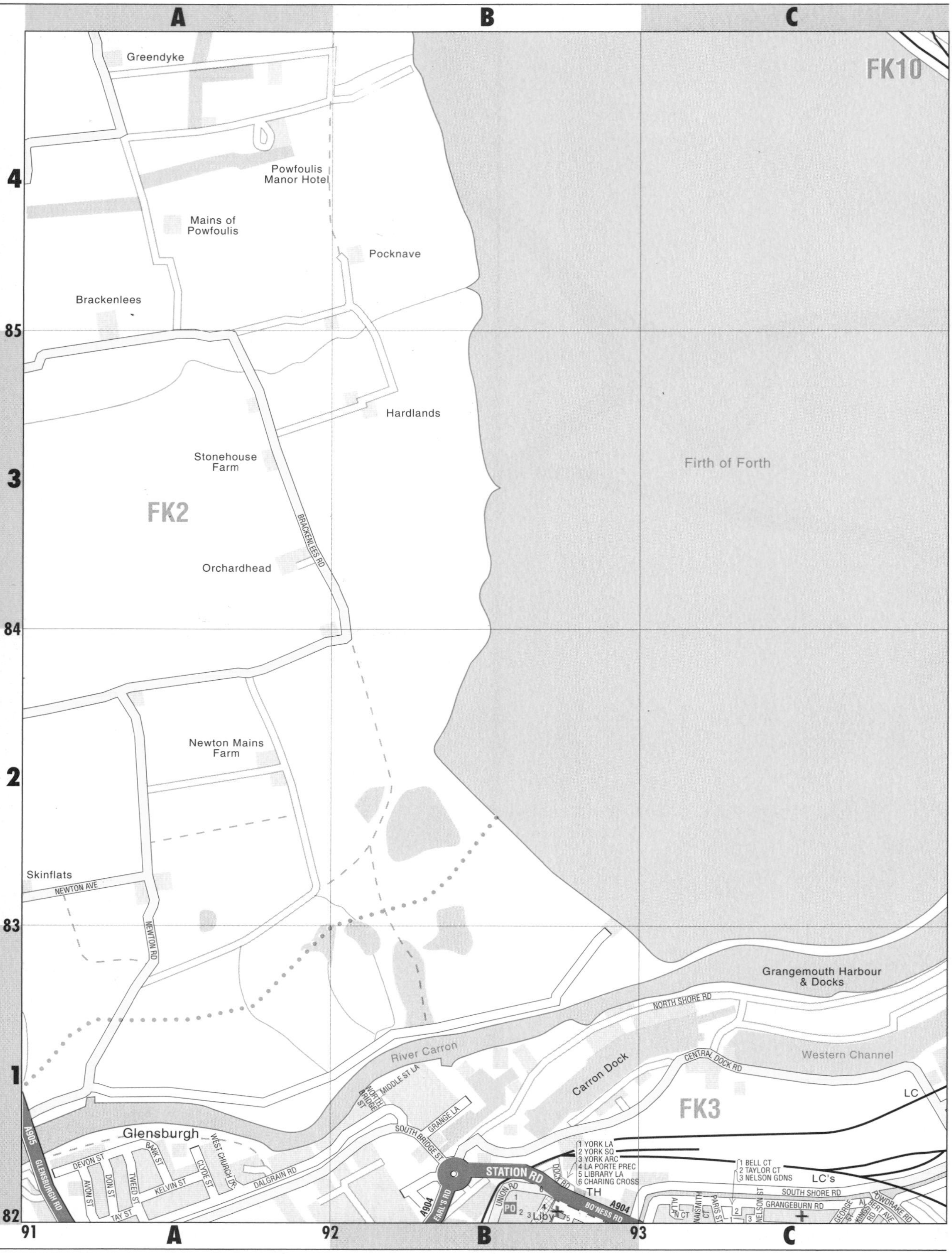

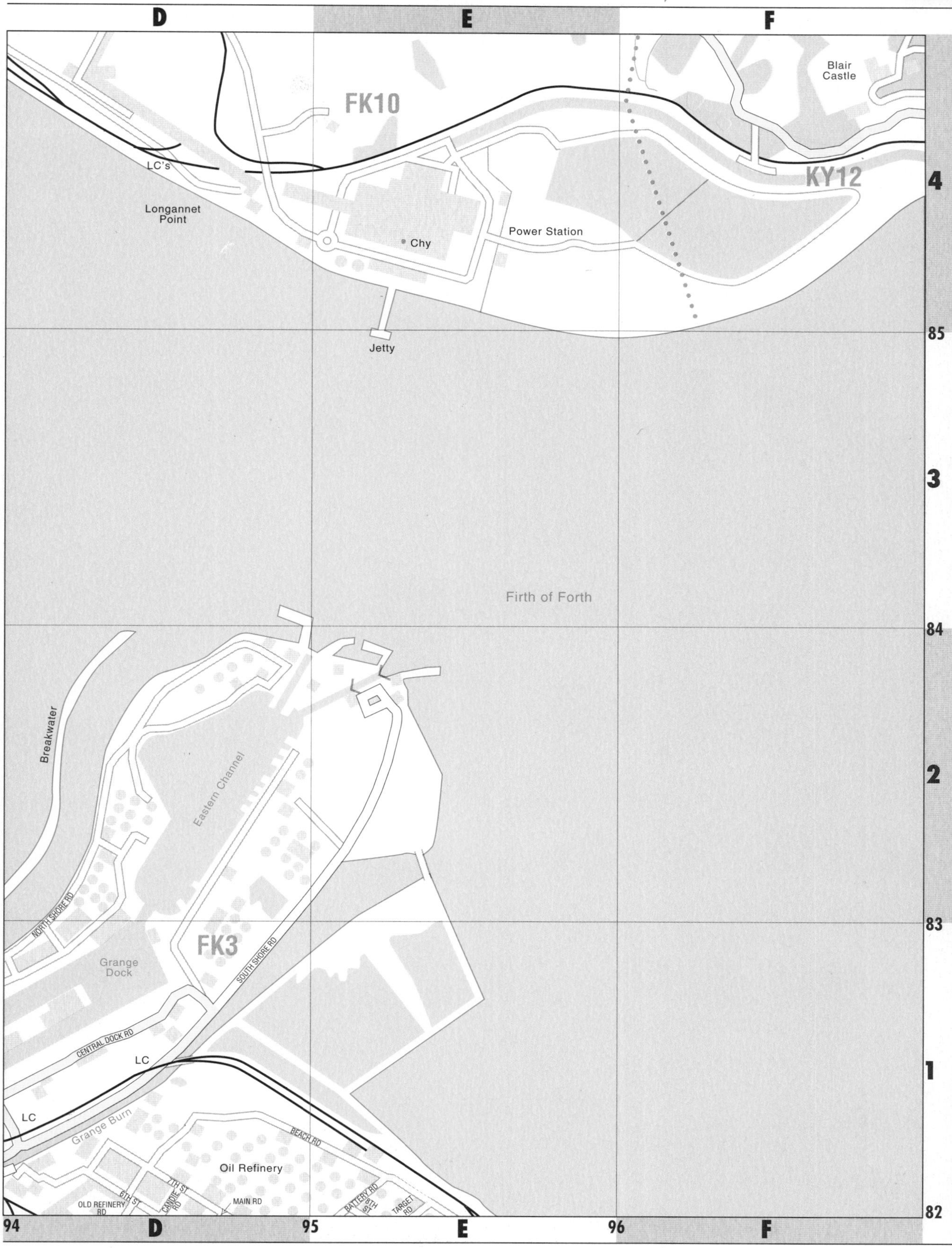

D
E
F

FK10

LC's
Longannet
Point

Chy

Power Station

Blair
Castle

KY12

4

Jetty

85

3

Firth of Forth

84

Breakwater

Eastern Channel

2

83

NORTH SHORE RD
SOUTH SHORE RD

FK3

Grange
Dock

CENTRAL DOCK RD

LC

LC

Grange Burn

BEACH RD

1

Oil Refinery

6TH ST
7TH ST
8TH ST
CANDIE RD
MAIN RD
OLD REFINERY RD
BATTERY RD
9TH
TARGET RD

82

94
D
95
E
96
F

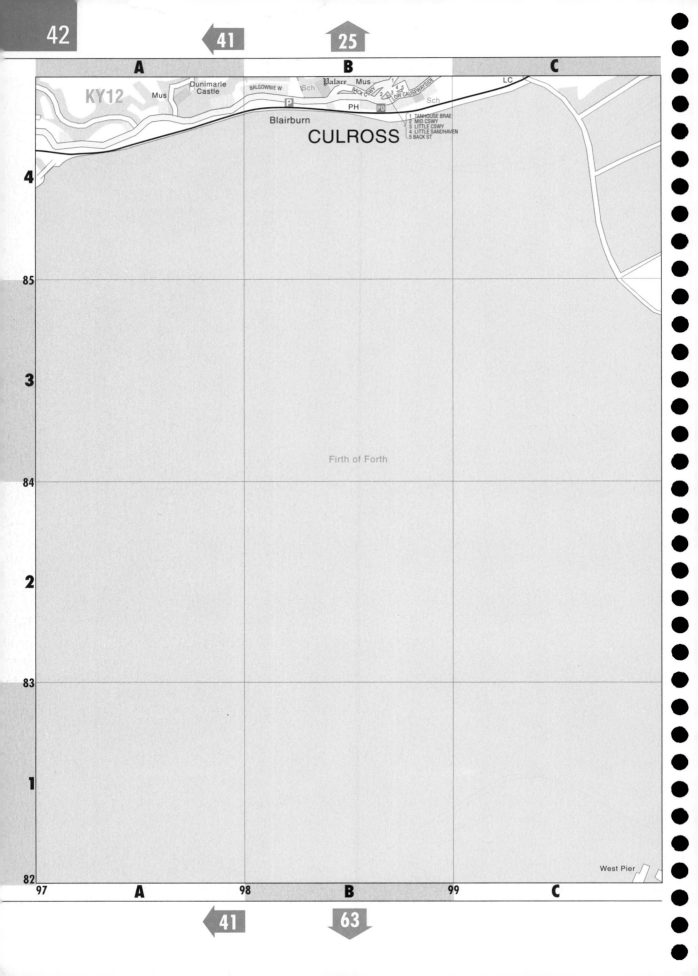

KY12

Mus

Dunimarle
Castle

Blairburn

BALGOWNIE W

Sch

Palace Mus

BACK CSWY

LOW CAUSEWAYSIDE

PH

PO

Sch

LC

A

B

C

CULROSS

1 TANHOUSE BRAE
2 MID CSWY
3 LITTLE CSWY
4 LITTLE SANDHAVEN
5 BACK ST

4

85

3

84

Firth of Forth

2

83

1

82

West Pier

97

A

98

B

99

C

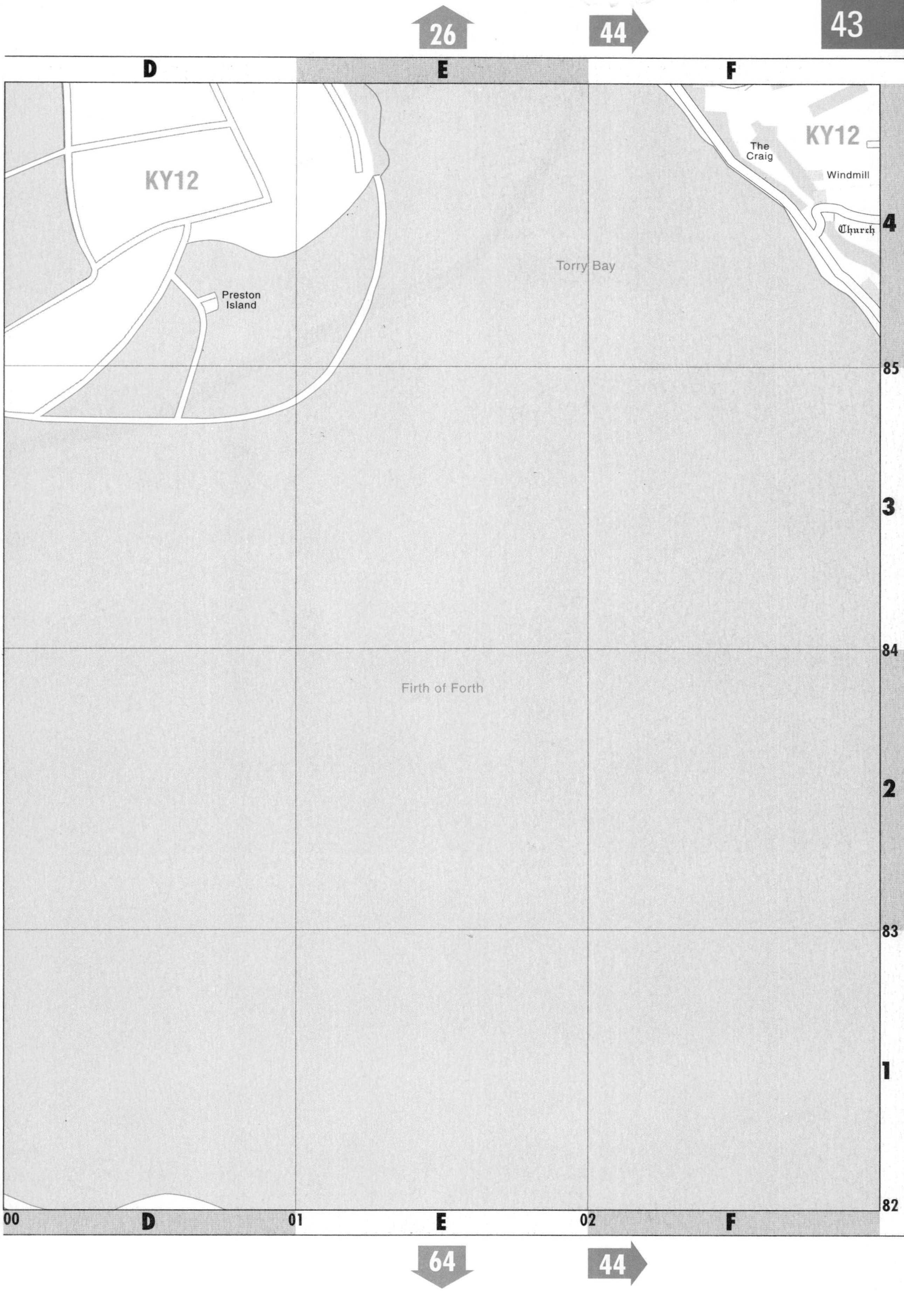

KY12

KY12
The Craig
Windmill
Church
4

Preston Island

Torry Bay

85

3

84

Firth of Forth

2

83

1

82

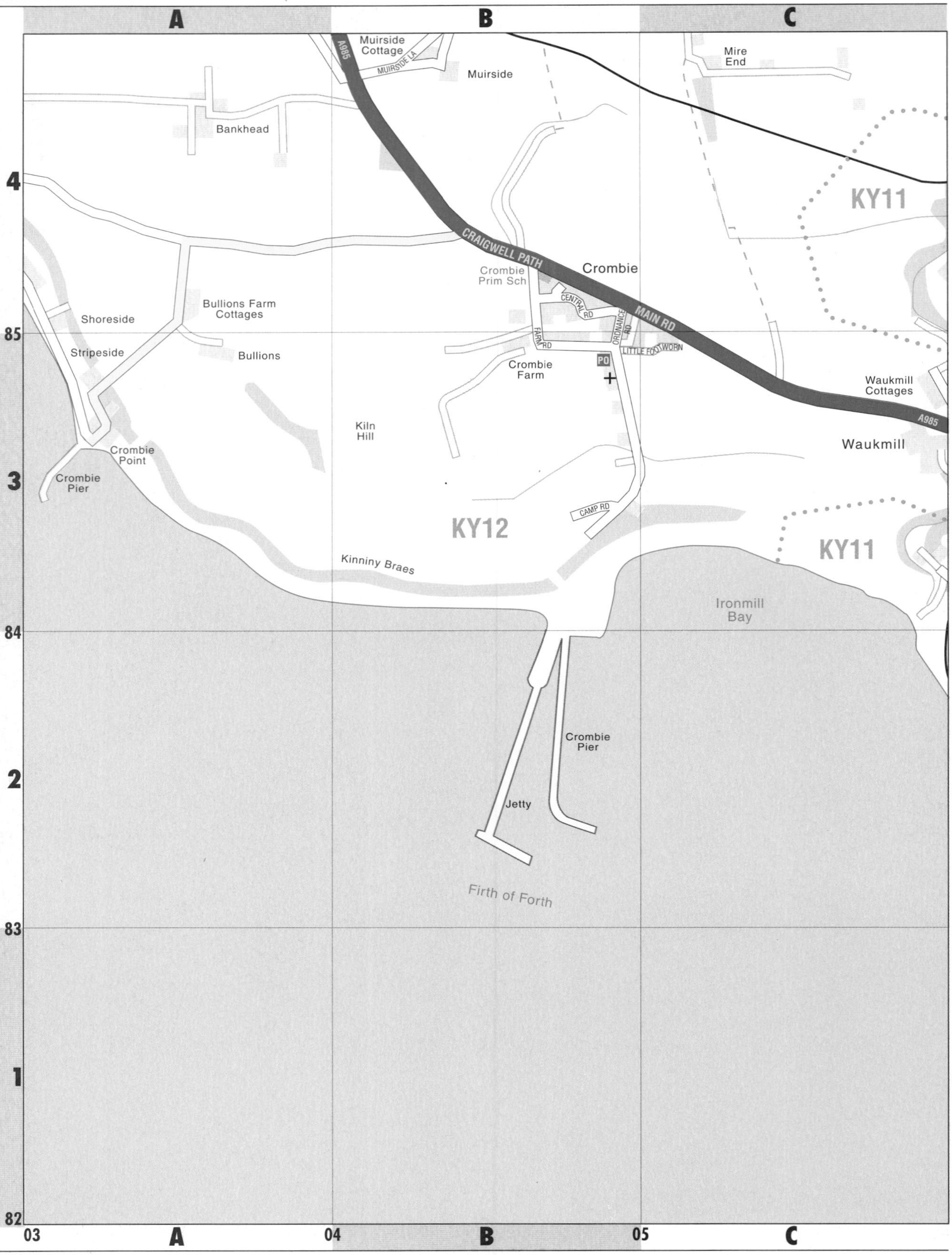

A   B   C

Muirside
Cottage

Muirside

MUIRSIDE LA

A985

Mire
End

Bankhead

KY11

4

CRAIGWELL PATH

Crombie

Crombie
Prim Sch

MAIN RD

CENTRAL RD

Shoreside

Bullions Farm
Cottages

85

ORDNANCE RD

FARM RD

LITTLE FOOTWORN

Stripeside

Bullions

Crombie
Farm

PO

Waukmill
Cottages

+

A985

Kiln
Hill

Waukmill

Crombie
Point

3

Crombie
Pier

KY12

CAMP RD

KY11

Kinniny Braes

Ironmill
Bay

84

2

Crombie
Pier

Jetty

Firth of Forth

83

1

82

03   A   04   B   05   C

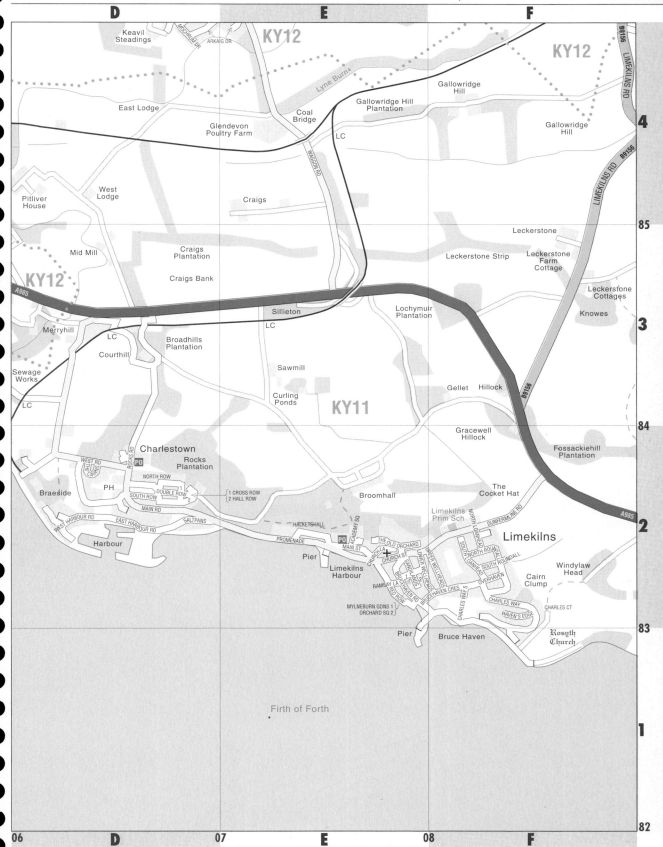

D   E   F

KY12

Keavil
Steadings

ARKAIG DR

Lyne Burn

East Lodge

Coal
Bridge

Gallowridge Hill
Plantation

Gallowridge
Hill

KY12

Gallowridge
Hill

4

Glendevon
Poultry Farm

WAGGON RD

LC

B9156   LIMEKILNS RD

West
Lodge

Pitliver
House

Craigs

85

Mid Mill

Craigs
Plantation

Leckerstone

Leckerstone Strip

Leckerstone
Farm
Cottage

KY12

Craigs Bank

Sillieton

Lochymuir
Plantation

Leckerstone
Cottages
Knowes

A985

Merryhill

LC

LC

Broadhills
Plantation

Sawmill

Gellet   Hillock

B9156

3

Courthill

Curling
Ponds

KY11

Sewage
Works

LC

Gracewell
Hillock

84

Charlestown

ROCKS RD

PO

Rocks
Plantation

Fossackiehill
Plantation

WEST RD

THE CRESS

Braeside

PH

NORTH ROW
DOUBLE ROW
SOUTH ROW
MAIN RD

1
2

1 CROSS ROW
2 HALL ROW

Broomhall

The
Cocket Hat

DUNFERMLINE RD

NORTH LOANHEAD

Limekilns
Prim Sch

Limekilns

2

WEST HARBOUR RD
EAST HARBOUR RD
SALTPANS

Harbour

PROMENADE

HALKETSHALL

PO

ACADEMY SQ

MAIN ST

CHURCH LA
CHURCH ST

THE OLD ORCHARD

UPPER WELLHEADS
LOWER WELLHEADS
SANDILANDS

SOUTH LOANHEAD
NORTH ROW
SOUTH ROUNDALL
MILL RD
OVERHAVEN

Cairn
Clump

Windylaw
Head

Pier

Limekilns
Harbour

RAMSAY LA
BRUCEHAVEN RD
RED ROW

BRUCEHAVEN CRES

CHARLES WAY S

CHARLES WAY

CHARLES CT

MYLNEBURN GDNS 1
ORCHARD SQ 2

HAVEN'S EDGE

83

Pier

Bruce Haven

Rosyth
Church

1

Firth of Forth

82

45
29

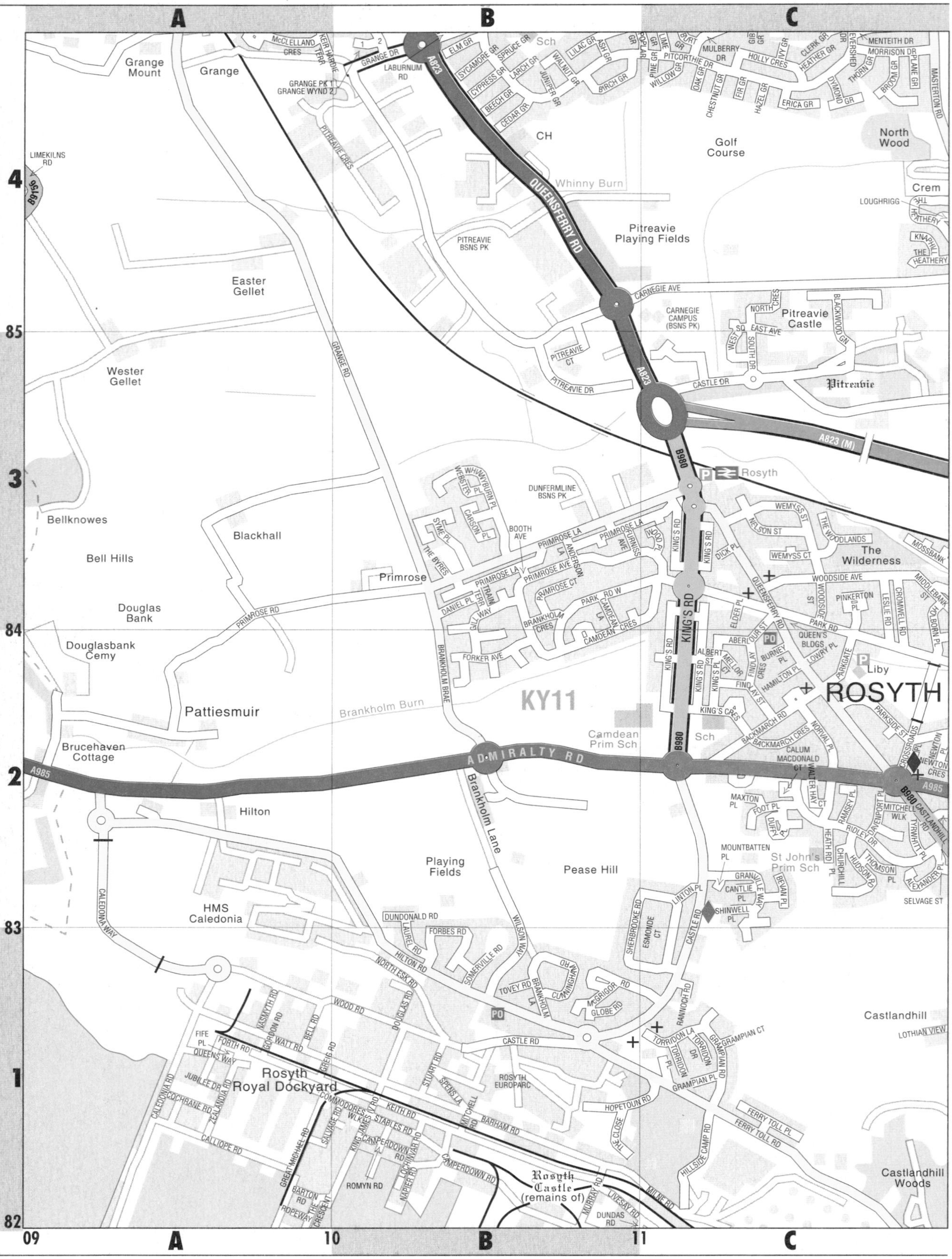
A
B
C
4
85
3
2
84
83
1
82
09
10
11
Grange Mount
Grange
McCLELLAND CRES
KEIR HARDIE TERR
GRANGE DR
GRANGE PK
GRANGE WYND
LABURNUM RD
A823
ELM GR
SYCAMORE GR
SPRUCE GR
CYPRESS GR
LARCH GR
BEECH GR
CEDAR GR
WALNUT GR
JUNIPER GR
LILAC GR
ASH GR
BIRCH GR
Sch
CH
POPLAR GR
PINE GR
LIME GR
WILLOW GR
PITCORTHIE DR
MULBERRY DR
OAK GR
CHESTNUT GR
FIR GR
HAZEL GR
HOLLY CRES
IVY GR
CLERK GR
HEATHER GR
ERICA GR
EVERSHED DR
DYMOND GR
THORN GR
BROOM GR
MENTEITH DR
MORRISON DR
PLANE GR
MASTERTON RD
Golf Course
North Wood
Crem
LOUGHRIGG
THE HEATHERY
KNAPHILL
LIMEKILNS RD
B9156
PITREAVIE CRES
QUEENSFERRY RD
Whinny Burn
PITREAVIE BSNS PK
Pitreavie Playing Fields
Easter Gellet
CARNEGIE AVE
CARNEGIE CAMPUS (BSNS PK)
NORTH CRES
Pitreavie Castle
BLACKWOOD GN
WEST SQ
EAST AVE
SOUTH DR
PITREAVIE CT
PITREAVIE DR
CASTLE DR
Pitreavie
Wester Gellet
GRANGE RD
A823 (M)
B980
Rosyth
WHINNYBURN PL
WEBSTER PL
CARSON PL
DUNFERMLINE BSNS PK
SYME PL
THE BYRES
BOOTH AVE
PRIMROSE LA
PRIMROSE AVE
PRIMROSE CT
ANDERSON LA
FURNISS AVE
WOOD PL
KING'S RD
DICK PL
WEMYSS ST
NELSON ST
WEMYSS CT
THE WOODLANDS
The Wilderness
MOSSBANK
Bellknowes
Blackhall
Bell Hills
Primrose
DANIEL PL
TRAIN TERR
GILL WAY
PARK RD W
CAMDEAN LA
BRANKHOLM CRES
CAMDEAN CRES
FORKER AVE
ELDER PL
QUEENSFERRY RD
WOODSIDE AVE
WOODSIDE ST
PINKERTON PL
LESLIE RD
CROMWELL RD
MIDDLEBANK ST
TOLBOOTH PL
PARK RD
Douglas Bank
PRIMROSE RD
ABERLOUR ST
QUEEN'S BLDGS
LOWRY PL
PARKGATE
Liby
ROSYTH
Douglasbank Cemy
BRANKHOLM BRAE
ALBERT ST
MELLOR CT
FINDLAY CRES
BURNEY PL
HAMILTON PL
FINDLAY ST
KING'S PL
KING'S CRES
KY11
Pattiesmuir
Brankholm Burn
Camdean Prim Sch
BACKMARCH RD
BACKMARCH CRES
NORVAL PL
PARKSIDE ST
Brucehaven Cottage
A985
ADMIRALTY RD
CALUM MACDONALD CT
WALTER HAY CT
CROSSROADS PL
NEWTON CRES
Hilton
Brankholm Lane
MAXTON PL
FOOT PL
DUFFY PL
RAMSEY PL
HEATH RD
DAVENPORT PL
MITCHELL WLK
CASTLANDHILL RD
RIDLEY DR
TYRWHITT PL
MOUNTBATTEN PL
St John's Prim Sch
CHURCHILL PL
HUDSON RD
THOMSON PL
ALEXANDER PL
SELVAGE ST
CALEDONIA WAY
Playing Fields
Pease Hill
HMS Caledonia
GRANVILLE WAY
CANTLIE PL
REVAN PL
LINTON PL
SHINWELL PL
DUNDONALD RD
LAUREL RD
FORBES RD
SHERBROOKE RD
ESMONDE CT
CASTLE RD
NORTH ESK RD
HILTON RD
SOMERVILLE RD
WILSON WAY
CUNNINGHAM RD
TOVEY RD
BRANKHOLM LA
McGRIGOR RD
GLOBE RD
RANNOCH RD
Castlandhill
LOTHIAN VIEW
NASMYTH RD
GORDON RD
WOOD RD
DOUGLAS RD
BELL RD
WATT RD
FIFE PL
FORTH RD
QUEENS WAY
PO
CASTLE RD
TORRIDON LA
TORRIDON DR
TORRIDON PL
GRAMPIAN CT
GRAMPIAN RD
GRAMPIAN PL
GREIG RD
JUBILEE DR
COCHRANE RD
ZEALANDIA RD
CALEDONIA RD
Rosyth Royal Dockyard
STUART RD
SPENS LA
ROSYTH EUROPARC
COMMODORES STABLES RD
WLKS
KEITH RD
MITCHELL RD
BARHAM RD
HOPETOUN RD
THE CLOSE
FERRY TOLL PL
FERRY TOLL RD
CALLIOPE RD
GREAT MICHAEL RD
SALVAGE RD
KING JAMES VI RD
CAMPERDOWN PL
LOCHNAGAR RD
CAMPERDOWN RD
Rosyth Castle (remains of)
MURRAY RD
LIVESAY RD
DUNDAS RD
MILNE RD
HILLSIDE CAMP RD
Castlandhill Woods
BARTON RD
ROPEWAY
THE CRESCENT
ROMYN RD
NAPIER RD

45
67

30
48

D E F

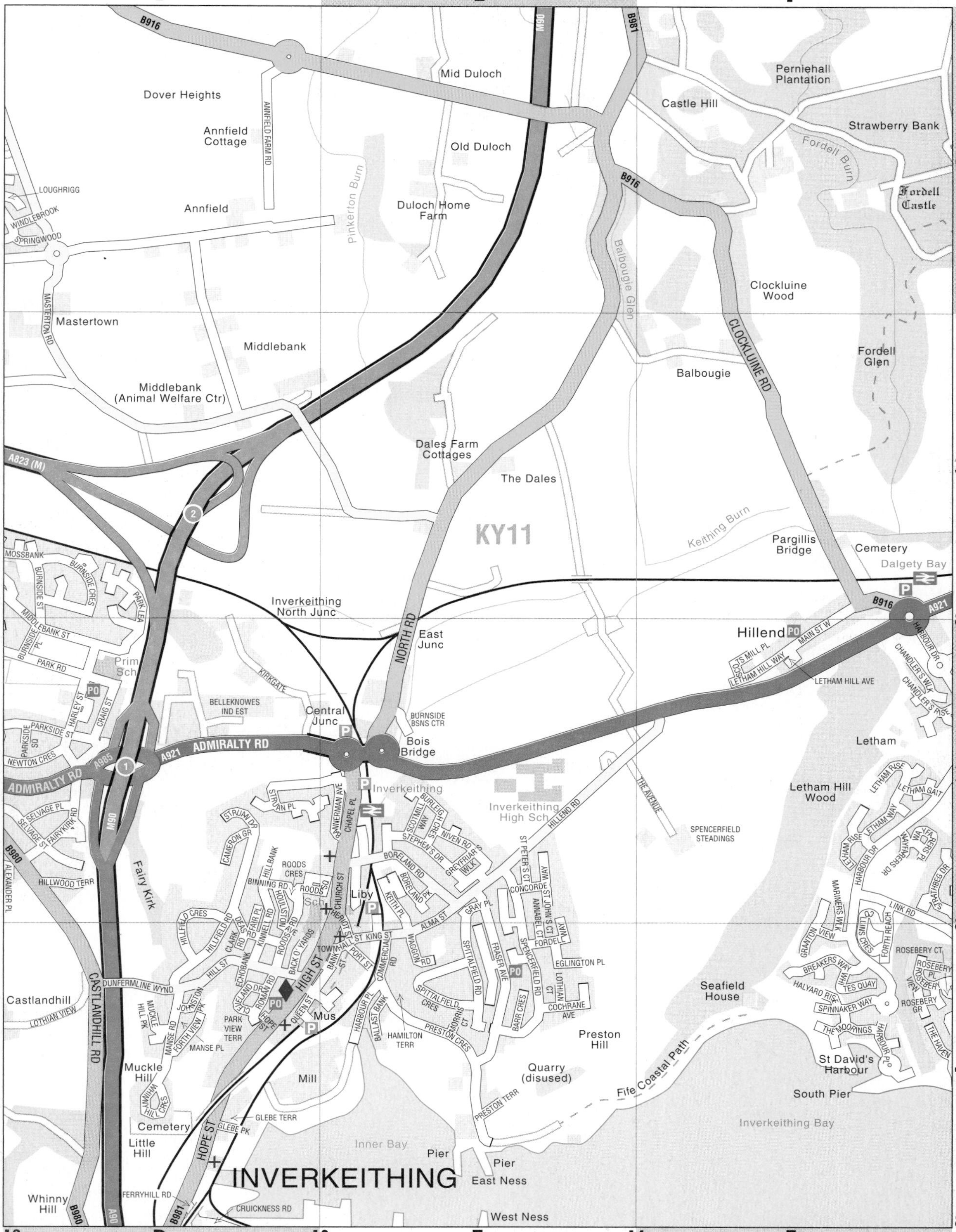
Dover Heights
Annfield Cottage
Annfield
Mid Duloch
Old Duloch
Duloch Home Farm
Pinkerton Burn
Perniehall Plantation
Castle Hill
Strawberry Bank
Fordell Burn
Fordell Castle
Clockluine Wood
Balbougie Glen
Fordell Glen
Balbougie
CLOCKLUINE RD
Mastertown
Middlebank
Middlebank (Animal Welfare Ctr)
Dales Farm Cottages
The Dales
KY11
Keithing Burn
Pargillis Bridge
Cemetery
Dalgety Bay
Inverkeithing North Junc
East Junc
NORTH RD
Hillend
Central Junc
Bois Bridge
ADMIRALTY RD
BELLEKNOWES IND EST
BURNSIDE BSNS CTR
Letham
Letham Hill Wood
Inverkeithing
Inverkeithing High Sch
SPENCERFIELD STEADINGS
Fairy Kirk
Castlandhill
CASTLANDHILL RD
HIGH ST
Seafield House
Preston Hill
Quarry (disused)
Fife Coastal Path
St David's Harbour
South Pier
Inverkeithing Bay
Muckle Hill
Mill
Cemetery
Little Hill
Inner Bay
Pier
East Ness
West Ness
Whinny Hill
INVERKEITHING
4
85
3
84
2
83
1
82
12
13
14

D E F

68
48

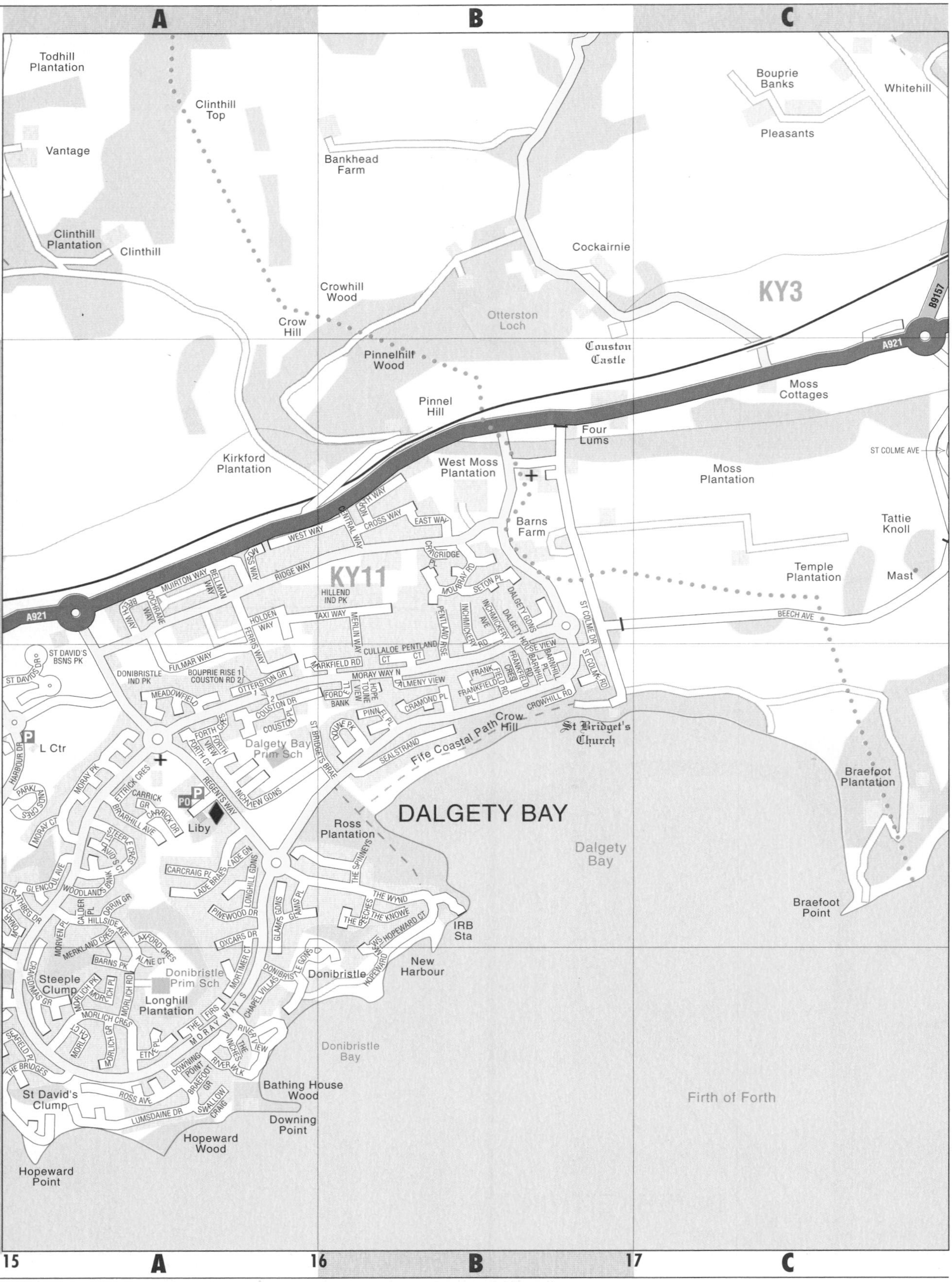

47 31

Todhill
Plantation

Clinthill
Top

Vantage

Bankhead
Farm

Bouprie
Banks

Whitehill

Pleasants

Clinthill
Plantation   Clinthill

Cockairnie

KY3

B9157

4

Crowhill
Wood

Otterston
Loch

85

Crow
Hill

Pinnelhill
Wood

Couston
Castle

Moss
Cottages

A921

Pinnel
Hill

Four
Lums

Moss
Plantation

ST COLME AVE

Kirkford
Plantation

West Moss
Plantation

Barns
Farm

Tattie
Knoll

3

WEST WAY
CENTRAL WAY
CROSS WAY
EAST WAY

BELLMAN WAY
MUIRTON WAY
RIDGE WAY

HILLEND
IND PK

KY11

CRAIGRIDGE
MOUNT PL

ST COLME DR

BEECH AVE

Temple
Plantation

Mast

84

ST DAVID'S
BSNS PK

FULMAR WAY
TAXI WAY
MERLIN WAY

HOLDEN
WAY

FERRIS WAY

PENTLAND RISE
INCHMICKERY
DALGETY GDNS
SETON PL

ST COLME RD

A921

ST DAVID'S

DONIBRISTLE
IND PK

MEADOWFIELD

BOUPRIE RISE 1
COUSTON RD 2

ARKFIELD RD

CULLALOE PENTLAND
CT

INCHKEITH AVE
FRANKE RD

MOSS VIEW
BARNHILL
CRES

L Ctr

OTTERSTON GR
COUSTON DR

MORAY WAY N

CRAMOND PL
ALMENY VIEW

FRANK
RD
FRANKFIELD

CROWHILL RD

Crow
Hill

Braefoot
Plantation

2

MORAY PK
PARK RD
MORAY CT

HARBOUR DR
PARK CRES

PATRICK CRES
CARRICK
GR
CARRICK DR

BARNHILL AVE
ST DAVID'S
ESK CT

FORTH GR
FORTH CT
REGENT'S WAY

ST BRIDGET'S BRAE

THE SALTINGS

Dalgety Bay
Prim Sch

LADE GN
NEW GDNS

Liby

SEALSTRAND

Fife Coastal Path

St Bridget's
Church

Ross
Plantation

DALGETY BAY

Dalgety
Bay

Braefoot
Point

83

STRATHBEG DR
GLENCOE LANE

CALDER PL
WOODLAND

CARRICK GR

BARNS PK

MERKLAND CRES
LAXFORD CRES
ALNE CT

CARCRAIG PL
LADE BRAES
PINEWOOD DR

LONGHILL GDNS
GLAMIS GDNS

MORTIMER CT

HOPEWARD CT
THE WYND
THE KNOWE
THE BEECHES
THE BIRCHES

IRB
Sta

Steeple
Clump

CRAIGDIMAS GR
MORLICH GR
MORLICH RD
CH PL

Donibristle
Prim Sch

DONIBRISTLE GDNS

CHAPEL VILLAS

MORAY WAY S

Donibristle

New
Harbour

Longhill
Plantation

THE FIRS
RIVER VIEW

RIVERWALK
INCHES

Donibristle
Bay

Firth of Forth

SEAFIELD CT
THE BRIDGES

MORLICH GR

MORDUN
ETNA

DOWNING POINT

BRAEFOOT GR
SWALLOW

RIVER VIEW

1

St David's
Clump

ROSS AVE

LUMSDAINE DR

CRAIG

Bathing House
Wood

Hopeward
Point

Hopeward
Wood

Downing
Point

82

15   **A**   16   **B**   17   **C**

47 69

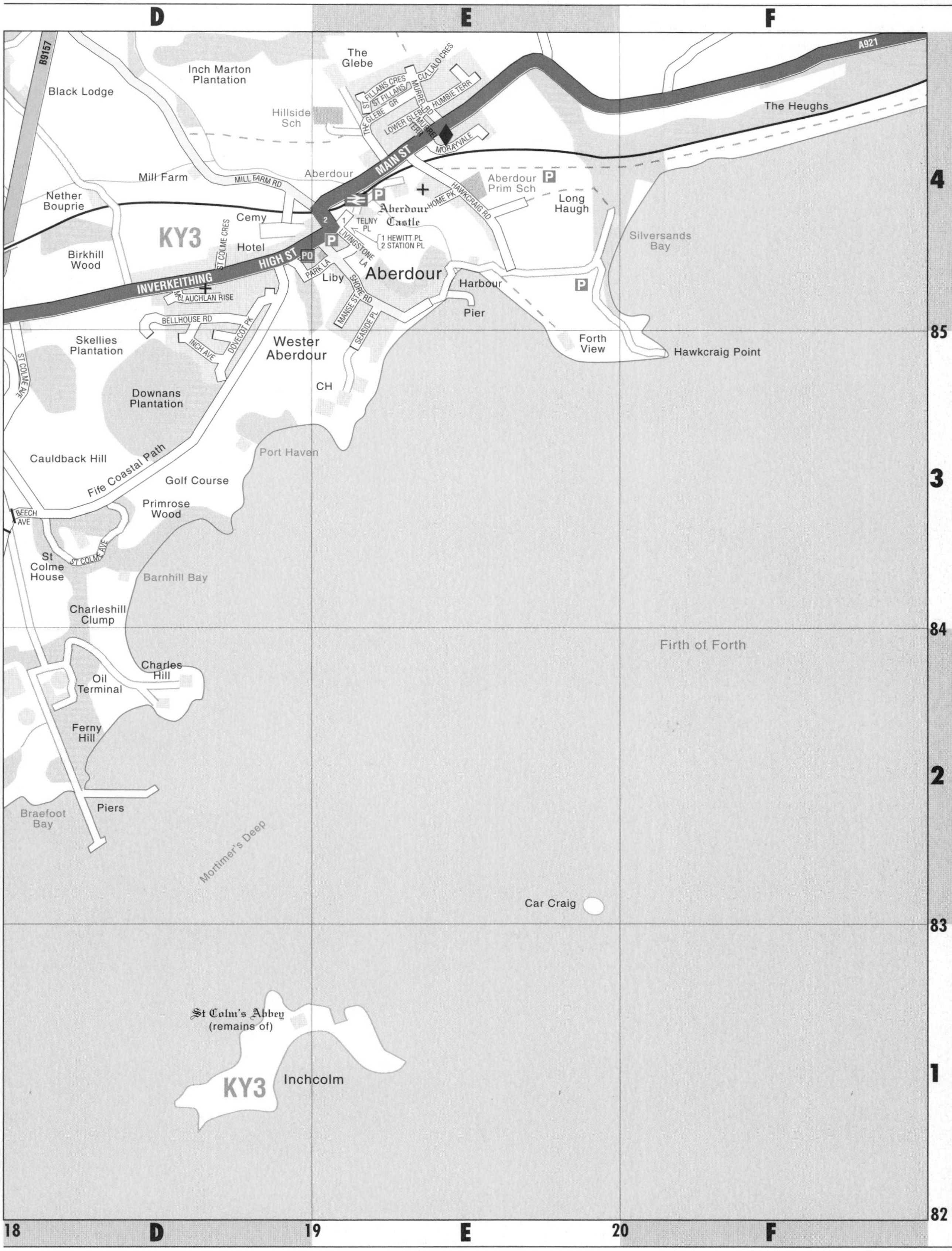

D   E   F

B9157

Inch Marton
Plantation

Black Lodge

The Glebe

ST FILLANS CRES
ST FILLANS ST
MORAY TERR
RUMBIE TERR
CLELALD CRES

Hillside
Sch

THE GLEBE
LOWER GLEBE
MAIN ST

MORAYVALE

Mill Farm

MILL FARM RD

Aberdour

4

Nether
Bouprie

Cemy

Aberdour
Prim Sch
P

Long
Haugh

HOME PK

HAWKCRAIG RD

KY3

ST COLME CRES

Hotel

Aberdour
Castle

Birkhill
Wood

HIGH ST

INVERKEITHING

PO

LIVINGSTONE

TELNY
PL

1 HEWITT PL
2 STATION PL

Silversands
Bay

The Heughs

A921

85

CLAUCHLAN RISE

PARK LA

Liby

Aberdour

BELLHOUSE RD

INCH AVE

DOVECOT PK

MANSE ST

SHORE RD

SEASIDE PL

Harbour

P

Skellies
Plantation

Wester
Aberdour

Pier

Forth
View

Hawkcraig Point

Downans
Plantation

CH

Cauldback Hill

Fife Coastal Path

Golf Course

Port Haven

3

ST COLME AVE

Primrose
Wood

BEECH
AVE

St
Colme
House

ST COLME AVE

Barnhill Bay

Firth of Forth

84

Charleshill
Clump

Oil
Terminal

Charles
Hill

Ferny
Hill

2

Braefoot
Bay

Piers

Mortimer's Deep

Car Craig

83

St Colm's Abbey
(remains of)

KY3

Inchcolm

1

82

18   D   19   E   20   F

49

33

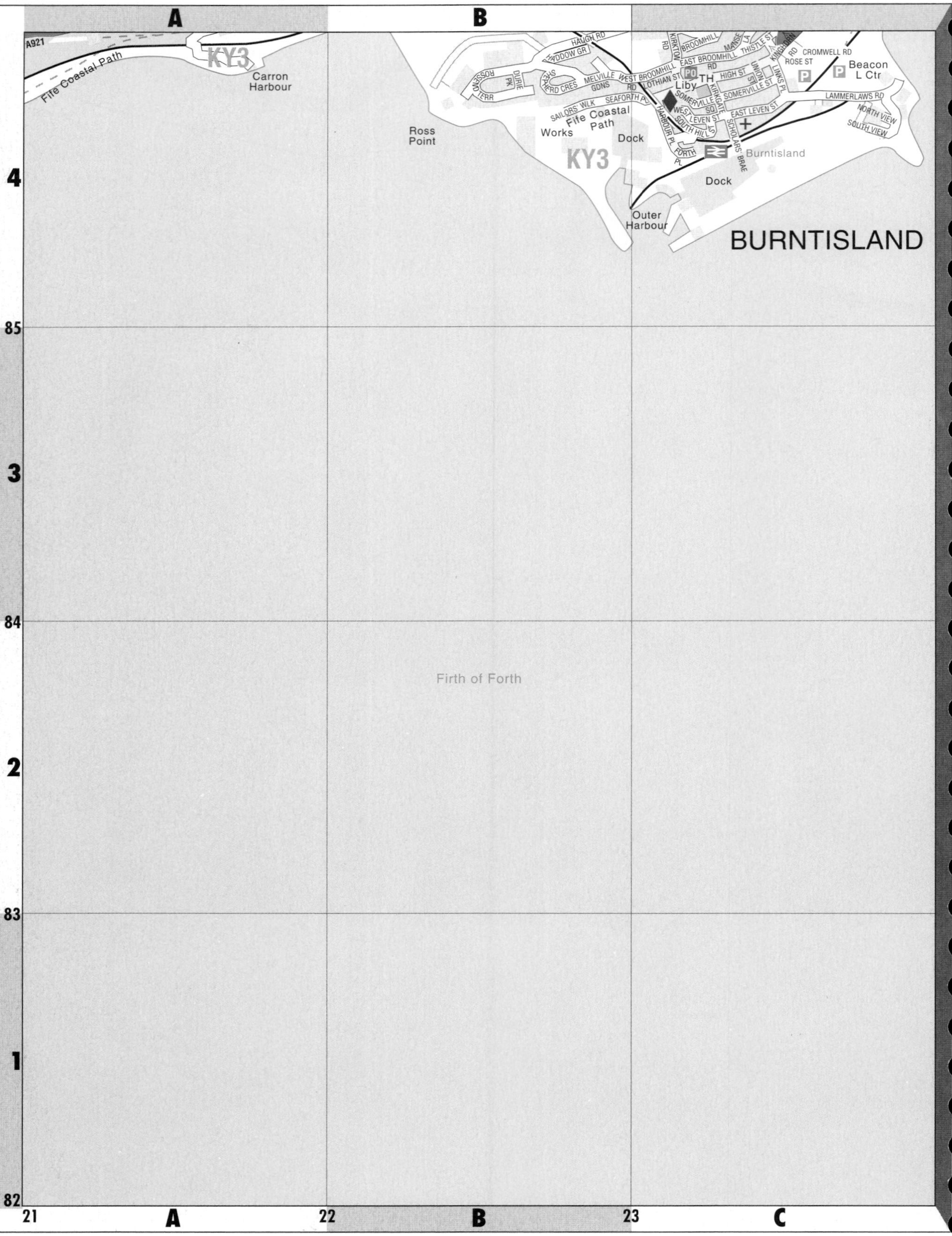

A   B

A921

KY3

Fife Coastal Path

Carron Harbour

HAUGH RD

WIDOW GR

ROSSEND TERR

DURIE ST

CHS

RD CRES

MELVILLE GDNS

SEAFORTH PL

SAILORS WLK

WEST BROOMHILL

LOTHIAN ST

BROOMHILL RD

EAST BROOMHILL

THISTLE ST

HIGH ST

SOMERVILLE ST

UNION ST

EAST LEVEN ST

WEST LEVEN ST

SOUTH HILL PL

HARBOUR PL

FORTH

KINGHORN

KIRKTON

BROOMHILL RD

MASSIE LA

KINGSLN

LINKS PL

CROMWELL RD

ROSE ST

Beacon L Ctr

LAMMERLAWS RD

NORTH VIEW

SOUTH VIEW

P

P

TH

Liby

SOMERVILLE SQ

SCHOLARS BRAE

Ross Point

Works

Fife Coastal Path

Dock

KY3

Burntisland

Dock

Outer Harbour

BURNTISLAND

4

85

3

84

Firth of Forth

2

83

1

82

21   A   22   B   23   C

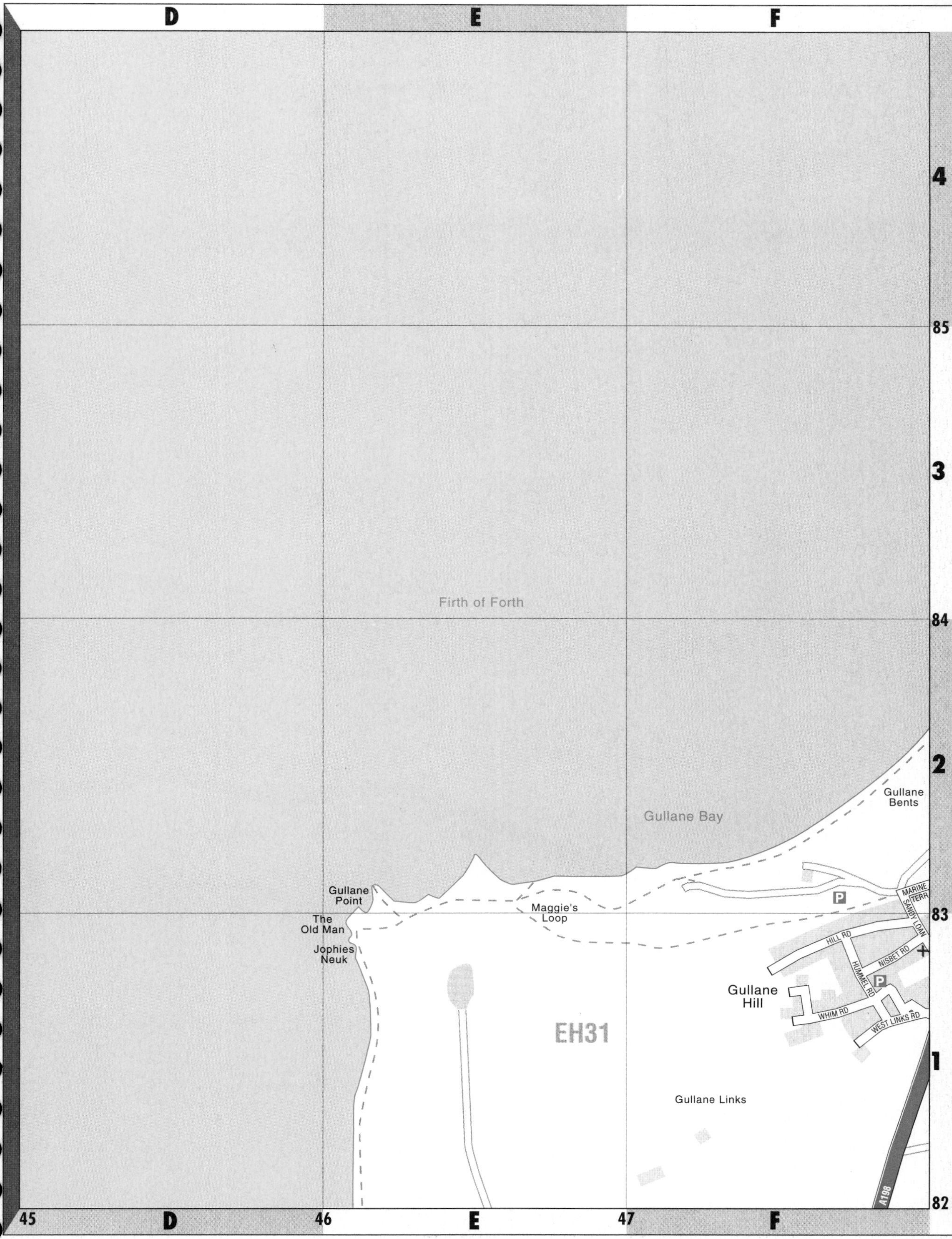

D   E   F

4

85

3

Firth of Forth

84

2

Gullane
Bents

Gullane Bay

Gullane
Point   Maggie's
                          Loop   MARINE
                                                                   TERR
The
Old Man   P   SANDY LOAN   83

Jophies   HILL RD
Neuk   NISBET RD

                                                    Gullane   P
EH31   Gullane   Hill   HUMMEL RD
                                                          WHIM RD
                                                              WEST LINKS RD   1

                          Gullane Links

A198

82

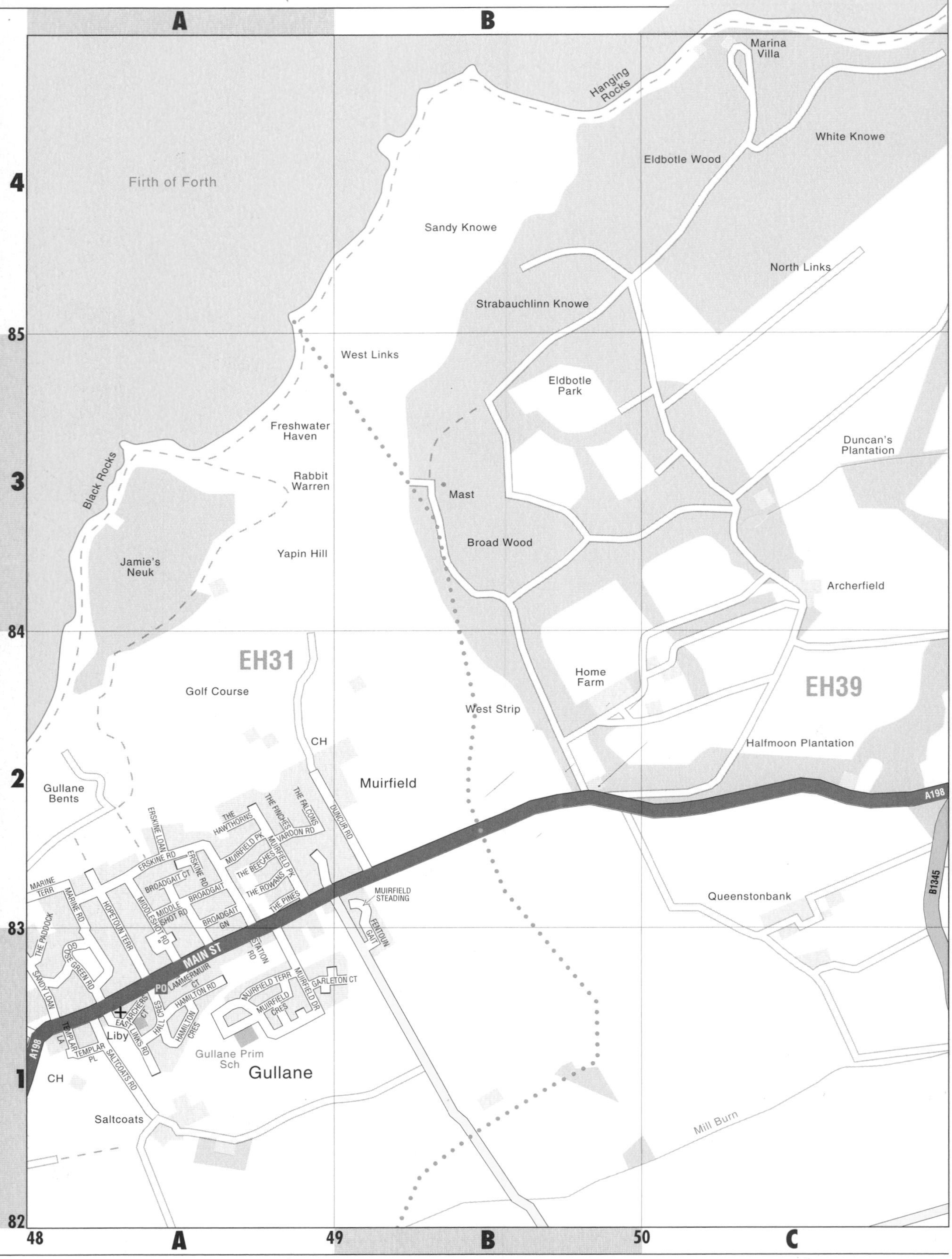

51

A
B

4

Firth of Forth

Marina Villa

Hanging Rocks

Eldbotle Wood

White Knowe

Sandy Knowe

North Links

85

Strabauchlinn Knowe

West Links

Eldbotle Park

Duncan's Plantation

Freshwater Haven

3

Rabbit Warren

Mast

Broad Wood

Archerfield

Black Rocks

Jamie's Neuk

Yapin Hill

84

Home Farm

EH31

EH39

Golf Course

West Strip

Halfmoon Plantation

CH

2

Muirfield

Gullane Bents

A198

B1345

ERSKINE LOAN
THE HAWTHORNS
THE FALCONS
THE FINCHES
VARDON RD
DUNCUR RD
Queenstonbank

MARINE TERR
ERSKINE RD
ERSKINE RD
MUIRFIELD PK
MUIRFIELD PK
THE BEECHES

BROADGAIT CT
BROADGAIT
THE ROWANS

MARINE RD
HOPETOUN TERR
MIDDLESHOT RD
MIDDLE SHOT RD
BROADGAIT GN
THE PINES

MUIRFIELD STEADING

83

THE PADDOCK
STATION RD
FENTON GAIT

MAIN ST

GREEN RD
PO
LAMMERMUIR CT
HAMILTON RD
MUIRFIELD TERR
CARLETON CT

SANDERS CT
HILL CT
HAMILTON CRES
MUIRFIELD CRES
MUIRFIELD DR

LYON CROSS RD
TEMPLAR PL
SALTCOATS RD
LINKS RD
EAST
Liby

1

CH

Gullane Prim Sch

Gullane

Saltcoats

Mill Burn

82

48
A
49
B
50
C

51
72

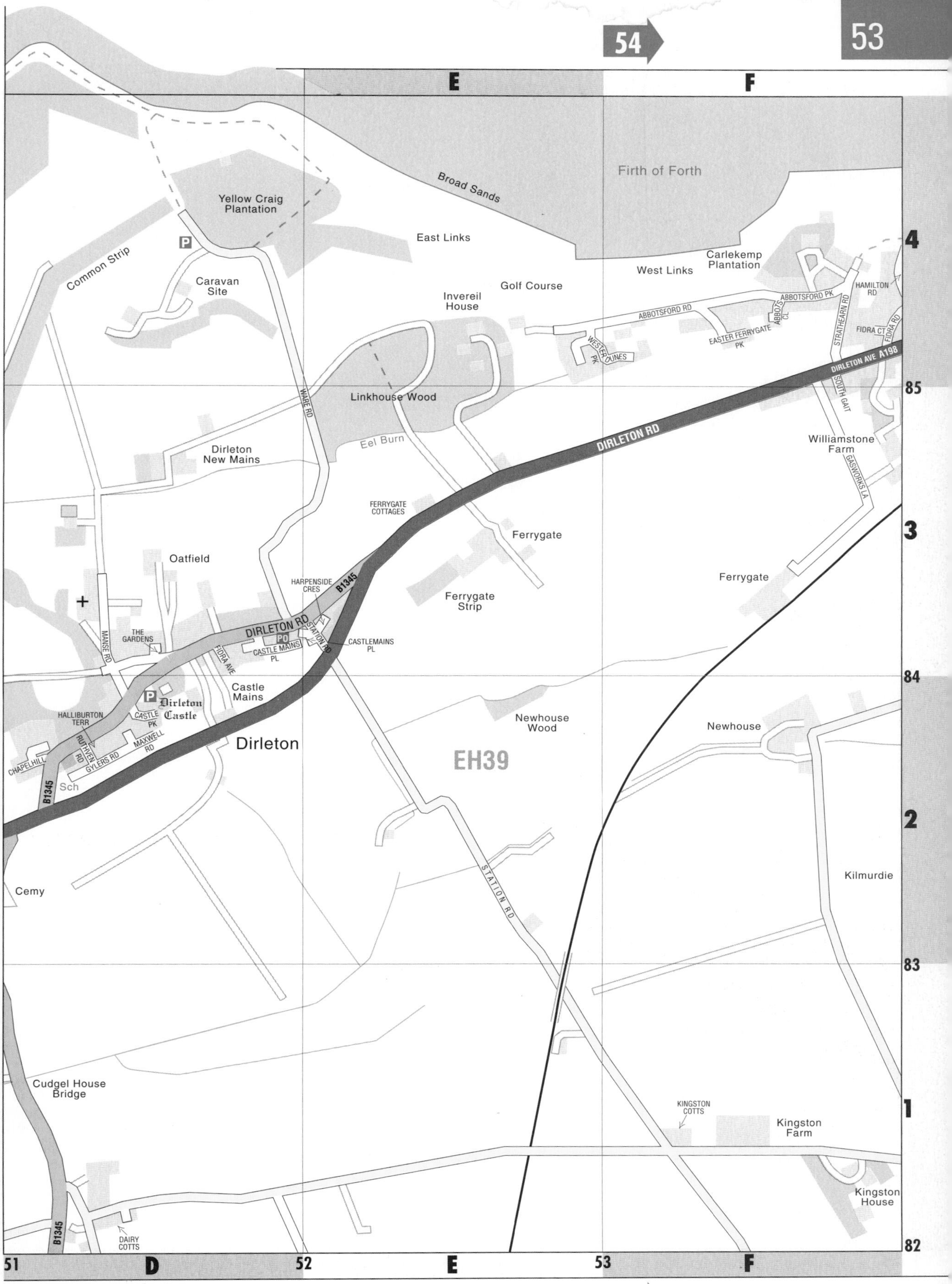

E

F

Firth of Forth

Broad Sands

Yellow Craig
Plantation

P

East Links

West Links

Carlekemp
Plantation

4

Common Strip

Caravan
Site

Golf Course

Invereil
House

ABBOTSFORD RD

ABBOTSFORD PK

HAMILTON
RD

ABBOTS
CT

STRATHEARN RD

FIDRA CT RD

WESTER
OUNES

PK

EASTER FERRYGATE
PK

DIRLETON AVE A198

SOUTH GAIT

85

WARE RD

Linkhouse Wood

DIRLETON RD

Williamstone
Farm

GASWORKS LA

Dirleton
New Mains

Eel Burn

FERRYGATE
COTTAGES

Ferrygate

Ferrygate

3

Oatfield

HARPENSIDE
CRES

B1345

Ferrygate
Strip

HALLIBURTON
TERR

MANSE RD

THE
GARDENS

DIRLETON RD

PO

CASTLE MAINS
PL

STATION RD

CASTLEMAINS
PL

84

FIDRA AVE

+

P

Castle
Mains

Newhouse
Wood

Newhouse

Dirleton
Castle

CASTLE
PK

Dirleton

EH39

Kilmurdie

CHAPELHILL

RUTHVEN RD

GYLERS RD

MAXWELL
RD

2

B1345

Sch

Cemy

STATION RD

83

Cudgel House
Bridge

KINGSTON
COTTS

Kingston
Farm

1

B1345

DAIRY
COTTS

Kingston
House

82

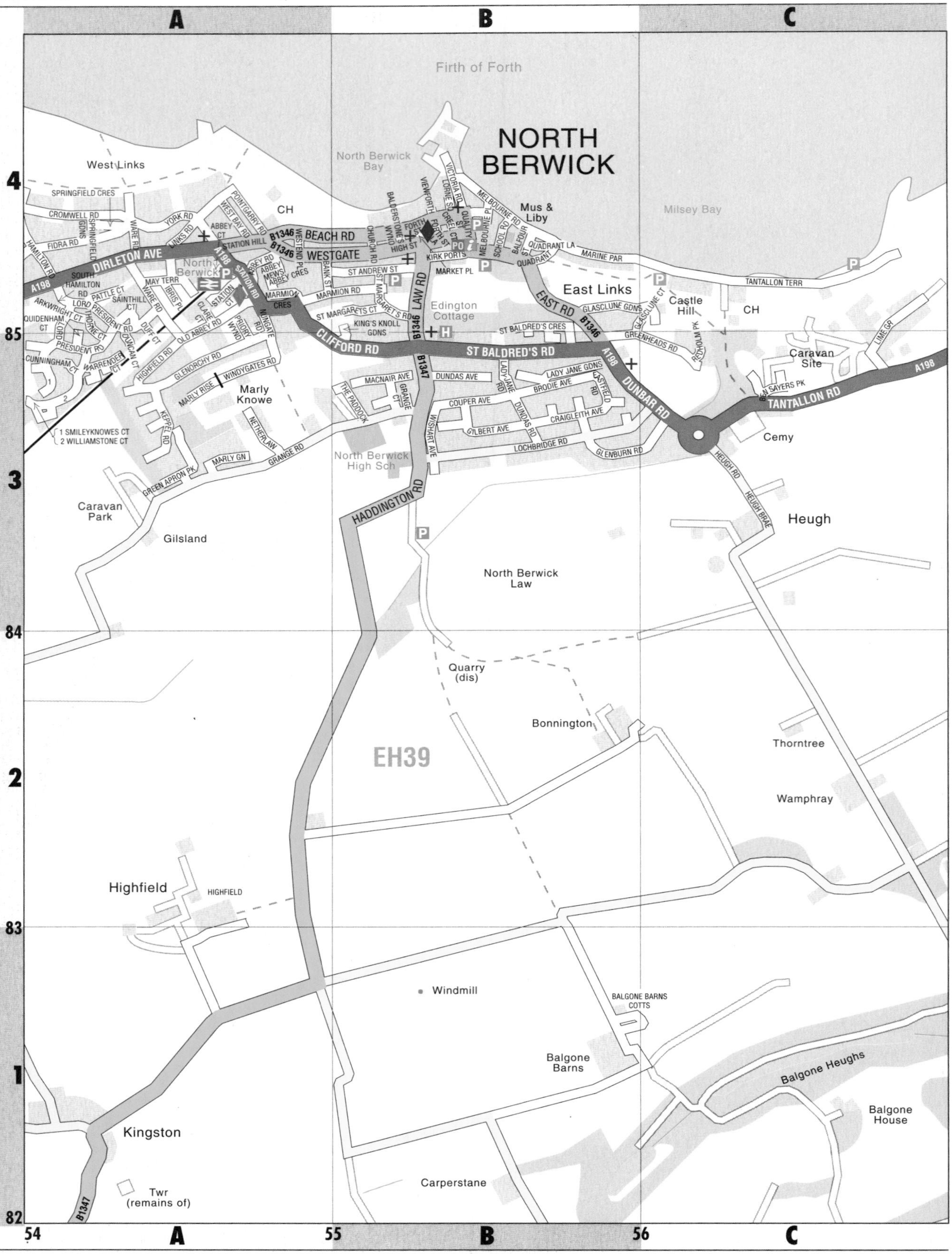

A   B   C

Firth of Forth

West Links

North Berwick Bay

**NORTH
BERWICK**

Milsey Bay

4

Springfield Cres
Cromwell Rd
Fidra Rd
York Rd
Links Rd
Abbey Ct
CH
B1346 BEACH RD
WESTGATE
Mus & Liby

DIRLETON AVE
Station Hill
B1346
CHURCH RD
VICTORIA RD
MELBOURNE RD
School Rd
BALFOUR
QUADRANT LA
MARINE PAR

Hamilton Rd
South Hamilton Rd
St Andrew St
Market Pl
QUADRANT

Tantallon Terr

85
Arkwright Ct
Quidenham Ct
President Rd
CLIFFORD RD
St Margaret's Ct
King's Knoll Gdns
ST BALDRED'S RD
Edington Cottage
H
EAST RD
East Links
Castle Hill
CH
Caravan Site

Cunningham Ct
Warrender
Highfield Rd
Old Abbey Rd
Marly Rise
Windygates Rd
Marly Knowe
MACNAIR AVE
DUNDAS AVE
Couper Ave
Gilbert Ave
Dundas Rd
Craigleith Ave
DUNBAR RD
TANTALLON RD
A198
Cemy

3
1 SMILEYKNOWES CT
2 WILLIAMSTONE CT
Nethereaw
Green Apron Pk
Marly Gn
Grange Rd
North Berwick High Sch
HADDINGTON RD
Lochbridge Rd
Glenburn Rd
HEUGH
Heugh

Caravan Park
Gilsland

Heugh

84

North Berwick Law

EH39

Quarry (dis)

Bonnington

2
Thorntree
Wamphray

Highfield
HIGHFIELD

83

Windmill
BALGONE BARNS COTTS

1
Balgone Barns
Balgone Heughs
Balgone House

Kingston

Twr
(remains of)

Carperstane

82
54   A   55   B   56   C

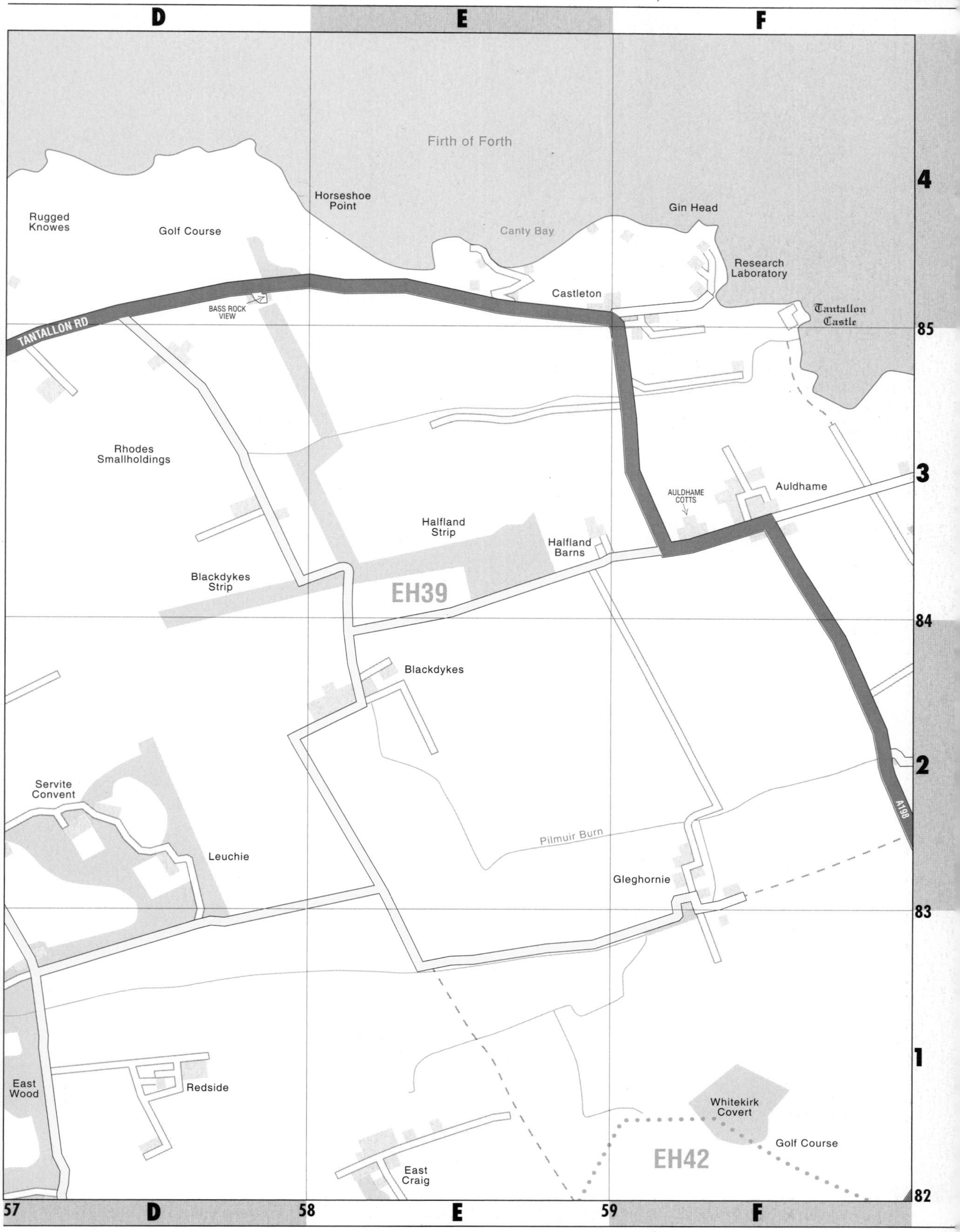

Firth of Forth

Rugged Knowes

Golf Course

Horseshoe Point

Canty Bay

Gin Head

Castleton

Research Laboratory

Tantallon Castle

TANTALLON RD

BASS ROCK VIEW

Rhodes Smallholdings

Halfland Strip

AULDHAME COTTS

Auldhame

Halfland Barns

Blackdykes Strip

EH39

Blackdykes

Servite Convent

Leuchie

Pilmuir Burn

Gleghornie

A198

East Wood

Redside

East Craig

Whitekirk Covert

Golf Course

EH42

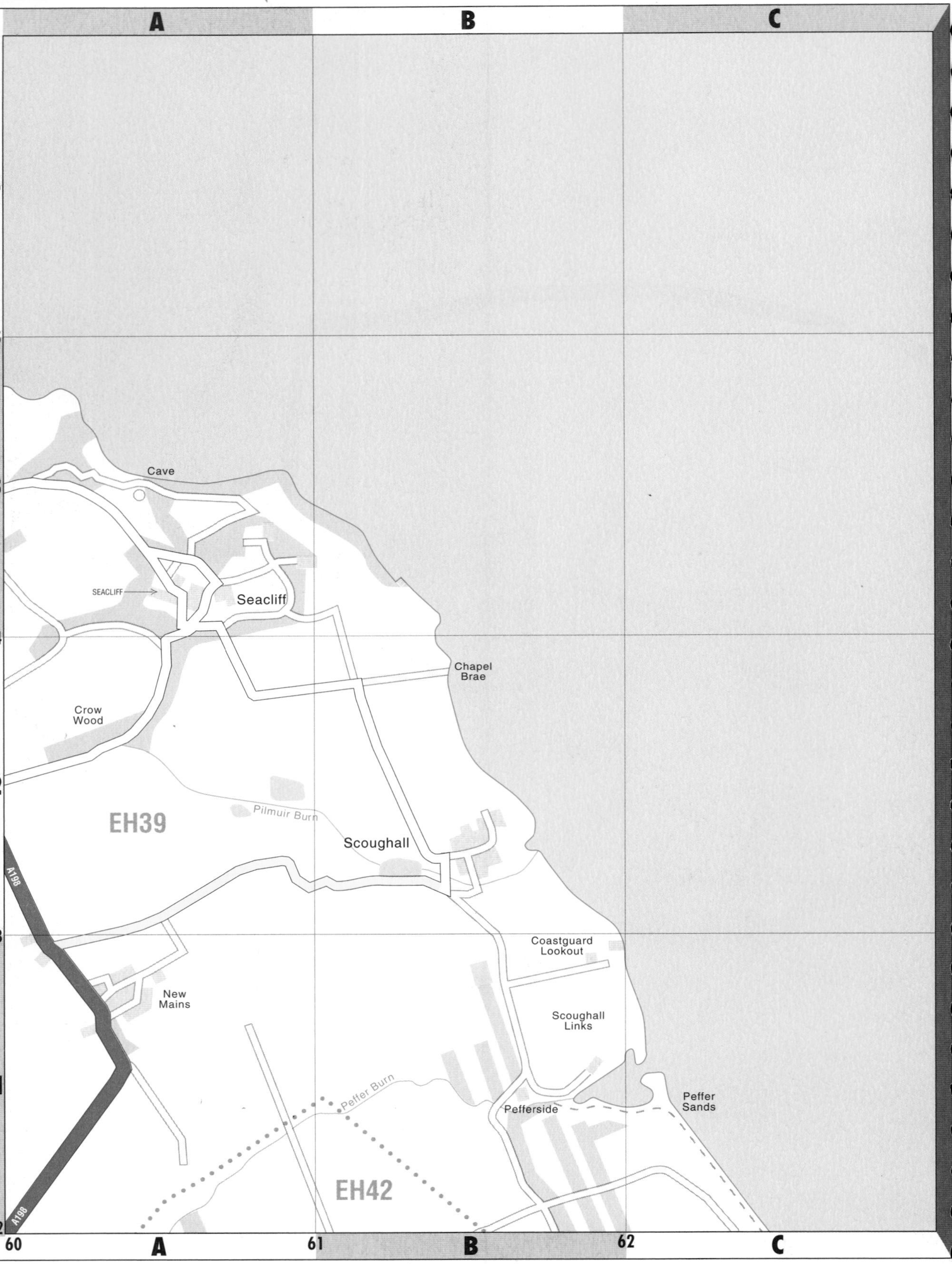

A   B   C

4

85

Cave

3

SEACLIFF →

Seacliff

Chapel
Brae

84

Crow
Wood

EH39

Pilmuir Burn

2

Scoughall

Coastguard
Lookout

83

New
Mains

Scoughall
Links

A198

1

Peffer Burn

Pefferside

Peffer
Sands

EH42

82

60   A   61   B   62   C

A198

36
58

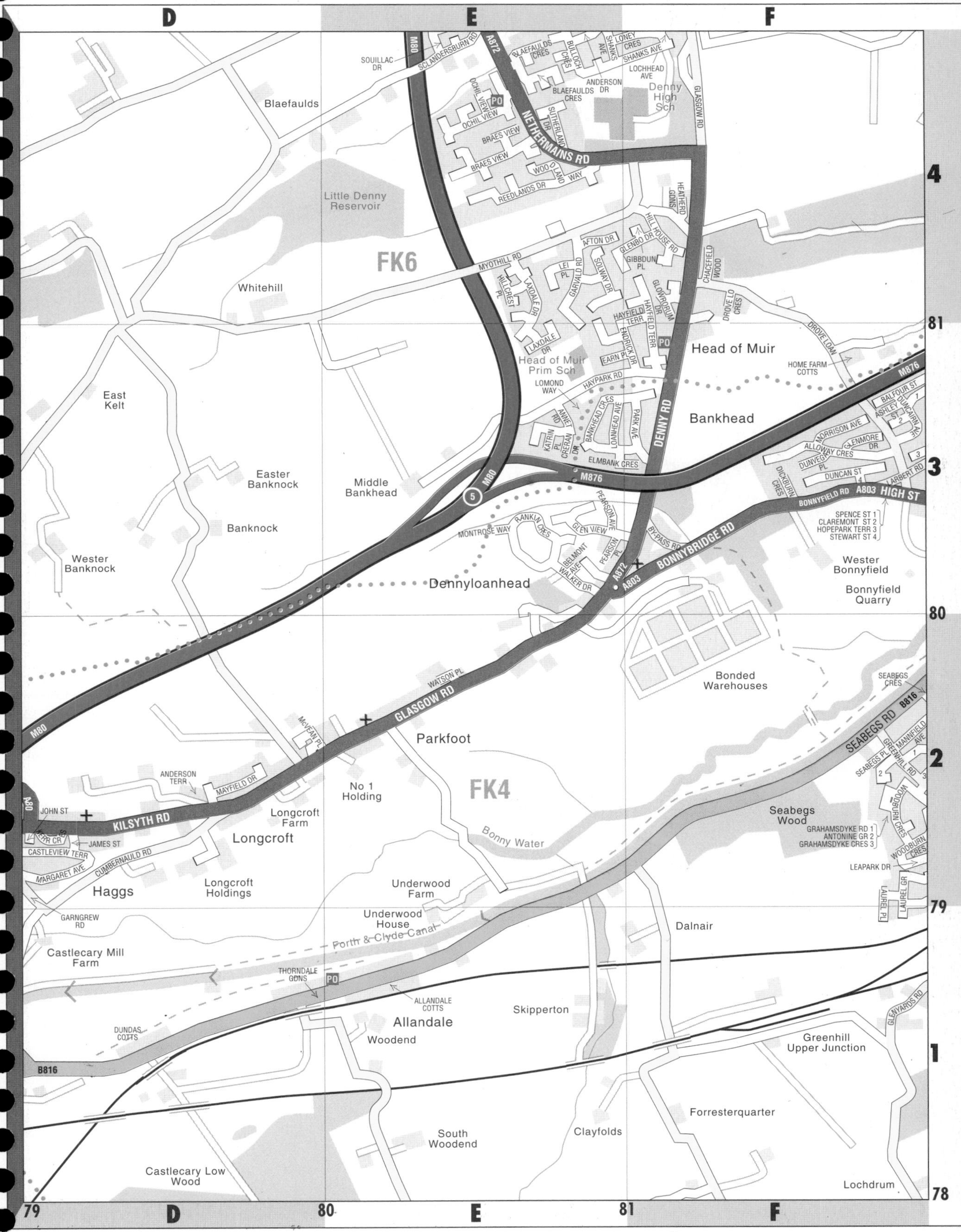
D
E
F
Blaefaulds
Little Denny Reservoir
FK6
Whitehill
East Kelt
Easter Banknock
Middle Bankhead
Banknock
Wester Banknock
Dennyloanhead
Head of Muir
Head of Muir Prim Sch
Bankhead
Denny High Sch
Wester Bonnyfield
Bonnyfield Quarry
Bonded Warehouses
Parkfoot
FK4
No 1 Holding
Longcroft Farm
Longcroft
Haggs
Longcroft Holdings
Underwood Farm
Underwood House
Bonny Water
Seabegs Wood
Dalnair
Castlecary Mill Farm
Forth & Clyde Canal
Skipperton
Allandale
Woodend
Greenhill Upper Junction
Forresterquarter
South Woodend
Clayfolds
Castlecary Low Wood
Lochdrum
M80
A872
M876
A803
A80
B816
DENNY RD
GLASGOW RD
KILSYTH RD
BONNYBRIDGE RD
NETHERMAINS RD
MYOTHILL RD
HIGH ST
SEABEGS RD
SOUILLAC DR
SCLANDERSBURN RD
BLAEFAULDS CRES
BULLOCH CRES
SHANKS AVE
LONEY CRES
LOCHHEAD AVE
ANDERSON DR
GLASGOW RD
OCHIL VIEW
BRAES VIEW
SUTHERLAND DR
WOODLAND WAY
REEDLANDS DR
HEATHERD GDNS
HILL HOUSE RD
AFTON DR
GLENBO DR
GIBBDUN PL
LEI PL
LAXDALE DR
HILLCREST PL
GARVALD RD
SOLWAY DR
GLOWRORUM DR
HAYFIELD TERR
ENDRICK DR
EARN PL
CHACEFIELD WOOD
DROVE LO CRES
DROVE LOAN
HOME FARM COTTS
LOMOND WAY
HAYPARK RD
ANNET RD
KATRIN PL
CREMAN DR
BANKHEAD CRES
LOANHEAD AVE
PARK AVE
ELMBANK CRES
BALFOUR ST
ASHLEY ST
DUNCAIRN AVE
MORRISON AVE
GLENMORE DR
ALLOWAY CRES
DUNVEG PL
DUNCAN ST
LARBERT RD
DICKBURN CRES
BONNYFIELD RD
SPENCE ST 1
CLAREMONT ST 2
HOPEPARK TERR 3
STEWART ST 4
PEARSON AVE
RANKIN CRES
GLEN VIEW
MONTROSE WAY
BY-PASS RD
BELMONT AVE
PEARSON PL
WALKER DR
WATSON PL
McVEAN PL
ANDERSON TERR
MAYFIELD DR
JOHN ST
KERR CR
JAMES ST
CASTLEVIEW TERR
CUMBERNAULD RD
MARGARET AVE
GARNGREW RD
SEABEGS CRES
SEABEGS PL
GREENHILL RD
MANNFIELD AVE
WOODBURN CRES
GRAHAMSDYKE RD 1
ANTONINE GR 2
GRAHAMSDYKE CRES 3
LEAPARK DR
LAUREL PL
LAUREL GR
THORNDALE GDNS
ALLANDALE COTTS
DUNDAS COTTS
GLENYARDS RD
PO
4
3
2
1
81
80
79
78
79
80
81

58

57

37

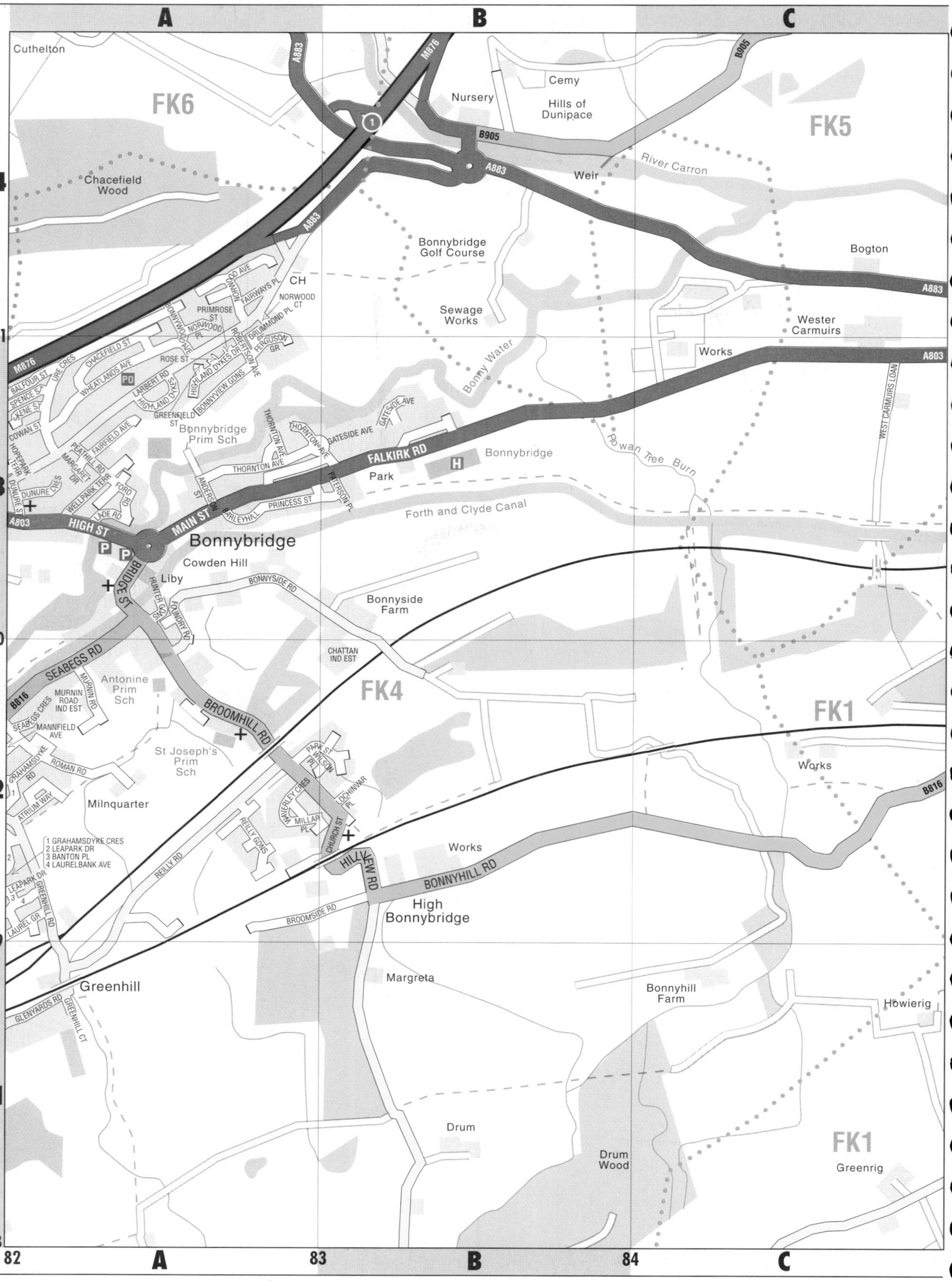
A
B
C
4
81
3
80
2
79
1
78
82
83
84
Cuthelton
FK6
Chacefield
Wood
M876
A883
B905
Cemy
Nursery
Hills of
Dunipace
FK5
River Carron
Weir
Bonnybridge
Golf Course
Bogton
CH
Sewage
Works
Bonny Water
Wester
Carmuirs
Works
A803
WEST CARMUIRS LOAN
PRIMROSE
ST
NORWOOD PL
NORWOOD CT
FAIRWAYS PL
DRUMMOND PL
FERGUSON GR
ROBERTSON AVE
ROSE ST
CHACEFIELD ST
WHEATLANDS AVE
PO
LARBERT RD
HIGHLAND DYKES DR
BONNYVIEW GDNS
BALFOUR ST
URE CRES
SPENCE ST
KEENE ST
COWAN ST
GREENFIELD ST
Bonnybridge
Prim Sch
FAIRFIELD AVE
THORNTON AVE
GATESIDE AVE
FALKIRK RD
H
Bonnybridge
Rowan Tree Burn
HOPEPARK TERR
PEATHILL RD
MARGARET DR
DUNURE CRES
WELLPARK TERR
FORD RD
Park
PATERSON PL
PRINCESS ST
ANDERSON ST
BARLEYHILL
Forth and Clyde Canal
HIGH ST
MAIN ST
P
Bonnybridge
Cowden Hill
BRIDGE ST
Liby
HUNTER GDNS
FOUNDRY RD
BONNYSIDE RD
Bonnyside
Farm
SEABEGS RD
B816
Antonine
Prim
Sch
MURNIN ROAD
IND EST
MURNIN RD
CHATTAN
IND EST
FK4
FK1
SEABEGS CRES
MANNFIELD AVE
BROOMHILL RD
St Joseph's
Prim
Sch
ROMAN RD
GRAHAMSDYKE RD
ATRIUM WAY
Milnquarter
PARK ST
WILSON PL
LOCHINVAR PL
WAVERLEY CRES
MILLAR PL
CHURCH ST
REILLY GDNS
REILLY RD
Works
1 GRAHAMSDYKE CRES
2 LEAPARK DR
3 BANTON PL
4 LAURELBANK AVE
HILLVIEW RD
BONNYHILL RD
High
Bonnybridge
BROOMSIDE RD
LEAPARK DR
GREENHILL RD
LAUREL GR
Greenhill
GLENYARDS RD
GREENHILL CT
Margreta
Bonnyhill
Farm
Howierig
Drum
Drum
Wood
FK1
Greenrig

57

38
60

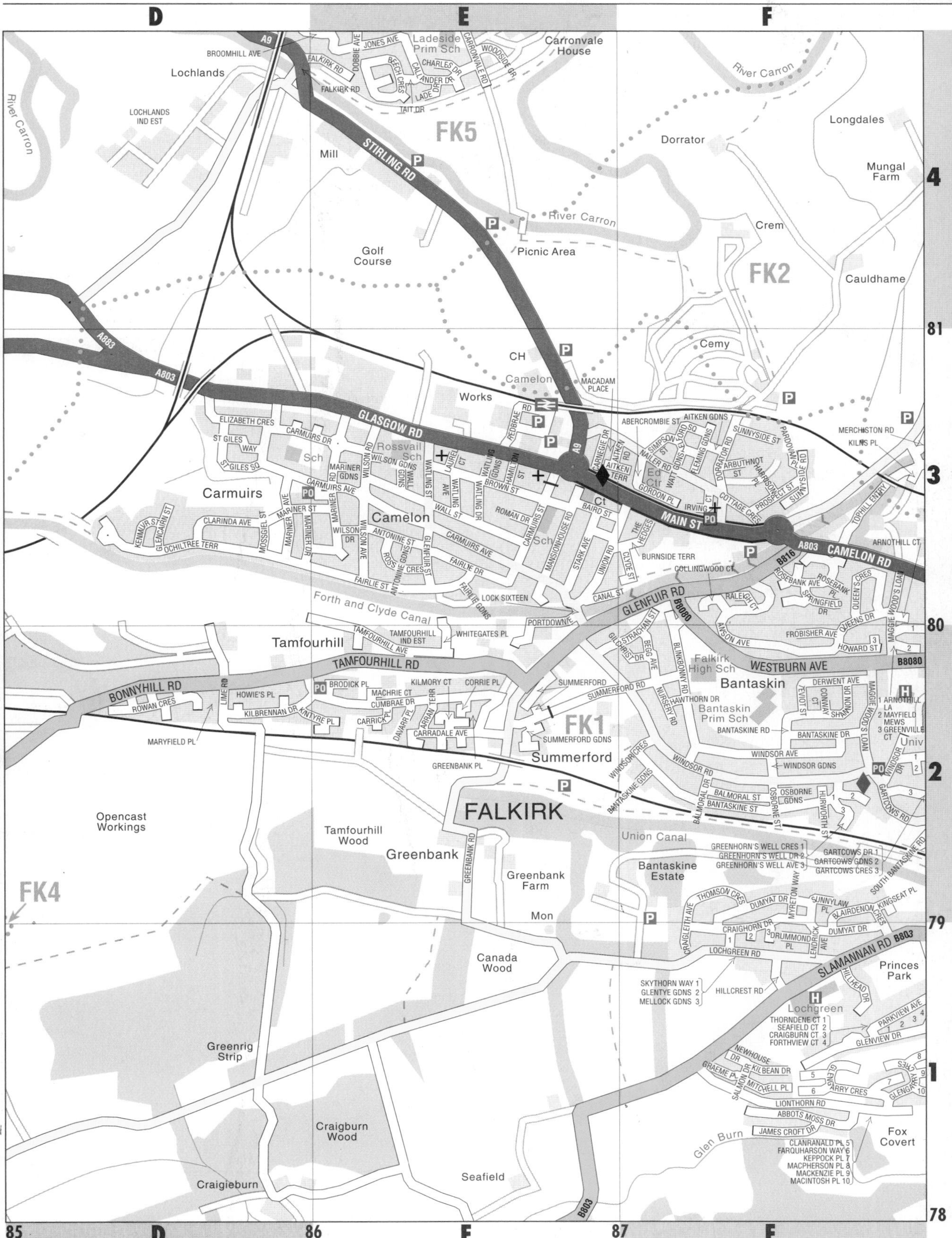
D
E
F
Lochlands
LOCHLANDS IND EST
River Carron
BROOMHILL AVE
A9
FALKIRK RD
Ladeside Prim Sch
JONES AVE
DOBBIE AVE
BEECH CRES
CALLANDER DR
CHARLES DR
CARRONVALE RD
WOODSIDE GR
LADE DR
TAIT DR
Carronvale House
River Carron
Longdales
FK5
Dorrator
Mill
STIRLING RD
Mungal Farm
4
River Carron
Crem
Golf Course
Picnic Area
FK2
Cauldhame
A883
81
CH
Cemy
Camelon
MACADAM PLACE
A803
Works
GLASGOW RD
ELIZABETH CRES
ST GILES WAY
ST GILES SQ
CARMUIRS DR
Rossvail Sch
Sch
WILSON GDNS
WILSON RD
MARINER GDNS
REDBRAE RD
ABERCROMBIE ST
AITKEN GDNS
SUNNYSIDE ST
MERCHISTON RD
KILNS PL
CARNEGIE DR
AITKEN RD
AITKEN TERR
SIMPSON ST
MAILER RD
WATT GDNS
ALFORD SQ
FLEMING GDNS
DORRATOR RD
ARBUTHNOT ST
HARRISON PL
PARDOVAN PL
SUNNYSIDE RD
PROSPECT ST
COTTAGE CRES
TOPHILL ENTRY
3
Ed Ctr
GORDON PL
IRVING CT
Carmuirs
CARMUIRS AVE
WATLING ST
LAUREL CT
WATLING AVE
WATLING DR
HAMILTON ST
BROWN ST
WALL GDNS
WALL ST
Ct
BAIRD ST
MAIN ST
PO
ARNOTHILL CT
CAMELON RD
Camelon
KENMUIR ST
GLENCAIRN ST
CLARINDA AVE
OCHILTREE TERR
MOSSGIEL ST
MARINER AVE
MARINER ST
MARINER DR
MARINER RD
WILSON DR
WILSON AVE
ANTONINE ST
ROSS CRES
ANTONINE GDNS
GLENFUIR ST
CARMUIRS AVE
FAIRLIE DR
FAIRLIE ST
FAIRLIE GDNS
ROMAN DR
CARMUIRS ST
MANSIONHOUSE RD
STARK AVE
UNION RD
THE HEDGES
CLYDE ST
BURNSIDE TERR
COLLINGWOOD CT
B816
ROSEBANK AVE
ROSEBANK PL
SPRINGFIELD DR
QUEEN'S CRES
MAGGIE WOOD'S LOAN
LOCK SIXTEEN
CANAL ST
GLENFUIR RD
B8080
RALEIGH CT
Forth and Clyde Canal
PORTDOWNIE
ANSON AVE
FROBISHER AVE
QUEENS DR
HOWARD ST
80
Tamfourhill
TAMFOURHILL AVE
TAMFOURHILL IND EST
WHITEGATES PL
STRACHAN ST
GILCHRIST DR
BEGG AVE
BLINKBONNY RD
Falkirk High Sch
WESTBURN AVE
B8080
TAMFOURHILL RD
Bantaskin
BONNYHILL RD
LIME RD
HOWIE'S PL
ROWAN CRES
BRODICK PL
MACHRIE CT
CUMBRAE DR
KINTYRE PL
KILBRENNAN DR
KILMORY CT
CORRIE PL
CARRICK PL
ARRAN TERR
DAVAAR PL
CARRADALE AVE
SUMMERFORD
SUMMERFORD RD
NURSERY RD
HAWTHORN DR
Bantaskin Prim Sch
DERWENT AVE
EVIOT ST
CONWAY CT
SHANNON DR
1 ARNOTHILL LA
2 MAYFIELD MEWS
3 GREENVILLE CT
MARYFIELD PL
FK1
SUMMERFORD GDNS
BANTASKINE RD
BANTASKINE DR
Univ
Summerford
WINDSOR CRES
WINDSOR AVE
WINDSOR GDNS
WINDSOR DR
GREENBANK PL
WINDSOR RD
2
WINDSOR GDNS
BANTASKINE GDNS
BALMORAL DR
BALMORAL ST
BANTASKINE ST
OSBORNE ST
OSBORNE GDNS
HURWORTH ST
GARTCOWS RD
Opencast Workings
FALKIRK
Tamfourhill Wood
Union Canal
GREENHORN'S WELL CRES 1
GREENHORN'S WELL DR 2
GREENHORN'S WELL AVE 3
GARTCOWS DR 1
GARTCOWS GDNS 2
GARTCOWS CRES 3
SOUTH BANTASKINE RD
Greenbank
GREENBANK RD
Bantaskine Estate
Greenbank Farm
FK4
THOMSON CRES
DUMYAT DR
MYRETON WAY
SUNNYLAW PL
BLAIRDENON CRES
KINGSEAT PL
Mon
79
CRAIGLEITH AVE
CRAIGHORN DR
DRUMMOND PL
LENDRICK AVE
DUMYAT DR
B803
LOCHGREEN RD
SLAMANNAN RD
Canada Wood
Princes Park
SKYTHORN WAY 1
GLENTYE GDNS 2
MELLOCK GDNS 3
HILLCREST RD
HILLHEAD DR
Lochgreen
THORNDENE CT 1
SEAFIELD CT 2
CRAIGBURN CT 3
FORTHVIEW CT 4
PARKVIEW AVE
GLENVIEW DR
Greenrig Strip
NEWHOUSE DR
KILBEAN DR
GRAEME PL
SALMOND PL
MITCHELL PL
GLENGARRY CRES
1
LIONTHORN RD
ABBOTS MOSS DR
Craigburn Wood
JAMES CROFT DR
Fox Covert
Glen Burn
CLANRANALD PL 5
FARQUHARSON WAY 6
KEPPOCK PL 7
MACPHERSON PL 8
MACKENZIE PL 9
MACINTOSH PL 10
Craigieburn
Seafield
B803
78
85
D
86
E
87
F

80
60

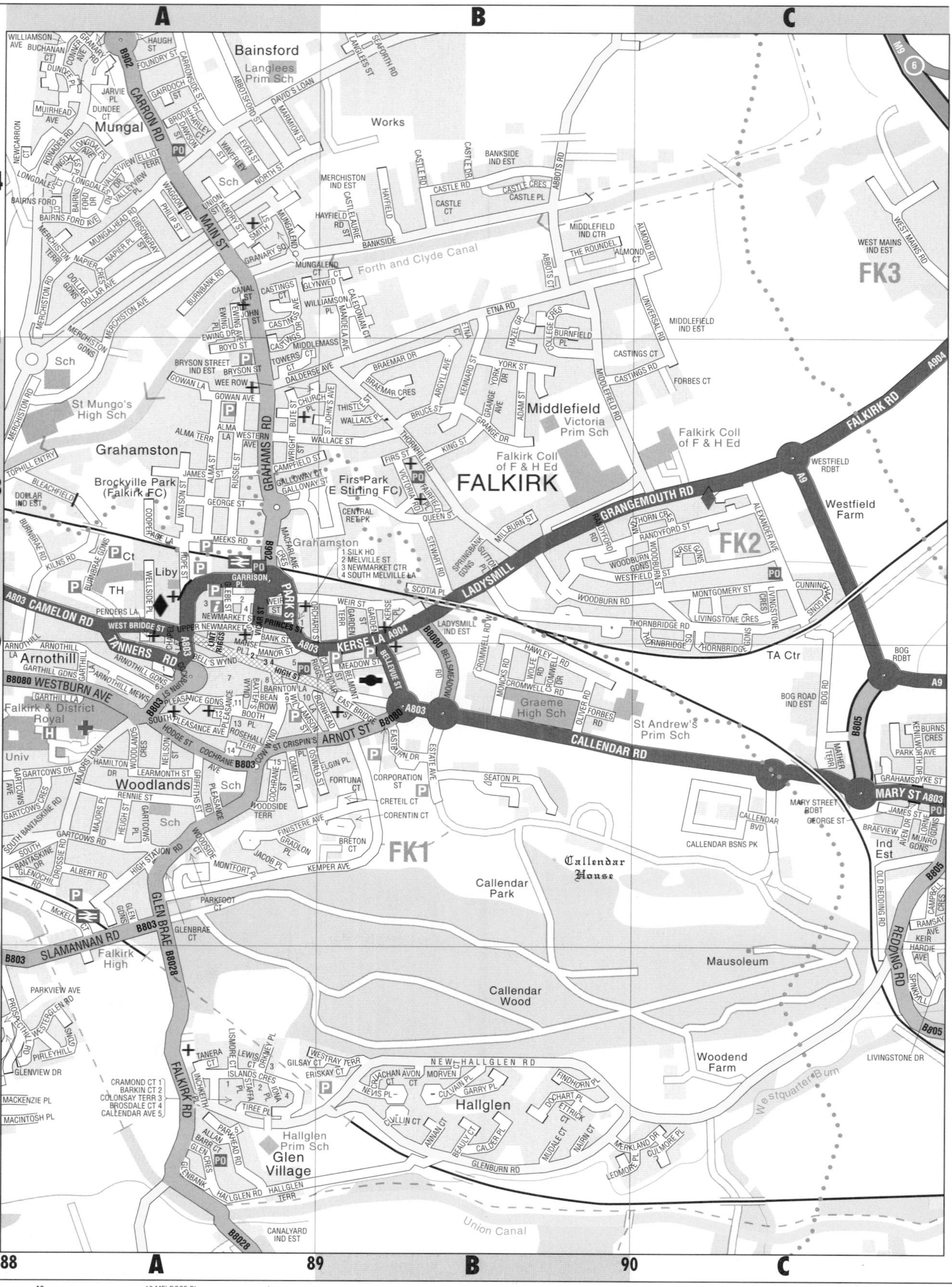

FK3

FK2

FALKIRK

FK1

Bainsford

Langlees Prim Sch

Works

Mungal

Grahamston

Brockville Park (Falkirk FC)

Middlefield

Victoria Prim Sch

Falkirk Coll of F & H Ed

Falkirk Coll of F & H Ed

Westfield Farm

Firs Park (E Stirling FC)

Central Ret Pk

Grahamston

1 SILK HO
2 MELVILLE ST
3 NEWMARKET CTR
4 SOUTH MELVILLE 4A

Arnothill

Falkirk & District Royal

Univ

Woodlands

Graeme High Sch

St Andrew's Prim Sch

Callendar Bsns Pk

Callendar Park

Callendar House

Callendar Wood

Mausoleum

Woodend Farm

Falkirk High

Hallglen Prim Sch

Glen Village

Hallglen

Union Canal

Forth and Clyde Canal

A2
1 BURNFOOT LA
2 KIRK WYND
3 TOLBOOTH ST
4 WOOER ST
5 CALLENDAR SQUARE SH CTR
6 ARNOTHILL BANK
7 HOWGATE SH CTR
8 KINGS CT
9 MISSION LA
10 MELROSE PL
11 ST ANDREWS PL
12 PLEASANCE SQ
13 PLEASANCE CT
14 ST MODANS CT
15 COMELY PARK TERR

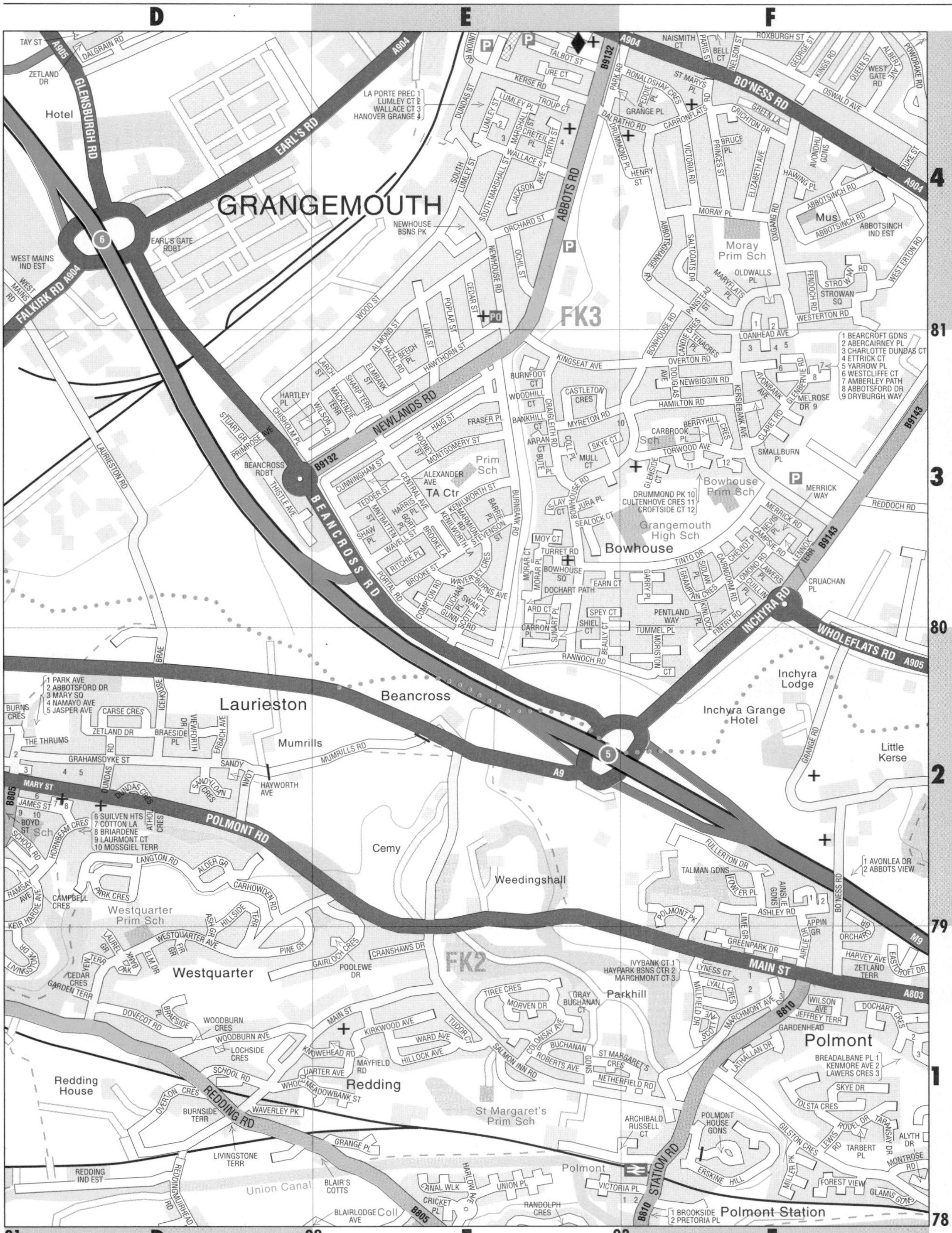
D
E
F
GRANGEMOUTH
FK3
FK2
Laurieston
Beancross
Mumrills
Westquarter
Redding
Redding House
Polmont
Parkhill
Weedingshall
Bowhouse
Inchyra Lodge
Inchyra Grange Hotel
Little Kerse
Cemy
Hotel
Mus
Moray Prim Sch
Bowhouse Prim Sch
Grangemouth High Sch
Westquarter Prim Sch
St Margaret's Prim Sch
Polmont Station
Union Canal
Coll
TA Ctr
Prim Sch
Sch
GLENSBURGH RD
EARL'S RD
EARL'S GATE RDBT
FALKIRK RD A904
WEST MAINS IND EST
A904
A905
BO'NESS RD
ABBOTS RD
B9132
NEWLANDS RD
BEANCROSS RDBT
BEANCROSS RD
NEWHOUSE BSNS PK
BOWHOUSE RD
INCHYRA RD
B9143
WHOLEFLATS RD A905
A9
M9
POLMONT RD
MAIN ST
A803
REDDING RD
B805
STATION RD
B810
GRAHAMSDYKE ST
MUMRILLS RD
LAURIESTON RD
GRANGE RD
BO'NESS RD
DUNDAS ST
KERSE RD
TALBOT ST
URE CT
TROUP CT
LUMLEY ST
SOUTH LUMLEY ST
MARSHALL ST
SOUTH MARSHALL ST
WALLACE ST
JACKSON AVE
ORCHARD ST
OCHIL ST
NEWHOUSE RD
CEDAR ST
POPLAR ST
LIME ST
HAWTHORN ST
WOOD ST
ALMOND ST
HAZEL RD
BEECH PL
ELMBANK ST
SHARP TERR
MACKENZIE TERR
WILSON ST
HARTLEY PL
CHISHOLM PL
PRIMROSE AVE
STUART GR
THISTLE AVE
HAIG ST
FRASER PL
RODNEY ST
MONTGOMERY ST
CUNNINGHAM ST
TEDDER ST
CENTRAL AVE
ALEXANDER AVE
KENILWORTH ST
MARMION ST
STEVENSON ST
BARRIE PL
BURNBANK RD
MOUNTBATTEN ST
HARRIS PL
GORT PL
WAVELL ST
RITCHIE PL
SHAW PL
BROOKE ST
BROOKE LA
WAVERLEY CRES
BURNS AVE
COMPTON RD
BUCHAN PL
SWAN PL
GUNN RD
SCOTT ST
PORTAL RD
BURNFOOT CT
WOODHILL CT
BANKHILL CT
ARRAN CT
BUTE PL
CRAIGLEITH RD
COLL PL
MULL CT
SKYE CT
MYRETON RD
CASTLETON CRES
KINGSEAT AVE
OVERTON RD
NEWBIGGIN RD
HAMILTON RD
DOUGLAS AVE
CANDIE CRES
TENACRES
BOWHOUSE RD
PANSTEAD ST
SALTCOATS DR
MARVELFLATS
OLDWALLS PL
LOANHEAD AVE
WESTERTON RD
STROWAN SQ
STROWAN RD
FENDOCH RD
ABBOTSINCH RD
ABBOTSINCH IND EST
HAWING PL
AVONDHU GDNS
OSWALD AVE
ROXBURGH ST
NAISMITH CT
PARIS ST
BELL CT
NELSON ST
GEORGE ST
KINGS RD
QUEEN ST
ALBERT AVE
WEST GATE RD
POWDRAKE RD
DUKE ST
ST MARYS PL
RONALDSHAY CRES
PEDDIE PL
GRANGE PL
CARRONFLATS RD
GREEN LA
CRICHTON DR
BRUCE PL
PRINCES ST
VICTORIA RD
ELIZABETH AVE
OXGANG RD
MORAY PL
HENRY ST
DALRATHO RD
DRUMMOND PL
ABBOTSGRANGE RD
PARK RD
LA PORTE PREC 1
LUMLEY CT 2
WALLACE CT 3
HANOVER GRANGE 4
1 BEARCROFT GDNS
2 ABERCAIRNEY PL
3 CHARLOTTE DUNDAS CT
4 ETTRICK CT
5 YARROW PL
6 WESTCLIFFE CT
7 AMBERLEY PATH
8 ABBOTSFORD DR
9 DRYBURGH WAY
GLENBERVIE RD
MELROSE DR
AVONBANK AVE
KERSEBANK AVE
CLARET RD
BERRYHILL CRES
CARBROOK PL
TORWOOD AVE
GLENSIDE CT
SMALLBURN PL
MERRICK WAY
MERRICK RD
REDDOCH RD
DRUMMOND PK 10
CULTENHOVE CRES 11
CROFTSIDE CT 12
CLAY CT
JURA PL
SEALOCK CT
NEVIS PL
CAMPSIE RD
LENNOX TERR
CRUACHAN PL
MOY CT
TURRET RD
BOWHOUSE SQ
MORAR CT
MORAR PL
EARN CT
DOCHART PATH
ARD CT
CARRON PL
SUNART PL
SHIEL CT
SPEY CT
BEAULY CT
TUMMEL PL
MORISTON CT
RANNOCH RD
GARRY PL
TINTO DR
SIDLAW PL
CAIRNGORM RD
CHEVIOT PL
GRAMPIAN CRES
LOMOND RD
KINLOCH PL
AWERS PL
CUILLIN PL
PENTLAND WAY
FINTRY RD
TAY ST
DALGRAIN RD
ZETLAND DR
1 PARK AVE
2 ABBOTSFORD DR
3 MARY SQ
4 NAMAYO AVE
5 JASPER AVE
BURNS CRES
THE THRUMS
CARSE CRES
ZETLAND DR
BRAESIDE PL
VIEWFORTH DR
ICEHOUSE BRAE
ERBACH AVE
SANDY LOAN
SANDYLOAN CRES
HAYWORTH AVE
MARY ST
JAMES ST
BOYD ST
SCHOOL RD
HORNBEAM CRES
DUNDAS CRES
ATHOL CRES
6 SUILVEN HTS
7 COTTON LA
8 BRIARDENE
9 LAURMONT CT
10 MOSSGIEL TERR
RAMSAY AVE
CAMPBELL CRES
PARK CRES
LANGTON RD
ALDER GR
CARHOWDEN RD
HILLSIDE TERR
ASH GR
WESTQUARTER AVE
LAUREL GR
FIR GR
ELM DR
OAK BANK
YEW TERR
PINE GR
CEDAR CRES
GARDEN TERR
KEIR HARDIE AVE
LIVINGSTONE DR
GAIRLOCH CRES
CRANSHAWS DR
POOLEWE DR
DOVECOT RD
BRAESIDE PL
WOODBURN CRES
WOODBURN AVE
LOCHSIDE CRES
SCHOOL RD
MAIN ST
KIRKWOOD AVE
KNOWEHEAD RD
MAYFIELD RD
QUARTER AVE
WHOLE
MEADOWBANK ST
WARD AVE
HILLOCK AVE
TUDOR CT
OVERTON CRES
BURNSIDE TERR
WAVERLEY PK
GRANGE PL
LIVINGSTONE TERR
REDDING IND EST
REDDINGMUIRHEAD RD
BLAIR'S COTTS
BLAIRLODGE AVE
CANAL WLK
CRICKET PL
HARLOW AVE
UNION PL
RANDOLPH CRES
VICTORIA PL
TIREE CRES
MORVEN DR
GRAY BUCHANAN CT
COLONSAY AVE
BUCHANAN GDNS
ROBERTS AVE
SALMON INN RD
ST MARGARET'S CRES
NETHERFIELD RD
ARCHIBALD RUSSELL CT
IVYBANK CT 1
HAYPARK BSNS CTR 2
MARCHMONT CT 3
LYNESS CT
LYALL CRES
MILLFIELD DR
MARCHMONT AVE
FULLERTON DR
TALMAN GDNS
FOWLER PL
AINSLIE GDNS
POLMONT PK
ASHLEY RD
LIME GR
GREENPARK DR
AIRLIE DR
APPIN GR
ORCHARD GR
HARVEY AVE
EASTCROFT DR
ZETLAND TERR
1 AVONLEA DR
2 ABBOTS VIEW
WILSON AVE
JEFFREY TERR
GARDENHEAD
DOCHART CRES
LATHALLAN DR
BREADALBANE PL 1
KENMORE AVE 2
LAWERS CRES 3
SKYE DR
TOLSTA CRES
POLMONT HOUSE GDNS
ERSKINE HILL
GILSTON CRES
LEWIS RD
RODEL DR
TARANSAY DR
TARBERT PL
ALYTH DR
MONTROSE RD
MILLER PK
FOREST VIEW
GLAMIS GDNS
1 BROOKSIDE
2 PRETORIA PL
91
92
93
78
79
80
81
1
2
3
4

61
41

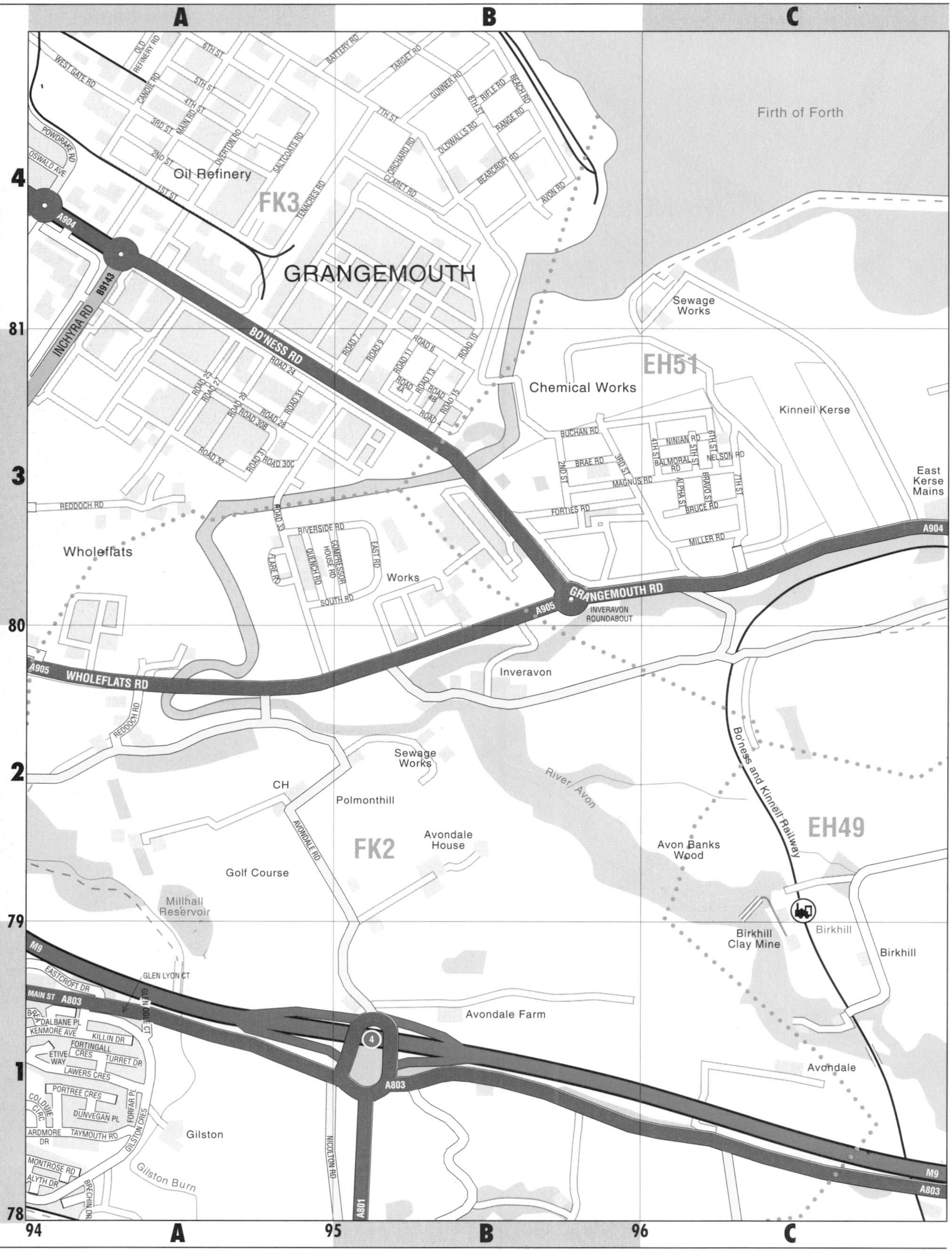
A
B
C
4
81
3
80
2
79
1
78
94
95
96
Firth of Forth
GRANGEMOUTH
Oil Refinery
FK3
OLD REFINERY RD
6TH ST
WEST GATE RD
5TH ST
CANDIE RD
4TH ST
3RD ST
MAIN RD ST
2ND ST
1ST ST
OVERTON RD
SALTCOATS RD
POWDRAKE RD
OSWALD AVE
BATTERY RD
TARGET RD
GUNNER RD
8TH ST
RIFLE RD
BEACH RD
7TH ST
ORCHARD RD
OLDWALLS RD
RANGE RD
CLARET RD
BEARCROFT RD
AVON RD
TENACRES RD
A904
B9143
INCHYRA RD
BO'NESS RD
ROAD 7
ROAD 9
ROAD 6
ROAD 10
ROAD 11
ROAD 13
ROAD 4A
ROAD 4B
ROAD 15
ROAD 4
ROAD 24
ROAD 25
ROAD 27
ROAD 29
ROAD 28
ROAD 30B
ROAD 31
ROAD 32
ROAD 30C
ROAD 33
Sewage Works
EH51
Chemical Works
Kinneil Kerse
BUCHAN RD
NINIAN RD
4TH ST
5TH ST
6TH ST
NELSON RD
2ND ST
BRAE RD
3RD ST
BALMORAL RD
MAGNUS RD
ALPHA ST
BRAVO ST
BRUCE RD
7TH ST
FORTIES RD
MILLER RD
East Kerse Mains
REDDOCH RD
Wholeflats
RIVERSIDE RD
FLARE RD
QUENCH RD
HOUSE RD
COMPRESSOR RD
EAST RD
SOUTH RD
Works
GRANGEMOUTH RD
A905
INVERAVON ROUNDABOUT
A905
WHOLEFLATS RD
Inveravon
REDDOCH RD
Sewage Works
CH
Polmonthill
River Avon
Bo'ness and Kinneil Railway
EH49
FK2
AVONDALE RD
Avondale House
Avon Banks Wood
Golf Course
Millhall Reservoir
Birkhill Clay Mine
Birkhill
Birkhill
M9
GLEN LYON CT
GLEN OGLE CT
EASTCROFT DR
MAIN ST
A803
BRAE
DALBANE PL
KENMORE AVE
KILLIN DR
FORTINGALL CRES
ETIVE WAY
TURRET DR
LAWERS CRES
Avondale Farm
4
A803
Avondale
PORTREE CRES
COLDUIE CIRC
DUNVEGAN PL
FORFAR PL
ARDMORE DR
TAYMOUTH RD
GILSTON CRES
Gilston
NICOLTON RD
MONTROSE RD
ALYTH DR
Gilston Burn
BRECHIN DR
A801
M9
A803

61
83

42
64

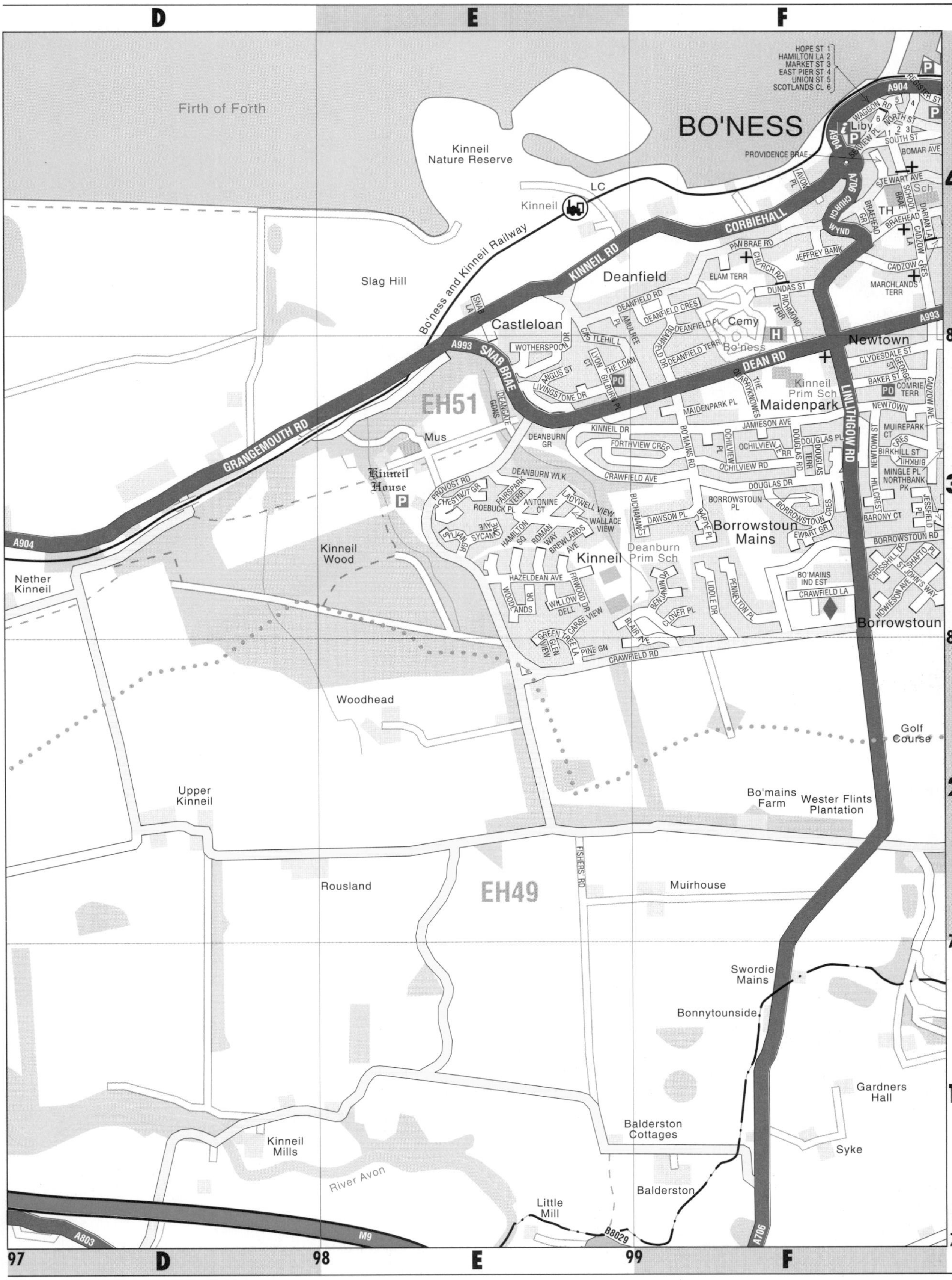
D
E
F
Firth of Forth
Kinneil Nature Reserve
BO'NESS
HOPE ST 1
HAMILTON LA 2
MARKET ST 3
EAST PIER ST 4
UNION ST 5
SCOTLANDS CL 6
A904
PROVIDENCE BRAE
Liby
Kinneil
LC
Bo'ness and Kinneil Railway
Slag Hill
KINNEIL RD
CORBIEHALL
Deanfield
Castleloan
Cemy
Newtown
A993
SNAB BRAE
DEAN RD
EH51
Maidenpark
Kinneil Prim Sch
LINLITHGOW RD
GRANGEMOUTH RD
Mus
Kinneil House
Kinneil Wood
Kinneil
Deanburn Prim Sch
Borrowstoun Mains
Borrowstoun
Nether Kinneil
CRAWFIELD RD
Woodhead
Golf Course
Upper Kinneil
Bo'mains Farm
Wester Flints Plantation
Rousland
EH49
FISHERS RD
Muirhouse
Swordie Mains
Bonnytounside
Gardners Hall
Balderston Cottages
Syke
Kinneil Mills
River Avon
Little Mill
Balderston
B8029
A706
M9
A803
4
81
3
80
2
79
1
78
97
98
99

84
64

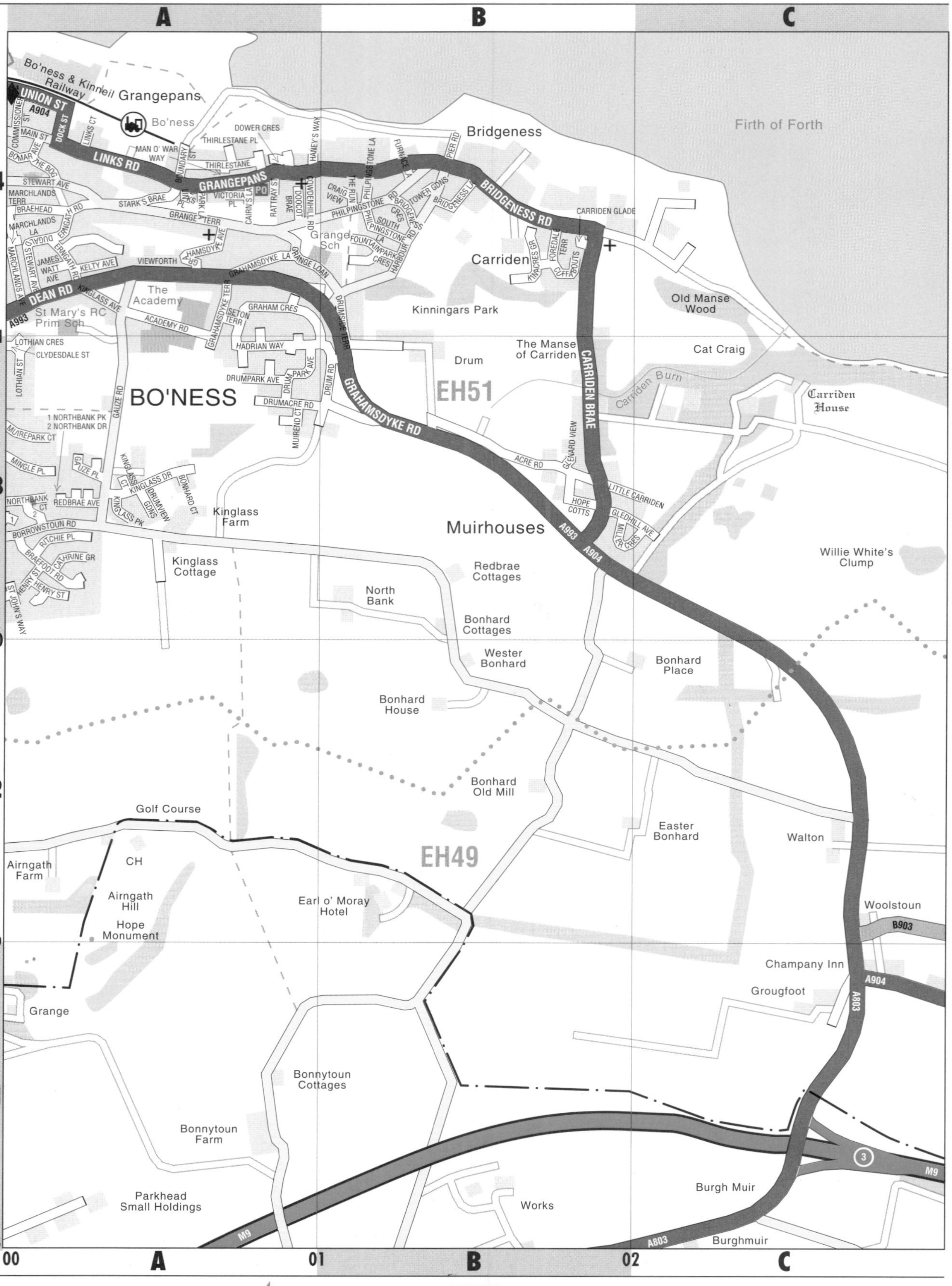

A | B | C

Bo'ness & Kinneil Railway | Grangepans
UNION ST
A904
COMMISSIONER
DOCK ST
LINKS CT
Bo'ness
Links Rd
MAIN ST
MAN O' WAR WAY
THE BY
BOMAR
DOWER CRES
THIRLESTANE PL
HANEY'S WAY
Bridgeness
PIER RD
Firth of Forth
4
STEWART AVE
MARCHLANDS TERR
BRAEHEAD
MARCHLANDS LA
MARCHLANDS RD
STARK'S BRAE
GRANGE TERR
GRANGEPANS
VICTORIA PL
THIRLESTANE
RATTRAY ST
THROWS
CRAIG VIEW
PHILPINGSTONE LA
THE RUN
TOWER GDNS
BRIDGENESS CRES
SOUTH PINGSTONE
FOUNTAINPARK CRES
Bridgeness Rd
CARRIDEN GLADE
KYACRES GR
FOREDALE TERR
DEAN RD
A993
St Mary's RC Prim Sch
Grange Sch
Grange Loan
DRUMACRE TERR
Grahamsdyke La
KELTY AVE
VIEWFORTH
GRAHAM CRES
Carriden
PROUTS
ORCHARD VIEW
Old Manse Wood
81
LOTHIAN CRES
CLYDESDALE ST
LOTHIAN PL
ACADEMY RD
HADRIAN WAY
The Academy
DRUMPARK RD
DRUM AVE
DRUM RD
Kinningars Park
Drum
The Manse of Carriden
EH51
Cat Craig
Carriden Burn
Carriden House
BO'NESS
GAUZE PL
KINGLASS DR
DRUMVIEW
BONHARD CT
DRUMACRE RD
MUIREND RD
Grahamsdyke Rd
ACRE RD
CARRIDEN BRAE
HOPE COTTS
LITTLE CARRIDEN
GLEDHILL AVE
3
NORTHBANK PK
NORTHBANK DR
MUIREPARK CT
REDBRAE AVE
KINGLASS GDNS
KINGLASS PK
Kinglass Farm
Muirhouses
A993
A904
MILLER CRES
Willie White's Clump
NORTHBANK CT
BORROWSTOUN RD
RITCHIE PL
BRAEFOOT RD
AHRINE GR
ST JOHN'S WAY
ST HENRY ST
HENRY ST
Kinglass Cottage
North Bank
Redbrae Cottages
Bonhard Cottages
80
Wester Bonhard
Bonhard Place
Bonhard House
2
Golf Course
Bonhard Old Mill
Easter Bonhard
Walton
Airngath Farm
CH
EH49
Airngath Hill
Hope Monument
Earl o' Moray Hotel
Woolstoun
B903
79
Champany Inn
A904
Grange
Grougfoot
A803
1
Bonnytoun Cottages
3
M9
Bonnytoun Farm
Burgh Muir
Parkhead Small Holdings
Works
A803
Burghmuir
78
00 | A | 01 | B | 02 | C

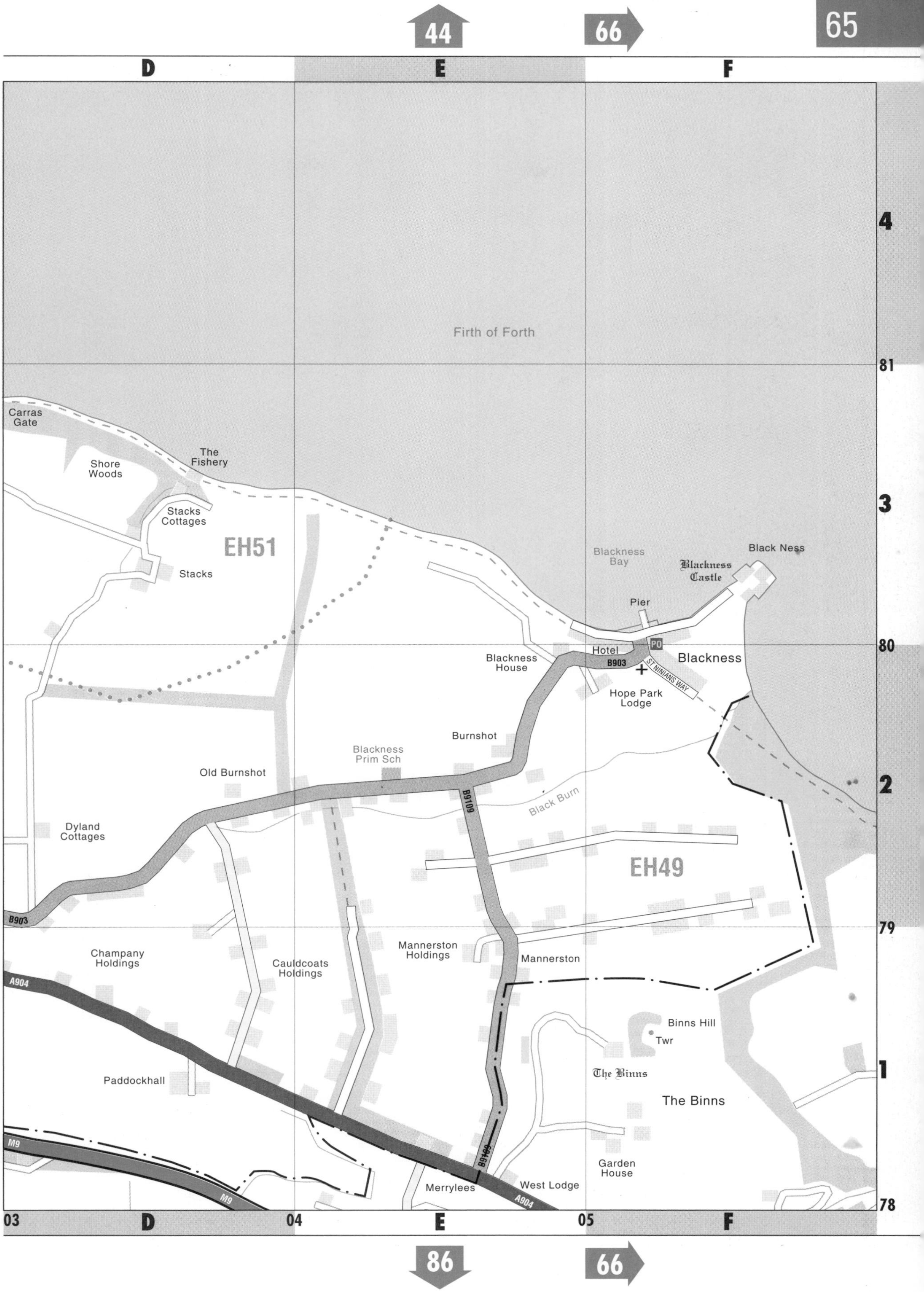

D
E
F

Firth of Forth

4

81

Carras Gate
Shore Woods
The Fishery
Stacks Cottages
EH51
Stacks

3

Blackness Bay
Blackness Castle
Black Ness

Pier

80

Hotel
Blackness House
B903
PO
ST NINIANS WAY
Blackness

Hope Park Lodge

Burnshot
Blackness Prim Sch
Old Burnshot
B9109
Black Burn

EH49

2

Dyland Cottages

B903

79

Champany Holdings
Cauldcoats Holdings
Mannerston Holdings
Mannerston

A904

Binns Hill
Twr
The Binns

1

Paddockhall

The Binns

M9

Garden House

Merrylees
West Lodge
A904

78

03
D
04
E
05
F

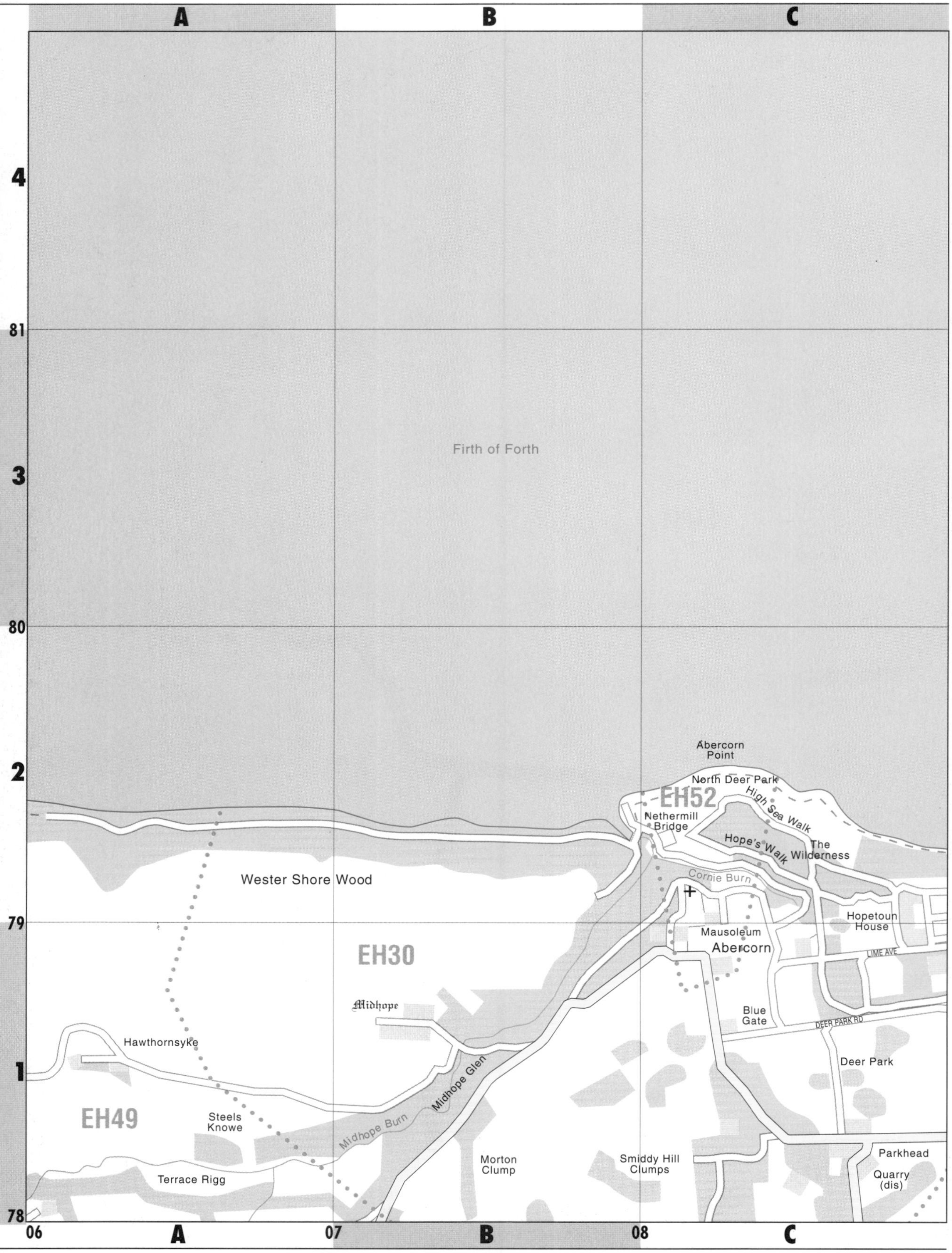
A   B   C

4

81

Firth of Forth

3

80

2

Abercorn
Point

North Deer Park

EH52

High Sea Walk

Nethermill
Bridge

Hope's Walk

The
Wilderness

Wester Shore Wood

Cornie Burn

79

Hopetoun
House

Mausoleum

Abercorn

LIME AVE

EH30

Midhope

Blue
Gate

DEER PARK RD

1

Hawthornsyke

Deer Park

EH49

Steels
Knowe

Midhope Burn

Midhope Glen

Morton
Clump

Smiddy Hill
Clumps

Parkhead

Quarry
(dis)

Terrace Rigg

78

06   A   07   B   08   C

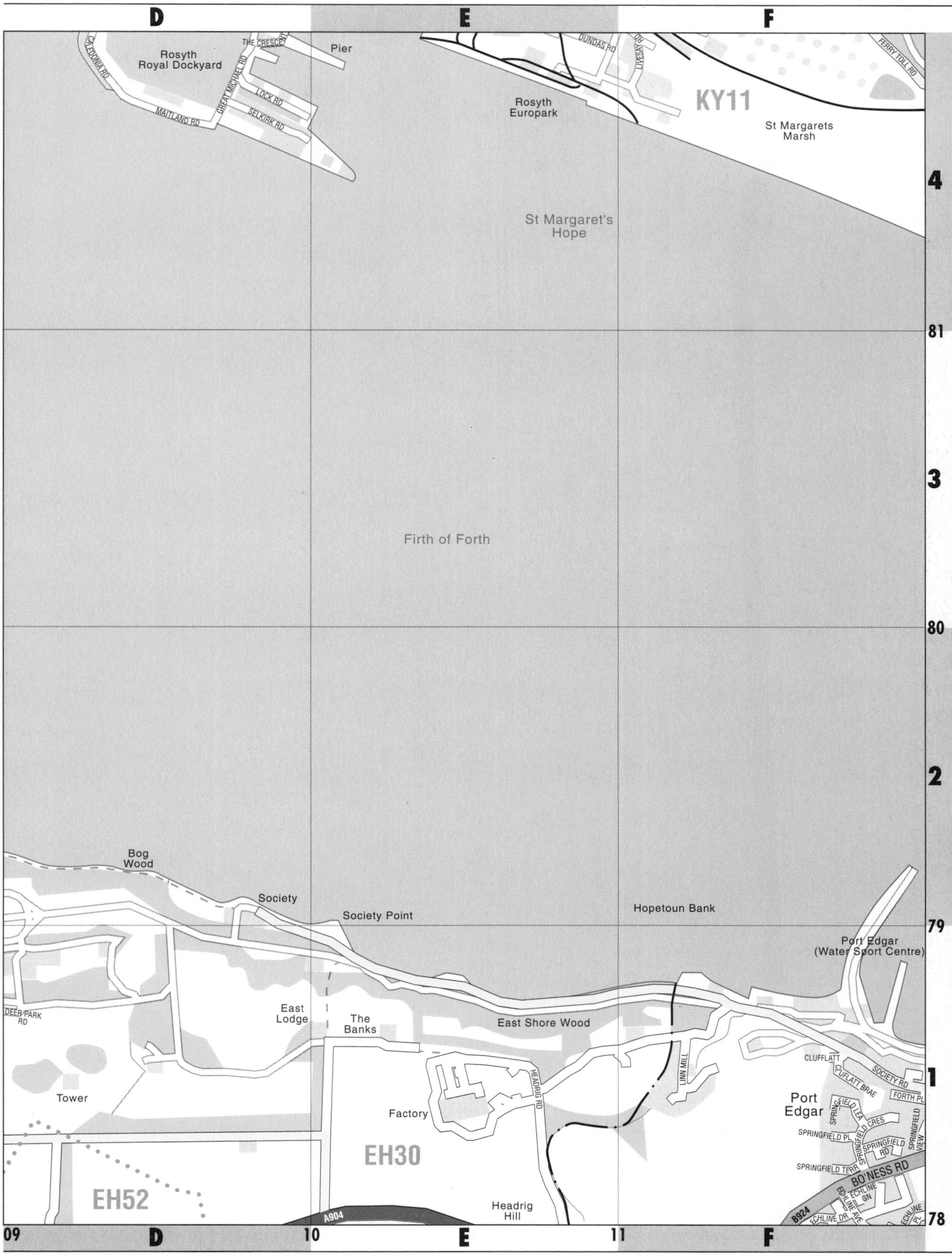

D · E · F

Rosyth
Royal Dockyard
Pier
THE CRESCENT
CALEDONIA RD
GREAT MICHAEL RD
LOCK RD
SELKIRK RD
MAITLAND RD

DUNDAS RD
LOVERS RD
FERRY TOLL RD

Rosyth
Europark

KY11

St Margarets
Marsh

St Margaret's
Hope

4

81

3

Firth of Forth

80

2

Bog
Wood

Society
Society Point

Hopetoun Bank

79

Port Edgar
(Water Sport Centre)

DEER PARK RD

East
Lodge

The
Banks

East Shore Wood

HEADRIG RD

LINN MILL

Port
Edgar

CLUFFLATT
CLUFLATT BRAE
SOCIETY RD
FORTH PL

Tower

Factory

EH30

SPRINGFIELD PL
SPRINGFIELD RD
SPRINGFIELD TERR
SPRINGFIELD CRES
SPRINGFIELD LEA
SPRINGFIELD VIEW
SPRINGFIELD PL

1

EH52

A904

Headrig
Hill

BO'NESS RD
B924
ECHLINE DR
ECHLINE AVE
ECHLINE GN
ECHLINE PL

78

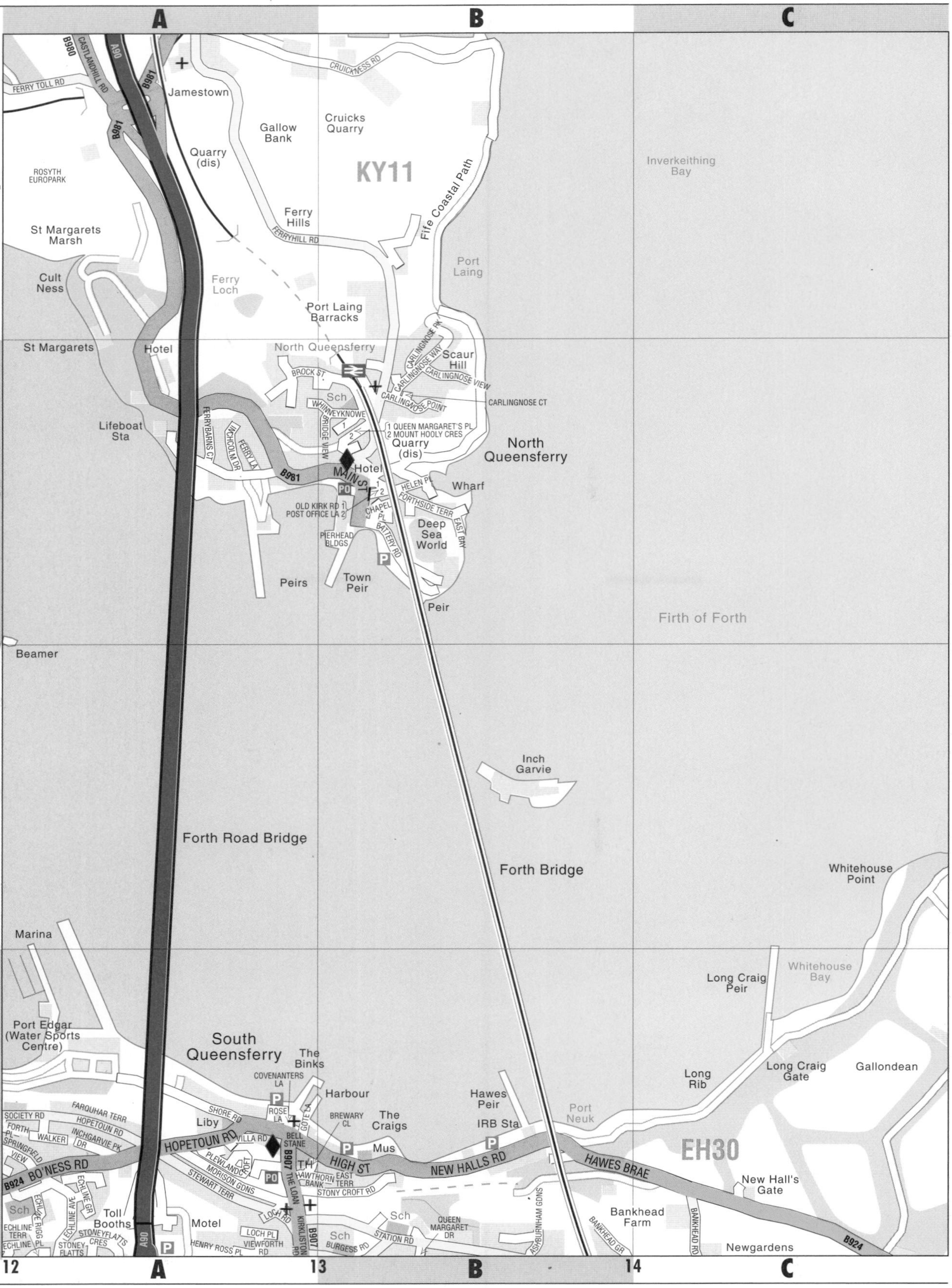

B980
CASTLANDHILL RD
A90
B981
FERRY TOLL RD

Jamestown

Gallow Bank

Cruicks Quarry

CRUICKNESS RD

KY11

Inverkeithing Bay

Quarry (dis)

ROSYTH EUROPARK

4

St Margarets Marsh

Ferry Hills

FERRYHILL RD

Cult Ness

Ferry Loch

Port Laing

Port Laing Barracks

81

St Margarets

Hotel

North Queensferry

BROCK ST

Sch

CARLINGNOSE WAY
CARLINGNOSE VIEW
Scaur Hill

CARLINGNOSE POINT
CARLINGHOSE

CARLINGNOSE CT

Lifeboat Sta

FERRYBARNS CT
INCHCOLM DR
FERRY LA

WHINNEYKNOWE
BRIDGE VIEW
1
2

1 QUEEN MARGARET'S PL
2 MOUNT HOOLY CRES
Quarry (dis)

North Queensferry

3

B981
MAIN ST
Hotel
PO
2
1
OLD KIRK RD 1
POST OFFICE LA 2
CHAPEL PL
BATTERY RD

HELEN PL
NORTHSIDE TERR
EAST BAY

Wharf

Peirs

PIERHEAD BLDGS

Town Peir

P

Deep Sea World

Peir

North Queensferry

80

Beamer

Firth of Forth

Inch Garvie

2

Forth Road Bridge

Forth Bridge

Whitehouse Point

Marina

79

Port Edgar (Water Sports Centre)

South Queensferry

The Binks

COVENANTERS LA

SHORE RD
ROSE LA

Harbour

BREWARY CL

The Craigs

Hawes Peir

IRB Sta

Port Neuk

Whitehouse Bay

Long Craig Peir

Long Rib

Long Craig Gate

Gallondean

1

SOCIETY RD
FARQUHAR TERR
FORTH PL
WALKER
SPRINGFIELD VIEW
INCHGARVIE PK
HOPETOUN PL
DR

Liby
HOPETOUN RD
VILLA RD
BELL STANE

Mus

HIGH ST
TH

Queen Margaret DR

NEW HALLS RD

HAWES BRAE

EH30

New Hall's Gate

BO'NESS RD
B924
ECHLINE AVE
ECHLINE GR
ECHLINE RIGG
STONEYFLATS
ECHLINE TERR
ECHLINE PL
STONEY FLATTS
STONEYFLATS CRES

Toll Booths
P

Motel

HENRY ROSS PL

PLEWLANDS
MORISON GDNS
STEWART TERR

PO
B907 THE LOAN
LOCH RD
KIRKLISTON RD
LOCH PL
VIEWFORTH RD

HAWTHORN BANK
STONY CROFT RD

Sch
STATION RD
BURGESS RD

Sch

ASHBURNHAM GDNS

BANKHEAD GR
Bankhead Farm

BANKHEAD RD

Newgardens

B924

78

48

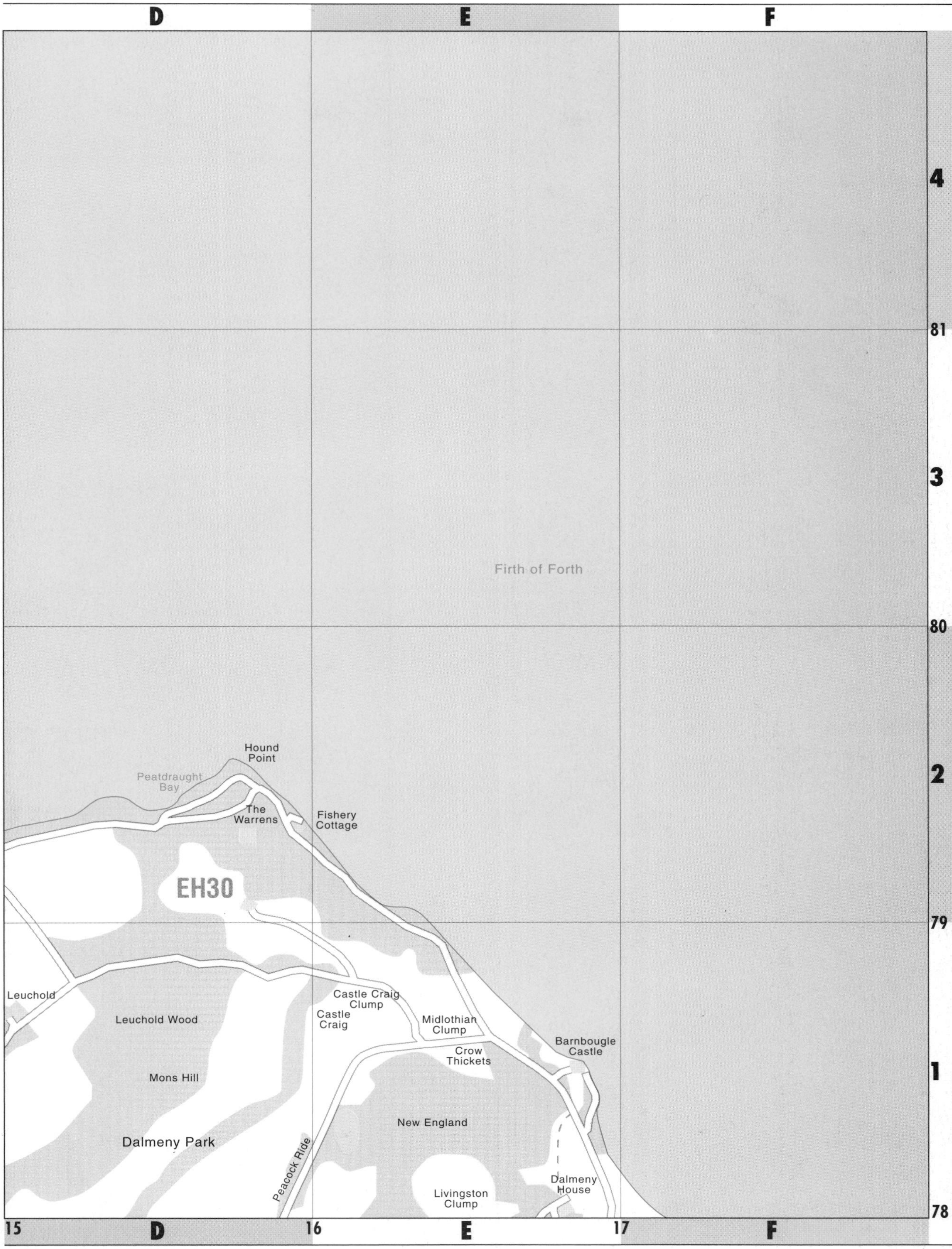
D
E
F
4
81
3
80
2
79
1
78
15
16
17
Firth of Forth
Hound Point
Peatdraught Bay
The Warrens
Fishery Cottage
EH30
Leuchold
Leuchold Wood
Castle Craig Clump
Castle Craig
Midlothian Clump
Crow Thickets
Barnbougle Castle
Mons Hill
New England
Dalmeny Park
Peacock Ride
Livingston Clump
Dalmeny House

90

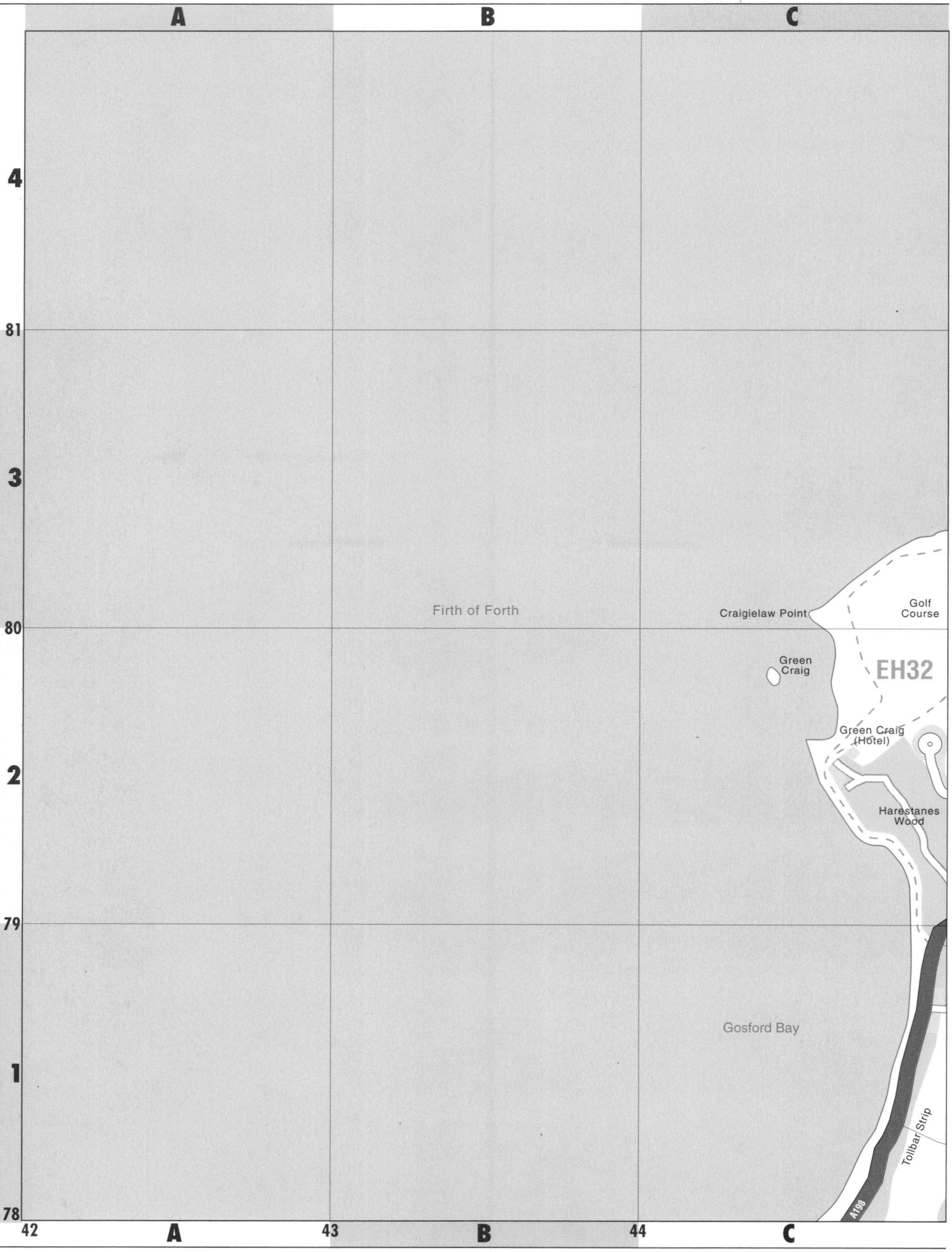

Firth of Forth

Craigielaw Point

Golf Course

Green Craig

EH32

Green Craig (Hotel)

Harestanes Wood

Gosford Bay

Tollbar Strip

A198

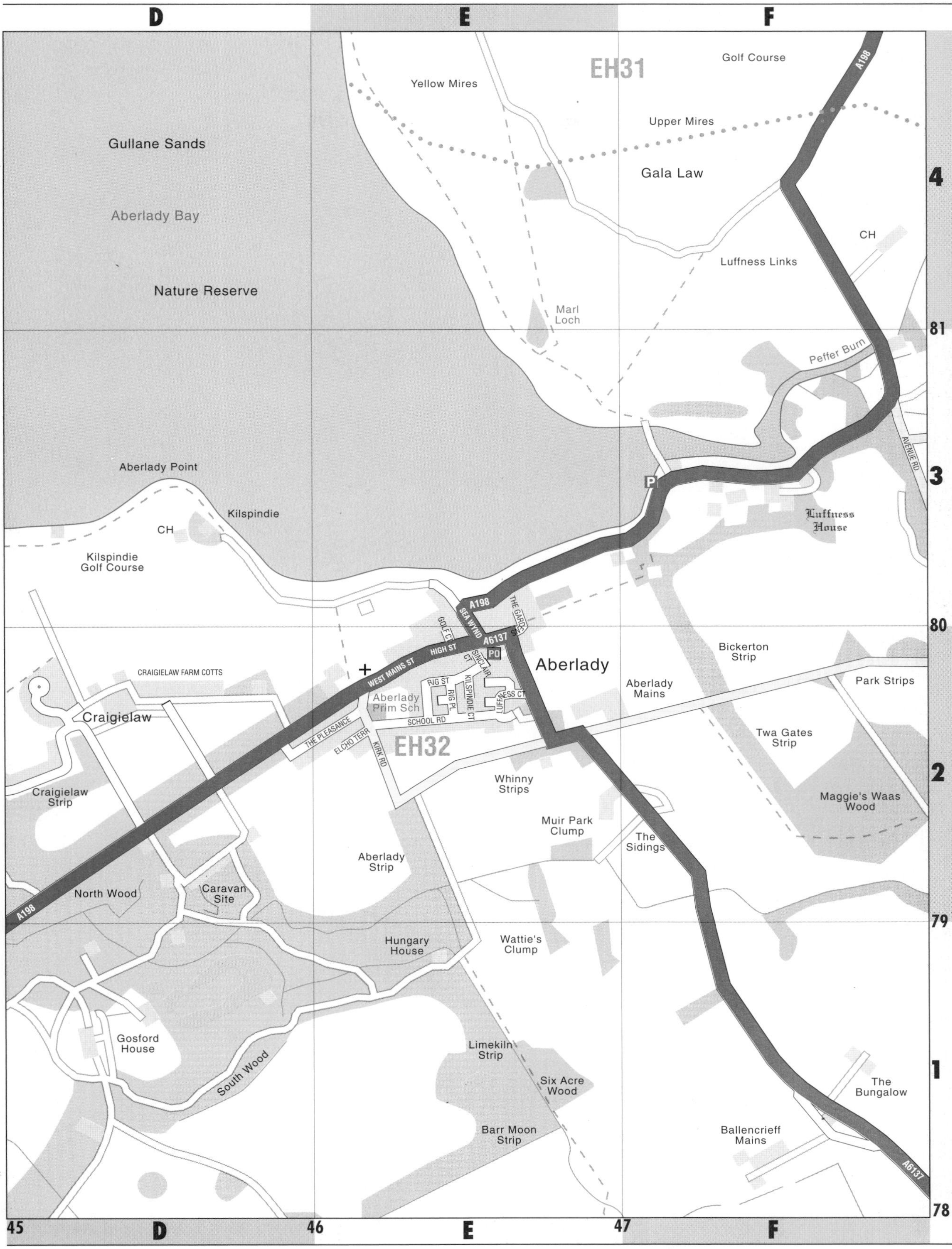

D E F

EH31

Gullane Sands

Yellow Mires

Golf Course

Upper Mires

Aberlady Bay

Gala Law

Nature Reserve

Luffness Links

CH

4

81

Marl Loch

Peffer Burn

3

Aberlady Point

P

Kilspindie

Luffness House

CH

Kilspindie Golf Course

A198

THE GARLE

A6137

SEA WYND

GOLF CT

HIGH ST

P

80

CRAIGIELAW FARM COTTS

WEST MAINS ST

Aberlady

Bickerton Strip

Park Strips

Craigielaw

Aberlady Prim Sch

THE PLEASANCE

RIG ST

RIG PL

SINCLAIR CT

KILSPINDIE CT

LUFFNESS CT

PO

Aberlady Mains

Twa Gates Strip

ELCHO TERR

KIRK RD

SCHOOL RD

EH32

Whinny Strips

Maggie's Waas Wood

2

Craigielaw Strip

Muir Park Clump

The Sidings

North Wood

A198

Caravan Site

Aberlady Strip

79

Hungary House

Wattie's Clump

Gosford House

South Wood

Limekiln Strip

Six Acre Wood

The Bungalow

1

Barr Moon Strip

Ballencrieff Mains

A6137

78

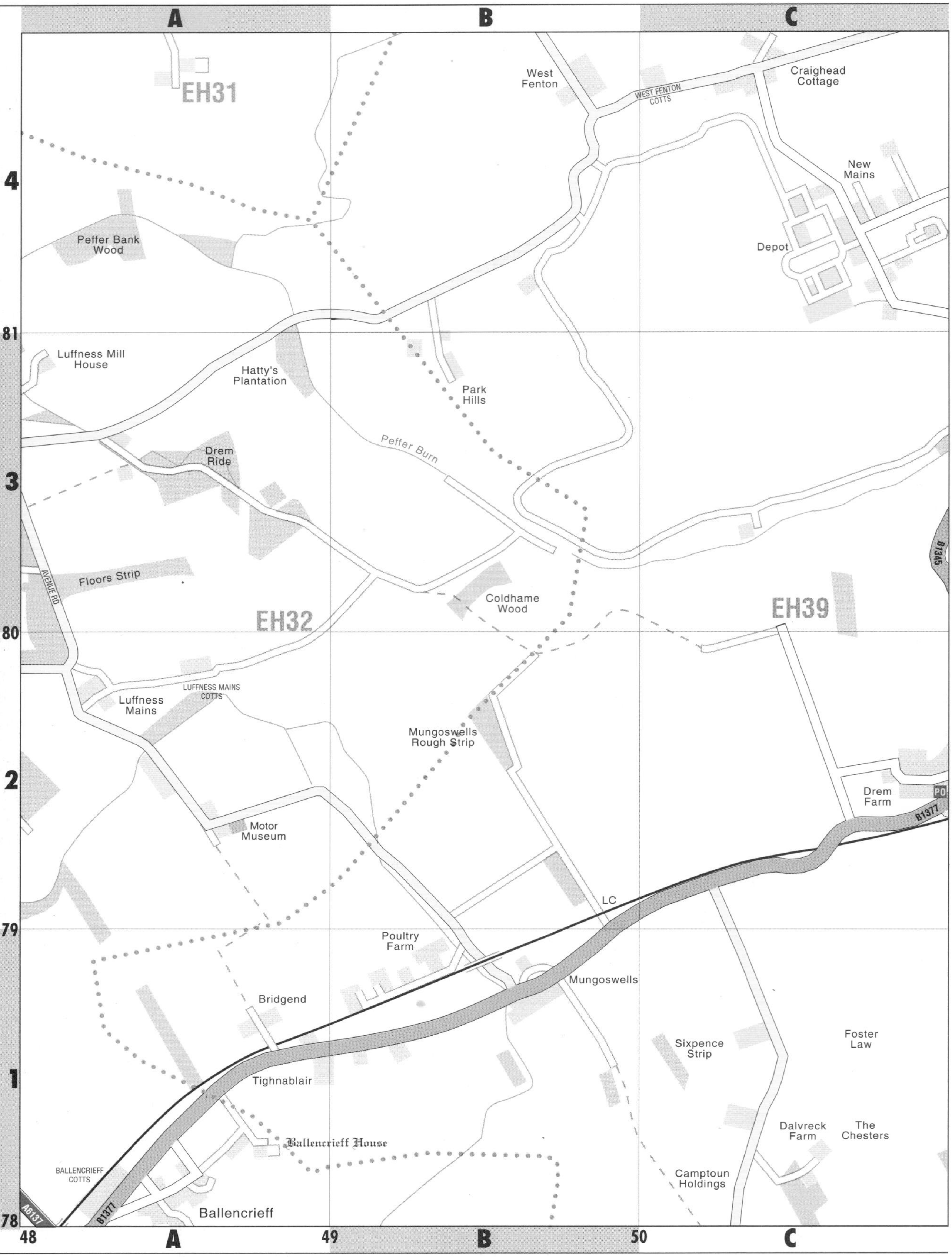

A   B   C

EH31

4

Peffer Bank
Wood

West
Fenton

WEST FENTON
COTTS

Craighead
Cottage

New
Mains

Depot

81

Luffness Mill
House

Hatty's
Plantation

Park
Hills

Peffer Burn

Drem
Ride

3

Floors Strip

EH32

Coldhame
Wood

EH39

B1345

80

Luffness Mains
Cotts

Luffness
Mains

Mungoswells
Rough Strip

Drem
Farm

PO

2

Motor
Museum

LC

B1377

79

Poultry
Farm

Mungoswells

Bridgend

Sixpence
Strip

Foster
Law

1

Tighnablair

Ballencrieff House

Dalvreck
Farm

The
Chesters

BALLENCRIEFF
COTTS

Camptoun
Holdings

A6137

B1377

Ballencrieff

78

48   A   49   B   50   C

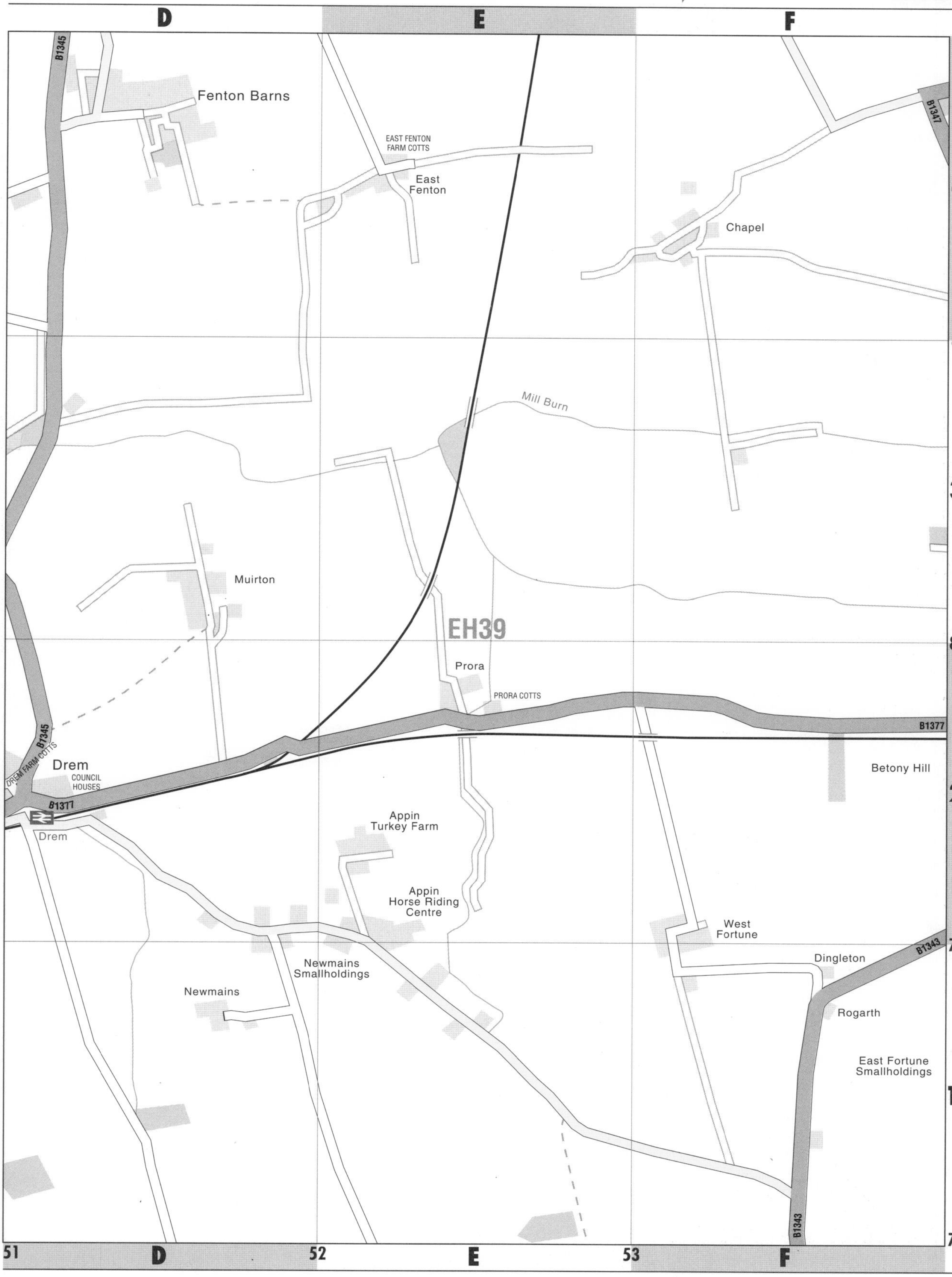
D
E
F
Fenton Barns
EAST FENTON
FARM COTTS
East
Fenton
Chapel
B1345
B1347
4
81
Mill Burn
3
Muirton
EH39
80
Prora
PRORA COTTS
B1377
B7345
DREM FARM COTTS
Drem
COUNCIL
HOUSES
B1377
Drem
Betony Hill
2
Appin
Turkey Farm
Appin
Horse Riding
Centre
West
Fortune
79
Dingleton
B1343
Newmains
Smallholdings
Newmains
Rogarth
East Fortune
Smallholdings
1
B1343
78
51
52
53
D
E
F

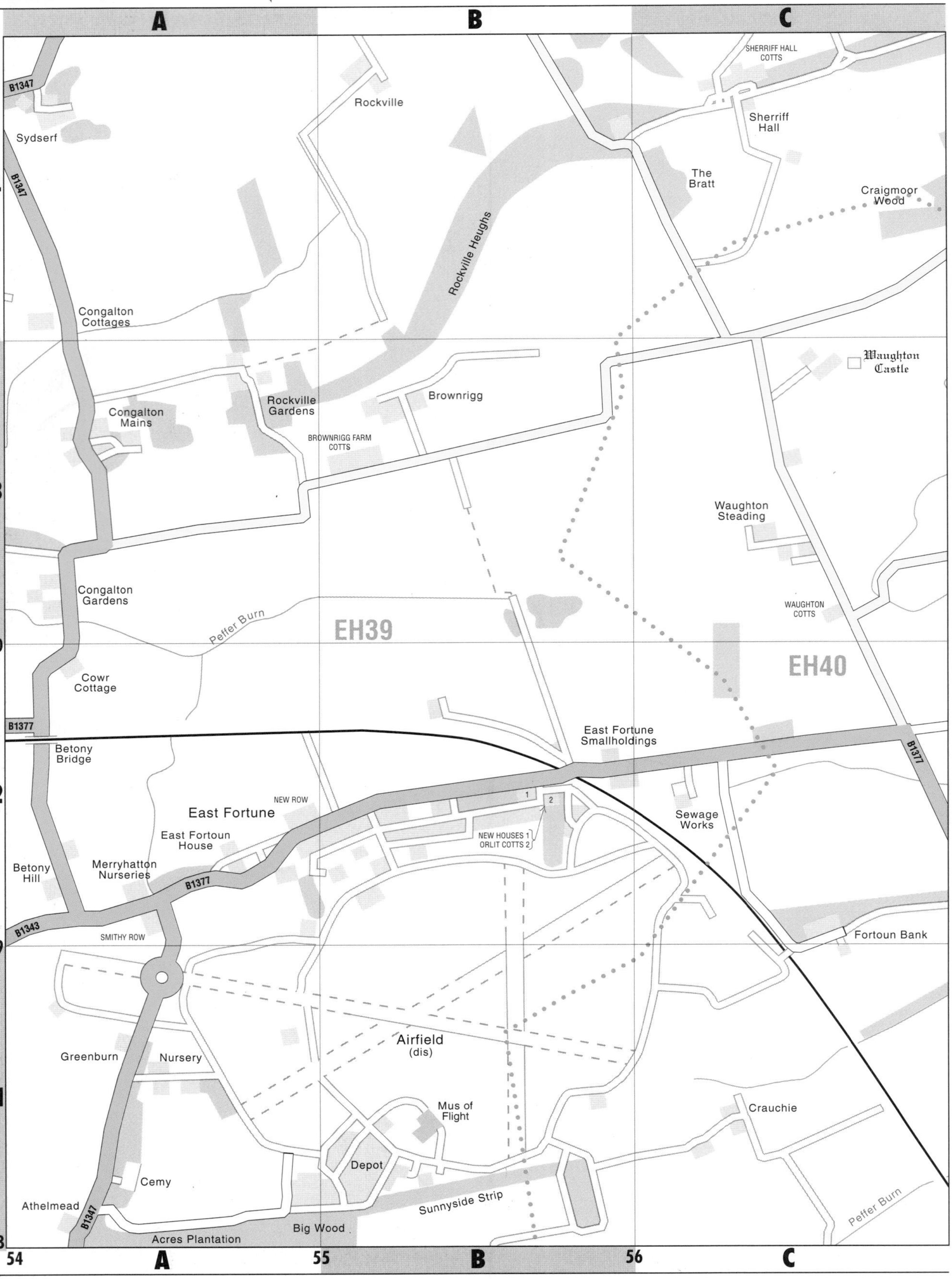

A

B

C

B1347

Rockville

SHERRIFF HALL COTTS

Sydserf

Sherriff Hall

4

The Bratt

Craigmoor Wood

B1347

Rockville Heughs

Congalton Cottages

81

Waughton Castle

Congalton Mains

Rockville Gardens

Brownrigg

BROWNRIGG FARM COTTS

Waughton Steading

3

Congalton Gardens

Peffer Burn

EH39

WAUGHTON COTTS

80

Cowr Cottage

EH40

B1377

Betony Bridge

East Fortune Smallholdings

2

NEW ROW

1

2

East Fortune

East Fortoun House

NEW HOUSES 1
ORLIT COTTS 2

Sewage Works

Betony Hill

Merryhatton Nurseries

B1377

B1343

79

SMITHY ROW

Fortoun Bank

1

Greenburn

Nursery

Airfield
(dis)

Crauchie

Mus of Flight

Cemy

Depot

Athelmead

B1347

Sunnyside Strip

Peffer Burn

78

Acres Plantation

Big Wood

54

A

55

B

56

C

55
76

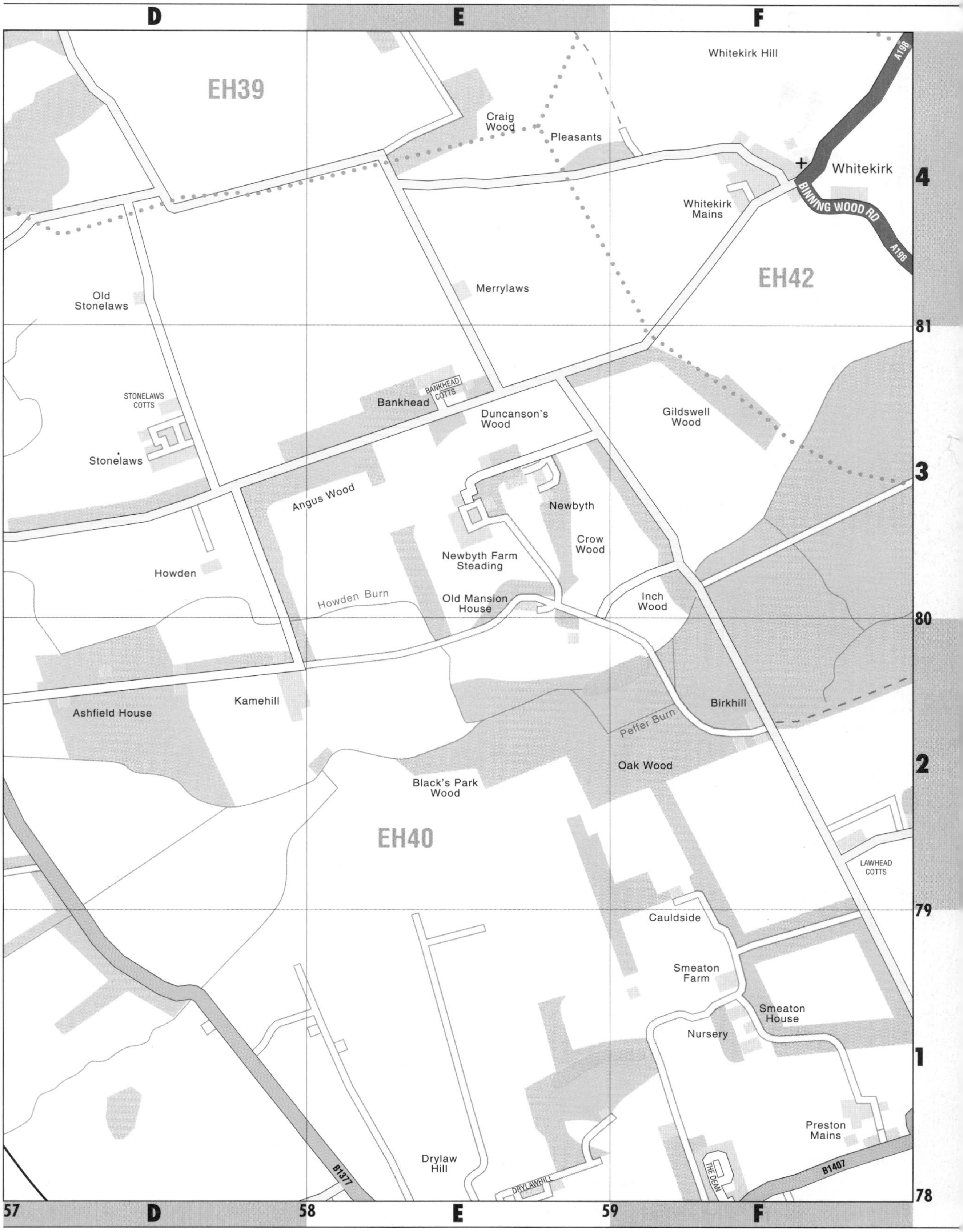
D
E
F
EH39
Craig Wood
Pleasants
Whitekirk Hill
A198
Whitekirk
BINNING WOOD RD
Whitekirk Mains
EH42
Old Stonelaws
Merrylaws
STONELAWS COTTS
BANKHEAD COTTS
Bankhead
Duncanson's Wood
Gildswell Wood
Stonelaws
Angus Wood
Newbyth
Crow Wood
Newbyth Farm Steading
Howden
Howden Burn
Old Mansion House
Inch Wood
Kamehill
Ashfield House
Birkhill
Peffer Burn
Oak Wood
Black's Park Wood
EH40
LAWHEAD COTTS
Cauldside
Smeaton Farm
Smeaton House
Nursery
Preston Mains
Drylaw Hill
DRYLAWHILL
THE DEAN
B1377
B1407
4
81
3
80
2
79
1
78
57
58
59

103
76

75
56

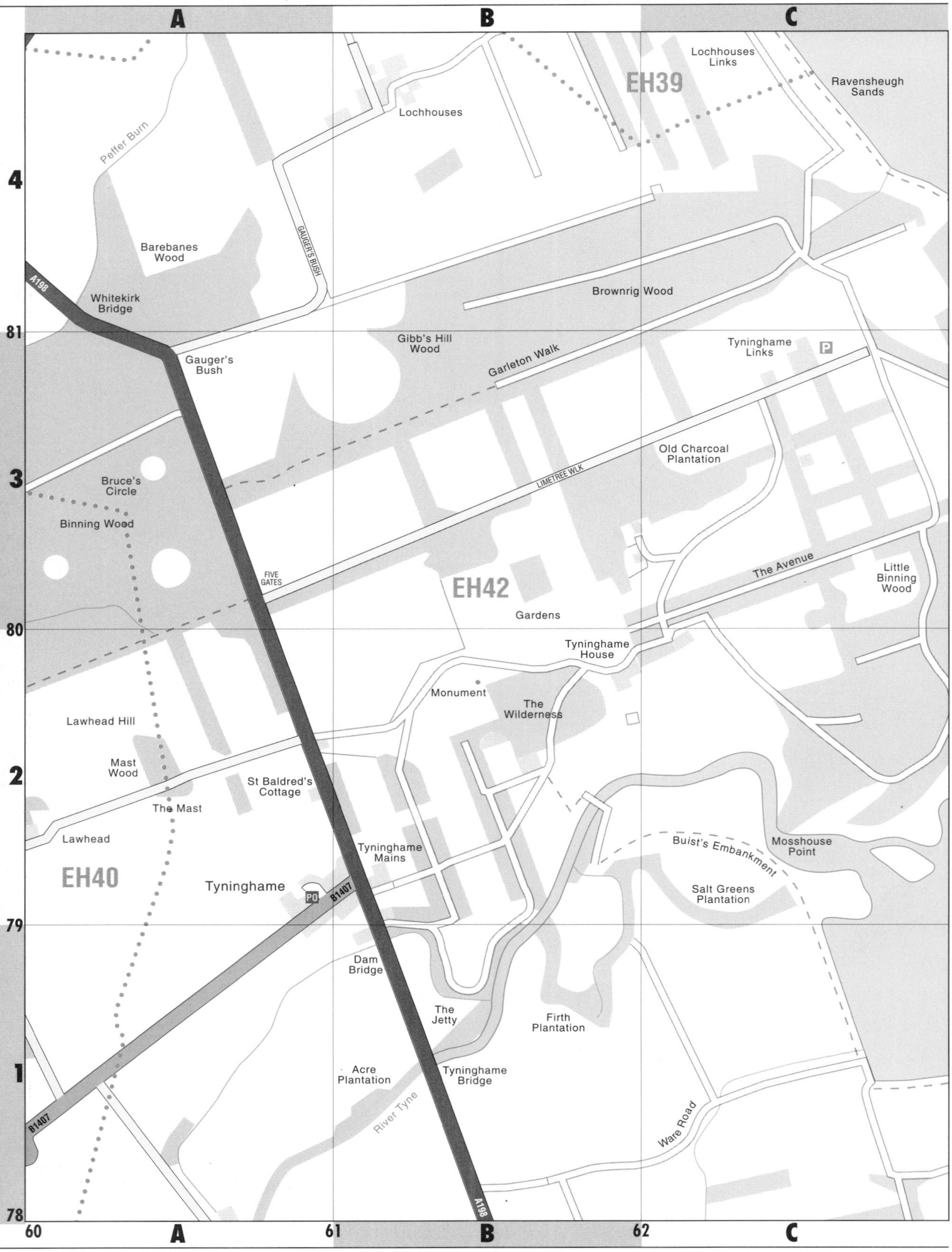
A
B
C
4
81
3
80
2
79
1
78
60
61
62
Lochhouses Links
Ravensheugh Sands
EH39
Lochhouses
Pefter Burn
Barebanes Wood
GAUGER'S BUSH
A198
Whitekirk Bridge
Brownrig Wood
Gibb's Hill Wood
Gauger's Bush
Tyninghame Links
P
Garleton Walk
Old Charcoal Plantation
LIMETREE WLK
Bruce's Circle
Binning Wood
FIVE GATES
EH42
The Avenue
Little Binning Wood
Gardens
Tyninghame House
Monument
The Wilderness
Lawhead Hill
Mast Wood
St Baldred's Cottage
The Mast
Lawhead
Buist's Embankment
Mosshouse Point
Tyninghame Mains
EH40
Tyninghame
PO
B1407
Salt Greens Plantation
Dam Bridge
The Jetty
Firth Plantation
Acre Plantation
Tyninghame Bridge
River Tyne
Ware Road
B1407
A198

75
104

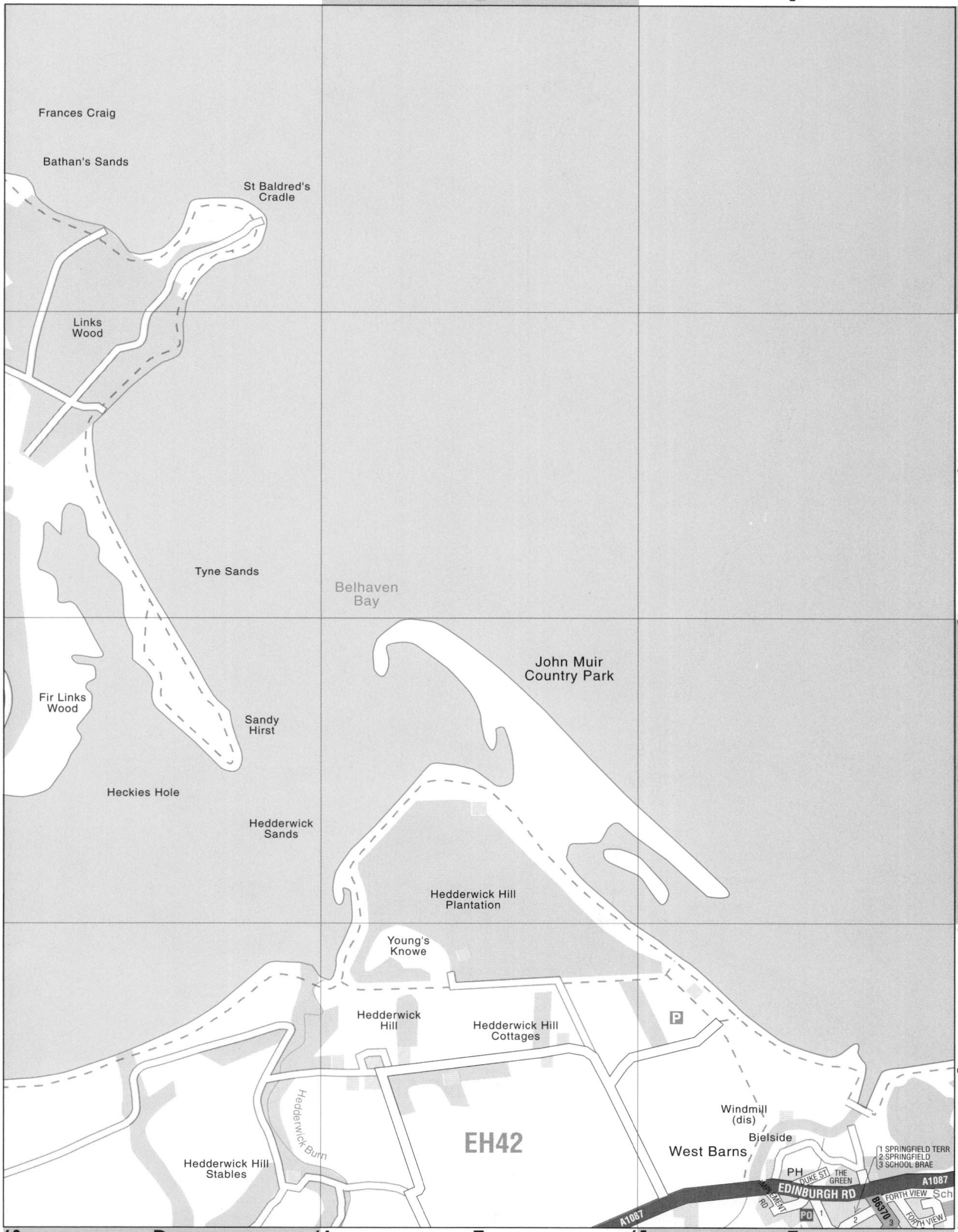

Frances Craig

Bathan's Sands

St Baldred's
Cradle

Links
Wood

Tyne Sands

Belhaven
Bay

Fir Links
Wood

Sandy
Hirst

John Muir
Country Park

Heckies Hole

Hedderwick
Sands

Hedderwick Hill
Plantation

Young's
Knowe

Hedderwick
Hill

Hedderwick Hill
Cottages

EH42

Windmill
(dis)

Bielside

West Barns

Hedderwick Hill
Stables

Hedderwick Burn

1 SPRINGFIELD TERR
2 SPRINGFIELD
3 SCHOOL BRAE

PH

DUKE ST

THE
GREEN

EDINBURGH RD

A1087

FORTH VIEW Sch

A1087

B6370

FORTH VIEW

4

81

3

80

2

79

1

78

77

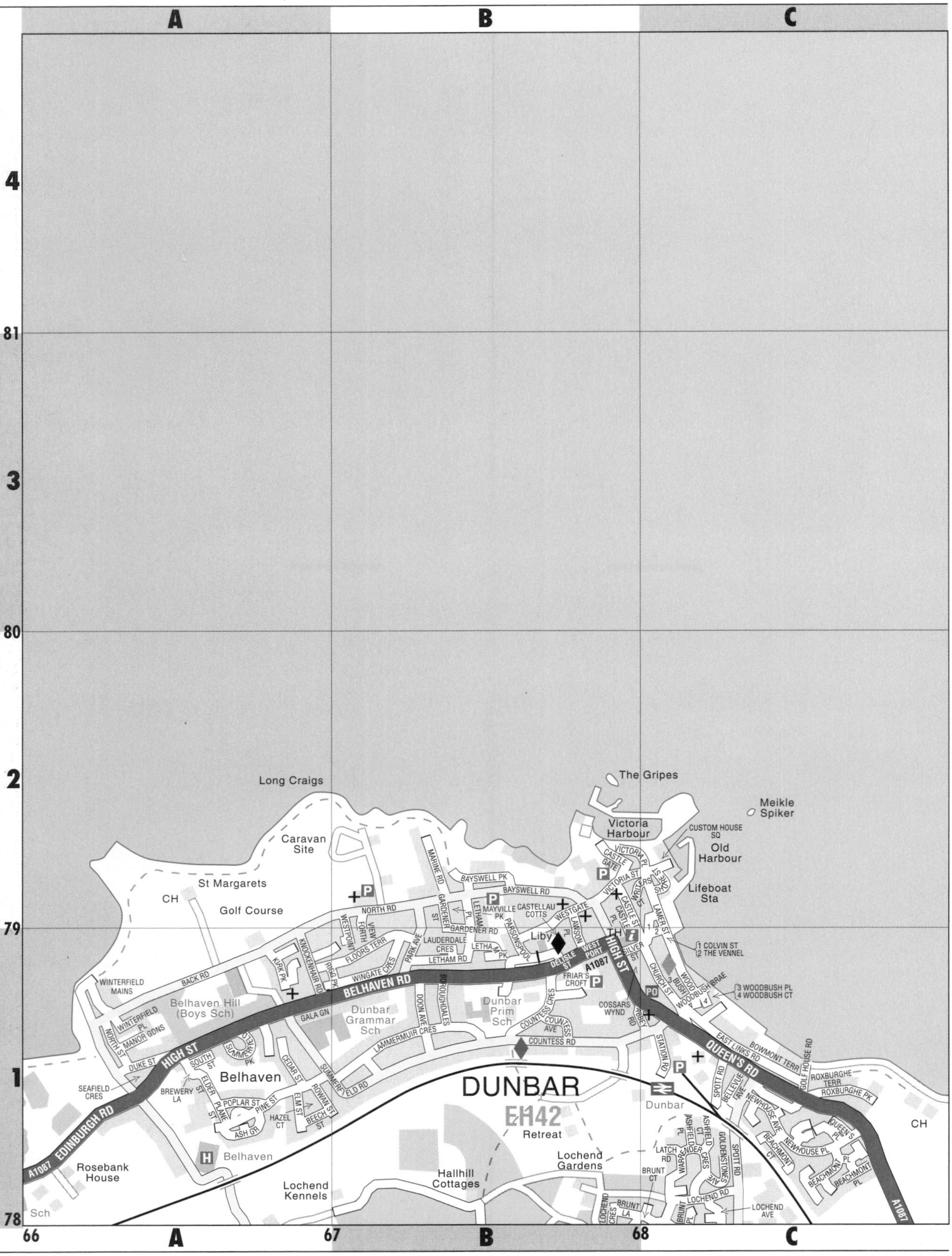

A
B
C
4
81
3
80
2
79
1
78
66
67
68
Long Craigs
The Gripes
Meikle Spiker
Victoria Harbour
CUSTOM HOUSE SQ
Old Harbour
Lifeboat Sta
Caravan Site
St Margarets
CH
Golf Course
NORTH RD
BAYSWELL PK
BAYSWELL RD
MARINE RD
MAYVILLE PK
CASTELLAU COTTS
WESTGATE
LAWSON PL
LETHAM PL
GARDENER RD
LAUDERDALE CRES
LETHAM RD
PARSONSPOOL
Liby
WEST PORT
DELISLE ST
A1087
HIGH ST
TH
VICTORIA ST
CASTLE ST
SILVER ST
CHURCH ST
LAMER ST
1 COLVIN ST
2 THE VENNEL
3 WOODBUSH PL
4 WOODBUSH CT
WOODBUSH BRAE
FRIAR'S CROFT
COSSARS WYND
PO
WESTPOINT
FORTH VIEW
FLOORS TERR
PARK AVE
WINGATE CRS
RIGG PK
KNOCKENHAIR RD
KIRK PK
BELHAVEN RD
BOROUGHDALES
DOON AVE
WINTERFIELD MAINS
BACK RD
Belhaven Hill (Boys Sch)
WINTERFIELD PL
MANOR GDNS
NORTH ST
GALA GN
Dunbar Grammar Sch
Dunbar Prim Sch
COUNTESS CRES
COUNTESS AVE
COUNTESS RD
LAMMERMUIR CRES
STATION RD
QUEEN'S RD
EAST LINKS RD
BOWMONT TERR
GOLF HOUSE RD
ROXBURGHE TERR
ROXBURGHE PK
SPOTT RD
BELLEVUE AVE
NEWHOUSE AVE
NEWHOUSE PL
BEACHMONT CT
BEACHMONT PL
QUEEN'S PL
CH
DUKE ST
SOUTH ST
SUMMERFIELD PK
CEDAR ST
SUMMERFIELD RD
Belhaven
SEAFIELD CRES
BREWERY LA
ELDER ST
PLANE ST
POPLAR ST
PINE ST
ASH GR
HAZEL CT
ELM ST
ROWAN ST
BEECH ST
DUNBAR
EH42
Dunbar
Retreat
EDINBURGH RD
A1087
Rosebank House
Belhaven
Sch
Lochend Kennels
Hallhill Cottages
Lochend Gardens
LATCH RD
BRUNT CT
WARRENDER CRES
ASHFIELD PL
ASHFIELD CT
GOLDENSTONES AVE
SPOTT RD
LOCHEND RD
LOCHEND CRES
BRUNT LA
BRUNT PL
LOCHEND AVE
A1087

77

106

D E F

4

81

3

80

2

79

1

78

69 70 71

D E F

Golf Course

Sports & Social
Centre

West Links

Fluke
Dub

EH42

The
Vaults

Vaults Wood

Lawrie's
Den

Mill Stone
Neuk

59

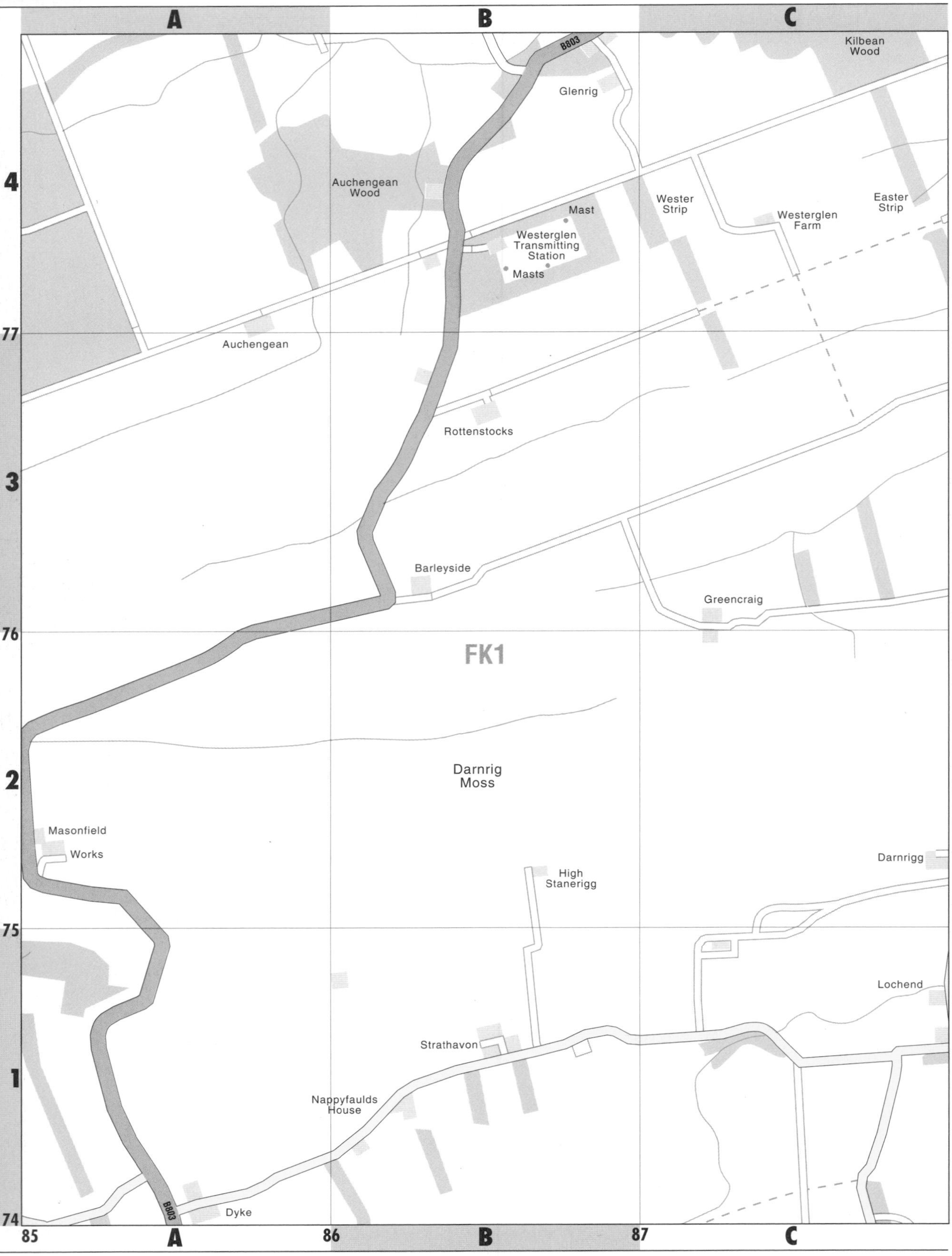
A
B
C
4
3
2
1
77
76
75
74
85
86
87
B803
Kilbean Wood
Glenrig
Auchengean Wood
Mast
Wester Strip
Westerglen Farm
Easter Strip
Westerglen Transmitting Station
Masts
Auchengean
Rottenstocks
Barleyside
Greencraig
FK1
Darnrig Moss
Masonfield
Works
Darnrigg
High Stanerigg
Lochend
Strathavon
Nappyfaulds House
Dyke

110

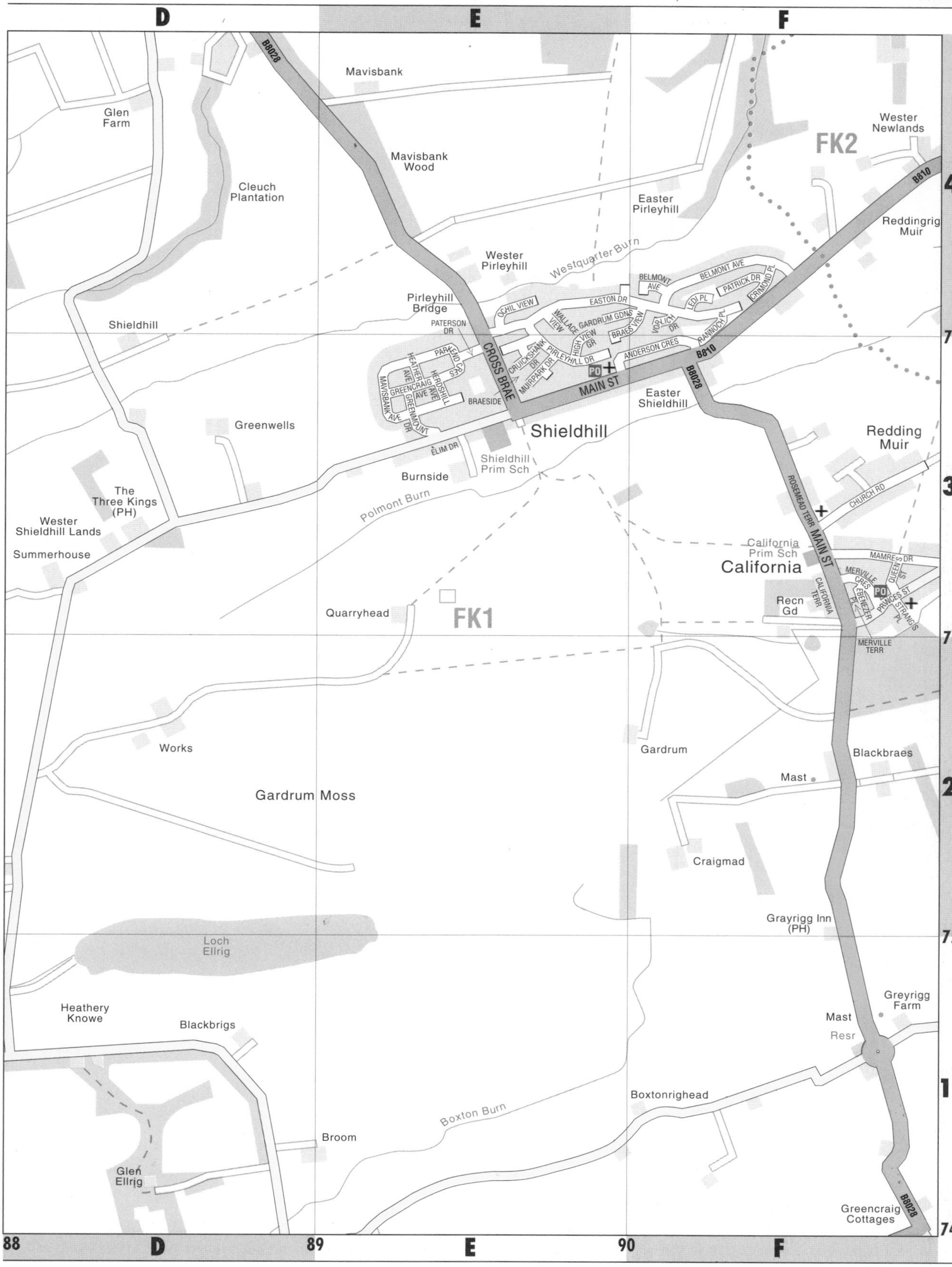

D
E
F

B8028

Mavisbank

Glen Farm

Mavisbank Wood

Cleuch Plantation

Easter Pirleyhill

FK2

Wester Newlands

B810

4

Reddingrig Muir

Westquarter Burn

Shieldhill

Wester Pirleyhill

Belmont Ave

Belmont Ave

Patrick Dr

Crinston Pl

Pirleyhill Bridge

Ochil View

Easton Dr

Ledi Pl

Paterson Dr

Wallace View

Gardrum Gdns

Braes View

Wallace Dr

Rannoch

77

Park Cres

Heather Ave

Hedishill Ave

Greencraig Ave

Greenmount Dr

Cruickshank Dr

High View Cres

Pirleyhill Dr

Muirpark Dr

CROSS BRAE

MAIN ST

Anderson Cres

B810

B8028

Greenwells

Elim Dr

Braeside

PO

Shieldhill

Easter Shieldhill

Redding Muir

Mavisbank Ave

Burnside

Shieldhill Prim Sch

Church Rd

3

The Three Kings (PH)

Rosebed Terr

Church Rd

Wester Shieldhill Lands

Polmont Burn

California Prim Sch

Mamre Dr

MAIN ST

Summerhouse

California

Merville Cres

Queen St

Quarryhead

FK1

California Terr

Ebenezer

Princes St

Recn Gd

PO

St Andrews Pl

76

Merville Terr

Works

Gardrum

Blackbraes

Gardrum Moss

Mast

2

Craigmad

Grayrigg Inn (PH)

75

Loch Ellrig

Greyrigg Farm

Heathery Knowe

Blackbrigs

Mast

Resr

1

Boxtonrighead

Boxton Burn

Broom

Glen Ellrig

B8028

Greencraig Cottages

74

88
D
89
E
90
F

81
61

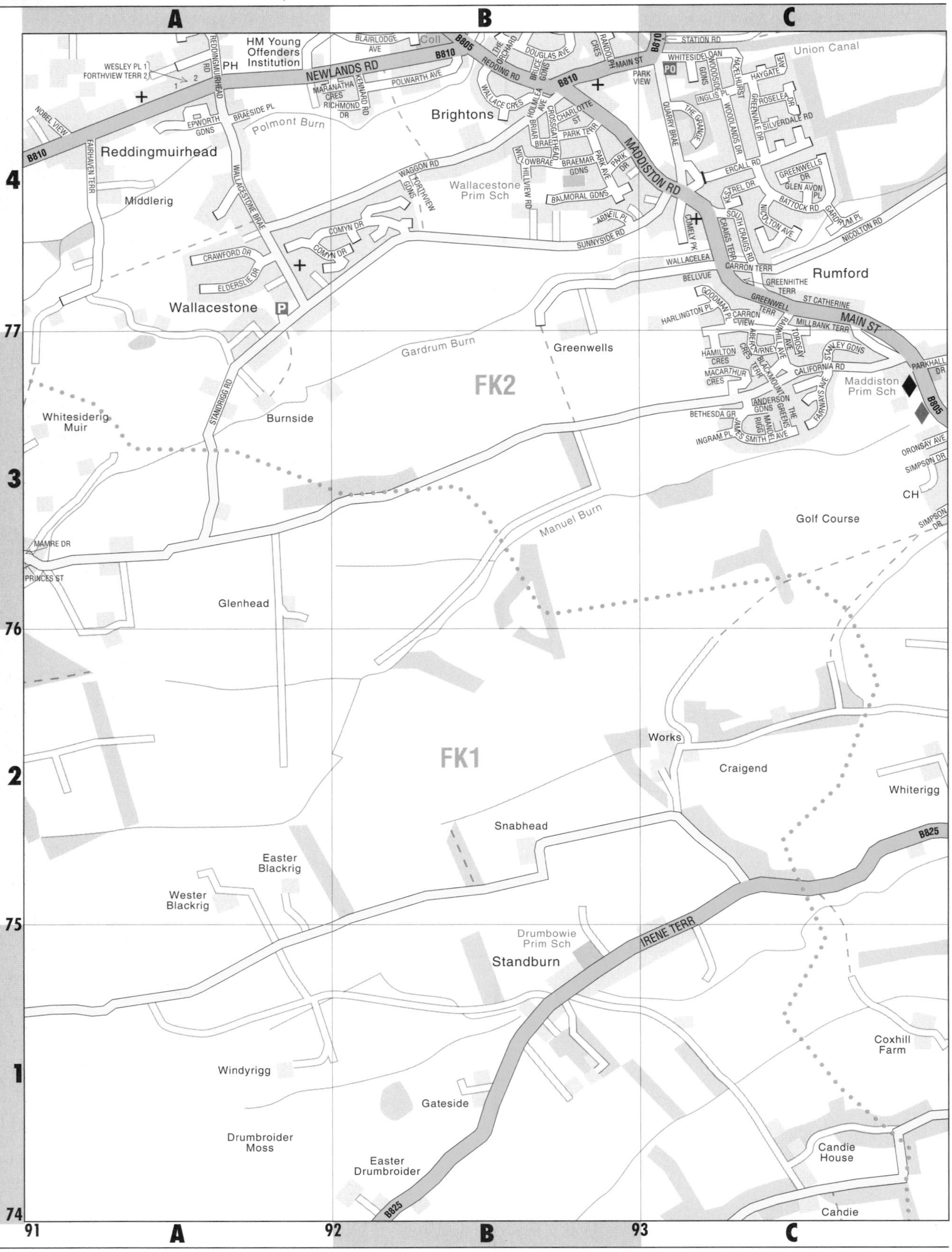
A
B
C
HM Young Offenders Institution
NEWLANDS RD
B810
B805
Coll
PH
WESLEY PL 1
FORTHVIEW TERR 2
REDDINGMUIRHEAD RD
NOBEL VIEW
Reddingmuirhead
FAIRHAVEN TERR
EPWORTH GDNS
BRAESIDE PL
Polmont Burn
MARANATHA CRES
RICHMOND DR
KENNARD RD
POLWARTH AVE
BLAIRLODGE AVE
Brightons
REDDING RD
DOUGLAS AVE
WALLACE CRES
MAIN ST
PARK VIEW
PO
STATION RD
WHITESIDELOAN
Union Canal
INGLIS PL
HAYGATE AVE
ROSELEA DR
SILVERDALE RD
WOODLANDS DR
GREENVALE DR
QUARRY BRAE
THE GRANGE
MADDISTON RD
ERCALL RD
GREENWELLS DR
GLEN AVON PL
BATTOCK RD
NICOLTON AVE
NICOLTON RD
GARDRUM PL
CHARLOTTE ST
PARK TERR
BRAEMAR GDNS
PARK AVE
PARK DR
BALMORAL GDNS
ARNEIL PL
SUNNYSIDE RD
Wallacestone Prim Sch
WAGGON RD
FORTHVIEW GDNS
Middlerig
WALLACESTONE BRAE
COMYN DR
CRAWFORD DR
ELDERSLIE DR
Wallacestone
P
COMELY PK
CRAIGS TERR
SOUTH CRAIGS RD
CARRON TERR
WALLACELEA
BELLVUE
Rumford
GREENHITHE TERR
GREENWELL TERR
ST CATHERINE
MAIN ST
MILLBANK TERR
HARLINGTON PL
CARRON VIEW
HAMILTON CRES
MACARTHUR CRES
CALIFORNIA RD
STANLEY GDNS
PARKHALL DR
Maddiston Prim Sch
Gardrum Burn
Greenwells
FK2
STANDRIGG RD
Burnside
Whitesiderig Muir
BETHESDA GR
INGRAM PL
ANDERSON GDNS
FAIRWAYS AVE
ORONSAY AVE
SIMPSON DR
CH
Golf Course
Manuel Burn
MAMRE DR
PRINCES ST
Glenhead
Works
Craigend
FK1
Whiterigg
Snabhead
B825
Easter Blackrig
Wester Blackrig
IRENE TERR
Drumbowie Prim Sch
Standburn
Coxhill Farm
Windyrigg
Gateside
Drumbroider Moss
Easter Drumbroider
Candie House
Candie
4
77
3
76
2
75
1
74
91
92
93

62
84

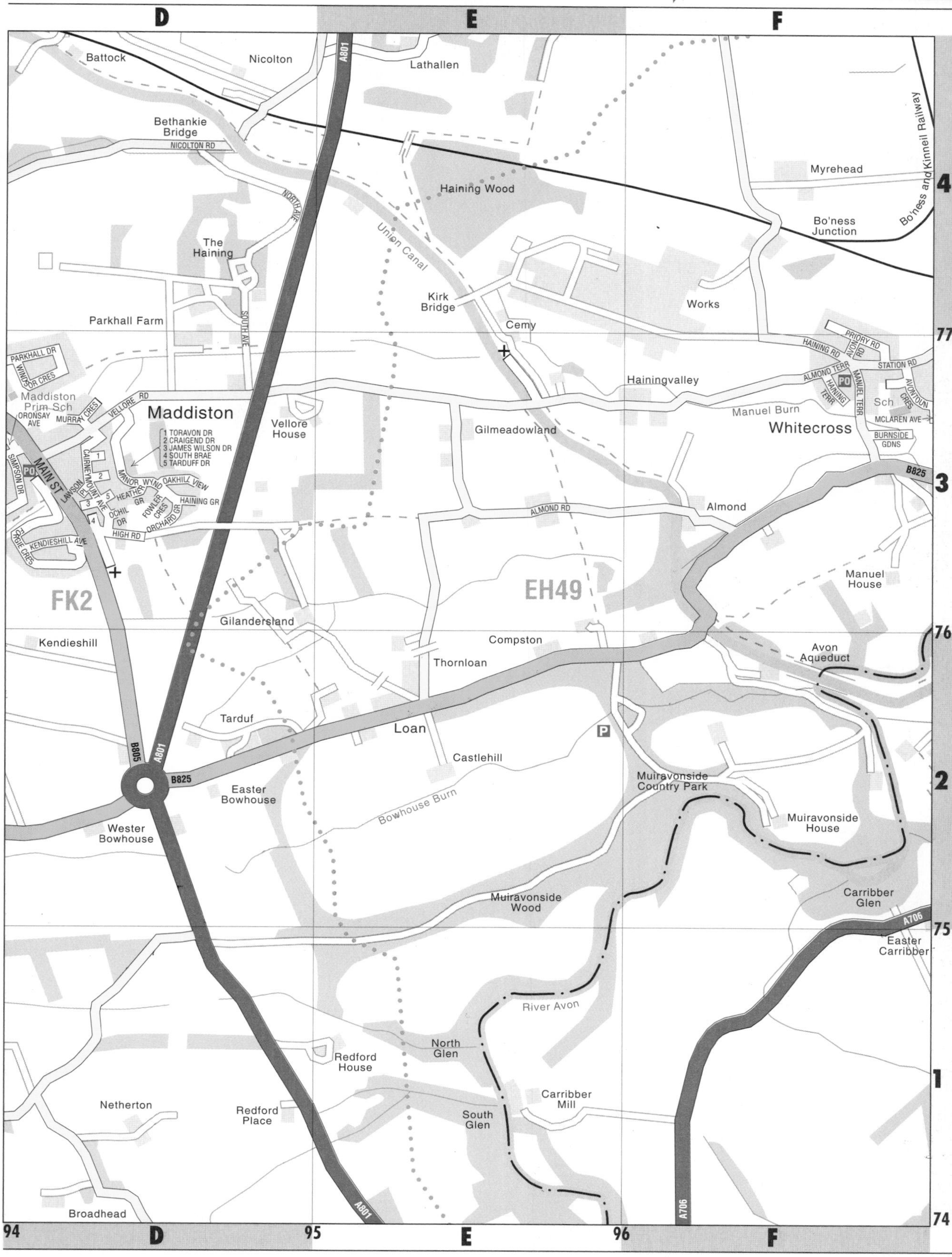
D
E
F
Battock
Nicolton
A801
Lathallen
Bethankie
Bridge
NICOLTON RD
Haining Wood
Myrehead
Bo'ness and Kinneil Railway
4
NORTH AVE
Union Canal
Bo'ness
Junction
The
Haining
Works
Kirk
Bridge
SOUTH AVE
Parkhall Farm
Cemy
77
PARKHALL DR
WINDSOR CRES
HAINING RD
PRIORY RD
AVON RD
STATION RD
Haininingvalley
ALMOND TERR
HAINING TERR
MANUEL TERR
AVONTOUN
Maddiston
Prim Sch
VELLORE RD
Maddiston
Vellore
House
Sch
CRES
ORONSAY
AVE
MURRAY CRES
Manuel Burn
MCLAREN AVE
1 TORAVON DR
2 CRAIGEND DR
3 JAMES WILSON DR
4 SOUTH BRAE
5 TARDUFF DR
Gilmeadowland
Whitecross
BURNSIDE
GDNS
MAIN ST
SIMPSON DR
PO
CAIRNEYMOUNT AVE
LAWSON PL
MANOR WYND
OAKHILL VIEW
B825
3
HEATHER GR
OCHIL DR
FOWLER CRES
HAINING GR
ORCHARD GR
ALMOND RD
Almond
HIGH RD
KENDIESHILL AVE
ARGYLE CRES
Manuel
House
FK2
EH49
Gilandersland
Kendieshill
Compston
76
Thornloan
Avon
Aqueduct
Tarduf
Loan
P
B805
A801
Castlehill
B825
Muiravonside
Country Park
2
Easter
Bowhouse
Bowhouse Burn
Muiravonside
House
Wester
Bowhouse
Carribber
Glen
Muiravonside
Wood
A706
75
Easter
Carribber
River Avon
North
Glen
Redford
House
1
Carribber
Mill
Netherton
Redford
Place
South
Glen
Broadhead
A801
A706
74
94
D
95
E
96
F

113
84

83
63

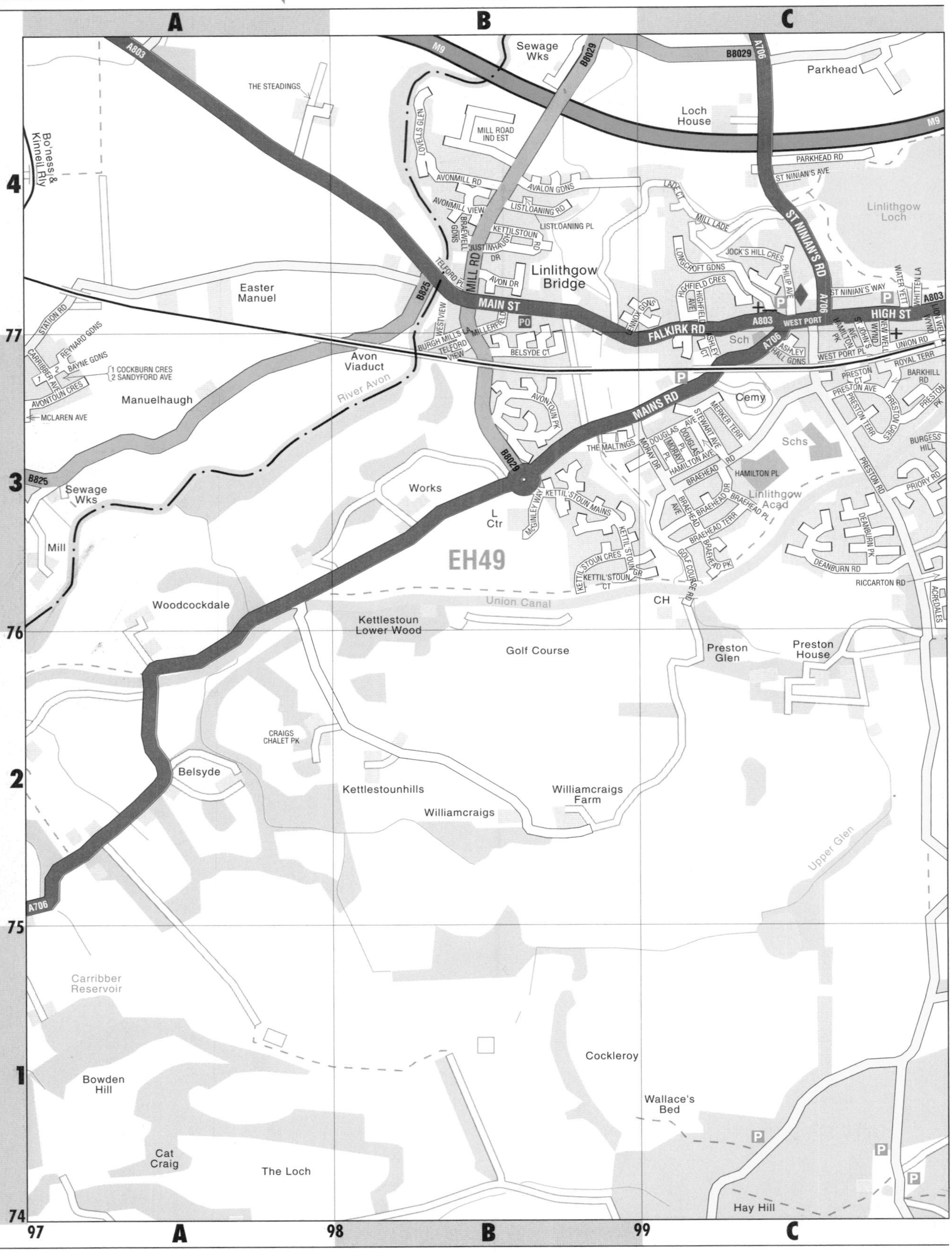
A
B
C
4
77
3
76
2
75
1
74
97
98
99
A803
M9
B8029
A706
Sewage Wks
Parkhead
Loch House
THE STEADINGS
Bo'ness & Kinneil Rly
MILL ROAD IND EST
LOVELLS GLEN
PARKHEAD RD
ST NINIAN'S AVE
AVONMILL RD
AVALON GDNS
AVONMILL VIEW
LISTLOANING RD
LISTLOANING PL
LADE CT
Linlithgow Loch
MILL LADE
BRAEWELL GDNS
KETTILSTOUN RD
JUSTINHAUGH DR
JOCK'S HILL CRES
ST NINIAN'S RD
LONGCROFT GDNS
Linlithgow Bridge
Easter Manuel
TELFORD PL
MILL RD
AVON DR
HIGHFIELD CRES
PHILIP AVE
ST NINIAN'S WAY
WATER YETT
WHITTEN LA
B825
MAIN ST
STATION RD
LENNOX GDNS
HIGHFIELD AVE
HIGH ST
PO
FALKIRK RD
A803
WEST PORT
REYNARD GDNS
BURGH MILLS LA
WESTVIEW
MILLERFIELD
Sch
HAMILTON PK
ST JOHN'S AVE
NEW WELL WYND
LION WELL WYND
UNION RD
CARRIBBER AVE
BAYNE GDNS
1 COCKBURN CRES
2 SANDYFORD AVE
TELFORD VIEW
BELSYDE CT
ASHLEY CT
ASHLEY HALL GDNS
WEST PORT PL
ROYAL TERR
AVONTOUN CRES
Avon Viaduct
PRESTON CT
PRESTON AVE
BARKHILL RD
Manuelhaugh
River Avon
AVONTOUN PK
MAINS RD
STEWART AVE
MERKER TERR
Cemy
PRESTON TERR
PRESTON CRES
PRESTON PK
MCLAREN AVE
DOUGLAS AVE
DOUGLAS PL
MORAY PL
MORAY DR
THE MALTINGS
HAMILTON AVE
Schs
BURGESS HILL
B8029
BRAEHEAD RD
HAMILTON PL
PRIORY RD
PRESTON RD
3
B825
Sewage Wks
Works
MCGINLEY WAY
KETTIL'STOUN MAINS
BRAEHEAD DR
BRAEHEAD PL
Linlithgow Acad
L Ctr
BRAEHEAD AVE
BRAEHEAD TERR
DEANBURN PK
Mill
EH49
KETTIL'STOUN CRES
KETTIL'STOUN GR
BRAEHEAD PK
DEANBURN RD
KETTIL'STOUN CT
GOLF COURSE RD
RICCARTON RD
ACREDALES
Woodcockdale
Union Canal
CH
Kettlestoun Lower Wood
Golf Course
Preston Glen
Preston House
CRAIGS CHALET PK
Belsyde
Kettlestounhills
Williamcraigs Farm
Williamcraigs
Upper Glen
A706
Carribber Reservoir
Cockleroy
Bowden Hill
Wallace's Bed
P
Cat Craig
The Loch
Hay Hill

83
114

64
86

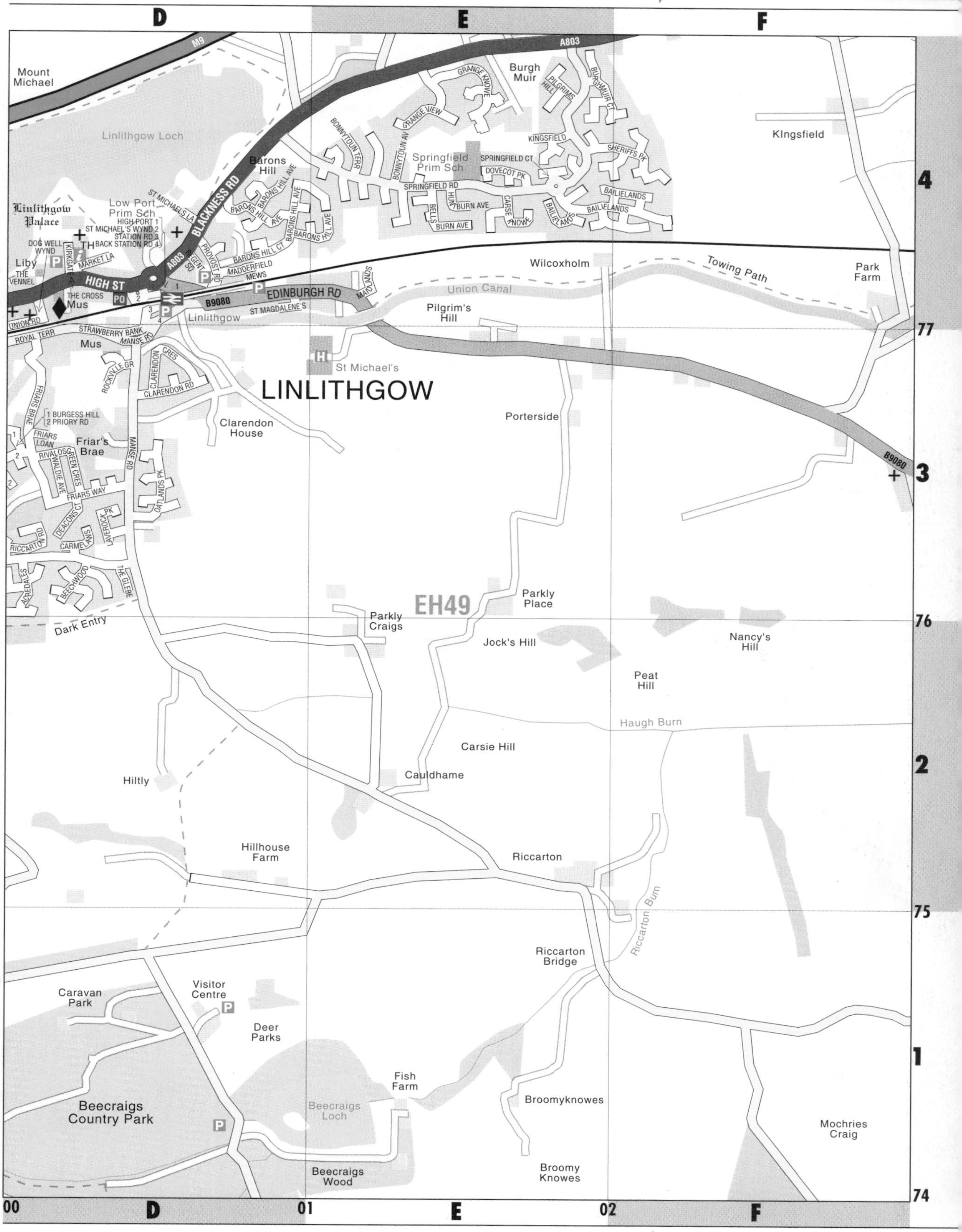
D
E
F
Mount Michael
M9
A803
Burgh Muir
Linlithgow Loch
Kingsfield
Barons Hill
Springfield Prim Sch
Linlithgow Palace
Low Port Prim Sch
BLACKNESS RD
GRANGE KNOWE
PILGRIMS HILL
BURGHMUIR CT
GRANGE VIEW
BONNYTOUN TERR
BONNYTOUN AV
KINGSFIELD
SHERIFFS PK
SPRINGFIELD CT
DOVECOT PK
SPRINGFIELD RD
BAILIELANDS
BARONS HILL AVE
BARONS HILL CT
BURN AVE
BELLS BURN AVE
CARSE KNOWE
ST MICHAEL'S LA
HIGH PORT 1
ST MICHAEL'S WYND 2
STATION RD 3
BACK STATION RD 4
DOG WELL WYND
KIRKGATE
MARKET LA
Liby
THE VENNEL
HIGH ST
THE CROSS
Mus
PO
REGENT SQ
PROVOST RD
MADDERFIELD MEWS
EDINBURGH RD
B9080
ST MAGDALENE'S
MAITLANDS
Wilcoxholm
Towing Path
Union Canal
Park Farm
Pilgrim's Hill
Linlithgow
UNION RD
ROYAL TERR
STRAWBERRY BANK
MANSE RD
St Michael's
LINLITHGOW
ROCKVILLE GR
CLARENDON CRES
CLARENDON RD
Porterside
FRIARS BRAE
1 BURGESS HILL
2 PRIORY RD
Clarendon House
FRIARS LOAN
Friar's Brae
RIVALDSGREEN CRES
WALDIE AVE
FRIARS WAY
OATLANDS PK
DEACONS CT
LAVEROCK PK
RICCARTON RD
CARMELAWS
ACREDALES
BEECHWOOD
THE GLEBE
EH49
Parkly Place
Parkly Craigs
Dark Entry
Jock's Hill
Nancy's Hill
Peat Hill
Haugh Burn
Carsie Hill
Cauldhame
Hiltly
Hillhouse Farm
Riccarton
Riccarton Burn
Riccarton Bridge
Caravan Park
Visitor Centre
Deer Parks
Fish Farm
Broomyknowes
Beecraigs Country Park
Beecraigs Loch
Beecraigs Wood
Broomy Knowes
Mochries Craig
4
77
3
76
2
75
1
74
00
01
02

115
86

85
65

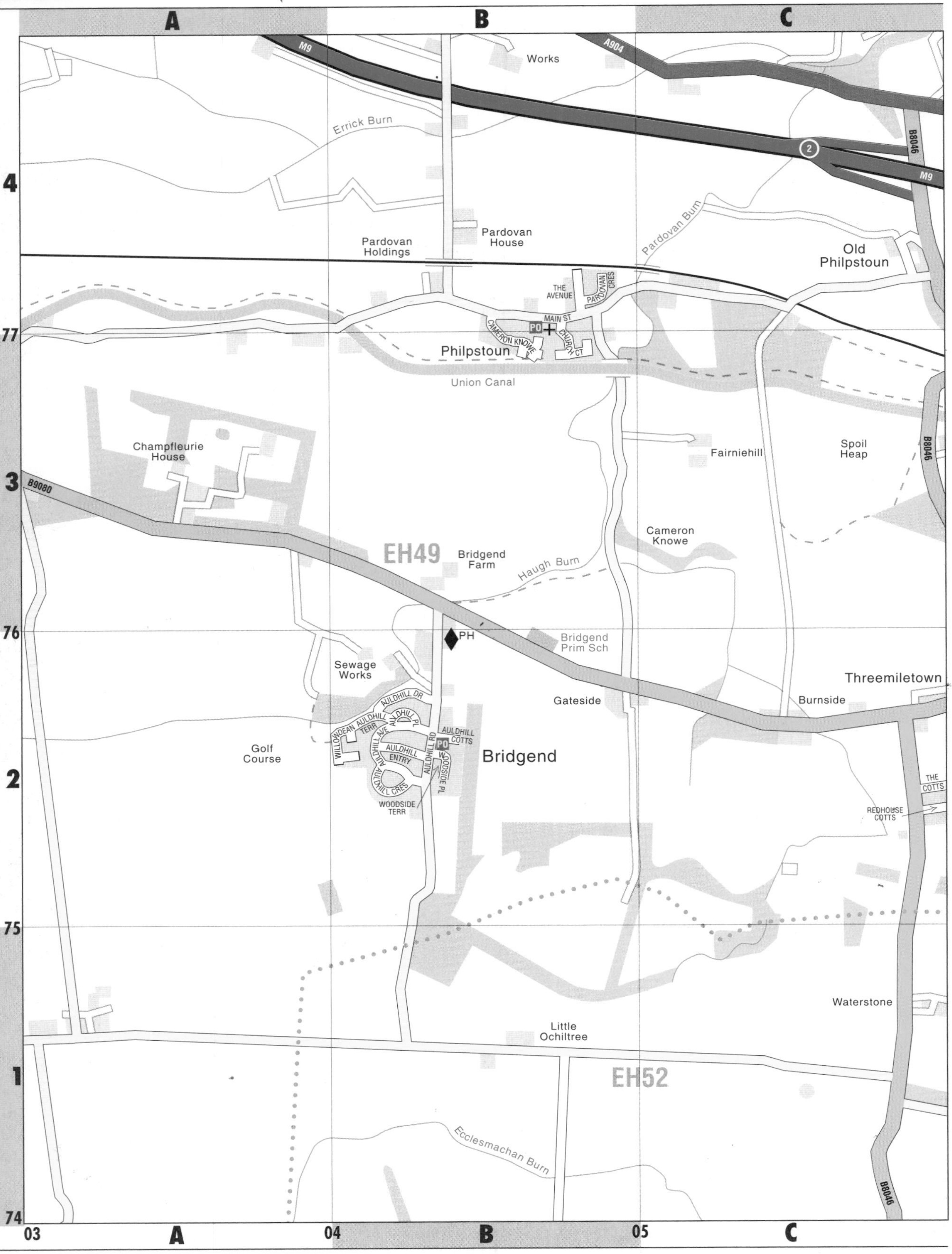
A
B
C
M9
A904
Works
Errick Burn
B8046
4
Pardovan Holdings
Pardovan House
Pardovan Burn
Old Philpstoun
THE AVENUE
PARDOVAN CRES
MAIN ST
CAMERON KNOWE
CHURCH CT
PO
77
Philpstoun
Union Canal
Champfleurie House
Fairniehill
Spoil Heap
3
B9080
Cameron Knowe
EH49
Bridgend Farm
Haugh Burn
76
PH
Bridgend Prim Sch
Sewage Works
Threemiletown
Gateside
Burnside
AULDHILL DR
WILLOWDEAN
AULDHILL TERR
AULDHILL PL
AULDHILL AVE
AULDHILL COTTS
AULDHILL ENTRY
AULDHILL RD
WOODSIDE PL
AULDHILL CRES
WOODSIDE TERR
Golf Course
Bridgend
2
THE COTTS
REDHOUSE COTTS
75
Waterstone
Little Ochiltree
1
EH52
Ecclesmachan Burn
74
03
04
05

85
116

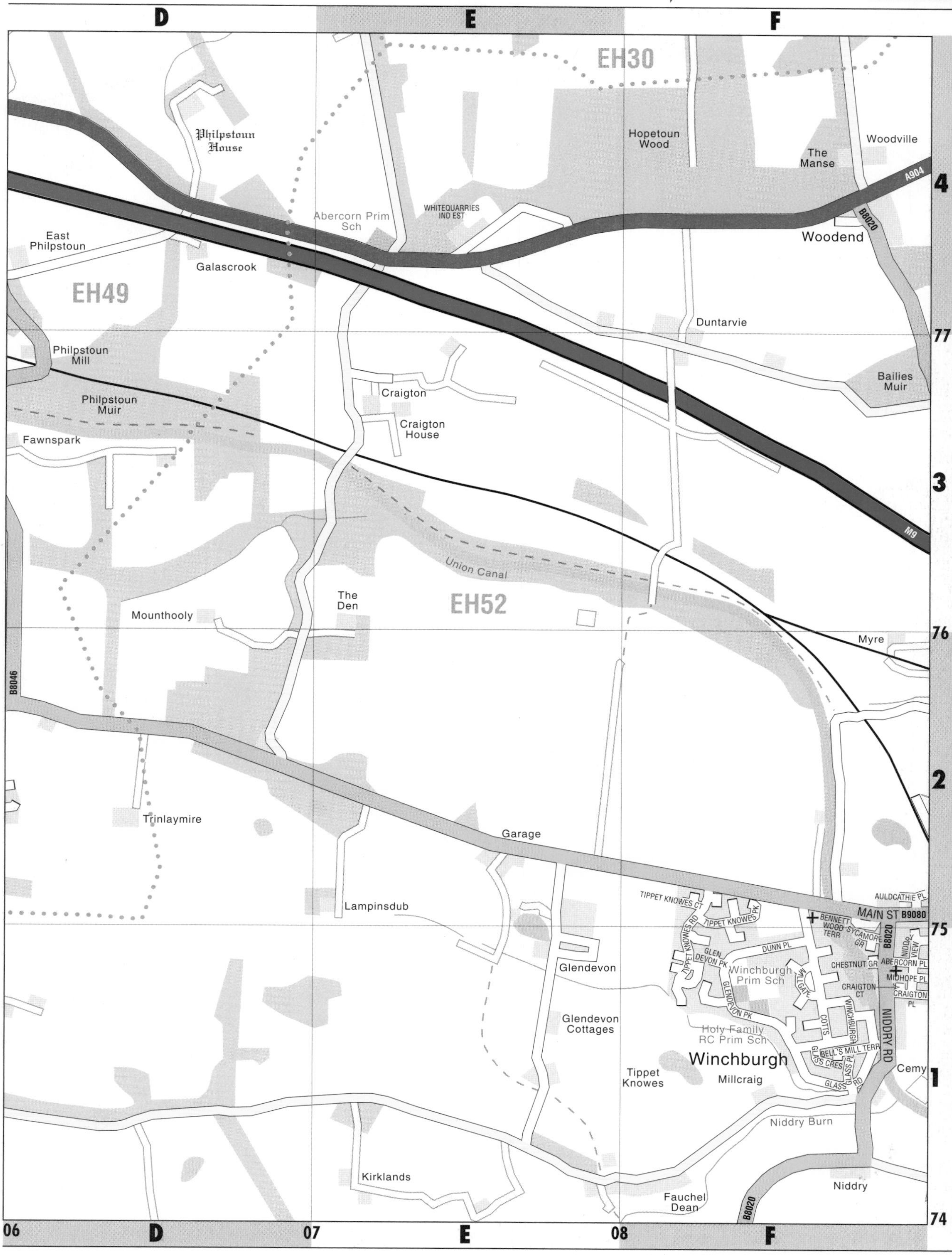

EH30

Philpstoun House

Hopetoun Wood

Woodville

The Manse

A904

4

Whitequarries Ind Est

Abercorn Prim Sch

B8020

Woodend

East Philpstoun

EH49

Galascrook

Duntarvie

77

Philpstoun Mill

Bailies Muir

Philpstoun Muir

Craigton

Fawnspark

Craigton House

3

Union Canal

M9

Mounthooly

The Den

EH52

Myre

76

B8046

2

Trinlaymire

Garage

Lampinsdub

TIPPET KNOWES CT

AULDCATHIE PL

MAIN ST B9080

75

Glendevon

Winchburgh Prim Sch

Holy Family RC Prim Sch

NIDDRY RD

Cemy

Glendevon Cottages

Winchburgh

1

Tippet Knowes

Millcraig

Niddry Burn

Niddry

Kirklands

Fauchel Dean

B8020

74

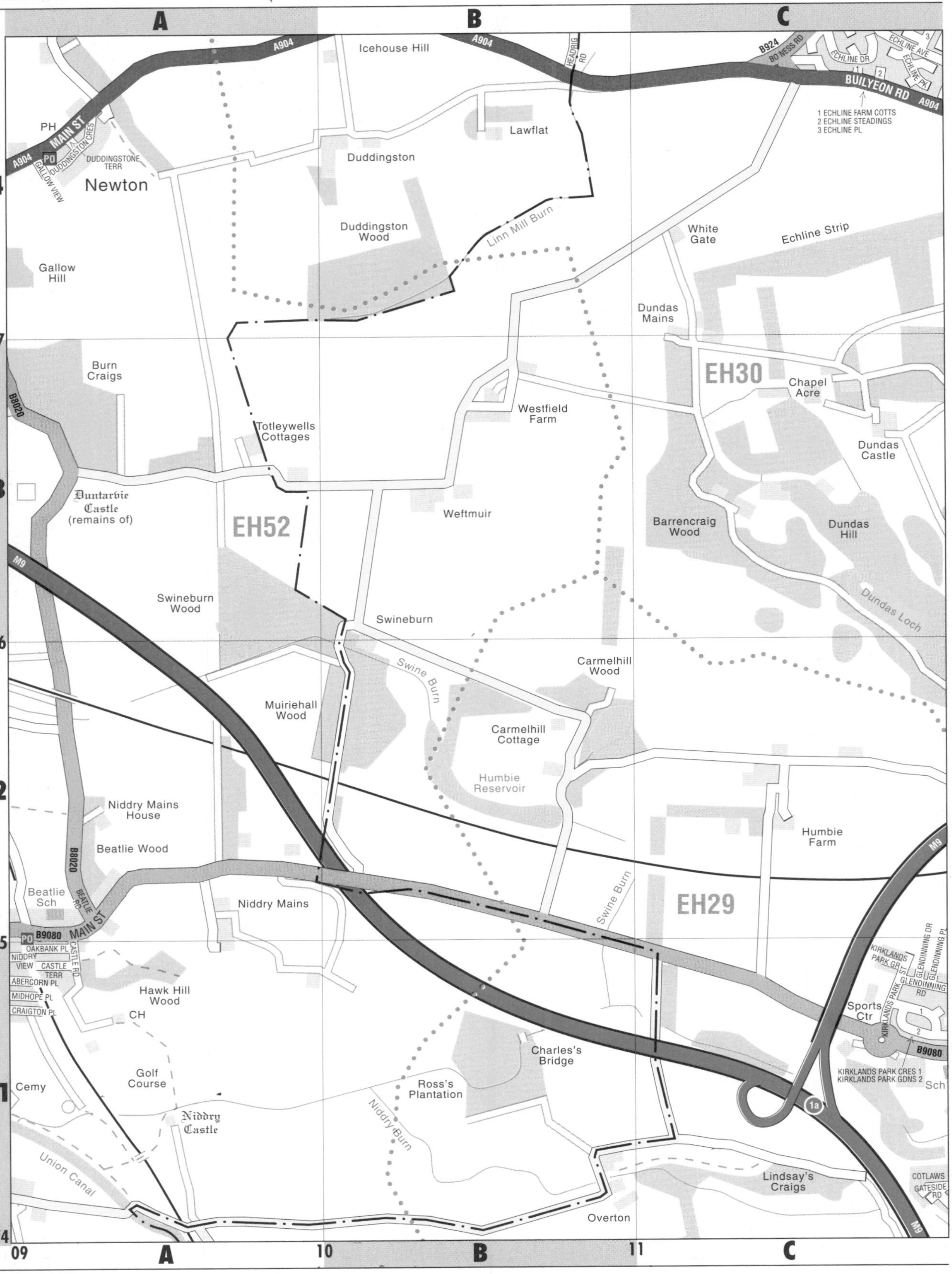

A904

A904

B924
BO NESS RD

BUILYEON RD
A904

ECHLINE AVE
ECHLINE DR
ECHLINE PK
3
2
1

Icehouse Hill

READRIG RD

Lawflat

1 ECHLINE FARM COTTS
2 ECHLINE STEADINGS
3 ECHLINE PL

MAIN ST
PH

DUDDINGSTON CRES

PO
DUDDINGSTONE TERR
GALLOW VIEW

Newton

Duddingston

White
Gate

Echline Strip

Duddingston
Wood

Linn Mill Burn

Dundas
Mains

4

Gallow
Hill

EH30

Chapel
Acre

77

B8020

Burn
Craigs

Westfield
Farm

Dundas
Castle

Totleywells
Cottages

Duntarvie
Castle
(remains of)

EH52

Weftmuir

Barrencraig
Wood

Dundas
Hill

3

M9

Dundas Loch

Swineburn
Wood

Swineburn

Swine Burn

Carmelhill
Wood

76

Muiriehall
Wood

Carmelhill
Cottage

2

Niddry Mains
House

Humbie
Reservoir

Humbie
Farm

B8020

M9

Beatlie Wood

BEATLIE RD

Beatlie
Sch

Niddry Mains

Swine Burn

EH29

KIRKLANDS
PARK GR

GLENDINNING DR

GLENDINNING PL

KIRKLANDS PARK ST

GLENDINNING
RD

PO
B9080

MAIN ST

CASTLE RD

75

NIDDRY
VIEW

OAKBANK PL

CASTLE
TERR

ABERCORN PL

MIDHOPE PL

CRAIGTON PL

Hawk Hill
Wood

CH

Sports
Ctr

2
1

B9080

KIRKLANDS PARK CRES 1
KIRKLANDS PARK GDNS 2

Sch

Cemy

Golf
Course

Charles's
Bridge

Ross's
Plantation

1a

1

Niddry
Castle

Niddry Burn

Lindsay's
Craigs

COTLAWS
GATESIDE
RD

Union Canal

Overton

M9

74

68
90

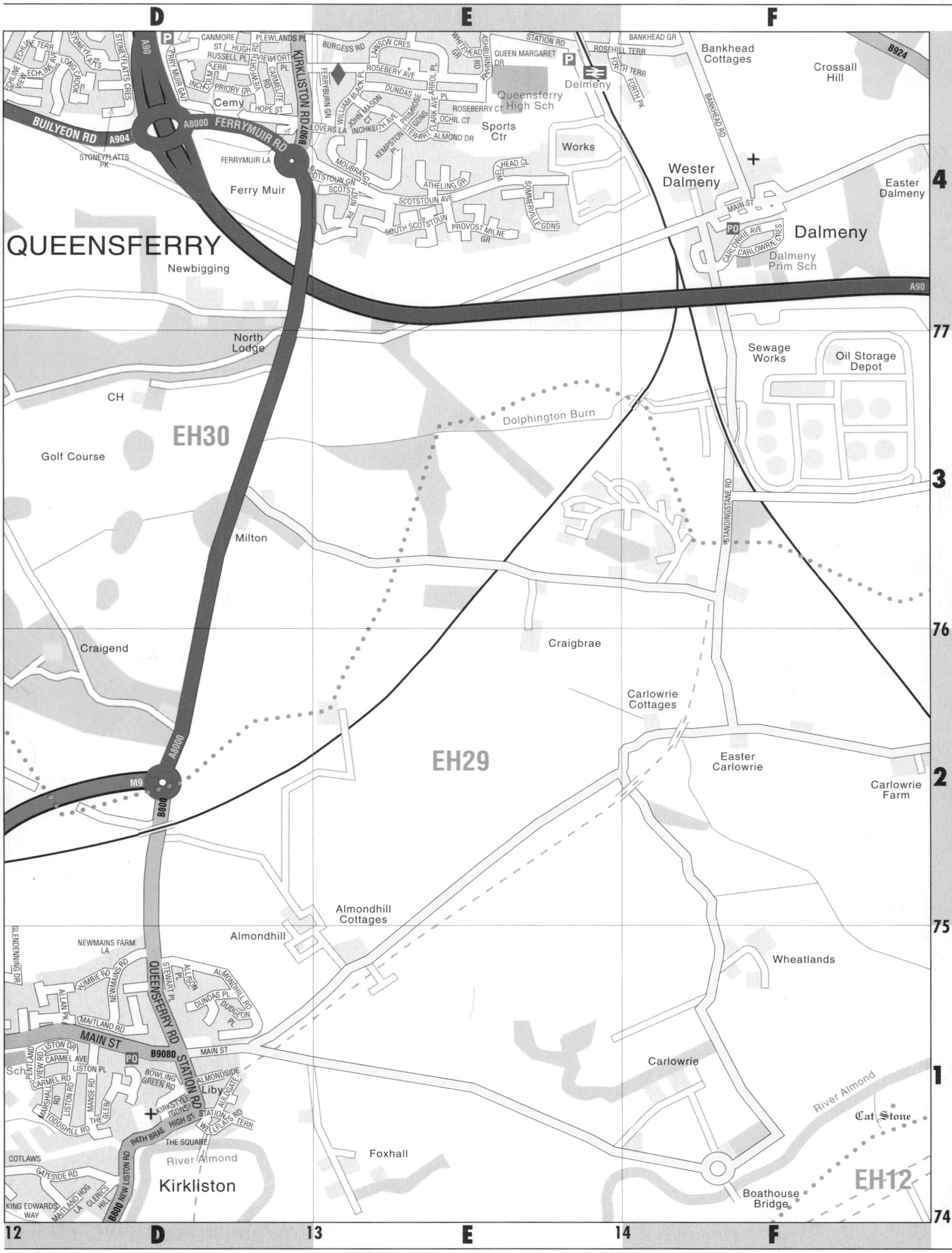
D
E
F
QUEENSFERRY
Newbigging
Ferry Muir
FERRYMUIR LA
STONEYFLATTS PK
BUILYEON RD
A904
A8000 FERRYMUIR RD
A90
B907 KIRKLISTON RD
CANMORE ST
PLEWLANDS PL
RUSSELL PL
VIEWFORTH
HUGH
PRIORY GR
HOPE ST
Cemy
BURGESS RD
LAWSON CRES
ROSEBERY AVE
DUNDAS
FERRYBURN GN
WILLIAM BLACK PL
JOHN MASON CT
INCHKEITH AVE
LOVERS LA
KEMPSTON PL
PRIMROSE GDNS
CLARK AVE
ARROL PL
ROSEBERY CT
OCHIL CT
ALMOND DR
MOUBRAY GR
SCOTSTOUN GN
SCOTSTOUN PK
SCOTSTOUN AVE
SOUTH SCOTSTOUN
ATHELING GR
WELLHEAD CL
PROVOST MILNE GR
SOMMERVILLE GDNS
WHITEHEAD GR
ASHBURNHAM RD
QUEEN MARGARET DR
Queensferry High Sch
Sports Ctr
Works
STATION RD
ROSEHILL TERR
FORTH TERR
FORTH PK
BANKHEAD GR
Delmeny
Bankhead Cottages
BANKHEAD RD
Crossall Hill
B924
Wester Dalmeny
MAIN ST
CARLOWRIE AVE
CARLOWRIE CRES
Dalmeny
Dalmeny Prim Sch
Easter Dalmeny
4
77
North Lodge
CH
EH30
Golf Course
Sewage Works
Oil Storage Depot
Dolphington Burn
STANDINGSTANE RD
3
Milton
76
Craigend
Craigbrae
Carlowrie Cottages
A8000
M9
B800
EH29
Easter Carlowrie
Carlowrie Farm
2
Almondhill Cottages
Almondhill
75
Wheatlands
GLENDENNING DR
NEWMAINS FARM LA
YUMBIE RD
NEWMAINS RD
ALLAN PK
MAITLAND RD
QUEENSFERRY RD
STEWART PL
ALLISON PL
ALMONDHILL RD
DUNDAS PL
DUDGEON PL
MAIN ST
B9080
Sch
PENTLAND VIEW RD
LISTON DR
CARMEL AVE
CARMEL RD
MARSHALL RD
LISTON PL
LISTON RD
MANSE RD
TODDSHILL RD
THE GLEBE
BOWLING GREEN RD
STATION RD
ALMONDSIDE
Liby
AULDGATE
KIRKSTYLE GDNS
HIGH ST
STATION
WELLFLATS RD
TERR
PATH BRAE
THE SQUARE
Carlowrie
1
River Almond
Cat Stone
COTLAWS
GATESIDE RD
KING EDWARDS WAY
MAITLAND HOG LA
CLERICS HILL
B800 NEW LISTON RD
Kirkliston
Foxhall
Boathouse Bridge
EH12
74
12
13
14

119
90

89
69

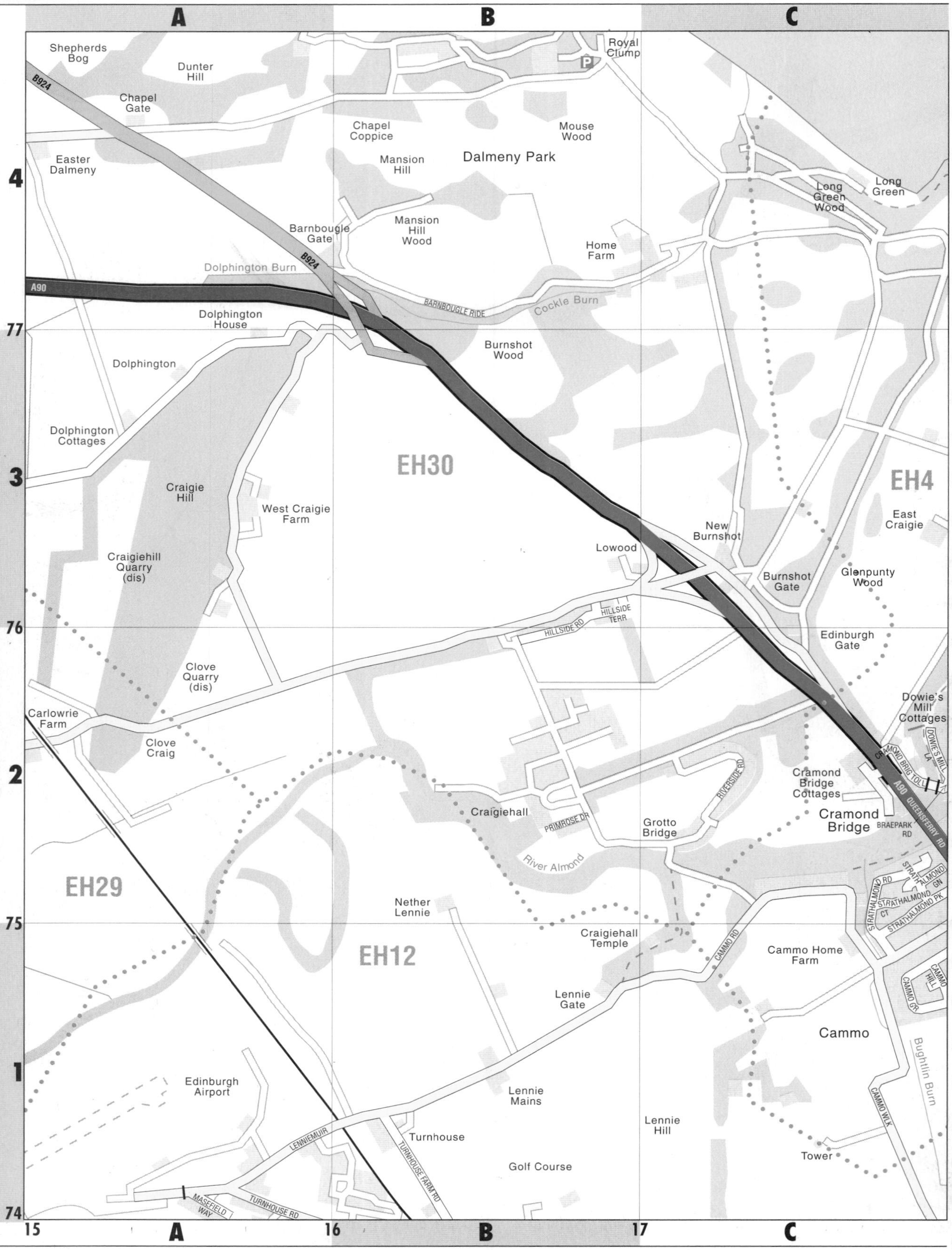

A   **B**   **C**

Shepherds Bog

Dunter Hill

Chapel Gate

B924

Royal Clump

P

Chapel Coppice

Mouse Wood

Mansion Hill

Dalmeny Park

4

Easter Dalmeny

Long Green Wood

Long Green

Barnbougle Gate

Mansion Hill Wood

Home Farm

Dolphington Burn

B924

Cockle Burn

A90

BARNBOUGLE RIDE

77

Dolphington House

Burnshot Wood

Dolphington

EH4

Dolphington Cottages

EH30

East Craigie

3

Craigie Hill

West Craigie Farm

New Burnshot

Lowood

Glenpunty Wood

Craigiehill Quarry (dis)

Burnshot Gate

Edinburgh Gate

76

Clove Quarry (dis)

HILLSIDE RD

HILLSIDE TERR

Dowie's Mill Cottages

Carlowrie Farm

DOWIE'S MILL LA

Clove Craig

CRAMOND BRIG TOLL

A90, QUEENSFERRY RD

Cramond Bridge Cottages

RUGBSIDE RD

2

EH29

Craigiehall

Grotto Bridge

Cramond Bridge

BRAEPARK RD

PRIMROSE DR

River Almond

STRATHALMOND RD

STRATHALMOND CT

STRATHALMOND PK

STRATHALMOND GN

Nether Lennie

CAMMO RD

Cammo Home Farm

CAMMO HILL

75

Craigiehall Temple

EH12

Lennie Gate

Cammo

CAMMO DR

Bughtlin Burn

1

Edinburgh Airport

Lennie Mains

Lennie Hill

Tower

CAMMO WLK

LENNIEMUIR

Turnhouse

TURNHOUSE FARM RD

Golf Course

74

MASEFIELD WAY

TURNHOUSE RD

15   **A**   **16**   **B**   **17**   **C**

89
120

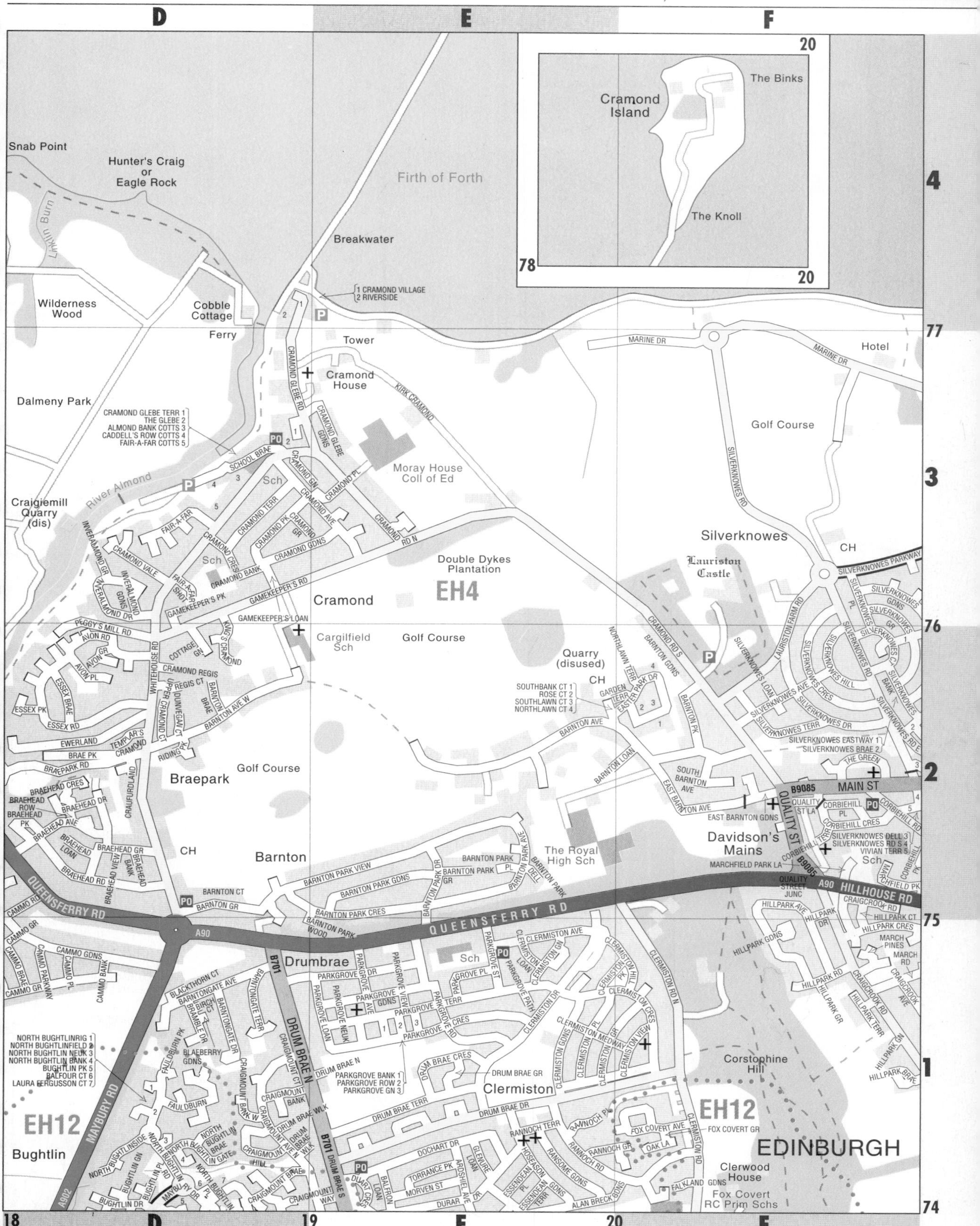
D
E
F
20
The Binks
Cramond Island
The Knoll
78
20
Snab Point
Hunter's Craig or Eagle Rock
Firth of Forth
Breakwater
Wilderness Wood
Cobble Cottage
Ferry
Tower
Hotel
Dalmeny Park
Cramond House
Golf Course
Moray House Coll of Ed
River Almond
Craigiemill Quarry (dis)
Silverknowes
Lauriston Castle
Double Dykes Plantation
Cramond
EH4
Cargilfield Sch
Golf Course
Quarry (disused)
Braepark
Golf Course
Davidson's Mains
Barnton
The Royal High Sch
QUEENSFERRY RD
Drumbrae
Clermiston
Corstophine Hill
EH12
EH12
Bughtlin
EDINBURGH
Clerwood House
Fox Covert RC Prim Schs
MAYBURY RD
DRUM BRAE N
4
3
77
76
2
75
1
74
18
19
20

91

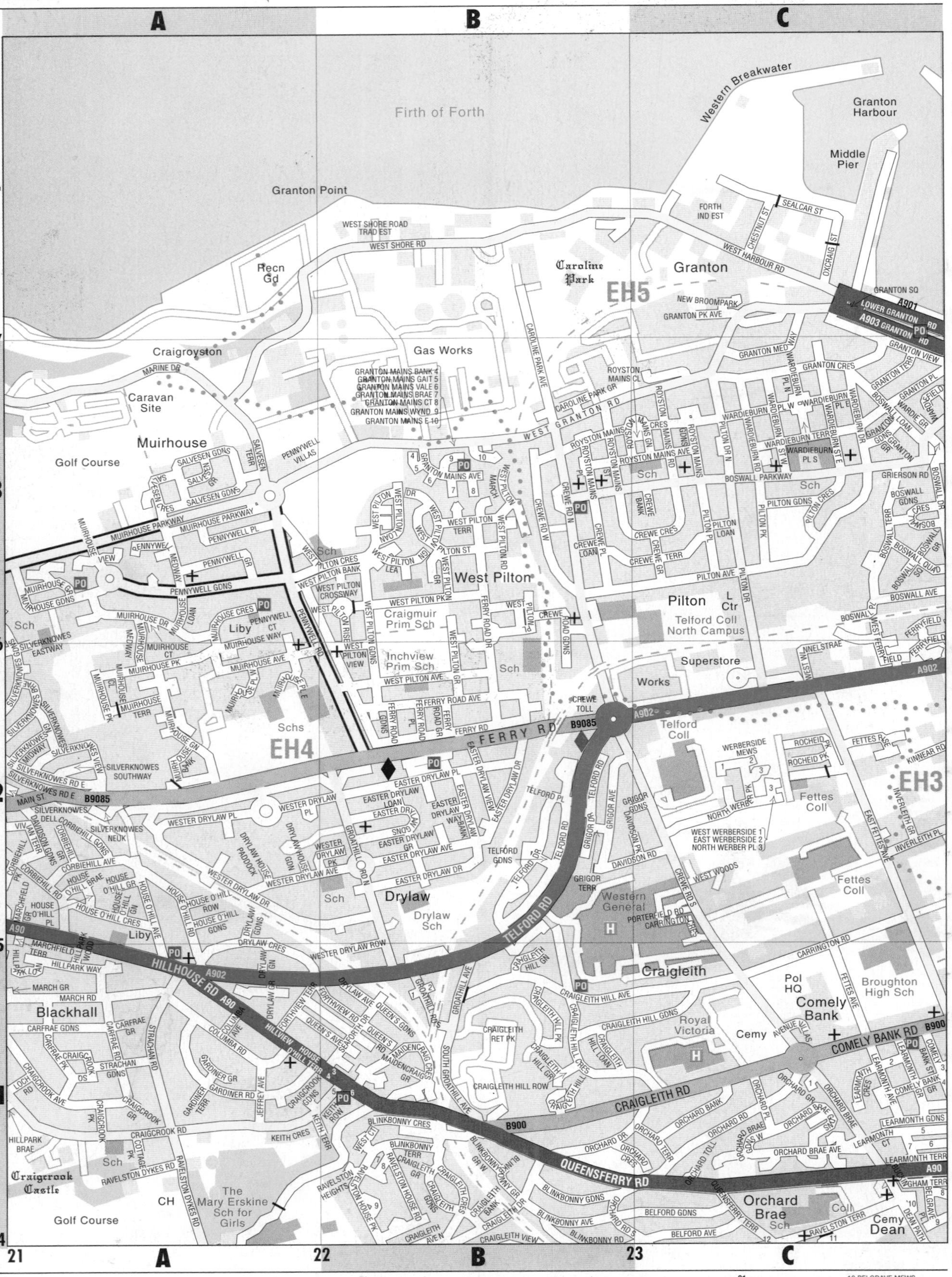

91

B1
1 GROATHILL GDNS W
2 GROATHILL GDNS E
3 SEAFORTH TERR
4 CRAIGCROOK TERR
5 CRAIGCROOK PL
6 MARISCHAL PL
7 EAST CT
8 RAVELSTON HOUSE LOAN
9 RAVELSTON HOUSE GR

122

C1
1 ORCHARD BRAE W
2 LEARMONTH PK
3 COMELY BANK TERR
4 LEARMONTH PL
5 LEARMONTH GDNS
6 LEARMONTH TERR LA
7 SOUTH LEARMONTH AVE
8 BELGRAVE CRESCENT LA
9 BELGRAVE CRES
10 BELGRAVE MEWS
11 BACK DEAN
12 RAVELSTON DYKES

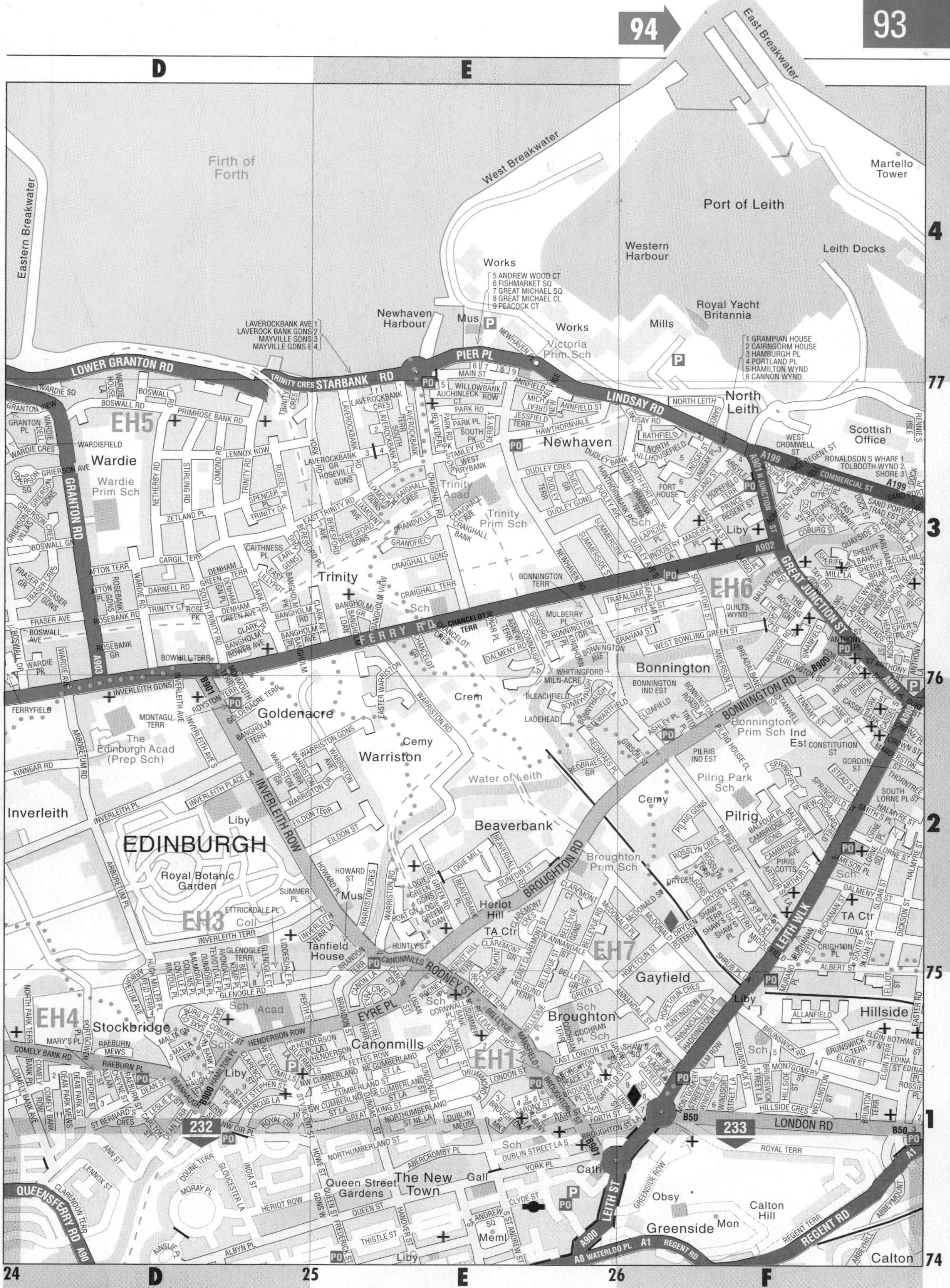

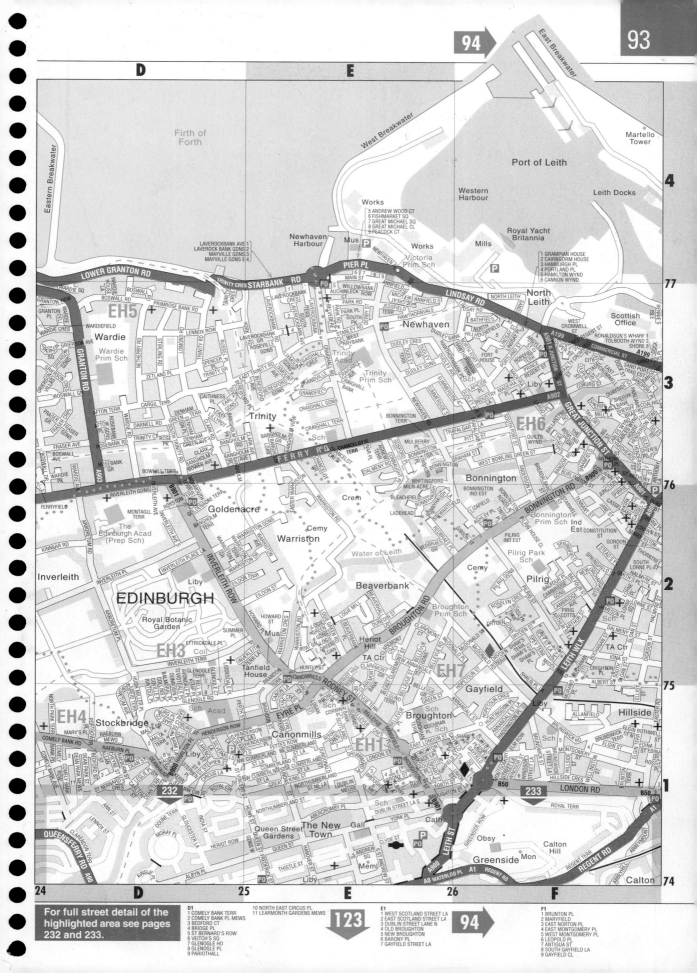

D   E   F

Firth of Forth

East Breakwater

Eastern Breakwater

West Breakwater

Port of Leith

Martello Tower

Western Harbour

Leith Docks

4

Works

5 ANDREW WOOD CT
6 FISHMARKET SQ
7 GREAT MICHAEL SQ
8 GREAT MICHAEL CL
9 PEACOCK CT

Newhaven Harbour

Mus

Works

Royal Yacht Britannia

Mills

1 GRAMPIAN HOUSE
2 CAIRNGORM HOUSE
3 HAMBURGH PL
4 PORTLAND PL
5 HAMILTON WYND
6 CANNON WYND

Scottish Office

LAVEROCKBANK AVE 1
LAVEROCK BANK GDNS 2
MAYVILLE GDNS 3
MAYVILLE GDNS E 4

Victoria Prim. Sch

PIER PL

LINDSAY RD

North Leith

77

LOWER GRANTON RD

TRINITY CRES STARBANK RD

MAIN ST

EH5

Wardie

Wardie Prim Sch

GRANTON RD

A903

Newhaven

A199

A902

EH6

3

Trinity Acad

Trinity Prim Sch

FERRY RD

Trinity

Craighall Bank

CHANCELOT TERR

Bonnington

Bonnington Ind Est

Bonnington Prim Sch Ind Est

GREAT JUNCTION ST

BONNINGTON RD

76

The Edinburgh Acad (Prep Sch)

Goldenacre

INVERLEITH ROW

Warriston

Crem

Cemy

Water of Leith

Pilrig Ind Est

Pilrig Park Sch

Cemy

Pilrig

2

Inverleith

EDINBURGH

Royal Botanic Garden

Liby

Beaverbank

Broughton Prim Sch

LEITH WLK

TA Ctr

EH3

Coll

Tanfield House

Heriot Hill

TA Ctr

EH7

Gayfield

75

EH4

Stockbridge

Liby

CANONMILLS

Canonmills

RODNEY ST

EYRE PL

Broughton

EH1

Sch Prim Sch

Hillside

Allanfield

232

QUEENSFERRY RD

A90

The New Town

Queen Street Gardens

233

LONDON RD

B50

1

Queen St

Calton Hill

LEITH ST

Greenside

Obsy

Mon

REGENT RD

Calton

74

24   D   25   E   26   F

For full street detail of the highlighted area see pages 232 and 233.

D1
1 COMELY BANK TERR
2 COMELY BANK PL MEWS
3 BEDFORD CT
4 BRIDGE PL
5 ST BERNARD'S ROW
6 VEITCH'S SQ
7 GLENOGLE HO
8 GLENOGLE PL
9 PARLIOTHALL

10 NORTH EAST CIRCUS PL
11 LEARMONTH GARDENS MEWS

123

94

E1
1 WEST SCOTLAND STREET LA
2 EAST SCOTLAND STREET LA
3 DUBLIN STREET LANE N
4 OLD BROUGHTON
5 NEW BROUGHTON
6 BARONY PL
7 GAYFIELD STREET LA

F1
1 BRUNTON PL
2 MARYFIELD
3 EAST NORTON PL
4 EAST MONTGOMERY PL
5 WEST MONTGOMERY PL
6 LEOPOLD PL
7 ANTIGUA ST
8 SOUTH GAYFIELD LA
9 GAYFIELD CL

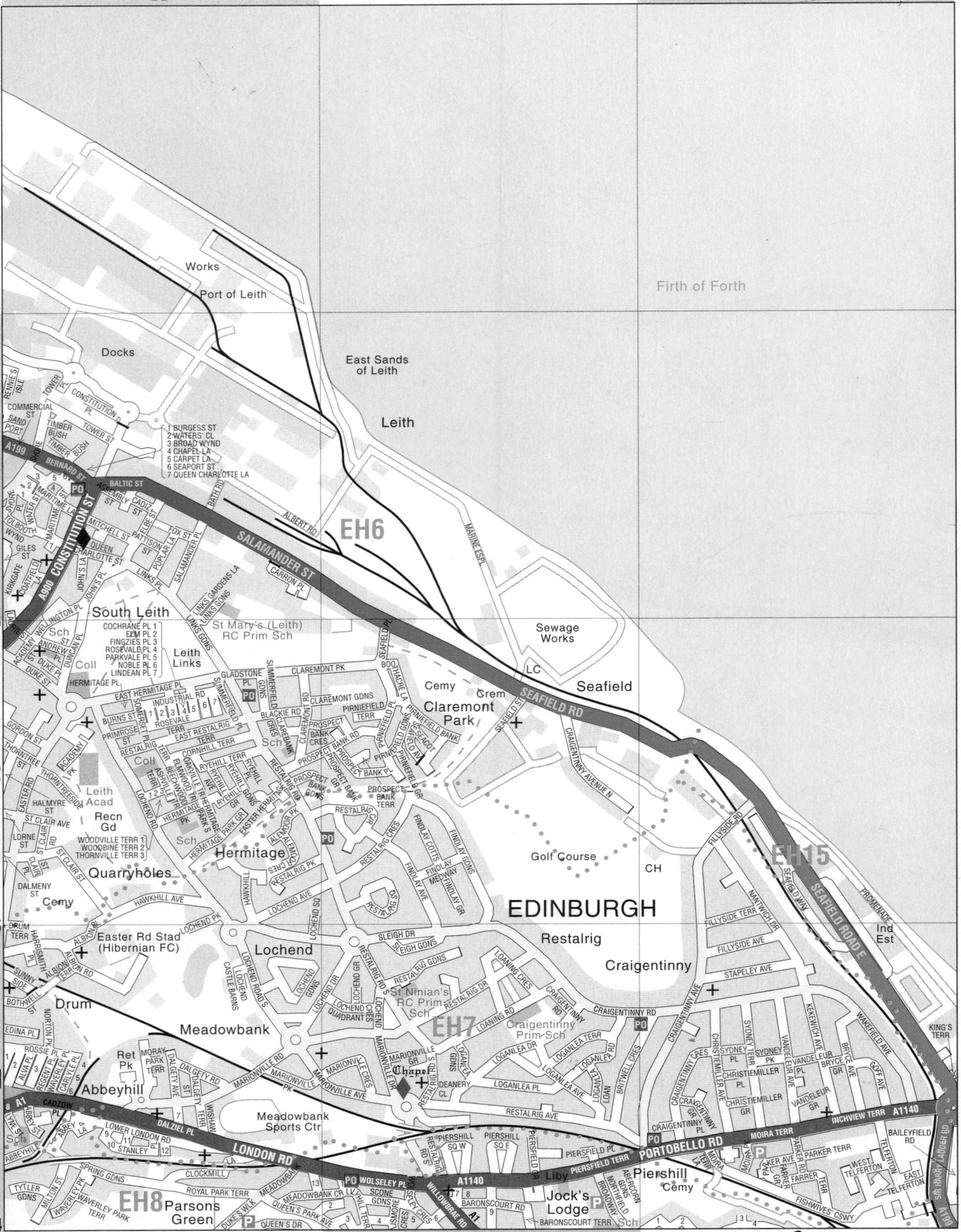

93   124

A1
1 MARYFIELD
2 MARYFIELD PL
3 LADY MENZIES PL
4 PITLOCHRY PL
5 SALMOND PL
6 EARLSTON PL
7 CAMBUSNETHAN ST
8 MONTROSE TERR
9 COMELEY GREEN PL
10 COMELEY GREEN CRES
11 WHYTE PL
12 SUNNYBANK PL
13 MEADOWBANK AVE

B1
1 PARSONS GREEN TERR
2 CONSIDINE TERR
3 CONSIDINE GDNS
4 LISMORE AVE
5 WILFRED TERR
6 ABERCORN RD
7 PIERSHILL LA
8 PIERSHILL PL
9 PIERSHILL TERR

C1
1 MOUNTCASTLE GN
2 MOUNTCASTLE PL
3 MOUNTCASTLE PK
4 MOUNTCASTLE CRES

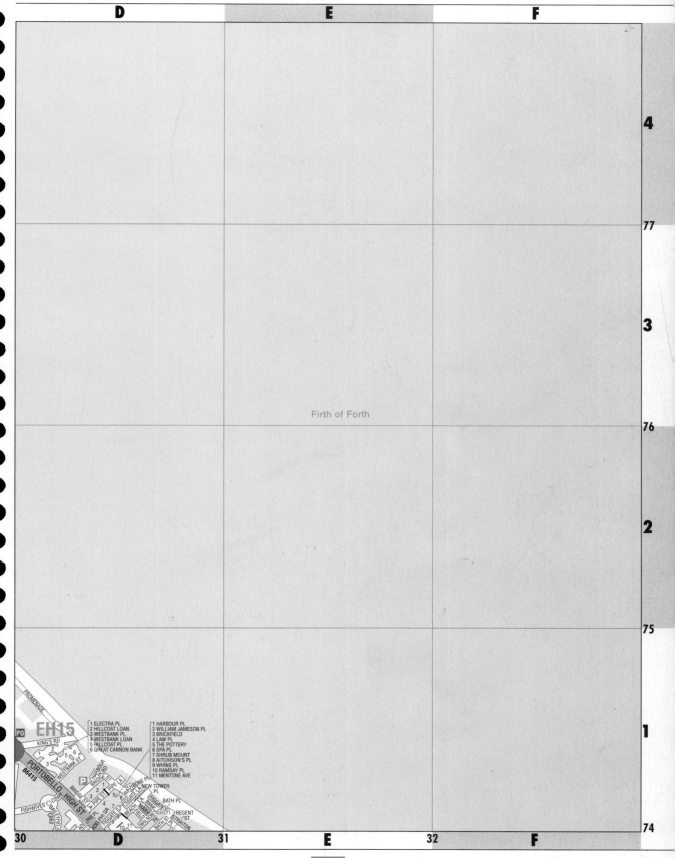

D   E   F

4

77

3

Firth of Forth

76

2

75

1

74

30   D   31   E   32   F

EH15

PO

KING'S RD

PORTOBELLO
B6415

PROMENADE

FISHWIVES'
CSWY

P

HARBOUR
BRIDGE ST

WESTBANK ST

HIGH ST

1 ELECTRA PL
2 HILLCOAT LOAN
3 WESTBANK PL
4 WESTBANK LOAN
5 HILLCOAT PL
6 GREAT CANNON BANK

1 HARBOUR PL
2 WILLIAM JAMESON PL
3 BRICKFIELD
4 LAW PL
5 THE POTTERY
6 SPA PL
7 SHRUB MOUNT
8 AITCHISON'S PL
9 WHINS PL
10 RAMSAY PL
11 MENTONE AVE

BRIDGE ST
PIPE ST
PIPE LA
RATHBONE PL
NEW TOWER PL
BATH PL
REGENT ST
STRAITON
BATH ST
MARLBOROUGH
BANK
BEACH LA

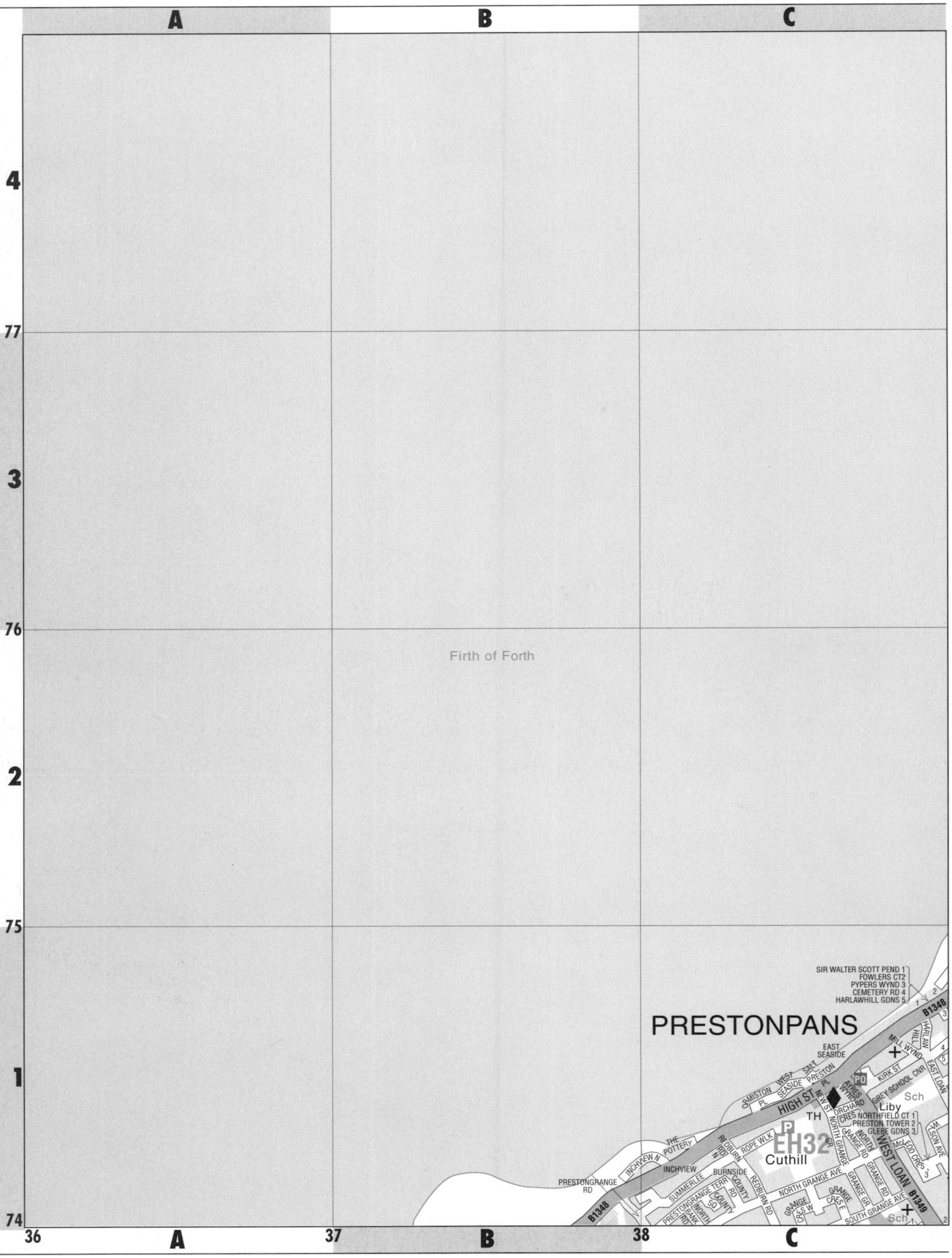

Firth of Forth

SIR WALTER SCOTT PEND 1
FOWLERS CT 2
PYPERS WYND 3
CEMETERY RD 4
HARLAWHILL GDNS 5

PRESTONPANS

EAST
SEASIDE

EH32
Cuthill

PRESTONGRANGE
RD

98

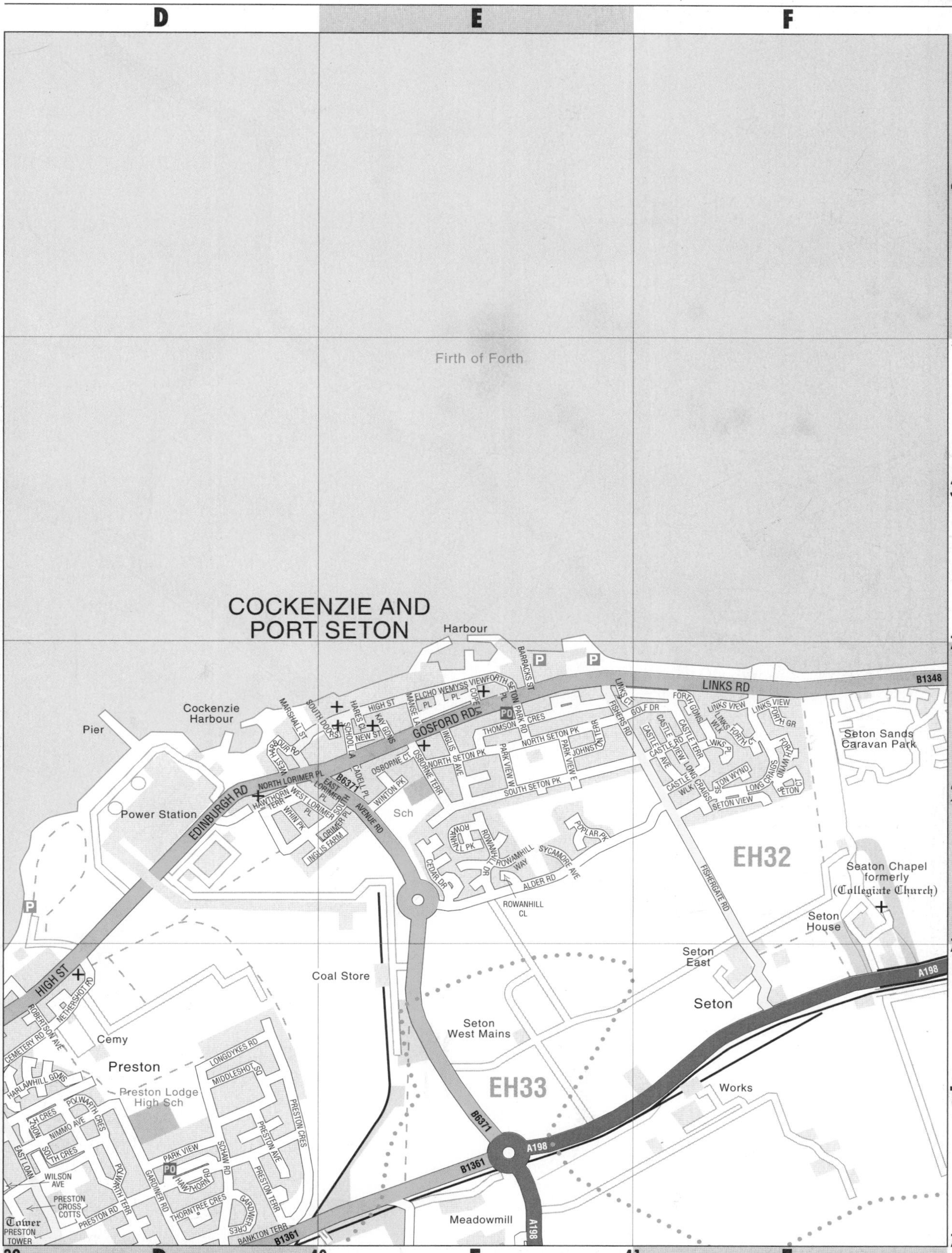
D
E
F
Firth of Forth
COCKENZIE AND PORT SETON
Harbour
Cockenzie Harbour
Pier
Power Station
LINKS RD
B1348
GOSFORD RD
EDINBURGH RD
B6371
AVENUE RD
HIGH ST
Sch
Seton Sands Caravan Park
EH32
Seaton Chapel formerly (Collegiate Church)
Seton House
Seton East
Seton
A198
Coal Store
Seton West Mains
EH33
Works
B1361
Meadowmill
Cemy
Preston
Preston Lodge High Sch
Tower
PRESTON TOWER
FISHERGATE RD
ROWANHILL CL
ALDER RD
SYCAMORE AVE
POPLAR PK
NORTH SETON PK
SOUTH SETON PK
SETON VIEW
LONGDYKES RD
MIDDLESHOT SQ
PRESTON CRES
PRESTON AVE
PRESTON TERR
BANKTON TERR
PRESTON RD
PARK VIEW
THORNTREE CRES
4
3
2
1
77
76
75
74
39
40
41

128

98

97
70

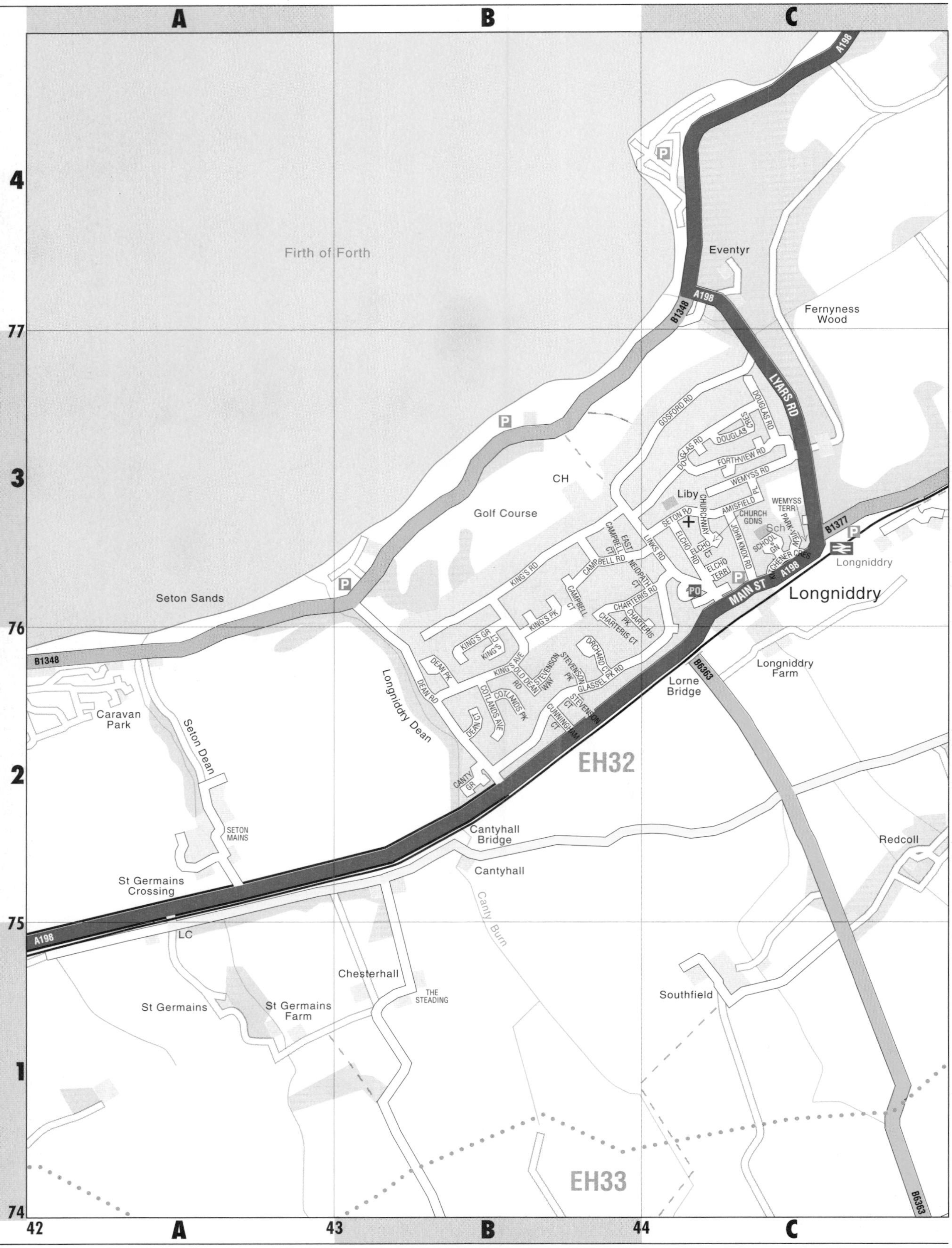
A
B
C
4
77
3
76
2
75
1
74
42
43
44
Firth of Forth
Eventyr
Fernyness
Wood
A198
B1348
LYARS RD
GOSFORD RD
DOUGLAS CRES
DOUGLAS RD
FORTHVIEW RD
WEMYSS RD
WEMYSS TERR
PARK VIEW
AMISFIELD
CHURCH GDNS
Sch
SCHOOL GN
KITCHENER CRES
Liby
SETON RD
CHURCHWAY
ELCHO RD
ELCHO CT
ELCHO TERR
JOHN KNOX RD
LINKS RD
EAST CAMPBELL CT
CAMPBELL RD
CAMPBELL CT
NEIDPATH CT
CHARTERIS RD
CHARTERIS PK
CHARTERIS CT
KING'S RD
KING'S PK
KING'S GR
KING'S CT
KING'S AVE
OLD DEAN RD
STEVENSON WAY
STEVENSON PK
STEVENSON GN
ORCHARD CT
GLASSEL PK RD
CUNNINGHAM CT
STEVENSON CT
DEAN PK
DEAN RD
DEAN CT
COTLANDS AVE
COTLANDS PK
CANTY GR
PO
P
MAIN ST
B1377
Longniddry
CH
Golf Course
Seton Sands
Caravan
Park
Seton Dean
Longniddry Dean
EH32
Lorne
Bridge
B6363
Longniddry
Farm
Cantyhall
Bridge
Cantyhall
SETON
MAINS
St Germains
Crossing
Redcoll
Canty Burn
LC
Chesterhall
THE
STEADING
Southfield
St Germains
St Germains
Farm
EH33

97
129

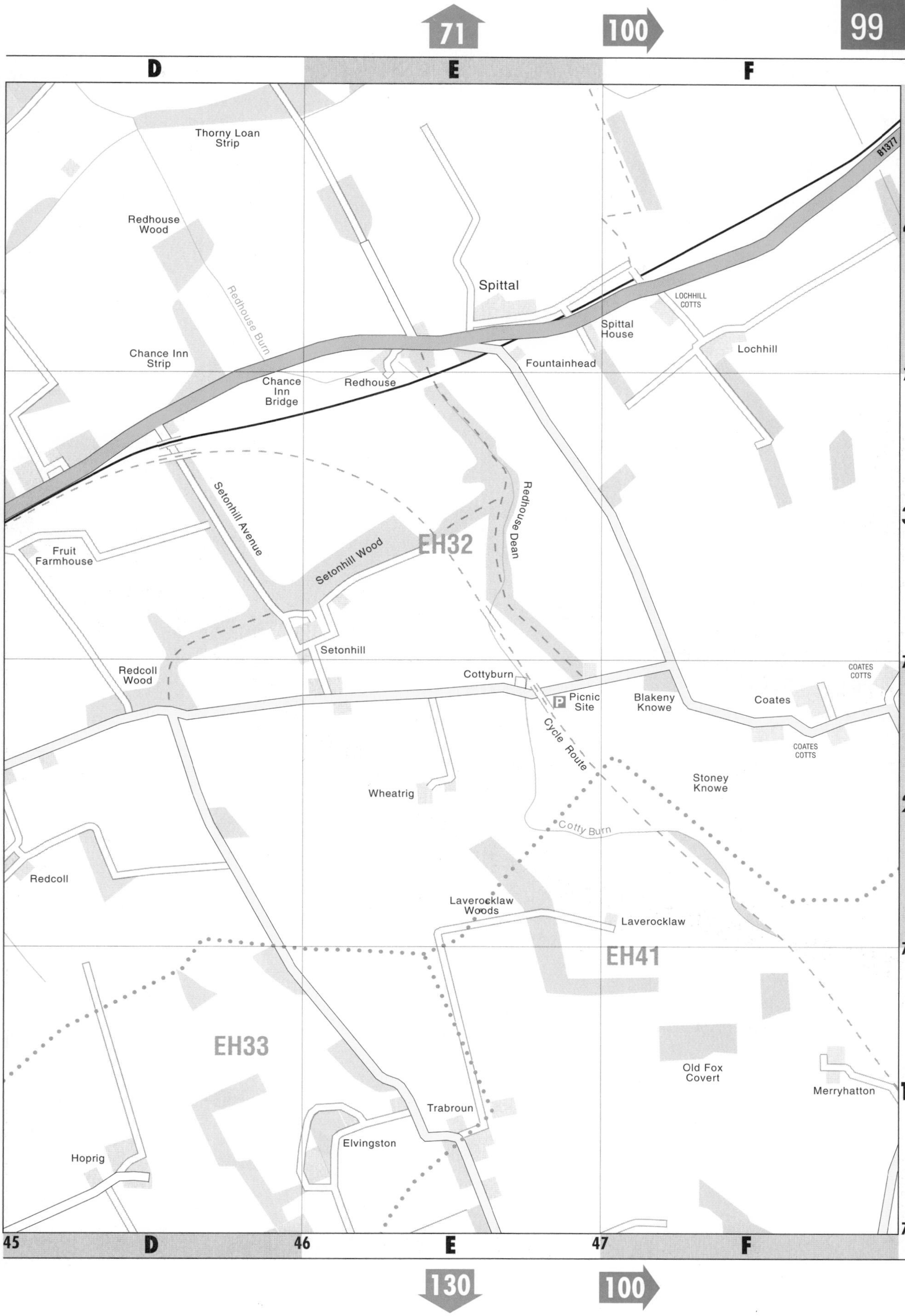
71
100
D
E
F
Thorny Loan Strip
Redhouse Wood
Redhouse Burn
Spittal
B1377
LOCHHILL COTTS
Spittal House
Lochhill
Chance Inn Strip
Chance Inn Bridge
Redhouse
Fountainhead
4
77
Setonhill Avenue
Redhouse Dean
Fruit Farmhouse
Setonhill Wood
EH32
3
Setonhill
Redcoll Wood
Cottyburn
Picnic Site
Blakeny Knowe
Coates
COATES COTTS
COATES COTTS
76
Cycle Route
Wheatrig
Stoney Knowe
Cotty Burn
2
Redcoll
Laverocklaw Woods
Laverocklaw
EH41
75
EH33
Old Fox Covert
Merryhatton
1
Trabroun
Elvingston
Hoprig
74
45
D
46
E
47
F
130
100

99
72

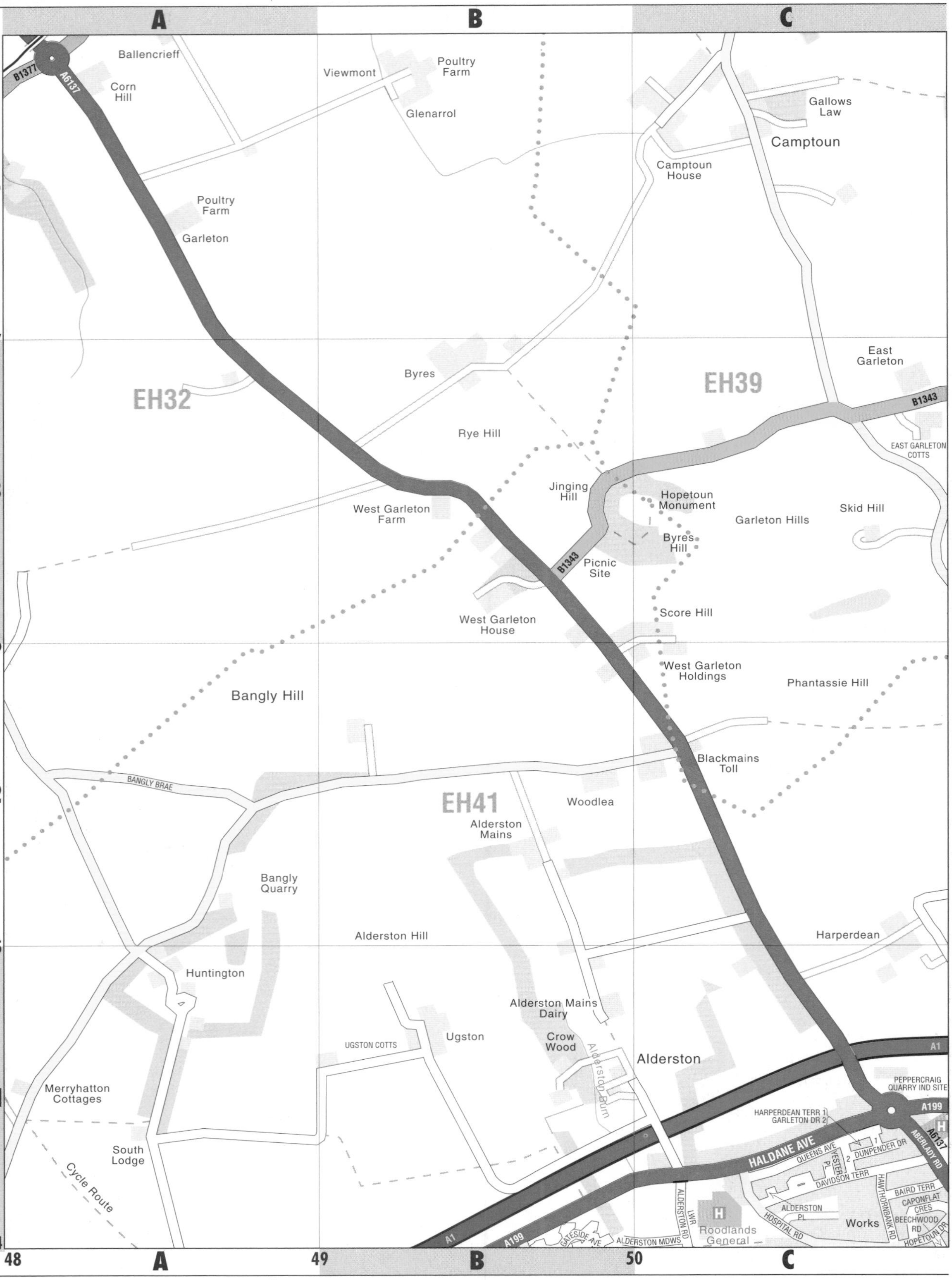

A

B

C

Ballencrieff

Corn Hill

B1377

A6137

Viewmont

Poultry Farm

Glenarrol

Gallows Law

Camptoun

Camptoun House

4

Poultry Farm

Garleton

East Garleton

77

EH32

Byres

EH39

B1343

Rye Hill

EAST GARLETON COTTS

3

West Garleton Farm

Jinging Hill

Hopetoun Monument

Skid Hill

Garleton Hills

B1343

Byres Hill

Picnic Site

West Garleton House

Score Hill

76

West Garleton Holdings

Phantassie Hill

Bangly Hill

BANGLY BRAE

Blackmains Toll

2

EH41

Woodlea

Alderston Mains

Bangly Quarry

Alderston Hill

Harperdean

75

Huntington

Alderston Mains Dairy

A1

Merryhatton Cottages

UGSTON COTTS

Ugston

Crow Wood

Alderston

PEPPERCRAIG QUARRY IND SITE

A199

A6137

H

1

HARPERDEAN TERR 1 GARLETON DR 2

HALDANE AVE

QUEENS AVE

WESTER PL

DUNPENDER DR

DAVIDSON TERR

BAIRD TERR

CAPONFLAT CRES

BEECHWOOD RD

South Lodge

Cycle Route

ALDERSTON PL

HOSPITAL RD

HAWTHORNBANK RD

Works

HOPETOUN DR

74

A1

A199

GATESIDE AVE

ALDERSTON MDWS

LWR

ALDERSTON RD

H

Roodlands General

48

A

49

B

50

C

99
131

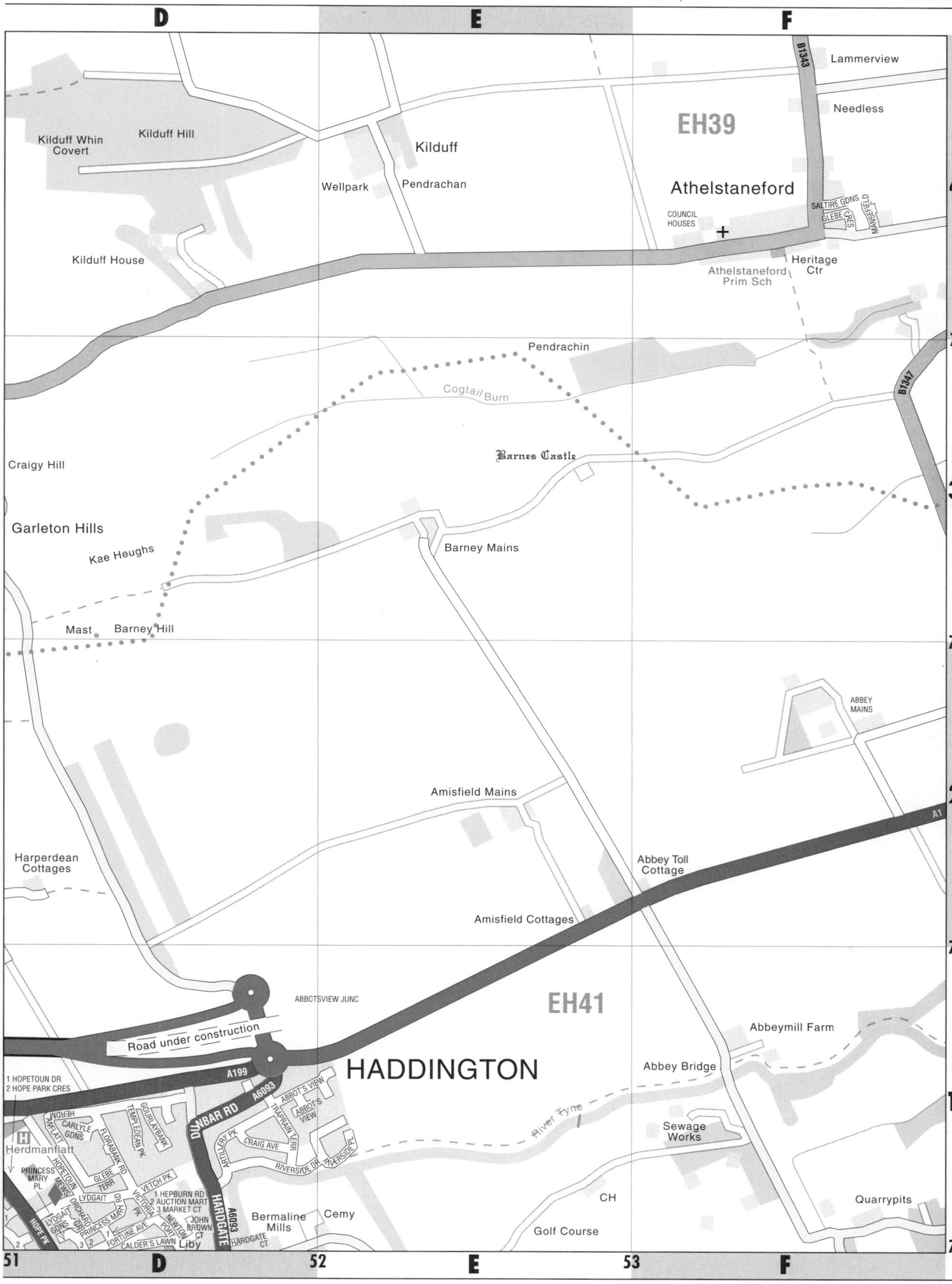

D
E
F

B1343
Lammerview
Needless

EH39

Kilduff Whin Covert
Kilduff Hill
Kilduff
Athelstaneford

4

Wellpark
Pendrachan

SALTIRE GDNS
GLEBE CRES
MARSFIELD

Kilduff House

COUNCIL HOUSES
+

Heritage Ctr

Athelstaneford Prim Sch

77

Pendrachin

Cogtail Burn

B1347

Craigy Hill

Barnes Castle

3

Garleton Hills

Kae Heughs

Barney Mains

Mast
Barney Hill

76

ABBEY MAINS

Amisfield Mains

2

A1

Harperdean Cottages

Abbey Toll Cottage

Amisfield Cottages

75

ABBOTSVIEW JUNC

EH41

Abbeymill Farm

Road under construction

HADDINGTON

Abbey Bridge

1

1 HOPETOUN DR
2 HOPE PARK CRES

A199
DUNBAR RD
A6093
ABBOT'S VIEW
ABBOT'S VIEW
TRAPRAIN TERR

River Tyne

Sewage Works

H
Herdmanflatt

CARLYLE GDNS
HEROW
FLORABANK RD

SERV PK
CRAIG AVE
RIVERSIDE DR
RIVERSIDE

PRINCESS MARY PL

LYDGAIT
VICTORIA
GLEBE TERR
FLORA TERR
VETCH PK
TEMPL EDEN PK

1 HEPBURN RD
2 AUCTION MART
3 MARKET CT
JOHN BROWN CT

CH

Quarrypits

HOPE PK
PRINCESS MARY
HOPETOUN CT
FORTUNE AVE
CALDER'S LAWN
Liby

HARDGATE
A6093
HARDGATE CT

Bermaline Mills
Cemy

Golf Course

74

51
D
52
E
53
F

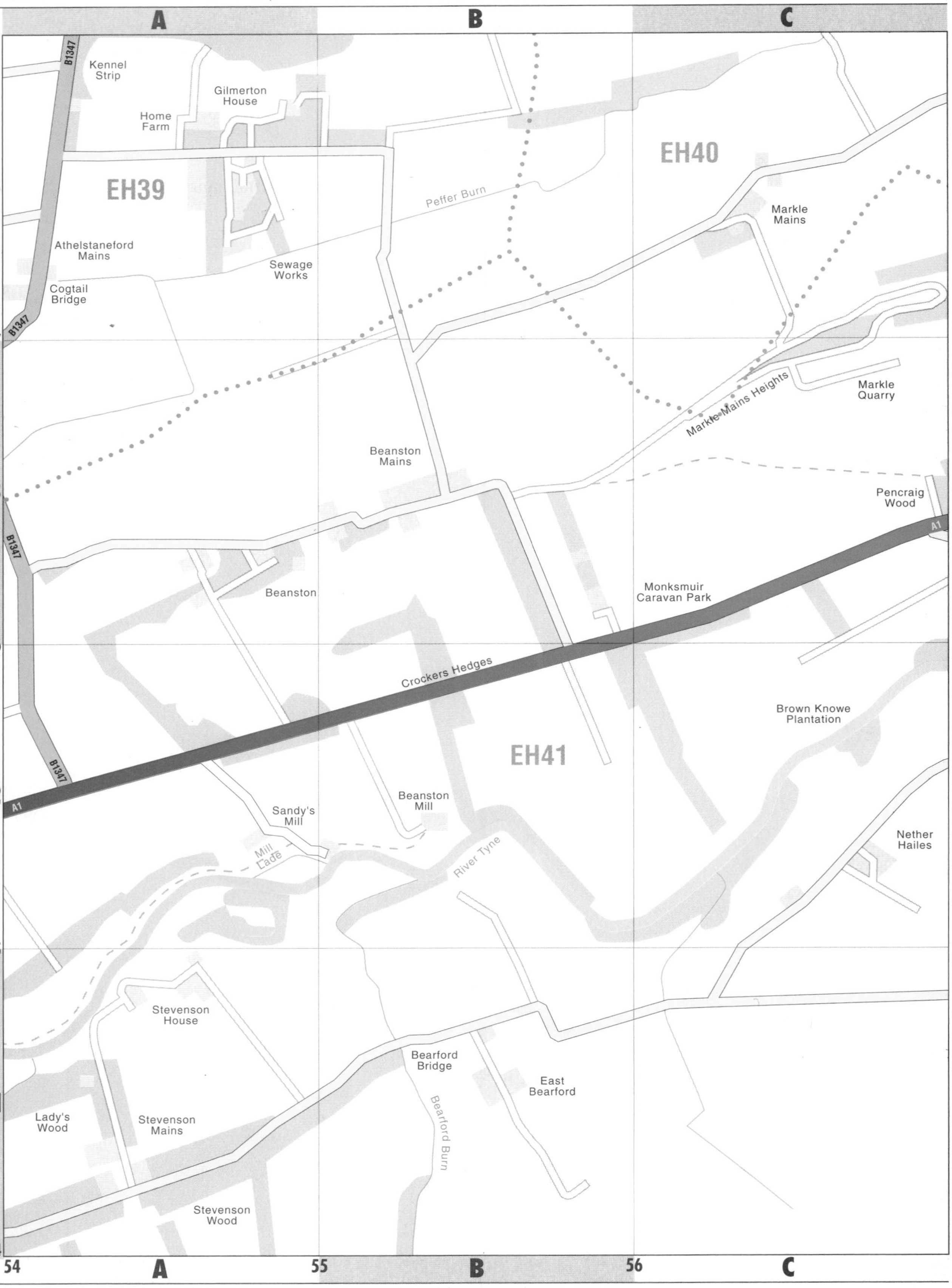

A   B   C

B1347

Kennel Strip

Gilmerton House

Home Farm

EH40

Peffer Burn

Markle Mains

4

EH39

Athelstaneford Mains

Sewage Works

Cogtail Bridge

B1347

Markle Mains Heights

Markle Quarry

77

Beanston Mains

Pencraig Wood

3

B1347

A1

Beanston

Monksmuir Caravan Park

76

Crockers Hedges

Brown Knowe Plantation

EH41

B1347

2

A1

Sandy's Mill

Beanston Mill

Nether Hailes

Mill Lade

River Tyne

75

Stevenson House

Bearford Bridge

East Bearford

1

Lady's Wood

Stevenson Mains

Bearford Burn

Stevenson Wood

74

54   A   55   B   56   C

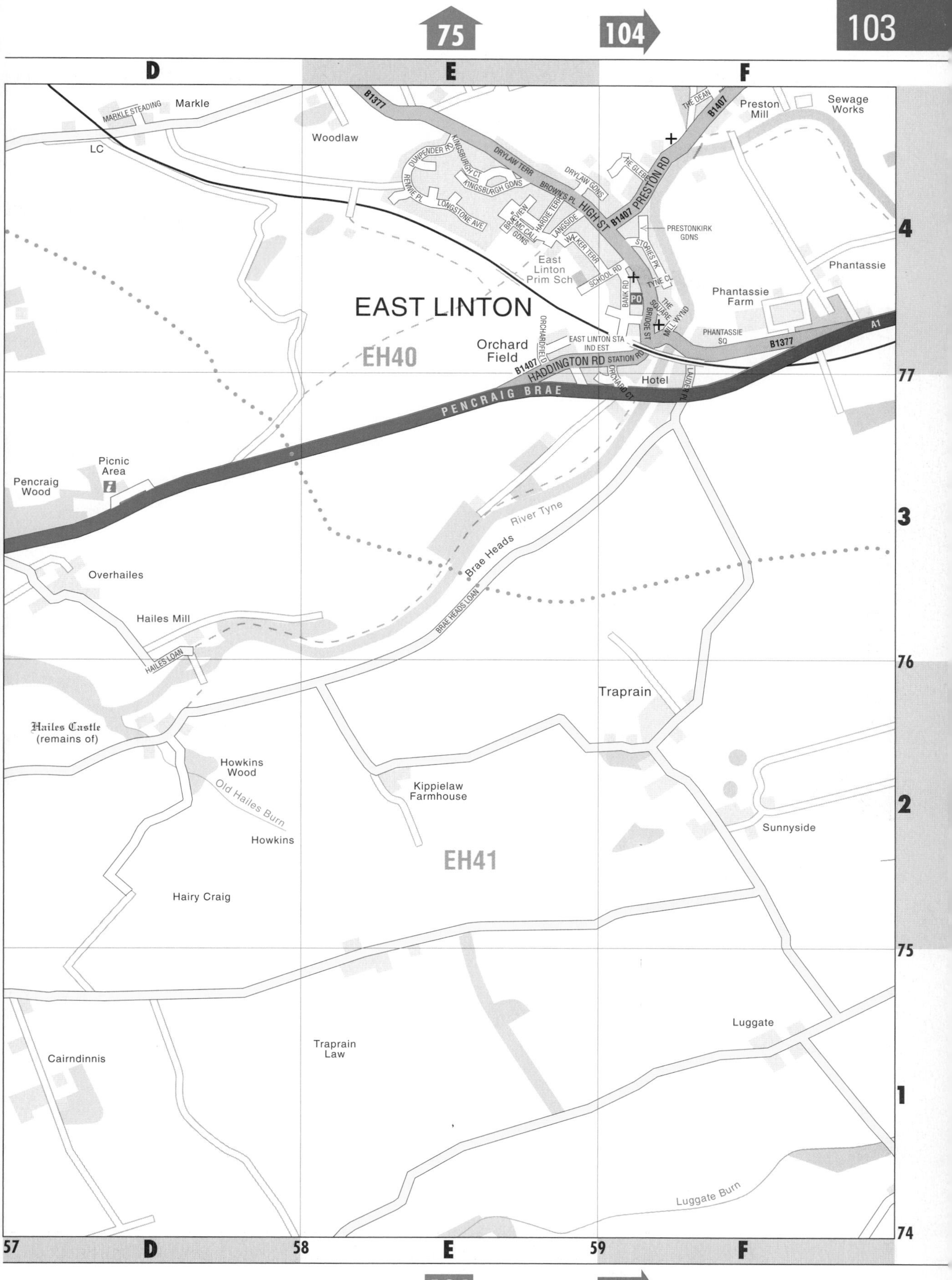
75
104
D
E
F
Markle
MARKLE STEADING
LC
Woodlaw
B1377
B1407
THE DEAN
Preston Mill
Sewage Works
DUNPENDER RD
KINGSBURGH RD
KINGSBURGH CT
KINGSBURGH GDNS
RENNIE PL
LONGSTONE AVE
DRYLAW TERR
DRYLAW GDNS
BROWN'S PL
HIGH ST
PRESTON RD
THE GLEBE
BRAE VIEW
MC CALL GDNS
HARDIE TERR
LANGSIDE
WALKER TERR
PRESTONKIRK GDNS
STORIES PK
East Linton Prim Sch
SCHOOL RD
BANK RD
PO
TYNE CL
THE SQUARE
BRIDGE ST
MILL WYND
Phantassie
Phantassie Farm
PHANTASSIE SQ
A1
EAST LINTON
EH40
ORCHARDFIELD
Orchard Field
EAST LINTON STA IND EST
HADDINGTON RD
STATION RD
ORCHARD CT
LAUDER PL
Hotel
PENCRAIG BRAE
Picnic Area
Pencraig Wood
River Tyne
Brae Heads
BRAE HEADS LOAN
Overhailes
Hailes Mill
HAILES LOAN
Traprain
Hailes Castle (remains of)
Howkins Wood
Old Hailes Burn
Kippielaw Farmhouse
Sunnyside
Howkins
EH41
Hairy Craig
Luggate
Cairndinnis
Traprain Law
Luggate Burn
4
77
3
76
2
75
1
74
57
58
59
134
104

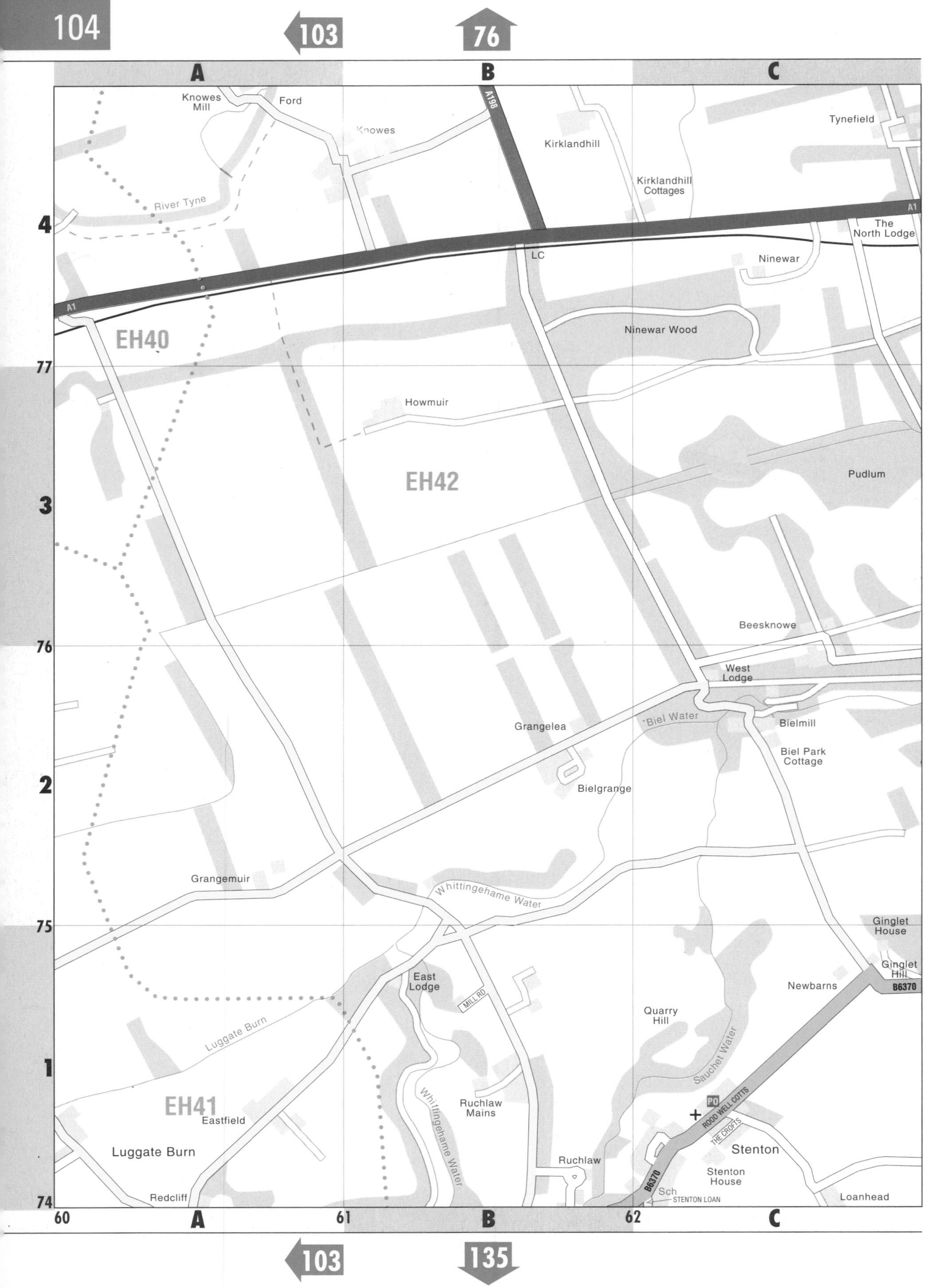

A   B   C

Knowes Mill
Ford
Knowes
Kirklandhill
Kirklandhill Cottages
Tynefield
River Tyne
A1
The North Lodge
4
LC
Ninewar
A1
EH40
Ninewar Wood
77
Howmuir
Pudlum
EH42
3
Beesknowe
76
West Lodge
Grangelea
Biel Water
Bielmill
Bielgrange
Biel Park Cottage
2
Grangemuir
Whittingehame Water
Ginglet House
75
Ginglet Hill
B6370
East Lodge
Newbarns
MILL RD
Quarry Hill
Sauchet Water
1
Luggate Burn
Whittingehame Water
PO
ROOD WELL COTTS
EH41
Ruchlaw Mains
THE CROFTS
Stenton
Eastfield
Luggate Burn
Ruchlaw
B6370
Stenton House
Sch
Loanhead
74
Redcliff
STENTON LOAN

60   A   61   B   62   C

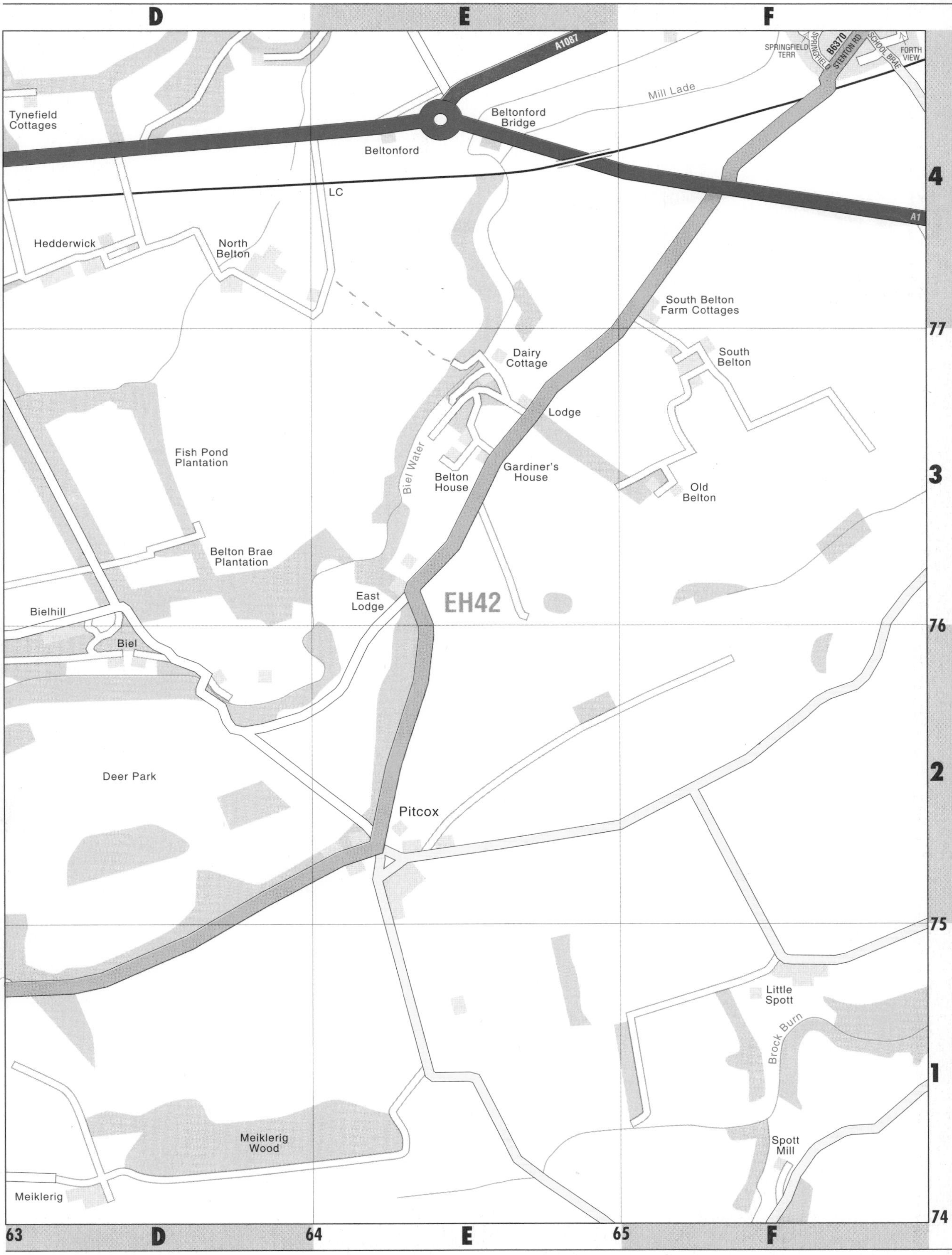

77
106
136
106

D
E
F

Tynefield
Cottages

A1087

SPRINGFIELD
TERR

B6370

STENTON RD

SCHOOL BRAE

FORTH
VIEW

Mill Lade

Beltonford
Bridge

Beltonford

A1

LC

4

Hedderwick

North
Belton

South Belton
Farm Cottages

77

Dairy
Cottage

South
Belton

Fish Pond
Plantation

Lodge

Belton
House

Gardiner's
House

Old
Belton

3

Biel Water

Belton Brae
Plantation

Bielhill

East
Lodge

EH42

Biel

76

Deer Park

2

Pitcox

75

Little
Spott

Brock Burn

1

Meiklerig
Wood

Spott
Mill

Meiklerig

74

63
64
65

105
78
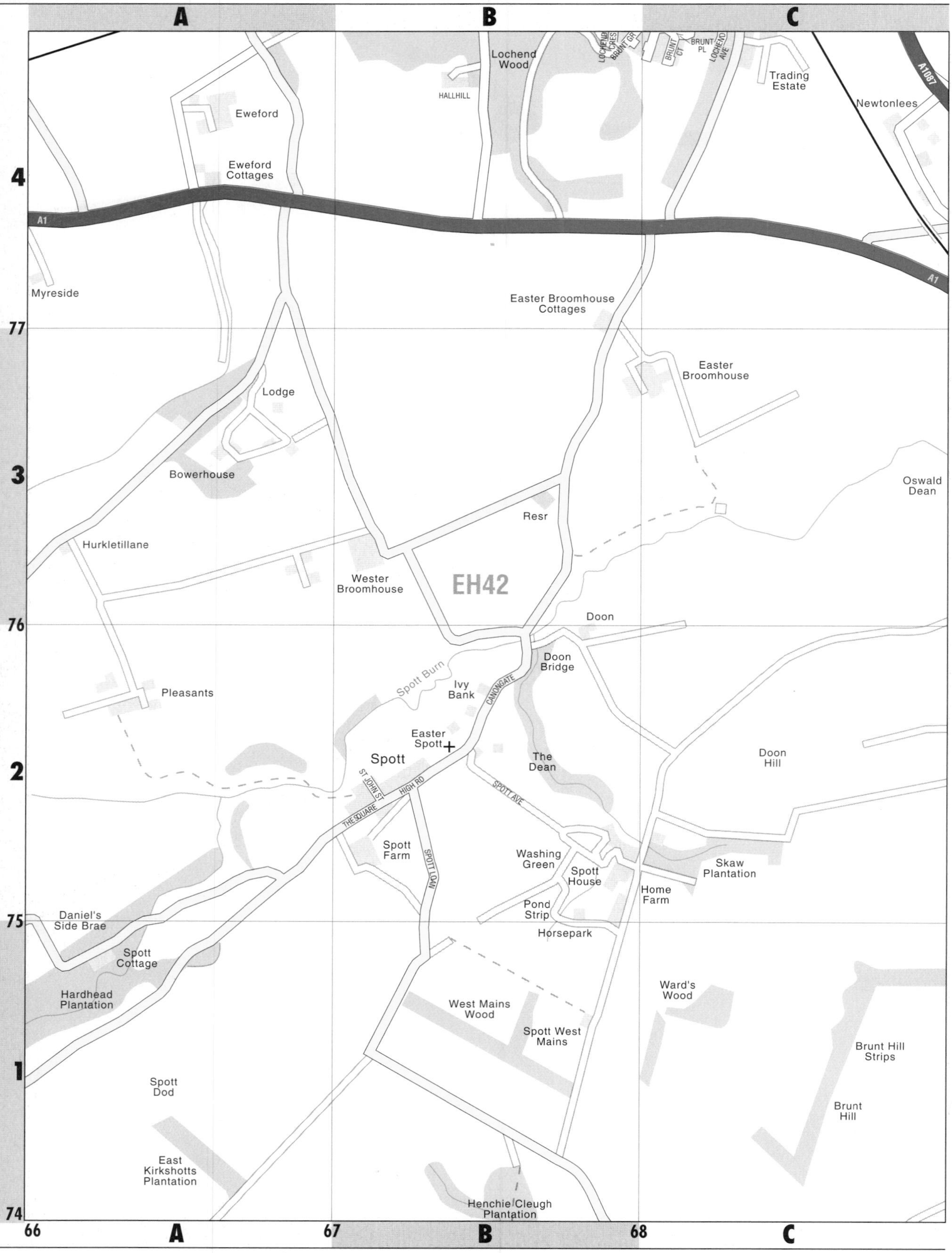
A
B
C
Lochend Wood
HALLHILL
LOCHEND CRES
BRUNT GR
BRUNT CT
BRUNT PL
LOCHEND AVE
Trading Estate
A1087
Newtonlees
Eweford
Eweford Cottages
4
A1
A1
Myreside
Easter Broomhouse Cottages
77
Easter Broomhouse
Lodge
3
Bowerhouse
Oswald Dean
Resr
Hurkletillane
Wester Broomhouse
EH42
76
Doon
Doon Bridge
Spott Burn
Ivy Bank
CANONGATE
Pleasants
Easter Spott
Spott
2
The Dean
Doon Hill
ST JOHN ST
HIGH RD
SPOTT AVE
THE SQUARE
Spott Farm
SPOTT LOAN
Washing Green
Spott House
Skaw Plantation
Home Farm
Daniel's Side Brae
Pond Strip
75
Horsepark
Spott Cottage
Ward's Wood
Hardhead Plantation
West Mains Wood
Spott West Mains
Brunt Hill Strips
1
Spott Dod
Brunt Hill
East Kirkshotts Plantation
Henchie Cleugh Plantation
74
66
A
67
B
68
C
105
137

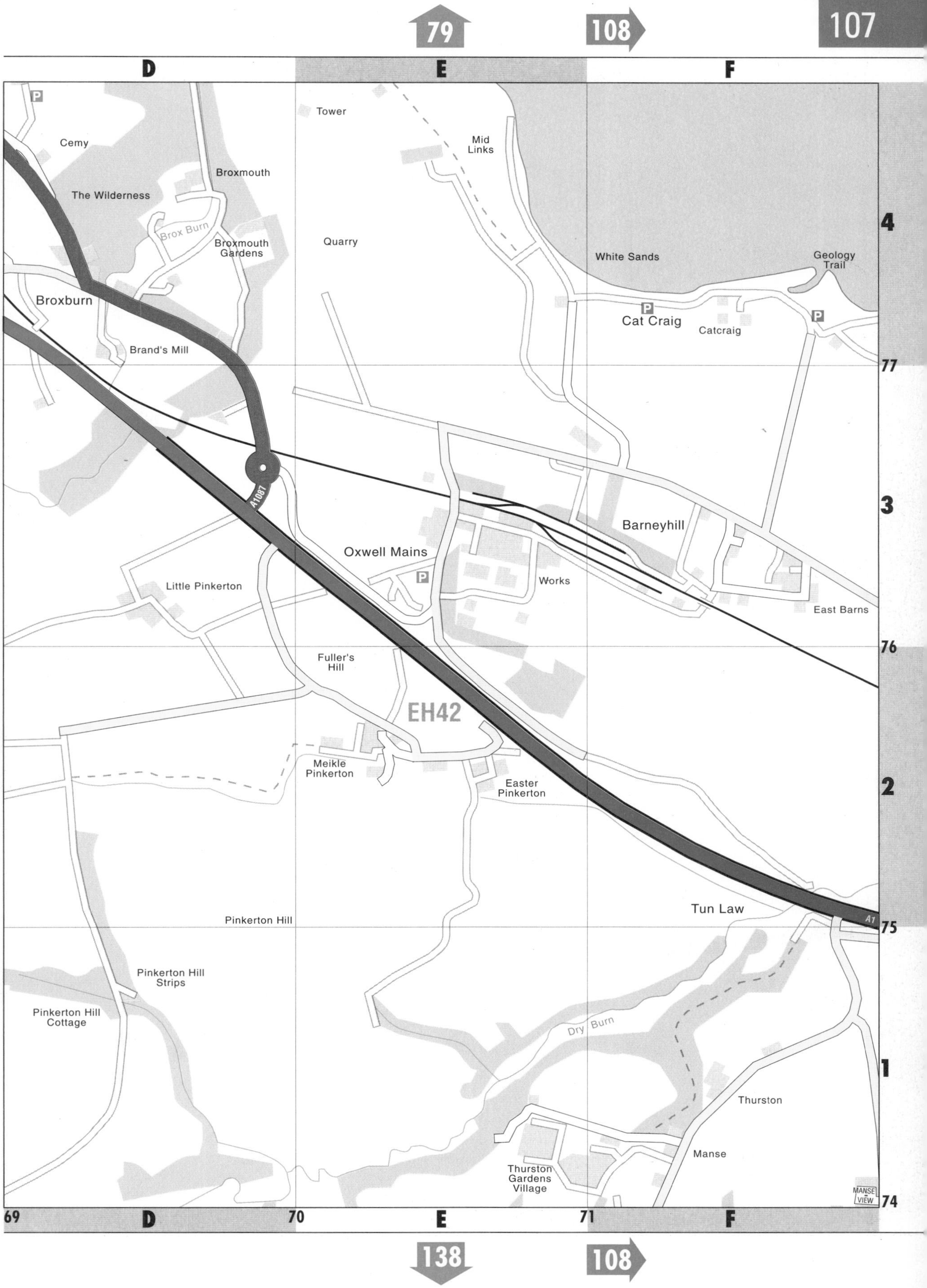
79
108
D
E
F
Tower
Cemy
Mid
Links
Broxmouth
The Wilderness
Brox Burn
Broxmouth
Gardens
Quarry
White Sands
Geology
Trail
Broxburn
Cat Craig
Catcraig
Brand's Mill
A1087
Barneyhill
Oxwell Mains
Works
Little Pinkerton
East Barns
Fuller's
Hill
EH42
Meikle
Pinkerton
Easter
Pinkerton
Tun Law
A1
Pinkerton Hill
Pinkerton Hill
Strips
Pinkerton Hill
Cottage
Dry Burn
Thurston
Manse
Thurston
Gardens
Village
MANSE
VIEW
4
77
3
76
2
75
1
74
69
70
71
138
108

107

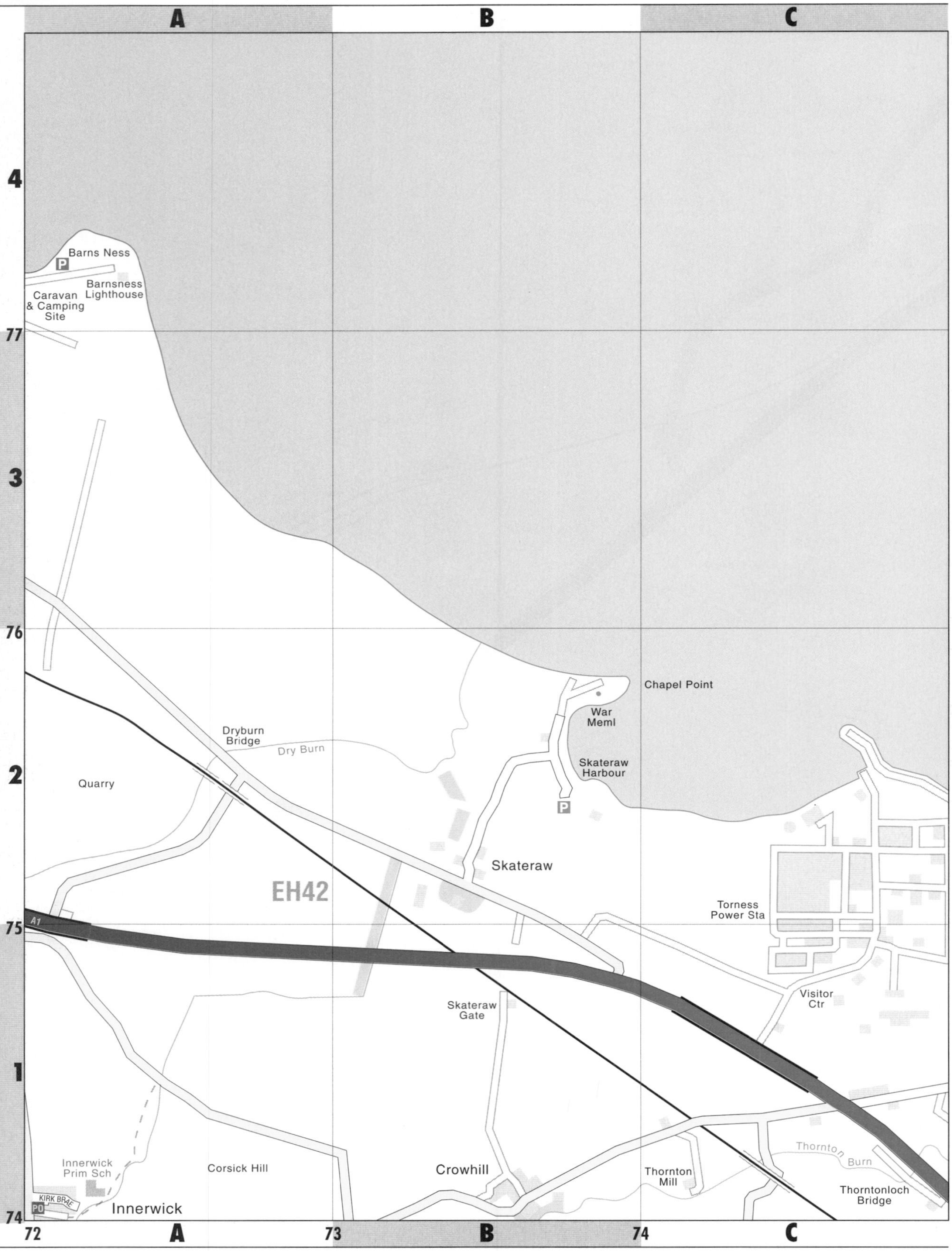
A
B
C
4
3
2
1
77
76
75
74
72
73
74
Barns Ness
P
Barnsness Lighthouse
Caravan & Camping Site
Chapel Point
War Meml
Skateraw Harbour
P
Dryburn Bridge
Dry Burn
Quarry
Skateraw
EH42
A1
Torness Power Sta
Visitor Ctr
Skateraw Gate
Crowhill
Corsick Hill
Innerwick Prim Sch
KIRK BRAE
PO
Innerwick
Thornton Mill
Thornton Burn
Thorntonloch Bridge

107
139

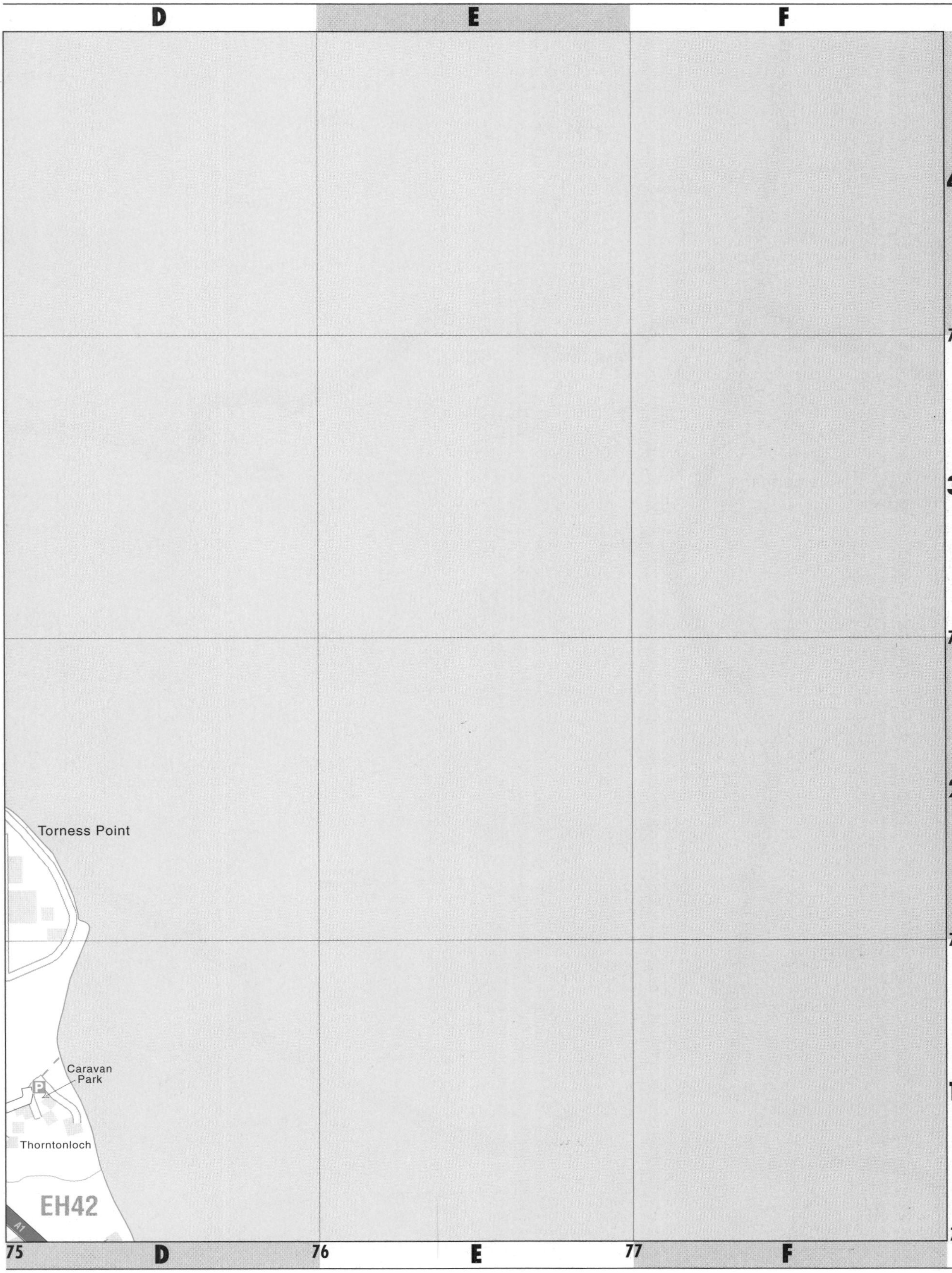
D
E
F
4
77
3
76
2
75
1
74
Torness Point
Caravan
Park
P
Thorntonloch
EH42
A1
75
76
77
D
E
F

140

80

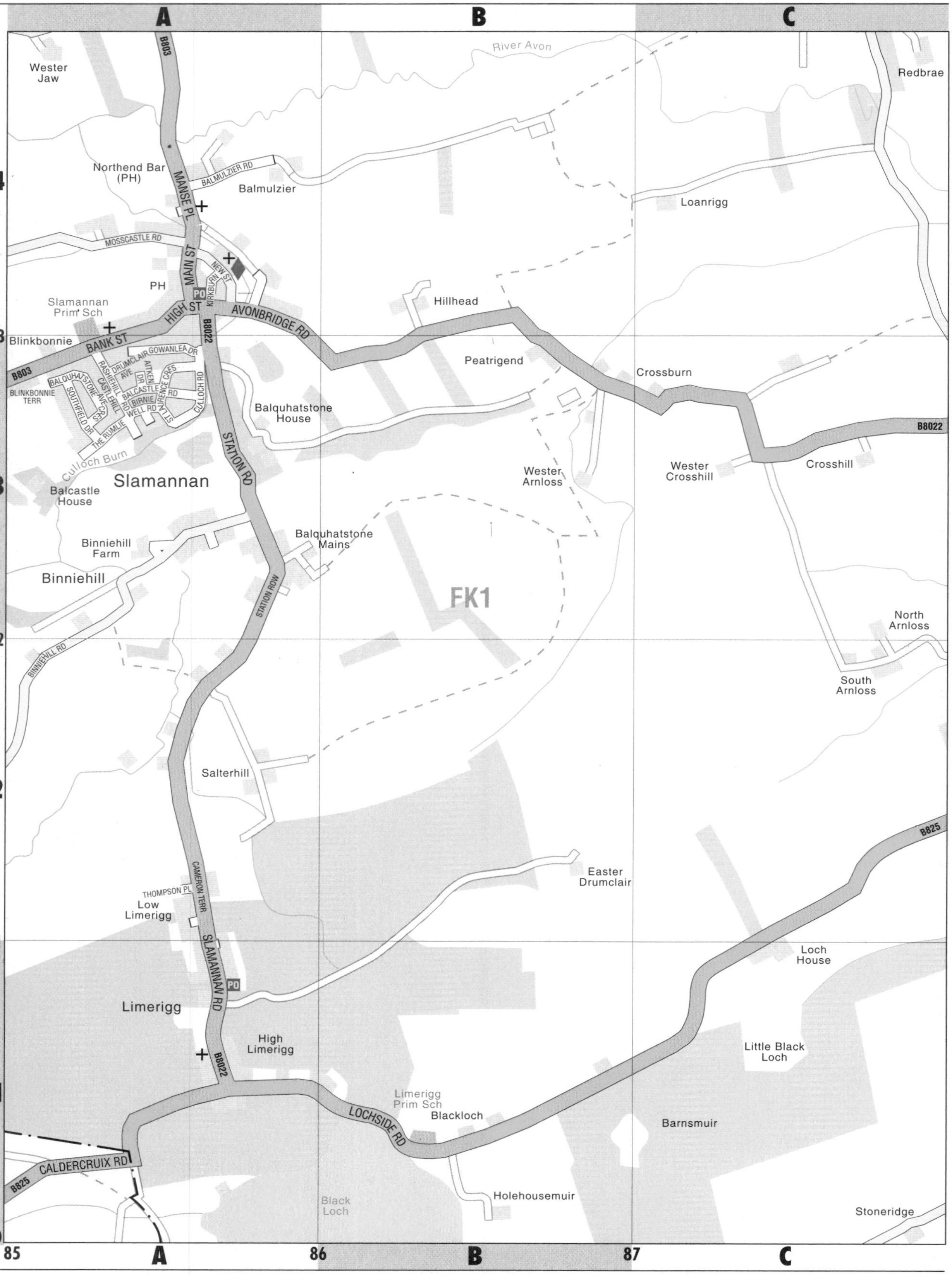
A
B
C
River Avon
Wester Jaw
Redbrae
B803
Northend Bar (PH)
BALMULZIER RD
Balmulzier
MANSE PL
Loanrigg
MOSSCASTLE RD
MAIN ST
NEW ST
KIRKBURN
PH
PO
Slamannan Prim Sch
HIGH ST
AVONBRIDGE RD
Hillhead
Blinkbonnie
BANK ST
B8022
GOWANLEA DR
DRUMCLAIR AVE
Peatrigend
Crossburn
BLINKBONNIE TERR
BALQUHATSTONE CRES
SOUTHFIELD DR
CASTLEHILL RD
RASHIEHILL RD
AITKEN DR
BALCASTLE RD
BIRNIE RD
WELL RD
ST LAURENCE CRES
CULLOCH RD
THE RUMLIE
Balquhatstone House
STATION RD
Culloch Burn
Slamannan
Balcastle House
Wester Arnloss
Wester Crosshill
Crosshill
Balquhatstone Mains
Binniehill Farm
Binniehill
FK1
STATION ROW
North Arnloss
BINNIEHILL RD
South Arnloss
Salterhill
B825
Easter Drumclair
THOMPSON PL
CAMERON TERR
Low Limerigg
SLAMANNAN RD
Loch House
Limerigg
High Limerigg
Little Black Loch
Limerigg Prim Sch
LOCHSIDE RD
Blackloch
Barnsmuir
CALDERCRUIX RD
Holehousemuir
Black Loch
Stoneridge
4
73
3
72
2
71
1
70
85
86
87

D E F

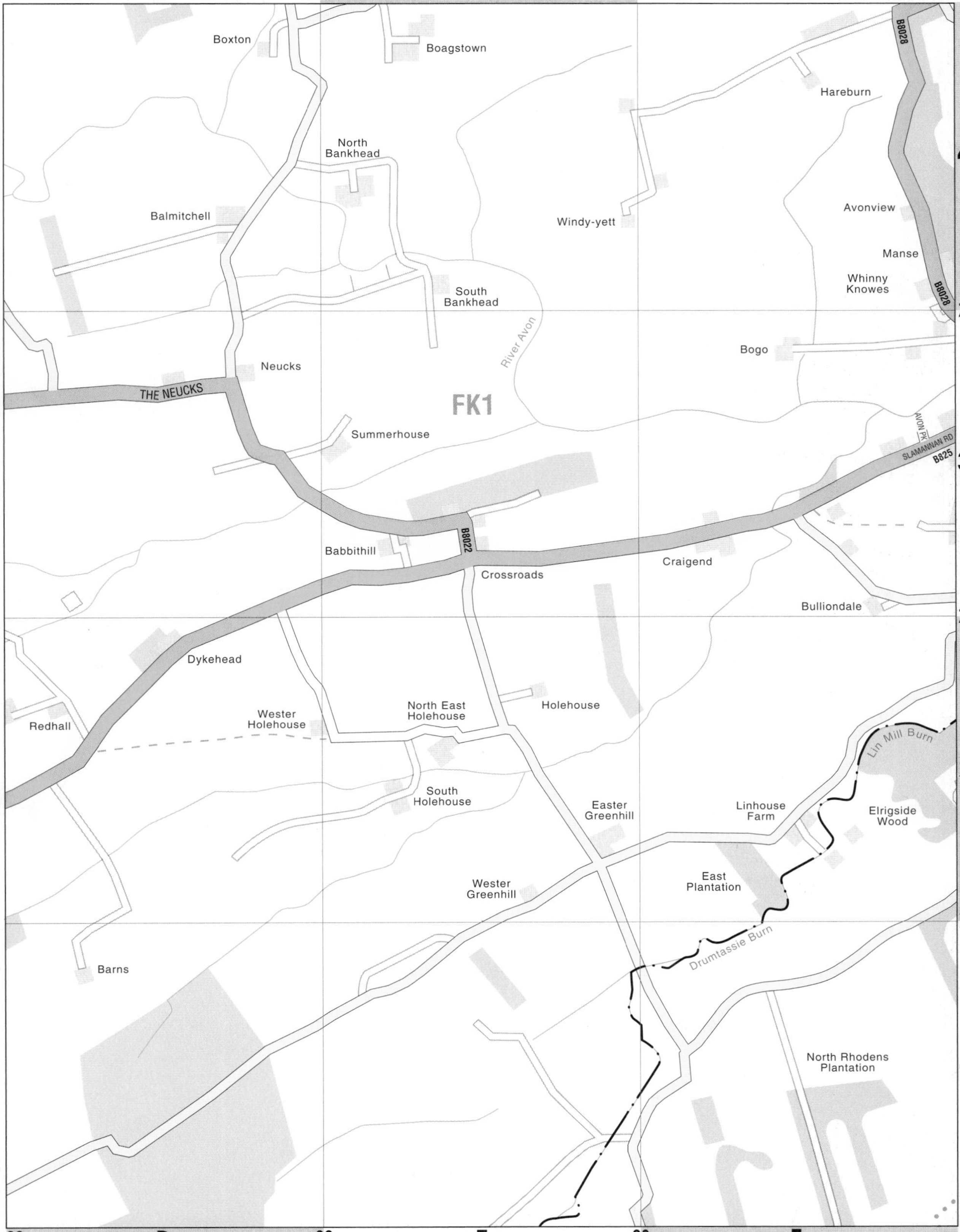
Boxton
Boagstown
Hareburn
B8028
North
Bankhead
Balmitchell
Windy-yett
Avonview
Manse
Whinny
Knowes
South
Bankhead
River Avon
Bogo
Neucks
THE NEUCKS
FK1
AVON PK
SLAMANNAN RD
B825
Summerhouse
B8022
Babbithill
Craigend
Crossroads
Bulliondale
Dykehead
Holehouse
North East
Holehouse
Wester
Holehouse
Redhall
Lin Mill Burn
South
Holehouse
Easter
Greenhill
Linhouse
Farm
Elrigside
Wood
Wester
Greenhill
East
Plantation
Drumtassie Burn
Barns
North Rhodens
Plantation
4
73
3
72
2
71
1
70
88
89
90

D E F

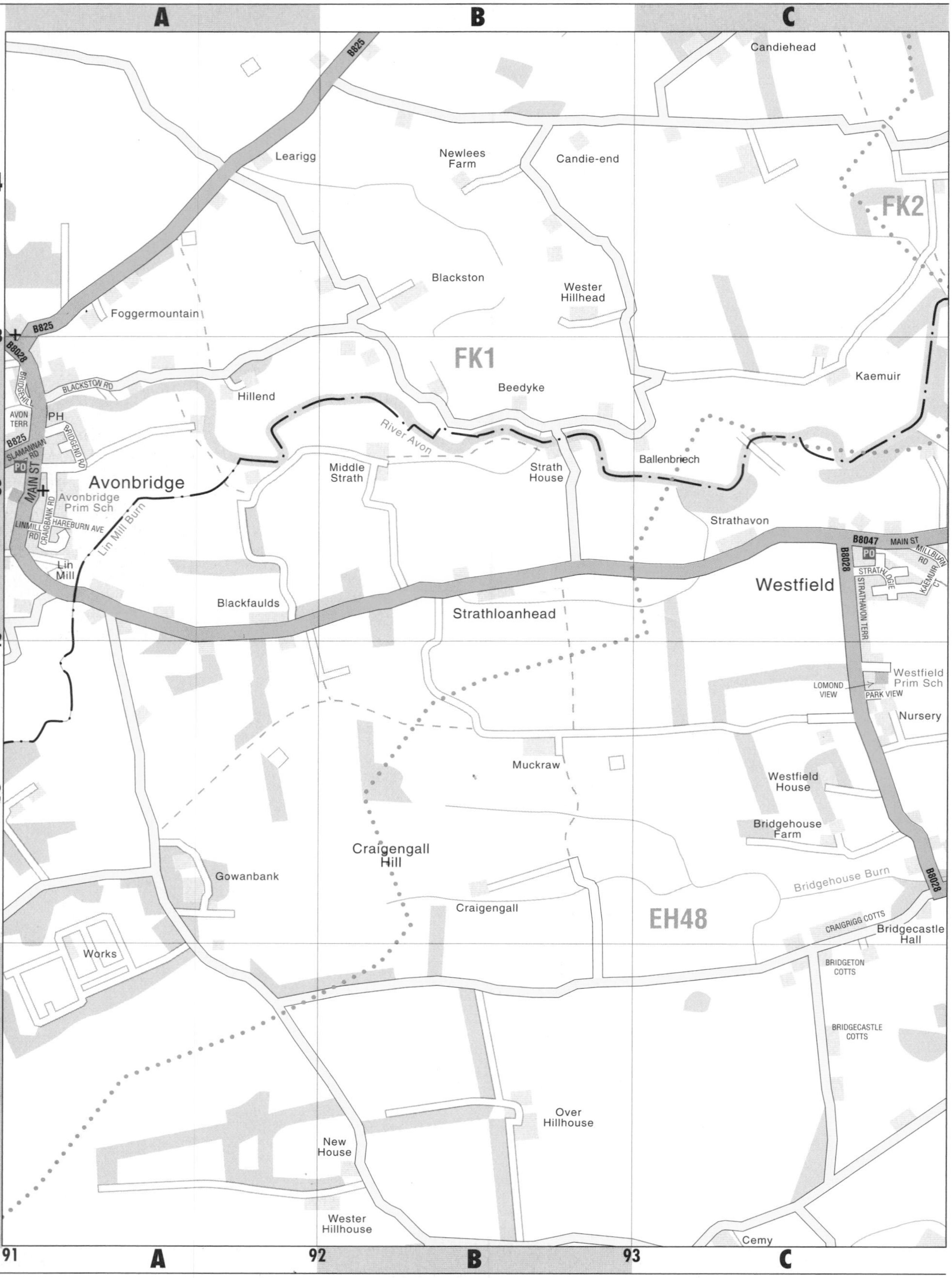

111
82

A
B
C

4

Candiehead

Learigg

Newlees Farm

Candie-end

FK2

Blackston

Wester Hillhead

Foggermountain

73

B825

B8028

FK1

Beedyke

Kaemuir

BRIDGEHILL

BLACKSTON RD

Hillend

River Avon

Ballenbriech

AVON TERR

PH

BRIDGEND RD

Middle Strath

Strath House

Strathavon

B8047

PO

MAIN ST

B825

SLAMANNAN RD

3

Avonbridge

B8028

STRATH AGE

Westfield

MILLBURN RD

KAEMUIR CT

PO

MAIN ST

Avonbridge Prim Sch

Lin Mill Burn

STRATHAVON TERR

CRAIGBANK RD

HAREBURN AVE

LINMILL RD

Lin Mill

Blackfaulds

Strathloanhead

LOMOND VIEW

PARK VIEW

Westfield Prim Sch

72

Nursery

Muckraw

Westfield House

2

Bridgehouse Farm

Gowanbank

Craigengall Hill

EH48

Bridgehouse Burn

B8028

Craigengall

CRAIGRIGG COTTS

Bridgecastle Hall

71

Works

BRIDGETON COTTS

Over Hillhouse

BRIDGECASTLE COTTS

1

New House

Wester Hillhouse

Cemy

70

91

A

92

B

93

C

111
143

83
114

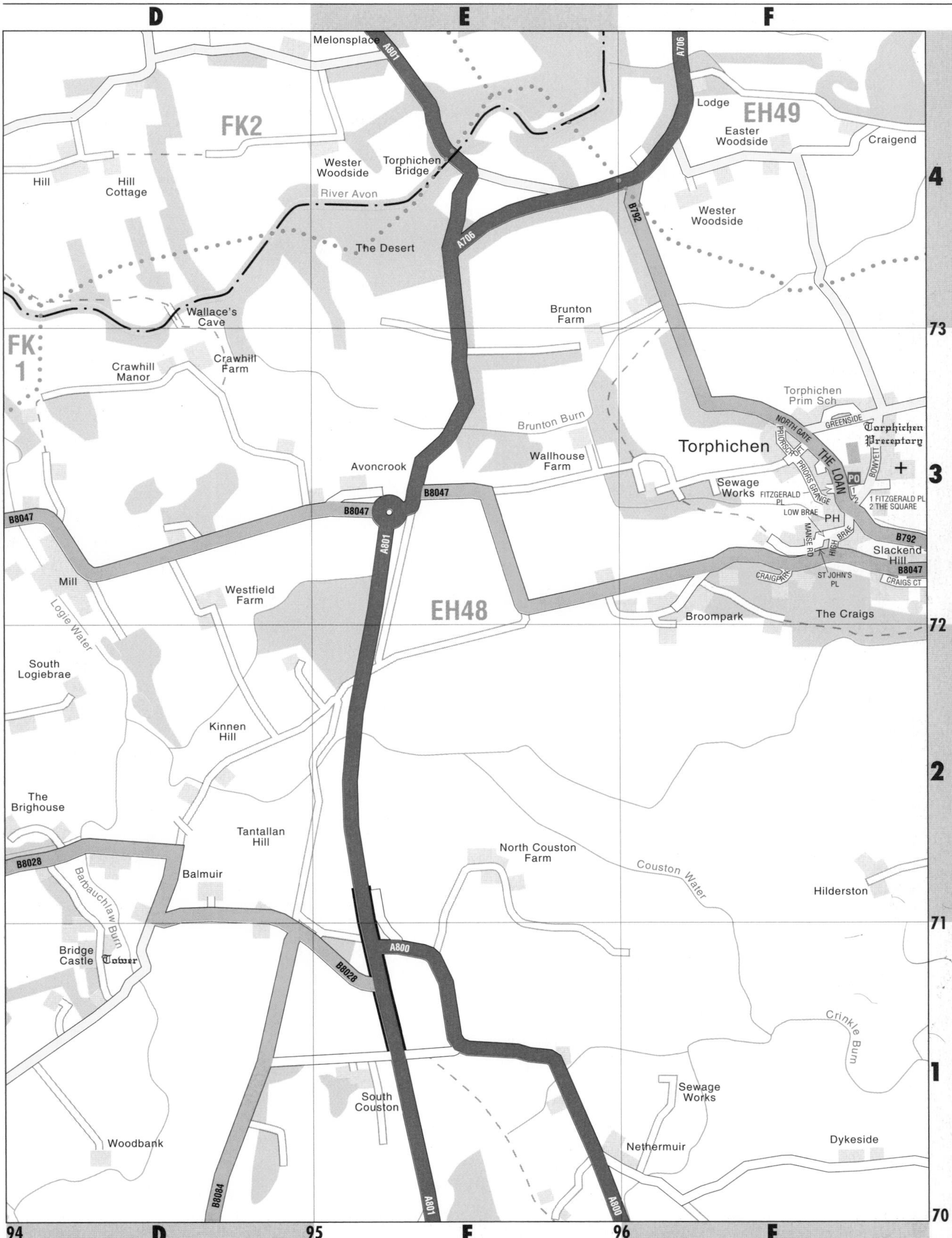
D
E
F
4
3
2
1
73
72
71
70
94
95
96
FK2
FK 1
EH49
EH48
Melonsplace
A801
A706
B792
Lodge
Easter Woodside
Craigend
Hill
Hill Cottage
Wester Woodside
Torphichen Bridge
River Avon
The Desert
Wester Woodside
Wallace's Cave
Brunton Farm
Crawhill Manor
Crawhill Farm
Torphichen Prim Sch
Brunton Burn
GREENSIDE
NORTH GATE
PRIORSCROFT
THE LOAN
PRIORS GRANGE
BOWYETT
Torphichen Preceptory
Torphichen
Wallhouse Farm
Avoncrook
PO
B8047
Sewage Works
FITZGERALD PL
LOW BRAE
PH
1 FITZGERALD PL
2 THE SQUARE
MANSE RD
HIGH BRAE
B792
Slackend Hill
B8047
Mill
CRAIGPARK
ST JOHN'S PL
CRAIGS CT
Westfield Farm
Logie Water
Broompark
The Craigs
South Logiebrae
Kinnen Hill
The Brighouse
Tantallan Hill
North Couston Farm
Couston Water
B8028
Balmuir
Barbauchlaw Burn
Hilderston
Bridge Castle
Tower
A800
B8028
Crinkle Burn
South Couston
Sewage Works
Woodbank
Nethermuir
Dykeside
B8084
A801
A800

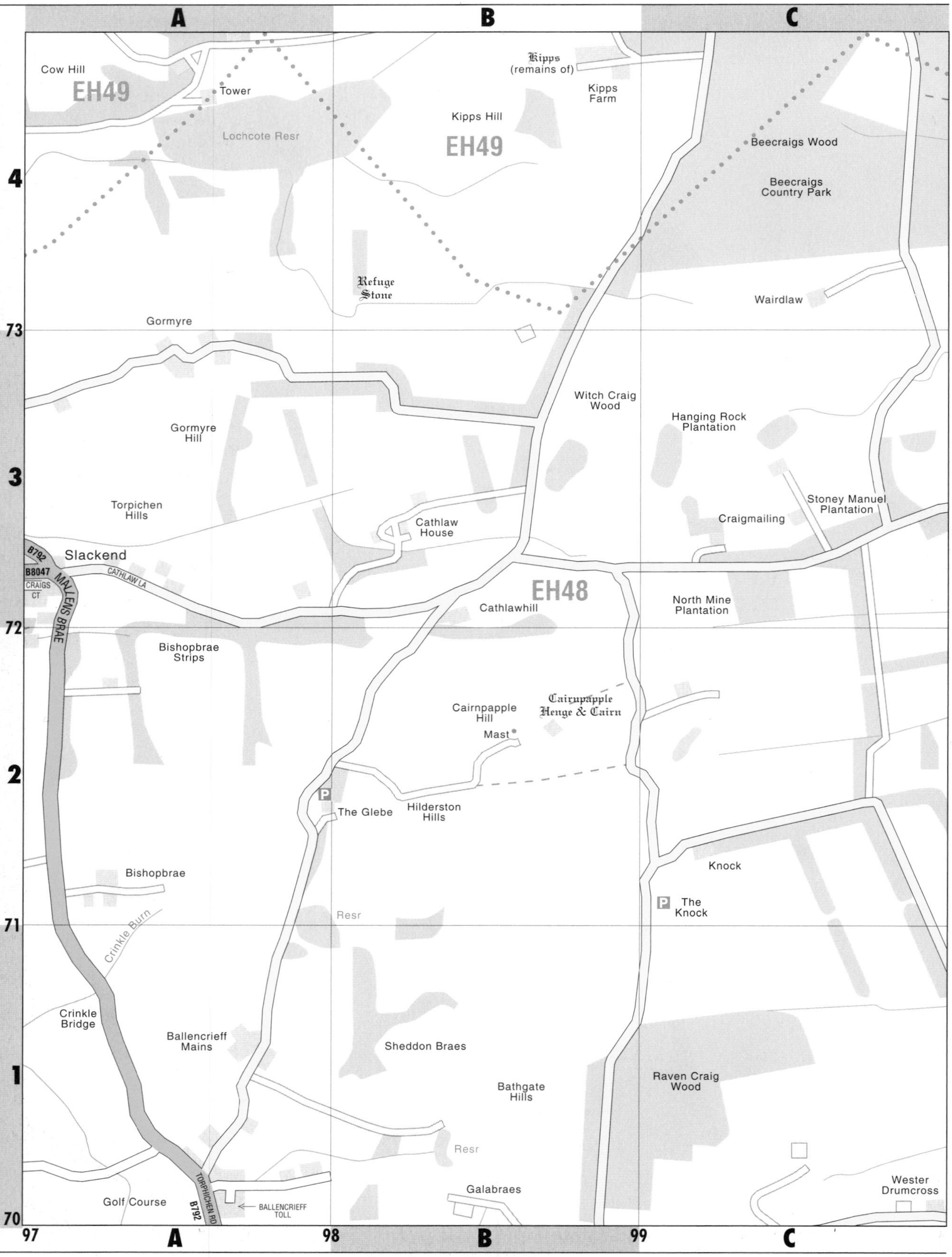

A   B   C

Cow Hill

EH49

Tower

Kipps
(remains of)

Kipps
Farm

Lochcote Resr

Kipps Hill

EH49

Beecraigs Wood

Beecraigs
Country Park

4

Refuge
Stone

Wairdlaw

Gormyre

73

Witch Craig
Wood

Hanging Rock
Plantation

Gormyre
Hill

3

Torpichen
Hills

Cathlaw
House

Craigmailing

Stoney Manuel
Plantation

Slackend

B792

B8047

CRAIGS
CT

CATHLAW LA

MALLENS BRAE

EH48

Cathlawhill

North Mine
Plantation

72

Bishopbrae
Strips

Cairnpapple
Hill

Cairnpapple
Henge & Cairn

Mast

2

P

The Glebe

Hilderston
Hills

Knock

Bishopbrae

P The
Knock

71

Resr

Crinkle Burn

Crinkle
Bridge

Ballencrieff
Mains

Sheddon Braes

Raven Craig
Wood

1

Bathgate
Hills

Resr

TORPICHEN RD

B792

Golf Course

BALLENCRIEFF
TOLL

Galabraes

Wester
Drumcross

70

97   A   98   B   99   C

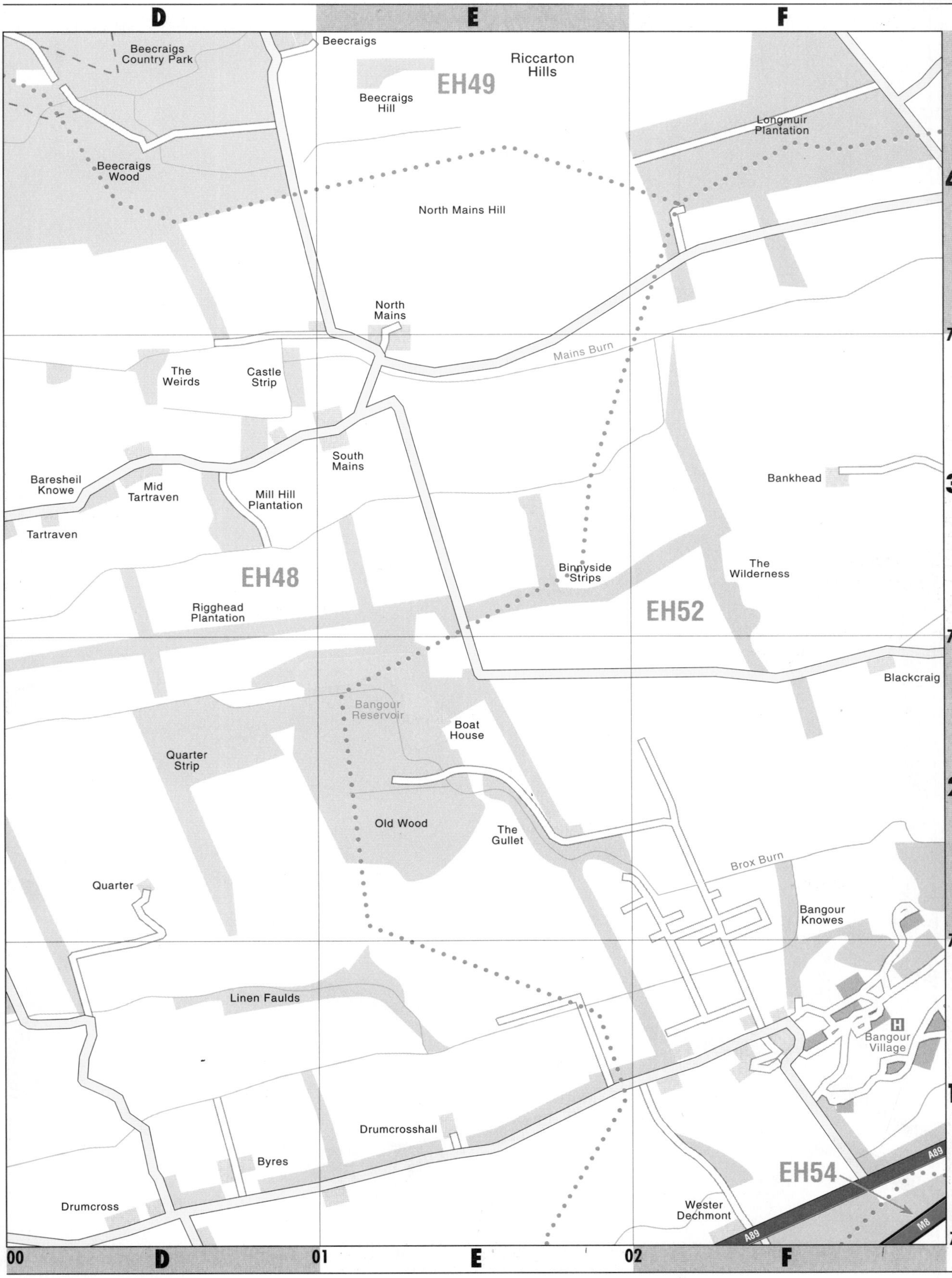

D
E
F

Beecraigs Country Park
Beecraigs
Beecraigs Hill
Riccarton Hills
EH49
Longmuir Plantation

Beecraigs Wood
North Mains Hill

4

North Mains
73
Mains Burn

The Weirds
Castle Strip

South Mains
Bankhead

Baresheil Knowe
Mid Tartraven
Mill Hill Plantation
The Wilderness
3

Tartraven

EH48
Binnyside Strips

Rigghead Plantation
EH52
72

Blackcraig

Bangour Reservoir
Boat House
Quarter Strip

2
Old Wood
The Gullet
Brox Burn

Quarter
Bangour Knowes
71

Linen Faulds

H
Bangour Village
1

Drumcrosshall

Byres
EH54
A89

Drumcross
Wester Dechmont
M8
70

115
86

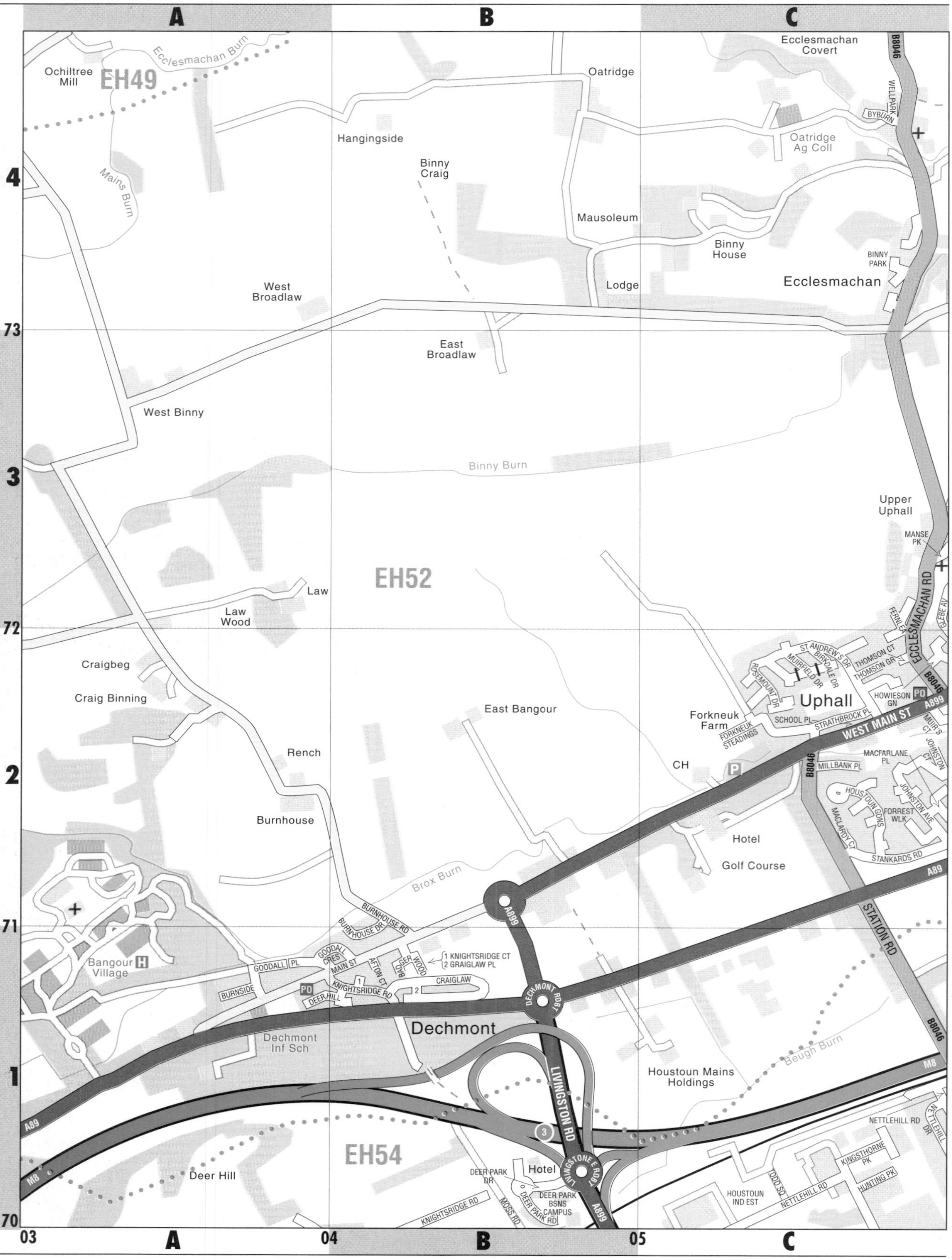
A
B
C
Ecclesmachan Covert
B8046
Ochiltree Mill
EH49
Ecclesmachan Burn
Oatridge
WELLPARK
BYBURN
Hangingside
Oatridge Ag Coll
Binny Craig
Mains Burn
4
Mausoleum
Binny House
BINNY PARK
West Broadlaw
Lodge
Ecclesmachan
73
East Broadlaw
West Binny
3
Binny Burn
Upper Uphall
MANSE PK
EH52
Law
Law Wood
ECCLESMACHAN RD
FERNLEA
GLEBE AV
72
Craigbeg
ST ANDREWS DR
BIRKDALE DR
MUIRFIELD DR
ROSEMOUNT DR
THOMSON CT
THOMSON GR
Craig Binning
HOWIESON GN
PO
Uphall
East Bangour
Forkneuk Farm
SCHOOL PL
STRATHBROCK PL
A899
WEST MAIN ST
MUIR'S CT
FORKNEUK STEADINGS
JOHNSTON CT
Rench
MACFARLANE PL
2
CH
P
B8046
MILLBANK PL
HOUSTOUN GDNS
JOHNSTON AVE
FORREST WLK
MACLARDY CT
Burnhouse
Hotel
STANKARDS RD
Golf Course
A89
Brox Burn
A899
STATION RD
BURNHOUSE RD
BURNHOUSE DR
71
GOODALL CRES
MAIN ST
AFTON CT
BADGER WOOD
1 KNIGHTSRIDGE CT
2 GRAIGLAW PL
GOODALL PL
Bangour Village
H
CRAIGLAW
BURNSIDE
PO
KNIGHTSRIDGE RD
DEER HILL
DECHMONT RDBT
Dechmont
Dechmont Inf Sch
B8046
LIVINGSTON RD
Beugh Burn
1
Houstoun Mains Holdings
M8
A89
3
NETTLEHILL RD
NETTLEHILL DR
EH54
LIVINGSTONE E RDBT
KINGSTHORNE PK
Hotel
DEER PARK DR
HUNTING PK
Deer Hill
M8
DEER PARK BSNS CAMPUS
DEER PARK RD
TODD SQ
HOUSTOUN IND EST
NETTLEHILL RD
KNIGHTSRIDGE RD
MOSS RD
A899
70
03
04
05

115
147

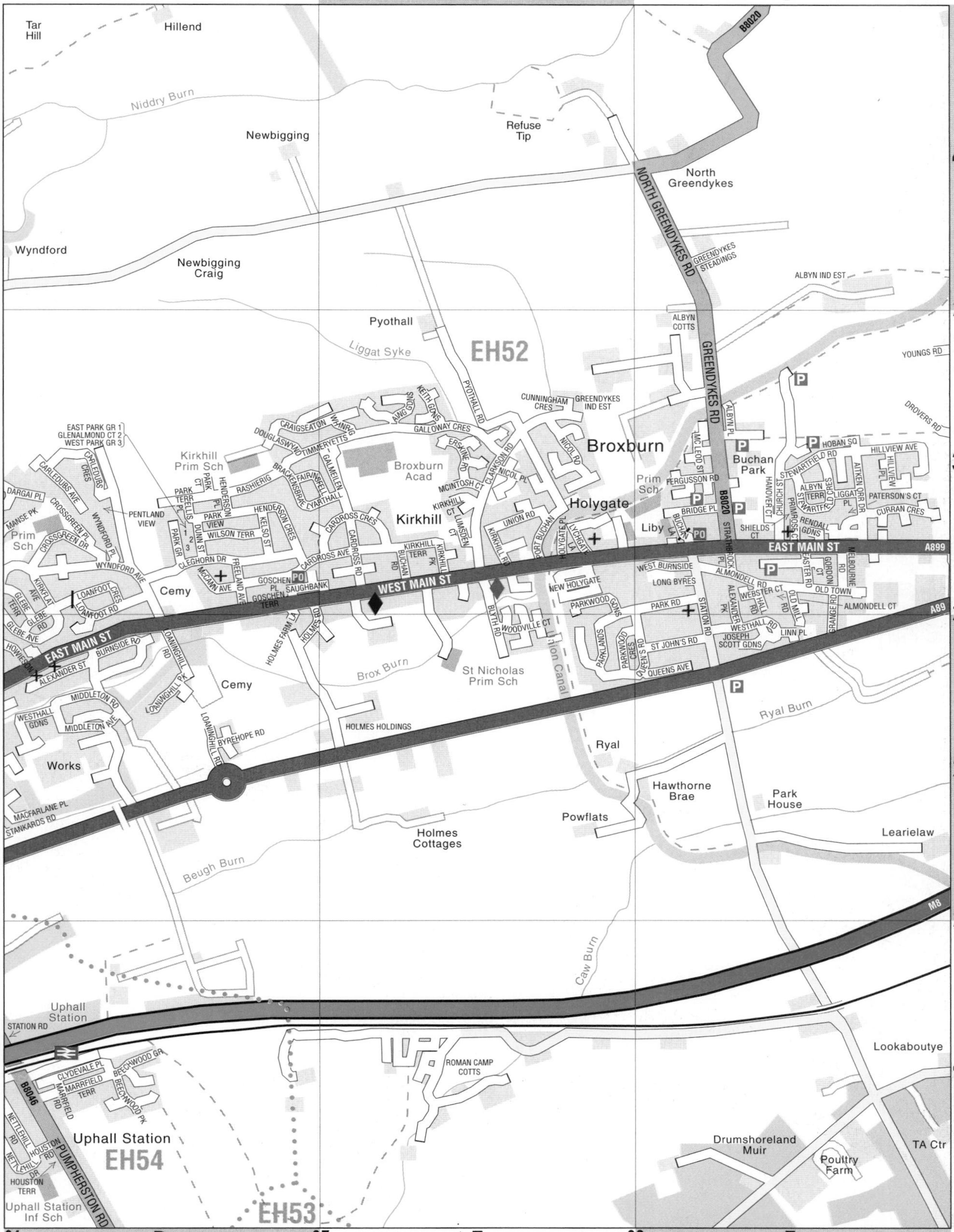

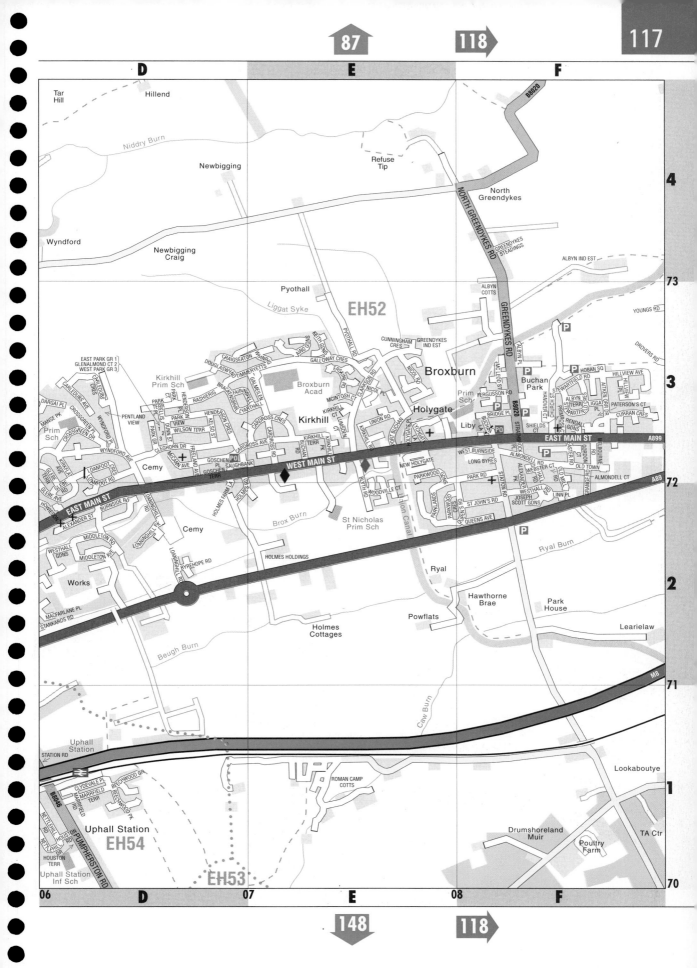

D
E
F

Tar Hill

Hillend

Niddry Burn

Newbigging

Refuse Tip

4

B8020

North Greendykes

NORTH GREENDYKES RD

Wyndford

Newbigging Craig

Pyothall

Liggat Syke

EH52

Albyn Cotts

GREENDYKES RD

ALBYN IND EST

73

YOUNGS RD

DROVERS RD

Cunningham Cres

GREENDYKES IND EST

Broxburn

Buchan Park

HOBAN SQ

HILLVIEW AVE

AITKEN DR

3

East Park Gr 1
Glenalmond Ct 2
West Park Gr 3

Craigseaton

Kirkhill Prim Sch

Douglaswd

Timmeryetts

Galmelen

Galloway Cres

Nicol Pl

Nicol Sq

Holygate

Prim Sch

FERGUSSON RD

STEWARTFIELD

ALBYN TERR

STEWARTFIELD

HANDVERE

RENDALL GDNS

CURRAN CRES

PATERSON'S CT

Dargai Pl

MANSE PK

CROSSGREEN DR

WYNDFORD AVE

PENTLAND VIEW

PARK GR

PARK TERR

PARK PL

CLEGHORN DR

HENDERSON ST

WILSON TERR

KELSO RD

RASHIERIG

BRACKENSBRAE

FAIRNSHELL

CYARTHALL

CARDROSS CRES

KIRKHILL TERR

KIRKHILL PL

CLUNSTEN

UNION RD

LYCHGATE

CLARKSON RD

KIRKHILL

Kirkhill

Prim Sch

Glebe Ave

GLEBE AVE

GLEBE RD

KIRKLA AVE

LOANFOOT RD

LOANFOOT PL

McCAIN AVE

GOSCHEN PL

GOSCHEN TERR

SAUGHBANK

CARDROSS AVE

FREELAND PL

HOLMES FARM LA

McINTOSH CT

PORT BUCHAN

BUCHAN CT

BLYTH RD

WOODVILLE CT

West Burnside

New Holygate

PARKWOOD GDNS

PARKWOOD

PARKWOOD

West Burnside

LONG BYRES

Park Rd

ALMONDELL RD

WEBSTER CT

OLD MILL

ALEXANDER PK

ALMONDELL CT

MELBOURNE

GORDON DR

FOSTER RD

OLD TOWN

A899

Prim Sch

Cemy

WEST MAIN ST

Liby

PO

STRATHBROCK

EAST MAIN ST

A899

SHIELDS CT

PRIMROSE CT

Cemy

EAST MAIN ST

ALEXANDER ST

BURNSIDE RD

DANINGHILL RD

HOLMES FARM LA

Brox Burn

St Nicholas Prim Sch

ST JOHN'S RD

JOSEPH SCOTT GDNS

WESTHALL

LINN PL

72

A89

WESTHALL GDNS

MIDDLETON RD

MIDDLETON

DANINGHILL PK

LONINGHILL RD

Cemy

Holmes Holdings

PEEL'S RD

QUEENS AVE

Works

BYREHOPE RD

LONINGHILL RD

Ryal

Hawthorne Brae

Ryal Burn

Park House

Learielaw

2

MACFARLANE PL

STANKARDS RD

Beugh Burn

Holmes Cottages

Powflats

71

Caw Burn

M8

Uphall Station

STATION RD

Roman Camp Cotts

Lookaboutye

1

B8046

CLYDEVALE PL

MARRFIELD TERR

MARRFIELD RD

BEECHWOOD GR

BEECHWOOD PK

Drumshoreland Muir

TA Ctr

NETTLEHILL RD

HOUSTON RD

PUMPHERSTON RD

Uphall Station

EH54

HOUSTON TERR

Uphall Station Inf Sch

EH53

Poultry Farm

70

06
D
07
E
08
F

117
88

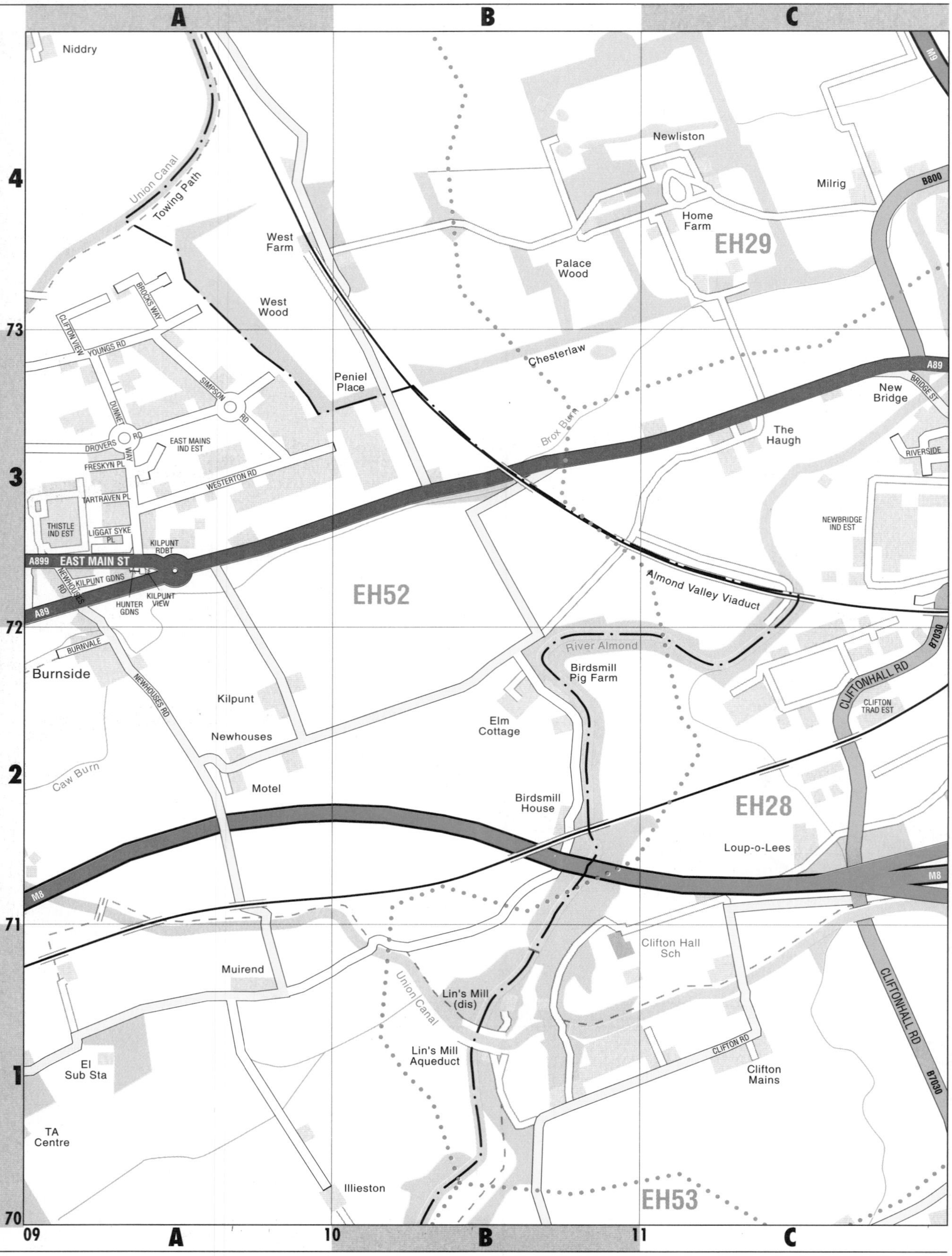

A **B** **C**

Niddry

Union Canal

Towing Path

West Farm

West Wood

CLIFTON VIEW

YOUNGS RD

BROCKS WAY

SIMPSON RD

DUNNE RD

Peniel Place

DROVERS WAY

FRESKYN PL

EAST MAINS IND EST

WESTERTON RD

TARTRAVEN PL

THISTLE IND EST

LIGGAT SYKE PL

KILPUNT RDBT

A899 **EAST MAIN ST**

NEWHOUSES RD

KILPUNT GDNS

HUNTER GDNS

KILPUNT VIEW

A89

Newliston

Milrig

Home Farm

Palace Wood

EH29

Chesterlaw

Brox Burn

The Haugh

A89

New Bridge

BRIDGE ST

RIVERSIDE

NEWBRIDGE IND EST

Almond Valley Viaduct

EH52

River Almond

Birdsmill Pig Farm

Elm Cottage

Birdsmill House

EH28

Loup-o-Lees

CLIFTONHALL RD

CLIFTON TRAD EST

B7030

Burnvale

Burnside

NEWHOUSES RD

Kilpunt

Newhouses

Caw Burn

Motel

M8

M8

Muirend

Union Canal

Lin's Mill (dis)

Lin's Mill Aqueduct

Clifton Hall Sch

CLIFTON RD

CLIFTON RD

Clifton Mains

CLIFTONHALL RD

B7030

El Sub Sta

TA Centre

Illieston

EH53

4

73

3

72

2

71

1

70

09 **A** 10 **B** 11 **C**

89
120

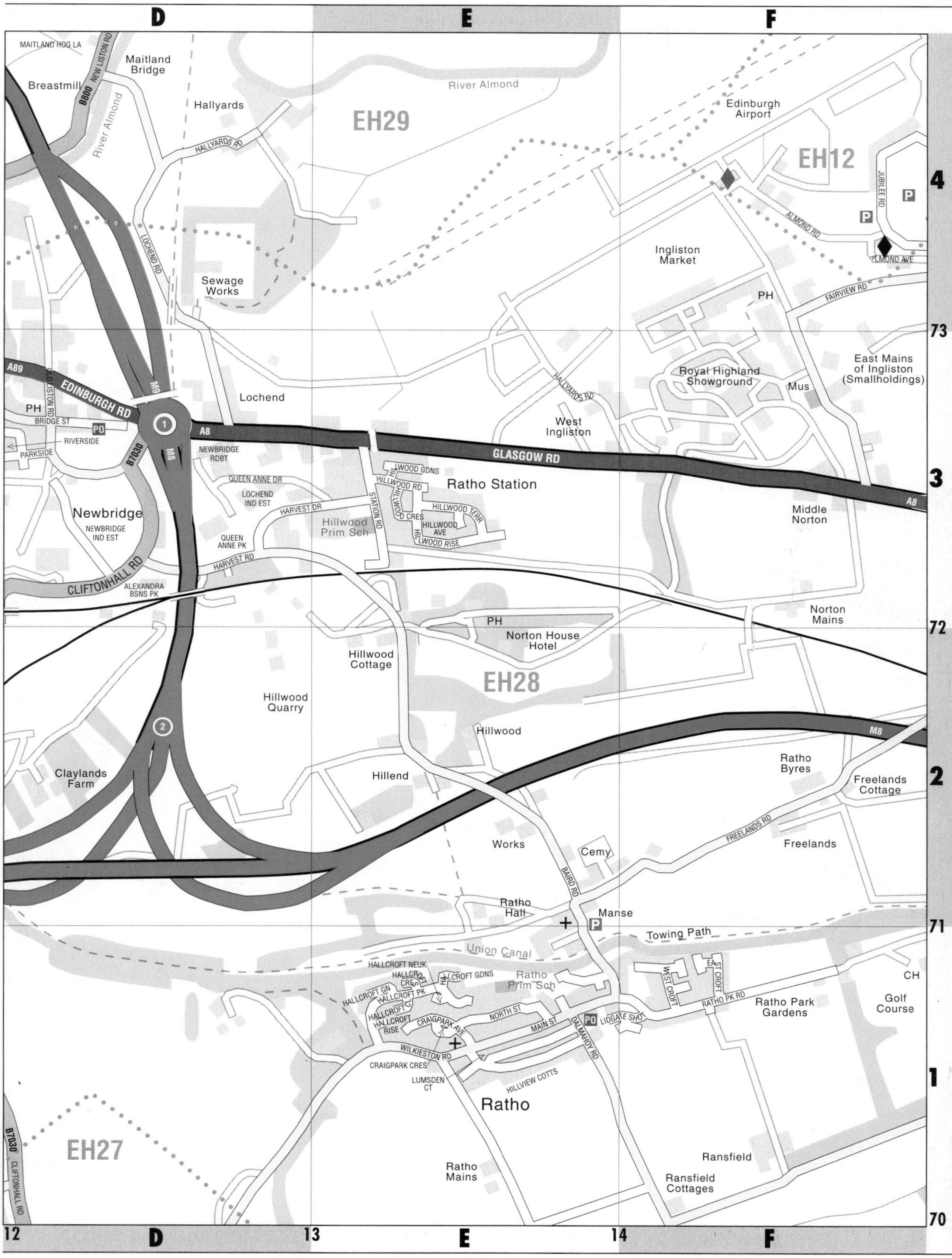
D
E
F
MAITLAND HOG LA
NEW LISTON RD
Maitland Bridge
Breastmill
B800
River Almond
Hallyards
River Almond
EH29
Edinburgh Airport
EH12
HALLYARDS RD
JUBILEE RD
P
P
ALMOND RD
LOCHEND RD
Ingliston Market
ALMOND AVE
Sewage Works
PH
FAIRVIEW RD
73
A89
OLD LISTON RD
EDINBURGH RD
M9
Lochend
HALLYARDS RD
Royal Highland Showground
East Mains of Ingliston (Smallholdings)
Mus
PH
BRIDGE ST
PO
A8
West Ingliston
RIVERSIDE
PARKSIDE
B7030
M8
NEWBRIDGE RDBT
GLASGOW RD
HILLWOOD GDNS
QUEEN ANNE DR
HILLWOOD RD
Ratho Station
LOCHEND IND EST
HARVEST DR
HILLWOOD CRES
HILLWOOD TERR
Newbridge
STATION RD
Hillwood Prim Sch
HILLWOOD AVE
HILLWOOD RISE
A8
Middle Norton
NEWBRIDGE IND EST
QUEEN ANNE PK
HARVEST RD
CLIFTONHALL RD
ALEXANDRA BSNS PK
Norton Mains
PH
Norton House Hotel
72
Hillwood Cottage
Hillwood Quarry
EH28
Hillwood
M8
Ratho Byres
Claylands Farm
Hillend
Freelands Cottage
2
FREELANDS RD
Works
Cemy
Freelands
BAIRD RD
Ratho Hall
Manse
P
71
Towing Path
Union Canal
HALLCROFT NEUK
HALLCROFT CRES
HALLCROFT GDNS
Ratho Prim Sch
EAST CROFT
WEST CROFT
CH
HALLCROFT GN
HALLCROFT PK
RATHO PK RD
Ratho Park Gardens
Golf Course
HALLCROFT CL
HALLCROFT RISE
CRAIGPARK AVE
NORTH ST
MAIN ST
PO
LIDGATE SHOT
DALMAHOY RD
WILKIESTON RD
CRAIGPARK CRES
LUMSDEN CT
HILLVIEW COTTS
1
Ratho
B7030
CLIFTONHALL RD
EH27
Ransfield
Ratho Mains
Ransfield Cottages
70
12
D
13
E
14
F
3
4

150
120

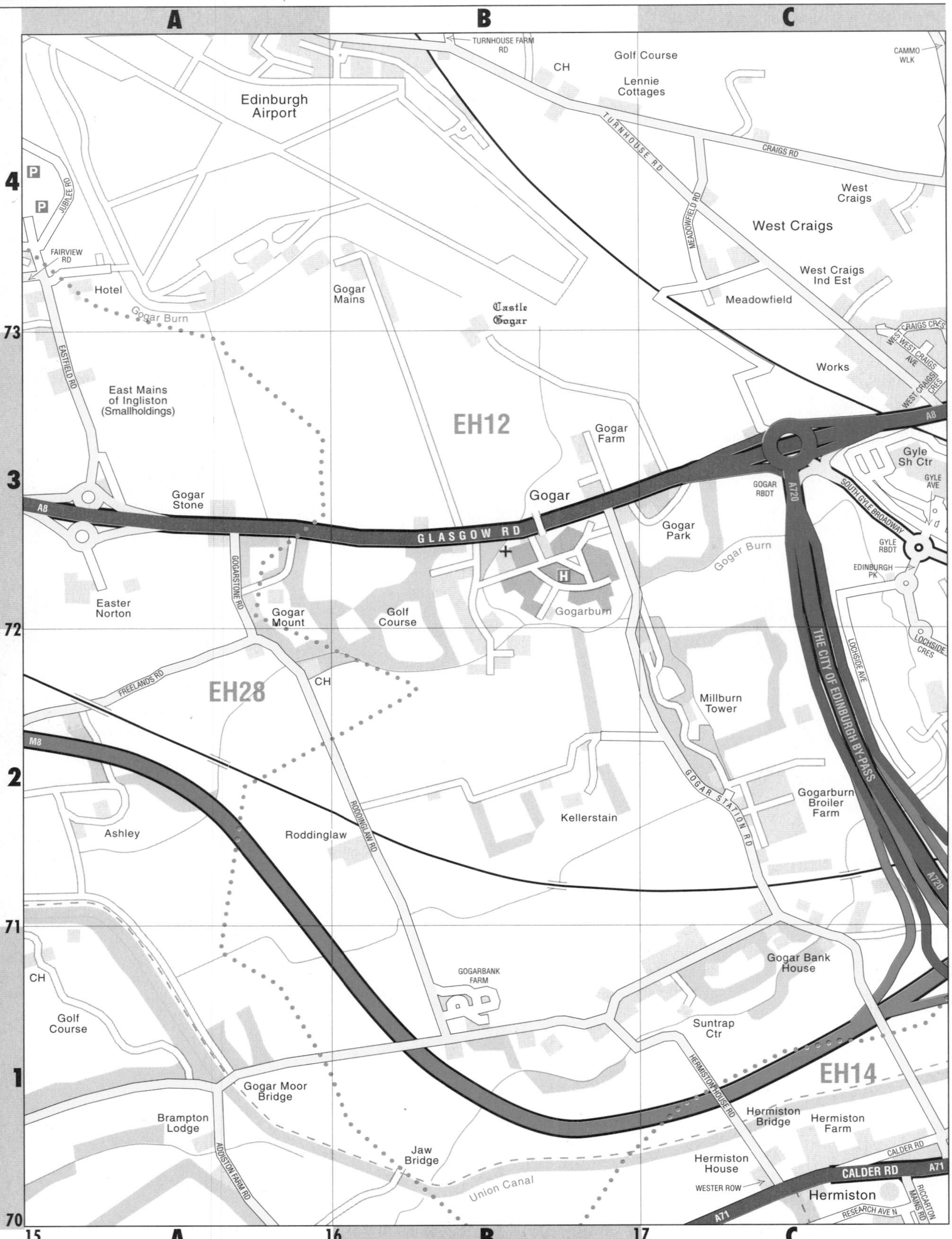

A   B   C

TURNHOUSE FARM RD

CH

Golf Course

Lennie Cottages

CAMMO WLK

TURNHOUSE RD

CRAIGS RD

Edinburgh Airport

MEADOWFIELD RD

West Craigs

West Craigs Ind Est

West Craigs

4

P

P

FAIRVIEW RD

JUBILEE RD

Hotel

Gogar Burn

Gogar Mains

Castle Gogar

Meadowfield

Works

W12 WEST CRAIGS AVE
WEST CRAIGS CRES
WEST CRAIGS CRES

A8

73

EASTFIELD RD

East Mains of Ingliston (Smallholdings)

EH12

Gogar Farm

Gogar

Gogar Park

Gogar RBDT

A720

SOUTH GYLE BROADWAY

Gyle Sh Ctr

GYLE AVE

3

A8

Gogar Stone

GOGARSTONE RD

GLASGOW RD

+

H

Gogarburn

Gogar Burn

GYLE RBDT

EDINBURGH PK

Edinburgh Pk

LOCHSIDE CRES

Easter Norton

Gogar Mount

Golf Course

CH

Millburn Tower

THE CITY OF EDINBURGH BY-PASS

LOCHSIDE AVE

72

EH28

FREELANDS RD

RODDINGLAW RD

GOGAR STATION RD

Gogarburn Broiler Farm

2

M8

Ashley

Roddinglaw

Kellerstain

A720

71

CH

Golf Course

GOGARBANK FARM

Gogar Bank House

Suntrap Ctr

HERMISTON HOUSE RD

EH14

1

Gogar Moor Bridge

Brampton Lodge

ADDISTON FARM RD

Jaw Bridge

Union Canal

Hermiston Bridge

Hermiston Farm

CALDER RD

Hermiston House

WESTER ROW

CALDER RD   A71

Hermiston

RICCARTON MAINS RD

A71

RESEARCH AVE N

70

15   A   16   B   17   C

91
122

D E F

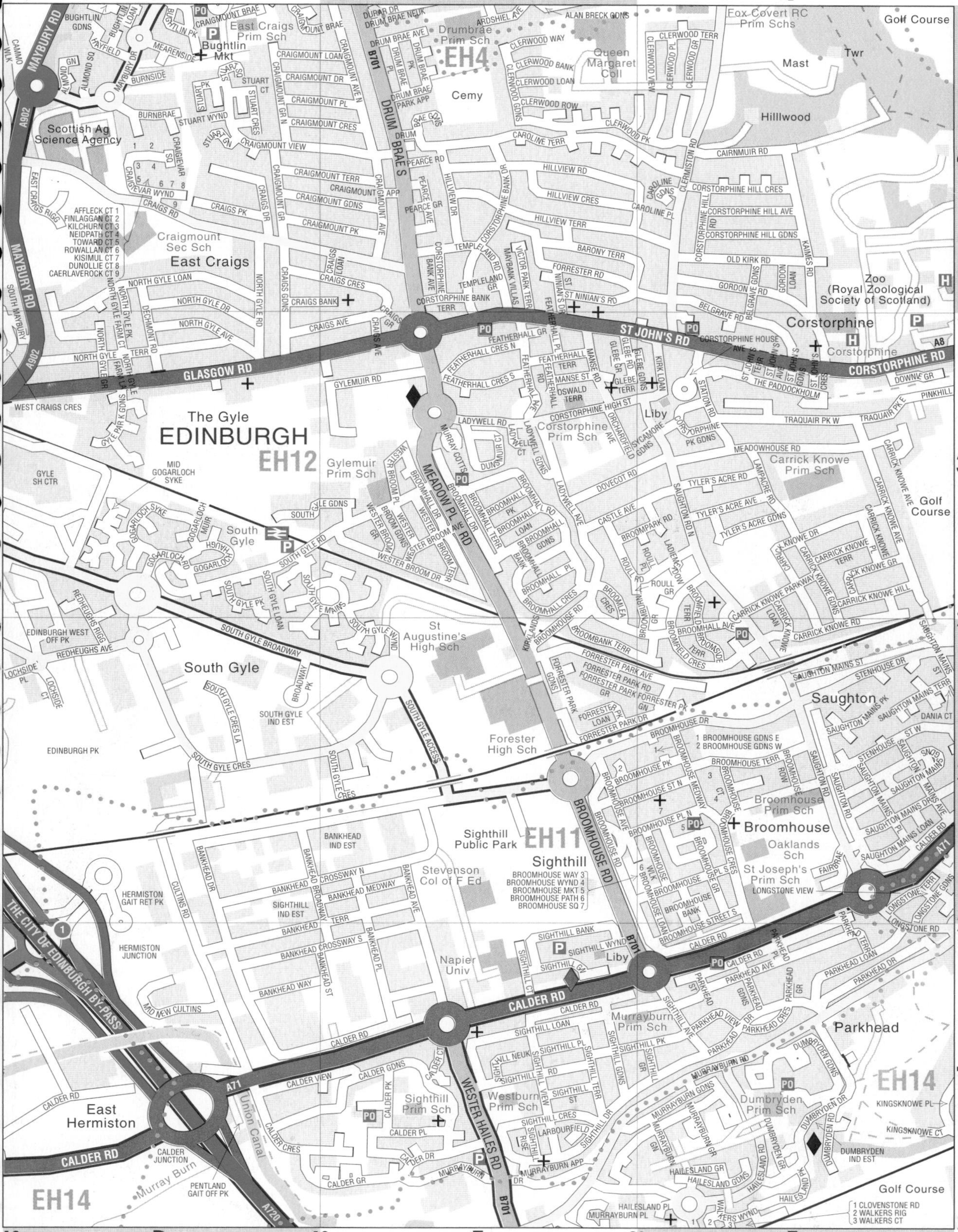
Golf Course
Fox Covert RC Prim Sch
Queen Margaret Coll
Drumbrae Prim Sch
EH4
Cemy
Mast
Twr
Hilllwood
Bughtlin Mkt
East Craigs Prim Sch
Scottish Ag Science Agency
Craigmount Sec Sch
East Craigs
Zoo (Royal Zoological Society of Scotland)
Corstorphine
GLASGOW RD
ST JOHN'S RD
CORSTORPHINE RD
MAYBURY RD
DRUM BRAES
The Gyle
EDINBURGH
EH12
Gylemuir Prim Sch
Corstorphine Prim Sch
Carrick Knowe Prim Sch
Liby
GYLE SH CTR
South Gyle
St Augustine's High Sch
MEADOW PL RD
BROOMHOUSE RD
Forester High Sch
Saughton
EDINBURGH PK
SOUTH GYLE IND EST
Sighthill Public Park
EH11
Sighthill
Broomhouse
Broomhouse Prim Sch
Oaklands Sch
St Joseph's Prim Sch
Stevenson Col of F Ed
Napier Univ
BANKHEAD IND EST
SIGHTHILL IND EST
HERMISTON GAIT RET PK
HERMISTON JUNCTION
THE CITY OF EDINBURGH BY-PASS
CALDER RD
Murrayburn Prim Sch
Parkhead
Sighthill Prim Sch
Westburn Prim Sch
Dumbryden Prim Sch
DUMBRYDEN IND EST
EH14
East Hermiston
CALDER JUNCTION
PENTLAND GAIT OFF PK
Union Canal
Murray Burn
WESTER HAILES RD
Golf Course
1 CLOVENSTONE RD
2 WALKERS RIG
3 WALKERS CT
4
73
3
72
2
71
1
70
18
19
20

D E F

152
122

121
92

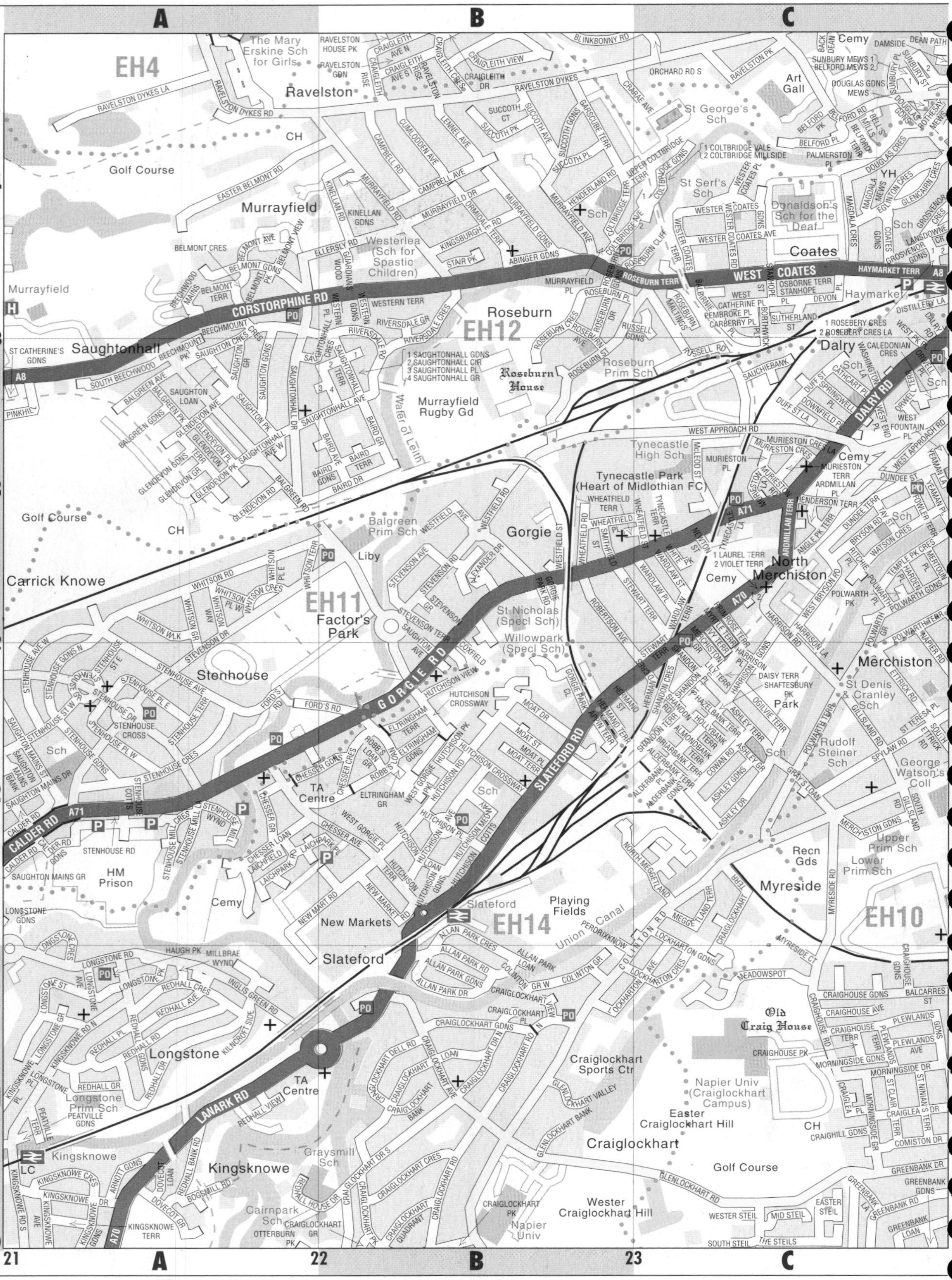
A
B
C
4
73
3
72
2
71
1
70
21
22
23
EH4
EH12
EH11
EH14
EH10
The Mary Erskine Sch for Girls
Ravelston
RAVELSTON DYKES LA
RAVELSTON DYKES RD
RAVELSTON DYKES
CH
Golf Course
EASTER BELMONT RD
Murrayfield
BELMONT CRES
BELMONT AVE
BELMONT GDNS
BELMONT VIEW
Murrayfield
H
Saughtonhall
CORSTORPHINE RD
A8
PO
BEECHMOUNT CRES
ST CATHERINE'S GDNS
SOUTH BEECHWOOD
BALGREEN AVE
BALGREEN GDNS
BALGREEN PK
GLENDEVON AVE
GLENDEVON GDNS
SAUGHTON LOAN
SAUGHTON PK
SAUGHTONHALL DR
SAUGHTONHALL AVE
PINKHILL
WESTERN TERR
RIVERSDALE GR
RIVERSDALE CRES
1 SAUGHTONHALL GDNS
2 SAUGHTONHALL CIR
3 SAUGHTONHALL PL
4 SAUGHTONHALL GR
Water of Leith
Murrayfield Rugby Gd
BAIRD AVE
BAIRD GDNS
BAIRD DR
BAIRD TERR
BAIRD GR
BALGREEN RD
GLENDEVON PK
CAMPBELL RD
CAMPBELL AVE
CUMLODDEN AVE
MURRAYFIELD RD
MURRAYFIELD DR
KINELLAN RD
KINELLAN GDNS
Westerlea (Sch for Spastic Children)
ELLERSLY RD
ABINGER GDNS
KINGSBURGH RD
STAIR PK
Roseburn
Roseburn House
ROSEBURN TERR
ROSEBURN CRES
Roseburn Prim Sch
RUSSELL GDNS
RUSSELL RD
SUCCOTH CT
SUCCOTH PK
SUCCOTH AVE
SUCCOTH PL
SUCCOTH GDNS
GARSCUBE TERR
CRAIGLEITH VIEW
CRAIGLEITH DR
CRAIGLEITH RISE
RAVELSTON HOUSE PK
RAVELSTON GDN
BLINKBONNY RD
ORCHARD RD S
St George's Sch
RAVELSTON PK
Art Gall
Cemy
DAMSIDE
DEAN PATH
SUNBURY MEWS
BELFORD MEWS
DOUGLAS GDNS MEWS
BELFORD RD
BELFORD PK
PALMERSTON PL
1 COLTBRIDGE VALE
2 COLTBRIDGE MILLSIDE
St Serf's Sch
WESTER COATES
Donaldson's Sch for the Deaf
COATES GDNS
WESTER COATES AVE
Coates
WEST COATES
HAYMARKET TERR
Haymarket
DISTILLERY LA
P
YH
Sch
MAGDALA CRES
GROSVENOR CRES
LANSDOWNE CRES
OSBORNE TERR
STANHOPE PL
WEST CATHERINE PL
PEMBROKE PL
CARBERRY PL
SUTHERLAND ST
DEVON PL
1 ROSEBERY CRES
2 ROSEBERY CRES LA
Dalry
CALEDONIAN CRES
DALRY RD
SAUCHIEBANK
DUFF ST
DUFF ST LA
DOWNFIELD PL
WEST APPROACH RD
Tynecastle High Sch
Tynecastle Park (Heart of Midlothian FC)
MURIESTON PL
MURIESTON CRES
MURIESTON TERR
Cemy
WHEATFIELD TERR
WHEATFIELD PL
WHEATFIELD RD
TYNECASTLE TERR
ARDMILLAN TERR
ARDMILLAN PL
HENDERSON TERR
DUNDEE ST
DUNDEE TERR
BRYSON RD
Sch
WATSON CRES
A71
Gorgie
1 LAUREL TERR
2 VIOLET TERR
Cemy
North Merchiston
A70
POLWARTH PK
POLWARTH GDNS
HARRISON RD
HARRISON LA
Merchiston
St Denis & Cranley Sch
DAISY TERR
SHAFTESBURY PK
Park
Rudolf Steiner Sch
George Watson's Coll
SPYLAW RD
Balgreen Prim Sch
Liby
WESTFIELD AVE
WESTFIELD RD
STEVENSON AVE
STEVENSON RD
STEVENSON GR
STEVENSON TERR
Factor's Park
St Nicholas (Specl Sch)
Willowpark (Specl Sch)
ROBERTSON AVE
STEWART TERR
WARDLAW PL
WARDLAW ST
Carrick Knowe
WHITSON RD
WHITSON CRES
WHITSON WALK
WHITSON GR
WHITSON WAY
STEVENSON DR
Stenhouse
STENHOUSE AVE
STENHOUSE CROSS
STENHOUSE GDNS
STENHOUSE CRES
STENHOUSE TERR
SAUGHTON MAINS DR
Sch
GORGIE RD
HUTCHISON VIEW
HUTCHISON CROSSWAY
FORD'S RD
ELTRINGHAM TERR
ELTRINGHAM GR
TA Centre
CHESSER GDNS
CHESSER CRES
CHESSER AVE
CHESSER GR
WEST GORGIE PL
MOAT DR
MOAT ST
MOAT PL
MOAT TERR
Sch
SLATEFORD RD
SHANDON CRES
SHANDON TERR
ASHLEY TERR
ASHLEY DR
GRAY'S LOAN
CALDER RD
STENHOUSE RD
HM Prison
SAUGHTON MAINS GR
Cemy
New Markets
NEW MART RD
Slateford
Playing Fields
Union Canal
Recn Gds
Myreside
Upper Prim Sch
Lower Prim Sch
MERCHISTON GDNS
LONGSTONE GDNS
LONGSTONE RD
HAUGH PK
MILLBRAE WYND
LONGSTONE ST
LONGSTONE PK
REDHALL CRES
REDHALL AVE
INGLIS GREEN RD
KILNCROFT SIDE
Slateford
ALLAN PARK CRES
ALLAN PARK RD
ALLAN PARK DR
COLINTON RD
COLINTON GR
CRAIGLOCKHART GDNS
LOCKHARTON AVE
LOCKHARTON CRES
MEADOWSPOT
MYRESIDE CT
CRAIGHOUSE GDNS
BALCARRES ST
Old Craig House
CRAIGHOUSE AVE
CRAIGHOUSE TERR
PLEWLANDS AVE
MORNINGSIDE DR
Longstone
REDHALL GR
Longstone Prim Sch
PEATVILLE GDNS
TA Centre
LANARK RD
Craiglockhart Sports Ctr
Napier Univ (Craiglockhart Campus)
Easter Craiglockhart Hill
Craiglockhart
CH
CRAIGHILL GDNS
COMISTON DR
Golf Course
GREENBANK DR
Kingsknowe
LC
Kingsknowe
Graysmill Sch
Cairnpark Sch
KINGSKNOWE CRES
KINGSKNOWE RD S
KINGSKNOWE TERR
DOVECOT GR
OTTERBURN PK
CRAIGLOCKHART DR S
CRAIGLOCKHART PK
Napier Univ
Wester Craiglockhart Hill
GLENLOCKHART RD
WESTER STEIL
MID STEIL
EASTER STEIL
SOUTH STEIL
THE STEILS
GREENBANK LOAN
A70

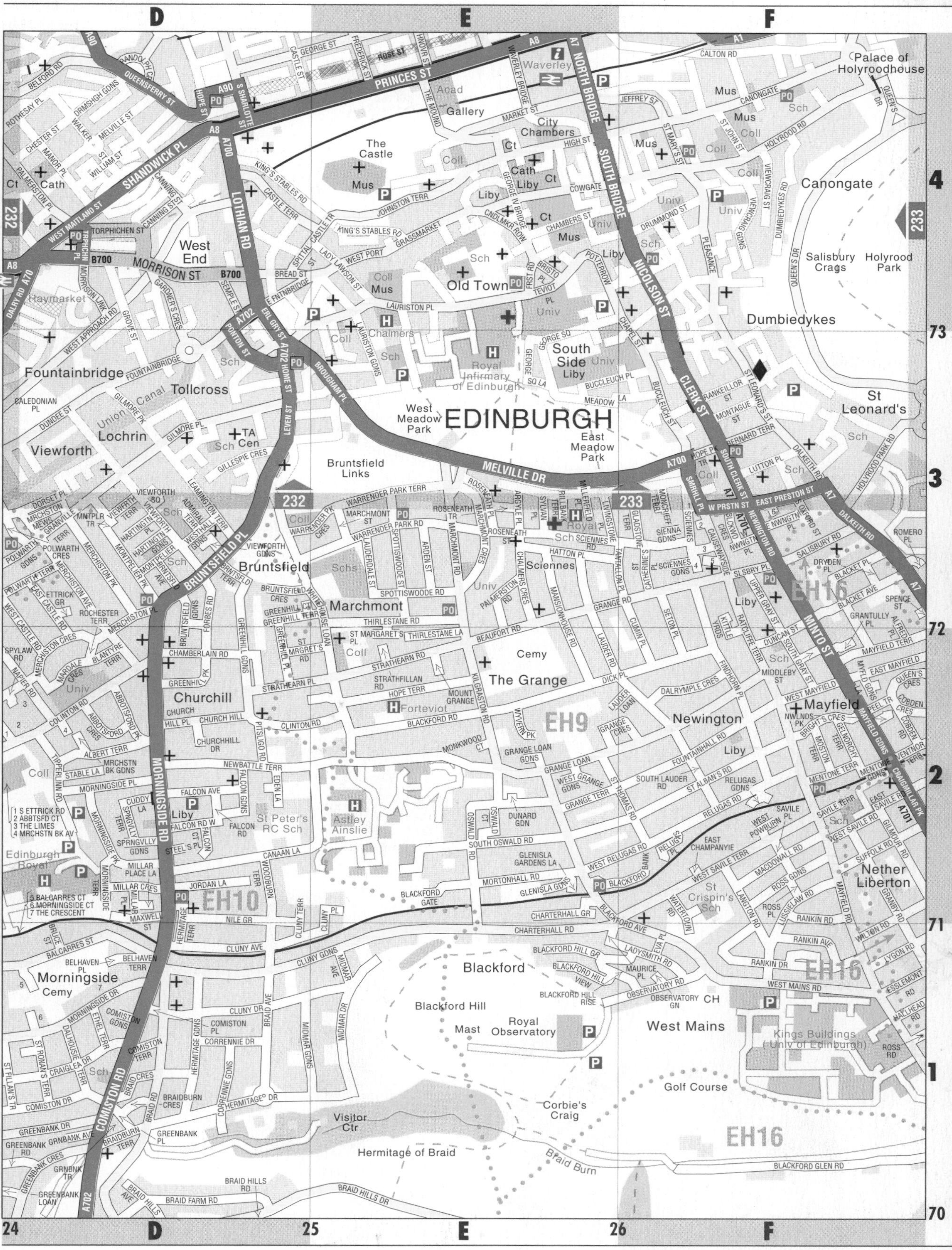

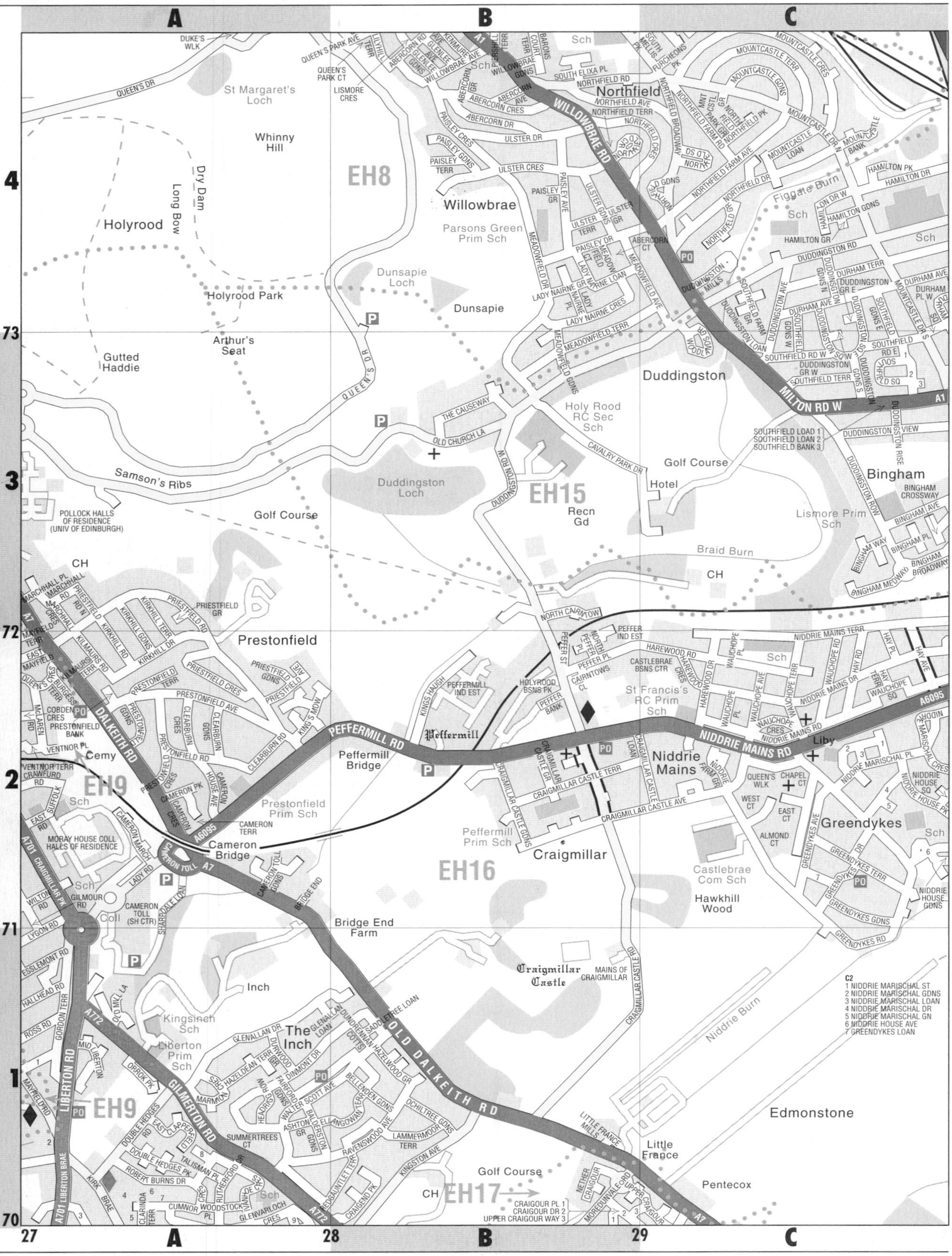

A1
1 BLACKBARONY RD
2 BRAEFOOT TERR
3 ORCHARDHEAD RD
4 MOSSGIEL WLK
5 ALLOWAY LOAN
6 JEAN ARMOUR AVE
7 SHANTER WAY
8 TRESSILIAN GDNS
9 GREENMANTLE LOAN

C2
1 NIDDRIE MARISCHAL ST
2 NIDDRIE MARISCHAL GDNS
3 NIDDRIE MARISCHAL LOAN
4 NIDDRIE MARISCHAL DR
5 NIDDRIE MARISCHAL GR
6 NIDDRIE HOUSE AVE
7 GREENDYKES LOAN

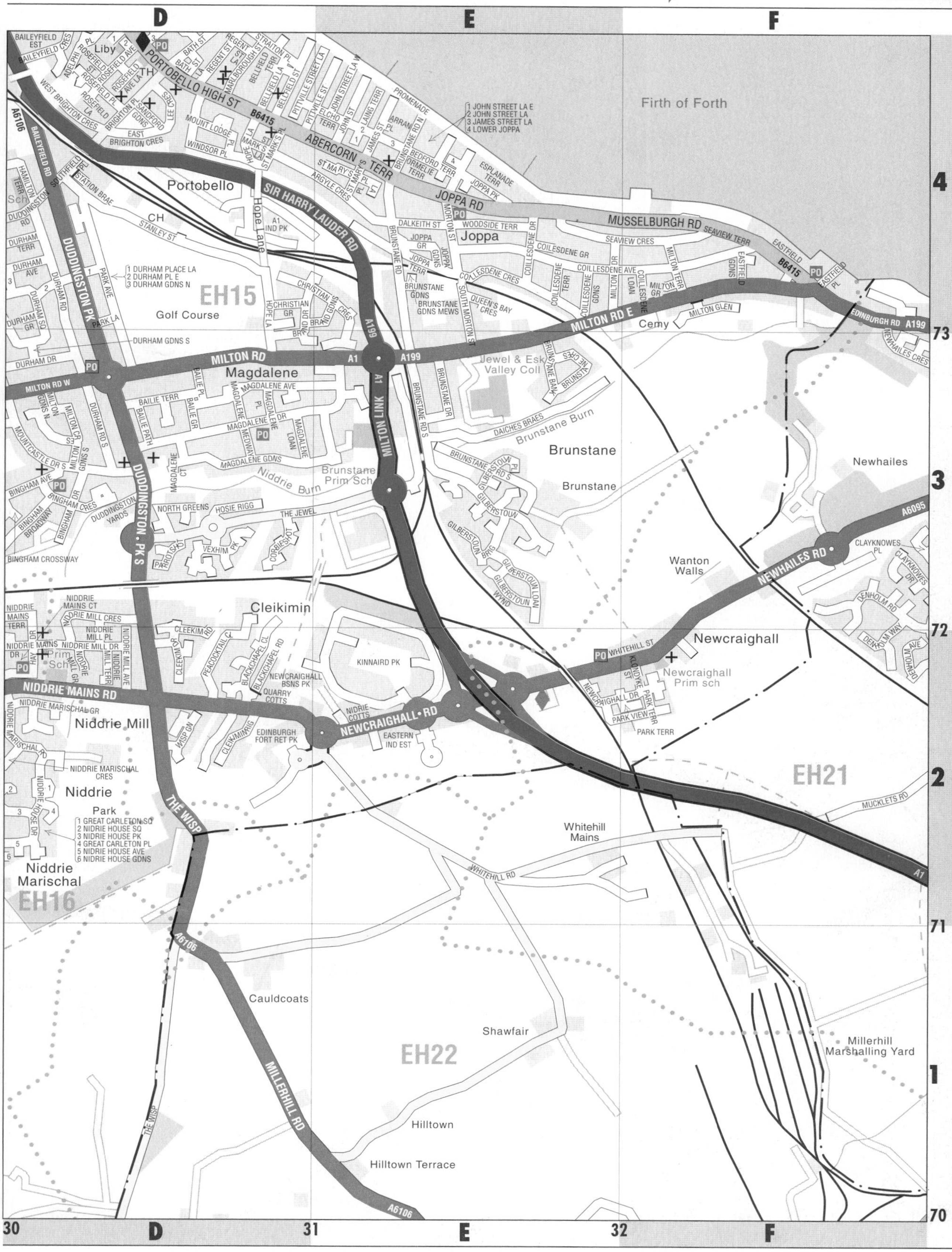

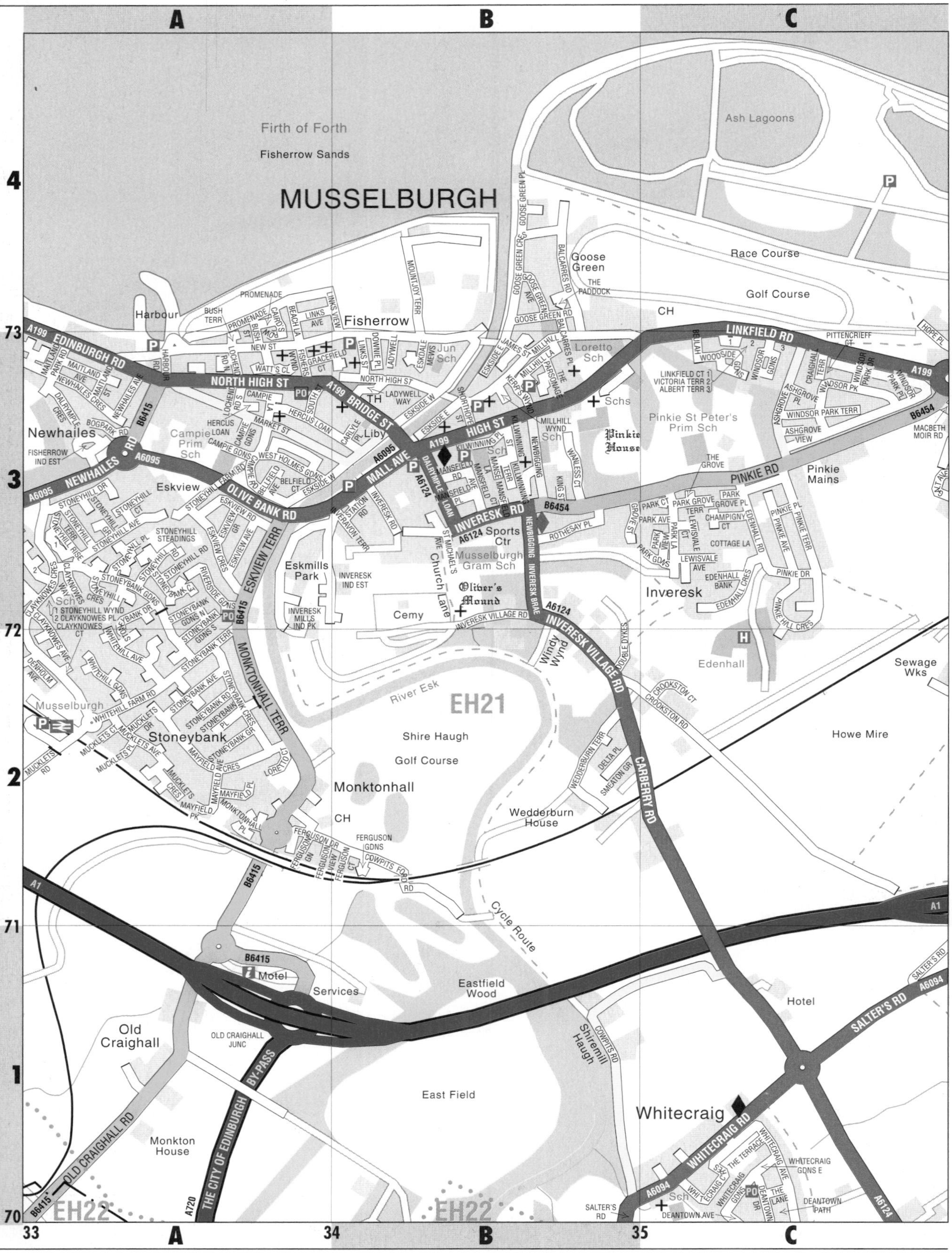

125

Firth of Forth

Fisherrow Sands

MUSSELBURGH

Ash Lagoons

Race Course

Golf Course

Goose Green

THE PADDOCK

CH

Harbour

PROMENADE

Fisherrow

Jun Sch

Loretto Sch

LINKFIELD RD

PITTENCRIEFF CT

HOPE PL

A199

Newhailes

EDINBURGH RD

NORTH HIGH ST

BRIDGE ST

HIGH ST

Pinkie St Peter's Prim Sch

MACBETH MOIR RD

B6454

Newhailes

Campie Prim Sch

Eskview

OLIVE BANK RD

Liby

MALL AVE

INVERESK RD

PINKIE RD

Pinkie Mains

Pinkie House

THE GROVE

Sports Ctr

Musselburgh Gram Sch

Inveresk

Eskmills Park

Inveresk Ind Est

Oliver's Mound

Cemy

Church Lane

INVERESK BRAE

Edenhall

Sewage Wks

River Esk

Shire Haugh

EH21

Golf Course

INVERESK VILLAGE RD

CARBERRY RD

Howe Mire

Stoneybank

MONKTONHALL TERR

Monktonhall

CH

Wedderburn House

Musselburgh

A1

Cycle Route

A1

SALTER'S RD

A6094

Motel

Services

Eastfield Wood

Hotel

SALTER'S RD

Old Craighall

OLD CRAIGHALL JUNC

BY-PASS

THE CITY OF EDINBURGH

East Field

Shiremill Haugh

Whitecraig

WHITECRAIG RD

A6124

Monkton House

A720

B6415

EH22

EH22

SALTER'S RD

A6094

Sch

DEANTOWN AVE

125
157

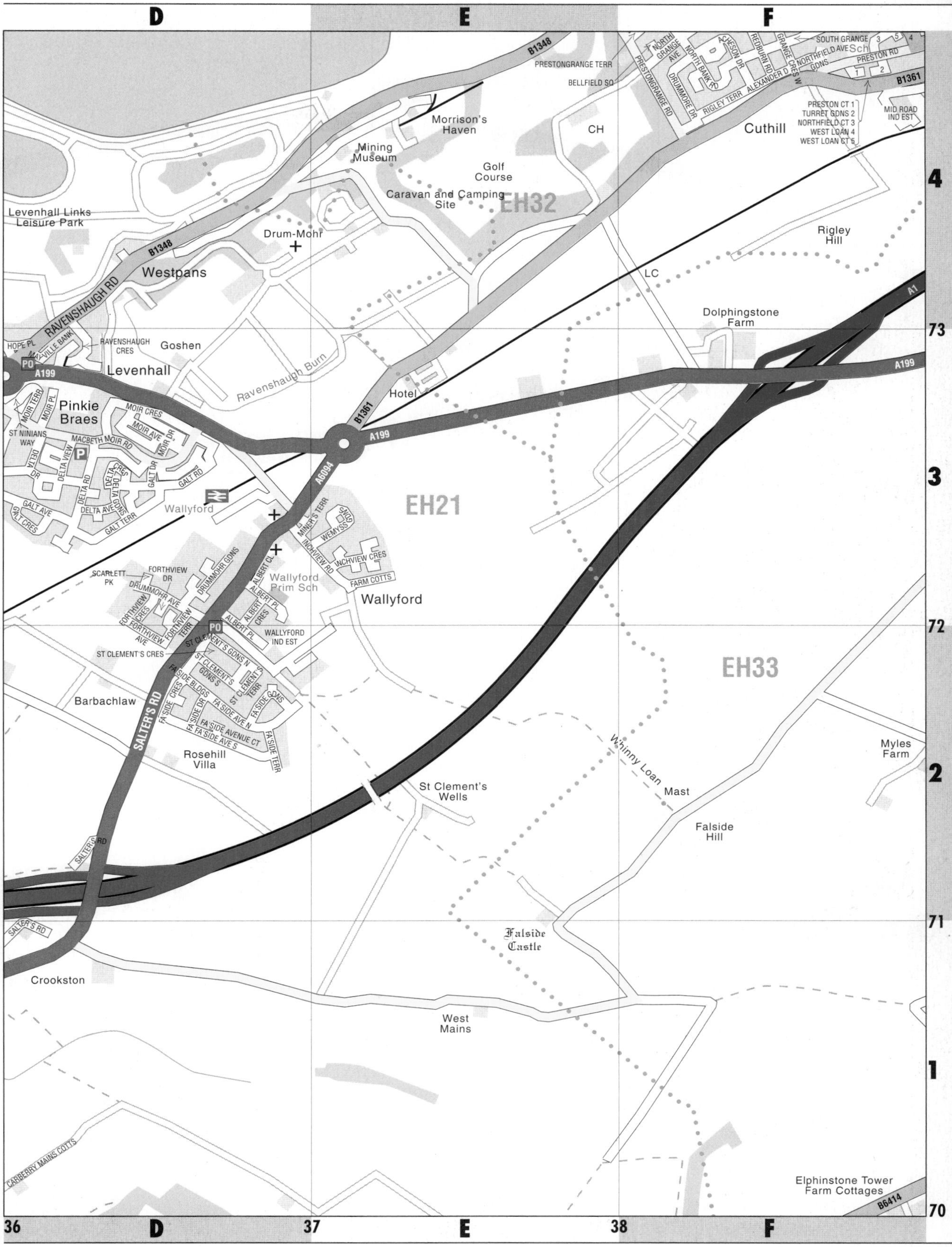

D   E   F

B1348
PRESTONGRANGE TERR
BELLFIELD SQ
SOUTH GRANGE AVE Sch
PRESTON RD
B1361

NORTH GRANGE AVE
NORTH BANK RD
PRESTONGRANGE RD
RIGLEY TERR
ALEXANDER D CR S
DRUMMORE DR
GRANGE CRES W

ACHESON DR
REDBURN RD

PRESTON CT 1
TURRET GDNS 2
NORTHFIELD CT 3
WEST LOAN 4
WEST LOAN CT 5

MID ROAD IND EST

Morrison's Haven
CH
Cuthill

Mining Museum
Golf Course
Caravan and Camping Site

EH32
Rigley Hill

4

Levenhall Links Leisure Park
Drum-Mohr
LC
Dolphingstone Farm

A1

Westpans
B1348
RAVENSHAUGH RD

73

Goshen
Ravenshaugh Burn
A199

Ravenshaugh Burn
Hotel

HOPE PL
MELVILLE BANK
RAVENSHAUGH CRES
Levenhall
PO
A199
B1361
A199

Pinkie Braes
MOIR TERR
ST NINIANS WAY
DELTA DR
MOIR CRES
MOIR AVE
MACBETH MOIR RD
GALT DR
GALT RD
P
A6094

3

DELTA VIEW
DELTA RD
DELTA CRES
DELTA AVE N
GALT AVE
GALT CRES
GALT TERR
Wallyford

EH21

SCARLETT PK
FORTHVIEW DR
DRUMMOHR AVE
MINER'S TERR
INCHVIEW RD
WEMYSS
SHED
INCHVIEW CRES
FARM COTTS

Wallyford Prim Sch

FORTHVIEW CRES
FORTHVIEW AVE
NORTHVIEW TERR
ALBERT GDNS
ALBERT CL
ALBERT PL
ALBERT CRES
Wallyford

ST CLEMENT'S CRES
PO
Wallyford IND EST

72

Barbachlaw
SALTER'S RD
ST CLEMENT'S GDNS N
ST CLEMENT'S GDNS S
ST CLEMENT'S BLDGS
ST CLEMENT'S TERR
FA SIDE CRES
FA SIDE DR
FA SIDE GDNS
FA SIDE AVE N
FA SIDE AVENUE CT
FA SIDE AVE S
FA SIDE TERR

EH33

Rosehill Villa
St Clement's Wells
Whinny Loan
Mast
Myles Farm

2

Falside Hill

SALTER'S RD
71

SALTER'S RD
Crookston

Falside Castle

West Mains

1

CARBERRY MAINS COTTS

Elphinstone Tower Farm Cottages
B6414

70

36   D   37   E   38   F

127
97

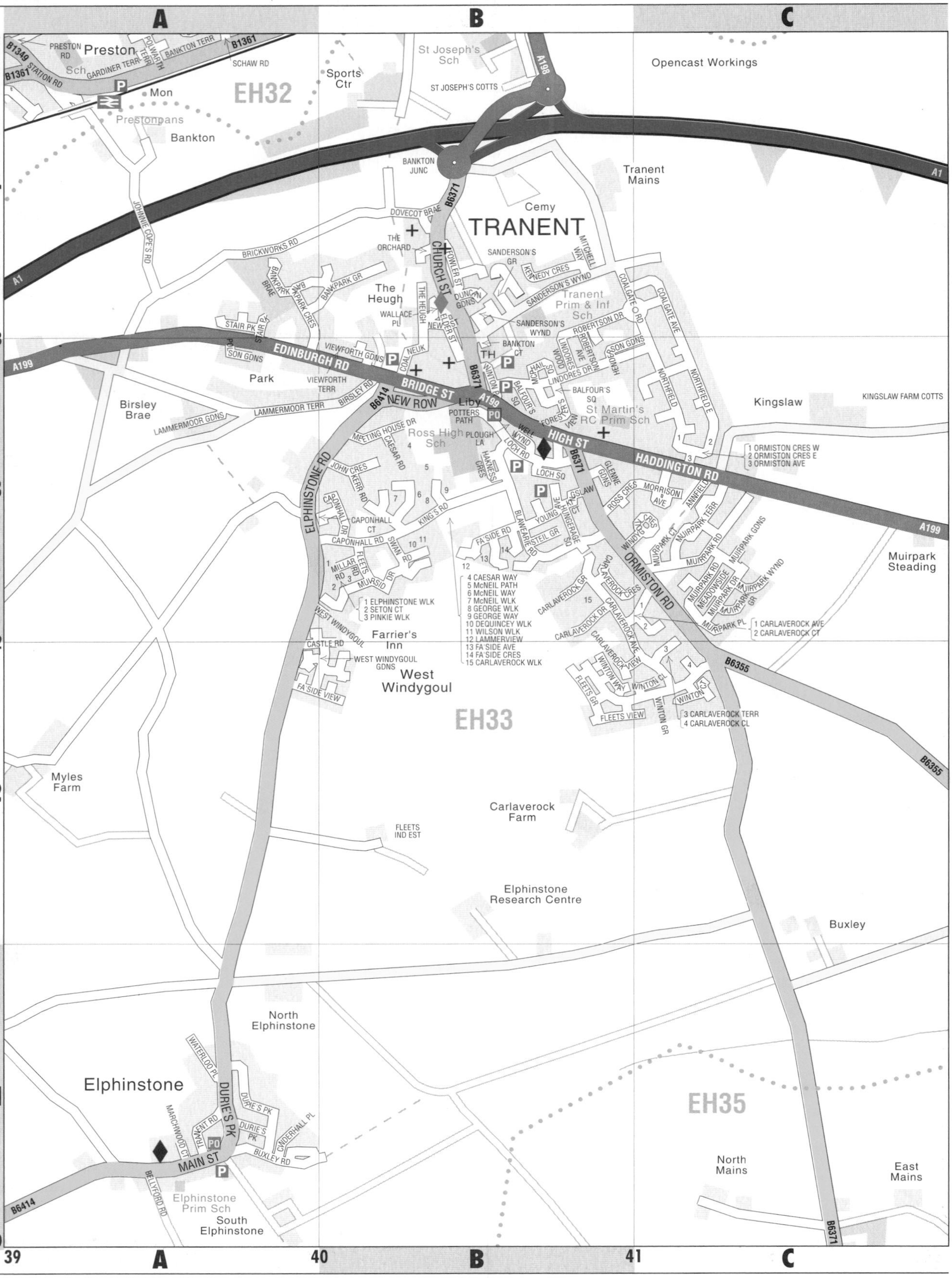
A
B
C
Preston
PRESTON RD
B1349
B1361
STATION RD
GARDINER TERR
POLWARTH TERR
BANKTON TERR
SCHAW RD
Sch
Mon
Prestonpans
Bankton
EH32
Sports Ctr
St Joseph's Sch
ST JOSEPH'S COTTS
A198
Opencast Workings
A1
BANKTON JUNC
B6371
Tranent Mains
Cemy
TRANENT
DOVECOT BRAE
THE ORCHARD
CHURCH ST
BRICKWORKS RD
JOHNNIE COPE'S RD
SANDERSON'S GR
KENNEDY CRES
MITCHELL WAY
SANDERSON'S WYND
Tranent Prim & Inf Sch
BANKPARK GR
BANKPARK BRAE
BANKPARK CRES
The Heugh
WALLACE PL
THE HEUGH
FOWLER ST
DUNCAN GDNS
ELDER ST
NEW ST
STAIR PK
SANDERSON'S WYND
ROBERTSON DR
COALGATE RD
COALGATE AVE
A199
EDINBURGH RD
VIEWFORTH GDNS
COAL NEUK
BANKTON CT
TH
LINDORES DR
ROBERTSON AVE
NORTHFIELD
NORTHFIELD E
Park
VIEWFORTH TERR
BIRSLEY RD
BRIDGE ST
BALFOUR'S SQ
St Martin's RC Prim Sch
Kingslaw
KINGSLAW FARM COTTS
Birsley Brae
LAMMERMOOR GDNS
LAMMERMOOR TERR
B6414
NEW ROW
Liby
POTTERS PATH
PO
HIGH ST
HADDINGTON RD
1 ORMISTON CRES W
2 ORMISTON CRES E
3 ORMISTON AVE
MEETING HOUSE DR
Ross High Sch
PLOUGH LA
WELL WYND
LOCH RD
LOCH SQ
CAESAR RD
JOHN CRES
ELPHINSTONE RD
HAKNESS CRES
GLENNIE GDNS
ROSS CRES
MORRISON AVE
ANNFIELD
MUIRPARK TERR
CAPONHALL DR
CAPONHALL CT
CAPONHALL RD
KING'S RD
YOUNG AVE
HUNGERAGE SQ
FA'SIDE RD
BLAWEARIE RD
STEIL GR
ORMISTON RD
MUIRPARK CT
MUIRPARK RD
MUIRPARK GDNS
Muirpark Steading
MILLAR RD
FLEETS RD
SWAN RD
MUIRSIDE DR
1 ELPHINSTONE WLK
2 SETON CT
3 PINKIE WLK
4 CAESAR WAY
5 McNEIL PATH
6 McNEIL WAY
7 McNEIL WLK
8 GEORGE WLK
9 GEORGE WAY
10 DEQUINCEY WLK
11 WILSON WLK
12 LAMMERVIEW
13 FA'SIDE AVE
14 FA'SIDE CRES
15 CARLAVEROCK WLK
CARLAVEROCK GR
CARLAVEROCK CRES
CARLAVEROCK DR
CARLAVEROCK AVE
CARLAVEROCK VIEW
MEADOWSIDE
MUIRPARK DR
MUIRPARK WYND
MUIRPARK PL
1 CARLAVEROCK AVE
2 CARLAVEROCK CT
WEST WINDYGOUL
Farrier's Inn
CASTLE RD
WEST WINDYGOUL GDNS
West Windygoul
FA'SIDE VIEW
WINTON WAY
WINTON CL
WINTON GR
FLEETS GR
FLEETS VIEW
B6355
3 CARLAVEROCK TERR
4 CARLAVEROCK CL
EH33
Myles Farm
Carlaverock Farm
FLEETS IND EST
Elphinstone Research Centre
Buxley
North Elphinstone
WATERLOO PL
DURIE'S PK
Elphinstone
EH35
MARCHWOOD CT
TRANENT RD
DURIE'S PK
CINDERHALL PL
BUXLEY RD
MAIN ST
BELLYFORD RD
Elphinstone Prim Sch
South Elphinstone
North Mains
East Mains
4
73
3
72
2
71
1
70
39
40
41

127
159

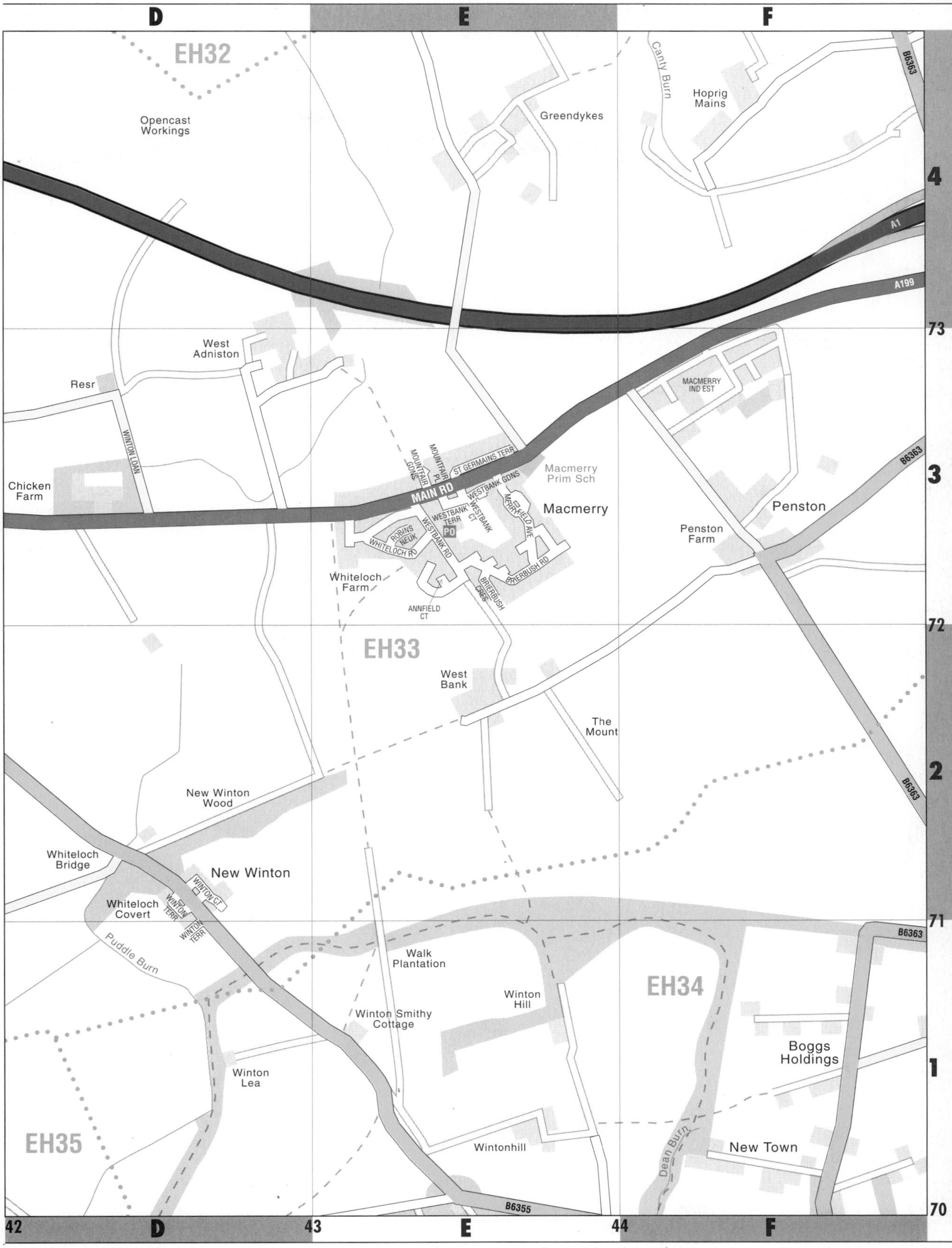

D
E
F

EH32

Opencast
Workings

Greendykes

Canty Burn

Hoprig
Mains

B6363

4

A1

A199

73

West
Adniston

Resr

WINTON LOAN

MACMERRY
IND EST

B6363

Chicken
Farm

MOUNTFAIR GDNS
MOUNTFAIR PL
ST GERMAINS TERR
MAIN RD
WESTBANK TERR
WESTBANK GDNS
WESTBANK CT
ROBINS NEUK
WHITELOCH RD
WESTBANK RD
PO
SHERBUSH GDNS
ASHERBUSH RD
ASHFIELD AVE

Macmerry
Prim Sch

Macmerry

Penston

Penston
Farm

3

Whiteloch
Farm

ANNFIELD
CT

EH33

West
Bank

The
Mount

72

B6363

2

New Winton
Wood

Whiteloch
Bridge

New Winton

WINTON PL CT
WINTON TERR

EH34

71

Whiteloch
Covert

Puddle Burn

Walk
Plantation

Winton
Hill

B6363

Boggs
Holdings

Winton Smithy
Cottage

Winton
Lea

EH35

Wintonhill

Dean Burn

New Town

1

42
D
43
E
44
F
70

B6355

129
99

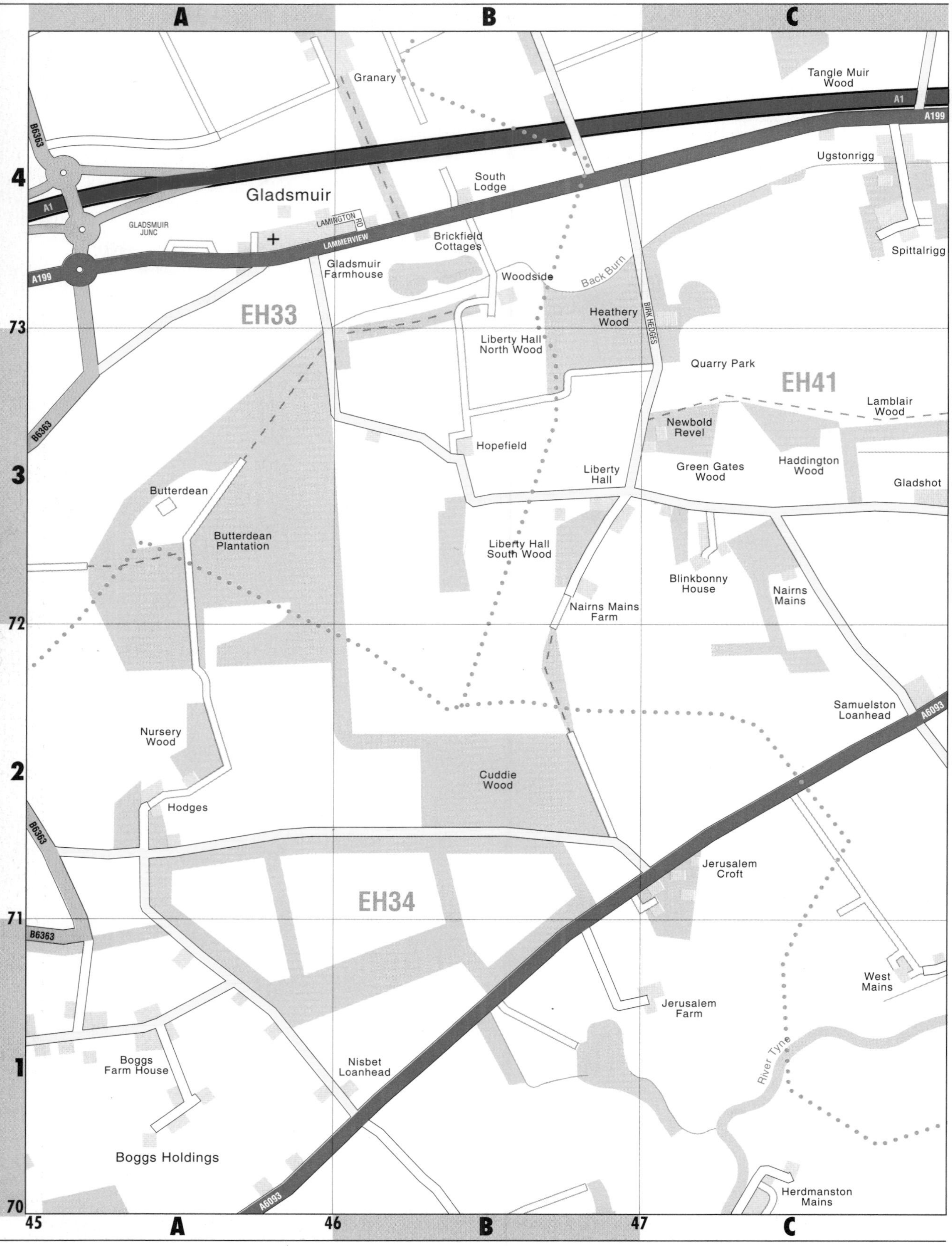

A   B   C

B6363

Granary

Tangle Muir Wood

A1

A199

4

A1

Gladsmuir

South Lodge

Ugstonrigg

GLADSMUIR JUNC

LAMINGTON RD

Spittalrigg

A199

+

LAMMERVIEW

Brickfield Cottages

Gladsmuir Farmhouse

Woodside

Back Burn

Heathery Wood

BIRK HEDGES

EH33

73

Liberty Hall North Wood

Quarry Park

EH41

B6363

Lamblair Wood

Newbold Revel

Hopefield

Liberty Hall

Green Gates Wood

Haddington Wood

Gladshot

3

Butterdean

Butterdean Plantation

Liberty Hall South Wood

Blinkbonny House

Nairns Mains

Nairns Mains Farm

72

Nursery Wood

Samuelston Loanhead

A6093

2

Hodges

Cuddie Wood

B6363

Jerusalem Croft

71

EH34

West Mains

B6363

Jerusalem Farm

River Tyne

1

Boggs Farm House

Nisbet Loanhead

Boggs Holdings

Herdmanston Mains

A6093

70

45   A   46   B   47   C

129
161

100
132

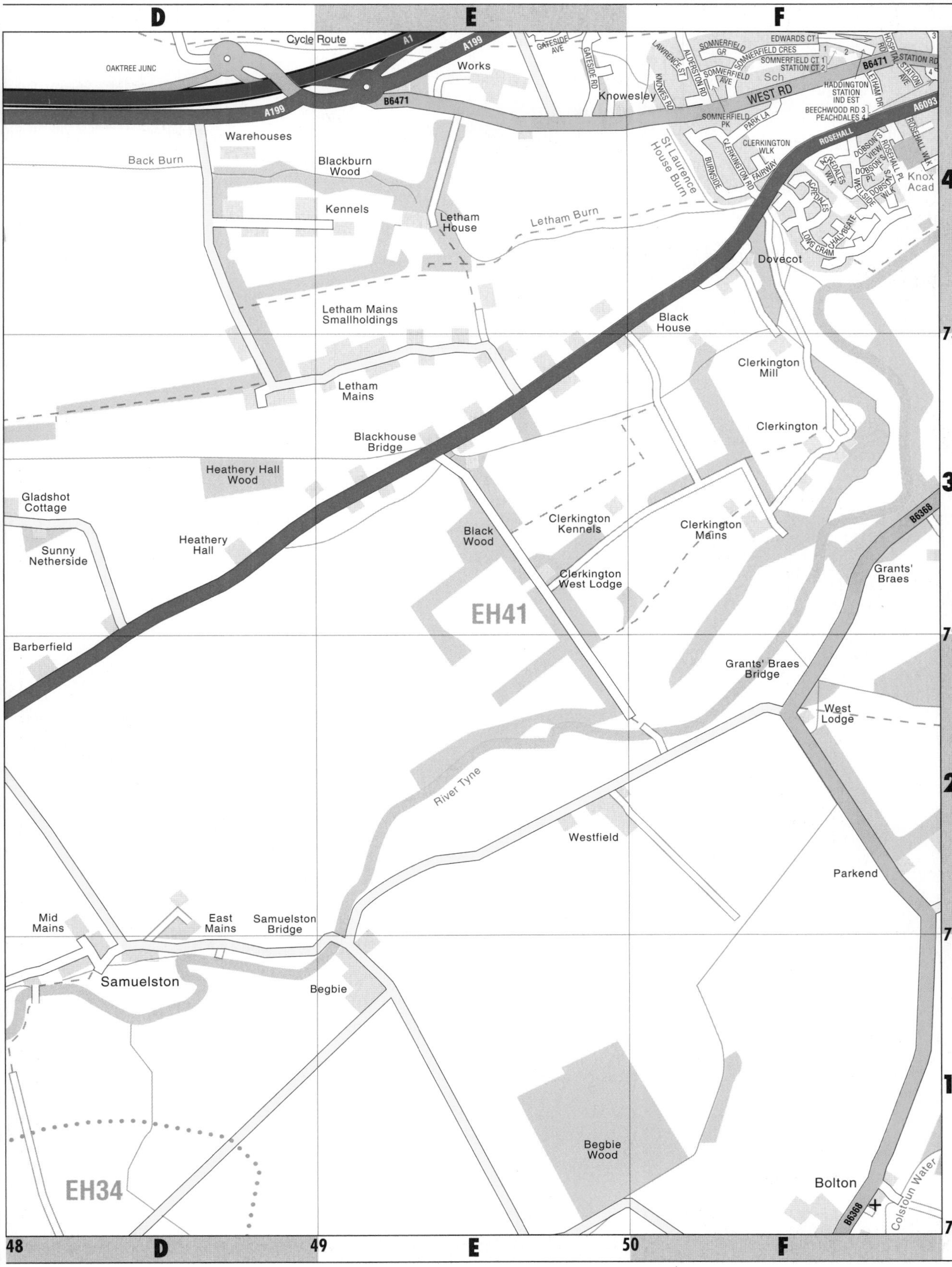
D
E
F
Cycle Route
A1
A199
OAKTREE JUNC
Works
B6471
GATESIDE AVE
GATESIDE RD
Knowesley
KNOWES RD
LAWRENCE ST
ALDERSTON RD
SOMNERFIELD GR
SOMNERFIELD CRES
SOMNERFIELD AVE
SOMNERFIELD CT 1
STATION CT 2
EDWARDS CT
Sch
WEST RD
HADDINGTON STATION IND EST
LETHAM DR
HOSPITAL RD
STATION RD
STATION AVE
BEECHWOOD RD 3
PEACHDALES 4
A6093
SOMNERFIELD PK
PARK LA
Warehouses
Back Burn
Blackburn Wood
St Laurence House Burn
CLERKINGTON WLK
ROSEHALL
BURNSIDE
CLERKINGTON RD
FAIRWAY
DOBSON'S VIEW
ROSEHALL PL
ROSEHALL WLK
Knox Acad
Kennels
Letham House
Letham Burn
Dovecot
LONG CRAM
CHALYBEATE
Letham Mains Smallholdings
Black House
73
Clerkington Mill
Letham Mains
Clerkington
Blackhouse Bridge
Heathery Hall Wood
3
Gladshot Cottage
Clerkington Kennels
Clerkington Mains
B6368
Black Wood
Heathery Hall
Sunny Netherside
Grants' Braes
Clerkington West Lodge
EH41
Barberfield
72
Grants' Braes Bridge
West Lodge
River Tyne
2
Westfield
Parkend
Mid Mains
East Mains
Samuelston Bridge
71
Samuelston
Begbie
1
Begbie Wood
EH34
Bolton
Colstoun Water
70
48
49
50

162
132

131
101

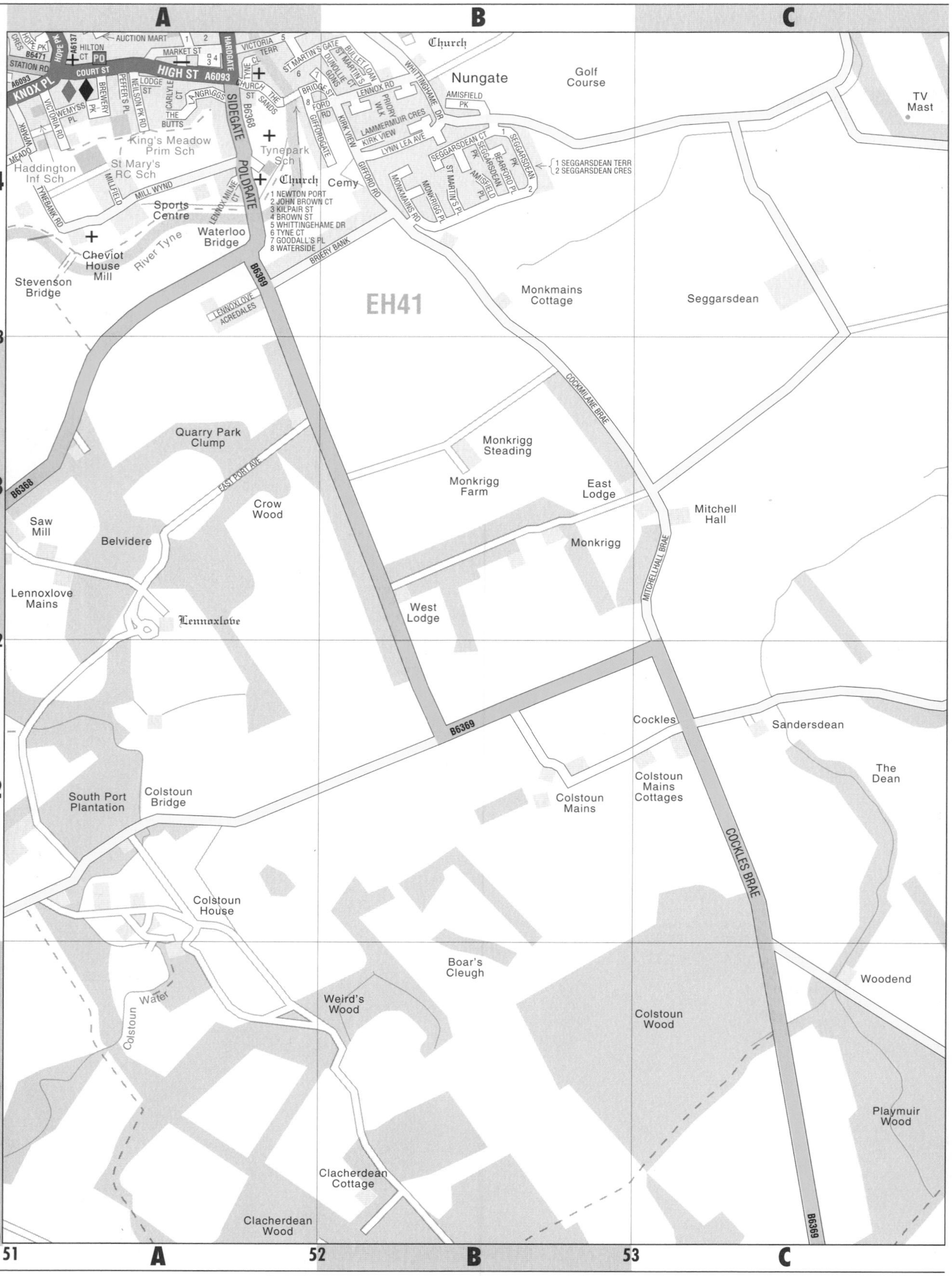
A
B
C
4
73
3
72
2
71
1
70
51
52
53
Church
Nungate
Golf Course
TV Mast
AUCTION MART
HILTON CT
PO
STATION RD
COURT ST
HIGH ST
A6093
KNOX PL
HOPE PK
A6137
B6471
MARKET ST
HARDGATE
VICTORIA TERR
TYNE CL
CHURCH ST
THE SANDS
ST MARTIN'S GATE
BULLET LOAN
DUNOLLIE CT
ST MARTIN'S GDNS
WHITTINGHAME DR
LENNOX RD
PRIORY WLK
AMISFIELD PK
LAMMERMUIR CRES
KIRK VIEW
LYNN LEA AVE
BRIDGE ST
FORD RD
GIFFORDGATE
SEGGARSDEAN CT
SEGGARSDEAN PK
BEARFORD PL
1 SEGGARSDEAN TERR
2 SEGGARSDEAN CRES
ST MARTIN'S PL
AMISFIELD PL
MONKRIGG RD
MONKMAINS RD
GIFFORD RD
WEMYSS PL
VICTORIA RD
BREWERY PK
PEFFER'S PL
NELSON PK RD
LODGE ST
CARLYLE CT
LANGRIGGS
THE BUTTS
SIDEGATE
B6368
King's Meadow Prim Sch
Haddington Inf Sch
St Mary's RC Sch
Tynepark Sch
Church
Cemy
POLDRATE
MILLFIELD
MILL WYND
TYNEBANK RD
LENNOX MILNE CT
Sports Centre
1 NEWTON PORT
2 JOHN BROWN CT
3 KILPAIR ST
4 BROWN ST
5 WHITTINGEHAME DR
6 TYNE CT
7 GOODALL'S PL
8 WATERSIDE
BRIERY BANK
Waterloo Bridge
Cheviot House Mill
River Tyne
Stevenson Bridge
B6369
EH41
LENNOXLOVE ACREDALES
Monkmains Cottage
Seggarsdean
COCKMILANE BRAE
Quarry Park Clump
Monkrigg Steading
Monkrigg Farm
East Lodge
Mitchell Hall
B6368
EAST PORT AVE
Crow Wood
Saw Mill
Belvidere
Monkrigg
MITCHELLHALL BRAE
Lennoxlove Mains
West Lodge
Lennoxlove
Cockles
Sandersdean
The Dean
South Port Plantation
Colstoun Bridge
Colstoun Mains
Colstoun Mains Cottages
COCKLES BRAE
Colstoun House
Boar's Cleugh
Woodend
Weird's Wood
Colstoun Water
Colstoun Wood
Playmuir Wood
Clacherdean Cottage
Clacherdean Wood

131
163

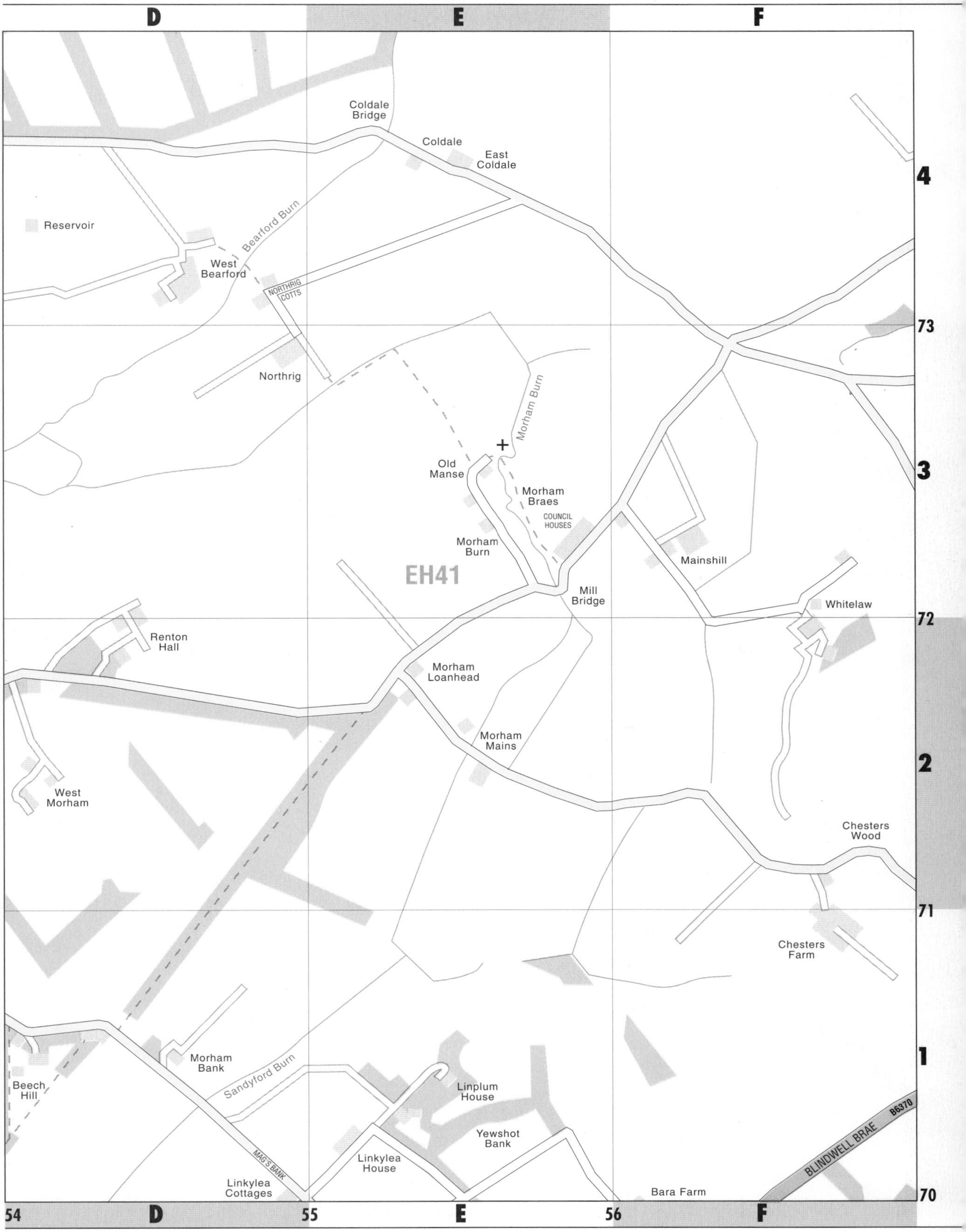

4

Coldale
Bridge
Coldale
East
Coldale

Reservoir

West
Bearford

Bearford Burn

NORTHRIG
COTTS

73

Northrig

Morham Burn

+

Old
Manse

Morham
Braes

COUNCIL
HOUSES

3

Morham
Burn

Mainshill

EH41

Mill
Bridge

Whitelaw

72

Renton
Hall

Morham
Loanhead

West
Morham

Morham
Mains

Chesters
Wood

2

71

Chesters
Farm

Morham
Bank

Sandyford Burn

Beech
Hill

1

Linplum
House

Yewshot
Bank

BLINDWELL BRAE B6370

MAG'S BANK

Linkylea
House

Bara Farm

Linkylea
Cottages

70

133
103

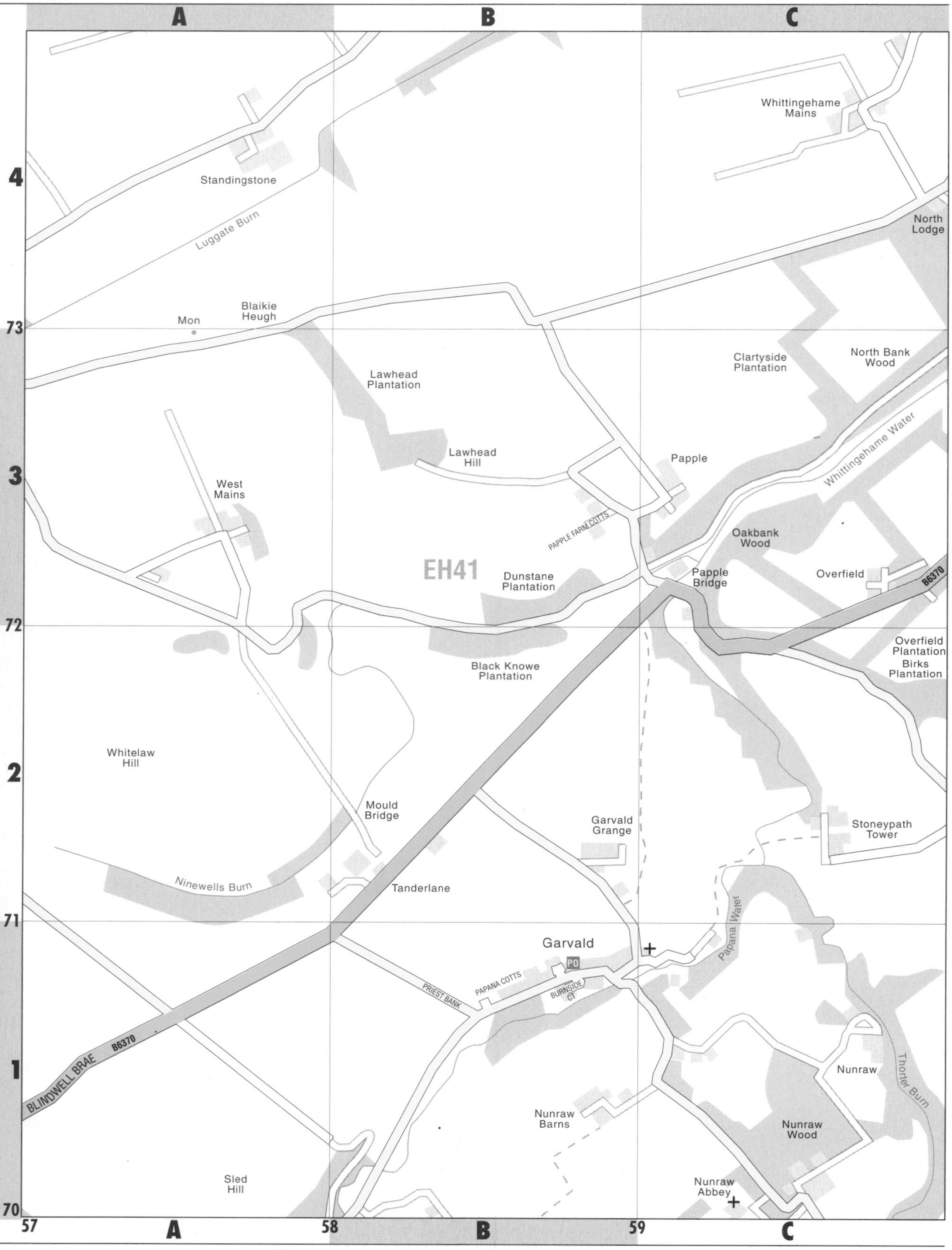

A
B
C

4

Standingstone

Whittingehame
Mains

Luggate Burn

North
Lodge

73

Mon

Blaikie
Heugh

Lawhead
Plantation

Clartyside
Plantation

North Bank
Wood

Whittingehame Water

3

West
Mains

Lawhead
Hill

Papple

Oakbank
Wood

Overfield

B6370

EH41

PAPPLE FARM COTTS

Dunstane
Plantation

Papple
Bridge

Overfield
Plantation
Birks
Plantation

72

Black Knowe
Plantation

2

Whitelaw
Hill

Garvald
Grange

Stoneypath
Tower

Mould
Bridge

Papana Water

Ninewells Burn

Tanderlane

71

Garvald

PO

Thorter Burn

Priest Bank

PAPANA COTTS

BURNSIDE
CT

1

BLINDWELL BRAE

B6370

Nunraw

Nunraw
Wood

Nunraw
Barns

Sled
Hill

Nunraw
Abbey

70

57

A

58

B

59

C

133
165

104
136

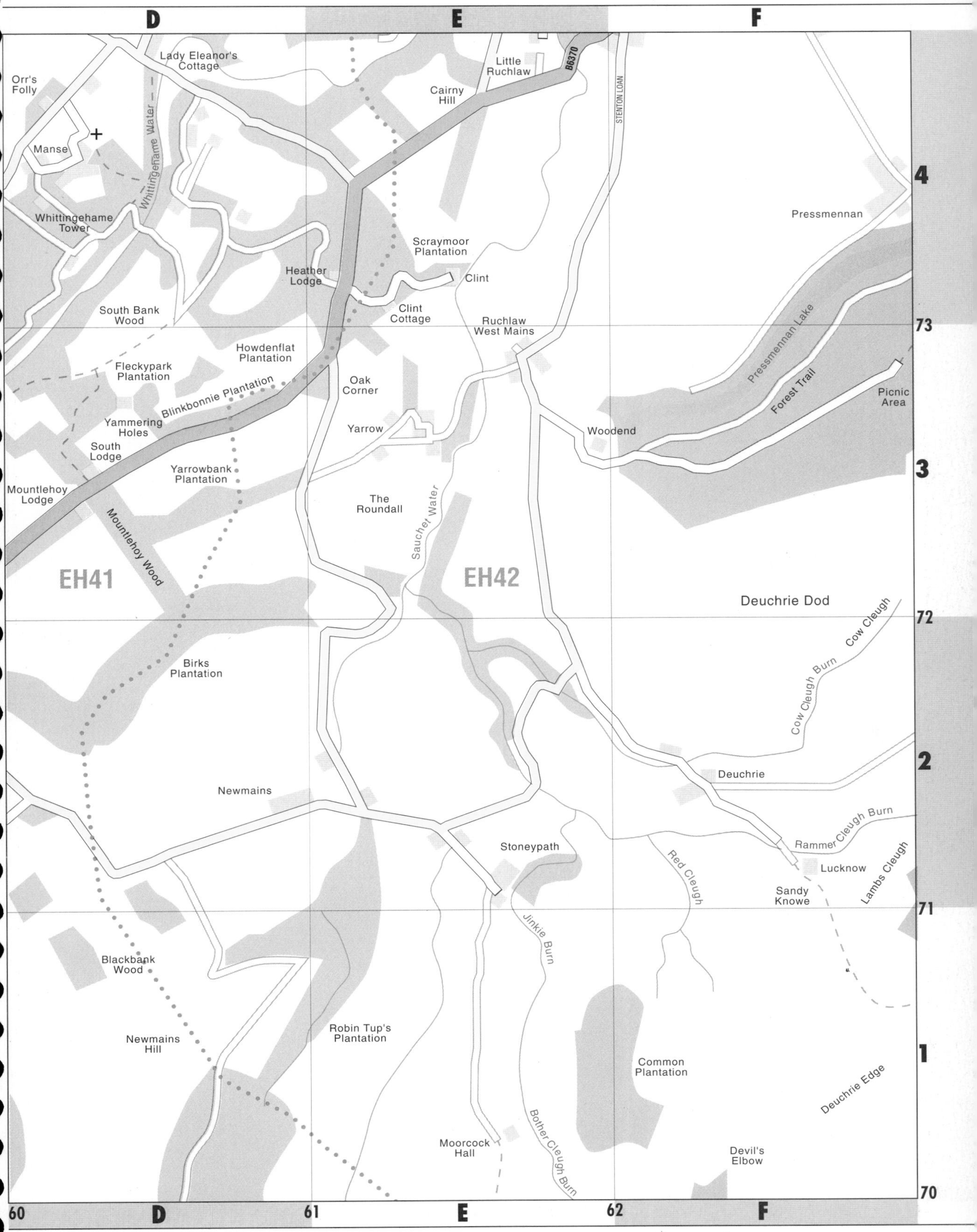
D
E
F
Lady Eleanor's Cottage
Orr's Folly
Manse
Whittingehame Water
Whittingehame Tower
Little Ruchlaw
Cairny Hill
B6370
STENTON LOAN
Pressmennan
Scraymoor Plantation
Heather Lodge
Clint
Clint Cottage
South Bank Wood
Ruchlaw West Mains
Howdenflat Plantation
Fleckypark Plantation
Blinkbonnie Plantation
Oak Corner
Pressmennan Lake
Forest Trail
Picnic Area
Yammering Holes
Yarrow
Woodend
South Lodge
Yarrowbank Plantation
Mountlehoy Lodge
The Roundall
Saucher Water
Mountlehoy Wood
EH41
EH42
Deuchrie Dod
Cow Cleugh
Cow Cleugh Burn
Birks Plantation
Deuchrie
Newmains
Rammer Cleugh Burn
Stoneypath
Red Cleugh
Lucknow
Lambs Cleugh
Sandy Knowe
Jinkie Burn
Blackbank Wood
Newmains Hill
Robin Tup's Plantation
Common Plantation
Deuchrie Edge
Moorcock Hall
Bother Cleugh Burn
Devil's Elbow
4
73
3
72
2
71
1
70
60
61
62

166
136

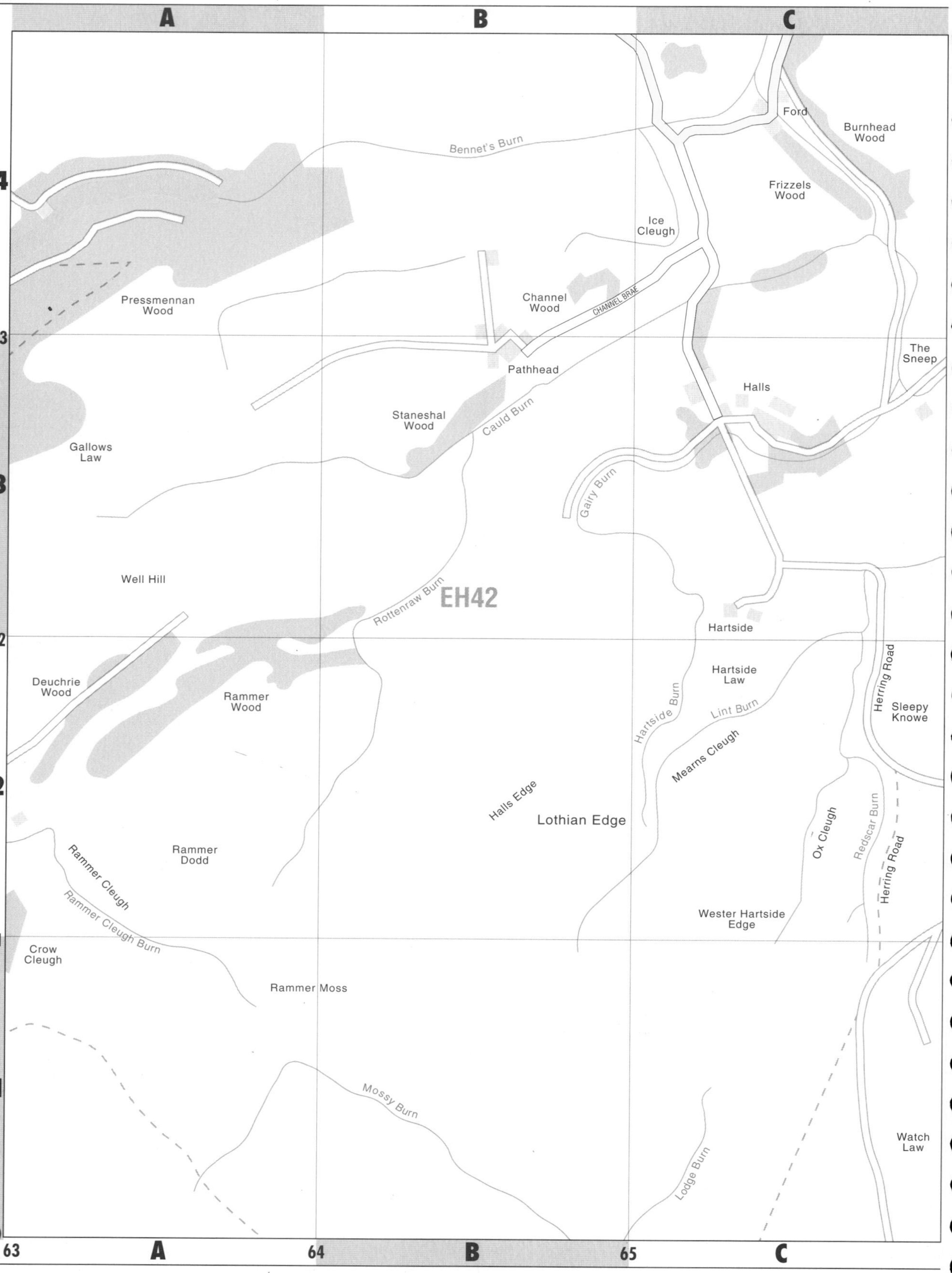

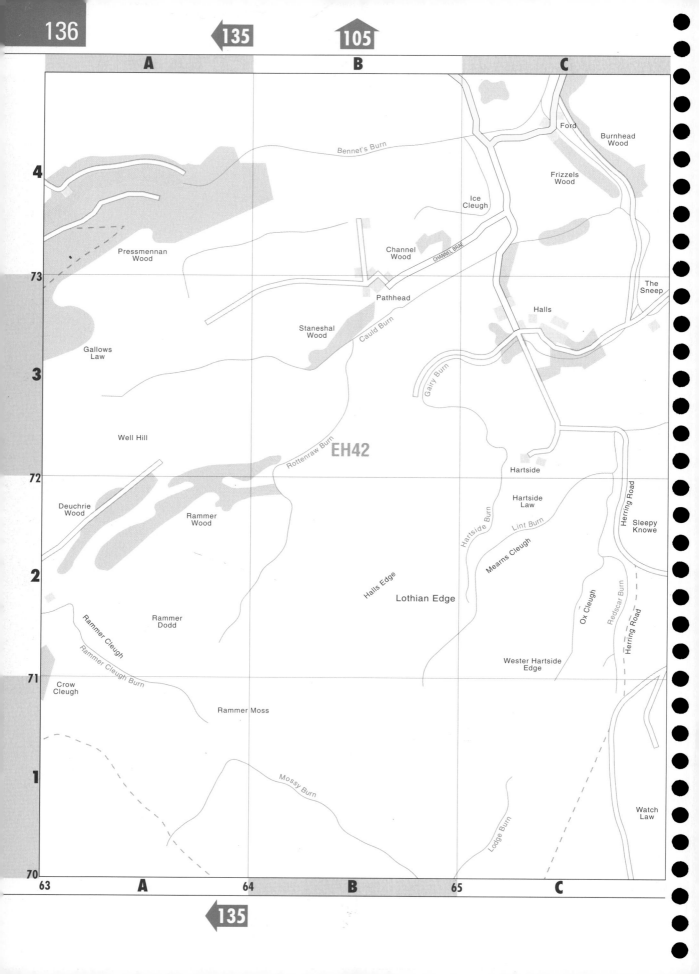

A　　　　　　　B　　　　　　　C

4

Bennet's Burn

Ford

Burnhead
Wood

Frizzels
Wood

Ice
Cleugh

Pressmennan
Wood

Channel
Wood

CHANNEL BRAE

The
Sneep

73

Pathhead

Halls

Staneshal
Wood

Cauld Burn

Gairy Burn

Gallows
Law

3

Well Hill

Rottenraw Burn

EH42

Hartside

72

Deuchrie
Wood

Rammer
Wood

Hartside
Law

Hartside Burn

Lint Burn

Herring Road

Sleepy
Knowe

2

Mearns Cleugh

Halls Edge

Lothian Edge

Ox Cleugh

Redscar Burn

Herring Road

Rammer
Dodd

Rammer Cleugh

Wester Hartside
Edge

71

Rammer Cleugh Burn

Crow
Cleugh

Rammer Moss

1

Mossy Burn

Lodge Burn

Watch
Law

70

63　　　A　　　64　　　B　　　65　　　C

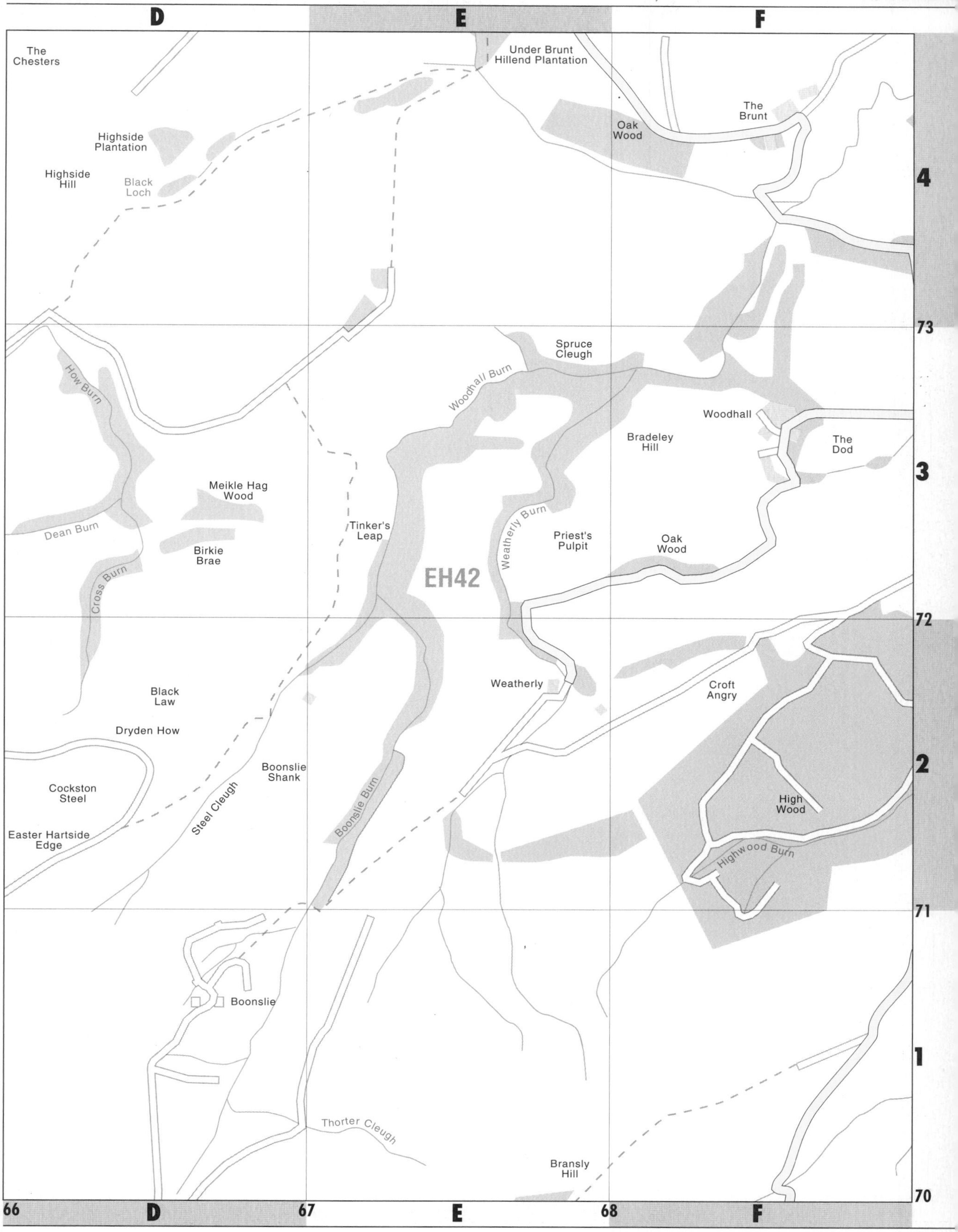
D
E
F
The Chesters
Under Brunt
Hillend Plantation
The Brunt
Oak Wood
Highside Plantation
Highside Hill
Black Loch
4
73
Spruce Cleugh
Woodhall Burn
How Burn
Woodhall
Bradeley Hill
The Dod
3
Meikle Hag Wood
Dean Burn
Tinker's Leap
Weatherly Burn
Priest's Pulpit
Oak Wood
Birkie Brae
Cross Burn
EH42
72
Weatherly
Croft Angry
Black Law
Dryden How
2
Boonslie Shank
Cockston Steel
Steel Cleugh
Boonslie Burn
High Wood
Easter Hartside Edge
Highwood Burn
71
Boonslie
1
Thorter Cleugh
Bransly Hill
70
66
D
67
E
68
F

137
107

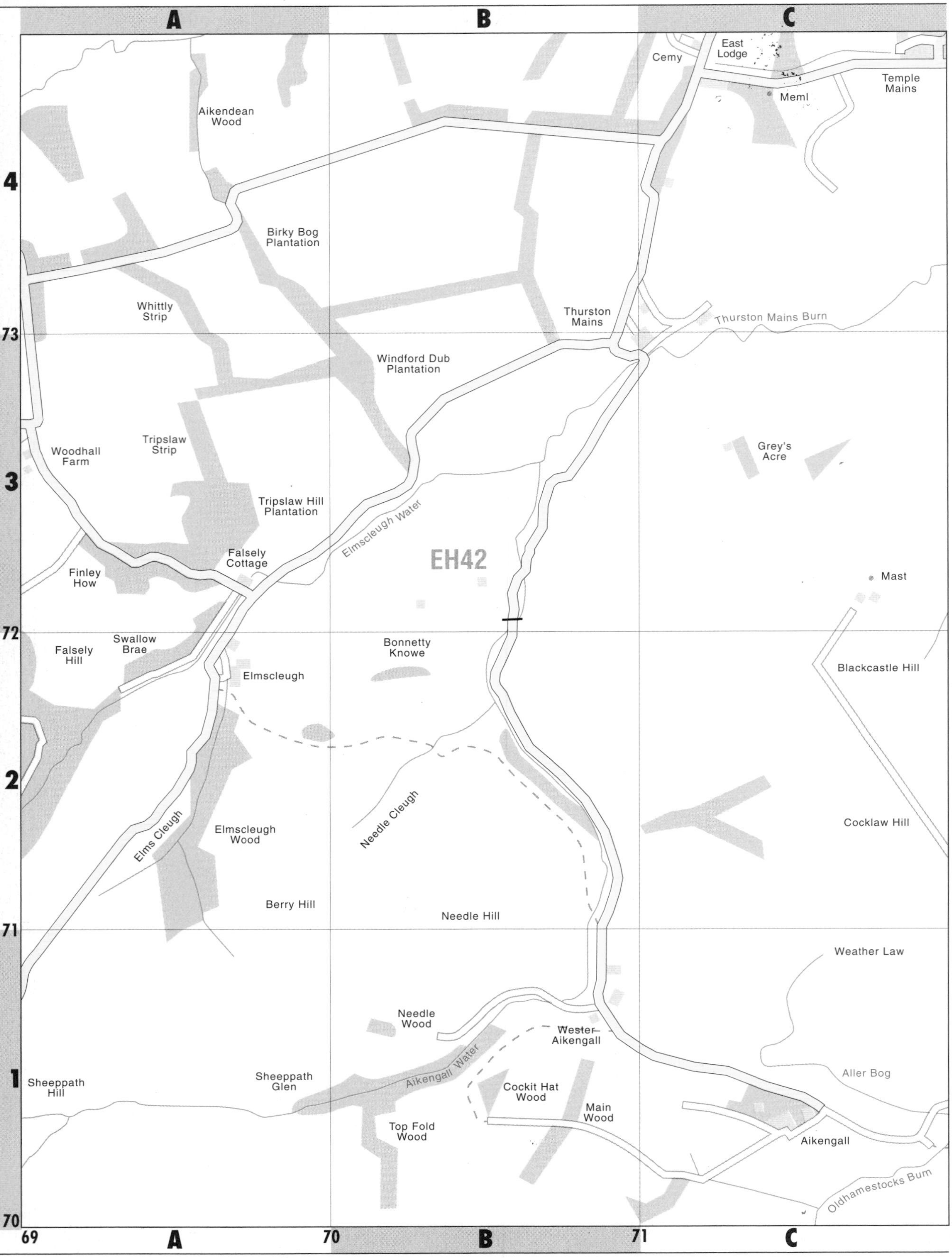
A
B
C
4
73
3
72
2
71
1
70
69
70
71
Cemy
East Lodge
Temple Mains
Meml
Aikendean Wood
Birky Bog Plantation
Whittly Strip
Thurston Mains
Thurston Mains Burn
Windford Dub Plantation
Woodhall Farm
Tripslaw Strip
Grey's Acre
Tripslaw Hill Plantation
Elmscleugh Water
Falsely Cottage
EH42
Finley How
Mast
Falsely Hill
Swallow Brae
Bonnetty Knowe
Elmscleugh
Blackcastle Hill
Elms Cleugh
Elmscleugh Wood
Needle Cleugh
Cocklaw Hill
Berry Hill
Needle Hill
Weather Law
Needle Wood
Wester Aikengall
Aikengall Water
Aller Bog
Sheeppath Hill
Sheeppath Glen
Cockit Hat Wood
Main Wood
Top Fold Wood
Aikengall
Oldhamestocks Burn

137

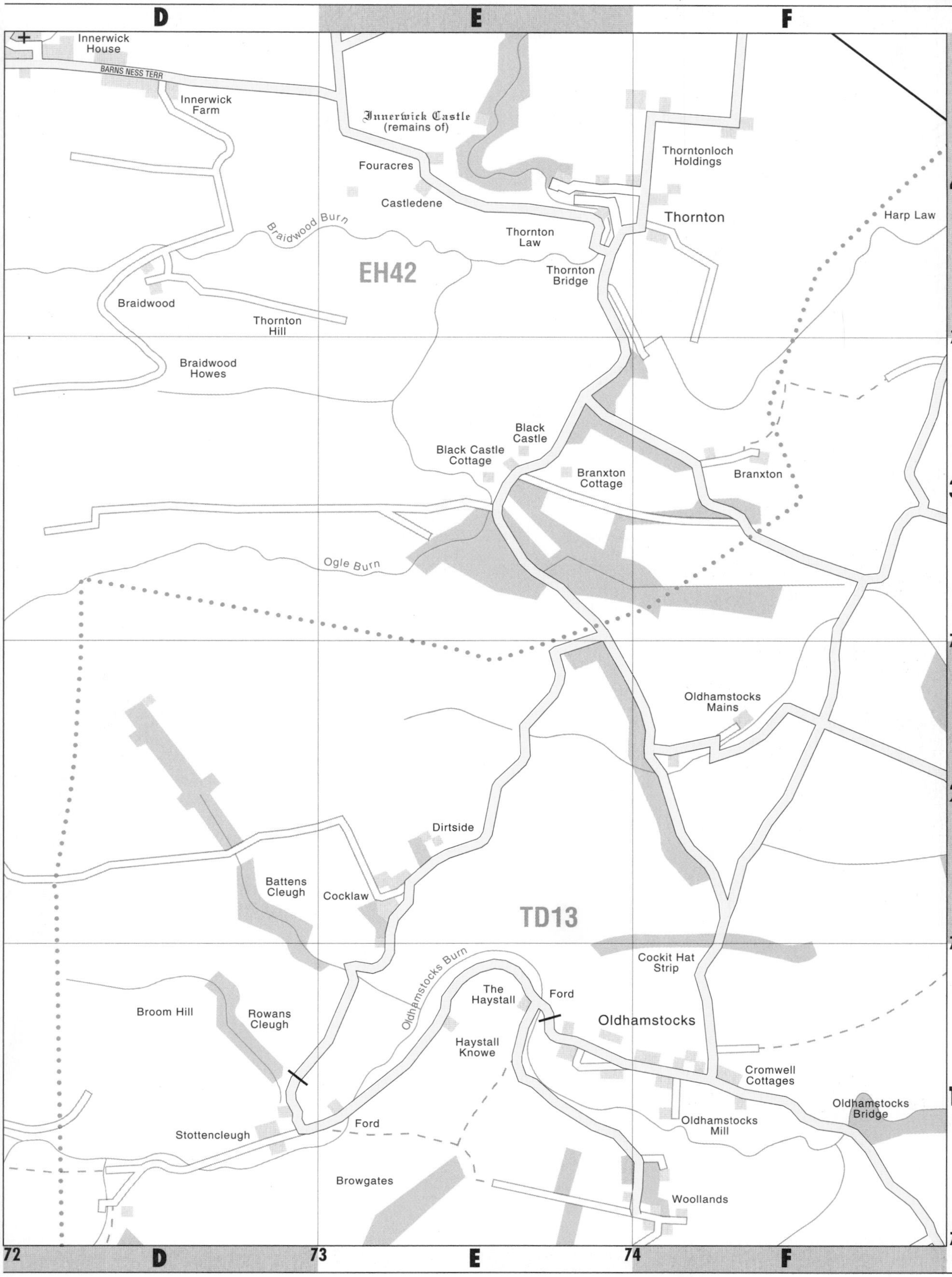
D
E
F
Innerwick House
BARNS NESS TERR
Innerwick Farm
Innerwick Castle (remains of)
Fouracres
Castledene
Thorntonloch Holdings
Thornton
Harp Law
Braidwood Burn
Thornton Law
Thornton Bridge
EH42
Braidwood
Thornton Hill
Braidwood Howes
Black Castle
Black Castle Cottage
Branxton Cottage
Branxton
Ogle Burn
Oldhamstocks Mains
Dirtside
Battens Cleugh
Cocklaw
TD13
Cockit Hat Strip
Oldhamstocks Burn
The Haystall
Ford
Oldhamstocks
Broom Hill
Rowans Cleugh
Haystall Knowe
Cromwell Cottages
Oldhamstocks Bridge
Oldhamstocks Mill
Stottencleugh
Ford
Browgates
Woollands
4
73
3
72
2
71
1
70
72
73
74

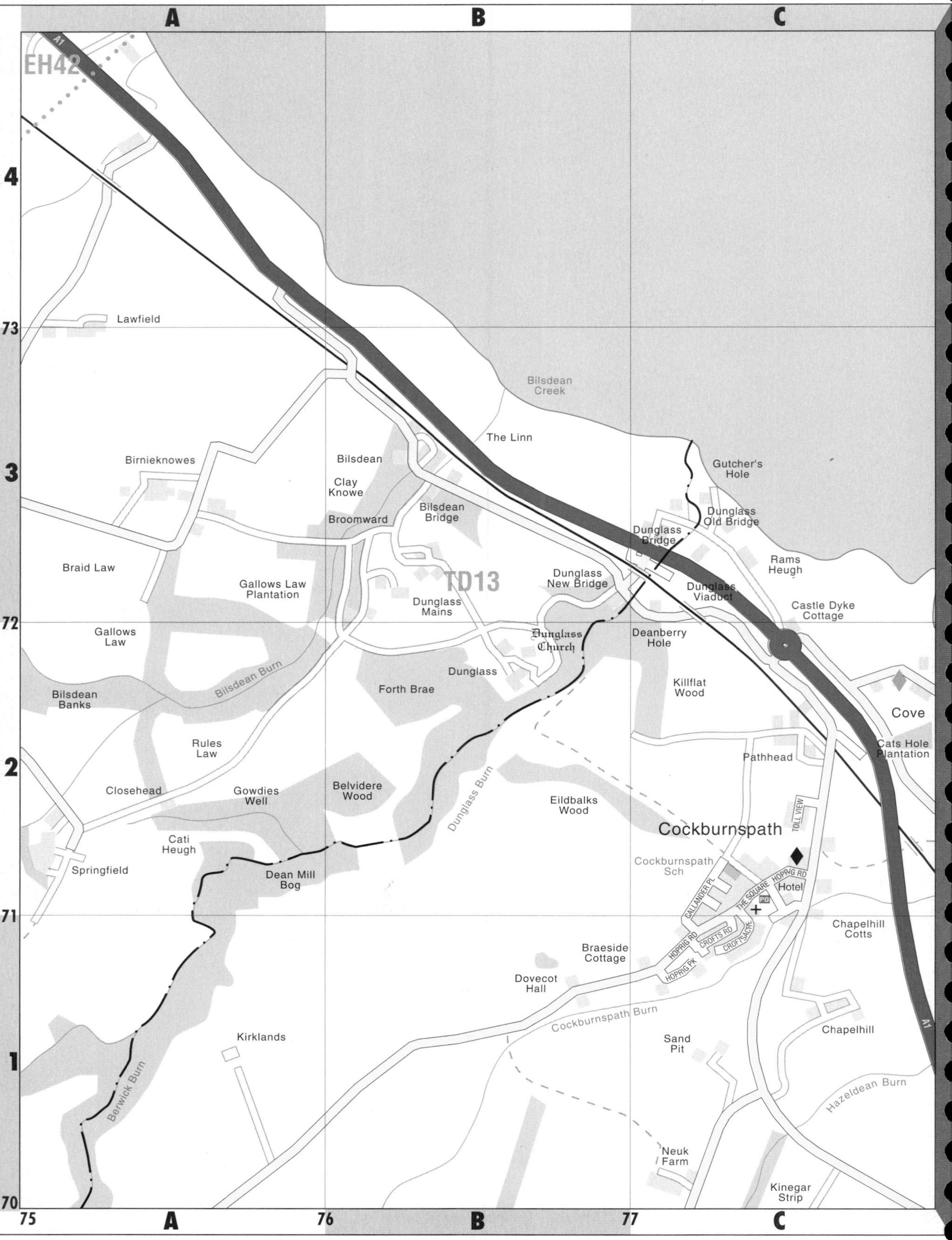

EH42

A1

Lawfield

4

73

Bilsdean
Creek

The Linn

Birnieknowes

3

Bilsdean

Gutcher's
Hole

Clay
Knowe

Dunglass
Old Bridge

Broomward

Bilsdean
Bridge

Dunglass
Bridge

Braid Law

Gallows Law
Plantation

TD13

Rams
Heugh

Dunglass
New Bridge

Dunglass Mains

Dunglass
Viaduct

Castle Dyke
Cottage

72

Gallows
Law

Dunglass
Church

Deanberry
Hole

Bilsdean
Burn

Forth Brae

Dunglass

Killflat
Wood

Cove

Bilsdean
Banks

Rules
Law

Dunglass Burn

Cats Hole
Plantation

Pathhead

2

Closehead

Gowdies
Well

Belvidere
Wood

Eildbalks
Wood

Cockburnspath

Cati
Heugh

Cockburnspath
Sch

TOLL VIEW

Springfield

Dean Mill
Bog

CALLANDER PL

THE SQUARE

HOPRIG RD

Hotel

Chapelhill
Cotts

71

HOPRIG RD

CROFTS RD

PO

CROFTS RD

Braeside
Cottage

HOPRIG PK

Dovecot
Hall

Kirklands

Cockburnspath Burn

Chapelhill

Berwick Burn

Sand
Pit

Hazeldean Burn

1

Neuk
Farm

A1

70

Kinegar
Strip

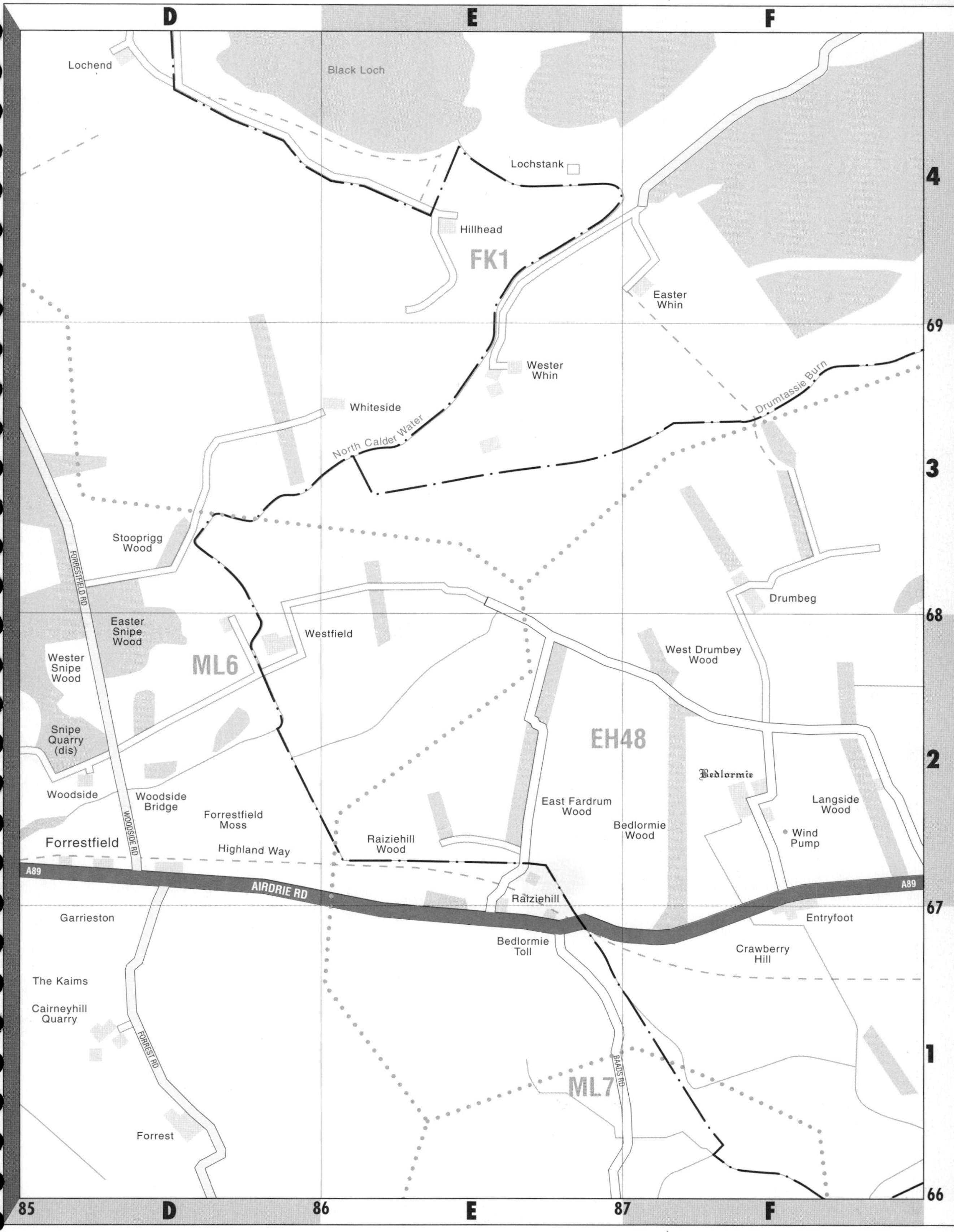

110
142
167
142

D

E

F

4

69

3

68

2

67

1

66

Lochend

Black Loch

Lochstank

Easter
Whin

Hillhead

FK1

Wester
Whin

Whiteside

North Calder Water

Drumtassie Burn

Stooprigg
Wood

Drumbeg

Easter
Snipe
Wood

Westfield

West Drumbey
Wood

Wester
Snipe
Wood

ML6

EH48

Bedlormie

Snipe
Quarry
(dis)

East Fardrum
Wood

Langside
Wood

Woodside

Woodside
Bridge

Forrestfield
Moss

Bedlormie
Wood

Wind
Pump

Forrestfield

Highland Way

Raiziehill
Wood

A89

AIRDRIE RD

A89

Garrieston

Raiziehill

Entryfoot

Bedlormie
Toll

Crawberry
Hill

The Kaims

Cairneyhill
Quarry

ML7

Forrest

FORRESTFIELD RD

WOODSIDE RD

FORREST RD

BAADS RD

85

86

87

141
111

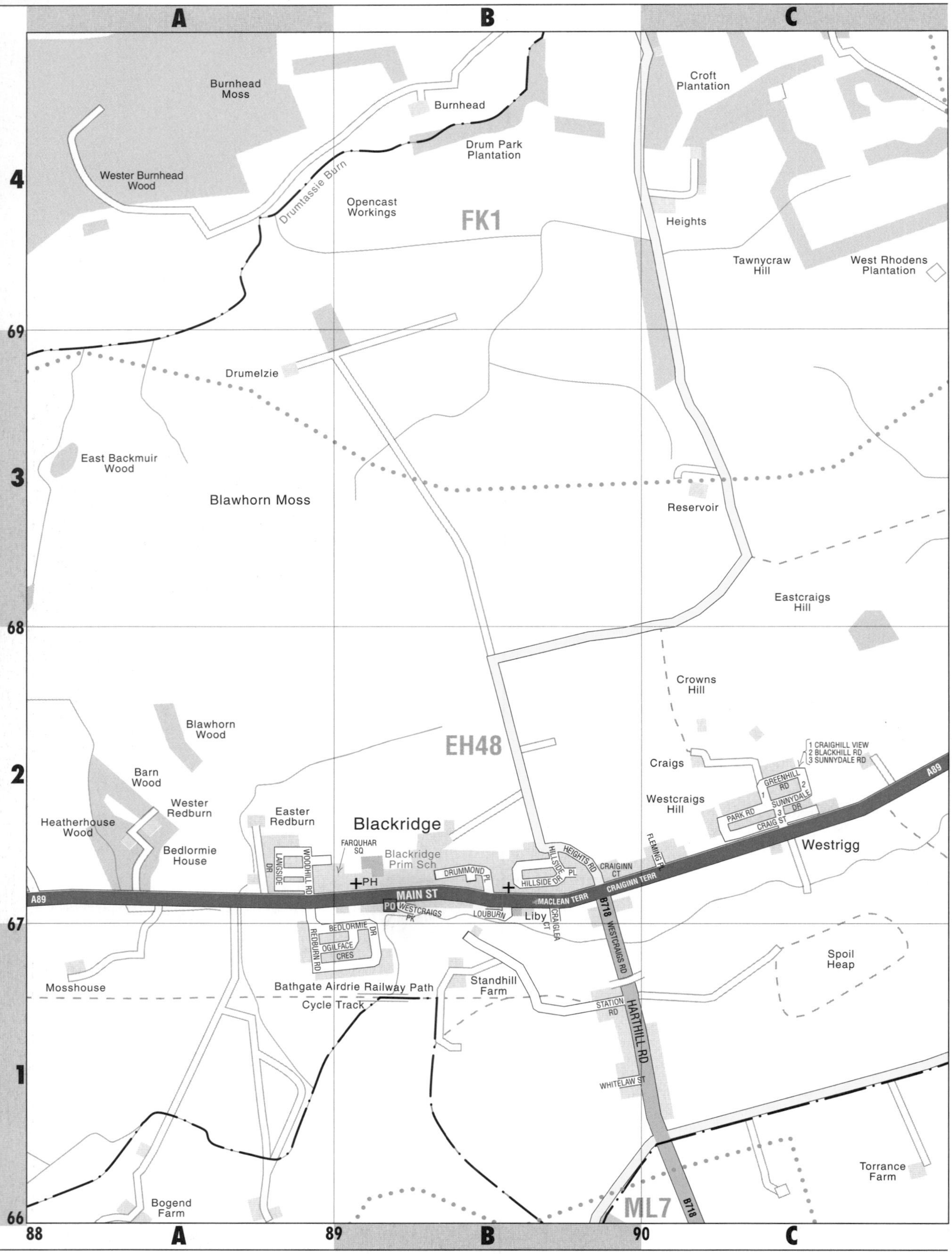

A B C

4

Burnhead Moss

Burnhead

Croft Plantation

Wester Burnhead Wood

Drum Park Plantation

Opencast Workings

Drumtassie Burn

FK1

Heights

Tawnycraw Hill

West Rhodens Plantation

69

Drumelzie

3

East Backmuir Wood

Blawhorn Moss

Reservoir

68

Eastcraigs Hill

Crowns Hill

2

Blawhorn Wood

Barn Wood

Wester Redburn

Heatherhouse Wood

Bedlormie House

Easter Redburn

FARQUHAR SQ

Blackridge

Blackridge Prim Sch

EH48

Craigs

Westcraigs Hill

1 CRAIGHILL VIEW
2 BLACKHILL RD
3 SUNNYDALE RD

GREENHILL RD

SUNNYDALE DR

PARK RD

CRAIG ST

Westrigg

A89

LANGSIDE DR

WOODHILL RD

DRUMMOND PL

HILLSIDE PL

HILLSIDE DR

HEIGHTS RD

CRAIGINN CT

CRAIGINN TERR

FLEMING PL

+PH

+

MACLEAN TERR

A89

67

PO

WESTCRAIGS PK

MAIN ST

LOUBURN

CRAIGLEA CT

Liby

BT18

WESTCRAIGS RD

BEDLORMIE DR

OGILFACE CRES

REDBURN RD

Mosshouse

Bathgate Airdrie Railway Path

Cycle Track

Standhill Farm

STATION RD

HARTHILL RD

Spoil Heap

1

WHITELAW ST

Torrance Farm

66

Bogend Farm

ML7

BT18

88 A 89 B 90 C

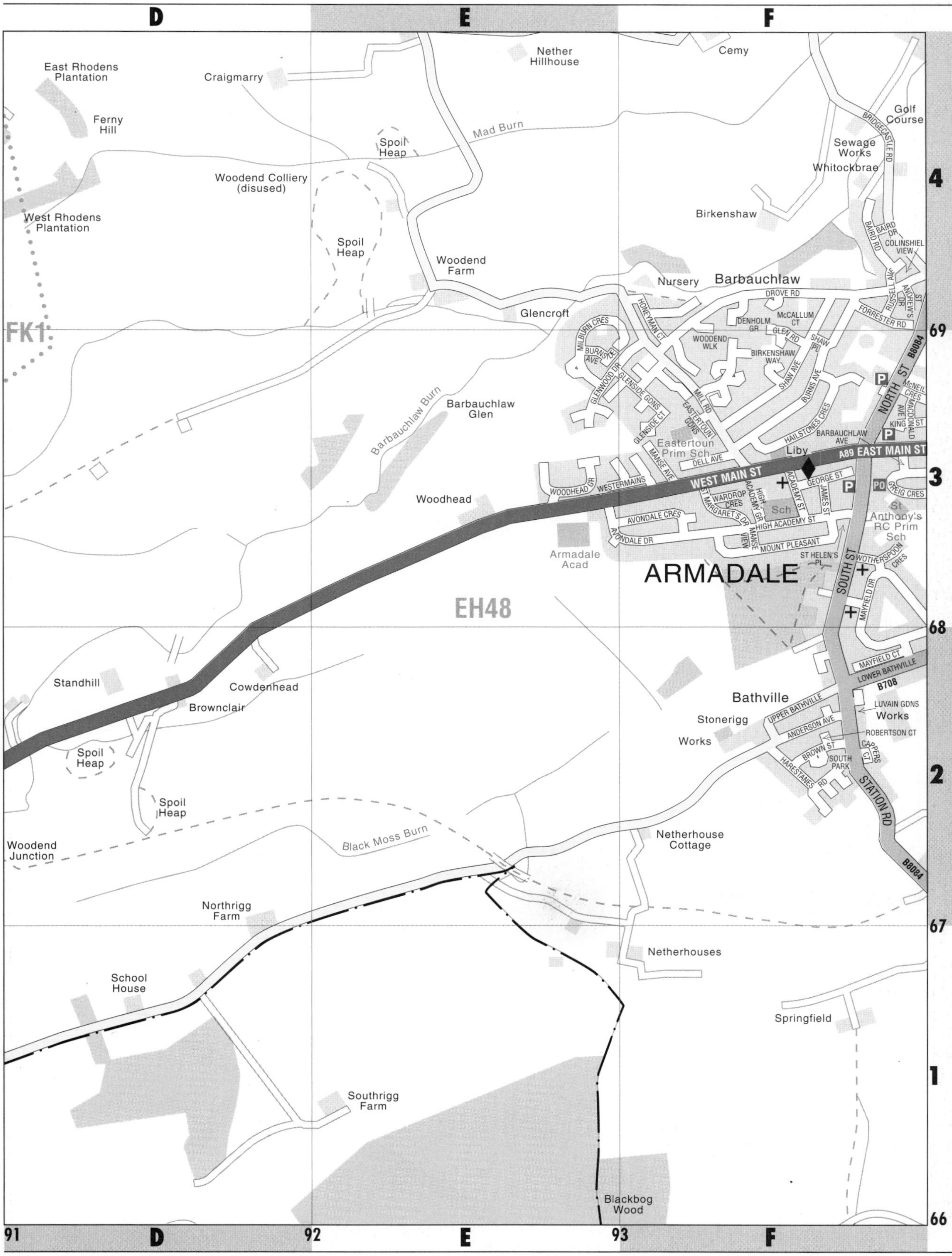

112
144

D
E
F

East Rhodens
Plantation
Craigmarry
Nether
Hillhouse
Cemy
Golf
Course
Ferny
Hill
Mad Burn
Spoil
Heap
BRIDGECASTLE RD
Sewage
Works
Whitockbrae
Woodend Colliery
(disused)
4
Birkenshaw
BAIRD DR
COLINSHIEL VIEW
West Rhodens
Plantation
Spoil
Heap
Nursery
Barbauchlaw
BAIRD RD
WHITBURN RD
ST ANDREW'S DR
FK1
Woodend
Farm
DROVE RD
McCALLUM
CT
FORRESTER RD
Glencroft
DENHOLM
GR
GLEN
RD
B8084
69
MILBURN CRES
HONEYMAN CT
WOODEND
WLK
SHAW
PL
69
Barbauchlaw Burn
Barbauchlaw
Glen
BURNS CT
GLENWOOD DR
GLENSIDE GDNS
EASTERTOUN
GDNS
MILL RD
BIRKENSHAW
WAY
SHAW AVE
BURNS AVE
NORTH ST
McNEIL
CRES
McDONALD
P
GLENSIDE CT
HAILSTONES CRES
BARBAUCHLAW
AVE
P
Eastertoun
Prim Sch
MANSE AVE
DELL AVE
Liby
Woodhead
WESTERMAINS
WOODHEAD
CRES
WEST MAIN ST
A89 EAST MAIN ST
GEORGE ST
P
PO
CREIG CRES
3
WARDROP
CRES
ST MARGARET'S DR
HIGH ACADEMY ST
ACADEMY ST
Sch
JAMES ST
St
Anthony's
RC Prim
Sch
AVONDALE CRES
MANSE
VIEW
HIGH ACADEMY ST
SOUTH ST
WOTHERSPOON
CRES
Armadale
Acad
AVONDALE DR
Mount Pleasant
St Helen's
Pl
ARMADALE
MAYFIELD DR
EH48
68
MAYFIELD CT
68
Standhill
Cowdenhead
LOWER BATHVILLE
B708
Brownclair
Bathville
LUVAIN GDNS
Works
Spoil
Heap
Stonerigg
UPPER BATHVILLE
ANDERSON AVE
ROBERTSON CT
CAPERS
CT
Works
2
Spoil
Heap
BROWN ST
SOUTH
PARK
STATION RD
Woodend
Junction
HARESTANES RD
Netherhouse
Cottage
Black Moss Burn
B8084
67
Northrigg
Farm
Netherhouses
67
School
House
Springfield
1
Southrigg
Farm
Blackbog
Wood
66
91
D
92
E
93
F
66

143
113

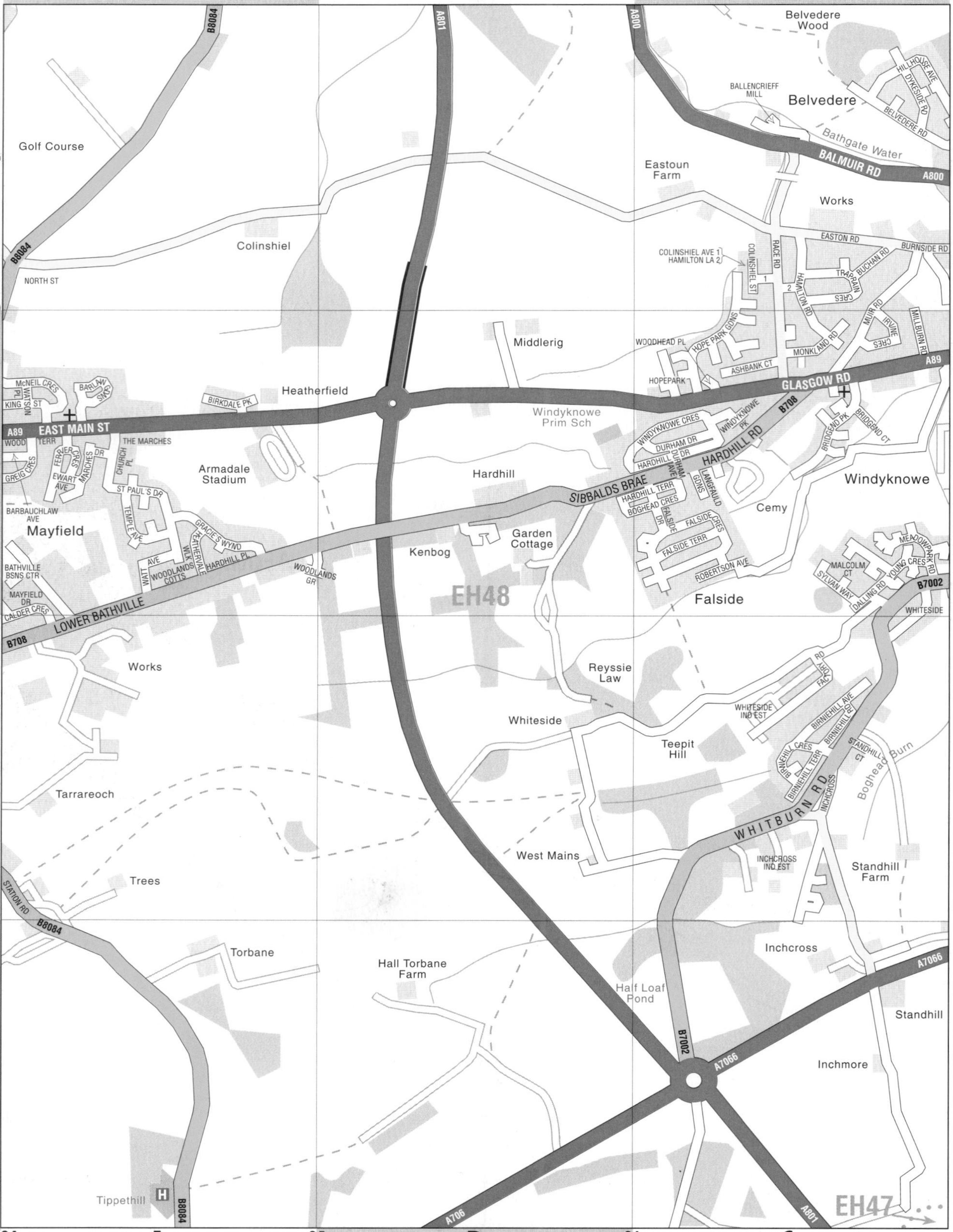
Golf Course
Colinshiel
NORTH ST
Heatherfield
Middlerig
Belvedere Wood
Belvedere
BALLENCRIEFF MILL
Bathgate Water
BALMUIR RD
Eastoun Farm
Works
EASTON RD
BURNSIDE RD
COLINSHIEL AVE 1
HAMILTON LA 2
RACE RD
HAMILTON RD
TRAPRAIN CRES
BUCHAN RD
MUIR RD
IRVINE CRES
MILLBURN RD
WOODHEAD PL
HOPE PARK GDNS
MONKLAND RD
ASHBANK CT
HOPEPARK
GLASGOW RD
EAST MAIN ST
BIRKDALE PK
Windyknowe Prim Sch
WINDYKNOWE CRES
WINDYKNOWE PK
DURHAM DR
HARDHILL RD
BRIDGEND PK
BRIDGEND CT
Windyknowe
Armadale Stadium
Hardhill
SIBBALDS BRAE
Cemy
Mayfield
Garden Cottage
Kenbog
EH48
Falside
ROBERTSON AVE
MEADOWPARK RD
MALCOLM CT
YOUNG CRES
SYLVAN WAY
DALLING RD
WHITESIDE
LOWER BATHVILLE
Works
Reyssie Law
Whiteside
WHITESIDE IND EST
Teepit Hill
BIRNIEHILL AVE
BIRNIEHILL CRES
BIRNIEHILL TERR
STANDHILL CT
Boghead Burn
Tarrareoch
WHITBURN RD
INCHCROSS
West Mains
INCHCROSS IND EST
Standhill Farm
Trees
STATION RD
Torbane
Hall Torbane Farm
Inchcross
Half Loaf Pond
Standhill
Inchmore
Tippethill
EH47
A801
A800
A89
B708
B7002
A7066
A706
B8084
A
B
C
94
95
96
66
67
68
69
1
2
3
4

143
170

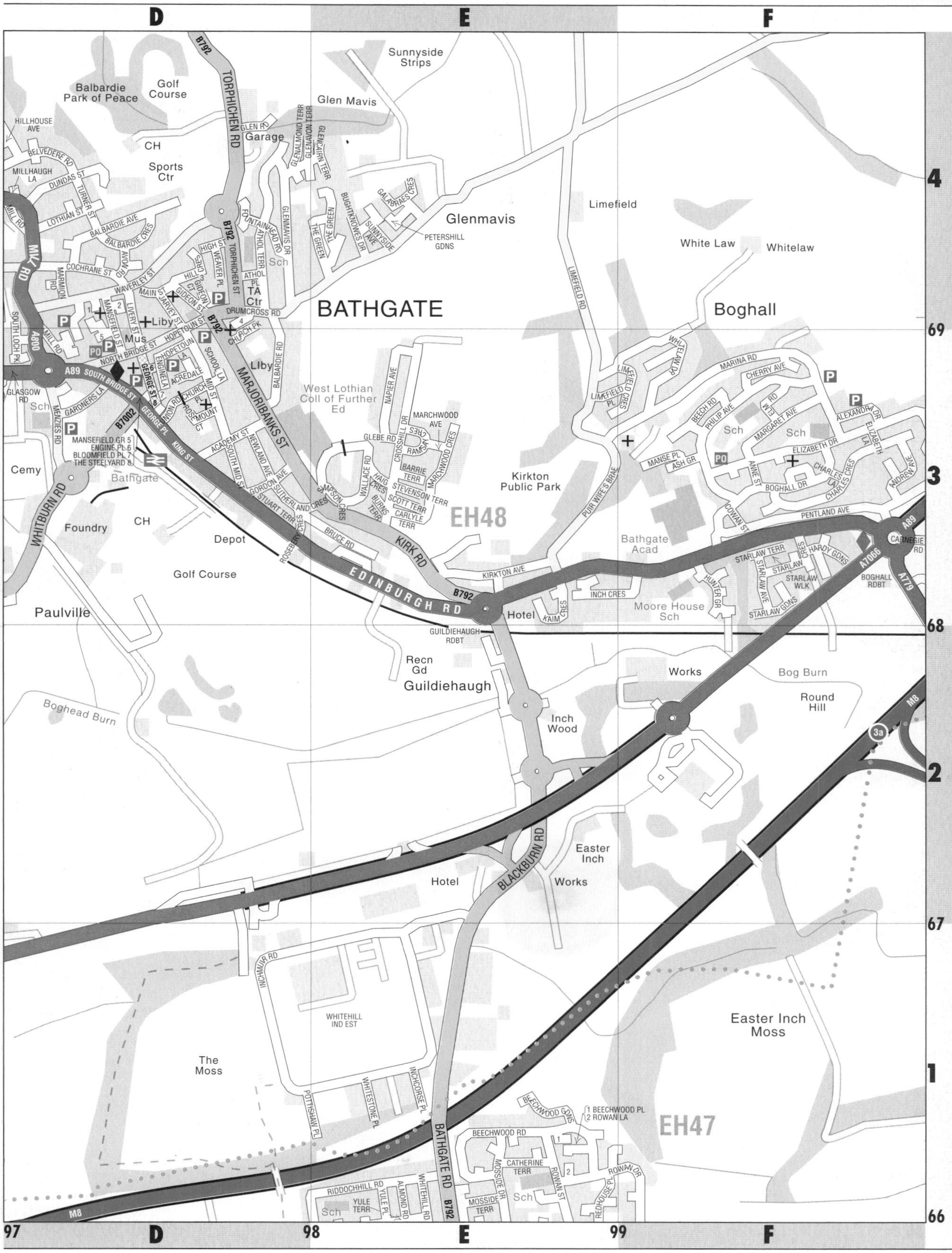

D4
1 WAVERLEY STREET IND UNITS
2 MANSEFIELD CT
3 GLEN WAY
4 HATFIELD PL

D   E   F

BATGATE

Boghall

EH48

Sunnyside Strips

Glen Mavis

Glenmavis

Limefield

White Law   Whitelaw

Balbardie Park of Peace

Golf Course

HILLHOUSE AVE

Sports Ctr

Garage

Kirkton Public Park

West Lothian Coll of Further Ed

Bathgate Acad

Moore House Sch

Cemy

Foundry

CH

Paulville

Golf Course

Boghead Burn

The Moss

WHITEHILL IND EST

Recn Gd

Guildiehaugh

GUILDIEHAUGH RDBT

Inch Wood

Hotel

Works

Bog Burn

Round Hill

Easter Inch

Works

Hotel

Easter Inch Moss

EH47

1 BEECHWOOD PL
2 ROWAN LA

Sch

CARNEGIE RD

BOGHALL RDBT

Mansfield GR 5
Engine PL 6
Bloomfield PL 7
The Steelyard 8

4

69

3

68

2

67

1

66

97   D   98   E   99   F

A   B   C

EH52   A89   M8

4

Drumcross
Cottages

Royston

DEANS
IND EST

ROYSTON RD

HERON
IND COMPLEX

Woodlands
Park

NORTHWOOD PK

WOODLANDS PK

EH48

MOSSGIEL
COTTS

ROYSTON
RDBT

HARDIE RD

MIDDLEWOOD PK

BEECHWOOD

Meldrum
Prim Sch

WESTWOOD PK

ELM
WOOD
PK

WESTWOOD PK

69

DEANS
IND EST

HARDIE RD

DEANSWOOD PK

PENWOOD PK

HARBURN AVE W

Sch

HARBURN AVE

Bog Burn

CARNEGIE RD

DEANS NORTH RD

WEST GLEN AVE

JUBILEE AVE

KILMORE AVE

NELBURN

HARBURN AVE

DEANS RD

GLEN
EAST

GLEN CRES

GLEN AVE

Neil Burn

Elizabeth
Dr

BURNKNOWE

GLEN TERR

GLEN RD

BROOM

Deans

A89

PENTLAND AVE

CAPUTHALL RD

DEANS
IND EST

CHRISTIE SQ

MANSON SQ

CHALMERS SQ

CULLEN SQ

GLEN CT

MAIN ST

ST ANDREWS WAY

PO

FIELD WAY

GLENEAGLES
WAY

MID ST

3MONS

3MONS

Sch

HUNTLY AVE

ELIE AVE

FLIE AVE

3

Carnegie Rd

NEILSON SQ

DEWAR SQ

LINDSAY SQ

DEANS
SERVICE UNITS

DEANS
RDBT

STAFFA

ARRAN

JURA

BUTE

ELIE AVE

Starlaw

DUNLOP SQ

EH54

AROL
SQ

DEANS SOUTH

DEANS SOUTH

68

A779

BARRACKS
RDBT

HOUSTOUN RD W

School House

HOUSTOUN RD

M8

TAILEND
IND PK

APPLETON PARKWAY
RDBT

Tailend Moss

DEANS RD

APPLETON PARKWAY

STARLAW
BSNS PK

2

STARLAW WEST
RDBT

A779

STARLAW RD

TAILEND
RDBT

STARLAW RD

A779

Starlaw

Lochshot Burn

Cousland
Wood

WILSON RD

SIMPSON PARKWAY

EH47

TOLL
RDBT

A705

67

West Long
Livingston

Cousland

P

FLEMING RD

Easter Inch
Moss

River Almond

PASSET RD

B7015

1

Seafield Inf
Sch

Kirkton
Campus

HEATHER PK

HARWOOD

BEECH PL

DEAN PL

DEAN BURN

MACINTOSH
RD

REDHOUSE RD

BYRE PK

HARWOOD

PO

BEECH

SEAFIELD
ROWS

COUSLAND TERR

COUSLAND CRES

ALMOND VIEW

MACINTOSH RD

A705

66

Seafield

EH55

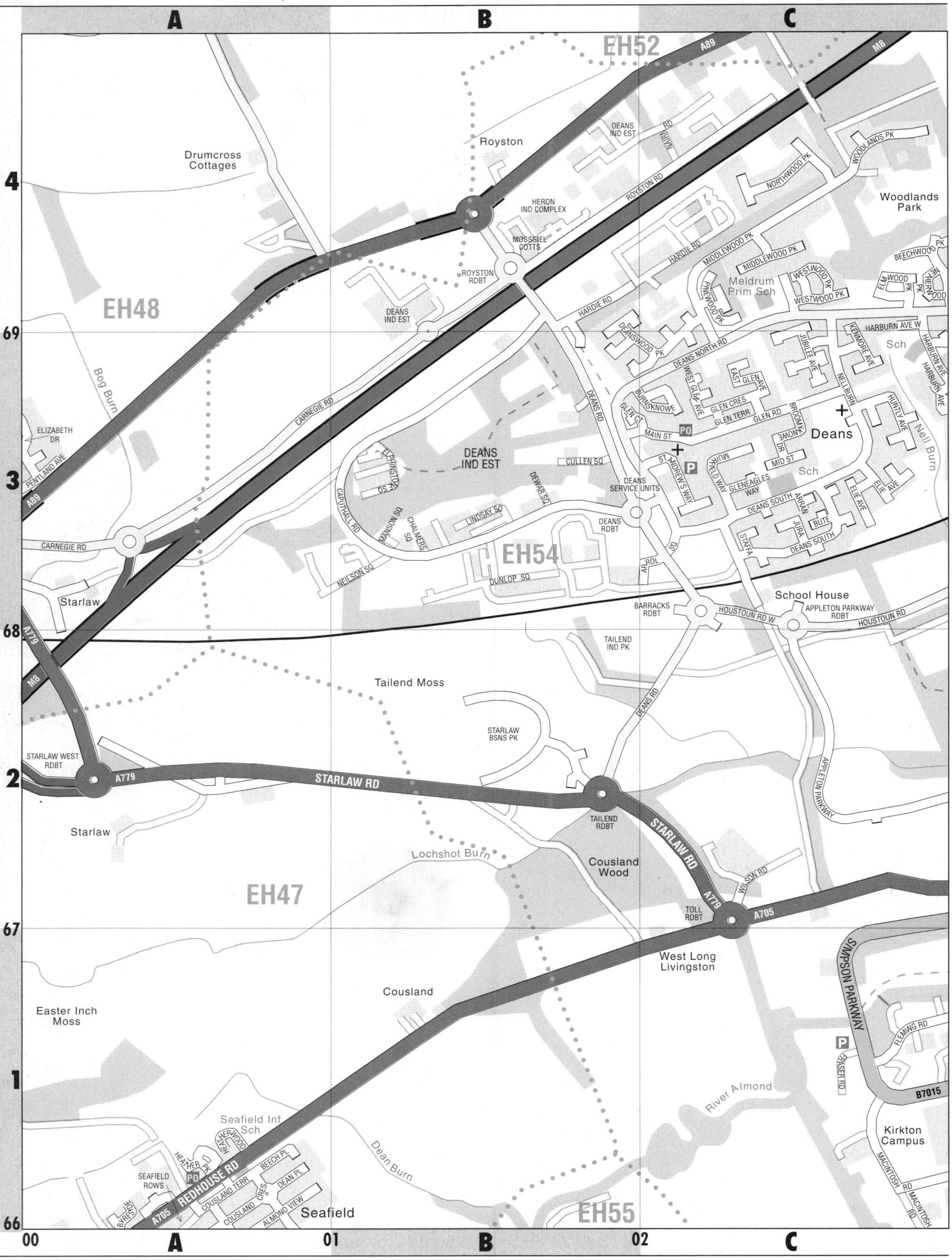

116
148

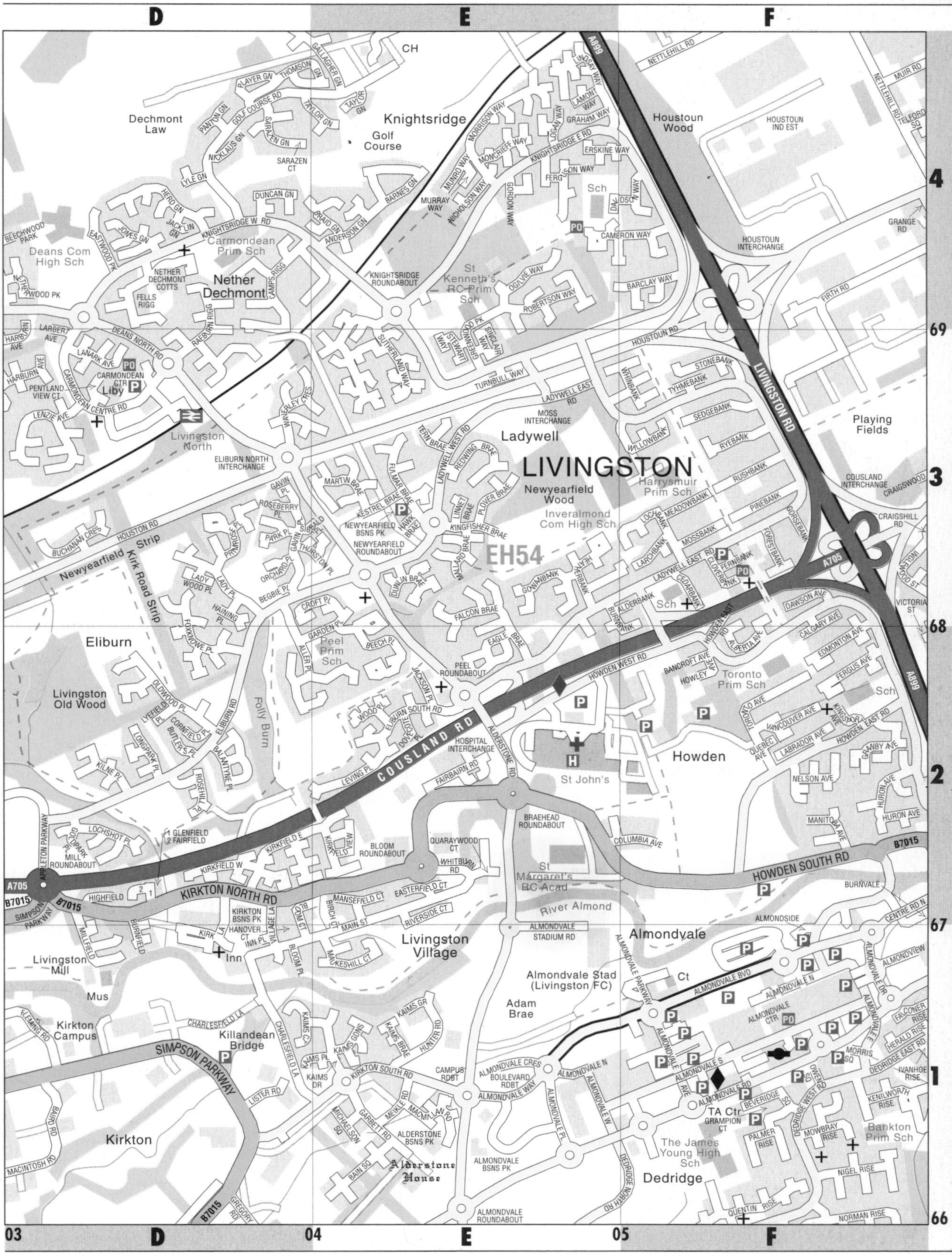
D
E
F
Dechmont Law
Knightsridge
Golf Course
CH
Houstoun Wood
HOUSTOUN IND EST
Deans Com High Sch
Carmondean Prim Sch
Nether Dechmont
St Kenneth's RC Prim Sch
KNIGHTSRIDGE ROUNDABOUT
HOUSTOUN INTERCHANGE
Liby
Livingston North
ELIBURN NORTH INTERCHANGE
MOSS INTERCHANGE
Ladywell
LIVINGSTON
Newyearfield Wood
Harrysmuir Prim Sch
Inveralmond Com High Sch
Playing Fields
COUSLAND INTERCHANGE
EH54
Newyearfield Strip
Kirk Road Strip
NEWYEARFIELD ROUNDABOUT
Eliburn
Peel Prim Sch
PEEL ROUNDABOUT
Livingston Old Wood
Folly Burn
COUSLAND RD
HOSPITAL INTERCHANGE
St John's
Howden
Toronto Prim Sch
BRAEHEAD ROUNDABOUT
BLOOM ROUNDABOUT
MILL ROUNDABOUT
KIRKTON NORTH RD
HOWDEN SOUTH RD
St Margaret's RC Acad
River Almond
Livingston Village
Livingston Mill
Inn
Mus
Almondvale
Almondvale Stad (Livingston FC)
Adam Brae
Kirkton Campus
Killandean Bridge
SIMPSON PARKWAY
Kirkton
CAMPUS RDBT
BOULEVARD RDBT
ALDERSTONE BSNS PK
Alderstone House
ALMONDVALE BSNS PK
ALMONDVALE ROUNDABOUT
TA Ctr
The James Young High Sch
Dedridge
Bankton Prim Sch
A899
A705
B7015
LIVINGSTON RD
4
69
3
68
2
67
1
66
03
04
05

173
148

147
117

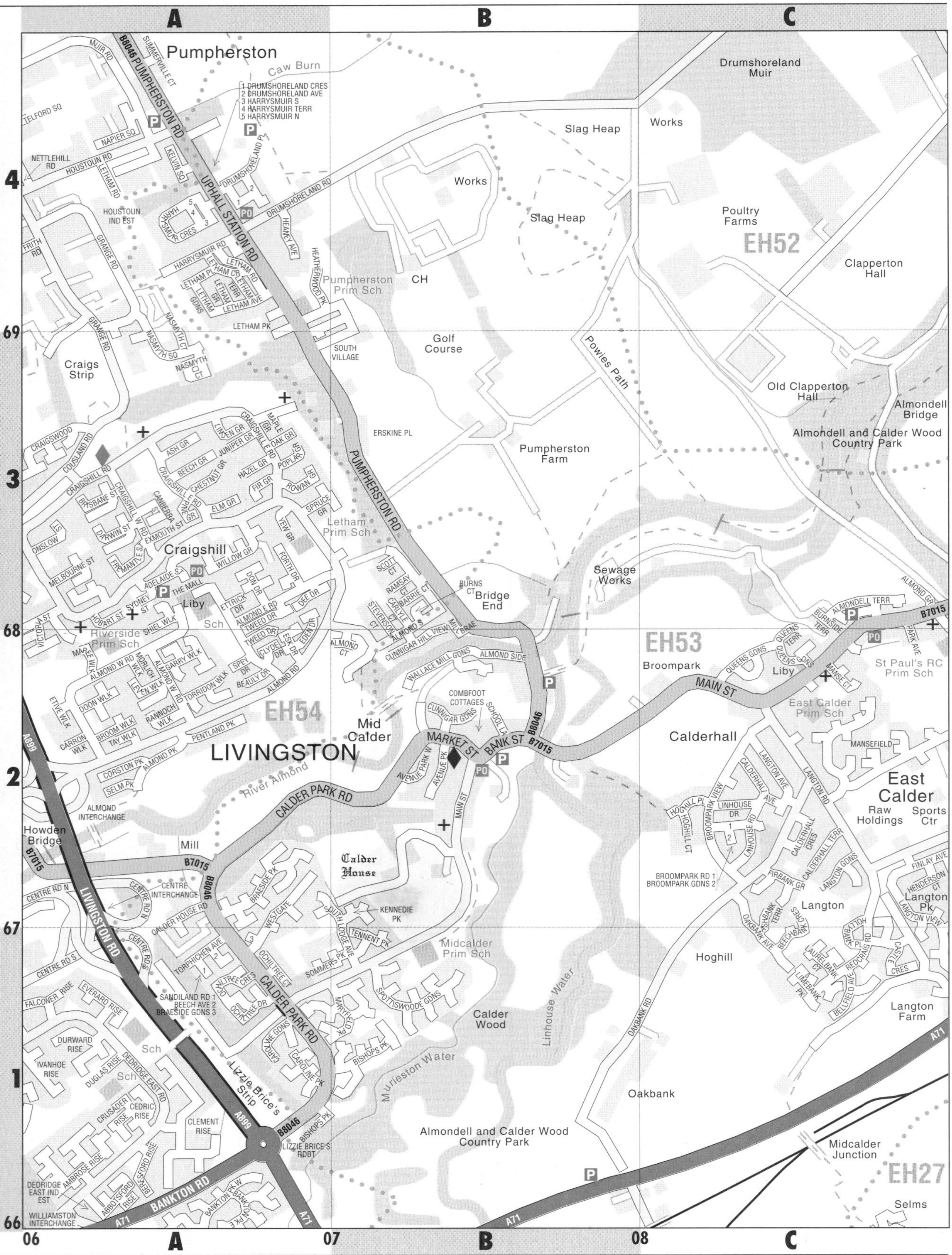
A
B
C
Pumpherston
Caw Burn
1 DRUMSHORELAND CRES
2 DRUMSHORELAND AVE
3 HARRYSMUIR S
4 HARRYSMUIR TERR
5 HARRYSMUIR N
PUMPHERSTON RD
UPHALL STATION RD
B8046
SUMMERVILLE CT
MUIR RD
TELFORD SQ
NAPIER SQ
NETTLEHILL RD
HOUSTOUN RD
LETHAM RD
KELVIN SQ
DRUMSHORELAND PL
DRUMSHORELAND RD
HEANEY AVE
HOUSTOUN IND EST
FRITH RD
GRANGE RD
HARRYSMUIR RD
HARRYSMUIR CRES
LETHAM PL
LETHAM CT
LETHAM TERR
LETHAM AVE
LETHAM GDNS
LETHAM PK
HEATHERWOOD PK
NASMYTH CT
NASMYTH SQ
Pumpherston Prim Sch
CH
Drumshoreland Muir
Slag Heap
Works
Works
Slag Heap
Poultry Farms
EH52
Clapperton Hall
Golf Course
SOUTH VILLAGE
Powies Path
Old Clapperton Hall
Almondell Bridge
Almondell and Calder Wood Country Park
Craigs Strip
CRAIGSWOOD
COUSLAND RD
CRAIGSHILL RD
CRAIGSHILL ST
CRAIGSHILL E RD
CRAIGSHILL W RD
ASH GR
LINDEN GR
JUNIPER GR
MAPLE GR
OAK GR
BEECH GR
CHESTNUT GR
HAZEL GR
POPLAR ST
ROWAN GR
FIR GR
PINE GR
ELM GR
SPRUCE GR
BRISBANE ST
CANBERRA ST
DARWIN ST
EXMOUTH ST
ERSKINE PL
Pumpherston Farm
Letham Prim Sch
ONSLOW ST
MELBOURNE ST
FREMANTLE ST
Craigshill
WILLOW GR
YEW GR
FORTH DR
ADELAIDE ST
THE MALL
Liby
Sch
DON DR
ETTRICK DR
ALMOND E RD
TWEED DR
DEE DR
SCOTT CT
RAMSAY CT
BARRIE CT
CARLYLE CT
STEVENSON CT
ALMOND S
BURNS CT
Bridge End
Sewage Works
VICTORIA ST
HOBART ST
SYDNEY ST
SHIEL WLK
Riverside Prim Sch
MARNE WLK
ALMOND W RD
MORLICH WLK
GARRY WLK
CLYDE DR
ESK DR
EDEN DR
ALMOND RD
ALMOND CT
CUNNIGAR HILL VIEW
MILL BRAE
ALMOND SIDE
WALLACE MILL GDNS
EH53
Broompark
QUEENS GDNS
QUEENS TERR
BURNSIDE TERR
ALMONDELL TERR
ALMOND GR
B7015
PARK AVE
St Paul's RC Prim Sch
Liby
MANSE CT
MAIN ST
ETTIVE WLK
DOON WLK
LEVEN WLK
TORRIDON WLK
SPEY DR
BEAULY DR
RANNOCH WLK
EH54
COMBFOOT COTTAGES
CUNNIGAR GDNS
SCHOOL LA
East Calder Prim Sch
Calderhall
BROOM WLK
TAY WLK
CARRON WLK
PENTLAND PK
CORSTON PK
ALMOND PK
SELM PK
LIVINGSTON
River Almond
Mid Calder
MARKET ST
BANK ST
B7015
PARK W
AVENUE PK
MAIN ST
CALDER PARK RD
MANSEFIELD
LANGTON AVE
CALDERHALL AVE
LANGTON RD
East Calder
Raw Holdings
Sports Ctr
A899
ALMOND INTERCHANGE
Howden Bridge
Mill
B7015
HOGHILL PL
HOGHILL CT
BROOMPARK VIEW
LINHOUSE DR
LINHOUSE RD
CALDERHALL CRES
CALDERHALL TERR
Calder House
BRAESIDE PK
BROOMPARK RD 1
BROOMPARK GDNS 2
FIRBANK GR
LANGTON GDNS
FINLAY AVE
HENDERSON CT
Langton Pk
LANGTON VIEW
CENTRE RD N
CENTRE INTERCHANGE
CALDER HOUSE RD
WESTGATE
SOUTH LODGE AVE
KENNEDIE PK
Langton
OAKBANK AVE
FIRBANK TERR
BEECHBANK CRES
PARK PL
REDCRAIG RD
CASTLE CRES
LAURELBANK CT
LIMEBANK PK
BELLFIELD AVE
LIVINGSTON RD
CENTRE RD S
TORPHICHEN AVE
TENNENT PK
SOMMERS PK
Midcalder Prim Sch
Hoghill
OCHILTREE CT
OCHILTREE CRES
OCHILTREE DR
SANDILAND RD 1
BEECH AVE 2
BRAESIDE GDNS 3
FALCONER RISE
EVERARD RISE
CALDER PARK RD
MARYFIELD PK
SPOTTISWOODE GDNS
Linhouse Water
Calder Wood
OAKBANK RD
Langton Farm
A71
DURWARD RISE
Sch
IVANHOE RISE
DUGLAS RISE
DEDRIDGE EAST RD
Sch
CARLOWRIE GDNS
CAROLINE PK
BISHOPS PK
Murieston Water
Lizzie Brice's Strip
Oakbank
CRUSADER RISE
CEDRIC RISE
CLEMENT RISE
B8046
BISHOPS PK
LIZZIE BRICE'S RDBT
Almondell and Calder Wood Country Park
Midcalder Junction
AMBROSE RISE
BLACKFORD RISE
ABBOTSFORD RISE
DEDRIDGE EAST IND EST
BANKTON RD
BANKTON PK W
BANKTON PK E
EH27
WILLIAMSTON INTERCHANGE
A71
A71
Selms
4
69
3
68
2
67
1
66
06
07
08

147
174

118
150

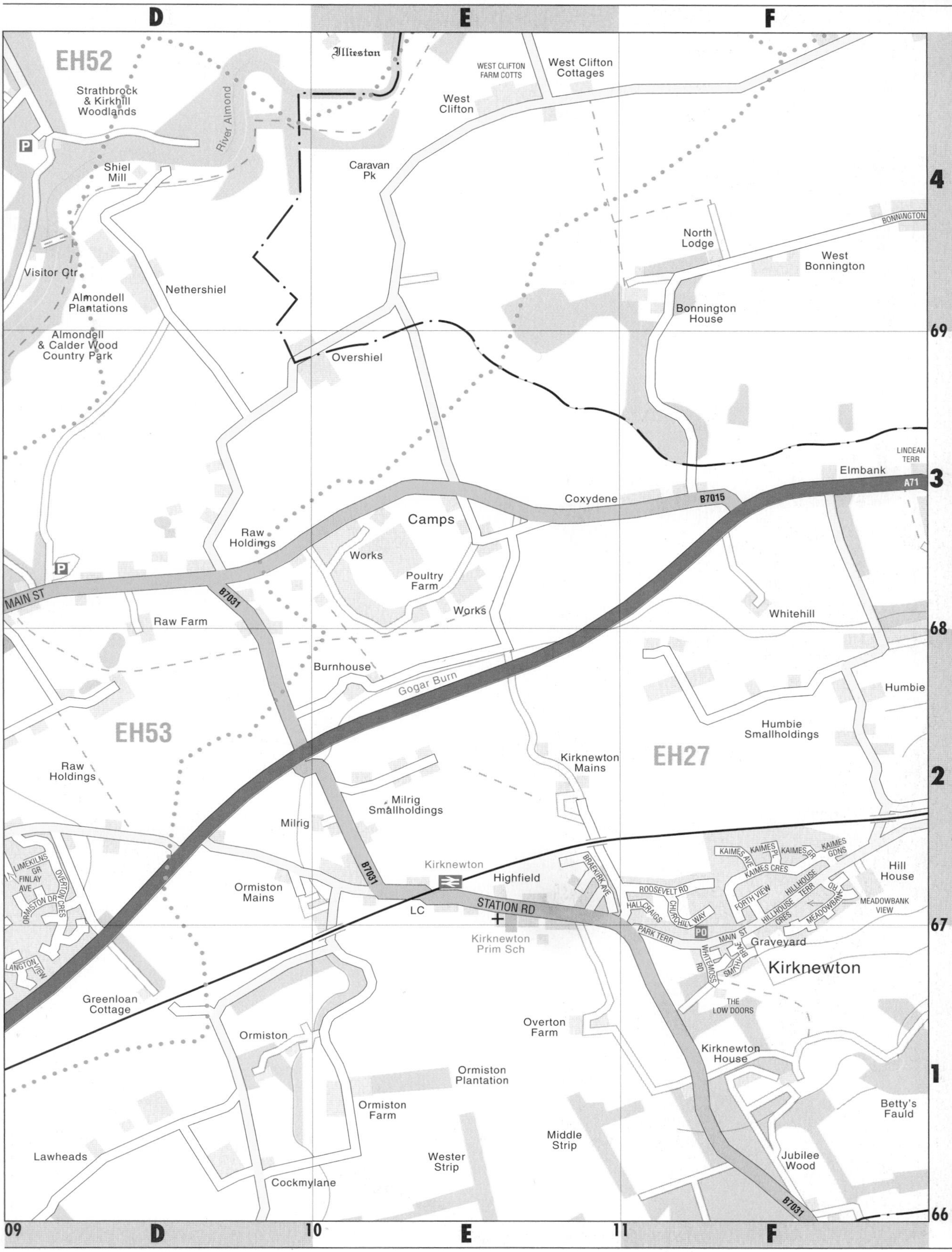
D
E
F
EH52
Illieston
WEST CLIFTON FARM COTTS
West Clifton Cottages
Strathbrock & Kirkhill Woodlands
River Almond
West Clifton
P
Shiel Mill
Caravan Pk
4
North Lodge
BONNINGTON
West Bonnington
Visitor Ctr
Nethershiel
Almondell Plantations
Bonnington House
69
Almondell & Calder Wood Country Park
Overshiel
LINDEAN TERR
Elmbank
A71
3
Coxydene
B7015
Camps
Raw Holdings
Works
P
Poultry Farm
MAIN ST
B7031
Works
Whitehill
Raw Farm
68
Burnhouse
Humbie
Gogar Burn
EH53
Humbie Smallholdings
Kirknewton Mains
EH27
Raw Holdings
2
Milrig Smallholdings
Milrig
KAIMES AVE
KAIMES PL
KAIMES GR
KAIMES GDNS
KAIMES CRES
LIMEKILNS GR
FINLAY AVE
OVERTON CRES
ORMISTON DR
Kirknewton
Hill House
BRAEKIRK AVE
Highfield
Ormiston Mains
B7031
ROOSEVELT RD
FORTH VIEW
HILLHOUSE TERR
MEADOWBANK RD
MEADOWBANK VIEW
LC
STATION RD
HALLCRAIGS
CHURCHILL WAY
HILLHOUSE CRES
67
PARK TERR
PO
MAIN ST
Graveyard
Kirknewton Prim Sch
WHITEMOSS RD
SMIDDY BRAE
LANGTON VIEW
Kirknewton
Greenloan Cottage
THE LOW DOORS
Overton Farm
Ormiston
Kirknewton House
1
Ormiston Plantation
Betty's Fauld
Ormiston Farm
Middle Strip
Lawheads
Wester Strip
Jubilee Wood
Cockmylane
B7031
66
09
10
11

175
150

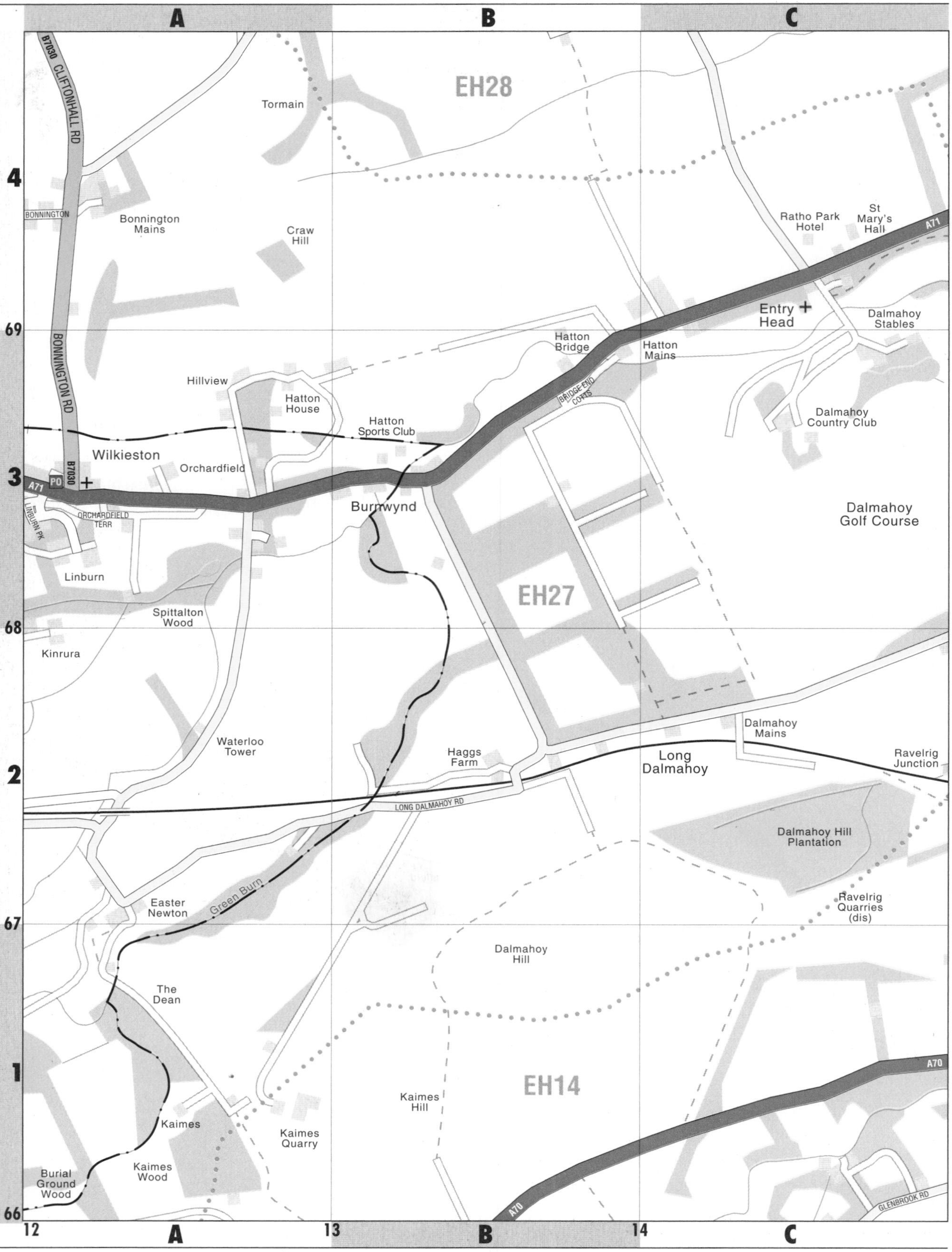
A
B
C
EH28
Tormain
B7030 CLIFTONHALL RD
BONNINGTON
Bonnington Mains
Craw Hill
Ratho Park Hotel
St Mary's Hall
A71
Entry Head
Dalmahoy Stables
BONNINGTON RD
Hatton Bridge
Hatton Mains
Hillview
Hatton House
BRIDGE END COTTS
Dalmahoy Country Club
Hatton Sports Club
Wilkieston
Orchardfield
B7030
PO
Burnwynd
Dalmahoy Golf Course
ORCHARDFIELD TERR
LINBURN PK
Linburn
EH27
Spittalton Wood
Kinrura
Waterloo Tower
Haggs Farm
Dalmahoy Mains
Long Dalmahoy
Ravelrig Junction
LONG DALMAHOY RD
Dalmahoy Hill Plantation
Green Burn
Easter Newton
Ravelrig Quarries (dis)
Dalmahoy Hill
The Dean
EH14
A70
Kaimes Hill
Kaimes
Kaimes Quarry
Kaimes Wood
Burial Ground Wood
GLENBROOK RD
4
69
3
68
2
67
1
66
12
13
14

120
152

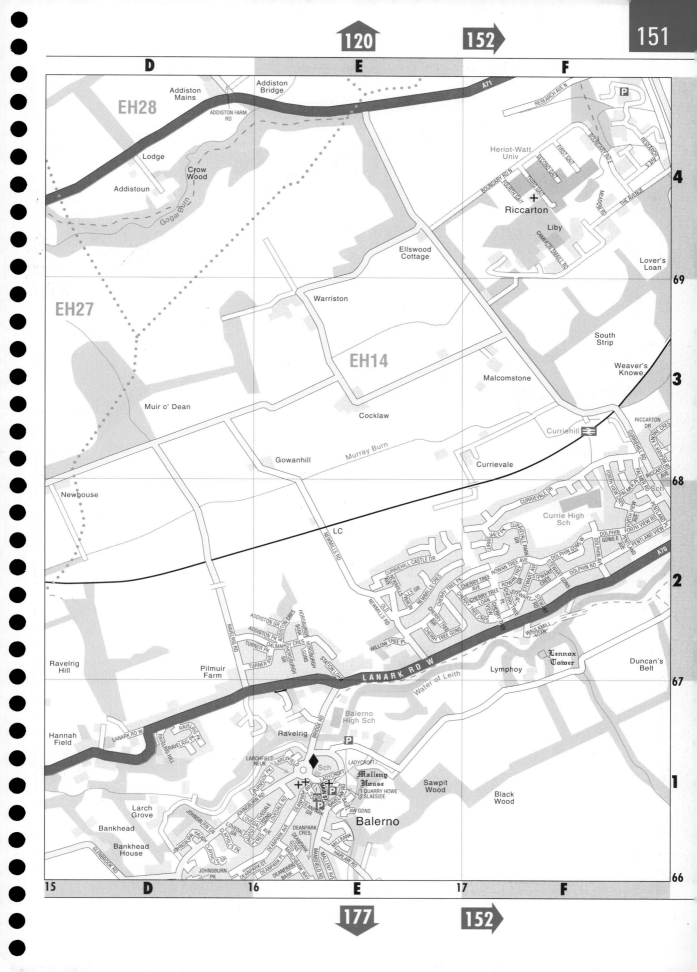
D
E
F
EH28
EH27
EH14
Addiston Mains
Addiston Bridge
ADDISTON FARM RD
A71
Lodge
Crow Wood
Addistoun
Gogar Burn
Heriot-Watt Univ
Riccarton
Liby
RESEARCH AVE N
BOUNDARY RD N
BOUNDARY RD E
FIRST GAIT
SECOND GAIT
THIRD GAIT
FOURTH GAIT
CAMERON SMAILL RD
MEADOW RD
THE AVENUE
RESEARCH AVE S
Ellswood Cottage
Lover's Loan
Warriston
South Strip
Weaver's Knowe
Malcomstone
Muir o' Dean
Cocklaw
Curriehill
RICCARTON DR
Gowanhill
Murray Burn
Currievale
Newhouse
CURRIEVALE DR
Currie High Sch
LC
NEWMILLS RD
CURRIEHILL CASTLE DR
ROWAN TREE AVE
CHERRY TREE AVE
CHERRY TREE LOAN
CHERRY TREE CRES
CHERRY TREE GDNS
CHERRY TREE PK
DOLPHIN GDNS W
DOLPHIN RD
DOLPHIN AVE
STEWART AVE
STEWART CRES
STEWART GDNS
STEWART RD
PENTLAND VIEW
FORTH VIEW RD
PALMER RD
A70
OLD NEWMILLS RD
WILLOW TREE PL
WAULKMILL LOAN
RAVELRIG RD
ADDISTON GR
ADDISTON CRES
ADDISTON PK
HORSBURGH BANK
HORSBURGH GDNS
HORSBURGH GR
DALMAHOY CRES
TURNER PK
TURNER AVE
STATION LOAN
LANARK RD W
Water of Leith
Lennox Tower
Lymphoy
Duncan's Belt
Ravelrig Hill
Pilmuir Farm
Balerno High Sch
Hannah Field
Ravelrig
BRIDGE RD
RAVELRIG PK
RAVELRIG HILL
LARCHFIELD NEUK
LARCHFIELD
Sch
LADYCROFT
Malleny House
1 QUARRY HOWE
2 SLAESIDE
MAIN ST
BAVELAW RD
Sawpit Wood
Black Wood
Larch Grove
Bankhead
Bankhead House
JOHNSBURN RD
JOHNSBURN GN
JOHNSBURN HAUGH
JOHNSBURN PK
LOVEDALE RD
LOVEDALE AVE
LOVEDALE CRES
CLAYHILLS GR
CLAYHILLS PK
DEANPARK BRAE
DEANPARK GR
DEANPARK AVE
DEANPARK CRES
DEANPARK GDNS
DEANPARK CT
DEANPARK PL
DEANPARK BANK
MARCHBANK WAY
MANSFIELD RD
MALLENY AVE
HARLAW RD
MILLBANK
Balerno
GLENBROOK RD
15
16
17
66
67
68
69
1
2
3
4

177
152

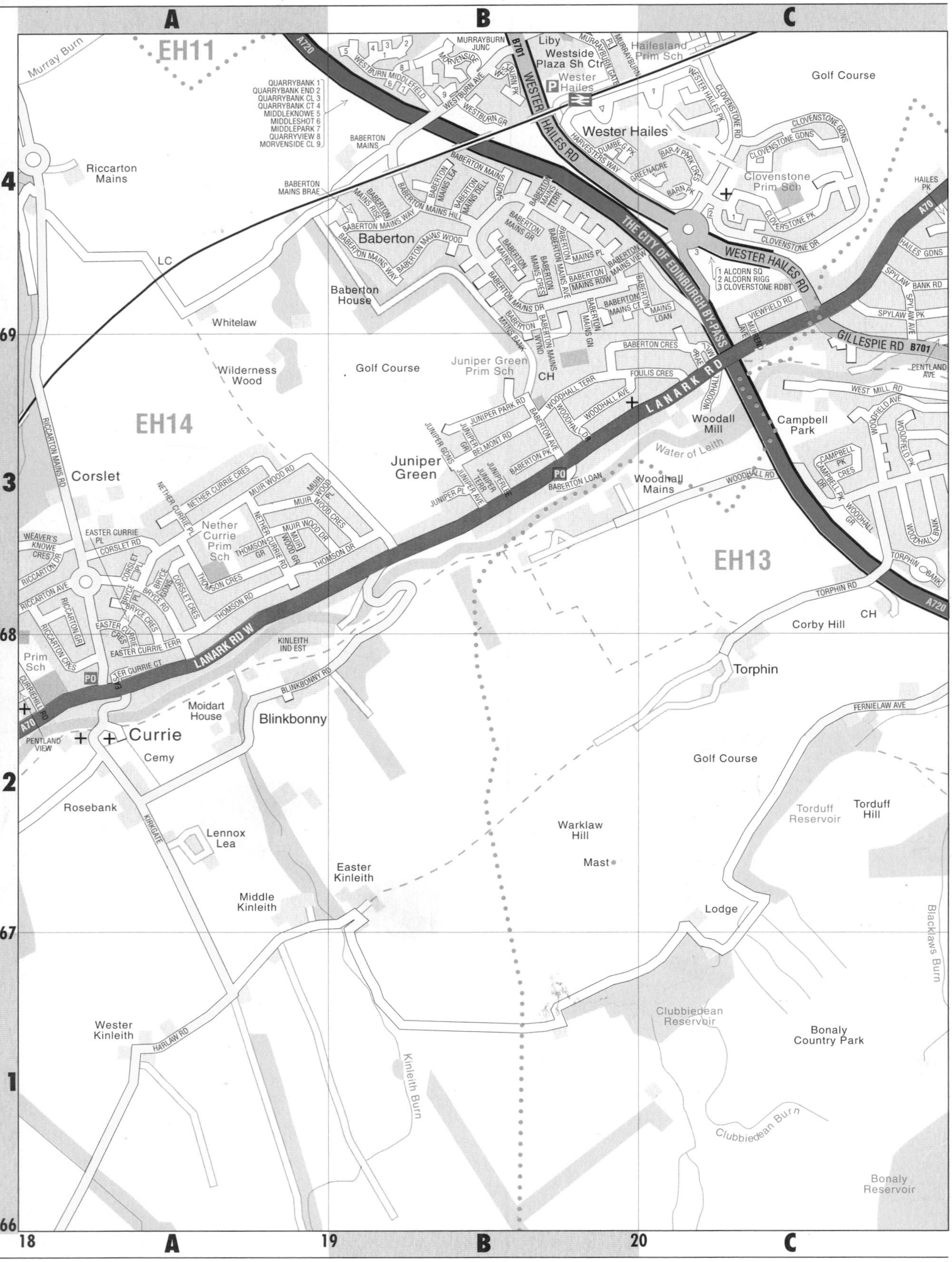

EH11

Murray Burn

A B C

QUARRYBANK 1
QUARRYBANK END 2
QUARRYBANK CL 3
QUARRYBANK CT 4
MIDDLEKNOWE 5
MIDDLESHOT 6
MIDDLEPARK 7
QUARRYVIEW 8
MORVENSIDE CL 9

Murrayburn Junc
Westburn Middlefield
Westburn Ave
Westburn Gr

Murrayburn Junc
Liby
Westside
Plaza Sh Ctr
Wester
Hailes
Hailesland
Prim Sch
Golf Course

Wester Hailes

Clovenstone Gdns
Clovenstone
Prim Sch
Clovenstone Pk
Clovenstone Dr

Hailes
Pk

A70

Hailes Gdns

Spylaw Bank Rd
Spylaw Pk

Riccarton
Mains

Baberton
Mains Brae

Baberton
Mains

Baberton Mains Way

Baberton

Baberton
House

LC

Whitelaw

Wilderness
Wood

Golf Course

Juniper Green
Prim Sch

CH

Baberton Cres

Foulis Cres

Lanark Rd

Viewfield Rd

Gillespie Rd B701

Pentland Ave

West Mill Rd

Woodall
Mill

Campbell
Park

1 ALCORN SQ
2 ALCORN RIGG
3 CLOVENSTONE RDBT

THE CITY OF EDINBURGH BY-PASS

WESTER HAILES RD

EH14

Corslet

Nether Currie
Prim Sch

Juniper
Green

Juniper Park Rd

Baberton Pk

Baberton Loan

Water of Leith

Woodhall
Mains

Woodhall Rd

EH13

Woodhall
Gr

Campbell
Pk Cres

Torphin Bank

A720

Riccarton Mains Rd

Weaver's
Knowe
Cres

Easter Currie
Pl

Corslet Rd

Bryce Cres

Thomson Dr

Muir Wood Rd
Muir Wood Cres

Lanark Rd W

Kinleith
Ind Est

PO

Torphin Rd

Corby Hill

CH

Torphin

Riccarton Ave

Prim
Sch

PO

A70

Pentland
View

Currie

Cemy

Moidart
House

Blinkbonny

Blinkbonny Rd

Fernielaw Ave

Rosebank

Lennox
Lea

Kirkgate

Easter
Kinleith

Middle
Kinleith

Golf Course

Warklaw
Hill

Mast

Lodge

Torduff
Reservoir

Torduff
Hill

Blacklaws Burn

Wester
Kinleith

Harlaw Rd

Kinleith Burn

Clubbiedean
Reservoir

Bonaly
Country Park

Clubbiedean Burn

Bonaly
Reservoir

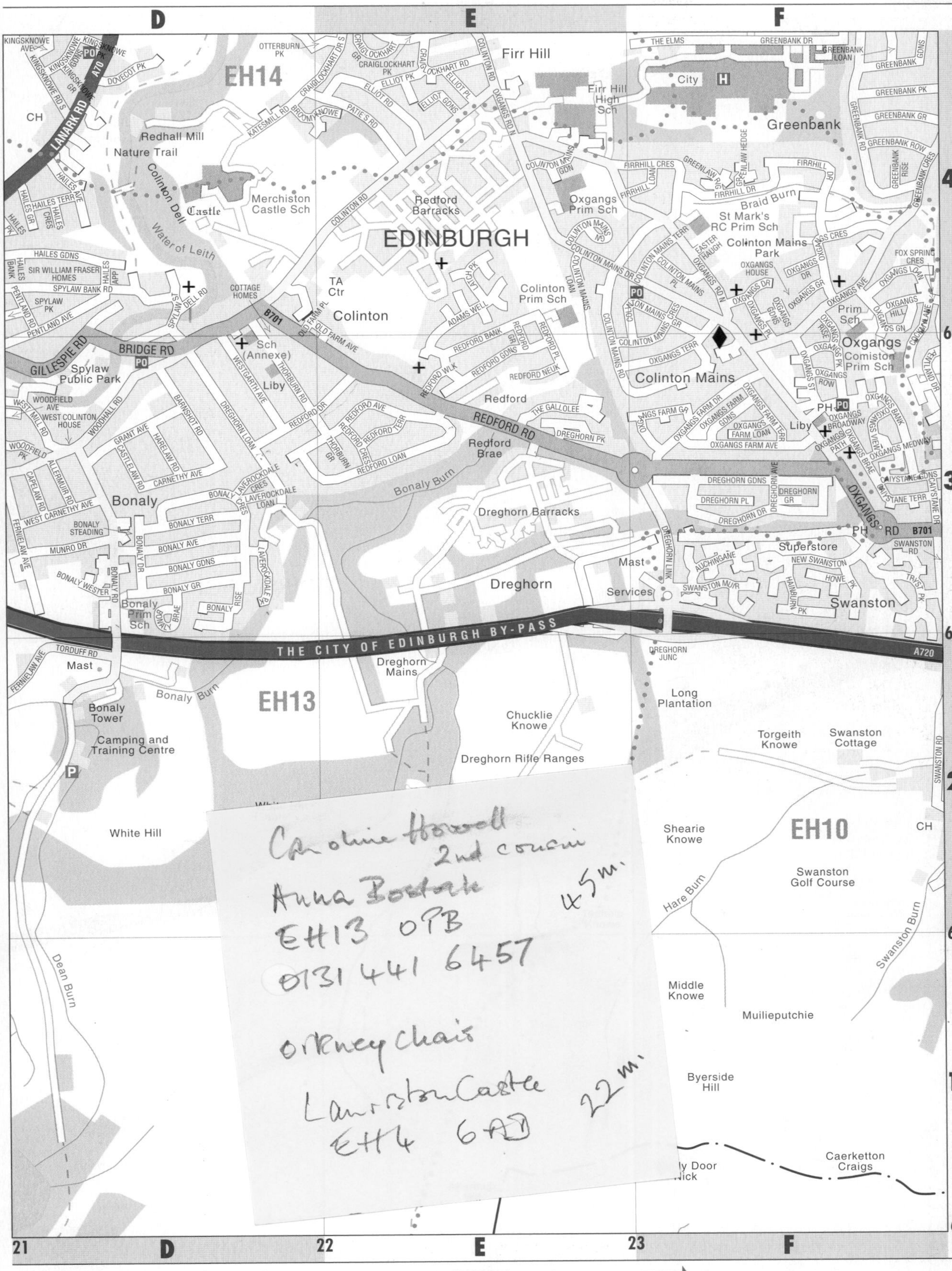

Handwritten note:

Caroline Howell
2nd cousin
Anna Bostock
EH13 0PB
0131 441 6457   45 m.

Orkney chairs

Lauriston Castle   22 m.
EH4 6AD

153
123

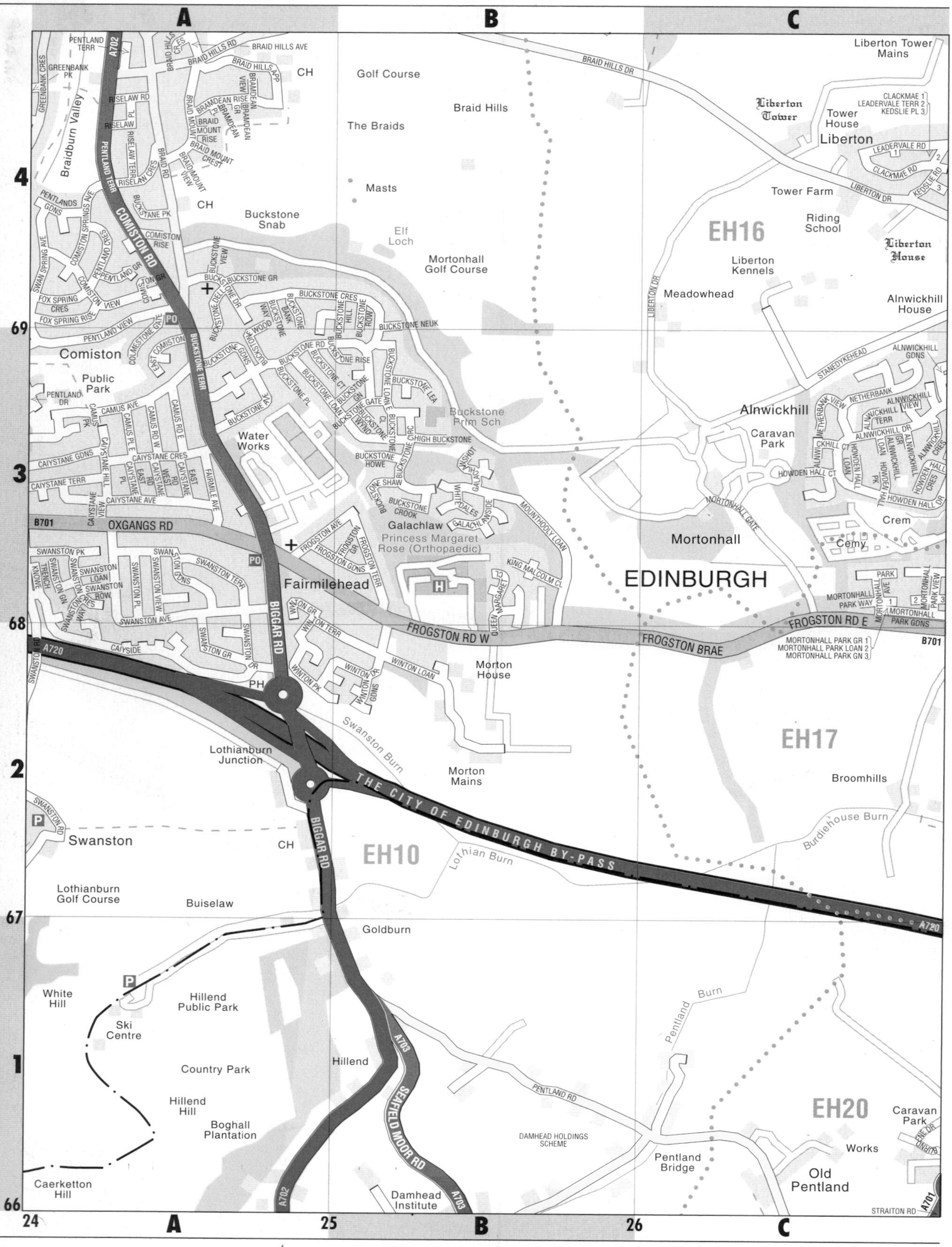
A
B
C
4
3
2
1
69
68
67
66
24
25
26
Liberton Tower Mains
Golf Course
Braid Hills
The Braids
Liberton Tower
Tower House
Liberton
Masts
Tower Farm
Buckstone Snab
Elf Loch
Mortonhall Golf Course
EH16
Riding School
Liberton House
Liberton Kennels
Meadowhead
Alnwickhill House
Comiston
Public Park
Braidburn Valley
Buckstone Prim Sch
Alnwickhill
Water Works
Caravan Park
Galachlaw
Princess Margaret Rose (Orthopaedic)
Mortonhall
Crem
Cemy
Fairmilehead
EDINBURGH
Morton House
EH17
Lothianburn Junction
Morton Mains
Broomhills
Swanston
EH10
Lothianburn Golf Course
Buiselaw
Goldburn
White Hill
Ski Centre
Hillend Public Park
Country Park
Hillend
Hillend Hill
Boghall Plantation
EH20
Caravan Park
Works
Pentland Bridge
Old Pentland
Caerketton Hill
Damhead Institute
DAMHEAD HOLDINGS SCHEME
COMISTON RD
BUCKSTONE TERR
BIGGAR RD
OXGANGS RD
FROGSTON RD W
FROGSTON BRAE
FROGSTON RD E
BRAID HILLS DR
LIBERTON DR
THE CITY OF EDINBURGH BY-PASS
SEAFIELD MOOR RD
PENTLAND RD
A702
A720
A703
B701
Swanston Burn
Lothian Burn
Burdiehouse Burn
Pentland Burn

153
180

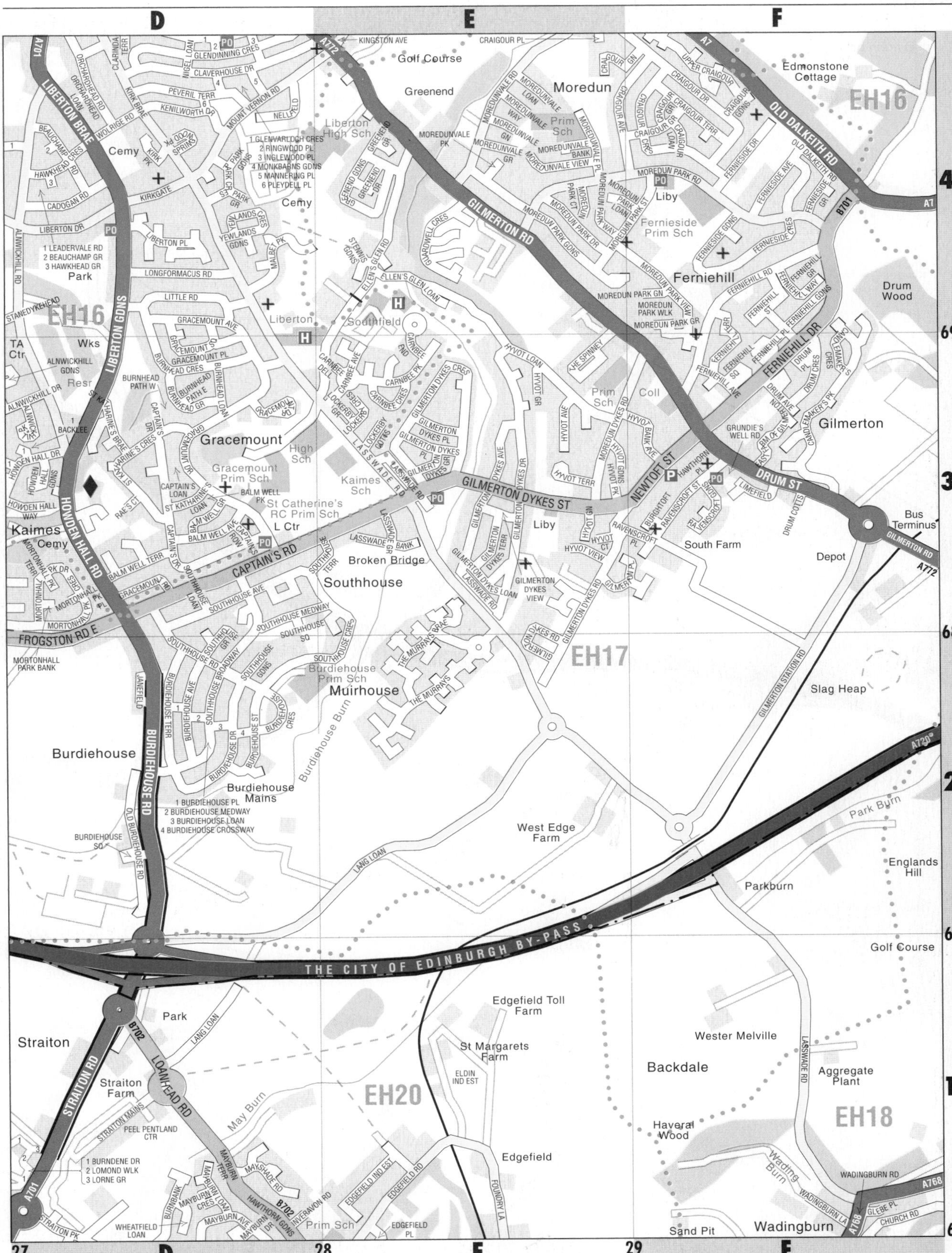
D
E
F
4
69
3
68
2
67
1
66
27
28
29
Golf Course
Greenend
Moredun
Edmonstone Cottage
EH16
OLD DALKEITH RD
LIBERTON BRAE
Cemy
KIRKGATE
Liberton High Sch
Cemy
1 GLENVARLOCH CRES
2 RINGWOOD PL
3 INGLEWOOD PL
4 MONKBARNS GDNS
5 MANNERING PL
6 PLEYDELL PL
GILMERTON RD
Prim Sch
Liby
Fernieside Prim Sch
Ferniehill
Drum Wood
1 LEADERVALE RD
2 BEAUCHAMP GR
3 HAWKHEAD GR
Park
LONGFORMACUS RD
LITTLE RD
GRACEMOUNT AVE
EH16
Wks
TA Ctr
Resr
Liberton
Southfield
LIBERTON GDNS
FERNIEHILL DR
Prim Sch
Coll
Gilmerton
Gracemount
High Sch
Gracemount Prim Sch
Kaimes Sch
St Catherine's RC Prim Sch
L Ctr
GILMERTON DYKES ST
NEWTOFT ST
DRUM ST
Liby
South Farm
Depot
Bus Terminus
Kaimes
Cemy
HOWDEN HALL RD
CAPTAIN'S RD
Broken Bridge
Southhouse
FROGSTON RD E
MORTONHALL PARK BANK
Burdiehouse Prim Sch
Muirhouse
EH17
Slag Heap
GILMERTON STATION RD
Burdiehouse
BURDIEHOUSE RD
Burdiehouse Mains
1 BURDIEHOUSE PL
2 BURDIEHOUSE MEDWAY
3 BURDIEHOUSE LOAN
4 BURDIEHOUSE CROSSWAY
Burdiehouse Burn
BURDIEHOUSE SQ
West Edge Farm
LANG LOAN
Park Burn
Englands Hill
Parkburn
THE CITY OF EDINBURGH BY-PASS
Golf Course
Edgefield Toll Farm
Park
Straiton
LANG LOAN
St Margarets Farm
ELDIN IND EST
Wester Melville
Backdale
Aggregate Plant
LASSWADE RD
Straiton Farm
STRAITON RD
LOANHEAD RD
EH20
May Burn
PEEL PENTLAND CTR
STRAITON MAINS
Haveral Wood
EH18
1 BURNDENE DR
2 LOMOND WLK
3 LORNE GR
Edgefield
Wading Burn
WADINGBURN RD
WHEATFIELD LOAN
Prim Sch
EDGEFIELD PL
Sand Pit
Wadingburn
CHURCH RD
GLEBE PL

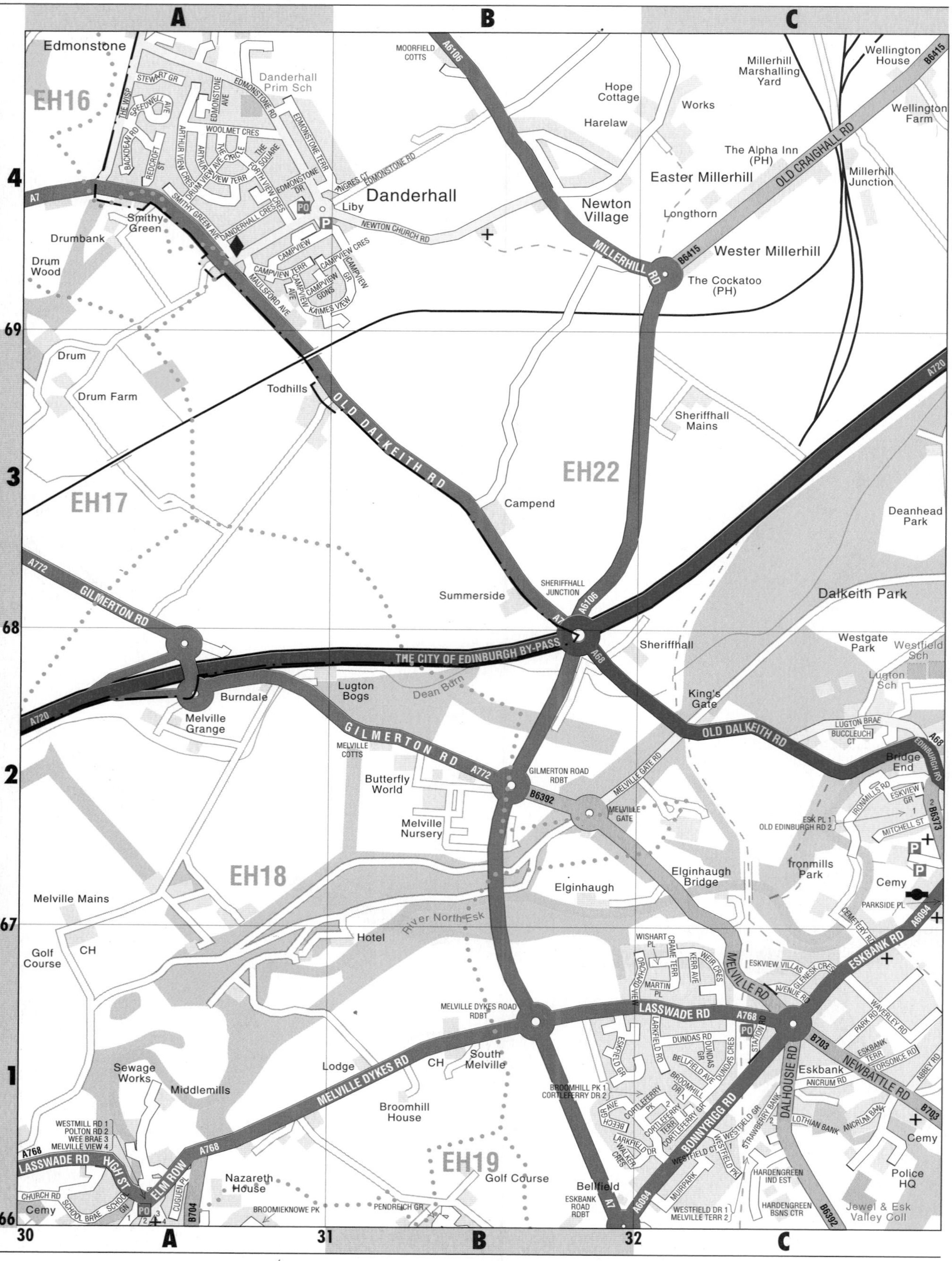

155 125

Edmonstone

EH16

Danderhall Prim Sch

STEWART GR

EDMONSTONE RD

EDMONSTONE AVE

THE WISP

BACKDEAN RD

GREENFIELD

REDFORD LOAN

ARTHUR VIEW CRES

ARTHUR VIEW TERR

THE CIRCLE

WOOLMET CRES

THE SQUARE

FORTH VIEW TERR

NORTH VIEW

INGRES CT

EDMONSTONE RD

MOORFIELD COTTS

A6106

Hope Cottage

Harelaw

Works

Millerhill Marshalling Yard

Wellington House

B6415

Easter Millerhill

The Alpha Inn (PH)

OLD CRAIGHALL RD

Wellington Farm

Millerhill Junction

Danderhall

Liby

Newton Village

Longthorn

Wester Millerhill

A7

Drumbank

Smithy Green

SMITHY GREEN AV

DANDERHALL CRES

PO

P

CAMPVIEW TERR

CAMPVIEW GDNS

CAMPVIEW

CAMPVIEW AVE

KAIMES VIEW

MULLSFORD AVE

CAMPVIEW CRES

NEWTON CHURCH RD

MILLERHILL RD

B6415

The Cockatoo (PH)

Drum Wood

Drum Farm

Drum

Todhills

OLD DALKEITH RD

Sheriffhall Mains

A720

EH17

EH22

Deanhead Park

GILMERTON RD

A772

Campend

Summerside

SHERIFFHALL JUNCTION

A6106

A7

Sheriffhall

Dalkeith Park

Westgate Park

Westfield Sch

Lugton Sch

69

68

67

66

4

3

2

1

Burndale

Melville Grange

THE CITY OF EDINBURGH BY-PASS

A68

A720

Lugton Bogs

Dean Burn

King's Gate

OLD DALKEITH RD

LUGTON BRAE

BUCCLEUCH CT

A68

EDINBURGH RD

Bridge End

GILMERTON RD

A772

MELVILLE COTTS

Butterfly World

B6392

GILMERTON ROAD RDBT

Melville Nursery

MELVILLE GATE RD

Melville Gate

IRONMILLS RD

ESKVIEW GR

OLD EDINBURGH RD 2

ESK PL 1

MITCHELL ST

P

P

Cemy

PARKSIDE PL

Ironmills Park

A6094

CEMETERY RD

EH18

Melville Mains

Golf Course

CH

Hotel

River North Esk

Elginhaugh Bridge

Elginhaugh

WISHART PL

CRANE TERR

ORCHARD FIELD

KERR AVE

MARTIN PL

ORCHARD VIEW

ESKVIEW VILLAS

GLENESK CRES

AVENUE RD

MELVILLE RD

ESKBANK RD

WAVERLEY RD

Park Ave

FORSONCE RD

NEWBATTLE RD

Eskbank

ANCRUM RD

B703

Sewage Works

Middlemills

MELVILLE DYKES RD

Lodge

CH

South Melville

MELVILLE DYKES ROAD RDBT

Broomhill House

LASSWADE RD

A768

DUNDAS RD

DUNDAS AVE

DUNDAS CRES

BROOMHILL PK 1

CORTLEFERRY DR 2

CORTLEFERRY PK

CORTLEFERRY TERR

BELLFIELD RD

ESTFEDER DR

LARKFIELD RD

LARKFIELD DR

BONNYRIGG RD

STATION RD

WESTFIELD CT

WESTFIELD PK

WESTFIELD AV

WATER CRES

STRAWBERRY BANK

STRAWBERRY GR

LOTHIAN BANK

DALHOUSIE RD

Eskbank

B703

ABBEY RD

EH19

Golf Course

Bellfield

ESKBANK ROAD RDBT

A7

A6094

MURRPARK

WESTFIELD DR 1

MELVILLE TERR 2

HARDENGREEN IND EST

HARDENGREEN BSNS CTR

B6392

Cemy

Police HQ

Jewel & Esk Valley Coll

LASSWADE RD

HIGH ST

ELM ROW

CUGUEN PL

B704

Nazareth House

BROOMIEKNOWE PK

PENDREICH GR

WESTMILL RD 1

POLTON RD 2

WEE BRAE 3

MELVILLE VIEW 4

A768

CHURCH RD

SCHOOL BRAE

Cemy

PO

A720

A7

Drum

EH16

A6106

30 31 32

A B C

155 182

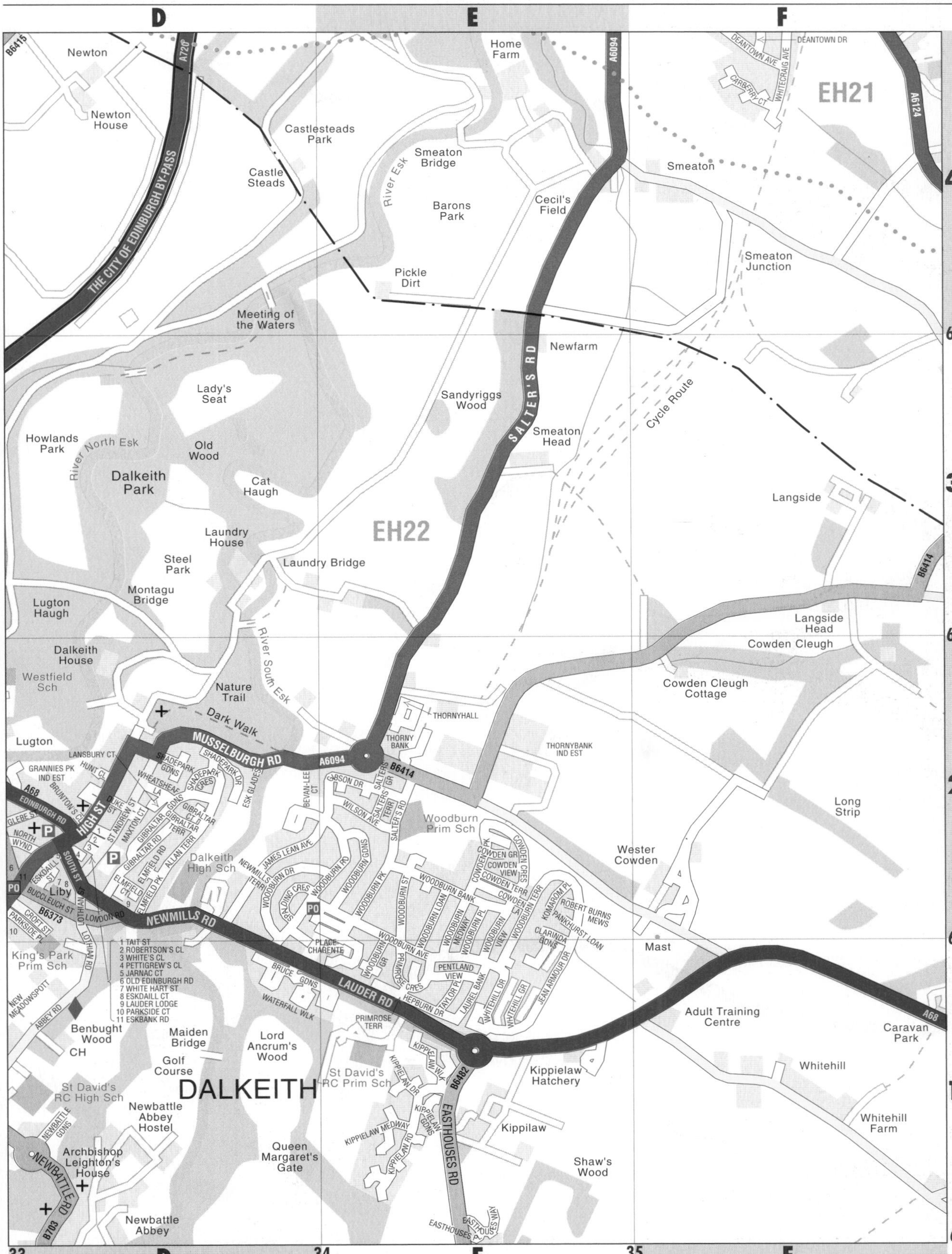
D
E
F
Newton
Newton House
THE CITY OF EDINBURGH BY-PASS
A720
B6415
Castlesteads Park
Castle Steads
Home Farm
Smeaton Bridge
River Esk
Barons Park
Cecil's Field
Pickle Dirt
Meeting of the Waters
A6094
DEANTOWN DR
DEANTOWN AVE
WHITECRAIG AVE
CARBERRY CT
EH21
A6124
Smeaton
Smeaton Junction
4
69
Newfarm
SALTER'S RD
Lady's Seat
Sandyriggs Wood
Cycle Route
Howlands Park
River North Esk
Old Wood
Smeaton Head
Dalkeith Park
Cat Haugh
Langside
3
EH22
Laundry House
Steel Park
Laundry Bridge
B6414
Montagu Bridge
Lugton Haugh
Langside Head
Cowden Cleugh
68
Dalkeith House
River South Esk
Westfield Sch
Nature Trail
Cowden Cleugh Cottage
Dark Walk
THORNYHALL
THORNY BANK
THORNYBANK IND EST
Lugton
MUSSELBURGH RD
LANSBURY CT
GRANNIES PK IND EST
HUNT CL
A68
EDINBURGH RD
HIGH ST
BRUNTON'S CL
SHADEPARK GDNS
SHADEPARK DR
SHADEPARK CRES
WHEATSHEAF LA
GIBRALTAR GDNS
GIBRALTAR CT
GIBRALTAR TERR
GIBRALTAR RD
ALLAN TERR
ESK GLADES
BEVAN-LEE CT
GIBSON DR
SALTERS GR
SALTERS TERR
SALTERS RD
WILSON AVE
Long Strip
2
GLEBE ST
NORTH WYND
DUKE ST
ST ANDREW ST
MAXTON CT
Woodburn Prim Sch
JAMES LEAN AVE
COWDEN PK
COWDEN GR
COWDEN VIEW
COWDEN CRES
COWDEN TERR
Wester Cowden
SOUTH ST
ESKDAILL ST
Dalkeith High Sch
NEWMILLS TERR
WOODBURN DR
WOODBURN RD
WOODBURN GDNS
WOODBURN PK
WOODBURN ST
WOODBURN BANK
WOODBURN LOAN
WOODBURN MEDWAY
WOODBURN PL
WOODBURN VIEW
WOODBURN TERR
KOMAROM PL
ROBERT BURNS MEWS
PANKHURST LOAN
CLARINDA GDNS
Liby
ELMFIELD CT
ELMFIELD RD
ELMFIELD PK
BUCCLEUCH ST
LOTHIAN ST
LONDON RD
NEWMILLS RD
SPALDING CRES
PO
B6373
CROFT ST
PARKSIDE PL
PLACE CHARENTE
WOODBURN AVE
WOODBURN GR
PRIMROSE CRES
PENTLAND VIEW
JEAN ARMOUR DR
Mast
67
1 TAIT ST
2 ROBERTSON'S CL
3 WHITE'S CL
4 PETTIGREW'S CL
5 JARNAC CT
6 OLD EDINBURGH RD
7 WHITE HART ST
8 ESKDAILL CT
9 LAUDER LODGE
10 PARKSIDE CT
11 ESKBANK RD
King's Park Prim Sch
LOTHIAN RD
BRUCE GDNS
LAUDER RD
TAYLOR PL
LAUREL BANK
WHITEHILL DR
WHITEHILL GR
HEPBURN DR
NEW MEADOWSPOTT
WATERFALL WLK
ABBEY RD
Adult Training Centre
A68
Caravan Park
Benbught Wood
CH
Maiden Bridge
Lord Ancrum's Wood
PRIMROSE TERR
KIPPIELAW WLK
B6482
Golf Course
St David's RC Prim Sch
KIPPIELAW DR
Kippielaw Hatchery
Whitehill
St David's RC High Sch
DALKEITH
1
Newbattle Abbey Hostel
KIPPIELAW GDNS
EASTHOUSES RD
Kippilaw
Whitehill Farm
NEWBATTLE GDNS
KIPPIELAW MEDWAY
KIPPIELAW RD
Archbishop Leighton's House
Queen Margaret's Gate
Shaw's Wood
NEWBATTLE RD
B703
Newbattle Abbey
EASTHOUSES WAY
EASTHOUSES PL
66
33
34
35

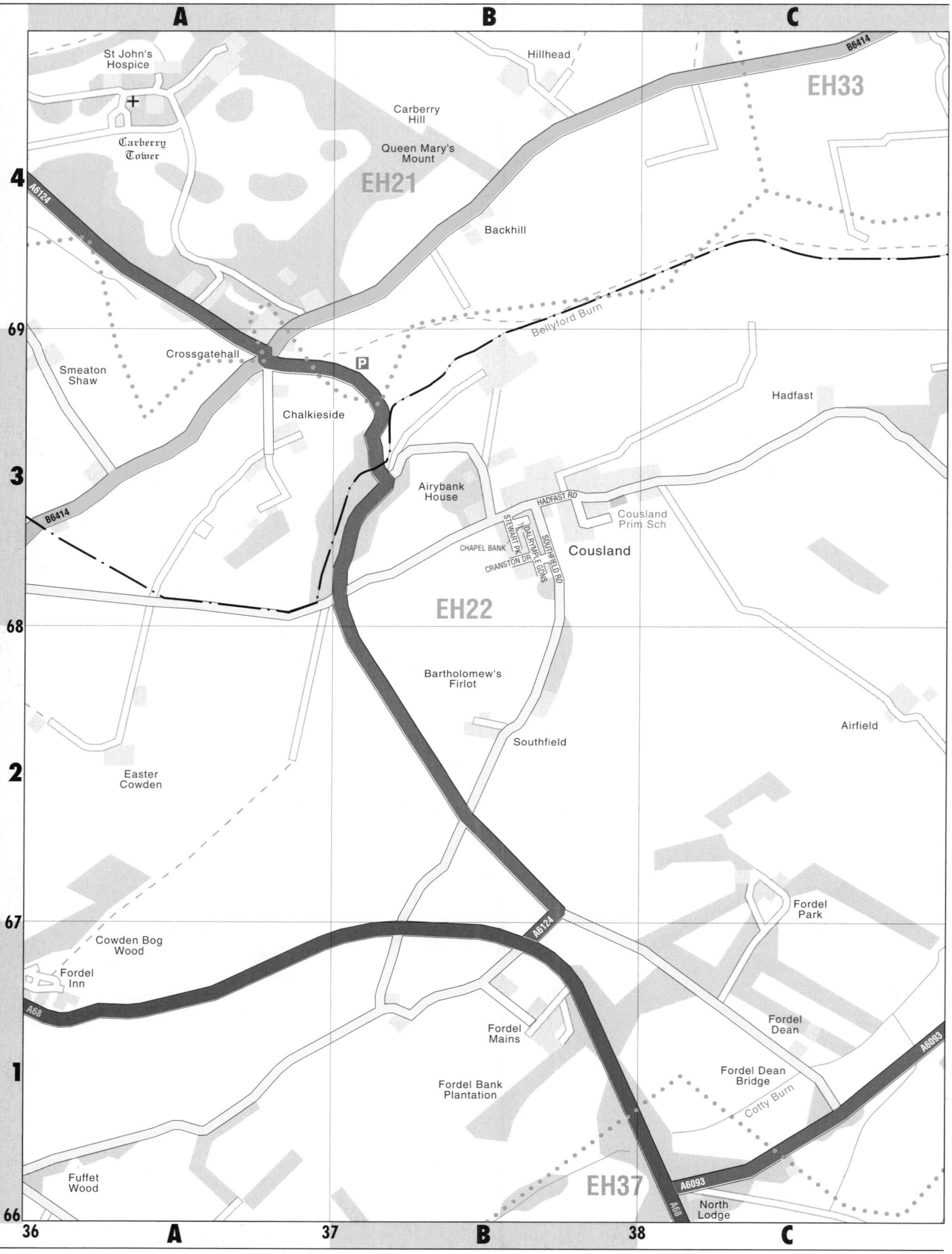

A B C

St John's Hospice

Hillhead

Carberry Hill

Carberry Tower

Queen Mary's Mount

EH21

EH33

B6414

4

A6124

Backhill

Bellyford Burn

69

Crossgatehall

P

Smeaton Shaw

Chalkieside

Hadfast

3

B6414

Airybank House

HADFAST RD

Cousland Prim Sch

CHAPEL BANK

CRANSTON DR

STEWART PK

DALRYMPLE GDNS

SOUTHFIELD RD

Cousland

EH22

68

Bartholomew's Firlot

Southfield

Airfield

2

Easter Cowden

67

Cowden Bog Wood

Fordel Park

Fordel Inn

A68

Fordel Mains

Fordel Dean

A6124

Fordel Dean Bridge

Cotty Burn

A6093

1

Fordel Bank Plantation

Fuffet Wood

EH37

A6093

North Lodge

A68

66

36 A 37 B 38 C

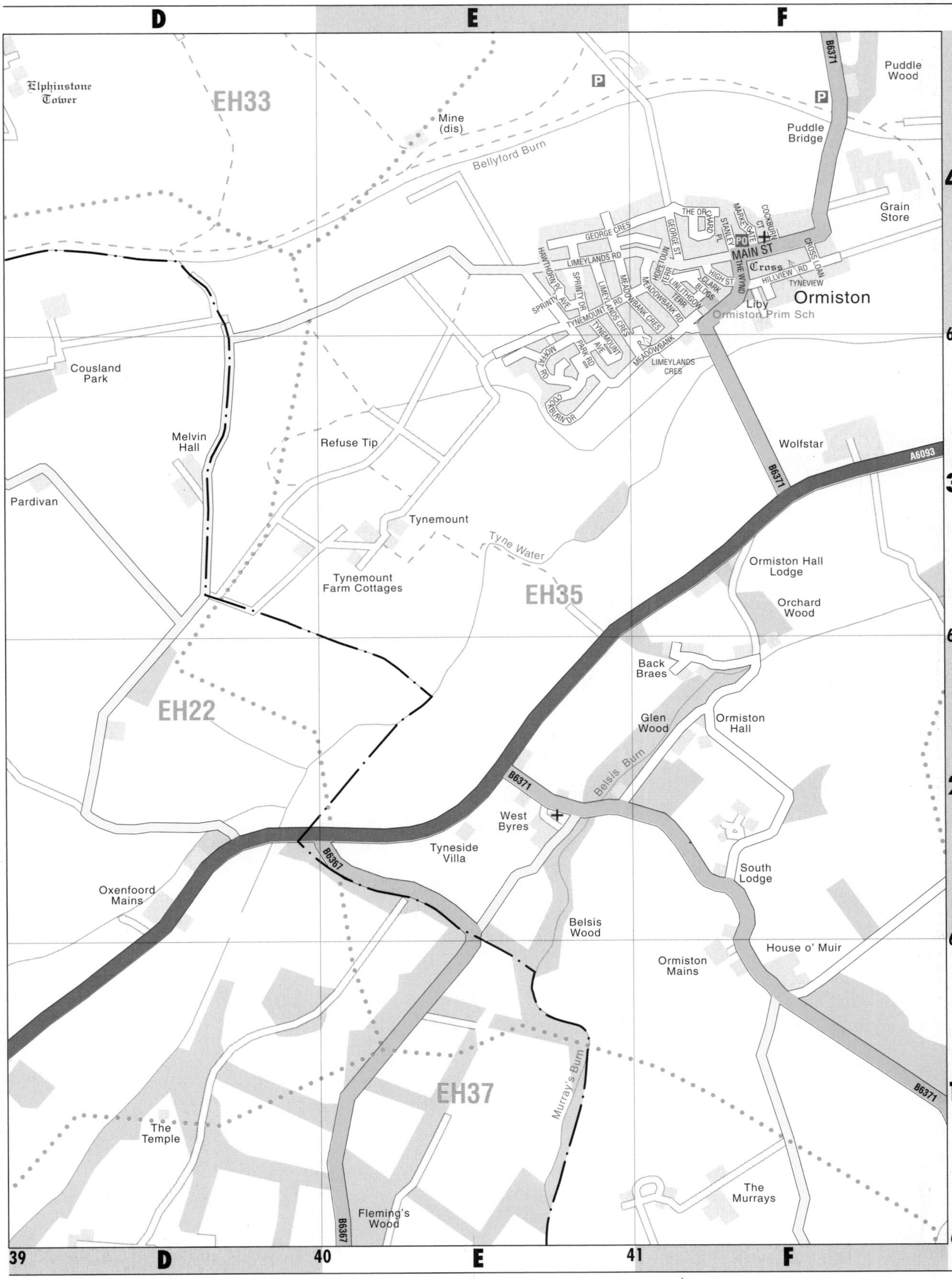

128
160

D E F

Elphinstone
Tower

EH33

Mine
(dis)

Bellyford Burn

P

P

Puddle
Wood

Puddle
Bridge

B6371

Grain
Store

4

THE ORCHARD CT

COCKBURN LN

George Cres

GEORGE ST

MARKET GATE

STANLEY PL

MAIN ST
POST

Cross

HIGH ST

HAWTHORN DR

LIMEYLANDS RD

SPRINTY DR

SPRINTY AVE

HOPETOUN

CLARK BLDGS

THE WYND

HILLVIEW RD

TYNEVIEW

CROSS LOAN

Ormiston

TYNEMOUNT AVE

LIMEYLANDS RD

MEADOWBANK CRES

HUTTON

Liby

MEADOWBANK RD

WILLOW

Ormiston Prim Sch

69

PARK RD

WOOD

LIMEYLANDS
CRES

TYNEMOUNT RD

HAWTHORN DR

Cousland
Park

Melvin
Hall

Refuse Tip

Wolfstar

A6093

B6371

3

Pardivan

Tynemount

Tyne Water

Ormiston Hall
Lodge

Orchard
Wood

Tynemount
Farm Cottages

EH35

Back
Braes

68

EH22

Glen
Wood

Ormiston
Hall

Belsis Burn

B6371

2

West
Byres

South
Lodge

Oxenfoord
Mains

Tyneside
Villa

B6367

Belsis
Wood

House o' Muir

67

Ormiston
Mains

The
Temple

EH37

Murray's Burn

B6371

1

Fleming's
Wood

B6367

The
Murrays

39 D 40 E 41 F 66

185
160

159
129

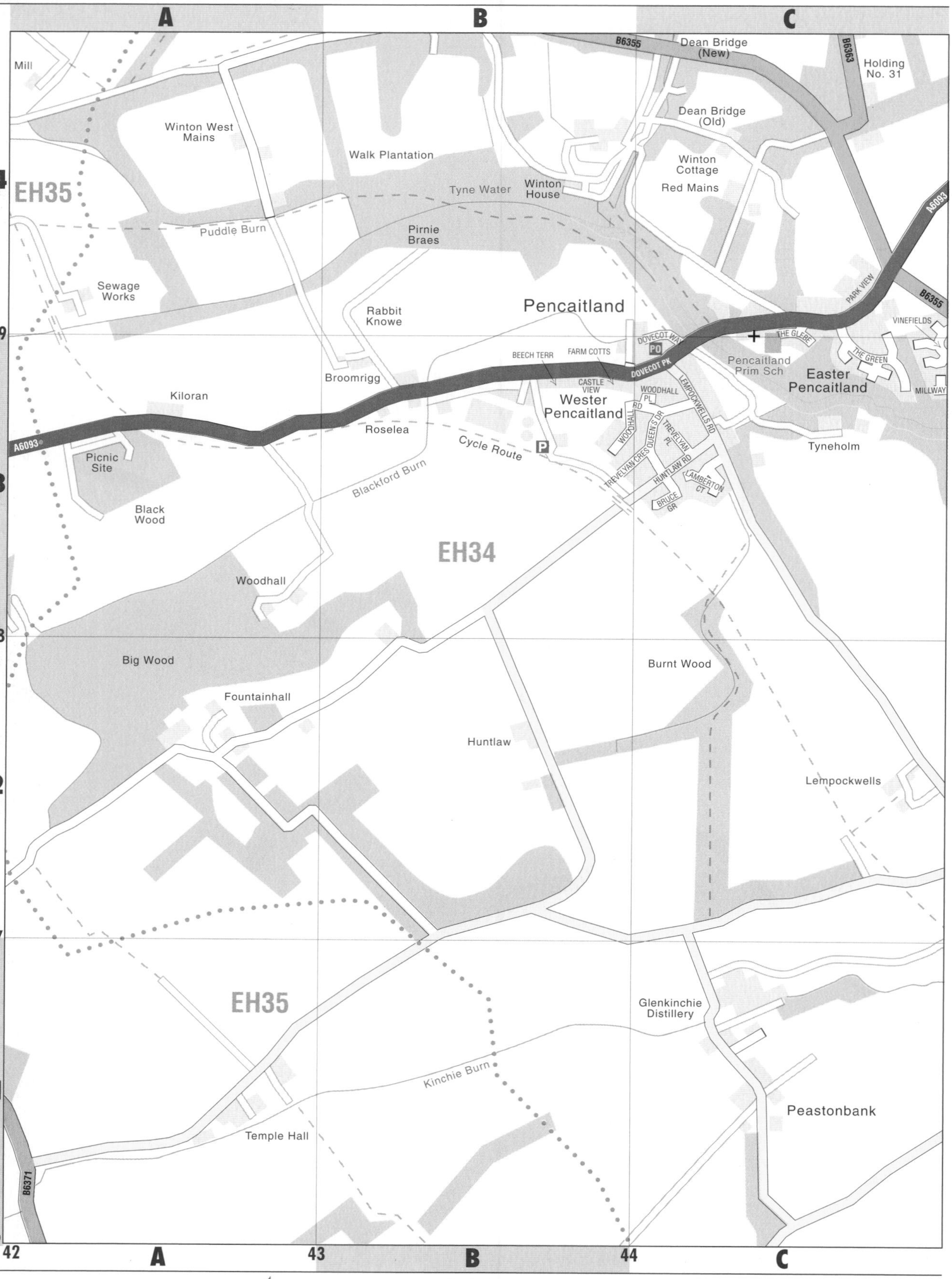

A **B** **C**

B6355
Dean Bridge (New)
B6363
Holding No. 31
Mill
Winton West Mains
Dean Bridge (Old)
Walk Plantation
Winton Cottage
A6093
4
EH35
Tyne Water
Winton House
Red Mains
Puddle Burn
Pirnie Braes
B6355
PARK VIEW
Sewage Works
VINEFIELDS
69
Rabbit Knowe
Pencaitland
DOVECOT WY
PO
THE GLEBE
THE GREEN
BEECH TERR
FARM COTTS
Pencaitland Prim Sch
Easter Pencaitland
Kiloran
Broomrigg
DOVECOT PK
CASTLE VIEW
LEMPOCKWELLS RD
MILLWAY
WOODHALL RD
A6093
Roselea
Wester Pencaitland
WOODHALL PL
Tyneholm
Picnic Site
Cycle Route
P
TREVELYAN PL
TREVELYAN CRES
QUEEN'S DR
3
Black Wood
Blackford Burn
HUNTLAW RD
LAMBERTON CT
BRUCE GR
EH34
Woodhall
68
Big Wood
Burnt Wood
Fountainhall
2
Huntlaw
Lempockwells
67
EH35
Glenkinchie Distillery
1
Kinchie Burn
Peastonbank
Temple Hall
B6371
66
42 **A** **43** **B** **44** **C**

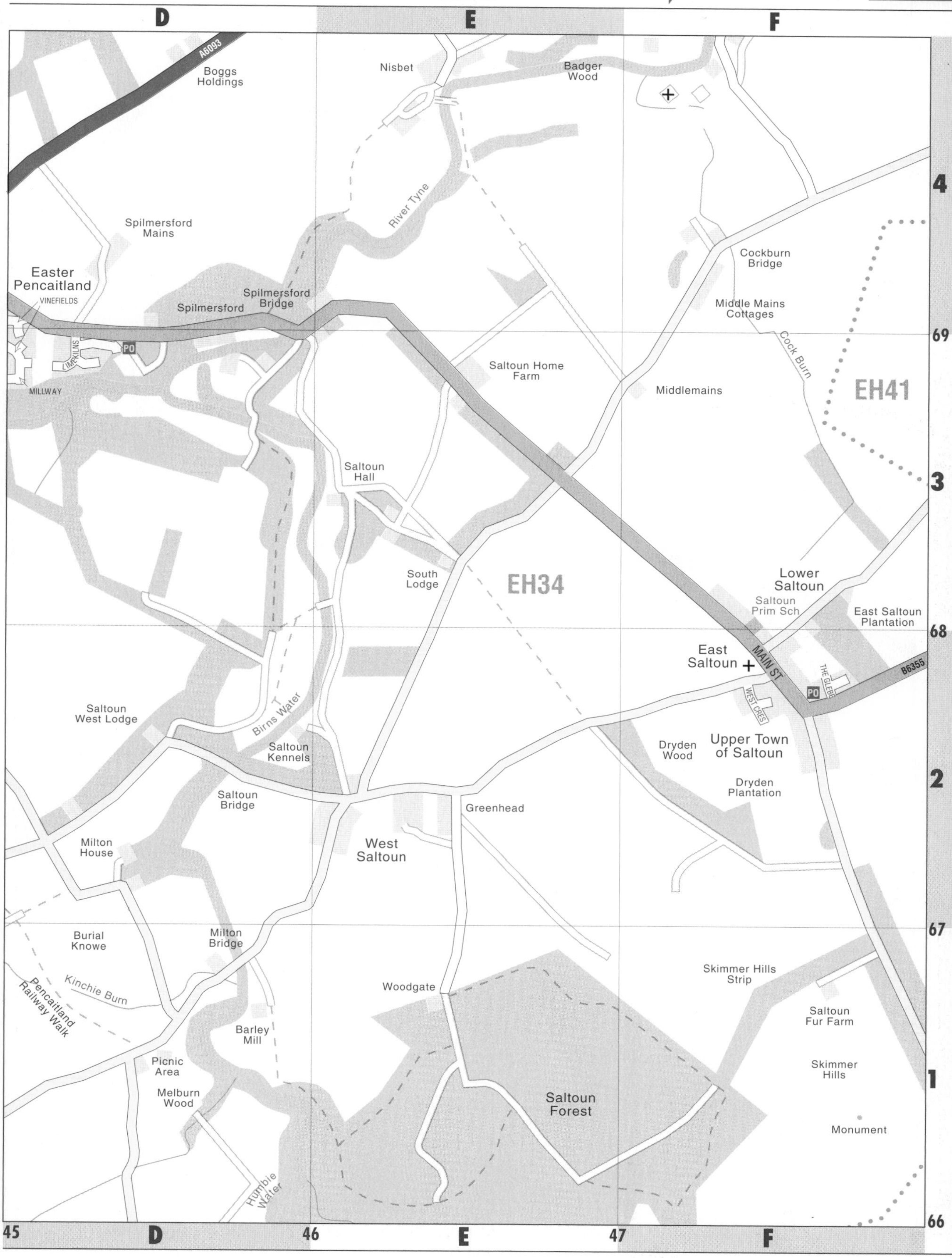

D
E
F

Boggs Holdings

A6093

Nisbet

Badger Wood

4

Spilmersford Mains

River Tyne

Cockburn Bridge

Easter Pencaitland

VINEFIELDS

Spilmersford Bridge

Spilmersford

Middle Mains Cottages

Cock Burn

69

PO

LIMEKILNS

Saltoun Home Farm

Middlemains

EH41

MILLWAY

Saltoun Hall

EH34

3

South Lodge

Lower Saltoun

Saltoun Prim Sch

East Saltoun Plantation

68

East Saltoun

MAIN ST

PO

THE GLEBE

B6355

Saltoun West Lodge

Birns Water

Saltoun Kennels

WEST CRES

Dryden Wood

Upper Town of Saltoun

Saltoun Bridge

Dryden Plantation

2

Milton House

Greenhead

West Saltoun

Burial Knowe

Milton Bridge

67

Kinchie Burn

Skimmer Hills Strip

Pencaitland Railway Walk

Woodgate

Saltoun Fur Farm

Barley Mill

Picnic Area

Skimmer Hills

Melburn Wood

Saltoun Forest

1

Monument

Humbie Water

66

45
D
46
E
47
F

161
131

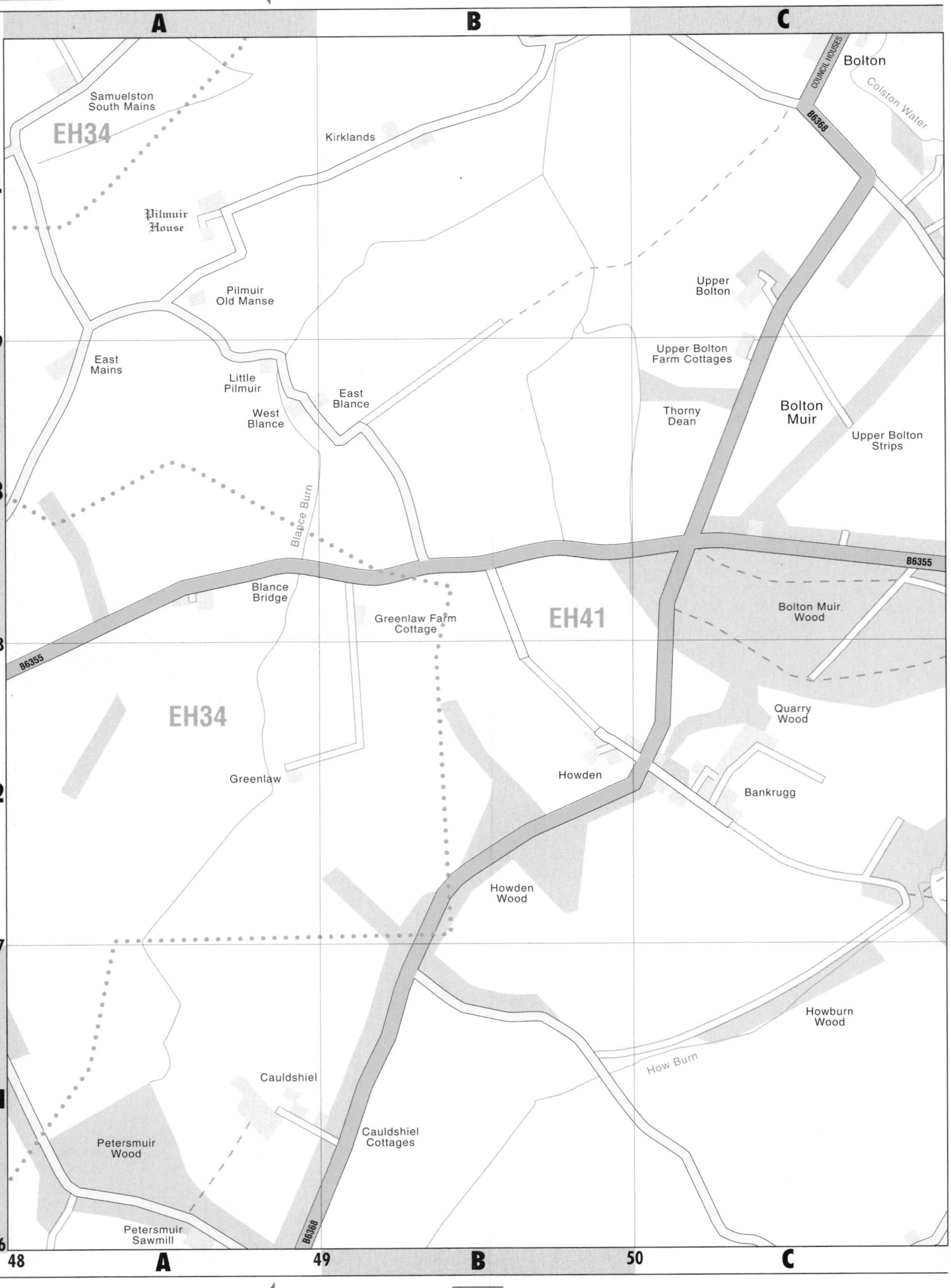

A | B | C

Bolton

COUNCIL HOUSES

Colston Water

Samuelston
South Mains

EH34

Kirklands

B6368

Pilmuir
House

Upper
Bolton

4

Upper Bolton
Farm Cottages

69

Pilmuir
Old Manse

East
Mains

Little
Pilmuir

East
Blance

West
Blance

Thorny
Dean

**Bolton
Muir**

Upper Bolton
Strips

3

Blance Burn

B6355

Bolton Muir
Wood

Blance
Bridge

Greenlaw Farm
Cottage

EH41

68

B6355

EH34

Quarry
Wood

Greenlaw

Howden

Bankrugg

2

Howden
Wood

67

Howburn
Wood

How Burn

Cauldshiel

1

Cauldshiel
Cottages

Petersmuir
Wood

B6368

66

Petersmuir
Sawmill

48 | A | 49 | B | 50 | C

132
164

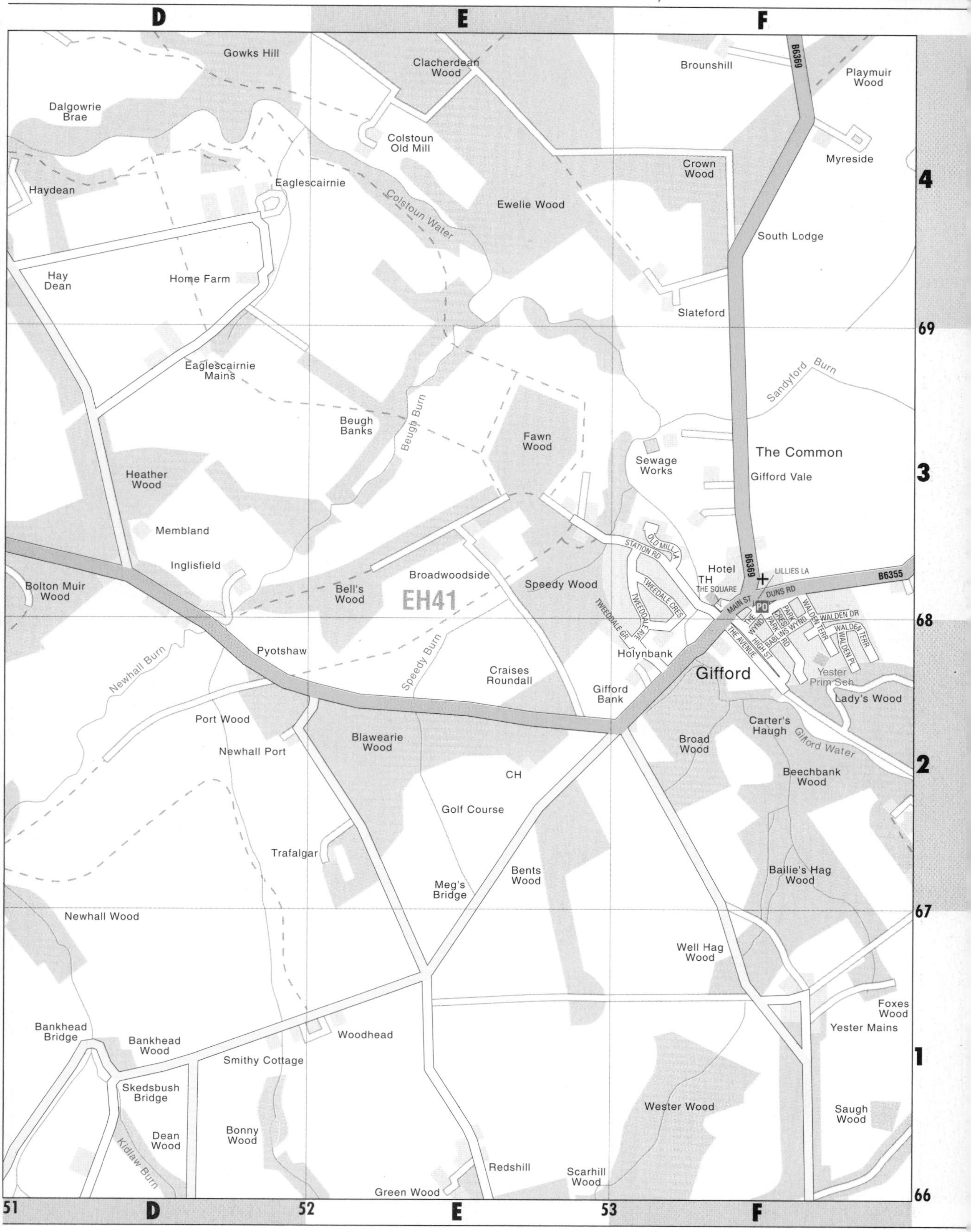
D
E
F
Gowks Hill
Clacherdean Wood
Brounshill
B6369
Playmuir Wood
Dalgowrie Brae
Colstoun Old Mill
Myreside
Crown Wood
4
Haydean
Eaglescairnie
Colstoun Water
Ewelie Wood
South Lodge
Hay Dean
Home Farm
Slateford
69
Eaglescairnie Mains
Sandyford Burn
Beugh Banks
Beugh Burn
Fawn Wood
Sewage Works
The Common
Heather Wood
Gifford Vale
3
Membland
OLD MILL LA
STATION RD
Inglisfield
Hotel
TH
THE SQUARE
B6369
LILLIES LA
Broadwoodside
B6355
Bolton Muir Wood
Bell's Wood
EH41
Speedy Wood
TWEEDALE CRES
DUNS RD
MAIN ST
PO
WALDEN DR
WALDEN TERR
TWEEDALE GR
TWEEDALE AVE
THE WYND
PARK CRES
PARK RD
HOPES WYND
WALDEN PL
68
THE AVENUE
HIGH ST
Pyotshaw
Holynbank
Newhall Burn
Speedy Burn
Craises Roundall
Gifford
Yester Prim Sch
Gifford Bank
Lady's Wood
Port Wood
Carter's Haugh
Blawearie Wood
Broad Wood
Gifford Water
Newhall Port
2
CH
Beechbank Wood
Golf Course
Trafalgar
Bents Wood
Baillie's Hag Wood
Meg's Bridge
Newhall Wood
67
Well Hag Wood
Foxes Wood
Bankhead Bridge
Yester Mains
Woodhead
Bankhead Wood
Smithy Cottage
1
Skedsbush Bridge
Wester Wood
Saugh Wood
Dean Wood
Bonny Wood
Kidlaw Burn
Redshill
Scarhill Wood
Green Wood
66
51
D
52
E
53
F

189
164

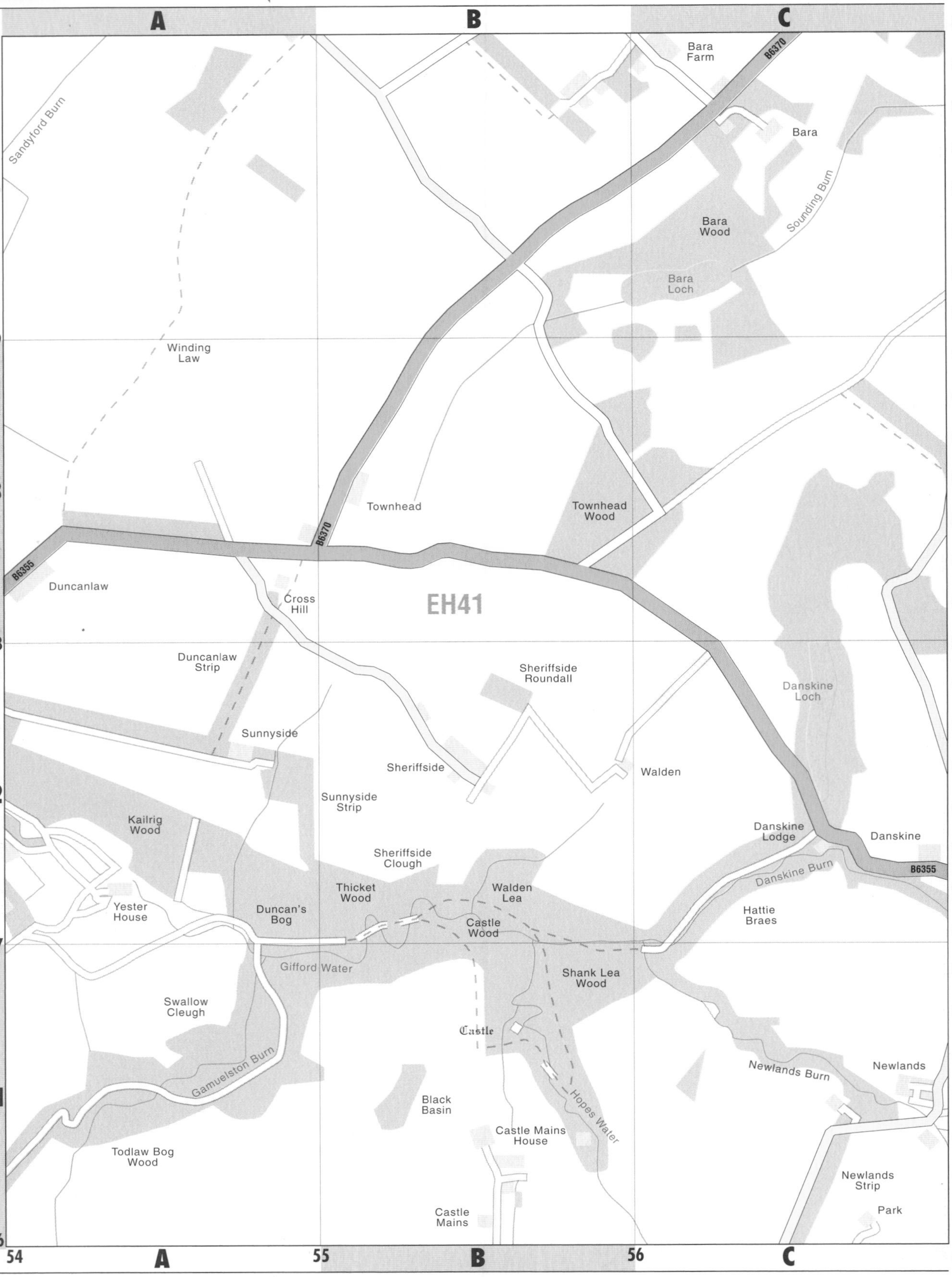

163
133

A · B · C

Sandyford Burn

B6370

Bara Farm

Bara

4

Winding Law

Bara Wood

Sounding Burn

Bara Loch

69

3

Townhead

Townhead Wood

B6370

B6355

Duncanlaw

Cross Hill

EH41

68

Duncanlaw Strip

Sheriffside Roundall

Danskine Loch

Sunnyside

Sheriffside

Walden

2

Kailrig Wood

Sunnyside Strip

Sheriffside Clough

Danskine Lodge

Danskine

Yester House

Duncan's Bog

Thicket Wood

Walden Lea

Danskine Burn

B6355

Castle Wood

Hattie Braes

67

Gifford Water

Shank Lea Wood

Swallow Cleugh

Castle

Newlands Burn

Newlands

Gamuelston Burn

Black Basin

Hopes Water

1

Todlaw Bog Wood

Castle Mains House

Newlands Strip

Park

66

54 · A · 55 · B · 56 · C

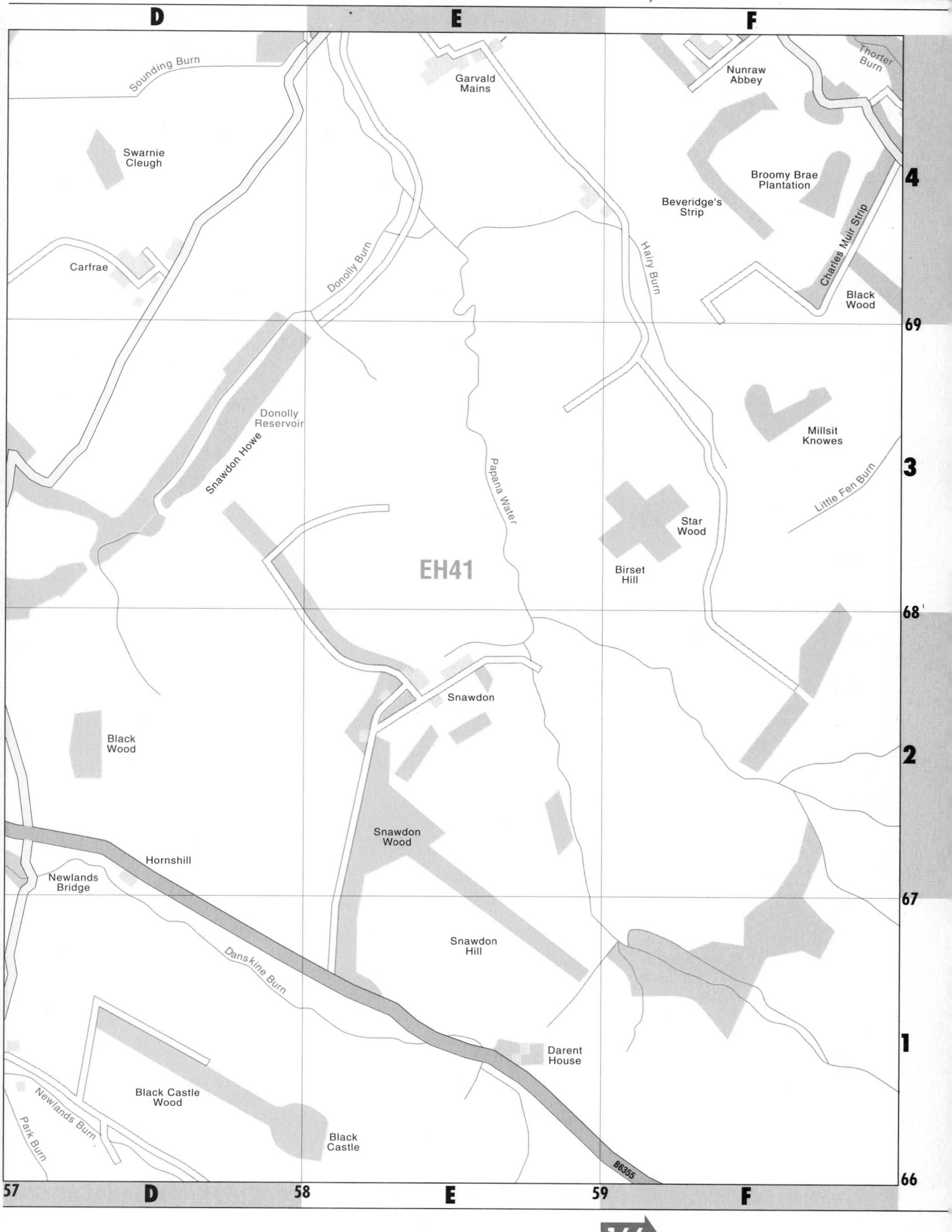
D
E
F
Sounding Burn
Garvald Mains
Nunraw Abbey
Thorter Burn
Swarnie Cleugh
Broomy Brae Plantation
Beveridge's Strip
Carfrae
Donolly Burn
Hairy Burn
Charles Muir Strip
Black Wood
Donolly Reservoir
Millsit Knowes
Snawdon Howe
Papana Water
Little Fen Burn
Star Wood
EH41
Birset Hill
Snawdon
Black Wood
Snawdon Wood
Hornshill
Newlands Bridge
Snawdon Hill
Danskine Burn
Darent House
Black Castle Wood
Newlands Burn
Park Burn
Black Castle
B6355
4
69
3
68
2
67
1
66
57
58
59

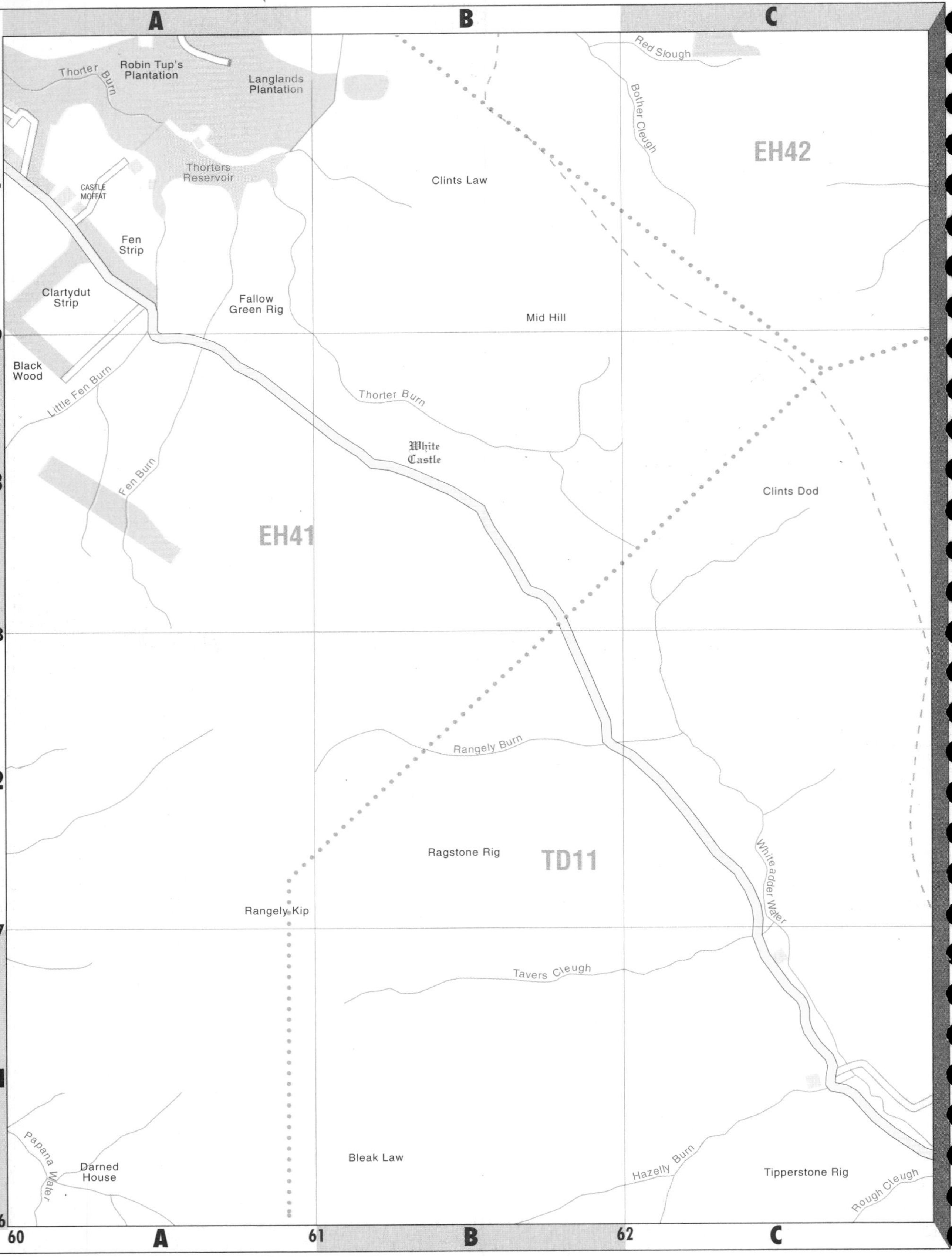

A   B   C

EH42

4

Red Slough

Bother Cleugh

Clints Law

Mid Hill

Thorter Burn

Robin Tup's Plantation

Langlands Plantation

Thorter Burn

Thorters Reservoir

CASTLE MOFFAT

Fen Strip

Clartydut Strip

Fallow Green Rig

69

Black Wood

Little Fen Burn

White Castle

Clints Dod

Fen Burn

3

EH41

68

Rangely Burn

2

Ragstone Rig

TD11

White adder Water

Rangely Kip

67

Tavers Cleugh

1

Papana Water

Darned House

Bleak Law

Hazelly Burn

Tipperstone Rig

Rough Cleugh

66
60   A   61   B   62   C

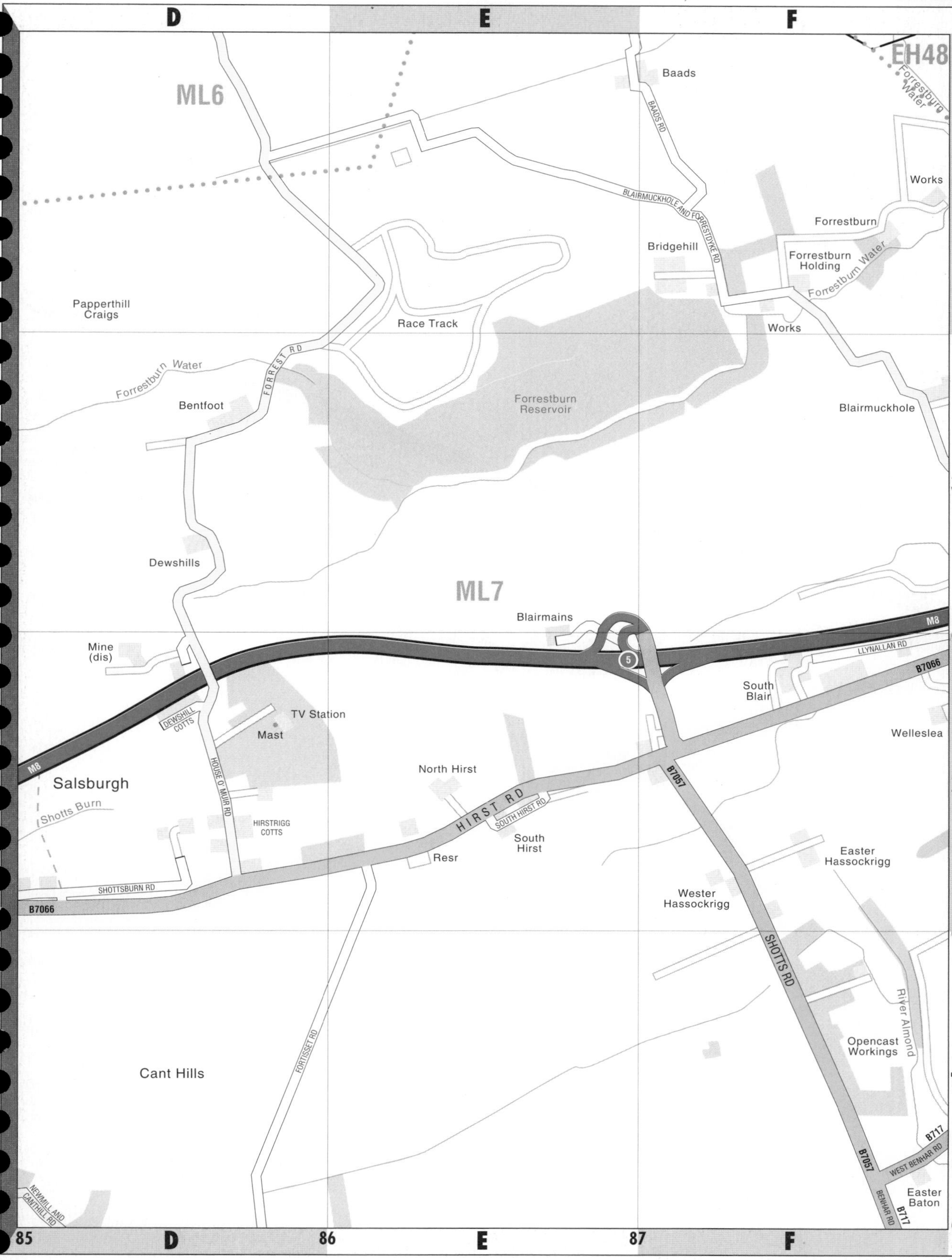

D   E   F

EH48

ML6

Baads

BAADS RD

Works

BLAIRMUCKHOLE AND FORRESTDYKE RD

Forrestburn

Forrestburn Water

Forrestburn
Holding

Bridgehill

4

Papperthill
Craigs

Forrestburn Water

FORREST RD

Works

65

Forrestburn Water

Bentfoot

Forrestburn
Reservoir

Blairmuckhole

3

Dewshills

ML7

Blairmains

M8

64

LLYNALLAN RD

Mine
(dis)

B7066

DEWSHILL COTTS

5

South
Blair

TV Station

Welleslea

HOUSE O MUIR RD

Mast

North Hirst

B7057

2

Salsburgh

HIRST RD

SOUTH HIRST RD

Easter
Hassockrigg

Shotts Burn

HIRSTRIGG
COTTS

South
Hirst

Resr

Wester
Hassockrigg

M8

SHOTTSBURN RD

SHOTTS RD

63

B7066

River Almond

FORTISSET RD

Opencast
Workings

Cant Hills

1

B7057

B717

Easter
Baton

NEWMILL AND CANTHILL RD

WEST BENHAR RD

BENHAR RD

B717

62

85   D   86   E   87   F

167
142

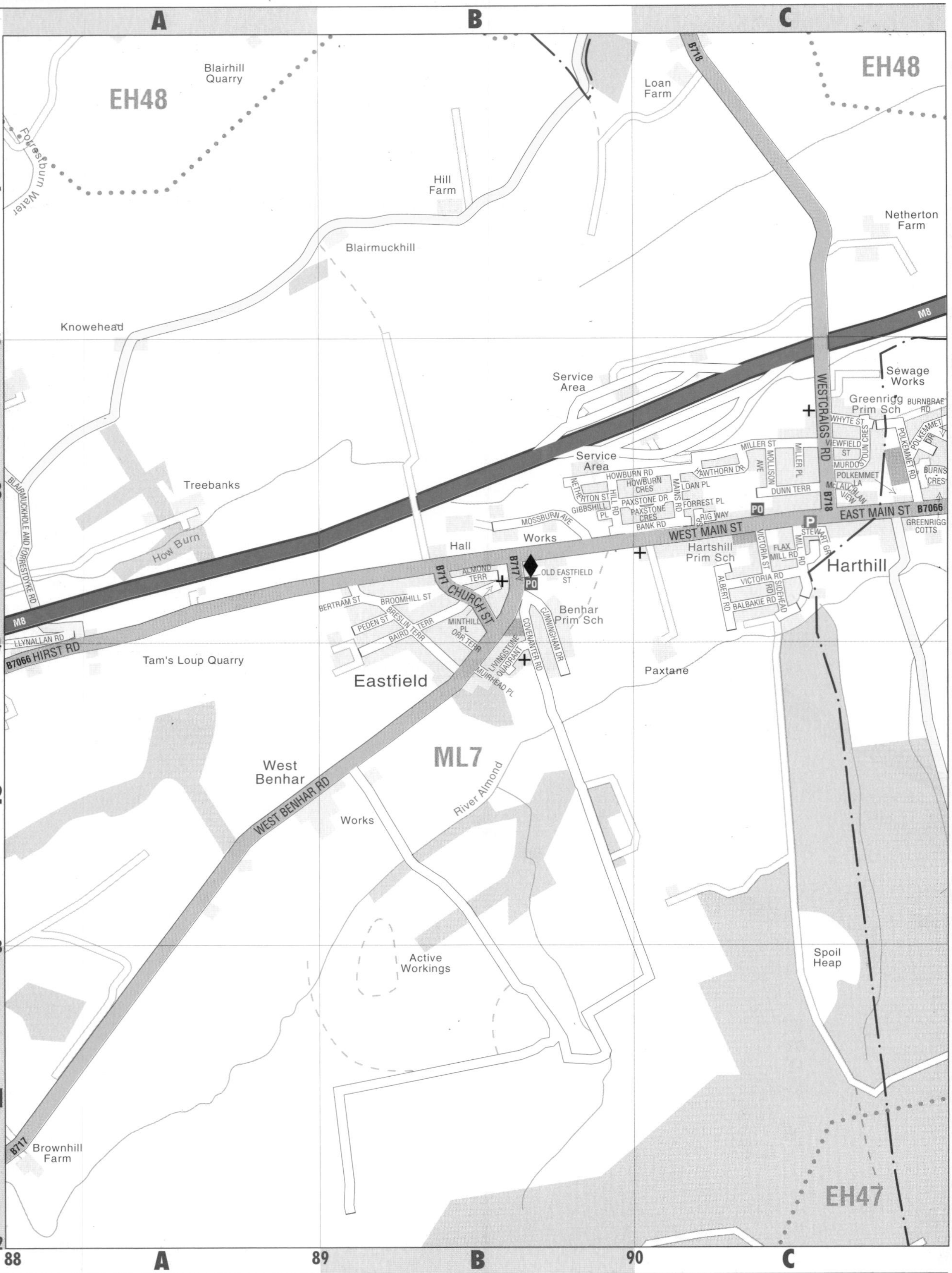

A   B   C

EH48

Blairhill Quarry

Loan Farm

EH48

B718

Hill Farm

Netherton Farm

Forresburn Water

Blairmuckhill

4

M8

Knowehead

65

Service Area

Sewage Works

Westcraigs Rd

Greenrigg Prim Sch

Burnbrae Rd

Treebanks

Service Area

Howburn Rd
Howburn Cres
Netherton St
Gibbshill Pl
Paxstone Dr
Paxstone Cres
Mossburn Ave
Bank Rd

Hawthorn Dr
Miller St
Loan Pl
Mains Rd
Forrest Pl
Rig Way

Miller St
Mollison Ave
Dunn Terr

Whyte St
Viewfield St
Murdos
Polkemmet View
McLauchlan
Polkemmet Rd

Burns Cres

3

How Burn

Works

West Main St

PO

East Main St

B7066

Greenrigg Cotts

B717

Hall

Almond Terr
B717 Church St
PO

Old Eastfield St

Hartshill Prim Sch
Victoria Rd
Albert St
Balbakie Rd

Flax Mill Rd
Stewart Gr
Mill Rd
Sid Head

P

Harthill

M8

Bertram St
Breslin Terr
Peden St
Baird Terr

Broomhill St

Minthill Pl
Orr Terr

Benhar Prim Sch

64

Llynallan Rd

B7066 Hirst Rd

Tam's Loup Quarry

Eastfield

Livingstone Pl
Muirhead Pl
Walpramt
Covenanter Rd
Cunningham Dr

Paxtane

ML7

West Benhar

West Benhar Rd

Works

River Almond

2

63

Active Workings

Spoil Heap

1

B717

Brownhill Farm

EH47

62

88   A   89   B   90   C

143 170

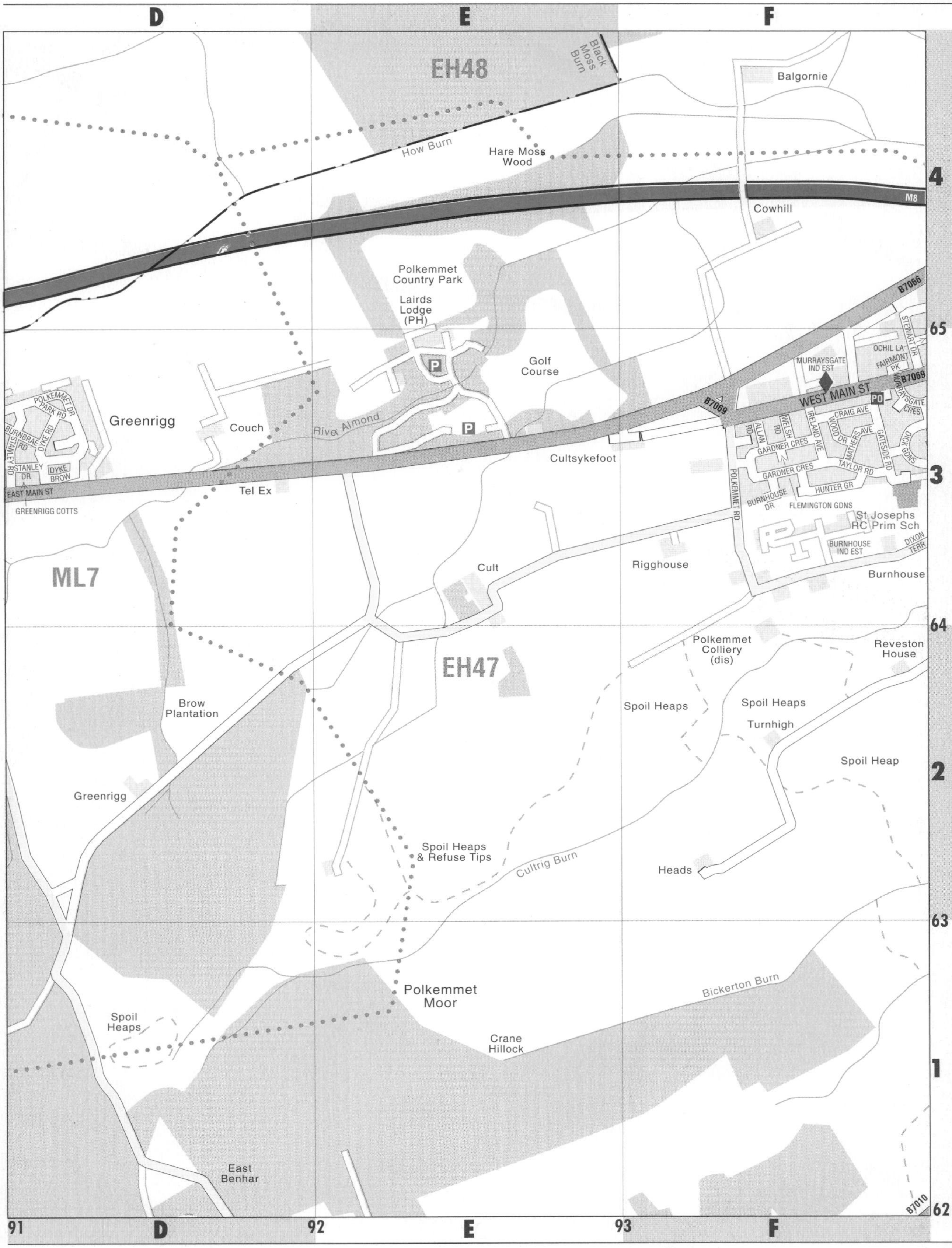
D
E
F
EH48
Black Moss Burn
Balgornie
How Burn
Hare Moss Wood
4
M8
Cowhill
Polkemmet Country Park
Lairds Lodge (PH)
B7066
65
Golf Course
STEWART DR
OCHIL LA
FAIRMONT PK
MURRAYSGATE IND EST
B7069
MURRAYSGATE CRES
WEST MAIN ST
PO
POLKEMMET DR
PARK RD
Greenrigg
Couch
River Almond
B7069
CRAIG AVE
ALLAN RD
WELSH RD
IRELAND AVE
WOOD DR
MATHERS AVE
GATESIDE RD
DICK GDNS
BURNBRAE RD
STANLEY RD
DYKE RD
GARDNER CRES
STANLEY DR
DYKE BROW
Cultsykefoot
GARDNER CRES
TAYLOR RD
3
EAST MAIN ST
Tel Ex
POLKEMMET RD
BURNHOUSE DR
HUNTER GR
FLEMINGTON GDNS
GREENRIGG COTTS
St Josephs RC Prim Sch
BURNHOUSE IND EST
DIXON TERR
ML7
Cult
Rigghouse
Burnhouse
64
Polkemmet Colliery (dis)
Reveston House
EH47
Brow Plantation
Spoil Heaps
Spoil Heaps
Turnhigh
Spoil Heap
2
Greenrigg
Spoil Heaps & Refuse Tips
Cultrig Burn
Heads
63
Polkemmet Moor
Bickerton Burn
Spoil Heaps
Crane Hillock
1
East Benhar
B7010
62
91
D
92
E
93
F

193 170

169
144

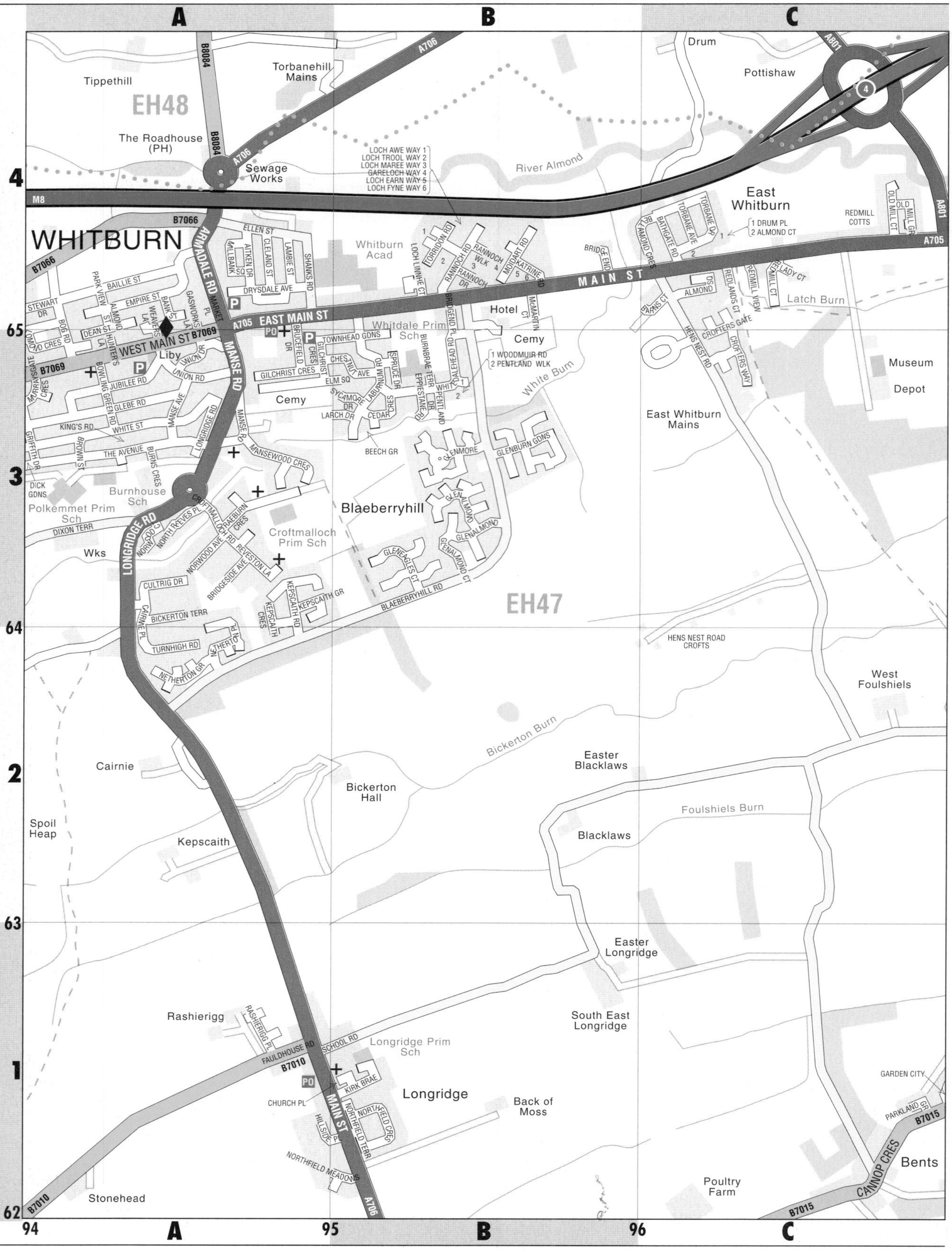
A
B
C
4
65
3
64
2
63
1
62
94
95
96
Tippethill
EH48
Torbanehill Mains
A706
B8084
Drum
Pottishaw
A801
4
The Roadhouse (PH)
Sewage Works
LOCH AWE WAY 1
LOCH TROOL WAY 2
LOCH MAREE WAY 3
GARELOCH WAY 4
LOCH EARN WAY 5
LOCH FYNE WAY 6
River Almond
East Whitburn
M8
B7066
WHITBURN
ELLEN ST
MILLBANK
AITKEN DR
CLELAND ST
LAMBIE ST
SHANKS RD
Whitburn Acad
LOCH LINNHIE CT
TORRIDON RD
RANNOCH RD
RANNOCH WLK
RANNOCH DR
MOIDART RD
KATRINE RD
TORBANE DR
TORBANE AVE
BATHGATE RD
ALMOND CRES
1 DRUM PL
2 ALMOND CT
REDMILL COTTS
OLD MILL CT
OLD MILL GR
A705
BRIDGE END
MAIN ST
BAILLIE ST
PARK VIEW
EMPIRE ST
BANK ST
GASWORKS LA
DRYSDALE AVE
STEWART DR
ALMOND ST
HUNTERS
WEAVERS LA
MARKET PL
EAST MAIN ST
Whitdale Prim Sch
Hotel
McMARTIN CT
ALMOND
REDLANDS CT
REDMILL VIEW
REDMILL CT
LADY CT
Latch Burn
DEAN ST
BOG RD
WEST MAIN ST
B7069
Liby
PO
BRUCEFIELD DR
GILCHRIST CRES
TOWNHEAD GDNS
BRIDGEND PL
BURNBRAE TERR
DALEHEAD RD
Cemy
1 WOODMUIR RD
2 PENTLAND WLK
FARMS CT
CROFTERS GATE
HENS NEST RD
CROFTERS WAY
Museum
Depot
MURRAYSIDE CRES
BOWLING GREEN RD
JUBILEE RD
UNION DR
UNION RD
MANSE RD
GILCHRIST CRES
CHESTNUT AVE
LABURNUM RD
SPRUCE DR
EPPIESTANE DR
PENTLAND DR
ELM SQ
SYCAMORE DR
CEDAR CRES
LARCH DR
White Burn
GLEBE RD
KING'S RD
WHITE ST
MANSE AVE
LONGRIDGE RD
BEECH GR
East Whitburn Mains
GRIFFITH DR
BROWN ST
THE AVENUE
BURNS CRES
MANSEWOOD CRES
GLENMORE
GLENBURN GDNS
DICK GDNS
Burnhouse Sch
Polkemmet Prim Sch
DIXON TERR
CROFTMALLOCH RD
NORTH REEVES PL
RAEBURN CRES
Blaeberryhill
GLENALMOND
Croftmalloch Prim Sch
Wks
NORWOOD AVE
REVESTON LA
BRIDGESIDE AVE
GLENEAGLES CT
GLENALMOND CT
CULTRIG DR
KEPSCAITH RD
KEPSCAITH GR
KEPSCAITH CRES
BLAEBERRYHILL RD
EH47
CAIRNIE PL
BICKERTON TERR
HENS NEST ROAD CROFTS
TURNHIGH RD
NETHERTON PL
NETHERTON GR
West Foulshiels
Bickerton Burn
Cairnie
Easter Blacklaws
Bickerton Hall
Foulshiels Burn
Spoil Heap
Kepscaith
Blacklaws
Easter Longridge
Rashierigg
RASHIERIGG PL
South East Longridge
FAULDHOUSE RD
SCHOOL RD
Longridge Prim Sch
B7010
KIRK BRAE
CHURCH PL
Longridge
Back of Moss
GARDEN CITY
NORTHFIELD CRES
HILLSIDE PL
NORTHFIELD TERR
PARKLAND GR
B7015
NORTHFIELD MEADOWS
CANNOP CRES
Bents
Poultry Farm
Stonehead
A706

169
194

145
172

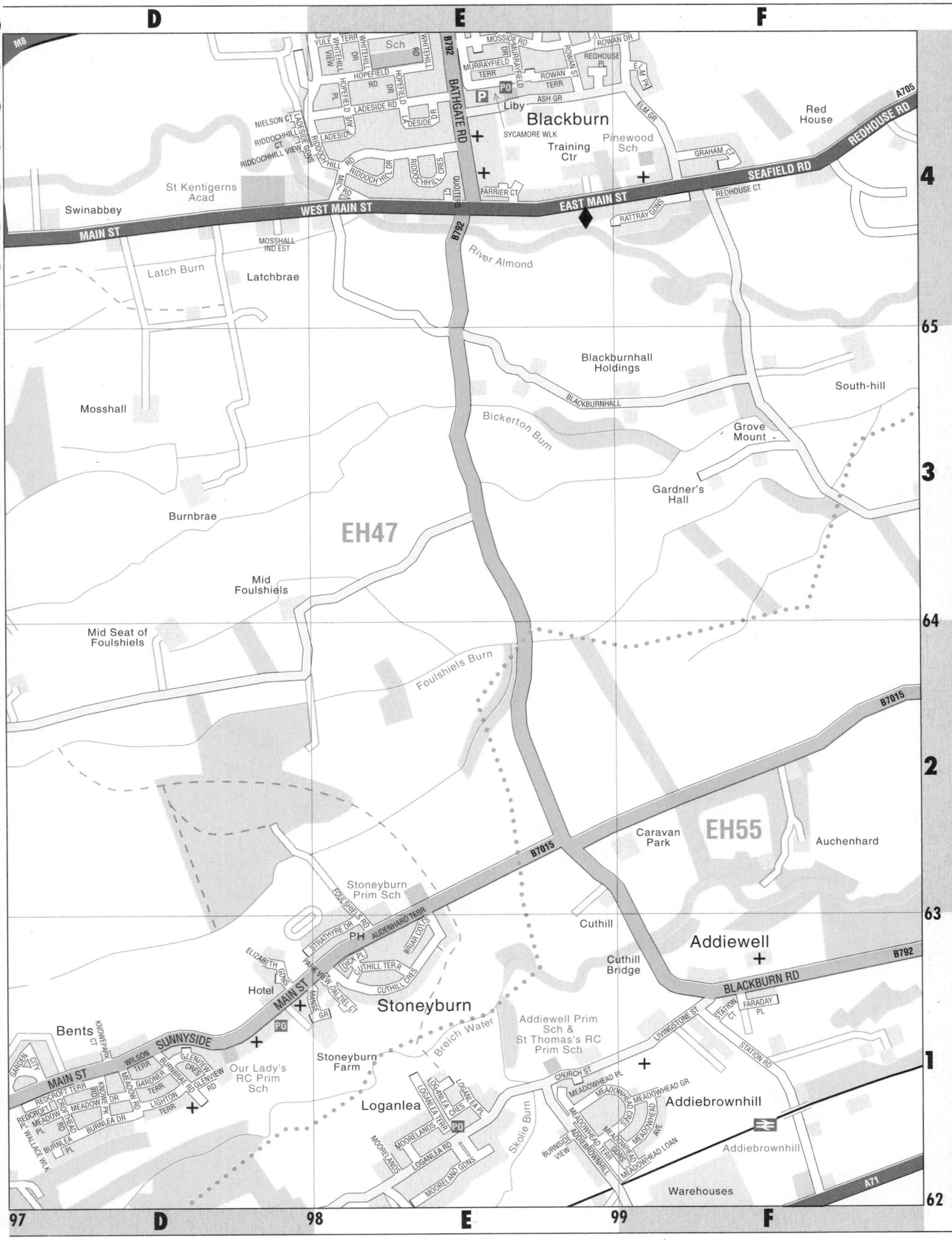
D
E
F
M8
Sch
YULE TERR
WHITEHILL VIEW
WHITEHILL DR
WHITEHILL RD
B792
BATHGATE RD
MOSSIDE RD
MURRAYFIELD DR
MURRAYFIELD TERR
ROWAN DR
ROWAN ST
ROWAN TERR
REDHOUSE PL
ELM PK
HOPEFIELD RD
HOPEFIELD DR
HOPEFIELD PL
LADESIDE RD
LADESIDE AVE
LADESIDE DR
LADESIDE
PO
P
Liby
ASH GR
Blackburn
A705
Red House
REDHOUSE RD
NIELSON CT
RIDDOCHHILL CT
RIDDOCHHILL VIEW
LADESIDE GDNS
RIDDOCHHILL RD
RIDDOCH HILL DR
RIDDOCHHILL CRES
QUITERS CT
MILL RD
SYCAMORE WLK
Training Ctr
Pinewood Sch
ELM GR
GRAHAM CT
SEAFIELD RD
FARRIER CT
REDHOUSE CT
St Kentigerns Acad
Swinabbey
WEST MAIN ST
EAST MAIN ST
RATTRAY GDNS
MAIN ST
MOSSHALL IND EST
River Almond
Latch Burn
Latchbrae
4
65
Blackburnhall Holdings
BLACKBURNHALL
South-hill
Mosshall
Bickerton Burn
Grove Mount
Gardner's Hall
3
Burnbrae
EH47
Mid Foulshiels
Mid Seat of Foulshiels
64
Foulshiels Burn
B7015
2
Caravan Park
EH55
Auchenhard
Stoneyburn Prim Sch
FOULSHIELS RD
STRATHYRE DR
AUDENHARD TERR
BRIAR COTS
PH
ELIZABETH GDNS
PARK VIEW
DICK PL
CUTHILL TERR
CUTHILL CRES
DALZIEL CT
MANSE GR
Hotel
MAIN ST
Cuthill
Cuthill Bridge
63
Addiewell
B792
BLACKBURN RD
FARADAY PL
STATION CT
Stoneyburn
Bents
KNOWEPARK CT
SUNNYSIDE
WILSON TERR
GLENVIEW CRES
GLENVIEW RD
BURNBRAE RD
GARDNER TERR
MEADOW RD
LIGHTON TERR
GARDEN CITY
REDCROFT TERR
REDCROFT PL
MEADOW PL
CROFTHEAD RD
KNOWE PK
MEADOW DR
BURNLEA DR
BURNLEA PL
WALLACE WLK
Our Lady's RC Prim Sch
Stoneyburn Farm
Breich Water
Addiewell Prim Sch & St Thomas's RC Prim Sch
LIVINGSTONE ST
STATION RD
1
CHURCH ST
MEADOWHEAD PL
MEADOWHEAD CRES
MEADOWHEAD GR
MEADOWHEAD AVE
MEADOWHEAD GDNS
MEADOWHEAD TERR
MEADOWHEAD LOAN
BURNSIDE VIEW
ADDIEBROWNHILL
Addiebrownhill
Loganlea
LOGANLEA TERR
LOGANLEA CRES
LOGANLEA PL
LOGANLEA RD
MOORELANDS
MOORELANDS TERR
MOORELAND GDNS
Skolie Burn
Warehouses
A71
62
97
98
99

195
172

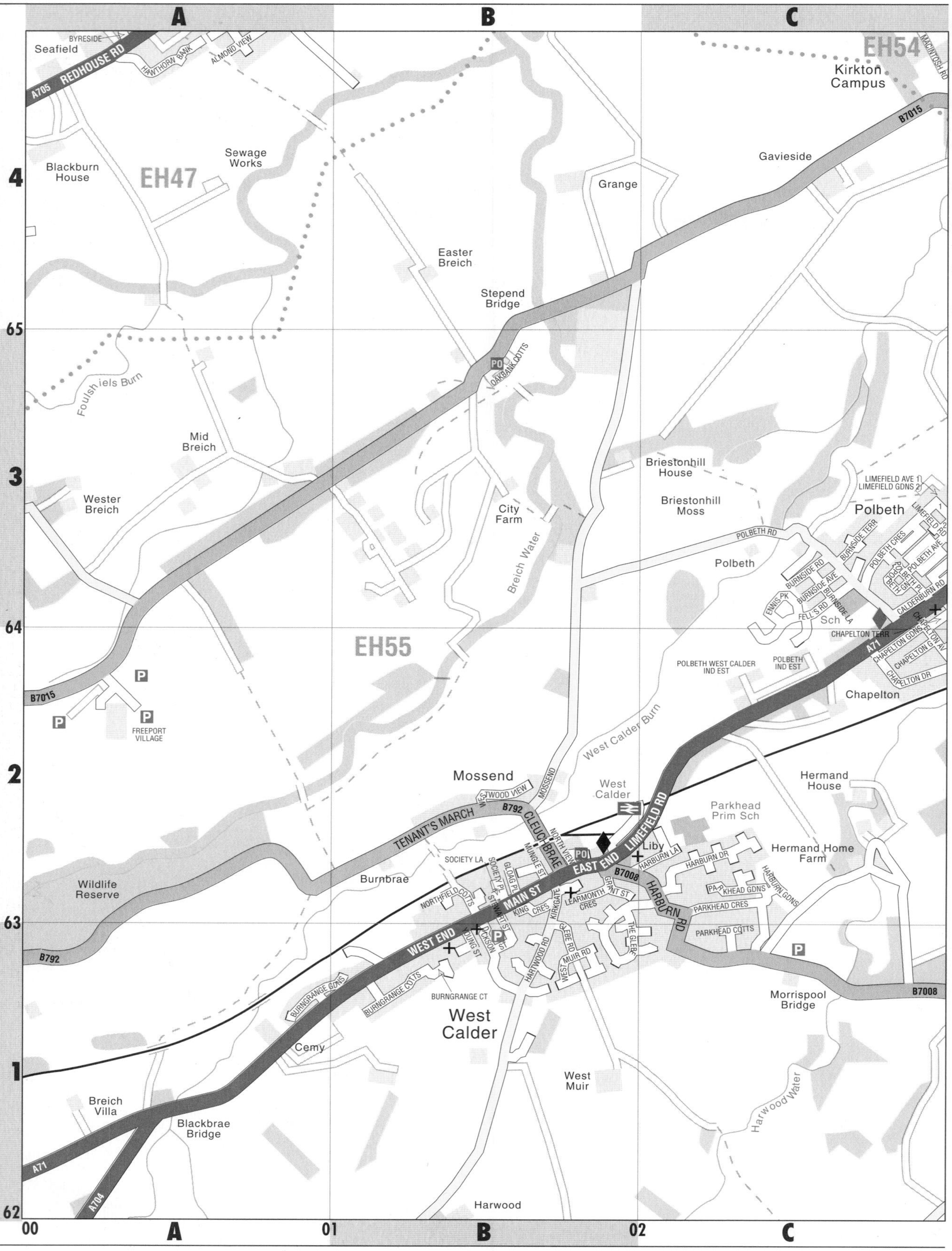

A B C

Seafield
BYRESIDE
REDHOUSE RD
A705
HAWTHORN BANK
ALMOND VIEW
Blackburn House
EH47
Sewage Works
EH54
Kirkton Campus
B7015
MACINTOSH RD

4

Easter Breich
Grange
Gavieside

Stepend Bridge

65

PO
OAKBANK COTTS

Foulshiels Burn

Mid Breich
Briestonhill House
LIMEFIELD AVE 1
LIMEFIELD GDNS 2

3

Wester Breich
City Farm
Briestonhill Moss
Polbeth
POLBETH RD
BURNSIDE RD
BURNSIDE TERR
POLBETH CRES
POLBETHANE
Polbeth

Breich Water
ENNIS PK
BURNSIDE AVE
FELL'S RD
BURNSIDE LA
Sch
CALDERBURN RD

64

EH55
CHAPELTON TERR
CHAPELTON GDNS 1
CHAPELTON GDNS 2
A71
CHAPELTON DR
Chapelton

B7015
POLBETH WEST CALDER IND EST
POLBETH IND EST

P
P
P
Freeport Village
West Calder Burn
Hermand House

2

Mossend
SPWOOD VIEW
MOSSEND
B792
CLEUGH BRAE
West Calder
Parkhead Prim Sch
Hermand Home Farm

Wildlife Reserve
TENANT'S MARCH
NORTH VIEW
PO
EAST END
LIMEFIELD RD
Liby
HARBURN LA
HARBURN DR
HARBURN GDNS
Burnbrae
SOCIETY LA
GLOVER PL
MUIR ST
B7008
PARKHEAD GDNS
Northfield COTTS
KING CRES
GRANT ST
HARBURN RD
PARKHEAD CRES
B792
MAIN ST
KINGSGATE
LEARMONTH CRES
THE GLEBE
PARKHEAD COTTS
WEST END
DICKSON
HARTWOOD RD
KING ST
MUIR RD
P
Morrispool Bridge
B7008

63

BURNGRANGE GDNS
BURNGRANGE COTTS
BURNGRANGE CT
West Calder

Cemy
West Muir

1

Breich Villa
Blackbrae Bridge
West Muir
Harwood Water

A71
A704
Harwood

62

00 A 01 B 02 C

147
174

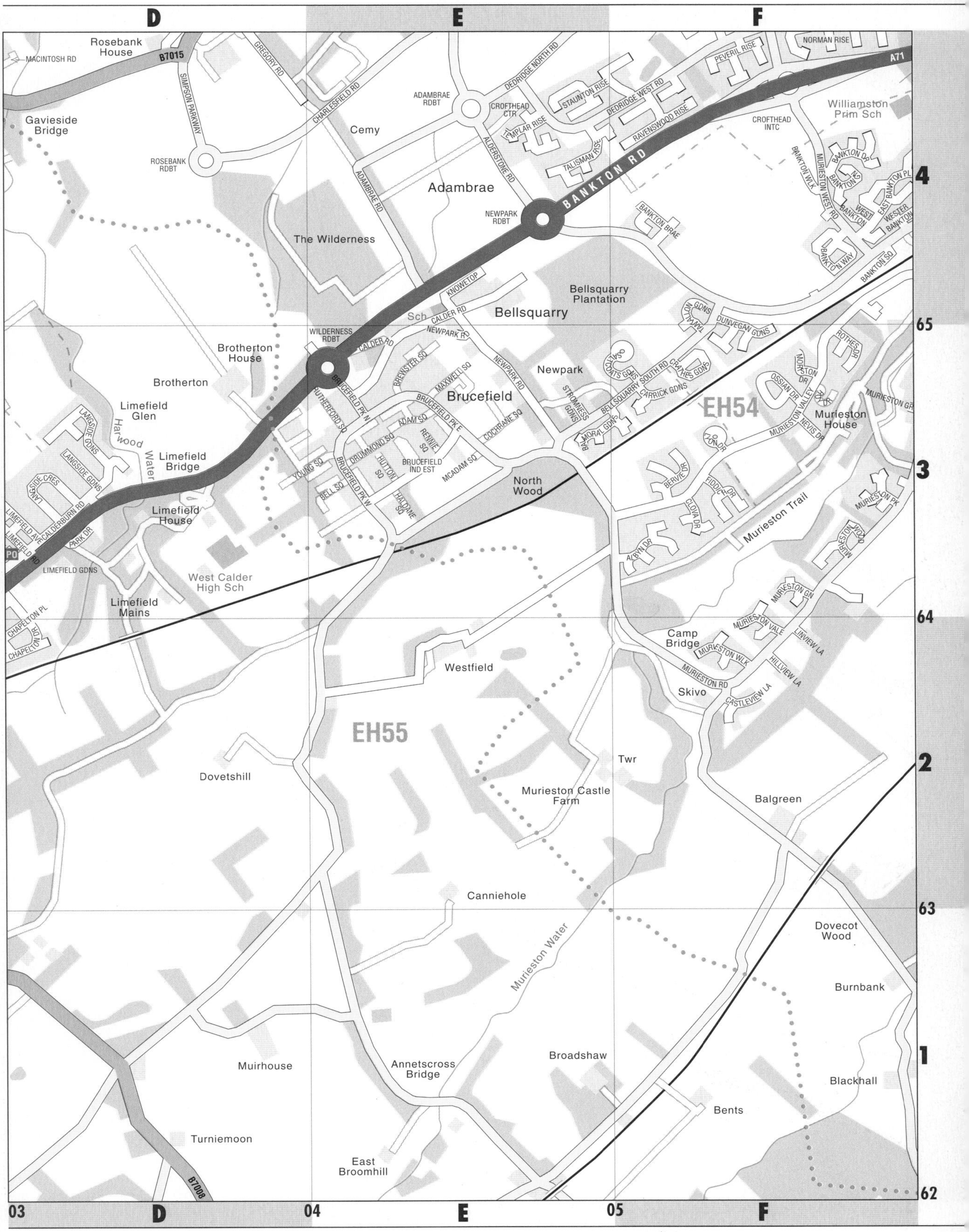
D
E
F
Rosebank House
MACINTOSH RD
B7015
GREGORY RD
SIMPSON PARKWAY
CHARLESFIELD RD
Gavieside Bridge
ROSEBANK RDBT
ADAMBRAE RDBT
Cemy
DEDRIDGE NORTH RD
CROFTHEAD CTR
STAUNTON RISE
PEVERIL RISE
NORMAN RISE
A71
DEDRIDGE WEST RD
RAVENSWOOD RISE
TEMPLAR RISE
TALISMAN RISE
ALDERSTONE RD
ADAMBRAE RD
Adambrae
BANKTON RD
NEWPARK RDBT
CROFTHEAD INTC
Williamston Prim Sch
BANKTON WLK
MURIESTON WEST RD
BANKTON DR
BANKTON SQ
BANKTON WAY
BANKTON BRAE
WESTER BANKTON
EAST BANKTON PL
The Wilderness
KNOWETOP
Bellsquarry Plantation
Bellsquarry
Sch
CALDER RD
NEWPARK RD
WILDERNESS RDBT
Brotherton House
Brotherton
TANNAHILL GDNS
DUNVEGAN GDNS
ROTHES DR
MORTON DR
OSSIAN DR
Newpark
CALDER RD
BREWSTER SQ
MAXWELL SQ
BRUCEFIELD PK N
RUTHERFORD SQ
BRUCEFIELD PK E
Brucefield
ADAM SQ
RENNIE SQ
COCHRANE SQ
DRUMMOND SQ
HUTTON SQ
YOUNG SQ
BELL SQ
BRUCEFIELD PK W
HALDANE SQ
BRUCEFIELD IND EST
MCADAM SQ
North Wood
CALCOTS GDNS
BELLSQUARRY SOUTH RD
CRAITHES GDNS
CARRICK GDNS
STROMNESS GDNS
BALMORAL GDNS
EH54
MURIESTON VALLEY
MURIESTON GR
Murieston House
NEVIS DR
DOON DR
BERVIE DR
FIDDICH DR
CLOVA DR
Murieston Trail
MURIESTON PK
MURIESTON WOOD
ALBYN DR
Limefield Glen
LANGSIDE GDNS
Harwood Water
Limefield Bridge
LANGSIDE CRES
CALDERBURN RD
LIMEFIELD AVE
LIMEFIELD RD
PARK DR
PO
Limefield House
LIMEFIELD GDNS
West Calder High Sch
Limefield Mains
CHAPELTON PL
CHAPELTON DR
MURIESTON GN
MURIESTON VALE
MURIESTON WLK
MURIESTON RD
LINVIEW LA
HILLVIEW LA
CASTLEVIEW LA
Camp Bridge
Skivo
Westfield
EH55
Twr
Dovetshill
Murieston Castle Farm
Balgreen
Canniehole
Dovecot Wood
Murieston Water
Burnbank
Muirhouse
Annetscross Bridge
Broadshaw
Blackhall
Bents
Turniemoon
B7008
East Broomhill
4
65
3
64
2
63
1
62
03
04
05
D
E
F

197
174

173
148

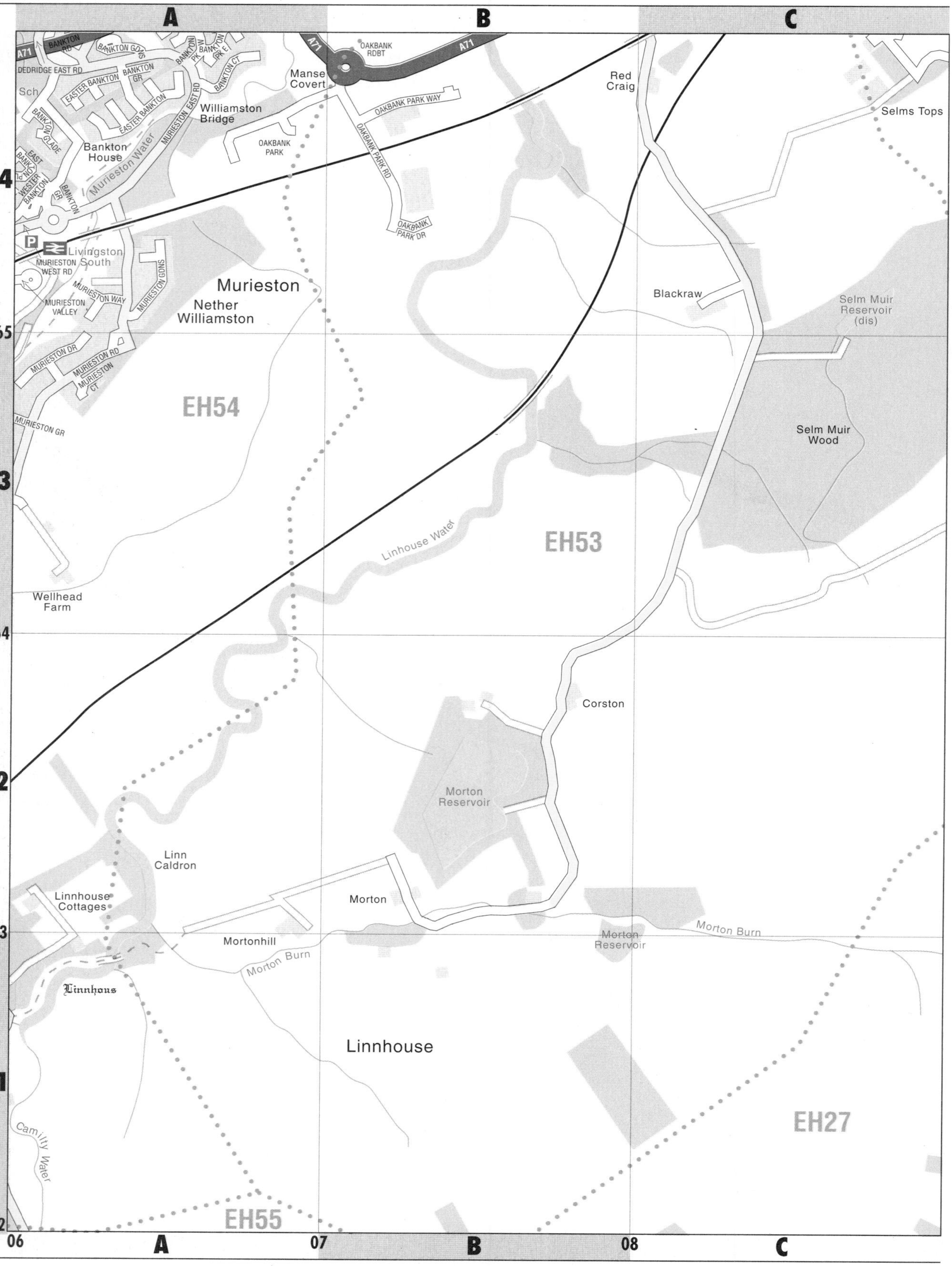

A **B** **C**

A71

BANKTON RD

DEDRIDGE EAST RD
EASTER BANKTON
BANKTON GDNS
BANKTON PK
BANKTON GR
BANKTON EAST RD
BANKTON CT
BANKTON PK E

Sch

OAKBANK RDBT

Manse
Covert

Williamston
Bridge

OAKBANK
PARK

OAKBANK PARK WAY

OAKBANK PARK RD

OAKBANK
PARK DR

Red
Craig

Selms Tops

4

Bankton
House

EAST BANKTON
EASTER BANKTON
WESTER BANKTON
BANKTON GR

Murieston Water

P

Livingston
South

MURIESTON
WEST RD

MURIESTON WAY

MURIESTON GDNS

MURIESTON VALLEY

MURIESTON DR

MURIESTON RD

MURIESTON CT

Murieston

Nether
Williamston

Blackraw

Selm Muir
Reservoir
(dis)

65

MURIESTON GR

EH54

Selm Muir
Wood

3

Linhouse Water

EH53

Wellhead
Farm

64

Corston

2

Morton
Reservoir

Linn
Caldron

Linnhouse
Cottages

Morton

Morton Burn

Morton
Reservoir

Morton Burn

63

Mortonhill

Morton Burn

Linnhous

Linnhouse

1

EH27

Camilty Water

62

06 **A** 07 **B** 08 **C**

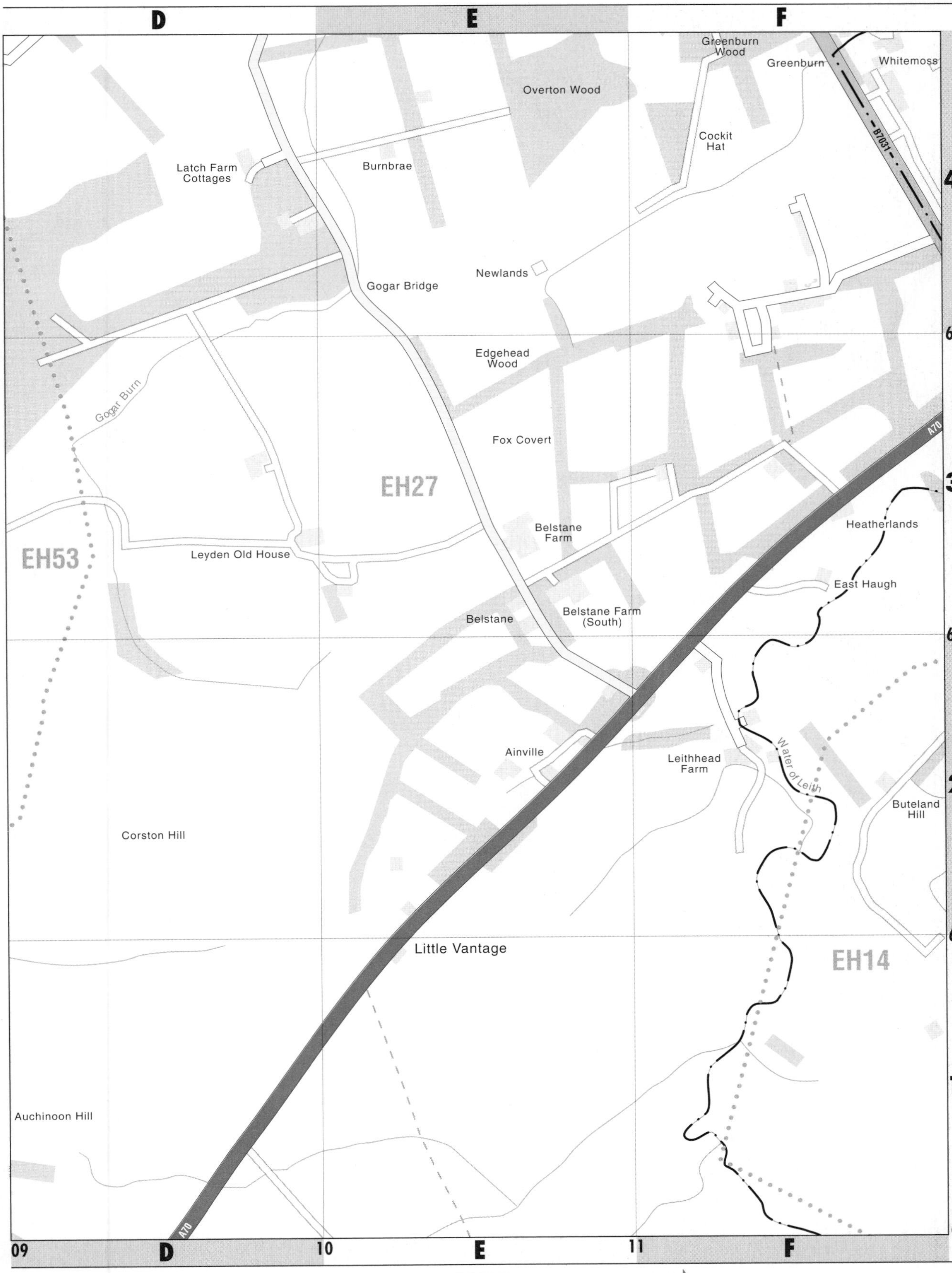

D E F

Greenburn
Wood
Greenburn
Whitemoss

Overton Wood

Cockit
Hat

B7031

Latch Farm
Cottages
Burnbrae

4

Gogar Bridge
Newlands

65

Edgehead
Wood

Gogar Burn

Fox Covert

A70

EH27

3

Heatherlands

EH53
Leyden Old House
Belstane
Farm

East Haugh

Belstane
Belstane Farm
(South)

64

Ainville
Leithhead
Farm

Water of Leith

Buteland
Hill

2

Corston Hill

63

Little Vantage

EH14

1

Auchinoon Hill

62

175
150

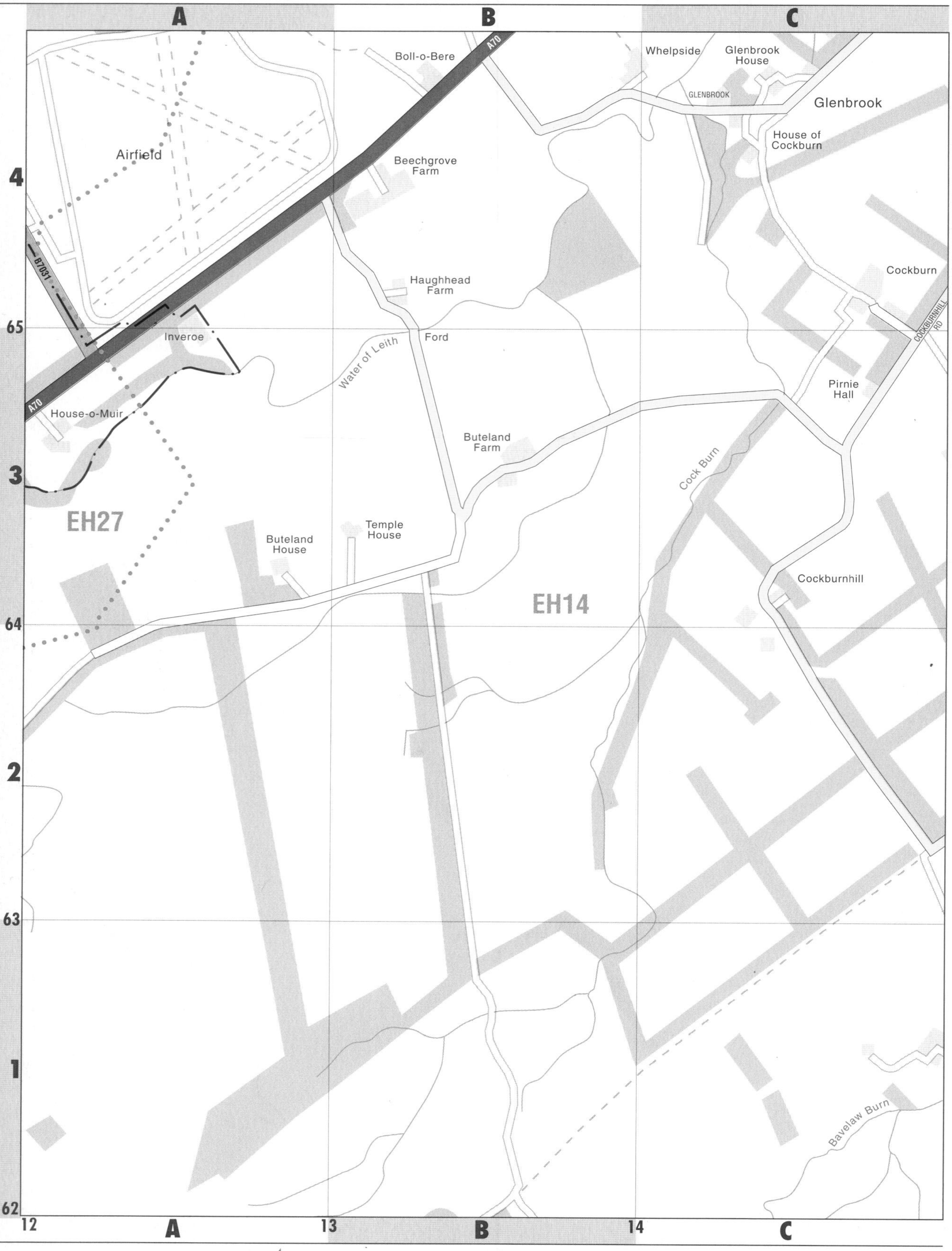

A B C

4

Airfield

Boll-o-Bere

A70

Whelpside

Glenbrook House

GLENBROOK

Glenbrook

House of Cockburn

Beechgrove Farm

B7031

Haughhead Farm

65

Inveroe

Ford

Water of Leith

Cockburn

COCKBURNHILL RD

House-o-Muir

A70

Pirnie Hall

3

EH27

Buteland Farm

Cock Burn

Buteland House

Temple House

Cockburnhill

64

EH14

2

63

1

Bavelaw Burn

62

12 A 13 B 14 C

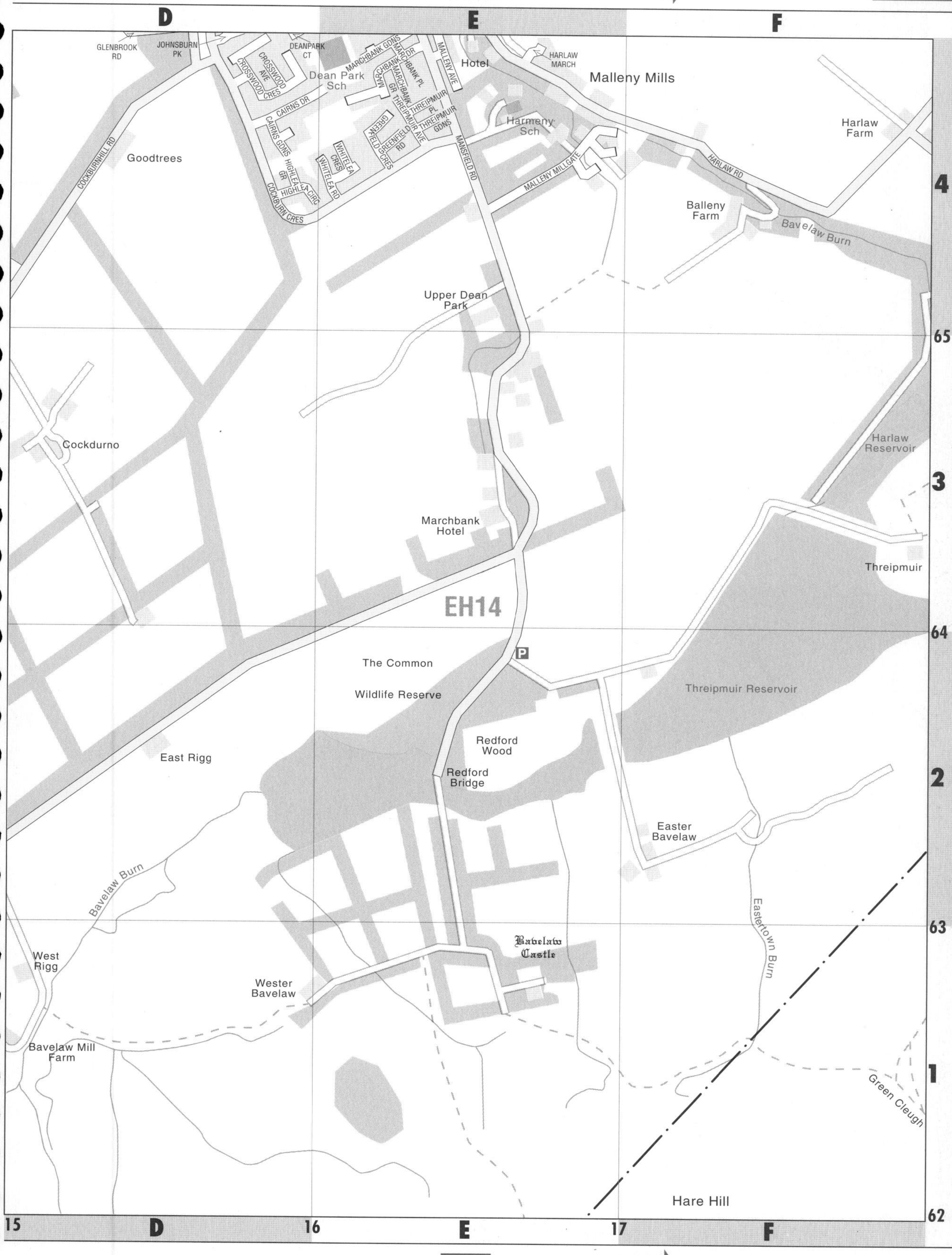

D E F

GLENBROOK RD
JOHNSBURN PK
DEANPARK CT
HARLAW MARCH
Malleny Mills
CROSSWOOD AVE
CROSSWOOD CRES
Dean Park Sch
MARCHBANK GDNS
MARCHBANK PL
MARCHBANK DR
MALLENY AVE
Hotel
Harmeny Sch
Harlaw Farm
Goodtrees
CAIRNS DR
CAIRNS GDNS
MARCHBANK WAY
MARCHBANK GR
THREIPMUIR PL
THREIPMUIR AVE
THREIPMUIR GDNS
MANSFIELD RD
MALLENY MILLGATE
HARLAW RD
Balleny Farm
Bavelaw Burn

HIGHLEA GR
HIGHLEA CIRC
WHITELEA RD
WHITELEA CRES
GREENFIELD CRES
GREENFIELD RD
COCKBURNHILL RD
COCKBURN CRES

4

Upper Dean Park

65

Cockdurno

Harlaw Reservoir

3

Marchbank Hotel

Threipmuir

EH14

64

The Common

Wildlife Reserve

Threipmuir Reservoir

Redford Wood

East Rigg

Redford Bridge

Easter Bavelaw

2

Bavelaw Burn

63

West Rigg

Wester Bavelaw

𝕭𝖆𝖛𝖊𝖑𝖆𝖜 𝕮𝖆𝖘𝖙𝖑𝖊

Easterton Burn

Bavelaw Mill Farm

1

Green Cleugh

Hare Hill

62

15 D 16 E 17 F

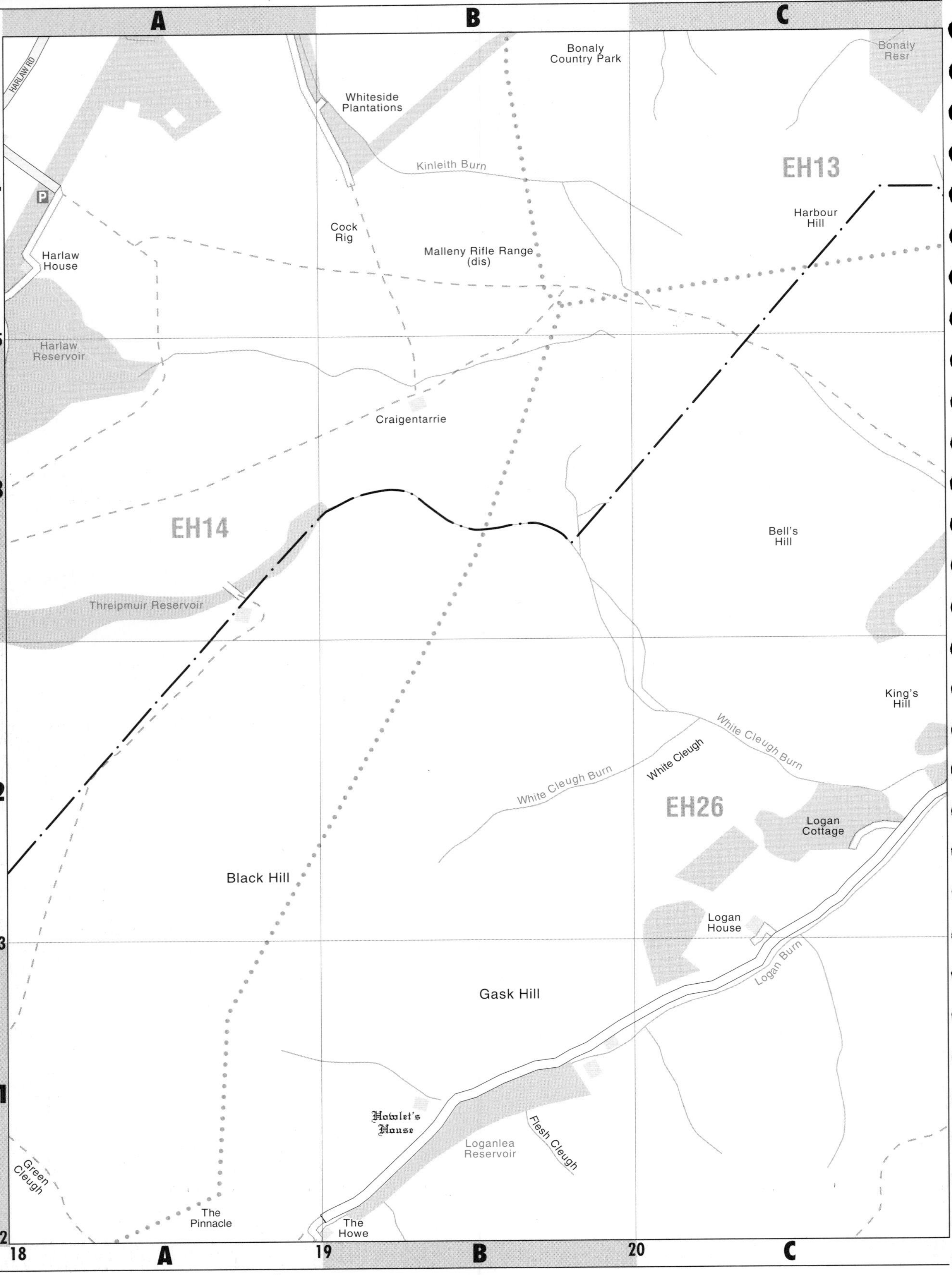

177
152

A   B   C

HARLAW RD

4

P

Harlaw
House

Whiteside
Plantations

Kinleith Burn

Cock
Rig

Malleny Rifle Range
(dis)

Bonaly
Country Park

Bonaly
Resr

EH13

Harbour
Hill

65

Harlaw
Reservoir

Craigentarrie

3

EH14

Threipmuir Reservoir

Bell's
Hill

King's
Hill

2

Black Hill

White Cleugh Burn

White Cleugh

White Cleugh Burn

EH26

Logan
Cottage

63

Logan
House

Logan Burn

Gask Hill

1

Howlet's
House

Loganlea
Reservoir

Flesh Cleugh

Green
Cleugh

The
Pinnacle

The
Howe

62

18   A   19   B   20   C

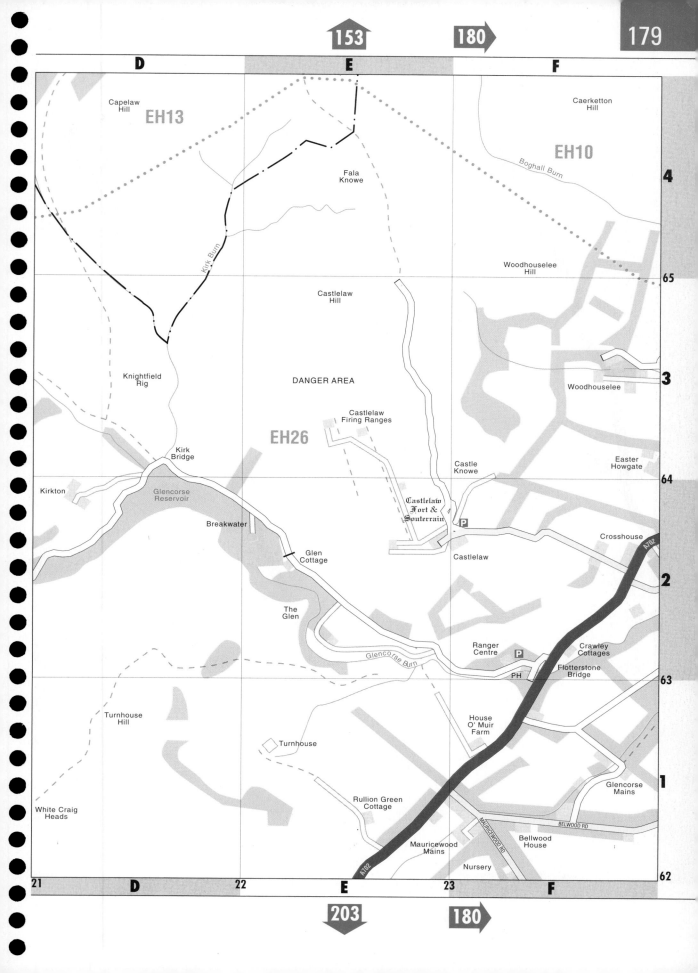

Capelaw
Hill
EH13

Caerketton
Hill

EH10

Boghall Burn

4

Fala
Knowe

Woodhouselee
Hill

65

Kirk Burn

Castlelaw
Hill

Knightfield
Rig

DANGER AREA

Woodhouselee

3

EH26

Castlelaw
Firing Ranges

Castle
Knowe

Easter
Howgate

Kirk
Bridge

64

Kirkton

Glencorse
Reservoir

Castlelaw
Fort &
Souterrain

P

Crosshouse

Breakwater

Glen
Cottage

Castlelaw

A702

2

The
Glen

Glencorse Burn

Ranger
Centre

P

Crawley
Cottages

Turnhouse
Hill

PH

Flotterstone
Bridge

63

Turnhouse

House
O' Muir
Farm

White Craig
Heads

Rullion Green
Cottage

Glencorse
Mains

1

MAURICEWOOD RD

BELWOOD RD

Mauricewood
Mains

Bellwood
House

A702

Nursery

62

179
154

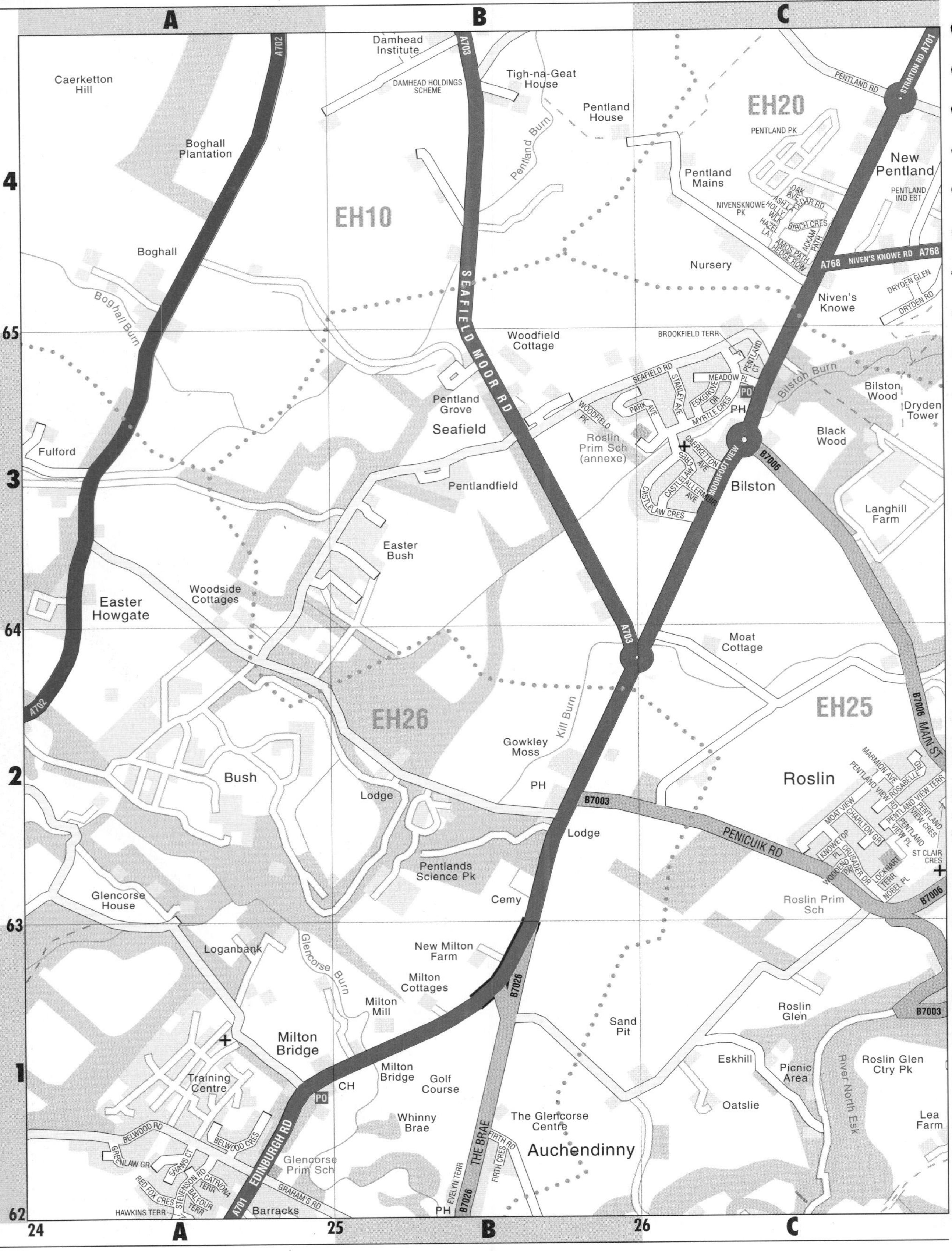
A
B
C
4
65
3
64
2
63
1
62
24
25
26
EH10
EH20
EH25
EH26
Caerketton Hill
Damhead Institute
DAMHEAD HOLDINGS SCHEME
Tigh-na-Geat House
Pentland House
Boghall Plantation
Boghall
Boghall Burn
Pentland Burn
Pentland Mains
PENTLAND PK
New Pentland
PENTLAND IND EST
PENTLAND RD
STRAITON RD A701
A702
A703
SEAFIELD MOOR RD
NIVENSKNOWE PK
OAK AVE
CEDAR RD
ASH LA
HOLLY WLK
HAZEL LA
BIRCH CRES
AMOS PATH
HEDGE ROW
ACKAM PATH
A768
NIVEN'S KNOWE RD
A768
Nursery
Niven's Knowe
DRYDEN GLEN
DRYDEN RD
Woodfield Cottage
BROOKFIELD TERR
PENTLAND CT
SEAFIELD RD
MEADOW PL
STANLEY AVE
PARK AVE
ESKGROVE DR
MYRTLE CRES
PO
PH
Bilston Burn
Bilston Wood
Dryden Tower
Black Wood
Pentland Grove
Seafield
WOODFIELD PK
Roslin Prim Sch (annexe)
CAERKETTON AVE
CAERKETTON CRES
CASTLELAW CRES
CALLERMUIR AVE
MOORFOOT VIEW
Bilston
B7006
Langhill Farm
Fulford
Pentlandfield
Easter Bush
Woodside Cottages
Easter Howgate
Moat Cottage
Kill Burn
Gowkley Moss
PH
Bush
Lodge
B7003
PENICUIK RD
Roslin
MAIN ST
MARMION AVE
ROSABELLE RD
PENTLAND VIEW RD
PENTLAND VIEW TERR
MOAT VIEW
CHARLTON GR
PENTLAND VIEW CRES
PENTLAND VIEW PL
KNOWETOP PL
CRUSADER DR
WOODEND PK
LOCKHART TERR
NOBEL PL
ST CLAIR CRES
Lodge
Pentlands Science Pk
Cemy
Glencorse House
Roslin Prim Sch
Loganbank
Glencorse Burn
New Milton Farm
Milton Cottages
Milton Mill
B7026
Roslin Glen
B7003
Sand Pit
Milton Bridge
Training Centre
Milton Bridge
Golf Course
Eskhill
Picnic Area
Roslin Glen Ctry Pk
River North Esk
CH
PO
Whinny Brae
Oatslie
Lea Farm
BELWOOD RD
BELWOOD CRES
GREENLAW GR
SHAWS CT
CATRIONA TERR
STEVENSON RD
RED FOX CRES
BALFOUR TERR
HAWKINS TERR
EDINBURGH RD
A701
GRAHAM'S RD
Barracks
Glencorse Prim Sch
THE BRAE
EVELYN TERR
FIRTH RD
FIRTH CRES
The Glencorse Centre
Auchendinny
PH
B7026

179
204

155
182

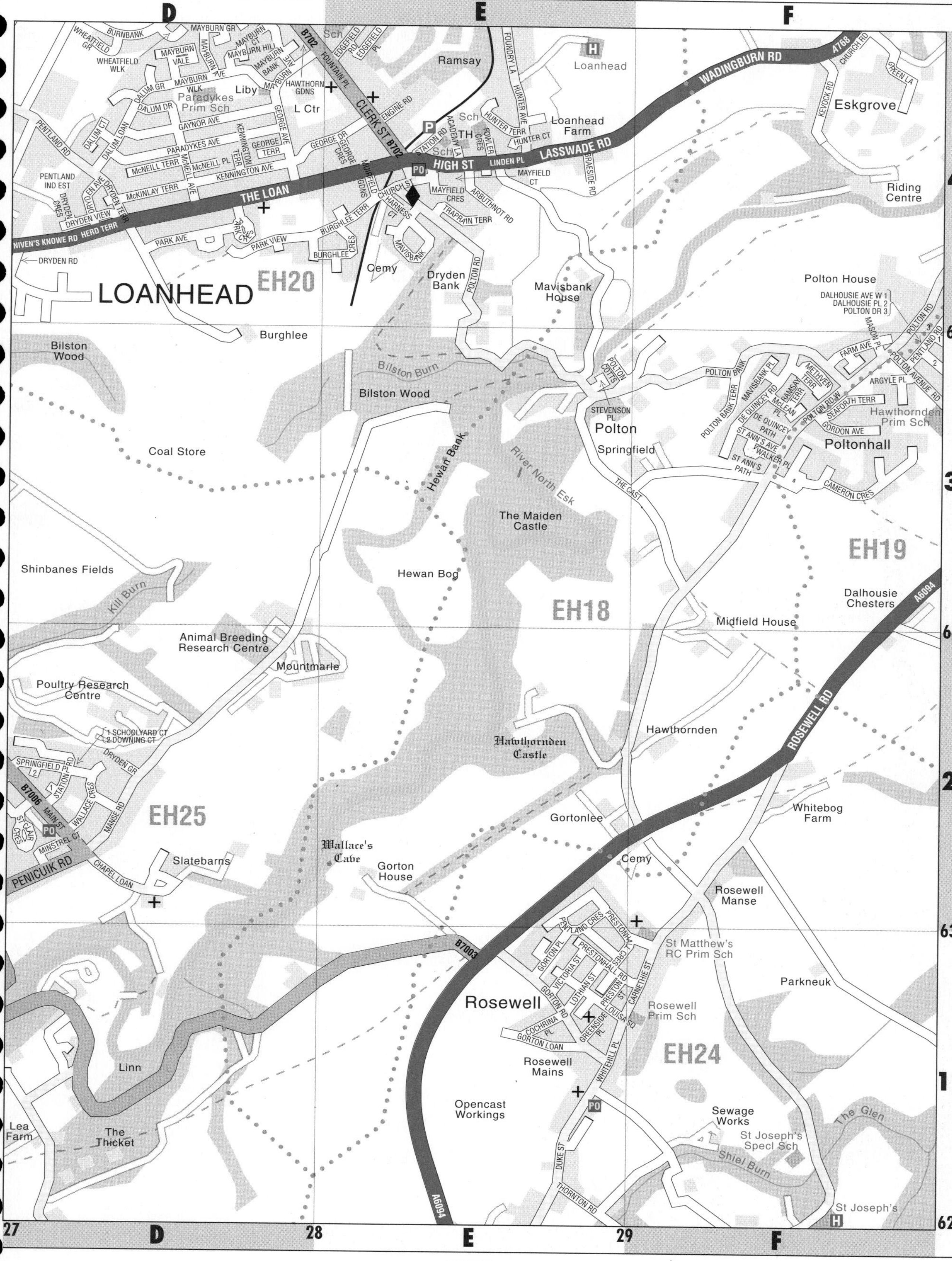
D
E
F
4
3
2
1
65
64
63
62
27
28
29
LOANHEAD
EH20
EH18
EH19
EH25
EH24
Loanhead
Ramsay
Liby
L Ctr
Paradykes Prim Sch
Sch
TH
PO
Cemy
Dryden Bank
Mavisbank House
Loanhead Farm
Eskgrove
Riding Centre
Polton House
Burghlee
Bilston Wood
Bilston Burn
Coal Store
Shinbanes Fields
Kill Burn
Hewan Bank
Hewan Bog
River North Esk
The Maiden Castle
Polton
Springfield
Poltonhall
Hawthornden Prim Sch
Dalhousie Chesters
Midfield House
Animal Breeding Research Centre
Mountmarle
Poultry Research Centre
Hawthornden Castle
Hawthornden
Gortonlee
Whitebog Farm
Wallace's Cave
Gorton House
Slatebarns
Rosewell Manse
St Matthew's RC Prim Sch
Parkneuk
Rosewell
Rosewell Prim Sch
Rosewell Mains
Opencast Workings
Sewage Works
St Joseph's Specl Sch
Shiel Burn
The Glen
St Joseph's
Linn
Lea Farm
The Thicket
THE LOAN
HIGH ST
LASSWADE RD
WADINGBURN RD
CLERK ST
ROSEWELL RD
PENICUIK RD
NIVEN'S KNOWE RD
HERD TERR
DRYDEN RD
PENTLAND RD
PENTLAND IND EST
B702
B7003
B7006
A6094
4768

181
156

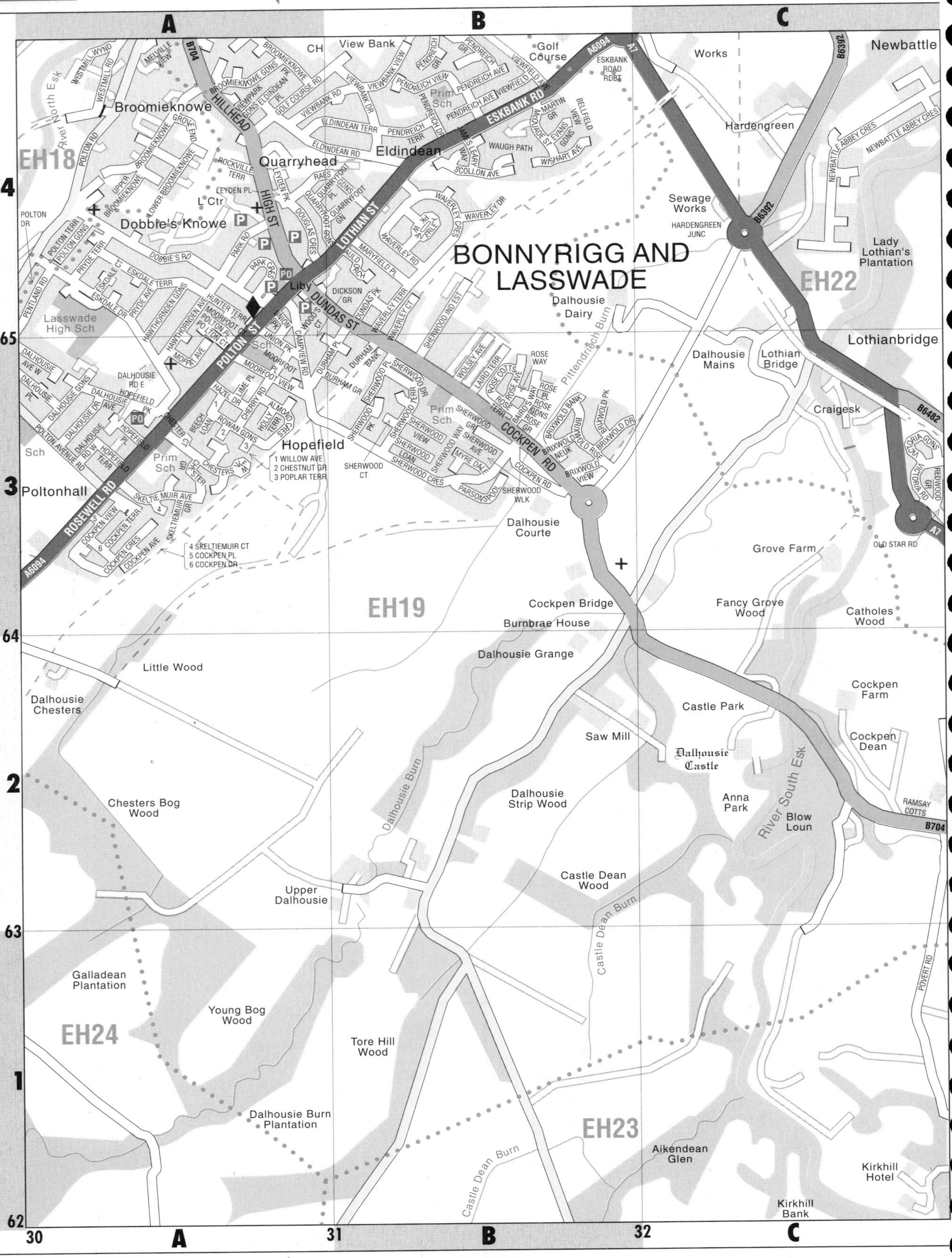
A
B
C
BONNYRIGG AND LASSWADE
Broomieknowe
Quarryhead
Eldindean
Dobbie's Knowe
L'Ctr
Lasswade High Sch
Hopefield
Poltonhall
Prim Sch
Sch
Liby
View Bank
Golf Course
CH
Works
Newbattle
Hardengreen
Sewage Works
HARDENGREEN JUNC
ESKBANK ROAD RDBT
Lady Lothian's Plantation
Lothianbridge
Dalhousie Mains
Lothian Bridge
Craigesk
Dalhousie Dairy
Pittendreich Burn
Dalhousie Courte
Grove Farm
Fancy Grove Wood
Catholes Wood
Cockpen Bridge
Burnbrae House
Dalhousie Grange
Little Wood
Dalhousie Chesters
Castle Park
Saw Mill
Dalhousie Castle
Cockpen Farm
Cockpen Dean
Anna Park
Blow Loun
River South Esk
Dalhousie Strip Wood
Dalhousie Burn
Chesters Bog Wood
Upper Dalhousie
Castle Dean Wood
Castle Dean Burn
Galladean Plantation
Young Bog Wood
Tore Hill Wood
Dalhousie Burn Plantation
Aikendean Glen
Kirkhill Hotel
Kirkhill Bank
RAMSAY COTTS
OLD STAR RD
POVERT RD
EH18
EH19
EH22
EH23
EH24
A6094
A7
B704
B6392
B6482
ESKBANK RD
LOTHIAN ST
DUNDAS ST
POLTON ST
ROSEWELL RD
COCKPEN RD
HIGH ST
HILLHEAD
1 WILLOW AVE
2 CHESTNUT GR
3 POPLAR TERR
4 SKELTIEMUIR CT
5 COCKPEN PL
6 COCKPEN DR
4
65
3
64
2
63
1
62
30
31
32

157
184

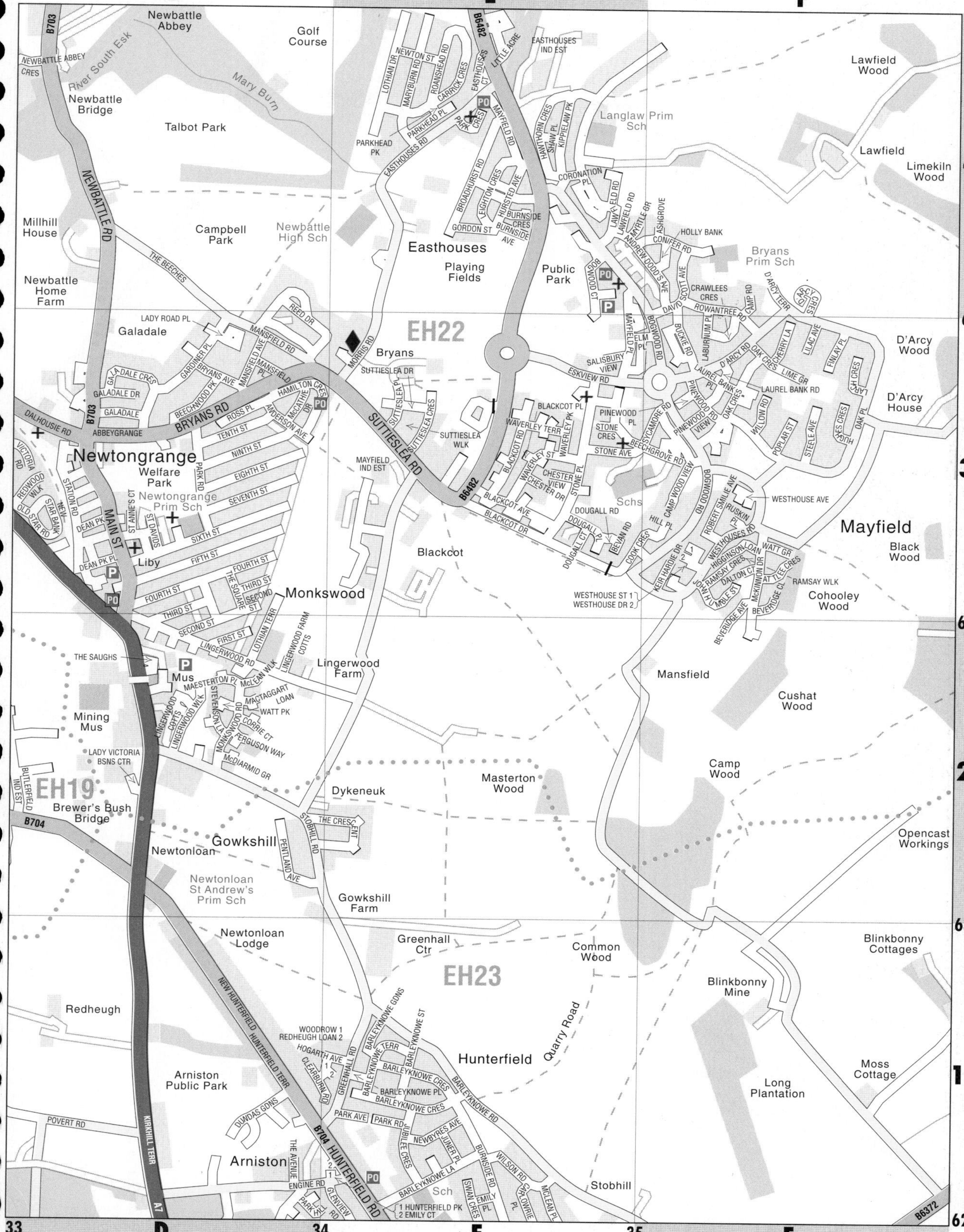
D
E
F
4
3
2
1
65
64
63
62
33
34
35
EH22
EH19
EH23
Newbattle Abbey
Golf Course
River South Esk
Mary Burn
Newbattle Bridge
Talbot Park
Lawfield Wood
Lawfield
Limekiln Wood
Langlaw Prim Sch
Easthouses Ind Est
Millhill House
Campbell Park
Newbattle High Sch
Easthouses
Playing Fields
Public Park
Bryans Prim Sch
Newbattle Home Farm
Galadale
Bryans
D'Arcy Wood
D'Arcy House
Newtongrange
Welfare Park
Newtongrange Prim Sch
Liby
Mayfield Ind Est
Suttieslea Wlk
Schs
Blackcot
Mayfield
Black Wood
Monkswood
Cohooley Wood
Mansfield
Lingerwood Farm
Mus
Mining Mus
Cushat Wood
Lady Victoria Bsns Ctr
Camp Wood
Masterton Wood
Dykeneuk
Brewer's Bush Bridge
Gowkshill
Newtonloan
Opencast Workings
Newtonloan St Andrew's Prim Sch
Gowkshill Farm
Newtonloan Lodge
Greenhall Ctr
Common Wood
Blinkbonny Cottages
Blinkbonny Mine
Redheugh
Quarry Road
Hunterfield
Moss Cottage
Long Plantation
Arniston Public Park
Arniston
Sch
Stobhill
B703
B6482
B704
B6372
A7
NEWBATTLE RD
MAIN ST
BRYANS RD
SUTTIESLEA RD
DALHOUSIE RD
ABBEYGRANGE
NEW HUNTERFIELD RD
HUNTERFIELD TERR
HUNTERFIELD RD
KIRKHILL TERR
POVERT RD
BARLEYKNOWE RD
EASTHOUSES RD
MAYFIELD RD
ESKVIEW RD
WESTHOUSE AVE
STOBHILL RD
THE BEECHES
LADY ROAD PL
MANSFIELD RD
REED DR
MORRIS RD
SUTTIESLEA DR
LINGERWOOD RD
PENTLAND AVE
THE CRESCENT
WOODROW 1
REDHEUGH LOAN 2
WESTHOUSE ST 1
WESTHOUSE DR 2
1 HUNTERFIELD PK
2 EMILY CT

207
184

183
158

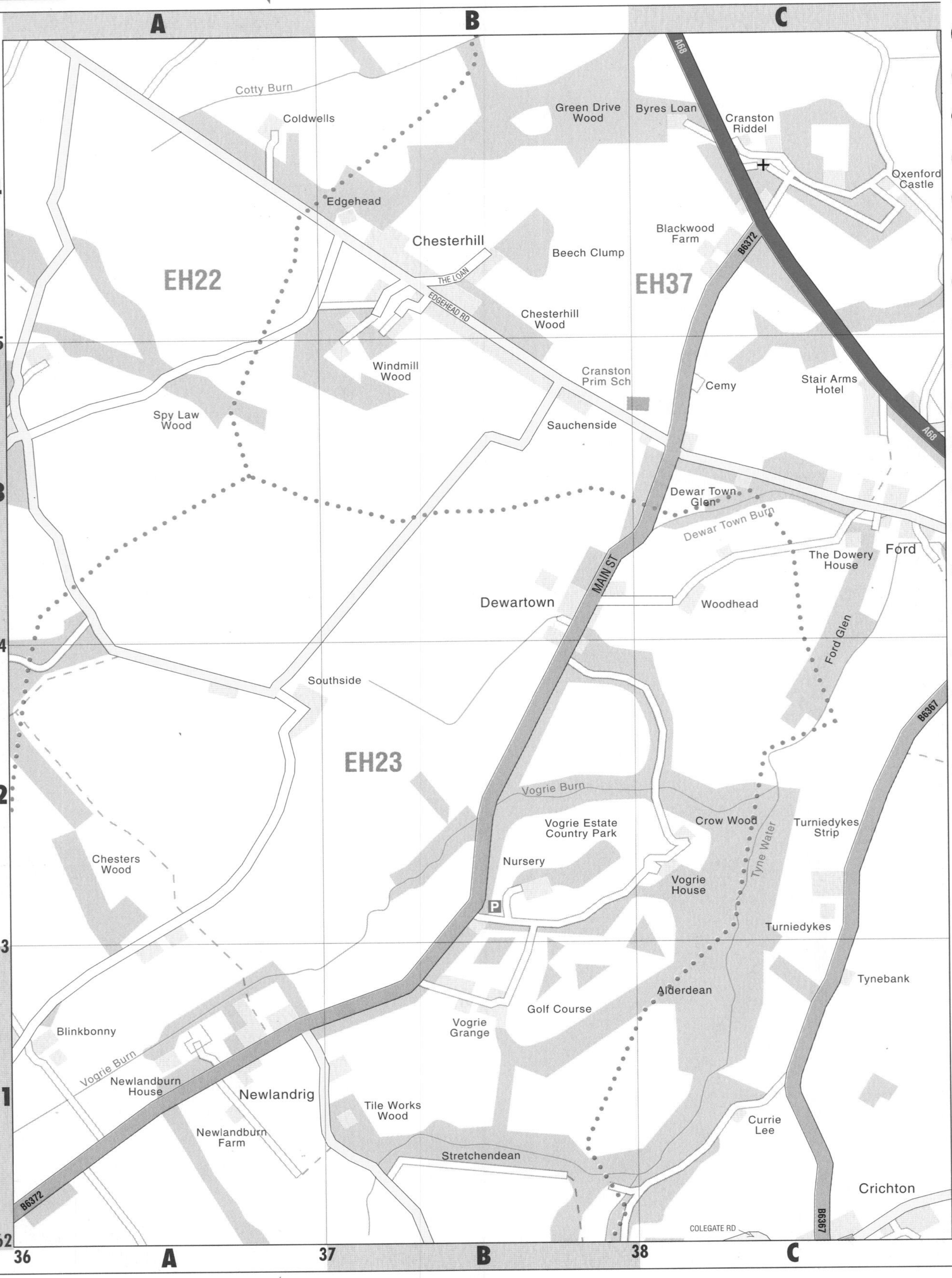

A   B   C

4

Cotty Burn

Coldwells

Green Drive Wood

Byres Loan

Cranston Riddel

Oxenford Castle

Edgehead

Chesterhill

Beech Clump

Blackwood Farm

EH37

EH22

THE LOAN

EDGEHEAD RD

Chesterhill Wood

Stair Arms Hotel

65

Windmill Wood

Cranston Prim Sch

Cemy

Spy Law Wood

Sauchenside

Dewar Town Glen

A68

B6372

3

Dewar Town Burn

The Dowery House

Ford

MAIN ST

Dewartown

Woodhead

Ford Glen

64

Southside

EH23

B6367

2

Chesters Wood

Vogrie Burn

Crow Wood

Turniedykes Strip

Vogrie Estate Country Park

Tyne Water

Nursery

Vogrie House

P

Turniedykes

63

Alderdean

Tynebank

Blinkbonny

Golf Course

Vogrie Grange

Newlandburn House

Newlandrig

1

Vogrie Burn

Tile Works Wood

Currie Lee

Newlandburn Farm

Stretchendean

Crichton

B6372

COLEGATE RD

B6367

62

36   A   37   B   38   C

159
186

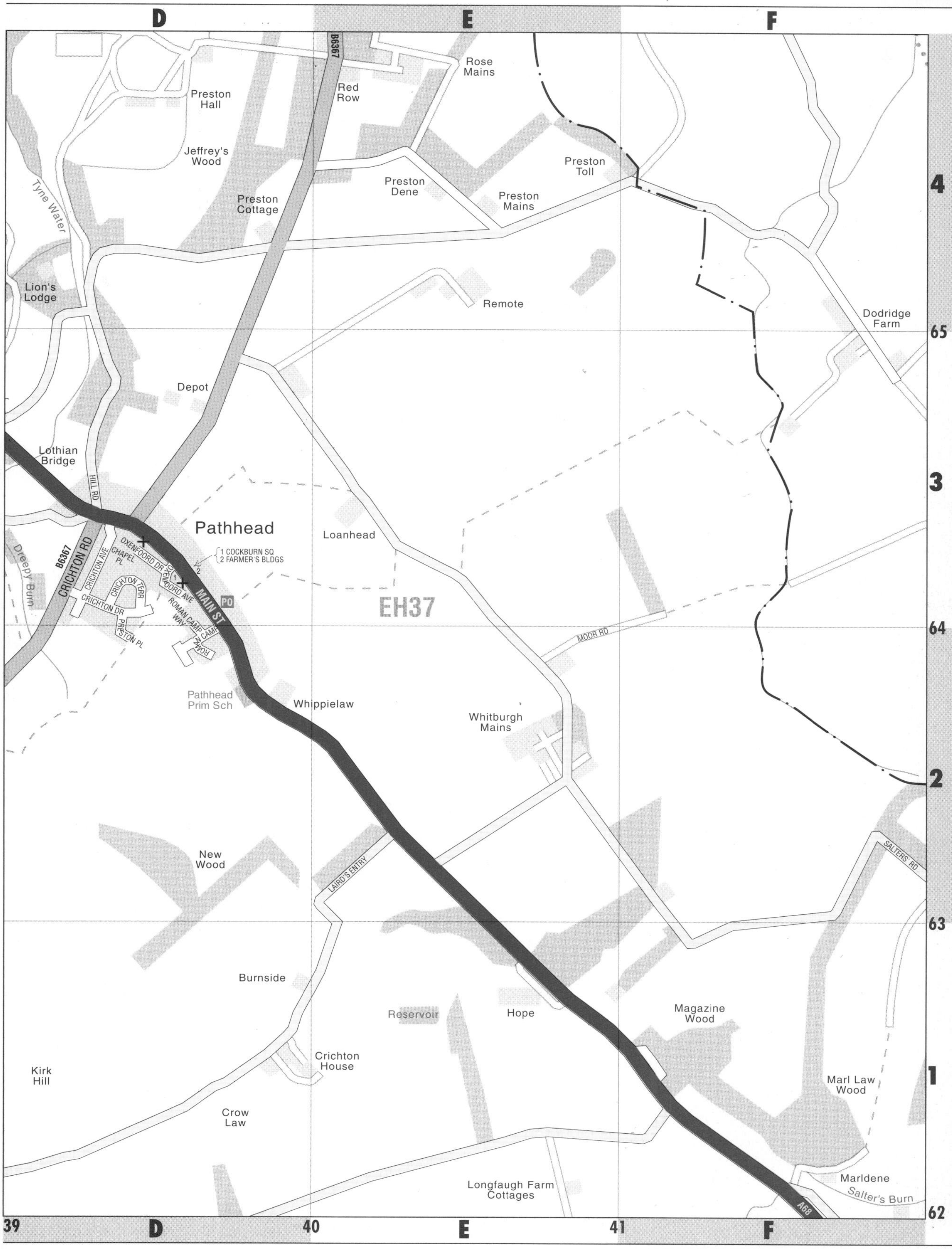
D
E
F
B6367
Rose Mains
Red Row
Preston Hall
Jeffrey's Wood
Tyne Water
Preston Cottage
Preston Dene
Preston Toll
Preston Mains
Lion's Lodge
Remote
Dodridge Farm
Depot
Lothian Bridge
HILL RD
Pathhead
Loanhead
1 COCKBURN SQ
2 FARMER'S BLDGS
OXENFOORD DR
CHAPEL PL
CRICHTON AVE
CRICHTON RD
B6367
Dreepy Burn
CRICHTON TERR
CRICHTON DR
PRESTON PL
OXENFOORD AVE
MAIN ST
ROMAN CAMP WAY
PO
EH37
MOOR RD
Pathhead Prim Sch
Whippielaw
Whitburgh Mains
New Wood
LAIRD'S ENTRY
SALTERS' RD
Burnside
Reservoir
Hope
Magazine Wood
Crichton House
Kirk Hill
Marl Law Wood
Crow Law
Longfaugh Farm Cottages
Marldene
Salter's Burn
A68
4
65
3
64
2
63
1
62
39
40
41

209
186

185
160

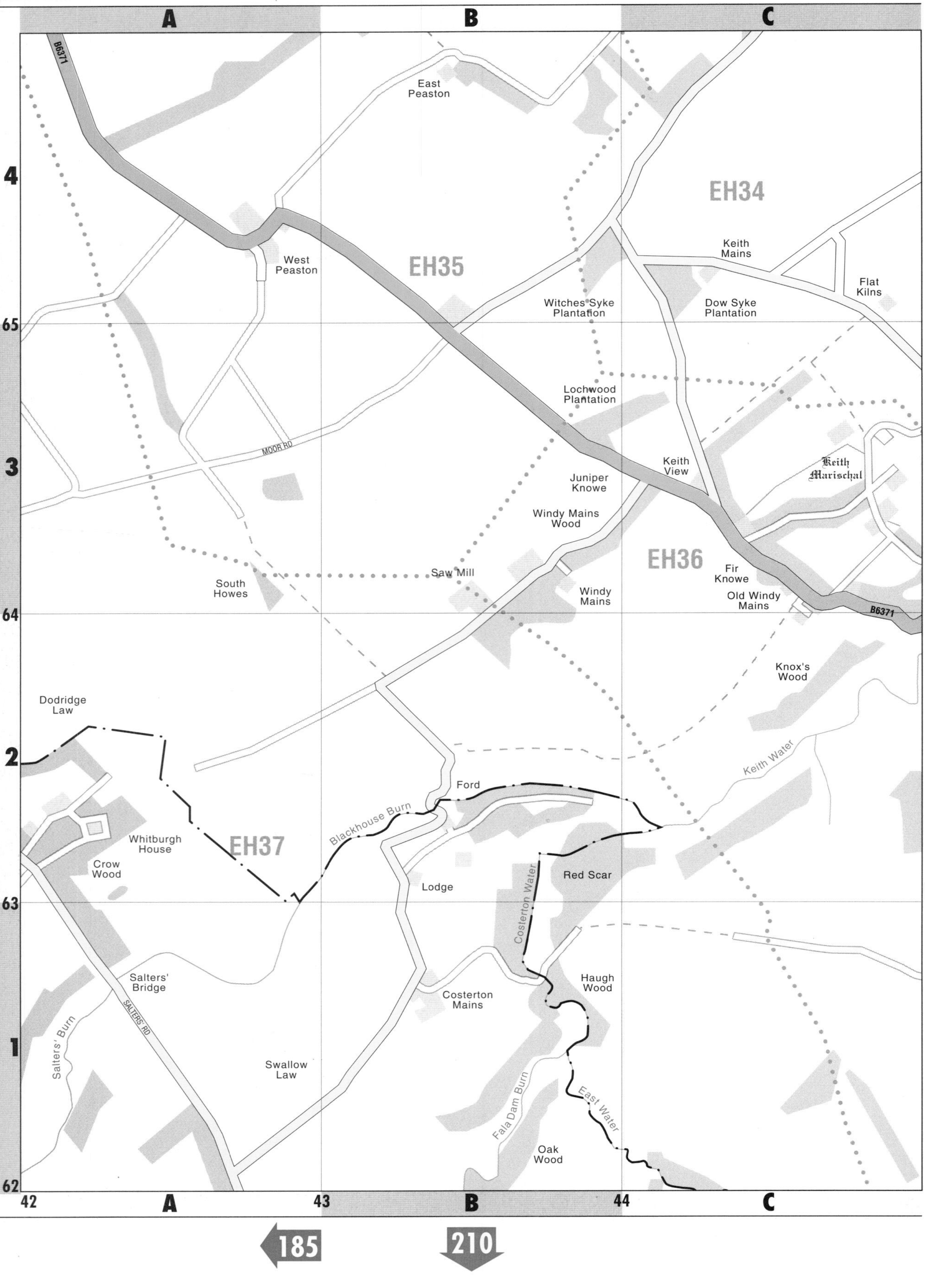
A
B
C
4
65
3
64
2
63
1
62
42
43
44
B6371
East Peaston
West Peaston
EH35
EH34
Keith Mains
Flat Kilns
Witches Syke Plantation
Dow Syke Plantation
Lochwood Plantation
MOOR RD
Keith View
Keith Marischal
Juniper Knowe
Windy Mains Wood
EH36
Fir Knowe
Saw Mill
South Howes
Windy Mains
Old Windy Mains
Knox's Wood
Dodridge Law
Keith Water
Ford
Blackhouse Burn
Whitburgh House
EH37
Crow Wood
Red Scar
Lodge
Costerton Water
Salters' Bridge
SALTERS RD
Haugh Wood
Costerton Mains
Salters' Burn
Swallow Law
Fala Dam Burn
East Water
Oak Wood

185
210

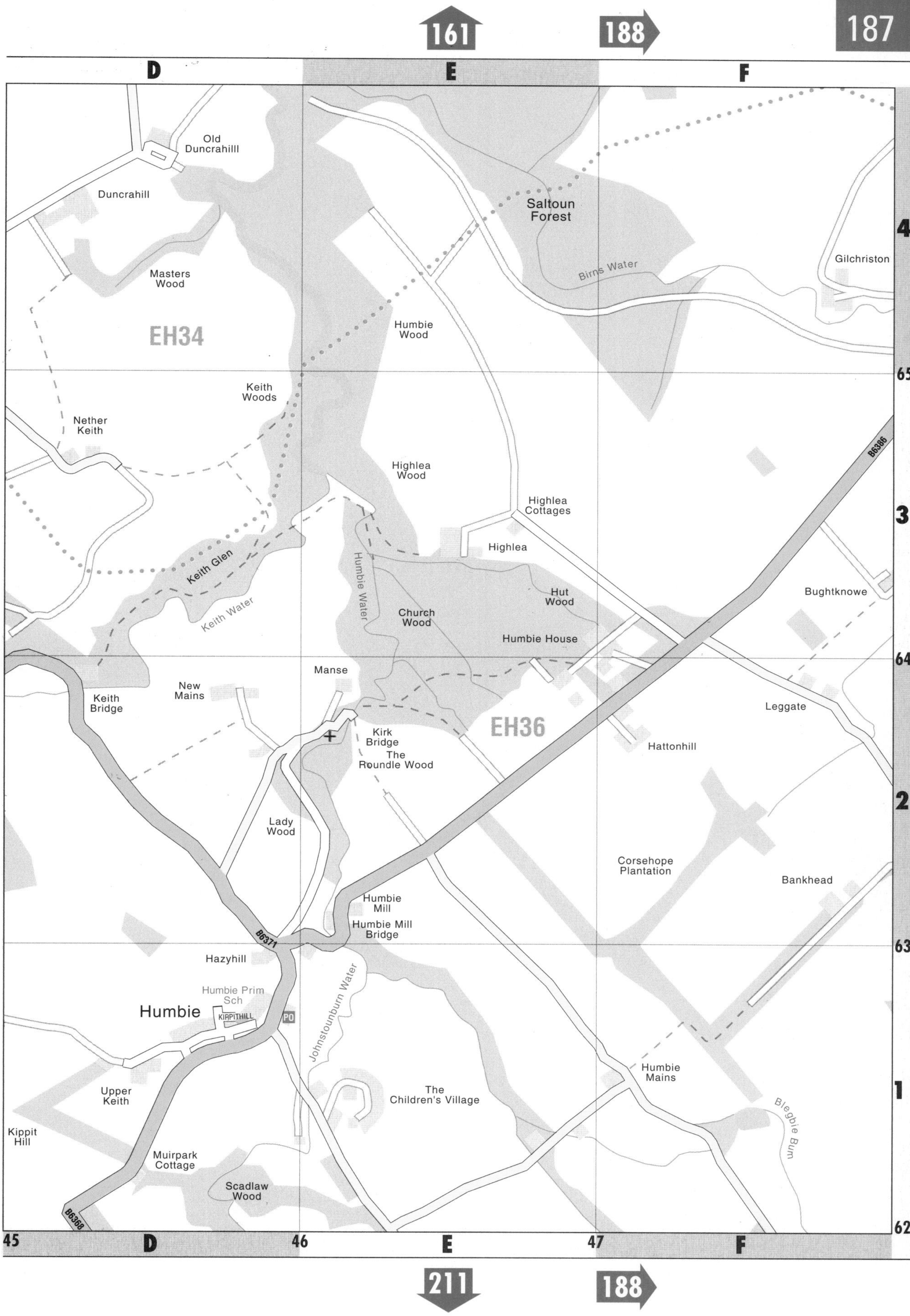

D   E   F

Old Duncrahilll

Duncrahill

Saltoun Forest

Birns Water

Gilchriston

Masters Wood

EH34

Humbie Wood

4

Keith Woods

65

Nether Keith

Highlea Wood

Highlea Cottages

3

Keith Glen

Highlea

Bughtknowe

Humbie Water

Hut Wood

Keith Water

Church Wood

Humbie House

64

New Mains

Manse

Leggate

Keith Bridge

Kirk Bridge
The Roundle Wood

EH36

Hattonhill

2

Lady Wood

Corsehope Plantation

Bankhead

Humbie Mill

Humbie Mill Bridge

63

Hazyhill

Johnstounburn Water

Humbie Prim Sch

Humbie

KIRPITHILL

PO

Blegbie Burn

Upper Keith

The Children's Village

Humbie Mains

1

Kippit Hill

Muirpark Cottage

Scadlaw Wood

B6371

B6368

B6368

B6368

45   D   46   E   47   F

62

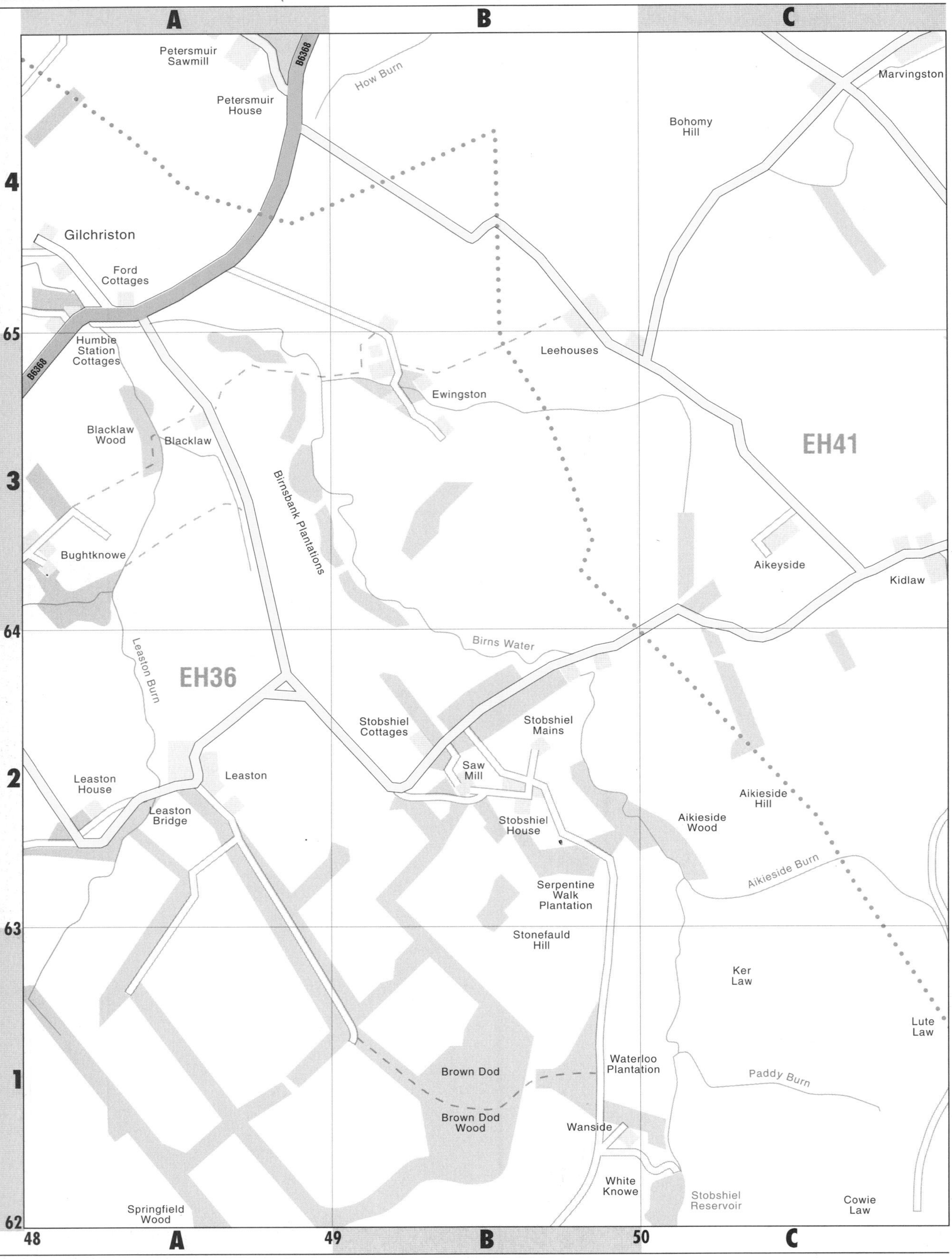

A   **B**   **C**

Petersmuir
Sawmill

B6368

How Burn

Petersmuir
House

Bohomy
Hill

Marvingston

4

Gilchriston

Ford
Cottages

65

Humbie
Station
Cottages

B6368

Leehouses

Ewingston

EH41

Blacklaw
Wood

Blacklaw

3

Birnsbank Plantations

Bughtknowe

Aikeyside

Kidlaw

64

Birns Water

Leaston Burn

EH36

Stobshiel
Cottages

Stobshiel
Mains

Aikieside
Hill

2

Leaston
House

Leaston

Saw
Mill

Aikieside
Wood

Aikieside Burn

Leaston
Bridge

Stobshiel
House

Serpentine
Walk
Plantation

63

Stonefauld
Hill

Ker
Law

Lute
Law

1

Brown Dod

Waterloo
Plantation

Paddy Burn

Brown Dod
Wood

Wanside

Springfield
Wood

White
Knowe

Stobshiel
Reservoir

Cowie
Law

62

48   **A**   49   **B**   50   **C**

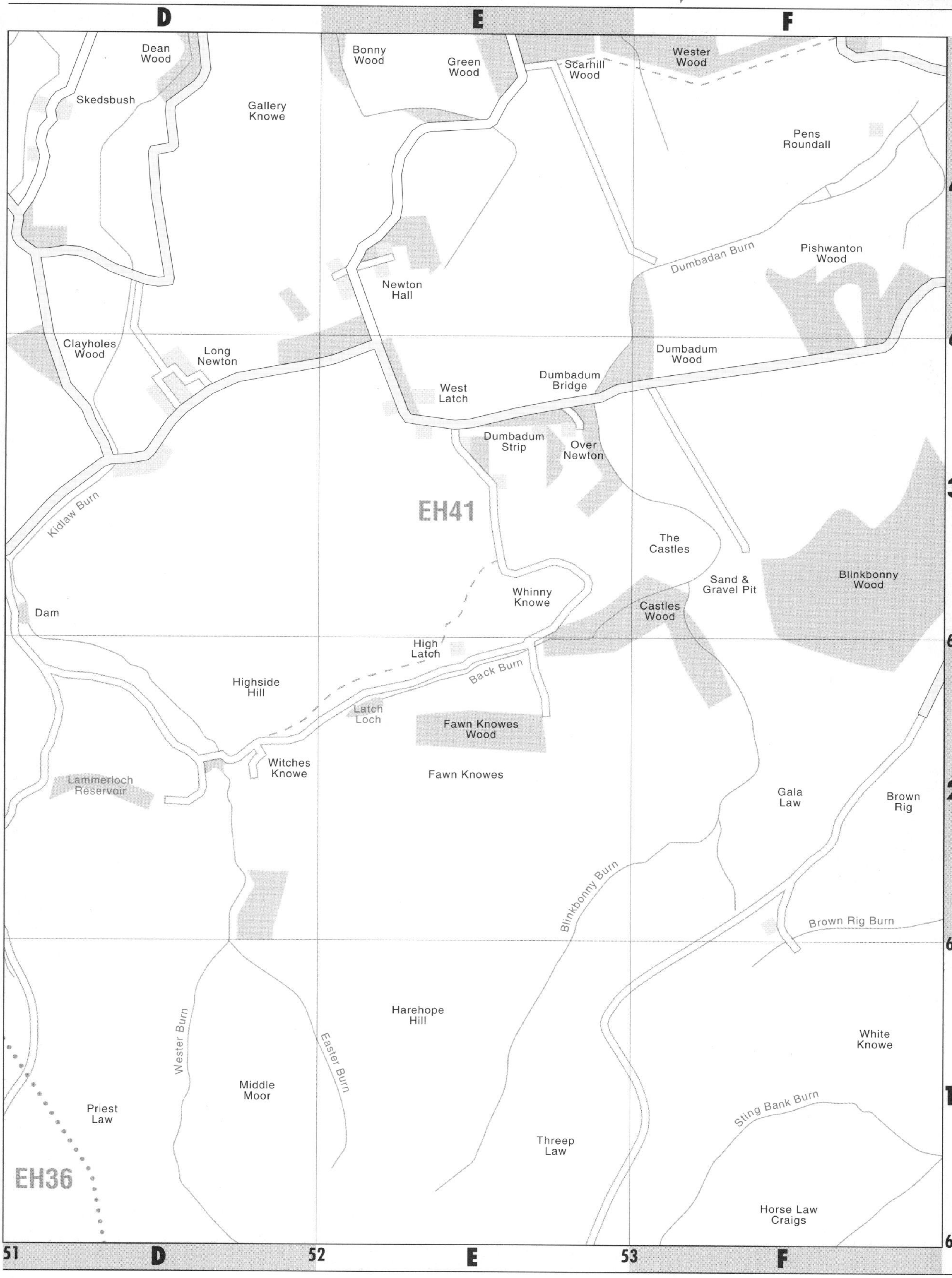

D   E   F

Dean Wood
Skedsbush
Gallery Knowe
Bonny Wood
Green Wood
Scarhill Wood
Wester Wood
Pens Roundall
4
Clayholes Wood
Long Newton
Newton Hall
Dumbadan Burn
Pishwanton Wood
Dumbadum Wood
65
West Latch
Dumbadum Bridge
Kidlaw Burn
Dumbadum Strip
Over Newton
EH41
The Castles
Blinkbonny Wood
3
Dam
Whinny Knowe
Sand & Gravel Pit
Castles Wood
High Latch
Back Burn
64
Highside Hill
Latch Loch
Fawn Knowes Wood
Lammerloch Reservoir
Witches Knowe
Fawn Knowes
Gala Law
Brown Rig
2
Blinkbonny Burn
Brown Rig Burn
63
Wester Burn
Easter Burn
Harehope Hill
White Knowe
Priest Law
Middle Moor
Sting Bank Burn
1
EH36
Threep Law
Horse Law Craigs
62

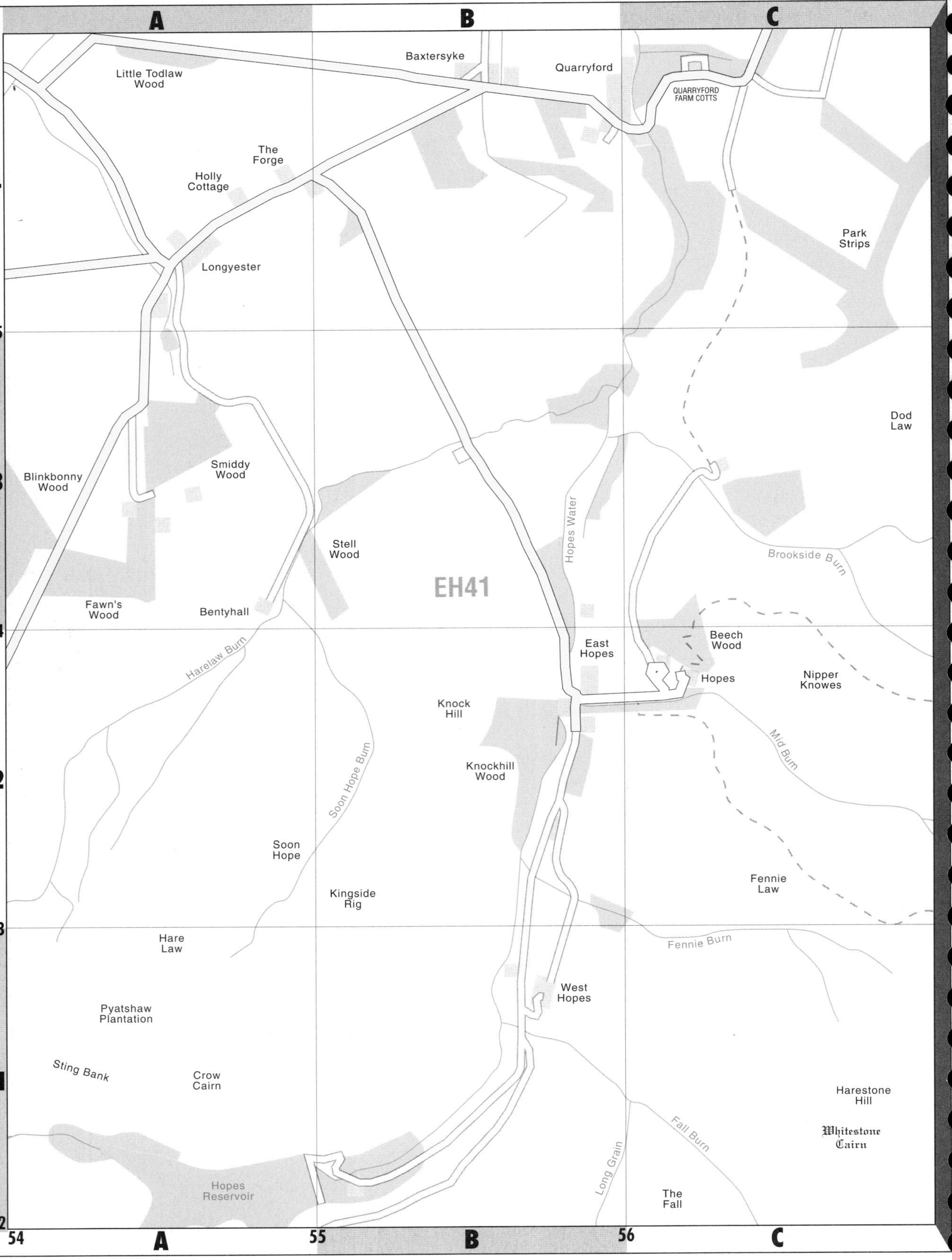

A   B   C

Little Todlaw
Wood

Baxtersyke

Quarryford

QUARRYFORD
FARM COTTS

The
Forge

Holly
Cottage

4

Park
Strips

Longyester

65

Dod
Law

Blinkbonny
Wood

Smiddy
Wood

3

Hopes Water

Brookside Burn

Stell
Wood

EH41

Fawn's
Wood

Bentyhall

64

East
Hopes

Beech
Wood

Harelaw Burn

Hopes

Nipper
Knowes

Knock
Hill

Soon Hope Burn

Knockhill
Wood

2

Mid Burn

Soon
Hope

Fennie
Law

Kingside
Rig

63

Fennie Burn

Hare
Law

Pyatshaw
Plantation

West
Hopes

Sting Bank

Crow
Cairn

1

Harestone
Hill

Fall Burn

Whitestone
Cairn

Long Grain

Hopes
Reservoir

The
Fall

62

54   A   55   B   56   C

167 192

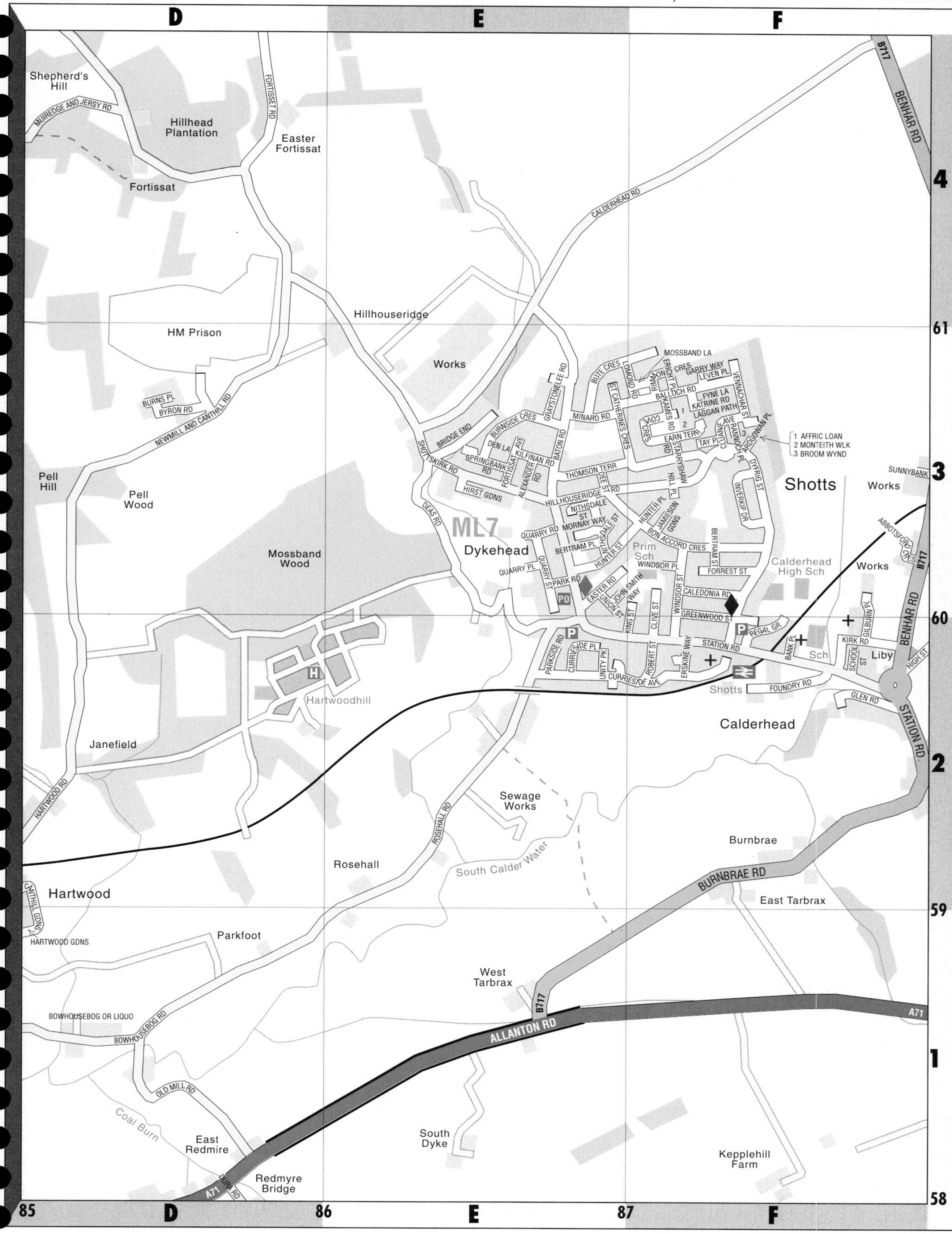

D
E
F
4
61
3
60
2
59
1
58
85
86
87
Shepherd's Hill
MUIREDGE AND JERSY RD
Hillhead Plantation
FORTISSAT RD
Easter Fortissat
Fortissat
CALDERHEAD RD
B717
BENHAR RD
HM Prison
Hillhouseridge
Works
BURNS PL
BYRON RD
NEWMILL AND CANTHILL RD
Pell Hill
Pell Wood
Mossband Wood
BRIDGE END
SHOTSKIRK RD
DEAS RD
ML7
Dykehead
MOSSBAND LA
BUTE CRES
LOMOND RD
GARRY WAY
LEVEN PL
BALLOCH RD
FYNE LA
KATRINE RD
LAGGAN PATH
VENNACHAR ST
ST CATHERINES CRES
MINARD RD
GRAYSTONE
LEE RD
BURNSIDE CRES
DEN LA
KILFINAN RD
BATON RD
SPRINGBANK RD
FORTISSAT AVE
ALEXANDER RD
HIRST GDNS
THOMSON TERR
DEE ST
HILLHOUSERIDGE RD
NITHSDALE ST
MORNAY WAY
QUARRY RD
BERTRAM PL
HUNTER ST
HUNTER PL
JAMIESON GDNS
BON ACCORD CRES
BERTRAM ST
FORREST ST
HILL PL
STARRYSHAW RD
EARN TERR
TAY PL
DYFRIG ST
INVERKIP DR
1 AFFRIC LOAN
2 MONTEITH WLK
3 BROOM WYND
Shotts
Works
SUNNYBANK
ABBOTSFORD CRES
Calderhead High Sch
Prim Sch
WINDSOR PL
QUARRY PL
QUARRY ST
PARK RD
PO
EASTER RD
UNION ST
JOHN SMITH WAY
KING ST
CLIVE ST
WINDSOR ST
CALEDONIA RD
GREENWOOD ST
REGAL GR
STATION RD
BANK PL
Sch
KIRK RD
GILBURN PL
SCHOOL ST
Liby
HIGH ST
P
PARKSIDE RD
CURRIESIDE PL
UNITY PK
ROBERT ST
ERSKINE WAY
CURRIESIDE AVE
FOUNDRY RD
Shotts
GLEN RD
STATION RD
H
Hartwoodhill
Janefield
Calderhead
HARTWOOD RD
Sewage Works
ROSEHALL RD
Rosehall
South Calder Water
Burnbrae
BURNBRAE RD
East Tarbrax
Hartwood
CANTHILL GDNS
HARTWOOD GDNS
Parkfoot
West Tarbrax
A71
BOWHOUSEBOG OR LIQUO
BOWHOUSEBOG RD
ALLANTON RD
OLD MILL RD
Coal Burn
East Redmire
South Dyke
Kepplehill Farm
Redmyre Bridge
DURA RD

212 192

A   B   C

4

61

B717

BENHAR RD

CH

Golf Course

Starryshaw Farm

South Calder Water

Stanebent

3

B717

Spoil Heap

Cairneyhead

ML7

Stane

STABLE RD

GRAY ST

HIGH ST

Torbothie

CEDAR WYND

ROWAN CRES

HAZEL GR

CHARLES ST

TORBOTHIE RD

CLYDE DR

KELVIN DR

CALDER DR

HAWTHORN DR

60

SOUTHFIELD RD

SOUTHFIELD LA

SOUTHFIELD CRES

Torbothie

Stane Prim Sch

MANSE RD

CEMETERY RD

Cemy

1 ETIVE WLK
2 ULG WAY
3 GAIR WYND
4 BOWMORE WLK
5 TORRIN LOAN
6 SPRINGHILL VIEW
7 DORNIE WYND
8 MORAR WAY
9 COIRE LOAN
10 SUNA PATH
11 SALEN LOAN

2

B7010

MAIN ST

CHARLOTTE ST

NEVIS PL

GARTEN DR

1

2

SMITHYHILL AVE

REDMANS RD

1

2

SANDYVALE PL

Stane

BLINNY CT 1
TARBRAX PATH 2

BRIDGE PL

KNOLL CROFT RD

NAVAR CT

SPEY GDNS

LOCHABER CRES

APPIN TERR

HUNTLY TERR

LANSDOWNE CRES

TULLOCH RD

MELFORD AVE

WYVIS PL

ONICH PL

LAGGAN AVE

9

10

11

7

6

EH47

SPRINGHILL RD

Springhill

B7010

59

STANE RD

BLACKHALL ST

BELMONT TERR

MULDRON CT

LARCHFIELD LA

NORTHFIELD AVE

DRUMOUNT CT

BERRYHILL PL

BROWN ST

ELMWOOD RD

Works

Springhill

SPRINGHILL AND LEADLOCH RD

Knowton Farm

B715 HEADLESSCROSS RD

B715

A71

Works

Lingore Linn

1

A71

58

88   A   89   B   90   C

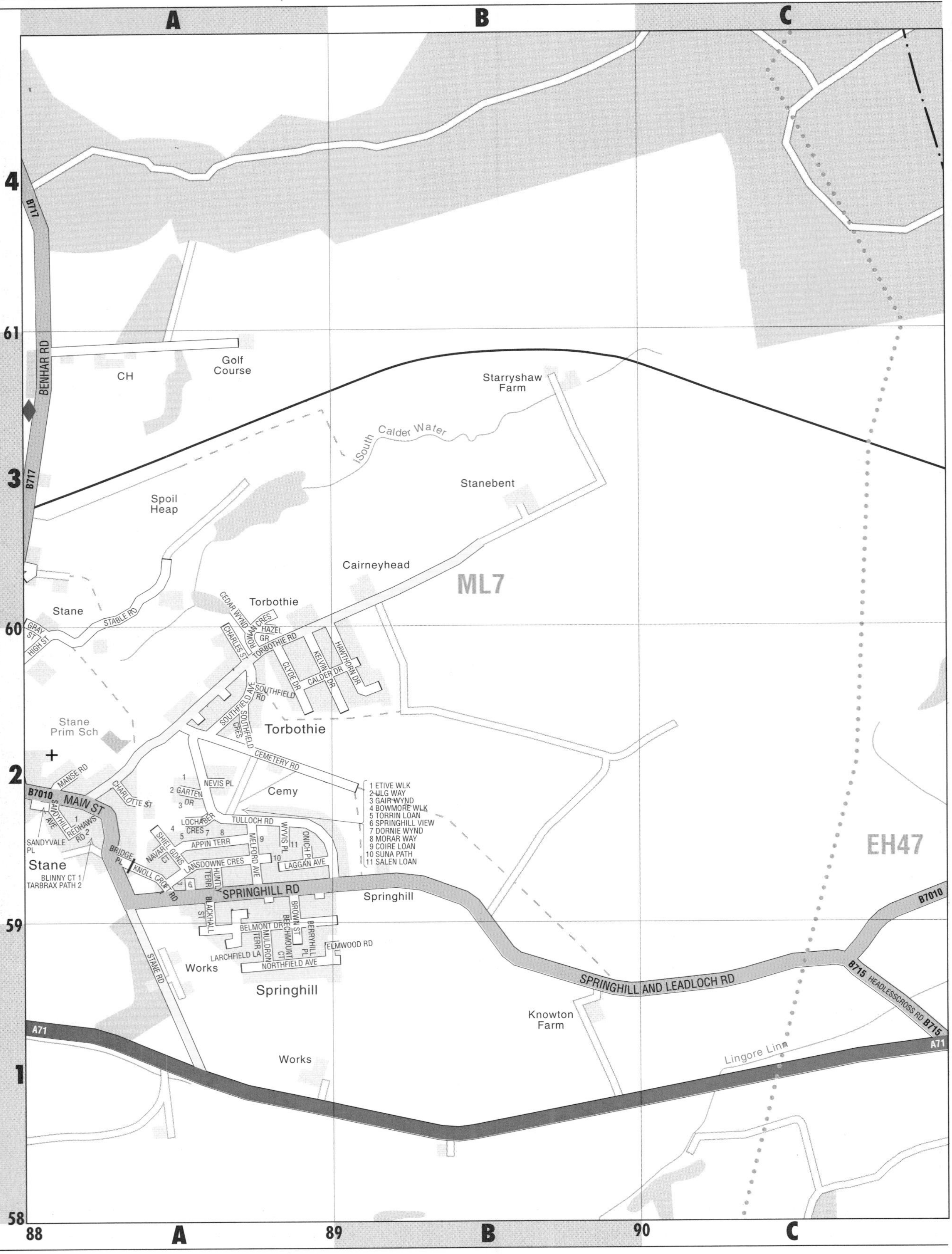

169
194

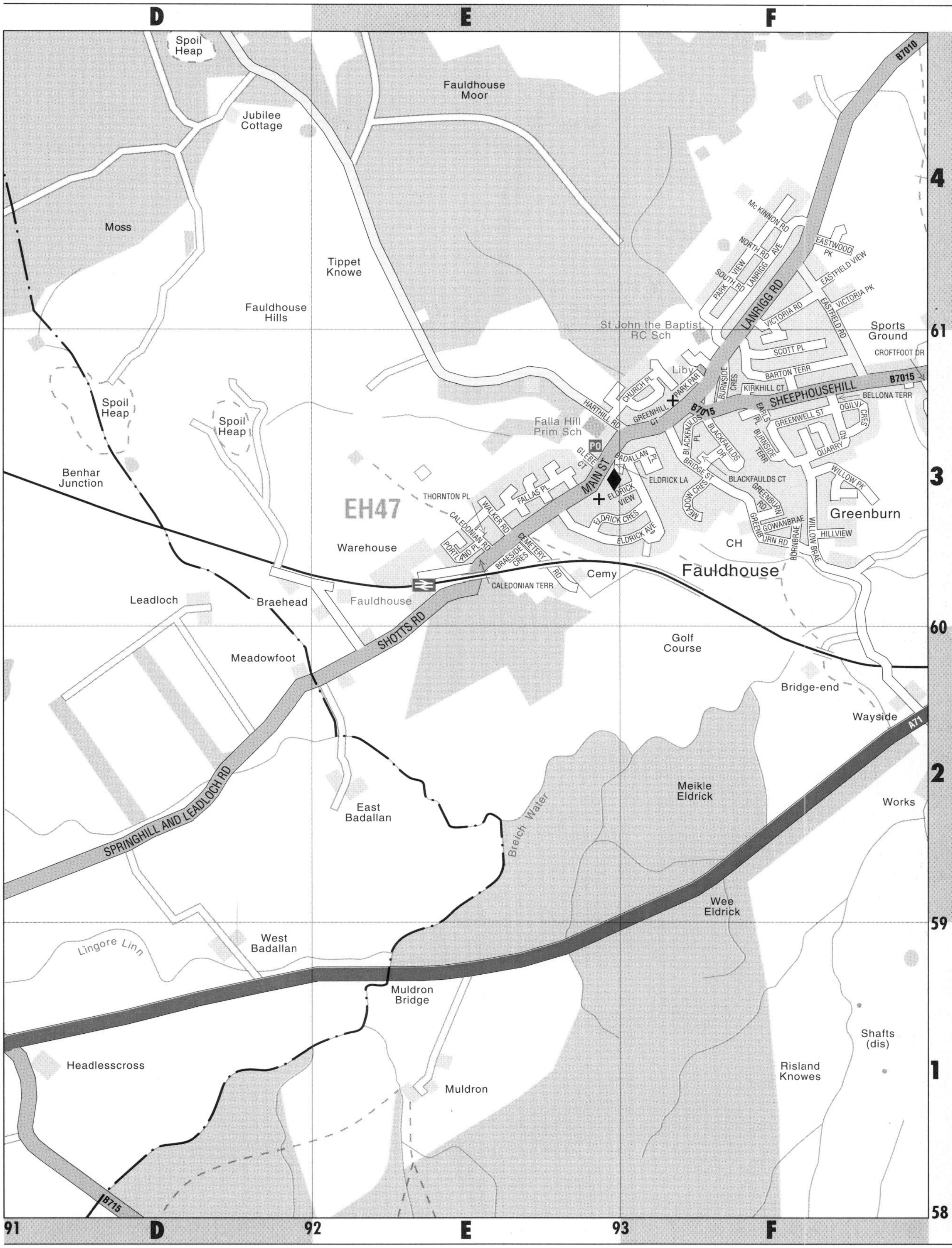
D
E
F
Spoil Heap
Fauldhouse Moor
Jubilee Cottage
B7010
Moss
Tippet Knowe
Fauldhouse Hills
4
Mc KINNON RD
NORTH RD
LANRIGG AVE
PARK VIEW
SOUTH RD
LANRIGG RD
EASTWOOD PK
EASTFIELD VIEW
VICTORIA PK
VICTORIA RD
EASTFIELD RD
St John the Baptist RC Sch
Sports Ground
61
SCOTT PL
CROFTFOOT DR
Liby
PARK PAR
CHURCH PL
BURNSIDE CRES
BARTON TERR
KIRKHILL CT
B7015
SHEEPHOUSEHILL
BELLONA TERR
HARTHILL RD
GREENHILL CT
B7015
EARLS PL
OGILVY CRES
GREENWELL ST
Spoil Heap
Spoil Heap
Falla Hill Prim Sch
BLACKFAULDS PL
BLACKFAULDS DR
BURNSIDE TERR
QUARRY RD
PO
GLEBE CT
BADALLAN PL
MAIN ST
ELDRICK LA
BRIDGE ST
BLACKFAULDS CT
WILLOW PK
Benhar Junction
3
THORNTON PL
FALLAS PL
ELDRICK VIEW
MEADOW CRES
GREENBURN RD
Greenburn
EH47
WALKER RD
CALEDONIAN RD
ELDRICK CRES
ELDRICK AVE
GREENBURN RD
GOWANBRAE
WILLOW BRAE
HILLVIEW
PORTLAND PL
CEMETERY RD
BRAESIDE CRES
Warehouse
CH
BORNBRAE
Cemy
Fauldhouse
CALEDONIAN TERR
Leadloch
Braehead
Fauldhouse
SHOTTS RD
60
Golf Course
Meadowfoot
Bridge-end
Wayside
A71
2
Meikle Eldrick
SPRINGHILL AND LEADLOCH RD
East Badallan
Works
Breich Water
Wee Eldrick
59
West Badallan
Lingore Linn
Muldron Bridge
Shafts (dis)
Headlesscross
Risland Knowes
1
Muldron
B715
58
91
D
92
E
93
F

214
194

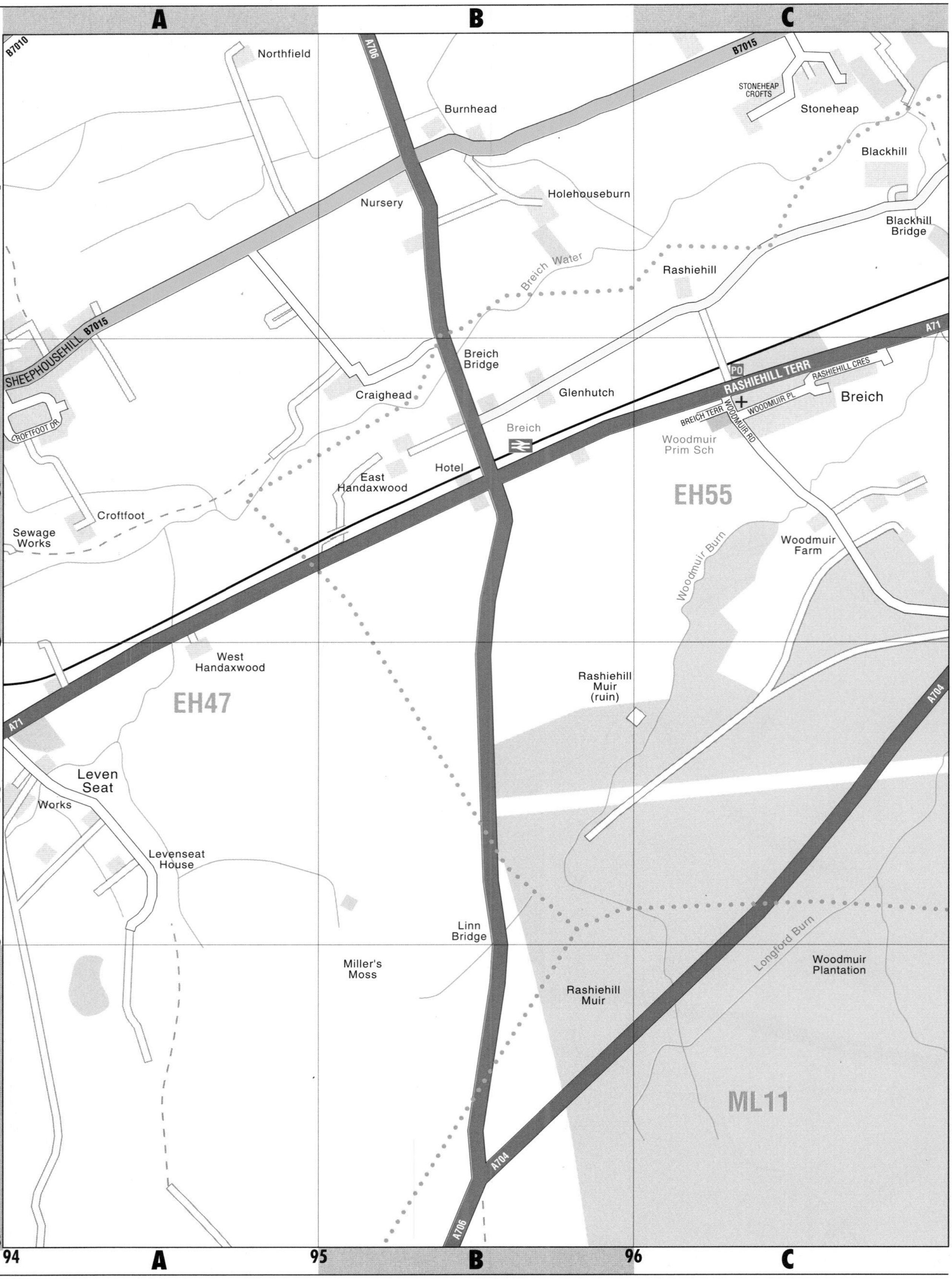
A
B
C
B7010
Northfield
A706
B7015
STONEHEAP CROFTS
Stoneheap
Burnhead
Blackhill
4
Holehouseburn
Nursery
Blackhill Bridge
Breich Water
Rashiehill
61
SHEEPHOUSEHILL
B7015
A71
Breich Bridge
PO
RASHIEHILL TERR
RASHIEHILL CRES
Breich
Glenhutch
Craighead
WOODMUIR PL
CROFTFOOT DR
BREICH TERR
WOODMUIR RD
Breich
Woodmuir Prim Sch
Hotel
East Handaxwood
3
EH55
Croftfoot
Sewage Works
Woodmuir Burn
Woodmuir Farm
60
West Handaxwood
Rashiehill Muir (ruin)
EH47
A71
A704
Leven Seat
2
Works
Levenseat House
Linn Bridge
59
Miller's Moss
Longford Burn
Woodmuir Plantation
Rashiehill Muir
1
ML11
A704
A706
58
94
95
96

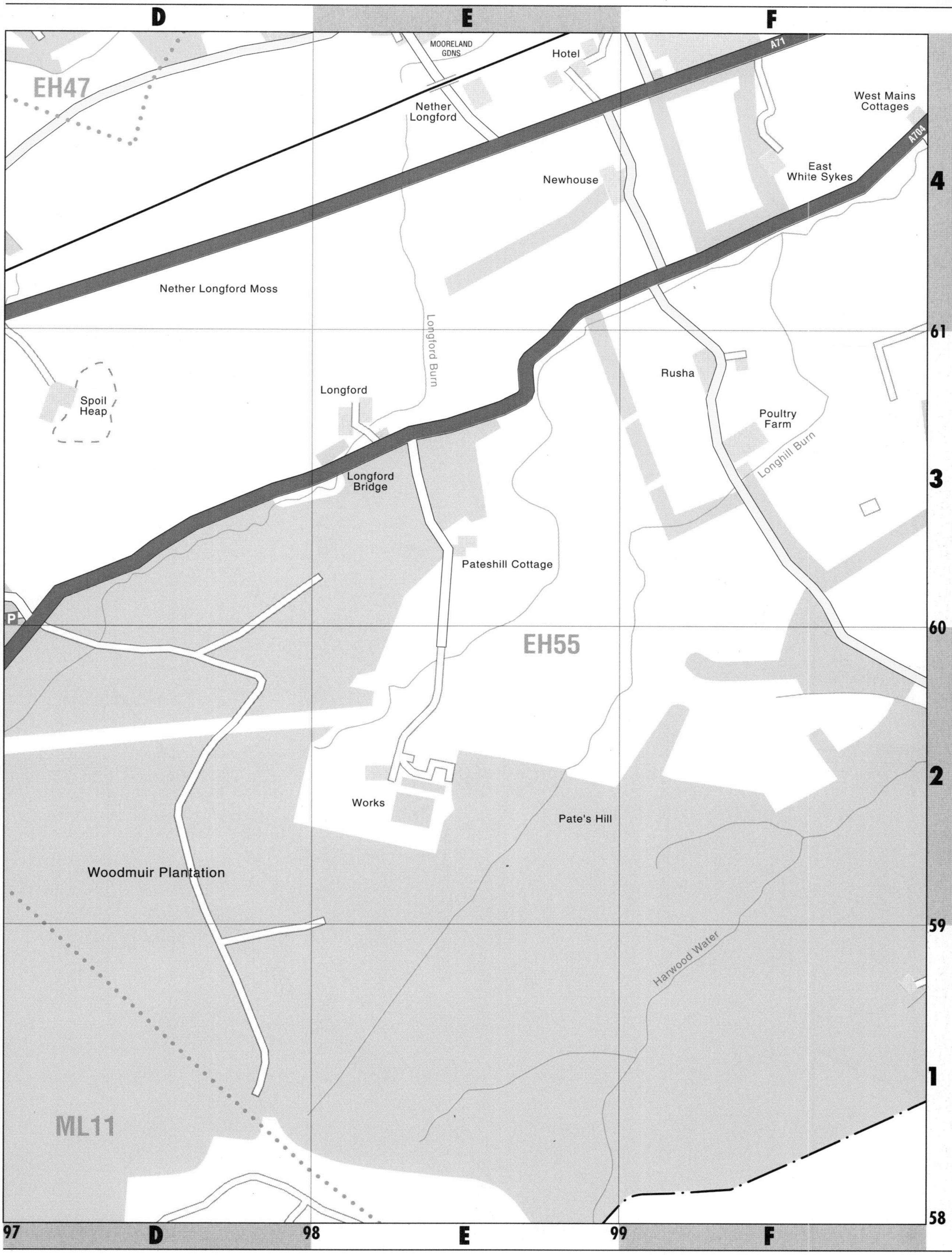

EH47

MOORELAND GDNS

Hotel

West Mains Cottages

Nether Longford

Newhouse

East White Sykes

Nether Longford Moss

Longford Burn

A71

A704

61

Longford

Rusha

Spoil Heap

Poultry Farm

Longhill Burn

Longford Bridge

3

Pateshill Cottage

60

EH55

Works

2

Pate's Hill

Woodmuir Plantation

59

Harwood Water

ML11

1

58

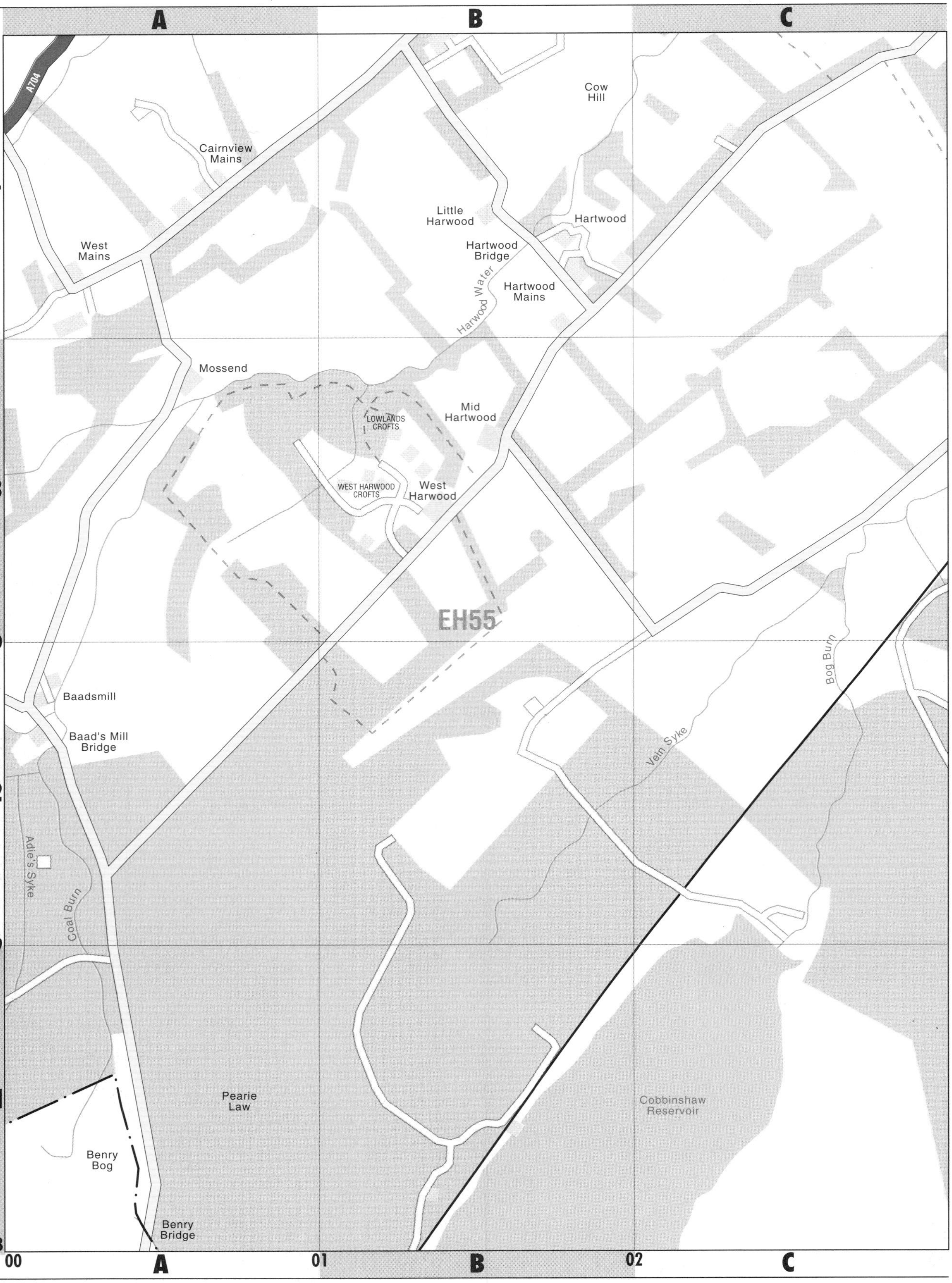

A   B   C

A704

Cow
Hill

Cairnview
Mains

Little
Harwood

Hartwood

4

West
Mains

Hartwood
Bridge

Hartwood
Mains

61

Harwood Water

Mossend

Mid
Hartwood

LOWLANDS
CROFTS

3

WEST HARWOOD
CROFTS

West
Harwood

Bog Burn

EH55

60

Baadsmill

Vein Syke

Baad's Mill
Bridge

2

Adie's Syke

Coal Burn

59

Pearie
Law

Cobbinshaw
Reservoir

1

Benry
Bog

Benry
Bridge

58

173 198

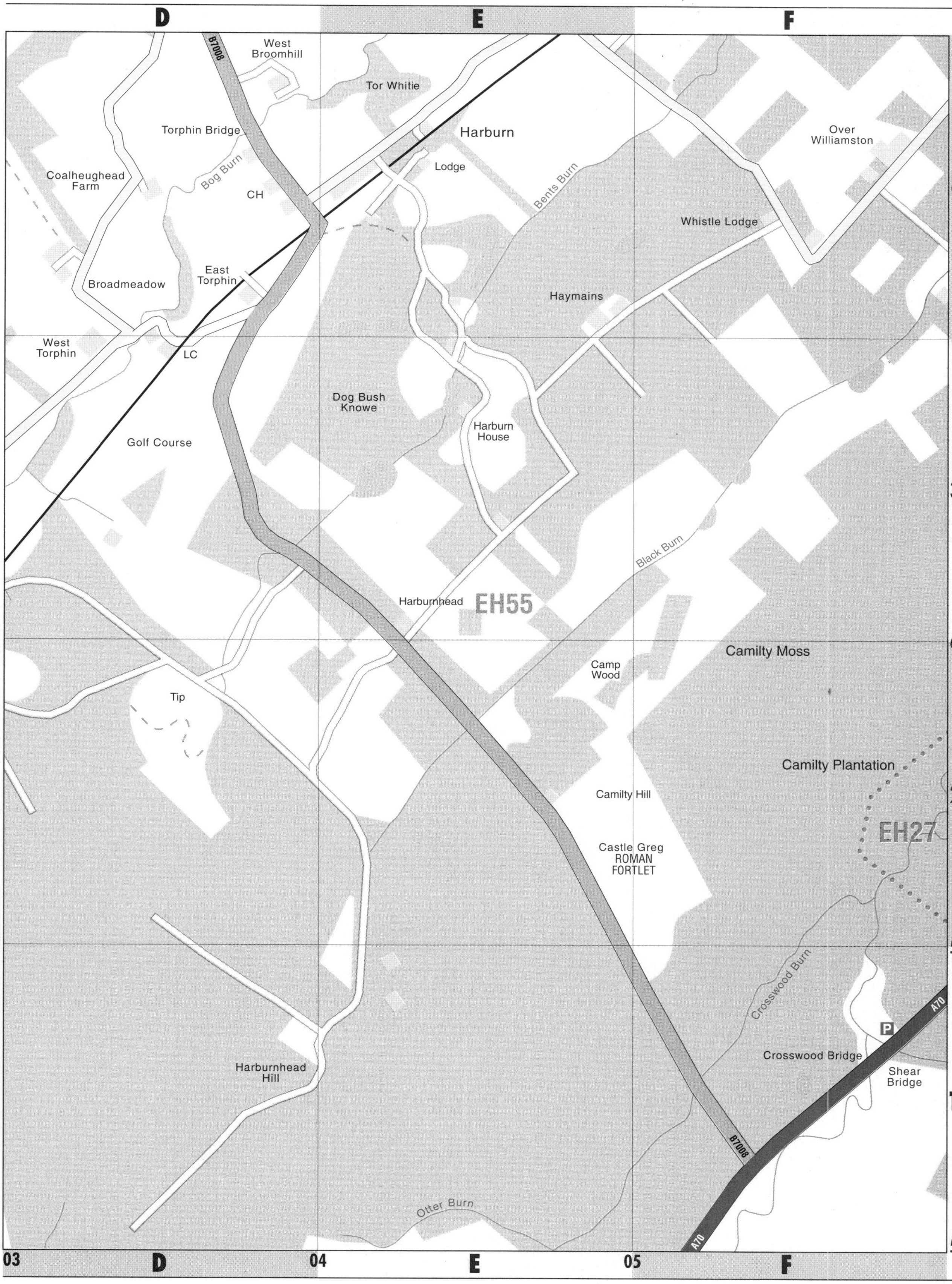
D
E
F
B7008
West Broomhill
Tor Whitie
Torphin Bridge
Harburn
Over Williamston
Coalheughead Farm
Bog Burn
CH
Lodge
Bents Burn
4
Whistle Lodge
Broadmeadow
East Torphin
Haymains
West Torphin
LC
61
Dog Bush Knowe
Harburn House
Golf Course
3
Black Burn
Harburnhead
EH55
60
Camp Wood
Camilty Moss
Tip
Camilty Plantation
Camilty Hill
2
EH27
Castle Greg ROMAN FORTLET
59
Crosswood Burn
A70
P
Crosswood Bridge
Shear Bridge
Harburnhead Hill
1
Otter Burn
58
03
04
05

218 198

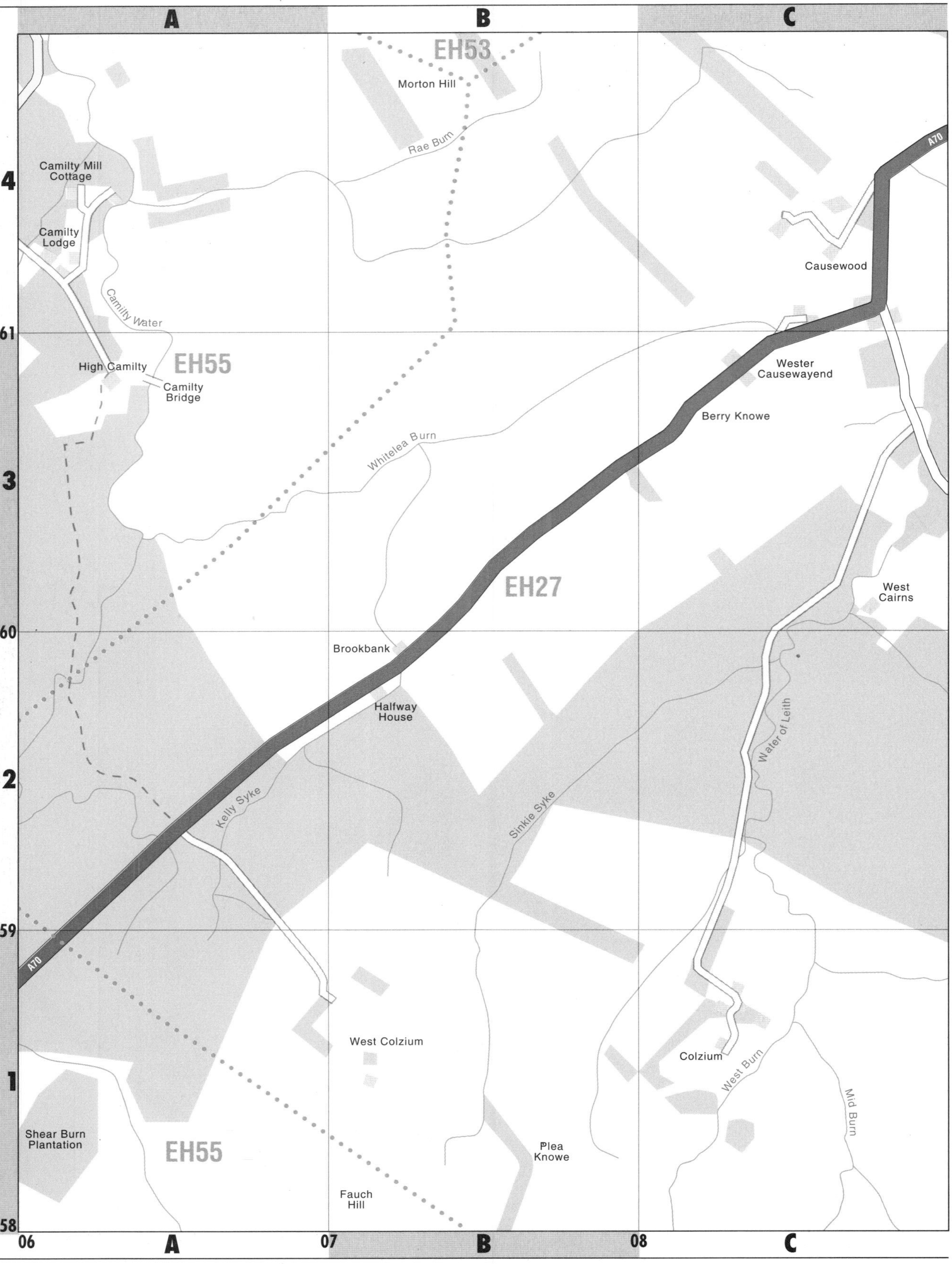

197
174
197

EH53

Morton Hill

Rae Burn

Camilty Mill
Cottage

4

Camilty
Lodge

Camilty Water

61

EH55

High Camilty

Camilty
Bridge

Whitelea Burn

3

EH27

60

Brookbank

Halfway
House

2

Kelly Syke

Sinkie Syke

59

A70

West Colzium

1

Shear Burn
Plantation

EH55

Fauch
Hill

Plea
Knowe

58

Causewood

Wester
Causewayend

Berry Knowe

West
Cairns

Water of Leith

Colzium

West Burn

Mid Burn

A70

A

B

C

06

07

08

A

B

C

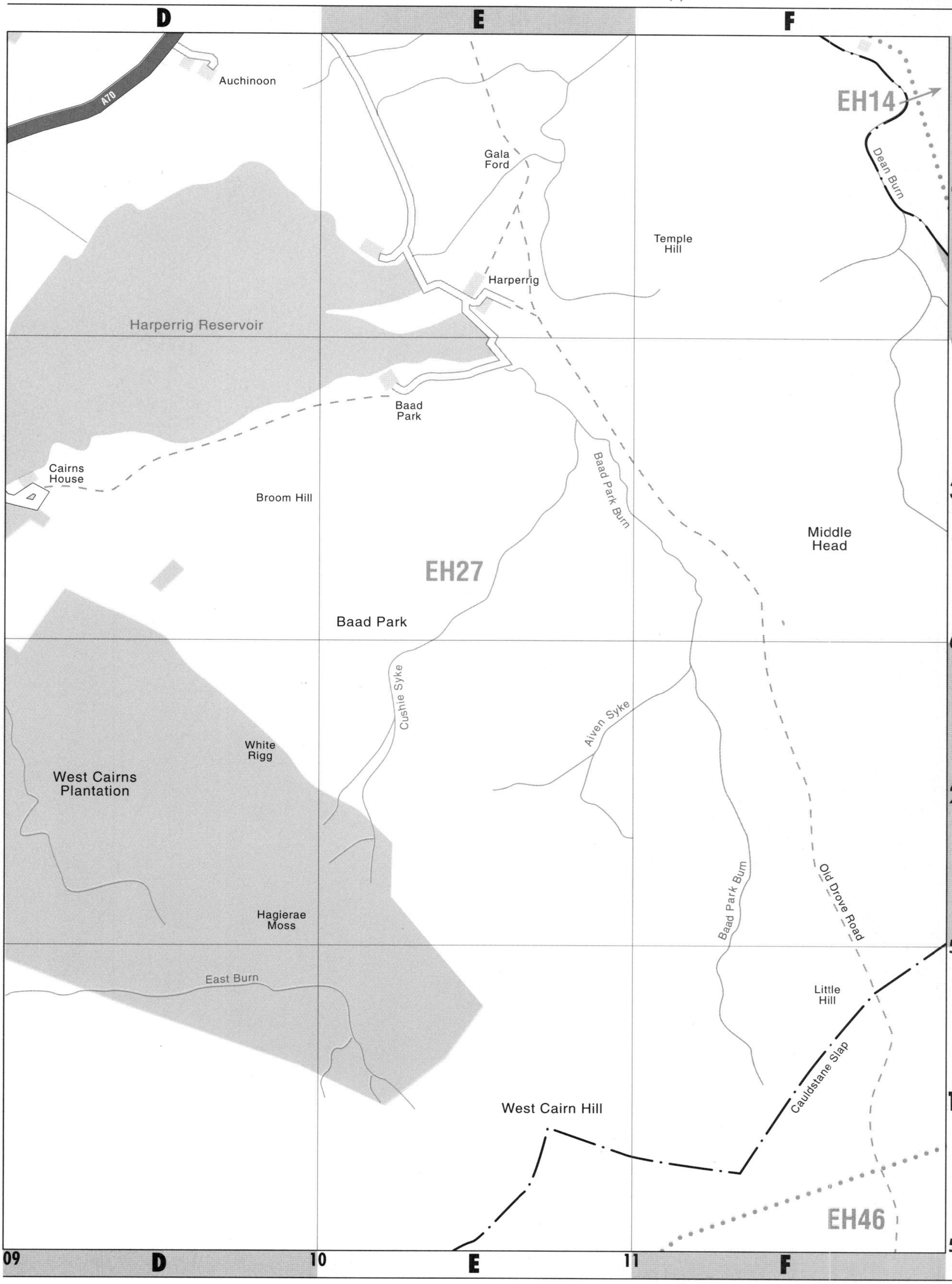

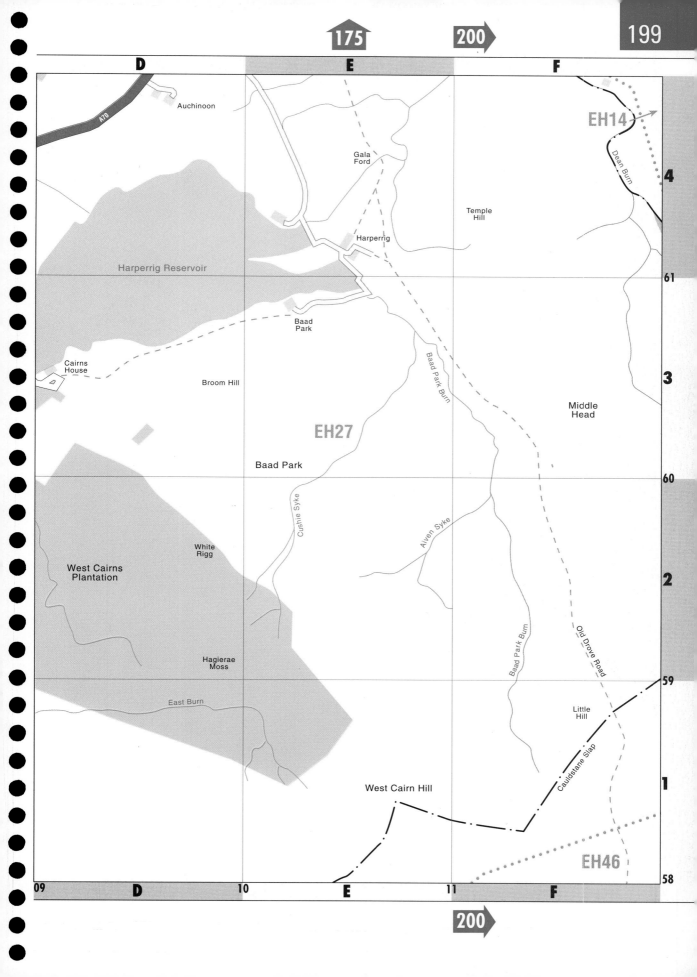

D
E
F

Auchinoon

EH14

Gala
Ford

Dean Burn

Temple
Hill

4

Harperrig

Harperrig Reservoir

61

Baad
Park

Baad Park Burn

Cairns
House

Broom Hill

3

Middle
Head

EH27

Baad Park

60

Cushie Syke

Aiven Syke

White
Rigg

West Cairns
Plantation

2

Baad Park Burn

Old Drove Road

Hagierae
Moss

59

East Burn

Little
Hill

West Cairn Hill

Cauldstane Slap

1

EH46

58

199
176

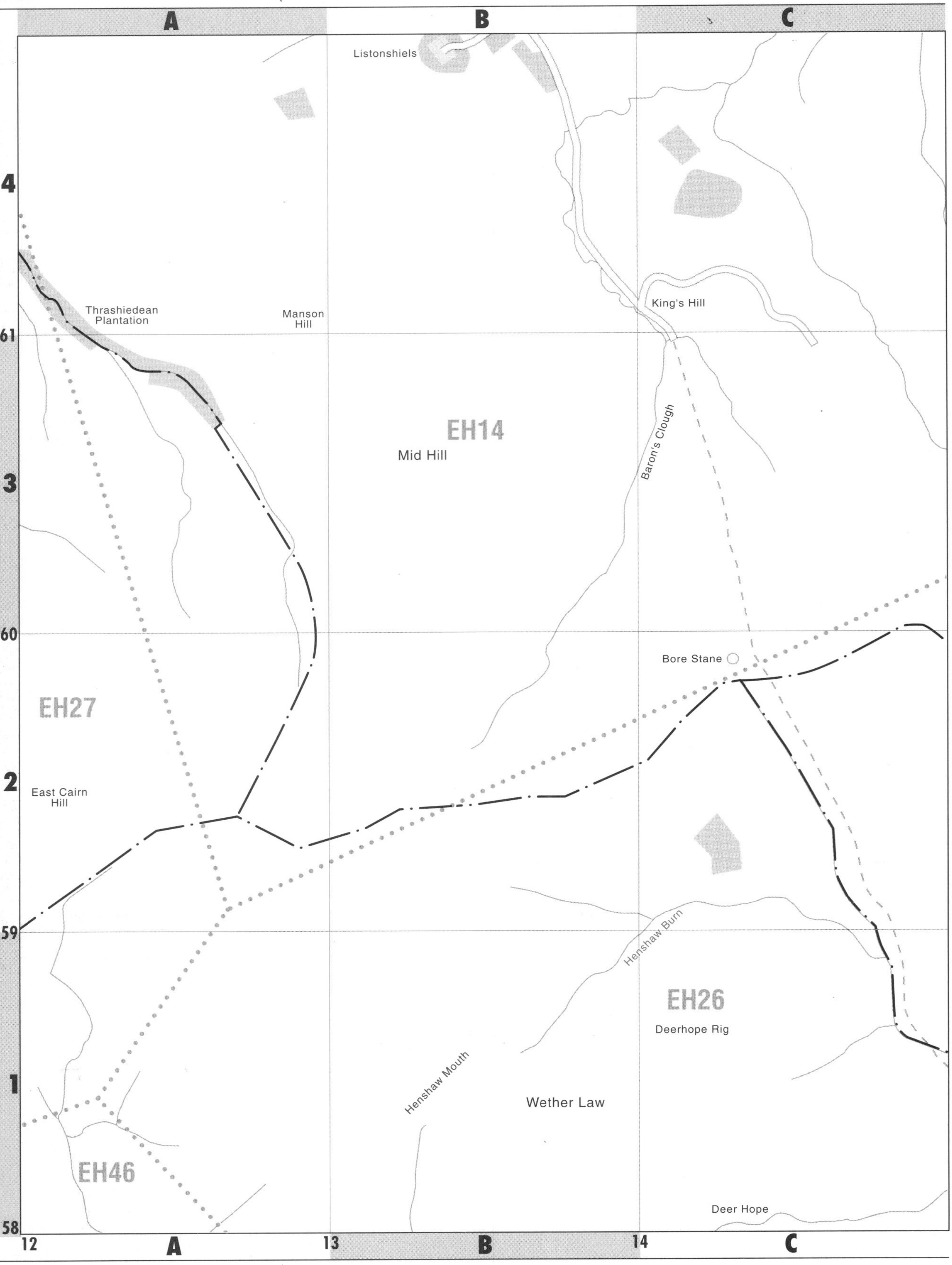
A
B
C
Listonshiels
4
Thrashiedean
Plantation
Manson
Hill
King's Hill
61
EH14
Mid Hill
Baron's Clough
3
60
Bore Stane
EH27
2
East Cairn
Hill
59
Henshaw Burn
EH26
Deerhope Rig
1
Henshaw Mouth
Wether Law
EH46
Deer Hope
58
12
13
14

199
219

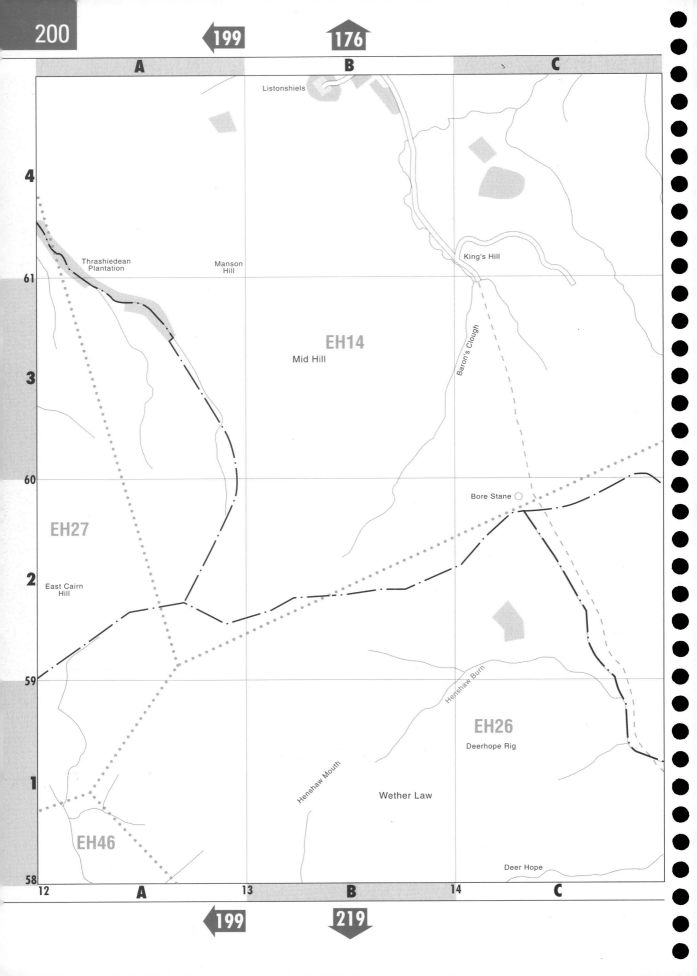

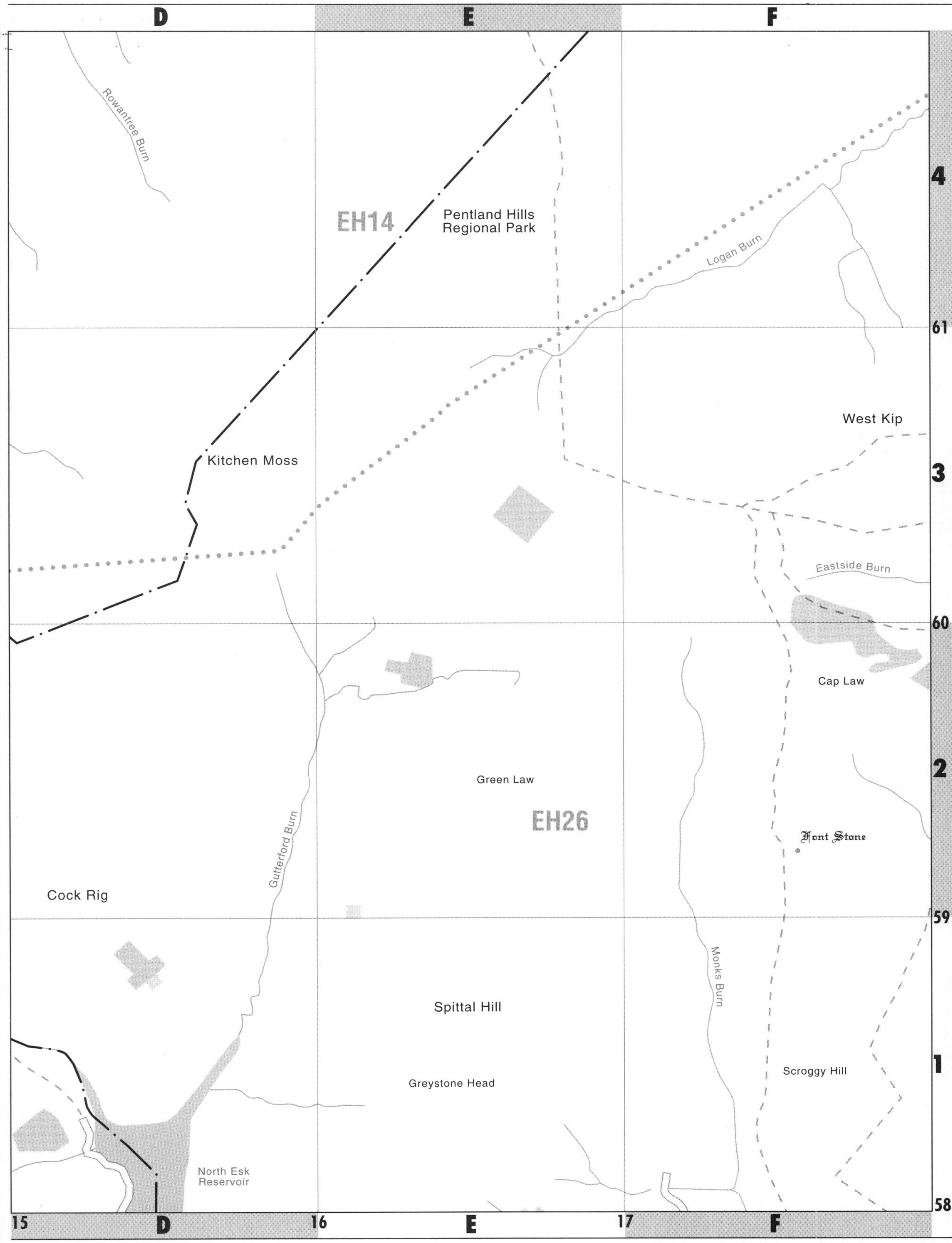
D
E
F
Rowantree Burn
EH14
Pentland Hills
Regional Park
Logan Burn
4
61
West Kip
Kitchen Moss
3
Eastside Burn
60
Cap Law
Green Law
2
EH26
Gutterford Burn
Font Stone
Cock Rig
59
Monks Burn
Spittal Hill
1
Scroggy Hill
Greystone Head
North Esk
Reservoir
58
15
16
17
D
E
F

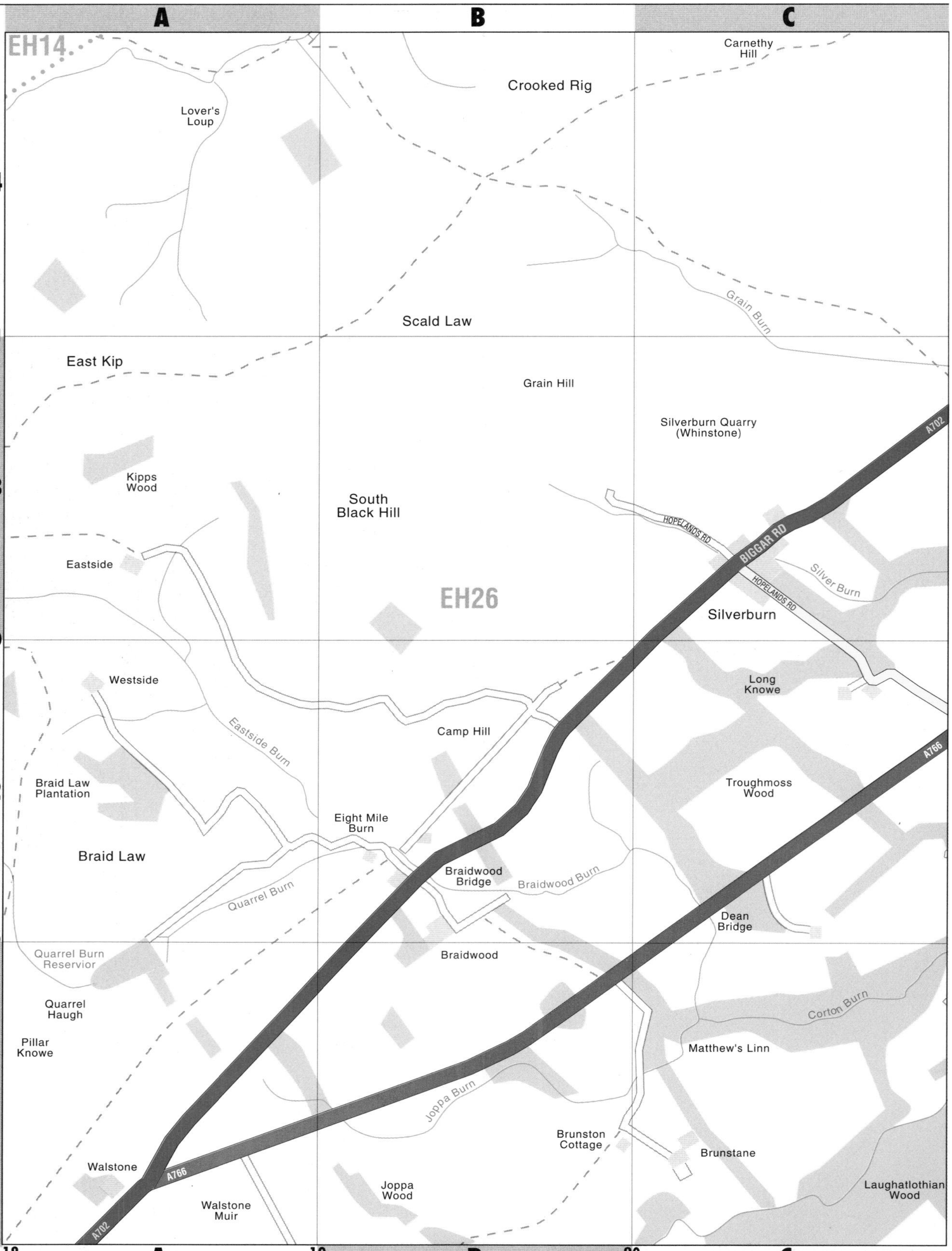

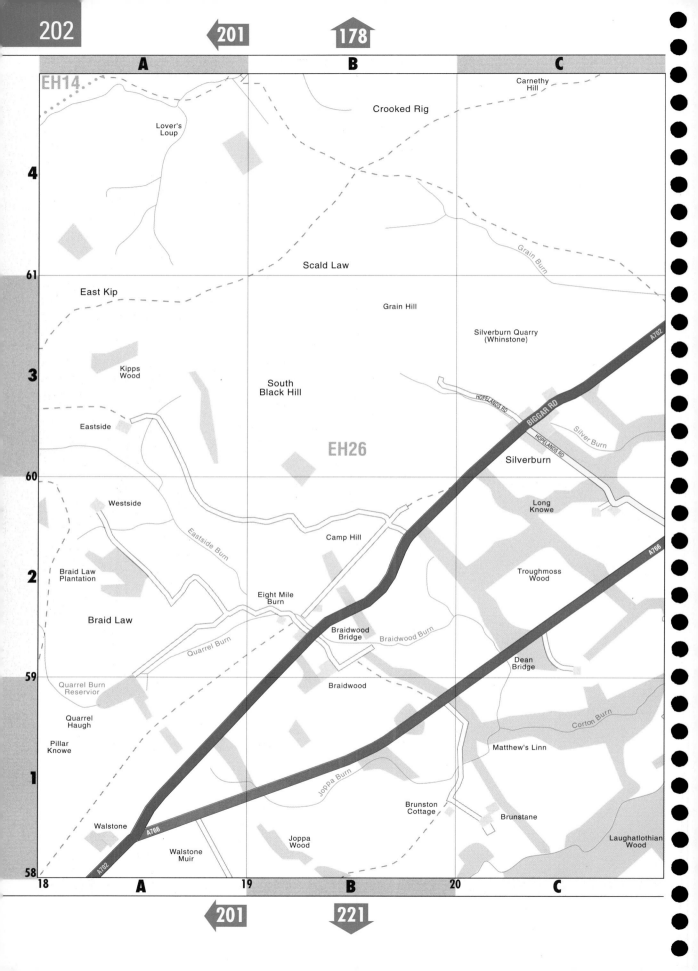

EH14

A

B

C

Carnethy Hill

Crooked Rig

Lover's Loup

4

Scald Law

Grain Burn

61

East Kip

Grain Hill

Silverburn Quarry (Whinstone)

Kipps Wood

3

South Black Hill

HOPELANDS RD

A702

BIGGAR RD

HOPELANDS RD

Silver Burn

Eastside

EH26

Silverburn

60

Westside

Long Knowe

Eastside Burn

Camp Hill

Braid Law Plantation

A766

Troughmoss Wood

2

Eight Mile Burn

Braidwood Bridge

Braidwood Burn

Braid Law

Dean Bridge

Quarrel Burn

59

Quarrel Burn Reservoir

Braidwood

Corton Burn

Quarrel Haugh

Pillar Knowe

Matthew's Linn

1

Joppa Burn

Brunston Cottage

Brunstane

Walstone

A766

Laughatlothian Wood

Walstone Muir

Joppa Wood

58

A702

18

A

19

B

20

C

D E F

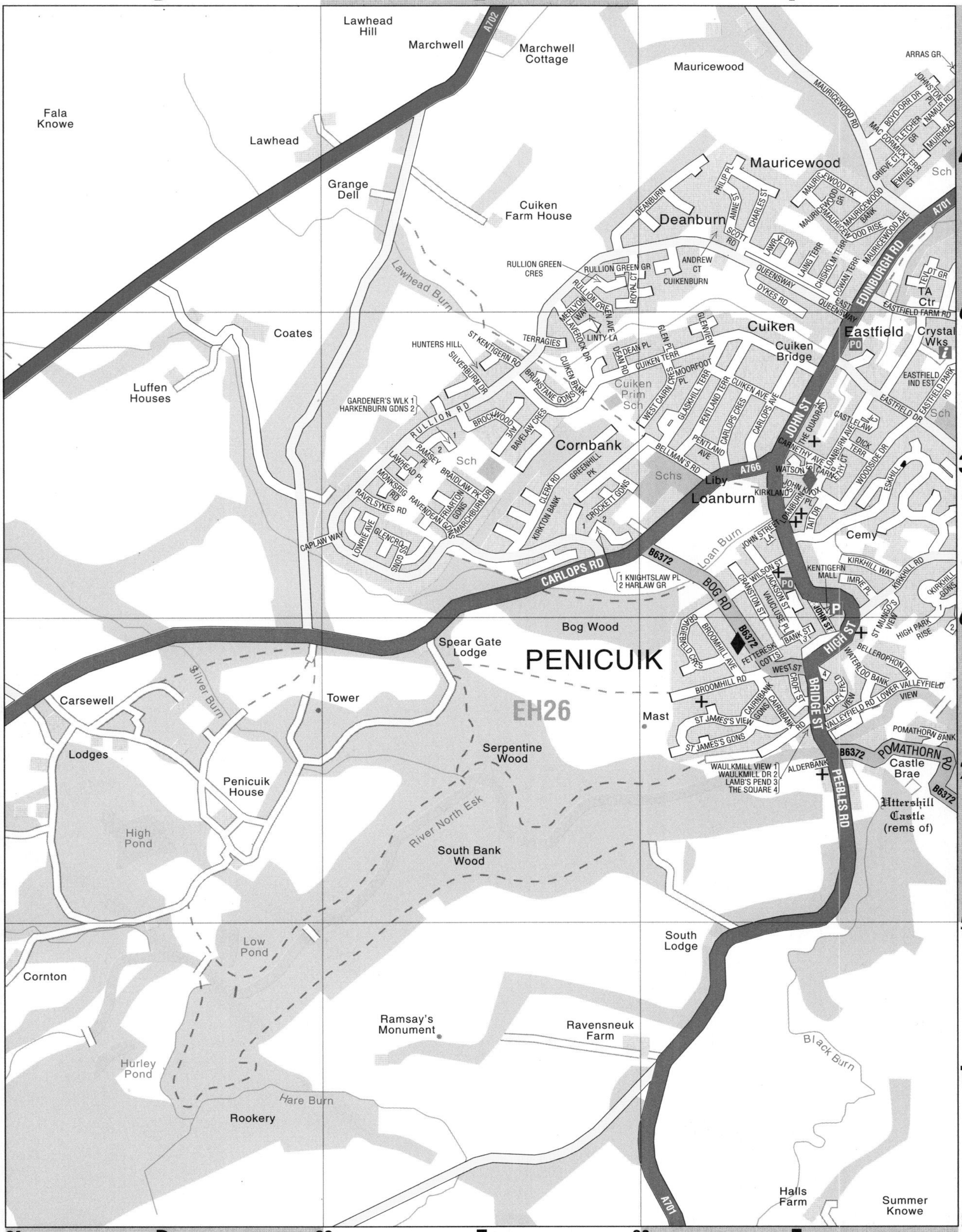
Lawhead Hill
Marchwell
Marchwell Cottage
Mauricewood
Fala Knowe
Lawhead
Grange Dell
Cuiken Farm House
Mauricewood
Deanburn
Coates
Luffen Houses
Cuiken
Cuiken Bridge
Eastfield
Crystal Wks
TA Ctr
Cornbank
Liby
Loanburn
Cemy
Bog Wood
Spear Gate Lodge
PENICUIK
EH26
Carsewell
Tower
Mast
Lodges
Serpentine Wood
Penicuik House
High Pond
River North Esk
South Bank Wood
Castle Brae
Uttershill Castle (rems of)
Low Pond
South Lodge
Cornton
Ramsay's Monument
Ravensneuk Farm
Black Burn
Hurley Pond
Hare Burn
Rookery
Halls Farm
Summer Knowe
Lawhead Burn
Silver Burn
Loan Burn
CARLOPS RD
EDINBURGH RD
JOHN ST
HIGH ST
BRIDGE ST
PEEBLES RD
BOG RD
A702
A701
A766
B6372
21 22 23
58 59 60 61
1 2 3 4

D E F

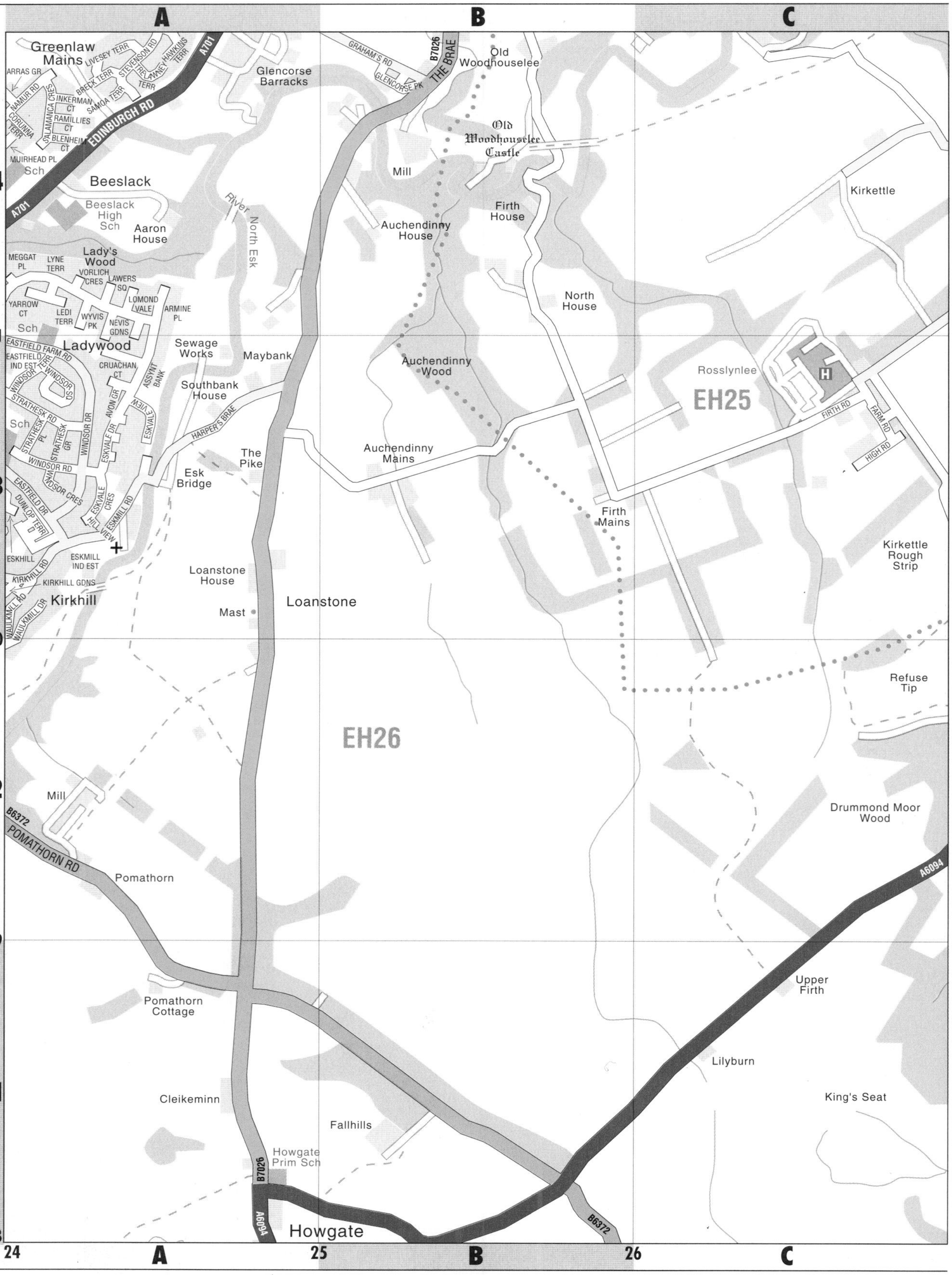

A B C

Greenlaw Mains
Glencorse Barracks
Old Woodhouselee
Old Woodhouselee Castle
Kirkettle

Beeslack
Beeslack High Sch
Aaron House
River North Esk
Mill
Auchendinny House
Firth House
North House

Lady's Wood
Ladywood
Sewage Works
Maybank
Auchendinny Wood
Rosslynlee
EH25

Southbank House
The Pike
Auchendinny Mains
Firth Mains
Kirkettle Rough Strip

Esk Bridge
Kirkhill
Loanstone House
Mast
Loanstone

EH26

Refuse Tip

Mill
Pomathorn
Drummond Moor Wood

Pomathorn Cottage
Upper Firth

Cleikeminn
Lilyburn
King's Seat

Fallhills
Howgate Prim Sch
Howgate

181 206

D E F

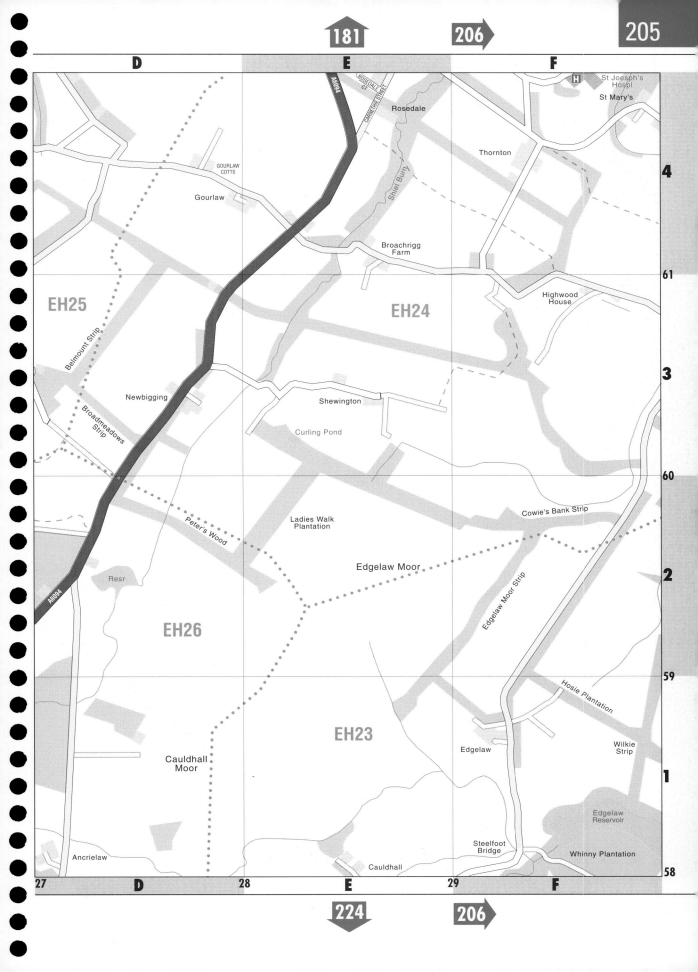
A6094
ROSEDALE CT
CARNETHIE STREET
Rosedale
St Joseph's Hospl
St Mary's
Thornton
GOURLAW COTTS
Gourlaw
Shiel Burn
Broachrigg Farm
EH25
EH24
Highwood House
Belmount Strip
Newbigging
Shewington
Broadmeadows Strip
Curling Pond
Ladies Walk Plantation
Cowie's Bank Strip
Peter's Wood
Edgelaw Moor
Resr
A6094
EH26
Edgelaw Moor Strip
Hosie Plantation
EH23
Edgelaw
Wilkie Strip
Cauldhall Moor
Edgelaw Reservoir
Steelfoot Bridge
Whinny Plantation
Ancrielaw
Cauldhall

4 61 3 60 2 59 1 58

27 D 28 E 29 F

224 206

205
182

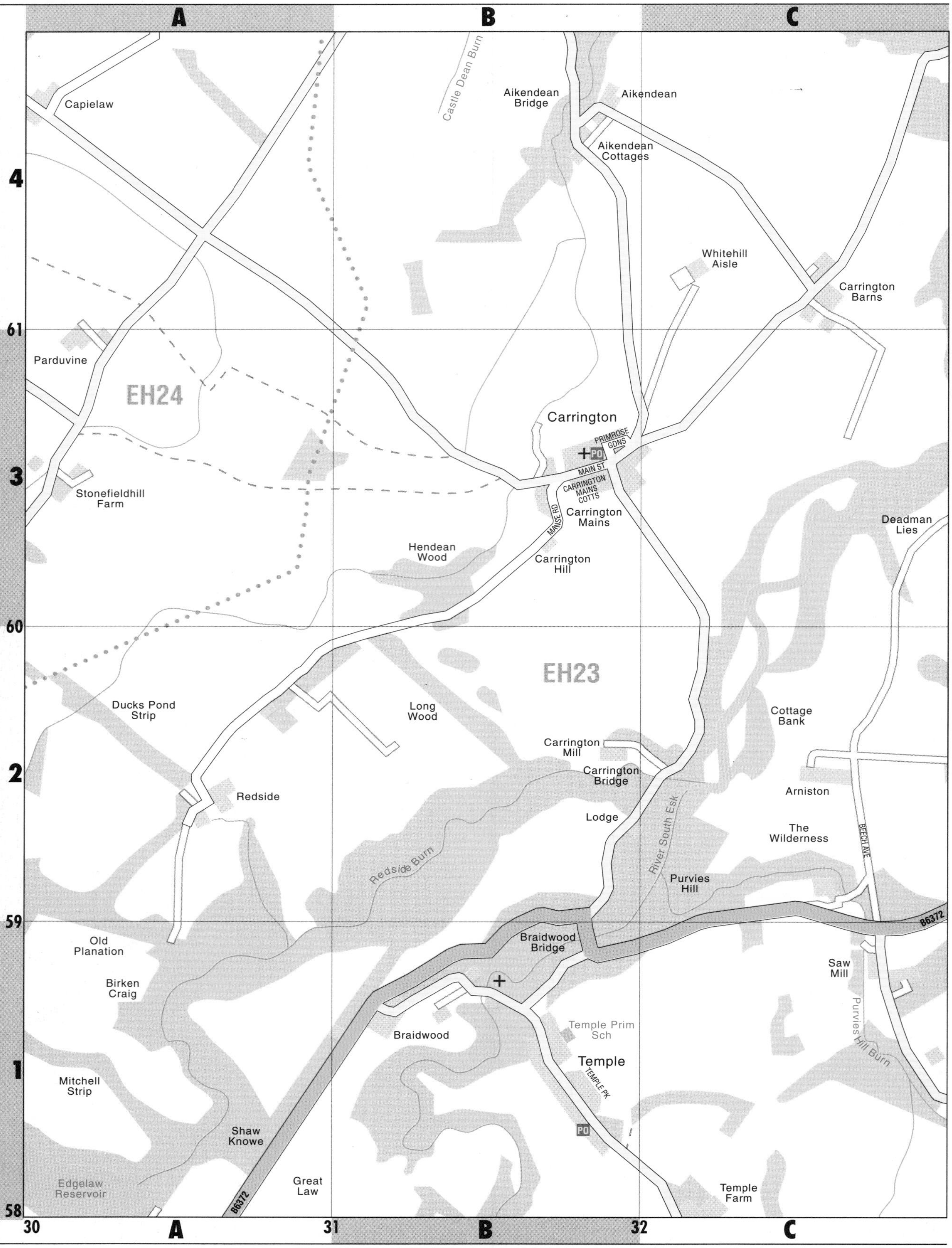
A
B
C
4
61
3
60
2
59
1
58
30
31
32
Castle Dean Burn
Capielaw
Aikendean Bridge
Aikendean
Aikendean Cottages
Whitehill Aisle
Carrington Barns
Parduvine
EH24
Carrington
PRIMROSE GDNS
PO
MAIN ST
CARRINGTON MAINS COTTS
Stonefieldhill Farm
MANSE RD
Carrington Mains
Deadman Lies
Hendean Wood
Carrington Hill
EH23
Ducks Pond Strip
Long Wood
Cottage Bank
Carrington Mill
Carrington Bridge
Arniston
Redside
Lodge
River South Esk
The Wilderness
BEECH AVE
Redside Burn
Purvies Hill
B6372
Old Planation
Braidwood Bridge
Saw Mill
Birken Craig
Temple Prim Sch
Braidwood
Temple
Purvies Hill Burn
TEMPLE PK
Mitchell Strip
PO
Shaw Knowe
Great Law
Temple Farm
Edgelaw Reservoir
B6372

205
225

183
208

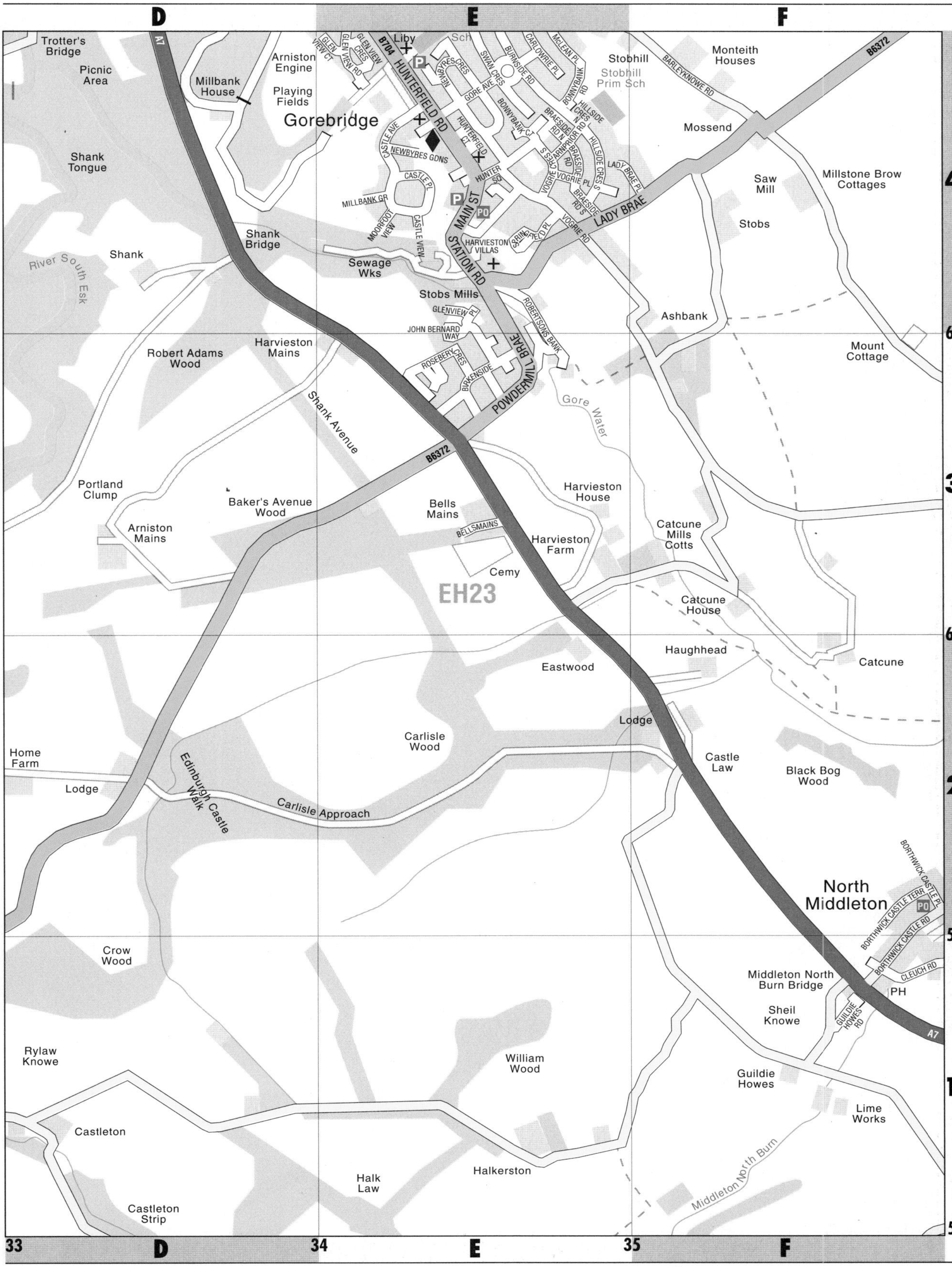
D
E
F
Trotter's Bridge
Picnic Area
Millbank House
Arniston Engine
Playing Fields
Gorebridge
Liby
Sch
Stobhill
Stobhill Prim Sch
Monteith Houses
Mossend
Shank Tongue
Shank
River South Esk
Shank Bridge
Sewage Wks
Stobs Mills
Saw Mill
Millstone Brow Cottages
Stobs
Ashbank
Mount Cottage
HUNTERFIELD RD
MAIN ST
STATION RD
LADY BRAE
POWDERMILL BRAE
ROBERTSONS BANK
GLENVIEW PL
JOHN BERNARD WAY
ROSEBERY CRES
BIRKENSIDE
NEWBYRES GDNS
CASTLE PL
MILLBANK GR
MOORFOOT VIEW
CASTLE VIEW
HARVIESTON VILLAS
SPRINGFIELD PL
VOGRIE RD
VOGRIE PL
HUNTER SQ
GORE AVE
SWAN CRES
BURNSIDE RD
CARLOWRIE PL
MCLEAN PL
BONNYBANK RD
BONNYBANK CT
HILLSIDE CRES
BRAESIDE RD
BARLEYKNOWE RD
B6372
B704
A7
Robert Adams Wood
Harvieston Mains
Shank Avenue
Gore Water
Portland Clump
Baker's Avenue Wood
Arniston Mains
Bells Mains
BELLSMAINS
Harvieston House
Harvieston Farm
Catcune Mills Cotts
Cemy
EH23
Catcune House
Haughhead
Catcune
Eastwood
Lodge
Carlisle Wood
Castle Law
Black Bog Wood
Home Farm
Lodge
Edinburgh Castle Walk
Carlisle Approach
North Middleton
BORTHWICK CASTLE PL
BORTHWICK CASTLE TERR
BORTHWICK CASTLE RD
CLEUCH RD
GUILDIE HOWES RD
PH
PO
Crow Wood
Middleton North Burn Bridge
Sheil Knowe
Rylaw Knowe
William Wood
Guildie Howes
Lime Works
Castleton
Halk Law
Halkerston
Middleton North Burn
Castleton Strip
4
61
3
60
2
59
1
58
33
34
35

226
208

207
184

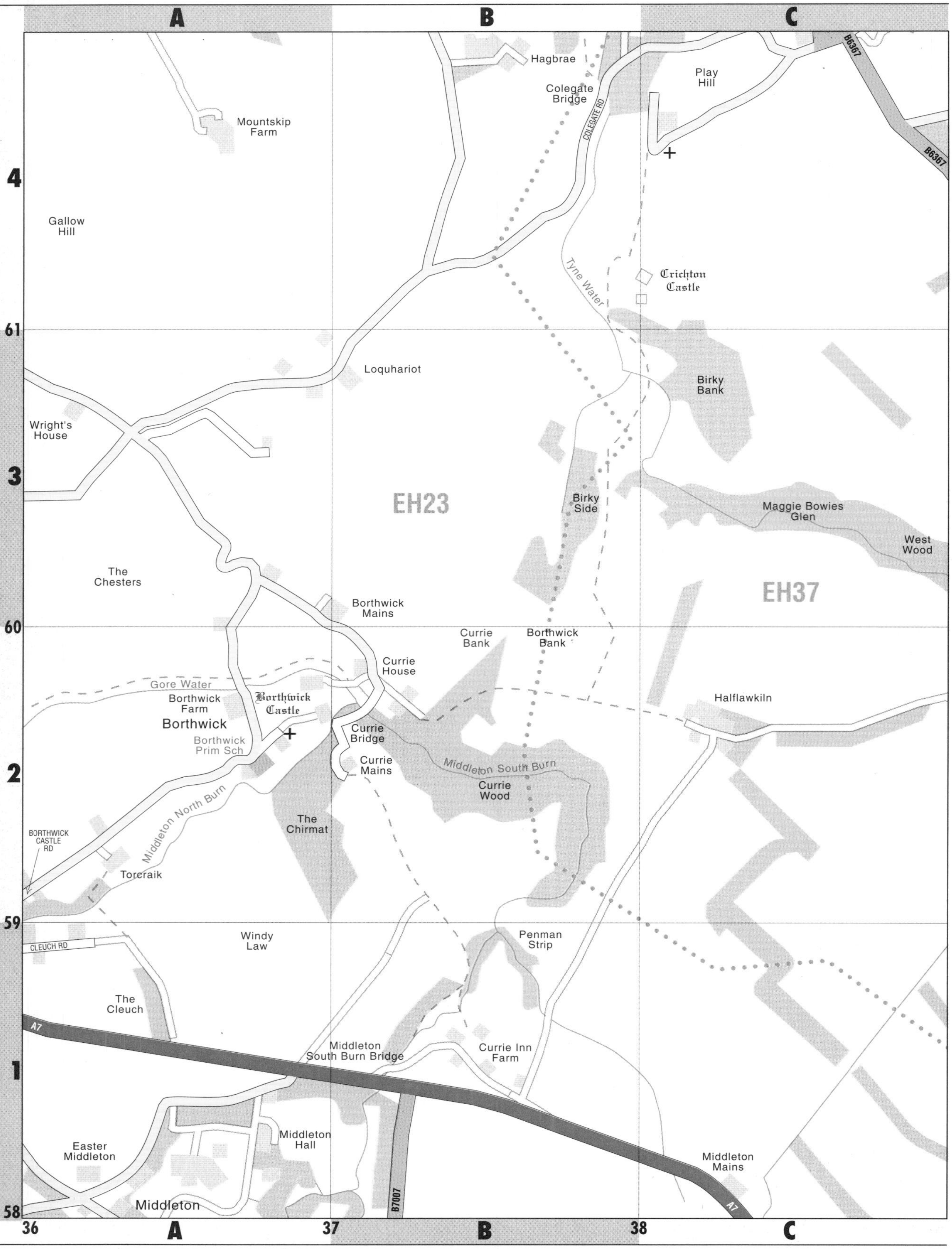

A **B** **C**

Mountskip
Farm

Hagbrae

Colegate
Bridge

COLGATE RD

Play
Hill

B6367

B6367

+

4

Gallow
Hill

Tyne Water

Crichton
Castle

61

Loquhariot

Birky
Bank

Wright's
House

EH23

Birky
Side

Maggie Bowies
Glen

West
Wood

3

EH37

The
Chesters

Borthwick
Mains

Currie
Bank

Borthwick
Bank

60

Currie
House

Halflawkiln

Gore Water

Borthwick
Farm

Borthwick
Castle

Borthwick

Currie
Bridge

Middleton South Burn

Borthwick
Prim Sch

+

Currie
Mains

Currie
Wood

2

BORTHWICK
CASTLE
RD

Middleton North Burn

The
Chirmat

Torcraik

59

Windy
Law

Penman
Strip

CLEUCH RD

The
Cleuch

A7

Middleton
South Burn Bridge

Currie Inn
Farm

1

Easter
Middleton

Middleton
Hall

Middleton
Mains

B7007

A7

58

36 **A** 37 **B** 38 **C**

Middleton

207
227

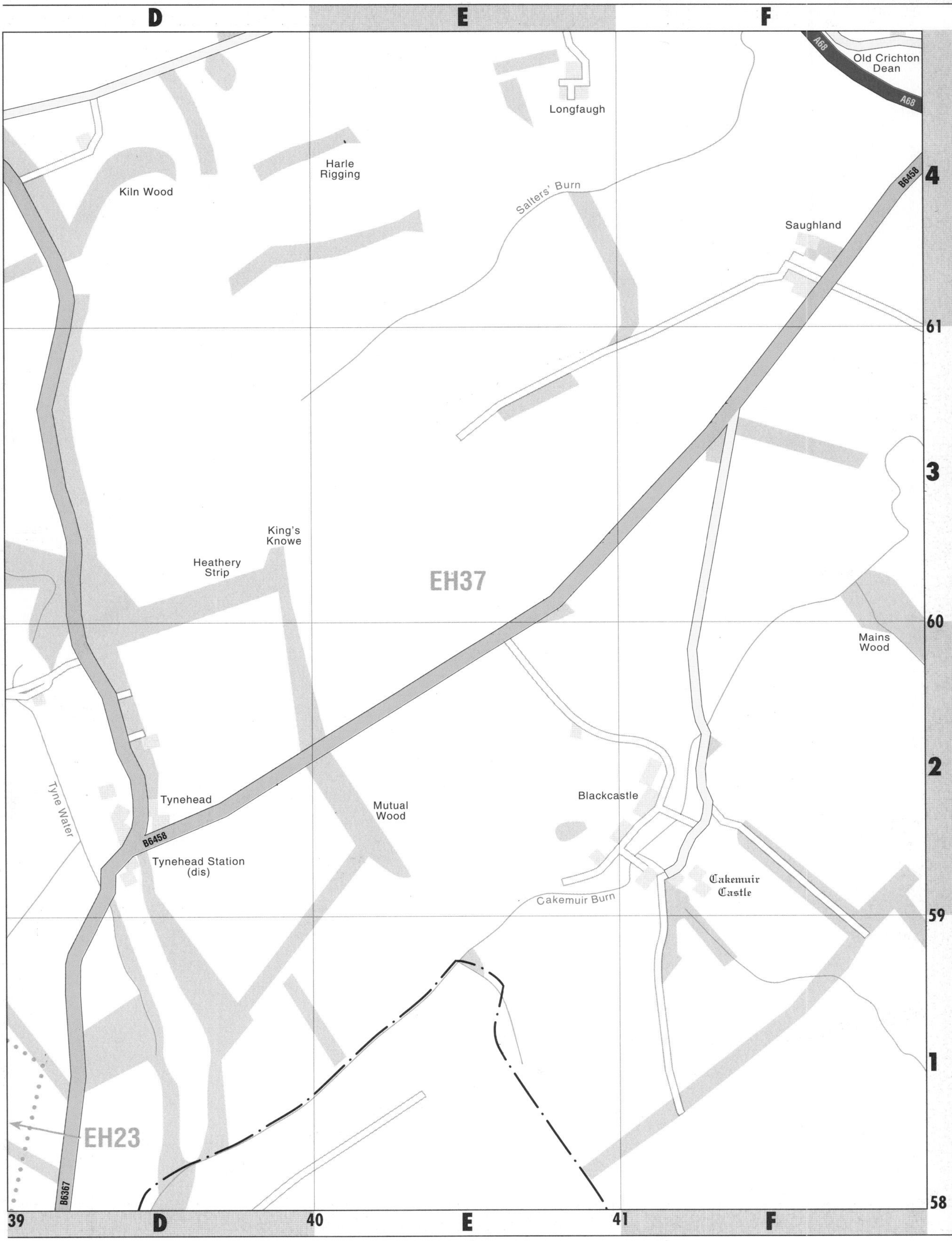

D   E   F

Old Crichton
Dean
A68

B6458
4

Longfaugh

Kiln Wood

Harle
Rigging

Salters' Burn

Saughland

61

3

King's
Knowe

Heathery
Strip

EH37

Mains
Wood

60

Tyne Water

Tynehead

Mutual
Wood

Blackcastle

2

B6458

Tynehead Station
(dis)

Cakemuir
Castle

Cakemuir Burn

59

1

EH23

B6367

58

39   D   40   E   41   F

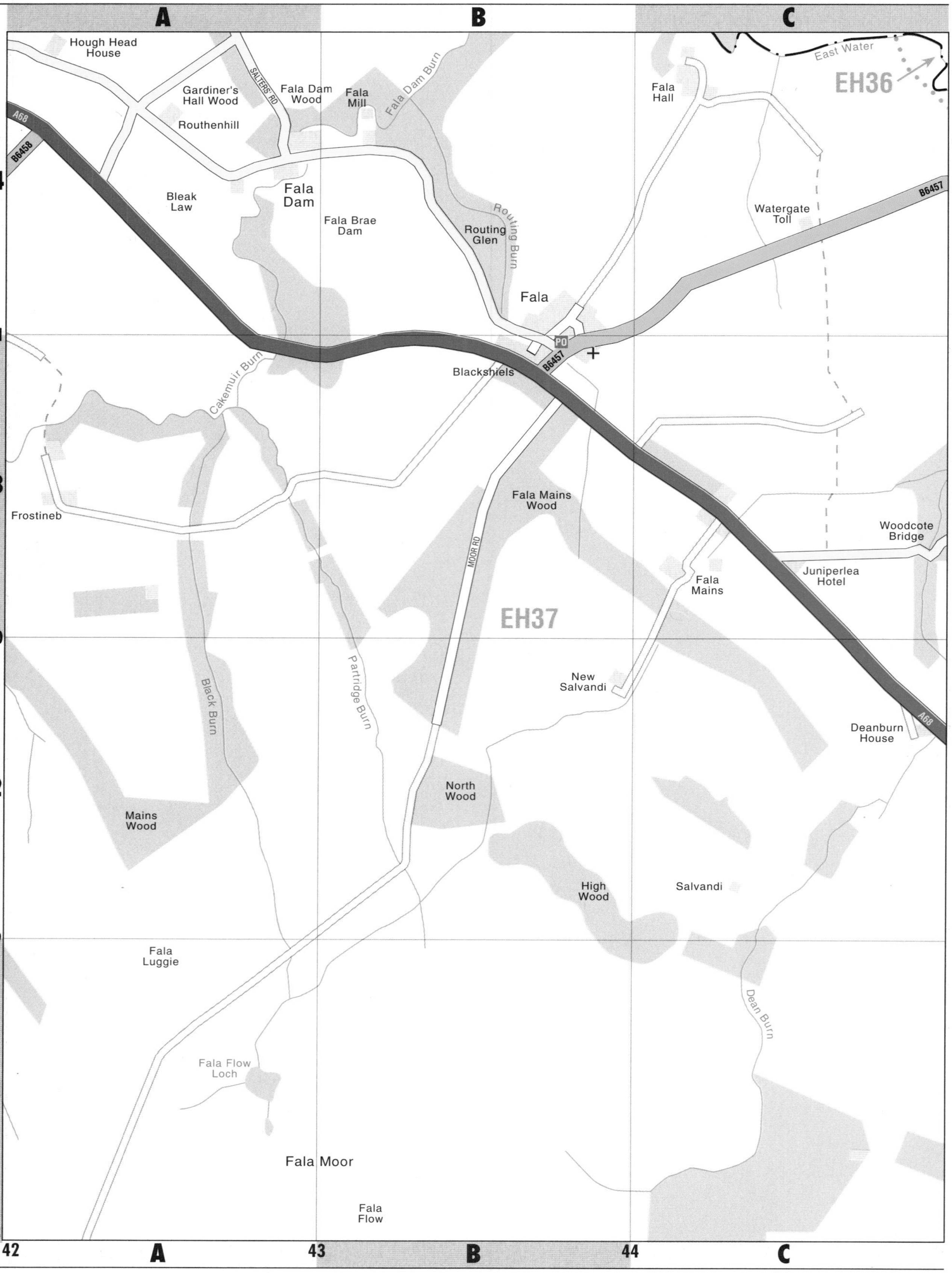

A   B   C

Hough Head House

Gardiner's Hall Wood

Fala Dam Wood

Fala Mill

Fala Hall

EH36

East Water

Routhenhill

B6458

A68

Fala Dam Burn

Watergate Toll

B6457

4

Bleak Law

Fala Dam

SALTERS RD

Fala Brae Dam

Routing Glen

Routing Burn

Fala

61

Cakemuir Burn

PO

Blackshiels

B6457

3

Frostineb

Fala Mains Wood

Woodcote Bridge

MOOR RD

Fala Mains

Juniperlea Hotel

EH37

60

Black Burn

Partridge Burn

New Salvandi

A68

Deanburn House

2

Mains Wood

North Wood

High Wood

Salvandi

59

Fala Luggie

Dean Burn

1

Fala Flow Loch

Fala Moor

58

Fala Flow

42   A   43   B   44   C

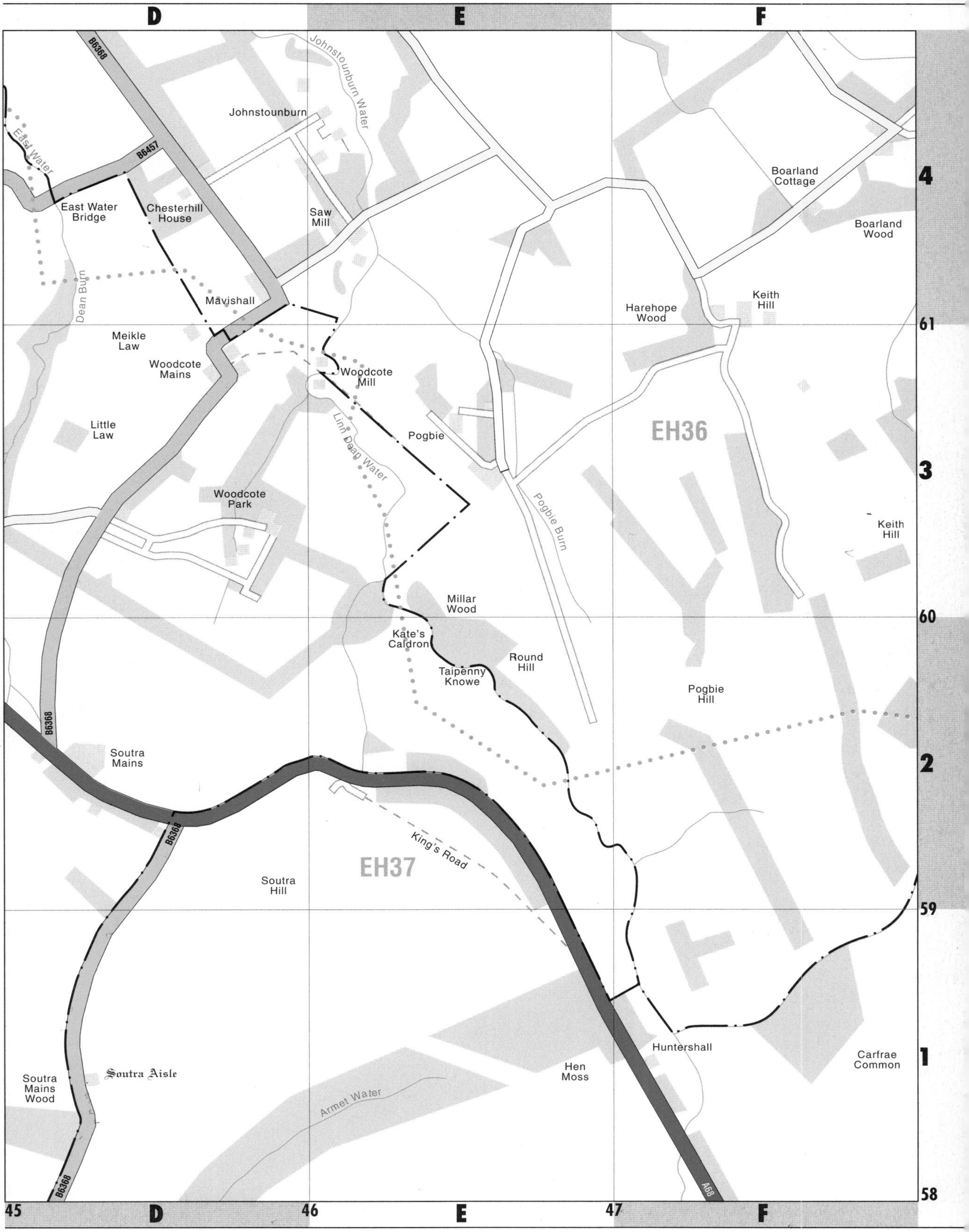

D

E

F

4

Boarland
Cottage

Boarland
Wood

Keith
Hill

Johnstounburn

Johnstounburn Water

Saw
Mill

East
Water

East Water
Bridge

Chesterhill
House

B6457

B6368

Dean Burn

Mavishall

Harehope
Wood

61

Meikle
Law

Woodcote
Mains

Woodcote
Mill

EH36

Little
Law

Linn Dean Water

Pogbie

Keith
Hill

3

Woodcote
Park

Pogbie Burn

60

Millar
Wood

Kate's
Caldron

Round
Hill

Pogbie
Hill

Taipenny
Knowe

B6368

Soutra
Mains

2

Soutra
Hill

King's Road

EH37

B6368

59

Huntershall

Carfrae
Common

1

Soutra
Mains
Wood

Soutra Aisle

Hen
Moss

Armet Water

A68

58

45

D

46

E

47

F

191
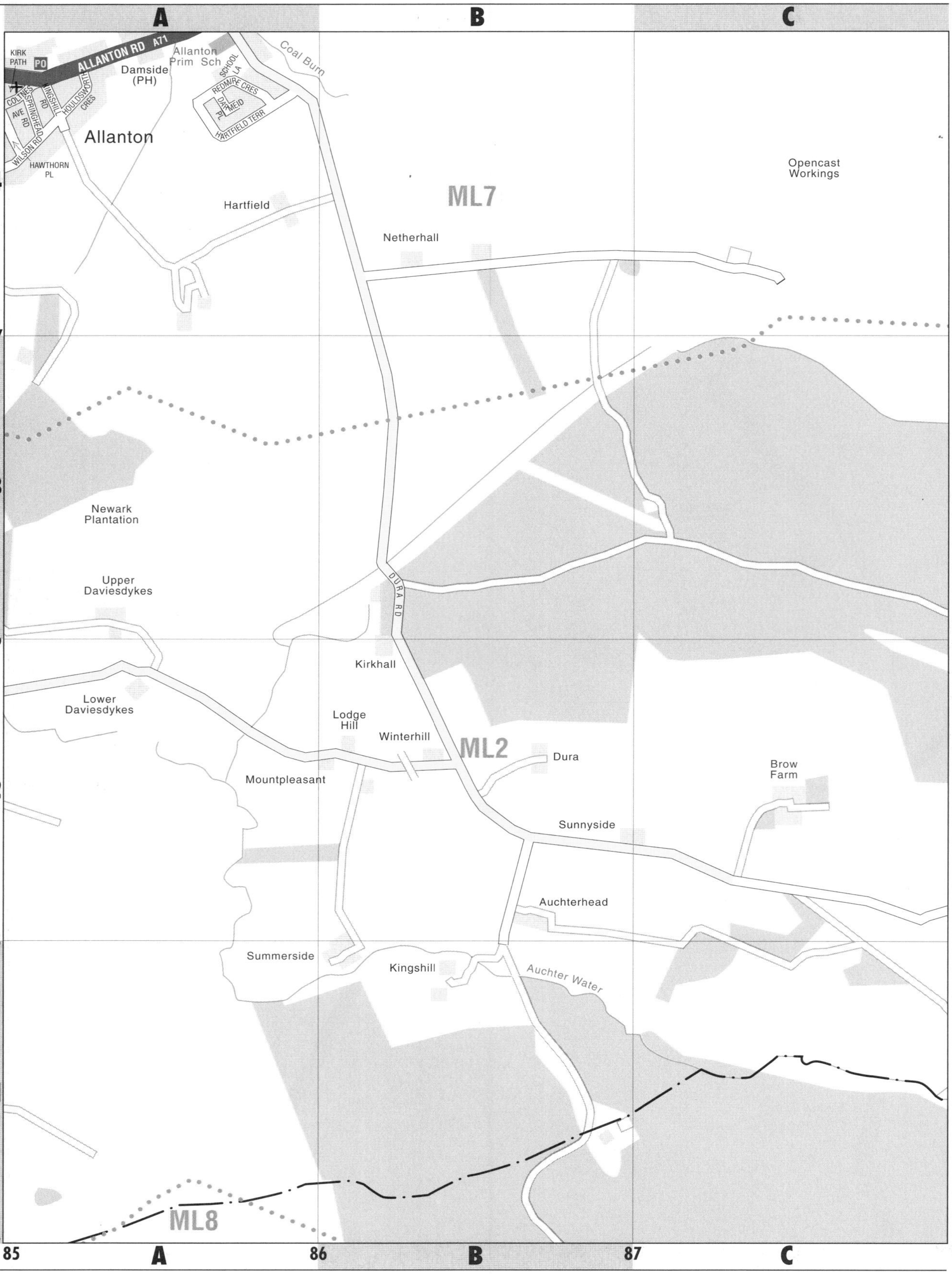
A
B
C
KIRK PATH
PO
ALLANTON RD
A71
Allanton Prim Sch
Damside (PH)
SCHOOL LA
Coal Burn
REDMIRE CRES
DALMEID PL
HARTFIELD TERR
KINGSHILL RD
HOULDSWORTH CRES
COLTNESS AVE
SPRINGHEAD RD
WILSON RD
HAWTHORN PL
Allanton
Opencast Workings
4
ML7
Hartfield
Netherhall
57
3
Newark Plantation
Upper Daviesdykes
DURA RD
56
Kirkhall
Lower Daviesdykes
Lodge Hill
Winterhill
ML2
Dura
Brow Farm
2
Mountpleasant
Sunnyside
Auchterhead
55
Summerside
Kingshill
Auchter Water
1
ML8
54
85
86
87
230

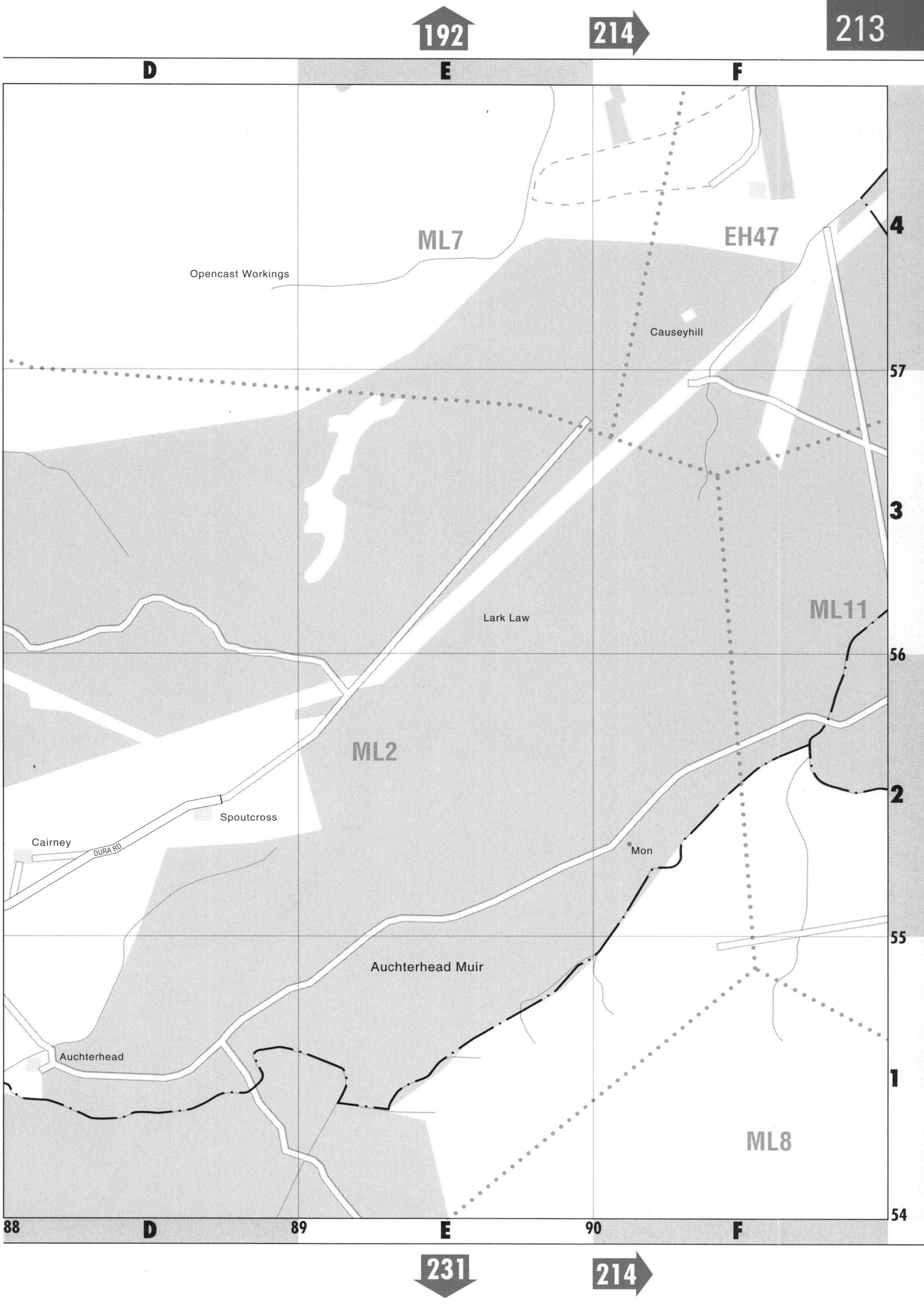

D E F

ML7

Opencast Workings

EH47

Causeyhill

4

57

3

Lark Law

ML11

56

ML2

Spoutcross

2

Cairney

DURA RD

Mon

55

Auchterhead Muir

1

Auchterhead

ML8

54

88 D 89 E 90 F

213
193

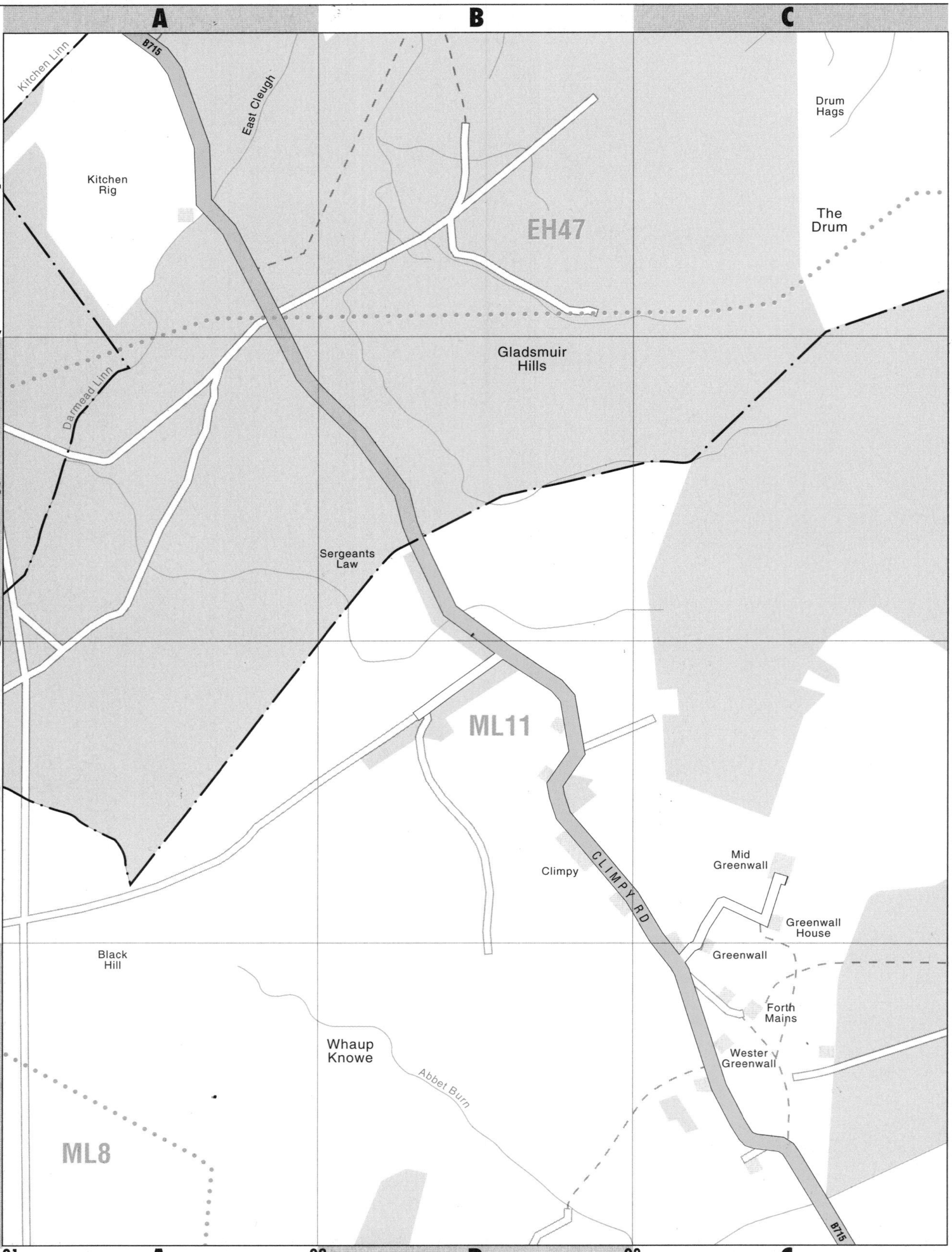
A
B
C
Kitchen Linn
B715
East Cleugh
Kitchen Rig
Drum Hags
The Drum
EH47
Gladsmuir Hills
Darmead Linn
Sergeants Law
ML11
CLIMPY RD
Climpy
Mid Greenwall
Greenwall House
Greenwall
Forth Mains
Wester Greenwall
Black Hill
Whaup Knowe
Abbet Burn
ML8
B715
4
3
2
1
57
56
55
54
91
92
93

213

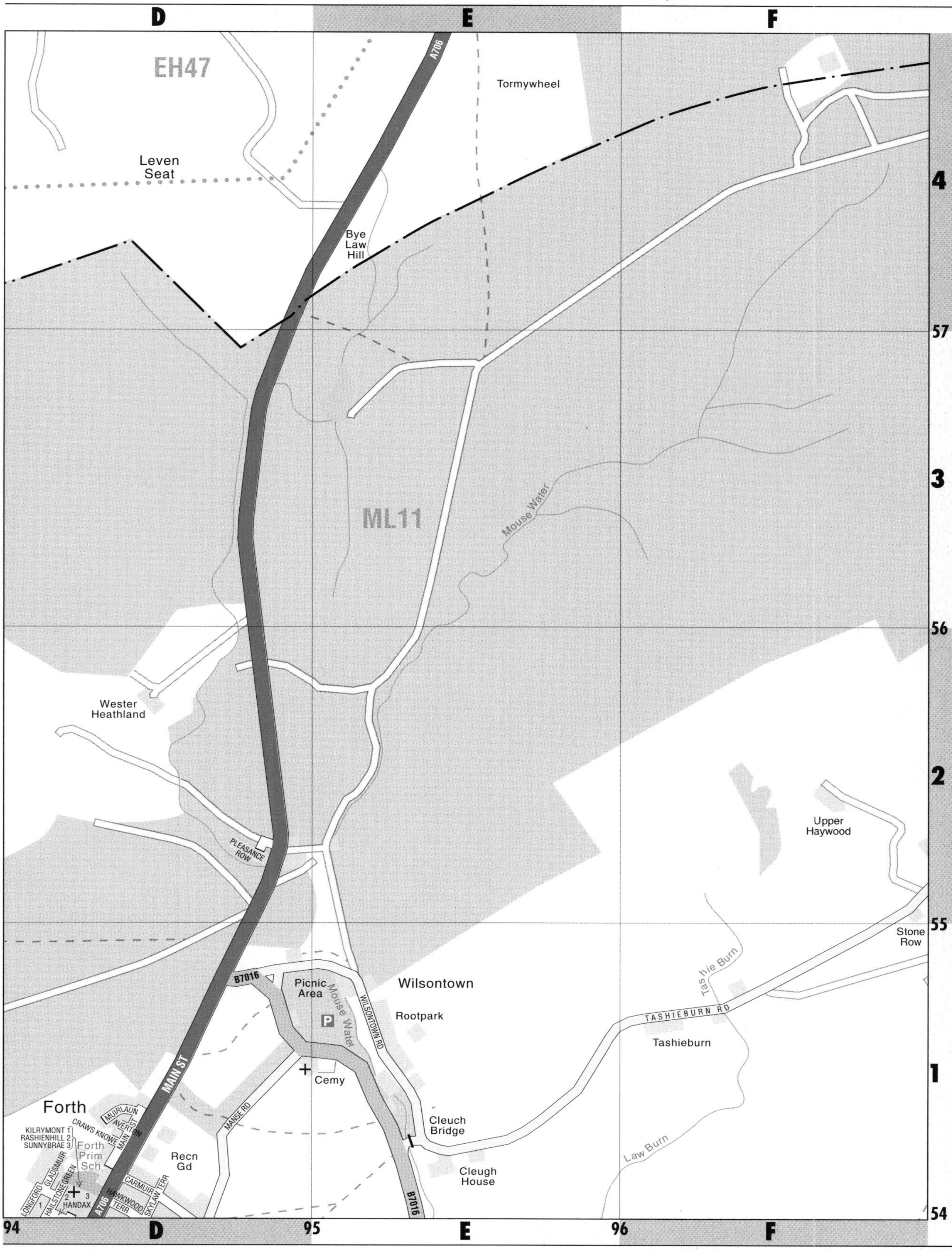
D
E
F
EH47
Tormywheel
A706
Leven
Seat
Bye
Law
Hill
4
57
3
ML11
Mouse Water
56
Wester
Heathland
2
Upper
Haywood
PLEASANCE ROW
55
Stone
Row
B7016
Picnic
Area
Mouse Water
WILSONTOWN RD
Wilsontown
Rootpark
Tashie Burn
TASHIEBURN RD
Tashieburn
MAIN ST
Cemy
1
Forth
MUIRLAUN
AVERTON
CRAWS KNOWE
MAIN ST
KILRYMONT 1
RASHIENHILL 2
SUNNYBRAE 3
Forth
Prim
Sch
MANSE RD
Cleuch
Bridge
Recn
Gd
Cleugh
House
Law Burn
LONGFORD
GLADSMUIR
HAILSTONEGREEN
HANDAX
CARMUIR
SKYLAW TERR
HAWKWOOD TERR
B7016
54
94
D
95
E
96
F

215
195

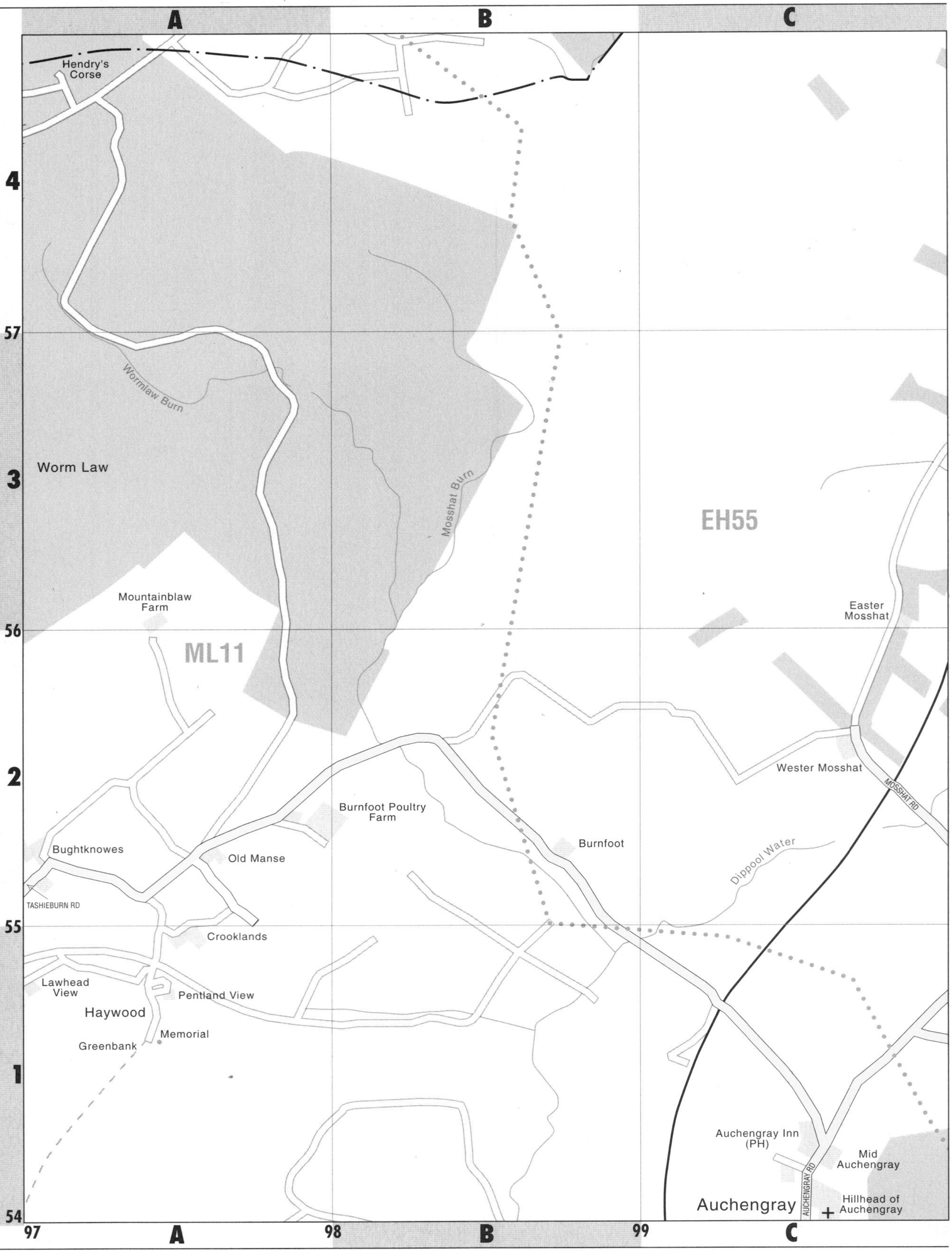

A **B** **C**

Hendry's Corse

4

57

Wormlaw Burn

Worm Law

3

EH55

Mountainblaw Farm

Easter Mosshat

56

ML11

Wester Mosshat

MOSSHAT RD

2

Burnfoot Poultry Farm

Burnfoot

Bughtknowes

Old Manse

Dippool Water

TASHIEBURN RD

55

Crooklands

Lawhead View

Pentland View

Haywood

Memorial

Auchengray Inn (PH)

Greenbank

Mid Auchengray

1

AUCHENGRAY RD

Auchengray

Hillhead of Auchengray

54

97 **A** 98 **B** 99 **C**

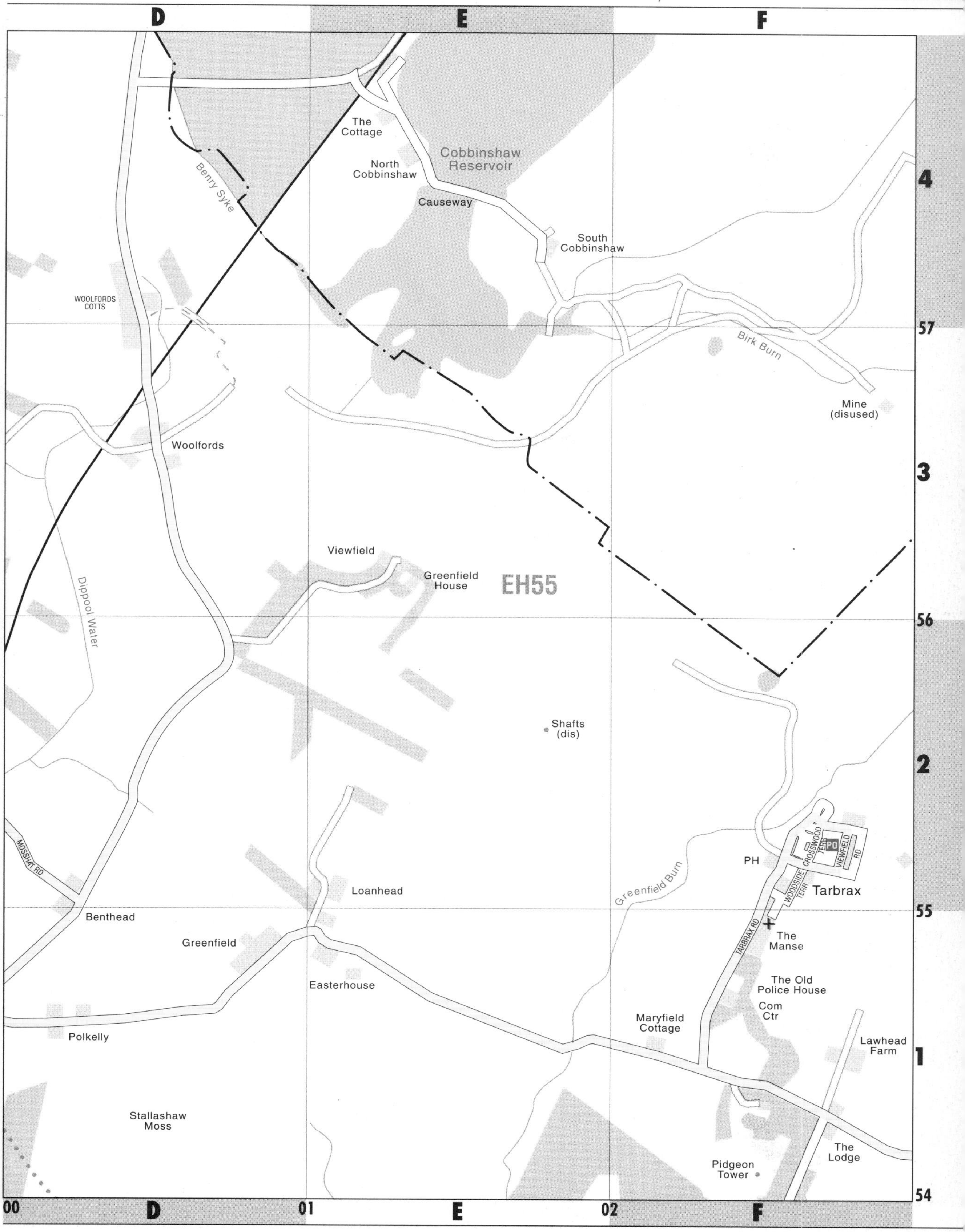

D E F

4

The Cottage
North Cobbinshaw
Cobbinshaw Reservoir
Causeway
South Cobbinshaw
Benty Syke
Birk Burn
57
WOOLFORDS COTTS
Mine (disused)
Woolfords
3
Viewfield
Greenfield House
EH55
Dippool Water
56
Shafts (dis)
2
Loanhead
Greenfield Burn
PH
Tarbrax
Benthead
Greenfield
55
The Manse
Easterhouse
Maryfield Cottage
The Old Police House
Com Ctr
Polkelly
Lawhead Farm
1
Stallashaw Moss
Pidgeon Tower
The Lodge
54

MOSSAT RD
TARBRAX RD
WOODSIDE CROSSWOOD TERR
PO TERR
VIEWFIELD RD

00 D 01 E 02 F

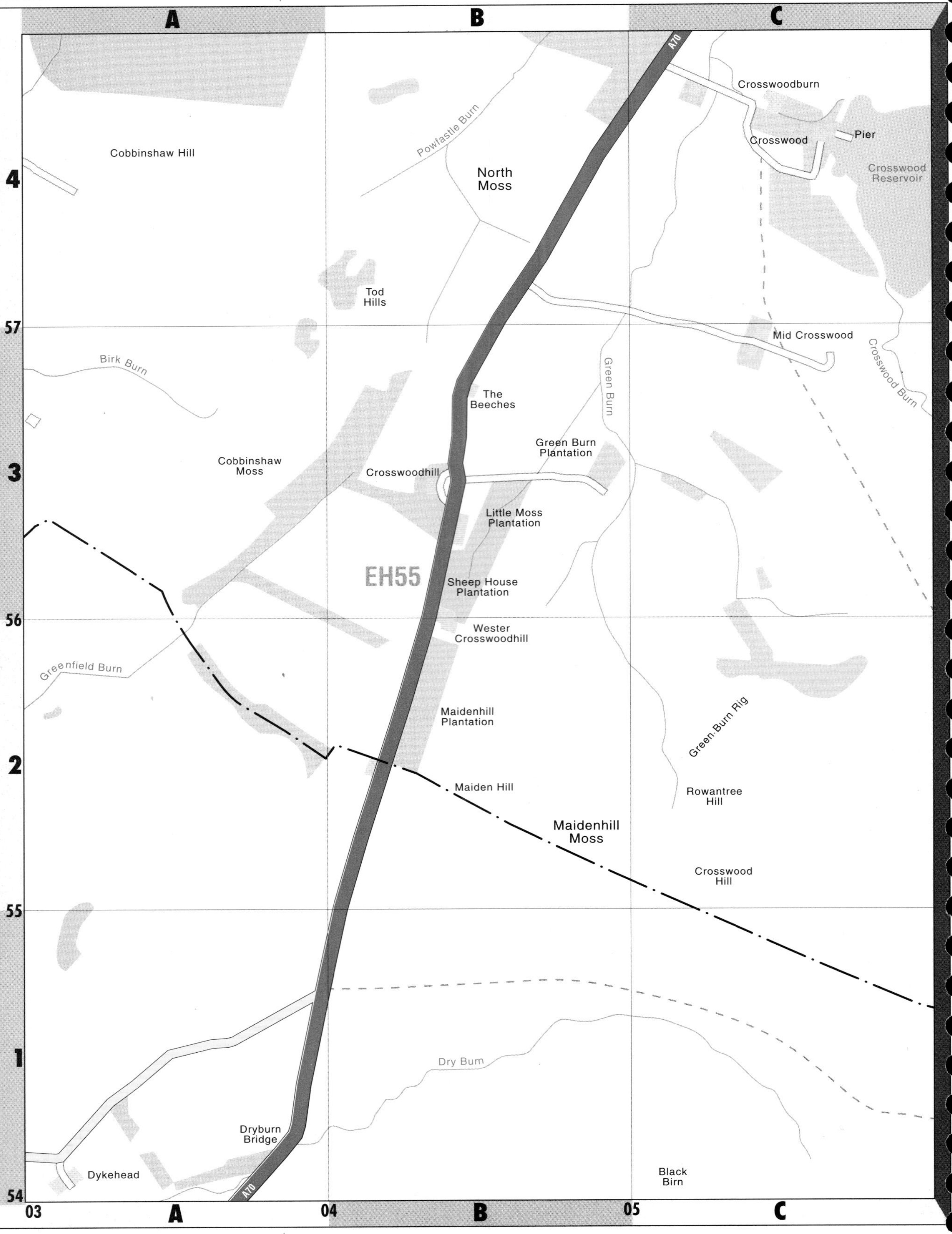

A B C

Cobbinshaw Hill

Powfastle Burn

North Moss

Crosswoodburn

Crosswood

Pier

Crosswood Reservoir

Tod Hills

Birk Burn

Mid Crosswood

Crosswood Burn

57

The Beeches

Green Burn

Cobbinshaw Moss

Crosswoodhill

Green Burn Plantation

3

Little Moss Plantation

EH55

Sheep House Plantation

56

Wester Crosswoodhill

Greenfield Burn

Green Burn Rig

Maidenhill Plantation

2

Maiden Hill

Maidenhill Moss

Rowantree Hill

Crosswood Hill

55

1

Dry Burn

Dryburn Bridge

Dykehead

A70

Black Birn

54

03 A 04 B 05 C

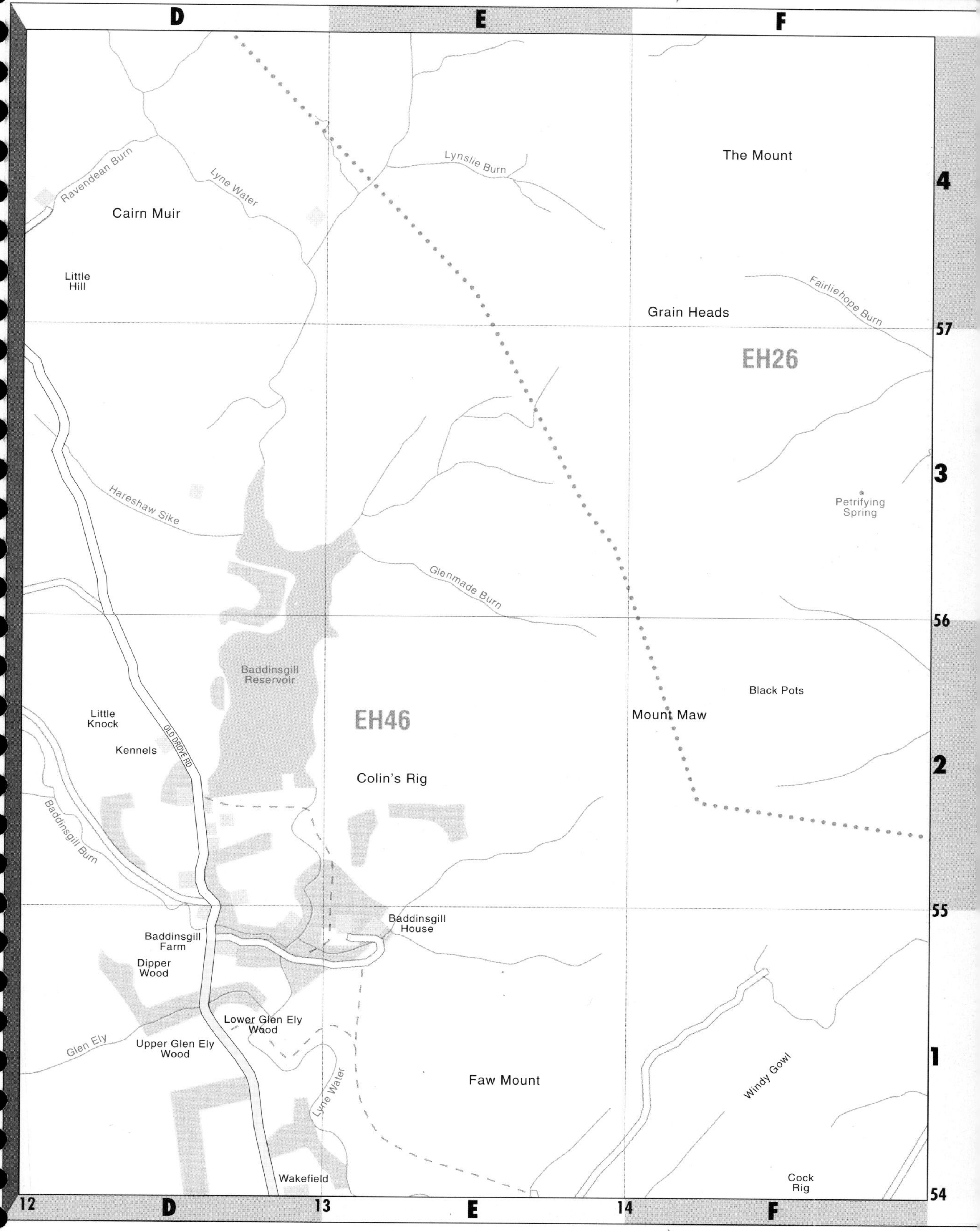

D

E

F

4

The Mount

Ravendean Burn

Lyne Water

Lynslie Burn

Cairn Muir

Little
Hill

Grain Heads

57

Fairliehope Burn

EH26

3

Hareshaw Sike

Petrifying
Spring

Glenmade Burn

56

Baddinsgill
Reservoir

Black Pots

Little
Knock

EH46

Mount Maw

2

Kennels

OLD DROVE RD

Colin's Rig

Baddinsgill
Burn

55

Baddinsgill
House

Baddinsgill
Farm

Dipper
Wood

Lower Glen Ely
Wood

Glen Ely

Lyne Water

1

Upper Glen Ely
Wood

Faw Mount

Windy Gowl

Wakefield

Cock
Rig

54

219
201

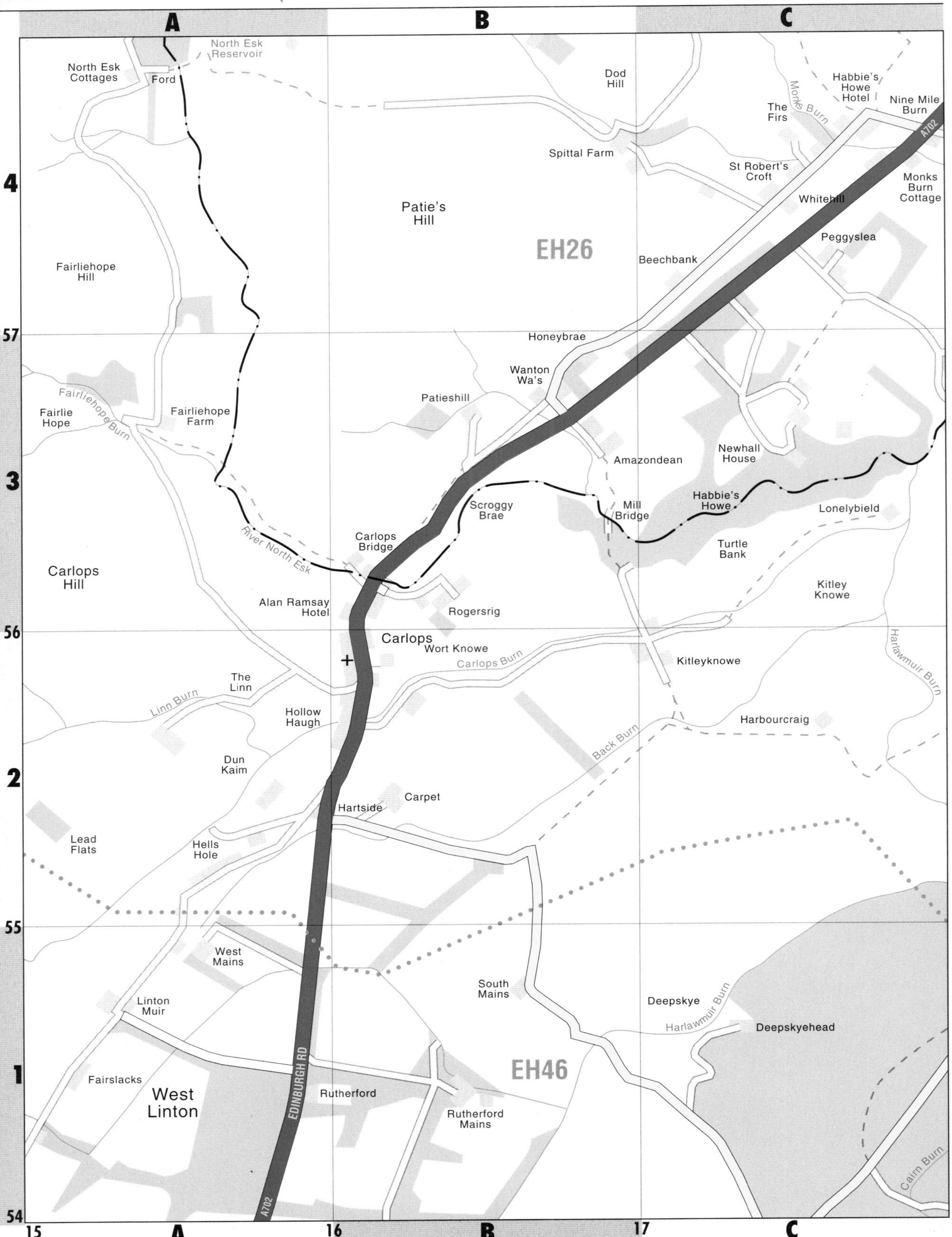

North Esk Reservoir

North Esk Cottages

Ford

Dod Hill

Spittal Farm

Habbie's Howe Hotel

The Firs

Nine Mile Burn

Monks Burn

A702

St Robert's Croft

Monks Burn Cottage

Patie's Hill

EH26

Whitehill

Beechbank

Peggyslea

Fairliehope Hill

Honeybrae

Wanton Wa's

Patieshill

Newhall House

Fairlie Hope

Fairliehope Burn

Fairliehope Farm

Amazondean

Habbie's Howe

Lonelybield

River North Esk

Scroggy Brae

Mill Bridge

Turtle Bank

Carlops Bridge

Carlops Hill

Kitley Knowe

Alan Ramsay Hotel

Rogersrig

Harlawmuir Burn

Carlops

Wort Knowe

Kitleyknowe

Carlops Burn

The Linn

Linn Burn

Hollow Haugh

Back Burn

Harbourcraig

Dun Kaim

Lead Flats

Carpet

Hartside

Hells Hole

Deepskye

West Mains

South Mains

Harlawmuir Burn

Deepskyehead

Linton Muir

EH46

Fairslacks

West Linton

EDINBURGH RD

Rutherford

Rutherford Mains

Cairn Burn

A702

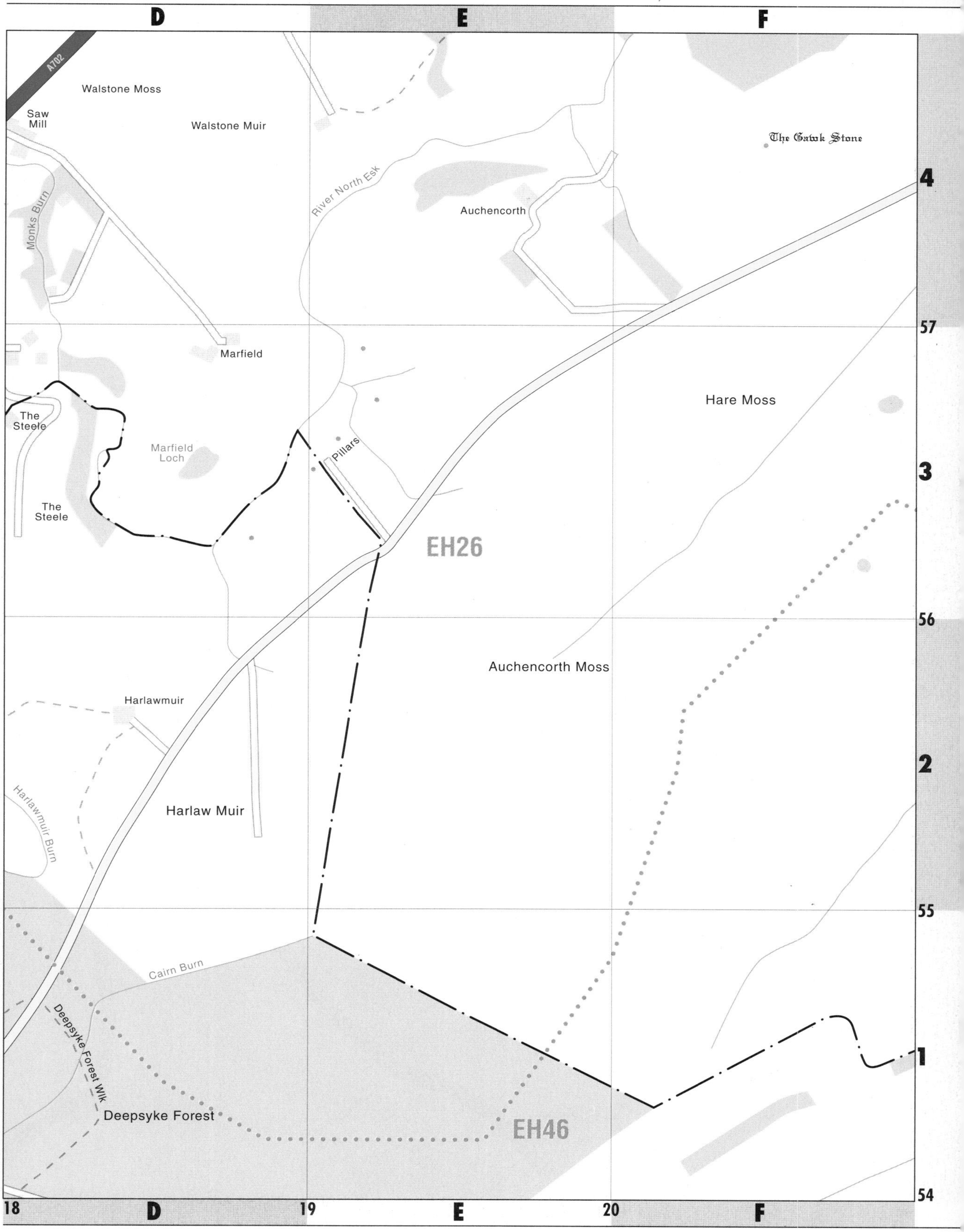

D   E   F

A702

Walstone Moss

Saw Mill

Walstone Muir

The Gawk Stone

Monks Burn

River North Esk

Auchencorth

4

Marfield

57

The Steele

Hare Moss

Marfield Loch

Pillars

3

The Steele

EH26

56

Auchencorth Moss

Harlawmuir

Harlawmuir Burn

2

Harlaw Muir

55

Cairn Burn

Deepsyke Forest Wlk

1

Deepsyke Forest

EH46

54

221
203

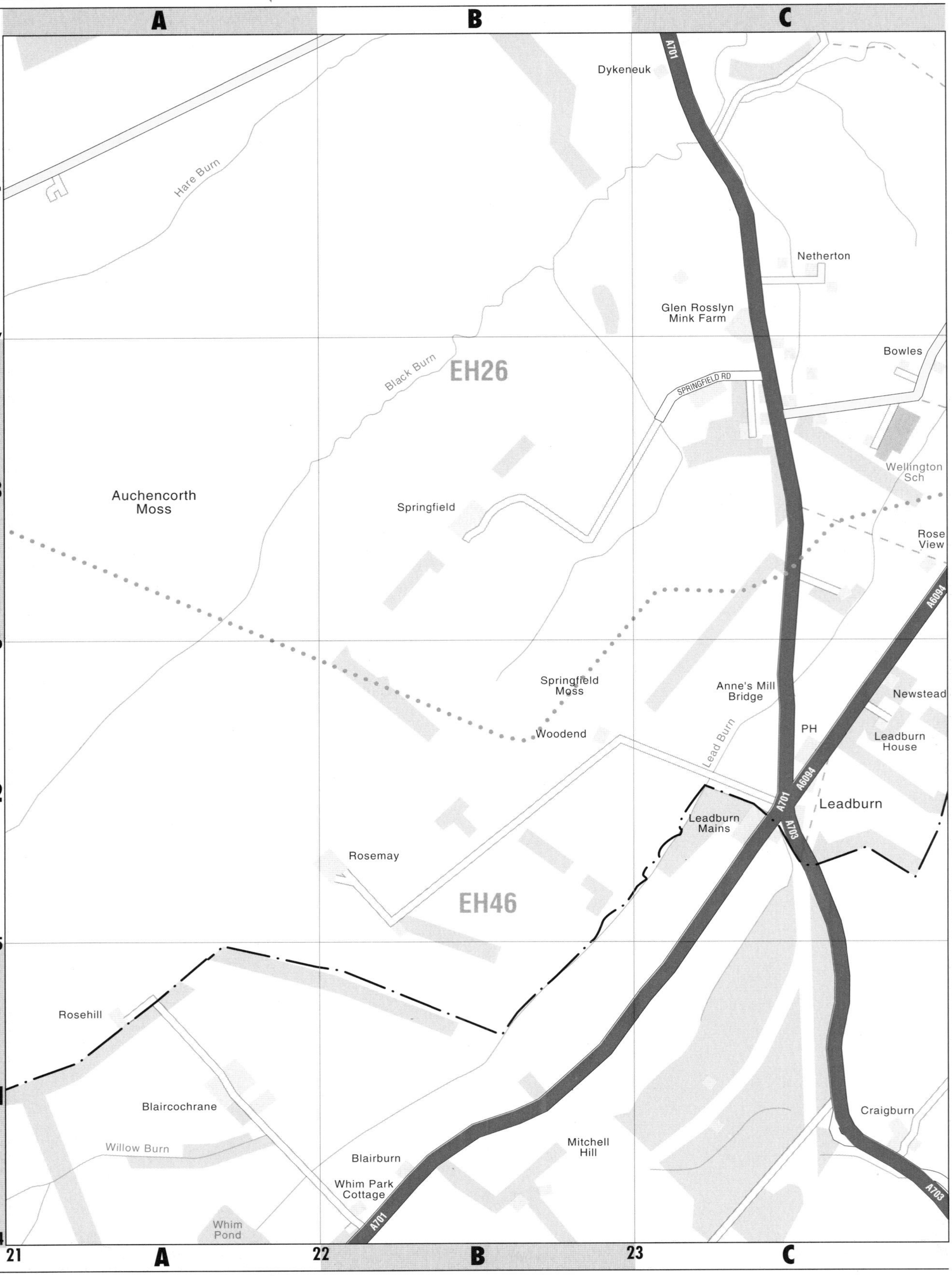

A **B** **C**

4

Dykeneuk

Hare Burn

Netherton

Glen Rosslyn
Mink Farm

57

Bowles

Black Burn

EH26

SPRINGFIELD RD

Wellington
Sch

3

Auchencorth
Moss

Springfield

Rose
View

56

Springfield
Moss

Anne's Mill
Bridge

Newstead

Woodend

Lead Burn

PH

Leadburn
House

2

Leadburn
Mains

Leadburn

Rosemay

EH46

55

Rosehill

1

Blaircochrane

Craigburn

Willow Burn

Mitchell
Hill

Blairburn

Whim Park
Cottage

54

Whim
Pond

21 **A** 22 **B** 23 **C**

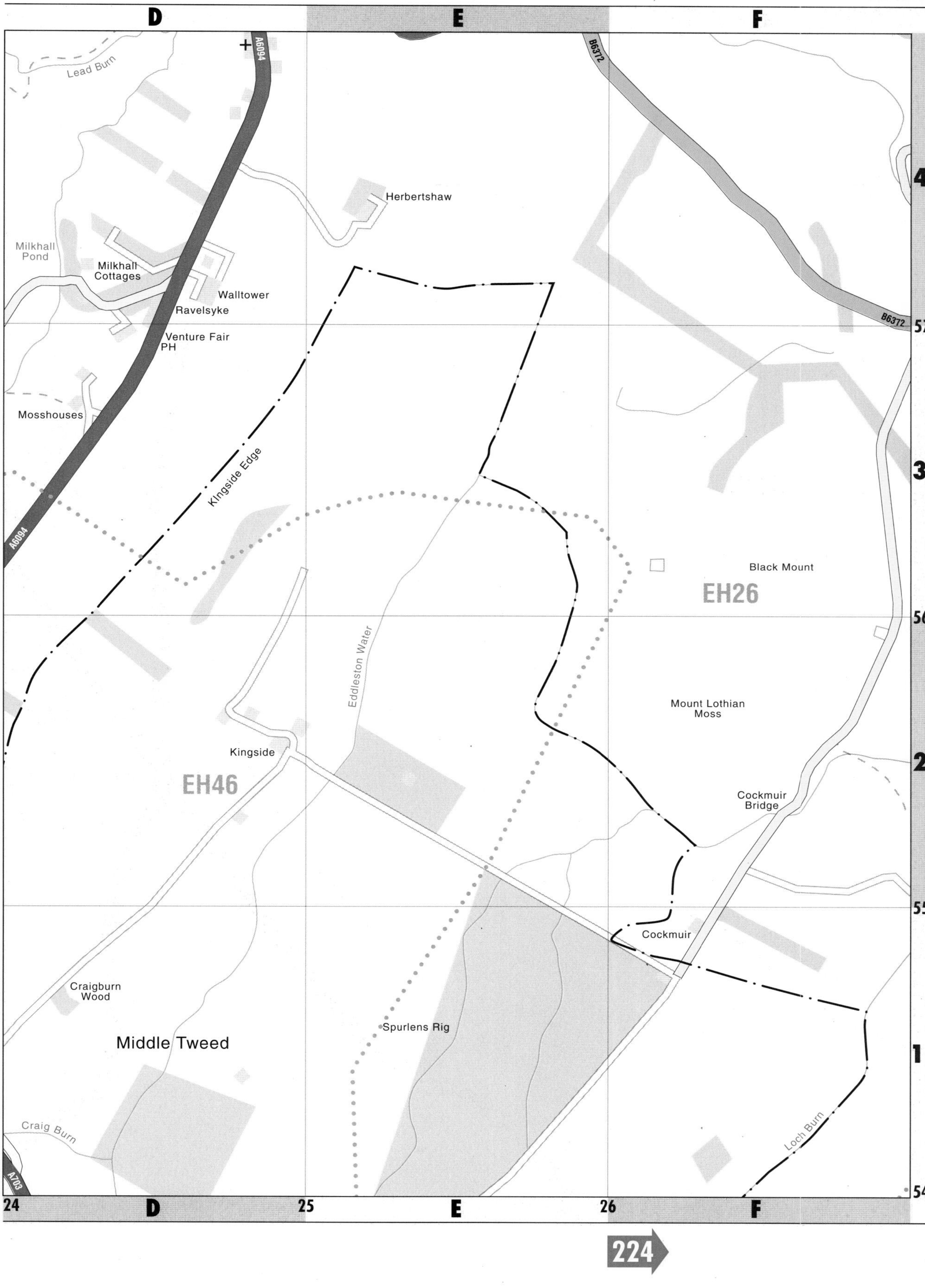

D
E
F

4

57

3

56

2

55

1

54

A6094

Lead Burn

Milkhall Pond

Milkhall Cottages

Walltower

Ravelsyke

Venture Fair PH

Mosshouses

Kingside Edge

A6094

B6372

B6372

Herbertshaw

Black Mount

EH26

Mount Lothian Moss

Cockmuir Bridge

Kingside

EH46

Eddleston Water

Cockmuir

Craigburn Wood

Middle Tweed

Spurlens Rig

Craig Burn

A703

Loch Burn

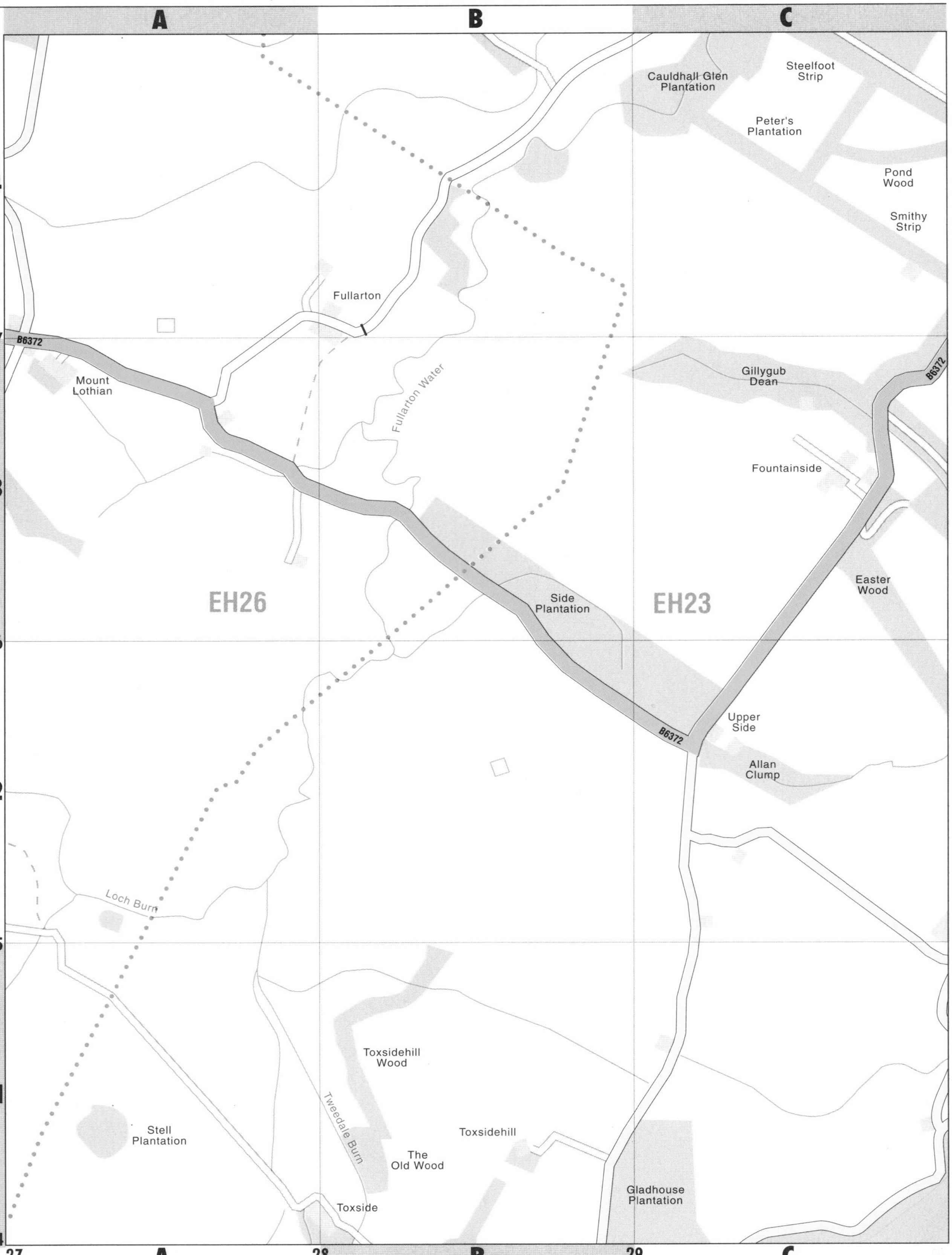

A   B   C

4

Cauldhall Glen Plantation

Steelfoot Strip

Peter's Plantation

Pond Wood

Smithy Strip

Fullarton

57

B6372

B6372

Mount Lothian

Fullarton Water

Gillygub Dean

Fountainside

3

EH26

Side Plantation

EH23

Easter Wood

56

Upper Side

B6372

Allan Clump

2

Loch Burn

55

Toxsidehill Wood

1

Tweedale Burn

Stell Plantation

The Old Wood

Toxsidehill

Gladhouse Plantation

Toxside

54

27   A   28   B   29   C

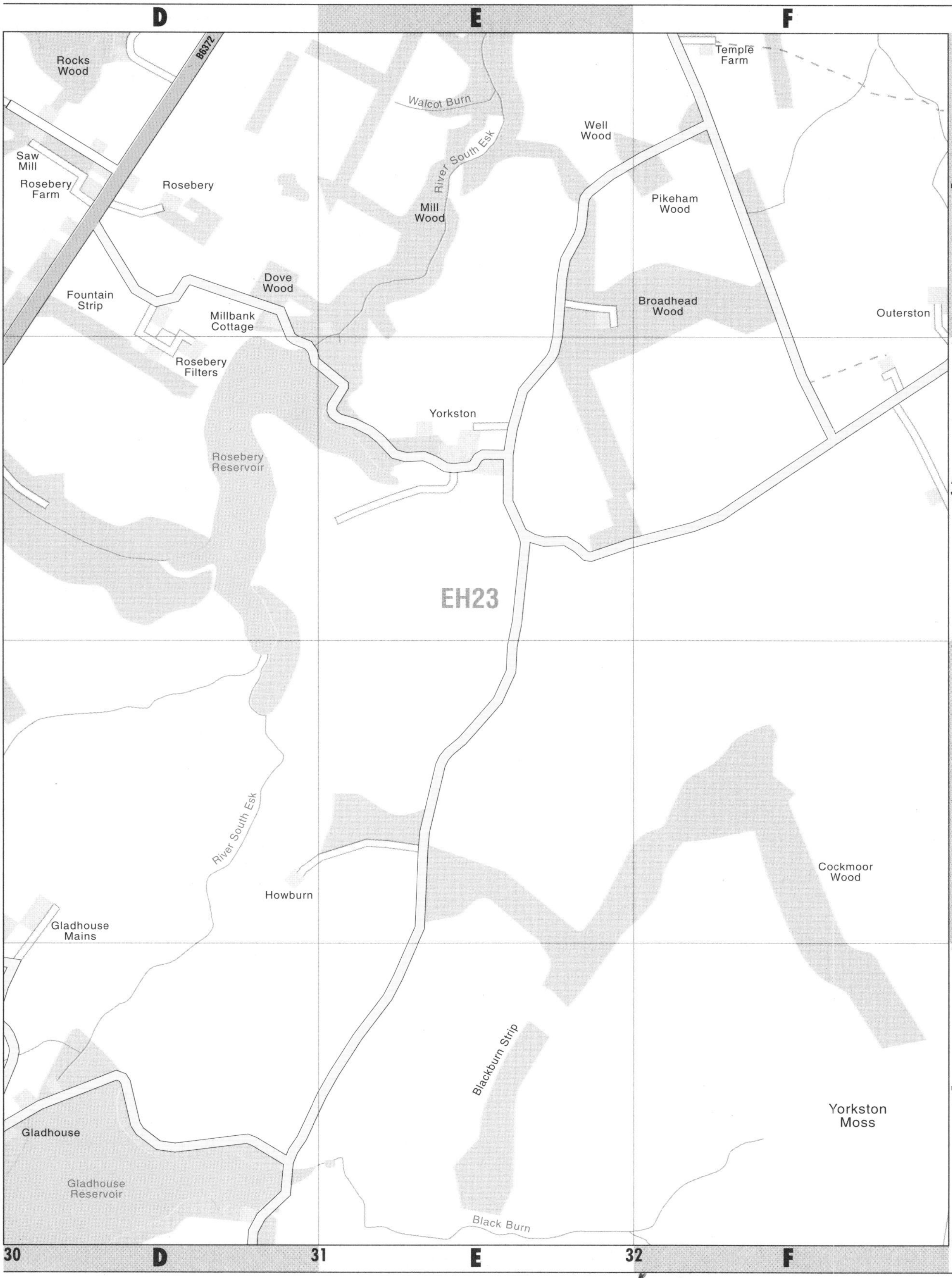

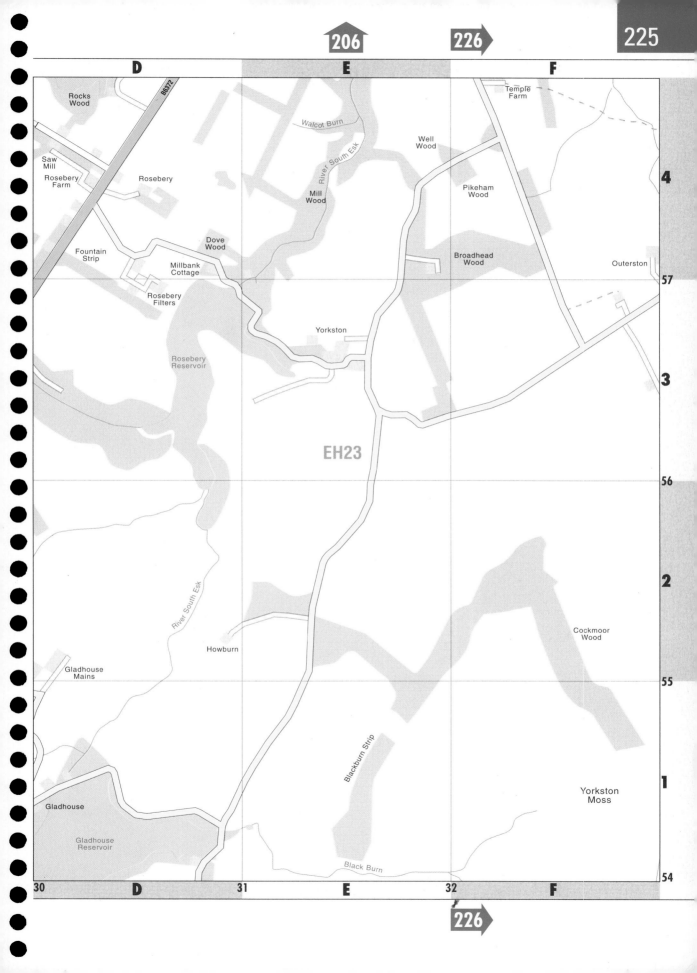

D

E

F

Rocks
Wood

B6372

Walcot Burn

River South Esk

Well
Wood

Temple
Farm

4

Saw
Mill

Rosebery
Farm

Rosebery

Mill
Wood

Pikeham
Wood

Outerston

Fountain
Strip

Dove
Wood

Millbank
Cottage

Broadhead
Wood

57

Rosebery
Filters

Yorkston

Rosebery
Reservoir

3

EH23

56

River South Esk

2

Cockmoor
Wood

Howburn

Gladhouse
Mains

55

Blackburn Strip

Gladhouse

Yorkston
Moss

1

Gladhouse
Reservoir

Black Burn

54

30

D

31

E

32

F

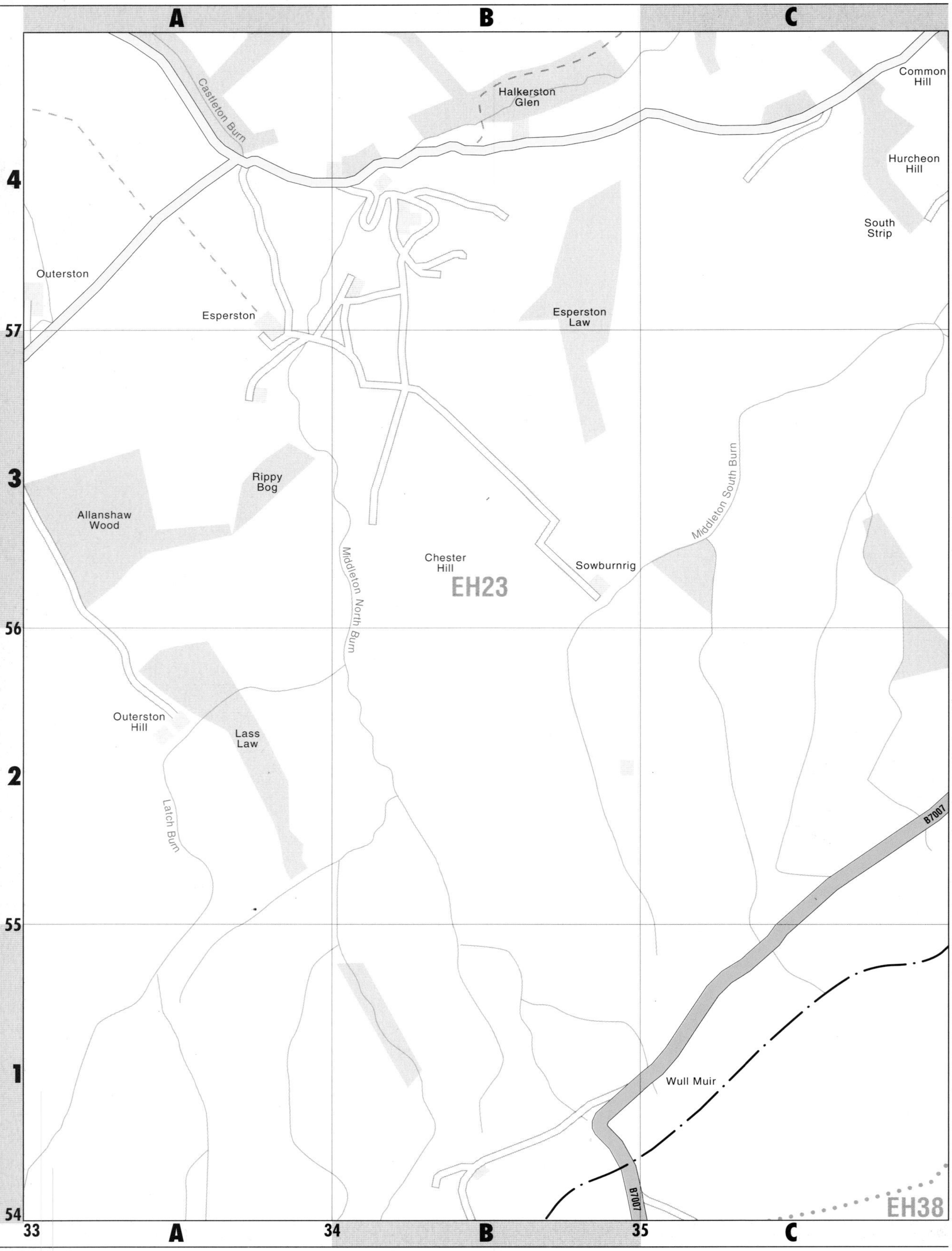
A
B
C
Halkerston Glen
Castleton Burn
Common Hill
Hurcheon Hill
South Strip
4
Outerston
Esperston
Esperston Law
57
3
Rippy Bog
Allanshaw Wood
Middleton South Burn
Chester Hill
Sowburnrig
EH23
Middleton North Burn
56
Outerston Hill
Lass Law
2
Latch Burn
B7007
55
1
Wull Muir
B7007
EH38
54
33
34
35

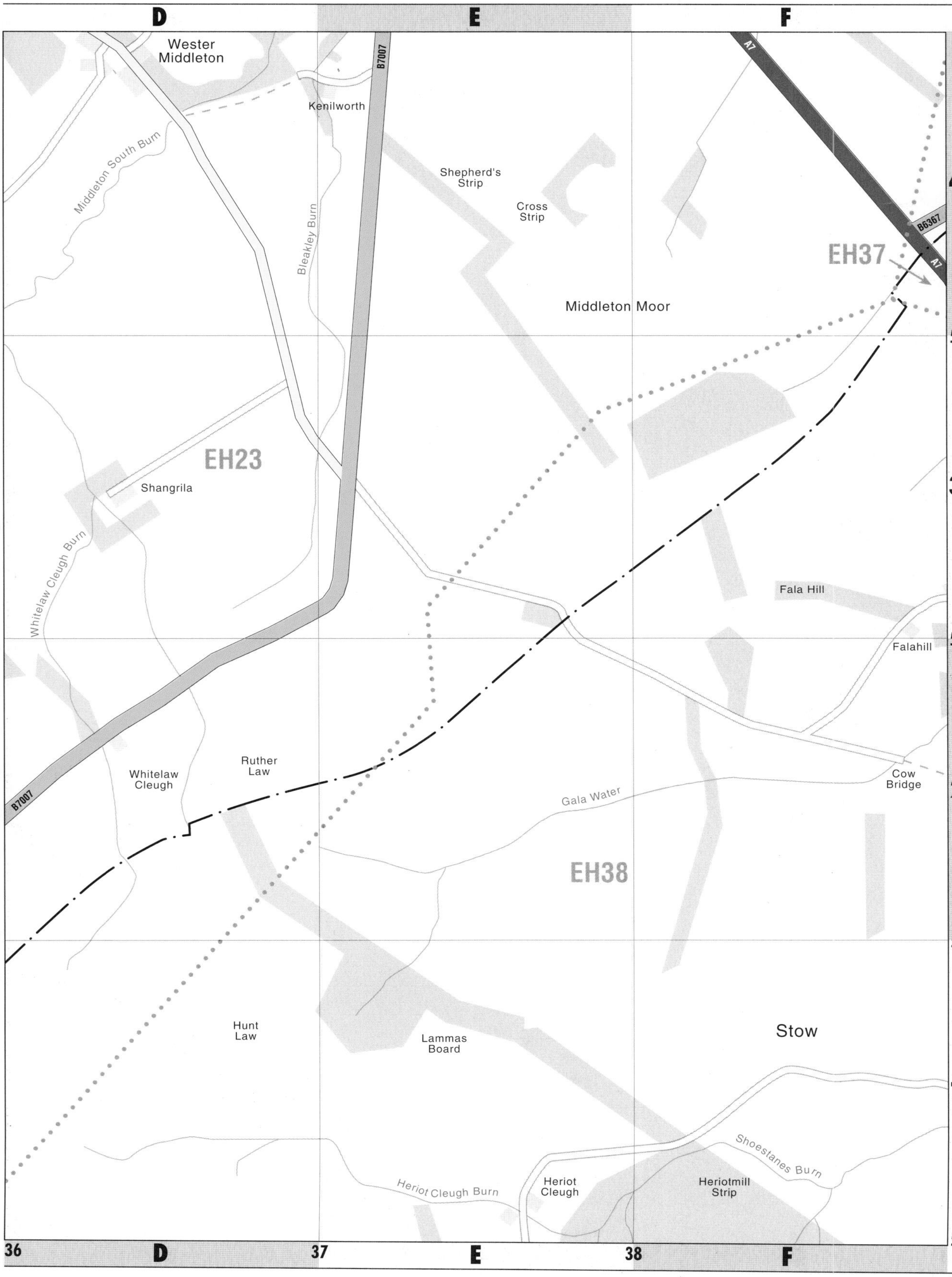

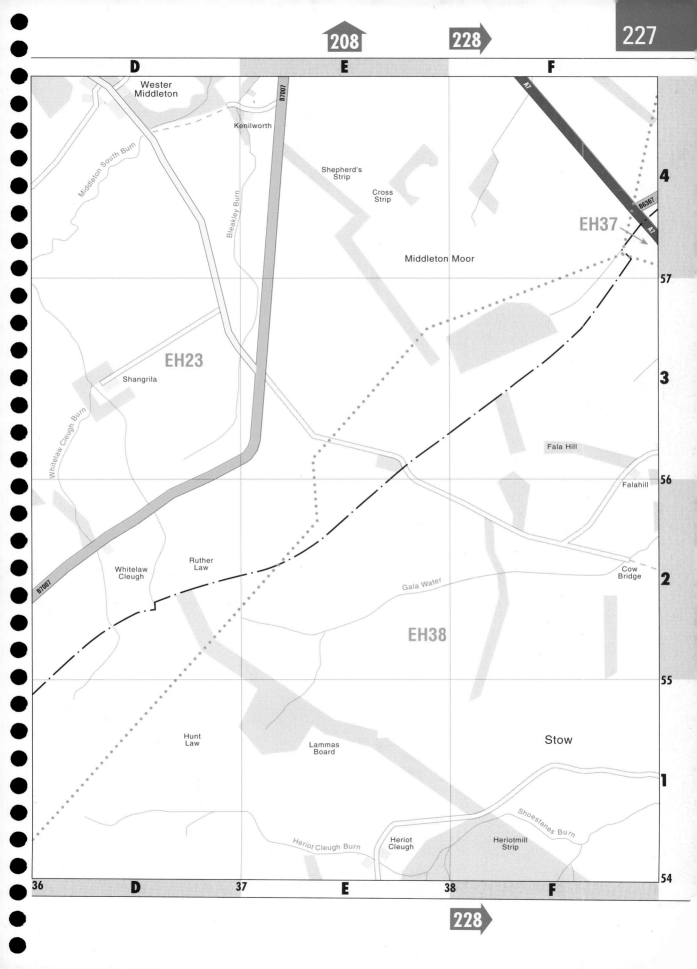

D
E
F

Wester Middleton

B7007

Kenilworth

A7

4

Shepherd's Strip

Cross Strip

B6367

EH37

Middleton Moor

A7

57

EH23

3

Shangrila

Fala Hill

Middleton South Burn

Bleakley Burn

56

Falahill

Whitelaw Cleugh Burn

Ruther Law

Whitelaw Cleugh

Cow Bridge

2

B7007

Gala Water

EH38

55

Hunt Law

Stow

Lammas Board

1

Shoestanes Burn

Heriot Cleugh Burn

Heriot Cleugh

Heriotmill Strip

54

36
D
37
E
38
F

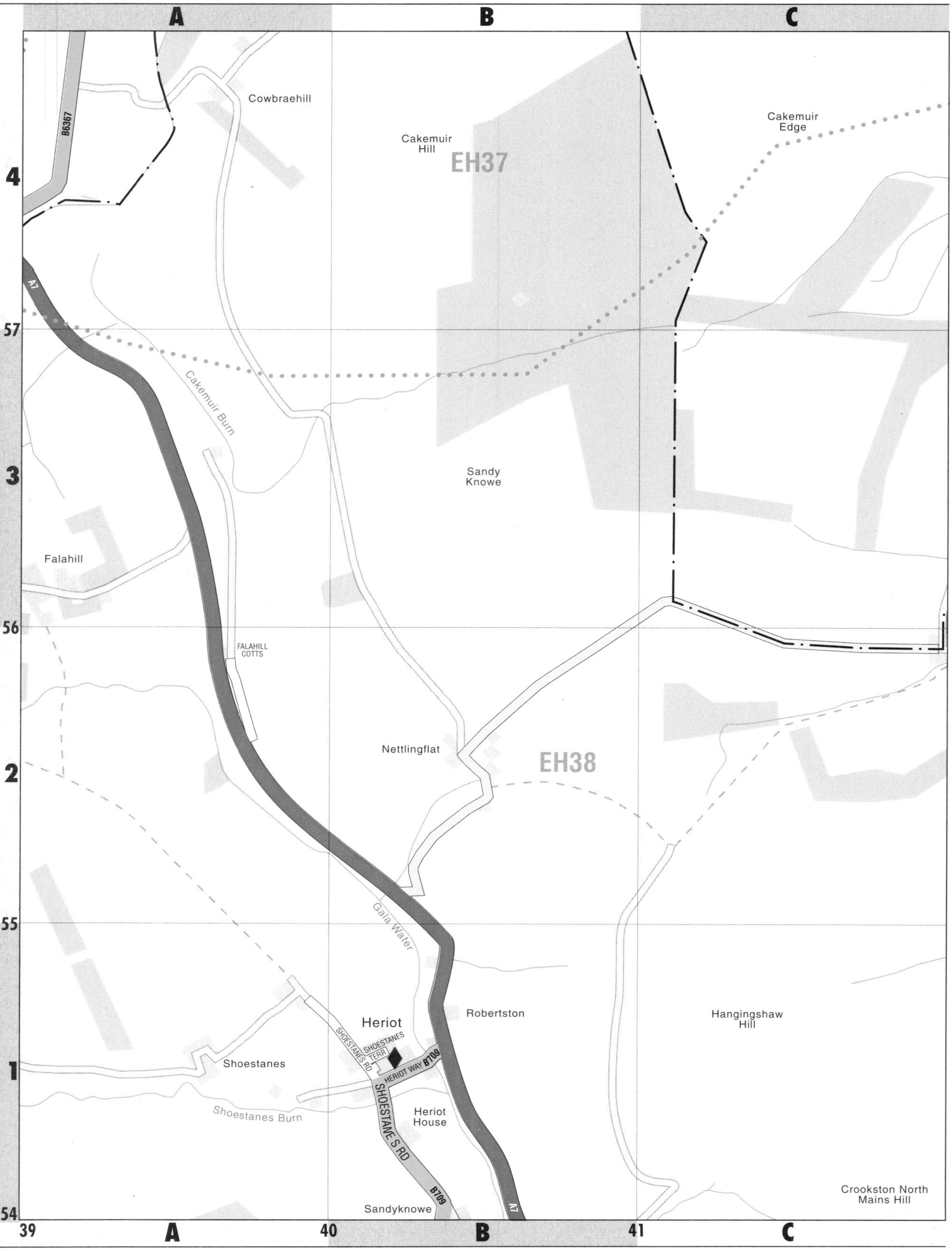

A B C

4

57

3

56

2

55

1

54

39 A 40 B 41 C

Cowbraehill

Cakemuir Hill

Cakemuir Edge

EH37

Cakemuir Burn

Sandy Knowe

Falahill

FALAHILL COTTS

Nettlingflat

EH38

Gala Water

Heriot

Robertston

Hangingshaw Hill

Shoestanes

SHOESTANES TERR.

HERIOT WAY B709

Heriot House

Shoestanes Burn

SHOESTANES RD

SHOESTANES RD

B709

A7

Sandyknowe

Crookston North Mains Hill

B6367

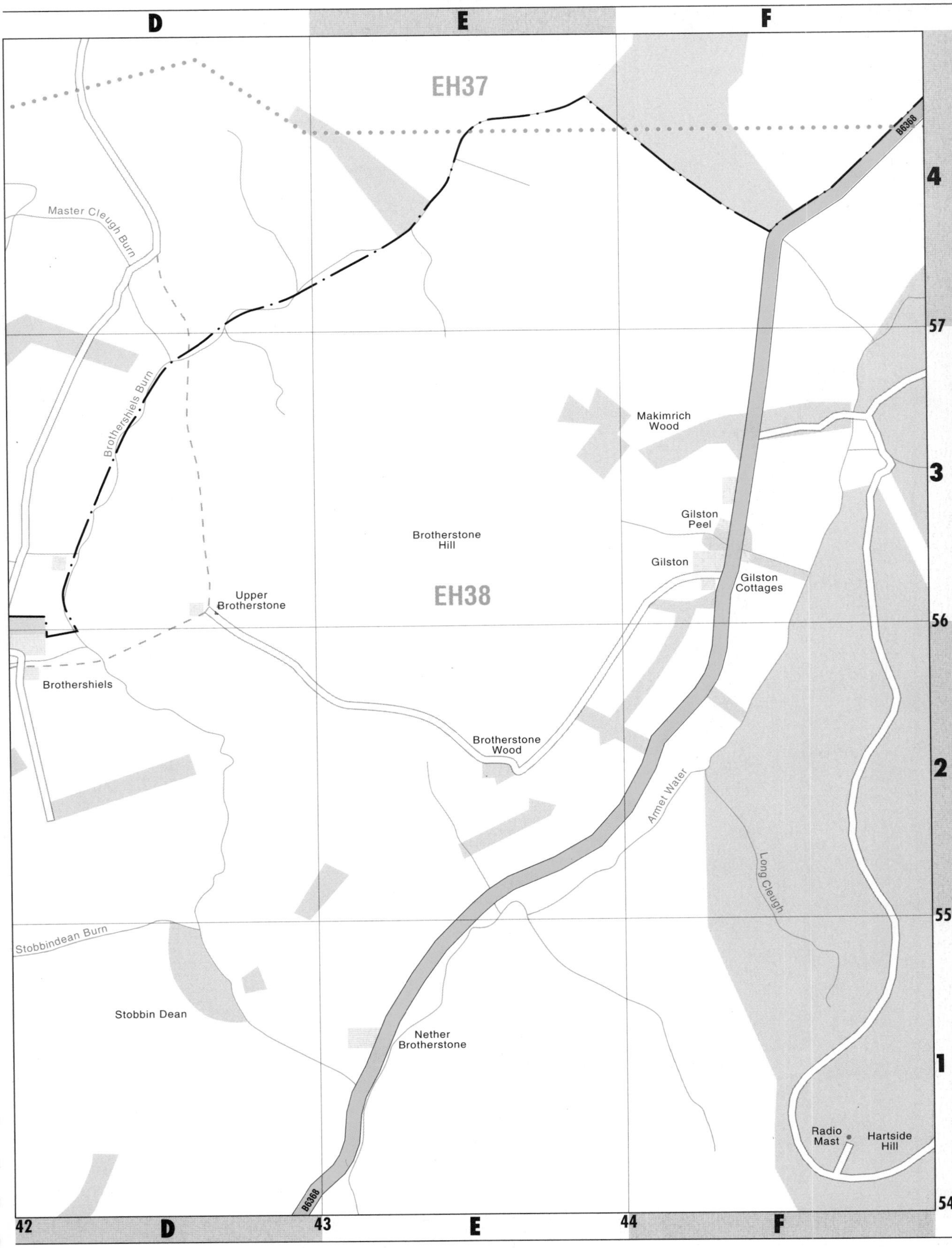

EH37

EH38

B6368

Master Cleugh Burn

Brothershiels Burn

Makimrich Wood

Brotherstone Hill

Gilston Peel

Gilston

Gilston Cottages

Upper Brotherstone

Brothershiels

Brotherstone Wood

Arnet Water

Long Cleugh

Stobbindean Burn

Stobbin Dean

Nether Brotherstone

Radio Mast

Hartside Hill

B6368

D   E   F

42   D   43   E   44   F

54   1   55   2   56   3   57   4

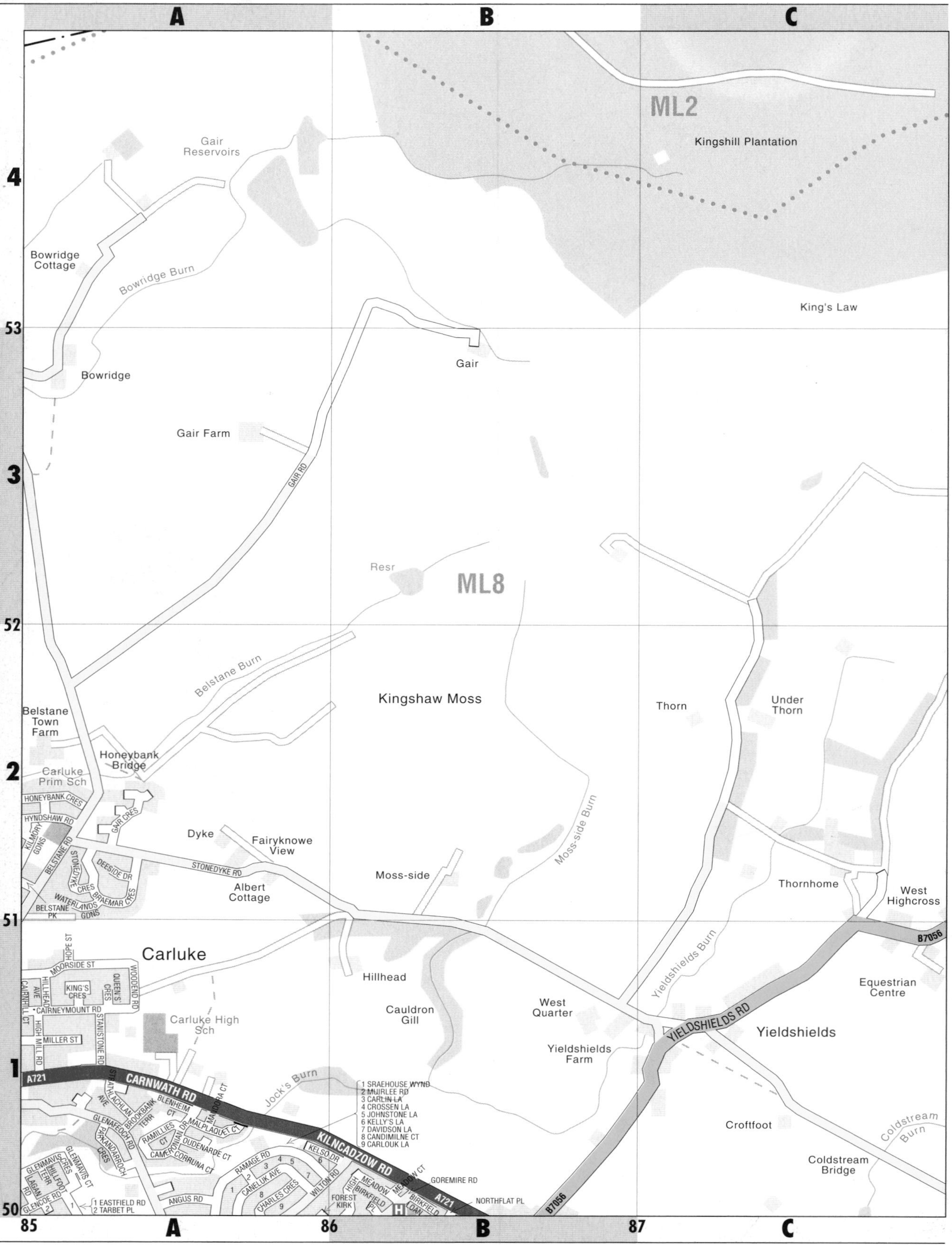

ML2

Kingshill Plantation

King's Law

A

B

C

4

Gair
Reservoirs

Bowridge
Cottage

Bowridge Burn

53

Bowridge

Gair

Gair Farm

GAIR RD

3

Resr

ML8

52

Belstane Burn

Kingshaw Moss

Thorn

Under
Thorn

Belstane
Town
Farm

Honeybank
Bridge

Carluke
Prim Sch

2

HONEYBANK CRES

HYNDSHAW RD

KILMORY GDNS

BELSTANE RD

GAIR CRES

STONEDYKE

DEESIDE DR

Dyke

Fairyknowe
View

STONEDYKE RD

Moss-side

Moss-side Burn

Thornhome

West
Highcross

WATERLANDS GDNS

CRES

BRAEMAR CRES

Albert
Cottage

Yieldshields Burn

BELSTANE
PK

51

ROE ST

Carluke

Hillhead

B7056

MOORSIDE ST

KING'S CRES

WOODEND ST

QUEEN'S CRES

Cauldron
Gill

West
Quarter

YIELDSHIELDS RD

Equestrian
Centre

HILLHEAD AVE

CAIRNEYMOUNT RD

Carluke High
Sch

Yieldshields
Farm

Yieldshields

CALDER ST

HIGH MILL RD

MILLER ST

STANISTONE RD

1

A721

CARNWATH RD

Jock's Burn

1 SRAEHOUSE WYND
2 MUIRLEE RD
3 CARLIN LA
4 CROSSEN LA
5 JOHNSTONE LA
6 KELLY'S LA
7 DAVIDSON LA
8 CANDIMILNE CT
9 CARLOUK LA

Croftfoot

Coldstream
Burn

ST ATHELACHAN AVE

BROOKBANK TERR

BLENHEIM CT

MALPLAQUET CT

MANORIA CT

KILNCADZOW RD

KELSO DR

Coldstream
Bridge

GLENAFEOCH RD

RAMILLIES DR

OUDENARDE CT

RAMAGE RD

CAMEL UK AVE

WILTON RD

GOREMIRE RD

A721

GLENMAVIS DR

HILLTOP

GLENANDERROCH

CORRUNA CT

CHARLES CRES

MEADOW

BIRKFIELD

B7056

GLENCOE RD

GLENMAVIS TERR

ANGUS RD

FOREST
KIRK

HIGH BIRKFIELD

NORTHFLAT PL

1 EASTFIELD RD
2 TARBET PL

H

50

85

A

86

B

87

C

213

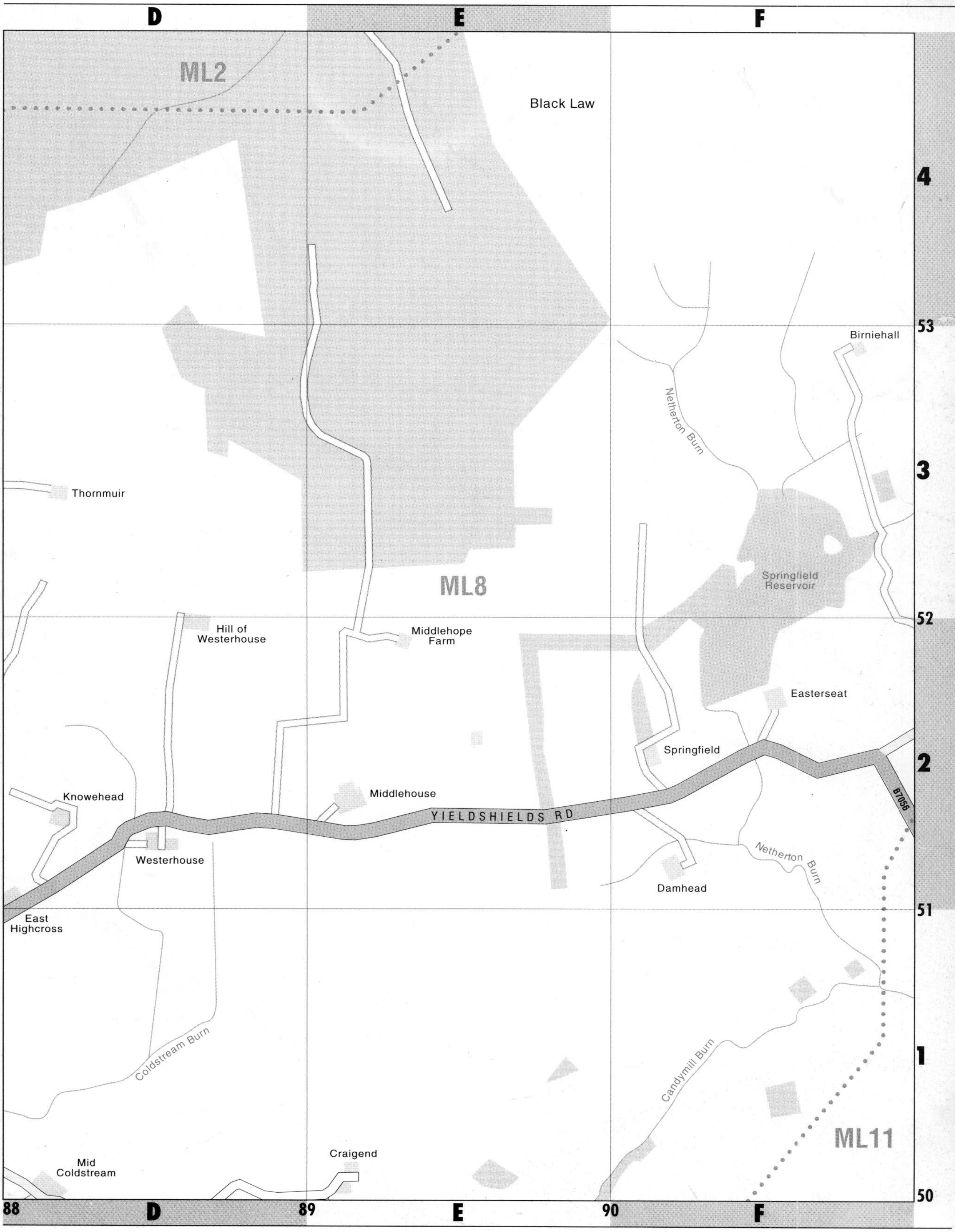
D
E
F
ML2
Black Law
4
53
Birniehall
Netherton Burn
3
Thornmuir
Springfield
Reservoir
ML8
52
Hill of
Westerhouse
Middlehope
Farm
Easterseat
Springfield
2
Knowehead
Middlehouse
YIELDSHIELDS RD
B7056
Westerhouse
Netherton Burn
Damhead
East
Highcross
51
Coldstream Burn
1
Candymill Burn
ML11
Craigend
Mid
Coldstream
50
88
89
90

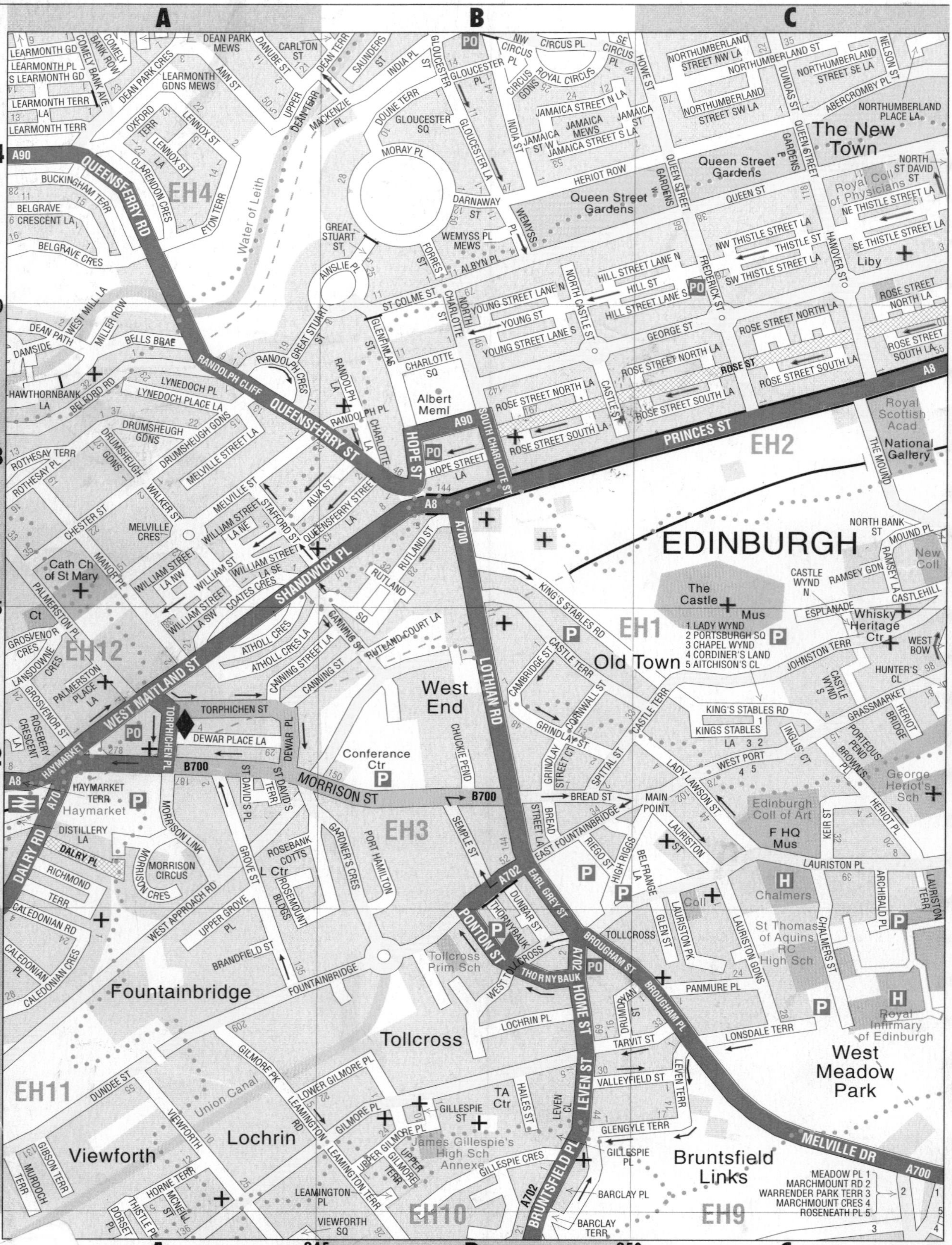

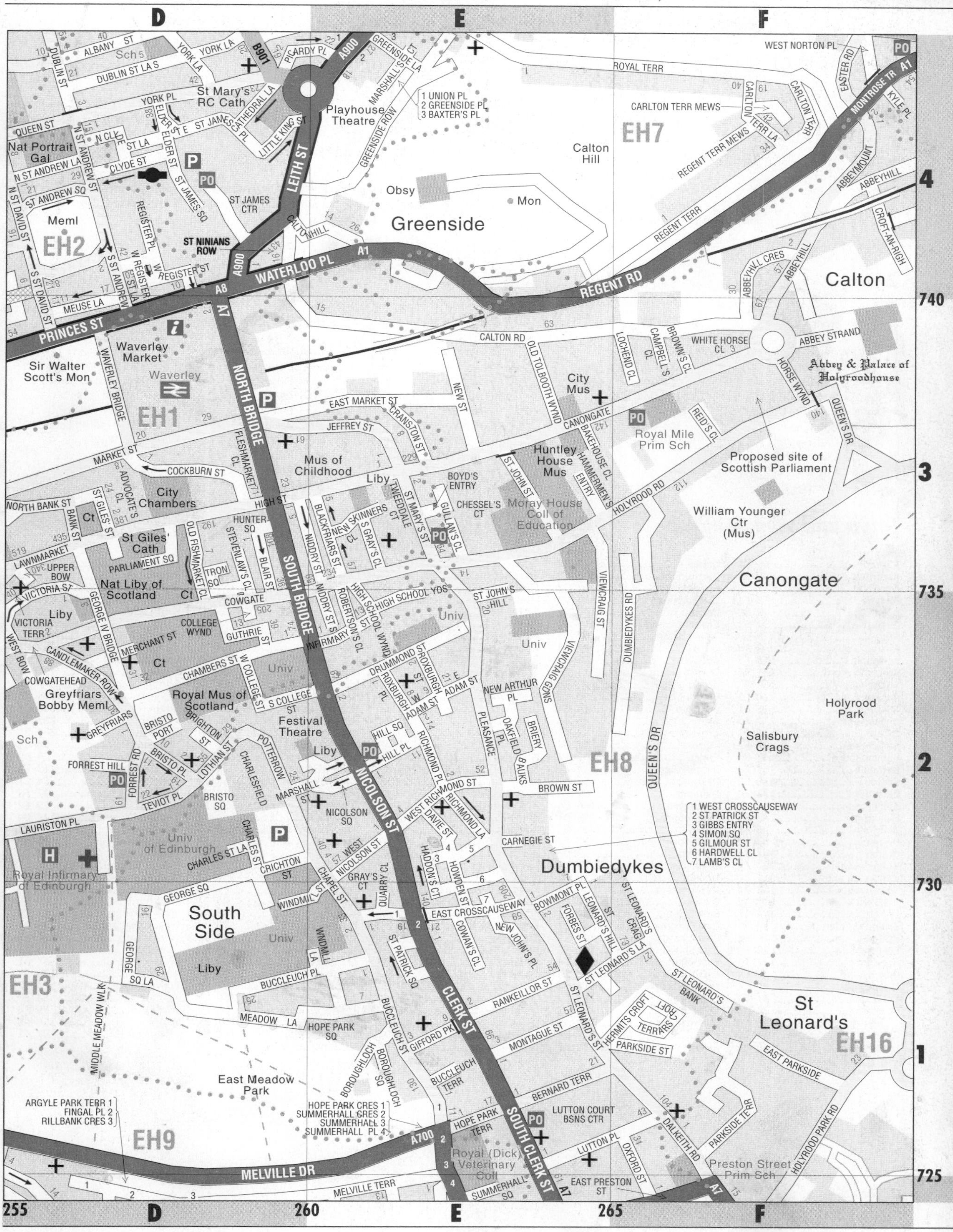

Index

Street names are listed alphabetically and show the locality, the Postcode District, the page number and a reference to the square in which the name falls on the map page

Mansefield Ct 2 Bathgate EH48 .. 145 D4

Full street name
This may have been abbreviated on the map

Location Number
If present, this indicates the street's position on a congested area of the map instead of the name

Town, village or locality in which the street falls.

Postcode District for the street name

Page number of the map on which the street name appears

Grid square in which the centre of the street falls

Schools, hospitals, sports centres, railway stations, shopping centres, industrial estates, public amenities and other places of interest are also listed. These are highlighted in magenta

Abbreviations used in the index

App	Approach	Cl	Close	Espl	Esplanade	Mdw	Meadows	S	South
Arc	Arcade	Comm	Common	Est	Estate	N	North	Sq	Square
Ave	Avenue	Cnr	Corner	Gdns	Gardens	Orch	Orchard	Strs	Stairs
Bvd	Boulevard	Cotts	Cottages	Gn	Green	Par	Parade	Stps	Steps
Bldgs	Buildings	Ct	Court	Gr	Grove	Pk	Park	St	Street, Saint
Bsns Pk	Business Park	Ctyd	Courtyard	Hts	Heights	Pas	Passage	Terr	Terrace
Bsns Ctr	Business Centre	Cres	Crescent	Ho	House	Pl	Place	Tk	Track
Bglws	Bungalows	Dr	Drive	Ind Est	Industrial Estate	Prec	Precinct	Trad Est	Trading Estate
Cswy	Causeway	Dro	Drove	Intc	Interchange	Prom	Promenade	Wlk	Walk
Ctr	Centre	E	East	Junc	Junction	Ret Pk	Retail Park	W	West
Circ	Circle	Emb	Embankment	La	Lane	Rd	Road	Yd	Yard
Cir	Circus	Ent	Enterprise	Mans	Mansions	Rdbt	Roundabout		

Town and village index

Abercorn	66 C1	Carnock	27 E3	Fallin	8 B2	Longcroft	57 D2
Aberdour	49 E4	Carrington	206 B3	Fauldhouse	193 F3	Longniddry	98 C3
Aberlady	71 E2	Charlestown	45 D2	Fishcross	5 F2	Longridge	170 B1
Addiewell	171 F1	Clackmannan	11 D2	Fordell	31 D3	Macmerry	129 E3
Airth	22 B2	Cockburnspath	140 C2	Forrestfield	141 D2	Maddiston	83 D3
Allandale	57 E1	Cockenzie and		Forth	215 D1	Manor Powis	3 D2
Alloa	10 B3	Port Seton	97 E3	Garvald	134 B1	Mayfield	183 F3
Alva	5 D3	Comrie	26 B4	Gifford	163 F2	Menstrie	3 F3
Armadale	143 F3	Cousland	158 B3	Gladsmuir	130 A4	Mid Calder	148 B2
Athelstaneford	101 F4	Cowdenbeath	13 F2	Gorebridge	207 E4	Musselburgh	126 B4
Auchendinny	180 B1	Cowie	20 B4	Gowkhall	27 F4	New Winton	129 D2
Auchengray	216 C1	Craigiehall	90 B2	Grangemouth	61 E4	Newbridge	119 D3
Auchtertool	15 D1	Crombie	44 B4	Gullane	52 A1	Newcraighall	125 F2
Avonbridge	112 A3	Crossford	28 A1	Haddington	101 E1	Newmills	26 B1
Balerno	151 E1	Crossgates	30 C3	Haggs	57 D2	Newton	88 A4
Bankhead	57 F3	Culross	42 B4	Halbeath	30 A3	Newtongrange	183 D3
Bannockburn	7 F1	Currie	152 A2	Harthill	168 C3	North Berwick	54 B4
Bathgate	145 E4	Dalgety Bay	48 B2	Hartwood	191 D1	North Middleton	207 F2
Bilston	180 C3	Dalkeith	157 D1	Heriot	228 B1	North Queensferry	68 B3
Blackburn	171 E4	Dalmeny	89 F4	High Bonnybridge	58 B2	Oakley	26 C4
Blackness	65 F2	Danderhall	156 B4	High Valleyfield	26 A1	Ormiston	159 F4
Blackridge	142 B2	Dechmont	116 B1	Hillend	47 F2	Pathhead	185 D3
Blairhall	26 A4	Denny	36 C1	Howgate	204 A1	Pencaitland	160 B4
Bo'ness	63 F4	Dennyloanhead	57 E3	Humbie	187 D1	Penicuik	203 E2
Bolton	162 C4	Dirleton	53 D2	Innerwick	108 A1	Philpstoun	86 B3
Bonnybridge	58 A3	Drem	73 D2	Inverkeithing	47 D1	Plean	20 B2
Bonnyrigg and		Dunbar	78 B1	Kelty	12 B4	Polbeth	172 C3
Lasswade	182 B4	Dunfermline	29 E3	Kincardine	23 F2	Polmont	61 F1
Borthwick	208 A2	Dysart	18 A4	Kinghorn	35 D2	Prestonpans	96 C1
Breich	194 C3	East Calder	148 C2	Kingseat	12 A1	Pumpherston	148 A4
Bridge of Allan	2 A4	East Fortune	74 A2	Kirkcaldy	17 E2	Queensferry	89 D4
Bridgend	86 B2	East Linton	103 E4	Kirkliston	89 D1	Ratho	119 E1
Brightons	82 B4	East Saltoun	161 F2	Kirknewton	149 F1	Ratho Station	119 E3
Broxburn	117 E3	East Whitburn	170 C4	Larbert	38 A1	Redding	61 E1
Burntisland	50 C4	Easthouses	183 D4	Laurieston	61 D2	Reddingmuirhead	82 A4
Cairneyhill	27 E1	Ecclesmachan	116 C4	Letham	39 E4	Rosewell	181 E1
California	81 F3	Edinburgh	123 E3	Limekilns	45 F2	Roslin	180 C2
Cambus	9 D4	Edinburgh	232 C3	Linlithgow	85 D3	Rosyth	46 C2
Cambusbarron	6 B3	Elphinstone	128 A1	Livingston	147 E3	Salsburgh	167 D2
Cardenden	15 E4	Fala	210 B4	Loanhead	181 D4	Seafield	146 A1
Carluke	230 A1	Falkirk	60 B3	Lochgelly	14 B4	Shieldhill	81 E3
						Shotts	191 F3
						Silverburn	202 C3
						Skinflats	39 F2
						Slamannan	110 A3
						South Alloa	9 F2
						Spittal	99 E4
						Spott	106 B2
						Standburn	82 B1
						Stenhousemuir	38 B2
						Stenton	104 C1
						Stirling	7 E4
						Stoneyburn	171 E1
						Straiton	155 D1
						Tarbrax	217 F2
						Temple	206 B1
						Threemiletown	86 C2
						Throsk	9 D2
						Torphichen	113 F3
						Torryburn	26 C1
						Torwood	37 F3
						Townhill	29 E4
						Tranent	128 B4
						Tullibody	4 B2
						Tyninghame	76 A2
						Uphall	116 C2
						Uphall Station	117 D1
						Wallacestone	82 A4
						Wallyford	127 E3
						Wellwood	29 D4
						West Barns	77 F1
						West Calder	172 B1
						West Linton	220 A1
						Westfield	112 C3
						Westquarter	61 D1
						Whitburn	170 A4
						Whitecraig	126 C1
						Whitecross	83 F3
						Whitekirk	75 F4
						Wilkieston	150 A3
						Winchburgh	87 F1

1st St FK3 62 A4
2nd St
Grangemouth, Chemical Works EH51 62 B3
Grangemouth, Oil Refinery FK3 62 A4
3rd St
Grangemouth, Chemical Works EH51 62 B3
Grangemouth, Oil Refinery FK3 62 A4
4th St
Grangemouth, Chemical Works EH51 62 C3
Grangemouth, Oil Refinery FK3 62 A4
5th St
Grangemouth, Chemical Works EH51 62 C3
Grangemouth, Oil Refinery FK3 62 A4
6th St
Grangemouth, Oil Refinery FK9 41 D1
Grangemouth, Chemical Works EH51 62 C3
7th St
Grangemouth, Chemical Works EH51 62 C3
Grangemouth, Oil Refinery FK3 62 B4
8th St FK3 62 B4
A1 Ind Pk EH15 125 D4
Abbey Craig Rd FK10 5 D1
Abbey Cres EH39 54 A4
Abbey Ct EH39 54 A4
Abbey La EH8 94 A1
Abbey Mains EH41 101 F2
Abbey Mews EH39 54 A4
Abbey Mill FK8 7 E4
Abbey & Palace of Holyroodhouse EH8 233 F3
Abbey Park Pl KY12 29 D2
Abbey Rd Dalkeith EH22 157 D1
Dunbar EH42 78 B1
North Berwick EH39 54 A4
Stirling FK8 2 B1
Abbey Rd Pl FK8 7 E4
Abbey St Edinburgh EH7 94 A1
High Valleyfield KY12 26 A1
Abbey Strand EH8 233 F3
Abbey View
Crossford KY12 28 B1
Dunfermline KY11 29 F1
Abbeygrange EH22 183 D3
Abbeyhill EH8 233 F4
Abbeyhill Cres EH8 233 F4
Abbeyhill Prim Sch EH7 94 A1
Abbeymount EH8 233 F4
Abbot Rd FK7 7 E2
Abbot St KY12 29 D2
Abbot's View EH41 101 D1
Abbots Cl EH39 53 F4
Abbots Ct FK2 60 B4
Abbots Mill KY2 17 D2
Abbots Moss Dr FK1 59 F1
Abbots Rd Falkirk FK2 60 B4
Grangemouth FK3 61 E4
Abbots View FK2 61 F2
Abbots Wlk KY2 16 C2
Abbotsford Cres
Edinburgh EH10 123 D2
Shotts ML7 191 F3
Abbotsford Ct EH10 123 D2
Abbotsford Dr
Grangemouth FK3 61 F3
Laurieston FK2 61 D2
Abbotsford Gdns FK2 39 D1
Abbotsford Pk
Edinburgh EH10 123 D2
North Berwick EH39 53 F4
Abbotsford Pl FK8 2 B1
Abbotsford Rd EH39 53 F4
Abbotsford Rise EH54 148 A1
Abbotsford St FK2 60 A4
Abbotsgrange Rd FK3 61 F4
Abbotshall Rd KY2, KY1 17 D1
Abbotsinch Ind Est FK3 61 F4
Abbotsinch Rd FK3 61 F4
Abbotsview Junc EH41 101 D1
Abden Ave KY3 35 D2
Abden Ct KY3 35 D2
Abden Pl KY3 35 D2
Abel Pl KY11 29 F2
Abercairney Cres FK1 82 C3
Abercairney Pl FK3 61 F4
Abercorn Ave EH8 124 B4
Abercorn Cres EH8 124 B4
Abercorn Ct EH8 124 B4
Abercorn Dr EH8 124 B4
Abercorn Gdns EH8 94 B1
Abercorn Gr EH8 124 B4
Abercorn Pl EH52 87 F1
Abercorn Prim Sch EH52 87 E4
Abercorn Rd EH8 124 B4
Abercorn Terr EH15 125 E4
Abercrombie Pl FK11 3 F3
Abercrombie St FK1 59 F3
Abercromby Dr FK9 2 A4
Abercromby Pl
Edinburgh EH3 232 C4
Stirling FK8 7 D4
Tullibody FK10 4 A1
Aberdour Castle KY3 49 E4
Aberdour Cres KY11 29 E1
Aberdour Pl KY11 29 E1
Aberdour Prim Sch KY3 49 E4
Aberdour Rd
Burntisland KY3 33 E1
Dunfermline KY11 29 F1
Aberdour Sta KY3 49 E4
Aberlady Prim Sch EH32 71 E2
Aberlady Rd EH41 100 C1
Aberlour St KY11 46 C2
Abinger Gdns EH12 122 B4
Abington Rd KY12 28 C1
Aboyne Ave FK9 2 B2
Aboyne Gdns KY2 16 C4
Academy La EH20 181 E4
Academy Pk EH6 94 A2
Academy Pl FK7 7 F1
Academy Rd
Bo'ness EH51 64 A4
Stirling FK8 7 D4
Academy Sq KY11 45 E2
Academy St Alloa FK10 9 F4
Armadale EH48 143 F3
Bathgate EH48 145 D3
Edinburgh EH6 94 A2
Academy The EH51 64 A4
Acheson Dr EH32 127 F4
Achray Ct FK10 10 B3
Achray Dr FK9 2 A2
Ackam Path EH20 180 C4
Acorn Cres FK5 38 B1
Acre Rd EH51 64 B3
Acredale Bathgate EH48 145 D3
Linlithgow EH49 85 D3
Acredales EH41 131 F4
Acredales Wlk EH41 131 F4
Adam Cres FK5 38 C1
Adam Pl KY5 14 A4
Adam Smith Cl KY1 17 E2
Adam Smith Ct KY1 17 E2
Adam Sq EH54 173 E3
Adam St FK2 60 B3
Adambrae Rd EH54 173 E4
Adambrae Rdbt EH54 173 E4
Adams Loan FK2 39 D1
Adams Well EH13 153 E4
Adamson Ave KY2 17 D3
Adamson Cres KY12 29 E3
Adamson Pl FK9 2 A2
Adamson Rd KY5 14 A4
Addiebrownhill EH55 171 E1
Addiebrownhill Sta EH55 171 F1
Addiewell Prim Sch & St Thomas's RC Prim Sch EH55 171 E1
Addiston Cres EH14 151 E2
Addiston Farm Rd EH28 120 A1
Addiston Gr EH14 151 E2
Addiston Pk EH14 151 E2
Adelaide St EH54 148 A3
Adelphi Gr 1 EH15 125 D4
Adelphi Pl EH15 125 D4
Admiral Terr EH10 123 D3
Admiralty Rd
Inverkeithing KY11 47 E2
Rosyth KY11 46 B2
Admiralty St EH6 93 F3
Advocate's Cl EH1 233 D3
Affleck Ct EH12 121 D4
Affric Dr FK2 39 E1
Affric Loan ML7 191 F3
Affric Way KY12 28 A1
Afton Ct Dechmont EH52 116 B1
Stirling FK7 7 E3
Afton Dr FK6 57 E4
Afton Gr KY11 29 F3
Afton Pl EH5 93 D3
Afton Terr EH5 93 D3
Agnew Terr EH6 93 E3
Ailsa Gr KY2 16 C4
Ainslie Gdns FK2 61 F2
Ainslie Pl EH3 232 B4
Airdrie Rd ML6 141 D2
Airlie Dr FK2 61 F1
Airth Dr FK7 7 E2
Airth Prim Sch FK2 22 C2
Airthrey Ave FK9 2 A3
Airthrey Dr FK5 39 D2
Airthrey Rd FK9 2 B3
Aitchison Dr FK5 38 A2
Aitchison's Cl EH1 232 C2
Aitchison's Pl EH15 95 D1
Aitken Cres FK7 7 D1
Aitken Ct KY1 17 D1
Aitken Dr Slamannan FK1 110 A3
Whitburn EH47 170 A4
Aitken Gdns FK1 59 F3
Aitken Orr Dr EH52 117 F3
Aitken Rd FK1 59 E3
Aitken St KY1 17 F4
Aitken Terr FK1 59 E3
Akarit Rd FK5 38 C1
Alan Breck Gdns EH4 91 E1
Alan Wlk FK9 1 C4
Albany Ind Est KY12 29 D2
Albany La EH1 93 E1
Albany St
Dunfermline KY12 29 D2
Edinburgh EH1 233 D4
Albert Ave FK3 61 F4
Albert Cl EH21 127 D3
Albert Cres EH21 127 D3
Albert Pl Stirling FK8 7 D4
Wallyford EH21 127 D3
Albert Rd Edinburgh EH6 94 A3
Falkirk FK1 60 A2
Harthill ML7 168 C3
Albert St Edinburgh EH7 93 F2
Rosyth KY11 46 C2
Albert Terr
Edinburgh EH10 123 D2
Musselburgh EH21 126 C3
Alberta Ave EH54 147 F2
Albion Pl EH7 94 A1
Albion Rd EH7 94 A1
Albion Terr EH7 94 A1
Albyn Cotts EH52 117 F3
Albyn Dr EH54 173 F3
Albyn Ind Est EH52 117 F4
Albyn Pl Broxburn EH52 117 F3
Edinburgh EH2 232 B4
Albyn Terr EH52 117 F3
Alcorn Rigg EH14 152 C4
Alcorn Sq EH14 152 C4
Alder Gr Dunfermline KY11 29 E1
Westquarter FK2 61 D2
Alderbank
Livingston EH54 147 F3
Penicuik EH26 203 F2
Alderbank Gdns EH11 122 C2
Alderbank Pl EH11 122 C2
Alderbank Terr EH11 122 C2
Alderston Dr KY12 29 E3
Alderston Mdws EH41 100 C1
Alderston Pl EH41 100 C1
Alderston Rd EH41 131 F4
Alderstone Bsns Pk EH54 147 E1
Alderstone Rd
Livingston, Adambrae EH54 173 E4
Livingston, Howden EH54 147 E2
Alemoor Cres EH7 94 A2
Alemoor Pk EH7 94 A2
Alexander Ave
Falkirk FK2 60 C3
Grangemouth FK3 61 E3
Alexander Dr
Bridge of A FK9 2 A4
Edinburgh EH11 122 B3
Prestonpans EH32 127 F4
Alexander McLeod Pl FK7 8 C2
Alexander Pk EH52 117 F2
Alexander Pl KY11 46 C2
Alexander Rd ML7 191 E3
Alexander St
Cowdenbeath KY4 13 E3
Dysart KY1 18 A4
Uphall EH52 117 D2
Alexander The Third St KY3 34 C1
Alexandra Bsns Pk EH28 119 D3
Alexandra Dr Alloa FK10 9 F4
Bathgate EH48 145 F3
Alexandra Pl FK8 2 B1
Alexandra St
Dunfermline KY12 29 D3
Kirkcaldy KY1 17 E3
Alford Ave KY2 16 C4
Alfred Pl EH9 123 F2
Alice Cox Wlk KY11 29 E1
Alice Gr KY4 30 C3
Aline Ct KY11 48 A1
Alison Gr KY12 28 A1
Alison St KY1 17 D1
Allan Barr Ct FK1 60 A1
Allan Cres Denny FK6 36 B2
Dunfermline KY11 29 F1
Allan Ct FK3 40 C1
Allan Park Cres EH14 122 B2
Allan Park Dr EH14 122 B1
Allan Park Gdns EH14 122 B1
Allan Park Loan EH14 122 B1
Allan Park Rd EH14 122 B1
Allan Pk
Cowdenbeath KY4 13 D1
Kirkliston EH29 89 D1
Stirling FK8 7 D4
Allan Rd EH47 169 F3
Allan St EH4 93 D1
Allan Terr EH22 157 D2
Allan's Prim Sch FK8 7 D4
Allanbank Rd FK5 38 B1
Allandale Cotts FK4 57 E1
Allanfield EH7 93 F1
Allanton Prim Sch ML7 212 A4
Allanton Rd ML7 191 E1
Allanvale Rd FK9 1 C4
Allanwater Gdns FK9 2 A4
Allanwood Ct FK9 2 A4
Allardice Cres KY2 16 B3
Allen Gr KY12 26 C4
Aller Pl EH54 147 D2
Allermuir Ave EH25 180 C3
Allermuir Rd EH13 153 D3
Allison Pl EH29 89 D1
Alloa Acad FK10 9 F4
Alloa Rd
Clackmannan FK10 11 D2
Falkirk FK2 39 D2
Fishcross FK10 5 E2
Manor Powis FK9 3 D2
Stenhousemuir FK5 38 C2
Tullibody FK10 4 B2
Alloa Twr FK10 10 A3
Alloway Cres FK4 57 F3
Alloway Dr FK7 20 B4
Alloway Loan 5 EH16 124 A1
Alma La FK2 60 A3
Alma St Falkirk FK2 60 A3
Inverkeithing KY11 47 E2
Alma Terr FK2 60 A3
Almond Ave HE12 119 F4
Almond Bank Cotts EH4 91 D3
Almond Cres EH19 182 A3
Almond Ct
East Whitburn EH47 170 C4
Edinburgh EH16 124 C2
Falkirk FK2 60 C4
Livingston EH54 148 B2
Stirling FK7 7 E3
Almond East Rd EH54 148 A3
Almond Gn EH12 121 D4
Almond Gr
East Calder EH53 148 C3
Queensferry EH30 89 E4
Almond Intc EH54 148 A2
Almond Pk EH54 148 A2
Almond Pl KY1 17 E4
Almond Rd
Blackburn EH47 145 E1
Dunfermline KY11 29 F1
Falkirk FK2 60 C4
Livingston EH54 148 A2
Maddiston FK2 83 E3
Newbridge HE12 119 F4
Almond S EH53 148 B3
Almond Side EH53 148 B2
Almond Sq
East Whitburn EH47 170 C4
Edinburgh EH12 121 D4
Almond St
Grangemouth FK3 61 E3
Whitburn EH47 170 A4
Almond Terr
Harthill ML7 168 B3
Whitecross EH49 83 F3
Almond View EH47 146 A1
Almond West Rd EH54 148 A2
Almondbank Prim Sch EH54 148 A3
Almondbank Terr EH11 122 C2
Almondell & Calder Wood Ctry Pk EH52 149 D4
Almondell Ct EH52 117 F3
Almondell Rd EH52 117 F3
Almondell Terr EH53 148 C3
Almondhill Rd EH29 89 D1
Almondside
Kirkliston EH29 89 D1
Livingston EH54 147 F1
Almondvale Ave EH54 147 F1
Almondvale Bsns Pk EH54 147 E1
Almondvale Bvd EH54 147 F1
Almondvale Cres EH54 147 E1
Almondvale Ctr EH54 147 F1
Almondvale Dr EH54 147 F1
Almondvale E EH54 147 F1
Almondvale N
Livingston EH54 147 E1
Livingston EH54 147 F1
Almondvale Parkway EH54 147 F1
Almondvale Pl EH54 147 E1
Almondvale Rd EH54 147 F1
Almondvale Rdbt EH54 147 F1
Almondvale S EH54 147 F1
Almondvale Stad (Livingston FC) EH54 147 E1
Almondvale Stadium Rd EH54 147 E1
Almondvale W EH54 147 E1
Almondvale Way EH54 147 E1
Almondview EH54 147 F1
Alness Gr KY12 28 C1
Alnwickhill Cres EH16 154 C3
Alnwickhill Ct EH16 154 C3
Alnwickhill Dr EH16 154 C3
Alnwickhill Gdns EH16 154 C3
Alnwickhill Gr EH16 154 C3
Alnwickhill Loan EH16 154 C3
Alnwickhill Pk EH16 155 D3
Alnwickhill Rd EH16 155 D4
Alnwickhill Terr EH16 154 C3
Alnwickhill View EH16 154 C3
Alpha St EH51 62 C3
Alva Acad FK12 5 D4
Alva Glen FK12 5 D4
Alva Ind Est FK12 5 E3
Alva Pl EH7 94 A1
Alva Prim Sch FK12 5 D3
Alva St EH2 232 A3
Alyth Dr FK2 62 A1
Amberley Path FK3 61 F3
Ambrose Rise EH54 148 A1
Amisfield Pk EH41 132 B4
Amisfield Pl
Haddington EH41 132 B4
Longniddry EH32 98 C3
Amos Path EH20 180 C4
Amulree Pl EH51 63 E4
Ancrum Bank EH22 156 C1
Ancrum Rd EH22 156 C1
Anderson Ave
Armadale EH48 143 F2
Crossford KY12 28 A1
Newtongrange EH22 183 D3
Anderson Cres FK1 81 F3
Anderson Dr
Cowdenbeath KY4 13 D1
Denny FK6 36 C1
Falkirk FK2 39 D1
Anderson Gdns FK2 82 C3
Anderson Gn EH54 147 E4
Anderson La
Kincardine FK10 23 F2
Rosyth KY11 46 B3
Anderson Park Rd FK6 36 C1
Anderson Pl
Edinburgh EH6 93 F3
Stirling FK7 7 D2
Anderson St
Bonnybridge FK4 58 A3
Dysart KY1 18 A4
Kirkaldy KY1 17 F3
Anderson Terr FK4 57 D2
Andrew Ave EH48 145 F3
Andrew Cres FK5 38 B2
Andrew Ct EH26 203 F4
Andrew Dodd's Ave EH22 183 F4
Andrew St KY5 14 A3
Andrew Wood Ct EH6 93 E3
Angle Park Terr EH11 122 C3
Angres Ct EH22 156 B4
Angus Rd ML8 230 A1
Angus St EH51 63 E3
Ann St EH4 232 A4
Annabel Ct KY11 47 E1
Annan Ct FK1 60 B1
Annandale St EH7 93 F1
Annandale Street La EH7 93 F1
Anne Dr Bridge of A FK9 2 A3
Stenhousemuir FK5 38 C2
Anne St Alloa FK10 9 F4
Bathgate EH48 145 F3
Penicuik EH26 203 F4
Annet Rd FK6 57 E3
Annfield Edinburgh EH6 93 E3
Tranent EH33 128 C3
Annfield Ct EH33 129 E3
Annfield Dr FK7 7 E3
Annfield Farm Rd KY11 47 D4
Annfield Gdns FK8 7 D3
Annfield St EH6 93 E3
Anson Ave FK1 59 F2
Antigua St 7 EH1 93 F1
Antonine Ct EH51 63 E3
Antonine Gdns FK1 59 E3
Antonine Gr FK4 57 F2
Antonine Prim Sch FK4 58 A2
Antonine St FK1 59 E3
Appin Cres
Dunfermline KY12 29 D2
Kircaldy KY2 16 C4
Appin Gr FK2 61 F2
Appin Terr
Edinburgh EH14 122 B2
Shotts ML7 192 A2
Appleton Parkway EH54 146 C2
Appleton Parkway Rdbt EH54 146 C3
Arboretum Ave EH4 93 D1
Arboretum Pl EH3 93 D2
Arboretum Rd EH3 93 D2
Arbroath Cres FK9 2 A2
Arbuthnot Rd EH20 181 E4
Arbuthnot St FK1 59 F3
Arcade FK8 7 D4
Archers Ave FK7 7 E2
Archers Ct EH31 52 A1
Archibald Pl EH3 232 C2
Archibald Russell Ct FK2 61 F1
Ard Ct FK3 61 E3
Ardeer Pl KY11 29 E1
Arden St EH9 123 E3
Ardgowan Pl ML7 191 F3
Ardmillan Pl EH11 122 C3
Ardmillan Terr EH11 122 C3
Ardmore Dr FK2 62 A1
Ardshiel Ave EH4 91 E1
Ardvreck Pl FK2 39 D2
Argyle Cres EH15 125 E4
Argyle Park Terr EH9 233 D1
Argyle Pl
Bonnyrigg and Lasswade EH19 181 F3
Edinburgh EH9 123 E3
Argyle St EH6 93 F3
Argyll Ave Falkirk FK2 60 B3
Stirling FK8 2 B1
Argyll Pl FK10 10 B4
Argyll St FK10 10 B4
Arkaig Dr KY12 28 B1
Arkwright Ct EH39 54 A4
Armadale Acad EH48 143 E3
Armadale Prim Sch EH48 143 F3
Armadale Rd EH47 170 A4
Armine Pl EH26 204 A4
Armour Ave FK7 20 B4
Arneil Pl FK2 82 B4
Arnot St FK1 60 B2
Arnothill FK1 60 A2
Arnothill Bank 6 FK1 60 A2
Arnothill Ct FK1 59 F3
Arnothill Gdns FK1 60 A2
Arnothill La FK1 59 F2
Arnothill Mews FK1 60 A2
Arnott Gdns EH14 122 A1
Arnprior Rd EH23 207 E4
Arns Gr FK10 9 F4
Arnswell FK10 5 E1
Arran EH54 146 C3
Arran Cres KY2 16 C4
Arran Ct Alloa FK10 10 A3
Grangemouth FK3 61 E3
Arran Pl EH15 125 E4
Arran Terr FK1 59 E2
Arras Gr EH26 204 A4
Arrol Cres FK10 10 B4
Arrol Pl EH30 89 E4
Arrol Sq EH54 146 C3
Arthur Pl KY4 13 E2

Arthur St
Cowdenbeath KY4 13 E2
Dunfermline KY12 29 D3
Edinburgh EH6 93 F2
Arthur Street La EH6 93 F2
Arthur View Cres
EH22 156 A4
Arthur View Terr EH22 156 A4
Arthur's Dr FK5 38 C1
Artillery Pk EH41 101 D1
Ash Braes FK10 23 E2
Ash Gr Alloa FK10 10 B3
Bathgate EH48 145 F3
Blackburn EH47 171 E4
Carnock KY12 27 E3
Cowdenbeath KY4 13 D2
Dunfermline KY11 46 B4
Dunbar EH42 78 A1
Livingston EH54 148 A3
Stenhousemuir FK5 38 C1
Westquarter FK2 61 D1
Ash La EH20 180 C4
Ash Terr FK8 6 C3
Ashbank Ct EH48 144 C3
Ashbank Terr EH53 148 C2
Ashbrae Gdns FK7 7 D1
Ashburnham Gdns EH30 68 B1
Ashburnham Rd EH30 89 E4
Ashfield Ct EH42 78 C1
Ashfield Pl EH42 78 C1
Ashgrove Mayfield EH22 183 F4
Musselburgh EH21 126 C3
Ashgrove Pl EH21 126 C3
Ashgrove View EH21 126 C3
Ashley Ct EH49 84 C3
Ashley Dr EH11 122 C2
Ashley Gdns EH11 122 C2
Ashley Gr EH11 122 C2
Ashley Hall Gdns EH49 84 C3
Ashley Pl EH6 93 F2
Ashley Rd FK2 61 F2
Ashley St FK4 57 F3
Ashley Terr Alloa FK10 10 A4
Edinburgh EH11 122 C2
Ashton Gr EH16 124 A1
Ashville Terr EH6 94 A2
Asquith St KY1 17 D2
Assembly St EH6 94 A3
Assynt Bank EH26 204 A3
Astley Ainslie Hospl
EH9 123 E2
Atheling Gr EH30 89 E4
Athelstaneford Prim Sch
EH39 101 F4
Athol Cres FK2 61 D2
Athol Pl Bathgate EH48 145 D4
Dunfermline KY12 29 E2
Athol Terr EH48 145 D4
Atholl Cres EH3 232 A2
Atholl Crescent La
EH3 232 A2
Atholl Pl FK8 1 C1
Atholl Terr KY2 16 B4
Atrium Way FK4 58 A2
Attlee Cres EH22 183 F3
Auchengray Rd ML11 216 C1
Auchentyre Pl FK2 39 E2
Auchinbaird FK10 5 E1
Auchingane EH10 153 F3
Auchinleck Ct EH6 93 E3
Auchterderran Rd KY5 14 A4
Auchtertool Prim Sch
KY2 15 D1
Auction Mart EH41 101 D1
Audenhard Terr EH47 171 E1
Auld Brig Rd FK10 10 A3
Auld Orch EH19 182 B4
Auldcathie Pl EH52 87 F2
Auldgate EH29 89 D1
Auldhame Cotts EH39 55 F3
Auldhill Ave EH49 86 B2
Auldhill Cotts EH49 86 B2
Auldhill Cres EH49 86 B2
Auldhill Dr EH49 86 B2
Auldhill Entry EH49 86 B2
Auldhill Pl EH49 86 B2
Auldhill Rd EH49 86 B2
Auldhill Terr EH49 86 B2
Ava St KY1 17 D1
Avalon Gdns EH49 84 B4
Aven Dr FK2 60 C2
Avenue Pk Bridge of A FK9 1 C4
Mid Calder EH53 148 B2
Avenue Pk W EH53 148 B2
Avenue Rd
Cockenzie & Port Seton
EH32 97 E2
Dalkeith EH22 156 C1
Avenue The Bridge of A FK9 2 A4
Currie EH14 151 F4
Dalgety Bay KY11 47 F2
Falkirk FK2 39 E1
Gifford EH41 163 F2
Gorebridge EH23 183 D1
Lochgelly KY5 14 B4
Philpstoun EH49 86 B4
Whitburn EH47 170 A3
Avenue Villas EH4 92 C1
Averton ML11 215 D1
Avon Ct FK1 60 B1
Avon Dr EH49 84 B4
Avon Gr
Edinburgh EH4 91 D2
Penicuik EH26 204 A3
Avon Pk FK1 111 F3
Avon Pl Bo'ness EH51 63 F4
Edinburgh EH4 91 D2
Avon Rd Bathgate EH48 145 D4
Edinburgh EH4 91 D2
Grangemouth FK3 62 B4
Whitecross EH49 83 F3
Avon St Denny FK6 36 B2
Grangemouth FK3 40 A1
Avon Terr FK1 112 A3
Avonbank Ave FK3 61 F3
Avonbridge Prim Sch
FK1 112 A3
Avonbridge Rd FK1 110 A4
Avondale Cres EH48 143 F3
Avondale Dr EH48 143 F3
Avondale Pl EH3 93 D1
Avondale Rd FK2 62 A2
Avondhu Gdns FK3 61 F4
Avonlea Dr FK2 61 F2
Avonmill Rd EH49 84 B4
Avonmill View EH49 84 B4
Avonside Dr FK6 36 B3
Avontoun Cres EH49 84 A3
Avontoun Pk EH49 84 B3
Ayres Wynd EH32 96 C1
Aytoun Cres KY3 33 F1
Aytoun Gr KY12 28 C3

Baads Rd ML7 141 E1
Baberton Ave EH14 152 B3
Baberton Cres EH14 152 C3
Baberton Loan EH14 152 B3
Baberton Mains EH14 152 B4
Baberton Mains Ave
EH14 152 B4
Baberton Mains Bank
EH14 152 B4
Baberton Mains Brae
EH14 152 B4
Baberton Mains Cres
EH14 152 B4
Baberton Mains Ct
EH14 152 B4
Baberton Mains Dell
EH14 152 B4
Baberton Mains Dr
EH14 152 B4
Baberton Mains Gdns
EH14 152 B4
Baberton Mains Gn
EH14 152 B4
Baberton Mains Gr
EH14 152 B4
Baberton Mains Hill
EH14 152 B4
Baberton Mains Lea
EH14 152 B4
Baberton Mains Loan
EH14 152 C4
Baberton Mains Pk
EH14 152 B4
Baberton Mains Pl
EH14 152 B4
Baberton Mains Rise
EH14 152 B4
Baberton Mains Row
EH14 152 B4
Baberton Mains Terr
EH14 152 B4
Baberton Mains View
EH14 152 C4
Baberton Mains Way EH14 152 B4
Baberton Mains Wood
EH14 152 B4
Baberton Mains Wynd
EH14 152 B4
Baberton Pk EH14 152 B3
Bablins Wynd EH41 163 F2
Back Cswy KY12 42 B4
Back Dean EH4 122 C4
Back O' Hill Ind Est FK8 2 A1
Back O' Hill Rd FK8 2 A1
Back O' Yds KY11 47 D1
Back Rd Alva FK12 4 C4
Dunbar EH42 78 A1
Back St KY12 42 B4
Back Station Rd EH49 85 D4
Backdean Rd EH22 156 A4
Backlee EH16 155 D3
Backmarch Cres KY11 46 C2
Backmarch Rd KY11 46 C2
Backwood Ct FK10 10 C3
Badallan Pl EH47 193 F3
Badger Wood EH52 116 B1
Baileyfield Cres EH15 125 D4
Baileyfield Est EH15 125 D4
Baileyfield Rd
Edinburgh, Northfield
EH15 94 C1
Edinburgh, Portobello
EH15 125 D4
Bailie Gr EH15 125 D3
Bailie Path EH15 125 D3
Bailie Pl EH15 125 D3
Bailie Terr EH15 125 D3
Bailielands EH49 85 E4
Baillie St EH47 170 A4
Baillie Waugh Rd FK7 7 E2
Bain Sq EH54 147 E1
Bain St KY5 14 A4
Baingle Brae FK10 4 A2
Baingle Cres FK10 4 A2
Bainsford Prim Sch
FK2 60 A4
Baird Ave EH12 122 B3
Baird Dr Armadale EH48 143 F4
Edinburgh EH12 122 B3
Baird Gdns EH12 122 B3
Baird Gr EH12 122 B3
Baird Rd Armadale EH48 143 F4
Livingston EH54 147 D1
Ratho EH28 119 E2
Baird St FK1 59 E3
Baird Terr
Edinburgh EH12 122 B3
Haddington EH41 100 C1
Harthill ML7 168 B3
Baird's Way EH19 182 B3
Bairns Ford Ave FK2 60 A4
Bairns Ford Ct FK2 60 A4
Bairns Ford Dr FK2 60 A4
Bakehouse Cl EH8 233 E3
Baker St Bo'ness EH51 63 F3
Stirling FK8 7 D4
Balantyne Pl EH54 147 D2
Balbakie Rd ML7 168 C3
Balbardie Ave EH48 145 D4
Balbardie Cres EH48 145 D4
Balbardie Prim Sch
EH48 145 D4
Balbardie Rd EH48 145 D3
Balbirnie Pl EH12 122 C4
Balcarres Ct EH10 123 D1
Balcarres Pl EH21 126 B4
Balcarres Rd EH21 126 B4
Balcarres St EH10 123 D1
Balcastle Rd FK1 110 A3
Balderston Gdns EH16 124 A1
Balderstone's Wynd
EH39 54 B4
Baldridgeburn KY12 28 C3
Baldwin Cres KY2 17 D3
Balerno High Sch EH14 151 E1
Balfour Cres Larbert FK5 38 B1
Plean FK7 20 B2
Balfour Ct
Dunfermline KY12 29 E3
Edinburgh EH12 91 D1
Balfour Pl EH6 93 F2
Balfour St Alloa FK10 10 B4
Bannockburn FK7 7 E1
Bonnybridge FK4 57 F3
Edinburgh EH6 93 F2
Kirkaldy KY2 17 D3
North Berwick EH39 54 B4
Stirling FK8 1 C1
Balfour Terr EH26 180 A1
Balfour's Sq EH33 128 B3
Balfron Loan EH4 91 E1
Balgone Barns Cotts
EH39 54 B1
Balgreen Ave EH12 122 A3
Balgreen Gdns EH12 122 A3
Balgreen Pk EH12 122 A3
Balgreen Prim Sch
EH11 122 B3
Balgreen Rd EH12 122 A3
Baliol St KY3 34 C1
Ballantyne Rd EH6 93 F3
Ballast Bank KY11 47 E1
Ballater Dr FK9 2 B2
Ballencrieff Mill EH48 144 C4
Ballencrieff Toll EH48 114 A1
Ballengeich Pass FK8 2 A1
Ballengeich Rd FK8 1 C1
Ballingry La KY5 14 A4
Ballingry St KY5 14 A4
Balloch Rd ML7 191 F3
Balm Well Ave EH16 155 D3
Balm Well Gr EH16 155 D3
Balm Well Pk EH16 155 D3
Balm Well Terr EH16 155 D3
Balmoral Dr Falkirk FK1 59 F2
Kircaldy KY2 16 B3
Balmoral Gdns
Brightons FK2 82 B4
Livingston EH54 173 E3
Balmoral Pl
Edinburgh EH3 93 D1
Stenhousemuir FK5 38 C2
Stirling FK8 7 D4
Balmoral Rd EH51 62 C3
Balmoral St FK1 59 F2
Balmuir Rd EH48 144 C4
Balmulzier Rd FK1 110 A4
Balnacraig KY12 28 A1
Balquhatstone Cres
FK1 110 A3
Balquhidderock FK7 7 E2
Balsusney Rd KY2 17 D3
Baltic St EH6 94 A3
Balure Cres FK7 8 B2
Balvaird Pl KY12 29 E3
Balwearie Cres KY2 17 D1
Balwearie Gdns KY2 16 C1
Balwearie Rd KY2 17 D1
Balwearie Sch KY2 17 D1
Banchory Cotts KY3 34 C3
Banchory Pl FK10 4 B2
Banchory Prim Sch FK10 4 B2
Bancroft Ave EH54 147 F2
Bandeath Ind Est FK7 9 D3
Bandeath Rd FK7 8 C3
Bandon Ave KY1 17 F4
Bangholm Ave EH5 93 D3
Bangholm Bower Ave
EH5 93 D3
Bangholm Gr EH5 93 E3
Bangholm Loan EH5 93 E3
Bangholm Pk EH5 93 D3
Bangholm Pl EH5 93 D3
Bangholm Rd EH5 93 D3
Bangholm Terr EH3 93 D2
Bangholm View EH5 93 E3
Bangly Brae EH41 100 A2
Bangor Rd EH6 93 F3
Bangour Village Hospl
EH52 116 A1
Bank Pl ML7 191 F2
Bank Rd East Linton EH40 103 F4
Harthill ML7 168 C3
Bank St Alloa FK10 10 A3
Edinburgh EH1 233 D3
Falkirk FK1 60 A3
Grangemouth FK3 40 A1
Inverkeithing KY11 47 E1
Kincardine FK10 23 E2
Kirkaldy KY1 17 F4
Lochgelly KY5 14 A4
Mid Calder EH53 148 B2
North Berwick EH39 54 A4
Penicuik EH26 203 F2
Slamannan FK1 110 A3
Stirling FK8 7 D4
Whitburn EH47 170 A4
Bankhead Ave EH11 121 E2
Bankhead Broadway
EH11 121 D2
Bankhead Cotts EH40 75 E3
Bankhead Cres FK4 57 E3
Bankhead Crossway N
EH11 121 D2
Bankhead Crossway S
EH11 121 E1
Bankhead Dr EH11 121 D2
Bankhead Gr EH30 68 B1
Bankhead Ind Est EH11 121 E2
Bankhead Medway
EH11 121 E2
Bankhead Pl EH11 121 E1
Bankhead Rd
Fishcross FK10 5 E2
Queensferry EH30 89 F4
Bankhead St EH11 121 E1
Bankhead Terr EH11 121 D1
Bankhead Way EH11 121 D1
Bankhill Ct FK3 61 E3
Bankpark Brae EH33 128 A4
Bankpark Cres EH33 128 A4
Bankpark Gr EH33 128 B4
Bankside FK2 60 B4
Bankside Ct FK6 36 C1
Bankside Ind Est FK2 60 B4
Bankton Brae EH54 173 F4
Bankton Ct
Livingston EH54 174 A4
Tranent EH33 128 B3
Bankton Dr EH54 173 F4
Bankton Gdns EH54 174 A4
Bankton Glade EH54 174 A4
Bankton Gn EH54 173 F4
Bankton Gr EH54 174 A4
Bankton Junc EH33 128 B4
Bankton Pk E EH54 148 A1
Bankton Pk W EH54 148 A1
Bankton Prim Sch
EH54 147 F1
Bankton Rd EH54 173 E4
Bankton Sq EH54 173 F4
Bankton Terr EH33 128 A4
Bankton Way EH54 173 F4
Bankton Wlk EH54 173 F4
Bannerman Ave KY11 47 E2
Bannerman St KY12 29 D3
Bannoch Brae KY12 29 E2
Bannock Rd FK7 8 B2
Bannockburn High Sch
FK7 7 E1
Bannockburn Hospl FK7 19 F4
Bannockburn Prim Sch
FK7 7 F1
Bannockburn Rd
Cowie FK7 20 B4
Stirling FK7 7 E2
Bannockburn Station Rd
FK7 8 A2
Bantaskin Prim Sch FK1 59 F2
Bantaskine Dr FK1 59 F2
Bantaskine Gdns FK1 59 F2
Bantaskine St FK1 59 F2
Banton Pl FK4 58 A2
Baptie Pl EH51 63 F3
Barassie Dr KY2 17 D4
Barbauchlaw Ave EH48 143 F3
Barbour Ave FK7 7 E2
Barbour Gr KY12 28 C3
Barclay Pl EH10 232 B1
Barclay Rd KY3 34 C2
Barclay St KY4 13 D2
Barclay Terr EH10 232 B1
Barclay Way EH54 147 F4
Barham Rd KY11 46 B1
Barkhill Rd EH49 84 C3
Barkin Ct FK1 60 A1
Barlaw Gdns EH48 144 A3
Barleyhill FK4 58 A3
Barleyknowe Cres
EH23 183 E1
Barleyknowe Gdns
EH23 183 E1
Barleyknowe La EH23 183 E1
Barleyknowe Pl EH23 183 E1
Barleyknowe Rd EH23 183 E1
Barleyknowe St EH23 183 E1
Barleyknowe Terr EH23 183 E1
Barn Park Cres EH14 152 C4
Barn Pk EH14 152 C4
Barn Rd FK8 7 D4
Barnbougle Ride EH30 90 B4
Barnego Rd FK6 36 B2
Barnes Gn EH54 147 E4
Barnet Cres KY1 17 D1
Barnhill Dr FK10 4 B1
Barnhill Pl KY11 48 B2
Barnhill Rd KY11 48 B2
Barns Ct EH47 170 C4
Barns Ness Terr EH42 139 D4
Barns Pk KY11 48 A1
Barnsdale Rd FK7 7 D2
Barnshot Rd EH13 153 D3
Barnton Ave EH4 91 E2
Barnton Ave W EH4 91 D2
Barnton Brae EH4 91 D2
Barnton Ct EH4 91 D2
Barnton Gdns EH4 91 F2
Barnton Gr EH4 91 D2
Barnton La FK1 60 A2
Barnton Loan EH4 91 F2
Barnton Park Ave EH4 91 E2
Barnton Park Cres EH4 91 E2
Barnton Park Dell EH4 91 E2
Barnton Park Dr EH4 91 E2
Barnton Park Gdns EH4 91 E2
Barnton Park Gr EH4 91 E2
Barnton Park Pl EH4 91 E2
Barnton Park View EH4 91 E2
Barnton Park Wood EH4 91 D1
Barnton Pk EH4 91 F2
Barnton St FK8 7 D4
Barntongate Ave EH4 91 D1
Barntongate Dr EH4 91 D1
Barntongate Terr EH4 91 D1
Barnwell Rd FK9 2 B2
Barons Hill Ave EH49 85 D4
Barons Hill Ct EH49 85 D4
Baronscourt Rd EH8 94 B1
Baronscourt Terr EH8 124 B4
Barony Ct EH51 63 F3
Barony Pl 6 EH3 93 E1
Barony St EH3 93 E1
Barony Terr EH12 121 E4
Barr Cres KY11 47 E1
Barra Pl FK5 39 D2
Barracks Rdbt EH54 146 C3
Barracks St EH32 97 E2
Barrie Ct EH54 148 B3
Barrie Pl
Dunfermline KY12 28 C3
Grangemouth FK3 61 E3
Barrie Rd FK5 38 C2
Barrie St KY12 28 C3
Barrie Terr EH48 145 E3
Barton Rd KY11 46 A1
Barton Terr EH47 193 F3
Bass Rock View EH39 55 D4
Bastion Wynd FK8 7 D4
Bath Pl EH15 95 D1
Bath Rd EH6 94 A3
Bath St EH15 125 D4
Bath Street La EH15 125 D4
Bathfield EH6 93 F3
Bathgate Acad EH48 145 F3
Bathgate Rd
Blackburn EH47 171 E4
East Whitburn EH47 170 C4
Bathgate Sta EH48 145 D3
Bathville Bsns Ctr EH48 144 A3
Baton Rd ML7 191 E3
Batterflats Gdns FK7 6 C3
Battery Rd
Grangemouth FK3 62 B4
North Queensferry KY11 68 B3
Battock Rd FK2 82 C4
Bavelaw Cres EH26 203 E3
Bavelaw Gdns EH14 151 E1
Bavelaw Rd EH14 151 E1
Baxter Cres FK6 36 B1
Baxter St FK7 8 B2
Baxter's Pl EH1 233 E4
Baxter's Wynd FK1 60 A2
Bayne Gdns EH49 84 A3
Bayne St FK8 2 A1
Bayswell Pk EH42 78 B2
Bayswell Rd EH42 78 B2
Beach La Edinburgh EH15 95 D1
Edinburgh EH15 125 D4
Musselburgh EH21 126 A4
Beach Rd Grangemouth FK9 41 D1
North Berwick EH39 54 A4
Beachmont Ct EH42 78 C1
Beachmont Pl EH42 78 C1
Beaconhurst Sch FK9 2 B3
Bean Row FK1 60 A2
Beancross Prim Sch FK3 61 E3
Beancross Rd FK3 61 E3
Beancross Rdbt FK3 61 D3
Bearcroft Gdns FK3 61 F4
Bearcroft Rd FK3 62 B4
Bearford Pl EH41 132 B4
Bearside Rd FK7 7 D2
Beath High Sch KY4 13 D2
Beath View KY11 29 F2
Beath View Rd KY4 13 D1
Beatlie Rd EH52 88 A2
Beatlie Sch EH52 88 A2
Beaton Ave FK7 7 E1
Beatty Ave FK8 2 A1
Beatty Cres KY1 17 E4
Beatty Ct KY1 17 E4
Beatty Pl KY12 29 E3
Beauchamp Gr EH16 155 D4
Beauchamp Rd EH16 155 D4
Beauclerc St FK12 5 D4
Beaufort Cres KY2 16 B3
Beaufort Dr FK2 39 D2
Beaufort Rd EH9 123 E2
Beauly Ct Falkirk FK1 60 B1
Grangemouth FK3 61 E2
Beauly Dr EH54 148 A2
Beauly Pl KY2 16 C4
Beaumont Dr FK2 39 D1
Beaverbank Pl EH7 93 E2

Beaverhall Rd EH7 93 E2
Beck Cres KY12 29 E3
Beda Pl FK7 8 B3
Bedford Ct Alloa FK10 10 A3
Edinburgh 3 EH4 93 D1
Bedford Pl FK10 10 A3
Bedford St EH4 93 D1
Bedford Terr EH15 125 E4
Bedlormie Dr EH48 142 B1
Beech Ave Carrington EH23 206 C2
Dalgety Bay KY11 48 C3
Mid Calder EH53 148 A1
Plean FK7 20 B2
Beech Cres Denny FK6 36 B2
Larbert FK5 59 E4
Beech Gr Dunfermline KY11 46 B4
Livingston EH54 148 A3
Whitburn EH47 170 B3
Beech Gr Ave EH22 156 B1
Beech La FK9 2 A2
Beech Loan EH19 182 A3
Beech Pl Grangemouth FK3 61 E3
Livingston EH54 147 E2
Seafield EH47 146 A1
Beech Rd EH48 145 F3
Beech St EH42 78 A1
Beech Terr EH34 160 B3
Beech Way KY11 48 A3
Beechbank Cres EH53 148 C1
Beeches The
Dalgety Bay KY11 48 B2
Gullane EH31 52 A2
Newtongrange EH22 183 D4
Beechgrove Rd EH22 183 F3
Beechmount Cres EH12 122 A4
Beechmount Ct ML7 192 A1
Beechmount Pk EH12 122 A3
Beechwood Alloa FK10 5 E1
Crossford KY12 28 A1
Linlithgow EH49 85 D3
Beechwood Gdns EH47 145 E1
Beechwood Gr EH54 117 D1
Beechwood Mains EH12 122 A4
Beechwood Pk
Livingston EH54 146 C4
Newtongrange EH22 183 D3
Uphall Station EH54 117 D1
Beechwood Pl EH47 145 E1
Beechwood Rd
Blackburn EH47 145 E1
Haddington EH41 131 F4
Beechwood Terr EH6 94 A2
Beecraigs Ctry Pk EH49 85 D1
Beeslack High Sch EH26 204 A4
Begbie Pl EH54 147 D3
Begg Ave FK1 59 F2
Beldorney Pl KY12 29 E3
Belfield Ct EH21 126 A3
Belford Ave EH4 92 C1
Belford Gdns EH4 92 C1
Belford Pk EH4 122 C4
Belford Pl EH4 122 C4
Belford Rd EH4 122 C4
Belford Terr EH4 122 C4
Belfrange La EH3 232 C2
Belgrave Cres EH4 232 A4
Belgrave Crescent La
EH4 232 A4
Belgrave Gdns EH12 121 F4
Belgrave Mews 10 EH4 92 C1
Belgrave Pl EH4 92 C1
Belgrave Rd EH12 121 F3
Belhaven Hill (Boys Sch)
EH42 78 A1
Belhaven Hospl EH42 78 A1
Belhaven Pl EH10 123 D1
Belhaven Rd EH42 78 B1
Belhaven Terr EH10 123 D1
Bell Ct FK3 40 C1
Bell Pl EH3 93 D1
Bell Rd KY11 46 A1
Bell Sq EH54 173 E3
Bell Stane EH30 68 A1
Bell's Mill Terr EH52 87 F1
Bell's Mills EH4 122 C4
Bell's Wynd FK1 60 A2
Bellamond Cres EH47 170 C4
Belleknowes Ind Est KY11 47 D2
Bellenden Gdns EH16 124 B1
Bellerophon Dr EH26 203 F2
Bellevue Edinburgh EH7 93 E1
Maddiston FK2 82 C4
Bellevue Ave EH42 78 C1
Bellevue Cres EH3 93 E1
Bellevue Gdns EH7 93 E2
Bellevue Gr EH7 93 E1
Bellevue Pl EH7 93 E1
Bellevue Rd Alloa FK10 9 F3
Edinburgh EH7 93 E2
Bellevue St Edinburgh EH7 93 E1
Falkirk FK1 60 B2
Bellevue Terr EH7 93 E1
Bellfield Ave
Dalkeith EH22 156 C1
East Calder EH53 148 C1
Musselburgh EH21 126 A3
Bellfield Cres KY1 18 A4
Bellfield La EH15 125 D4
Bellfield Rd Bannockburn FK7 7 F1
Stirling FK8 7 D3
Bellfield Sq EH32 127 F4
Bellfield St EH15 125 D4
Bellfield Terr EH15 125 D4
Bellfield View EH19 182 B4
Bellhouse Rd KY3 49 D4
Bellman Way KY11 48 A3
Bellman's Rd EH26 203 F3
Bellona Terr EH47 193 F3
Bells Brae EH4 232 A3
Bells Burn Ave EH49 85 E4
Bellsdyke Hospl FK5 38 B3
Bellsdyke Rd Falkirk FK2 39 E3
Larbert FK5 38 B2
Bellsmains EH23 207 E3
Bellsmeadow Rd FK1 60 B2
Bellsquarry Prim Sch
EH54 173 E4
Bellsquarry South Rd
EH54 173 F3
Bellyeoman La KY12 29 E3
Bellyeoman Prim Sch
KY12 29 E3
Bellyeoman Rd KY12 29 E3
Bellyford Rd EH33 128 A1
Belmont Ave
Dennyloanhead FK4 57 E3
Edinburgh EH12 122 A4
Shieldhill FK1 81 F4
Belmont Cres EH12 122 A4
Belmont Dr ML7 192 A1
Belmont Gdns EH12 122 A4
Belmont Pk EH12 122 A4
Belmont Rd EH14 152 B3
Belmont St FK1 60 B2
Belmont Terr EH12 122 A4
Belmont View EH12 122 A4
Belstane Pk ML8 230 A2
Belstane Rd ML8 230 A2
Belsyde Ct EH49 84 B3
Belvedere Pk EH6 93 E3
Belvedere Rd EH48 144 C4
Belwood Cres EH26 180 A1
Belwood Rd EH26 179 F1
Ben Alder Pl KY2 16 C3
Ben Ledi Rd KY2 16 C3
Ben Lomond View KY12 27 D3
Ben Nevis Pl KY2 16 C3
Ben Sayers Pk EH39 54 C3
Benarty St KY2 16 C3
Bendachin Dr KY12 29 F3
Bendameer Rd KY3 33 E1
Benhar Prim Sch ML7 168 B3
Benhar Rd Harthill ML7 167 F1
Shotts ML7 192 A3
Benjamin Dr EH51 63 F3
Bennett Wood Terr EH52 87 F2
Bennie Mus EH48 145 D3
Bennochy Ave KY2 17 D3
Bennochy Ct KY2 17 D3
Bennochy Gdns KY2 17 D3
Bennochy Rd KY2 16 C3
Bentheads FK7 19 F4
Benview FK7 7 E1
Benview Terr FK10 5 F2
Beresford Ave EH5 93 E3
Beresford Gdns EH5 93 E3
Beresford Pl EH5 93 D3
Beresford Rise EH54 148 A1
Berkeley St FK7 7 D2
Bernard Shaw St KY12 28 C3
Bernard St EH6 94 A3
Bernard Terr EH8 233 E1
Berry St KY5 14 A4
Berryhill FK7 20 C4
Berryhill Cres FK3 61 F3
Berryhill Pl ML7 192 A1
Berrylaw Pl KY12 28 C2
Berrylaw Rd KY12 28 B2
Bertram Pl ML7 191 E3
Bertram St Harthill ML7 168 B3
Shotts ML7 191 F3
Bervie Dr EH54 173 F3
Berwick Pl Dysart KY1 18 A4
Kirkaldy KY1 17 E3
Bethesda Gr FK2 82 C3
Beulah EH21 126 C3
Bevan Dr FK12 5 E4
Bevan Pl KY11 46 C2
Bevan Rd EH22 183 E3
Bevan-lee Ct EH22 157 D2
Beveridge Ave EH22 183 F3
Beveridge Cl EH22 183 F3
Beveridge Rd KY1 17 D2
Beveridge Sq EH54 147 F1
Beveridge St KY11 29 E1
Bickerton Terr EH47 170 A3
Bickram Cres KY12 26 B4
Biggar Rd Edinburgh EH10 154 A2
Silverburn EH26 202 C3
Biggin Wa's KY1 17 F4
Bingham Ave EH15 124 C3
Bingham Broadway EH15 125 D3
Bingham Cres EH15 125 D3
Bingham Crossway EH15 124 C3
Bingham Dr EH15 125 D3
Bingham Medway EH15 124 C3
Bingham Pl EH15 124 C3
Bingham Way EH15 124 C3
Binn Ave KY3 33 F1
Binnie Pl FK2 39 F1
Binniehill Rd FK1 110 A2
Binning Rd KY11 47 D2
Binning Wood Rd EH42 75 F4
Binns The EH49 65 F1
Binny Pk EH52 116 C4
Birch Ave FK8 6 C3
Birch Cres EH20 180 C4
Birch Ct Edinburgh EH4 91 D1
Livingston EH54 147 E1
Birch Gr KY11 46 B4
Birchbank KY4 13 D1
Birchwood FK10 5 E1
Birk Hedges EH41 130 C3
Birkdale Dr EH52 116 C2
Birkdale Pk EH48 144 A3
Birkenshaw Way EH48 143 F3
Birkenside EH23 207 E3
Birkfield Loan ML8 230 B1
Birkfield Pl ML8 230 B1
Birkhill Clay Mine EH49 62 C1
Birkhill Cres EH51 63 F3
Birkhill Rd FK7 6 C3
Birkhill St EH51 63 F3
Birkhill Sta EH49 62 C2
Birnam Ct FK2 39 E1
Birnam Rd KY2 16 C4
Birnie Brae KY5 14 A4
Birnie St KY5 14 A4
Birniehill Ave EH48 144 C2
Birniehill Cres EH48 144 C2
Birniehill Rd EH48 144 C2
Birniehill Terr EH48 144 C2
Birniewell Rd FK1 110 A3
Birrell Dr KY11 29 E1
Birrell Street Wynd KY1 17 E3
Birrell's La KY1 17 F4
Birsley Rd EH33 128 B3
Bishops Pk EH53 148 B1
Black Craigs KY2 16 B4
Blackbarony Rd 1 EH16 124 A1
Blackburn Ave KY12 28 B3
Blackburn Dr KY4 13 D2
Blackburn Prim Sch EH47 145 E1
Blackburn Rd
Addiewell EH55 171 F1
Blackburn EH48 145 E2
Blackburnhall EH47 171 E3
Blackchapel Cl EH15 125 D2
Blackchapel Rd EH15 125 D2
Blackcot Ave EH22 183 E3
Blackcot Dr EH22 183 E3
Blackcot Pl EH22 183 E3
Blackcot Rd EH22 183 E3
Blacket Ave EH9 123 F3
Blacket Pl EH9 123 F3
Blackfaulds Ct EH47 193 F3
Blackfaulds Dr EH47 193 F3
Blackfaulds Pl EH47 193 F3
Blackford Ave EH9 123 E2
Blackford Bank EH9 123 E2
Blackford Gate EH9 123 E2
Blackford Glen Rd EH16 123 F1
Blackford Hill Gr EH9 123 E1
Blackford Hill Rise EH9 123 E1
Blackford Hill View EH9 123 E1
Blackford Rd EH9 123 E2
Blackfriars St EH1 233 E3
Blackhall Prim Sch EH4 92 A1
Blackhall St ML7 192 A2
Blackhill Rd EH48 142 C2
Blackie Rd EH6 94 A2
Blacklaw Prim Sch KY11 29 E1
Blacklaw Rd KY11 29 E1
Blackmill Cres FK2 39 D2
Blackmount Terr FK2 82 C3
Blackmuir Pl FK10 4 B2
Blackness Castle EH49 65 F3
Blackness Prim Sch EH49 65 E2
Blackness Rd EH49 85 D4
Blackridge Prim Sch EH48 142 B2
Blackston Rd FK1 112 A3
Blackthorn Ct EH4 91 D1
Blackwood Cres EH9 123 F3
Blackwood Gn KY11 46 C4
Blaeberry Gdns EH4 91 D1
Blaeberryhill Rd EH47 170 B3
Blaefaulds Cres FK6 57 E4
Blair Ave EH51 63 F3
Blair Dr Dunfermline KY12 29 D3
Kelty KY4 12 B4
Blair Pl KY2 16 B3
Blair St Edinburgh EH1 233 D3
Kelty KY4 12 B4
Blair Terr FK5 39 D2
Blair's Cotts FK2 61 E1
Blairdenon Cres FK1 59 F2
Blairdenon Dr FK10 5 D1
Blairdenon Rd FK12 4 C3
Blairforkie Dr FK9 1 C4
Blairhall Prim Sch KY12 26 A4
Blairlodge Ave FK2 82 B4
Blairmore Rd KY2 16 B4
Blairmuckhole
and Forrestdyke Rd
ML7 167 F4
Blairwood Wlk KY12 26 C4
Blake St KY11 29 E1
Blamey Cres KY4 13 D1
Blantyre Terr EH10 123 D2
Blawearie Rd EH33 128 B3
Bleachfield Edinburgh EH6 93 E2
Falkirk FK2 60 A3
Blenheim Ct Carluke ML8 230 A1
Penicuik EH26 204 A4
Blenheim Pl FK5 38 C3
Blindwell Brae EH41 133 F1
Blindwells FK12 4 C3
Blinkbonnie Terr FK1 110 A3
Blinkbonny Ave EH4 92 B1
Blinkbonny Cres EH4 92 B1
Blinkbonny Gdns EH4 92 B1
Blinkbonny Gr EH4 92 B1
Blinkbonny Gr W EH4 92 B1
Blinkbonny Rd Currie EH14 152 A2
Falkirk FK1 59 F2
Blinkbonny Terr EH4 92 B1
Blinny Ct ML7 192 A2
Bloom Ct EH54 147 D2
Bloom Pl EH54 147 D1
Bloom Rdbt EH54 147 E2
Bloomfield Pl EH48 145 D3
Blyth Rd EH52 117 E2
Blyth St KY1 17 F4
Bo'mains Ind Est EH51 63 F3
Bo'mains Rd EH51 63 F3
Bo'ness Hospl EH51 63 F4
Bo'ness & Kinneil Railway
EH51 63 E4
Bo'ness Public Sch (Prim)
EH51 63 F4
Bo'ness Rd
Grangemouth FK3, EH51 62 A3
Polmont FK2 61 F2
Queensferry EH30 67 F1
Bo'ness Sta EH51 64 A4
Boat Gn EH3 93 E2
Bog Rd Laurieston FK2 60 C2
Penicuik EH26 203 F3
Whitburn EH47 170 A3
Bog Rdbt FK2 60 C2
Bog Road Ind Est FK2 60 C2
Bog The EH51 64 A4
Bogend Rd Bannockburn FK7 19 F4
Larbert FK2 38 A4
Torwood FK5 37 F4
Boghall Dr EH48 145 F3
Boghall Prim Sch EH48 145 F3
Boghall Rdbt EH48 145 F3
Boghead Cres EH48 144 C3
Bogies Wynd KY1 17 E3
Boglily Rd KY2 16 C2
Bogpark Rd EH21 126 A3
Bogsmill Rd EH14 122 A1
Bogwood Ct EH22 183 E4
Bogwood Dr KY12 28 A1
Bogwood Rd EH22 183 F3
Bohun Ct FK7 7 E2
Bolam Dr KY3 33 F1
Bolan Sq KY5 14 A4
Bomar Ave EH51 64 A4
Bon Accord Cres ML7 191 F3
Bonaly Ave EH13 153 D3
Bonaly Brae EH13 153 D3
Bonaly Cres EH13 153 D3
Bonaly Ctry Pk EH13 152 C1
Bonaly Dr EH13 153 D3
Bonaly Gdns EH13 153 D3
Bonaly Gr EH13 153 D3
Bonaly Prim Sch EH13 153 D3
Bonaly Prim Sch (Annexe)
EH13 153 D3
Bonaly Rd EH13 153 D3
Bonaly Rise EH13 153 D3
Bonaly Steading EH13 153 D3
Bonaly Terr EH13 153 D3
Bonaly Wester EH13 153 D3
Bonar Pl EH6 93 E3
Bonhard Ct EH51 64 A3
Bonnar St KY12 29 D2
Bonnington EH27 150 A4
Bonnington Ave EH6 93 E3
Bonnington Gr EH6 93 E3
Bonnington Ind Est EH6 93 F2
Bonnington Prim Sch EH6 93 F2
Bonnington Rd
Edinburgh EH6 93 F2
Wilkieston EH27 150 A3
Bonnington Road La EH6 93 F2
Bonnington Terr EH6 93 E3
Bonnybank Ct EH23 207 E4
Bonnybank Rd EH23 207 E4
Bonnybridge Hospl FK4 58 B3
Bonnybridge Prim Sch
FK4 58 A3
Bonnybridge Rd FK4 57 F3
Bonnyfield Rd FK4 57 F3
Bonnyhaugh EH6 93 E2
Bonnyhaugh La EH6 93 E2
Bonnyhill Rd Falkirk FK1 59 D2
High Bonnybridge FK4 58 B2
Bonnyrigg Prim Sch EH19 182 B3
Bonnyrigg Rd EH22 156 C1
Bonnyside Rd FK4 58 A3
Bonnyton Pl KY11 29 E2
Bonnytoun Ave EH49 85 E4
Bonnytoun Terr EH49 85 E4
Bonnyview Gdns FK4 58 A3
Bonnywood Ave FK4 58 A4
Booth Ave KY11 46 B3
Booth Pl FK1 60 A2
Boothacre La EH6 94 B2
Boreland Pk KY11 47 E2
Boreland Rd Dysart KY1 18 A4
Inverkeithing KY11 47 E2
Borestone Cres FK7 7 D2
Borestone Ct FK7 7 D1
Borestone Pl FK7 7 D1
Borestone Prim Sch FK7 7 D1
Boroughdales EH42 78 B1
Boroughloch EH8 233 E1
Boroughloch Sq EH8 233 E1
Boroughmuir High Sch
EH10 123 D1
Boroughmuir Sec Sch (Annexe)
EH11 122 C3
Borrowlea Rd FK7 7 E4
Borrowmeadow Rd FK7 7 F4
Borrowstoun Cres EH51 63 F3
Borrowstoun Pl EH51 63 F3
Borrowstoun Rd EH51 64 A3
Borthwick Castle Pl EH23 207 F2
Borthwick Castle Rd
EH23 207 F1
Borthwick Castle Terr
EH23 207 F2
Borthwick Pl EH12 122 C4
Borthwick Prim Sch EH23 208 A2
Boswall Ave EH5 92 C3
Boswall Cres EH5 92 C3
Boswall Dr EH5 93 D3
Boswall Gdns EH5 92 C3
Boswall Gn EH5 93 D3
Boswall Gr EH5 92 C3
Boswall Loan EH5 92 C3
Boswall Parkway EH5 92 C3
Boswall Pl EH5 92 C3
Boswall Quadrant EH5 92 C3
Boswall Rd EH5 93 D3
Boswall Sq EH5 92 C3
Boswall Terr EH5 92 C3
Boswell Dr Kinghorn KY3 35 D2
Oakley KY12 26 C3
Boswell Rd KY5 14 A4
Bothkennar Prim Sch FK2 39 F2
Bothkennar Rd FK2 39 F2
Bothwell Gdns KY11 29 D1
Bothwell St
Dunfermline KY11 29 D1
Edinburgh EH7 94 A1
Boulevard Rdbt EH54 147 E1
Boundary Rd E EH14 151 F4
Boundary Rd N EH14 151 F4
Boundary St EH51 64 A4
Bouprie Rise KY11 48 A2
Bourtree Gr KY12 26 B4
Bow Butts KY12 29 D1
Bow St FK8 7 D4
Bowhill Terr EH5 93 D3
Bowhouse Dr KY1 35 D4
Bowhouse Gdns FK10 10 A3
Bowhouse Prim Sch FK3 61 F3
Bowhouse Rd Alloa FK10 10 A3
Grangemouth FK3 61 F3
Bowhouse Sq FK3 61 E3
Bowhousebog or Liquo
ML7 191 D1
Bowhousebog Rd ML7 191 D1
Bowling Green Rd
Kirkliston EH29 89 D1
Whitburn EH47 170 A3
Bowling Green St KY4 13 E2
Bowling Green The EH6 93 F3
Bowmont Pl EH8 233 E1
Bowmont Terr EH42 78 C1
Bowmore Wlk ML7 192 A2
Bowyett EH48 113 F3
Boyd Pl KY5 14 A4
Boyd St Falkirk FK2 60 A3
Laurieston FK2 61 D2
Boyd's Entry EH1 233 E3
Boyd-Orr Dr EH26 203 F4
Brackenlees Rd FK2 40 A3
Brackensbrae EH52 117 D3
Bradbury St FK2 39 D1
Brae Heads Loan EH40 103 E3
Brae Pk EH4 91 D2
Brae Rd EH51 62 B3
Brae The Bannockburn FK7 7 E1
Cambusbarron FK7 6 B3
Penicuik EH26 180 B1
Braefoot Gr KY11 48 A1
Braefoot Rd EH51 64 A3
Braefoot Terr 2 EH16 124 A1
Braehead Alloa FK10 4 B1
Alva FK12 5 D4
Bo'ness EH51 63 F4
Braehead Ave
Edinburgh EH4 91 D2
Linlithgow EH49 84 C3
Tullibody FK10 4 B1
Braehead Bank EH4 91 D2
Braehead Cres EH4 91 D2
Braehead Dr Edinburgh EH4 91 D2
Linlithgow EH49 84 C3
Braehead Gr Bo'ness EH51 63 F4
Edinburgh EH4 91 D2
Braehead Loan EH4 91 D2
Braehead Pk Edinburgh EH4 91 D2
Linlithgow EH49 84 C3
Braehead Pl EH49 84 C3
Braehead Prim Sch FK7 7 E2
Braehead Rd
Edinburgh EH4 91 D2
Linlithgow EH49 84 C3
Stirling FK7 7 E2
Braehead Rdbt EH54 147 E2
Braehead Row EH4 91 D2
Braehead Terr EH49 84 C3
Braehead View EH4 91 D2
Braekirk Ave EH27 149 E1
Braemar Cres
Carluke ML8 230 A2
Falkirk FK2 60 B3
Braemar Dr FK2 60 B3
Braemar Gdns
Brightons FK2 82 B4
Denny FK6 36 B2
Braemar Pl FK5 39 D2
Braemount KY4 13 D1
Braepark Rd EH4 91 D2
Braes The Lochgelly KY5 14 A4
Tullibody FK10 4 B2
Braes View Denny FK6 57 E4
Shieldhill FK1 81 F4
Braeside Alloa FK10 5 E1
Shieldhill FK1 81 E3
Braeside Cres EH47 193 E3
Braeside Gdns EH53 148 A1
Braeside Pk EH53 148 A2
Braeside Pl Laurieston FK2 61 D2
Redding FK2 61 D1
Reddingmuirhead FK2 82 A4
Braeside Rd
Gorebridge EH37 207 E4
Loanhead EH20 181 E4
Braeside Rd N EH23 207 E4
Braeside Rd S EH23 207 E4

Braeview
East Linton EH40 103 E4
Laurieston FK2 60 C2
Stenhousemuir FK5 38 B1
Braewell Gdns EH49 84 B4
Braid Ave EH10 123 D1
Braid Cres EH10 123 D1
Braid Farm Rd EH10 123 D1
Braid Gn EH54 147 E4
Braid Hills App EH10 154 A4
Braid Hills Ave EH10 123 D1
Braid Hills Cres EH10 154 A4
Braid Hills Dr EH16 154 B4
Braid Hills Rd EH10 154 A4
Braid Mount EH10 154 A4
Braid Mount Crest EH10 154 A4
Braid Mount Rise EH10 154 A4
Braid Mount View EH10 154 A4
Braidburn Cres EH10 123 D1
Braidburn Terr EH10 123 D1
Braidlaw Pk EH26 203 E3
Braigh Gdns KY12 28 B3
Bramble Dr EH4 91 D1
Bramdean Gr EH10 154 A4
Bramdean Pl EH10 154 A4
Bramdean Rise EH10 154 A4
Bramdean View EH10 154 A4
Brand Dr EH15 125 D4
Brand Gdns EH15 125 E4
Brandfield St EH3 232 A1
Brandon St EH3 93 E1
Brandon Terr EH3 93 E2
Brands Row KY4 30 C4
Brandy Riggs KY12 27 E1
Brandy Wells KY12 27 E1
Brandyhill FK10 5 F2
Brankholm Brae KY11 46 B2
Brankholm Cres KY11 46 B3
Brankholm La KY11 46 B1
Branning Ct KY1 17 E3
Branshill Pk FK10 10 A4
Branshill Rd FK10 10 A4
Branxton Wynd KY1 35 D4
Bravo St EH51 62 C3
Bread St EH3 232 B2
Bread Street La EH3 232 B2
Breadalbane Pl FK2 61 F1
Breadalbane St EH6 93 F2
Breakers Way KY11 47 F1
Brechin Dr FK2 62 A1
Breck Terr EH26 204 A4
Breich Sta EH55 194 B3
Breich Terr EH55 194 C3
Brentham Ave FK8 7 D3
Brentham Cres FK8 7 D3
Breslin Terr ML7 168 B3
Breton Ct FK1 60 B2
Brewary Cl EH30 68 A1
Brewery La EH42 78 A1
Brewery Pk EH41 132 A4
Brewlands Ave EH51 62 B3
Brewster Pl FK6 36 B1
Brewster Sq EH54 173 E3
Briar Brae FK2 82 B4
Briar Cotts EH47 171 E1
Briar Pl KY11 29 E2
Briarbank EH54 147 E3
Briarbank Terr EH11 122 C2
Briarcliff St KY1 17 F3
Briardene FK2 61 D2
Briarhill Ave KY11 48 A2
Briars Rd FK10 4 C1
Brickfield EH15 95 D1
Brickworks Rd EH33 128 A4
Bridge Cres FK6 36 B1
Bridge End
East Whitburn EH47 170 B4
Edinburgh EH16 124 A2
Shotts ML7 191 E3
Bridge End Cotts EH27 150 B3
Bridge of Allan Prim Sch
FK9 2 A3
Bridge of Allan Sta FK9 1 C4
Bridge Pl Broxburn EH52 117 F3
Denny FK6 36 B1
Edinburgh 4 EH3 93 D1
Shotts ML7 192 A2
Bridge Rd Balerno EH14 151 E1
Edinburgh EH13 153 D3
Bridge St Bonnybridge FK4 58 A3
Cowdenbeath KY4 13 E2
Dunfermline KY12 28 C2
East Linton EH40 103 F4
Edinburgh EH15 95 D1
Fauldhouse EH47 193 F3
Haddington EH41 132 B4
Kincardine FK10 23 E2
Kirkaldy KY1 17 D1
Musselburgh EH21 126 B3
Newbridge EH28 119 D3
Penicuik EH26 203 F2
Tranent EH33 128 B3
Bridge Street La EH15 95 D1
Bridge Terr FK10 10 A3
Bridge View KY11 68 B3
Bridgecastle Cotts EH48 112 C1
Bridgecastle Rd EH48 143 F4
Bridgehaugh Rd FK9 2 A1
Bridgehill FK1 112 A3
Bridgend Ct EH48 144 C3
Bridgend Pk EH48 144 C3
Bridgend Pl EH47 170 B4
Bridgend Prim Sch EH49 86 B2
Bridgend Rd FK1 112 A3
Bridgeness Cres EH51 64 B4
Bridgeness La EH51 64 B4
Bridgeness Rd EH51 64 B4
Bridges The KY11 48 A1
Bridgeside Ave EH47 170 A3
Bridgeton Cotts EH48 112 C1
Brierbush Cres EH33 129 E3
Brierbush Rd EH33 129 E3
Briery Bank EH41 132 B4
Briery Bauks EH8 233 E2
Brig-O-Doon Gr FK7 20 C4
Bright's Cres EH9 123 F2
Brighton Pl EH15 125 D4
Brighton St EH1 233 D2
Brisbane St EH54 148 A3
Bristo Pl EH1 233 D2
Bristo Port EH1 233 D2
Bristo Sq EH8 233 D2
Britwell Cres EH7 94 B1
Brixwold Bank EH19 182 B3
Brixwold Dr EH19 182 B3
Brixwold Neuk EH19 182 B3
Brixwold Pk EH19 182 B3
Brixwold Rise EH19 182 B3
Brixwold View EH19 182 B3
Broad St Alloa FK10 10 A3
Cowdenbeath KY4 13 E1
Denny FK6 36 C1
Stirling FK8 7 D4
Broad Wynd Edinburgh EH6 94 A3
Kirkaldy KY1 17 E3
Broadgait EH31 52 A2
Broadgait Ct EH31 52 A2
Broadgait Gn EH31 52 A2
Broadhurst Rd EH22 183 E4
Broadleys Rd FK7 7 E4
Broadleys Rdbt FK7 7 E3
Brock Pl FK7 7 D1
Brock St KY11 68 A3
Brocks Way EH52 118 A4
Brockville Pk (Falkirk FC)
FK1 60 A3
Brockwood Ave EH26 203 E3
Brodick Pl FK1 59 E2
Brodick Rd KY2 16 C4
Brodie Ave EH39 54 B3
Brodie St FK2 60 A4
Broich The FK12 4 C4
Bronte Pl FK5 39 D2
Brook St Alva FK12 5 D3
Menstrie FK11 3 F3
Brookbank Terr ML8 230 A1
Brooke La FK3 61 E3
Brooke St FK3 61 E3
Brookfield Pl FK12 5 D3
Brookfield Terr EH25 180 C3
Brookside FK2 61 F1
Broom Ct FK7 7 E2
Broom Gr KY11 46 C4
Broom Pk E FK11 4 A3
Broom Pk W FK11 4 A3
Broom Pl KY2 16 B4
Broom Rd Kircaldy KY2 16 B4
Stirling FK7 7 E2
Broom Wlk EH54 148 A2
Broom Wynd ML7 191 F3
Broomage Ave FK5 38 A2
Broomage Cres FK5 38 A2
Broomage Dr FK5 38 A2
Broomage Pk FK5 38 B1
Broombank Terr EH12 121 E2
Broomburn Gr EH12 121 F2
Broomfield Cres EH12 121 F2
Broomfield Dr KY12 29 D3
Broomfield Rd KY4 13 E3
Broomfield Terr EH12 121 F3
Broomhall Ave EH12 121 F2
Broomhall Bank EH12 121 E3
Broomhall Cres EH12 121 E3
Broomhall Dr EH12 121 E3
Broomhall Gdns EH12 121 E3
Broomhall Loan EH12 121 E3
Broomhall Pk EH12 121 E3
Broomhall Pl EH12 121 E3
Broomhall Rd EH12 121 E3
Broomhall Terr EH12 121 E3
Broomhead Dr KY12 28 C3
Broomhead Pk KY12 28 C3
Broomhill KY3 50 C4
Broomhill Ave
Burntisland KY3 33 F1
Larbert FK5 38 A1
Penicuik EH26 203 F2
Broomhill Dr EH22 156 C1
Broomhill Pk EH22 156 C1
Broomhill Pl Denny FK6 36 B2
Stirling FK7 6 C3
Broomhill Rd
Bonnybridge FK4 58 A2
Penicuik EH26 203 F2
Broomhill St ML7 168 B3
Broomhouse Ave EH11 121 E2
Broomhouse Bank EH11 121 F2
Broomhouse Cres EH11 121 F2
Broomhouse Ct EH11 121 F2
Broomhouse Dr EH11 121 F2
Broomhouse Gdns E EH11 121 F2
Broomhouse Gdns W EH11 121 E2
Broomhouse Gr EH11 121 F2
Broomhouse Loan EH11 121 F2
Broomhouse Medway
EH11 121 F2
Broomhouse Mkt EH11 121 F2
Broomhouse Path EH11 121 F2
Broomhouse Pk EH11 121 F2
Broomhouse Pl N EH11 121 F2
Broomhouse Pl S EH11 121 F2
Broomhouse Prim Sch
EH11 121 F2
Broomhouse Rd EH11 121 E2
Broomhouse Row EH11 121 F2
Broomhouse Sq EH11 121 F2
Broomhouse St N EH11 121 F2
Broomhouse St S EH11 121 F1
Broomhouse Terr EH11 121 F2
Broomhouse Way EH11 121 F2
Broomhouse Wlk EH11 121 F2
Broomhouse Wynd EH11 121 F2
Broomieknowe
Bonnyrigg and
Lasswade EH18 182 A4
Dunfermline KY11 29 E2
Tullibody FK10 4 B2
Broomieknowe Gdns
EH19 182 A4
Broomieknowe Pk EH19 182 A4
Broomknowe Dr FK10 23 E3
Broomlea Cres EH12 121 E3
Broompark Gdns
Denny FK6 36 C1
East Calder EH53 148 C2
Broompark Rd
East Calder EH53 148 C2
Edinburgh EH12 121 F3
Broompark View EH53 148 C2
Broomridge Rd FK7 7 E2
Broomside KY2 16 B4
Broomside Pl FK5 38 B1
Broomside Rd FK4 58 A2
Broomside Terr EH12 121 F2
Broomyknowe EH14 153 D4
Broomyknowe Dr EH54 146 C3
Brora Pl KY12 28 B1
Brosdale Ct FK1 60 A1
Brougham Pl EH3 232 C1
Brougham St EH3 232 B1
Broughton High Sch EH4 92 C1
Broughton Market EH3 93 E1
Broughton Pl EH1 93 E1
Broughton Place La EH1 93 E1
Broughton Prim Sch EH7 93 E2
Broughton Rd EH7 93 E2
Broughton St EH1 93 E1
Broughton Street La EH1 93 E1
Brown Ave Alloa FK10 4 C1
Stirling FK9 2 A1
Brown St Armadale EH48 143 F2
Edinburgh EH8 233 E2
Falkirk FK1 59 E3
Haddington EH41 132 A4
Shotts ML7 192 A2
Whitburn EH47 170 A3
Brown's Cl EH8 233 F3
Brown's Pl
East Linton EH40 103 E4
Edinburgh EH1 232 C2
Brownrigg Farm Cotts
EH39 74 B3
Broxburn Acad EH52 117 E3
Broxburn Prim Sch EH52 117 F3
Bruart Ave FK5 38 C2
Bruce Cres Falkirk FK2 39 D2
Plean FK7 20 B2
Bruce Dr Fallin FK7 8 B3
Stenhousemuir FK5 38 C2
Bruce Gdns Brightons FK2 82 B4
Dalkeith EH22 157 D1
Bruce Gr EH34 160 C3
Bruce Pl FK3 61 F4
Bruce Rd Bathgate EH48 145 E3
Grangemouth EH51 62 C3
Bruce St Alloa FK10 10 B4
Bannockburn FK7 7 F1
Clackmannan FK10 11 D2
Dunfermline KY12 28 C2
Edinburgh EH10 123 D1
Falkirk FK2 60 B3
Kinghorn KY3 35 D2
Plean FK7 20 B2
Stirling FK8 2 A1
Bruce Terr Cambusbarron FK7 6 B3
Kinghorn KY3 35 D2
Bruce View FK7 7 D1
Brucefield Ave KY11 29 D1
Brucefield Cres FK10 11 D2
Brucefield Dr EH47 170 A3
Brucefield Feus KY11 29 E2
Brucefield Ind Est EH54 173 E3
Brucefield Pk E EH54 173 E3
Brucefield Pk N EH54 173 E3
Brucefield Pk W EH54 173 E3
Brucefield Terr KY4 13 F3
Brucehaven Cres KY11 45 F2
Brucehaven Rd KY11 45 E2
Brunstane Bank EH15 125 E3
Brunstane Cres EH15 125 E3
Brunstane Dr EH15 125 E3
Brunstane Gardens Mews
EH15 125 E4
Brunstane Gdns
Edinburgh EH15 125 E4
Penicuik EH26 203 E3
Brunstane Prim Sch EH15 125 E3
Brunstane Rd EH15 125 E4
Brunstane Rd N EH15 125 E4
Brunstane Rd S EH15 125 E3
Brunswick Rd EH7 93 F1
Brunswick St EH7 93 F1
Brunswick Street La EH7 93 F1
Brunswick Terr EH7 93 F1
Brunt Gr EH42 106 B4
Brunt La EH42 78 B1
Brunt Pl EH42 106 C4
Brunton Pl 1 EH7 93 F1
Brunton Terr EH7 93 F1
Brunton's Cl EH22 157 D2
Bruntsfield Ave EH10 123 D3
Bruntsfield Cres EH10 123 D3
Bruntsfield Gdns EH10 123 D3
Bruntsfield Pl EH10 232 B1
Bruntsfield Prim Sch
EH10 123 D3
Bruntsfield Terr EH10 123 D3
Bryans Ave EH22 183 D3
Bryans Prim Sch EH22 183 F4
Bryans Rd EH22 183 D3
Bryce Ave Edinburgh EH7 94 C1
Falkirk FK2 39 D1
Bryce Cres EH14 152 A3
Bryce Gdns EH14 152 A3
Bryce Gr EH7 94 C1
Bryce Pl EH14 152 A3
Bryce Rd EH14 152 A3
Bryony The FK10 4 A1
Bryson Rd EH11 122 C3
Bryson St FK2 60 A3
Bryson Street Ind Est FK2 60 A3
Buccleuch Ct EH22 156 C2
Buccleuch Pl EH8 233 D1
Buccleuch St
Dalkeith EH22 157 D2
Edinburgh EH8 233 E1
Buccleuch Terr EH8 233 E1
Buchan La EH52 117 F3
Buchan Pl FK3 61 E3
Buchan Rd Bathgate EH48 144 C4
Broxburn EH52 117 E3
Grangemouth EH51 62 B3
Buchanan Cres EH54 147 D3
Buchanan Ct Bo'ness EH51 63 F3
Falkirk FK2 60 A4
Kirkaldy KY1 17 D1
Buchanan Dr FK9 2 A2
Buchanan Gdns FK2 61 E1
Buchanan St
Dunfermline KY12 29 D2
Edinburgh EH6 93 F2
Buckie Rd EH22 183 F3
Buckingham Terr EH4 232 A4
Buckstane Pk EH10 154 A4
Buckstone Ave EH10 154 A3
Buckstone Bank EH10 154 A4
Buckstone Circ EH10 154 B3
Buckstone Cl EH10 154 B3
Buckstone Cres EH10 154 A4
Buckstone Crook EH10 154 B3
Buckstone Ct EH10 154 A3
Buckstone Dell EH10 154 A4
Buckstone Dr EH10 154 A4
Buckstone Gate EH10 154 B3
Buckstone Gdns EH10 154 A3
Buckstone Gn EH10 154 B3
Buckstone Gr EH10 154 A4
Buckstone Hill EH10 154 B4
Buckstone Howe EH10 154 B3
Buckstone Lea EH10 154 B3
Buckstone Loan EH10 154 B3
Buckstone Loan E EH10 154 B3
Buckstone Neuk EH10 154 B4
Buckstone Pl EH10 154 A3
Buckstone Prim Sch
EH10 154 B3
Buckstone Rd EH10 154 A3
Buckstone Rise EH10 154 B3
Buckstone Row EH10 154 B4
Buckstone Shaw EH10 154 B3
Buckstone Terr EH10 154 A3
Buckstone View EH10 154 A4
Buckstone Way EH10 154 A4
Buckstone Wood EH10 154 A3
Buckstone Wynd EH10 154 B3
Buffies Brae KY12 28 C2
Bughtknowes Dr EH48 145 E4
Bughtlin Dr EH12 91 D1
Bughtlin Gdns EH12 121 D4
Bughtlin Gn EH12 91 D1
Bughtlin Loan EH12 121 D4
Bughtlin Mkt EH12 121 D4
Bughtlin Pk EH12 121 D4
Bughtlin Pl EH12 91 D1
Builyeon Rd EH30 89 D4
Buller St KY5 14 A4
Bullet Loan EH41 132 B4
Bulloch Cres FK6 36 B1
Bungalows The FK5 38 A1
Buntine Cres FK7 7 D2
Burdiehouse Ave EH17 155 D2
Burdiehouse Cres EH17 155 D2
Burdiehouse Crossway
EH17 155 D2
Burdiehouse Dr EH17 155 D2
Burdiehouse Loan EH17 155 D2
Burdiehouse Medway
EH17 155 D2
Burdiehouse Pl EH17 155 D2
Burdiehouse Prim Sch
EH17 155 D2
Burdiehouse Rd EH17 155 D2
Burdiehouse Sq EH17 155 D2
Burdiehouse St EH17 155 D2
Burdiehouse Terr EH17 155 D2
Burgess Hill EH49 85 D3
Burgess Rd EH30 89 E4
Burgess St EH6 94 A3
Burgess Terr EH9 124 A2
Burgh Mews FK10 10 A3
Burgh Mills La EH49 84 B3
Burgh Rd KY4 13 E2
Burghlee Cres EH20 181 E4
Burghlee Terr EH20 181 E4
Burghmuir Ct EH49 85 E4
Burghmuir Ind Est FK8 7 D3
Burghmuir Rd FK7 7 D3
Burghtoft EH17 155 F3
Burleigh Cres KY11 47 E2
Burleigh Way FK10 10 B3
Burlington St EH6 93 F3
Burn Dr FK7 7 E2
Burnbank Carnock KY12 27 E4
Livingston EH54 147 E3
Loanhead EH20 181 D4
Burnbank Rd Falkirk FK2 60 A4
Grangemouth FK3 61 E3
Burnbrae Alloa FK10 10 B4
Edinburgh EH12 121 D4
Fauldhouse EH47 193 F3
Burnbrae Gdns Alva FK12 5 D3
Falkirk FK1 60 A3
Burnbrae Pk FK10 23 F2
Burnbrae Rd Falkirk FK1 60 A3
Harthill ML7 169 D3
Shotts ML7 191 F2
Stoneyburn EH47 171 D1
Burnbrae Terr EH47 170 B3
Burndene Dr EH20 155 D1
Burnee FK10 5 F2
Burney Pl KY11 46 C2
Burnfield EH54 147 D1
Burnfield Pl FK2 60 B4
Burnfoot Ct FK3 61 E3
Burnfoot La 1 FK1 60 A2
Burngrange Cotts EH55 172 B1
Burngrange Ct EH55 172 B1
Burngrange Gdns EH55 172 A1
Burnhead Cres EH16 155 D3
Burnhead Gr EH16 155 D3
Burnhead La FK1 60 B2
Burnhead Loan EH16 155 D3
Burnhead Path E EH16 155 D3
Burnhead Path W EH16 155 D3
Burnhead Rd FK5 38 B2
Burnhouse Dr
Dechmont EH52 116 B1
Whitburn EH47 169 F3
Burnhouse Ind Est EH47 169 F3
Burnhouse Rd EH52 116 B2
Burnhouse Sch EH47 170 A3
Burnlea Dr EH47 171 D1
Burnlea Pl EH47 171 D1
Burns Ave Armadale EH48 143 F3
Grangemouth FK3 61 E3
Burns Cres Harthill ML7 168 C3
Laurieston FK2 60 C2
Whitburn EH47 170 A3
Burns Ct EH54 148 B3
Burns Pl ML7 191 D3
Burns St Dunfermline KY12 28 C3
Edinburgh EH6 94 A2
High Valleyfield KY12 26 A1
Stirling FK8 2 A1
Burns Terr Bathgate EH48 145 E3
Cowie FK7 20 B4
Burnside Dechmont EH52 116 A1
Edinburgh EH12 121 D4
Haddington EH41 131 F4
Prestonpans EH32 96 C1
Burnside Ave
Armadale EH48 143 E3
Easthouses EH22 183 E4
Kinghorn KY3 34 C2
Polbeth EH55 172 C3
Burnside Bsns Ctr KY11 47 E2
Burnside Cres
Clackmannan FK10 11 D3
Easthouses EH22 183 E4
Fauldhouse EH47 193 F3
Plean FK7 20 B2
Rosyth KY11 47 D3
Shotts ML7 191 E3
Burnside Ct EH41 134 B1
Burnside Gdns EH49 83 F3
Burnside La EH55 172 C3
Burnside Pk EH14 151 E1
Burnside Pl Falkirk FK2 39 D2
Rosyth KY11 47 D2
Burnside Rd
Bathgate EH48 144 C4
Gorebridge EH23 183 E1
Menstrie FK11 3 F3
Polbeth EH55 172 C3
Uphall EH52 117 D2
Burnside St Alloa FK10 5 E1
Rosyth KY11 47 D3
Stirling FK7 7 E3
Burnside Terr
Cowdenbeath KY4 13 D1
East Calder EH53 148 C3
Falkirk FK1 59 F3
Fauldhouse EH47 193 F3
Oakley KY12 27 D4
Polbeth EH55 172 C3
Redding FK2 61 D1
Burnside View EH55 171 E1
Burnsknowe EH54 146 C3
Burntisland Prim Sch KY3 33 F1
Burntisland Rd KY3 34 C1
Burntisland Sta KY3 50 C4
Burnvale Broxburn EH52 118 A2
Livingston EH54 147 F2
Burt Ave KY3 34 C2
Burt Gr KY11 29 F1
Burt St KY12 29 D3
Bush St EH21 126 A3
Bush Terr EH21 126 A3
Bute EH54 146 C3
Bute Cres Dunfermline KY11 29 F2
Shotts ML7 191 E3
Bute Pl FK3 61 E3
Bute St FK2 60 A3
Bute Wynd KY1 17 D1
Butler's Pl EH54 147 D2
Butlerfield Ind Est EH19 183 D2
Butterfly World EH18 156 B2

Butts The EH41 132 A4
Buxley Rd EH33 128 A1
By-Pass Rd FK4 57 F3
Byburn EH52 116 C4
Byrehope Rd EH52 117 D2
Byres The KY11 46 B3
Byreside EH47 146 A1
Byron Rd ML7 191 D3

Cables Wynd EH6 93 F3
Caddell's Row Cotts EH4 91 D3
Cadell Dr FK2 39 D3
Cadell Pl EH32 97 E2
Cadgers Loan FK7 20 A1
Cadiz St EH6 94 A3
Cadogan Rd EH16 155 D4
Cadzow Ave EH51 63 F3
Cadzow Cres EH51 63 F4
Cadzow La EH51 63 F4
Cadzow Pl EH7 94 A1
Caerketton Ave EH25 180 C3
Caerlaverock Ct EH12 121 D4
Caesar Rd EH33 128 B3
Caesar Way EH33 128 B3
Caird's Row EH21 126 A4
Cairn Gr KY12 28 B1
Cairn's La EH51 64 A4
Cairnbank Gdns EH26 203 F2
Cairnbank Rd EH26 203 F2
Cairncubie Rd KY12 29 E4
Cairneyhill Prim Sch KY12 27 E1
Cairneyhill Rd KY12 28 A1
Cairneymount Ave FK2 83 D3
Cairneymount Rd ML8 230 A1
Cairngorm Cres KY2 16 C3
Cairngorm Ho EH6 93 F3
Cairngorm Rd FK3 61 F3
Cairnhill Ct ML8 230 A1
Cairnie Pl EH47 170 A3
Cairnmuir Rd EH12 121 F4
Cairnoch Way FK7 7 F1
Cairnoch Wlk FK6 36 B1
Cairnpapple Henge & Cairn EH48 114 B2
Cairnpark Sch EH14 122 A1
Cairns Dr EH14 177 D4
Cairns Gdns EH14 177 D4
Cairns St E KY1 17 F4
Cairns St W KY1 17 E4
Cairns The
Charlestown KY11 45 D2
Menstrie FK11 4 A3
Cairntows Cl EH16 124 B2
Cairnwell Pl
Cairneyhill KY12 27 E1
Kircaldy KY2 16 C4
Caithness Ct KY1 17 F4
Caithness Pl Edinburgh EH5 93 D3
Kirkaldy KY1 17 F4
Caiyside EH10 154 A2
Caiystane Ave EH10 154 A3
Caiystane Cres EH10 154 A3
Caiystane Dr EH10 153 F3
Caiystane Gdns EH10 154 A3
Caiystane Hill EH10 154 A3
Caiystane Terr EH10 154 A3
Caiystane View EH10 154 A3
Calais View KY11 29 F1
Calaisburn Pl KY11 29 F1
Calder Cres
Armadale EH48 144 A3
Edinburgh EH11 121 D1
Calder Ct Edinburgh EH11 121 E1
Stirling FK7 7 E3
Calder Dr Edinburgh EH11 121 E1
Shotts ML7 192 A2
Calder Gdns EH11 121 E1
Calder Gr EH11 121 E1
Calder House Rd EH53 148 A2
Calder Junc EH11 121 D1
Calder Park Rd EH53 148 A1
Calder Pk EH11 121 E1
Calder Pl Dalgety Bay KY11 48 A2
Edinburgh EH11 121 E1
Falkirk FK1 60 B1
Calder Rd
Edinburgh, East Hermiston EH14 121 D1
Edinburgh, Sighthill EH11 121 E1
Livingston EH54 173 E3
Calder Rd Gdns EH11 122 A2
Calder View EH11 121 D1
Calder's Lawn EH41 101 D1
Calderburn Rd EH55 173 D3
Caldercruix Rd FK1 110 A1
Calderhall Ave EH53 148 C2
Calderhall Cres EH53 148 C2
Calderhall Terr EH53 148 C2
Calderhead High Sch ML7 191 F3
Calderhead Rd ML7 191 E4
Caledonia Rd Rosyth KY11 46 A1
Shotts ML7 191 F3
Caledonia Way KY11 46 A2
Caledonian Cres EH11 232 A1
Caledonian Ct FK2 60 B4
Caledonian Gdns FK10 9 F3
Caledonian Pl EH11 232 A1
Caledonian Rd Alloa FK10 9 F3
Edinburgh EH11 232 A1
Fauldhouse EH47 193 E3
Caledonian Terr EH47 193 E3
Calgary Ave EH54 147 F2
California Prim Sch FK1 81 F3
California Rd FK2 82 C3
California Terr FK1 81 F3
Callander Dr FK5 59 E4
Callander Pl TD13 140 C2
Callendar Ave FK1 60 A1
Callendar Bsns Pk FK1 60 C2
Callendar Bvd FK1 60 C2
Callendar Ho FK1 60 B2
Callendar Rd FK1 60 B2
Callendar Riggs FK1 60 B2
Callendar Square Sh Ctr 5 FK1 60 A2
Calliope Rd KY11 46 A1
Calton Cres FK7 7 D2
Calton Hill EH1 233 E4
Calton Rd EH8 233 E3
Caltrop Pl FK7 7 F2
Calum Macdonald Ct KY11 46 C2
Cambridge Ave EH6 93 F2
Cambridge Gdns EH6 93 F2
Cambridge St EH1 232 B2
Cambusbarron Prim Sch FK7 6 B3
Cambusnethan St 7 EH7 94 A1
Camdean Cres KY11 46 B3
Camdean La KY11 46 B3
Camdean Prim Sch KY11 46 B2
Camelon Ed Ctr FK1 59 F3
Camelon Rd FK1 59 F3
Camelon Sta FK1 59 E3
Cameron Cres
Bonnyrigg and Lasswade EH19 181 F3
Edinburgh EH16 124 A2
Cameron Gr KY11 47 D2
Cameron House Ave EH16 124 A2
Cameron Knowe EH49 86 B3
Cameron March EH16 124 A2
Cameron Pk EH16 124 A2
Cameron Pl FK2 39 D1
Cameron Smaill Rd EH14 151 F4
Cameron St KY12 28 C2
Cameron Terr
Edinburgh EH16 124 A2
Slamannan FK1 110 A2
Cameron Toll EH16 124 A2
Cameron Toll Gdns EH16 124 A2
Cameron Toll (Sh Ctr) EH16 124 A2
Cameron Way EH54 147 F4
Cameronian Dr ML8 230 A1
Cameronian St FK8 7 D4
Camilla Gr KY2 15 E1
Cammo Bank EH4 91 D1
Cammo Brae EH4 91 D1
Cammo Gdns EH4 91 D1
Cammo Hill EH4 90 C1
Cammo Parkway EH4 91 D1
Cammo Pl EH4 91 D1
Cammo Rd EH12 90 C1
Cammo Wlk EH4 90 C1
Camp Rd Crombie KY12 44 B3
Mayfield EH22 183 F4
Camp Wood View EH22 183 F3
Campbell Ave EH12 122 B4
Campbell Cres
Laurieston FK2 60 C2
Lochgelly KY5 14 A4
Campbell Ct
Longniddry EH32 98 B3
Stirling FK7 6 C2
Campbell Dr FK5 38 A1
Campbell Park Cres EH13 152 C3
Campbell Park Dr EH13 152 C3
Campbell Rd
Edinburgh EH12 122 B4
Longniddry EH32 98 B3
Campbell St KY12 29 D2
Campbell's Cl EH8 233 F3
Camperdown Rd KY11 46 B1
Campfield St FK2 60 A3
Campie Gdns EH21 126 A3
Campie La EH21 126 A3
Campie Prim Sch EH21 126 A3
Campie Rd EH21 126 A3
Campie Terr FK2 39 F1
Camps Rd KY12 27 E3
Camps Rigg EH54 147 D4
Campsie Cres KY2 16 C4
Campsie Rd FK3 61 F3
Campus Rdbt EH54 147 E1
Campview EH22 156 A4
Campview Ave EH22 156 A4
Campview Cres EH22 156 B4
Campview Gdns EH22 156 A4
Campview Gr EH22 156 B4
Campview Rd EH19 182 A3
Campview Terr EH22 156 A4
Camus Ave EH10 154 A3
Camus Pk EH10 154 A3
Camus Pl E EH10 154 A3
Camus Rd E EH10 154 A3
Camus Rd W EH10 154 A3
Canaan La EH10 123 D2
Canal St
Falkirk, Camelon FK1 59 E3
Falkirk, Grahamston FK2 60 A4
Canal Wlk FK2 61 E1
Canalyard Ind Est FK1 60 A1
Canavan Ct FK7 7 E2
Canberra St EH54 148 A3
Candie Cres FK3 61 F3
Candie Rd FK3 62 A4
Candimilne Ct ML8 230 A1
Candlemaker Row EH1 233 D2
Candlemaker's Cres EH17 155 F3
Candlemaker's Pk EH17 155 F3
Candleriggs FK10 10 A3
Candleriggs Ct FK10 10 A3
Caneluk Ave ML8 230 A1
Canmore Dr FK5 38 C2
Canmore Gr KY12 29 D3
Canmore St
Dunfermline KY12 29 D2
Kinghorn KY3 34 C1
Queensferry EH30 89 D4
Canmore Terr KY12 29 D4
Canmore Prim Sch KY11 29 F1
Canning St EH3 232 B2
Canning Street La EH3 232 A2
Cannon Wynd EH6 93 F3
Cannonmills Sch (Specl) EH7 93 E1
Cannons Way FK2 39 D1
Cannop Cres EH47 170 C1
Canon La EH3 93 E1
Canon Lynch Ct KY12 28 C2
Canon St EH3 93 E1
Canongate EH8 233 E3
Canonmills EH3 93 E2
Canthill Gdns ML7 191 D2
Cantlie Pl KY11 46 C2
Cantsdam Rd KY4 12 C4
Canty Gr EH32 98 B2
Capelaw Rd EH13 153 D3
Caplaw Way EH26 203 E3
Caponflat Cres EH41 100 C1
Caponhall Ct EH33 128 B3
Caponhall Dr EH33 128 B3
Caponhall Rd EH33 128 B3
Cappers Ct EH48 143 F2
Captain's Dr EH16 155 D3
Captain's Loan EH16 155 D3
Captain's Rd EH17 155 D3
Captain's Row EH16 155 D3
Caputhall Rd EH54 146 B3
Carberry Ct EH21 157 F4
Carberry Mains Cotts EH21 127 D1
Carberry Pl EH12 122 C4
Carberry Rd EH21 126 C2
Carbrook Dr FK7 20 B2
Carbrook Pl FK3 61 F3
Carcraig Pl KY11 48 A2
Cardross Ave EH52 117 D3
Cardross Cres EH52 117 E3
Cardross Rd EH52 117 E3
Cardrowan Rd FK7 20 B1
Carfrae Gdns EH4 92 A1
Carfrae Gr EH4 92 A1
Carfrae Pk EH4 92 A1
Carfrae Rd EH4 92 A1
Cargil Terr EH5 93 D3
Cargilfield Sch EH4 91 D2
Carhowden Rd FK2 61 D2
Carlaverock Ave EH33 128 B3
Carlaverock Cres EH33 128 B3
Carlaverock Ct EH33 128 C3
Carlaverock Dr EH33 128 B3
Carlaverock Gr EH33 128 B3
Carlaverock Terr EH33 128 C2
Carlaverock View EH33 128 B2
Carlaverock Wlk EH33 128 B3
Carledubs Ave EH52 117 D3
Carledubs Cres EH52 117 D3
Carlie Ave FK9 2 A3
Carlin Craig KY3 34 C1
Carlin Cres KY3 34 C1
Carlin La ML8 230 A1
Carlingnose Ct KY11 68 B3
Carlingnose Pk KY11 68 B3
Carlingnose Point KY11 68 B3
Carlingnose View KY11 68 B3
Carlingnose Way KY11 68 B3
Carlops Ave EH26 203 F3
Carlops Cres EH26 203 F3
Carlops Rd EH26 203 E3
Carlouk La ML8 230 A1
Carlowrie Ave EH30 89 F4
Carlowrie Cres EH30 89 F4
Carlowrie Pl EH23 207 E4
Carlton St EH4 93 D1
Carlton Terr EH7 233 F4
Carlton Terrace La EH7 233 F4
Carlton Terrace Mews EH7 233 F4
Carluke High Sch ML8 230 A1
Carluke Prim Sch ML8 230 A2
Carlyle Ct
Haddington EH41 132 A4
Livingston EH54 148 B3
Carlyle Gdns EH41 101 D1
Carlyle La KY12 28 C3
Carlyle Pl Edinburgh EH7 94 A1
Musselburgh EH21 126 B3
Carlyle Rd KY1 17 D2
Carlyle St KY12 26 A1
Carlyle Terr EH48 145 E3
Carmel Ave EH29 89 D1
Carmel Rd EH29 89 D1
Carmelaws EH49 85 D3
Carmelite Rd EH30 89 D4
Carmondean Centre Rd EH54 147 D3
Carmondean Ctr EH54 147 D3
Carmondean Prim Sch EH54 147 D4
Carmuir ML11 215 D1
Carmuirs Ave FK1 59 E3
Carmuirs Dr FK1 59 E3
Carmuirs Prim Sch FK1 59 E3
Carmuirs St FK1 59 E3
Carnaughton Pl FK12 4 C3
Carnbee Ave EH16 155 E3
Carnbee Cres EH16 155 E3
Carnbee Dell EH16 155 E3
Carnbee End EH16 155 E3
Carnbee Pk EH16 155 E3
Carnbee Pl KY12 29 E2
Carnegie Ave KY11 46 C4
Carnegie Birthplace Mus KY12 29 D2
Carnegie Campus (Bsns Pk) KY11 46 C4
Carnegie Dr
Dunfermline KY12 29 D2
Falkirk FK1 59 E3
Carnegie Rd EH48 146 A3
Carnegie St EH8 233 E2
Carneil Rd KY12 27 E4
Carneil Terr KY12 27 E3
Carnethie St EH24 181 F1
Carnethy Ave
Edinburgh EH13 153 D3
Penicuik EH26 203 F3
Carnethy Cres KY2 16 C4
Carnethy Ct EH26 203 F3
Carnock Prim Sch KY12 27 E4
Carnock Rd KY12 28 A3
Carnock St FK7 20 C4
Carnwath Rd ML8 230 A1
Caroline Cres FK12 4 C3
Caroline Gdns
Edinburgh EH12 121 F4
Mid Calder EH53 148 A1
Caroline Park Ave EH5 92 B3
Caroline Park Gr EH5 92 B3
Caroline Pk EH53 148 A1
Caroline Pl EH12 121 F4
Caroline Terr EH12 121 E4
Carpet La EH6 94 A3
Carradale Ave FK1 59 E2
Carribber Ave EH49 84 A3
Carrick Cres EH22 183 E4
Carrick Ct FK7 7 E3
Carrick Dr KY11 48 A2
Carrick Gdns EH54 173 F3
Carrick Gr KY11 48 A2
Carrick Knowe Ave EH12 121 F3
Carrick Knowe Dr EH12 121 F3
Carrick Knowe Gdns EH12 121 F3
Carrick Knowe Gr EH12 121 F3
Carrick Knowe Hill EH12 121 F3
Carrick Knowe Loan EH12 121 F3
Carrick Knowe Parkway EH12 121 F3
Carrick Knowe Pl EH12 121 F3
Carrick Knowe Prim Sch EH12 121 F3
Carrick Knowe Rd EH12 121 F2
Carrick Knowe Terr EH12 121 F3
Carrick Pl
Falkirk, Roughlands FK2 39 D2
Falkirk, Tamfourhill FK1 59 E2
Carriden Brae EH51 64 B3
Carriden Glade EH51 64 B4
Carrington Cres EH4 92 C2
Carrington Mains Cotts EH23 206 B3
Carrington Rd EH4 92 C1
Carron Ind Est FK2 39 D1
Carron La KY11 29 F2
Carron Pl Edinburgh EH6 94 A3
Grangemouth FK3 61 E2
Kircaldy KY2 16 C4
Stirling FK7 7 D1
Carron Prim Sch FK2 39 D1
Carron Rd FK2 60 A4
Carron Terr FK2 82 C4
Carron View FK2 82 C4
Carron Wlk EH54 148 A2
Carronbank Ave FK2 39 D1
Carronbank Cres FK6 36 C2
Carronbank Ct FK2 39 D1
Carronflats Rd FK3 61 F4
Carrongrove Ave FK2 39 D1
Carrongrove Rd FK2 39 D1
Carronhall Ave FK2 39 E2
Carronlea Dr FK2 39 D1
Carronshore Prim Sch FK2 39 E2
Carronshore Rd FK2 39 D1
Carronside Pl FK6 36 C2
Carronside St FK2 60 A4
Carronvale Ave FK5 38 B1
Carronvale Rd FK5 38 B1
Carronview FK5 38 B1
Carsaig Ct FK9 2 A3
Carse Cres FK2 61 D2
Carse Knowe EH49 85 E4
Carse Terr FK10 9 F4
Carse View Airth FK2 22 C2
Bo'ness EH51 63 E3
Carsebridge Rd FK10 10 B4
Carseview Bannockburn FK7 7 F1
Tullibody FK10 4 A1
Carson Pl KY11 46 B3
Carswell Pl KY12 28 C3
Cartmore Rd KY5 14 A4
Cassel's La EH6 93 F2
Casselbank St EH6 93 F2
Cast The EH18 181 E3
Castellau Cotts EH42 78 B1
Castings Ave FK2 60 A4
Castings Ct
Falkirk, Grahamston FK2 60 A4
Falkirk, Middlefield FK2 60 C3
Castings Dr FK2 60 A3
Castings Rd FK2 60 C3
Castings The KY12 28 B3
Castlandhill Rd KY11 47 D1
Castle Ave Airth FK2 22 C2
Cockenzie & Port Seton EH32 97 F2
Edinburgh EH12 121 E3
Falkirk FK2 39 E2
Gorebridge EH23 207 E4
Castle Bsns Pk The FK8 1 C1
Castle Cres Denny FK6 36 B1
East Calder EH53 148 C1
Falkirk FK2 60 B4
Torwood FK5 37 F4
Castle Ct Falkirk FK2 60 B4
Menstrie FK11 3 F3
Stirling FK8 7 D4
Castle Dr Airth FK2 22 C2
Dunfermline KY11 46 C3
Falkirk FK2 60 B4
Stenhousemuir FK5 38 C1
Castle Gate EH42 78 B2
Castle Gogar EH12 120 B4
Castle Mains Pl EH39 53 D3
Castle Moffat EH14 166 A4
Castle Pk EH39 53 D2
Castle Pl Dunbar EH42 78 B2
Falkirk FK2 60 B4
Gorebridge EH23 207 E4
Castle Rd
Cockenzie & Port Seton EH32 97 F2
Falkirk FK2 60 B4
Menstrie FK11 3 F3
Rosyth KY11 46 C1
Stirling FK9 2 B2
Tranent EH33 128 B3
Winchburgh EH52 88 A1
Castle Row KY12 28 B3
Castle St Alloa FK10 10 A3
Clackmannan FK10 11 D2
Dunbar EH42 78 B2
Edinburgh EH2 232 B3
Castle Terr
Clackmannan FK10 11 D2
Cockenzie & Port Seton EH32 97 F2
Denny FK6 36 B1
Edinburgh EH2 232 B2
Winchburgh EH52 88 A1
Castle View
Cockenzie & Port Seton EH32 97 F2
Fallin FK7 8 B2
Gorebridge EH23 207 E4
Pencaitland EH34 160 B3
Castle Wlk EH32 97 F2
Castle Wynd FK8 7 D4
Castle Wynd N EH1 232 C2
Castle Wynd S EH1 232 C2
Castleblair KY12 28 C2
Castleblair La KY12 28 C3
Castleblair Mews KY12 28 C3
Castleblair Pk KY12 28 C3
Castlebrae Bsns Ctr EH16 124 C2
Castlebrae Com Sch EH16 124 C2
Castlegait FK8 7 D4
Castlehill Bo'ness EH51 63 E4
Edinburgh EH1 232 C3
Castlehill Ave FK1 110 A3
Castlelaurie St FK2 60 B4
Castlelaw Cres EH25 180 C3
Castlelaw Ct EH26 203 F3
Castlelaw Fort & Souterrain EH26 179 E2
Castlelaw Rd EH13 153 D3
Castlemains Pl EH39 53 E3
Castlemount Terr KY2 16 B4
Castlepark FK10 23 E3
Castlerig KY3 34 C1
Castleton Cres FK3 61 E3
Castleview FK9 2 A2
Castleview Dr FK9 2 A4
Castleview La EH54 173 F2
Castleview Terr FK4 57 D2
Cath Church of St Mary EH12 232 A3
Cathcart Pl EH11 122 C3
Cathedral La EH1 233 D4
Catherine St FK7 7 E1
Catherine Terr EH47 145 E1
Cathlaw La EH48 114 A3
Cathrine Gr EH51 64 A3
Catriona Terr EH26 180 A1
Cattle Market FK10 11 D3
Cauldhame Cres FK7 6 B3
Causeway The
Bridge of A FK9 2 B3
Edinburgh EH15 124 B3
Causewayhead Rd FK9 2 B2
Causewayside EH9 123 F3
Cavalry Park Dr EH15 124 B3
Cawder Gdns FK9 1 C4
Cawder Rd FK9 1 C4
Cawdor Cres KY2 16 C3
Cecil St FK7 7 D3
Cedar Ave Kirkaldy KY1 17 E4
Stirling FK8 6 C3
Cedar Cres
Cowdenbeath KY4 13 E3
Westquarter FK2 61 D1
Whitburn EH47 170 B3
Cedar Dr EH32 97 E2
Cedar Gr
Dunfermline KY11 46 B4
Stenhousemuir FK5 38 B1
Cedar Rd EH20 180 C4
Cedar St Dunbar EH42 78 A1
Grangemouth FK3 61 E4
Cedar Wynd ML7 192 A3
Cedarbank EH54 147 F3
Cedarbank Sch EH54 147 F3
Cedars The FK10 4 A1
Cedric Rise EH54 148 A1

Cemetery Rd Dalkeith EH22 156 C1
Fauldhouse EH47 193 E3
Prestonpans EH32 96 C1
Shotts ML7 192 A2
Central Ave FK3 61 E3
Central Bvd FK5 38 A2
Central Dock Rd FK3 40 C1
Central Dr FK5 38 C2
Central Park Ave FK5 38 A2
Central Park Bsns Pk FK5 38 A2
Central Pk (Cowdenbeath FC) KY4 13 E2
Central Rd KY12 44 B4
Central Ret Pk FK1 60 B3
Central Way KY11 48 B3
Centre Intc EH54 148 A1
Chacefield St FK4 58 A3
Chacefield Wood FK6 57 F4
Chalmers Cres EH9 123 E3
Chalmers Hospl EH3 232 C2
Chalmers Sq EH54 146 B3
Chalmers St
Dunfermline KY12 28 C2
Edinburgh EH3 232 C1
Chalmerston Rd FK9 1 A2
Chalton Rd FK9 2 A4
Chalybeate EH41 131 F4
Chamberfield Rd KY12 29 E3
Chamberlain Rd EH10 123 D2
Chambers Dr FK2 39 D1
Chambers St EH1 233 D2
Chamfron Gdns FK7 7 F2
Champigny Ct EH21 126 C3
Chancelot Cres EH6 93 E3
Chancelot Gr EH5 93 E3
Chancelot Terr EH6 93 E3
Chandler's Rise KY11 47 F2
Chandler's Wlk KY11 47 F2
Channel Brae EH42 136 B4
Chapel Bank EH22 158 B3
Chapel Cres FK2 39 D2
Chapel Ct EH16 124 C2
Chapel Dr FK5 38 C2
Chapel Gr KY2 16 B4
Chapel La Edinburgh EH6 94 A3
Falkirk FK1 60 A3
Chapel Level KY2 16 C4
Chapel Loan EH25 181 D2
Chapel Pl
High Valleyfield KY12 26 A1
Inverkeithing KY11 47 E2
Kircaldy KY2 16 B4
North Queensferry KY11 68 B3
Pathhead EH37 185 D3
Chapel Rd KY2 16 B4
Chapel St Cowdenbeath KY4 13 E2
Dunfermline KY12 28 C2
Edinburgh EH8 233 E1
High Valleyfield KY12 26 A1
Kincardine FK10 23 F2
Lochgelly KY5 14 A4
Chapel Villas KY11 48 A1
Chapel Wynd EH1 232 C2
Chapelfauld Gn KY11 29 F2
Chapelhill
Clackmannan FK10 11 D2
Dirleton EH39 53 D2
Kircaldy KY2 16 B4
Chapelhill St FK10 23 E3
Chapelton Ave EH55 172 C2
Chapelton Dr EH55 172 C2
Chapelton Gdns EH55 172 C2
Chapelton Gr EH55 172 C2
Chapelton Pl EH55 173 D2
Chapelton Terr EH55 172 C3
Chapelwell Pl KY11 29 F2
Charing Cross FK3 40 B1
Charles Ave FK9 2 A3
Charles Cres
Bathgate EH48 145 F3
Carluke ML8 230 A1
Charles Ct KY11 45 F2
Charles Dr FK5 59 E4
Charles La EH48 145 F3
Charles Rodger Pl FK9 2 A3
Charles St Alloa FK10 9 F4
Dunfermline KY11 29 D1
Edinburgh EH8 233 D2
Penicuik EH26 203 F4
Shotts ML7 192 A2
Stirling FK8 7 D3
Charles Street La EH1 233 D2
Charles Way KY11 45 F2
Charles Way S KY11 45 F2
Charlesfield EH8 123 E4
Charlesfield La EH54 147 D1
Charlesfield Rd EH54 173 E4
Charlotte Dundas Ct FK3 61 F3
Charlotte Hill Ct FK5 38 A2
Charlotte La EH2 232 B3
Charlotte Sq EH2 232 B3
Charlotte St Brightons FK2 82 B4
Kirkaldy KY1 17 D2
Shotts ML7 192 A2
Charlton Gr EH25 180 C2
Charter St FK7 7 D2
Charterhall Gr EH9 123 E2
Charterhall Rd EH9 123 E1
Charteris Ct EH32 98 B3
Charteris Pk EH32 98 B3
Charteris Rd EH32 98 B3
Chartershall Rd FK7 7 D1
Chattan Ave FK9 2 A2
Chattan Ind Est FK4 58 B2
Cherry Ave EH48 145 F3
Cherry La EH22 183 F3
Cherry Pl KY4 13 E2
Cherry Rd EH19 182 A3
Cherry Tree Ave EH14 151 F2
Cherry Tree Cres EH14 151 F2
Cherry Tree Gdns EH14 151 E2
Cherry Tree Gr EH14 151 E2
Cherry Tree Loan EH14 151 F2
Cherry Tree Pk EH14 151 E2
Cherry Tree Pl EH14 151 F2
Cherry Tree View EH14 151 F2
Cherrybank KY12 29 E3
Cherryton Dr FK10 11 D3
Chessel's Ct EH8 233 E3
Chesser Ave EH14 122 B2
Chesser Cres EH14 122 B2
Chesser Gdns EH14 122 A2
Chesser Gr EH14 122 A2
Chesser Loan EH14 122 A2
Chester Ct EH19 182 A3
Chester Dr EH22 183 E3
Chester Gr EH19 182 A3
Chester St EH3 232 A3
Chester View EH22 183 E3
Chesters View EH19 182 A3
Chestnut Ave Kirkaldy KY1 17 E4
Whitburn EH47 170 B3
Chestnut Cres FK6 36 B2
Chestnut Gr Bo'ness EH51 63 E3
Bonnyrigg and Lasswade EH19 182 A3
Dunfermline KY11 46 C4
Livingston EH54 148 A3
Stenhousemuir FK5 38 C2
Winchburgh EH52 87 F1
Chestnut St EH5 92 C4
Cheviot Pl FK3 61 F3
Cheviot Rd KY2 16 C4
Cheyne St EH4 93 D1
Chief's Cl KY1 17 E3
Chisholm Ave FK9 2 A2
Chisholm Cres KY5 14 A4
Chisholm Pl FK3 61 D3
Chisholm St KY12 29 E4
Chisholm Terr EH26 203 F4
Christian Cres EH15 125 E4
Christian Gr EH15 125 D4
Christie Pl KY1 17 E4
Christie St KY12 29 D3
Christie Terr FK5 38 C2
Christiemiller Ave EH7 94 C1
Christiemiller Gr EH7 94 C1
Christiemiller Pl EH7 94 C1
Chuckie Pend EH3 232 B2
Church Ct Kirkaldy KY1 17 E2
Philpstoun EH49 86 B3
Church Gdns EH32 98 C3
Church Gr Alloa FK10 5 E1
Burntisland KY3 33 E1
Church Hill EH10 123 D2
Church Hill Pl EH10 123 D2
Church La Denny FK6 36 B2
Kirkaldy KY1 17 E2
Limekilns KY11 45 E2
Church Pk EH48 145 D3
Church Pl Armadale EH48 144 A3
Bathgate EH48 145 D3
Crossgates KY4 30 C4
Falkirk FK2 60 A3
Fauldhouse EH47 193 F3
Longridge EH47 170 B1
Church Rd Bo'ness EH51 63 F4
Bonnyrigg and Lasswade EH18 155 F1
California FK1 81 F3
North Berwick EH39 54 B4
Church St Addiewell EH55 171 E1
Alloa FK10 10 A3
Broxburn EH52 117 F3
Burntisland KY3 33 E1
Cowdenbeath KY4 13 E2
Dunbar EH42 78 C1
Falkirk FK2 39 E1
Haddington EH41 132 A4
Harthill ML7 168 B3
High Bonnybridge FK4 58 B2
Inverkeithing KY11 47 E2
Kingseat KY12 12 A1
Kirkaldy KY1 17 F3
Limekilns KY11 45 E2
Loanhead EH20 181 E4
Lochgelly KY5 14 A4
Stenhousemuir FK5 38 C2
Tranent EH33 128 B4
Church Wlk Denny FK6 36 C1
Kinghorn KY3 35 D2
Church Wynd EH51 63 F4
Churchhill Dr EH10 123 D2
Churchill Dr FK9 2 A3
Churchill Pl KY11 46 C2
Churchill St FK10 9 F4
Churchill Way EH27 149 F2
Churchway EH32 98 C3
Cinderhall Pl EH33 128 A1
Circle The EH22 156 A4
Circus Gdns EH3 232 B4
Circus La EH3 93 D1
Circus Pl EH3 232 B4
Citadel Pl EH6 93 F3
Citadel St EH6 93 F3
City Hospl EH14 153 F4
City Mus EH8 233 E3
City Of Edinburgh By-Pass
The Dalkeith EH22 157 D4
Edinburgh EH10 154 B2
Whitecraig EH21 126 A1
Clackmae Gr EH16 154 C4
Clackmae Rd EH16 154 C4
Clackmannan Coll of F Ed FK10 10 A4
Clackmannan Prim Sch FK10 11 D2
Clackmannan Rd FK10 10 B3
Clanranald Pl FK1 59 F1
Clare Ct EH39 54 A4
Clarebank Cres EH6 94 A2
Claremont FK10 9 F4
Claremont Bank EH7 93 E2
Claremont Cres EH7 93 E2
Claremont Ct EH7 93 E2
Claremont Dr FK9 2 B4
Claremont Gdns EH6 94 B2
Claremont Gr EH7 93 E2
Claremont Ind Est FK10 10 A3
Claremont Pk EH6 94 A2
Claremont Prim Sch FK10 9 F4
Claremont Rd EH6 94 A2
Claremont St FK4 57 F3
Clarence St EH3 93 D1
Clarendon Cres
Edinburgh EH4 232 A4
Linlithgow EH49 85 D3
Clarendon Pl FK8 7 D4
Clarendon Rd
Linlithgow EH49 85 D3
Stirling FK8 7 D4
Claret Rd
Grangemouth, Bowhouse FK3 61 F3
Grangemouth, Oil Refinery FK3 62 B4
Clarinda Ave FK1 59 D3
Clarinda Gdns EH22 157 E2
Clarinda Terr EH16 124 A1
Clark Ave EH5 93 E3
Clark Bldgs EH35 159 F4
Clark Pl Edinburgh EH5 93 D3
Kirkaldy KY2 17 D3
Clark Rd Edinburgh EH5 93 D3
Inverkeithing KY11 47 D1
Clark St FK7 7 D1
Clarkson Rd EH52 117 E3
Claverhouse Dr EH16 155 D4
Claycrofts Pl FK7 7 D3
Clayhills Gr EH14 151 D1
Clayhills Pk EH14 151 D1
Clayknowes Ave EH21 126 A3
Clayknowes Cres EH21 126 A3
Clayknowes Ct EH21 126 A2
Clayknowes Dr EH21 125 F3
Clayknowes Pl EH21 126 A3
Clayknowes Way EH21 126 A3
Claymore Dr FK7 7 E2
Clearburn Cres EH16 124 A2
Clearburn Gdns EH16 124 A2
Clearburn Rd
Edinburgh EH16 124 A2
Gorebridge EH23 183 D1
Cleaves The FK10 4 A1
Cleekim Dr EH15 125 D2
Cleekim Rd EH15 125 D2
Cleghorn Dr EH52 117 D3
Cleikiminrig EH15 125 D2
Cleish Gdns KY2 16 C3
Cleish Pl KY11 29 F1
Cleish Rd KY11 29 F1
Cleland St EH47 170 A4
Clement Rise EH54 148 A1
Clerics Hill EH29 89 D1
Clerk Gr KY11 29 F1
Clerk Rd EH26 203 E3
Clerk St Edinburgh EH8 233 E1
Loanhead EH20 181 F4
Clerkington Rd EH41 131 F4
Clerkington Wlk EH41 131 F4
Clermiston Ave EH4 91 E1
Clermiston Cres EH4 91 E1
Clermiston Dr EH4 91 E1
Clermiston Gdns EH4 91 E1
Clermiston Gn EH4 91 E1
Clermiston Gr EH4 91 E1
Clermiston Hill EH4 91 F1
Clermiston Loan EH4 91 E1
Clermiston Medway EH4 91 E1
Clermiston Pk EH4 91 E1
Clermiston Pl EH4 91 E1
Clermiston Prim Sch EH4 91 E1
Clermiston Rd EH12 121 F4
Clermiston Rd N EH4 91 F1
Clermiston View EH4 91 F1
Clerwood Bank EH12 121 E4
Clerwood Gdns EH12 121 E4
Clerwood Gr EH12 121 F4
Clerwood Loan EH12 121 E4
Clerwood Pk EH12 121 E4
Clerwood Pl EH12 121 F4
Clerwood Row EH12 121 E4
Clerwood Terr EH12 121 F4
Clerwood View EH12 121 F4
Clerwood Way EH12 121 E4
Cleuch Ave FK10 4 A1
Cleuch Dr FK12 4 C4
Cleuch Rd EH23 207 F1
Cleuchbrae EH55 172 B2
Cleveland Dr KY11 47 D1
Clifford Rd
North Berwick EH39 54 B3
Stirling FK8 7 D3
Clifton Hall Sch EH28 118 B1
Clifton Rd EH28 118 C1
Clifton Trad Est EH28 118 C2
Clifton View EH52 118 A3
Cliftonhall Rd EH28 119 D3
Climpy Rd ML11 214 B2
Clinkum Bank KY12 26 B2
Clinton Rd EH9 123 D2
Clive St ML7 191 F3
Cloanden Pl KY2 17 D2
Clockluine Rd KY11 47 F3
Clockmill La EH7, EH8 94 A1
Close The KY11 46 B1
Clova Dr EH54 173 F3
Clovenstone Dr EH14 152 C4
Clovenstone Gdns EH14 152 C4
Clovenstone Pk EH14 152 C4
Clovenstone Prim Sch EH14 152 C4
Clovenstone Rd EH14 152 C4
Clover Pl EH51 63 F3
Cloverbank EH54 147 F3
Cloverstone Pk EH14 152 C4
Cloverstone Rdbt EH14 152 C4
Cloves The FK11 4 A3
Cluanie Ave ML7 191 F3
Clufflatt EH30 67 F1
Cluflatt Brae EH30 67 F1
Clune Rd KY12 27 F4
Clunie Rd KY11 29 F2
Clunivar St KY12 28 B3
Cluny Ave EH10 123 D1
Cluny Dr Edinburgh EH10 123 D1
Stenhousemuir FK5 38 C2
Cluny Gdns EH10 123 E1
Cluny Pl EH10 123 E2
Cluny Terr EH10 123 D1
Clyde Cres Dunfermline KY11 29 F1
Larbert FK5 38 A2
Clyde Dr Livingston EH54 148 A2
Shotts ML7 192 A2
Clyde St Edinburgh EH1 233 D4
Falkirk FK1 59 F3
Grangemouth FK3 40 A1
Clydesdale St EH51 63 F3
Clydevale Pl EH54 117 D1
Coal Neuk EH33 128 B3
Coal Rd KY12 28 C2
Coal Wynd Bannockburn FK7 7 E1
Kirkaldy KY1 17 E2
Coalgate FK10 10 A3
Coalgate Ave EH33 128 C4
Coalgate Rd EH33 128 C4
Coalhill EH6 93 F3
Coalpots Way FK10 5 F2
Coates Cotts EH32 99 F2
Coates Cres EH3 232 A3
Coates Gdns EH12 122 C4
Coatfield La EH6 94 A3
Cobblebrae Cres FK2 39 D1
Cobden Cres EH9 123 F2
Cobden Rd EH9 123 F2
Cobden St Alva FK12 5 D4
Alva, The Boll FK12 5 D3
Coblecrook Gdns FK12 4 C3
Coblecrook La FK12 4 C3
Coblecrook Pl FK12 4 C3
Coburg St EH6 93 F3
Cochran Pl EH7 93 E1
Cochran Terr EH7 93 E1
Cochrane Ave Falkirk FK2 60 A2
Inverkeithing KY11 47 E1
Cochrane Cres FK12 4 C4
Cochrane Pl EH6 94 A2
Cochrane Rd KY11 46 A1
Cochrane Sq EH54 173 E3
Cochrane St
Bathgate EH48 145 D4
Falkirk FK1 60 A2
Cochrane Way KY11 48 A3
Cochrane Wlk KY11 29 F2
Cochranes The FK12 5 D4
Cochrie Pl FK10 4 B1
Cochrina Pl EH24 181 E1
Cockburn Cres
Balerno EH14 177 D4
Whitecross EH49 84 A3
Cockburn Ct EH35 159 F4
Cockburn Dr EH35 159 E3
Cockburn Sq EH37 185 D3
Cockburn St
Edinburgh EH1 233 D3
Falkirk FK1 60 A2
Cockburnhill Rd EH14 177 D4
Cockburnspath Sch TD13 140 C2
Cockenzie Prim Sch EH32 97 E2
Cocklaw St KY4 12 B4
Cockles Brae EH41 132 C2
Cockmilane Brae EH41 132 B3
Cockmylane EH13, EH10 153 F4
Cockpen Ave EH19 182 A3
Cockpen Cres EH19 182 A3
Cockpen Dr EH19 182 A3
Cockpen Pl EH19 182 A3
Cockpen Rd EH19 182 B3
Cockpen Terr EH19 182 A3
Cockpen View EH19 182 A3
Coilesdene Gr EH15 125 E4
Coillesdene Ave EH15 125 E4
Coillesdene Cres EH15 125 E4
Coillesdene Dr EH15 125 E4
Coillesdene Gdns EH15 125 E4
Coillesdene Loan EH15 125 F4
Coillesdene Terr EH15 125 E4
Coire Loan ML7 192 A2
Coldingham Pl KY12 29 E2
Colduie Circ FK2 62 A1
Colegate Rd EH37 208 B4
Coles Pl KY4 31 D3
Colinshiel Ave EH48 144 C4
Colinshiel St EH48 144 C4
Colinshiel View EH48 143 F4
Colinswell Rd KY3 33 E1
Colinton Gr EH14 122 B1
Colinton Gr W EH14 122 B1
Colinton Mains Cres EH13 153 F3
Colinton Mains Dr EH13 153 E4
Colinton Mains Gdns EH13 153 E4
Colinton Mains Gn EH13 153 E4
Colinton Mains Gr EH13 153 F4
Colinton Mains Loan EH13 153 E4
Colinton Mains Pl EH13 153 F4
Colinton Mains Rd EH13 153 E3
Colinton Mains Terr EH13 153 F4
Colinton Prim Sch EH13 153 E4
Colinton Rd EH10, EH13 122 C2
Coll Pl FK3 61 E3
College Cres FK2 60 B4
College Wynd EH1 233 D2
Colliers Rd FK7 8 B2
Collingwood Ct FK1 59 F3
Collins Cres KY11 47 F1
Collins Pl EH3 93 D1
Colliston Rd KY12 29 E3
Collyland Rd FK10 5 E2
Colmestone Gate EH10 154 A3
Colonsay Ave FK2 61 E1
Colonsay Terr FK1 60 A1
Colquhoun St FK7 7 E3
Colquhoun Terr FK7 7 E3
Colsnaur FK11 4 A3
Coltbridge Ave EH12 122 B4
Coltbridge Gdns EH12 122 C4
Coltbridge Millside EH12 122 C4
Coltbridge Terr EH12 122 B4
Coltbridge Vale EH12 122 C4
Coltnes Ave ML7 212 A4
Colton Ct KY12 28 C2
Columba Ave EH4 92 A1
Columba Rd EH4 92 A1
Columbia Ave EH54 147 F2
Colvin St EH42 78 C1
Combfoot Cotts EH53 148 B2
Comeley Green Cres 10 EH7 94 A1
Comeley Green Pl 9 EH7 94 A1
Comely Bank Ave EH4 93 D1
Comely Bank Gr EH4 92 C1
Comely Bank Pl EH4 93 D1
Comely Bank Place Mews 2 EH4 93 D1
Comely Bank Rd EH4 92 C1
Comely Bank Row EH4 93 D1
Comely Bank St EH4 92 C1
Comely Bank Terr 1 EH4 93 D1
Comely Park La KY12 29 D2
Comely Park Prim Sch FK1 60 A2
Comely Park Terr 15 FK1 60 A2
Comely Pk Dunfermline KY12 29 D2
Maddiston FK2 82 C4
Comely Pl FK1 60 A2
Comiston Dr EH10 123 D1
Comiston Gdns EH10 123 D1
Comiston Gr EH10 154 A4
Comiston Pl EH10 123 D1
Comiston Prim Sch EH13 153 F3
Comiston Rd EH10 154 A4
Comiston Rise EH10 154 A4
Comiston Springs Ave EH10 154 A4
Comiston Terr EH10 123 D1
Comiston View EH10 154 A4
Commercial Prim Sch KY11 29 E2
Commercial Rd KY11 47 E1
Commercial School La KY12 29 D2
Commercial St
Edinburgh EH6 93 F3
Kirkaldy KY1 17 E3
Commissioner St EH51 64 A4
Commodores Wlk KY11 46 B1
Compass Sch EH41 131 F4
Compressor House Rd FK2 62 B3
Compton Rd FK3 61 E3
Comrie Terr EH51 63 F3
Comyn Dr FK2 82 B4
Concorde Way KY11 47 E2
Coneyhill Rd FK9 2 A4
Coneypark FK7 6 C3
Conifer Rd EH22 183 F4
Coningsby Pl FK10 10 A3
Connaught Pl EH6 93 E3
Conner Ave FK2 60 A4
Considine Gdns 3 EH8 94 B1
Considine Terr 2 EH8 94 B1
Constable Rd FK7 7 D3
Constitution Pl EH6 94 A3
Constitution St EH6 94 A3
Conway Ct FK1 59 F2
Cook Cres EH22 183 E3
Cook Pl KY1 18 A4
Cook Sq KY5 14 A4
Cook St KY1 18 A4
Cooper's La FK10 23 F2
Cooperage La FK1 60 A3
Cope La EH32 97 E2
Copeland Cres KY4 13 D1
Copland Pl FK12 4 C4
Copper Beech Wynd KY12 27 E1
Corbett Pl KY11 29 F1
Corbiehall EH51 63 F4
Corbiehill Ave EH4 92 A2
Corbiehill Cres EH4 91 F2
Corbiehill Gdns EH4 92 A2
Corbiehill Gr EH4 92 A2
Corbiehill Pk EH4 92 A2
Corbiehill Pl EH4 91 F2
Corbiehill Terr EH4 91 F2
Corbieshot EH15 125 D3
Corbiewood Dr FK7 19 F4

Cordiner's Land EH1 232 C2
Corentin Ct FK1 60 B2
Cormailin Pl KY12 26 A1
Corn Exchange Rd FK8 7 D4
Cornbank-St James' Prim Sch EH26 203 E3
Cornfield Pl EH54 147 D2
Cornhill Cres FK7 7 D2
Cornhill Terr EH6 94 A2
Cornton Bsns Pk FK9 2 A2
Cornton Cres FK9 2 A3
Cornton Prim Sch FK9 2 A2
Cornton Rd FK9 2 A2
Cornwall St EH1 232 B2
Cornwallis Pl EH3 93 E1
Coronation Pl
  Mayfield EH22 183 E4
  Skinflats FK2 39 F2
Corpach Dr KY12 28 C1
Corporation St FK1 60 B2
Correnie Dr EH10 123 D1
Correnie Gdns EH10 123 D1
Corrie Ave FK5 38 C2
Corrie Ct EH22 183 D2
Corrie Pl FK1 59 E2
Corruna Ct ML8 230 A1
Corslet Cres EH14 152 A3
Corslet Pl EH14 152 A3
Corslet Rd EH14 152 A3
Corston Pk EH54 148 A2
Corstorphine Bank Ave EH12 121 E4
Corstorphine Bank Dr EH12 121 E4
Corstorphine Bank Terr EH12 121 E4
Corstorphine High St EH12 121 E3
Corstorphine Hill Ave EH12 121 F4
Corstorphine Hill Cres EH12 121 F4
Corstorphine Hill Gdns EH12 121 F4
Corstorphine Hill Rd EH12 121 F4
Corstorphine Hospl EH12 121 F3
Corstorphine House Ave EH12 121 F3
Corstorphine Park Gdns EH12 121 F3
Corstorphine Prim Sch EH12 121 E3
Corstorphine Rd EH12 122 A4
Cortachy Ave FK2 39 D2
Cortleferry Dr EH22 156 C1
Cortleferry Gr EH22 156 C1
Cortleferry Pk EH22 156 C1
Cortleferry Terr EH22 156 C1
Corunna Pl EH6 93 F3
Corunna Terr EH26 204 A4
Cossars Wynd EH42 78 B1
Cotburn Cres KY3 33 F1
Cotlands Ave EH32 98 B2
Cotlands Pk EH32 98 B2
Cotlaws EH29 89 D1
Cottage Cres FK1 59 F3
Cottage Gn EH4 91 D2
Cottage Homes EH13 153 D4
Cottage La EH21 126 C3
Cottage Pk EH4 92 A1
Cotton La FK2 61 D2
Cotts The EH49 86 C2
Coulport Pl KY12 28 C1
Council Houses
  Athelstaneford EH39 101 F4
  Bolton EH41 162 C4
  Drem EH39 73 D2
  Gifford EH41 133 E3
Countess Ave EH42 78 B1
Countess Cres EH42 78 B1
Countess Rd EH42 78 B1
County Hospl FK10 10 A4
County Houses KY4 31 D3
County Rd EH32 96 C1
County Sq EH32 96 C1
Couper Ave EH39 54 B3
Couper Gr KY11 29 F1
Couper St EH6 93 F3
Court St EH41 132 A4
Courthill FK12 5 D4
Cousin's La KY12 28 C2
Cousland Cres EH47 146 A1
Cousland Intc EH54 147 F3
Cousland Prim Sch EH22 158 B3
Cousland Rd EH54 147 E2
Cousland Terr EH47 146 A1
Couston Dr KY11 48 A2
Couston Pl KY11 48 A2
Couston Rd KY11 48 A2
Couston St KY12 29 D2
Cove Cres ML7 191 F3
Covenanter Rd ML7 168 B2
Covenanters La EH30 68 A1
Coville Pl EH3 93 D1
Cow Wynd FK1 60 A2
Cowan Rd EH11 122 C2
Cowan St Bathgate EH48 145 F3
  Bonnybridge FK4 58 A3
Cowan Terr EH26 203 F4
Cowan's Cl EH8 233 E1
Cowane St FK8 7 D4
Cowden Cres EH22 157 E2
Cowden Gr EH22 157 E2
Cowden La EH22 157 E2
Cowden Pk EH22 157 E2
Cowden Terr EH22 157 E2
Cowden View EH22 157 E2
Cowdenbeath Prim Sch KY4 13 E2
Cowdenbeath Rd KY3 33 F1
Cowdenbeath Sta KY4 13 E2
Cowdenhill Rd EH51 64 A4
Cowgate EH1 233 D2
Cowgatehead EH1 233 D2
Cowie Prim Sch FK7 20 B4
Cowie Rd FK7 20 A4
Cowiehall Rd FK7 20 B4
Cowpits Ford Rd EH21 126 B2
Cowpits Rd EH21 126 B1
Coxfield EH11 122 B2
Coxithill Rd FK7 7 D2
Craig Ave Haddington EH41 101 D1
  Whitburn EH47 169 F3
Craig Cres FK9 2 B2
Craig Ct Bridge of A FK9 2 A3
  Burntisland KY3 33 E1
Craig Leith Rd FK7 7 E3
Craig St Blackridge EH48 142 C2
  Rosyth KY11 47 D2
Craigbank Alloa FK10 5 E1
  Crossford KY12 28 B1
Craigbank Prim Sch FK10 5 E1
Craigbank Rd FK1 112 A3
Craigbeath Ct KY4 13 D3
Craigburn Ct FK1 59 F1
Craigcrook Ave EH4 92 A1
Craigcrook Gdns EH4 92 A1
Craigcrook Gr EH4 92 A1
Craigcrook Pk EH4 92 A1
Craigcrook Pl 5 EH4 92 B1
Craigcrook Rd EH4 92 A1
Craigcrook Sq EH4 92 A1
Craigcrook Terr 4 EH4 92 B1
Craigdimas Gr KY11 48 A1
Craigearn Ave KY2 16 A4
Craigend Dr FK2 83 D3
Craigend Pk EH16 124 B1
Craigend Rd FK7 7 D2
Craigentinny Ave EH7 94 C1
Craigentinny Ave N EH6 94 B2
Craigentinny Cres EH7 94 C1
Craigentinny Gr EH7 94 C1
Craigentinny Pl EH7 94 C1
Craigentinny Prim Sch EH7 94 B1
Craigentinny Rd EH7 94 B1
Craigford Dr FK7 7 E1
Craigforth Cres FK8 1 C1
Craighall Ave EH6 93 E3
Craighall Bank EH6 93 E3
Craighall Cres EH6 93 E3
Craighall Gdns EH6 93 E3
Craighall Rd EH6 93 E3
Craighall St FK8 1 C1
Craighall Terr
  Edinburgh EH6 93 E3
  Musselburgh EH21 126 C3
Craighill Gdns EH10 122 C1
Craighill View EH48 142 C2
Craigholm La KY3 33 F1
Craighorn FK11 4 A3
Craighorn Dr FK1 59 F1
Craighorn Rd FK12 4 C3
Craighouse Ave EH10 122 C1
Craighouse Gdns EH10 122 C1
Craighouse Pk EH10 122 C1
Craighouse Rd EH10 122 C1
Craighouse Terr EH10 122 C1
Craigie Ct FK5 38 A1
Craigiebield Cres EH26 203 F2
Craigielaw Farm Cotts EH32 71 D2
Craigievar Ave FK2 39 D2
Craigievar Gdns KY2 16 C3
Craigievar Sq EH12 121 D4
Craigievar Wynd EH12 121 D4
Craiginn Ct EH48 142 B2
Craiginn Terr EH48 142 B2
Craigkennochie Terr KY3 33 F1
Craiglaw EH52 116 B1
Craiglea Ct EH48 142 B2
Craiglea Dr EH10 123 D1
Craiglea Pl EH10 122 C1
Craigleith FK10 5 F2
Craigleith Ave Falkirk FK1 59 F1
  North Berwick EH39 54 B3
Craigleith Ave N EH4 122 B4
Craigleith Ave S EH4 122 B4
Craigleith Bank EH4 92 B1
Craigleith Cres EH4 92 B1
Craigleith Dr EH4 92 B1
Craigleith Gdns EH4 92 B1
Craigleith Gr EH4 92 B1
Craigleith Hill EH4 92 B1
Craigleith Hill Ave EH4 92 B1
Craigleith Hill Cres EH4 92 B1
Craigleith Hill Gdns EH4 92 C1
Craigleith Hill Gn EH4 92 B1
Craigleith Hill Gr EH4 92 B1
Craigleith Hill Loan EH4 92 B1
Craigleith Hill Pk EH4 92 B1
Craigleith Hill Row EH4 92 B1
Craigleith Rd Edinburgh EH4 92 C1
  Grangemouth FK3 61 E3
Craigleith Ret Pk EH4 92 B1
Craigleith Rise EH4 122 B4
Craigleith View EH4 122 B4
Craiglockhart Ave EH14 122 B1
Craiglockhart Bank EH14 122 B1
Craiglockhart Cres EH14 122 B1
Craiglockhart Dell Rd EH14 122 B1
Craiglockhart Dr N EH14 122 B1
Craiglockhart Dr S EH14 122 B1
Craiglockhart Gdns EH14 122 B1
Craiglockhart Gr EH14 153 E4
Craiglockhart Loan EH14 122 B1
Craiglockhart Pk EH14 122 B1
Craiglockhart Pl EH14 122 B1
Craiglockhart Prim Sch EH11 122 C2
Craiglockhart Quadrant EH14 122 B1
Craiglockhart Rd EH14 122 B1
Craiglockhart Rd N EH14 122 B1
Craiglockhart Sports Ctr EH14 122 B1
Craiglockhart Terr EH14 122 C2
Craiglockhart View EH14 122 B1
Craigluscar Ct KY12 28 A4
Craigluscar Rd KY12 28 A4
Craigmillar Castle EH16 124 B1
Craigmillar Castle Ave EH16 124 C2
Craigmillar Castle Gdns EH16 124 B2
Craigmillar Castle Gr EH16 124 B2
Craigmillar Castle Loan EH16 124 C2
Craigmillar Castle Rd EH16 124 B1
Craigmillar Castle Terr EH16 124 B2
Craigmillar Pk EH16 124 A2
Craigmillar Pl FK5 38 C2
Craigmillar Prim Sch EH16 124 C2
Craigmore Gdns KY12 26 C1
Craigmount KY2 16 A4
Craigmount App EH12 121 E4
Craigmount Ave EH12 121 E4
Craigmount Ave N EH12 91 D1
Craigmount Bank EH4 91 D1
Craigmount Bank W EH4 91 D1
Craigmount Brae EH12 91 D1
Craigmount Cres EH12 121 E4
Craigmount Ct EH4 91 D1
Craigmount Dr EH12 121 D4
Craigmount Gdns EH12 121 E4
Craigmount Gr EH12 121 D4
Craigmount Gr N EH12 121 D4
Craigmount Hill EH4 91 D1
Craigmount Loan EH12 121 D4
Craigmount Pk EH12 121 E4
Craigmount Pl EH12 121 E4
Craigmount Sec Sch EH12 121 D4
Craigmount Terr EH12 121 E4
Craigmount View EH12 121 D4
Craigmount Way EH12 91 E1
Craigmuir Prim Sch EH4 92 B3
Craigmyle St KY12 29 E3
Craigomus Cres FK11 3 F3
Craigour Ave EH17 155 E4
Craigour Cres EH17 155 F4
Craigour Dr EH17 155 F4
Craigour Gdns EH17 155 F4
Craigour Gn EH17 155 E4
Craigour Gr EH17 155 F4
Craigour Loan EH17 155 F4
Craigour Pl EH17 155 E4
Craigour Terr EH17 155 F4
Craigpark EH48 113 F3
Craigpark Ave EH28 119 E1
Craigpark Cres EH28 119 E1
Craigridge Pl KY11 48 B3
Craigrie Terr FK10 11 D2
Craigrigg Cotts EH48 112 C2
Craigroyston Com High Sch EH4 92 A2
Craigs Ave EH12 121 E3
Craigs Bank EH12 121 D4
Craigs Chalet Pk EH49 84 A2
Craigs Cres EH12 121 E4
Craigs Ct EH48 113 F3
Craigs Dr EH12 121 D4
Craigs Gdns EH12 121 D4
Craigs Gr EH12 121 E4
Craigs Loan EH12 121 E4
Craigs Pk EH12 121 D4
Craigs Rd EH12 121 D4
Craigs Terr FK2 82 C4
Craigseaton EH52 117 D3
Craigshill East Rd EH54 148 A3
Craigshill Rd EH54 148 A3
Craigshill West Rd EH54 148 A3
Craigston Dr KY12 29 E3
Craigswood EH54 148 A3
Craigton Cres FK12 4 C3
Craigton Ct EH52 87 F1
Craigton Pl KY4 13 E1
Craigview Alloa FK10 5 E1
  Bo'ness EH51 64 B4
Craigward FK10 10 A3
Craigwell Path KY12 44 B4
Crame Terr EH22 156 C1
Cramond Ave EH4 91 E3
Cramond Bank EH4 91 D3
Cramond Brig Toll EH4 90 C2
Cramond Cres EH4 91 D3
Cramond Ct FK1 60 A1
Cramond Gdns
  Edinburgh EH4 91 D3
  Kircaldy KY2 16 C4
Cramond Glebe Gdns EH4 91 E3
Cramond Glebe Rd EH4 91 D3
Cramond Glebe Terr EH4 91 D3
Cramond Gn EH4 91 D3
Cramond Gr EH4 91 D3
Cramond Pk EH4 91 D3
Cramond Pl
  Dalgety Bay KY11 48 B2
  Edinburgh EH4 91 E3
Cramond Prim Sch EH4 91 D3
Cramond Rd N EH4 91 E3
Cramond Rd S EH4 91 F2
Cramond Regis EH4 91 D2
Cramond Terr EH4 91 D3
Cramond Vale EH4 91 D3
Cramond Village EH4 91 D4
Cranshaws Dr FK2 61 E1
Cranston Dr EH22 158 B3
Cranston Prim Sch EH37 184 C3
Cranston St Edinburgh EH8 233 E3
  Penicuik EH26 203 F3
Crarae Ave EH4 122 B4
Crathes Ave FK5 39 D2
Crathes Gdns EH54 173 F3
Crathie Dr FK6 36 B2
Craufurdland EH4 91 D2
Crawfield Ave EH51 63 F3
Crawfield La EH51 63 F3
Crawfield Rd EH51 63 F2
Crawford Dr FK2 82 A4
Crawford Pl KY12 29 E4
Crawford Sq FK2 22 B2
Crawfurd Rd EH16 124 A2
Crawlees Cres EH22 183 F3
Craws Knowe ML11 215 D1
Creel Ct EH39 54 B4
Creran Dr FK6 57 E3
Crescent The
  Edinburgh EH10 123 D1
  Gowkshill EH23 183 E2
  Rosyth KY11 46 A1
Creteil Ct FK1 60 B2
Creteil Pl FK3 61 E4
Crewe Bank EH5 92 C3
Crewe Cres EH5 92 C3
Crewe Gr EH5 92 C3
Crewe Loan EH5 92 B3
Crewe Pl EH5 92 B3
Crewe Rd N EH5 92 B3
Crewe Rd S EH4 92 C2
Crewe Rd W EH5 92 B3
Crewe Road Gdns EH5 92 B3
Crewe Terr EH5 92 C3
Crewe Toll EH4 92 B2
Crichton Ave EH37 185 D3
Crichton Castle EH37 208 C4
Crichton Dr
  Grangemouth FK3 61 F4
  Pathhead EH37 185 D3
Crichton Rd EH37 185 D3
Crichton St EH8 233 D2
Crichton Terr EH37 185 D3
Cricket Pl FK2 61 E1
Crighton Pl EH6 93 F2
Crimond Pl FK1 81 F4
Cringate Gdns FK7 7 F1
Crockett Gdns EH26 203 E3
Croft An Righ KY3 35 D2
Croft Pl EH54 147 E3
Croft St Dalkeith EH22 157 D2
  Penicuik EH26 203 F2
Croft's Rd FK10 4 A2
Croft-An-Righ EH8 233 F4
Crofters Gate EH47 170 C4
Crofters Way EH47 170 C3
Croftfoot Dr EH47 194 A3
Croftfoot Pl FK6 36 B2
Crofthead Ct FK8 2 A1
Crofthead Ctr EH54 173 E4
Crofthead Intc EH54 173 F4
Crofthead Rd Stirling FK8 2 A1
  Stoneyburn EH47 171 D1
Croftmalloch Prim Sch EH47 170 A3
Croftmalloch Rd EH47 170 A3
Crofts Rd TD13 140 C1
Crofts The EH42 104 C1
Croftsacre TD13 140 C1
Croftshaw Rd FK12 5 D4
Croftside Ct FK3 61 F3
Cromarty Pl KY1 17 F4
Crombie Prim Sch KY12 44 B4
Cromwell Dr FK1 60 B2
Cromwell Pl EH6 93 F3
Cromwell Rd
  Burntisland KY3 33 F1
  Falkirk FK1 60 B2
  North Berwick EH39 54 A4
  Rosyth KY11 46 C3
Cromwell Rd W FK1 60 B2
Crookston Ct EH21 126 C2
Crookston Rd EH21 126 C2
Crophill FK10 5 E1
Crosford Prim Sch KY12 28 A1
Cross Brae FK1 81 E3
Cross Loan EH35 159 F4
Cross Row KY11 45 D2
Cross St Dysart KY1 18 A4
  Falkirk FK2 39 D1
Cross The Linlithgow EH49 85 D4
  Lochgelly KY5 14 A4
Cross Way KY11 48 B3
Cross Wynd KY12 29 D2
Crossen La ML8 230 A1
Crossgatehead Rd FK2 82 B4
Crossgates Prim Sch KY4 30 C3
Crossgreen Dr EH52 117 D3
Crossgreen Pl EH52 117 D3
Crosshill Dr
  Bathgate EH48 145 E3
  Bo'ness EH51 63 F3
Crossroads Pl KY11 46 C2
Crosswood Ave EH14 177 D4
Crosswood Cres EH14 177 D4
Crosswood Terr EH55 217 F2
Crowhill Rd KY11 48 B2
Crown Gdns FK10 9 F4
Crown Pl EH6 93 F2
Crown St EH6 93 F2
Crownest Loan FK5 38 C1
Cruachan Ave FK9 2 A2
Cruachan Ct Falkirk FK1 60 B1
  Penicuik EH26 204 A3
Cruachan Pl FK3 61 F3
Cruckburn Wynd FK7 6 C2
Cruickness Rd KY11 68 B4
Cruickshank Dr FK1 81 E3
Cruikshank's Ct FK6 36 C1
Crum Cres FK7 7 E1
Crusader Dr EH25 180 C2
Crusader Rise EH54 148 A1
Crystal Works EH26 203 F3
Cuddy La EH10 123 D2
Cuddyhouse Rd KY12 12 B2
Cuffabouts EH51 64 B4
Cuguen Pl EH18 156 A1
Cuiken Ave EH26 203 F3
Cuiken Bank EH26 203 E3
Cuiken Prim Sch EH26 203 E3
Cuiken Terr EH26 203 F3
Cuikenburn EH26 203 F4
Cuil Gr KY12 28 B3
Cuillin Ct FK1 60 B1
Cuillin Pl FK3 61 F3
Cullalo Cres KY3 49 E4
Cullaloe Ct KY11 48 B2
Cullaloe Nature Reserve KY3 32 A2
Cullaloe View KY4 13 E1
Cullen Cres KY2 16 C4
Cullen Sq EH54 146 B3
Culloch Rd FK1 110 A3
Culmore Pl FK1 60 C1
Culross Abbey KY12 25 E1
Culross Palace KY12 42 B4
Culross Prim Sch KY12 42 B4
Cultenhove Cres
  Grangemouth FK3 61 F3
  Stirling FK7 6 C2
Cultenhove Pl FK7 7 D2
Cultenhove Rd FK7 7 D2
Cultins Rd EH11 121 D2
Cultrig Dr EH47 170 A3
Culvain Pl FK1 60 B1
Culzean Cres KY2 16 B4
Culzean Pl FK5 38 C2
Cumberland St EH3 93 E1
Cumbernauld Rd FK4 57 D2
Cumbrae Ct KY2 17 D4
Cumbrae Dr FK1 59 E2
Cumbrae Terr KY2 17 D4
Cumin Pl EH9 123 F2
Cumlodden Ave EH12 122 B4
Cumnor Cres EH16 124 A1
Cunnigar Gdns EH53 148 B2
Cunnigar Hill View EH53 148 B2
Cunningham Cres EH52 117 E3
Cunningham Ct
  Longniddry EH32 98 B2
  North Berwick EH39 54 A3
Cunningham Dr ML7 168 B3
Cunningham Gdns FK2 60 C3
Cunningham Rd
  Rosyth KY11 46 B1
  Stenhousemuir FK5 39 D2
  Stirling FK7 7 E4
Cunningham St FK3 61 E3
Curling Knowe KY4 31 D3
Curling Pk KY4 30 C3
Curran Cres EH52 117 F3
Currie High Sch EH14 151 F2
Curriehill Castle Dr EH14 151 E2
Curriehill Prim Sch EH14 152 A2
Curriehill Rd EH14 151 F3
Curriehill Sta EH14 151 F3
Currieside Ave ML7 191 F2
Currieside Pl ML7 191 E2
Currievale Dr EH14 151 F2
Currievale Park Gr EH14 151 F2
Currievale Pk EH14 151 F2
Cushenquarter Dr FK7 20 B2
Custom House Sq EH42 78 C2
Custonhall Pl FK6 36 B1
Cuthill Cres EH47 171 E1
Cuthill Terr EH47 171 E1
Cuttyfield Pl FK2 39 E2
Cypress Gr KY11 46 B4

D'arcy Cres EH22 183 F4
D'arcy Rd EH22 183 F3
D'arcy Terr EH22 183 F4
Daiches Braes EH15 125 E3
Dairy Cotts EH39 53 D1
Dairy Prim Sch EH11 122 C3
Daisy Terr EH11 122 C2
Dalachy Cotts KY3 32 C1
Dalbeath Cres KY4 13 D1
Dalbeath Gdns KY4 12 C1
Dalcross Way KY12 29 F3
Dalderse Ave FK2 60 A3
Dalgety Ave EH7 94 A1
Dalgety Bay Prim Sch KY11 48 A2
Dalgety Bay Sta KY11 47 F3
Dalgety Gdns KY11 48 B3
Dalgety House View KY11 48 B3
Dalgety Rd EH7 94 A1
Dalgety St EH7 94 A1
Dalgleish Ct FK8 7 D4

Dalgrain Rd FK3 40 A1
Dalhousie Ave EH19 182 A3
Dalhousie Ave W EH19 182 A3
Dalhousie Dr EH19 182 A3
Dalhousie Gdns EH19 182 A3
Dalhousie Rd EH22 156 C1
Dalhousie Rd E EH19 182 A3
Dalhousie Rd W EH19 182 A3
Dalhousie Terr EH10 123 D1
Dalkeith High Sch EH22 157 D2
Dalkeith Rd EH16 233 F1
Dalkeith St EH15 125 E4
Dallas Ave KY3 33 F1
Dallas Dr KY2 16 C4
Dalling Rd EH48 144 C3
Dalmahoy Cres EH14 151 E2
Dalmahoy Rd EH28 119 E1
Dalmeny Ho EH30 69 E1
Dalmeny Prim Sch EH30 89 F4
Dalmeny Rd EH6 93 E3
Dalmeny St EH6 93 F2
Dalmeny Sta EH30 89 E4
Dalmeny View KY11 48 B2
Dalmore Dr FK12 4 C3
Dalmorglen Pk FK7 6 C3
Dalratho Rd FK3 61 F4
Dalry Pl EH11 232 A2
Dalry Rd EH11 122 C4
Dalrymple Cres
Edinburgh EH9 123 F2
Musselburgh EH21 126 A3
Dalrymple Gdns EH22 158 B3
Dalrymple Loan EH21 126 B3
Dalton Ct EH22 183 F3
Dalum Ct EH20 181 D4
Dalum Dr EH20 181 D4
Dalum Gr EH20 181 D4
Dalum Loan EH20 181 D4
Dalziel Ct EH47 171 E1
Dalziel Pl EH7 94 A1
Damhead
Holdings Scheme EH10 154 B1
Damside EH4 232 A3
Danderhall Cres EH22 156 A4
Danderhall Prim Sch
EH22 156 A4
Dania Ct EH11 121 F2
Daniel Pl KY11 46 B3
Daniel Stewart's
& Melville Coll EH4 92 C1
Danube St EH4 232 A4
Dargai Pl EH52 117 D3
Darian La EH51 63 F4
Darmeid Pl ML7 212 A4
Darnaway St EH3 232 B4
Darnell Rd EH5 93 D3
Darney Terr KY3 34 C1
Darnley St FK8 7 D4
Darrach Dr FK6 36 A1
Darwin St EH54 148 A3
Davaar Dr KY2 16 C4
Davarr Pl FK1 59 E2
Davenport Pl KY11 46 C2
David Henderson Ct KY12 29 D2
David Millar Pl KY12 28 C3
David Scott Ave EH22 183 F4
David St Dunfermline KY12 29 D3
Kirkaldy KY1 17 D2
Lochgelly KY5 14 A4
David The First St KY3 34 C1
David's Loan FK2 39 E1
Davids Mains Prim Sch
EH4 91 F2
Davidson Gdns EH4 92 A2
Davidson La ML8 230 A1
Davidson Pk EH4 92 C2
Davidson Rd EH4 92 C2
Davidson St FK7 7 E1
Davidson Terr EH41 100 C1
Davidson Way EH54 147 F4
Davie St EH8 233 E2
Daviot Rd KY12 29 F3
Dawson Ave Alloa FK10 9 F4
Livingston EH54 147 F3
Dawson Park Sch FK2 39 D1
Dawson Pl EH51 63 F3
Dawson St FK2 60 A4
De Quincey Path EH18 181 F3
De Quincey Rd EH18 181 F3
Deacons Ct EH49 85 D3
Dean Bank La EH3 93 D1
Dean Cres FK8 2 B1
Dean Ct EH32 98 B2
Dean Dr KY12 28 A1
Dean Gr KY12 28 A1
Dean Park Cres EH4 232 A4
Dean Park Mews EH4 93 D1
Dean Park Prim Sch
EH14 151 E1
Dean Park Sch EH14 177 E4
Dean Path EH4 92 C1
Dean Pk Gowkhall KY12 27 F4
Longniddry EH32 98 B2
Newtongrange EH22 183 D3
Dean Park Pl EH22 183 D3
Dean Park St EH4 93 D1
Dean Pl Penicuik EH26 203 E3
Seafield EH47 146 A1
Dean Rd Bo'ness EH51 63 F3
Kirkaldy KY2 17 D2
Longniddry EH32 98 B2
Penicuik EH26 203 E3
Dean Ridge KY12 27 F4
Dean St Edinburgh EH4 93 D1
Whitburn EH47 170 A4
Dean Terr EH4 232 A4
Dean The EH40 75 F1
Deanburn EH26 203 F4
Deanburn Gr EH51 63 E3
Deanburn Pk EH49 84 C3
Deanburn Prim Sch EH51 63 E3
Deanburn Rd EH49 84 C3
Deanburn Wlk EH51 63 E3
Deanery Cl EH7 94 B1
Deanfield Cres EH51 63 F4
Deanfield Dr EH51 63 F3
Deanfield Pl EH51 63 F4
Deanfield Rd EH51 63 F4
Deanfield Terr EH51 63 F3
Deangate Gdns EH51 63 E3
Deanhaugh St EH4 93 D1
Deanpark Ave EH14 151 E1
Deanpark Bank EH14 151 E1
Deanpark Brae EH14 151 E1
Deanpark Cres EH14 151 E1
Deanpark Ct EH14 151 D1
Deanpark Gdns EH14 151 E1
Deanpark Gr EH14 151 E1
Deanpark Pl EH14 151 E1
Deans Com High Sch
EH54 147 D4
Deans Ind Est EH54 146 B3
Deans North Rd EH54 146 C4
Deans Prim Sch EH54 146 C3
Deans Rd EH54 146 B3
Deans Rdbt EH54 146 B3
Deans Service Units EH54 146 C3
Deans South EH54 146 C3
Deanswood Pk EH54 146 C3
Deantown Ave EH21 157 F4
Deantown Dr EH21 126 C1
Deantown Path EH21 126 C1
Deas Rd Inverkeithing KY11 47 D1
Shotts ML7 191 E3
Dechmont Inf Sch EH52 116 A1
Dechmont Rd EH12 121 D3
Dechmont Rdbt EH52 116 B1
Dedridge East Ind Est
EH54 148 A1
Dedridge East Rd EH54 148 A1
Dedridge North Rd EH54 147 F1
Dedridge Prim Sch EH54 148 A1
Dedridge West Rd EH54 173 F4
Dee Dr EH54 148 A3
Dee Pl KY11 29 F1
Dee St ML7 191 E3
Deep Sea World KY11 68 B3
Deer Park Bsns Campus
EH54 116 B1
Deer Park Dr EH54 116 B1
Deer Park Rd Abercorn EH30 66 C1
Dechmont EH54 116 B1
Deerhill EH52 116 B1
Deerpark FK10 5 F1
Deerpark Prim Sch FK10 5 F1
Deeside Dr ML8 230 A2
Delisle St EH42 78 B1
Dell Ave EH48 143 F3
Dell Rd EH13 153 D4
Delph Rd FK10 4 B1
Delphwood Cres FK10 4 B1
Delta Ave EH21 127 D3
Delta Cres EH21 127 D3
Delta Dr EH21 127 D3
Delta Gdns EH21 127 D3
Delta Pl EH21 126 B2
Delta Rd EH21 127 D3
Delta View EH21 127 D3
Dempster Pl KY12 28 C3
Den La ML7 191 E3
Den Rd KY2, KY1 17 E3
Denburn Pl KY2 17 E3
Denburn Rd KY1 17 E4
Denend Cres KY2 17 D3
Denham Green Ave EH5 93 D3
Denham Green Pl EH5 93 D3
Denham Green Terr EH5 93 D3
Denholm Ave EH21 125 F2
Denholm Gr EH48 143 F4
Denholm Rd EH21 125 F3
Denholm Way EH21 125 F3
Denny High Sch FK6 57 F4
Denny Prim Sch FK6 36 B1
Denny Rd Bankhead FK4 57 F3
Larbert FK5 38 A1
Denovan Rd FK6 36 C2
Dequincey Wlk EH33 128 B3
Derby St EH6 93 E3
Deroran Pl FK8 6 C3
Derwent Ave FK1 59 F2
Devon Ct FK10 4 A1
Devon Dr FK10 4 C2
Devon Pl Edinburgh EH12 122 C4
Tullibody FK10 4 A1
Devon Rd FK10 10 B3
Devon St FK3 40 A1
Devon Terr KY11 29 F1
Devon Village FK10 5 F2
Devonbank FK10 5 F2
Devonway FK10 11 D3
Dewar Ave FK10 23 F2
Dewar Pl EH3 232 A2
Dewar Place La EH3 232 A2
Dewar Sq EH54 146 B3
Dewar St Dunfermline KY12 28 C2
Lochgelly KY5 14 A4
Dewshill Cotts ML7 167 D2
Dick Cres KY3 33 F1
Dick Gdns EH47 169 F3
Dick Pl Edinburgh EH9 123 E2
Rosyth KY11 46 C3
Stoneyburn EH47 171 E1
Dick St KY12 29 E3
Dick Terr EH26 203 F3
Dickburn Cres FK4 57 F3
Dickies Wells FK12 5 E4
Dickson Ct KY5 14 A4
Dickson St
Dunfermline KY12 29 D1
Edinburgh EH6 93 F2
West Calder EH55 172 B1
Dicksons Gr EH19 182 A4
Dinmont Dr EH16 124 A1
Dirleton Ave EH39 54 A4
Dirleton Castle EH39 53 D2
Dirleton Gdns FK10 9 F4
Dirleton La FK10 9 F3
Dirleton Prim Sch EH39 53 D2
Dirleton Rd Dirleton EH39 53 D3
North Berwick EH39 53 F3
Distillery La EH11 122 C4
Diverswell FK10 5 E1
Dixon Terr EH47 170 A3
Dobbie Ave FK5 38 B1
Dobbie's Rd EH19 182 A4
Dobson's Pl EH41 131 F4
Dobson's View EH41 131 F4
Dobson's Wlk EH41 131 F4
Dochart Cres FK2 61 F1
Dochart Dr EH4 91 E1
Dochart Path FK3 61 E3
Dochart Pl FK1 60 B1
Dock Pl EH6 93 F3
Dock Rd FK3 40 B1
Dock St Bo'ness EH51 64 A4
Edinburgh EH6 93 F3
Falkirk FK2 39 E1
Doctor's Row KY1 17 F4
Dog Well Wynd EH49 85 D4
Dollar Ave FK2 60 A4
Dollar Cres KY2 16 B4
Dollar Ct KY12 28 C3
Dollar Gdns FK2 60 A4
Dollar Gr KY3 33 F1
Dollar Ind Est FK1 60 A3
Dollar Rd KY3 33 F1
Dolphin Ave EH14 151 F2
Dolphin Gdns E EH14 151 F2
Dolphin Gdns W EH14 151 F2
Dolphin Rd EH14 151 F2
Don Dr EH54 148 A3
Don Rd KY11 29 F1
Don St FK3 40 A1
Donald St KY12 29 E3
Donaldson Ct FK10 23 F2
Donaldson Pl FK7 6 B3
Donaldson's Sch
for the Deaf
Edinburgh, Coates EH12 122 C4
Edinburgh, Stockbridge EH4 93 D1
Donibristle Gdns KY11 48 A1
Donibristle Ind Pk KY11 48 A2
Donibristle Prim Sch
KY11 48 A1
Doo Dells La KY3 34 C1
Doo'cot Brae FK10 10 A4
Doocot Brae EH51 64 A4
Doon Ave EH42 78 B1
Doon Wlk EH54 148 A2
Dora Ct KY4 13 E3
Dornie Wynd ML7 192 A2
Dorrator Rd FK1 59 F3
Dorset Pl EH11 123 D3
Double Dykes EH21 126 B2
Double Hedges Pk EH16 124 A1
Double Hedges Rd EH16 124 A1
Double Row KY11 45 D2
Dougall Ct EH22 183 E3
Dougall Pl EH22 183 E3
Dougall Rd EH22 183 E3
Douglas Ave Brightons FK2 82 B4
Crossford KY12 28 A1
Grangemouth FK3 61 F3
Linlithgow EH49 84 C3
Douglas Cres
Bonnyrigg and Lasswade
EH19 182 A4
Edinburgh EH12 122 C4
Longniddry EH32 98 C3
Douglas Dr Bo'ness EH51 63 F3
Dunfermline KY12 28 C3
Stirling FK7 7 E2
Douglas Gardens Mews
EH4 122 C4
Douglas Gdns EH4 122 C4
Douglas Pk KY12 28 C3
Douglas Pl Bo'ness EH51 63 F3
Linlithgow EH49 84 C3
Stenhousemuir FK5 38 C2
Douglas Rd Bo'ness EH51 63 F3
Longniddry EH32 98 C3
Rosyth KY11 46 B1
Douglas St Bannockburn FK7 7 F1
Dunfermline KY12 29 D2
Kirkaldy KY1 17 D2
Stirling FK8 2 A1
Douglas Terr
Bo'ness EH51 63 F3
Stirling FK7 6 C3
Douglaswynd EH52 117 D3
Doune Cres FK5 39 D2
Doune Pk KY11 48 B2
Doune Terr EH3 232 B4
Dovecot Brae EH33 128 B4
Dovecot Gr EH14 122 A1
Dovecot Loan EH14 122 A1
Dovecot Pk Aberdour KY3 49 D3
Edinburgh EH14 153 D4
Linlithgow EH49 85 E4
Pencaitland EH34 160 C3
Dovecot Pl FK10 4 A2
Dovecot Rd
Edinburgh EH12 121 E3
Tullibody FK10 4 A2
Westquarter FK2 61 D1
Dovecot Way EH34 160 C4
Dovecote Pl EH54 147 E2
Dovehill FK10 10 A4
Dowan Pl FK7 6 C3
Dower Cres EH51 64 A4
Dowie's Mill La EH4 90 C2
Downfield KY4 13 E3
Downfield Pl EH11 122 C3
Downie Gr EH12 121 F3
Downie Pl EH21 126 B3
Downing Ct EH25 181 D2
Downing Point KY11 48 A1
Downs Cres FK10 9 F3
Dreghorn Ave EH13 153 F3
Dreghorn Dr EH13 153 F3
Dreghorn Gdns EH13 153 F3
Dreghorn Gr EH13 153 F3
Dreghorn Junc EH10 153 F3
Dreghorn Link EH10 153 F3
Dreghorn Loan EH13 153 D3
Dreghorn Pk EH13 153 E3
Dreghorn Pl EH13 153 F3
Drem Farm Cotts EH39 73 D2
Drem Sta EH39 73 D2
Drip Rd FK8 1 C1
Dronachy Rd KY2 16 C2
Drossie Rd FK1 60 A2
Drove Loan FK6 57 F3
Drove Loan Cres FK6 57 F4
Drove Rd EH48 143 F4
Droverhall Ave KY4 31 D3
Droverhall Pl KY4 31 D3
Drovers Rd EH52 118 A3
Drum Ave EH17 155 F3
Drum Brae Ave EH12 121 E4
Drum Brae Cres EH4 91 E1
Drum Brae Dr EH4 91 E1
Drum Brae Gdns EH12 121 E4
Drum Brae Gr EH4 91 E1
Drum Brae N EH4 91 D1
Drum Brae Neuk EH12 121 E4
Drum Brae Park App
EH12 121 E4
Drum Brae Pk EH12 121 E4
Drum Brae Pl EH12 121 E4
Drum Brae S EH12 121 E4
Drum Brae Terr EH4 91 E1
Drum Brae Wlk EH4 91 D1
Drum Cotts EH17 155 F3
Drum Cres EH17 155 F3
Drum Pl
East Whitburn EH47 170 C4
Edinburgh EH17 155 F3
Drum Rd Bo'ness EH51 64 B3
Dunfermline KY11 29 F1
Drum St EH17 155 F3
Drum Terr EH7 94 A1
Drum View Ave EH22 156 A4
Drumacre Rd EH51 64 A3
Drumbowie Prim Sch
FK1 82 B1
Drumbrae Prim Sch EH4 121 E4
Drumclair Ave FK1 110 A3
Drumcross Rd EH48 145 D4
Drumdryan St EH3 232 B1
Drumlanrig Pl FK5 38 C2
Drummohr Ave EH21 127 D3
Drummohr Gdns EH21 127 D3
Drummond Com High Sch
EH7 93 E1
Drummond La FK8 7 D3
Drummond Pk FK3 61 F3
Drummond Pl
Blackridge EH48 142 B2
Bonnybridge FK4 58 A4
Dunfermline KY12 29 E3
Edinburgh EH3 93 E1
Falkirk FK1 59 F2
Grangemouth FK3 61 F4
Stirling FK8 7 D3
Drummond Place La FK8 7 D3
Drummond Sq
Livingston EH54 173 E3
Lochgelly KY5 14 A4
Drummond St EH8 233 E2
Drummore Dr EH32 127 F4
Drummormie Rd KY12 27 E1
Drumpark Ave EH51 64 A3
Drumpark St FK7 7 D2
Drumsheugh Gdns EH3 232 A3
Drumshoreland Ave
EH53 148 A4
Drumshoreland Cres
EH53 148 A4
Drumshoreland Pl EH53 148 A4
Drumshoreland Rd EH53 148 A4
Drumside Terr EH51 64 B4
Drumview Gdns EH51 64 A3
Dryburgh Ave FK6 36 B1
Dryburgh Pl KY5 14 A4
Dryburgh Way FK3 61 F3
Dryden Ave EH20 181 D4
Dryden Cres EH20 181 D4
Dryden Gdns EH7 93 F2
Dryden Glen EH20 180 C4
Dryden Gr EH25 181 D2
Dryden Pl EH9 123 F3
Dryden Rd EH20 180 C4
Dryden St EH7 93 F2
Dryden Terr Edinburgh EH7 93 F2
Loanhead EH20 181 D4
Dryden View EH20 181 D4
Drylaw Ave EH4 92 B1
Drylaw Cres EH4 92 A1
Drylaw Gdns
East Linton EH40 103 E4
Edinburgh EH4 92 A2
Drylaw Gn EH4 92 A1
Drylaw Gr EH4 92 A1
Drylaw House Gdn EH4 92 A2
Drylaw House Paddock
EH4 92 A2
Drylaw Sch EH4 92 B2
Drylaw Terr EH40 103 E4
Drylawhill EH40 75 E1
Drylie St KY4 13 D2
Drysdale Ave EH47 170 A4
Drysdale St FK10 10 A3
Duart Cres EH4 91 E1
Dublin Meuse EH3 93 E1
Dublin St EH1 233 D4
Dublin Street La N 3 EH3 93 E1
Dublin Street La S EH1 233 D4
Duddingston Ave EH15 124 C4
Duddingston Cres EH52 88 A4
Duddingston Gdns S EH15 124 C3
Duddingston Gr E EH15 124 C4
Duddingston Gr W EH15 124 C3
Duddingston Loan EH15 124 C3
Duddingston Mills EH8 124 C4
Duddingston Pk EH15 125 D4
Duddingston Pk S EH15 125 D3
Duddingston Prim Sch
EH15 124 C4
Duddingston Rd EH15 124 C4
Duddingston Rd W EH15 124 B3
Duddingston Rise EH15 124 C3
Duddingston Row EH15 124 C3
Duddingston Sq E EH15 124 C4
Duddingston Sq W EH15 124 C3
Duddingston View EH15 124 C3
Duddingston Yds EH15 125 D3
Duddingstone Terr EH52 88 A4
Duddington Gdns N EH15 124 C4
Dudgeon Pl EH29 89 D1
Dudley Ave EH6 93 E3
Dudley Ave S EH6 93 F3
Dudley Bank EH6 93 E3
Dudley Cres EH6 93 E3
Dudley Gdns EH6 93 E3
Dudley Gr EH6 93 E3
Dudley Terr EH6 93 E3
Duff Cres FK8 1 C1
Duff Ct EH39 54 A4
Duff St EH11 122 C3
Duff Street La EH11 122 C3
Duffy Pl KY11 46 C2
Dugald Stewart Ave EH51 64 A4
Duglas Rise EH54 148 A1
Duke Pl EH6 94 A2
Duke St Alva FK12 5 D4
Bannockburn FK7 7 E1
Clackmannan FK10 11 D2
Dalkeith EH22 157 D2
Denny FK6 36 B1
Dunbar EH42 78 A1
Edinburgh EH6 94 A2
Grangemouth FK3 61 F4
Rosewell EH24 181 E1
West Barns EH42 77 F1
Duke's Wlk EH8 94 A1
Dumbarton Rd FK8 6 C4
Dumbeg Pk EH14 152 B4
Dumbiedykes Rd EH8 233 F2
Dumbryden Dr EH14 121 F1
Dumbryden Gdns EH14 121 F1
Dumbryden Gr EH14 121 F1
Dumbryden Prim Sch
EH14 121 F1
Dumbryden Rd EH14 121 F1
Dumyat Ave FK10 4 A1
Dumyat Dr FK1 59 F2
Dumyat Rd Alva FK12 4 C3
Menstrie FK11 3 F3
Stirling FK9 2 B2
Dumyat St FK10 4 C1
Dunard Gdn EH9 123 E2
Dunbar Ave FK5 38 C2
Dunbar Gate FK6 36 C2
Dunbar Gram Sch EH42 78 A1
Dunbar Pl KY2 16 C3
Dunbar Prim Sch EH42 78 B1
Dunbar Rd
Haddington EH41 101 D1
North Berwick EH39 54 C3
Dunbar St EH3 232 B1
Dunbar Sta EH42 78 C1
Duncairn Ave FK4 57 F3
Duncan Ave FK2 39 D2
Duncan Cres KY11 29 F1
Duncan Ct EH39 54 A3
Duncan Gdns EH33 128 B4
Duncan Gn EH54 147 D4
Duncan Pl EH6 94 A2
Duncan St Bonnybridge FK4 57 F3
Edinburgh EH9 123 F2
Kirkaldy KY2 17 D2
Duncanson Ave FK10 10 A4
Duncanson Dr KY3 34 A1
Duncarron Ind Est FK6 36 C1
Duncarron Pl FK6 36 C1
Duncur Rd EH31 52 B2
Dundaff Ct FK6 36 B1
Dundarroch St FK5 38 A1
Dundas Ave
North Berwick EH39 54 B3
Queensferry EH30 89 E4
Dundas Cotts FK4 57 D1
Dundas Cres
Clackmannan FK10 11 D2
Dalkeith EH22 156 C1
Laurieston FK2 61 D2

Dundas Gdns EH23 183 D1
Dundas Gr EH22 156 C1
Dundas Pk EH19 182 B4
Dundas Pl EH29 89 D1
Dundas Rd Dalkeith EH22 156 C1
Laurieston FK2 61 D2
North Berwick EH39 54 B3
Rosyth KY11 67 E4
Stirling FK9 2 A2
Dundas St Bathgate EH48 145 D4
Bo'ness EH51 63 F4
Bonnyrigg and Lasswade
EH19 182 B4
Edinburgh EH3 93 E1
Grangemouth FK3 61 E4
Lochgelly KY5 14 A4
Townhill KY12 29 E4
Dundee Ct FK2 60 A4
Dundee Pl FK2 60 A4
Dundee St EH11 232 A1
Dundee Terr EH11 122 C3
Dundonald Rd KY11 46 B2
Dundonald St EH3 93 E1
Dundrennan Cotts EH16 124 B1
Dunearn Bank KY3 33 E1
Dunearn Dr KY2 16 C3
Dunearn Sch KY2 16 C4
Dunedin St EH7 93 E2
Dunfermline Abbey KY12 28 C2
Dunfermline Bsns Ctr
KY11 29 D1
Dunfermline Bsns Pk
KY11 46 B3
Dunfermline High Sch
KY11 29 D1
Dunfermline Mus KY12 29 D2
Dunfermline Rd
Crossgates KY4 30 C3
Limekilns KY11 45 F2
Dunfermline Sta KY12 29 D2
Dunfermline Wynd KY11 47 D1
Dunglass Church TD13 140 B2
Dunimarle St KY12 26 A1
Dunipace Cres KY12 29 F3
Dunipace Prim Sch FK6 36 B2
Dunkeld Pl FK2 39 E1
Dunlin Brae EH54 147 E3
Dunlop Sq EH54 146 B3
Dunlop Terr EH26 204 A3
Dunmar Cres FK10 4 C1
Dunmar Dr FK10 4 C1
Dunn Cres KY11 29 F2
Dunn Pl EH52 87 F1
Dunn St EH52 117 D3
Dunn Terr ML7 168 C3
Dunnet Way EH52 118 A3
Dunnikier Prim Sch KY2 17 D3
Dunnikier Rd KY1 17 E3
Dunnikier Way KY1 17 E4
Dunning Pl FK2 39 E1
Dunnottar Dr FK5 38 C2
Dunnottar Pl KY2 16 C2
Dunollie Ct EH12 121 D4
Dunollie Gdns EH41 132 B4
Dunpender Dr EH41 100 C1
Dunpender Rd EH40 103 E4
Dunrobin Ave FK5 38 C3
Dunrobin Pl EH3 93 D1
Dunrobin Rd KY2 16 C2
Duns Rd EH41 163 F3
Dunsire St KY1 17 F4
Dunsmuir Ct EH12 121 E3
Dunster Rd FK9 2 B2
Dunure Cres FK4 58 A3
Dunure Pl KY2 16 C2
Dunure St FK4 58 A3
Dunvegan Ave Kircaldy KY2 16 B3
Stenhousemuir FK5 38 C2
Dunvegan Ct Alloa FK10 10 A3
Crossford KY12 28 A1
Edinburgh EH4 91 D2
Dunvegan Dr Falkirk FK2 39 E1
Stirling FK9 2 A2
Dunvegan Gdns EH54 173 F3
Dunvegan Pl
Bonnybridge FK4 57 F3
Polmont FK2 62 A1
Dura Rd ML7 212 B3
Durar Dr EH4 91 E1
Durham Ave
Bathgate EH48 144 C3
Edinburgh EH15 124 C4
Durham Bank EH19 182 B3
Durham Dr Bathgate EH48 144 C3
Edinburgh EH15 125 D3
Durham Gdns N EH15 125 D4
Durham Gdns S EH15 125 D3
Durham Gr
Bonnyrigg and Lasswade
EH19 182 B3
Edinburgh EH15 125 D4
Durham Pl EH19 182 B3
Durham Pl E EH15 125 D4
Durham Pl W EH15 124 C4
Durham Place La EH15 125 D4
Durham Rd EH15 125 D4
Durham Rd S EH15 125 D3
Durham Sq EH15 125 D4
Durham Terr
Edinburgh EH15 124 C4
Newmills KY12 26 B1
Durie Pk KY3 50 B4
Durie Pl KY11 29 F2
Durie's Pk EH33 128 A1
Durward Rise EH54 148 A1
Durwood Gr EH16 124 A1
Dyfrig St ML7 191 F3
Dyke Brow ML7 169 D3
Dyke Rd ML7 169 D3
Dykehead Prim Sch ML7 191 F3
Dykes Rd EH26 203 F4
Dykeside Rd EH48 144 C4
Dymond Gr KY11 46 C4
Dysart Prim Sch KY1 18 A4
Dysart Rd KY1 17 F3

Eagle Brae EH54 147 E2
Eagle Rock EH4 91 D4
Earl Grey St EH3 232 B2
Earl Haig Gdns EH5 93 D3
Earl Of Mar Ct FK10 10 A3
Earl's Gate Rdbt FK3 61 D4
Earl's Rd FK3 61 D4
Earls Ct FK10 10 A3
Earls Pl EH47 193 F3
Earlsburn Ave FK7 7 D2
Earlshill Dr FK7 7 F1
Earlston Pl 6 EH7 94 A1
Earn Ct Alloa FK10 10 B3
Grangemouth FK3 61 E3
Earn Gr KY11 29 F2
Earn Pl FK6 57 E3
Earn Rd KY1 17 E4
Earn Terr ML7 191 F3
East Adam St EH8 233 E2
East Albert Rd KY1 17 E3
East Ave Blairhall KY12 26 A4
Dunfermline KY11 46 C4
East Baldridge Dr KY12 28 C3
East Bankton Pl EH54 173 F4
East Barnton Ave EH4 91 F2
East Barnton Gdns EH4 91 F2
East Bay KY11 68 B3
East Boreland Pl FK6 36 C1
East Bridge St FK1 60 B2
East Brighton Cres EH15 125 D4
East Broomhill Rd KY3 50 C4
East Caiystane Pl EH10 154 A3
East Caiystane Rd EH10 154 A3
East Calder Prim Sch
EH53 148 C2
East Campbell Ct EH32 98 B3
East Castle Rd EH10 123 D3
East Castle St FK10 10 A3
East Champanyie EH9 123 F2
East Clapperfield EH16 124 A1
East Claremont St EH7 93 E2
East Comiston EH10 154 A3
East Craigs Prim Sch
EH12 121 D4
East Craigs Rigg EH12 121 D4
East Croft EH28 119 F1
East Cromwell St EH6 93 F3
East Crosscauseway EH8 233 E1
East Ct
Edinburgh, Greendykes
EH16 124 C2
Edinburgh, Ravelston 7 EH4 92 B1
East Dr FK5 38 B1
East End EH55 172 B2
East End Park
(Dunfermline Athletic FC)
KY12 29 E2
East Farm Of Gilmerton
EH17 155 F3
East Fenton Farm Cotts
EH39 73 E4
East Fergus Pl KY1 17 D2
East Fettes Ave EH4 92 C2
East Fountainbridge EH3 232 B2
East Garleton Cotts EH39 100 C3
East Glen Ave EH54 146 C3
East Harbour Rd KY11 45 D2
East Hermitage Pl EH6 94 A2
East Leven St KY3 50 C4
East Lillypot EH5 93 D3
East Link Rd FK9 2 B3
East Links Rd Dunbar EH42 78 C1
Gullane EH31 52 A1
East Linton Prim Sch EH40 103 E4
East Linton Station Ind Est
EH40 103 F4
East Loan EH32 97 D1
East London St EH7 93 E1
East Lorimer Pl EH32 97 E2
East Main St
Armadale EH48 144 A3
Blackburn EH47 171 E4
Broxburn EH52 117 F3
Harthill ML7 168 C3
Uphall EH52 117 D2
Whitburn EH47 170 A4
East Mains FK11 4 A3
East Mains Ind Est EH52 118 A3
East March St KY1 17 F4
East Market St EH8 233 E3
East Mayfield EH9 123 F2
East Montgomery Pl 4
EH7 93 F1
East Murrayfield FK7 7 F1
East Newington Pl EH9 123 F3
East Norton Pl 3 EH7 93 F1
East Park Gr EH52 117 D3
East Parkside EH16 233 F1
East Pier St EH51 63 F4
East Plean Prim Sch FK7 20 B2
East Port KY12 29 D2
East Port Ave EH41 132 A3
East Preston St EH8 233 F1
East Preston Street La 6
EH8 123 F3
East Quality St KY1 18 A4
East Queensway EH26 203 F3
East Rd Grangemouth FK2 62 B3
North Berwick EH39 54 B4
East Restalrig Terr EH6 94 A2
East Savile Rd EH16 123 F2
East Sciennes St 2 EH9 123 F3
East Scotland Street La 2
EH3 93 E1
East Seaside EH32 96 C1
East Silvermills La EH3 93 D1
East Stirling St FK12 5 D4
East Suffolk Rd EH16 124 A2
East Telferton EH7 94 C1
East Terr EH30 68 B1
East Toll KY3 33 F1
East Trinity Rd EH5 93 E3
East Vennel FK10 10 A3
East Vows Wlk KY1 35 D4
East Way KY11 48 B3
East Werberside EH4 92 C2
East Whitefield KY12 29 F3
Eastburn Dr FK1 60 B2
Eastcroft Dr FK2 62 A1
Eastcroft St FK5 38 A1
Easter Bankton EH54 174 A4
Easter Belmont Rd EH12 122 A4
Easter Carmuirs Prim Sch
FK1 59 D3
Easter Cornton Rd FK9 2 A2
Easter Currie Cres EH14 152 A3
Easter Currie Ct EH14 152 A2
Easter Currie Pl EH14 152 A3
Easter Currie Terr EH14 152 A2
Easter Drylaw Ave EH4 92 B2
Easter Drylaw Bank EH4 92 B2
Easter Drylaw Dr EH4 92 B2
Easter Drylaw Gdns EH4 92 B2
Easter Drylaw Gr EH4 92 B2
Easter Drylaw Loan EH4 92 B2
Easter Drylaw Pl EH4 92 B2
Easter Drylaw View EH4 92 B2
Easter Drylaw Way EH4 92 B2
Easter Ferrygate Pk EH39 53 F4
Easter Haugh EH13 153 F4
Easter Hermitage EH6 94 A2
Easter Livilands FK7 7 E2
Easter Park Dr EH4 91 F2
Easter Rd Broxburn EH52 117 F3
Edinburgh EH6 94 A2
Shotts ML7 191 E3
Easter Road Stad
(Hibernian FC) EH7 94 A1
Easter Steil EH10 122 C1
Easter Warriston EH7 93 E2
Easterfield Ct EH54 147 E2
Eastern Ind Est EH15 125 E2
Easterton Cres FK7 20 C4
Easterton Dr FK7 20 C4
Easterton Gr FK7 20 C4
Eastertoun Gdns EH48 143 F3
Eastertoun Prim Sch
EH48 143 F3
Eastfield EH15 125 F4
Eastfield Dr EH26 203 F3
Eastfield Farm Rd EH26 203 F4
Eastfield Gdns EH15 125 F4
Eastfield Ind Est EH26 203 F3
Eastfield Park Rd EH26 203 F3
Eastfield Pl EH15 125 F4
Eastfield Rd Carluke ML8 230 A1
Edinburgh EH28 120 A3
Fauldhouse EH47 193 F4
North Berwick EH39 54 B3
Eastfield View EH47 193 F4
Easthouses Ct EH22 183 E4
Easthouses Ind Est
EH22 183 E4
Easthouses Pl EH22 157 E1
Easthouses Rd
Dalkeith EH22 157 E1
Easthouses EH22 183 E4
Easthouses Way EH22 157 E1
Easton Ct FK8 2 A1
Easton Dr FK1 81 E4
Easton Rd EH48 144 C4
Eastwood Pk
Fauldhouse EH47 193 F4
Livingston EH54 147 D4
Ebenezer Pl FK1 81 F3
Eccles Ct FK7 7 D2
Ecclesmachan Rd EH52 116 C3
Echline Ave EH30 89 D4
Echline Dr EH30 88 C4
Echline Farm Cotts EH30 88 C4
Echline Gdns EH30 67 F1
Echline Gn EH30 67 F1
Echline Gr EH30 68 A1
Echline Pk EH30 88 C4
Echline Prim Sch EH30 68 A1
Echline Rigg EH30 68 A1
Echline Steadings EH30 88 C4
Echline Terr EH30 89 D4
Echline View EH30 89 D4
Echobank KY11 47 D1
Eden Dr EH54 148 A2
Eden La EH10 123 D2
Eden Rd Alloa FK10 9 F4
Dunfermline KY11 29 F1
Edenhall Bank EH21 126 C3
Edenhall Cres EH21 126 C3
Edenhall Hospl EH21 126 C2
Edenhall Rd EH21 126 C3
Edgefield Ind Est EH20 155 E1
Edgefield Pl EH20 181 E4
Edgefield Rd EH20 155 E1
Edgehead Rd EH37 184 B4
Edina Pl EH7 94 A1
Edina St EH7 93 F1
Edinburgh Acad EH3 93 D1
Edinburgh Acad
(Prep Sch) The EH3 93 D2
Edinburgh Castle EH1 232 C3
Edinburgh Fort Ret Pk
EH15 125 D2
Edinburgh Pk
Edinburgh EH12 120 C3
Edinburgh EH12 121 D2
Edinburgh Rd
Bathgate EH48 145 E3
Cockenzie & Port Seton EH32 97 D2
Dalkeith EH22 157 D2
Harthill ML7 168 B3
Linlithgow EH49 85 D4
Musselburgh EH21 126 A3
Newbridge EH28 119 D3
Penicuik EH26 204 A4
Tranent EH33 128 A3
West Barns EH42 77 F1
West Linton EH46 220 A1
Edinburgh West Off Pk
EH12 121 D2
Edinburgh Coll of Art
EH3 232 C2
Edinburgh Rd EH48 145 E3
Edington Cottage Hospl
EH39 54 B4
Edington Pl KY1 18 A4
Edmonstone Ave EH22 156 A4
Edmonstone Dr EH22 156 A4
Edmonstone Rd EH22 156 B4
Edmonstone Terr EH22 156 A4
Edmonton Ave EH54 147 F2
Edward Ave
Stenhousemuir FK5 38 C2
Stirling FK8 2 B1
Edward Pl FK2 39 F2
Edward Rd FK8 2 A1
Edward St Dunfermline KY12 29 D3
Kirkcaldy KY2 17 D4
Eglington Pl KY11 47 E1
Eglingtoun Dr KY12 28 C3
Eglinton Cres EH12 122 C4
Eighth St EH22 183 D3
Eildon St EH3 93 E2
Eildon Terr EH3 93 E2
Eilean La KY12 26 C1
Elam Terr EH51 63 F4
Elbe St EH6 94 A3
Elcho Ct EH32 98 C3
Elcho Pl EH32 97 E2
Elcho Rd EH32 98 C3
Elcho Terr Aberlady EH32 71 E2
Edinburgh EH15 125 E4
Longniddry EH32 98 C3
Elder Pl KY11 46 C3
Elder St Dunbar EH42 78 A1
Edinburgh EH1 233 D4
Tranent EH33 128 B4
Elder St E EH1 233 D4
Elderslie Dr FK2 82 A4
Eldin Ind Est EH20 155 E1
Eldindean Pl EH19 182 A4
Eldindean Rd EH19 182 B4
Eldindean Terr EH19 182 B4
Eldrick Ave EH47 193 F3
Eldrick Cres EH47 193 E3
Eldrick La EH47 193 E3
Eldrick View EH47 193 F3
Electra Pl EH15 95 D1
Elgin Ct KY12 29 D1
Elgin Dr FK7 7 E2
Elgin Pl FK1 60 B2
Elgin Rd KY4 13 E2
Elgin St Dunfermline KY12 29 D1
Edinburgh EH7 93 F1
Kirkcaldy KY2 17 D3
Elgin St N EH7 93 F1
Elgin Terr EH7 93 F1
Eliburn North Intc EH54 147 D3
Eliburn Rd EH54 147 D2
Eliburn South Rd EH54 147 E2
Elie Ave EH54 146 C3
Elim Dr FK1 81 E3
Elizabeth Ave
Grangemouth FK3 61 F4
Larbert FK5 38 B1
Elizabeth Cres FK1 59 D3
Elizabeth Dr EH48 145 F3
Elizabeth Gdns EH47 171 D1
Elizabeth La EH48 145 F3
Elizabeth St Dunfermline KY11 29 E1
Stirling FK8 7 D3
Elizafield EH6 93 F2
Ellaleen Gr KY12 28 A1
Ellangowan Terr EH16 124 B1
Ellen St EH47 170 A4
Ellen's Glen Loan EH17 155 E4
Ellen's Glen Rd EH17 155 E4
Ellersly Rd EH12 122 B4
Elliot Gdns EH14 153 E4
Elliot Pk EH14 153 E4
Elliot Pl EH14 153 E4
Elliot Rd EH14 153 E4
Elliot St Dunfermline KY11 29 D1
Edinburgh EH7 93 F1
Elliot Terr FK2 60 A4
Elliothill St KY11 29 D1
Ellis Pl EH52 117 D3
Ellon Pl KY12 29 E3
Ellon Rd KY2 16 B4
Elm Dr FK2 61 D1
Elm Gr Alloa FK10 10 B3
Blackburn EH47 171 F4
Dunfermline KY11 46 B4
Larbert FK5 38 B1
Livingston EH54 148 A3
Elm Pk EH47 171 F4
Elm Pl Edinburgh EH6 94 A2
Kirkcaldy KY2 16 C3
Mayfield EH22 183 E3
Elm Rd EH48 145 F3
Elm Row
Bonnyrigg and Lasswade
EH18 156 A1
Edinburgh EH7 93 F1
Elm Sq EH47 170 B3
Elm St Dunbar EH42 78 A1
Stirling FK8 1 C1
Elmbank FK11 4 A3
Elmbank Cres FK4 57 E3
Elmbank Rd FK7 7 D2
Elmbank St FK3 61 E3
Elmfield Ct EH22 157 D2
Elmfield Pk EH22 157 D2
Elmfield Rd EH22 157 D2
Elms The EH10 153 F4
Elmwood Pk EH54 146 C4
Elmwood Rd ML7 192 A1
Elmwood Terr EH6 94 A2
Elphinstone Cres FK2 22 C2
Elphinstone Prim Sch
EH33 128 A1
Elphinstone Rd EH33 128 A3
Elphinstone Sq EH54 146 B3
Elphinstone St FK10 23 F2
Elphinstone Wlk EH33 128 B3
Eltringham Gdns EH14 122 B2
Eltringham Gr EH14 122 B2
Eltringham Terr EH14 122 B2
Emily Ct EH23 183 E1
Emily Pl EH23 183 E1
Empire St EH47 170 A4
Endrick Dr FK6 57 F3
Endrick Pl FK7 7 D2
Engelen Dr FK10 10 A3
Engine La EH48 145 D3
Engine Pl EH48 145 D3
Engine Rd Gorebridge EH23 183 D1
Loanhead EH20 181 E4
Engineering Training Sch
KY2 17 D2
Ennis Pk EH55 172 C3
Eppiestane Rd EH47 170 B3
Epworth Gdns FK2 82 A4
Erbach Ave FK2 61 D2
Ercall Rd FK2 82 C4
Erica Gr KY11 46 C4
Ericht Pl ML7 191 F3
Eriskay Ct FK1 60 B1
Erngath Rd EH51 64 A4
Erskine Brae KY12 25 E1
Erskine Hill FK2 61 F1
Erskine Loan EH31 52 A2
Erskine Pl
Clackmannan FK10 10 C3
Mid Calder EH53 148 B3
Erskine Rd Broxburn EH52 117 E3
Gullane EH31 52 A2
Erskine Sq KY11 29 E1
Erskine St Alloa FK10 10 A4
Alva FK12 5 D4
Lochgelly KY5 14 A3
Erskine Way
Livingston EH54 147 E4
Shotts ML7 191 F2
Erskine Wynd KY12 27 D4
Esk Dr EH54 148 A2
Esk Glades EH22 157 D2
Esk Pl EH22 156 C2
Eskbank Rd
Bonnyrigg and Lasswade
EH19 182 B4
Dalkeith EH22 156 C1
Eskbank Road Rdbt EH22 156 B1
Eskbank Terr EH22 156 C1
Eskdaill Ct EH22 157 D2
Eskdaill St EH22 157 D2
Eskdale Ct EH19 182 A4
Eskdale Dr EH19 182 A4
Eskdale Mews EH21 126 B3
Eskdale Terr EH19 182 A4
Eskfield Gr EH22 156 B1
Eskgrove Dr EH25 180 C3
Eskhill EH26 203 F3
Eskmill Ind Est EH26 204 A3
Eskmill Rd EH26 204 A3
Eskside E EH21 126 B3
Eskside W EH21 126 B3
Eskvale Cres EH26 204 A3
Eskvale Dr EH26 204 A3
Eskvale View EH26 204 A3
Eskview Ave EH21 126 A3
Eskview Cres EH21 126 A3
Eskview Gr Dalkeith EH22 156 C2
Musselburgh EH21 126 A3
Eskview Rd Mayfield EH22 183 E3
Musselburgh EH21 126 A3
Eskview Terr EH21 126 A3
Eskview Villas EH22 156 C1
Esmonde Ct KY11 46 C1
Esplanade Edinburgh EH1 232 C3
Kirkcaldy KY1 17 E1
Esplanade Terr EH15 125 E4
Essendean Pl EH4 91 E1
Essendean Terr EH4 91 E1
Essex Brae EH4 91 D2
Essex Pk EH4 91 D2
Essex Rd EH4 91 D2
Esslemont Rd EH16 124 A1
Estate Ave FK1 60 B2
Ethel Terr EH10 123 D1
Etive Pl Dalgety Bay KY11 48 A1
Stirling FK9 2 A2
Etive Way Polmont FK2 62 A1
Shotts ML7 192 A2

Etive Wlk EH54 148 A2
Etna Ct FK2 60 B4
Etna Rd FK2 60 B4
Eton Terr EH4 232 A4
Ettrick Cres KY11 48 A2
Ettrick Ct Falkirk FK1 60 B1
Grangemouth FK3 61 F3
Ettrick Dr EH54 148 A3
Ettrick Gr EH10 123 D3
Ettrick Rd EH10 122 C2
Ettrickdale Pl EH3 93 D2
Eva Pl EH9 123 F1
Evans Gdns EH19 182 B4
Evans St FK5 38 B2
Evelyn Terr EH26 180 B1
Everard Rise EH54 148 A1
Evershed Ct KY11 29 F1
Evershed Dr KY11 29 F1
Ewart Ave EH48 144 A3
Ewart Gr EH51 63 F3
Ewerland EH4 91 D2
Ewing Ave FK2 60 A4
Ewing Ct FK7 7 E2
Ewing Dr FK2 60 A4
Ewing Pl FK2 60 A4
Ewing St Cowdenbeath KY4 13 D1
Lochgelly KY5 14 A3
Penicuik EH26 203 F4
Excise La FK10 23 F2
Excise St FK10 23 F2
Exmouth St EH54 148 A3
Eyre Cres EH3 93 E1
Eyre Pl EH3 93 E1
Eyre Terr EH3 93 E1

Fa'side Ave EH33 128 B3
Fa'side Ave N EH21 127 D2
Fa'side Ave S EH21 127 D2
Fa'side Avenue Ct EH21 127 D2
Fa'side Bldgs EH21 127 D2
Fa'side Cres Tranent EH33 128 B3
Wallyford EH21 127 D2
Fa'side Dr EH21 127 D2
Fa'side Gdns EH21 127 D2
Fa'side Rd EH33 128 B3
Fa'side Terr EH21 127 D2
Fa'side View EH33 128 B3
Factory Rd Bathgate EH48 144 C2
Cowdenbeath KY4 13 E2
Kirkcaldy KY1 17 E3
Fair Isle Prim Sch KY2 16 C4
Fair Isle Rd KY2 16 C4
Fair Pl KY11 47 D2
Fair-a-Far EH4 91 D3
Fair-a-Far Cotts EH4 91 D3
Fair-a-Far Shot EH4 91 D3
Fairbairn Rd EH54 147 E2
Fairbrae EH11 121 F2
Fairfax Ct KY3 33 F1
Fairfield Alloa FK10 5 E1
Livingston EH54 147 D2
Fairfield Ave FK4 58 A3
Fairfield Pl FK2 60 B3
Fairfield Sch FK10 5 D1
Fairford Gdns EH16 124 A1
Fairgreen Pl FK7 19 F4
Fairhaven Terr FK2 82 A4
Fairhill Rd FK7 7 D1
Fairinsfell EH52 117 D3
Fairley Ct KY12 27 E1
Fairlie Dr FK1 59 E3
Fairlie Gdns FK1 59 E3
Fairlie St FK1 59 E3
Fairmile Ave EH10 154 A3
Fairmont Pk EH47 169 F3
Fairmount Dr FK10 5 D1
Fairspark Terr EH51 63 E3
Fairview Rd EH28 119 F4
Fairview Terr FK2 82 A4
Fairway EH41 131 F4
Fairway The KY1 17 F4
Fairways KY12 29 D3
Fairways Ave FK2 82 C3
Fairways Pl FK4 58 A4
Fairy Fa' Cres KY4 30 C3
Fairyburn Rd FK10 9 F4
Fairykirk Rd KY11 47 D2
Faith Mission Coll The
EH17 155 F3
Falahill Cotts EH38 228 A2
Falcon Ave EH10 123 D2
Falcon Brae EH54 147 E3
Falcon Ct EH10 123 D2
Falcon Dr FK5 38 A2
Falcon Gdns EH10 123 D2
Falcon Rd EH10 123 D2
Falcon Rd W EH10 123 D2
Falconer Ct FK7 7 E2
Falconer Rise EH54 147 F1
Falcons The EH31 52 A2
Falkirk Coll of F & H Ed
Flexible Learning Ctr
FK2 60 C3
Falkirk & District
Royal Infmy FK1 60 A2
Falkirk High Sch FK1 59 F2
Falkirk High Sta FK1 60 A2
Falkirk Rd Bannockburn FK7 19 F4
Bonnybridge FK4 58 B3
Falkirk, Glen Village FK1 60 A1
Falkirk, Westfield FK1 60 C3
Grangemouth FK3 61 D4
Larbert FK5 59 E4
Linlithgow EH49 84 C4
Falkland Gdns EH12 91 F1
Falkland Pl FK5 38 C2
Falla Hill Prim Sch EH47 193 E3
Fallas Pl EH47 193 E3
Fallin Prim Sch FK7 8 B3
Fallodon Cres KY2 17 D2
Falside Cres EH48 144 C3
Falside Dr EH48 144 C3
Falside Terr EH48 144 C3
Faraday Pl EH55 171 F1
Farm Ave EH18 181 F3
Farm Cotts
Pencaitland EH34 160 B3
Wallyford EH21 127 E3
Farm Rd Cowdenbeath KY4 13 D2
Cowie FK7 20 B4
Crombie KY12 44 B3
Fallin FK7 8 B3
Roslin EH25 204 C3
Farm Row KY12 30 A3
Farm St FK2 39 D1
Farmer's Bldgs EH37 185 D3
Farne Ct KY2 16 C4
Farnell Way KY12 29 E3
Farquhar Sq EH48 142 B2
Farquhar Terr EH30 68 A1
Farquharson Way FK1 59 F1
Farrer Gr EH7 94 C1
Farrer Terr EH7 94 C1
Farrier Ct EH47 171 E4
Farteviot Royal Hospl
for Sick Children EH9 123 E2
Fauldburn EH12 91 D1
Fauldburn Pk EH12 91 D1
Fauldhouse Rd EH47 170 A1
Fauldhouse Sta EH47 193 E3
Featherhall Ave EH12 121 E3
Featherhall Cres EH12 121 E3
Featherhall Cres N EH12 121 E3
Featherhall Cres S EH12 121 E3
Featherhall Gr EH12 121 E3
Featherhall Pl EH12 121 E3
Featherhall Rd EH12 121 E3
Featherhall Terr EH12 121 E3
Fell's Rd EH55 172 C3
Fells Rigg EH54 147 D4
Fendoch Rd FK3 61 F4
Fenton St FK10 10 A4
Fentoun Gait EH31 52 B1
Fere Gait FK10 23 F2
Fergus Ave EH54 147 F2
Fergus Pl KY11 29 E1
Fergus Wynd KY1 17 D1
Ferguson Ct EH21 126 B2
Ferguson Dr Denny FK6 36 B1
Falkirk FK2 39 D3
Musselburgh EH21 126 A2
Ferguson Gdns EH21 126 B2
Ferguson Gn EH21 126 A2
Ferguson Gr FK4 58 A3
Ferguson Pl KY3 33 F1
Ferguson St FK8 1 C1
Ferguson View EH21 126 A2
Ferguson Way
Livingston EH54 147 E4
Newtongrange EH22 183 D2
Fergusson Rd EH52 117 F3
Fern Lea Gr FK2 39 E2
Fernbank EH54 147 F3
Fernie Pl KY12 28 C3
Ferniehill Ave EH17 155 F3
Ferniehill Dr EH17 155 F3
Ferniehill Gdns EH17 155 F4
Ferniehill Gr EH17 155 F4
Ferniehill Pl EH17 155 F3
Ferniehill Rd EH17 155 F4
Ferniehill Sq EH17 155 F3
Ferniehill St EH17 155 F4
Ferniehill Terr EH17 155 F3
Ferniehill Way EH17 155 F4
Fernielaw Ave
Edinburgh EH13 152 C2
Edinburgh, Bonaly EH13 153 D3
Fernieside Ave EH17 155 F4
Fernieside Cres EH17 155 F4
Fernieside Dr EH17 155 F4
Fernieside Gdns EH17 155 F4
Fernieside Gr EH17 155 F4
Fernieside Prim Sch
EH17 155 F4
Fernlea EH52 116 C3
Ferrard Rd KY2 17 D2
Ferrier Cres EH48 144 A3
Ferris Way KY11 48 A2
Ferry La KY11 68 A3
Ferry Muir Gait EH30 89 D4
Ferry Orch FK9 2 B1
Ferry Rd Edinburgh EH4, EH5 92 B2
South Alloa FK7 9 F2
Stirling FK9 2 B1
Ferry Road Ave EH4 92 B2
Ferry Road Dr EH4 92 B3
Ferry Road Gdns EH4 92 B2
Ferry Road Gr EH4 92 B2
Ferry Road Pl EH4 92 B2
Ferry Toll Pl KY11 46 C1
Ferry Toll Rd KY11 46 C1
Ferrybarns Ct KY11 68 A3
Ferryburn Gn EH30 89 E4
Ferryfield EH5 93 D2
Ferrygate Cotts EH39 53 E3
Ferryhill Prim Sch EH4 92 B2
Ferryhill Rd KY11 68 B4
Ferrymuir La EH30 89 D4
Ferrymuir Rd EH30 89 D4
Fetteresk Cotts EH26 203 F2
Fettes Ave EH4 92 C1
Fettes Coll EH4 92 C2
Fettes Rise EH4 92 C2
Fettes Row EH3 93 E1
Fiddich Dr EH54 173 F3
Fidra Ave EH39 53 D3
Fidra Ct EH39 53 F4
Fidra Rd EH39 54 A4
Fife Coll of F & H Ed KY1 17 D2
Fife Coll Priory Campus
KY1 17 E3
Fife Pl KY11 46 A1
Fifth St EH22 183 D3
Figgate Bank EH15 95 D1
Figgate La EH15 95 D1
Figgate St EH15 95 D1
Fillyside Ave EH7 94 C1
Fillyside Rd EH7 94 C2
Fillyside Terr EH7 94 C2
Finches The EH31 52 A2
Findhorn Pl Edinburgh EH9 123 F2
Falkirk FK1 60 B1
Kircaldy KY2 16 C4
Findlay Ave EH7 94 B2
Findlay Cotts EH7 94 B2
Findlay Cres KY11 46 C2
Findlay Gdns EH7 94 B2
Findlay Gr EH7 94 B2
Findlay Medway EH7 94 B2
Findlay St KY11 46 C2
Fingal Pl EH9 233 D1
Fingzies Pl EH6 94 A2
Finistere Ave FK1 60 A2
Finlaggan Ct EH12 121 D4
Finlarig Ct FK5 38 C2
Finlay Ave EH53 148 C2
Finlay Pl EH22 183 F3
Fintry Rd FK3 61 F3
Fir Gr Dunfermline KY11 46 C4
Livingston EH54 148 A3
Westquarter FK2 61 D1
Fir La FK5 38 B1
Firbank Gr EH53 148 C2
Firpark Terr FK7 6 B3
Firr Hill High Sch EH14 153 E4
Firrhill Cres EH13 153 F4
Firrhill Dr EH13 153 F4
Firrhill Loan EH13 153 F4
Firs Cres FK7 7 E1
Firs Entry FK7 7 E1
Firs Pk
(East Stirlingshire FC)
FK2 60 B3
Firs Rd FK10 4 B1
Firs St FK2 60 B3
Firs The Bannockburn FK7 7 E1
Dalgety Bay KY11 48 A1
First Gait EH14 151 F4
First St EH22 183 D2
Firth Cres EH26 180 B1
Firth Rd Auchendinny EH26 180 B1
Livingston EH54 147 F4
Roslin EH25 204 C3
Firwood Dr EH51 63 E3
Fishcross Prim Sch FK10 5 E2
Fishergate Rd EH32 97 F2
Fisherrow Ind Est EH21 126 A3
Fishers' Rd EH51 63 E2
Fishers Rd EH32 97 E2
Fishers Wynd EH21 126 A3
Fishmarket Sq EH6 93 E4
Fishwives' Cswy EH7, EH15 94 C1
Fitzgerald Pl EH48 113 F3
Fitzroy Sq KY1 18 A4
Fitzroy St KY1 18 A4
Five Gates EH42 76 A3
Flare Rd FK2 62 A3
Flax Mill Rd ML7 168 C3
Fleets Gr EH33 128 B2
Fleets Ind Est EH33 128 B2
Fleets Rd EH33 128 B3
Fleets View EH33 128 B2
Fleming Dr FK5 39 D2
Fleming Gdns FK1 59 F3
Fleming Pl EH48 142 C2
Fleming Rd EH54 146 C1
Fleming Way KY3 33 F1
Flemington Gdns EH47 169 F3
Flesh Wynd KY1 17 E3
Fleshmarket Cl EH1 233 D3
Fletcher Gr EH26 203 F4
Flint Cres FK7 20 B4
Floors Pl KY2 16 B3
Floors Terr EH42 78 B1
Florabank Rd EH41 101 D1
Flower Pl KY4 12 C4
Fod St KY11 30 A3
Fodbank View KY11 29 F2
Foot Pl KY11 46 C2
Foote St KY5 14 A3
Forbes Cres FK5 38 B1
Forbes Ct FK2 60 C3
Forbes Rd Edinburgh EH10 123 D3
Falkirk FK1 60 B2
Rosyth KY11 46 B1
Forbes St Alloa FK10 9 F3
Edinburgh EH8 233 E1
Forbeslea Gdns KY12 27 F4
Ford Rd Bonnybridge FK4 58 A3
Haddington EH41 132 B4
Ford View KY12 27 E1
Ford's Rd EH11 122 A2
Fordell Bank KY11 48 B2
Fordell Gdns KY2 16 B3
Fordell Way KY11 47 E1
Forebraes FK10 10 A4
Foredale Terr EH51 64 B4
Forest Kirk ML8 230 A1
Forest Pl KY12 29 E4
Forest Rd KY12 29 E4
Forest View FK2 61 F1
Forestbank EH54 147 F3
Forester Gr FK10 4 C1
Forester High Sch EH12 121 E2
Forester's Lea Cres KY12 29 F2
Forester's View EH33 128 B3
Forfar Pl FK2 62 A1
Forgie Cres FK2 83 D3
Forglen Cres FK9 2 A3
Forglen Rd FK9 2 A3
Forker Ave KY11 46 B2
Forkneuk Rd EH52 116 C2
Forkneuk Steadings
EH52 116 C3
Forman Gr KY11 29 F1
Forres Dr KY2 16 B4
Forres St EH3 232 B4
Forrest Hill EH1 233 D2
Forrest Pl ML7 168 C3
Forrest Rd Edinburgh EH1 233 D2
Forrestfield ML6 141 D1
Salsburgh ML7 167 D3
Stirling FK8 2 A1
Forrest St ML7 191 F3
Forrest Wlk EH52 116 C2
Forrester Ct KY5 14 A4
Forrester Park Ave EH12 121 E2
Forrester Park Dr EH12 121 E2
Forrester Park Gdns
EH12 121 E2
Forrester Park Gn EH12 121 F2
Forrester Park Gr EH12 121 E2
Forrester Park Loan EH12 121 E2
Forrester Park Rd EH12 121 E2
Forrester Pl FK2 22 B2
Forrester Rd
Armadale EH48 143 F4
Edinburgh EH12 121 E4
Forrestfield Rd ML6 141 D3
Fort Ho EH6 93 F3
Fort Prim Sch EH6 93 F3
Forth Ave Kirkaldy KY2 17 D2
Larbert FK5 38 A2
Forth Ave Ind Est KY2 17 D2
Forth Cres Alloa FK10 10 B3
Dalgety Bay KY11 48 A2
High Valleyfield KY12 26 A1
Stirling FK8 7 E4
Forth Ct
Cockenzie & Port Seton EH32 97 F2
Dalgety Bay KY11 48 A2
Dunfermline KY12 29 D1
Stirling FK8 2 A1
Forth Dr EH54 148 A3
Forth Gdns
Cockenzie & Port Seton EH32 97 F2
Oakley KY12 26 C4
Forth Gr EH32 97 F2
Forth Ind Est EH5 92 C4
Forth Park Dr KY2 17 D3
Forth Park Gdns KY2 17 D3
Forth Park Maternity Hospl
KY2 17 D3
Forth Pk Bridge of A FK9 2 A3
Queensferry EH30 89 F4
Forth Pl Burntisland KY3 50 C4
Queensferry EH30 68 A1
Forth Prim Sch ML11 215 D1
Forth Rd KY11 46 A1
Forth Reach KY11 47 F1
Forth St Cambus FK10 9 D4
Dunfermline KY12 29 D1
Edinburgh EH1 93 E1
Fallin FK7 8 B2
Grangemouth FK3 61 E4
Kincardine FK10 23 E2
Stirling FK8 2 A1
Forth Street La EH39 54 B4
Forth Terr EH30 89 E4
Forth View
Dalgety Bay KY11 48 A2
Inverkeithing KY11 47 D1
Kincardine FK10 23 F2
Kirknewton EH27 149 F2
Stirling FK8 2 A1
West Barns EH42 77 F1
Forth View Ave EH14 151 F2
Forth View Cotts KY12 26 A1
Forth View Cres
Currie EH14 151 F2
Danderhall EH22 156 A4
Forth View Ind Est KY12 26 A1
Forth View Rd EH14 151 F2
Forth Wynd EH32 97 F2
Forthbank Ind Est FK10 10 A2
Forthbank Pl KY12 25 F1
Forthbank
(Stirling Albion FC) FK7 7 F4
Forthside Terr KY11 68 B3
Forthvale FK11 4 A3
Forthview FK7 7 F1
Forthview Ave EH21 127 D2
Forthview Cres
Bo'ness EH51 63 F3
Musselburgh EH21 127 D3
Forthview Ct FK1 59 F1
Forthview Dr EH21 127 D3
Forthview Gdns FK2 82 B4
Forthview Rd
Edinburgh EH4 92 B1
Longniddry EH32 98 C3
Forthview Terr
Edinburgh EH4 92 A1
Reddingmuirhead FK2 82 A4
Wallyford EH21 127 D2
Forties Rd EH51 62 B3
Fortingall Cres FK2 62 A1
Fortissat Ave ML7 191 E3
Fortisset Rd ML7 167 D1
Fortuna Ct FK1 60 B2
Fortune Ave EH41 101 D1
Foulden Pl KY12 29 E2
Foulford Pl KY4 13 D2
Foulford Prim Sch KY4 13 D3
Foulford Rd KY4 13 D2
Foulford St KY4 13 E2
Foulis Cres EH14 152 C3
Foulshiels Rd EH47 171 E1
Foundry La EH20 155 E1
Foundry Loan FK5 38 A1
Foundry Rd
Bonnybridge FK4 58 A3
Shotts ML7 191 F2
Foundry St
Dunfermline KY12 29 D2
Falkirk FK2 60 A4
Fountain Pl EH20 181 E4
Fountain Rd FK9 2 A4
Fountainbridge EH3 232 A1
Fountainhall Rd EH9 123 F2
Fountainhead Rd EH48 145 D4
Fountainpark Cres EH51 64 B4
Fourth Gait EH14 151 F4
Fourth St EH22 183 D3
Fowler Cres
Loanhead EH20 181 E4
Maddiston FK2 83 D3
Fowler Pl FK2 61 F2
Fowler St EH33 128 B4
Fowler Terr EH11 122 C3
Fowlers Ct EH32 96 C1
Fox Covert Ave EH12 91 F1
Fox Covert Gr EH12 91 F1
Fox Covert RC Prim Schs
EH12 91 F1
Fox Spring Cres EH10 154 A4
Fox Spring Rise EH10 154 A4
Fox St EH6 94 A3
Foxknowe Pl EH54 147 D2
Franchi Dr FK5 38 C3
Francis Ct KY12 28 B3
Francis St KY5 14 A4
Frankfield Cres KY11 48 B2
Frankfield Pl KY11 48 B2
Frankfield Rd KY11 48 B2
Fraser Ave Edinburgh EH5 93 D3
Inverkeithing KY11 47 E1
Fraser Cres EH5 93 D3
Fraser Dr KY5 14 A4
Fraser Gdns EH5 93 D3
Fraser Gr EH5 93 D3
Fraser Pl Dysart KY1 18 A4
Grangemouth FK3 61 E3
Stirling FK9 2 A2
Fraser Rd EH54 146 C1
Frederick Cres KY11 29 D1
Frederick St EH2 232 C4
Freeland Ave EH52 117 D3
Freelands Rd
Edinburgh EH28 120 A2
Ratho EH28 119 F2
Freeport Village EH55 172 A2
Fremantle St EH54 148 A3
Freskyn Pl EH52 118 A3
Frew Ct KY11 29 E1
Friar's Croft EH42 78 B1
Friars Brae EH49 85 D3
Friars Loan EH49 85 D3
Friars St FK8 7 D4
Friars Way EH49 85 D3
Friarton Gdns EH26 203 E3
Friendship Gdns FK2 39 E2
Frobisher Ave FK1 59 F2
Frogston Ave EH10 154 A3
Frogston Brae EH17 154 C2
Frogston Gdns EH10 154 B3
Frogston Gr EH10 154 B3
Frogston Rd E EH17 154 C3
Frogston Rd W EH10 154 B2
Frogston Terr EH10 154 B3
Fullerton Dr FK2 61 F2
Fulmar Brae EH54 147 E3
Fulmar Way KY11 48 A2
Furcheons Pk EH8 124 C4
Furnace La EH51 64 B4
Furnace Pl KY4 13 F3
Furniss Ave KY11 46 B3
Fyne La ML7 191 F3

Gaberston Ave FK10 10 B4
Gagarin Way KY4 13 F3
Gair Cres ML8 230 A2
Gair Rd ML8 230 A3
Gair Wynd ML7 192 A2
Gairdoch Dr FK2 39 E2
Gairdoch St FK2 60 A4
Gairloch Cres FK2 61 E1
Gala Gn EH42 78 A1
Galabraes Cres EH48 145 E4
Galachlawshot EH10 154 B3
Galachlawside EH10 154 B3
Galadale EH22 183 D3
Galadale Cres EH22 183 D3
Galadale Dr EH22 183 D3
Gallacher Pl KY4 13 F3
Gallagher Gn EH54 147 E4
Gallamuir Dr FK7 20 B2
Gallamuir Rd FK7 20 B3
Gallolee The EH13 153 E3
Gallow View EH52 88 A4
Galloway Ct FK1 60 A3
Galloway St FK1 60 A3
Gallows Loan KY12 25 E1
Galmeilen EH52 117 E3
Galt Ave EH21 127 D3
Galt Cres EH21 127 D3
Galt Dr EH21 127 D3

Galt Rd EH21 127 D3
Galt Terr EH21 127 D3
Gambeson Cres FK7 7 E2
Gamekeeper's Loan EH4 91 D3
Gamekeeper's Pk EH4 91 D3
Gamekeeper's Rd EH4 91 D3
Garbett Rd EH54 147 E1
Garden City EH47 171 D1
Garden Ct KY12 29 E4
Garden Pl Cairneyhill KY12 27 E1
  Clackmannan FK10 11 D2
  Livingston EH54 147 E2
  Townhill KY12 29 E4
Garden St FK1 60 B3
Garden Terr
  Clackmannan FK10 11 D2
  Edinburgh EH4 91 F2
  Falkirk FK1 60 B3
  Westquarter FK2 61 D1
Gardener Rd EH42 78 B1
Gardener St EH42 78 B2
Gardener's Wlk EH26 203 E3
Gardeners Ct KY12 29 D2
Gardeners' St KY12 29 D2
Gardenhead FK2 61 F1
Gardens The Aberlady EH32 71 E3
  Dirleton EH39 53 D3
Gardiner Cres EH32 97 D1
Gardiner Gr EH4 92 A1
Gardiner Pl
  Cowdenbeath KY4 13 D1
  Newtongrange EH22 183 D3
Gardiner Rd
  Cowdenbeath KY4 13 E1
  Edinburgh EH4 92 A1
  Prestonpans EH32 97 D1
Gardiner St KY5 14 A4
Gardiner Terr
  Edinburgh EH4 92 A1
  Tranent EH33 128 A4
Gardner Cres EH47 169 F3
Gardner Terr EH47 171 D1
Gardner's Cres EH3 232 B2
Gardners La EH48 145 D3
Gardrum Gdns FK1 81 E4
Gardrum Pl FK2 82 C4
Gareloch Way EH47 170 B4
Garleton Ct EH31 52 A1
Garleton Dr EH41 100 C1
Garngrew Rd FK4 57 D2
Garrison Pl FK1 60 A3
Garry Pl Falkirk FK1 60 B1
  Grangemouth FK3 61 F3
Garry St KY5 14 A4
Garry Way ML7 191 F3
Garry Wlk EH54 148 A2
Garscube Terr EH12 122 B4
Gartclush Gdns FK7 19 F4
Gartcows Ave FK1 60 A2
Gartcows Cres FK1 60 A2
Gartcows Dr FK1 60 A2
Gartcows Gdns FK1 59 F2
Gartcows Pl FK1 60 A2
Gartcows Rd FK1 60 A2
Garten Dr ML7 192 A2
Garthill Gdns FK1 60 A2
Garthill La FK1 60 A2
Gartmorn Rd FK10 5 E1
Garvald La FK6 36 B1
Garvald Rd FK6 57 E4
Garvally Cres FK10 10 A4
Garvock Bank KY11 29 F2
Garvock Hill KY12 29 E2
Garvock Terr KY12 29 E2
Gas Wynd KY1 17 D1
Gasworks La
  North Berwick EH39 53 F3
  Whitburn EH47 170 A4
Gateside Ave
  Bonnybridge FK4 58 B3
  Haddington EH41 100 B1
Gateside Ct KY4 13 D2
Gateside Ind Est KY4 13 D2
Gateside Rd
  Haddington EH41 131 E4
  Kirkliston EH29 89 D1
  Stirling FK7 7 D2
  Whitburn EH47 169 F3
Gauger's Bush EH42 76 A4
Gauze Pl EH51 64 A3
Gauze Rd EH51 64 A3
Gavin Pl EH54 147 D3
Gavins Rd FK10 4 C1
Gayfield Cl [9] EH1 93 F1
Gayfield Place La EH1 93 F1
Gayfield Sq EH1 93 F1
Gayfield St EH1 93 F1
Gayfield Street La [7] EH1 93 F1
Gaynor Ave EH20 181 D4
Gean Rd FK10 9 F4
Gellatly Rd KY11 29 E1
Gelnorchy Terr EH9 123 F2
George Ave EH20 181 D4
George Cres
  Loanhead EH20 181 E4
  Ormiston EH35 159 E4
George Dr EH20 181 E4
George Heriot's Sch EH3 232 C2
George IV Bridge EH1 233 D2
George Sq EH8 233 D1
George Square La EH8 233 D1
George St Alva FK12 5 D3
  Armadale EH48 143 F3
  Bathgate EH48 145 D3
  Bo'ness EH51 63 F3
  Cowdenbeath KY4 13 D2
  Dunfermline KY11 29 D1
  Edinburgh EH2 232 C3
George St continued
  Falkirk FK2 60 A3
  Grangemouth FK3 61 F4
  Kincardine FK10 23 F2
  Kirkaldy KY1 17 D2
  Larbert FK5 38 B2
  Laurieston FK2 60 C2
  Ormiston EH35 159 F4
George Terr EH20 181 D4
George Watson's Coll EH10 122 C2
George Watson's Coll Lower Prim Sch EH10 122 C2
George Watson's Coll Upper Prim Sch EH10 122 C2
George Way EH33 128 B3
George Wlk EH33 128 B3
Gerald Terr FK5 38 C2
Gib Gr KY11 29 F1
Gibbdun Pl FK6 57 F4
Gibbs Entry EH8 233 E2
Gibbshill Pl ML7 168 B3
Gibraltar Ct EH22 157 D2
Gibraltar Gdns EH22 157 D2
Gibraltar Rd EH22 157 D2
Gibraltar Terr EH22 157 D2
Gibson Dr EH22 157 E2
Gibson St EH7 93 F2
Gibson Terr EH11 232 A1
Gibsongray St FK2 60 A4
Gideon Ct EH48 145 D4
Gideon St EH48 145 D4
Gifford Pk EH8 233 E1
Gifford Rd EH41 132 B4
Giffordgate EH41 132 A4
Gilberstoun EH15 125 E3
Gilberstoun Brig EH15 125 E3
Gilberstoun Loan EH15 125 E3
Gilberstoun Pl EH15 125 E3
Gilberstoun Wynd EH15 125 E3
Gilbert Ave EH39 54 B3
Gilburn Pl Bo'ness EH51 63 E3
  Shotts ML7 191 F2
Gilchrist Cres EH47 170 A3
Gilchrist Dr FK1 59 F2
Giles St EH6 93 F3
Gilfillan Pl FK2 39 E1
Gilfillan Rd KY11 29 F2
Gill Pk FK6 36 C1
Gill Way KY11 46 B3
Gillespie Cres EH10 232 B1
Gillespie Gr KY12 26 C4
Gillespie Pl Bannockburn FK7 7 D1
  Edinburgh EH11 232 B1
Gillespie Rd EH13 152 C3
Gillespie St EH3 232 B1
Gillespie Terr FK7 20 B1
Gillie Ct KY11 29 E1
Gillies Dr FK7 7 E2
Gillies Hill FK7 6 B3
Gillsland Rd EH10 122 C2
Gilmerton Dykes Ave EH17 155 E3
Gilmerton Dykes Cres EH17 155 E3
Gilmerton Dykes Dr EH17 155 E3
Gilmerton Dykes Gr EH17 155 E3
Gilmerton Dykes Loan EH17 155 E3
Gilmerton Dykes Pl EH17 155 E3
Gilmerton Dykes Rd EH17 155 E3
Gilmerton Dykes St EH17 155 E3
Gilmerton Dykes Terr EH17 155 E3
Gilmerton Dykes View EH17 155 E3
Gilmerton Pl EH17 155 E3
Gilmerton Prim Sch EH17 155 E3
Gilmerton Rd EH16, EH17 155 E4
Gilmerton Road Rdbt EH22 156 B2
Gilmerton Station Rd EH17 155 F2
Gilmore Pk EH11 232 A1
Gilmore Pl EH3 123 D3
Gilmour Rd EH16 123 F2
Gilmour St
  Cowdenbeath KY4 13 E3
  Edinburgh EH8 233 E2
Gilsay Ct FK1 60 B1
Gilston Cres FK2 62 A1
Gladney Sq KY1 17 D1
Gladsmuir ML11 215 D1
Gladsmuir Junc EH33 130 A4
Gladstone Pl
  Dunfermline KY12 29 D3
  Edinburgh EH6 94 A2
  Stirling FK8 7 D3
Gladstone Rd FK5 38 B2
Gladstone Terr EH9 123 F3
Glaive Ave FK7 7 E2
Glamis Gdns
  Dalgety Bay KY11 48 A2
  Polmont FK2 61 F1
Glamis Pl KY11 48 A2
Glamis Rd Kinghorn KY3 34 C2
  Kircaldy KY2 16 B4
Glamis Terr KY3 34 C2
Glasclune Ct EH39 54 B4
Glasclune Gdns EH39 54 B4
Glasgow Rd
  Bannockburn FK7 19 E4
  Bathgate EH48 144 C3
  Denny FK6 36 C1
  Edinburgh EH12 120 B3
  Falkirk FK1 59 E3
  Longcroft FK4 57 E2
  Ratho Station EH28 119 E3
  Stirling FK7 7 D1
Glaskhill Terr EH26 203 F3
Glass Cres EH52 87 F1
Glass Pl EH52 87 F1
Glass Rd EH52 87 F1
Glassel Park Rd EH32 98 B2
Glasshouse Loan FK10 10 A3
Glasswork St KY1 17 D2
Glebe Ave Stirling FK8 7 D4
  Uphall EH52 117 D2
Glebe Cres Alva FK12 5 D4
  Athelstaneford EH39 101 F4
  Stirling FK8 7 D4
Glebe Ct EH47 193 E3
Glebe Gdns
  Edinburgh EH12 121 E3
  Prestonpans EH32 96 C1
Glebe Gr EH12 121 E3
Glebe Pk Inverkeithing KY11 47 D1
  Kirkaldy KY1 17 E3
Glebe Pl
  Bonnyrigg and Lasswade EH18 155 F1
  Burntisland KY3 33 F1
  Kinghorn KY3 34 C2
Glebe Rd Bathgate EH48 145 E3
  Edinburgh EH12 121 E3
  Kincardine FK10 23 F3
  Uphall EH52 117 D2
  West Calder EH55 172 B1
  Whitburn EH47 170 A3
Glebe St Dalkeith EH22 157 D2
  Denny FK6 36 C1
  Falkirk FK1 60 A3
Glebe Terr Alloa FK10 10 A3
  Edinburgh EH12 121 E3
  Haddington EH41 101 D1
  Inverkeithing KY11 47 D1
  Uphall EH52 117 D3
Glebe The Aberdour KY3 49 E4
  Alva FK12 5 D4
  Clackmannan FK10 11 D2
  East Linton EH40 103 F4
  East Saltoun EH34 161 F2
  Edinburgh EH4 91 D3
  Kirkliston EH29 89 D1
  Linlithgow EH49 85 D3
  Pencaitland EH34 160 C4
  West Calder EH55 172 B1
Gledhill Ave EH51 64 B3
Glen Albyn Dr KY2 16 A4
Glen Artney Gr KY11 29 E1
Glen Avon Pl FK2 82 C4
Glen Beasdale Ct KY11 29 E1
Glen Brae FK1 60 A2
Glen Bridge KY12 28 C2
Glen Bruar Pl KY2 16 A4
Glen Clova Cres KY12 27 E1
Glen Cres Falkirk FK1 60 A1
  Livingston EH54 146 C3
Glen Ct EH54 146 B3
Glen Fruin Gr KY11 29 E1
Glen Gdns FK1 60 A2
Glen Isla Gr KY11 29 E1
Glen Isla Rd KY2 16 B4
Glen Lyon Ct FK2 62 A1
Glen Moriston Dr KY12 27 E1
Glen Nevis Dr KY11 29 E1
Glen Ogle Ct FK2 62 A1
Glen Pl EH26 203 F3
Glen Rd Armadale EH48 143 F3
  Bathgate EH48 145 D4
  Livingston EH54 146 C3
  Plean FK7 20 B1
  Shotts ML7 191 F2
  Torwood FK5 37 E4
Glen St EH3 232 C1
Glen Terr Denny FK6 36 B1
  Livingston EH54 146 C3
Glen Tye Rd FK7 7 E3
Glen View Bo'ness EH51 63 E2
  Dennyloanhead FK4 57 E3
Glen View Cres EH23 207 E4
Glen View Ct EH23 207 E4
Glen View Rd EH23 207 E4
Glen Way [3] EH48 145 D4
Glenafeoch Rd ML8 230 A1
Glenallan Dr EH16 124 A1
Glenallan Loan EH16 124 A1
Glenalmond EH47 170 B3
Glenalmond Ct
  Broxburn EH52 117 D3
  Whitburn EH47 170 B3
Glenalmond Terr EH48 145 D4
Glenard View EH51 64 B3
Glenavon Dr KY12 27 E1
Glenavon Terr EH48 145 D4
Glenbank FK1 60 A1
Glenbervie Ave FK5 38 A2
Glenbervie Cres FK5 38 A2
Glenbervie Dr FK5 38 A2
Glenbervie Gr KY11 29 E1
Glenbervie Rd FK3 61 F3
Glenbo Dr FK6 57 F4
Glenbrae Ct FK1 60 A2
Glenbridge Ct KY12 28 C2
Glenbrook EH14 176 C4
Glenburn Gdns EH47 170 B3
Glenburn Gr KY12 26 C4
Glenburn Rd Falkirk FK1 60 B1
  North Berwick EH39 54 B3
Glencairn Cres EH12 122 C4
Glencairn St Falkirk FK1 59 D3
  Stirling FK7 7 D2
Glencairn Terr EH48 145 E4
Glencoe Rd Carluke ML8 230 A1
  Stirling FK8 2 A1
Glencorse Pk EH26 204 B4
Glencorse Prim Sch EH26 180 A1
Glencoul Ave KY11 48 A2
Glencross Gdns EH26 203 E3
Glendenning Dr EH29 89 D1
Glendevon Ave EH12 122 A3
Glendevon Dr FK8 1 C1
Glendevon Gdns EH12 122 A3
Glendevon Gr EH12 122 A3
Glendevon Pk
  Edinburgh EH12 122 A3
  Winchburgh EH52 87 F1
Glendevon Pl EH12 122 A3
Glendevon Rd EH12 122 A3
Glendevon Terr EH12 122 A3
Glendinning Cres EH16 155 D4
Glendinning Dr EH29 88 C1
Glendinning Pl EH29 88 C1
Glendinning Rd EH29 88 C1
Gleneagles Ct EH47 170 B3
Gleneagles Way EH54 146 C3
Glenesk Cres EH22 156 C1
Glenfield Carnock KY12 27 E3
  Livingston EH54 147 D2
Glenfield Ave KY4 13 E3
Glenfield Cres KY4 13 E3
Glenfield Ct KY4 13 E3
Glenfield Gdns KY4 13 E3
Glenfield Ind Est KY4 13 E3
Glenfield Rd KY4 13 E3
Glenfinlas St EH3 232 B3
Glenfuir Rd FK1 59 F3
Glenfuir St FK1 59 E3
Glengairn Wlk KY11 29 E1
Glengarry Cres FK1 59 F1
Glengyle Terr EH3 232 C1
Glenisla Gardens La EH9 123 E2
Glenisla Gdns EH9 123 E2
Glenkinchie Distillery EH34 160 C1
Glenlee Ave EH8 124 B4
Glenlee Gdns EH8 124 B4
Glenlockhart Bank EH14 122 B1
Glenlockhart Rd EH10 122 C1
Glenlockhart Valley EH14 122 B1
Glenmavis Cres ML8 230 A1
Glenmavis Ct ML8 230 A1
Glenmavis Dr EH48 145 D4
Glenmore EH47 170 B3
Glenmore Dr FK4 57 F3
Glennie Gdns EH33 128 B3
Glenochil Pk FK10 4 C2
Glenochil Rd FK1 60 A2
Glenochil Terr FK10 4 C2
Glenogle Ct EH3 93 D1
Glenogle Ho [7] EH3 93 D1
Glenogle Pl [8] EH3 93 D1
Glenogle Rd EH3 93 D1
Glenogle Terr EH3 93 D2
Glenorchy Rd EH39 54 A3
Glensburgh Rd FK3 61 D4
Glenshiel Gr KY11 29 E1
Glenside Ct
  Armadale EH48 143 F3
  Grangemouth FK3 61 F3
Glenside Gdns EH48 143 F3
Glentye Gdns FK1 59 F1
Glenure Loan EH4 91 E1
Glenvarloch Cres EH16 155 D4
Glenview Denny FK6 36 A2
  Menstrie FK11 4 A3
  Penicuik EH26 203 F3
Glenview Cres EH47 171 D1
Glenview Dr FK1 59 F1
Glenview Rd EH47 171 D1
Glenwinnel Rd FK12 4 C4
Glenwood Dr EH48 143 E3
Glenyards Rd FK4 58 A1
Gloag Pl EH55 172 B2
Globe Rd KY11 46 B1
Gloucester La EH3 232 B4
Gloucester Pl EH3 232 B4
Gloucester Sq EH3 232 B4
Gloucester St EH3 232 B4
Glover's Ct KY3 35 D2
Glowrorum Dr FK6 57 F4
Glynwed Ct FK2 60 B4
Godfrey Ave FK6 36 B1
Godfrey Cres FK5 38 B1
Goff Ave EH7 94 C1
Gogar Loan FK9 3 E3
Gogar Pl FK7 7 E1
Gogar Rbdt HE12 120 C3
Gogar Station Rd EH12 120 C2
Gogarbank Farm EH12 120 B1
Gogarburn Hospl EH12 120 B3
Gogarloch Haugh EH12 121 D3
Gogarloch Muir EH12 121 D3
Gogarloch Rd EH12 121 D3
Gogarloch Syke EH12 121 D3
Gogarstone Rd EH28 120 A3
Goldenacre Terr EH3 93 D2
Goldenstones Ave EH42 78 C1
Goldpark Pl EH54 147 D2
Golf Course Rd
  Bonnyrigg and Lasswade EH19 182 A4
  Cowdenbeath KY4 13 E3
  Linlithgow EH49 84 C3
  Livingston EH54 147 D4
Golf Ct EH32 71 E2
Golf Dr EH32 97 F2
Golf House Rd EH42 78 C1
Golfdrum St KY12 28 C2
Goodall Cres EH52 116 B1
Goodall Pl EH52 116 A1
Goodall's Pl EH41 132 B4
Goodman Pl FK2 82 C4
Goose Green Ave EH21 126 B4
Goose Green Cres EH21 126 B4
Goose Green Pl EH21 126 B4
Goose Green Rd
  Gullane EH31 52 A1
  Musselburgh EH21 126 B4
Goosecroft Rd FK8 7 D4
Gordon Ave
  Bathgate EH48 145 D3
  Bonnyrigg and Lasswade EH19 181 F3
Gordon Cres Bridge of A FK9 2 A4
  Stirling FK8 1 C1
Gordon Ct EH52 117 F3
Gordon Dr FK10 10 B4
Gordon Loan EH12 121 F4
Gordon Pl FK1 59 F3
Gordon Rd
  Edinburgh EH12 121 F4
  Rosyth KY11 46 A1
Gordon St
  Cowdenbeath KY4 13 E3
  Easthouses EH22 183 E4
  Edinburgh EH6 94 A2
  Lochgelly KY5 14 A4
Gordon Terr
  Dunfermline KY11 29 D1
  Edinburgh EH16 124 A1
Gordon Way EH54 147 E4
Gore Ave EH23 207 E4
Gorebridge Prim Sch EH23 207 E4
Goremire Rd ML8 230 A1
Gorgie Park Cl EH14 122 B2
Gorgie Park Rd EH11 122 B3
Gorgie Rd EH11 122 B2
Gorrie St Denny FK6 36 B1
  Dunfermline KY11 29 E1
Gorsebank EH54 147 F3
Gort Pl FK3 61 E3
Gorton Loan EH24 181 E1
Gorton Pl EH24 181 E1
Gorton Rd EH24 181 E1
Goschen Pl EH52 117 D3
Goschen Terr EH52 117 D3
Gosford Ho EH32 71 D1
Gosford Pl EH6 93 E3
Gosford Rd
  Cockenzie & Port Seton EH32 97 E2
  Kircaldy KY2 16 B4
  Longniddry EH32 98 C3
Gote La EH30 68 A1
Gourlaw Cotts EH24 205 D4
Gourlay St KY2 17 D2
Gourlaybank EH41 101 D1
Gow Cres KY1 17 D2
Gowan Ave FK2 60 A3
Gowan La FK2 60 A3
Gowanbank EH54 147 E3
Gowanbrae EH47 193 F3
Gowanbrae Dr KY12 29 E2
Gowanbrae Pl KY12 29 E2
Gowanbrae Terr KY12 29 E2
Gowanhill Gdns FK8 1 C1
Gowanlea Dr FK1 110 A3
Grace St KY5 14 B4
Gracefield Ct EH21 126 A3
Gracemount Ave EH16 155 D4
Gracemount Dr EH16 155 D3
Gracemount High Sch EH16 155 D3
Gracemount Pl EH16 155 D3
Gracemount Prim Sch EH16 155 D3
Gracemount Rd EH16 155 D3
Gracemount Sq EH16 155 D3
Gracie Cres FK7 8 B2
Gracie's Wynd EH48 144 A3
Gradlon Pl FK1 60 A2
Graeme High Sch FK1 60 B2
Graeme Pl FK1 59 F1
Graham Ave Larbert FK5 38 A2
  Stirling FK9 2 B2
Graham Cres EH51 64 A4
Graham Ct EH47 171 F4
Graham St Bridge of A FK9 2 A4
  Edinburgh EH6 93 F3
Graham Terr FK2 22 B2
Graham Way EH54 147 E4
Graham's Rd EH26 204 B4
Grahams Rd FK2 60 A3
Grahamsdyke Ave EH51 64 A4
Grahamsdyke Cres FK4 58 A2
Grahamsdyke La EH51 64 A4
Grahamsdyke Rd
  Bo'ness EH51 64 B3
  Bonnybridge FK4 58 A2
Grahamsdyke St FK2 61 D2
Grahamsdyke Terr EH51 64 A4
Grahamston Sta FK1 60 A3
Graiglaw Pl EH52 116 B1
Graigleith View FK10 4 B2
Grainger St KY5 14 A4
Grampian Cres FK3 61 F3
Grampian Ct KY11 46 C1
Grampian Gdns KY2 16 C3
Grampian Ho EH6 93 F3
Grampian Pl KY11 46 C1
Grampian Rd Rosyth KY11 46 C1
  Stirling FK7 6 C3
Grampion Ct EH54 147 F1
Granary Rd FK2 60 A4
Granary Sq FK2 60 A4
Granby Ave EH54 147 F2
Granby Rd EH16 123 F2
Grandfield EH6 93 E3
Grandville EH6 93 E3

Grange Ave FK2 60 B3
Grange Cotts KY3 34 C3
Grange Cres EH9 123 E2
Grange Cres E EH32 96 C1
Grange Cres W EH32 127 F4
Grange Ct
5 Edinburgh EH9 123 F3
North Berwick EH39 54 B3
Grange Dr
Dunfermline KY11 46 B4
Falkirk FK2 60 B3
Grange Gdns FK9 2 B4
Grange Gr EH32 96 C1
Grange Knowe EH49 85 E4
Grange La FK3 40 B1
Grange Loan Bo'ness EH51 64 A4
Edinburgh EH9 123 E2
Grange Loan Gdns EH9 123 E2
Grange Pk KY11 46 B4
Grange Pl Grangemouth FK3 61 E4
Redding FK2 61 E1
Grange Rd Alloa FK10 9 F3
Bridge of A FK9 2 B3
Broxburn EH52 117 F2
Burntisland KY3 33 E1
Dunfermline KY11 46 B3
Edinburgh EH9 123 E3
Livingston EH54 148 A4
North Berwick EH39 54 A3
Polmont FK2, FK3 61 F2
Prestonpans EH32 96 C1
Grange Sch EH51 64 A4
Grange Terr Bo'ness EH51 64 A4
Edinburgh EH9 123 E2
Grange The FK2 82 C4
Grange View EH49 85 E4
Grange Wynd KY11 46 B4
Grangeburn Rd FK3 40 C1
Grangemouth High Sch
FK3 61 F3
Grangemouth Rd FK2 60 C3
Grangepans EH51 64 A4
Grangeview FK5 38 C1
Grannies Park Ind Est
EH22 157 D2
Grant Ave EH13 153 D3
Grant Pl FK9 2 A2
Grant St Alloa FK10 9 F3
West Calder EH55 172 B2
Granton Cres EH5 92 C3
Granton Gdns EH5 92 C3
Granton Gr EH5 92 C3
Granton Mains Ave EH4 92 B3
Granton Mains Bank EH4 92 B3
Granton Mains Brae EH4 92 B3
Granton Mains Ct EH4 92 B3
Granton Mains E EH4 92 B3
Granton Mains Gait EH4 92 B3
Granton Mains Vale EH4 92 B3
Granton Mains Wynd EH4 92 B3
Granton Medway EH5 92 C3
Granton Park Ave EH5 92 C4
Granton Pl EH5 92 C3
Granton Prim Sch EH5 92 C3
Granton Rd EH5 93 D3
Granton Sq EH5 92 C4
Granton Terr EH5 92 C3
Granton View
Dalgety Bay KY11 47 F1
Edinburgh EH5 92 C3
Grants Bank KY12 29 D2
Grantully Pl EH9 123 F2
Granville Terr EH10 123 D3
Granville Way KY11 46 C2
Grassmarket EH1 232 C2
Gray Buchanan Ct FK2 61 E1
Gray Pk KY4 13 E3
Gray Pl KY11 47 E2
Gray St ML7 192 A2
Gray's Ct EH8 233 E2
Gray's Loan EH10 122 C2
Graysmill Sch EH14 122 B1
Graystale Rd FK7 7 D2
Graystonelee Rd ML7 191 E3
Great Cannon Bank EH15 95 D1
Great Carleton Pl EH16 125 D2
Great Carleton Sq EH16 125 D2
Great Junction St EH6 93 F3
Great King St EH3 93 E1
Great Michael Cl EH6 93 E4
Great Michael Rd KY11 46 A1
Great Michael Rise EH6 93 E3
Great Michael Sq EH6 93 E4
Great Stuart St EH3 232 A3
Green Apron Pk EH39 54 A3
Green La
Bonnyrigg and Lasswade
EH18 181 F4
Grangemouth FK3 61 F4
Green St Edinburgh EH7 93 E1
Townhill KY12 29 E4
Green The Alva FK12 5 D4
Bathgate EH48 145 E4
Edinburgh EH4 91 F2
Pencaitland EH34 160 C3
West Barns EH42 77 F1
Green Tree La EH51 63 E3
Greenacre EH14 152 C4
Greenacre Ct FK7 7 F1
Greenacre Pl FK7 7 F1
Greenbank Ave EH10 123 D1
Greenbank Cres EH10 154 A4
Greenbank Dr
Cowdenbeath KY4 13 D1
Edinburgh EH10 123 D1
Greenbank Gdns EH10 153 F4
Greenbank Gr EH10 153 F4
Greenbank La EH10 122 C1
Greenbank Loan EH10 122 C1
Greenbank Pk EH10 153 F4
Greenbank Pl
Edinburgh EH10 123 D1
Falkirk FK1 59 E2
Greenbank Rd
Edinburgh EH10 122 C1
Falkirk FK1 59 E2
Greenbank Rise EH10 153 F4
Greenbank Row EH10 153 F4
Greenbank Terr EH10 123 D1
Greenburn Rd EH47 193 F3
Greencraig Ave FK1 81 E3
Greendykes Ave EH16 124 C2
Greendykes Dr EH16 124 C2
Greendykes Gdns EH16 124 C2
Greendykes Ind Est EH52 117 E3
Greendykes Loan 7
EH16 124 C2
Greendykes Prim Sch
EH16 124 C2
Greendykes Rd
Broxburn EH52 117 F3
Edinburgh EH16 124 C1
Greendykes Steadings
EH52 117 F4
Greendykes Terr EH16 124 C2
Greenend Dr EH17 155 E4
Greenend Gdns EH17 155 E4
Greenend Gr EH17 155 E4
Greenfield Cres EH14 177 E4
Greenfield Rd EH14 177 E4
Greenfield St Alloa FK10 10 A4
Bonnybridge FK4 58 A3
Greenhall Rd EH23 183 E1
Greenhead FK12 5 D3
Greenheads Rd EH39 54 C3
Greenhill Ct
Bonnybridge FK4 58 A1
Edinburgh EH10 123 D3
Fauldhouse EH47 193 F3
Greenhill Gdns EH10 123 D2
Greenhill Pk
Edinburgh EH10 123 D2
Penicuik EH26 203 E3
Greenhill Pl EH10 123 D2
Greenhill Rd
Blackridge EH48 142 C2
Bonnybridge FK4 58 A2
Greenhill Terr EH10 123 D3
Greenhithe Terr FK2 82 C4
Greenhorn's Well Ave FK1 59 F2
Greenhorn's Well Cres
FK1 59 F2
Greenhorn's Well Dr FK1 59 F2
Greenlaw Gr EH26 180 A1
Greenlaw Hedge EH13 153 F4
Greenlaw Rig EH13 153 F4
Greenloanings KY2 16 B4
Greenmantle Loan 9
EH16 124 A1
Greenmount KY4 13 D1
Greenmount Dr
Burntisland KY3 33 F1
Shieldhill FK1 81 E3
Greenmount Rd N KY3 33 F1
Greenmount Rd S KY3 34 A1
Greenpark Dr FK2 61 F1
Greenrigg Cotts ML7 169 D3
Greenrigg Prim Sch ML7 168 C3
Greens The FK2 82 C3
Greenside EH48 113 F3
Greenside La EH1 233 E4
Greenside Pl
Edinburgh EH1 233 E4
Rosewell EH24 181 E1
Greenside Row EH1 233 E4
Greenside St FK10 10 A3
Greenvale Dr FK2 82 C4
Greenville Ct FK1 59 F2
Greenwell St EH47 193 F3
Greenwell Terr FK2 82 C4
Greenwells Dr FK2 82 C4
Greenwood Ave FK8 7 D4
Greenwood Pk EH54 147 E3
Greenwood St ML7 191 F3
Gregory Rd EH54 173 D4
Greig Cres EH48 144 A3
Greig Pl KY5 14 A4
Greig Rd KY11 46 A1
Grendon Ct FK8 7 D3
Grendon Gdns FK8 7 D3
Grey Craigs KY12 27 E1
Grey School Cnr EH32 96 C1
Greyfriar's Wlk KY11 47 E2
Greyfriars EH1 233 D2
Greyfriars Bobby Meml
EH1 233 D2
Greygoran FK10 5 E1
Grierson Ave EH5 93 D3
Grierson Cres
Cambusbarron FK7 6 B3
Edinburgh EH5 93 D3
Grierson Gdns EH5 93 D3
Grierson Rd EH5 92 C3
Grierson Sq EH5 93 D3
Grierson Villas EH5 93 D3
Grieve Ct EH26 203 F4
Grieve St Dunfermline KY12 28 C2
Kirkaldy KY2 17 D3
Griffith Dr EH47 170 A3
Griffiths St FK1 60 A2
Grigor Ave EH4 92 B2
Grigor Dr EH4 92 B2
Grigor Gdns EH4 92 C2
Grigor Terr EH4 92 B2
Grindlay St EH3 232 B2
Grindlay Street Ct EH3 232 B2
Groathill Ave EH4 92 B1
Groathill Gdns E 2 EH4 92 B1
Groathill Gdns W 1 EH4 92 B1
Groathill Rd N EH4 92 B2
Groathill Rd S EH4 92 B1
Grodwell Dr FK12 4 C4
Grosvenor Gdns EH12 122 C4
Grosvenor St EH12 232 A2
Grove Cres FK2 39 D1
Grove End EH18 182 A4
Grove St Denny FK6 36 B1
Edinburgh EH3 232 A2
Musselburgh EH21 126 B3
Grove The EH21 126 C3
Grundie's Well Rd EH17 155 F3
Guardians Wood EH12 122 B4
Guardwell Cres EH17 155 E4
Guildhall St KY12 29 D2
Guildie Howes Rd EH23 207 F1
Guildiehaugh Rdbt EH48 145 E3
Guildry Gr KY12 29 F2
Gullan's Cl EH1 233 E3
Gullane Prim Sch EH31 52 A1
Gunn Rd FK3 61 E3
Gunner Rd FK3 62 B4
Guthrie St EH1 233 D2
Guttergates Rd KY11 30 A3
Gyle Ave EH12 120 C3
Gyle Park Gdns EH12 121 D3
Gyle Rbdt EH12 120 C3
Gyle Sh Ctr EH12 121 D3
Gylemuir Prim Sch EH12 121 E3
Gylemuir Rd EH12 121 E3
Gylers Rd EH39 53 D2

Haddington Inf Sch
EH41 132 A4
Haddington Pl EH7 93 F1
Haddington Rd
East Linton EH40 103 E4
Musselburgh EH21 127 D3
North Berwick EH39 54 B3
Tranent EH33 128 C3
Haddington Station
Ind Est EH41 131 F4
Haddon's Ct EH8 233 E2
Haddow Gr KY3 50 B4
Hadfast Rd EH22 158 B3
Hadrian Way EH51 64 A3
Haig Ave Kirkaldy KY1 17 E4
Stirling FK8 2 A1
Haig Cres Bathgate EH48 145 E3
Dunfermline KY12 29 E3
Haig St FK3 61 E3
Hailes App EH13 153 D4
Hailes Ave EH13 153 D4
Hailes Bank EH13 153 D4
Hailes Castle EH41 103 D2
Hailes Cres EH13 153 D4
Hailes Gdns EH13 153 D4
Hailes Gr EH13 153 D4
Hailes Loan EH41 103 D2
Hailes Pk EH13 152 C4
Hailes Pl KY12 29 E2
Hailes St EH3 232 B1
Hailes Terr EH13 153 D4
Hailesland Gdns EH14 121 F1
Hailesland Gr EH14 121 F1
Hailesland Pk EH14 121 F1
Hailesland Pl EH14 121 F1
Hailesland Prim Sch
EH14 152 C4
Hailesland Rd EH14 121 F1
Hailstonegreen ML11 215 D1
Hailstones Cres EH48 143 F3
Hainburn Pk EH10 153 F3
Haining Gr FK2 83 D3
Haining Pl
Grangemouth FK3 61 F4
Livingston EH54 147 D3
Haining Rd EH49 83 F3
Haining Terr EH49 83 F3
Hakness Cres EH33 128 B3
Halbeath Dr KY11 29 F3
Halbeath Pl KY11 29 F3
Halbeath Rd
Dunfermline KY11 29 F3
Halbeath KY11 30 A3
Halbeath Ret Pk KY11 30 A3
Halberts Cres FK7 7 D1
Haldane Ave Bridge of A FK9 2 A3
Haddington EH41 100 C1
Haldane Gr KY12 26 B4
Haldane Sq EH54 173 E3
Halketshall KY11 45 E2
Halkett Cres KY11 29 E1
Hall Cres EH31 52 A1
Hall La KY5 14 A4
Hall Rd EH52 117 F3
Hall Row KY11 45 D2
Hall St Cowdenbeath KY4 13 E2
Lochgelly KY5 14 A4
Hallcraigs EH27 149 F2
Hallcroft Cl EH28 119 E1
Hallcroft Cres EH28 119 E1
Hallcroft Gdns EH28 119 E1
Hallcroft Gn EH28 119 E1
Hallcroft Neuk EH28 119 E1
Hallcroft Pk EH28 119 E1
Hallcroft Rise EH28 119 E1
Hallglen Prim Sch FK1 60 A1
Hallglen Rd FK1 60 A1
Hallglen Terr FK1 60 A1
Hallhead Rd EH16 123 F1
Hallhill EH42 106 B4
Halliburton Terr EH39 53 D2
Hallows The KY1 17 F4
Hallpark FK10 10 B4
Hallyards Rd
Newbridge HE29 119 D4
Ratho Station EH28 119 E3
Halmyre St EH6 94 A2
Halyard Rise KY11 47 F1
Halyard Terr KY2 15 D1
Hamburgh Pl EH6 93 F3
Hamilton Ave
Linlithgow EH49 84 C3
Stenhousemuir FK5 38 C2
Hamilton Cres
Gullane EH31 52 A1
Maddiston FK2 82 C3
Newtongrange EH22 183 D3
Hamilton Dr
Edinburgh EH15 124 C4
Falkirk FK1 60 A2
Stirling FK9 2 B2
Hamilton Dr W EH15 124 C4
Hamilton Gdns EH15 124 C4
Hamilton Gr EH15 124 C4
Hamilton La
Bathgate EH48 144 C4
Bo'ness EH51 63 F4
Hamilton Pk
Edinburgh EH15 124 C4
Linlithgow EH49 84 C3
Hamilton Pl Edinburgh EH3 93 D1
Linlithgow EH49 84 C3
Rosyth KY11 46 C2
Hamilton Rd
Bathgate EH48 144 C4
Grangemouth FK3 61 F3
Gullane EH31 52 A1
Larbert FK2 38 B3
North Berwick EH39 54 A4
Hamilton Sq EH51 63 E3
Hamilton St Falkirk FK1 59 E3
Lochgelly KY5 14 A3
Hamilton Terr
Edinburgh EH15 125 D4
High Valleyfield KY12 26 A1
Inverkeithing KY11 47 E1
Hamilton Wynd EH6 93 F3
Hammermen's Entry EH8 233 E3
Handax ML11 215 D1
Haney's Way EH51 64 A4
Hanover Ct Broxburn EH52 117 F3
Livingston EH54 147 D2
Hanover Grange FK3 61 E4
Hanover St EH2 232 C4
Harbour Dr KY11 47 F2
Harbour Pl Burntisland KY3 50 C4
Dalgety Bay KY11 47 F1
Edinburgh EH15 95 D1
Inverkeithing KY11 47 E1
Harbour Rd Bo'ness EH51 64 B4
Edinburgh EH15 95 D1
Kinghorn KY3 35 D1
Musselburgh EH21 126 A3
Harburn Ave EH54 146 C3
Harburn Ave W EH54 146 C4
Harburn Dr EH55 172 C2
Harburn Gdns EH55 172 C2
Harburn La EH55 172 C2
Harburn Rd EH55 172 C2
Harcourt Rd KY2 17 D3
Harden Pl EH11 122 C3
Hardengreen Bsns Ctr
EH22 156 C1
Hardengreen Ind Est
EH22 156 C1
Hardengreen Junc EH22 182 C4
Hardgate EH41 101 D1
Hardgate Ct EH41 101 D1
Hardhill Dr EH48 144 C3
Hardhill Pl EH48 144 A3
Hardhill Rd EH48 144 C3
Hardhill Terr EH48 144 C3
Hardie Cres FK7 8 B2
Hardie Ct FK7 7 E2
Hardie Rd EH54 146 B4
Hardie Terr EH40 103 E4
Hardwell Cl EH8 233 E2
Hardy Gdns EH48 145 F3
Hareburn Ave FK1 112 A3
Harelaw Rd EH13 153 D3
Hares Cl EH32 97 E2
Harestanes Rd EH48 143 F2
Harewood Cres EH16 124 C2
Harewood Dr EH16 124 C2
Harewood Rd EH16 124 C2
Harkenburn Gdns EH26 203 E3
Harlaw Gr EH26 203 E3
Harlaw Hill EH32 96 C1
Harlaw March EH14 177 E4
Harlaw Rd Balerno EH14 177 F4
Currie EH14 152 A1
Harlawhill Gdns EH32 97 D1
Harley Ct FK2 60 A4
Harley St KY11 47 D2
Harlington Pl FK2 82 C4
Harlow Ave FK2 61 E1
Harmeny Sch EH14 177 E4
Harness Ct EH20 181 E4
Harpenside Cres EH39 53 E3
Harper's Brae EH26 204 A3
Harperdean Terr EH41 100 C1
Harriebrae Pk KY12 28 C2
Harriet St KY1 17 F3
Harris Ct FK10 10 A3
Harris Dr KY2 16 C4
Harris Pl Dunfermline KY11 29 E1
Grangemouth FK3 61 E3
Harrismith Pl EH7 94 A1
Harrison Gdns EH11 122 C2
Harrison La EH11 122 C3
Harrison Pl
Edinburgh EH11 122 C2
Falkirk FK1 59 F3
Harrison Rd EH11 122 C3
Harrysmuir Cres EH53 148 A4
Harrysmuir N EH53 148 A4
Harrysmuir Prim Sch EH54 147 F3
Harrysmuir Rd EH53 148 A4
Harrysmuir S EH53 148 A4
Harrysmuir Terr EH53 148 A4
Hart St EH1 93 E1
Hart Street La EH1 93 E1
Hart Wynd FK7 7 F1
Hartfield Terr ML7 212 A4
Harthill Rd
Blackridge EH48 142 B1
Fauldhouse EH47 193 E3
Hartington Gdns EH10 123 D3
Hartington Pl EH10 123 D3
Hartley Pl FK3 61 D3
Hartshill Prim Sch ML7 168 C3
Hartwood Gdns ML7 191 D1
Hartwood Rd Shotts ML7 191 D2
West Calder EH55 172 B1
Hartwoodhill Hospl ML7 191 D2
Harvest Dr EH28 119 D3
Harvest Rd EH28 119 D3
Harvesters Way EH14 152 B4
Harvey Ave FK2 61 F1
Harvey Wynd FK8 2 A1
Harvieston Villas EH23 207 E4
Hatfield Pl 4 EH48 145 D4
Hatton Pl EH9 123 E3
Haugh Gdns FK2 39 D1
Haugh Park EH14 122 A1
Haugh Rd Burntisland KY3 50 B4
Stirling FK9 2 A1
Haugh St Edinburgh EH4 93 D1
Falkirk FK2 39 D1
Haven The KY11 47 F1
Haven's Edge KY11 45 F2
Hawes Brae EH30 68 B1
Hawk Brae EH54 147 E3
Hawkcraig Rd KY3 49 E4
Hawkhead Cres EH16 155 D4
Hawkhead Gr EH16 155 D4
Hawkhill EH7 94 A2
Hawkhill Ave EH7 94 A2
Hawkhill Rd Alloa FK10 10 B3
Kincardine FK10 23 E3
Hawkins Terr EH26 204 A4
Hawksmuir KY1 17 E3
Hawkwood Terr ML11 215 D1
Hawley Rd FK1 60 B2
Hawthorn Bank
Carnock KY12 27 E3
Queensferry EH30 68 A1
Seafield EH47 172 A4
Hawthorn Cres
Easthouses EH22 183 E4
Fallin FK7 8 B2
Hill of B KY4 12 C1
Stirling FK8 1 C1
Hawthorn Dr Denny FK6 36 B2
Falkirk FK1 59 F2
Fallin FK7 8 B2
Harthill ML7 168 C3
Shotts ML7 192 B2
Hawthorn Gdns EH20 155 D1
Hawthorn Pl
Edinburgh EH17 155 F3
Ormiston EH35 159 E4
Shotts ML7 212 A4
Uphall EH52 116 C2
Hawthorn Rd EH32 97 D1
Hawthorn St FK3 61 E3
Hawthorn Terr EH32 97 D2
Hawthornbank La EH4 232 A3
Hawthornbank Pl EH6 93 E3
Hawthornbank Rd EH41 100 C1
Hawthornbank Terr EH6 93 F3
Hawthornden Ave EH19 182 A4
Hawthornden Gdns EH19 182 A4
Hawthornden Prim Sch
EH19 181 F3
Hawthorne Pl FK5 38 B1
Hawthorns The EH31 52 A2
Hawthornvale EH6 93 E3
Hay Ave EH16 124 C2
Hay Dr EH16 125 D2
Hay Gr KY11 29 F1
Hay Pl EH16 124 C2
Hay Rd EH16 124 C2
Hay Terr EH16 124 C2
Hayfield Edinburgh EH12 121 D4
Falkirk FK2 60 B4
Hayfield Ind Est KY2 17 D4
Hayfield Pl KY2 17 D4
Hayfield Rd Falkirk FK2 60 B4
Kirkaldy KY1 17 E4
Hayfield Terr FK6 57 F4
Haygate Ave FK2 82 C4
Haymarket EH12 232 A2
Haymarket Sta EH12 232 A2
Haymarket Terr EH12 122 C4
Haypark Bsns Ctr FK2 61 F1
Haypark Rd FK6 57 E3
Hayworth Ave FK2 61 D2
Hazel Ave KY2 17 D3
Hazel Cres FK6 36 B2
Hazel Ct EH42 78 A1
Hazel Dr EH19 182 A3
Hazel Gr Dunfermline KY11 46 C4
Falkirk FK2 60 B4
Livingston EH54 148 A3
Shotts ML7 192 A2

Hazel La EH20 ...... 180 C4
Hazel Rd FK3 ...... 61 E3
Hazelbank Gdns FK8 ...... 2 A1
Hazelbank Terr EH11 ...... 122 C2
Hazeldean Ave EH51 ...... 63 E3
Hazeldean Terr EH16 ...... 124 A1
Hazelhurst FK2 ...... 82 C4
Hazelwood Gr EH16 ...... 124 B1
Head of Muir Prim Sch 57 E3
Headlesscross Rd ML7 ...... 192 C1
Headrig Rd EH30 ...... 67 E3
Headrigg Row EH14 ...... 124 A1
Headwell Ave KY12 ...... 29 D3
Headwell Rd KY12 ...... 29 D3
Heaney Ave EH53 ...... 148 A4
Heath Rd KY11 ...... 46 C2
Heather Ave FK1 ...... 81 E3
Heather Gr
  Dunfermline KY11 ...... 46 C4
  Maddiston FK2 ...... 83 D3
Heather Pk EH47 ...... 146 A1
Heatherbank EH54 ...... 147 E3
Heatherdale Gdns FK6 ...... 57 F4
Heathervale Wlk EH48 ...... 144 A4
Heatherwood EH47 ...... 146 A1
Heatherwood Pk EH53 ...... 148 A4
Heathery The KY11 ...... 46 C4
Hedge Row EH20 ...... 180 C4
Hedges The FK1 ...... 59 F3
Heggie's Wynd KY1 ...... 17 D1
Heights Rd EH48 ...... 142 B2
Helen Pl KY11 ...... 68 B3
Helmsdale Pk KY12 ...... 28 C1
Henderland Rd EH12 ...... 122 B4
Henderson Ave FK10 ...... 10 A4
Henderson Cres EH52 ...... 117 D3
Henderson Ct EH53 ...... 148 C2
Henderson Gdns
  Edinburgh EH6 ...... 93 F3
  Tranent EH33 ...... 128 B3
Henderson Pl Alva FK12 ...... 5 D4
  Broxburn EH52 ...... 117 D3
  Edinburgh EH3 ...... 93 D1
Henderson Place La EH3 ...... 93 D1
Henderson Row EH3 ...... 93 D1
Henderson St
  Bridge of A FK9 ...... 2 A4
  Edinburgh EH6 ...... 93 F3
  Kingseat KY12 ...... 12 A1
  Lochgelly KY5 ...... 14 A4
Henderson Terr EH11 ...... 122 C3
Hendry Cres KY2 ...... 17 D3
Hendry Rd KY2 ...... 17 D3
Hendry St FK2 ...... 60 A4
Hendry's Wynd KY1 ...... 17 D1
Hennings The FK10 ...... 5 E1
Henry Ross Pl EH30 ...... 68 A1
Henry St Alva FK12 ...... 5 D3
  Bo'ness FK3 ...... 64 A3
  Grangemouth FK3 ...... 61 F4
Henryson Rd KY11 ...... 29 F2
Hens Nest Rd EH47 ...... 170 C1
Hens Nest Road Crofts EH47 ...... 170 C2
Hepburn Dr EH22 ...... 157 E1
Hepburn Rd EH41 ...... 101 D1
Herald Rise EH54 ...... 147 F1
Herbertshire St FK6 ...... 36 C1
Hercus Loan EH21 ...... 126 A3
Herd Gn EH54 ...... 147 D4
Herd Terr EH20 ...... 181 D4
Herdmanflatt EH41 ...... 101 D1
Herdmanflatt Hospl EH41 ...... 101 D1
Herdshill Ave FK1 ...... 81 E3
Heriot Bridge EH1 ...... 232 C2
Heriot Gdns KY3 ...... 33 F1
Heriot Hill Terr EH7 ...... 93 E2
Heriot Pl EH3 ...... 232 C2
Heriot Row EH3 ...... 232 B4
Heriot St KY11 ...... 47 E1
Heriot Way EH38 ...... 228 B1
Heriot-Watt Univ EH14 ...... 151 F4
Heritage Dr FK2 ...... 39 D2
Hermand Cres EH11 ...... 122 C2
Hermand St EH11 ...... 122 B2
Hermand Terr EH11 ...... 122 B2
Hermiston Gait Ret Pk 121 D2
Hermiston House Rd EH14 ...... 120 C1
Hermiston Junc EH11 ...... 121 D1
Hermitage Dr EH10 ...... 123 D1
Hermitage Gdns EH10 ...... 123 D1
Hermitage Park Gr EH6 ...... 94 A2
Hermitage Park Prim Sch EH6 ...... 94 A2
Hermitage Pk EH6 ...... 94 A2
Hermitage Pk S EH6 ...... 94 A2
Hermitage Pl EH6 ...... 94 A2
Hermitage Rd FK9 ...... 2 C3
Hermitage Terr EH10 ...... 123 D1
Hermits Croft EH8 ...... 233 F1
Heron Ind Complex EH54 ...... 146 B4
Hervey St EH6 ...... 10 A4
Heugh Brae EH39 ...... 54 C3
Heugh Rd EH39 ...... 54 C3
Heugh St FK1 ...... 60 A2
Heugh The EH33 ...... 128 B4
Hewitt Pl KY11 ...... 49 E4
Heyford Pl FK7 ...... 6 B3
Higginson La EH22 ...... 183 F3
High Academy Gr EH48 ...... 143 F3
High Academy La EH48 ...... 143 F3
High Beveridgewell KY12 ...... 28 C3
High Brae EH48 ...... 113 F3
High Buckstone EH10 ...... 154 B3

High Meadow ML8 ...... 230 B1
High Mill Rd ML8 ...... 230 A1
High Park Rise EH26 ...... 203 F2
High Port EH49 ...... 85 D4
High Rd Maddiston FK2 ...... 83 D3
  Roslin EH25 ...... 204 C3
  Spott EH42 ...... 106 B2
High Riggs EH3 ...... 232 B2
High School Wynd EH1 ...... 233 E2
High School Yds EH1 ...... 233 E2
High St Aberdour KY3 ...... 49 D4
  Aberlady EH32 ...... 71 E2
  Airth FK2 ...... 22 B2
  Alloa FK10 ...... 10 A3
  Bathgate EH48 ...... 145 D4
  Bonnybridge FK4 ...... 58 A3
  Bonnyrigg and Lasswade EH18 ...... 156 A1
  Bonnyrigg and Lasswade EH19 ...... 182 A4
  Burntisland KY3 ...... 50 C4
  Clackmannan KY10 ...... 10 C2
  Cockenzie & Port Seton EH32 ...... 97 E2
  Cowdenbeath KY4 ...... 13 E2
  Dalkeith EH22 ...... 157 D2
  Dunbar EH42 ...... 78 B1
  Dunbar, Belhaven EH42 ...... 78 A1
  Dunfermline KY12 ...... 29 D2
  Dysart KY1 ...... 18 A4
  East Linton EH40 ...... 103 E4
  Edinburgh EH1 ...... 233 D3
  Falkirk FK1 ...... 60 A2
  Gifford EH41 ...... 163 F2
  Haddington EH41 ...... 132 A4
  Inverkeithing KY11 ...... 47 D1
  Kincardine FK10 ...... 23 F2
  Kinghorn KY3 ...... 34 C1
  Kirkcaldy KY1 ...... 17 E2
  Kirkliston EH29 ...... 89 D1
  Linlithgow EH49 ...... 85 D4
  Loanhead EH20 ...... 181 E4
  Lochgelly KY5 ...... 14 A4
  Musselburgh EH21 ...... 126 B3
  North Berwick EH39 ...... 54 B4
  Ormiston EH35 ...... 159 F4
  Penicuik EH26 ...... 203 F2
  Prestonpans FK32 ...... 96 C1
  Queensferry EH30 ...... 68 B1
  Shotts ML7 ...... 191 F2
  Slamannan FK1 ...... 110 A4
  Tranent EH33 ...... 128 B3
High Station Rd FK1 ...... 60 A2
High View Gr FK1 ...... 81 E3
Highfield Livingston EH54 ...... 147 D2
  North Berwick EH39 ...... 54 A2
Highfield Ave EH49 ...... 84 C4
Highfield Cres EH49 ...... 84 C4
Highfield Rd EH49 ...... 54 A3
Highland Dr FK5 ...... 38 B2
Highland Dykes Cres FK4 ...... 58 A3
Highland Dykes Dr FK4 ...... 58 A3
Highlea Circ EH14 ...... 177 D4
Highlea Gr EH14 ...... 177 D4
Hill Cres EH48 ...... 145 D4
Hill Gr KY12 ...... 26 B4
Hill House Rd FK6 ...... 57 F4
Hill of Beath Prim Sch KY4 ...... 12 C1
Hill Pk FK10 ...... 10 A4
Hill Pl Alloa FK10 ...... 10 A4
  Edinburgh EH8 ...... 233 E2
  Kirkcaldy KY1 ...... 17 E2
  Mayfield KY22 ...... 183 F3
  Shotts ML7 ...... 191 F3
Hill Rd Gullane EH31 ...... 51 F1
  Harthill ML7 ...... 168 B3
  Pathhead EH37 ...... 185 D3
Hill Sq EH8 ...... 233 E2
Hill St Alloa FK10 ...... 10 A4
  Cowdenbeath KY4 ...... 13 E2
  Dunfermline KY12 ...... 29 D2
  Dysart KY1 ...... 18 A4
  Edinburgh EH2 ...... 232 C4
  Inverkeithing KY11 ...... 47 D1
  Kirkcaldy KY1 ...... 17 D2
  Stirling FK7 ...... 7 D2
Hill Street La N EH2 ...... 232 C4
Hill Street La S EH2 ...... 232 C4
Hill View EH54 ...... 204 A3
Hillary Rd FK5 ...... 38 C2
Hillbank KY11 ...... 47 D2
Hillcoat Loan EH15 ...... 95 D1
Hillcoat Pl EH15 ...... 95 D1
Hillcrest Bo'ness EH51 ...... 63 F3
  Cowdenbeath KY4 ...... 13 D2
Hillcrest Ave KY2 ...... 16 C3
Hillcrest Dr EH10 ...... 10 B3
Hillcrest Pl FK6 ...... 57 E4
Hillcrest Rd FK1 ...... 59 F1
Hillend Ind EH11 ...... 48 B3
Hillfield Cres KY11 ...... 47 D2
Hillfield Rd KY11 ...... 47 D1
Hillfoot Terr EH22 ...... 230 A1
Hillfoots Rd FK9 ...... 2 C2
Hillhead EH19 ...... 182 A4
Hillhead Ave ML8 ...... 230 A1
Hillhead Dr FK1 ...... 59 F1
Hillhouse Ave EH48 ...... 144 C4
Hillhouse Cres EH27 ...... 149 F2
Hillhouse Rd EH4 ...... 92 A1
Hillhouse Terr EH27 ...... 149 F2
Hillhouseridge Rd ML7 ...... 191 E3
Hillock Ave FK2 ...... 61 D1
Hillpark Ave EH4 ...... 91 F1
Hillpark Brae EH4 ...... 91 F1
Hillpark Cres Bannockburn FK7 ...... 7 E1
  Edinburgh EH4 ...... 91 F1

Hillpark Ct EH4 ...... 91 F2
Hillpark Dr Bannockburn FK7 ...... 7 E1
  Edinburgh EH4 ...... 91 F2
Hillpark Gdns EH4 ...... 91 F1
Hillpark Gn EH4 ...... 91 F1
Hillpark Gr EH4 ...... 91 F1
Hillpark Loan EH4 ...... 92 A1
Hillpark Rd EH4 ...... 91 F1
Hillpark Terr EH4 ...... 91 F1
Hillpark Way EH4 ...... 92 A1
Hillpark Wood EH4 ...... 92 A1
Hillside EH10 ...... 5 E1
Hillside Ave KY11 ...... 48 A2
Hillside Camp Rd KY11 ...... 46 C1
Hillside Cres EH7 ...... 93 F1
Hillside Cres N EH23 ...... 207 E4
Hillside Cres S EH23 ...... 207 E4
Hillside Dr EH48 ...... 142 B2
Hillside Pl Blackridge EH48 ...... 142 B2
  Longridge EH47 ...... 170 B1
Hillside Rd EH30 ...... 90 B2
Hillside St KY3 ...... 49 E4
Hillside St EH7 ...... 93 F1
Hillside Terr Alloa FK10 ...... 10 A4
  Craigiehall EH30 ...... 90 B3
  Westquarter FK2 ...... 61 D2
Hillview Cowdenbeath KY4 ...... 13 D2
  Edinburgh EH4 ...... 92 A1
  Fauldhouse EH47 ...... 193 F3
  Oakley KY12 ...... 26 C4
Hillview Ave EH12 ...... 117 F3
Hillview Cotts EH28 ...... 119 E1
Hillview Cres
  Crossgates KY4 ...... 30 C3
  Edinburgh EH12 ...... 121 E4
Hillview Dr Bridge of A FK9 ...... 2 A3
  Edinburgh EH12 ...... 121 E4
Hillview La FK10 ...... 173 F2
Hillview Pl Broxburn EH52 ...... 117 F3
  Crossgates KY4 ...... 30 C3
  Fallin FK7 ...... 8 B2
Hillview Rd Brightons FK2 ...... 82 B4
  Edinburgh EH12 ...... 121 E4
  High Bonnybridge FK4 ...... 58 B2
  Larbert FK5 ...... 38 B2
  Ormiston EH35 ...... 159 F4
Hillview Terr Alloa FK10 ...... 10 B3
  Edinburgh EH12 ...... 121 E4
Hillwood Ave EH28 ...... 119 E3
Hillwood Cres EH28 ...... 119 E3
Hillwood Gdns EH28 ...... 119 E3
Hillwood Prim Sch EH28 ...... 119 E3
Hillwood Rd EH28 ...... 119 E3
Hillwood Rise EH28 ...... 119 E3
Hillwood Terr
  Ratho Station EH28 ...... 119 E3
  Rosyth KY11 ...... 47 D2
Hilton EH7 ...... 20 C4
Hilton Cres FK10 ...... 10 B4
Hilton Ct EH14 ...... 132 A4
Hilton Rd Alloa FK10 ...... 10 B4
  Cairneyhill KY12 ...... 27 F1
  Rosyth KY11 ...... 46 B1
Hilton Terr FK7 ...... 8 B2
Hilton View KY4 ...... 13 F3
Hirst Cres FK7 ...... 8 B2
Hirst Ct FK7 ...... 8 B2
Hirst Gdns ML7 ...... 191 E3
Hirst Rd ML7 ...... 167 E2
Hirstrigg Cotts ML7 ...... 167 D2
Hoban St EH52 ...... 117 F3
Hobart St EH54 ...... 148 A3
Hodge St KY1 ...... 60 A2
Hogarth Ave EH23 ...... 183 E1
Hoggan Cres KY11 ...... 29 E1
Hoghill Ct EH53 ...... 148 C2
Hoghill Pl EH53 ...... 148 C2
Holborn Pl KY11 ...... 46 C3
Holbourne Pl FK11 ...... 4 A4
Holden Way KY11 ...... 48 A3
Holly Ave FK5 ...... 38 C2
Holly Bank EH22 ...... 183 F4
Holly Cres KY11 ...... 46 C4
Holly Pl KY1 ...... 17 E4
Holly Terr EH19 ...... 182 A3
Holly Wlk EH20 ...... 180 C4
Hollybank Pl EH53 ...... 148 C1
Hollybank Terr EH11 ...... 122 C2
Holmes Farm La EH52 ...... 117 D3
Holmes Holdings EH52 ...... 117 E2
Holmes Rd EH52 ...... 117 D2
Holmlea Ave FK2 ...... 82 B4
Holton Cres EH15 ...... 5 E1
Holton Sq FK10 ...... 5 E1
Holy Cross Prim Sch EH6 ...... 93 E3
Holy Family RC Prim Sch EH52 ...... 87 F1
Holy Rood RC Sec Sch 124 B3
Holy Trinity Episcopal Prim Sch FK8 ...... 7 D4
Holygate Pl EH52 ...... 117 E3
Holyrood Bsns Pk EH16 ...... 124 B2
Holyrood Park Rd EH16 ...... 233 F1
Holyrood Pl
  Dunfermline KY12 ...... 29 D2
  Stenhousemuir FK5 ...... 38 C2
Holyrood Rd EH8 ...... 233 F3
Home Farm Cotts FK6 ...... 57 F3
Home Pk KY3 ...... 49 E4
Home St EH3 ...... 232 B1
Homesteads The FK8 ...... 6 B4
Honeybank Cres ML8 ...... 230 A1
Honeyman Ct EH48 ...... 143 F4
Hookney Terr FK6 ...... 36 C1
Hope Cotts EH51 ...... 64 B3
Hope La EH15 ...... 125 D4

Hope Park Cres
  Edinburgh EH8 ...... 233 E1
  Haddington EH41 ...... 101 E1
Hope Park Gdns EH48 ...... 144 C3
Hope Park Sq EH8 ...... 233 E1
Hope Park Terr EH8 ...... 233 E1
Hope Pk EH41 ...... 101 D1
Hope Pl EH21 ...... 126 C3
Hope St Bo'ness EH51 ...... 63 F4
  Carluke ML8 ...... 230 A1
  Cowdenbeath KY4 ...... 13 F3
  Edinburgh EH2 ...... 232 B3
  Falkirk FK1 ...... 60 A3
  Inverkeithing KY11 ...... 47 D1
  Queensferry EH30 ...... 89 D4
  Stirling FK8 ...... 1 C1
Hope Street La EH2 ...... 232 B3
Hope Terr EH9 ...... 123 E2
Hopefield Dr EH47 ...... 171 E4
Hopefield Pk EH19 ...... 182 A3
Hopefield Pl
  Blackburn EH47 ...... 171 E4
  Bonnyrigg and Lasswade EH19 ...... 182 A3
Hopefield Prim Sch EH19 ...... 182 A3
Hopefield Rd EH47 ...... 171 E4
Hopefield Terr
  Bonnyrigg and Lasswade EH19 ...... 182 A3
  Edinburgh EH6 ...... 93 F3
Hopelands Rd EH26 ...... 202 C3
Hopepark EH48 ...... 144 C3
Hopepark Terr FK6 ...... 57 F3
Hopetoun Cres EH7 ...... 93 F1
Hopetoun Dr
  Bridge of A FK9 ...... 2 A4
  Haddington EH41 ...... 100 C1
Hopetoun Ho EH30 ...... 66 C1
Hopetoun La EH48 ...... 145 D3
Hopetoun Mews KY11 ...... 101 D1
Hopetoun Mon EH39 ...... 100 C3
Hopetoun Pl KY2 ...... 16 B3
Hopetoun Rd
  Queensferry EH30 ...... 68 A1
  Rosyth KY11 ...... 46 B1
Hopetoun St
  Bathgate EH48 ...... 145 D3
  Edinburgh EH7 ...... 93 F2
Hopetoun Terr
  Gullane EH31 ...... 52 A2
  Ormiston EH35 ...... 159 F4
Hopetoune View KY11 ...... 48 B2
Hopeward Ct KY11 ...... 48 B2
Hopeward Mews KY11 ...... 48 B1
Hoprig Pk TD13 ...... 140 C1
Hoprig Rd TD13 ...... 140 C1
Hornbeam Cres FK2 ...... 61 D2
Horne Terr EH11 ...... 232 A1
Horsburgh Bank EH14 ...... 151 E2
Horsburgh Gdns EH14 ...... 151 E2
Horsburgh Gr EH14 ...... 151 E2
Horse Wynd EH8 ...... 233 F3
Hoseason Gdns EH4 ...... 91 E1
Hosie Rigg EH15 ...... 125 D3
Hospital Hill KY11 ...... 29 D1
Hospital Intc EH54 ...... 147 E2
Hospital Rd EH41 ...... 100 C1
Hot Pot Wynd FK2 ...... 18 A3
Houldsworth Cres ML7 ...... 212 A4
Houldsworth St KY2 ...... 26 A4
Houliston Ave KY11 ...... 47 D2
House O' Muir Rd ML7 ...... 167 D2
House O'Hill Ave EH4 ...... 92 A1
House O'Hill Brae EH4 ...... 92 A1
House O'Hill Cres EH4 ...... 92 A1
House O'Hill Gdns EH4 ...... 92 A1
House O'Hill Gn EH4 ...... 92 A1
House O'Hill Gr EH4 ...... 92 A1
House O'Hill Pl EH4 ...... 92 A1
House O'Hill Rd EH4 ...... 92 A1
House O'Hill Row EH4 ...... 92 A1
House O'Hill Terr EH4 ...... 92 A1
Houston Ct KY12 ...... 28 C2
Houston Rd
  Livingston EH54 ...... 147 D3
  Uphall Station EH54 ...... 117 D1
Houstoun Gdns EH52 ...... 116 C2
Houstoun Ind Est
  Dechmont EH52 ...... 116 C1
  Livingston EH54 ...... 147 F4
Houstoun Intc EH54 ...... 147 F4
Houstoun Rd EH54 ...... 147 F3
Houstoun Rd W EH54 ...... 146 C3
Howard Cres KY11 ...... 29 E1
Howard Pl Dysart KY1 ...... 18 A4
  Edinburgh EH3 ...... 93 E2
Howard St Edinburgh EH3 ...... 93 E2
  Falkirk FK1 ...... 59 F2
Howburn Cres ML7 ...... 168 C3
Howburn Rd ML7 ...... 168 B3
Howden East Rd EH54 ...... 147 F3
Howden Hall Cres EH16 ...... 154 C3
Howden Hall Ct EH16 ...... 154 C3
Howden Hall Dr EH16 ...... 154 C3
Howden Hall Gdns EH16 ...... 155 D3
Howden Hall Loan EH16 ...... 154 C3
Howden Hall Pk EH16 ...... 154 C3
Howden Hall Rd EH16 ...... 155 D3
Howden Hall Way EH16 ...... 155 D3
Howden South Rd EH54 ...... 147 F2
Howden St EH8 ...... 233 E1
Howden St Andrew's RC Prim Sch EH54 ...... 147 F2
Howden West Rd EH54 ...... 147 F3
Howe Pk EH10 ...... 153 F2
Howe St EH3 ...... 232 C4
Howetown FK10 ...... 5 E2
Howgate Prim Sch EH26 ...... 204 A1

Howgate Sh Ctr 7 FK1 ...... 60 A2
Howie's Pl FK1 ...... 59 D2
Howieson Ave EH51 ...... 63 F3
Howieson Gn EH52 ...... 116 C3
Howlands Rd FK7 ...... 7 D2
Howley Ave EH54 ...... 147 F2
Hudson Rd KY11 ...... 46 C2
Hugh Ave KY5 ...... 14 A4
Hugh Miller Pl EH3 ...... 93 D1
Hugh Pl KY5 ...... 14 A4
Hugh Russell Pl EH30 ...... 89 D4
Hughes Cres EH22 ...... 183 F3
Humbie Prim Sch EH36 ...... 187 D1
Humbie Rd EH29 ...... 89 D1
Humbie Terr KY3 ...... 49 E4
Hume Cres FK9 ...... 2 A3
Hume Ct FK7 ...... 7 D2
Hummel Rd EH31 ...... 51 F1
Hungerage Sq EH33 ...... 128 B3
Hunt Cl EH22 ...... 157 D2
Hunt Pl KY11 ...... 28 A1
Huntburn Ave EH49 ...... 85 E4
Hunter Ave EH20 ...... 181 E4
Hunter Ct EH20 ...... 181 E4
Hunter Gdns
  Bonnybridge FK4 ...... 58 A3
  Broxburn EH52 ...... 118 A3
  Denny FK6 ...... 36 B1
Hunter Gr Bathgate EH48 ...... 145 F3
  Whitburn EH47 ...... 169 F3
Hunter Hospl KY1 ...... 17 D2
Hunter Pl Dunfermline KY12 ...... 28 C3
  Kirkcaldy KY1 ...... 17 D3
  Shotts ML7 ...... 191 F3
  Stenhousemuir FK2 ...... 39 D2
Hunter Rd EH54 ...... 147 E1
Hunter Sq Edinburgh EH1 ...... 233 D3
  Gorebridge EH23 ...... 207 E4
Hunter St Kirkcaldy KY1 ...... 17 D2
  Shotts ML7 ...... 191 F3
Hunter Terr
  Bonnyrigg and Lasswade EH19 ...... 182 A4
  Loanhead EH20 ...... 181 E4
Hunter's Cl EH1 ...... 232 C2
Hunter's La EH47 ...... 170 A3
Hunter's Tryst Prim Sch EH13 ...... 153 F2
Hunterfield Ct EH23 ...... 207 E4
Hunterfield Pk EH23 ...... 183 E1
Hunterfield Rd EH23 ...... 207 E4
Hunterfield Terr EH23 ...... 183 D1
Hunters Hill EH26 ...... 203 E3
Hunting Pk EH54 ...... 116 C1
Huntingdon Pl EH7 ...... 93 F1
Huntlaw Rd EH34 ...... 160 C3
Huntley Cres FK8 ...... 1 C1
Huntley House Mus EH8 ...... 233 E3
Huntly Ave EH54 ...... 146 C3
Huntly Cres KY2 ...... 16 B4
Huntly St EH3 ...... 93 E2
Huntly Terr ML7 ...... 192 A2
Huron Ave EH54 ...... 147 F2
Hursted Ave EH22 ...... 183 F4
Hurworth St FK1 ...... 59 F2
Husband Pl KY11 ...... 29 F1
Hutchison Ave EH14 ...... 122 B2
Hutchison Cotts EH14 ...... 122 B2
Hutchison Crossway EH14 ...... 122 B2
Hutchison Gdns EH14 ...... 122 B2
Hutchison Loan EH14 ...... 122 B2
Hutchison Medway EH14 ...... 122 B2
Hutchison Pk EH14 ...... 122 B2
Hutchison Pl EH14 ...... 122 B2
Hutchison Rd EH14 ...... 122 B2
Hutchison Terr EH14 ...... 122 B2
Hutchison View EH14 ...... 122 B2
Hutton Pk FK10 ...... 10 B4
Hutton Sq EH54 ...... 173 E3
Hyndshaw Rd ML8 ...... 230 A2
Hyvot Ave EH17 ...... 155 E3
Hyvot Bank Ave EH17 ...... 155 E3
Hyvot Ct EH17 ...... 155 E3
Hyvot Gdns EH17 ...... 155 E3
Hyvot Gn EH17 ...... 155 E3
Hyvot Gr EH17 ...... 155 E3
Hyvot Loan EH17 ...... 155 E3
Hyvot Pk EH17 ...... 155 E3
Hyvot Terr EH17 ...... 155 E3
Hyvot View EH17 ...... 155 E3

Ibris Pl EH39 ...... 54 A4
Icehouse Brae FK2 ...... 61 D2
Implement Rd EH42 ...... 77 F1
Imrie Pl EH26 ...... 203 F3
Inch Ave KY3 ...... 49 D3
Inch Cres EH48 ...... 145 E4
Inch View KY3 ...... 34 C1
Inchcolm Dr KY11 ...... 68 A3
Inchcolm Rd KY11 ...... 29 F2
Inchcolm Terr EH30 ...... 89 D4
Inchcorse Pl EH48 ...... 145 E4
Inchcross EH48 ...... 144 C2
Inchcross Ind Est EH48 ...... 144 C2
Inches The KY11 ...... 48 A1
Inchgarvie Cres KY11 ...... 29 F2
Inchgarvie Pk EH30 ...... 68 A1
Inchgarvie Rd KY2 ...... 16 C4
Inchkeith Ave EH30 ...... 89 E4
Inchkeith Ct KY11 ...... 29 F2
Inchkeith Dr KY11 ...... 29 F2
Inchkeith Pl KY11 ...... 60 A1
Inchkeith Sch KY12 ...... 42 B4
Inchmickery Ave KY11 ...... 48 B3
Inchmickery Rd KY11 ...... 48 B3

Inchmuir Rd EH48 145 D1
Inchna FK11 4 A3
Inchview EH32 96 C1
Inchview Cres EH21 127 E3
Inchview Gdns KY11 48 A2
Inchview N EH32 96 C1
Inchview Prim Sch EH4 92 B2
Inchview Rd EH21 127 E3
Inchview Terr EH7 94 C1
Inchyra Rd FK3 61 F3
India Pl EH3 232 B4
India St EH3 232 B4
Industrial Rd EH6 94 A2
Industry La EH6 93 F3
Infirmary St EH1 233 E2
Ingleston Ave FK6 36 B3
Inglewood FK10 9 F4
Inglewood Pl EH16 155 D4
Inglewood Rd FK10 9 F4
Inglewood St EH54 147 F3
Inglis Ave EH32 97 E2
Inglis Cres KY3 34 C2
Inglis' Ct EH1 232 C2
Inglis Dr FK2 39 E1
Inglis Farm EH32 97 E2
Inglis Green Rd EH14 122 A1
Inglis Pl FK2 82 C4
Inglis St KY12 29 D2
Ingram Pl FK2 82 C3
Inkerman Ct EH26 204 A4
Inn Pl EH54 147 D1
Innerpeffray Dr FK2 39 D2
Innerwick Prim Sch EH42 108 A1
Institution St KY1 17 F4
Inver Ct FK2 39 E1
Inverallan Ct FK9 1 C4
Inverallan Dr FK9 1 C4
Inverallan Rd FK9 1 C4
Inveralmond Com High Sch EH54 147 E3
Inveralmond Dr EH4 91 D3
Inveralmond Gdns EH4 91 D3
Inveralmond Gr EH4 91 D3
Inverary Dr FK5 38 C3
Inveravon Rd EH20 155 D1
Inveravon Rdbt EH51 62 B3
Inveravon Terr EH21 126 B3
Inveresk Brae EH21 126 B3
Inveresk Ind Est EH21 126 B3
Inveresk Mills Ind Pk EH21 126 A3
Inveresk Rd EH21 126 B3
Inveresk Village Rd EH21 126 B2
Inverkeithing High Sch KY11 47 E2
Inverkeithing Mus KY11 47 D1
Inverkeithing Prim Sch KY11 47 D2
Inverkeithing Rd
Aberdour KY3 49 D4
Crossgates KY4 30 C3
Inverkeithing Sta KY11 47 E2
Inverkip Dr ML7 191 F3
Inverleith Ave EH3 93 D2
Inverleith Ave S EH3 93 D2
Inverleith Gr EH3 92 C2
Inverleith Pl EH3 93 D2
Inverleith Place La EH3 93 D2
Inverleith Row EH3 93 D2
Inverleith Terr EH3 93 D2
Inverleith Terrace La EH3 93 E2
Invertiel Rd KY1 35 D4
Invertiel Terr KY1 17 D1
Inzievar Prim Sch KY12 26 C4
Inzievar Terr KY12 27 D3
Iona Pl FK1 60 A1
Iona Rd KY11 29 F2
Iona St EH6 93 F2
Ireland Ave EH47 169 F3
Irene Terr FK1 82 C1
Ironmills Rd EH22 156 C2
Irvine Cres EH48 144 C3
Irvine Pl FK8 7 D4
Irving Ct FK1 59 F3
Islands Cres FK1 60 A1
Islay Ct FK3 61 E3
Islay Rd KY11 29 F1
Ivanhoe Cres EH16 124 A1
Ivanhoe Pl FK8 2 A1
Ivanhoe Rise EH54 148 A1
Ivy Gr KY11 46 C4
Ivy La KY1 18 A4
Ivy Terr EH11 122 C3
Ivybank Ct FK2 61 F1
Izatt Ave KY11 29 D1
Izatt St FK10 10 A4
Izatt Terr FK10 11 D2

Jacklin Gn EH54 147 D4
Jackson Ave FK3 61 E4
Jackson Pl EH54 147 E2
Jackson St EH26 203 F3
Jacob Pl FK1 60 A2
Jail Wynd FK8 7 D4
Jamaica Mews EH3 232 B4
Jamaica St EH3 232 B4
Jamaica St W EH3 232 B4
Jamaica Street North La EH3 232 B4
Jamaica Street South La EH3 232 B4
James Croft Dr FK1 59 F1
James Ct KY4 13 E1
James Gillespie's High Sch EH9 123 E3
James Gillespie's High Sch Annexe EH3 232 B1
James Gillespie's Prim Sch EH9 123 E3
James Gr KY1 17 D1
James Hog Cres KY12 26 C3
James Lean Ave EH22 157 D2
James Leary Way EH19 182 B4
James' Park La KY3 33 F1
James' Pk KY3 33 F1
James Smith Ave FK2 82 C3
James St Alva FK12 5 D3
Armadale EH48 143 F3
Bannockburn FK7 7 E1
Cowdenbeath KY4 13 E1
Dunfermline KY12 29 D2
Edinburgh EH15 125 E4
Falkirk FK2 60 A3
Haggs FK4 57 D2
Laurieston FK2 60 C2
Musselburgh EH21 126 B3
Stenhousemuir FK5 38 B1
Stirling FK8 2 A1
James Street La EH15 125 E4
James Watt Ave EH51 64 A4
James Wilson Dr FK2 83 D3
James Young High Sch The EH54 147 F1
Jameson Pl EH6 93 F2
Jamieson Ave Bo'ness EH51 63 F3
Stenhousemuir FK5 38 C2
Jamieson Gdns ML7 191 F3
Jane St EH6 93 F2
Janefield EH17 155 D2
Jarnac Ct EH22 157 D2
Jarvey St EH48 145 D4
Jarvie Pl FK2 60 A4
Jasper Ave FK2 61 D2
Jawbanes Rd KY2 35 D4
Jean Armour Ave 6 EH16 124 A1
Jean Armour Dr EH22 157 E1
Jeffrey Ave EH4 92 A1
Jeffrey Bank EH51 63 F4
Jeffrey St EH1 233 E3
Jeffrey Terr FK2 61 F1
Jellyholm Rd FK10 10 C4
Jennie Rennie's Rd KY11 29 D1
Jessfield Pl EH51 63 F3
Jessfield Terr EH6 93 E3
Jewel & Esk Valley Coll
Dalkeith EH22 156 C1
Edinburgh EH15 125 E3
Jewel The EH15 125 D3
Jock's Hill Cres EH49 84 C4
John Bernard Way EH23 207 E3
John Brown Ct EH41 132 A4
John Cres EH33 128 B3
John Davidson Dr FK6 36 B2
John Humble St EH22 183 F3
John Knox Pl EH26 203 F3
John Knox Rd EH32 98 C3
John Mason Ct EH30 89 E4
John Muir Ctry Pk EH42 77 E2
John Murray Dr FK9 2 A4
John Row Pl KY12 27 D4
John Rushforth Pl FK8 1 C1
John Smith Way ML7 191 E3
John St Dunfermline KY11 29 D1
Edinburgh EH15 125 E4
Falkirk FK2 60 A4
Haggs FK4 57 D2
Kincardine FK10 23 E2
Kirkcaldy KY2 17 D3
Penicuik EH26 203 F3
Stirling FK8 7 D4
John Street La
Edinburgh EH15 125 E4
Penicuik EH26 203 F3
John Street La E EH15 125 E4
John Street La W EH15 125 E4
John Stuart Gait KY12 26 C3
John Woods Pl KY4 30 C4
John's La EH6 94 A3
John's Pl EH6 94 A3
Johnnie Cope's Rd EH33 128 A4
Johnsburn Gn EH14 151 D1
Johnsburn Haugh EH14 151 D1
Johnsburn Pk EH14 177 D4
Johnsburn Rd EH14 151 D1
Johnston Ave
Stenhousemuir FK5 38 C2
Stirling FK9 2 A2
Uphall EH52 116 C2
Johnston Cres
Dunfermline KY11 29 D1
Lochgelly KY5 14 A4
Johnston Ct EH52 116 C2
Johnston Pk
Cowdenbeath KY4 13 E3
Inverkeithing KY11 47 D1
Johnston Pl Denny FK6 36 B1
Penicuik EH26 203 F4
Johnston St FK7 7 E1
Johnston Terr
Cockenzie & Port Seton EH32 97 E2
Edinburgh EH1 232 C2
Johnstone La ML8 230 A1
Johnstone St Alva FK12 5 D3
Menstrie FK11 3 F3
Jones Ave FK5 59 E4
Jones Gn EH54 147 D4
Joppa Gdns EH15 125 E4
Joppa Gr EH15 125 E4
Joppa Pk EH15 125 E4
Joppa Rd EH15 125 E4
Joppa Terr EH15 125 E4
Jordan La EH10 123 D2
Joseph Scott Gdns EH52 117 F2
Jubilee Ave EH54 146 C3
Jubilee Cres EH23 183 E1
Jubilee Dr KY11 46 A1
Jubilee Rd Denny FK6 36 C2
Newbridge EH12 119 F4
Whitburn EH47 170 A3
Junction Pl EH6 93 F3
Junction Rd KY1 17 E4
Juner Pl EH23 183 E1
Juniper Ave EH14 152 B3
Juniper Gdns EH14 152 B3
Juniper Gr
Dunfermline KY11 46 B4
Edinburgh EH14 152 B3
Livingston EH54 148 A3
Juniper Green Prim Sch EH14 152 B3
Juniper Park Rd EH14 152 B3
Juniper Pl EH14 152 B3
Juniper Terr EH14 152 B3
Juniperlee EH14 152 B3
Jura EH54 146 C3
Jura Pl FK3 61 E3
Justinhaugh Dr EH49 84 B4

Kaemuir Ct EH48 112 C3
Kaim Cres EH48 145 E3
Kaimes Ave EH27 149 F2
Kaimes Cres EH27 149 F2
Kaimes Gdns EH27 149 F2
Kaimes Gr EH27 149 F2
Kaimes Pl EH27 149 F2
Kaimes Rd EH12 121 F4
Kaimes Sch EH16 155 E3
Kaimes View EH22 156 A4
Kaims Brae EH54 147 E1
Kaims Ct EH54 147 D1
Kaims Dr EH54 147 E1
Kaims Gdns EH54 147 E1
Kaims Gr EH54 147 E1
Kaims Pl EH54 147 E1
Kames Pl KY12 29 E3
Kames Rd ML7 191 F3
Katesmill Rd EH14 153 D4
Katherine St
Kirkcaldy KY2 17 D3
Livingston EH54 148 A3
Katrine Cres KY2 16 C4
Katrine Ct FK10 10 B3
Katrine Dr KY12 28 A1
Katrine Pl FK6 57 E3
Katrine Rd Shotts ML7 191 F3
Whitburn EH47 170 B4
Kay Gdns EH32 97 E2
Keavil Pl KY12 28 A1
Kedslie Pl EH16 154 C4
Kedslie Rd EH16 154 C4
Keilarsbrae FK10 5 E1
Keir Ave FK8 2 A1
Keir Gdns FK9 2 A4
Keir Hardie Ave FK2 61 D2
Keir Hardie Dr EH22 183 F3
Keir Hardie Rd FK12 5 E4
Keir Hardie Terr KY11 29 D1
Keir St Bridge of A FK9 2 A4
Cowdenbeath KY4 13 D2
Edinburgh EH3 232 C2
Keirsbeath Ct KY12 12 A1
Keith Ave FK7 7 E2
Keith Cres EH4 92 A1
Keith Gdns EH52 117 E3
Keith Pl Dunfermline KY12 29 E2
Inverkeithing KY11 47 E2
Keith Rd KY11 46 B1
Keith Row EH4 92 B1
Keith St FK10 23 F2
Keith Terr EH4 92 A1
Kekewich Ave EH7 94 C1
Kellie Pl FK10 10 A4
Kelliebank FK10 9 F3
Kelly Dr FK6 36 C2
Kelly's La ML8 230 A1
Kellywood Cres FK10 23 F2
Kelso Dr ML8 230 B1
Kelso Pl KY2 17 D3
Kelso St EH52 117 D3
Kelty Ave EH51 64 A4
Kelvin Dr ML7 192 A2
Kelvin Sq EH54 148 A4
Kelvin St FK3 40 A1
Kemp Pl EH3 93 D1
Kemper Ave FK1 60 B2
Kempston Pl EH30 89 E4
Kendieshill Ave FK2 83 D3
Kenilworth Dr
Edinburgh EH16 155 D4
Laurieston FK2 60 C2
Kenilworth La FK3 61 E3
Kenilworth Rd FK9 2 A4
Kenilworth Rise EH54 147 F1
Kenilworth St FK3 61 E3
Kenmore Ave
Livingston EH54 146 C3
Polmont FK2 62 A1
Kenmore Terr KY2 16 C4
Kenmuir St FK1 59 D3
Kenmure Ave EH8 124 B4
Kenmure Pl
Dunfermline KY12 29 E3
Stenhousemuir FK5 38 C2
Kennard Rd FK2 82 B4
Kennard St Falkirk FK2 60 B3
Lochgelly KY5 14 A4
Kennedie Pk EH53 148 B2
Kennedy Cres
Dunfermline KY12 29 D3
Kirkcaldy KY2 17 D3
Tranent EH33 128 B4
Kenningknowes Rd FK7 6 C3
Kennington Ave EH20 181 D4
Kennington Terr EH20 181 D4
Kent Rd Alloa FK10 9 F4
Stirling FK7 7 D3
Kent St KY12 29 E3
Kentigern Mall EH26 203 F3
Keppel Rd EH39 54 A3
Keppock Pl FK1 59 F1
Kepscaith Cres EH47 170 A3
Kepscaith Gr EH47 170 A3
Kepscaith Rd EH47 170 A3
Kerr Ave EH22 156 C1
Kerr Cres FK4 57 D2
Kerr Pl Denny FK6 36 B1
Dunfermline KY11 29 F1
Kerr Rd EH33 128 B3
Kerr St EH3 93 D1
Kerr's Wynd EH21 126 B3
Kerrisk Dr KY11 29 F1
Kerse Gdns FK2 60 C3
Kerse Green Rd FK10 10 C3
Kerse La FK1 60 B3
Kerse Pl FK1 60 B3
Kerse Rd Grangemouth FK3 61 E4
Stirling FK7 7 E3
Kersebonny Rd FK8 6 B4
Kersie Rd FK7 9 D2
Kersie Terr FK7 9 F2
Kersiebank Ave FK3 61 F3
Kestrel Brae EH54 147 E3
Kestrel Dr FK2 82 C4
Kettil'stoun Cres EH49 84 B3
Kettil'stoun Ct EH49 84 B3
Kettil'stoun Gr EH49 84 B3
Kettil'stoun Mains EH49 84 B3
Kettilstoun Rd EH49 84 B4
Keverkae FK10 9 F3
Kevock Rd EH18 181 F4
Kidd St KY1 17 E4
Kilbagie St FK10 23 E2
Kilbean Dr FK1 59 F1
Kilbirnie Terr FK6 36 B2
Kilbrennan Dr FK1 59 D2
Kilburn Rd KY12 28 A1
Kilchurn Ct EH12 121 D4
Kilcruik Rd KY3 34 C2
Kildean Hospl FK8 1 C1
Kildean Sch FK8 1 C1
Kildonan Pk KY12 28 C1
Kildrummy Ave FK5 38 C2
Kilduthie Pl FK10 23 F3
Kilfinan Rd ML7 191 E3
Kilgour Ave KY1 17 E4
Kilgraston Rd EH9 123 E2
Killin Ct KY12 28 C1
Killin Dr FK2 62 A1
Killochan Way KY12 29 E3
Kilmartin Way KY12 29 E3
Kilmaurs Rd EH16 124 A2
Kilmaurs Terr EH16 124 A2
Kilmory Ct FK1 59 E2
Kilmory Gdns ML8 230 A2
Kilmun Rd KY2 16 B4
Kilmundy Dr KY3 33 E1
Kilncraigs Ct FK10 10 B3
Kilncraigs Rd FK10 10 B3
Kilncroft Side EH14 122 A1
Kilne Pl EH54 147 D2
Kilns Pl FK2 59 F3
Kilns Rd FK1 60 A3
Kilpair St EH41 132 A4
Kilpunt Gdns EH52 118 A3
Kilpunt Rdbt EH52 118 A3
Kilpunt View EH52 118 A3
Kilrie Cotts KY2 33 F4
Kilrymont ML1 215 D1
Kilspindie Ct EH32 71 E2
Kilsyth Rd FK4 57 D2
Kilwinning Pl EH21 126 B3
Kilwinning St EH21 126 B3
Kilwinning Terr EH21 126 B3
Kinacres Gr EH51 64 B4
Kincairne Ct FK10 23 F2
Kincardine Rd FK2 39 E2
Kincraig Pl KY12 28 C1
Kinellan Gdns EH12 122 B4
Kinellan Rd EH12 122 B4
King Cres EH55 172 B2
King Edwards Way EH29 89 D1
King James IV Rd KY11 46 B1
King Malcolm Cl EH10 154 B3
King O' Muirs Ave FK10 4 C2
King St Armadale EH48 144 A3
Bathgate EH48 145 D3
Cowdenbeath KY4 13 E2
Edinburgh EH6 93 F3
Falkirk FK2 60 B3
Fallin FK7 8 B2
Inverkeithing KY11 47 E1
Kirkcaldy KY2 17 D3
Musselburgh EH21 126 B3
Shotts ML7 191 F2
Stenhousemuir FK5 38 C2
Stirling FK8 7 D4
King's Ave EH32 98 B2
King's Court EH32 98 B2
King's Cramond EH4 91 D2
King's Cres Carluke ML8 230 A1
Rosyth KY11 46 C2
King's Dr KY3 34 C2
King's Gr EH32 98 B2
King's Knoll Gdns EH39 54 B3
King's Mdw EH16 124 A2
King's Meadow Prim Sch EH41 132 A4
King's Park Prim Sch EH22 157 D1
King's Park Rd FK8 7 D4
King's Pk EH32 98 B3
King's Pl KY11 46 C2
King's Rd Edinburgh EH15 95 D1
Longniddry EH32 98 B3
Rosyth KY11 46 C3
Tranent EH33 128 B3
King's Rd EH47 170 A3
King's Road Prim Sch KY11 46 C2
King's Stables La EH1 232 C2
King's Stables Rd EH1 232 C2
King's Terr EH15 94 C1
Kingfisher Brae EH54 147 E3
Kinghorn Pl EH6 93 E3
Kinghorn Prim Sch KY3 34 C1
Kinghorn Rd Burntisland KY3 34 A1
Kirkcaldy KY1, KY2 35 D4
Kinghorn Sta KY3 34 C1
Kinglass Ave EH51 64 A4
Kinglass Ct EH51 64 A3
Kinglass Dr EH51 64 A3
Kinglass Pk EH51 64 A3
Kings Bldgs (Univ of Edinburgh) EH9 123 E1
Kings Ct Alloa FK10 10 A4
8 Falkirk FK1 60 A2
Stenhousemuir FK5 38 B1
Kings Haugh EH16 124 B2
Kings Park Hospl FK7 6 C3
Kings Rd FK3 61 F4
Kingsburgh Ct EH40 103 E4
Kingsburgh Gdns EH40 103 E4
Kingsburgh Rd EH12 122 B4
Kingseat Ave FK3 61 E3
Kingseat Pl FK1 59 F2
Kingseat Rd
Dunfermline KY12 29 E3
Halbeath KY11, KY12 30 A3
Kingsfield EH49 85 E4
Kingsgate KY12 29 D2
Kingshill Rd ML7 212 A4
Kingsinch Sch EH16 124 A1
Kingsknowe Ave EH14 122 A1
Kingsknowe Cres EH14 122 A1
Kingsknowe Ct EH14 121 F1
Kingsknowe Dr EH14 122 A1
Kingsknowe Gdns EH14 153 D4
Kingsknowe Gr EH14 153 D4
Kingsknowe Pk EH14 153 D4
Kingsknowe Pl EH14 121 F1
Kingsknowe Rd N EH14 122 A1
Kingsknowe Rd S EH14 122 A1
Kingsknowe Sta EH14 122 A1
Kingsknowe Terr EH14 122 A1
Kingslaw Ct EH33 128 B3
Kingslaw Farm Cotts EH33 128 C3
Kingsley Ave FK5 38 C2
Kingsport Ave EH54 147 F2
Kingstables La FK8 7 D4
Kingsthorne Pk EH54 116 C1
Kingston Ave EH16 124 B1
Kingston Cotts EH39 53 F1
Kingswell Pk FK10 10 B4
Kininmonth St KY1 17 D1
Kinleith Ind Est EH14 152 A2
Kinloch Pl FK3 61 F3
Kinloss Ct KY12 26 A1
Kinnaird Ave FK2 39 D2
Kinnaird Dr FK5 38 C2
Kinnaird Pk EH15 125 E2
Kinnaird Pl Dunfermline KY12 29 E3
Kirkcaldy KY2 16 B2
Kinnear Rd EH3 93 D2
Kinneil Dr EH51 63 E3
Kinneil Prim Sch EH51 63 F3
Kinneil Rd EH51 63 E4
Kinneil Sta EH51 63 E4
Kinnell Rd KY11 47 D1
Kinnis Ct KY11 29 F1
Kinnonmonth Ave KY3 33 E1
Kintyre Pl FK1 59 E2
Kippielaw Dr EH22 157 E1
Kippielaw Gdns EH22 157 E1
Kippielaw Medway EH22 157 E1
Kippielaw Pk EH22 183 E4
Kippielaw Rd EH22 157 E1
Kippielaw Wlk EH22 157 E1
Kippithill EH36 187 D1
Kirk Ave FK5 38 C1
Kirk Brae Edinburgh EH16 155 D4
Innerwick EH42 108 A1
Kincardine FK10 23 F3
Longridge EH47 170 B1
Kirk Cramond EH4 91 E3
Kirk La EH54 147 D1
Kirk Loan EH12 121 F3
Kirk Path ML7 212 A4
Kirk Pk Dunbar EH42 78 A1
Edinburgh EH16 155 D4
Kirk Ports EH39 54 B4
Kirk Rd Aberlady EH32 71 E2
Bathgate EH48 145 E3
Shotts ML7 191 F2
Kirk St Culross KY12 25 E1
Edinburgh EH6 93 F2
Kincardine FK10 23 F2
Prestonpans EH32 96 C1
Kirk View EH41 132 B4
Kirk Wynd
Clackmannan FK10 11 D3
2 Falkirk FK1 60 A2
Kirkcaldy KY1 17 E2
Stirling FK7 7 D2
Kirkcaldy High Sch KY1 17 D4

Kirkcaldy Mus & Art Gallery KY1 17 D2
Kirkbank Rd KY3 33 F1
Kirkbrae FK10 10 C2
Kirkbride Terr FK7 20 B2
Kirkburn FK1 110 A4
Kirkcaldy Rd
Burntisland KY3 33 F1
Kinghorn KY3 35 D2
Kirkcaldy Sta KY1 17 D2
Kirkfield E EH54 147 D2
Kirkfield View EH54 147 E2
Kirkfield W EH54 147 D2
Kirkflat EH52 117 D3
Kirkford Ct KY4 13 D2
Kirkgate Alloa FK10 10 A3
Burntisland KY3 50 C4
Currie EH14 152 A2
Dunfermline KY12 28 C2
Edinburgh EH16 155 D4
Inverkeithing KY11 47 D2
Linlithgow EH49 85 D4
West Calder EH55 172 B2
Kirkhall Pl FK6 36 C1
Kirkhill Ct Broxburn EH52 117 E3
Fauldhouse EH47 193 F3
Kirkhill Dr EH16 124 A2
Kirkhill Gdns
Edinburgh EH16 124 A3
Penicuik EH26 203 F3
Kirkhill Pk EH52 117 E3
Kirkhill Prim Sch EH52 117 D3
Kirkhill Rd Broxburn EH52 117 E3
Edinburgh EH16 124 A2
Penicuik EH26 203 F3
Kirkhill Terr
Broxburn EH52 117 E3
Edinburgh EH16 124 A3
Gorebridge EH23 183 D1
Kirkhill Way EH26 203 F3
Kirkland Dr FK6 36 A1
Kirklands Dunfermline KY12 29 D1
Edinburgh EH12 121 E2
Penicuik EH26 203 F3
Kirklands Park Cres EH29 88 C1
Kirklands Park Gdns EH29 88 C1
Kirklands Park Gr EH29 88 C1
Kirklands Park St EH29 88 C1
Kirkliston Prim Sch EH29 89 D1
Kirkliston Rd EH30 89 D4
Kirknewton Prim Sch EH27 149 E2
Kirknewton Sta EH27 149 E2
Kirkslap FK6 36 C1
Kirkstyle Gdns EH29 89 D1
Kirkton Ave EH48 145 E3
Kirkton Bank EH26 203 E3
Kirkton Bsns Pk EH54 147 D2
Kirkton N EH54 147 D2
Kirkton Pl Cowdenbeath KY4 13 D3
Falkirk FK2 39 E2
Kirkton Rd KY3 33 F1
Kirkton South Rd EH54 147 E1
Kirkway FK2 22 B2
Kirkwood Ave FK2 61 E1
Kirkwood Cres KY12 28 A1
Kisimul Ct EH12 121 D4
Kitchener Cres EH32 98 C3
Kittle Yds EH9 123 F2
Knaphill KY11 46 C4
Knights Way FK6 36 B1
Knightsbridge Rd
Livingston EH54 147 E4
Uphall EH52 116 B1
Knightsiaw Pl EH26 203 E3
Knightsridge Ct EH52 116 B1
Knightsridge East Rd EH54 147 E4
Knightsridge Prim Sch EH54 147 E4
Knightsridge Rd EH52 116 B1
Knightsridge Rdbt EH54 147 E4
Knightsridge West Rd EH54 147 D4
Knockenhair Rd EH42 78 A1
Knockhill Cl KY5 14 A4
Knockhouse Gdns KY12 28 A1
Knockhouse Rd KY12 28 A1
Knoll Croft Rd ML7 192 A2
Knowe Park Rd EH47 171 D1
Knowe The Alloa FK10 5 E1
Dalgety Bay KY11 48 B2
Knowefaulds Rd FK10 4 A2
Knowehead Rd FK2 61 E1
Knowepark Ct EH47 171 D1
Knowes Rd EH41 131 F4
Knowetop EH54 173 E4
Knowetop Pl EH25 180 C2
Knowhead Rd KY12 28 A1
Knox Acad EH41 131 F4
Knox Pl EH41 132 A4
Komarom Pl EH22 157 E2
Kyle Ave FK7 20 C4
Kyle Pl EH7 233 F4
Kyles The KY1 17 F3

La Porte Prec FK3 61 E4
Labrador Ave EH54 147 F2
Laburnum Dr KY1 17 E4
Laburnum Gr
Burntisland KY3 33 F1
Stirling FK8 6 C3
Laburnum Pl EH22 183 F3
Laburnum Rd
Dunfermline KY11 29 E1
Whitburn EH47 170 B3
Lade Braes KY11 48 A2
Lade Ct EH49 84 C4
Lade Dr FK5 59 E4
Lade Gn KY11 48 A2
Lade Mill FK7 7 E1
Lade Rd FK4 58 A3
Ladehead EH6 93 E2
Ladeside Ave EH47 171 E4
Ladeside Cres FK5 38 C1
Ladeside Dr EH47 171 E4
Ladeside Gdns EH47 171 D4
Ladeside Prim Sch FK5 59 E4
Ladeside Rd EH47 171 E4
Ladiemeadow EH12 121 F3
Lady Anne Ct KY4 30 C3
Lady Brae EH23 207 E4
Lady Brae Pl EH23 207 F4
Lady Ct EH47 170 B4
Lady Helen Cotts KY5 15 D4
Lady Helen St KY1 17 D1
Lady Jane Gdns EH39 54 B3
Lady Jane Rd EH39 54 B3
Lady Lawson St EH3 232 C2
Lady Menzies Pl 3 EH7 94 A1
Lady Nairn Ave KY1 17 F3
Lady Nairne Cres EH8 124 B4
Lady Nairne Gr EH8 124 B4
Lady Nairne Loan EH8 124 B4
Lady Nairne Pl EH8 124 B4
Lady Nairne Rd KY12 28 C3
Lady Pl EH54 147 D3
Lady Rd EH16 124 A2
Lady Road Pl EH22 183 D3
Lady Victoria Bsns Ctr EH22 183 D2
Lady Wood Pl EH54 147 D3
Lady Wynd EH1 232 C2
Ladyburn Pl KY3 35 D2
Ladycroft EH14 151 E1
Ladysgate Ct FK2 39 D2
Ladysmill FK2 60 B3
Ladysmill Ct KY12 29 D1
Ladysmill Ind Est FK1 60 B3
Ladysmith Rd EH9 123 F1
Ladysneuk Rd FK9 2 B1
Ladywell EH21 126 B3
Ladywell Ave EH12 121 E3
Ladywell Ct
Edinburgh EH12 121 E3
Larbert FK5 38 A2
Ladywell Dr FK10 4 A2
Ladywell E EH54 147 E3
Ladywell East Rd EH54 147 F3
Ladywell Gdns EH12 121 E3
Ladywell Gr FK10 11 D2
Ladywell Pl FK10 4 A2
Ladywell Rd EH12 121 E3
Ladywell View EH51 63 E3
Ladywell Way EH21 126 B3
Ladywell West Rd EH54 147 E3
Ladywood FK10 11 E2
Ladywood Prim Sch EH26 204 A4
Lagan Rd ML8 230 A1
Laggan Ave ML7 192 A2
Laggan Path ML7 191 F3
Laichfield EH14 122 A2
Laichpark Pl EH14 122 A2
Laichpark Rd EH14 122 A2
Laing Gdns EH52 117 E3
Laing Terr Edinburgh EH15 125 E4
Penicuik EH26 203 F4
Laird Terr EH19 182 B3
Laird's Entry EH37 185 E2
Lakeside Rd KY2 16 C2
Lamb's Cl EH8 233 E1
Lamb's Pend EH26 203 F2
Lambert Dr KY12 29 E2
Lambert Terr FK10 10 B4
Lamberton Ave FK7 7 E2
Lamberton Ct EH34 160 C3
Lambie St EH47 170 A4
Lamer St EH42 78 C2
Lamington Rd EH33 130 B4
Lammerlaws Rd KY3 50 C4
Lammermoor Gdns EH33 128 A3
Lammermoor Terr
Edinburgh EH16 124 B1
Tranent EH33 128 A3
Lammermuir Cres
Dunbar EH42 78 B1
Haddington EH41 132 B4
Lammermuir Ct EH31 52 A1
Lammermuir Pl KY2 16 C3
Lammerview
Gladsmuir EH33 130 B4
Tranent EH33 128 B3
Lamond View FK5 38 B1
Lamont Cres FK7 8 B3
Lamont Way EH54 147 E4
Lampacre Rd EH12 121 F3
Lanark Ave EH54 147 D3
Lanark Rd
Edinburgh, Kingsknowe EH14 122 A1
Edinburgh, Westerhailes EH13 152 C3
Landale Gdns KY3 33 F1
Landale Pl KY3 33 F1
Landale St KY5 14 A4
Lane The EH21 126 C1
Lang Loan EH17 155 E2
Langfauld Gdns EH48 144 C3
Langhill Pl FK6 36 B1
Langlaw Prim Sch EH22 183 E4
Langlaw Rd EH22 183 E4
Langlees Prim Sch FK2 60 A4
Langlees St FK2 39 E1
Langriggs EH41 132 A4
Langside EH40 103 E4
Langside Cres EH55 173 D3
Langside Dr EH48 142 A2
Langside Gdns EH55 173 D3
Langton Ave EH53 148 C2
Langton Gdns EH53 148 C2
Langton Rd
East Calder EH53 148 C2
Edinburgh EH9 123 F2
Westquarter FK2 61 D2
Langton View EH53 148 C2
Lanrigg Ave EH47 193 F4
Lanrigg Rd EH47 193 F4
Lansbury Ct EH22 157 D2
Lansbury St KY1 17 F4
Lansdowne Cres
Edinburgh EH12 232 A2
Kincardine FK10 23 F2
Shotts ML7 192 A2
Lapicide Pl EH6 93 F3
Larbert Ave EH54 147 D4
Larbert High Sch FK5 38 C1
Larbert High Sch (Annexe) FK5 38 C1
Larbert Rd FK4 58 A3
Larbert Sta FK5 38 B1
Larbert Village Prim Sch FK5 38 A1
Larbourfield EH11 121 E1
Larch Cres EH22 183 F3
Larch Dr EH47 170 B3
Larch Gr Dunfermline KY11 46 B4
Stenhousemuir FK5 38 C2
Larch St FK3 61 E3
Larchbank EH54 147 F3
Larches The FK10 10 A4
Larchfield EH14 151 E1
Larchfield La ML7 192 A1
Larchfield Neuk EH14 151 E1
Largo Pl EH6 93 F3
Larkfield Dr EH22 156 C1
Larkfield Rd EH22 156 C1
Lasswade Bank EH17 155 E3
Lasswade Gr EH17 155 E3
Lasswade High Sch EH19 182 A4
Lasswade Prim Sch EH19 182 B4
Lasswade Rd
Bonnyrigg and Lasswade EH18 156 A1
Dalkeith EH22 156 C1
Edinburgh EH16, EH17 155 E3
Loanhead EH20 181 E4
Latch Pk EH13 153 E4
Latch Rd EH42 78 C1
Latch The KY12 27 E1
Lathallan Dr FK2 61 F1
Lauder Coll KY11 30 A3
Lauder Loan EH9 123 F2
Lauder Lodge EH22 157 D2
Lauder Pl EH40 103 F4
Lauder Rd Dalkeith EH22 157 E1
Edinburgh EH9 123 E2
Kirkcaldy KY2 17 E3
Lauder St KY12 29 E3
Lauderdale Cres EH42 78 B1
Lauderdale St EH9 123 E3
Laurel Bank EH22 157 E1
Laurel Bank Pl EH22 183 F3
Laurel Bank Rd EH22 183 F3
Laurel Cres KY2 17 D4
Laurel Ct FK1 59 E3
Laurel Gr Bonnybridge FK4 57 F2
Westquarter FK2 61 D1
Laurel Pl FK4 57 F2
Laurel Rd KY11 46 B1
Laurel Terr EH11 122 C3
Laurelbank Ave FK4 58 A2
Laurelbank Ct EH53 148 C1
Laurelhill Gdns FK8 6 C3
Laurelhill Pl FK8 7 D3
Laurels The FK10 4 A1
Laurencecroft Rd FK8 2 A1
Laurie St EH6 94 A2
Laurieston Prim Sch FK2 61 D2
Laurieston Rd FK3 61 D3
Lauriston Castle EH4 91 F3
Lauriston Dr KY12 29 E3
Lauriston Farm Rd EH4 91 F2
Lauriston Gdns EH3 232 C1
Lauriston Pk EH3 232 C1
Lauriston Pl EH3 232 C2
Lauriston St EH3 232 C2
Lauriston Terr EH3 232 C2
Laurmont Ct FK2 61 D2
Laverock Dr EH26 203 E3
Laverock Pk EH49 85 D3
Laverockbank Ave EH5 93 E3
Laverockbank Cres EH5 93 E3
Laverockbank Gdns EH5 93 E3
Laverockbank Gr EH5 93 E3
Laverockbank Rd EH5 93 E3
Laverockbank Terr EH5 93 E3
Laverockdale Cres EH13 153 D3
Laverockdale Loan EH13 153 D3
Laverockdale Pk EH13 153 D3
Law Pl EH15 95 D1
Law Rd Dunfermline KY11 29 F2
North Berwick EH39 54 B4
Lawers Cres FK2 62 A1
Lawers Pl FK3 61 F3
Lawers Sq EH26 204 A4
Lawfield Rd EH22 183 E4
Lawhead Cotts EH40 75 F2
Lawhead Pl EH26 203 E3
Lawnmarket EH1 233 D3
Lawrence St EH41 131 F4
Lawrie Dr EH26 203 F4
Lawson Cres EH30 89 E4
Lawson Gdns KY1 17 F4
Lawson Pl Dunbar EH42 78 B1
Maddiston FK2 83 D3
Lawson St KY1 17 F4
Lawswell FK10 5 F2
Laxdale Dr FK6 57 E4
Laxford Cres KY11 48 A2
Leadburn Ave KY12 29 D4
Leadervale Rd EH16 154 C4
Leadervale Terr EH16 154 C4
Leadside Cres KY12 29 D4
Leamington Pl EH10 232 B1
Leamington Rd EH3 232 A1
Leamington Terr EH10 123 D3
Learmonth Ave EH4 92 C1
Learmonth Cres
Edinburgh EH4 92 C1
West Calder EH55 172 B2
Learmonth Ct EH4 92 C1
Learmonth Gardens Mews 11 EH4 93 D1
Learmonth Gdns 5 EH4 92 C1
Learmonth Gr EH4 92 C1
Learmonth Pk 2 EH4 92 C1
Learmonth Pl EH4 232 A4
Learmonth St FK1 60 A2
Learmonth Terr EH4 232 A4
Learmonth Terrace La EH4 232 A4
Ledi Ave FK10 4 A1
Ledi Pl FK1 81 F4
Ledi Terr EH26 204 A4
Ledi View FK9 2 A2
Ledmore Pl FK1 60 C1
Lee Cres EH15 125 D4
Leighton Cres EH22 183 E4
Leighton St KY12 26 A1
Leith Acad EH6 94 A2
Leith Ave KY3 33 F1
Leith Pl FK6 57 E4
Leith Prim Sch EH6 94 A2
Leith St EH1 233 D4
Leith Walk Prim Sch EH7 93 F1
Leith Wlk EH6, EH7 93 F2
Lempockwells Rd EH34 160 C3
Lendrick Ave FK1 59 F1
Lennel Ave EH12 122 B4
Lenniemuir EH12 90 A1
Lennox Ave FK7 7 D2
Lennox Gdns EH49 84 B4
Lennox Milne Ct EH41 132 A4
Lennox Rd EH41 132 B4
Lennox Row EH5 93 D3
Lennox St EH4 232 A4
Lennox Street La EH4 232 A4
Lennox Terr FK3 61 F3
Lennoxlove EH41 132 A3
Lennoxlove Acredales EH41 132 A4
Leny Pl KY12 29 D3
Lenzie Ave EH54 147 D3
Leopold Pl 6 EH7 93 F1
Leslie Pl EH4 93 D1
Leslie Rd KY11 46 C3
Leslie St KY1 35 D4
Lestrange Terr FK12 5 D4
Letham Ave EH53 148 A4
Letham Cotts FK2 39 E4
Letham Cres EH53 148 A4
Letham Dr EH41 131 F4
Letham Gait KY11 47 F2
Letham Gdns EH53 148 A4
Letham Gr EH53 148 A4
Letham Hill Ave KY11 47 F2
Letham Hill Way KY11 47 F2
Letham Pk Dunbar EH42 78 B1
Pumpherston EH53 148 A4
Letham Pl Dunbar EH42 78 B2
Pumpherston EH53 148 A4
Letham Prim Sch EH54 148 A3
Letham Rd Dunbar EH42 78 B1
Livingston EH54 148 A4
Letham Rise KY11 47 F2
Letham Terr EH53 148 A4
Letham Terrs FK2 22 B1
Letham Way KY11 47 F2
Leuchatsbeath Dr KY4 13 D3
Leven Cl EH3 232 B1
Leven Ct FK10 10 B3
Leven Pl ML7 191 F3
Leven St Edinburgh EH3 232 B1
Falkirk FK2 60 A4
Leven Terr EH3 232 C1
Leven Wlk EH54 148 A2
Leving Pl EH54 147 E2
Lewis Ct Alloa FK10 10 A3
Falkirk FK1 60 A1
Lewis Rd FK2 61 F1
Lewisvale Ave EH21 126 C3
Lewisvale Ct EH21 126 C3
Leyden Pk EH19 182 A4
Leyden Pl EH19 182 A4
Leys Park Rd KY12 29 D2
Liberton Brae EH16 155 D4
Liberton Dr EH16 154 C4
Liberton Gdns EH16 155 D4
Liberton High Sch EH17 155 E4
Liberton Hospl EH16 155 D4
Liberton Pl EH16 155 D4
Liberton Prim Sch EH16 124 A1
Liberton Rd EH16 124 A1
Library La FK3 40 B1
Liddesdale Pl EH3 93 D1
Liddle Dr EH51 63 F3
Lidgate Shot EH28 119 F1
Liggar's Pl KY12 28 C1
Liggat Pl EH52 117 F3
Liggat Syke Pl EH52 118 A3
Lighton Terr EH47 171 D1
Lilac Ave EH22 183 F3
Lilac Cres KY1 17 E4
Lilac Gr KY11 46 B4
Lillies La EH41 163 F3
Lilly's La KY11 29 D1
Lily Terr EH11 122 C2
Lilybank Ct FK10 5 E1
Lilyhill Terr EH8 94 B1
Lime Ave EH30 66 C1
Lime Gr Dunfermline KY11 29 F1
Larbert FK5 38 B1
Mayfield EH22 183 F3
North Berwick EH39 54 C3
Polmont FK2 61 F1
Lime Pl EH19 182 A3
Lime Rd FK1 59 D2
Lime St FK3 61 E3
Limebank Pk EH53 148 C1
Limefield EH17 155 F3
Limefield Ave EH55 173 D3
Limefield Cres EH48 145 F3
Limefield Gdns EH55 173 D3
Limefield Pl EH48 145 E3
Limefield Rd
Bathgate EH48 145 E4
West Calder EH55 173 D3
Limekilns EH34 161 D3
Limekilns Gr EH53 149 D2
Limekilns Prim Sch KY11 45 F2
Limekilns Rd KY12 28 C1
Limerigg Prim Sch FK1 110 B1
Limes The EH10 123 D2
Limetree Wlk EH42 76 B3
Limeylands Cres EH35 159 E4
Limeylands Rd EH35 159 E4
Lina St KY2 17 D3
Linburn Gr KY11 29 F2
Linburn Pk EH27 150 A3
Linburn Pl KY11 29 F2
Linburn Rd KY11 29 F2
Lindean Pl EH6 94 A2
Lindean Terr EH27 149 F3
Linden Ave Denny FK6 36 B2
Stirling FK7 7 E3
Linden Gr EH54 148 A3
Linden Pl EH20 181 E4
Lindores Dr Kirkcaldy KY2 16 C4
Tranent EH33 128 B3
Lindsay Dr FK9 2 A2
Lindsay Pl Edinburgh EH6 93 F3
Lochgelly KY5 14 A4
Lindsay Rd EH6 93 F3
Lindsay Sq EH54 146 B3
Lindsay St EH6 93 F3
Lindsay Way EH54 147 E4
Lindsay's Wynd KY12 26 C3
Lingerwood Farm Cotts EH22 183 D2
Lingerwood Rd EH22 183 D2
Lingerwood Wlk EH22 183 D2
Linhouse Dr EH53 148 C2
Linhouse Rd EH53 148 C2
Link Rd KY11 47 F2
Linkfield Ct EH21 126 C3
Linkfield Rd EH21 126 C3
Links Ave EH21 126 A4
Links Ct Bo'ness EH51 64 A4
Cockenzie & Port Seton EH32 97 E2
Links Dr KY12 28 A1
Links Gardens La EH6 94 A3
Links Gdns EH6 94 A2
Links Pl Bo'ness EH51 64 A4
Burntisland KY3 50 C4
Cockenzie & Port Seton EH32 97 F2
Edinburgh EH6 94 A3
Links Rd Bo'ness EH51 64 A4
Cockenzie & Port Seton EH32 97 F2
Longniddry EH32 98 C3
North Berwick EH39 54 A4
Links St Kirkaldy KY1 17 D1
Musselburgh EH21 126 B3
Links View
Cockenzie & Port Seton EH32 97 F2
Musselburgh EH21 126 B4
Links Wlk EH32 97 F2
Linlithgow Acad EH49 84 C3
Linlithgow Canal Mus EH49 85 D3
Linlithgow Palace EH49 85 D4
Linlithgow Pl FK5 38 C2
Linlithgow Prim Sch EH49 84 C3
Linlithgow Prim Sch West Port Annexe EH49 84 C3
Linlithgow Rd EH51 63 F3
Linlithgow Sta EH49 85 D4
Linlithgow Story (Mus) The EH49 85 D4
Linlithgow Terr EH35 159 F4
Linmill Rd FK1 112 A3
Linn Mill EH30 67 F1
Linn Pl EH52 117 F2
Linnet Brae EH54 147 E3
Linsay Macdonald Ct KY12 29 E2
Lint Riggs FK1 60 A3
Linton La KY2 16 C3
Linton Pl KY11 46 C2
Linty La EH26 203 E3
Linview La EH54 173 F2
Lion Well Wynd EH49 84 C4
Lionthorn Rd FK1 59 F1
Lipney FK11 4 A3

Lismore Ave
4 Edinburgh EH8 94 B1
Kirkcaldy KY2 16 C4
Lismore Cres EH8 94 B1
Lismore Ct FK1 60 A1
Lismore Pl KY2 16 C4
Lismore Prim Sch EH15 124 C3
Lister Ct FK9 2 A3
Lister Rd EH54 147 D1
Listloaning Pl EH49 84 B4
Listloaning Rd EH49 84 B4
Liston Dr EH29 89 D1
Liston Pl EH29 89 D1
Liston Rd EH29 89 D1
Little Acre EH22 183 E4
Little Carriden EH51 64 B3
Little Cswy KY12 42 B4
Little Denny Rd FK6 36 B1
Little Footworn KY12 44 C3
Little France Mills EH16 124 B1
Little King St EH1 233 D4
Little Rd EH16 155 D4
Little Sandhaven KY12 42 B4
Livery St EH48 145 D4
Livesay Rd KY11 46 B1
Livesey Terr EH26 204 A4
Livilands Ct FK8 7 D3
Livilands Gate FK8 7 D3
Livilands La FK8 7 D3
Livingston Mill EH54 147 D1
Livingston North Sta
EH54 147 D3
Livingston Rd EH54 147 F3
Livingston South Sta
EH54 174 A4
Livingstone Cres FK2 60 C3
Livingstone Dr
Bo'ness EH51 63 E3
Burntisland KY3 33 F1
Laurieston FK2 61 D1
Livingstone E Rdbt EH54 116 B1
Livingstone La KY3 49 E4
Livingstone Pl EH9 123 E3
Livingstone Quadrant
ML7 168 B2
Livingstone St EH55 171 F1
Livingstone Terr FK2 61 D1
Lixmount Ave EH5 93 E3
Lixmount Gdns EH5 93 E3
Lizzie Brice's Rdbt EH54 148 A1
Llynallan Rd ML7 168 A3
Loan Pl ML7 168 C3
Loan The Bo'ness EH51 63 E3
Loanhead EH20 181 D4
Pathhead EH37 184 B4
Queensferry EH30 68 A1
Torphichen EH48 113 F3
Loanburn EH26 203 F3
Loanburn Ave EH26 203 F3
Loanfoot Cres EH52 117 D3
Loanfoot Gdns FK7 20 B2
Loanfoot Rd EH52 117 D2
Loanhead Ave
Bankhead FK4 57 E3
Grangemouth FK3 61 F3
Loanhead Hospl EH20 181 E4
Loanhead Pl KY2 17 D3
Loanhead Prim Sch EH20 181 E4
Loanhead Prim Sch
(Annexe) EH20 181 E4
Loanhead Rd EH20 155 D1
Loaning Cres EH7 94 B1
Loaning Rd EH7 94 B1
Loaninghill Pk EH52 117 D2
Loaninghill Rd EH52 117 D2
Loch Awe Way EH47 170 B4
Loch Earn Way EH47 170 B4
Loch Fyne Way EH47 170 B4
Loch Linnhe Ct EH47 170 B4
Loch Maree Way EH47 170 B4
Loch Pl EH30 68 A1
Loch Rd Edinburgh EH4 92 A1
Queensferry EH30 68 A1
Tranent EH33 128 B3
Loch Sq EH33 128 B3
Loch St KY12 29 E4
Loch Trool Way EH47 170 B4
Lochaber Cres ML7 192 A2
Lochaber Dr FK5 38 C2
Lochbank EH54 147 F3
Lochbrae FK10 5 E1
Lochbridge Rd EH39 54 B3
Lochend Ave Dunbar EH42 78 C1
Edinburgh EH7 94 A2
Lochend Castle Barns EH7 94 A1
Lochend Cl EH8 233 F3
Lochend Cres Dunbar EH42 78 B1
Edinburgh EH7 94 B1
Lochend Dr EH7 94 B1
Lochend Gdns EH7 94 A1
Lochend Gr EH7 94 B1
Lochend Ind Est EH28 119 D3
Lochend Pk EH7 94 A2
Lochend Quadrant EH7 94 B1
Lochend Rd Dunbar EH42 78 C1
Edinburgh EH6 94 A2
Ratho Station EH28 119 D4
Lochend Rd N EH21 126 A3
Lochend Rd S
Edinburgh EH7 94 A1
Musselburgh EH21 126 A3
Lochend Sq EH7 94 A1
Lochgelly Ind Pk KY5 14 B4
Lochgelly North
Specl Sch (Prim) KY5 14 A4
Lochgelly Rd KY4 13 E3
Lochgelly South Prim Sch
KY5 14 A4
Lochgelly West Prim Sch
KY5 14 A4
Lochgreen Hospl FK1 59 F1
Lochgreen Rd FK1 59 F1
Lochhead Ave FK6 36 C1
Lochhill Cotts EH32 99 F4
Lochies Rd Burntisland KY3 34 A1
Clackmannan FK10 11 D2
Lochinvar Pl FK4 58 B2
Lochinvar Rd KY11 46 B1
Lochlands Ind Est FK5 59 D4
Lochmaben Dr FK5 38 C2
Lochpark Pl FK6 36 C1
Lochridge Pl FK6 36 B1
Lochrin Pl EH3 232 B1
Lochshot Pl EH54 147 D2
Lochside Ave EH12 120 C2
Lochside Cres
Edinburgh EH12 120 C2
Redding FK2 61 D1
Lochside Ct EH12 121 D2
Lochside Pl EH12 121 D2
Lochside Rd FK1 110 B1
Lock Rd KY11 67 D4
Lock Sixteen FK1 59 E3
Lockerby Cotts EH16 155 E3
Lockerby Cres EH16 155 E3
Lockerby Gr EH16 155 E3
Lockhart Terr EH25 180 C2
Lockharton Ave EH10 122 C1
Lockharton Cres EH10 122 C1
Lockharton Gdns EH14 122 C2
Lodge Dr FK5 38 C1
Lodge St EH41 132 A4
Logan St EH3 93 E1
Logan Way EH54 147 E4
Loganlea Ave EH7 94 B1
Loganlea Cres EH55 171 E1
Loganlea Dr EH7 94 B1
Loganlea Gdns EH7 94 B1
Loganlea Loan EH7 94 B1
Loganlea Pl EH7 94 B1
Loganlea Rd
Addiewell EH55 171 E1
Edinburgh EH7 94 B1
Loganlea Terr
Addiewell EH55 171 E1
Edinburgh EH7 94 B1
Logie Dr FK5 38 A2
Logie Green Gdns EH7 93 E2
Logie Green Loan EH7 93 E2
Logie Green Rd EH7 93 E2
Logie La FK9 2 B4
Logie Mill EH7 93 E2
Logie Pl KY12 28 B3
Logie Rd FK9 2 B2
Lomond Cres
Dunfermline KY11 29 F1
Stenhousemuir FK5 38 C2
Stirling FK9 2 A2
Whitburn EH47 170 A3
Lomond Ct FK10 10 B3
Lomond Dr Bannockburn FK7 7 F1
Falkirk FK2 39 E1
Lomond Gdns KY2 16 C3
Lomond Rd Edinburgh EH5 93 D3
Grangemouth FK3 61 F3
Shotts ML7 191 F3
Lomond St FK10 4 C1
Lomond Vale EH26 204 A4
Lomond View EH48 112 C2
Lomond Way FK6 57 E3
Lomond Wlk EH20 155 D1
London Rd Dalkeith EH22 157 D2
Edinburgh EH7 94 A1
London St EH3 93 E1
London Street Prim Sch
EH7 93 E1
Loney Cres FK6 57 F4
Long Byres EH52 117 F3
Long Craig Wlk KY1 35 D4
Long Craigs EH32 97 F2
Long Craigs Terr KY3 35 D2
Long Cram EH41 131 F4
Long Crook EH30 89 D4
Long Dalmahoy Rd EH27 150 B2
Long Row Halbeath KY12 30 A4
Menstrie FK11 4 A4
Longannet Cotts FK10 24 A1
Longbraes Gdns KY2 16 B3
Longcroft Gdns EH49 84 C4
Longdales Ave FK2 60 A4
Longdales Ct FK2 60 A4
Longdales Pl FK2 60 A4
Longdales Rd FK2 60 A4
Longdyke Pl FK2 39 E2
Longdykes Rd EH32 97 D1
Longford ML11 215 D1
Longformacus Rd EH16 155 D4
Longhill Gdns KY11 48 A2
Longniddry Prim Sch
EH32 98 C3
Longniddry Sta EH32 98 C3
Longpark Pl EH54 147 D2
Longridge Prim Sch
EH47 170 B1
Longridge Rd EH47 170 A3
Longstone Ave
East Linton EH40 103 E4
Edinburgh EH14 122 A1
Longstone Cres EH14 122 A2
Longstone Gdns EH14 121 F2
Longstone Gr EH14 122 A1
Longstone Pk EH14 122 A1
Longstone Pl EH14 122 A1
Longstone Prim Sch
EH14 122 A1
Longstone Rd EH14 122 A1
Longstone St EH14 122 A1
Longstone Terr EH14 121 F2
Longstone View EH14 121 F2
Lonsdale Cres KY3 33 F1
Lonsdale Terr EH3 232 C1
Lookaboutye Brae FK10 11 D2
Loom Rd KY2 17 D3
Lord President Rd EH39 54 A4
Loretto Ct EH21 126 A2
Loretto RC Prim Sch
EH21 126 B3
Loretto Sch EH21 126 B3
Lorimar Pl FK2 39 D1
Lorne Gdns FK2 60 C2
Lorne Gr EH20 155 D1
Lorne Pl EH6 93 F2
Lorne Prim Sch EH6 93 F2
Lorne Rd FK5 38 B1
Lorne Sq Edinburgh EH6 93 F2
North Berwick EH39 54 B4
Lorne St Edinburgh EH6 93 F2
Kirkcaldy KY1 17 F4
Lornshill Acad FK10 4 C1
Lornshill Cres FK10 9 F4
Losshill FK11 4 A3
Lothian Bank EH22 156 C1
Lothian Coll of Nursing &
Midwifery EH3 232 C2
Lothian Cres Bo'ness EH51 64 A3
Stirling FK9 2 B2
Lothian Ct KY11 47 E1
Lothian Dr EH22 183 E4
Lothian Rd Dalkeith EH22 157 D2
Edinburgh EH1 232 B2
Lothian St Bathgate EH48 145 D4
Bo'ness EH51 64 A3
Bonnyrigg and Lasswade
EH19 182 B4
Burntisland KY3 50 C4
Dalkeith EH22 157 D2
Edinburgh EH1 123 E4
Rosewell EH24 181 E1
Lothian Terr Kirkcaldy KY2 17 D4
Newtongrange EH22 183 D2
Lothian View KY11 47 D1
Louburn EH48 142 B2
Loudens Wlk FK6 36 B3
Loughborough Rd KY1 17 F4
Loughrig KY11 47 D4
Louisa Sq EH24 181 E1
Louise St KY11 29 E1
Lovedale Ave EH14 151 D1
Lovedale Cres EH14 151 D1
Lovedale Gdns EH14 151 E1
Lovedale Gr EH14 151 D1
Lovedale Rd EH14 151 E1
Lovells Glen EH49 84 B4
Lovers La EH30 89 E4
Lovers Loan Alva FK12 5 D4
Dunfermline KY12 28 C1
Lovers Wlk FK8 2 A1
Low Brae EH48 113 F3
Low Causewayside
Culross KY12 42 B4
Newmills KY12 26 B1
Low Cswy Culross KY12 25 F1
Torryburn KY12 26 C1
Low Doors The EH27 149 F1
Low Port Prim Sch EH49 85 D4
Lower Alderston Rd
EH41 100 C1
Lower Bathville EH48 144 A3
Lower Bridge St FK8 2 A1
Lower Broomieknowe
EH18 182 A4
Lower Castlehill FK8 2 A1
Lower Gilmore Pl EH3 232 B1
Lower Glebe KY3 49 E4
Lower Granton Rd EH5 93 D3
Lower Joppa EH15 125 E4
Lower London Rd EH7 94 A1
Lower Valleyfield View
EH26 203 F2
Lower Wellheads KY11 45 E2
Lowlands Crofts EH55 196 B2
Lowrie Ave EH26 203 E3
Lowry Pl KY11 46 C2
Ludgate FK10 10 A3
Luffness Ct EH32 71 E2
Luffness Mains Cotts
EH39 72 A2
Lugton Brae EH22 156 C2
Lugton Sch EH22 156 C2
Lumley Ct FK3 61 E4
Lumley Pl FK3 61 E4
Lumley St FK3 61 E4
Lumphinnans
Prim & Com Sch KY4 13 E3
Lumphinnans Rd KY5 14 A4
Lumsdaine Dr KY11 48 A1
Lumsden Ct
Broxburn EH52 117 E3
Ratho EH28 119 E1
Lundin Rd KY12 28 A2
Lussielaw Rd EH9 123 F2
Lutton Court Bsns Ctr
EH8 233 E1
Lutton Pl EH8 233 E1
Luvain Gdns EH48 143 F2
Lyall Cres FK2 61 F1
Lyars Rd EH32 98 C3
Lyarthall EH52 117 E3
Lychgate Rd FK10 4 A1
Lydgait EH41 101 D1
Lydgait Gdns EH41 101 D1
Lyefield Pl EH54 147 D2
Lygon Rd EH16 123 F1
Lyle Gn EH54 147 D4
Lynburn Sch KY11 29 F1
Lyne Gr KY12 28 B1
Lyne St EH7 94 A1
Lyne Terr EH26 204 A4
Lynebank
(Psychiatric) Hospl KY11 30 A3
Lyneburn Cres KY11 30 A3
Lynedoch Pl EH3 232 A3
Lynedoch Place La EH3 232 A3
Lyness Ct FK2 61 F1
Lynn Lea Ave EH41 132 B4
Lyon Cres FK9 2 A3
Lyon Ct EH51 63 E3
Lyon Dr EH54 173 F3

Mac Cormick Terr EH26 203 F4
Macadam Pl FK1 59 E3
Macarthur Cres FK2 82 C3
Macbeth Moir Rd EH21 127 D3
Macbeth Rd KY11 29 F2
Macdonald Ave EH48 143 F3
Macdonald Dr FK7 7 D2
Macdonald Pl KY3 34 A1
Macdonald Sq KY11 30 A3
Macdowall Rd EH9 123 F2
Macduff Cres KY3 34 C1
Mace Ct FK7 7 E2
Macfarlane Cres FK1 60 A3
Macfarlane Pl EH52 116 C2
Machrie Ct FK1 59 E2
Macindoe Cres KY1 17 E4
Macintosh Pl FK1 60 A1
Macintosh Rd EH54 146 C1
Mackenzie Cres KY5 14 B4
Mackenzie Pl
Edinburgh EH3 232 B4
Falkirk FK1 60 A1
Mackenzie Terr FK3 61 E3
Mackie Pl KY11 29 F1
Maclachlan Ave FK6 36 B1
Maclardy Ct EH52 116 C2
Maclaren Terr FK2 39 D1
Maclean Cres FK12 5 E4
Maclean Ct FK7 7 E2
Maclean Terr EH48 142 B2
Macmerry Ind Est EH33 129 F3
Macmerry Prim Sch
EH33 129 E3
Macmillan Rd EH54 147 E1
Macnair Ave EH39 54 B3
Macpherson Pl FK1 59 F1
Mactaggart Loan EH22 183 D2
Madderfield Mews EH49 85 D4
Maddiston Prim Sch FK2 82 C3
Maddiston Rd FK2 82 C4
Madeira Pl EH6 93 F3
Madeira St EH6 93 F3
Madill Pl FK5 38 C2
Maesterton Pl EH22 183 D2
Mag's Brae EH41 133 D1
Magdala Cres EH12 122 C4
Magdala Mews EH12 122 C4
Magdalene Ave EH15 125 D3
Magdalene Ct EH15 125 D3
Magdalene Dr EH15 125 D3
Magdalene Gdns EH15 125 D3
Magdalene Loan EH15 125 D3
Magdalene Medway EH15 125 D3
Magdalene Pl EH15 125 D3
Maggie Wood's Loan FK1 59 F3
Magnus Rd EH51 62 B3
Maidencraig Cres EH4 92 B1
Maidencraig Gr EH4 92 B1
Maidenpark Pl EH51 63 F3
Maidlands EH49 85 E4
Main Point EH3 232 C2
Main Rd Charlestown KY11 45 D2
Crombie KY12 44 C4
Grangemouth FK3 62 A4
Macmerry EH33 129 E3
Main St Aberdour KY3 49 E4
Airth FK2 22 B2
Alloa FK10 5 E1
Auchtertool KY2 15 D1
Avonbridge FK1 112 A3
Balerno EH14 151 E1
Bannockburn FK7 7 E1
Bathgate EH48 145 D4
Blackridge EH48 142 B2
Bo'ness EH51 64 A4
Bonnybridge FK4 58 A3
Brightons FK2 82 B4
Cairneyhill KY12 27 E1
California FK1 81 F3
Cambus FK10 9 D4
Carnock KY12 27 E4
Carrington EH23 206 B3
Clackmannan FK10 11 D2
Comrie KY12 26 B4
Cowdenbeath, Hill of Beath
KY4 13 D1
Cowdenbeath, Lumphinnans
KY4 13 F3
Cowie FK7 20 B4
Crossford KY12 28 B1
Crossgates KY4 30 C3
Dalmeny EH29, EH30 89 F4
Dechmont EH52 116 B1
East Calder EH53 148 C2
East Saltoun EH34 161 F2
East Whitburn EH47 170 B4
Edinburgh EH6 93 E4
Edinburgh, Davidsons Mains
EH4 91 F2
Elphinstone EH33 128 A1
Main St continued
Falkirk FK1 59 F3
Falkirk, Bainsford FK2 60 A4
Falkirk, Carronshore FK2 39 E2
Fallin FK7 8 C2
Fauldhouse EH47 193 E3
Forth ML11 215 D1
Gifford EH41 163 F3
Gorebridge EH23 207 E4
Gullane EH31 52 A1
Halbeath KY11 30 A3
High Valleyfield KY12 25 F1
Kirkliston EH29, EH30 89 D1
Kirknewton EH53, EH27 149 F1
Larbert FK5 38 B1
Limekilns KY11 45 E2
Linlithgow EH49 84 B4
Livingston,Deans EH54 146 C3
Livingston, Livingston Village
EH54 147 E1
Lochgelly KY5 14 A4
Longniddry EH32 98 C3
Longridge EH47 170 B1
Mid Calder EH53 148 B2
Newton EH52 88 A4
Newtongrange EH22 183 D3
North Queensferry KY11 68 B3
Ormiston EH35 159 F4
Pathhead EH37 185 D3
Pathhead, Dewartown EH37 184 B3
Philpstoun EH49 86 B4
Plean FK7 20 B2
Polmont FK2 61 F1
Ratho EH28 119 E1
Redding FK2 61 E1
Roslin EH25 181 D2
Shieldhill FK1 81 E3
Shotts ML7 192 A2
Slamannan FK1 110 A4
Stenhousemuir FK5 38 C1
Stirling, Cambusbarron FK7 6 B3
Stirling, St Ninians FK7 7 D2
Stoneyburn EH47 171 D1
Torryburn KY12 26 B1
Townhill KY12 29 E4
Tullibody FK10 4 A1
West Calder EH55 172 B2
Westfield EH48 112 C3
Winchburgh EH52 87 F2
Main St E FK11 4 A3
Main St W Hillend KY11 47 F2
Menstrie FK11 3 F3
Mains Of Craigmillar
EH16 124 B1
Mains Rd Harthill ML7 168 C3
Linlithgow EH49 84 C3
Maitland Ave
Bannockburn FK7 7 E1
Musselburgh EH21 126 A3
Maitland Cres FK7 7 D2
Maitland Hog La EH29 89 D1
Maitland Park Rd EH21 126 A3
Maitland Rd
Kirkliston EH29 89 D1
Rosyth KY11 67 D4
Maitland St
Dunfermline KY12 28 C2
Musselburgh EH21 126 A3
Majors Loan FK1 60 A2
Majors Pl FK1 60 A2
Malbet Pk EH16 155 D4
Malcolm Ct EH48 144 C3
Malcolm Dr FK5 38 C2
Malcolm St KY11 29 D1
Mall Ave EH21 126 B3
Mall The EH54 148 A3
Mallard Brae EH54 147 E3
Mallens Brae EH48 114 A3
Malleny Millgate EH14 177 E4
Malplaquet Ct ML8 230 A1
Malta Gn EH4 93 D1
Malta Terr EH4 93 D1
Maltings The
Auchtertool KY2 15 D1
Linlithgow EH49 84 B3
Mamre Dr FK1 81 F3
Man O' War Way EH51 64 A4
Mandel Rigg FK2 82 C3
Mandela Ave FK2 60 B4
Manderston St EH6 93 F2
Mandora Ct ML8 230 A1
Manitoba Ave EH54 147 F2
Mannan Dr FK10 11 D2
Mannering Pl EH16 155 D4
Mannfield Ave FK4 57 F2
Manor Cres FK10 4 A1
Manor Gdns EH42 78 A1
Manor Loan FK11 3 D2
Manor Pl EH3 232 A3
Manor Powis Cotts FK11 3 D2
Manor St FK1 60 A2
Manor Wynd FK2 83 D3
Manse Ave
Armadale EH48 143 F3
Whitburn EH47 170 A3
Manse Cres FK7 7 D2
Manse Ct EH53 148 C2
Manse Gr EH47 171 E1
Manse La Burntisland KY3 33 F1
Cockenzie & Port Seton
EH32 97 E2
Musselburgh EH21 126 B3
Manse Pk EH52 116 C3
Manse Pl Bannockburn FK7 7 F1
Bathgate EH48 145 F3
Falkirk FK1 60 A2
Inverkeithing KY11 47 D1
Slamannan FK1 110 A4

Manse Rd Carrington EH23 .. 206 B3
Crossgates KY4 30 C4
Dirleton EH39 53 D3
Edinburgh EH12 121 E3
Forth ML11 215 D1
Inverkeithing KY11 47 D1
Kincardine FK10 23 F3
Kinghorn KY3 34 C2
Kirkliston EH29 89 D1
Linlithgow EH49 85 D3
Roslin EH25 181 D2
Shotts ML7 192 A2
Torphichen EH48 113 F3
Whitburn EH47 170 A3
Manse St Aberdour KY3 49 E4
Edinburgh EH12 121 E3
Manse View
Armadale EH48 143 F3
Innerwick EH42 107 F1
Mansefield
Athelstaneford EH39 101 F4
East Calder EH53 148 C2
Mansefield Ct
2 Bathgate EH48 145 D4
Livingston EH54 147 E2
Mansefield Gr EH48 145 D3
Mansefield St EH48 145 D4
Mansewood Cres EH47 170 A3
Mansfield Ave Alloa FK10 5 E1
Musselburgh EH21 126 B3
Newtongrange EH22 183 D3
Mansfield Ct EH21 126 B3
Mansfield Pl
Edinburgh EH3 93 E1
Musselburgh EH21 126 B3
Newtongrange EH22 183 D3
Mansfield Rd
Balerno EH14 177 E4
Musselburgh EH21 126 B3
Newtongrange EH22 183 D3
Mansionhouse Rd
Edinburgh EH9 123 E3
Falkirk FK1 59 E3
Manson Sq EH54 146 B3
Manuel Terr EH49 83 F3
Maple Ave FK5 38 C2
Maple Ct FK10 10 A3
Maple Gr EH54 148 A3
Maple Pl FK6 36 B2
Maple St KY2 17 D4
Mar Pl Alloa FK10 5 E1
Stirling FK8 7 D4
Mar St FK10 10 A3
Mar Terr FK10 11 D2
Maranatha Cres FK2 82 B4
March Gr EH4 92 A1
March Pines EH4 91 F1
March Rd EH4 92 A1
Marchbank Dr EH14 177 E4
Marchbank Gdns EH14 177 E4
Marchbank Gr EH14 177 E4
Marchbank Pl EH14 177 E4
Marchbank Way EH14 151 E1
Marchburn Dr EH26 203 E3
Marches Dr EH48 144 A3
Marches The
Armadale EH48 144 A3
Stirling FK8 7 D4
Marchfield Gr EH4 92 A2
Marchfield Park La EH4 91 F2
Marchfield Pk EH4 91 F2
Marchfield Terr EH4 92 A2
Marchglen FK13 5 F3
Marchhall Cres EH16 124 A3
Marchhall Pl EH16 124 A3
Marchhall Rd EH16 124 A3
Marchlands Ave EH51 64 A4
Marchlands La EH51 64 A4
Marchmont Ave FK2 61 F1
Marchmont Cres EH9 123 E3
Marchmont Ct FK2 61 F1
Marchmont Rd EH9 123 E3
Marchmont St EH9 123 E3
Marchside Ct FK10 5 E1
Marchwood Ave EH48 145 E3
Marchwood Cres EH48 145 E3
Marchwood Ct EH33 128 A1
Mardale Cres EH10 123 D2
Maree Ct FK10 10 B3
Maree Pl Crossford KY12 28 A1
Kircaldy KY2 16 C4
Maree Wlk EH54 148 A2
Margaret Ave
Bathgate EH48 145 F3
Haggs FK4 57 D2
Margaret Ct FK6 36 C1
Margaret Dr FK4 58 A3
Margaret Rd FK7 7 E1
Margaret Terr FK5 38 C2
Maria St KY1 17 E3
Marina Rd EH48 145 F3
Marine Dr EH4, EH5 92 A3
Marine Espl EH6 94 B3
Marine Par EH39 54 B4
Marine Rd Dunbar EH42 78 B2
Gullane EH31 52 A2
Marine Terr EH31 52 A2
Mariner Ave FK1 59 D3
Mariner Dr FK1 59 D3
Mariner Gdns FK1 59 E3
Mariner Rd FK1 59 E3
Mariner St FK1 59 D3
Mariners St KY2 17 D3
Mariners Wlk KY11 47 F2
Marion St KY1 17 D1
Marionville Ave EH7 94 B1
Marionville Cres EH7 94 B1
Marionville Dr EH7 94 B1
Marionville Gr EH7 94 B1
Marionville Pk EH7 94 A1
Marionville Rd EH7 94 A1
Marischal Dr EH16 124 C2
Marischal Pl 6 EH4 92 B1
Maritime La EH6 94 A3
Maritime St EH6 94 A3
Marjoribanks St EH48 145 D3
Market Ct EH41 101 D1
Market La EH49 85 D4
Market Pl
North Berwick EH39 54 B4
Whitburn EH47 170 A4
Market St Bo'ness EH51 63 F4
Dunfermline KY12 29 D2
Edinburgh EH1 233 D3
Haddington EH41 132 A4
Mid Calder EH53 148 B2
Musselburgh EH21 126 A3
Marketgate EH35 159 F4
Markfield Rd KY11 48 B2
Markle Steading EH40 103 D4
Marlborough Dr FK9 2 B2
Marlborough St EH15 125 D4
Marly Gn EH39 54 A3
Marly Rise EH39 54 A3
Marmion Ave EH25 180 C2
Marmion Cres
Edinburgh EH16 124 A1
North Berwick EH39 54 A4
Marmion Rd
Bathgate EH48 145 D4
Grangemouth FK3 61 E3
North Berwick EH39 54 A4
Marmion St FK2 60 A4
Marquis Dr FK10 11 D2
Marrfield Rd EH54 117 D1
Marrfield Terr EH54 117 D1
Marschal Ct FK7 7 E2
Marshall Pl KY11 29 D1
Marshall Rd EH29 89 D1
Marshall St
Cockenzie & Port Seton EH32 . 97 D2
Cowdenbeath KY4 13 E2
Edinburgh EH8 233 D2
Grangemouth FK3 61 E4
Marshall's Ct EH1 233 E4
Marshill FK10 10 A3
Martin Brae EH54 147 E3
Martin Gr EH19 182 B4
Martin Pl EH22 156 C1
Mary Erskine
Sch for Girls The EH4 92 A1
Mary Erskine & Stewart's
Melville Jun Sch The EH4 92 C1
Mary Pl Clackmannan FK10 11 D3
Dunfermline KY11 29 D1
Mary Sq FK2 61 D2
Mary St FK2 60 C2
Mary Stevenson Dr FK10 10 A4
Mary Street Rdbt FK2 60 C2
Mary's Pl EH4 93 D1
Maryburn Rd EH22 183 E4
Maryfield 2 EH7 93 F1
Maryfield Pk EH53 148 B1
Maryfield Pl
Bonnyrigg and Lasswade
EH19 182 B4
2 Edinburgh EH7 94 A1
Falkirk FK1 59 D2
Maryflats Pl FK3 61 F4
Maryhall St KY1 17 E3
Marywell KY1 17 E3
Masefield Way EH12 90 A1
Mason Pl EH18 181 F3
Masserene Rd KY2 16 C3
Masterton Rd KY11 47 D4
Mather Terr FK2 60 C2
Mathers Ave EH47 169 F3
Mathieson Pl KY11 29 F1
Matthew St KY2 17 D3
Maukeshill Ct EH54 147 E1
Maulsford Ave EH22 156 A4
Maurice Ave FK7 7 E2
Maurice Pl EH9 123 E1
Mauricewood Ave EH26 203 F4
Mauricewood Bank EH26 203 F4
Mauricewood Gr EH26 203 F4
Mauricewood Pk EH26 203 F4
Mauricewood Prim Sch
EH26 204 A4
Mauricewood Rd EH26 203 F4
Mauricewood Rise EH26 203 F4
Mavisbank EH20 181 E4
Mavisbank Ave FK1 81 E3
Mavisbank Pl EH18 181 F3
Maxton Cres FK12 5 E4
Maxton Ct EH22 157 D2
Maxton Pl KY11 46 C2
Maxwell Cres KY4 13 D1
Maxwell Pl FK8 7 D4
Maxwell Rd EH39 53 D2
Maxwell Sq EH54 173 E3
Maxwell St EH10 123 D2
May Terr EH39 54 A4
Maybank Villas EH12 121 E4
Mayburn Ave EH20 155 D1
Mayburn Bank EH20 181 D4
Mayburn Cres EH20 155 D1
Mayburn Ct EH20 181 D4
Mayburn Dr EH20 155 D1
Mayburn Gr EH20 181 D4
Mayburn Hill EH20 181 D4
Mayburn Loan EH20 155 D1
Mayburn Terr EH20 155 D1
Mayburn Vale EH20 181 D4
Mayburn Wlk EH20 181 D4
Maybury Rd EH12 121 D4
Mayfield Ave EH21 126 A2
Mayfield Cres
Clackmannan FK10 11 D3
Loanhead EH20 181 E4
Musselburgh EH21 126 A2
Mayfield Ct Armadale EH48 . 143 F2
Loanhead EH20 181 E4
Stirling FK7 7 D2
Mayfield Dr
Armadale EH48 143 F3
Longcroft FK4 57 D2
Mayfield Gdns EH9 123 F2
Mayfield Gdns La EH9 123 F2
Mayfield Ind Est EH22 183 E3
Mayfield Mews FK1 59 F2
Mayfield Pk EH21 126 A2
Mayfield Pl Mayfield EH22 183 E3
Musselburgh EH21 126 A2
Mayfield Prim Sch EH22 183 E3
Mayfield Rd
Easthouses EH22 183 E4
Edinburgh EH9 123 F2
Redding FK2 61 E1
Mayfield St FK7 7 D2
Mayfield Terr EH9 123 F2
Mayflower St KY12 29 E4
Maygate KY12 29 D2
Mayne Ave FK9 2 A3
Mayshade Rd EH20 155 D1
Mayville Bank EH21 127 D3
Mayville Gdns EH5 93 E3
Mayville Gdns E EH5 93 E3
Mayville Pk EH42 78 B2
McAdam Sq EH54 173 E3
McAlley Ct FK9 1 C4
McAllister Ct FK7 7 E1
McCall Gdns EH40 103 E4
McCallum Ct EH48 143 F4
McCann Ave EH52 117 D3
McCathie Dr EH22 183 D3
McClelland Cres KY11 29 D1
McDiarmid Gr EH22 183 D2
McDonald Pl EH7 93 F2
McDonald Rd EH7 93 F2
McDonald St EH7 93 F2
McDouall Stewart Mus
KY1 18 A4
McDouall Stuart Pl KY1 18 A4
McGinley Way EH49 84 B3
McGregor Ave KY5 14 A4
McGrigor Rd Rosyth KY11 46 B1
Stirling FK7 7 D2
McIntosh Ct EH52 117 E3
McKane Pl KY12 28 C1
McKay Dr KY11 29 F1
McKell Ct FK1 60 A2
McKenzie St KY1 17 F4
McKinlay Cres FK10 10 B4
McKinlay Terr EH20 181 D4
McKinnon Dr EH22 183 F3
McKinnon Rd EH47 193 F4
McLachlan Ave FK7 7 D1
McLachlan St FK5 38 B1
McLaren Ave EH49 84 A3
McLaren Ct FK5 38 B1
McLaren Rd EH9 124 A2
McLaren Terr FK7 7 D2
McLauchlan Rise KY3 49 D4
McLauchlan View ML7 168 C3
McLean Pl
Bonnyrigg and Lasswade
EH18 181 F3
Gorebridge EH23 207 E4
McLean Sch KY12 28 C3
McLean Wlk EH22 183 D2
McLeod Cres EH32 96 C1
McLeod St Broxburn EH52 117 F3
Edinburgh EH11 122 C3
McMartin Ct EH47 170 B4
McNeil Cres EH48 144 A3
McNeil Path EH33 128 B3
McNeil Way EH33 128 B3
McNeil Wlk EH33 128 B3
McNeill Ave EH20 181 D4
McNeill Pl EH20 181 D4
McNeill St EH11 232 A1
McNeill Terr EH20 181 D4
McPhail Sq EH33 128 B3
McPherson Dr FK8 2 A1
McQuade St EH19 182 B4
McRae Cres KY3 33 F1
McTaggart Ave FK6 36 C1
McVean Pl FK4 57 D2
Meadow Cres EH47 193 F3
Meadow Ct
Burntisland KY3 33 F1
Carluke ML8 230 B1
Meadow Dr EH47 171 D1
Meadow Gn FK10 5 D1
Meadow La EH8 233 D1
Meadow Pk FK10 5 D3
Meadow Pl Bilston EH25 180 C3
Dunfermline KY11 29 F2
Edinburgh EH9 232 C1
Stirling FK8 2 B1
Stoneyburn EH47 171 D1
Meadow Place Rd EH12 121 E3
Meadow Rd Currie EH14 151 F4
Stoneyburn EH47 171 D1
Meadow St FK1 60 B2
Meadowbank
Edinburgh EH8 94 A1
Livingston EH54 147 F3
Ormiston EH35 159 F3
Meadowbank Ave 13 EH8 94 A1
Meadowbank Cres
Edinburgh EH8 94 A1
Ormiston EH35 159 E4
Meadowbank Rd
Kirknewton EH27 149 F2
Ormiston EH35 159 F4
Meadowbank Sports Ctr
EH7 94 A1
Meadowbank St FK2 61 E1
Meadowbank View EH27 149 F2
Meadowend KY12 28 B1
Meadowfield
Burntisland KY3 33 F1
Cowdenbeath KY4 13 E3
Dalgety Bay KY11 48 A2
Meadowfield Ave EH8 124 C4
Meadowfield Ct EH8 124 B4
Meadowfield Dr EH8 124 B4
Meadowfield Gdns EH8 124 B3
Meadowfield Ind Est KY3 33 F1
Meadowfield Rd EH12 120 C4
Meadowfield Terr EH8 124 B3
Meadowforth Rd FK7 7 E4
Meadowhead Ave EH55 171 F1
Meadowhead Cres EH55 171 F1
Meadowhead Gdns EH55 171 F1
Meadowhead Gr EH55 171 F1
Meadowhead Loan EH55 171 F1
Meadowhead Pl EH55 171 E1
Meadowhead Terr EH55 171 E1
Meadowhouse Rd EH12 121 F3
Meadowland Rd FK9 2 A3
Meadowpark EH41 132 A4
Meadowpark Rd EH48 144 C3
Meadowside EH33 128 C3
Meadowspot EH10 122 C1
Meadowview KY12 28 A1
Mearenside EH12 121 D4
Medwyn Pl FK10 9 F3
Meeks Rd FK2 60 A3
Meeting House Dr EH33 128 B3
Meggat Pl EH26 204 A4
Meggetland Terr EH14 122 C2
Meikle Rd EH54 147 E1
Melbourne Pl EH39 54 B4
Melbourne Rd
Broxburn EH52 117 F3
North Berwick EH39 54 B4
Melbourne St EH54 148 A3
Meldrum Cres KY3 33 E1
Meldrum Ct KY11 29 F1
Meldrum Prim Sch EH54 146 C4
Meldrum Rd KY2 17 D3
Melford Ave ML7 192 A2
Melfort Dr FK7 7 D2
Melgund Pl KY5 14 A4
Melgund Terr EH7 93 E1
Mellerstain Rd KY2 16 B3
Mellock Gdns FK1 59 F1
Mellor Ct KY11 46 C2
Melrose Cres KY2 17 E3
Melrose Dr FK3 61 F3
Melrose Pl 10 FK1 60 A2
Melville Cotts EH18 156 B2
Melville Cres EH3 232 A3
Melville Dr EH9 233 D1
Melville Dykes Rd EH18 156 B1
Melville Gate EH22 156 B2
Melville Gate Rd EH22 156 C2
Melville Gdns KY3 50 B4
Melville Pl Bridge of A FK9 2 A4
Kircaldy KY2 16 B3
Melville Rd EH22 156 C1
Melville St Edinburgh EH3 232 A3
Falkirk FK1 60 A3
Lochgelly KY5 14 A4
Melville Street La EH3 232 A3
Melville Terr
Dalkeith EH22 156 C1
Edinburgh EH9 233 E1
Stirling FK8 7 D3
Melville View EH18 182 A4
Menstrie Castle FK11 3 F3
Menstrie Pl FK11 4 A3
Menstrie Prim Sch FK11 4 A3
Menteith Ct FK10 10 B3
Menteith Dr KY11 29 F1
Menteith Rd FK9 2 A2
Mentone Ave EH15 95 D1
Mentone Gdns EH9 123 F2
Mentone Terr EH9 123 F2
Menzies Cres KY2 16 C3
Menzies Dr FK8 2 A1
Menzies Rd EH48 145 D3
Mercat Pl FK10 11 D2
Mercat The KY1 17 E2
Mercer Pl KY11 29 F2
Mercer St FK10 23 F2
Merchant St EH1 233 D2
Merchiston Ave
Edinburgh EH10 123 D3
Falkirk FK2 60 A4
Merchiston Bank Ave
EH10 123 D2
Merchiston Bank Gdns
EH10 123 D2
Merchiston Castle Sch
EH14 153 D4
Merchiston Cres EH10 123 D2
Merchiston Gdns
Edinburgh EH10 122 C2
Falkirk FK2 60 A3
Merchiston Gr EH11 122 C2
Merchiston Ind Est FK2 60 B4
Merchiston Mews EH10 123 D3
Merchiston Pk EH10 123 D3
Merchiston Pl EH10 123 D3
Merchiston Rd
Falkirk, Grahamston FK2 60 A3
Falkirk, Mungal FK2 60 A4
Merchiston Terr FK2 60 A4
Meredith Dr FK5 38 C2
Merker Terr EH49 84 C3
Merkland Cres KY11 48 A2
Merkland Dr FK1 60 C1
Merlin Way KY11 48 B3
Merlyon Way EH26 203 E4
Merrick Rd FK3 61 F3
Merrick Way FK3 61 F3
Merryfield Ave EH33 129 E3
Mertoun Pl EH11 122 C3
Merville Cres FK1 81 F3
Merville Terr FK1 81 F3
Methven Dr KY12 29 D3
Methven Pl KY1 17 D1
Methven Rd KY1 17 D1
Methven Terr EH18 181 F3
Meuse La EH2 233 D3
Michaelson Sq EH54 147 E1
Mid Beveridgewell KY12 28 C3
Mid Brae KY12 28 C3
Mid Cswy KY12 42 B4
Mid Gogarloch Syke
EH12 121 D3
Mid Liberton EH16 124 A1
Mid New Cultins EH11 121 D1
Mid Rd KY3 34 C2
Mid Road Ind Est EH32 127 F4
Mid St Bathgate EH48 145 D3
Kirkaldy KY1 17 E3
Livingston EH54 146 C3
Lochgelly KY5 14 A4
Mid Steil EH10 122 C1
Midcalder Prim Sch EH53 148 B1
Middle Meadow Wlk EH8 233 D1
Middle Street La FK3 40 B1
Middlebank St KY11 46 C3
Middleby St EH9 123 F2
Middlefield EH7 93 F2
Middlefield Ind Ctr FK2 60 B4
Middlefield Ind Est FK2 60 C4
Middlefield Rd FK2 60 B3
Middleknowe EH14 152 B4
Middlemass Ct FK2 60 A3
Middlemuir Rd FK7 7 E3
Middlepark EH14 152 B4
Middleshot EH14 152 B4
Middleshot Rd EH31 52 A2
Middleshot Sq EH32 97 D1
Middleton FK11 4 A3
Middleton Ave EH52 117 D2
Middleton Rd EH52 117 D2
Middlewood Pk EH54 146 C4
Midhope Pl EH52 88 A1
Midmar Ave EH10 123 E1
Midmar Dr EH10 123 E1
Midmar Gdns EH10 123 D1
Midthorn Cres FK2 60 C3
Midtown FK11 3 F3
Milburn Cres EH48 143 E3
Milesmark Ct KY12 28 B3
Milesmark Prim Sch KY12 28 B3
Mill Farm Rd KY3 49 D4
Mill Hill FK7 6 B3
Mill La Edinburgh EH6 93 F3
Kincardine FK10 23 F2
Mill Lade EH49 84 C4
Mill Rd Alloa FK10 10 A3
Armadale EH48 143 F3
Bathgate EH48 145 D4
Blackburn EH47 171 E4
Cambusbarron FK7 6 B3
Clackmannan FK10 11 D3
Dunfermline KY11 29 D1
Falkirk FK2 39 D2
Harthill ML7 168 C3
Linlithgow EH49 84 B4
Stenton EH42 104 B1
Mill Rdbt EH54 147 D2
Mill Road Ind Est EH49 84 B4
Mill St Alloa FK10 10 A3
Dunfermline KY12 28 C2
Kirkcaldy KY1 17 D1
Mill Wynd
East Linton EH40 103 F4
Haddington EH41 132 A4
Prestonpans EH32 96 C1
Millar Cres EH10 123 D2
Millar Pl Edinburgh EH10 123 D2
High Bonnybridge FK4 58 A2
Stenhousemuir FK2 39 D3
Stirling FK8 2 B1
Millar Place La EH10 123 D2
Millar Rd EH33 128 B3
Millars Wynd FK10 5 E1
Millbank EH14 151 E1
Millbank Gr EH23 207 E4
Millbank Pl EH52 116 C2
Millbank Sq EH47 170 A4
Millbank Terr FK2 82 C4
Millbrae EH53 148 B3
Millbrae Wynd EH14 122 A1
Millbrook Pl FK11 3 F3
Millburn Rd
Bathgate EH48 144 C3
Westfield EH48 112 C3
Millburn St FK2 60 B3
Milldean Gr KY12 29 E3
Miller Ave KY12 28 A1
Miller Cres EH51 64 B3
Miller Pk FK2 61 F1
Miller Pl Airth FK2 22 C2
Harthill ML7 168 C3
Miller Rd Dunfermline KY12 28 C3
Grangemouth EH51 62 C3
Miller Row EH4 232 A3

Miller St Carluke ML8 .... 230 A1
  Harthill ML7 .... 168 C3
  Kirkcaldy KY1 .... 17 F4
Millerfield EH49 .... 84 B4
Millerfield Pl EH9 .... 123 E3
Millerhill Rd Dalkeith EH22 . 125 D1
  Danderhall EH22 .... 156 B4
Millfield Haddington EH41 .. 132 A4
  Livingston EH54 .... 147 D1
Millfield Dr FK2 .... 61 F1
Millflats St FK2 .... 39 D1
Millgate EH52 .... 87 F1
Millhall Rd FK7 .... 7 E3
Millhaugh La EH48 .... 145 D4
Millhill EH21 .... 126 B3
Millhill La EH21 .... 126 B3
Millhill St KY11 .... 29 D1
Millhill Wynd EH21 .... 126 B3
Millie St KY1 .... 17 E3
Millway EH34 .... 161 D3
Miln-acre EH6 .... 93 E2
Milne Cres KY4 .... 13 E2
Milne Rd KY11 .... 46 C1
Milnepark Rd FK7 .... 19 F4
Milton Brae FK7 .... 7 D1
Milton Cl FK6 .... 36 B2
Milton Cres
  Bannockburn FK7 .... 7 E1
  Edinburgh EH15 .... 125 D3
Milton Dr EH15 .... 125 E4
Milton Gdns FK7 .... 7 D1
Milton Gdns N EH15 .... 125 D3
Milton Gdns S EH15 .... 125 D3
Milton Glen EH15 .... 125 F4
Milton Gn KY12 .... 29 D1
Milton Gr Bannockburn FK7 .. 7 E1
  Edinburgh EH15 .... 125 E4
Milton Link EH15 .... 125 E3
Milton Pl FK6 .... 36 B2
Milton Rd Bannockburn FK7 .. 7 E1
  Edinburgh EH15 .... 125 D3
  Kirkcaldy KY1 .... 17 D1
Milton Rd E EH15 .... 125 E4
Milton Rd W EH15 .... 124 C3
Milton Row FK6 .... 36 C2
Milton St EH8 .... 94 A1
Milton Terr
  Bannockburn FK7 .... 7 D1
  Edinburgh EH15 .... 125 E4
Minard Rd ML7 .... 191 E3
Mine Rd FK9 .... 2 A4
Miner's Terr EH21 .... 127 D3
Mingle Pl EH51 .... 64 A3
Minstrel Ct EH25 .... 181 D2
Minthill Pl ML7 .... 168 B3
Minto Ct FK12 .... 5 D3
Minto Gdns FK12 .... 5 D3
Minto Pl KY2 .... 16 C2
Minto St Edinburgh EH9 ..... 123 F2
  Lochgelly KY5 .... 14 A4
Mission La 9 FK1 .... 60 A2
Mitchell Cres Alloa FK10 ...... 9 F4
  Cowdenbeath KY4 .... 13 D1
Mitchell Pl Falkirk FK1 .... 59 F1
  Kirkcaldy KY1 .... 17 E3
Mitchell Rd KY11 .... 46 B1
Mitchell St Dalkeith EH22 ... 156 C2
  Edinburgh EH6 .... 94 A3
  Kirkcaldy KY1 .... 17 E2
Mitchell Way EH33 .... 128 B4
Mitchell Wlk KY11 .... 46 C2
Mitchellhall Brae EH41 ...... 132 C3
Moat Dr EH14 .... 122 B2
Moat Pl EH14 .... 122 B2
Moat St EH14 .... 122 B2
Moat Terr EH14 .... 122 B2
Moat View EH17 .... 180 C2
Mochrum Dr KY12 .... 45 D4
Modan Rd FK7 .... 7 D2
Moffat Ave
  Bonnyrigg and Lasswade
  EH19 .... 182 A3
  Falkirk FK2 .... 39 E2
Moffat Cres KY5 .... 14 A4
Moffat Rd EH35 .... 159 E3
Moidart Rd EH47 .... 170 B4
Moir Ave EH21 .... 127 D3
Moir Cres EH21 .... 127 D3
Moir Ct KY4 .... 12 C4
Moir Dr EH21 .... 127 D3
Moir Pl EH21 .... 127 D3
Moir St FK10 .... 10 A4
Moir Terr EH21 .... 127 D3
Moira Pk EH7 .... 94 C1
Moira Terr EH7 .... 94 C1
Moira Terrace La EH7 .... 94 C1
Mollison Ave ML7 .... 168 C3
Monar Ct KY11 .... 48 A2
Monastery St KY12 .... 29 D2
Moncks Rd KY11 .... 60 B2
Moncrieff Terr EH9 .... 123 F3
Moncrieff Way EH54 .... 147 E4
Moncur St KY12 .... 29 E4
Monkbarns Gdns EH16 .... 155 D4
Monkland Rd EH48 .... 144 C3
Monkmains Rd EH41 .... 132 B4
Monkrigg Pl EH41 .... 132 B4
Monksrig Rd EH26 .... 203 D2
Monkswood Rd EH22 .... 183 D2
Monktonhall Pl EH21 .... 126 A2
Monktonhall Terr EH21 ..... 126 A2
Monkwood Ct EH9 .... 123 E2
Monmouth Terr EH3 .... 93 D2
Montagu Terr EH3 .... 93 D2
Montague St EH8 .... 233 E1

Monteith Wlk ML7 .... 191 F3
Montfort Pl FK1 .... 60 A2
Montgomery Cres FK2 .... 39 D1
Montgomery Dr FK2 .... 39 D1
Montgomery St
  Edinburgh EH7 .... 93 F1
  Falkirk FK2 .... 60 C3
  Grangemouth FK3 .... 61 E3
  Kirkcaldy KY2 .... 17 D3
Montgomery Street La
  EH7 .... 93 F1
Montgomery Way FK9 .... 2 A2
Montgomery Well FK2 .... 39 D1
Montpelier EH10 .... 123 D3
Montpelier Pk EH10 .... 123 D3
Montpelier Terr EH10 .... 123 D3
Montrose Rd Polmont FK2 .... 62 A1
  Stirling FK8 .... 2 B2
Montrose Terr EH7 .... 233 F4
Montrose Way FK4 .... 57 E3
Moodie St KY12 .... 29 D2
Moor Rd Fala EH37 .... 210 B3
  Pathhead EH37 .... 185 E2
  Pencaitland EH35 .... 186 A3
Moore House Sch EH14 .... 121 E1
Mooreland Gdns EH55 .... 171 E1
Moorelands EH55 .... 171 E1
Moorfield Cotts EH22 .... 156 B4
Moorfoot Ct EH19 .... 182 A4
Moorfoot Pl
  Bonnyrigg and Lasswade
  EH19 .... 182 A3
  Penicuik EH26 .... 203 F3
Moorfoot View
  Bilston EH26 .... 180 C3
  Bonnyrigg and Lasswade
  EH19 .... 182 A3
  Gorebridge EH23 .... 207 E4
Moorings The KY11 .... 47 F1
Moorside St ML8 .... 230 A1
Morar Ct FK3 .... 61 E3
Morar Dr FK2 .... 39 E1
Morar Pl FK3 .... 61 E3
Morar Rd KY12 .... 28 A1
Moray Way FK2 .... 192 A2
Moray Ct Auchtertool KY2 .... 15 D1
  Dalgety Bay KY11 .... 48 A2
Moray Dr EH49 .... 84 C3
Moray House Coll
  Halls Of Residence
  EH16 .... 124 A2
Moray House Coll of Ed
  Edinburgh, Canongate EH8 .. 233 E3
  Edinburgh, Cramond EH4 ... 91 E2
Moray Park Terr EH7 .... 94 A1
Moray Pk KY11 .... 48 A2
Moray Pl Edinburgh EH3 ..... 232 B4
  Grangemouth FK3 .... 61 F4
  Linlithgow EH49 .... 84 C3
Moray Prim Sch FK3 .... 61 F4
Moray Way N KY11 .... 48 B2
Moray Way S KY11 .... 48 A1
Morayvale KY11 .... 49 E4
Moredun Dykes Rd EH17 .... 155 E4
Moredun Park Ct EH17 .... 155 E4
Moredun Park Dr EH17 ...... 155 E4
Moredun Park Gdns
  EH17 .... 155 E4
Moredun Park Gn EH17 ..... 155 E4
Moredun Park Gr EH17 ...... 155 E4
Moredun Park Loan
  EH17 .... 155 E4
Moredun Park Rd EH17 ...... 155 E4
Moredun Park St EH17 .... 155 E4
Moredun Park View
  EH17 .... 155 F4
Moredun Park Way EH17 .... 155 F4
Moredun Park Wlk EH17 .... 155 F4
Moredun Prim Sch EH17 .... 155 E4
Moredunvale Bank EH17 .... 155 F4
Moredunvale Gn EH17 .... 155 F4
Moredunvale Gr EH17 .... 155 F4
Moredunvale Loan EH17 .... 155 F4
Moredunvale Pk EH17 .... 155 F4
Moredunvale Pl EH17 .... 155 F4
Moredunvale Rd EH17 .... 155 F4
Moredunvale View EH17 .... 155 F4
Moredunvale Way EH17 ..... 155 F4
Morgan Ct FK7 .... 7 E2
Morison Gdns EH30 .... 68 A1
Moriston Ct FK3 .... 61 F2
Moriston Dr EH54 .... 173 F3
Morley Cres FK7 .... 7 D2
Morlich Cres KY11 .... 48 A1
Morlich Ct KY11 .... 48 A1
Morlich Gr KY11 .... 48 A1
Morlich Pk KY11 .... 48 A1
Morlich Pl KY11 .... 48 A1
Morlich Rd KY11 .... 48 A1
Morlich Wlk EH54 .... 148 A2
Mornay Way ML7 .... 191 E3
Morningside Ct EH10 .... 123 D1
Morningside Dr EH10 .... 123 D1
Morningside Gdns EH10 .... 122 C1
Morningside Gr EH10 .... 122 C1
Morningside Pk EH10 .... 123 D2
Morningside Pl EH10 .... 123 D2
Morningside Rd EH10 .... 123 D2
Morningside Terr EH10 ...... 123 D2
Morris Ct KY11 .... 47 E1
Morris Rd EH22 .... 183 E3
Morris Sq EH54 .... 147 F1
Morris Terr FK8 .... 7 D4
Morrison Ave
  Bonnybridge FK4 .... 57 F3
  Tranent EH33 .... 128 C3
Morrison Circ EH3 .... 232 A2
Morrison Cres EH3 .... 232 A2

Morrison Dr
  Bannockburn FK7 .... 7 E1
  Dunfermline KY11 .... 46 C4
Morrison Link EH3 .... 232 A2
Morrison St EH3 .... 232 A2
Morrison Way EH54 .... 147 E4
Mortimer Ct KY11 .... 48 A1
Morton St EH15 .... 125 E4
Mortonhall Gate EH16 .... 154 C3
Mortonhall Park Ave
  EH17 .... 154 C3
Mortonhall Park Bank
  EH17 .... 155 D3
Mortonhall Park Cres
  EH17 .... 155 D3
Mortonhall Park Dr
  EH17 .... 155 D3
Mortonhall Park Gdns
  EH17 .... 154 C3
Mortonhall Park Gr
  EH17 .... 154 C3
Mortonhall Park Pl
  EH17 .... 155 D3
Mortonhall Park Terr
  EH17 .... 155 D3
Mortonhall Park View
  EH17 .... 154 C3
Mortonhall Park Way
  EH17 .... 154 C3
Mortonhall Rd EH9 .... 123 E2
Morven Ct FK1 .... 60 B1
Morven Dr FK2 .... 61 E1
Morven Gr KY2 .... 16 C4
Morven Pl KY11 .... 48 A2
Morven St EH4 .... 91 E1
Morvenside EH14 .... 152 B4
Morvenside Cl EH14 .... 152 B4
Moss Intc EH54 .... 147 E3
Moss Rd FK7 .... 8 B2
Moss Way KY11 .... 48 A3
Moss-side Rd KY4 .... 13 D2
Mossband La ML7 .... 191 F3
Mossbank
  Cowdenbeath KY4 .... 13 D1
  Livingston EH54 .... 147 F3
  Rosyth KY11 .... 46 C3
Mossburn Ave ML7 .... 168 B3
Mosscastle Rd FK1 .... 110 A4
Mossend EH55 .... 172 B2
Mossend Terr KY4 .... 13 D1
Mossgiel Ave Cowie FK7 ...... 20 B4
  Stirling FK8 .... 2 A1
Mossgiel Cotts EH54 .... 146 B4
Mossgiel St FK1 .... 59 D3
Mossgiel Terr FK2 .... 61 D2
Mossgiel Wlk 4 EH16 .... 124 A1
Mosshall Ind Est EH47 .... 171 D4
Mosshat Rd EH55 .... 216 C2
Mosshouse FK7 .... 6 C2
Mosside Dr EH47 .... 145 E1
Mosside Rd EH47 .... 171 E4
Mosside Terr EH47 .... 145 E1
Moston Terr EH9 .... 123 F2
Motion St KY5 .... 14 A4
Moubray Ave EH30 .... 89 E4
Moubray Rd KY11 .... 48 B3
Moulin Way KY12 .... 29 F3
Mound Pl EH1 .... 232 C3
Mound The EH2 .... 232 C3
Mount Grange EH9 .... 123 E2
Mount Hooly Cres KY11 .... 68 B3
Mount Hope FK9 .... 2 B4
Mount Lodge Pl EH15 .... 125 D4
Mount Oliphant FK7 .... 20 B4
Mount Pleasant EH48 .... 143 F3
Mount Vernon Rd EH16 ..... 155 D4
Mount William FK10 .... 5 F1
Mountbatten Pl KY11 .... 46 C2
Mountbatten St FK3 .... 61 E3
Mountcastle Bank EH8 ...... 124 C4
Mountcastle Cres EH8 .... 124 C4
Mountcastle Dr N EH15 ..... 124 C4
Mountcastle Dr S EH15 ..... 124 C3
Mountcastle Gdns EH8 ...... 124 C4
Mountcastle Gn 1 EH8 .... 94 C1
Mountcastle Gr EH8 .... 124 C4
Mountcastle Loan EH8 ...... 124 C4
Mountcastle Pl 3 EH8 .... 94 C1
Mountcastle Pl 2 EH8 .... 94 C1
Mountcastle Terr EH8 .... 124 C4
Mountfair Gdns EH33 .... 129 E3
Mountfair Pl EH33 .... 129 E3
Mounthooly Loan EH10 ..... 154 B3
Mountjoy Terr EH21 .... 126 B4
Mowbray Ct FK7 .... 7 E2
Mowbray Gdns KY4 .... 30 C3
Mowbray Rise EH54 .... 147 F1
Moy Ct FK3 .... 61 E3
Muckle Hill Pk KY11 .... 47 D1
Mucklets Ave EH21 .... 126 A2
Mucklets Cres EH21 .... 126 A2
Mucklets Ct EH21 .... 126 A2
Mucklets Dr EH21 .... 126 A2
Mucklets Pl EH21 .... 126 A2
Mucklets Rd EH21 .... 125 F2
Mudale Ct FK1 .... 60 B1
Muia's Ct EH52 .... 116 C2
Muir Ct KY4 .... 30 C3
Muir Rd Bathgate EH48 ...... 144 C4
  Livingston EH54 .... 148 A4
  Townhill KY12 .... 29 E4
Muir St KY5 .... 38 B1
Muir Wood Cres EH14 .... 152 A3
Muir Wood Dr EH14 .... 152 A3
Muir Wood Gr EH14 .... 152 A3
Muir Wood Pl EH14 .... 152 A3
Muir Wood Rd EH14 .... 152 A3
Muiralehouse Rd FK7 .... 19 F4

Muiravonside Ctry Pk
  EH49 .... 83 F2
Muirdyke Ave FK2 .... 39 E2
Muiredge & Jersey Rd
  ML7 .... 191 D4
Muirend Ave EH14 .... 152 C4
Muirend Ct EH51 .... 64 A3
Muirend Rd FK7 .... 7 D3
Muirepark Ct EH51 .... 64 A3
Muirfield Cres EH31 .... 52 A1
Muirfield Dr Gullane EH31 ... 52 A1
  Uphall EH52 .... 116 C2
Muirfield Gdns EH20 .... 181 E4
Muirfield Pk EH31 .... 52 A1
Muirfield Rd FK5 .... 38 C1
Muirfield Steading EH31 ..... 52 B2
Muirfield Terr EH31 .... 52 A1
Muirfield Way EH54 .... 146 C3
Muirhall Pl FK5 .... 38 B2
Muirhall Rd FK5 .... 38 B2
Muirhead Ave FK2 .... 60 A4
Muirhead Pl Harthill ML7 .. 168 B2
  Penicuik EH26 .... 203 F4
Muirhead Rd FK5 .... 38 C2
Muirhouse Ave EH4 .... 92 A2
Muirhouse Bank EH4 .... 92 A2
Muirhouse Cl EH4 .... 92 A2
Muirhouse Cres EH4 .... 92 A2
Muirhouse Dr EH4 .... 92 A3
Muirhouse Gdns EH4 .... 92 A3
Muirhouse Gn EH4 .... 92 A2
Muirhouse Gr EH4 .... 92 A3
Muirhouse Loan EH4 .... 92 A3
Muirhouse Medway EH4 ..... 92 A3
Muirhouse Parkway EH4 ..... 92 A3
Muirhouse Pk EH4 .... 92 A2
Muirhouse Pl E EH4 .... 92 A2
Muirhouse Pl W EH4 .... 92 A2
Muirhouse Prim Sch EH4 .... 92 A2
Muirhouse Terr EH4 .... 92 A2
Muirhouse View EH4 .... 92 A2
Muirhouse Way EH4 .... 92 A2
Muirlaun ML11 .... 215 D1
Muirlee Rd ML8 .... 230 A1
Muirpark EH22 .... 156 C1
Muirpark Ct EH33 .... 128 C3
Muirpark Dr Shieldhill FK1 ... 81 E3
  Tranent EH33 .... 128 C3
Muirpark Gdns
  Tranent EH33 .... 128 C3
  Tullibody FK10 .... 4 C2
Muirpark Gr EH33 .... 128 C3
Muirpark Pl EH33 .... 128 C3
Muirpark Rd EH33 .... 128 C3
Muirpark Terr EH33 .... 128 C3
Muirpark Wynd EH33 .... 128 C3
Muirside Dr KY12 .... 27 E1
Muirside Gr EH33 .... 128 B3
Muirside Gr KY12 .... 27 E1
Muirside La KY12 .... 44 B4
Muirside Rd FK10 .... 4 B2
Muirton Rd FK7 .... 7 F3
Muirton Rdbt FK7 .... 7 F4
Muirton Way KY11 .... 48 A3
Mulberry Dr KY11 .... 29 F1
Mulberry Pl EH6 .... 93 E3
Muldron Terr ML7 .... 192 A1
Mull Ct Alloa FK10 .... 10 A3
  Grangemouth FK3 .... 61 E3
Mumrills Rd FK2 .... 61 E2
Mungalend FK2 .... 60 A4
Mungalend Ct FK2 .... 60 A4
Mungalhead Rd FK2 .... 60 A4
Mungle St EH55 .... 172 B2
Munro Ave FK9 .... 2 A2
Munro Dr EH13 .... 153 D3
Munro Gdns FK2 .... 60 C2
Munro Pl KY11 .... 9 F3
Munro Rd FK7 .... 7 F3
Munro St Kirkcaldy KY1 ...... 17 D1
  Stenhousemuir FK5 .... 38 C2
Munro Way EH54 .... 147 E4
Murano Pl EH7 .... 93 F1
Murderdean Rd EH22 .... 183 D3
Murdoch Terr EH11 .... 232 A1
Murdostoun Cres ML7 .... 168 C3
Murieston Cres EH11 .... 122 C3
Murieston Crescent La
  EH11 .... 122 C3
Murieston Ct EH54 .... 174 A3
Murieston Dr EH54 .... 174 A3
Murieston East Rd EH54 .... 174 A4
Murieston Gdns EH54 .... 174 A4
Murieston Gn EH54 .... 173 F3
Murieston Gr EH54 .... 174 A3
Murieston La EH11 .... 122 C3
Murieston Pk EH54 .... 173 F3
Murieston Pl EH11 .... 122 C3
Murieston Rd
  Edinburgh EH11 .... 122 C3
  Livingston EH54 .... 173 F2
Murieston Terr EH11 .... 122 C3
Murieston Vale EH54 .... 173 F2
Murieston Valley EH54 ...... 173 F3
Murieston West Rd EH54 ... 173 F4
Murieston Wlk EH54 .... 173 F2
Murieston Wood EH54 .... 173 F3
Murnin Ct FK7 .... 7 E2
Murnin Rd FK4 .... 58 A2
Murnin Road Ind Est FK4 .... 58 A2
Murray Cotts EH12 .... 121 E3
Murray Cres FK2 .... 83 D3
Murray Pl Cambusbarron FK7 . 6 B4
  Stirling FK8 .... 7 D4
Murray Rd KY11 .... 46 B1
Murray Way EH54 .... 147 E4
Murray Wlk KY11 .... 29 F2

Murrayburn App EH14 .... 121 E1
Murrayburn Dr EH14 .... 121 E1
Murrayburn Gate EH14 ...... 152 B4
Murrayburn Gdns EH14 ..... 121 E1
Murrayburn Gn EH14 .... 121 E1
Murrayburn Gr EH14 .... 121 E1
Murrayburn Junc EH14 ...... 152 B4
Murrayburn Pk EH14 .... 121 E1
Murrayburn Pl EH14 .... 121 E1
Murrayburn Prim Sch
  EH11 .... 121 E1
Murrayburn Rd EH14 .... 121 E1
Murrayfield Ave EH12 .... 122 B4
Murrayfield Dr
  Blackburn EH47 .... 171 E4
  Edinburgh EH12 .... 122 B4
Murrayfield Gdns EH12 ...... 122 B4
Murrayfield Hospl EH12 ..... 122 A4
Murrayfield Pl
  Bannockburn FK7 .... 7 E1
  Edinburgh EH12 .... 122 B4
Murrayfield Prim Sch
  EH47 .... 145 E1
Murrayfield Rd EH12 .... 122 B4
Murrayfield Rugby Gd
  EH12 .... 122 B3
Murrayfield Terr
  Bannockburn FK7 .... 7 E1
  Blackburn EH47 .... 171 E4
Murrays Brae The EH17 ..... 155 E2
Murrays The EH17 .... 155 E2
Murraysgate Cres EH47 ..... 169 F3
Murraysgate Ind Est
  EH47 .... 169 F3
Murrayshall Rd FK7 .... 7 D2
Murrel Rd KY3 .... 49 E4
Murrel Terr KY3 .... 49 E4
Mus of Childhood EH1 ...... 233 E3
Mus of Flight EH39 .... 74 B1
Music Hall La KY12 .... 29 D2
Musselburgh Burgry
  Prim Sch EH21 .... 126 B3
Musselburgh Gram Sch
  EH21 .... 126 B3
Musselburgh Rd
  Dalkeith EH22 .... 157 D2
  Edinburgh EH15 .... 125 F4
Musselburgh Sta EH21 ...... 126 A2
Myers Ct KY12 .... 29 E3
Mylne Pl FK2 .... 39 D1
Mylneburn Gdns KY11 .... 45 E2
Myothill Rd FK6 .... 57 E4
Myre Cres KY3 .... 35 D2
Myre Dale EH19 .... 182 B3
Myreside Ct EH10 .... 122 C1
Myreside Rd EH10 .... 122 C2
Myreton FK11 .... 4 A3
Myreton Dr FK7 .... 19 F4
Myreton Rd FK3 .... 61 E3
Myreton Way FK2 .... 59 F2
Myretoungate FK12 .... 4 C3
Myrtle Cres
  Bilston EH25 .... 180 C3
  Kirkcaldy KY2 .... 17 D4
Myrtle Gr EH22 .... 183 E4
Myrtle Terr EH11 .... 122 C3

Nailer Rd Falkirk FK1 .... 59 F3
  Stirling FK7 .... 7 D1
Nairn Ct FK1 .... 60 B1
Nairn Rd EH54 .... 146 C4
Nairn St KY1 .... 17 E3
Naismith Ct FK3 .... 40 C1
Namayo Ave FK2 .... 61 D2
Namur Rd EH26 .... 204 A4
Nantwich Dr EH7 .... 94 C2
Napier Ave EH48 .... 145 E3
Napier Cres FK2 .... 60 A4
Napier Pl FK2 .... 60 A4
Napier Rd
  Edinburgh EH10 .... 123 D2
  Rosyth KY11 .... 46 B1
Napier Sq EH54 .... 148 A4
Napier St KY1 .... 17 F4
Napier Univ
  Edinburgh EH10 .... 123 D2
  Edinburgh, Craiglockhart
  EH14 .... 122 B1
  Edinburgh, Sighthill EH11 .... 121 E1
Napier Univ
  (Craiglockhart Campus)
  EH10 .... 122 C1
Nasmyth Ct EH54 .... 148 A3
Nasmyth Rd KY11 .... 46 A1
Nasmyth Sq EH54 .... 148 A3
Natal Pl KY4 .... 13 E2
National Gallery EH2 .... 232 C3
National Liby of Scotland
  EH1 .... 233 D3
National Portrait Gallery
  EH2 .... 233 D4
Navar Ct ML7 .... 192 A2
Nebit The FK12 .... 4 C3
Neidpath Ct
  Edinburgh EH21 .... 121 D4
  Longniddry EH32 .... 98 C3
Neidpath Dr FK5 .... 38 C2
Neidpath Pl KY12 .... 29 E3
Neilson Gr KY3 .... 33 F1
Neilson Park Rd EH41 .... 132 A4
Neilson Sq EH54 .... 146 B3
Neilson St FK1 .... 60 A2
Nellburn EH16 .... 146 C3
Nellfield EH16 .... 155 D4
Nelson Ave EH54 .... 147 F2
Nelson Gdns FK3 .... 40 C1
Nelson Pl FK7 .... 7 E3
Nelson Rd EH51 .... 62 C3

Nelson St Edinburgh EH3 ... 232 C4
Grangemouth FK3 ... 61 F4
Kirkcaldy KY2 ... 17 D3
Rosyth KY11 ... 46 C3
Ness The KY12 ... 26 C1
Nether Craigour EH17 ... 124 B1
Nether Currie Cres EH14 .. 152 A3
Nether Currie Pl EH14 ... 152 A3
Nether Currie Prim Sch
EH14 ... 152 A3
Nether Currie Rd EH14 ... 152 A3
Nether Dechmont Cotts
EH54 ... 147 D4
Nether St Dysart KY1 ... 18 A4
Kirkcaldy KY1 ... 17 E3
Netherbank EH16 ... 154 C3
Netherbank View EH16 ... 154 C3
Netherbeath Rd KY4 ... 30 C4
Netherby Rd Airth FK2 ... 22 B2
Edinburgh EH5 ... 93 D3
Netherfield Rd FK2 ... 61 E1
Nethergate KY3 ... 35 D1
Nethergate The FK12 ... 4 C3
Netherlaw EH39 ... 54 A3
Nethermains Prim Sch
FK6 ... 36 B1
Nethermains Rd FK6 ... 36 B1
Nethershot Rd EH32 ... 97 D1
Netherton Gr EH47 ... 170 A2
Netherton Pl EH47 ... 170 A2
Netherton St ML7 ... 168 B3
Nethertown Broad St
KY12 ... 29 D1
Netherwood Pk EH54 ... 147 D4
Nettlehill Dr EH54 ... 116 C1
Nettlehill Rd
Livingston EH54 ... 147 F4
Uphall Station EH54 ... 117 D1
Neucks The FK1 ... 111 D3
Nevis Cres FK10 ... 10 A4
Nevis Dr EH54 ... 173 F3
Nevis Gdns EH26 ... 204 A4
Nevis Pl Falkirk FK1 ... 60 B1
Grangemouth FK3 ... 61 F3
Shotts ML7 ... 192 A2
New Arthur Pl EH8 ... 233 E2
New Broompark EH5 ... 92 C4
New Broughton 5 EH3 ... 93 E1
New Carron Rd FK5 ... 39 D2
New Coll EH1 ... 232 C3
New Hallglen Rd FK1 ... 60 B1
New Halls Rd EH30 ... 68 B1
New Holygate EH52 ... 117 E3
New Houses EH39 ... 74 B2
New Hunterfield EH23 ... 183 D1
New John's Pl EH8 ... 233 E1
New La EH6 ... 93 E3
New Line Rd FK7 ... 19 D4
New Liston Rd EH29 ... 89 D1
New Market Rd EH14 ... 122 B2
New Mart Rd EH14 ... 122 A2
New Meadowspott
EH22 ... 157 D1
New Orchardfield EH6 ... 93 F2
New Rd FK7 ... 7 E1
New Row Dunfermline KY12 ... 29 D2
East Fortune EH39 ... 74 A2
Kincardine FK10 ... 24 A2
Tranent EH33 ... 128 B3
New Skinners Cl EH1 ... 233 E3
New St Bridge of A FK9 ... 1 C4
Cockenzie & Port Seton
EH32 ... 97 E2
Edinburgh EH8 ... 233 E3
Musselburgh EH21 ... 126 A3
Prestonpans EH32 ... 96 C1
Slamannan FK1 ... 110 A4
Tranent EH33 ... 128 B4
New Star Bank EH22 ... 183 D3
New Swanston EH10 ... 153 F3
New Tower Pl EH15 ... 95 D1
New Well Wynd EH49 ... 84 C3
Newbattle Abbey Cres
EH22 ... 182 C4
Newbattle Gdns EH22 ... 157 D1
Newbattle High Sch
EH22 ... 183 E4
Newbattle Terr EH10 ... 123 D2
Newbiggin Cres FK10 ... 4 B1
Newbiggin Rd FK3 ... 61 F3
Newbigging
Auchtertool KY2 ... 15 E1
Musselburgh EH21 ... 126 B3
Newbigging Terr KY2 ... 15 E1
Newbridge Ind Est EH28 ... 118 C3
Newbridge Rdbt EH28 ... 119 D3
Newburn Pl KY12 ... 29 E2
Newbyres Ave EH23 ... 183 E1
Newbyres Cres EH23 ... 207 E4
Newbyres Gdns EH23 ... 207 E4
Newcarron Ct FK2 ... 60 A4
Newcraighall Bsns Pk
EH15 ... 125 D2
Newcraighall Dr EH21 ... 125 E2
Newcraighall Prim sch
EH21 ... 125 F2
Newcraighall Rd EH15 ... 125 D2
Newhailes Ave EH21 ... 126 A3
Newhailes Cres EH21 ... 126 A3
Newhailes Rd EH15 ... 125 F3
Newhaven Pl EH6 ... 93 E4
Newhaven Rd EH6 ... 93 E3
Newhouse FK8 ... 7 D3
Newhouse Ave EH42 ... 78 C1
Newhouse Bsns Pk FK3 ... 61 E4
Newhouse Dr FK1 ... 59 F1
Newhouse Pl EH42 ... 78 C1
Newhouse Rd FK3 ... 61 E4
Newhouses Rd EH52 ... 118 A2
Newington Rd EH9 ... 123 F3
Newland Ave EH48 ... 145 D3
Newlands Pk
Dunfermline KY12 ... 29 D3
Edinburgh EH9 ... 123 F2
Newlands Pl FK10 ... 4 B2
Newlands Rd
Bannockburn FK7 ... 19 E4
Brightons FK2 ... 82 B4
Grangemouth FK3 ... 61 E3
Newliston Dr KY2 ... 16 B4
Newmains Farm La EH29 ... 89 D1
Newmains Rd EH29 ... 89 D1
Newmarket FK7 ... 7 F1
Newmarket Ctr FK1 ... 60 A3
Newmarket St FK1 ... 60 A3
Newmill & Canthill Rd
ML7 ... 191 D3
Newmills FK10 ... 4 A2
Newmills Ave EH14 ... 151 E2
Newmills Cres EH14 ... 151 E2
Newmills Gr EH14 ... 151 E2
Newmills Rd Currie EH14 ... 151 E2
Dalkeith EH22 ... 157 D2
Newmills Terr EH22 ... 157 D2
Newpark Cres FK7 ... 7 D1
Newpark Rd
Livingston EH54 ... 173 E3
Stirling FK7 ... 7 D1
Newpark Rdbt EH54 ... 173 E4
Newtoft St EH17 ... 155 F3
Newton Ave FK2 ... 40 A2
Newton Church Rd EH22 ... 156 B4
Newton Cres KY11 ... 47 D2
Newton Pl KY11 ... 46 C2
Newton Port EH41 ... 101 D1
Newton Rd FK3 ... 40 A1
Newton St
Easthouses EH22 ... 183 E4
Edinburgh EH11 ... 122 C3
Newtongrange Prim Sch
EH22 ... 183 D3
Newtonloan St Andrew's
Prim Sch EH23 ... 183 D2
Newtonshaw FK10 ... 5 E1
Newtown EH51 ... 63 F3
Newtown St EH51 ... 63 F3
Newyearfield Bsns Pk
EH54 ... 147 E3
Newyearfield Rdbt EH54 ... 147 E3
Nicholson Way EH54 ... 147 E4
Nicklaus Gn EH54 ... 147 D4
Nicol Pl EH52 ... 117 E3
Nicol Rd EH52 ... 117 E3
Nicol St KY1 ... 17 D2
Nicolson Sq EH8 ... 233 E2
Nicolson St EH8 ... 233 E2
Nicolton Ave FK2 ... 82 C4
Nicolton Rd FK2 ... 62 A1
Niddrie Farm Gr EH16 ... 124 C2
Niddrie House Ave 6
EH16 ... 124 C2
Niddrie House Dr EH16 ... 125 D2
Niddrie House Gdns
EH16 ... 124 C2
Niddrie House Pk EH16 ... 124 C2
Niddrie House Sq EH16 ... 124 C2
Niddrie Mains Ct EH16 ... 125 D2
Niddrie Mains Dr EH16 ... 124 C2
Niddrie Mains Rd EH16 ... 124 C2
Niddrie Mains Terr EH16 ... 124 C2
Niddrie Marischal Cres
EH16 ... 124 C2
Niddrie Marischal Dr 4
EH16 ... 124 C2
Niddrie Marischal Gdns 2
EH16 ... 124 C2
Niddrie Marischal Gn 5
EH16 ... 124 C2
Niddrie Marischal Gr
EH16 ... 125 D2
Niddrie Marischal Loan 3
EH16 ... 124 C2
Niddrie Marischal Pl
EH16 ... 124 C2
Niddrie Marischal Rd
EH16 ... 125 D2
Niddrie Marischal St 1
EH16 ... 124 C2
Niddrie Mill Ave EH15 ... 125 D2
Niddrie Mill Cres EH15 ... 125 D3
Niddrie Mill Dr EH15 ... 125 D2
Niddrie Mill Gr EH15 ... 125 D2
Niddrie Mill Pl EH15 ... 125 D2
Niddrie Mill Prim Sch
EH15 ... 125 D2
Niddrie Mill Terr EH15 ... 125 D2
Niddry Rd EH52 ... 87 F1
Niddry St EH1 ... 233 D3
Niddry St S EH1 ... 233 E2
Niddry View EH52 ... 87 F1
Nidrie Cotts EH15 ... 125 E2
Nielson Ct EH47 ... 171 D4
Nigel Loan EH16 ... 155 D4
Nigel Rise EH54 ... 147 F1
Nile Gr EH10 ... 123 D2
Nile St KY2 ... 17 D3
Nimmo Ave EH32 ... 97 D1
Ninian Rd EH51 ... 62 C3
Ninth St EH22 ... 183 D3
Nisbet Dr FK6 ... 36 B1
Nisbet Rd EH31 ... 51 F1
Nith St KY11 ... 29 F1
Nithsdale St ML7 ... 191 E3
Niven Rd KY11 ... 47 E2
Niven's Knowe Rd EH20 ... 180 C4
Nivensknowe Pk EH20 ... 180 C4
No 7 Pit Rd KY4 ... 13 E2
Nobel Pl EH25 ... 180 C2
Nobel View FK2 ... 82 A4
Noble Pl EH6 ... 94 A2
Norman Rise EH54 ... 147 F1
Normand Brae KY1 ... 18 A4
Normand Rd KY1 ... 18 A4
North Approach Rd FK10 ... 23 F2
North Ave FK2 ... 83 D4
North Bank Rd EH32 ... 127 F4
North Bank St EH1 ... 233 D3
North Berwick High Sch
EH39 ... 54 B3
North Bridge EH1 ... 233 D3
North Bridge St
Bathgate EH48 ... 145 D3
Grangemouth FK3 ... 40 B1
North Bughtlin Bank EH12 .. 91 D1
North Bughtlin Brae EH12 .. 91 D1
North Bughtlin Gate EH12 ... 91 D1
North Bughtlin Neuk
EH12 ... 91 D1
North Bughtlin Pl EH12 ... 91 D1
North Bughtlin Rd EH12 ... 91 D1
North Bughtlinfield EH12 ... 91 D1
North Bughtlinrig EH12 ... 91 D1
North Bughtlinside EH12 ... 91 D1
North Cairntow EH16 ... 124 B3
North Castle St Alloa FK10 ... 10 A3
Edinburgh EH2 ... 232 B4
North Charlotte St EH2 ... 232 B3
North Clyde Street La
EH1 ... 233 D4
North Cres
Dunfermline KY11 ... 46 C4
Prestonpans EH32 ... 97 D1
North East Circus Pl 10
EH3 ... 93 D1
North East Cumberland
Street La EH3 ... 93 E1
North East Thistle
Street La EH2 ... 232 C4
North Esk Lodge
(Loretto Jun Sch) EH21 .. 126 B3
North Esk Rd KY11 ... 46 B1
North Fort St EH6 ... 93 F3
North Gate EH48 ... 113 F3
North Grange Ave EH32 ... 96 C1
North Grange Gr EH32 ... 96 C1
North Grange Rd EH32 ... 96 C1
North Greendykes Rd
EH52 ... 117 F4
North Greens EH15 ... 125 D3
North Gyle Ave EH12 ... 121 D3
North Gyle Dr EH12 ... 121 D4
North Gyle Farm Ct
EH12 ... 121 D3
North Gyle Farm La
EH12 ... 121 D3
North Gyle Gr EH12 ... 121 D3
North Gyle Loan EH12 ... 121 D4
North Gyle Pk EH12 ... 121 D4
North Gyle Rd EH12 ... 121 D4
North Gyle Terr EH12 ... 121 D3
North High St EH21 ... 126 A3
North Hillhousefield EH6 ... 93 F3
North Junction St EH6 ... 93 F3
North Larches KY11 ... 29 F2
North Leith Sands EH6 ... 93 F3
North Loanhead KY11 ... 45 F2
North Lorimer Pl EH32 ... 97 D2
North Main St FK2 ... 39 E2
North Meggetland EH14 ... 122 C2
North Overgate KY3 ... 34 C2
North Park Terr EH4 ... 93 D1
North Peffer Pl EH16 ... 124 B2
North Prim Sch KY2 ... 17 D3
North Queensferry Sta
KY11 ... 68 B3
North Rd Dunbar EH42 ... 78 B2
Fauldhouse EH47 ... 193 F4
Inverkeithing KY11 ... 47 E2
North Reeves Pl EH47 ... 170 A3
North Roundall KY11 ... 45 F2
North Row KY11 ... 45 D2
North Seton Pk EH32 ... 97 E2
North Shore Rd FK3 ... 40 C1
North St Alloa FK10 ... 10 A4
Armadale EH48 ... 143 F3
Bo'ness EH51 ... 63 F4
Clackmannan FK10 ... 11 D2
Dunbar EH42 ... 78 A1
Falkirk FK2 ... 60 A4
Lochgelly KY5 ... 14 A4
Ratho EH28 ... 119 E1
Stirling FK9 ... 2 B1
North St Andrew La EH2 .. 233 D4
North St Andrew St EH2 ... 233 D4
North St David St EH2 ... 233 D4
North View Burntisland KY3 ... 50 C4
West Calder EH55 ... 172 B2
North Way KY11 ... 48 B3
North Werber Pk EH4 ... 92 C2
North Werber Pl EH4 ... 92 C2
North West Circus Pl
EH3 ... 93 D1
North West Cumberland
Street La EH3 ... 93 E1
North West Thistle
Street La
EH2 ... 232 C4
North Wood Rd FK10 ... 4 B1
North Wynd EH22 ... 157 D2
Northbank Ct EH51 ... 64 A3
Northbank Dr EH51 ... 64 A3
Northbank Pk EH51 ... 63 F3
Northbank Rd KY12 ... 27 E1
Northend FK7 ... 6 B3
Northfield
Cowdenbeath KY4 ... 13 E3
Tranent EH33 ... 128 C3
Northfield Ave
Edinburgh EH8 ... 124 B4
Shotts ML7 ... 192 A1
Northfield Broadway
EH8 ... 124 C4
Northfield Cir EH8 ... 124 B4
Northfield Cotts EH55 ... 172 B2
Northfield Cres
Edinburgh EH8 ... 124 C4
Longridge EH47 ... 170 B1
Northfield Ct EH32 ... 127 F4
Northfield Dr EH8 ... 124 C4
Northfield E EH33 ... 128 C3
Northfield Farm Ave
EH8 ... 124 C4
Northfield Farm Rd EH8 ... 124 C4
Northfield Gdns
Clackmannan FK10 ... 11 D2
Edinburgh EH8 ... 124 C4
Prestonpans EH32 ... 127 F4
Northfield Gr EH8 ... 124 C4
Northfield Mdws EH47 ... 170 B1
Northfield Park Gr EH8 ... 124 C4
Northfield Pk EH8 ... 124 C4
Northfield Rd Denny FK6 ... 36 B2
Edinburgh EH8 ... 124 B4
Northfield Sq EH8 ... 124 C4
Northfield Terr
Edinburgh EH8 ... 124 B4
Longridge EH47 ... 170 B1
Northflat Pl ML8 ... 230 A1
Northlawn Ct EH4 ... 91 F2
Northlawn Terr EH4 ... 91 F2
Northrig Cotts EH41 ... 133 D4
Northumberland
Place La EH3 ... 232 C4
Northumberland St EH3 ... 232 C4
Northumberland Street
North East La EH3 ... 93 E1
Northumberland Street
North West La EH3 ... 232 C4
Northumberland Street
South East La EH3 ... 232 C4
Northumberland Street
South West La EH3 ... 232 C4
Northwood Pk EH54 ... 146 C4
Norton Pk EH7 ... 94 A1
Norton Pl KY11 ... 29 F1
Norton St FK12 ... 5 D4
Norval Pl KY11 ... 46 C2
Norwood Ave Alloa FK10 ... 9 F4
Bonnybridge FK4 ... 58 A4
Whitburn EH47 ... 170 A3
Norwood Cres FK10 ... 9 F4
Norwood Ct
Bonnybridge FK4 ... 58 A4
Whitburn EH47 ... 170 A3
Norwood Gr FK10 ... 9 F4
Norwood Pl FK4 ... 58 A4
Novar Cres KY1 ... 17 D1
Nungate Rd EH39 ... 54 A4
Nunraw Abbey EH41 ... 134 C1
Nursery Rd FK1 ... 59 F2

Oak Ave EH20 ... 180 C4
Oak Bank FK2 ... 61 D1
Oak Cres Mayfield EH22 ... 183 F3
Plean FK7 ... 20 B2
Oak Dr Fallin FK7 ... 8 B2
Larbert FK5 ... 38 B1
Oak Gr Dunfermline KY11 ... 46 C4
Livingston EH54 ... 148 A3
Oak La EH12 ... 91 F1
Oak Pl EH22 ... 183 F3
Oak St FK8 ... 1 C1
Oakbank Ave EH53 ... 148 C1
Oakbank Cotts EH55 ... 172 B3
Oakbank Park Dr EH53 ... 174 B4
Oakbank Park Rd EH53 ... 174 B4
Oakbank Park Way EH54 ... 174 B4
Oakbank Pk EH54 ... 174 A4
Oakbank Pl EH52 ... 88 A1
Oakbank Rd EH53 ... 148 C1
Oakbank Rdbt EH53 ... 174 B4
Oakfield Pl EH8 ... 233 E2
Oakfield St KY4 ... 12 C4
Oakhill View FK2 ... 83 D3
Oaklands Sch EH11 ... 121 F2
Oaktree Ct KY1 ... 17 E4
Oaktree Junc EH41 ... 131 D4
Oaktree Sq KY1 ... 17 E4
Oakville Terr EH6 ... 94 A2
Oatlands Pk EH49 ... 85 D3
Oatridge Ag Coll EH52 ... 116 C4
Oberon FK10 ... 9 F4
Observatory Gn EH9 ... 123 F1
Observatory Rd EH9 ... 123 F1
Ochil Ave KY2 ... 16 C3
Ochil Cres FK8 ... 2 A1
Ochil Ct Queensferry EH30 ... 89 E4
Tullibody FK10 ... 4 B2
Ochil Dr Maddiston FK2 ... 83 D3
Stenhousemuir FK5 ... 38 C2
Ochil La EH47 ... 169 F3
Ochil Rd Alva FK12 ... 5 D4
Menstrie FK11 ... 4 A4
Stirling FK9 ... 2 B2
Ochil St Alloa FK10 ... 10 A4
Fallin FK7 ... 8 B2
Grangemouth FK3 ... 61 E4
Tullibody FK10 ... 4 A2
Ochil Terr KY11 ... 29 F1
Ochil View Denny FK6 ... 57 E4
Kincardine FK10 ... 23 E2
Shieldhill FK1 ... 81 E4
Ochilmount FK7 ... 7 F1
Ochiltree Cres EH53 ... 148 A1
Ochiltree Ct EH53 ... 148 A1
Ochiltree Dr EH53 ... 148 A1
Ochiltree Gdns EH16 ... 124 B1
Ochiltree Terr FK1 ... 59 D3
Ochilview Alva FK12 ... 5 D4
Cowdenbeath KY4 ... 13 F3
Cowie FK7 ... 20 C3
Ochilview Dr KY12 ... 26 A1
Ochilview Pk
(Stenhousemuir FC)
FK5 ... 38 B2
Ochilview Pl EH51 ... 63 F3
Ochilview Rd EH51 ... 63 F3
Ochilview Terr EH51 ... 63 F3
Ochville Terr FK10 ... 5 E2
Octavia St KY2 ... 17 D3
Ogilface Cres EH48 ... 142 B1
Ogilvie Pl FK9 ... 2 A3
Ogilvie Rd FK8 ... 7 D3
Ogilvie Terr EH11 ... 122 C2
Ogilvie Way EH54 ... 147 E4
Ogilvy Cres EH47 ... 193 F3
Old Abbey Rd EH39 ... 54 A4
Old Bellsdyke Rd FK5 ... 38 A2
Old Bridge St FK10 ... 10 A3
Old Broughton 4 EH3 ... 93 E1
Old Burdiehouse Rd
EH17 ... 155 D2
Old Church La EH15 ... 124 B3
Old Craighall Junc EH21 .. 126 A1
Old Craighall Rd EH22 ... 156 C4
Old Dalkeith Rd EH22 ... 156 B3
Old Dean Rd EH32 ... 98 B2
Old Denny Rd FK5 ... 38 A2
Old Drove Rd
Cambusbarron FK7 ... 6 B3
West Linton EH46 ... 219 D2
Old Eastfield St ML7 ... 168 B3
Old Edinburgh Rd EH22 ... 156 C2
Old Farm Ave EH13 ... 153 E4
Old Farm Pl EH13 ... 153 D4
Old Fishmarket Cl EH1 ... 233 D3
Old Forge Gr KY12 ... 26 C4
Old Hillview Pl KY4 ... 30 C3
Old Kirk Pl KY12 ... 29 E2
Old Kirk Rd
Dunfermline KY12 ... 29 E2
Edinburgh EH12 ... 121 F4
North Queensferry KY11 .. 68 B3
Old Linbun Rd KY11 ... 29 F2
Old Liston Rd EH28 ... 119 D3
Old Mill Ct EH47 ... 170 C4
Old Mill Ctyd The KY11 ... 29 D1
Old Mill Gr EH47 ... 170 C4
Old Mill La
Edinburgh EH16 ... 124 A1
Gifford EH41 ... 163 F3
Oakley KY12 ... 26 C3
Old Mill Rd
Broxburn EH52 ... 117 F3
Shotts ML7 ... 191 D1
Old Newmills Rd EH14 ... 151 E2
Old Orch The KY11 ... 45 E2
Old Perth Rd KY4 ... 13 D2
Old Redding Rd FK2 ... 60 C2
Old Refinery Rd FK3 ... 62 A4
Old School Ct FK10 ... 4 A1
Old Star Rd EH22 ... 183 D3
Old Tolbooth Wynd EH8 ... 233 E3
Old Town Bannockburn FK7 ... 7 E1
Broxburn EH52 ... 117 F3
Oldwalls Pl FK3 ... 61 F4
Oldwalls Rd FK3 ... 62 B4
Oldwood Pl EH54 ... 147 D2
Olive Bank Rd EH21 ... 126 A3
Oliver Rd FK1 ... 60 B2
Olympia Arc KY1 ... 17 D2
Onich Pl ML7 ... 192 A2
Onslow St EH54 ... 148 A3
Orchard Bank EH4 ... 92 C1
Orchard Brae EH4 ... 92 C1
Orchard Brae Ave EH4 ... 92 C1
Orchard Brae Gdns EH4 ... 92 C1
Orchard Brae Gdns W 1
EH4 ... 92 C1
Orchard Brae W EH4 ... 92 C1
Orchard Cres
Edinburgh EH4 ... 92 B1
Prestonpans EH32 ... 96 C1
Orchard Ct
East Linton EH40 ... 103 F4
Kinghorn KY3 ... 35 D2
Longniddry EH32 ... 98 B2
Orchard Dr EH4 ... 92 B1
Orchard Gdns KY3 ... 35 D2
Orchard Gr Edinburgh EH4 ... 92 C1
Haddington EH41 ... 101 D1
Kincardine FK10 ... 23 F2
Maddiston FK2 ... 83 D3
Polmont FK2 ... 61 F1
Orchard House Hospl FK8 ... 2 A1
Orchard La
Dunfermline KY11 ... 29 E1
Dysart KY1 ... 18 A4
Orchard Pl Dysart KY1 ... 18 A4
Edinburgh EH4 ... 92 C1
Livingston EH54 ... 147 D3
Orchard Rd Bridge of A FK9 ... 2 A3
Edinburgh EH4 ... 92 C1
Grangemouth FK3 ... 62 B4
Kinghorn KY3 ... 34 C2
Orchard Rd S EH4 ... 92 B1
Orchard Sq KY11 ... 45 E2

Orchard St Falkirk FK1 60 A3
Grangemouth FK3 61 E4
Orchard Terr
Clackmannan FK10 11 E1
Edinburgh EH4 92 C1
Kinghorn KY3 34 C2
Torryburn KY12 26 C1
Orchard The
Brightons FK2 82 B4
Crossford KY12 28 A1
Ormiston EH35 159 F4
Tranent EH33 128 B4
Tullibody FK10 4 A1
Orchard Toll EH4 92 C1
Orchard View EH22 156 C1
Orchardcroft FK8 7 D4
Orchardfield EH40 103 E4
Orchardfield Ave EH12 121 E3
Orchardfield Terr EH27 150 A3
Orchardhead Loan EH16 155 D4
Orchardhead Rd EH16 155 D4
Ordnance Rd KY12 44 B4
Oriel Cres KY2 17 D2
Oriel Rd KY2 16 C3
Orkney Ct FK10 10 A3
Orkney Pl Falkirk FK1 60 A1
Kirkcaldy KY1 17 F4
Orlit Cotts EH39 74 B2
Ormelie Terr EH15 125 E4
Ormidale Terr EH12 122 B4
Ormiston Ave EH33 128 C3
Ormiston Cres E EH33 128 C3
Ormiston Cres W EH33 128 C3
Ormiston Dr Alloa FK10 4 C1
East Calder EH53 149 D2
Ormiston Pk KY12 29 E3
Ormiston Pl EH32 96 C1
Ormiston Prim Sch EH35 159 F4
Ormiston Rd EH33 128 B3
Orr Terr ML7 168 B2
Orrin Gr KY11 48 A2
Orrock Dr KY3 33 F1
Orrok Pk EH16 124 A1
Orwell Pl
Dunfermline KY12 29 E2
Edinburgh EH11 122 C3
Orwell Prim Sch EH10 122 C3
Orwell Terr EH11 122 C3
Osborne Ct EH32 97 E2
Osborne Dr FK10 23 F2
Osborne Gdns FK1 59 F2
Osborne St FK1 59 F2
Osborne Terr
Cockenzie & Port Seton
EH32 97 E2
Edinburgh EH12 122 C4
Ossian Dr EH54 173 F3
Oswald Ave FK3 61 F4
Oswald Ct EH9 123 E2
Oswald Rd EH9 123 E2
Oswald St FK1 60 A2
Oswald Terr EH12 121 E3
Oswalds Wynd KY1 17 E2
Otterburn Pk EH14 153 D4
Otterston Gr KY11 48 A2
Otterston Pl KY2 16 C4
Oudenarde Ct ML8 230 A1
Our Lady of Lourdes
RC Prim Sch EH47 171 E4
Our Lady's RC Prim Sch
EH47 171 D1
Overhaven KY11 45 F2
Overton Cres Denny FK6 36 B1
East Calder EH53 149 D2
Redding FK2 61 D1
Overton Mains KY1 17 F4
Overton Rd
Grangemouth, Bowhouse
FK3 61 F3
Grangemouth, Oil Refinery
FK3 62 A4
Kirkcaldy KY1 17 E4
Owen sq EH54 147 F1
Oxcars Dr KY11 48 A2
Oxcraig St EH5 92 C4
Oxenfoord Ave EH37 185 D3
Oxenfoord Dr EH37 185 D3
Oxford St EH8 233 F1
Oxford Terr EH4 232 A4
Oxgang Rd FK3 61 F4
Oxgangs Ave EH13 153 F4
Oxgangs Bank EH13 153 F3
Oxgangs Brae EH13 153 F3
Oxgangs Broadway EH13 153 F3
Oxgangs Cres EH13 153 F4
Oxgangs Dr EH13 153 F4
Oxgangs Farm Ave EH13 153 F3
Oxgangs Farm Dr EH13 153 F3
Oxgangs Farm Gdns
EH13 153 F3
Oxgangs Farm Gr EH13 153 F3
Oxgangs Farm Loan
EH13 153 F3
Oxgangs Farm Terr EH13 153 F3
Oxgangs Gdns EH13 153 F4
Oxgangs Gn EH13 153 F4
Oxgangs Gr EH13 153 F4
Oxgangs Hill EH13 153 F4
Oxgangs Ho EH13 153 F4
Oxgangs Loan EH13 153 F4
Oxgangs Medway EH13 153 F3
Oxgangs Path EH13 153 F3
Oxgangs Pk EH13 153 F3
Oxgangs Pl EH13 153 F4
Oxgangs Prim Sch EH13 153 E4
Oxgangs Rd EH10 154 A3
Oxgangs Rd N EH13 153 F4
Oxgangs Rise EH13 153 F4
Oxgangs Row EH13 153 F3
Oxgangs St EH13 153 F3
Oxgangs Terr EH13 153 F3
Oxgangs View EH13 153 F3

Paddock The Gullane EH31 52 A1
Musselburgh EH21 126 B4
North Berwick EH39 54 B3
Paddockholm The EH12 121 F3
Page St KY5 14 A4
Paisley Ave EH8 124 B4
Paisley Cres EH8 124 B4
Paisley Dr EH8 124 B4
Paisley Gdns EH8 124 B4
Paisley Gr EH8 124 B4
Paisley Terr EH8 124 B4
Palmer Pl EH14 151 F2
Palmer Rd EH14 151 F2
Palmer Rise EH54 147 F1
Palmerston Pl EH12 232 A3
Palmerston Place La
EH12 232 A2
Palmerston Rd EH9 123 E3
Pan Ha' KY1 18 A3
Panbrae Rd EH51 63 F4
Pankhurst Loan EH22 157 E2
Panmure Pl EH3 232 C1
Pannie Rd KY1 17 E4
Panstead St FK3 61 F4
Panton Gn EH54 147 D4
Papana Cotts EH41 134 B1
Papple Farm Cotts EH41 134 B3
Paradise La FK10 23 F2
Paradykes Ave EH20 181 D4
Paradykes Prim Sch EH20 181 D4
Pardovan Cres EH49 86 B4
Pardovan Pl FK1 59 F3
Pariothall 9 EH3 93 D1
Paris Ave FK6 36 C1
Paris St FK3 61 F4
Park Ave Bankhead FK4 57 F3
Bilston EH25 180 B3
Brightons FK2 82 B4
Cowdenbeath KY4 13 E2
Dunbar EH42 78 B1
Dunfermline KY12 29 D2
Edinburgh EH15 125 D4
Gorebridge EH23 183 E1
Laurieston FK2 60 C2
Loanhead EH20 181 D4
Musselburgh EH21 126 C3
Stenhousemuir FK5 38 B1
Stirling FK8 7 D3
Park Cres Alloa FK10 5 E1
Bannockburn FK7 7 E1
Bonnyrigg and Lasswade
EH19 182 A4
Easthouses EH22 183 E4
Edinburgh EH16 155 D4
Falkirk FK2 39 D1
Gifford EH41 163 F3
Loanhead EH20 181 D4
Westquarter FK2 61 D2
Park Ct Broxburn EH52 117 D3
Musselburgh EH21 126 C3
Park Dr Bannockburn FK7 7 E1
Brightons FK2 82 B4
Stenhousemuir FK5 38 B1
West Calder EH55 173 D3
Park Gdns Bannockburn FK7 7 E1
Edinburgh EH16 155 D4
Musselburgh EH21 126 C3
Park Gr Broxburn EH52 117 D3
Edinburgh EH16 155 D4
Park Grove Pl EH21 126 C3
Park Grove Terr EH21 126 C3
Park Hill EH23 183 D1
Park La Aberdour KY3 49 D4
Bo'ness EH51 64 A4
Edinburgh EH15 125 D4
Haddington EH41 131 F4
Musselburgh EH21 126 C3
Stirling FK8 7 D4
Park Lea KY11 47 D3
Park Par EH47 193 F3
Park Pl Alloa FK10 10 B4
Clackmannan FK10 11 D2
Dunfermline KY12 29 D2
Edinburgh EH6 93 E3
Hill of B KY4 30 C4
Kinghorn KY3 34 C1
Kirkcaldy KY1 17 D2
Livingston EH54 147 D3
Stirling FK7 6 C3
Park Prim Sch FK10 10 A3
Park Rd Blackridge EH48 142 C2
Bonnyrigg and Lasswade
EH19 182 A4
Broxburn EH52 117 F3
Cockenzie & Port Seton
EH32 97 E2
Cowdenbeath KY4 13 D2
Dalkeith EH22 156 C1
Edinburgh EH6 93 E3
Falkirk FK2 39 D1
Gifford EH41 163 F2
Gorebridge EH23 183 E1
Grangemouth FK3 61 E4
Harthill ML7 169 D3
Kirkcaldy KY1 17 F4
Menstrie FK11 4 A3
Newtongrange EH22 183 D3
Ormiston EH35 159 E3
Rosyth KY11 46 C3
Shotts ML7 191 E3
Park Rd W KY11 46 B3
Park Road Prim Sch KY11 47 D2
Park St Alva FK12 5 D4
Cowdenbeath KY4 13 E2
Cowie FK7 20 C4
Falkirk FK1 60 A3
High Bonnybridge FK4 58 B2
Lochgelly KY5 14 A4
Park Terr Brightons FK2 82 B4
Broxburn EH52 117 D3
Kirknewton EH27 149 F1
Newcraighall EH21 125 F2
Stirling FK8 7 D3
Tullibody FK10 4 A1
Park View Brightons FK2 82 C4
Broxburn EH52 117 D3
Fauldhouse EH47 193 F4
Kirkcaldy KY2 16 C3
Loanhead EH20 181 D4
Musselburgh EH21 126 C3
Pencaitland EH34 160 C4
Prestonpans EH32 97 D1
Stoneyburn EH47 171 E1
Westfield EH48 112 C2
Whitburn EH47 170 A4
Park View E EH32 97 E2
Park View Terr KY11 47 D1
Park View W EH32 97 E2
Park-View EH32 98 C3
Parkandarroch Cres
ML8 230 A1
Parkdyke FK7 6 C3
Parkend Cres FK1 81 E3
Parker Ave EH7 94 C1
Parker Rd EH7 94 C1
Parker Terr EH7 94 C1
Parkfoot Ct FK1 60 A2
Parkgate Alva FK12 4 C3
Rosyth KY11 46 C2
Parkgrove Ave EH4 91 E1
Parkgrove Bank EH4 91 E1
Parkgrove Cres EH4 91 E1
Parkgrove Dr EH4 91 E1
Parkgrove Gdns EH4 91 E1
Parkgrove Gn EH4 91 E1
Parkgrove Loan EH4 91 E1
Parkgrove Neuk EH4 91 E1
Parkgrove Path EH4 91 E1
Parkgrove Pl EH4 91 E1
Parkgrove Rd EH4 91 E1
Parkgrove Row EH4 91 E1
Parkgrove St EH4 91 E1
Parkgrove Terr EH4 91 E1
Parkgrove View EH4 91 E1
Parkhall Dr FK2 83 D3
Parkhead Ave EH11 121 F1
Parkhead Cotts EH55 172 C1
Parkhead Cres
Edinburgh EH11 121 F1
West Calder EH55 172 C2
Parkhead Ct FK10 10 B4
Parkhead Dr EH11 121 F1
Parkhead Gdns
Edinburgh EH11 121 F1
West Calder EH55 172 C2
Parkhead Gr EH11 121 F1
Parkhead Loan EH11 121 F1
Parkhead Pk EH22 183 E4
Parkhead Pl
Easthouses EH22 183 E4
Edinburgh EH11 121 F1
Parkhead Prim Sch
EH55 172 C2
Parkhead Rd Alloa FK10 10 B4
Falkirk FK1 60 A1
Linlithgow EH49 84 C4
Parkhead St EH11 121 F1
Parkhead Terr EH11 121 F1
Parkhead View EH11 121 F1
Parkland Gr Comrie KY12 26 B4
Stoneyburn EH47 170 C1
Parklands EH52 117 E2
Parklands Cres KY11 48 A2
Parkneuk Rd KY12 28 B3
Parkside EH28 119 D3
Parkside Ct Dalkeith EH22 157 D2
Plean FK7 20 B2
Parkside Pl EH22 157 D2
Parkside Rd ML7 191 E2
Parkside Sq KY11 47 D2
Parkside St
Edinburgh EH8 233 F1
Rosyth KY11 46 C2
Parkside Terr EH16 233 F1
Parkvale Pl EH6 94 A2
Parkview Ave FK1 59 F1
Parkway FK10 10 A4
Parkwood Cres EH52 117 E2
Parkwood Gdns EH52 117 E3
Parliament Sq EH1 233 D3
Parliament St EH6 93 F3
Parrotshot EH15 125 D3
Parsonage The EH21 126 B3
Parsons Green Prim Sch
EH8 124 B4
Parsons Green Terr 1
EH8 94 B1
Parsonspool
Bonnyrigg and Lasswade
EH19 182 B3
Dunbar EH42 78 B1
Paterson Dr FK1 81 E3
Paterson Pl Bonnybridge
FK4 58 B3
Bridge of A FK9 2 A3
Paterson Way KY11 29 D1
Paterson's Ct EH52 117 F3
Path Brae EH29 89 D1
Path The Bannockburn FK7 7 E1
Kirkcaldy KY1 17 E3
Pathead Prim Sch KY1 17 D1
Pathfoot Ave FK9 2 B4
Pathfoot Dr FK9 2 B4
Pathfoot Rd FK9 2 B3
Pathhead Ct KY1 17 E3
Pathhead Prim Sch
EH37 185 D2
Patie's Rd EH14 153 E4
Paton St Alloa FK10 10 A4
Dunfermline KY12 29 E3
Patrick Dr FK1 81 F4
Patterson La KY4 13 E2
Patterson Pl KY2 17 D3
Patterson St KY2 17 D3
Pattison St EH6 94 A3
Pattle Ct EH39 54 A4
Paul Dr FK2 22 C2
Paul Pl KY4 13 E2
Paul St KY5 14 A3
Pavilion View FK10 9 F4
Paxstone Cres ML7 168 C3
Paxstone Dr ML7 168 C3
Paxton Cres KY5 14 A4
Paxton Pl KY5 14 A4
Peachdales EH41 131 F4
Peacock Ct EH6 93 E4
Peacocktail Cl EH15 125 D2
Pearce Ave EH12 121 E4
Pearce Gr EH12 121 E4
Pearce Rd EH12 121 E4
Pearson Ave FK4 57 E3
Pearson Pl FK4 57 E3
Peathill Rd FK4 58 A3
Peatville Gdns EH14 122 A1
Peatville Terr EH14 122 A1
Peddie Pl FK3 61 F4
Peden St ML7 168 B3
Peebles Rd EH26 203 F2
Peebles St KY1 35 D4
Peel Pentland Ctr
EH20 155 D1
Peel Prim Sch EH54 147 E2
Peel Rdbt EH54 147 E2
Peel Terr EH9 123 F2
Peffer Bank EH16 124 B2
Peffer Ind Est EH16 124 B2
Peffer Pl EH16 124 B2
Peffer St EH16 124 B2
Peffer's Pl EH41 132 A4
Peffermill Ind Est EH16 124 B2
Peffermill Prim Sch
EH16 124 B2
Peffermill Rd EH16 124 B2
Peggy's Mill Rd EH4 91 D2
Peirson Rd KY11 29 F2
Pelstream Ave FK7 7 D2
Pembroke Pl EH12 122 C4
Pembroke St FK5 38 B2
Pencaitland Prim Sch
EH34 160 C3
Pencraig Brae EH40 103 E3
Penders La FK1 60 A3
Pendreich Ave EH19 182 B4
Pendreich Dr EH19 182 B4
Pendreich Gr EH19 182 B4
Pendreich Terr EH19 182 B4
Pendreich View EH19 182 B4
Pendreich Way FK9 2 A2
Penicuik High Sch EH26 203 F3
Penicuik Rd EH25 180 C2
Pennelton Pl EH51 63 F3
Pennyschool Pl FK10 11 D2
Pennywell Ct EH4 92 A3
Pennywell Gdns EH4 92 A3
Pennywell Gr EH4 92 A3
Pennywell Medway EH4 92 A3
Pennywell Pl EH4 92 A3
Pennywell Rd EH4 92 A3
Pennywell Villas EH4 92 A3
Pentland Ave
Bathgate EH48 145 F3
Currie EH14 151 F2
Edinburgh EH13 153 D4
Newton Grange EH23 183 D2
Penicuik EH26 203 F3
Pentland Cres
Edinburgh EH10 154 A4
Rosewell EH24 181 E2
Pentland Ct Bilston EH25 180 C3
Dalgety Bay KY11 48 B2
Pentland Dr
Edinburgh EH10 153 F3
Whitburn EH47 170 B3
Pentland Gait Off Pk
EH11 121 D1
Pentland Gr EH10 154 A4
Pentland Hills
Regional Pk EH14, EH26 201 E4
Pentland Ind Est EH20 181 D4
Pentland Pk
Livingston EH54 148 A2
Loanhead EH20 180 C4
Pentland Pl Currie EH14 151 F2
Kirkcaldy KY2 16 C3
Pentland Rd
Bonnyrigg and Lasswade
EH19 182 A4
Edinburgh EH13 153 D4
Edinburgh, Old Pentland
EH10 154 B1
Pentland Rise KY11 48 B3
Pentland Terr
Dunfermline KY11 29 F1
Edinburgh EH10 154 A4
High Valleyfield KY12 26 A1
Penicuik EH26 203 F3
Pentland View Currie EH14 151 F2
Dalkeith EH22 157 E1
Edinburgh EH10 154 A3
Uphall EH52 117 D3
Pentland View Cres
EH25 180 C2
Pentland View Ct EH54 147 D3
Pentland View Pl EH25 180 C2
Pentland View Rd
Kirkliston EH29 89 D1
Roslin EH25 180 C2
Pentland View Terr EH25 180 C2
Pentland Way FK3 61 F3
Pentland Wlk EH47 170 B3
Pentlands Gdns EH10 154 A4
Peppercraig Quarry
Ind Site EH41 100 C1
Percival St KY2 17 D3
Perdieus Mount KY12 29 D1
Perdrixknowe EH14 122 B1
Perth Rd KY4 13 E3
Perth St EH3 93 D1
Petershill Gdns EH48 145 E4
Peterswell Brae FK7 7 F1
Pettigrew's Cl EH22 157 D2
Pettycur Bay KY3 34 C1
Pettycur Rd KY3 34 C1
Peveril Rise EH54 173 F4
Peveril Terr EH16 155 D4
Phantassie Sq EH40 103 F4
Philip Ave Bathgate EH48 145 F3
Linlithgow EH49 84 C4
Philip Dr FK5 38 B1
Philip Pl EH26 203 F4
Philip St FK2 60 A4
Philpingstone La EH51 64 B4
Philpingstone Rd EH51 64 B4
Phoenix La KY12 28 C2
Picardy Pl EH1 233 D4
Pier Pl EH6 93 E4
Pier Rd EH51 64 B4
Pierhead Bldgs KY11 68 B3
Piersfield Gr EH8 94 B1
Piersfield Pl EH8 94 B1
Piersfield Terr EH8 94 B1
Piershill La 7 EH8 94 B1
Piershill Pl 8 EH8 94 B1
Piershill Sch EH8 124 B4
Piershill Sq E EH8 94 B1
Piershill Sq W EH8 94 B1
Piershill Terr 9 EH8 94 B1
Pike Rd FK7 7 E2
Pilgrims Hill EH49 85 E4
Pilkham Ct KY4 13 E2
Pilmuir St KY12 29 D3
Pilrig Gdns EH6 93 F2
Pilrig House Cl EH6 93 F2
Pilrig Ind Est EH6 93 F2
Pilrig Park Sch EH6 93 F2
Pilrig St EH6 93 F2
Pilton Ave EH5 92 C3
Pilton Cres EH5 92 C3
Pilton Dr EH5 92 C3
Pilton Dr N EH5 92 C3
Pilton Gdns EH5 92 C3
Pilton Loan EH5 92 C3
Pilton Pk EH5 92 C3
Pilton Pl EH5 92 C3
Pine Gn EH51 63 E2
Pine Gr Alloa FK10 10 B3
Dunfermline KY11 46 C4
Livingston EH54 148 A3
Westquarter FK2 61 D1
Pine St EH42 78 A1
Pine Wlk FK5 38 B1
Pineapple The FK2 22 A3
Pinebank EH54 147 F3
Pines The EH31 52 A2
Pinewood Dr KY11 48 A2
Pinewood Pk EH54 146 C4
Pinewood Pl EH22 183 F3
Pinewood Rd EH22 183 F3
Pinewood Sch EH47 171 F4
Pinewood View EH22 183 F3
Pinkerton Pl KY11 46 C3
Pinkhill EH12 122 A3
Pinkie Ave EH21 126 C3
Pinkie Dr EH21 126 C3
Pinkie Hill Cres EH21 126 C3
Pinkie Pl EH21 126 C3
Pinkie Rd EH21 126 C3
Pinkie St Peter's Prim Sch
EH21 126 C3
Pinkie Terr EH21 126 C3
Pinkie Wlk EH33 128 B3
Pinnel Pl KY11 48 B2
Pipe La EH15 95 D1
Pipe St EH15 95 D1
Piper Cres KY3 33 E1
Pirig Cotts EH6 93 F2
Pirleyhill Dr FK1 81 E3
Pirleyhill Gdns FK1 60 A1
Pirnhall Rd FK7 19 D4
Pirniefield Bank EH6 94 B2
Pirniefield Gdns EH6 94 B2
Pirniefield Gr EH6 94 B2
Pirniefield Pl EH6 94 B2
Pirniefield Terr EH6 94 B2
Pirniehall Prim Sch EH4 92 B3
Pirrie St EH6 93 F2
Pitbauchlie Bank KY11 29 E1
Pitcairn St KY11 29 E1
Pitcorthie Dr KY11 46 C4
Pitcorthie Prim Sch KY11 29 F1
Pitcorthie Rd KY11 29 E1
Pitdinnie Pl KY12 27 E1
Pitdinnie Rd KY12 27 E1
Pitfairn Rd FK10 5 F2

Pitfirane Pk KY12 28 A1
Pitfour Pl KY2 16 B4
Pitlochry Pl 4 EH7 94 A1
Pitreavie Bsns Pk KY11 46 B4
Pitreavie Cres KY11 46 B4
Pitreavie Ct KY11 46 B3
Pitreavie Dr KY11 46 B3
Pitreavie Prim Sch KY11 46 B4
Pitsligo Rd EH10 123 D2
Pitt St EH6 93 F3
Pitt Terr FK8 7 D3
Pittencrieff Ct EH21 126 C3
Pittencrieff House Mus KY12 28 C2
Pittencrieff Prim Sch KY12 28 C2
Pittencrieff St KY12 28 C2
Pittville St EH15 125 E4
Pittville Street La EH15 125 D4
Place Charente EH22 157 E1
Plane Gr KY11 46 C4
Plane St EH42 78 A1
Plantation St KY5 14 A4
Player Gn EH54 147 D4
Players Rd FK7 7 E4
Plean Ctry Pk FK7 20 A1
Pleasance Edinburgh EH8 233 E2
Falkirk FK1 60 A2
Pleasance Brae KY12 27 F1
Pleasance Ct
13 Falkirk FK2 60 A2
Halbeath KY12 30 A4
Pleasance Gdns FK1 60 A2
Pleasance Rd
Dunfermline KY12 29 F3
Falkirk FK2 60 A2
Halbeath KY12 30 A3
Pleasance Row ML11 215 D2
Pleasance Sq 12 FK1 60 A2
Pleasance The EH32 71 E2
Plewlandcroft EH30 68 A1
Plewlands Ave EH10 122 C1
Plewlands Gdns EH10 122 C1
Plewlands Pl EH30 89 D4
Plewlands Terr EH10 122 C1
Pleydell Pl EH16 155 D4
Plough La EH33 128 B3
Plover Brae EH54 147 E3
Poachers Gn FK10 11 D3
Pointgarry Rd EH39 54 A4
Polbeth Ave EH55 172 C3
Polbeth Cres EH55 172 C3
Polbeth Gdns EH55 172 C3
Polbeth Ind Est EH55 172 C3
Polbeth Pl EH55 172 C3
Polbeth Rd EH55 172 C3
Polbeth West Calder Ind Est EH55 172 C3
Poldrate EH41 132 A4
Polkemmet Ctry Pk EH47 169 E4
Polkemmet Dr ML7 169 D3
Polkemmet La ML7 168 C3
Polkemmet Prim Sch EH47 170 A3
Polkemmet Rd
Harthill ML7 168 C3
Whitburn EH47 169 F3
Pollock Halls of Residence (Univ of Edinburgh) EH16 124 A3
Pollock Wlk KY12 28 C3
Polmaise Ave FK7 7 D2
Polmaise Cres FK7 8 B3
Polmaise Ct FK7 7 D2
Polmaise Rd
Cambusbarron FK7 6 C2
Stirling FK7 6 C3
Polmont House Gdns FK2 61 F1
Polmont Pk FK2 61 F2
Polmont Rd FK2 61 D2
Polmont Sta FK2 61 F1
Polson Gdns EH33 128 A3
Polton Avenue Rd EH19 182 A3
Polton Bank EH18 181 F3
Polton Bank Terr EH18 181 F3
Polton Cotts EH18 181 E3
Polton Ct EH19 182 A4
Polton Gdns EH18 182 A4
Polton Pl EH19 182 A4
Polton Rd
Bonnyrigg and Lasswade EH18 182 A4
Loanhead EH20, EH18 181 E4
Polton Rd W EH18 181 F3
Polton St EH19 182 A3
Polton Terr EH18 182 A4
Polwarth Ave FK2 82 B4
Polwarth Cres
Edinburgh EH11 123 D3
Prestonpans EH32 97 D1
Polwarth Gdns EH11 122 C3
Polwarth Gr EH11 122 C3
Polwarth Pk EH11 122 C3
Polwarth Pl EH11 122 C3
Polwarth Terr
Edinburgh EH11 122 C2
Prestonpans EH32 97 D1
Polworth Pl KY4 13 E2
Pomathorn Bank EH26 203 F2
Pomathorn Rd EH26 203 F2
Pompee Rd FK10 5 D1
Ponton St EH3 232 B1
Poolewe Dr FK2 61 E1
Poplar Cres KY2 17 D4
Poplar Gr
Dunfermline KY11 46 C4
Livingston EH54 148 A3
Poplar La EH6 94 A3
Poplar St Dunbar EH42 78 A1
Grangemouth FK3 61 E4
Mayfield EH22 183 F3
Poplar Terr EH19 182 A3
Poplars The FK10 4 A1
Port Buchan EH52 117 E3
Port Edgar Water Sports Ctr EH30 67 F1
Port Hamilton EH3 232 B2
Port St Clackmannan FK10 11 D2
Inverkeithing KY11 47 E1
Stirling FK8 7 D4
Portal Rd FK3 61 E3
Portdownie FK1 59 E3
Porteous' Pend EH1 232 C2
Porterfield KY12 26 C4
Porterfield Rd EH4 92 C2
Portgower Pl EH4 93 D1
Portland Pl Edinburgh EH6 93 F3
Fauldhouse EH47 193 E3
Portland St EH6 93 F3
Portobello High Sch EH15 124 C4
Portobello Rd EH8 94 C1
Portree Cres FK2 62 A1
Portsburgh Sq EH1 232 C2
Post Office La KY11 68 B3
Posthill FK10 5 E1
Potter Pl FK2 39 F2
Potterrow EH8 233 D2
Potters Path EH33 128 B3
Pottery St KY1 17 F4
Pottery The
Edinburgh EH15 95 D1
Prestonpans EH32 96 C1
Pottis Rd FK7 7 E2
Pottishaw Pl EH48 145 E1
Povert Rd EH19, EH23 182 C1
Powdermill Brae EH23 207 E3
Powdrake Rd FK3 61 F4
Pratt St KY1 17 D1
President Kennedy Dr FK7 20 B2
Preston Ave
Linlithgow EH49 84 C3
Prestonpans EH32 97 D1
Preston Cres
Inverkeithing KY11 47 E1
Linlithgow EH49 84 C3
Prestonpans EH32 97 D1
Preston Cross Cotts EH32 97 D1
Preston Ct
Linlithgow EH49 84 C3
Prestonpans EH32 127 F4
Preston Lodge High Sch EH32 97 D1
Preston Mill EH40 103 F4
Preston Pk EH49 84 C3
Preston Pl EH37 185 D2
Preston Rd
East Linton EH40 103 F4
Linlithgow EH49 84 C3
Prestonpans EH32 97 D1
Preston St
High Valleyfield KY12 26 A1
Rosewell EH24 181 E1
Preston Street Prim Sch EH8 233 F1
Preston Terr
Inverkeithing KY11 47 E1
Linlithgow EH49 84 C3
Prestonpans EH32 97 D1
Preston Tower EH32 97 D1
Prestonfield Ave EH16 124 A2
Prestonfield Bank EH16 124 A2
Prestonfield Cres EH16 124 A2
Prestonfield Gdns EH16 124 A2
Prestonfield Prim Sch EH16 124 A2
Prestonfield Rd EH16 124 A2
Prestonfield Terr EH16 124 A2
Prestongrange Rd EH32 127 F4
Prestongrange Terr EH32 96 C1
Prestonhall Cres EH24 181 E1
Prestonhall Rd EH24 181 E1
Prestonkirk Gdns EH40 103 F4
Prestonpans Prim Sch
Prestonpans, Cuthill EH32 96 C1
Prestonpans, Preston EH32 128 A4
Prestonpans Sta EH32 128 A4
Pretoria Pl
Cowdenbeath KY4 13 D2
Polmont FK2 61 F1
Pretoria Rd FK5 38 A1
Priest Bank EH41 134 B1
Priestfield Ave EH16 124 A2
Priestfield Cres EH16 124 A2
Priestfield Gdns EH16 124 A2
Priestfield Gr EH16 124 A3
Priestfield Rd EH16 124 A3
Priestfield Rd N EH16 124 A3
Prime Gilt Box St KY2 17 D3
Primmer Pl KY4 13 E2
Primrose Ave
Grangemouth FK3 61 D3
Rosyth KY11 46 B3
Primrose Bank Rd EH5 93 D3
Primrose Cres EH22 157 E1
Primrose Ct
Broxburn EH52 117 F3
Rosyth KY11 46 B3
Primrose Dr EH30 90 B2
Primrose Gdns
Carrington EH23 206 B3
Queensferry EH30 89 E4
Primrose La
Cowdenbeath KY4 13 E3
Kincardine FK10 23 F2
Rosyth KY11 46 B3
Primrose Pl Alloa FK10 10 A3
Livingston EH54 147 D3
Primrose Rd KY11 46 A3
Primrose St Alloa FK10 10 A4
Bonnybridge FK4 58 A3
Edinburgh EH6 94 A2
Primrose Terr
Dalkeith EH22 157 E1
Edinburgh EH11 122 C3
Prince Regent St EH6 93 F3
Princes St California FK1 81 F3
Edinburgh EH2 232 C3
Falkirk FK1 60 A3
Grangemouth FK3 61 F4
Stirling FK8 7 D4
Princess Margaret Rose Hospl (Orthopaedic) EH10 154 B3
Princess Mary Pl EH41 101 D1
Princess Mary Rd EH41 101 D1
Princess St FK4 58 A3
Priors Grange EH48 113 F3
Priorscroft EH48 113 F3
Priory Gr EH30 89 D4
Priory La KY12 29 D2
Priory Rd Linlithgow EH49 84 C3
Whitecross EH49 83 F3
Priory Sq FK10 23 F2
Priory Wlk EH41 132 B4
Priory Wynd EH39 54 A4
Promenade
Edinburgh EH15 95 D1
Limekilns KY11 45 E2
Musselburgh EH21 126 A4
Prora Cotts EH39 73 E2
Prospect Bank Cres EH6 94 B2
Prospect Bank Gdns EH6 94 A2
Prospect Bank Gr EH6 94 B2
Prospect Bank Pl EH6 94 B2
Prospect Bank Rd EH6 94 B2
Prospect Bank Sch EH6 94 A2
Prospect Bank Terr EH6 94 B2
Prospect St
Cowdenbeath KY4 13 D2
Falkirk FK1 59 F3
Prospecthill Rd FK1 60 A1
Providence Brae EH51 63 F4
Provost Hunter Ave FK12 5 E4
Provost Milne Gr EH30 89 E4
Provost Rd Bo'ness EH51 63 E3
Linlithgow EH49 85 D4
Pryde Ave EH19 182 A4
Pryde Terr EH19 182 A4
Puir Wife's Brae EH48 145 E3
Pullar Ave FK9 2 A3
Pullar Ct FK9 2 A3
Pumpherston Prim Sch EH53 148 A4
Pumpherston Rd EH54, EH53 148 B3
Pyothall Rd EH52 117 E3
Pypers Wynd EH32 96 C1

Quadrant EH39 54 B4
Quadrant La EH39 54 B4
Quadrant The EH26 203 F3
Quakerfield FK7 7 F1
Quality St Dysart KY1 18 A4
Edinburgh EH4 91 F2
North Berwick EH39 54 B4
Quality Street Junc EH4 91 F2
Quality Street La EH4 91 F2
Quaraywood Ct EH54 147 E2
Quarrolhall Cres FK2 39 D2
Quarry Brae Brightons FK2 82 C4
Kirkcaldy KY1 17 F4
Quarry Cl EH8 233 E1
Quarry Cotts EH15 125 D2
Quarry Ct KY4 13 D2
Quarry Howe EH14 151 E1
Quarry Knowe FK7 19 F4
Quarry Pl Alloa FK10 10 B4
Shotts ML7 191 E3
Quarry Rd
Cambusbarron FK7 6 B3
Fauldhouse EH47 193 F3
Shotts ML7 191 E3
Quarry St ML7 191 E3
Quarrybank EH14 152 B4
Quarrybank Cl EH14 152 B4
Quarrybank Ct EH14 152 B4
Quarrybank End EH14 152 B4
Quarryfoot Gdns EH19 182 B4
Quarryfoot Gn EH19 182 B4
Quarryfoot Pl EH19 182 A4
Quarryford Farm Cotts EH41 190 C4
Quarryknowes The EH51 63 F3
Quarryside Ct KY12 28 B3
Quarryview EH14 152 B4
Quayside St EH6 93 F3
Quebec Ave EH54 147 F2
Queen Anne Dr EH28 119 D3
Queen Anne High Sch KY12 28 C3
Queen Anne Pk EH28 119 D3
Queen Anne St KY12 29 D2
Queen Charlotte La EH6 94 A3
Queen Charlotte St EH6 94 A3
Queen Margaret Cl EH10 154 B3
Queen Margaret Coll EH12 121 E4
Queen Margaret Coll (Leith Campus) EH6 94 A2
Queen Margaret Dr EH30 89 E4
Queen Margaret Fauld KY12 29 F3
Queen Margaret Hospl KY12 29 F3
Queen Margaret St KY3 34 C1
Queen Margaret's Pl KY11 68 B3
Queen St Alloa FK10 10 A4
Alva FK12 5 D4
Bannockburn FK7 7 E1
Edinburgh EH2 232 C4
Falkirk FK2 60 B3
Fallin FK7 8 B2
Grangemouth FK3 61 F4
Inverkeithing KY11 47 D1
Stirling FK8 7 D4
Queen Street Gdns E EH3 232 C4
Queen Street Gdns W EH3 232 C4
Queen's Ave
Bridge of A FK9 2 A3
Edinburgh EH4 92 A1
Queen's Ave S EH4 92 B1
Queen's Bay Cres EH15 125 E4
Queen's Bldgs KY11 46 C3
Queen's Cres
Carluke ML8 230 A1
Edinburgh EH9 123 F2
Falkirk FK1 59 F3
Queen's Ct FK9 1 C4
Queen's Dr EH8 233 F2
Queen's Dr Larbert FK5 38 B1
Pencaitland EH34 160 C3
Queen's Gdns EH4 92 B1
Queen's La FK9 2 A4
Queen's Park Ave EH8 94 A1
Queen's Park Ct EH8 124 B4
Queen's Pl EH42 78 C1
Queen's Rd
Broxburn EH52 117 F2
Dunbar EH42 78 C1
Edinburgh EH4 92 B1
Stirling FK8 6 C4
Queen's St FK1 81 F3
Queen's Wlk EH16 124 C2
Queens Ave
Broxburn EH52 117 F2
Haddington EH41 100 C1
Queens Cres KY3 34 C1
Queens Ct FK5 38 B2
Queens Dr Denny FK6 36 C2
Falkirk FK1 59 F3
Queens Gdns EH53 148 C2
Queens Terr EH53 148 C2
Queens Way KY11 46 A1
Queensferry High Sch EH30 89 E4
Queensferry Mus EH30 68 B1
Queensferry Rd
Dunfermline KY11 46 B4
Edinburgh, Braepark EH4 91 D2
Edinburgh, Orchard Brae EH4 92 B1
Kirkliston EH29 89 D1
Rosyth KY11 46 C3
Queensferry St EH2 232 A3
Queensferry Street La EH2 232 B3
Queensferry Terr EH4 92 C1
Queenshaugh KY12 27 E4
Queenshaugh Dr FK8 2 B1
Queensway EH26 203 F4
Quench Rd FK2 62 A3
Quentin Rise EH54 147 F1
Quidenham Ct EH39 54 A3
Quilts The EH6 93 F3
Quilts Wynd EH6 93 F3
Quoiters Ct EH47 171 E4

R L Stevenson's Birthplace & Mus EH3 93 E2
Race Rd EH48 144 C4
Rae Ct FK2 39 E2
Rae St Cowdenbeath KY4 13 E1
Stenhousemuir FK5 38 B2
Rae's Ct EH16 155 D3
Raeburn Cres
Kirkcaldy KY2 17 D2
Whitburn EH47 170 A3
Raeburn Mews EH4 93 D1
Raeburn Pl EH4 93 D1
Raeburn Rigg EH54 147 D3
Raeburn St EH4 93 D1
Raes Gdns EH19 182 B4
Rainhill Ave FK2 82 C3
Raith Ave KY4 13 E2
Raith Cres KY2 17 D2
Raith Dr KY2 17 D2
Raith Gdns KY2 16 C2
Raleigh Ct FK1 59 F3
Ramage Rd ML8 230 A1
Ramillies Ct Carluke ML8 230 A1
Penicuik EH26 204 A4
Ramsay Ave FK2 61 D2
Ramsay Cotts EH19 182 C2
Ramsay Cres
Bathgate EH48 145 E3
Burntisland KY3 34 A1
Mayfield EH22 183 F3
Ramsay Ct EH54 148 B3
Ramsay La
Kincardine FK10 23 F2
Limekilns KY11 45 E2
Ramsay Pl Edinburgh EH15 95 D1
Stirling FK8 2 A1
Ramsay Rd KY1 17 D1
Ramsay Terr EH18 181 F3
Ramsay Wlk EH22 183 F3
Ramsey Ct FK10 23 F2
Ramsey Gdn EH1 232 C3
Ramsey La EH1 232 C3
Ramsey Pl Penicuik EH26 203 E3
Rosyth KY11 46 C2
Ramsey Tullis Ave FK10 4 B1
Ramsey Tullis Dr FK10 4 B1
Randolph Cliff EH3 232 A3
Randolph Cres
Bannockburn FK7 7 E1
Brightons FK2 82 B4
Edinburgh EH3 232 A3
Randolph Ct FK8 7 D3
Randolph Gdns FK6 36 B1
Randolph Ind Est KY1 18 A4
Randolph La EH3 232 B3
Randolph Pl
Bannockburn FK7 7 E1
Edinburgh EH3 232 B3
Kirkcaldy KY1 18 A4
Randolph Rd FK8 7 D3
Randolph St
Cowdenbeath KY4 13 E2
Dunfermline KY12 29 D2
Randolph Terr FK7 7 D2
Randyford Rd FK2 60 B3
Randyford St FK2 60 C3
Range Rd FK3 62 B4
Rankeillor St EH8 233 E1
Rankin Ave EH9 123 F1
Rankin Cres FK4 57 E3
Rankin Dr EH9 123 F1
Rankin Rd EH9 123 F2
Rannoch Ct FK10 10 B3
Rannoch Dr
Crossford KY12 28 A1
Whitburn EH47 170 B4
Rannoch Gr EH4 91 E1
Rannoch Pl Edinburgh EH4 91 E1
Shieldhill FK1 81 F4
Shotts ML7 191 F3
Stenhousemuir FK5 38 C2
Rannoch Rd
Edinburgh EH4 91 E1
Grangemouth FK3 61 E2
Kirkcaldy KY2 16 C4
Rosyth KY11 46 C1
Whitburn EH47 170 B4
Rannoch Terr EH4 91 E1
Rannoch Wlk
Livingston EH54 148 A2
Whitburn EH47 170 B4
Ransome Gdns EH4 91 E1
Raploch Prim Sch FK8 1 C1
Raploch Rd FK8 1 C1
Rashiehill Cres EH55 194 C3
Rashiehill Rd FK1 110 A3
Rashiehill Terr EH55 194 C3
Rashienhill ML11 215 D1
Rashierig EH52 117 D3
Rashierigg Pl EH47 170 A1
Ratcliffe Terr EH9 123 F2
Rathbone Pl EH15 95 D1
Ratho Park Rd EH28 119 F1
Ratho Pl KY11 29 E2
Ratho Prim Sch EH28 119 E1
Rattray Gdns EH47 171 F4
Rattray St EH51 64 A4
Rattray Terr KY5 14 A4
Ravelrig Hill EH14 151 D1
Ravelrig Pk EH14 151 D1
Ravelrig Rd EH14 151 D2
Ravelston Dykes EH12 122 B4
Ravelston Dykes La EH4 122 A4
Ravelston Dykes Rd EH4 122 A4
Ravelston Gdn EH4 122 B4
Ravelston Hts EH4 92 B1
Ravelston House Gr 9 EH4 92 B1
Ravelston House Loan 8 EH4 92 B1
Ravelston House Pk EH4 92 B1
Ravelston House Rd EH4 92 B1
Ravelston Pk EH4 122 C4
Ravelston Rise EH4 122 B4
Ravelston Terr EH4 92 C1
Ravelsykes Rd EH26 203 E3
Ravendean Gdns EH26 203 E3
Ravens Craig KY1 17 E3
Ravenscraig Park Nature Trail KY1 17 F3
Ravenscraig St KY1 17 F3
Ravenscroft Gdns EH17 155 F3
Ravenscroft Pl EH17 155 F3
Ravenscroft St EH17 155 F3
Ravenshaugh Cres EH21 127 D3
Ravenshaugh Rd EH21 127 D4
Ravenswood Ave EH16 124 B1
Ravenswood Rise EH54 173 F4
Rectory La KY1 18 A4
Red Craigs KY2 16 B4
Red Fox Cres EH26 180 A1
Red Row KY11 45 E2
Redbrae Ave EH51 64 A3
Redbrae Rd FK1 59 E3
Redbraes Gr EH7 93 E2
Redbraes Pl EH7 93 E2
Redburn Rd
Blackridge EH48 142 A1
Prestonpans EH32 96 C1
Redburn Rd N EH32 96 C1
Redburn Wynd KY1 17 E2
Redcraig Rd EH53 148 C1

Redcroft Pl EH47 171 D1
Redcroft St EH22 156 A4
Redcroft Terr EH47 171 D1
Redding Ind Est FK2 61 D1
Redding Rd Brightons FK2 82 B4
Redding FK2 61 D1
Reddingmuirhead Rd
FK2 61 D1
Reddoch Rd FK2 62 A2
Redford Ave EH13 153 E3
Redford Bank EH13 153 E3
Redford Cres EH13 153 E3
Redford Dr EH13 153 D3
Redford Gdns EH13 153 E3
Redford Gr EH13 153 E3
Redford Loan EH13 153 E3
Redford Neuk EH13 153 E3
Redford Pl EH13 153 E3
Redford Rd EH13 153 E3
Redford Terr EH13 153 E3
Redford Wlk EH13 153 E3
Redgauntlet Terr EH16 124 B1
Redhall Ave EH14 122 A1
Redhall Bank Rd EH14 122 A1
Redhall Cres EH14 122 A1
Redhall Dr EH14 122 A1
Redhall Gdns EH14 122 A1
Redhall Gr EH14 122 A1
Redhall House Dr
EH14 122 A1
Redhall Pl EH14 122 A1
Redhall Rd EH14 122 A1
Redhall View EH14 122 A1
Redhaws Rd ML7 192 A2
Redheugh Loan EH23 183 E1
Redheughs Ave EH12 121 D2
Redheughs Rigg EH12 121 D2
Redholm Pk EH39 54 C3
Redhouse Cotts EH49 86 C2
Redhouse Ct EH47 171 F4
Redhouse Pl EH47 145 E1
Redhouse Rd EH47 172 A4
Redlands Ct EH47 170 C4
Redlands Rd FK10 4 A2
Redmill Cotts EH47 170 C4
Redmill Ct EH47 170 C4
Redmill View EH47 170 C4
Redmire Cres ML7 212 A4
Redpath Dr FK2 39 D2
Redwell Pl FK10 9 F4
Redwing Brae EH54 147 E3
Redwood Gr EH22 182 C3
Redwood Wlk EH22 183 D3
Reed Dr EH22 183 D4
Reedlands Dr FK6 57 E4
Regal Gr ML7 191 F2
Regent Pl EH7 94 A1
Regent Rd EH7, EH8 233 E4
Regent Sq EH49 85 D4
Regent St
Edinburgh EH15 125 D4
Kincardine FK10 23 F2
Regent Street La EH15 125 D4
Regent Terr EH7 233 F4
Regent Terrace Mews
EH7 233 F4
Regents Way KY11 48 A2
Regis Ct EH4 91 D2
Register Pl EH2 233 D4
Register St EH51 63 F4
Reid Ave KY4 30 C3
Reid St
Dunfermline KY12 29 D2
Lochgelly KY5 14 A4
Reid Terr EH3 93 D1
Reid's Cl EH8 233 F3
Reilly Gdns FK4 58 A2
Reilly Rd FK4 58 A2
Relugas Gdns EH9 123 F2
Relugas Pl EH9 123 F2
Relugas Rd EH9 123 F2
Rendall Gdns EH52 117 F3
Rennie Pl EH40 103 E4
Rennie Sq EH54 173 E3
Rennie St FK1 60 A2
Rennie's Isle EH6 93 F3
Research Ave N
Currie EH14 151 F4
Edinburgh EH14 120 C1
Research Ave S EH14 151 F4
Restalrig Ave EH7 94 B1
Restalrig Cir EH7 94 B2
Restalrig Cres EH7 94 B2
Restalrig Dr EH7 94 B1
Restalrig Gdns EH7 94 B1
Restalrig Pk EH7 94 A2
Restalrig Rd EH6 94 A2
Restalrig Rd S EH7 94 B1
Restalrig Sq EH7 94 B2
Restalrig Terr EH6 94 A2
Reveston La EH47 170 A3
Reynard Gdns EH49 84 A3
Rhodders Gr FK12 5 D4
Rhodes St KY11 29 D1
Riccarton Ave EH14 152 A3
Riccarton Cres EH14 152 A2
Riccarton Dr EH14 152 A3
Riccarton Gr EH14 152 A3
Riccarton Mains Rd
EH14 152 A3
Riccarton Prim Sch
EH14 151 F2
Riccarton Rd EH49 84 C3
Richmond Dr FK2 82 B4
Richmond La EH8 233 E2
Richmond Pl
Edinburgh EH8 233 E2
Lochgelly KY5 14 A4
Richmond Terr
Bo'ness EH51 63 F4
Edinburgh EH11 232 A2
Riddochhill Cres EH47 171 E4
Riddochhill Ct EH47 171 D4
Riddochhill Dr EH47 171 E4
Riddochhill Rd EH47 171 E4
Riddochhill View EH47 171 D4
Ridge Way KY11 48 A3
Riding Pk EH4 91 D2
Ridley Dr KY11 46 C2
Riego St EH3 232 B2
Rifle Rd FK3 62 B4
Rig Pl EH32 71 E2
Rig St EH32 71 E2
Rigg Pk EH42 78 B1
Riggs View KY12 27 E1
Rigley Terr EH32 127 F4
Rillbank Cres EH9 233 D1
Rillbank Terr EH9 123 E3
Rimmon Cres ML7 191 F3
Ring Rd FK10 10 A4
Ringwood Pl EH16 155 D4
Rintoul Ave KY12 26 A4
Rintoul Pl Blairhall KY12 26 A4
Edinburgh EH3 93 D1
Riselaw Cres EH10 154 A4
Riselaw Pl EH10 154 A4
Riselaw Rd EH10 154 A4
Riselaw Terr EH10 154 A4
Ritchie Pl Bo'ness EH51 64 A3
Edinburgh EH11 122 C3
Grangemouth FK3 61 E3
Rivaldsgreen Cres EH49 85 D3
River St FK2 39 D1
River View KY11 48 A1
River Wlk KY11 48 A1
Riverbank View FK8 7 E4
Riversdale Cres EH12 122 B4
Riversdale Gr EH12 122 B4
Riversdale Rd EH12 122 B4
Riverside Edinburgh EH4 91 E4
Newbridge EH28 118 C3
Riverside Ct EH54 147 E2
Riverside Dr
Haddington EH41 101 D1
Stirling FK8 2 B1
Riverside Gdns EH21 126 A3
Riverside Pl EH41 101 E1
Riverside Prim Sch
Livingston EH54 148 A2
Stirling FK8 2 A1
Riverside Rd
Craigiehall EH30 90 C2
Grangemouth FK2 62 A3
Riverside Terr FK10 23 F2
Riverside View FK10 10 A2
Road 10 FK3 62 B3
Road 11 FK3 62 B3
Road 13 FK3 62 B3
Road 15 FK3 62 B3
Road 24 FK3 62 A3
Road 25 FK3 62 A3
Road 27 FK3 62 A3
Road 28 FK3 62 A3
Road 29 FK3 62 A3
Road 30b FK3 62 A3
Road 30c FK3 62 A3
Road 31 FK3 62 A3
Road 32 FK3 62 A3
Road 33 FK2, FK3 62 A3
Road 4 FK3 62 B3
Road 4a FK3 62 B3
Road 4b FK3 62 B3
Road 6 FK3 62 B3
Road 7 FK3 62 B3
Road 9 FK3 62 B3
Roanhead Terr FK10 23 F2
Roanshead Rd EH22 183 E4
Robb's Loan EH14 122 B2
Robb's Loan Gr EH14 122 B2
Robert Bruce Ct FK5 38 A1
Robert Burns Dr EH16 124 A1
Robert Burns Mews
EH22 157 E2
Robert Dick Ct FK10 4 B1
Robert Hardie Ct FK5 38 B1
Robert Kinmond Ave FK10 4 B1
Robert Knox Ave FK10 4 B1
Robert Smillie Ave EH22 183 F3
Robert Smith Ct KY4 13 F3
Robert St ML7 191 F2
Roberts Ave FK2 61 E1
Roberts St KY1 17 F4
Robertson Ave
Bathgate EH48 144 C3
Bonnybridge FK4 58 A3
Edinburgh EH11 122 B3
Prestonpans EH32 97 D1
Tranent EH33 128 B3
Robertson Bank EH23 207 E3
Robertson Ct EH48 143 F2
Robertson Dr EH33 128 B4
Robertson Pl FK7 7 D2
Robertson Rd KY12 29 E3
Robertson St FK12 5 D4
Robertson Way EH54 147 E4
Robertson's Cl
Dalkeith EH22 157 D2
Edinburgh EH1 233 E2
Robertsons Bank EH37 207 E4
Robins Neuk EH33 129 E3
Rocheid Pk EH4 92 C2
Rochester Terr EH10 123 D2
Rocks Rd KY11 45 D2
Rockville Gr EH49 85 D3
Rockville Terr EH19 182 A4
Roddinglaw Rd EH12 120 B2
Rodel Dr FK2 61 F1
Rodney Pl EH7 93 E1
Rodney St Edinburgh EH7 93 E1
Grangemouth FK3 61 E3
Roebuck Pl EH51 63 E3
Rolland St KY12 29 D2
Roman Camp EH37 185 D2
Roman Camp Cotts
EH52 117 E1
Roman Camp Way
EH37 185 D2
Roman Dr FK1 59 E3
Roman Rd
Bonnybridge FK4 58 A2
Inverkeithing KY11 47 D1
Roman Way EH51 63 E3
Romero Pl EH16 123 F3
Romyn Rd KY11 46 B1
Ronades Rd FK2 60 A4
Ronald Cres FK5 38 A1
Ronald Pl FK8 7 D4
Ronaldshay Cres FK3 61 F4
Ronaldson Gr KY12 29 E3
Ronaldson's Wharf EH6 93 F3
Rood Well Cotts EH42 104 C1
Roodlands General Hospl
EH41 100 C1
Roods Cres KY11 47 D2
Roods Rd KY11 47 D1
Roods Sq KY11 47 E2
Roomlin Gdns KY1 17 F4
Roosevelt Rd EH27 149 F2
Rope Wlk EH32 96 C1
Ropeway KY11 46 A1
Rosabelle Rd EH25 180 C2
Rosabelle St KY1 17 F4
Rose Ave EH19 182 B3
Rose Cotts EH19 182 B3
Rose Cres KY12 29 D2
Rose Ct EH4 91 F2
Rose Gdns
Bonnyrigg and Lasswade
EH19 182 B3
Cairneyhill KY12 27 E1
Rose Gr EH19 182 B3
Rose La Lochgelly KY5 14 A4
Queensferry EH30 68 A1
Torryburn KY12 26 C1
Rose Pk EH5 93 D3
Rose Pl EH19 182 B3
Rose St Alloa FK10 4 C1
Bonnybridge FK4 58 A3
Burntisland KY3 50 C4
Cowdenbeath KY4 13 E2
Dunfermline KY12 29 D2
Edinburgh EH2 232 C3
Rose Street North La
EH2 232 C3
Rose Street South La
EH2 232 C3
Rose Terr
Bonnyrigg and Lasswade
EH19 182 B3
Denny FK6 36 B1
Stenhousemuir FK5 38 C2
Rose Way EH19 182 B3
Rosebank Alloa FK10 5 E1
Cowdenbeath KY4 13 E2
Dunfermline KY11 29 E1
Rosebank Ave FK1 59 F3
Rosebank Cotts EH3 232 A2
Rosebank Gdns
Alloa FK10 10 B4
Dunfermline KY12 28 B3
Edinburgh EH5 93 D3
Kincardine FK10 23 F2
Rosebank Gr EH5 93 D3
Rosebank Pl FK1 59 F3
Rosebank Rd EH5 93 D3
Rosebank Rdbt EH54 173 D4
Roseberry Ct EH30 89 E4
Roseberry Pl EH54 147 D3
Rosebery Ave EH30 89 E4
Rosebery Cres
Bathgate EH48 145 D3
Edinburgh EH12 122 C4
Gorebridge EH23 207 E3
Rosebery Crescent La
EH12 122 C4
Rosebery Ct
Dalgety Bay KY11 47 F1
Kirkcaldy KY1 17 D3
Rosebery Gr KY11 47 F1
Rosebery Pl
Dalgety Bay KY11 47 F1
Stirling FK8 2 A1
Rosebery Terr KY1 17 D3
Rosebery View KY11 47 F1
Roseburn Ave EH12 122 B4
Roseburn Cliff EH12 122 C4
Roseburn Cres EH12 122 B4
Roseburn Dr EH12 122 B4
Roseburn Gdns EH12 122 B4
Roseburn Maltings
EH12 122 C4
Roseburn Pl EH12 122 B4
Roseburn Prim Sch
EH12 122 B3
Roseburn St EH12 122 B3
Roseburn Terr EH12 122 C4
Rosebush Cres KY11 29 E2
Rosedale Ct EH24 205 E4
Rosefield Ave EH15 125 D4
Rosefield Avenue La EH15 125 D4
Rosefield La EH15 125 D4
Rosefield Pl EH15 125 D4
Rosefield St EH15 125 D4
Rosehall Pl EH41 131 F4
Rosehall Rd ML7 191 E2
Rosehall Terr FK1 60 A2
Rosehall Wlk EH41 131 F4
Rosehill Cres KY4 13 D2
Rosehill Pl EH54 147 D2
Rosehill Terr EH30 89 E4
Roselea Dr FK2 82 C4
Rosemead Terr FK1 81 F3
Rosemill Ct KY12 26 B1
Rosemount Ave KY2 17 D4
Rosemount Bldgs EH3 232 A2
Rosemount Ct EH48 145 D3
Rosemount Dr EH52 116 C2
Roseneath Pl EH9 123 E3
Roseneath St EH9 123 E3
Roseneath Terr EH9 123 E3
Rosevale Pl EH6 94 A2
Rosevale Terr EH6 94 A2
Roseville Gdns EH5 93 E3
Rosewell Prim Sch
EH24 181 F1
Rosewell Rd EH19 181 F2
Roslin Glen Ctry Pk
EH25 180 C1
Roslin Prim Sch EH25 180 C2
Roslin Prim Sch (Annexe)
EH25 180 B3
Ross Ave KY11 48 A1
Ross Cres Falkirk FK1 59 E3
Tranent EH33 128 B3
Ross Ct FK7 7 D2
Ross Gdns Edinburgh EH9 123 F2
Kirkcaldy KY1 17 F4
Ross High Sch EH33 128 B3
Ross La KY12 28 C2
Ross Pl Edinburgh EH9 123 F2
Kinghorn KY3 34 C1
Newtongrange EH22 183 D3
Ross Rd EH16 123 F1
Ross St KY12 29 D3
Rossend Terr KY3 50 B4
Rossie Pl EH7 94 A1
Rossland Pl KY3 34 C1
Rosslyn Cres EH6 93 F2
Rosslyn St KY1 17 F4
Rosslyn Terr EH6 93 F2
Rosslynlee Hospl EH25 204 C3
Rossness Dr KY3 34 C1
Rossvail Sch FK1 59 E3
Rosyth Europarc
North Queensferry KY11 68 A4
Rosyth KY11 46 B1
Rosyth Sta KY11 46 C3
Rothes Dr EH54 173 F3
Rothesay Mews EH3 122 C4
Rothesay Pl
Edinburgh EH3 232 A3
Musselburgh EH21 126 B3
Rothesay Terr EH3 232 A3
Roughburn Rd FK9 2 A3
Roughlands Cres FK2 39 D2
Roughlands Dr FK2 39 D2
Roull Gr EH12 121 E3
Roull Pl EH12 121 F3
Roull Rd EH12 121 E3
Round The KY12 29 E2
Roundel The FK2 60 B4
Roundelwood FK10 5 D1
Roundhouse FK7 20 B4
Rowallan Ct EH12 121 D4
Rowallan Dr FK7 19 F4
Rowan Cres Falkirk FK1 59 D2
Shotts ML7 192 A2
Rowan Ct FK7 7 F1
Rowan Dr EH47 145 F1
Rowan Gdns EH19 182 A3
Rowan Gr
Dunfermline KY11 29 E1
Livingston EH54 148 A3
Rowan La EH47 145 E1
Rowan St Blackburn EH47 145 E1
Dunbar EH42 78 A1
Rowan Terr
Blackburn EH47 171 E4
Cowdenbeath KY4 13 E2
Rowan Tree Ave EH14 151 F2
Rowan Tree Gr EH14 151 F2
Rowanhill Cl EH32 97 E2
Rowanhill Dr EH32 97 E2
Rowanhill Pk EH32 97 E2
Rowanhill Way EH32 97 E2
Rowans The Alloa FK10 5 E1
Gullane EH31 52 A2
Rowantree Rd EH22 183 F4
Roxburgh Pl
Edinburgh EH8 233 E2
Stenhousemuir FK5 38 C2
Roxburgh St
Edinburgh EH8 233 E2
Grangemouth FK3 61 F4
Roxburghe Pk EH42 78 C1
Roxburghe Terr EH42 78 C1
Roy Dr EH54 173 F3
Royal Blind Sch EH16 123 F2
Royal Botanic Garden
EH3 93 D2
Royal Cir EH3 232 B4
Royal Coll of Physicians
EH2 232 C4
Royal Cres EH3 93 E1
Royal Ct EH26 203 E4
Royal (Dick)
Veterinary Coll EH8 233 e1
Royal Edinburgh Hospl
EH10 123 D2
Royal Gdns FK8 7 D4
Royal High Prim Sch
EH8 124 B4
Royal High Sch The EH4 91 E2
Royal Hospl
for Sick Children EH9 123 E3
Royal Infirmary
of Edinburgh EH3 233 D2
Royal Mile Prim Sch
EH8 233 F3
Royal Mus of Scotland
EH1 233 D2
Royal Observatory EH9 123 E1
Royal Park Terr EH8 94 A1
Royal Scot Way KY12 29 D3
Royal Scottish Acad
EH2 232 C3
Royal Scottish
National Hospl The
FK5 37 F2
Royal Terr
Edinburgh EH7 233 E4
Linlithgow EH49 84 C3
Royal Victoria Hospl EH4 92 C1
Royal Yacht Britannia
EH6 93 F4
Royston Mains Ave EH5 92 C3
Royston Mains Cl EH5 92 C3
Royston Mains Cres EH5 92 C3
Royston Mains Gdns EH5 92 C3
Royston Mains Gn EH5 92 C3
Royston Mains Pl EH5 92 B3
Royston Mains Rd EH5 92 C3
Royston Mains St EH5 92 B3
Royston Prim Sch EH5 92 C3
Royston Rd EH54 146 C4
Royston Rdbt EH54 146 B4
Royston Terr EH3 93 D2
Rudolf Steiner Sch
EH10 122 C2
Rulley View FK6 36 B2
Rullion Green Ave EH26 203 E4
Rullion Green Cres EH26 203 E4
Rullion Green Gr EH26 203 E4
Rullion Rd EH26 203 E3
Rumblingwell KY12 28 B3
Rumlie The FK1 110 A3
Run The EH51 64 B4
Rushbank EH54 147 F3
Ruskie Rd FK9 2 A2
Ruskin Pl EH22 183 F3
Russel Ct KY5 14 A4
Russel Pl EH5 93 D3
Russel St FK2 60 A3
Russell Ave EH48 143 F4
Russell Ct KY11 29 F1
Russell Gdns EH12 122 C4
Russell Gr KY3 33 F1
Russell Pl Kirkcaldy KY1 17 E3
Oakley KY12 26 C4
Russell Rd EH11 122 C3
Russell St
Cowdenbeath KY4 13 D2
Lochgelly KY5 14 A4
Rutherford Ct
Bridge of A FK9 2 A4
Kirkcaldy KY1 17 F4
Rutherford Dr EH16 124 A1
Rutherford Sq EH54 173 E3
Ruthven Rd EH39 53 D2
Rutland Court La EH3 232 B2
Rutland Sq EH1 232 B3
Rutland St EH1 232 B3
Ryebank EH54 147 F3
Ryehill Ave EH6 94 A2
Ryehill Gdns EH6 94 A2
Ryehill Gr EH6 94 A2
Ryehill Pl EH6 94 A2
Ryehill Terr EH6 94 A2
Rymalton KY1 17 E3

Sacred Heart RC Prim Sch
Grangemouth FK3 61 F3
Penicuik EH26 203 F3
Saddletree Loan EH16 124 B1
Sailors' Wlk KY3 50 B4
Sainford Cres FK2 39 D1
Sainthill Ct EH39 54 A4
St Alban's Rd EH9 123 F2
St Andrew Pl EH6 94 A2
St Andrew Sq EH2 233 D4
St Andrew St
Dalkeith EH22 157 D2
Dunfermline KY11 29 E1
North Berwick EH39 54 B4
St Andrew's Ct FK5 38 A2
St Andrew's Dr Airth FK2 22 A4
Armadale EH48 143 F4
Uphall EH52 116 C2
St Andrew's High Sch
KY2 17 E4
St Andrew's Prim Sch
FK1 60 B2
St Andrews Way EH54 146 C3
St Andrews Pl 11 FK1 60 A2
St Ann's Ave EH18 181 F3
St Ann's Path EH18 181 F3
St Anne's Cres FK7 7 F1
St Anne's Ct EH22 183 D3
St Anthony La EH6 93 F3
St Anthony Pl EH6 93 F3
St Anthony St EH6 93 F3
St Anthony's RC Prim Sch
EH48 143 F3
St Augustine's High Sch
EH12 121 E2
St Baldred's Cres EH39 54 B4
St Baldred's Rd EH39 54 B3

St Bernadette's RC Prim Sch FK10 4 A1
St Bernard's Cres EH4 93 D1
St Bernard's Row 5 EH4 93 D1
St Bride's RC Prim Sch KY4 13 E2
St Bridget's Church KY11 48 B2
St Bridgets Brae KY11 48 B2
St Brycedale Ave KY1 17 D2
St Brycedale Rd KY1 17 D2
St Catherine FK2 82 C4
St Catherine's Gdns EH12 122 A3
St Catherine's Pl EH9 123 F3
St Catherine's RC Prim Sch EH16 155 D3
St Catherine's Wynd KY12 28 C2
St Catherines Cres ML7 191 F3
St Clair Ave EH6 94 A2
St Clair Cres EH25 181 D2
St Clair Pl EH6 94 A2
St Clair Rd EH6 94 A2
St Clair St Edinburgh EH6 94 A2
Kirkcaldy KY1 17 F4
St Clair Terr EH10 122 C1
St Clement's Cres EH21 127 D2
St Clement's Gdns N EH21 127 D2
St Clement's Gdns S EH21 127 D2
St Clement's Terr EH21 127 D2
St Colm's Abbey KY3 49 D1
St Colm's Ed Ctr & Coll EH3 93 D2
St Colme Ave KY3 49 D3
St Colme Cres KY3 49 D4
St Colme Dr KY11 48 B3
St Colme Rd KY11 48 B2
St Colme St EH3 232 B4
St Columba's High Sch KY11 29 F2
St Columba's RC Prim Sch EH48 145 F3
St Crispin's Pl FK1 60 A2
St Crispin's Sch EH16 123 F2
St Cuthbert's RC Prim Sch EH14 122 B2
St David's Bsns Pk KY11 48 A2
St David's Ct
Dalgety Bay KY11 48 A2
Larbert FK5 38 A1
St David's Pl EH3 232 A2
St David's RC High Sch EH22 157 D1
St David's RC Prim Sch
Dalkeith EH22 157 E1
Edinburgh EH4 92 B2
St David's Terr EH3 232 A2
St Davids EH22 183 D3
St Davids Dr KY11 48 A2
St Denis & Cranley Sch EH10 122 C2
St Fillan's Terr EH10 123 D1
St Fillans Cres KY3 49 E4
St Fillans Gr KY3 49 E4
St Fillans Pl KY2 16 B4
St Fillans Rd KY2 16 B4
St Francis' RC Prim Sch FK2 60 A3
St Francis's RC Prim Sch EH16 124 C2
St Gabrial's RC Prim Sch EH32 96 C1
St Gabriel's RC Prim Sch EH32 127 F4
St George's Ct FK5 38 A1
St George's Sch EH12 122 C4
St Georges Sch for girls EH12 122 B4
St Germains Terr EH33 129 E3
St Giles' Cath EH1 233 D3
St Giles Sq FK1 59 D3
St Giles St EH1 233 D3
St Giles Way FK1 59 D3
St Helen's Pl EH48 143 F3
St James Ctr EH1 233 D4
St James' Orch FK9 2 B1
St James' Pl EH1 233 D4
St James Pl KY3 35 D1
St James Sq EH1 233 D4
St James's Gdns EH26 203 F2
St James's View EH26 203 F2
St Joesph's Hospl EH24 205 F4
St John Ogilvie RC Prim Sch EH54 146 C3
St John St
Edinburgh EH8 233 E3
Spott EH42 106 B2
Stirling FK8 7 D4
St John the Baptist RC Sch EH47 193 F3
St John Vianney Prim Sch EH16 124 A1
St John's Ave
Edinburgh EH12 121 F3
Falkirk FK2 60 B3
Linlithgow EH49 84 C3
St John's Cres EH12 121 F3
St John's Ct KY11 47 E2
St John's Dr KY12 29 E2
St John's Gate FK6 36 B1
St John's Gdns Denny FK6 36 B1
Edinburgh EH12 121 F3
St John's Gr FK6 36 B1
St John's Hill EH8 233 E2
St John's Hospl EH54 147 E2
St John's Pl KY12 29 E2
St John's Pl EH48 113 F3
St John's Prim Sch
Edinburgh EH15 125 D4
Rosyth KY11 46 C2
St John's Rd
Broxburn EH52 117 F2
Edinburgh EH12 121 E3
St John's Terr EH12 121 F3
St John's Way EH51 63 F3
St Joseph's Cotts EH33 128 B4
St Joseph's Prim Sch
Bonnybridge FK4 58 A2
Edinburgh EH11 121 F2
St Joseph's RC Prim Sch EH49 84 C3
St Joseph's Sch EH32 128 B4
St Joseph's Specl Sch EH24 181 F1
St Josephs RC Prim Sch EH47 169 F3
St Katharine's Brae EH16 155 D3
St Katharine's Cres EH16 155 D3
St Katharine's Loan EH16 155 D3
St Kenneth's RC Prim Sch EH54 147 E4
St Kentigern Rd EH26 203 E3
St Kentigerns Acad EH47 171 D4
St Kilda Cres KY2 16 C4
St Laurence Cres FK1 110 A3
St Lawrence St KY11 29 E1
St Leonard's EH8 123 F3
St Leonard's Bank EH8 233 F1
St Leonard's Crag EH8 233 F1
St Leonard's Ct KY3 35 D2
St Leonard's Hill EH8 233 E1
St Leonard's La EH8 233 E1
St Leonard's Pl
Dunfermline KY11 29 D1
Kinghorn KY3 34 C2
St Leonard's Prim Sch KY11 29 D1
St Leonard's St
Dunfermline KY11 29 D1
Edinburgh EH8 233 E1
St Lukes Prim Sch EH22 183 E3
St Magdalene's EH49 85 D4
St Margaret St KY12 29 D2
St Margaret's Cres FK2 61 F1
St Margaret's Dr EH48 143 F3
St Margaret's Pl EH9 123 E2
St Margaret's Prep Sch EH16 124 A2
St Margaret's Prim Sch KY11 29 E2
St Margaret's Prim Sch FK2 61 E1
St Margaret's RC Acad EH54 147 E2
St Margaret's RC Prim Sch
Cowie FK7 20 B4
Loanhead EH20 155 E1
Queensferry EH30 68 B1
St Margaret's Rd
Edinburgh EH9 123 D2
North Berwick EH39 54 B4
St Margaret's Sch EH16 124 A2
St Margaret's Sch Sen Coll EH16 124 A2
St Margarets Ct EH39 54 B4
St Margarets Dr KY12 29 D2
St Marie's Prim Sch KY2 17 E4
St Mark's La EH15 125 D4
St Mark's Pl EH15 125 D4
St Mark's RC Prim Sch EH14 153 F4
St Martin's Ct EH41 132 B4
St Martin's Gate EH41 132 A4
St Martin's Pl EH41 132 B4
St Martin's RC Prim Sch EH33 128 B3
St Mary's (Leith) RC Prim Sch EH6 94 A3
St Mary's Music Sch EH12 122 C4
St Mary's Pl
Edinburgh EH15 125 E4
Kirkcaldy KY1 17 E3
St Mary's Place La EH15 125 E4
St Mary's RC Cath EH1 233 D4
St Mary's RC Prim Sch
Bannockburn FK7 7 E1
Bathgate EH48 145 D3
Bo'ness EH51 64 A4
Bonnyrigg and Lasswade EH19 182 A3
Edinburgh EH1 93 E1
Polbeth EH55 172 C3
Stirling FK8 1 C1
St Mary's RC Sch EH41 132 A4
St Mary's Rd KY1 17 E3
St Mary's St EH1 233 E3
St Mary's Wynd FK8 7 D4
St Marys Pl FK3 61 F4
St Matthew's RC Prim Sch EH24 181 F1
St Michael's Ave EH21 126 B3
St Michael's Hospl EH49 85 E3
St Michael's Wynd EH49 85 D4
St Michaels La EH49 85 D4
St Modan's High Sch FK7 7 D2
St Modans Ct 14 FK1 60 A2
St Mungo's High Sch FK2 60 A3
St Mungo's Prim Sch FK10 10 B3
St Mungo's View EH26 203 F3
St Mungo's Wynd FK10 10 A3
St Nicholas Prim Sch EH52 117 E2
St Nicholas (Specl Sch) EH11 122 B3
St Ninian's Ave EH49 84 C4
St Ninian's Dr EH12 121 E4
St Ninian's RC Prim Sch
Edinburgh EH7 94 B1
Livingston EH54 148 A1
St Ninian's Rd
Edinburgh EH12 121 E4
Linlithgow EH49 84 C4
St Ninian's Row EH1 233 D4
St Ninian's Terr EH10 122 C1
St Ninian's Way EH49 84 C4
St Ninians Prim Sch FK7 7 D2
St Ninians Rd
Cambusbarron FK7 6 C3
Stirling FK8 7 D3
St Ninians Row EH1 93 E1
St Ninians Way
Blackness EH49 65 F2
Musselburgh EH21 127 D3
St Patrick Sq EH8 233 E1
St Patrick St EH8 233 E1
St Patrick's RC Prim Sch FK6 36 C2
St Patrick's RC Prim Sch ML7 191 F2
St Paul's Dr EH48 144 A3
St Paul's RC Prim Sch EH53 148 C2
St Peter's Ct KY11 47 E2
St Peter's RC Sch EH10 123 D2
St Ronan's Terr EH10 123 D1
St Serf's Pl FK10 4 A2
St Serf's Prim Sch
High Valleyfield KY12 26 A1
Tullibody FK10 4 A2
St Serf's Rd FK10 4 A2
St Serf's Sch EH12 122 C4
St Serf's Wlk FK12 4 C3
St Serfs Gr FK10 11 D2
St Stephen Pl EH3 93 D1
St Stephen St EH3 93 D1
St Teresa Pl EH10 122 C2
St Thomas of Aquins RC High Sch EH3 232 C1
St Thomas Rd EH9 123 F2
St Thomas's Pl FK7 6 C3
St Thomas's Well FK7 6 B4
St Valery Dr FK7 7 D2
St Vincent St EH3 93 D1
Salamanca Cres EH26 204 A4
Salamander Pl EH6 94 A3
Salamander St EH6 94 A3
Salen Loan ML7 192 A2
Salisbury Pl EH9 123 F3
Salisbury Rd EH16 123 F3
Salisbury St KY2 17 D3
Salisbury View EH22 183 E3
Salmon Dr FK1 59 F1
Salmon Inn Rd FK2 61 E1
Salmond Pl 5 EH7 94 A1
Salt Preston Pl EH32 96 C1
Saltcoats Dr FK3 61 F4
Saltcoats Gdns EH54 173 F3
Saltcoats Rd
Grangemouth FK3 62 A4
Gullane EH31 52 A1
Salter's Rd Dalkeith EH22 157 E3
Wallyford EH21 127 D2
Salters'Gr EH22 157 E2
Salters' Rd Dalkeith EH22 157 E2
Pathhead EH37 186 A1
Salters' Terr EH22 157 E2
Saltire Gdns EH39 101 F4
Saltoun Prim Sch EH34 161 F3
Saltpans KY11 45 D2
Salvage Rd KY11 46 B1
Salvesen Cres EH4 92 A3
Salvesen Gdns EH4 92 A3
Salvesen Gr EH4 92 A3
Salvesen Terr EH4 92 A3
Samoa Terr EH26 204 A4
Sand Port EH6 94 A3
Sandport Trad Est EH6 93 F3
Sandeman Ct FK10 23 F2
Sanderson Terr KY2 15 D1
Sanderson's Gr EH33 128 B4
Sandersons Wynd EH33 128 B4
Sandford Gdns EH15 125 D4
Sandiland Dr EH53 148 A1
Sandilands KY11 45 E2
Sandport Pl EH6 93 F3
Sandport St EH6 93 F3
Sands The EH41 132 A4
Sandy Loan Gullane EH31 52 A1
Laurieston FK2 61 D2
Sandy Rd KY3 32 B3
Sandyford Ave EH49 84 A3
Sandyhill Ave ML7 192 A2
Sandyloan Cres FK2 61 D2
Sandyvale Pl ML7 192 A2
Sang Pl KY1 17 D2
Sang Rd KY1 17 D2
Sarazen Ct EH54 147 D4
Sarazen Gn EH54 147 D4
Sauchenbush Rd KY2 16 C3
Sauchie Ct FK7 7 F1
Sauchie Hospl FK10 10 B4
Sauchie St FK7 7 D1
Sauchiebank EH11 122 C3
Saughbank EH52 117 D3
Saughs The EH22 183 D2
Saughton Ave EH11 122 B2
Saughton Cres EH12 122 A3
Saughton Gdns EH12 122 A3
Saughton Gr EH12 122 A3
Saughton Loan EH12 122 A3
Saughton Mains Ave EH11 121 F2
Saughton Mains Bank EH11 122 A2
Saughton Mains Dr EH11 121 F2
Saughton Mains Gdns EH11 121 F2
Saughton Mains Gr EH11 122 A2
Saughton Mains Loan EH11 121 F2
Saughton Mains Pk EH11 121 F2
Saughton Mains Pl EH11 121 F2
Saughton Mains St EH11 122 A2
Saughton Mains Terr EH11 121 F2
Saughton Pk EH12 122 A3
Saughton Rd EH11 121 F2
Saughton Rd N EH12 121 F3
Saughtonhall Ave EH12 122 B3
Saughtonhall Ave W EH12 122 A3
Saughtonhall Cir EH12 122 B3
Saughtonhall Cres EH12 122 A3
Saughtonhall Dr EH12 122 A3
Saughtonhall Gdns EH12 122 B3
Saughtonhall Gr EH12 122 B3
Saughtonhall Pl EH12 122 B3
Saughtonhall Terr EH12 122 B3
Saunders St
Edinburgh EH3 232 B4
Kirkcaldy KY1 17 D1
Savile Pl EH9 123 F2
Savile Terr EH9 123 F2
Sawers Ave FK6 36 B1
Saxe Coburg Pl EH3 93 D1
Saxe Coburg St EH3 93 D1
Scarlett Pk EH21 127 D3
Schaw Ct FK10 5 E1
Schaw Rd EH32 97 D1
Schawpark Ave FK10 5 E1
Schiltron Way FK7 7 E2
Scholars' Brae KY3 50 C4
School Brae Bo'ness EH51 63 F4
Bonnyrigg and Lasswade EH18 156 A1
Dysart KY1 18 A4
Edinburgh EH4 91 D3
West Barns EH42 105 F4
School Gn
Bonnyrigg and Lasswade EH18 156 A1
Longniddry EH32 98 C3
School La Bathgate EH48 145 D3
Cockenzie & Port Seton EH32 97 E2
Menstrie FK11 4 A4
Mid Calder EH53 148 B2
Shotts ML7 212 A4
School Pl EH52 116 C2
School Rd Aberlady EH32 71 E2
East Linton EH40 103 F4
Laurieston FK2 61 D2
Longridge EH47 170 B1
North Berwick EH39 54 B4
Redding FK2 61 D1
Tullibody FK10 4 A1
School Row KY12 28 B3
School St
Cowdenbeath KY4 13 E2
Shotts ML7 191 F2
School Wlk FK5 38 B2
School Wynd KY1 17 D1
Schoolyard Ct EH25 181 D2
Sciennes EH9 123 F3
Sciennes Gdns EH9 123 F3
Sciennes Hill Pl 4 EH9 123 F3
Sciennes House Pl 3 EH9 123 F3
Sciennes Pl 1 EH9 123 F3
Sciennes Prim Sch EH9 123 E3
Sciennes Rd EH9 123 E3
Sclandersburn Rd FK6 57 E4
Scobie Pl KY12 29 E2
Scollon Ave EH19 182 B4
Scone Gdns EH8 94 B1
Scotch Whisky Heritage Ctr The EH1 123 E4
Scotia Pl FK2 60 B3
Scotland Dr KY12 29 F2
Scotland St EH3 93 E1
Scotlands Cl EH51 63 F4
Scotmill Way KY11 47 E2
Scots Mill Pl KY11 47 F2
Scotstoun Ave EH30 89 E4
Scotstoun Gn EH30 89 D4
Scotstoun Pk EH30 89 E4
Scotstoun Rd FK7 20 C4
Scott Ave FK2 61 F1
Scott Cres FK10 10 A3
Scott Ct EH54 148 B3
Scott Pl EH47 193 F3
Scott Rd EH26 203 F4
Scott St Dunfermline KY12 28 C3
Grangemouth FK3 61 E3
Kirkcaldy KY1 17 D1
Stirling FK8 2 A1
Scott Terr EH48 145 E3
Scottish Ag Mus EH28 119 F3
Scottish Ag Science Agency EH12 121 D4
Scottish Mining Mus Lady Victoria Colliery EH22 183 D2
Scottish Nat Gall of Mod Art EH4 122 C4
Scottish Pol Coll FK10 23 F3
Scottish Prison Service Coll FK2 82 B4
Sea Wynd EH32 71 E3
Seabegs Cres FK4 58 A2
Seabegs Pl FK4 57 F2
Seabegs Rd FK4 57 F2
Seacliff EH39 56 A3
Seacot EH6 94 B2
Seafield Ave EH6 94 B2
Seafield Cres EH42 78 A1
Seafield Ct FK1 59 F1
Seafield Inf Sch EH54 146 C3
Seafield Moor Rd EH25 180 B3
Seafield Pl
Dalgety Bay KY11 48 A1
Edinburgh EH6 94 B2
Seafield Rd Bilston EH25 180 C3
Blackburn EH47 171 F4
Edinburgh EH6 94 B2
Kirkcaldy KY1 35 D4
Seafield Rd E EH15 94 C2
Seafield Rows EH47 146 A1
Seafield St EH6 94 B2
Seafield View
Kinghorn KY3 35 D2
Kirkcaldy KY1 35 D4
Seafield Way EH15 94 C2
Seaforth Dr EH4 92 B1
Seaforth Pl Burntisland KY3 50 C4
Kirkaldy KY1 17 F4
Stirling FK8 7 D4
Seaforth Rd FK2 39 E1
Seaforth Terr
Bonnyrigg and Lasswade EH19 181 F3
3 Edinburgh EH4 92 B1
Sealcar St EH5 92 C4
Sealock Ct FK3 61 E3
Sealstrand KY11 48 B2
Seaport St EH6 94 A3
Seaside Pl KY3 49 E4
Seaton Pl FK1 60 B2
Seaview Cres EH15 125 F4
Seaview Pl EH51 63 F4
Seaview Terr EH15 125 F4
Seco Pl KY4 13 E2
Second Gait EH14 151 F4
Second St EH22 183 D2
Sedgebank EH54 147 F3
Seggarsdean Ct EH41 132 B4
Seggarsdean Pk EH41 132 B4
Seggarsdean Terr EH41 132 B4
Selkirk Ave KY4 13 E1
Selkirk Rd KY11 67 D4
Selm Pk EH54 148 A2
Selvage Pl KY11 47 D2
Selvage St KY11 47 D2
Semple St EH3 232 B2
Seton Chapel EH32 97 F2
Seton Ct
Cockenzie & Port Seton EH32 97 F2
Tranent EH33 128 B3
Seton Dr FK7 7 E2
Seton Mains EH32 98 A2
Seton Pl
Cockenzie & Port Seton EH32 97 E2
Dalgety Bay KY11 48 B3
Edinburgh EH9 123 F3
Kirkcaldy KY2 16 B4
Seton Rd EH32 98 C3
Seton Terr EH51 64 A4
Seton View EH32 97 F2
Seton Wynd EH32 97 F2
Seventh St EH22 183 D3
Shadepark Cres EH22 157 D2
Shadepark Dr EH22 157 D2
Shadepark Gdns EH22 157 D2
Shaftesbury Pk EH11 122 C2
Shaftesbury St FK10 10 A4
Shafto Pl EH51 63 F3
Shamrock St KY12 29 D3
Shandon Cres EH11 122 C2
Shandon Pl EH11 122 C2
Shandon Rd EH11 122 C2
Shandon St EH11 122 C2
Shandon Terr EH11 122 C2
Shandwick Pl EH2 232 A3
Shanks Ave FK6 57 F4
Shanks Rd EH47 170 A4
Shannon Dr FK1 59 F2
Shanter Way 7 EH16 124 A1
Sharp Terr FK3 61 E3
Sharpdale Loan EH16 124 A2
Shaw Ave EH48 143 F3
Shaw Cres KY5 14 A4
Shaw Pl Armadale EH48 143 F3
Grangemouth FK3 61 E3
Mayfield EH22 183 E4
Shaw St KY11 29 E1
Shaw's Pl EH7 93 F2
Shaw's Sq EH1 93 F1
Shaw's St EH7 93 F2
Shaw's Terr EH7 93 F2
Shaws Ct EH26 180 A1
Sheephousehill FK1 193 F3
Sheperdlands Gr KY12 26 B4
Shepherd Cres KY3 50 B4
Sherbrooke Rd KY11 46 B2
Sheriff Bank EH6 93 F3
Sheriff Brae EH6 93 F3

Sheriff Pk EH6 93 F3
Sheriffhall Junc EH22 156 B3
Sheriffmuir Rd FK9 2 B4
Sheriffmuirlands FK9 2 B2
Sheriffs Pk EH49 85 F4
Sherriff Hall Cotts EH39 74 C4
Sherriff La FK5 38 C2
Sherwood Ave EH19 182 B3
Sherwood Cres EH19 182 B3
Sherwood Ct EH19 182 B3
Sherwood Dr EH19 182 B3
Sherwood Gr EH19 182 B3
Sherwood Ind Est EH19 182 B4
Sherwood Loan EH19 182 B3
Sherwood Pk EH19 182 B3
Sherwood Pl EH19 182 B3
Sherwood Terr EH19 182 B3
Sherwood View EH19 182 B3
Sherwood Way EH19 182 B3
Sherwood Wlk EH19 182 B3
Shetland Ct FK10 10 A3
Shetland Pl KY1 17 F4
Shiel Ct FK3 61 E2
Shiel Gdns Falkirk FK2 39 E1
Shotts ML7 192 A2
Shiel Wlk EH54 148 A3
Shieldhill Prim Sch FK1 81 E3
Shields Ct EH52 117 F3
Shields Rd KY11 29 F2
Shieling The KY12 27 F1
Shillinghill FK10 10 A3
Shinwell Pl KY11 46 C2
Shiphaugh Pl FK8 2 B1
Shire Way FK10 9 F3
Shirra's Brae Rd FK7 7 E2
Shoestanes Rd EH38 228 B1
Shoestanes Terr EH38 228 B1
Shore EH6 94 A3
Shore Pl EH6 94 A3
Shore Rd Aberdour KY3 49 E4
Airth FK2 22 B2
Dysart KY1 18 A3
Queensferry EH30 68 A1
Stirling FK8 7 D4
Shore St EH42 78 C2
Shore The FK10 10 A3
Shorthope St EH21 126 B3
Shotts Rd
Fauldhouse EH47 193 E2
Harthill ML7 167 F1
Shotts Sta ML7 191 F2
Shottsburn Rd ML7 167 D2
Shottskirk Rd ML7 191 E3
Shrub Mount EH15 95 D1
Shrub Place La EH7 93 F1
Sibbald Pl EH54 147 D3
Sibbalds Brae EH48 144 B3
Sidegate EH41 132 A4
Sidehead Rd ML7 168 C3
Sidlaw Pl FK3 61 F3
Sidlaw St KY2 16 C4
Sienna Gdns EH9 123 F3
Sighthill Ave EH11 121 F1
Sighthill Bank EH11 121 E1
Sighthill Cres EH11 121 E1
Sighthill Ct EH11 121 E1
Sighthill Dr EH11 121 E1
Sighthill Gdns EH11 121 E1
Sighthill Gn EH11 121 E1
Sighthill Gr EH11 121 F1
Sighthill Ind Est EH11 121 D2
Sighthill Loan EH11 121 E1
Sighthill Neuk EH11 121 E1
Sighthill Pk EH11 121 F1
Sighthill Pl EH11 121 E1
Sighthill Prim Sch EH11 121 E1
Sighthill Rd EH11 121 E1
Sighthill Rise EH11 121 E1
Sighthill St EH11 121 E1
Sighthill Terr EH11 121 E1
Sighthill View EH11 121 E1
Sighthill Wynd EH11 121 E1
Silk Ho FK1 60 A3
Silver St Dunbar EH42 78 B1
Kincardine FK10 23 F2
Silverbarton Terr KY3 33 E1
Silverburn Dr EH26 203 E3
Silverdale Rd FK2 82 C4
Silverknowes Ave EH4 91 F2
Silverknowes Bank EH4 91 F2
Silverknowes Brae EH4 92 A2
Silverknowes Cres EH4 91 F2
Silverknowes Ct EH4 91 F2
Silverknowes Dell EH4 91 F2
Silverknowes Dr EH4 91 F2
Silverknowes Eastway
EH4 91 F2
Silverknowes Gdns EH4 92 A2
Silverknowes Gn EH4 92 A2
Silverknowes Gr EH4 91 F2
Silverknowes Hill EH4 91 F2
Silverknowes Loan EH4 91 F2
Silverknowes Midway
EH4 92 A2
Silverknowes Neuk EH4 92 A2
Silverknowes Parkway
EH4 91 F3
Silverknowes Pl EH4 91 F3
Silverknowes Prim Sch
EH4 92 A3
Silverknowes Rd EH4 91 F3
Silverknowes Rd E EH4 92 A2
Silverknowes Rd S EH4 91 F2
Silverknowes Southway
EH4 92 A2
Silverknowes Terr EH4 91 F2
Silverknowes View EH4 92 A2
Simon Sq EH8 233 E2
Simpson Cres EH48 145 E3
Simpson Dr FK2 83 D3
Simpson Parkway EH54 147 D1
Simpson Rd EH52 118 A3
Simpson St FK1 59 F3
Simpson Wlk KY11 29 F1
Sinclair Cres FK6 36 B1
Sinclair Ct Aberlady EH32 71 E2
Bannockburn FK7 7 F1
Sinclair Dr
Cowdenbeath KY4 13 D1
Fallin FK7 8 B2
Sinclair Gdns KY12 29 D2
Sinclair Pl FK2 39 D1
Sinclair Way EH54 147 E3
Sinclairtown Prim Sch
KY1 17 F4
Sir George Bruce Rd
KY12 26 C4
Sir Harry Lauder Rd
EH15 125 D4
Sir James Black Gait KY5 14 A4
Sir Walter Scott Pend
EH32 96 C1
Sir Walter Scott's Mon
EH2 233 D3
Sir William Fraser Homes
EH13 153 D4
Sir William Wallace Ct
FK5 38 A2
Sivewright Ct FK10 23 F2
Sixth St EH22 183 D3
Skaithmuir Ave FK2 39 D2
Skaithmuir Cres FK2 39 D2
Skelmorlie Pl FK5 38 C2
Skeltie Muir Ave EH19 182 A3
Skeltiemuir Ct EH19 182 A3
Skeltiemuir Gr EH19 182 A3
Skene St FK4 58 A3
Skibo Ct KY12 29 D2
Skibo Pl KY2 16 B3
Skye Ct FK3 61 E3
Skye Dr FK2 61 F1
Skye Rd KY11 29 F1
Skylaw Terr ML11 215 D1
Skythorn Way FK1 59 F1
Slaeside EH14 151 E1
Slamannan Prim Sch
FK1 110 A4
Slamannan Rd
Avonbridge FK1 112 A3
Falkirk FK1 60 A1
Slamannan FK1 110 A1
Slateford Rd EH14 122 B2
Slateford Sta EH14 122 B2
Sleigh Dr EH7 94 B1
Sleigh Gdns EH7 94 B1
Sligo St KY12 26 C4
Sloan St EH6 93 F2
Small St KY5 14 A3
Smallburn Pl FK3 61 F3
Smeaton Gdns KY2 17 E3
Smeaton Gr EH21 126 B2
Smeaton Ind Site KY1 17 E4
Smeaton Rd KY1 17 E3
Smiddy Wynd FK12 5 D3
Smileyknowes Ct EH39 54 A3
Smith Art Gallery & Mus
FK8 7 D4
Smith Ave KY4 13 D2
Smith Pl FK6 36 B1
Smith St FK2 60 A4
Smith's Pl EH6 93 F2
Smith's Terr KY1 17 E3
Smithfield Loan FK10 9 F3
Smithfield St EH11 122 B3
Smithy Brae EH27 149 F1
Smithy Green Ave EH22 156 A4
Smithy Row EH39 74 A2
Snab Brae EH51 63 E3
Snab La EH51 63 E4
Snowden Sch Ltd FK8 7 D4
Snowdon Pl FK8 7 D3
Snowdon Place La FK7 7 D3
Society La EH55 172 B2
Society Pl EH55 172 B2
Society Rd EH30 67 F1
Solway Dr FK6 57 E4
Somerset Pl EH6 94 A2
Somerville Rd KY11 46 B1
Somerville Sq KY3 50 C4
Somerville St KY3 50 C4
Sommers Pk EH53 148 B1
Sommerville Gdns EH30 89 E4
Somnerfield Ave EH41 131 F4
Somnerfield Cres EH41 131 F4
Somnerfield Ct EH41 131 F4
Somnerfield Gr EH41 131 F4
Somnerfield Pk EH41 131 F4
Souillac Dr FK6 36 B1
South Acres KY12 27 E1
South Approach Rd FK2 23 D1
South Ave Blairhall KY12 26 A4
Maddiston FK2 83 D4
South Bantaskine Dr FK1 60 A2
South Bantaskine Rd FK1 60 A2
South Barnton Ave EH4 91 F2
South Beechwood EH12 122 A3
South Brae FK2 83 D3
South Bridge EH1 233 D3
South Bridge St
Bathgate EH48 145 D3
Grangemouth FK3 40 B1
South Broomage Ave FK5 38 B1
South Charlotte St EH2 232 B3
South Clerk St EH8 233 E1
South College St EH8 233 D2
South Craigs Rd FK2 82 C4
South Cres EH32 97 D1
South Dewar St KY12 28 C2
South Doors EH32 97 E2
South Dr KY11 46 C3
South East Circus Pl
EH3 232 B4
South East Cumberland
Street La EH3 93 E1
South East Thistle
Street La EH2 232 C4
South Elixa Pl EH8 124 B4
South Ettrick Rd EH10 122 C2
South Fergus Pl KY1 17 D2
South Fort St EH6 93 F3
South Gait EH39 53 F4
South Gayfield La 8 EH1 93 F1
South Gillsland Rd EH10 122 C2
South Grange Ave EH32 127 F4
South Gray St EH9 123 F2
South Gray's Cl EH1 233 E3
South Green Dr FK2 22 C2
South Groathill Ave EH4 92 B1
South Gyle Access EH12 121 E2
South Gyle Broadway
EH12 121 D2
South Gyle Cres EH12 121 D2
South Gyle Crescent La
EH12 121 D2
South Gyle Gdns EH12 121 D3
South Gyle Ind Est EH12 121 D2
South Gyle Loan EH12 121 D3
South Gyle Mains EH12 121 D3
South Gyle Pk EH12 121 D3
South Gyle Rd EH12 121 D3
South Gyle Sta EH12 121 D3
South Gyle Wynd EH12 121 E2
South Hamilton Rd EH39 54 A4
South Hill St KY3 50 C4
South Hirst Rd ML7 167 E2
South Knowe KY4 30 C3
South Larch Rd KY11 29 F2
South Lauder Rd EH9 123 F2
South Laverockbank Ave
EH5 93 E3
South Learmonth Ave 7
EH4 92 C1
South Loanhead KY11 45 F2
South Loch Pk EH48 145 D3
South Lodge Ave EH53 148 B1
South Lorimer Pl EH32 97 E2
South Lorne Pl EH6 93 F2
South Lumley St FK3 61 E4
South Marshall St FK3 61 E4
South Maybury EH12 121 D3
South Mellis Pk EH8 124 C4
South Melville La FK1 60 A3
South Mid St EH48 145 D3
South Morningside
Prim Sch EH10 123 D1
South Morton St EH15 125 E4
South Oswald Rd EH9 123 E2
South Overgate KY3 35 D2
South Oxford St EH8 123 F3
South Philpingstone La
EH51 64 B4
South Pilmuir Rd FK10 11 D2
South Pk Armadale EH48 143 F2
Edinburgh EH6 93 E3
South Pleasance Ave FK1 60 A2
South Queensferry
Prim Sch EH30 68 B1
South Rd
Fauldhouse EH47 193 F4
Grangemouth FK2 62 A3
South Roundall KY11 45 F2
South Row
Charlestown KY11 45 D2
Kirkcaldy KY1 17 F4
South Scotstoun EH30 89 E4
South Seton Pk EH32 97 E2
South Shore Rd FK3 41 D1
South Sloan St EH6 93 F2
South St Armadale EH48 143 F3
Bo'ness EH51 63 F4
Cambus FK10 9 D4
Cowdenbeath KY4 13 E1
Dalkeith EH22 157 D2
Dunbar EH42 78 A1
Lochgelly KY5 14 A3
Musselburgh EH21 126 A3
Stirling FK9 2 B1
South St Andrew St EH2 233 D4
South St David St EH2 233 D3
South Steil EH10 122 C1
South Trinity Rd EH5 93 D3
South View
Burntisland KY3 50 C4
Stenhousemuir FK5 38 B1
South Village EH53 148 B3
South West Cumberland
Street La EH3 93 E1
South West Thistle
Street La EH2 232 C4
Southbank Ct EH4 91 F2
Southcroft FK12 4 C3
Southerton Cres KY2 16 C2
Southerton Gdns KY2 16 C2
Southerton Rd KY2 16 C2
Southfield KY4 13 E3
Southfield Ave ML7 192 A2
Southfield Bank EH15 124 C3
Southfield Cres
Shotts ML7 192 A2
Stirling FK8 7 D3
Southfield Dr FK1 110 A3
Southfield Farm Gr
EH15 124 C4
Southfield Gdns E EH15 124 C4
Southfield Gdns W EH15 124 C3
Southfield Hospl EH17 155 E4
Southfield Load EH15 124 C3
Southfield Loan EH15 124 C3
Southfield Pl EH15 125 D4
Southfield Rd
Cousland EH22 158 B3
Shotts ML7 192 A2
Southfield Rd E EH15 124 C3
Southfield Rd W EH15 124 C3
Southfield Sq EH15 124 C3
Southfield Terr EH15 124 C3
Southhouse Ave EH17 155 D3
Southhouse Broadway
EH17 155 D2
Southhouse Cres EH17 155 E2
Southhouse Gdns EH17 155 D2
Southhouse Gr EH17 155 D2
Southhouse Loan EH17 155 D3
Southhouse Medway
EH17 155 D3
Southhouse Rd EH17 155 D2
Southhouse Sq EH17 155 D3
Southhouse Terr EH17 155 E3
Southlawn Ct EH4 91 F2
Spa Pl EH15 95 D1
Spalding Cres EH22 157 D2
Speedwell Ave EH22 156 A4
Spence Ave KY3 33 F1
Spence St
Bonnybridge FK4 58 A3
Edinburgh EH16 123 F3
Spencer Pl Edinburgh EH5 93 D3
Kirkcaldy KY1 17 F4
Spencerfield Rd KY11 47 E1
Spencerfield Steadings
KY11 47 F2
Spens La KY11 46 B1
Spey Ct Grangemouth FK3 61 E3
Stirling FK7 7 E3
Spey Dr EH54 148 A2
Spey St EH7 93 F2
Spey Street La EH7 93 F2
Spey Terr EH7 93 F2
Spier's Pl EH6 93 F3
Spinkhill FK2 60 C1
Spinnaker Way KY11 47 F1
Spinner's Ct KY12 27 E1
Spinney The EH17 155 E3
Spinneys The KY11 48 B2
Spittal Hill FK9 2 B2
Spittal St Edinburgh EH3 232 B2
Stirling FK8 7 D4
Spittalfield Cres KY11 47 E1
Spittalfield Rd KY11 47 E1
Spott Ave EH42 106 B2
Spott Loan EH42 106 B2
Spott Rd EH42 78 C1
Spottiswoode Gdns
EH53 148 B1
Spottiswoode Rd EH9 123 E3
Spottiswoode St EH9 123 E3
Sprig Way ML7 168 C3
Spring Gdns EH8 94 A1
Springbank Gdns FK2 60 B3
Springbank Rd
Shotts ML7 191 E3
Stirling FK7 7 E3
Springbank Terr KY12 29 D3
Springfield Edinburgh EH6 93 F2
West Barns EH42 105 F4
Springfield Cres
North Berwick EH39 54 A4
Queensferry EH30 67 F1
Springfield Ct EH49 85 E4
Springfield Dr FK1 59 F3
Springfield Gdns EH39 54 A4
Springfield Lea EH30 67 F1
Springfield Pl
Gorebridge EH23 207 E4
Queensferry EH30 67 F1
Roslin EH25 181 D2
Springfield Prim Sch
EH49 85 E4
Springfield Rd Alloa FK10 10 B4
Denny FK6 36 C1
Linlithgow EH49 85 E4
Penicuik EH26 222 C3
Queensferry EH30 67 F1
Stirling FK7 7 E3
Springfield St EH6 93 F2
Springfield Terr
Queensferry EH30 67 F1
West Barns EH42 77 F1
Springfield View EH30 68 A1
Springhead Rd ML7 212 A4
Springhill Brae KY4 30 C3
Springhill & Leadloch Rd
ML7 192 C1
Springhill Rd ML7 192 A2
Springhill View ML7 192 A2
Springkerse Ind Est FK7 7 E3
Springkerse Rd FK7 7 E3
Springkerse Rdbt FK7 7 F4
Springvalley Gdns
EH10 123 D2
Springvalley Terr EH10 123 D2
Springwell Pl EH11 122 C3
Springwood KY11 47 D4
Springwood Ave FK8 6 C3
Springwood Pk EH16 155 D4
Sprinty Ave EH35 159 E4
Sprinty Dr EH35 159 E4
Sprotwell Terr FK10 5 E1
Spruce Dr EH47 170 B3
Spruce Gr
Dunfermline KY11 46 B4
Livingston EH54 148 A3
Spylaw Ave EH13 152 C4
Spylaw Bank Rd EH13 153 D4
Spylaw Pk EH13 152 C4
Spylaw Rd EH10 122 C2
Spylaw St EH13 153 D4
Square The
Cockburnspath TD13 140 C2
Danderhall EH22 156 A4
East Linton EH40 103 F4
Fallin FK7 8 B2
Gifford EH41 163 F3
Kirkliston EH29 89 D1
Newtongrange EH22 183 D3
Penicuik EH26 203 F2
Spott EH42 106 B2
Torphichen EH48 113 F3
Sraehouse Wynd ML8 230 A1
Stable La EH10 123 D2
Stable Rd ML7 192 A3
Stables Rd KY11 46 B1
Staffa EH54 146 C3
Staffa Pl FK1 60 A1
Stafford St EH3 232 A3
Stair Pk Edinburgh EH12 122 B4
Tranent EH33 128 A4
Standalane FK10 23 F2
Standhill Ct EH48 144 C2
Standing Stone Wlk KY11 29 F1
Standingstane Rd EH30 89 F3
Standrigg Rd FK2 82 A3
Stane Prim Sch ML7 192 A2
Stane Rd ML7 192 A1
Stanedykehead EH16 154 C3
Stanhope Pl EH12 122 C4
Stanhope St EH12 122 C4
Stanistone Rd ML8 230 A1
Stankards Rd EH52 116 C2
Stanley Ave EH25 180 C3
Stanley Dr Bridge of A FK9 2 A4
Harthill ML7 169 D3
Stanley Gdns FK2 82 C3
Stanley Pl Edinburgh EH7 94 A1
Ormiston EH35 159 F4
Stanley Rd Edinburgh EH6 93 E3
Harthill ML7 169 D3
Stanley St EH15 125 D4
Stanley Terr KY12 27 D3
Stanton Ave FK10 9 F3
Stanwell St EH6 93 F2
Stapeley Ave EH7 94 C1
Starbank Rd EH5 93 E3
Stark Ave FK1 59 E3
Stark's Brae EH51 64 A4
Stark's Park
(Raith Rovers FC) KY1 17 D1
Starlaw Ave EH48 145 F3
Starlaw Bsns Pk EH54 146 B2
Starlaw Cres EH48 145 F3
Starlaw Gdns EH48 145 F3
Starlaw Rd EH54, EH47 146 B2
Starlaw Terr EH48 145 F3
Starlaw West Rdbt
EH47 146 A2
Starlaw Wlk EH48 145 F3
Starryshaw Rd ML7 191 F3
Station Ave EH41 131 F4
Station Brae
Edinburgh EH15 125 D4
Kinghorn KY3 34 C1
Station Ct Addiewell EH55 171 F1
Haddington EH41 131 F4
North Berwick EH39 54 A4
Station Hill EH39 54 A4
Station Loan EH14 151 E2
Station Pl KY3 49 E4
Station Rd
Addiewell EH55 171 F1
Armadale EH48 143 F2
Bannockburn FK7 7 F1
Blackridge EH48 142 B1
Bridge of A FK9 1 C4
Brightons FK2 61 F1
Broxburn EH52 117 F3
Cambus FK10 4 A1
Cowdenbeath KY4 13 E2
Cowie FK7 20 B3
Dalkeith EH22 156 C1
Dirleton EH39 53 E2
Dunbar EH42 78 C1
Dysart KY1 18 A4
East Linton EH40 103 F4
Edinburgh EH12 121 F3
Gifford EH41 163 F3
Gorebridge EH23 207 E4
Grangemouth FK3 40 B1
Gullane EH31 52 A1
Kincardine FK10 23 E2
Kirkcaldy KY2, KY1 17 D2
Kirkliston EH29 89 D1
Kirknewton EH27 149 E2
Linlithgow EH49 85 D4
Loanhead EH20 181 E4
Lochgelly KY5 14 A4
Musselburgh EH21 126 B3
Newtongrange EH22 183 D3
North Berwick EH39 54 A4
Oakley KY12 26 C3
Prestonpans EH32 128 A4
Queensferry EH30 68 B1
Ratho Station EH28 119 E3
Roslin EH25 181 D2
Shotts ML7 191 F2
Slamannan FK1 110 A3
Stirling FK8 7 D4
Uphall EH52 116 C2

Station Rd continued
Uphall Station EH54 117 D1
Whitecross EH49 83 F3
Station Row FK1 110 A3
Station Terr EH29 89 D1
Staunton Rise EH54 173 E4
Stead's Pl EH6 93 F2
Steading The EH32 98 B1
Steadings The EH49 84 A4
Steel Gr KY12 26 B4
Steel's Pl EH10 123 D2
Steele Ave EH22 183 F3
Steelyard The EH48 145 D3
Steeple Cres KY11 48 A2
Steil Gr EH33 128 B3
Steils The EH10 122 C1
Stein Sq FK7 7 F1
Stein's Pl KY4 13 E2
Stenhouse Ave EH11 122 A2
Stenhouse Ave W EH11 122 A2
Stenhouse Cotts EH11 122 A2
Stenhouse Cres EH11 122 A2
Stenhouse Cross EH11 122 A2
Stenhouse Dr
Burntisland KY3 33 E1
Edinburgh EH11 122 A2
Stenhouse Gdns EH11 122 A2
Stenhouse Gdns N EH11 122 A2
Stenhouse Gr EH11 122 A2
Stenhouse Mill Cres EH11 122 A2
Stenhouse Mill La EH11 122 A2
Stenhouse Mill Wynd
EH11 122 A2
Stenhouse Pl E EH11 122 A2
Stenhouse Pl W EH11 122 A2
Stenhouse Prim Sch
EH11 122 A2
Stenhouse Rd
Edinburgh EH11 122 A2
Stenhousemuir FK5 38 C1
Stenhouse St KY4 13 D2
Stenhouse St E EH11 122 A2
Stenhouse St W EH11 121 F2
Stenhouse Terr EH11 122 A2
Stenhousemuir Prim Sch
FK5 38 B2
Stennis Gdns EH17 155 E4
Stenton Loan EH42 135 F4
Stenton Prim Sch EH42 104 C1
Stenton Rd EH42 105 F4
Stephen Pl KY5 14 A4
Stephen's Dr KY11 47 E2
Steps St FK5 38 C2
Steuart Rd FK9 1 C4
Stevenlaw's Cl EH1 233 D3
Stevenson Ave EH11 122 B3
Stevenson Coll of F Ed
EH11 121 E2
Stevenson Ct Bridge of A FK9 2 A3
Livingston EH54 148 B3
Longniddry EH32 98 B2
Stevenson Dr EH11 122 A2
Stevenson Gr EH11 122 B3
Stevenson La EH22 183 D2
Stevenson Pk EH32 98 B2
Stevenson Pl EH18 181 E3
Stevenson Rd
Edinburgh EH11 122 B3
Penicuik EH26 204 A4
Stevenson St FK3 61 E3
Stevenson Terr
Bathgate EH48 145 E3
Edinburgh EH11 122 B3
Stevenson Way EH32 98 B2
Stewart Ave Bo'ness EH51 63 F4
Currie EH14 151 F2
Linlithgow EH49 84 C3
Stewart Clark Ave EH30 89 E4
Stewart Cres Currie EH14 151 F2
Lochgelly KY5 14 A4
Stewart Dr EH47 169 F4
Stewart Gdns EH14 151 F2
Stewart Gr
Danderhall EH22 156 A4
Harthill ML7 168 C3
Stewart Pk EH22 158 B3
Stewart Pl Currie EH14 151 F2
Kirkliston EH29 89 D1
Stewart Rd Currie EH14 151 F2
Falkirk FK2 60 B3
Stewart Sq FK8 2 A1
Stewart St
Bonnybridge FK4 57 F3
Cambusbarron FK7 6 B3
Dysart KY1 18 A4
Townhill KY12 29 E4
West Calder EH55 172 B1
Stewart Terr
Edinburgh EH11 122 C3
Queensferry EH30 68 A1
Stewart Way EH54 147 E3
Stewartfield EH6 93 E2
Stewartfield Cres EH52 117 F3
Stewartfield Rd EH52 117 F3
Stirling Castle FK8 1 C1
Stirling Ent Pk FK7 7 E4
Stirling F Ed Ctr FK7 7 E3
Stirling High Sch FK8 7 D3
Stirling Pl FK7 20 B2
Stirling Rd Alloa FK10 9 F4
Alva FK12 4 C4
Edinburgh EH5 93 D3
Falkirk FK1 59 E4
Fallin FK7 8 B2
Larbert FK5 37 F3
Torwood FK5 37 F3
Tullibody FK10 4 A2
Stirling Royal Infmy FK8 7 D3
Stirling St Alva FK12 5 D4
Denny FK6 36 B2
Stirling Sta FK8 7 D4
Stobhill Prim Sch EH23 207 E4
Stobhill Rd EH23 183 D2
Stobie Pl KY12 26 C4
Stobs Pl KY2 16 B4
Stockbridge Prim Sch
EH3 93 D1
Stone Ave EH22 183 E3
Stone Cres EH22 183 E3
Stone Pl EH22 183 E3
Stonebank EH54 147 F3
Stonedyke Cres ML8 230 A2
Stonedyke Rd ML8 230 A2
Stoneheap Crofts EH47 194 C4
Stonelaws Cotts EH40 75 D3
Stoneybank Ave EH21 126 A2
Stoneybank Cres EH21 126 A2
Stoneybank Ct EH21 126 A3
Stoneybank Dr EH21 126 A3
Stoneybank Gdns EH21 126 A3
Stoneybank Gdns N
EH21 126 A3
Stoneybank Gdns S
EH21 126 A3
Stoneybank Gr EH21 126 A2
Stoneybank Pl EH21 126 A2
Stoneybank Rd EH21 126 A2
Stoneybank Terr EH21 126 A2
Stoneyburn Prim Sch
EH47 171 E2
Stoneyflatts EH30 89 D4
Stoneyflatts Cres EH30 89 D4
Stoneyflatts Pk EH30 89 D4
Stoneyhill Ave EH21 126 A3
Stoneyhill Cres EH21 126 A3
Stoneyhill Ct EH21 126 A3
Stoneyhill Dr EH21 126 A3
Stoneyhill Farm Rd
EH21 126 A3
Stoneyhill Gr EH21 126 A3
Stoneyhill Pl EH21 126 A3
Stoneyhill Rd EH21 126 A3
Stoneyhill Rise EH21 126 A3
Stoneyhill Steading
EH21 126 A3
Stoneyhill Terr EH21 126 A3
Stoneyhill Wynd EH21 126 A3
Stoneywood Pk FK6 36 A1
Stony Brae FK10 24 B1
Stony Croft Rd EH30 68 B1
Stories Pk EH40 103 F4
Strachan Gdns EH4 92 A1
Strachan Rd EH4 92 A1
Strachan St FK1 59 F2
Straiton Mains EH20 155 D1
Straiton Pk EH20 155 D1
Straiton Pl EH15 125 D4
Straiton Rd
Loanhead EH20 180 C4
Straiton EH20 155 D1
Strang's Pl FK1 81 F3
Strathallan Ct FK9 2 A3
Strathallan Dr KY2 16 C3
Strathallan Rd FK9 2 A3
Strathalmond Ct EH4 90 C2
Strathalmond Gn EH4 90 C2
Strathalmond Pk EH4 90 C2
Strathalmond Rd EH4 90 C2
Strathavon Terr EH48 112 C3
Strathbeg Dr KY11 47 F2
Strathbrock Pl
Broxburn EH52 117 F3
Uphall EH52 116 C2
Strathearn Pl EH9 123 D2
Strathearn Rd
Edinburgh EH9 123 E2
Kirkcaldy KY1 17 F4
North Berwick EH39 53 F4
Strathesk Gr EH26 204 A3
Strathesk Pl EH26 204 A3
Strathfillan Rd EH9 123 E2
Strathkinnes Rd KY2 17 D2
Strathlachlan Ave ML8 230 A1
Strathlogie EH48 112 C3
Strathmiglo Pl FK5 38 C2
Strathmore Cres FK9 2 A2
Strathmore Dr
Dunfermline KY12 29 E3
Stirling FK9 2 A2
Strathmore St KY3 34 C2
Strathyre Dr EH47 171 E1
Strawberry Bank
Dalkeith EH22 156 C1
Linlithgow EH49 85 D3
Streets Pl KY12 29 E4
Stripehead FK10 10 A3
Striven Dr FK2 39 E1
Striven Pl KY2 16 C4
Stromness Gdns EH54 173 E3
Strowan Rd FK3 61 F4
Strowan Sq FK3 61 F4
Struan Dr KY11 47 D2
Struan Pl KY11 47 D2
Strude Howe FK12 5 D4
Strude Mill FK12 5 D4
Strude St FK12 5 D4
Stuart Cres EH12 121 D4
Stuart Ct EH12 121 D4
Stuart Gn EH12 121 D4
Stuart Gr FK3 61 D3
Stuart Pk EH12 121 D4
Stuart Pl KY4 13 E3
Stuart Rd KY11 46 B1
Stuart Sq EH12 121 D4
Stuart Terr EH48 145 D3
Stuart Wynd EH12 121 D4
Succoth Ave EH12 122 B4
Succoth Ct EH12 122 B4
Succoth Gdns EH12 122 B4
Succoth Pk EH12 122 B4
Succoth Pl EH12 122 B4
Suffolk Rd EH16 123 F2
Suilven Hts FK2 61 D2
Summer Bank EH3 93 E1
Summer Pl EH3 93 E2
Summerfield Gdns EH6 94 A2
Summerfield Pk EH42 78 A1
Summerfield Pl EH6 94 A2
Summerfield Rd EH42 78 B1
Summerford FK1 59 E2
Summerford Gdns FK1 59 E2
Summerford Rd FK1 59 E2
Summerhall EH8 233 E1
Summerhall Cres EH9 233 E1
Summerhall Pl EH9 233 E1
Summerhall Sq EH9 233 E1
Summerlee EH32 96 C1
Summerside Pl EH6 93 E3
Summerside St EH6 93 E3
Summertrees Ct EH16 124 A1
Summerville Ct EH54 148 A4
Suna Path ML7 192 A2
Sunart Pl FK3 61 E3
Sunbury Mews EH4 122 C4
Sunbury Pl EH4 122 C4
Sunningdale La KY12 28 B3
Sunnybank ML7 191 F3
Sunnybank Pl 12 EH7 94 A1
Sunnybank Rd FK7 7 D2
Sunnybrae ML11 215 D1
Sunnydale Dr EH48 142 C2
Sunnydale Rd EH48 142 C2
Sunnylaw Pl FK1 59 F2
Sunnylaw Rd FK9 2 A4
Sunnyside Edinburgh EH7 94 A1
Stirling FK7 7 D2
Stoneyburn EH47 171 D1
Sunnyside Ave EH48 145 E4
Sunnyside Ct FK10 10 A4
Sunnyside Pl KY5 14 A3
Sunnyside Prim Sch FK10 10 A4
Sunnyside Rd Alloa FK10 10 A4
Brightons FK2 82 B4
Falkirk FK1 59 F3
Sunnyside St FK1 59 F3
Surcoat Loan FK7 7 F2
Sutherland Ave Alloa FK10 10 B4
Stirling FK8 2 B1
Sutherland Cres EH48 145 D3
Sutherland Dr FK6 57 E4
Sutherland Pl KY1 17 F4
Sutherland St EH12 122 C4
Sutherland Way EH54 147 E3
Suttie Way FK9 1 C4
Suttieslea Cres EH22 183 E3
Suttieslea Dr EH22 183 E3
Suttieslea Pl EH22 183 E3
Suttieslea Rd EH22 183 E3
Suttieslea Wlk EH22 183 E3
Sutton Park Cres FK5 38 C2
Sutton Pl FK2 60 B3
Swallow Craig KY11 48 A1
Swallowdrum Rd KY12 28 B3
Swan Cres EH23 207 E4
Swan Pl FK3 61 E3
Swan Rd Kirkcaldy KY1 17 D2
Tranent EH33 128 B3
Swan Spring Ave EH10 154 A4
Swanfield EH6 93 F3
Swanston Ave EH10 154 A3
Swanston Cres EH10 154 A3
Swanston Dr EH10 154 A2
Swanston Gdns EH10 154 A3
Swanston Gn EH10 154 A3
Swanston Gr EH10 154 A2
Swanston Loan EH10 154 A3
Swanston Muir EH10 153 F3
Swanston Pk EH10 154 A3
Swanston Pl EH10 154 A3
Swanston Rd EH10 154 A2
Swanston Row EH10 154 A3
Swanston Terr EH10 154 A3
Swanston View EH10 154 A3
Swanston Way EH10 154 A3
Swinburne Dr FK10 5 D1
Swintons Pl KY4 12 C1
Sword's Way FK2 39 D1
Sycamore Ave
Bo'ness EH51 63 E3
Cockenzie & Port Seton
EH32 97 E2
Kirkcaldy KY1 17 E4
Sycamore Cres KY4 13 E3
Sycamore Dr EH47 170 B3
Sycamore Gdns EH12 121 F3
Sycamore Gr
Dunfermline KY11 46 B4
Winchburgh EH52 87 F1
Sycamore Pl FK8 6 C3
Sycamore Rd EH22 183 F3
Sycamore Wlk EH47 171 E4
Sycamores The FK10 4 A1
Sydney Pk EH7 94 C1
Sydney Pl EH7 94 C1
Sydney St EH54 148 A3
Sydney Terr EH7 94 C1
Sylvan Gr EH51 63 E3
Sylvan Pl EH9 123 E3
Sylvan Way EH48 144 C3
Syme Pl KY11 46 B3
Symington Pl FK2 39 D2
Ta-Verne La KY11 29 E1
Tailend Ind Pk EH54 146 B2
Tailend Rdbt EH54 146 B2
Tait Dr Larbert FK5 59 E4
Penicuik EH26 203 F3
Tait St EH22 157 D2
Talbot St FK3 61 E4
Talisman Pl EH16 124 A1
Talman Gdns FK2 61 F2
Tam O'Shanter Dr FK7 20 B4
Tamfourhill Ave FK1 59 E2
Tamfourhill Ind Est FK1 59 E2
Tamfourhill Rd FK1 59 E2
Tanera Ct FK1 60 A1
Tanhouse Brae KY12 42 B4
Tanners Rd FK1 60 A2
Tannery La FK8 2 A1
Tantallon Castle EH39 55 F4
Tantallon Dr FK2 39 D2
Tantallon Gdns EH54 173 F4
Tantallon Pl EH9 123 E3
Tantallon Rd EH39 54 C3
Tantallon Terr EH39 54 C4
Tapitlaw Gr KY12 26 B4
Tappoch Pl FK5 38 A2
Taransay Dr FK2 61 F1
Tarbert Pl FK2 61 F1
Tarbert Terr FK10 23 F2
Tarbet Pl ML8 230 A1
Tarbrax Path ML7 192 A2
Tarbrax Rd EH55 217 F1
Tarduff Dr FK2 83 D3
Tarduff Pl FK6 36 A1
Targate Rd KY12 28 B3
Targe Wynd FK7 7 F2
Target Rd FK3 62 B4
Tartraven Pl EH52 118 A3
Tarvit St EH3 232 C1
Tashieburn Rd ML11 215 F1
Tavern Cotts KY4 30 C4
Taxi Way KY11 48 B3
Tay Ct FK10 10 B3
Tay Pl ML7 191 F3
Tay St Edinburgh EH11 122 C3
Falkirk FK2 39 E1
Grangemouth FK3 40 A1
Tay Terr KY11 29 F1
Tay Wlk EH54 148 A2
Taylor Ave KY4 13 E2
Taylor Ct FK3 40 C1
Taylor Gdns EH6 93 F3
Taylor Gn EH54 147 E4
Taylor Pl EH22 157 E1
Taylor Rd EH47 169 F3
Taylor's Rd FK5 38 B1
Taymouth Rd FK2 62 A1
Tedder St FK3 61 E3
Telferton EH7 94 C1
Telford Coll EH4 92 C2
Telford Coll
Lochend Annexe EH6 94 A2
Telford Coll North Campus
EH5 92 C3
Telford Ct FK7 7 E1
Telford Dr EH4 92 B2
Telford Gdns EH4 92 B2
Telford Pl Edinburgh EH4 92 B2
Linlithgow EH49 84 B4
Telford Rd EH4 92 B2
Telford Sq Falkirk FK1 59 F3
Livingston EH54 147 F4
Telford View EH49 84 B3
Telny Pl KY3 49 E4
Templar La EH31 52 A1
Templar Pl EH31 52 A1
Templar Rise EH54 173 E4
Templar's Cramond EH4 91 D2
Templars Cres KY3 34 C2
Temple Ave EH48 144 A3
Temple Denny Rd FK6 36 B1
Temple Park Cres EH11 122 C3
Temple Pk EH23 206 B1
Temple Prim Sch EH23 206 B1
Templedean Pk EH41 101 D1
Templehall Ave KY2 16 C4
Templeland Gr EH12 121 E4
Templeland Rd EH12 121 E4
Ten Acres FK10 5 D1
Tenacres Pl FK3 61 F3
Tenacres Rd FK3 62 A4
Tenant's March EH55 172 B2
Tennant St EH6 93 F2
Tennent Pk EH53 148 B1
Tenth St EH22 183 D3
Tern Brae EH54 147 E3
Terrace St KY1 18 A4
Terrace The EH21 126 C1
Terragies EH26 203 E3
Terrars Croft EH8 233 F1
Terris St KY4 13 E2
Teviot Gr EH26 203 F4
Teviot Pl EH1 233 D2
Teviot St FK1 59 F2
Teviotdale Pl EH3 93 D1
Thane Pl KY11 29 F1
Thimblehall Dr KY12 29 E2
Thimblehall Pl KY12 29 E2
Thimblehall Rd KY12 29 F2
Third Gait EH14 151 F4
Third St EH22 183 D3
Thirlestane EH51 64 A4
Thirlestane La EH9 123 E2
Thirlestane Pl EH51 64 A4
Thirlestane Rd EH9 123 E3
Thistle Ave Denny FK6 36 B2
Grangemouth FK3 61 D3
Thistle Ind Est
Broxburn EH52 118 A3
Cowdenbeath KY4 13 F2
Stirling FK7 7 E3
Thistle Pl EH11 232 A1
Thistle St Alloa FK10 10 B3
Burntisland KY3 50 C4
Cowdenbeath KY4 13 E2
Dunfermline KY12 29 D3
Edinburgh EH2 232 C4
Falkirk FK2 60 B3
Kirkcaldy KY1 17 E2
Thompson Pl FK1 110 A2
Thomson Cres
Cockenzie & Port Seton
EH32 97 E2
Currie EH14 152 A3
Falkirk FK1 59 F2
Thomson Ct EH52 116 C2
Thomson Dr EH14 152 B3
Thomson Gn EH54 147 D4
Thomson Gr Currie EH14 152 A3
Uphall EH52 116 C2
Thomson Pl
Cambusbarron FK7 6 B3
Rosyth KY11 46 C2
Thomson Rd EH14 152 A3
Thomson Terr ML7 191 E3
Thorburn Gr EH13 153 E3
Thorburn Rd EH13 153 D3
Thorn Gr KY11 46 C4
Thorn Tree Pl KY12 26 C3
Thornbridge Gdns FK2 60 C2
Thornbridge Rd FK2 60 C3
Thornbridge Sq FK2 60 C3
Thorndale Gdns FK4 57 D1
Thorndene Ct FK1 59 F1
Thorne Ct EH39 54 A4
Thorne Rd FK10 4 C1
Thornhill Dr KY2 17 D3
Thornhill Rd Falkirk FK2 60 B3
Kirkcaldy KY2 17 E3
Thornton Ave FK4 58 A3
Thornton Pl EH47 193 E3
Thornton Rd EH24 181 E1
Thorntree Cres EH32 97 D1
Thorntree St EH6 94 A2
Thorntreeside EH6 94 A2
Thornville Terr EH6 94 A2
Thorny Bank EH22 157 E2
Thornybank Ind Est
EH22 157 E2
Thornybauk EH3 232 B1
Thornyhall EH22 157 E2
Threipmuir Ave EH14 177 E4
Threipmuir Gdns EH14 177 E4
Threipmuir Pl EH14 177 E4
Thrums The FK2 61 D2
Thurston Pl EH54 147 E3
Timber Bush EH6 94 A3
Timmeryetts EH52 117 E3
Timmons Pk KY5 14 A4
Timmons Pl FK6 36 B1
Tinian Cres KY12 26 B1
Tinto Dr FK3 61 F3
Tinto Pl Dunfermline KY11 29 F1
Edinburgh EH6 93 F2
Tipperlinn Rd EH10 123 D2
Tippet Knowes Ct EH52 87 F2
Tippet Knowes Pk EH52 87 F2
Tippet Knowes Rd EH52 87 F1
Tippethill Hospl EH48 144 A1
Tiree Cres FK2 61 E1
Tiree Pl Falkirk FK1 60 A1
Kirkcaldy KY2 16 C4
Titania FK10 10 A4
Todd Sq EH54 116 C1
Toddshill Rd EH29 89 D1
Tolbooth St
3 Falkirk FK1 60 A2
Kirkcaldy KY1 17 E2
Tolbooth Wynd EH6 94 A3
Toll Rd FK10 23 F2
Toll Rdbt EH54 146 C2
Toll View TD13 140 C2
Tollcross EH3 232 B1
Tollcross Prim Sch
EH3 232 B1
Tollgate KY11 29 D1
Tolmount Dr KY12 29 E2
Tolsta Cres FK2 61 F1
Tophill Entry FK1 59 F3
Toravon Dr FK2 83 D3
Torbain KY2 16 B4
Torbain Prim Sch KY2 16 B4
Torbain Rd KY2 16 A3
Torbane Ave EH47 170 C4
Torbane Dr EH47 170 C4
Torbeith Gdns KY4 12 C1
Torbothie Rd ML7 192 A2
Torbrex Farm Rd FK7 7 D2
Torbrex La FK7 7 D3
Torbrex Rd FK7 6 C2
Torburn Ave FK7 20 B2
Torduff Rd EH13 153 D2
Torlea Pl FK5 38 A2
Torness Power Sta
Visitor Ctr EH42 108 C2
Toronto Ave EH54 147 F2
Toronto Prim Sch
EH54 147 F2
Torosay Ave FK2 82 C3
Torphichen Ave EH53 148 A1
Torphichen Pl EH3 232 A2
Torphichen Preceptory
EH48 113 F3
Torphichen Prim Sch
EH48 113 F3
Torphichen Rd EH48 145 D4

Torphichen St
Bathgate EH48 145 D4
Edinburgh EH3 232 A2
Torphin Bank EH13 152 C3
Torphin Rd EH13 152 C3
Torrance Pk EH4 91 E1
Torridon Ave FK2 39 E1
Torridon Ct FK10 10 B3
Torridon Dr KY11 46 C1
Torridon La KY11 46 C1
Torridon Pl Kirkcaldy KY2 16 C4
Rosyth KY11 46 C1
Torridon Rd EH47 170 B4
Torridon Wlk EH54 148 A2
Torrin Loan ML7 192 A2
Torry Dr FK12 4 C4
Torryburn Prim Sch KY12 26 C1
Torsonce Rd EH22 156 C1
Torvean Pl KY11 29 E1
Torwood Ave
Grangemouth FK3 61 F3
Larbert FK5 38 A1
Torwood Pl KY12 29 E3
Torwood Sch FK5 37 F3
Touch Prim Sch KY11 29 F2
Touch Rd FK7 6 A3
Touch Wards KY12 29 F2
Touchhill Cres FK7 20 B2
Tovey Rd KY11 46 B1
Toward Ct EH12 121 D4
Tower Gdns EH51 64 B4
Tower Pl
Clackmannan FK10 10 C3
Edinburgh EH6 94 A3
Tower St Alloa FK10 10 A4
Edinburgh EH6 94 A3
Tower Terr KY1 17 F4
Tower View FK10 5 F1
Towerbank Prim Sch
EH15 95 D1
Towers Ct FK2 60 A3
Towers Pl FK9 2 B2
Town Burn FK7 6 C2
Town House St FK6 36 C1
Townhall St KY11 47 E1
Townhead Dysart KY1 18 A4
Kinghorn KY3 34 C2
Townhead Gdns EH47 170 B3
Townhill Ctry Pk KY12 29 E4
Townhill Prim Sch KY12 29 E4
Townhill Rd KY12 29 D3
Townsend Cres KY1 17 E2
Townsend Pl KY1 17 E2
Trafalgar La EH6 93 F3
Trafalgar St EH6 93 F3
Train Terr KY11 46 B3
Tranent Inf Sch EH33 128 B4
Tranent Prim Sch EH33 128 B4
Tranent Rd EH33 128 A1
Transy Gr KY12 29 E2
Transy Pl KY12 29 E2
Traprain Cres EH48 144 C4
Traprain Terr
Haddington EH41 101 D1
Loanhead EH20 181 E4
Traquair Pk E EH12 121 F3
Traquair Pk W EH12 121 F3
Trelawney Terr EH26 204 A4
Tremayne Pl KY12 28 C3
Trench Knowe EH10 154 A3
Trenchard Pl KY12 28 C3
Tressilian Gdns 8 EH16 124 A1
Trevelyan Cres EH34 160 C3
Trevelyan Pl EH34 160 C3
Trinity Acad EH6 93 E3
Trinity Cres EH5 93 D3
Trinity Ct EH5 93 D3
Trinity Gr EH5 93 D3
Trinity Prim Sch EH6 93 E3
Trinity Rd EH5 93 D3
Tron Ct FK10 4 A1
Tron Sq EH1 233 D3
Trondheim Parkway KY11 29 F1
Trondheim Pl KY11 29 F1
Trongate KY3 35 D2
Troup Ct FK3 61 E4
Tryst Pk EH10 153 F3
Tryst Rd FK5 38 B2
Tudor Ct FK2 61 E1
Tuke St KY12 29 D3
Tulliallan Castle FK10 23 E3
Tulliallan Pl FK5 39 D2
Tulliallan Prim Sch FK10 23 F2
Tulliallan Terr FK10 23 F3
Tullibody Rd FK10 4 C1
Tulligarth Pk FK10 10 A4
Tulloch Ct KY4 13 E3
Tulloch Rd ML7 192 A2
Tummel Dr KY2 16 B4
Tummel Pl
Grangemouth FK3 61 F2
Stenhousemuir FK5 38 C2
Turnbull Gr KY11 29 F1
Turnbull Way EH54 147 E3
Turner Ave EH14 151 E2
Turner Pk EH14 151 E2
Turner St EH48 145 D4
Turnhigh Rd EH47 170 A2
Turnhouse Farm Rd EH12 90 B1
Turnhouse Rd EH12 120 B4
Turret Ct FK10 10 B3
Turret Dr FK2 62 A1
Turret Gdns EH32 127 F4
Turret Rd FK3 61 E3
Turriff Pl KY2 16 C4
Twain Ave FK5 39 D2
Tweed Dr EH54 148 A3
Tweed St Dunfermline KY11 29 F1
Grangemouth FK3 40 A1
Tweedale Cres EH41 163 F3
Tweeddale Ave EH41 163 F3
Tweeddale Ct EH1 233 E3
Tweeddale Dr KY11 29 F1
Tweeddale Gr EH41 163 F2
Tyhmebank EH54 147 F3
Tyler's Acre Ave EH12 121 F3
Tyler's Acre Gdns EH12 121 F3
Tyler's Acre Rd EH12 121 F3
Tyndrum Pl KY2 16 C4
Tyne Cl East Linton EH40 103 F4
Haddington EH41 132 A4
Tynebank Rd EH41 132 A4
Tynecastle High Sch
EH11 122 C3
Tynecastle La EH11 122 C3
Tynecastle Pk (Heart of
Midlothian FC) EH11 122 C3
Tynecastle Terr EH11 122 C3
Tynemount Ave EH35 159 E3
Tynemount Rd EH35 159 E4
Tyneview EH35 159 F4
Tyrwhitt Pl KY11 46 C2
Tytler Gdns EH8 94 A1

Ugston Cotts EH41 100 B1
Ulg Way ML7 192 A2
Ulster Cres EH8 124 B4
Ulster Dr EH8 124 B4
Ulster Gdns EH8 124 B4
Ulster Gr EH8 124 B4
Ulster Terr EH8 124 B4
Underwood Cotts FK7 6 B3
Underwood Rd FK7 6 B3
Union Dr EH47 170 A3
Union Pk EH19 182 A3
Union Pl Brightons FK2 61 E1
Edinburgh EH1 233 E4
Larbert FK5 38 A1
Union Rd Bathgate EH48 145 D3
Broxburn EH52 117 E3
Falkirk FK1 59 E3
Grangemouth FK3 40 B1
Linlithgow EH49 84 C3
Whitburn EH47 170 A3
Union St Alloa FK10 10 A3
Bo'ness EH51 64 A4
Bridge of A FK9 2 A4
Burntisland KY3 50 C4
Cowdenbeath KY4 13 E2
Edinburgh EH1 93 F1
Falkirk FK2 60 A4
Kirkcaldy KY1 17 F4
Lochgelly KY5 14 A4
Shotts ML7 191 E3
Stenhousemuir FK5 38 C2
Stirling FK8 2 A1
Unity Pk ML7 191 E2
Univ of Dundee Sch of
Nursing & Midwifery
Fife Campus KY2 17 D2
Univ of Edinburgh EH8 233 D2
Univ of Stirling
(Dept of Nursing &
Midwifery, Forth Valley
Campus) FK1 60 A2
Universal Rd FK2 60 C4
University of Stirling FK9 2 B3
University Rd W FK9 2 B3
Uphall Prim Sch EH52 117 D3
Uphall Station Inf Sch
EH54 117 D1
Uphall Station Rd EH53 148 A4
Uphall Station Sta EH54 117 D1
Upper Bathville EH48 143 F2
Upper Bow EH1 233 D3
Upper Bridge St FK8 2 A1
Upper Broomieknowe
EH18 182 A4
Upper Castlehill FK8 7 D4
Upper Coltbridge Terr
EH12 122 C4
Upper Craigour EH17 155 F4
Upper Craigour Way
EH17 124 B1
Upper Craigs FK8 7 D4
Upper Cramond Ct EH4 91 D2
Upper Dean Terr EH4 232 A4
Upper Gilmore Pl EH3 232 B1
Upper Gilmore Terr EH3 232 B1
Upper Gray St EH9 123 F3
Upper Grove Pl EH3 232 A1
Upper Millhill St KY11 29 D2
Upper Newmarket St FK1 60 A3
Upper Wellheads KY11 45 F2
Ure Cres FK4 58 A3
Ure Ct FK3 61 E4
Urquhart Cres KY12 28 C2
Urquhart Ct KY2 16 B3
Urquhart Cut KY12 28 C2
Urquhart Farm Cotts KY12 28 B1

Vale Gr FK9 1 C3
Vale Pl FK6 36 C2
Valeview FK5 38 B1
Valley Field View EH26 203 F2
Valley Gdns KY2 16 C3
Valley Gdns S KY2 16 C3
Valley Prim Sch KY2 17 D4
Valley View KY2 16 C3
Valleyfield Ave KY12 26 A1
Valleyfield Pl
Cowdenbeath KY4 13 E3
Stirling FK7 7 E3
Valleyfield Rd EH26 203 F2
Valleyfield St EH3 232 C1
Valleyfield Woodland Pk
KY12 26 A1
Valleyview Dr FK2 60 A4
Valleyview Pl FK2 60 A4
Vancouver Ave EH54 147 F2
Vandeleur Ave EH7 94 C1
Vandeleur Gr EH7 94 C1
Vandeleur Pl EH7 94 C1
Vardon Rd EH31 52 A2
Vaucluse Pl EH26 203 F2
Veere Pk KY12 25 F1
Veitch's Sq 6 EH4 93 D1
Vellore Rd FK2 83 D3
Venachar Pl KY12 28 A1
Vennachar St ML7 191 F3
Vennel The Denny FK6 36 C1
Dunbar EH42 78 C1
Linlithgow EH49 85 D4
Ventnor Pl EH9 124 A2
Ventnor Terr EH9 123 F2
Venturefair Ave KY12 29 D3
Veronica Cres KY1 17 E4
Vetch Pk EH41 101 D1
Vexhim Pk EH15 125 D3
Vicar St FK1 60 A3
Viceroy St KY2 17 D3
Victor Park Terr EH12 121 E4
Victoria Gdns
Kirkcaldy KY1 17 D2
Newtongrange EH22 182 C3
Victoria Hospl KY2 17 D4
Victoria Pk
Fauldhouse EH47 193 F4
Haddington EH41 101 D1
Victoria Pl Bo'ness EH51 64 A4
Brightons FK2 61 E1
Dunbar EH42 78 B2
Stirling FK8 7 D4
Victoria Prim Sch
Edinburgh EH6 93 E4
Falkirk FK2 60 B3
Victoria Rd Falkirk FK2 60 B3
Fauldhouse EH47 193 F4
Grangemouth FK3 61 F4
Haddington EH41 132 A4
Harthill ML7 168 C3
Kirkcaldy KY1 17 E3
Larbert FK5 38 A1
Newtongrange EH22 182 C3
North Berwick EH39 54 B4
Stirling FK8 7 D4
Victoria Sq FK8 7 D4
Victoria St Alloa FK10 10 A4
Dunbar EH42 78 B2
Dunfermline KY12 29 D3
Dysart KY1 18 A4
Edinburgh EH1 233 D3
Harthill ML7 168 C3
Livingston EH54 148 A2
Rosewell EH24 181 E1
Victoria Terr
Dunfermline KY12 29 D3
Edinburgh EH1 233 D2
Haddington EH41 132 A4
Menstrie FK11 4 A4
Musselburgh EH21 126 C3
Viewbank Dr EH19 182 B4
Viewbank Rd EH19 182 A4
Viewbank View EH19 182 B4
Viewcraig Gdns EH8 233 E2
Viewcraig St EH8 233 E2
Viewfield EH19 182 B4
Viewfield Ave EH19 182 B4
Viewfield Dr FK12 4 C3
Viewfield Rd
Edinburgh EH14 152 C4
Tarbrax EH55 217 F2
Viewfield St Harthill ML7 168 C3
Stirling FK8 7 D4
Viewfield Terr
Cowdenbeath KY4 13 F3
Dunfermline KY12 29 D2
Viewforth Bo'ness EH51 64 A4
Cockenzie & Port Seton
EH32 97 E2
Dunbar EH42 78 B2
Edinburgh EH10 123 D3
North Berwick EH39 54 B4
Viewforth Ave KY1 17 F4
Viewforth Dr FK2 61 D2
Viewforth Gdns
Edinburgh EH10 123 D3
Kirkcaldy KY1 17 F4
Tranent EH33 128 B3
Viewforth Pl EH30 89 D4
Viewforth Rd EH30 89 D4
Viewforth Sq EH10 123 D3
Viewforth St KY1 17 F4
Viewforth Terr
Edinburgh EH10 123 D3
Kirkcaldy KY1 17 F4
Tranent EH33 128 B3
Viewpark Gdns EH19 182 A4
Villa Bank FK6 36 C1
Villa Rd EH30 68 A1
Village La EH54 147 D2
Vinefields EH34 160 C3
Violet Terr EH11 122 C3
Vivian Terr EH4 92 A2
Vogrie Cres S EH23 207 E4
Vogrie Estate Ctry Pk
EH23 184 B2
Vogrie Pl EH23 207 E4
Vogrie Rd EH23 207 E4
Voil Rd FK9 2 A2
Volunteer's Gn KY1 17 E2
Vorlich Cres EH26 204 A4
Vorlich Dr FK1 81 F4
Vorlich Pl FK9 2 A2

Waddell St FK2 39 E1
Wadingburn La EH18 155 F1
Wadingburn Rd EH18 181 F4
Waggon Rd Bo'ness EH51 63 F4
Brightons FK2 82 B4
Crossford KY11 45 E4
Falkirk FK2 60 A4
Inverkeithing KY11 47 E1
Wakefield Ave EH7 94 C1
Walden Dr EH41 163 F3
Walden Pl EH41 163 F2
Walden Terr EH41 163 F2
Waldie Ave EH49 85 D3
Walk The Alloa FK10 10 A3
Dysart KY1 18 A4
Walker Cres EH22 156 C1
Walker Dr
Dennyloanhead FK4 57 E3
Queensferry EH30 68 A1
Walker Pl
Bonnyrigg and Lasswade
EH18 181 F3
Dunfermline KY11 29 F1
Walker Rd EH47 193 E3
Walker St
Cowdenbeath KY4 13 D2
Edinburgh EH3 232 A3
Kincardine FK10 23 F2
Kirkcaldy KY2 17 D3
Lochgelly KY5 14 A3
Walker Terr EH40 103 E4
Walkers Ct EH14 121 F1
Walkers Rig EH14 121 F1
Walkers Wynd EH14 121 F1
Wall Gdns FK1 59 E3
Wall St FK1 59 E3
Wallace Cres Brightons FK2 82 B4
Denny FK6 36 B1
Plean FK7 20 B2
Roslin EH25 181 D2
Wallace Ct
Grangemouth FK3 61 E4
Stirling FK8 2 A1
Wallace Gdns FK9 2 B2
Wallace High Sch FK9 2 A2
Wallace Mill Gdns EH53 148 B2
Wallace Mon FK9 2 C2
Wallace Pl
Cambusbarron FK7 6 B3
Falkirk FK2 60 B3
Fallin FK7 8 B2
Tranent EH33 128 B4
Wallace Rd EH48 145 E3
Wallace St Alloa FK10 10 B4
Bannockburn FK7 7 F1
Cowdenbeath KY4 13 E2
Dunfermline KY11 29 E1
Falkirk FK2 60 B3
Grangemouth FK3 61 E4
Stirling FK8 2 A1
Wallace View
Bo'ness EH51 63 E3
Shieldhill FK1 81 E4
Tullibody FK10 4 B2
Wallace Wlk EH47 171 D1
Wallacelea FK2 82 C4
Wallacestone Brae FK2 82 A4
Wallacestone Prim Sch
FK2 82 B4
Walls Pl KY11 29 F1
Wallsend Ct KY12 28 B3
Wallstale Rd FK7 7 D2
Wallyford Ind Est EH21 127 D2
Wallyford Prim Sch
EH21 127 D3
Wallyford Sta EH21 127 D3
Walmer Dr KY12 29 D2
Walnut Gr KY11 46 B4
Walter Hay Ct KY11 46 C2
Walter Scott Ave EH16 124 A1
Wanless Ct EH21 126 B3
Ward Ave FK2 61 E1
Ward St FK10 10 A3
Warden's Cl EH1 123 E4
Wardie Ave EH5 93 D3
Wardie Cres EH5 93 D3
Wardie Dell EH5 93 D3
Wardie Gr EH5 92 C3
Wardie House La EH5 93 D3
Wardie Pk EH5 93 D3
Wardie Prim Sch EH5 93 D3
Wardie Rd EH5 93 D3
Wardie Sq EH5 93 D3
Wardieburn Dr EH5 92 C3
Wardieburn Pl E EH5 92 C3
Wardieburn Pl N EH5 92 C3
Wardieburn Pl S EH5 92 C3
Wardieburn Pl W EH5 92 C3
Wardieburn Rd EH5 92 C3
Wardieburn St E EH5 92 C3
Wardieburn St W EH5 92 C3
Wardieburn Terr EH5 92 C3
Wardiefield EH5 93 D3
Wardlaw Cres
Dunfermline KY11 29 E1
Oakley KY12 26 C4
Wardlaw Pl
Edinburgh EH11 122 C3
Falkirk FK2 39 E1
Wardlaw St
Cowdenbeath KY4 13 E2
Edinburgh EH11 122 C3
Wardlaw Terr EH11 122 C3
Wardlaw Way KY12 26 C4
Wardrop Cres EH48 143 F3
Ware Rd Dirleton EH39 53 E3
North Berwick EH39 54 A4
Warrender Cres EH42 78 C1
Warrender Ct EH39 54 A3
Warrender Park Cres
EH9 123 E3
Warrender Park Rd EH9 123 E3
Warrender Park Terr
EH9 123 E3
Warriston Ave EH3 93 E2
Warriston Cres EH3 93 E2
Warriston Dr EH3 93 E2
Warriston Gdns EH3 93 E2
Warriston Gr EH3 93 D2
Warriston Rd EH3, EH7 93 E2
Warriston Terr EH3 93 D2
Washington La EH11 122 C3
Water St EH6 94 A3
Water Yett EH49 84 C4
Waterfall Wlk EH22 157 D1
Waterlands Gdns ML8 230 A2
Waterloo Bank EH26 203 F2
Waterloo Pl
Edinburgh EH1 233 D4
Elphinstone EH33 128 A1
Waters' Cl EH6 94 A3
Waterside EH41 132 A4
Watertoun Rd EH9 123 F2
Watling Ave FK1 59 E3
Watling Dr FK1 59 E3
Watling Gdns FK1 59 E3
Watling St FK1 59 E3
Watson Cres EH11 122 C3
Watson Pl
Armadale EH48 144 A3
Dennyloanhead FK4 57 E2
Dunfermline KY12 29 D3
Watson St
Cowdenbeath KY4 13 E2
Falkirk FK2 60 A3
Penicuik EH26 203 F3
Watt Ave EH48 144 A3
Watt Gdns FK1 59 F3
Watt Gr EH22 183 F3
Watt Pk EH22 183 D2
Watt Rd KY11 46 A1
Watt St KY1 18 A4
Watt's Cl EH21 126 A3
Watters Cres KY5 14 A3
Wauchope Ave EH16 124 C2
Wauchope Cres EH16 124 C2
Wauchope Pl EH16 124 C2
Wauchope Rd EH16 124 C2
Wauchope Sq EH16 124 C2
Wauchope Terr EH16 124 C2
Waugh Path EH19 182 B4
Waughton Cotts EH40 74 C3
Waulkmill Dr EH26 204 A3
Waulkmill Loan EH14 151 F2
Waulkmill Rd EH26 204 A3
Waulkmill View EH26 203 F3
Wavell St FK3 61 E3
Waverley Bridge EH1 233 D3
Waverley Cres
Bonnyrigg and Lasswade
EH19 182 B4
Grangemouth FK3 61 E3
High Bonnybridge FK4 58 A2
Livingston EH54 147 D3
Stirling FK8 2 B1
Waverley Ct EH19 182 B4
Waverley Dr EH19 182 B4
Waverley Park Terr EH8 94 A1
Waverley Pk
Bonnyrigg and Lasswade
EH19 182 B4
Edinburgh EH8 94 A1
Mayfield EH22 183 E3
Redding FK2 61 D1
Waverley Pl EH7 94 A1
Waverley Rd
Bonnyrigg and Lasswade
EH19 182 B4
Dalkeith EH22 156 C1
Stenhousemuir FK5 38 B1
Waverley St
Bathgate EH48 145 D4
Falkirk FK2 60 A4
Mayfield EH22 183 E3
Waverley St Ind Units 1
EH48 145 D4
Waverley Sta EH1 233 D3
Waverley Terr
Bonnyrigg and Lasswade
EH19 182 B4
Mayfield EH22 183 E3
Stenhousemuir FK5 38 B1
Wayfarers Dr KY11 47 F2
Wayfarers Pl KY11 47 F2
Weaver Pl EH48 145 D4
Weaver Row FK7 7 D2
Weaver's Knowe Cres
EH14 151 F3
Weavers Cres KY2 17 D3
Weavers La EH47 170 A3
Weavers Wlk KY12 29 D1
Webster Ave FK2 39 D2
Webster Ct EH52 117 F3
Webster Pl KY11 46 B3
Wedderburn Cres KY11 29 F1
Wedderburn Pl KY11 29 E1
Wedderburn Rd KY2 16 B4
Wedderburn St KY11 29 E1
Wedderburn Terr EH21 126 B2
Wee Brae EH18 156 A1
Wee Row FK2 60 A3
Weir Ave KY4 13 D1

Weir Cres EH22 156 C1
Weir Dr FK7 8 B2
Weir St Falkirk FK1 60 B3
Stirling FK8 1 C1
Well Rd Bridge of A FK9 2 A4
Lochgelly KY5 14 A4
Well Wynd EH33 128 B3
Wellflats Rd EH29 89 D1
Wellgate Dr FK9 2 B4
Wellgreen Pl FK8 7 D3
Wellhead Cl EH30 89 E4
Wellington Pl EH6 94 A3
Wellington Sch EH26 222 C3
Wellington St EH7 93 F1
Wellmyre FK10 11 D2
Wellpark EH52 116 C4
Wellpark Cres FK7 6 C2
Wellpark Terr FK4 58 A3
Wellside EH41 131 F4
Wellside Pl FK1 60 A3
Welsh Gdns FK9 2 A4
Welsh Rd EH47 169 F3
Wemyss Ct KY11 46 C3
Wemyss Gdns EH21 127 E3
Wemyss Pl
Cockenzie & Port Seton
EH32 97 E2
Edinburgh EH3 232 B4
Haddington EH41 132 A4
Wemyss Place Mews
EH3 232 B4
Wemyss Rd EH32 98 C3
Wemyss St
Cowdenbeath KY4 13 E2
Rosyth KY11 46 C3
Wemyss Terr EH32 98 C3
Wemyssfield KY1 17 D2
Werberside Mews EH4 92 C2
Wes Twindygoul Gdns
EH33 128 B3
Wesley Pl FK2 82 A4
West Adam St EH8 233 E2
West Albert Rd KY1 17 D2
West Annandale St EH7 93 E2
West Approach Rd
EH3 EH11 232 A2
West Baldridge Rd KY12 28 C3
West Bankton EH54 173 F4
West Barns Prim Sch
EH42 77 F1
West Bay Rd EH39 54 A4
West Benhar Rd ML7 168 A2
West Boreland Rd FK6 36 B1
West Bow EH1 233 D2
West Bowling Green St
EH6 93 F3
West Bridge St FK1 60 A3
West Brighton Cres
EH15 125 D4
West Broomhill Rd KY3 50 C4
West Bryson Rd EH11 122 C3
West Burnside EH52 117 F3
West Cairn Cres EH26 203 F3
West Caiystane Rd EH10 154 A3
West Calder High Sch
EH55 173 D3
West Calder Sta EH55 172 B2
West Carmuirs Loan FK5 58 C3
West Carnethy Ave
EH13 153 D3
West Castle Rd EH10 123 D3
West Catherine Pl EH12 122 C4
West Cherrybank EH6 93 E3
West Church Dr FK3 40 A1
West Clifton Farm Cotts
EH53 149 E4
West Coates EH12 122 C4
West Colinton Ho EH13 153 D3
West College St EH1 233 D2
West Craigs Ave EH12 120 C3
West Craigs Cres EH12 120 C4
West Cres EH34 161 F2
West Croft EH28 119 F1
West Cromwell St EH6 93 F3
West Crosscauseway
EH8 233 E1
West Ct
Edinburgh, Niddrie Mains
EH16 124 C2
Edinburgh, Ravelston EH4 92 B1
West Dr Dunfermline KY12 29 D2
Larbert FK5 38 B1
West End EH55 172 B1
West End Gdns FK10 10 A3
West End Pl EH11 122 C3
West Fenton Cotts EH32 72 C4
West Fergus Pl KY1 17 D2
West Ferryfield EH5 92 C2
West Fountain Pl EH11 122 C3
West Gate Rd FK3 62 A4
West Glen Ave EH54 146 C3
West Gorgie Pk EH14 122 B2
West Gorgie Pl EH14 122 B2
West Grange Gdns EH9 123 E2
West Granton Rd EH5 92 B3
West Harbour Rd
Charlestown KY11 45 D2
Cockenzie & Port Seton
EH32 97 D2
Edinburgh EH5 92 C4
West Harwood Crofts
EH55 196 B3
West Holmes Gdns
EH21 126 A3
West James St FK12 5 D3
West Johnstone St FK12 5 D3
West La KY4 13 D1
West Leven St KY3 50 C4
West Link Rd FK9 2 B3
West Links Rd EH31 51 F1
West Loan EH32 96 C1
West Loan Ct EH32 127 F4
West Lodge Gdns FK10 9 F4
West Lorimer Pl EH32 97 D2
West Lothian Coll of F Ed
EH48 145 E3
West Main St
Armadale EH48 143 F3
Blackburn EH47 171 E4
Broxburn EH52 117 E3
Harthill ML7 168 C3
Uphall EH52 116 C2
Whitburn EH47 169 F3
West Mains Ind Est FK3 61 D4
West Mains Rd EH9 123 F1
West Mains St EH32 71 E2
West Maitland St EH12 232 A2
West March St KY1 17 E4
West Mayfield EH9 123 F2
West Mill La EH4 232 A3
West Mill Rd EH13 152 C3
West Montgomery Pl 5
EH7 93 F1
West Muir Rd EH55 172 B1
West Murrayfield FK7 7 E1
West Nethertown St
KY12 29 D1
West Newington Pl EH9 123 F3
West Nicolson St EH8 233 E2
West Norton Pl EH7 233 F4
West Park Gr EH52 117 D3
West Park Pl EH11 122 C3
West Pilton Ave EH4 92 B2
West Pilton Bank EH4 92 B3
West Pilton Cres EH4 92 A3
West Pilton Crossway
EH4 92 B3
West Pilton Dr EH4 92 B3
West Pilton Gdns EH4 92 B3
West Pilton Gn EH4 92 B3
West Pilton Gr EH4 92 B2
West Pilton Lea EH4 92 B3
West Pilton Loan EH4 92 B3
West Pilton March EH4 92 B3
West Pilton Pk EH4 92 B3
West Pilton Pl EH4 92 B3
West Pilton Rd EH4 92 B3
West Pilton Rise EH4 92 B3
West Pilton St EH4 92 B3
West Pilton Terr EH4 92 B3
West Pilton View EH4 92 B2
West Pk Carnock KY12 27 E3
Lochgelly KY5 14 A4
West Port Dunbar EH42 78 B1
Dysart KY1 18 A4
Edinburgh EH1 232 C2
Linlithgow EH49 84 C4
West Port Pl EH49 84 C3
West Powburn EH9 123 F2
West Preston St EH8 123 F3
West Prim Sch KY1 17 D1
West Quality St KY1 18 A4
West Rd Charlestown KY11 45 D2
Haddington EH41 131 F4
West Register St EH2 233 D4
West Register Street La
EH2 233 D4
West Relugas Rd EH9 123 E2
West Richmond St EH8 233 E2
West Savile Rd EH16 123 F2
West Savile Terr EH9 123 F2
West Scotland Street La 1
EH3 93 E1
West Seaside EH32 96 C1
West Shore Rd EH5 92 B4
West Shore Road Trad Est
EH5 92 B4
West Silvermills La EH3 93 D1
West Sq KY11 46 C3
West St EH26 203 F2
West Stirling St FK12 4 C4
West Telferton EH7 94 C1
West Tollcross EH3 232 B1
West Torbain KY2 16 B4
West Vennel FK10 10 A3
West Way KY11 48 A3
West Werberside EH4 92 C2
West Windygoul EH33 128 A3
West Windygoul Gdns
EH33 128 A2
West Winnelstrae EH5 92 C2
West Woods EH4 92 C2
West Wynd KY1 17 E3
Westbank Ct EH33 129 E3
Westbank Gdns EH33 129 E3
Westbank Loan EH15 95 D1
Westbank Pl EH15 95 D1
Westbank Rd EH33 129 E3
Westbank St EH15 95 D1
Westbank Terr EH33 129 E3
Westburn Ave
Cowdenbeath KY4 13 D1
Edinburgh EH14 152 B4
Falkirk FK1 59 F2
Westburn Gdns EH14 152 B4
Westburn Gr EH14 152 B4
Westburn Middlefield
EH14 152 B4
Westburn Pk EH14 152 B4
Westburn Prim Sch
EH11 121 E1
Westcliffe Ct FK3 61 F3
Westcraigs Pk EH48 142 B2
Westcraigs Rd
Blackridge EH48 142 B2
Harthill ML7 168 C3
Westend Pl EH39 54 A4
Wester Bankton EH54 174 A4
Wester Bogie Rd KY2 16 A4
Wester Broom Ave EH12 121 E3
Wester Broom Dr EH12 121 E3
Wester Broom Gdns
EH12 121 E3
Wester Broom Gr EH12 121 E3
Wester Broom Pl EH12 121 E3
Wester Broom Terr EH12 121 E3
Wester Coates Ave EH12 122 C4
Wester Coates Gdns
EH12 122 C4
Wester Coates Pl EH12 122 C4
Wester Coates Rd EH12 122 C4
Wester Coates Terr EH12 122 C4
Wester Drylaw Ave EH4 92 A2
Wester Drylaw Dr EH4 92 A2
Wester Drylaw Pk EH4 92 B2
Wester Drylaw Pl EH4 92 A2
Wester Drylaw Row EH4 92 B1
Wester Hailes Pk EH14 152 C4
Wester Hailes Rd EH14 152 B4
Wester Hailes Sta EH14 152 B4
Wester Row EH14 120 C1
Wester Steil EH10 122 C1
Westerdunes Pk EH39 53 E4
Westerglen Rd FK1 60 A1
Westerlands Dr FK8 7 D3
Westerlea Ct FK9 2 A3
Westerlea Dr FK9 2 A3
Westerlea (Sch for
Spastic Children) EH12 122 B4
Westermains EH48 143 F3
Western Ave Crossford KY12 28 A1
Falkirk FK2 60 A3
Western Gdns EH12 122 B4
Western General Hospl
EH4 92 B2
Western Pl EH12 122 B4
Western Terr EH12 122 B4
Westerton FK7 20 B4
Westerton Dr FK9 2 A4
Westerton Rd
Broxburn EH52 118 A3
Grangemouth FK3 61 F4
Westerton Terr FK2 39 E2
Westfield FK10 24 A2
Westfield Ave EH11 122 B3
Westfield Ct EH22 156 C1
Westfield Dr EH22 156 C1
Westfield Gr
Crossgates KY4 30 C3
Dalkeith EH22 156 C1
Westfield Pk EH22 156 C1
Westfield Pl FK6 36 C1
Westfield Prim Sch EH48 112 C2
Westfield Rd EH11 122 B3
Westfield Rdbt FK2 60 C3
Westfield Sch EH22 157 D2
Westfield St
Edinburgh EH11 122 B3
Falkirk FK2 60 C3
Westgarth Ave EH13 153 D3
Westgate Dunbar EH42 78 B2
Mid Calder EH53 148 A2
North Berwick EH39 54 A4
Westhall Cres KY12 27 E1
Westhall Gdns
Edinburgh EH10 123 D3
Uphall EH52 117 D2
Westhall Rd EH52 117 F2
Westhouse Ave EH22 183 F3
Westhouse Dr EH22 183 F3
Westhouse St EH22 183 F3
Westhouses Rd EH22 183 F3
Westmill Rd EH18 182 A4
Westmill Wynd EH18 182 A4
Westminster Pl FK5 38 C2
Westpoint EH42 78 B1
Westquarter Ave FK2 61 D1
Westquarter Prim Sch
FK2 61 D1
Westray Terr FK1 60 B1
Westside Plaza Sh Ctr
EH14 152 B4
Westview EH49 84 B4
Westview Cres FK10 4 B1
Westwater St KY5 14 A4
Westwood Ave KY1 17 F4
Westwood Pk EH54 146 C4
Westwood Pl KY11 29 F2
Westwood View EH55 172 B2
Wharry Rd FK12 4 C4
Wheatfield Gr EH20 181 D4
Wheatfield Loan EH20 155 D1
Wheatfield Pl EH11 122 B3
Wheatfield Rd EH11 122 B3
Wheatfield St EH11 122 C3
Wheatfield Terr EH11 122 B3
Wheatfield Wlk EH20 181 D4
Wheatlands Ave FK4 58 A3
Wheatsheaf La EH22 157 D2
Whim Rd EH31 51 F1
Whin Park Ind Est EH32 97 D2
Whin Pk EH32 97 D2
Whinbank EH54 147 F3
Whinhill KY11 29 E2
Whinneyknowe KY11 68 B3
Whinniehill Terr KY12 27 E3
Whinny Hill Cres KY11 47 D1
Whinnyburn Pl KY11 46 B3
Whinrig EH52 117 E3
Whins of Milton Sch FK7 7 D1
Whins Pl EH15 95 D1
Whins Rd Alloa FK10 10 B4
Stirling FK7 7 D1
Whinwell Rd FK8 2 A1
Whirlbut Cres KY11 29 D1
Whirlbut St KY11 29 D1
Whitburn Acad EH47 170 B4
Whitburn Rd
Bathgate EH48 144 C2
Livingston EH54 147 E2
Whitdale Prim Sch EH47 170 B3
White Castle EH14 166 B3
White Hart St EH22 157 D2
White Horse Cl EH8 233 F3
White Pk EH11 122 C3
White St EH47 170 A3
White's Cl EH22 157 D2
Whitecraig Ave EH21 126 C1
Whitecraig Cres EH21 126 C1
Whitecraig Gdns EH21 126 C1
Whitecraig Gdns E EH21 126 C1
Whitecraig Prim Sch
EH21 126 C1
Whitecraig Rd EH21 126 C1
Whitecross Prim Sch
EH49 83 F3
Whitedalehead Rd EH47 170 B3
Whitedales EH10 154 B3
Whitefield Neuk KY12 29 F3
Whitefield Rd KY12 29 F3
Whitegates Pl FK1 59 E2
Whitehead Gr EH30 89 E4
Whitehill Ave EH21 126 A2
Whitehill Dr
Blackburn EH47 171 E4
Dalkeith EH22 157 E1
Whitehill Farm Rd EH21 126 A2
Whitehill Gdns EH21 126 A2
Whitehill Gr EH22 157 E1
Whitehill Ind Est EH48 145 E1
Whitehill Pl
Rosewell EH24 181 E1
Stirling FK8 7 D3
Whitehill Rd
Blackburn EH47 145 E1
Edinburgh EH21 125 E2
Whitehill St EH21 125 F2
Whitehill View EH47 171 E4
Whitehouse Loan EH9 123 E3
Whitehouse Rd
Edinburgh EH4 91 D2
Stirling FK7 7 E4
Whitelaw Cres KY11 29 E1
Whitelaw Dr EH48 145 F3
Whitelaw Pl KY11 29 E1
Whitelaw Rd KY11 29 E1
Whitelaw St EH48 142 B1
Whitelea Cres EH14 177 E4
Whitelea Rd EH14 177 E4
Whiteloch Rd EH33 129 E3
Whitemoss Rd EH27 149 F1
Whitemyre Ct KY12 28 B3
Whitequarries Ind Est
EH52 87 E4
Whites Quay KY11 47 F1
Whiteside EH48 144 C3
Whiteside Ind Est EH48 144 C2
Whitesideloan FK2 82 C4
Whitestone Pl EH48 145 E1
Whitingford EH6 93 E3
Whitson Cres EH11 122 A3
Whitson Gr EH11 122 A3
Whitson Pl E EH11 122 A3
Whitson Pl W EH11 122 A3
Whitson Rd EH11 122 A3
Whitson Terr EH11 122 A3
Whitson Way EH11 122 A3
Whitson Wlk EH11 122 A3
Whitten La EH49 84 C4
Whittingehame Dr EH41 132 A4
Whittinghame Dr EH41 132 B4
Wholeflats Rd FK2 61 F2
Wholequarter Ave FK2 61 E1
Whyte Pl 11 EH7 94 A1
Whyte St Harthill ML7 168 C3
Lochgelly KY5 14 A4
Whyte Wlk KY11 29 F2
Whytehouse Ave KY1 17 D2
Whyteman's Brae KY1 17 E4
Whytemans Brae Hospl
KY1 17 D4
Whytescauseway KY1 17 D2
Wilderness Rdbt EH54 173 E3
Wilderness The FK2 22 B2
Wildridge Way KY5 14 A4
Wilfred Terr 5 EH8 94 B1
Wilkieston Rd EH28 119 E1
William Black Pl EH30 89 E4
William Booth Pl FK7 7 D2
William Jameson Pl EH15 95 D1
William St
Dunfermline KY12 28 C2
Edinburgh EH3 232 A3
Kirkcaldy KY1 17 D1
William Street La NE EH3 232 A3
William Street La NW EH3 232 A3
William Street La SE EH3 232 A3
William Street La SW EH3 232 A2
William Younger Ctr
(Mus) EH8 233 F3
Williamfield Ave FK7 7 D2
Williamfield Sq 2 EH15 125 D4
Williamson Ave FK2 39 D1
Williamson Pl FK2 60 B4
Williamson St FK1 60 A2
Williamston Intc EH54 148 A1
Williamston Prim Sch
EH54 173 F4
Williamstone Ct EH39 54 A3
Willow Ave EH19 182 A3
Willow Brae EH47 193 F3
Willow Dell EH51 63 E3
Willow Dr KY1 17 D4
Willow Gr Dunfermline KY11 46 C4
Livingston EH54 148 A3
Willow Pk EH47 193 F3
Willow Rd EH22 183 F3
Willow Tree Pl EH14 151 E2
Willowbank EH54 147 F3
Willowbank Row EH6 93 E3
Willowbrae FK2 82 B4
Willowbrae Ave EH8 124 B4
Willowbrae Gdns EH8 124 B4
Willowbrae Rd EH8 124 B4
Willowdean EH49 86 B2
Willowpark (Specl Sch)
EH11 122 B3
Willows The
Cairneyhill KY12 27 E1
Tullibody FK10 4 A1
Wilson Ave Dalkeith EH22 157 E2
Denny FK6 36 B1
Falkirk FK1 59 E3
Kirkcaldy KY2 17 D3
Polmont FK2 61 F1
Prestonpans EH32 96 C1
Wilson Dr Bannockburn FK7 7 E1
Falkirk FK1 59 E3
Wilson Gdns FK1 59 E3
Wilson Pl FK4 58 B2
Wilson Rd Falkirk FK1 59 E3
Gorebridge EH23 183 E1
Livingston EH54 146 C2
Shotts ML7 212 A4
Wilson St Blairhall KY12 26 A4
Cowdenbeath KY4 13 E2
Grangemouth FK3 61 E3
Penicuik EH26 203 F3
Townhill KY12 29 E4
Wilson Terr
Broxburn EH52 117 D3
Stoneyburn EH47 171 D1
Wilson Way KY11 46 B1
Wilson Wlk EH33 128 B3
Wilson's Cl KY12 29 D2
Wilson's Pk EH15 95 D1
Wilsontown Rd ML11 215 E1
Wilton Rd Carluke ML8 230 A1
Edinburgh EH16 123 F2
Winchburgh Cotts EH52 87 F1
Winchburgh Prim Sch
EH52 87 F1
Winchester Ave FK6 36 C2
Winchester Avenue
Ind Est FK6 36 C2
Windlebrook KY11 47 D4
Windmill Gn KY1 17 F4
Windmill Knowe KY4 30 C3
Windmill La EH8 233 E1
Windmill Pl KY1 18 A4
Windmill Rd KY1 17 F4
Windmill St EH8 233 D1
Windsor Ave FK1 59 F2
Windsor Cres Falkirk FK1 59 F2
Maddiston FK2 83 D3
Penicuik EH26 204 A3
Windsor Dr Denny FK6 36 B2
Falkirk FK1 59 F2
Penicuik EH26 204 A3
Windsor Gdns Alloa FK10 9 F4
Falkirk FK1 59 F2
Musselburgh EH21 126 C3
Windsor Park Dr EH21 126 C3
Windsor Park Pl EH21 126 C3
Windsor Park Terr EH21 126 C3
Windsor Pk EH21 126 C3
Windsor Pl
Edinburgh EH15 125 D4
Shotts ML7 191 F3
Stirling FK8 7 D4
Windsor Rd Falkirk FK1 59 F2
Penicuik EH26 204 A3
Windsor Sq EH26 204 A3
Windsor St Edinburgh EH7 93 F1
Menstrie FK11 3 F3
Shotts ML7 191 F3
Windsor Street La EH7 93 F1
Windsor Terr EH26 204 A3
Windygate KY2 16 C1
Windygates Rd EH39 54 A3
Windygoul Cres EH33 128 C3
Windyhill Ave FK10 23 E3
Windyknowe Cres EH48 144 C3
Windyknowe Pk EH48 144 C3
Windyknowe Prim Sch
EH48 144 B3
Wingate Cres EH42 78 B1
Winifred Cres KY2 17 D3
Winifred St KY2 17 D3
Winterfield Mains EH42 78 A1
Winterfield Pl EH42 78 A1
Winton Cl EH33 128 C2
Winton Ct
New Winton EH33 129 D2
Tranent EH33 128 C2
Winton Dr EH10 154 B2
Winton Gdns EH10 154 B2
Winton Gr Edinburgh EH10 154 A3
Tranent EH33 128 C2
Winton Loan
Edinburgh EH10 154 B2
Macmerry EH33 129 D3
Winton Pk
Cockenzie & Port Seton
EH32 97 E2
Edinburgh EH10 154 A2
Winton Pl EH33 128 B3

Winton Terr
Edinburgh EH10 .... **154** A3
New Winton EH33 .... **129** D2
Winton Way EH33 .... **128** B2
Wishart Ave
Bonnyrigg and Lasswade
EH19 .... **182** B4
North Berwick EH39 .... **54** B3
Wishart Dr FK7 .... **7** E2
Wishart Pl
Dalkeith EH22 .... **156** C1
Kirkcaldy KY1 .... **17** F3
Wishaw Terr EH7 .... **94** A1
Wisp Gn EH15 .... **125** D2
Wisp The EH15 .... **125** D2
Witchbrae KY12 .... **29** D2
Wolfe Rd FK1 .... **60** B2
Wolrige Rd EH16 .... **155** D4
Wolseley Cres EH8 .... **94** B1
Wolseley Pl EH8 .... **94** B1
Wolsey Ave EH19 .... **182** B3
Wood Avens FK10 .... **4** B1
Wood Dr EH47 .... **169** F3
Wood Lea FK10 .... **23** F3
Wood Pl Livingston EH54 ...... **147** E2
Rosyth KY11 .... **46** C3
Wood Rd KY11 .... **46** B1
Wood St FK3 .... **61** E4
Wood's Ct EH19 .... **182** A4
Woodbank KY4 .... **13** D1
Woodbank Gr KY12 .... **26** B4
Woodbine Terr EH6 .... **94** A2
Woodburn Ave
Dalkeith EH22 .... **157** E1
Redding FK2 .... **61** D1
Woodburn Bank EH22 .... **157** E2
Woodburn Cres
Bonnybridge FK4 .... **57** F2
Oakley KY12 .... **26** C4
Redding FK2 .... **61** D1
Woodburn Dr
Alloa FK10 .... **4** C1
Dalkeith EH22 .... **157** D2

Woodburn Gdns
Dalkeith EH22 .... **157** E2
Falkirk FK2 .... **60** C3
Woodburn Gr EH22 .... **157** E1
Woodburn Loan EH22 .... **157** E2
Woodburn Medway EH22 .. **157** E2
Woodburn Pk EH22 .... **157** E2
Woodburn Pl EH22 .... **157** E2
Woodburn Prim Sch
EH22 .... 157 E2
Woodburn Rd
Dalkeith EH22 .... **157** E2
Falkirk FK2 .... **60** B3
Woodburn St
Dalkeith EH22 .... **157** E2
Falkirk FK2 .... **60** C3
Woodburn Terr
Dalkeith EH22 .... **157** E2
Edinburgh EH10 .... **123** D2
Woodburn View EH22 .... **157** E2
Woodburn Way FK12 .... **5** D3
Woodbush EH42 .... **78** C1
Woodbush Brae EH42 .... **78** C1
Woodbush Ct EH42 .... **78** C1
Woodbush Pl EH42 .... **78** C1
Woodend Pk EH25 .... **180** C2
Woodend Ind Est KY4 .... 13 D1
Woodend Pl KY4 .... **13** D1
Woodend Rd ML8 .... **230** A1
Woodend Wlk EH48 .... **143** F3
Woodfield Ave EH13 .... **152** C3
Woodfield Pk
Bilston EH25 .... **180** B3
Edinburgh EH13 .... **152** C3
Woodhall Ave EH14 .... **152** B3
Woodhall Bank EH13 .... **152** C3
Woodhall Dr EH14 .... **152** B3
Woodhall Gr EH13 .... **152** C3
Woodhall Millbrae EH14 ... **152** C3
Woodhall Pl EH34 .... **160** C3
Woodhall Rd EH34 .... **160** B3
Woodhall Terr EH14 .... **152** B3
Woodhead Farm Rd KY12 ... **25** F1
Woodhead Gr EH48 .... **143** E3
Woodhead Pl EH48 .... **144** C3
Woodhead St KY12 .... **26** A1

Woodhill Ct FK3 .... **61** E3
Woodhill Gr KY12 .... **28** A1
Woodhill Rd EH48 .... **142** A2
Woodland Way FK6 .... **57** E4
Woodlands FK10 .... **5** F1
Woodlands Bank KY11 .... **48** A2
Woodlands Cotts EH48 ...... **144** A3
Woodlands Cres FK1 .... **60** A2
Woodlands Dr
Bo'ness EH51 .... **63** E3
Brightons FK2 .... **82** C4
Crossford KY12 .... **28** A1
Woodlands Gr
Armadale EH48 .... **144** A4
Edinburgh EH15 .... **124** C3
Townhill KY12 .... **29** E4
Woodlands High Sch FK1 ... 60 A2
Woodlands Pk EH54 .... **146** C4
Woodlands Rd KY2 .... **16** B3
Woodlands Terr KY12 .... **26** A4
Woodlands The KY11 .... **46** C3
Woodlea Gdns FK10 .... **5** D1
Woodlea Pk FK10 .... **10** A4
Woodmill Cres KY11 .... **29** E2
Woodmill High Sch KY11 .... 29 F2
Woodmill Pl KY11 .... **29** F2
Woodmill Rd KY11 .... **29** E2
Woodmill St KY11 .... **29** D2
Woodmill Terr KY11 .... **29** D2
Woodmuir Pl EH55 .... **194** C3
Woodmuir Prim Sch
EH55 .... 194 C3
Woodmuir Rd
Breich EH55 .... **194** C3
Whitburn EH47 .... **170** B3
Woodrow EH23 .... **183** E1
Woodside KY4 .... **13** E2
Woodside Ave KY11 .... **46** C3
Woodside Ct
Cambusbarron FK7 .... **6** B3
Falkirk FK1 .... **60** A2
Woodside Dr EH26 .... **203** F3
Woodside Gdns
Brightons FK2 .... **82** C4
Musselburgh EH21 .... **126** C3
Woodside Gr FK5 .... **59** E4

Woodside Pl
Bridgend EH49 .... **86** B2
Fallin FK7 .... **8** B2
Woodside Rd Alloa FK10 .... **4** C1
Forrestfield ML6 .... **141** D2
Stirling FK8 .... **2** A2
Tullibody FK10 .... **4** A1
Woodside St KY11 .... **46** C3
Woodside Terr
Bridgend EH49 .... **86** B2
Clackmannan FK10 .... **10** C2
Edinburgh EH15 .... **125** E4
Falkirk FK1 .... **60** A2
Tarbrax EH55 .... **217** F2
Woodstock Pl EH16 .... **124** A1
Woodville Ct EH52 .... **117** E2
Woodville Terr EH6 .... **94** A2
Wooer St [4] FK1 .... **60** A2
Woolfords Cotts EH55 ...... **217** D4
Woolmet Cres EH22 .... **156** A4
Wordie Rd FK7 .... **6** C2
Wotherspoon Cres EH48 ... **143** F3
Wotherspoon Dr EH51 .... **63** E3
Wright Pl Kirkcaldy KY1 .... **17** E4
Lochgelly KY5 .... **14** A4
Wright St FK2 .... **60** A3
Writers Ct EH42 .... **78** B2
Wynd The Alva FK12 .... **5** D4
Dalgety Bay KY11 .... **48** B2
Gifford EH41 .... **163** F3
Ormiston EH35 .... **159** F4
Wyndford Ave EH52 .... **117** D3
Wyndford Pl EH52 .... **117** D3
Wyvern Pk EH9 .... **123** E2
Wyvis Pk EH26 .... **204** A4
Wyvis Pl ML7 .... **192** A2

Yardheads EH6 .... **93** F3
Yardley Pl FK2 .... **39** D1
Yarrow Ct EH26 .... **204** A4
Yarrow Pl FK3 .... **61** F3
Yeaman La EH11 .... **122** C3
Yeaman Pl EH11 .... **122** C3
Yester Pl EH41 .... **100** C1
Yester Prim Sch EH41 ...... 163 F2
Yetholm Pk KY12 .... **28** C1

Yetts The FK7 .... **6** B3
Yew Gr EH54 .... **148** A3
Yew Terr FK2 .... **61** D1
Yewlands Cres EH16 .... **155** D4
Yewlands Gdns EH16 .... **155** D4
Yieldshields Rd ML8 .... **231** E2
York Arc FK3 .... **40** B1
York Dr FK2 .... **60** B3
York La Edinburgh EH1 ...... **233** D4
Grangemouth FK3 .... **40** B1
York Pl Dunfermline KY12 ...... **29** E3
Edinburgh EH1 .... **233** D4
Kirkcaldy KY1 .... **17** F4
York Rd Edinburgh EH5 .... **93** E3
North Berwick EH39 .... **54** A4
York Sq FK3 .... **40** B1
York St FK2 .... **60** B3
Young Ave EH33 .... **128** B3
Young Cres EH48 .... **144** C3
Young Ct KY4 .... **13** E2
Young Sq EH54 .... **173** E3
Young St Edinburgh EH2 .... **232** B3
West Calder EH55 .... **172** B1
Young Street La N EH2 ...... **232** B3
Young Street La S EH2 ...... **232** B3
Young Terr KY4 .... **13** D2
Young's Terr KY1 .... **17** E3
Youngs Rd EH52 .... **118** A3
Yule Pl EH47 .... **145** E1
Yule Terr EH47 .... **171** E4

Zealandia Rd KY11 .... **46** A1
Zetland Dr
Grangemouth FK3 .... **61** D4
Laurieston FK2 .... **61** D2
Zetland Pl Edinburgh EH5 ...... **93** D3
Lochgelly KY5 .... **14** A4
Skinflats FK2 .... **39** F2
Zetland St FK10 .... **11** D2
Zetland Terr FK2 .... **61** F1
**Zoo (Royal Zoological
Society of Scotland)**
EH12 .... **121** F4

The Street Atlases are available from all good bookshops or by mail order direct from the publisher. Orders can be made in the following ways. **By phone** Ring our special Credit Card Hotline on **01933 443863** during office hours (9am to 5pm) or leave a message on the answering machine, quoting your full credit card number plus expiry date and your full name and address. **By post or fax** Fill out the order form below (you may photocopy it) and post it to: **Philip's Direct, 27 Sanders Road, Wellingborough, Northants NN8 4NL** or fax it to: **01933 443849**. Before placing an order by post, by fax or on the answering machine, please telephone to check availability and prices.

STREET ATLASES ORDER FORM

COLOUR LOCAL ATLASES

	PAPERBACK	
	Quantity @ £3.50 each	£ Total
CANNOCK, LICHFIELD, RUGELEY	☐ 0 540 07625 2	➤ ☐
DERBY AND BELPER	☐ 0 540 07608 2	➤ ☐
NORTHWICH, WINSFORD, MIDDLEWICH	☐ 0 540 07589 2	➤ ☐
PEAK DISTRICT TOWNS	☐ 0 540 07609 0	➤ ☐
STAFFORD, STONE, UTTOXETER	☐ 0 540 07626 0	➤ ☐
WARRINGTON, WIDNES, RUNCORN	☐ 0 540 07588 4	➤ ☐

COLOUR REGIONAL ATLASES

	HARDBACK	SPIRAL	POCKET	
	Quantity @ £10.99 each	Quantity @ £8.99 each	Quantity @ £5.99 each	£ Total
BERKSHIRE	☐ 0 540 06170 0	☐ 0 540 06172 7	☐ 0 540 06173 5	➤ ☐
	Quantity @ £10.99 each	Quantity @ £8.99 each	Quantity @ £4.99 each	£ Total
MERSEYSIDE	☐ 0 540 06480 7	☐ 0 540 06481 5	☐ 0 540 06482 3	➤ ☐
	Quantity @ £12.99 each	Quantity @ £9.99 each	Quantity @ £4.99 each	£ Total
DURHAM	☐ 0 540 06365 7	☐ 0 540 06366 5	☐ 0 540 06367 3	➤ ☐
EAST KENT	☐ 0 540 07483 7	☐ 0 540 07276 1	☐ 0 540 07287 7	➤ ☐
WEST KENT	☐ 0 540 07366 0	☐ 0 540 07367 9	☐ 0 540 07369 5	➤ ☐
EAST SUSSEX	☐ 0 540 07306 7	☐ 0 540 07307 5	☐ 0 540 07312 1	➤ ☐
WEST SUSSEX	☐ 0 540 07319 9	☐ 0 540 07323 7	☐ 0 540 07327 X	➤ ☐
	Quantity @ £12.99 each	Quantity @ £9.99 each	Quantity @ £5.50 each	£ Total
GREATER MANCHESTER	☐ 0 540 06485 8	☐ 0 540 06486 6	☐ 0 540 06487 4	➤ ☐
TYNE AND WEAR	☐ 0 540 06370 3	☐ 0 540 06371 1	☐ 0 540 06372 X	➤ ☐
	Quantity @ £12.99 each	Quantity @ £9.99 each	Quantity @ £5.99 each	£ Total
BIRMINGHAM & WEST MIDLANDS	☐ 0 540 07603 1	☐ 0 540 07604 X	☐ 0 540 07605 8	➤ ☐
BUCKINGHAMSHIRE	☐ 0 540 07466 7	☐ 0 540 07467 5	☐ 0 540 07468 3	➤ ☐
CHESHIRE	☐ 0 540 07507 8	☐ 0 540 07508 6	☐ 0 540 07509 4	➤ ☐
DERBYSHIRE	☐ 0 540 07531 0	☐ 0 540 07532 9	☐ 0 540 07533 7	➤ ☐
EDINBURGH & East Central Scotland	☐ 0 540 07653 8	☐ 0 540 07654 6	☐ 0 540 07656 2	➤ ☐

STREET ATLASES ORDER FORM

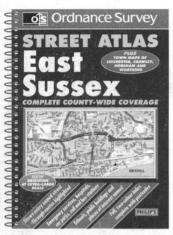

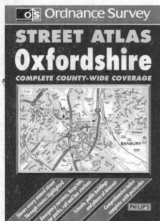

COLOUR REGIONAL ATLASES

	HARDBACK Quantity @ £12.99 each	SPIRAL Quantity @ £9.99 each	POCKET Quantity @ £5.99 each	£ Total
GLASGOW & West Central Scotland	☐ 0 540 07648 1	☐ 0 540 07649 X	☐ 0 540 07651 1	➤ ☐
NORTH HAMPSHIRE	☐ 0 540 07471 3	☐ 0 540 07472 1	☐ 0 540 07473 X	➤ ☐
SOUTH HAMPSHIRE	☐ 0 540 07476 4	☐ 0 540 07477 2	☐ 0 540 07478 0	➤ ☐
HERTFORDSHIRE	☐ 0 540 06174 3	☐ 0 540 06175 1	☐ 0 540 06176 X	➤ ☐
OXFORDSHIRE	☐ 0 540 07512 4	☐ 0 540 07513 2	☐ 0 540 07514 0	➤ ☐
SURREY	☐ 0 540 06435 1	☐ 0 540 06436 X	☐ 0 540 06438 6	➤ ☐
WARWICKSHIRE	☐ 0 540 07560 4	☐ 0 540 07561 2	☐ 0 540 07562 0	➤ ☐
SOUTH YORKSHIRE	☐ 0 540 06330 4	☐ 0 540 06331 2	☐ 0 540 06332 0	➤ ☐
WEST YORKSHIRE	☐ 0 540 06329 0	☐ 0 540 06327 4	☐ 0 540 06328 2	➤ ☐
	Quantity @ £14.99 each	Quantity @ £9.99 each	Quantity @ £5.99 each	£ Total
LANCASHIRE	☐ 0 540 06440 8	☐ 0 540 06441 6	☐ 0 540 06443 2	➤ ☐
NOTTINGHAMSHIRE	☐ 0 540 07541 8	☐ 0 540 075426 6	☐ 0 540 07543 4	➤ ☐
STAFFORDSHIRE	☐ 0 540 07549 3	☐ 0 540 07550 7	☐ 0 540 07551 5	➤ ☐

BLACK AND WHITE REGIONAL ATLASES

	HARDBACK Quantity @ £11.99 each	SOFTBACK Quantity @ £8.99 each	POCKET Quantity @ £3.99 each	£ Total
BRISTOL AND AVON	☐ 0 540 06140 9	☐ 0 540 06141 7	☐ 0 540 06142 5	➤ ☐
	Quantity @ £12.99 each	Quantity @ £9.99 each	Quantity @ £4.99 each	£ Total
CARDIFF, SWANSEA & GLAMORGAN	☐ 0 540 06186 7	☐ 0 540 06187 5	☐ 0 540 06207 3	➤ ☐
EAST ESSEX	☐ 0 540 05848 3	☐ 0 540 05866 1	☐ 0 540 05850 5	➤ ☐
WEST ESSEX	☐ 0 540 05849 1	☐ 0 540 05867 X	☐ 0 540 05851 3	➤ ☐

Post to: Philip's Direct, 27 Sanders Road, Wellingborough, Northants NN8 4NL

◆ Free postage and packing

◆ All available titles will normally be dispatched within 5 working days of receipt of order but please allow up to 28 days for delivery

☐ Please tick this box if you do not wish your name to be used by other carefully selected organisations that may wish to send you information about other products and services

Registered Office: Michelin House, 81 Fulham Road, London SW3 6RB

Registered in England number: 3597451

I enclose a cheque / postal order, for a **total** of ☐
made payable to *Octopus Publishing Group Ltd*, or please debit my
☐ Access ☐ American Express ☐ Visa ☐ Diners

account by ☐

Account no
☐☐☐☐☐ ☐☐☐☐☐ ☐☐☐☐ ☐☐☐☐

Expiry date ☐☐ ☐☐

Signature..

Name..

Address..

....

....

....POSTCODE